THE LAW OF TORTS

AUSTRALIA
The Law Book Company Ltd.
Sydney : Melbourne : Brisbane

CANADA AND U.S.A.
The Carswell Company Ltd.
Agincourt, Ontario

INDIA
N. M. Tripathi Private Ltd.
Bombay
and
Eastern Law House Private Ltd.
Calcutta
M.P.P. House
Bangalore

ISRAEL
Steimatzky's Agency Ltd.
Jerusalem : Tel Aviv : Haifa

MALAYSIA : SINGAPORE : BRUNEI
Malayan Law Journal (Pte.) Ltd.
Singapore

NEW ZEALAND
Sweet & Maxwell (N.Z.) Ltd.
Auckland

PAKISTAN
Pakistan Law House
Karachi

SALMOND AND HEUSTON
on the
LAW OF TORTS

EIGHTEENTH EDITION

by
R. F. V. HEUSTON
D.C.L. (Oxon.); M.A., LL.B. (Dublin)
Regius Professor of Laws in the University of Dublin
Of Gray's Inn and King's Inns, Dublin, Barrister

and
R. S. CHAMBERS
LL.B. (Hons.) (Auckland); D.PHIL. (Oxon.)
Lecturer in Law in the University of Auckland
Barrister, New Zealand

LONDON
Sweet & Maxwell
1981

Published by
Sweet & Maxwell Ltd.
11 New Fetter Lane, London
Printed in Great Britain by
Richard Clay (The Chaucer Press) Ltd.
Bungay, Suffolk

First Edition	(1907) The Author
Second Edition	(1910) The Author
Third Edition	(1912) The Author
Fourth Edition	(1916) The Author
Fifth Edition	(1920) The Author
Sixth Edition	(1924) The Author
Seventh Edition	(1928) W. T. S. Stallybrass
Eighth Edition	(1934) W. T. S. Stallybrass
Ninth Edition	(1936) W. T. S. Stallybrass
Tenth Edition	(1945) W. T. S. Stallybrass
Eleventh Edition	(1953) R. F. V. Heuston
Twelfth Edition	(1957) R. F. V. Heuston
Second Impression	(1959)
Thirteenth Edition	(1961) R. F. V. Heuston
Second Impression	(1962)
Fourteenth Edition	(1965) R. F. V. Heuston
Second Impression	(1967)
Fifteenth Edition	(1969) R. F. V. Heuston
Sixteenth Edition	(1973) R. F. V. Heuston
Seventeenth Edition	(1977) R. F. V. Heuston

British Library Cataloguing in Publication Data

Salmond, *Sir* John William
   Salmond and Heuston on the law of torts.—18th ed.
     1. Torts—Great Britain
     I. Title   II. Heuston, R.F.V.
     III. Chambers, R.S.
     344.106'3   KD1949

     ISBN 0-421-28700-4
     ISBN 0-421-28710-1 Pbk

©
Mrs. A. L. Gillingham
Wellington, New Zealand
1981

PREFACE

The scope and object of this work remain as they were stated by Sir John Salmond in the preface to the first edition in which he said: "I have endeavoured in this book to set forth the principles of the law of torts with as much precision, coherence, and system as the subject admits of, and with as much detailed consideration as is necessary to make the work one of practical utility."

For this edition, published nearly 75 years after the first by the original author, my name has been joined with his on the title page. The decision to do this (which was not made at my request) has naturally been a source of pleasure to me. It has also been a pleasure to be joined for the first time by an assistant editor, Dr. R. S. Chambers, from Sir John Salmond's own country. Dr. Chambers has undertaken primary responsibility for Chapter 4 (Nuisance) and Chapter 13 (Rylands v. Fletcher and Fire), as well as for Section 7 of Chapter 2 (Insurance). I have had primary responsibility for the other chapters. But each of us has read and commented on the first drafts of the other's chapters.

To me it is important that the book continues to be trusted by judges and practitioners throughout the common law world. I have notes of nearly 300 judgments in which different passages (or sometimes the same passage) in the text have been approved. A prominent academic has said that "the criteria of relevance of *Salmond on Torts* are very close, but not identical, to the criteria of a rather formalistic appellate court judge dealing with questions of law within that general area" (W. L. Twining (1974) *British Journal of Law and Society* 148, at p. 154). I regard this statement as being complimentary and not critical. While attention has been paid to the social implications of decisions, there are limits to what can be done within the limits of what is intended to be a readable legal textbook and not a volume in an encyclopedia of the social sciences.

Events have made it unnecessary to consider in much detail one social change which five years ago was being confidently forecast — the replacement of torts by some system of insurance. The cool reception given by Parliament to the Pearson Report (see below, §7), while very disappointing to those who had worked so hard for so long to improve the admittedly unsatisfactory state of the law relating to compensation for personal injuries, has at least meant that the present structure will remain for the foreseeable future. I may be permitted to draw attention, approvingly, to the remarks of the Minister of State for Consumer Affairs (Mrs. Sally Oppenheim, M.P.) in the House of Commons on November 4, 1980: "In no way would she wish to see any reform which undermined the law of tort in this country. That law was part of the fabric of society, depending as it did on the philosophy of duty and personal responsibility."

In the text the law is stated in the light of the reports and other literature available to me on December 31, 1980, although it has occasionally been possible to note briefly later developments. But experience has taught me the importance of adhering to the cut-off date and resisting the temptation to make changes in the text without full consideration. Some other points of editorial technique may be mentioned. First, the relevant periodical literature is cited at the beginning of each section and thereafter referred to only when really necessary. I hope this will achieve brevity in the footnotes without being unfair to the many authors who will find their ideas reproduced in the following pages. Secondly, there has been a slight decrease in the number of Commonwealth and Irish cases cited. Twenty years ago it was not so easy to find significant judgments from those jurisdictions. Now there are helpful publications like *Canadian Cases on the Law of Torts*, and the (forthcoming) textbook on the Irish Law of Torts by Professor B. McMahon and Mr. W. Binchy. Thirdly, the present edition attempts to take proper account of all recent decisions (including the very important *Anns* v. *Merton L.B.C.* [1978] A.C. 727) and statutes. But there has been an exceptional number of complex and difficult statutes since the last edition, *e.g.* the Civil Liability (Contribution) Act 1978, and the Limitation (Amendment) Act 1980, and I confess that I have left the Unfair Contract Terms Act 1977 to be dealt with in textbooks on contracts.

My sincere thanks are due to Mr. A. Kerr, LL.M., of University College, Dublin, and Mr. P. Ward-Perkins, M.A. of the Middle Temple, for help with the proofs. My thanks are also due to the Law Library, St. Cross, Oxford, for special facilities. Dr. Chambers in his turn would like to acknowledge his debt to New College, Oxford, of which he was Salvesen Fellow while working on his chapters.

R. F. V. HEUSTON

Trinity College,
Dublin
May 1981

CONTENTS

6. REVERSIONARY INTERESTS

7. TRESPASS TO THE PERSON

8. DEFAMATION

9. NEGLIGENCE

10. STATUTORY DUTIES

16. ECONOMIC RELATIONS

17. TRADE DISPUTES

18. DECEIT AND INJURIOUS FALSEHOOD

19. WRONGFUL PROCESS OF LAW

20. PARTIES

25. EXTRAJUDICIAL REMEDIES

TABLE OF CASES

TABLE OF STATUTES

CHAPTER 1

INTRODUCTORY

§ 1. THE FORMS OF ACTION[1]

In the fourteenth century remedies for wrongs were dependent upon writs. No one could bring an action in the king's common law courts without the king's writ and the number of writs available was very limited. Where there was no writ there was no right. One of Sir Henry Maine's most famous generalisations explains our early law: "So great is the ascendancy of the law of actions in the infancy of courts of justice, that substantive law has at first the look of being gradually secreted in the interstices of procedure."[2] Every plaintiff had to bring his cause of action within a recognised form of action, and "the key-note of the form of action is struck by the original writ, the writ whereby the action is begun."[3] Although modern research is inclined to minimise the importance of the writ system, it can be said that for five hundred years the writ determined the right. After some preliminary amendments of the law in 1832 and 1833, the Common Law Procedure Act 1852, provided that "it shall not be necessary to mention any form or cause of action in any writ of summons." Yet the most recent version of the English Rules of Court[4] has been interpreted to mean that even if it is not necessary to state the cause of action in the writ it is very desirable to do so.[5] Today "a cause of action" means a factual situation which entitles one person to obtain a remedy from another person in the courts.[6] So that it is unnecessary to attach a specific label such as "conversion" or "trespass," if the pleaded facts sufficiently support either claim.[7] Today the fundamental principle is that wherever a man has a right the law should give a remedy.[8] "This principle enables us to step over the tripwires of previous cases and to bring the law into accord with the needs of to-day."[9] The absence of a remedy is evidence, but no more than evidence, that no right exists.[10]

The forms of action

Yet "an English lawsuit is not a moot or a debate, but an attempt to arrive at a result on the facts before the court: broad academic arguments are quite unsuited to the processes of the English law."[11] So it is still necessary to know something of the nature and scope of the forms of action. "The forms of action," said Maitland at the beginning of this century,[12] "we

---

[1] Maitland, *Forms of Action*, lect. 1; Sutton, *Personal Action*, Chaps. 2 and 4; Milsom, *Historical Foundations of the Common Law*, Chaps. 1, 2, and 11.
[2] *Early Law and Custom*, p. 389.
[3] Maitland, *Forms of Action*, p. 299.
[4] Ord. 18, r. 15 (2). But in 1979 an amendment of the Rules of Court (S.I. 1979 No. 1716) replaced the original writ by a document to be described as a writ of summons.
[5] *Sterman* v. *E. W. and W. J. Moore Ltd.* [1970] 1 Q.B. 596, 603–604.
[6] *Letang* v. *Cooper* [1965] 1 Q.B. 232, 242–243.
[7] *Hesperides Hotels* v. *Aegean Turkish Holidays Ltd.* [1979] A.C. 508, 538.
[8] *Letang* v. *Cooper* [1965] 1 Q.B. 232. But see the criticism of this case below, § 221.
[9] *Hill* v. *Parsons (C. A.) & Co. Ltd.* [1972] Ch. 305, 316, *per* Lord Denning, M.R.
[10] *Dies* v. *British and International Mining Corporation* [1939] 1 K.B. 724, 738–739; *Sales Affiliates Ltd.* v. *Le Jean* [1947] Ch. 295, 305; *Nelson* v. *Larholt* [1948] 1 K.B. 339, 343; *Abbott* v. *Sullivan* [1952] 1 K.B. 189, 200.
[11] *Duple Motor Bodies* v. *I.R.C.* [1960] 1 W.L.R. 510 526, *per* Harman L.J.
[12] *Forms of Action*, p. 296.

1

have buried, but they still rule us from their graves"—perhaps less imperiously today than when Maitland wrote, for Lord Atkin said[13] that "When these ghosts of the past stand in the path of justice clanking their medieval chains the proper course for the judge is to pass through them undeterred." A knowledge of the forms of action is necessary for the following three reasons.

First, to one who is wholly ignorant of the old learning many of the older authorities on liability for civil injuries are unintelligible and misleading.

Secondly, questions as to the existence, nature, and extent of liability depend even yet in some instances on the particular kind of writ or remedy that would have been available for the plaintiff under the old practice.[14] An illustration is *Esso Petroleum Co. Ltd.* v. *Southport Corporation.*[15] The defendants' oil tanker *Inverpool* ran aground on a revetment wall in the Ribble estuary. There was a danger that she might break her back, with the probable loss of the ship herself and the lives of her crew. In order to prevent this the master decided to lighten the ship by jettisoning some of her cargo. The 400 tons of oil so discharged were carried by the action of the wind and tide on to the premises of the Southport Corporation. "Gratitude for deliverance, apart from other instincts, might have inspired a desire to reimburse the Corporation of Southport the amount of the expense to which they were put in cleaning the oil which came unwanted and unwelcome to their shore and to their lake."[16] Esso Petroleum took a different view. As events turned out they were legally justified in doing so. For although the plaintiffs alleged that the deposit of oil on the foreshore gave rise to three distinct causes of action—trespass, nuisance, and negligence—the trial judge decided each one of these allegations adversely to them and his judgment was approved by the House of Lords. A second illustration is the litigation arising out of another escape of oil at sea, this time from the *Wagon Mound* in Sydney Harbour. In one action the owners of a damaged wharf failed to recover,[17] but in another action, differently framed, the owners of ships moored to that wharf did recover.[18] Again as the same facts may support an action either in tort or in contract, and as there are different periods of limitation for tort and contract, the choice of remedy may be of great practical importance.[19] The choice between trespass and case[20] may have similar consequences.[21]

Thirdly, as Maitland pointed out, a lawyer can still "do his client a great deal of harm by advising a bad or inappropriate course of procedure, though it is true he cannot bring about a total shipwreck of a good cause so easily as he might have done some years ago."[22] The Esso Petroleum case again provides an example. The plaintiffs' case before and at the trial was that the defendants were vicariously responsible for the negligent conduct of the master of the *Inverpool* in his navigation of the vessel. As the master was

[13] *United Australia Ltd.* v. *Barclays Bank* [1941] A.C. 1, 29.
[14] *Contra,* Diplock L.J. in *Letang* v. *Cooper* [1965] 1 Q.B. 232, 243.
[15] [1956] A.C. 218 (H.L.).
[16] [1954] 2 Q.B. 182, 203, *per* Morris L.J.
[17] [1961] A.C. 388.
[18] [1967] 1 A.C. 617.
[19] See below, § 3, and 165.
[20] For this, see below, § 2.
[21] *Letang* v. *Cooper* [1965] 1 Q.B. 232.
[22] *Forms of Action,* p. 303. Sutton, *Personal Actions,* pp. 58–62, gives some practical illustrations.

acquitted of negligence it logically followed that the defendants also went free. The House of Lords (reversing the Court of Appeal) held that it was not then open to the Southport Corporation to allege that Esso Petroleum must discharge the onus of showing that they had not negligently sent the vessel to sea in an unseaworthy condition. Adherence to the pleadings is not 'pedantry[23] or mere formalism.'[24] It is bad law and bad practice to shrug off a criticism as "a mere pleading point."[25] These statements are of particular importance today, when the expansion of the tort of negligence, with its emphasis on the foresight of the hypothetical reasonable man, has tended to emphasise vagueness, informality and imprecision in the law.

Justice according to law

"The law of tort has fallen into great confusion, but, in the main, what acts and omissions result in responsibility and what do not are matters defined by long-established rules of law from which judges ought not wittingly to depart and no light is shed upon a given case by large generalisations about them."[26] It is better that the law should be clear than that it should be clever.[27] As it was put in a more recent American case: "rather than add to the already existing confusion with the formulation of a new rule, we conclude that the wisest approach is to return to the traditional principle, theories and standards of tort law."[28] For it must always be borne in mind that justice according to law is the common law ideal. "The qualities that saved English law when the day of trial came in the Tudor age were not vulgar common sense and the reflection of the layman's unanalysed instincts: rather they were strict logic and high technique, rooted in the Inns of Court, rooted in the Year Books, rooted in the centuries."[29] Sentiment is a poor guide to decision. So when in 1401 the defendant was about to be held liable for the escape of his fire, his counsel argued that he would be "undone and impoverished all his days if this action is to be maintained against him; for then twenty other such suits will be brought against him," but met with the reply: "What is that to us? It is better that he should be utterly undone than that the law should be changed for him."[30] The same answer would be given today. So it is not open to a modern judge to create a new remedy, and accordingly a new right, simply on the grounds of economy or convenience.[31] Sympathy for a morally meritorious plaintiff is sometimes judicially expressed, especially when he is a workman injured in the course of his employment.[32] On the other hand, a court should try not to be

---

[23] It should be remembered that a pedant may be right: *The Merak* [1965] P. 223, 260.
[24] [1956] A.C. 218, 241, *per* Lord Radcliffe. In general it is not possible to raise on appeal a point not taken in the court below: *Perkowski* v. *Wellington Corporation* [1959] A.C. 53. Yet in *Carmarthenshire C.C.* v. *Lewis* [1955] A.C. 549 the House of Lords appears to have allowed the appeal on a ground which was not argued at the trial.
[25] *Farrell* v. *Secretary of State* [1980] 1 W.L.R. 172, 180.
[26] *Victoria Park Racing and Recreation Grounds Co. Ltd.* v. *Taylor* (1937) 58 C.L.R. 479, 505 *per* Dixon J.
[27] *Parsons* v. *B.N.M. Laboratories Ltd.* [1964] 1 Q.B. 95, 102.
[28] *Hunsley* v. *Giard* 553 P. (2d) 1096 (1976).
[29] Maitland, Selden Society, Vol. 17, p. xviii.
[30] *Beaulieu* v. *Finglam* (1401) Y.B. 2 Hen. IV, f. 18, pl. 6 (reprinted in Fifoot, *History and Sources*, p. 166).
[31] *Re Wykeham Terrace* [1971] 1 Ch. 204, 213.
[32] *Chapman* v. *Oakleigh Animal Products Ltd.* (1970) 8 K.I.R. 1063, 1067.

influenced against the plaintiff by the fact that he is a disagreeable person standing on his legal rights.[33]

§ 2. TRESPASS AND CASE[34]

The term trespass has been used by lawyers and laymen in three senses of varying degrees of generality. (1) In its widest and original signification it includes any wrongful act—any infringement or transgression of the rule of right. This use is common in the Authorised Version of the Bible, and was presumably familiar when that version was first published. But it never obtained recognition in the technical language of the law,[35] and is now archaic even in popular speech. (2) In a second and narrower signification—its true legal sense—the term means any legal wrong for which the appropriate remedy was a writ of trespass—viz. any direct and forcible injury to person, land or chattels. (3) The third and narrowest meaning of the term is that in which, in accordance with popular speech, it is limited to one particular kind of trespass in the second sense—viz. the tort of trespass to land (trespass *quare clausum fregit*).

Under the old practice the remedies for torts were in general two in number—namely, the action of trespass and that of trespass on the case[36] (commonly called by way of abbreviation "case" simply). Trespass—"that fertile mother of actions"[37]—was the remedy for all forcible and direct injuries, whether to person, land, or chattels. Case, on the other hand, provided for all injuries not amounting to trespasses—that is to say, for all injuries which were either not forcible or not direct, but merely consequential.[38] An injury is an actionable wrong.

"Forcible"

The term "forcible" is used in a wide and somewhat unnatural sense to include any act of physical interference with the person or property of another. To lay one's finger on another person without lawful justification is as much a forcible injury in the eye of the law, and therefore a trespass, as to beat him with a stick. To walk peacefully across another man's land is a forcible injury and a trespass, no less than to break into his house *vi et armis*. So also it is probably a trespass deliberately to put matter where natural forces will take it on to the plaintiff's land.[39] But when there is no

---

[33] As in *Withers* v. *Perry Chain Co. Ltd.* [1961] 1 W.L.R. 1314, 316, or in some of the leading cases on wrongful imprisonment (see below, § 44).

[34] See Winfield and Goodhart, "Trespass and Negligence" (1933) 49 L.Q.R. 359; Prichard, "Trespass, Case, and the Rule in *Williams* v. *Holland*" [1964] C.L.J. 234; Trindade, "Some Curiosities of Negligent Trespass to the Person" (1971) 20 I.C.L.Q. 706; Fridman, "Trespass or Negligence" (1971) 9 Alberta L. Rev. 250.

[35] But Professor Milsom has contended ((1958) 74 L.Q.R. 407) that "had there been a medieval Salmond or Winfield trespass would have been the title, not of a chapter, but of the book."

[36] The action on the case (*super casum*), so called because the particular circumstances of the case are set out in the writ, goes back at least to the thirteenth century. For its relation to the Statute of Westminster II—a controversial matter—see Plucknett, *Concise History*, pp. 372–373.

[37] Maitland, *Forms of Action*, p. 342. The importance of the distinction was that in trespass if the plaintiff recovered less than 40 shillings he was entitled to no more costs than damages, whereas nominal damages in case carried costs with them.

[38] See Winfield, *Province*, pp. 11–14.

[39] See below, § 11.

physical interference there is no trespass and the proper remedy is case: as, for example, in libel, malicious prosecution or deceit.

"*Direct*"

To constitute a trespass, however, it is not enough that the injury should be forcible; it must also be direct and not merely consequential. An injury is said to be direct when it follows so immediately upon the act of the defendant that it may be termed part of that act; it is consequential, on the other hand, when, by reason of some obvious and visible intervening cause, it is regarded, not as part of the defendant's act, but merely as a consequence of it. In direct injuries the defendant is charged in an action of trespass with having done the thing complained of; in consequential injuries he is charged in an action of case with having done something else, by reason of which (*per quod*) the damage complained of has come about.[40] "And the distinction is well instanced by the example put[41] of a man throwing a log into the highway: if at the time of its being thrown it hit any person, it is trespass; but if after it be thrown, any person going along the road receive an injury by falling over it as it lies there, it is case. Neither does the degree of violence with which the act is done make any difference: for if the log were put down in the most quiet way upon a man's foot it is trespass; but if thrown into the road with whatever violence, and one afterwards falls over it, it is case and not trespass."[42] To take other illustrations of the distinction: the act of throwing water into one's neighbour's premises is a trespass; but to fix a spout in such fashion that rain water is discharged by it into those premises is a mere nuisance actionable in case,[43] and to discharge water on to A's property so that it is carried down to B's property is a mere nuisance as regards B.[44]

This distinction between direct and consequential injury is not identical with that between intentional and accidental or negligent injury. These are cross-divisions. Trespass lies for all direct injuries, whether wilful or merely negligent. Case is the appropriate remedy for all consequential injuries. This was settled by *Leame* v. *Bray*,[45] in which it was held that the act of the defendant in negligently driving his carriage so as to bring it into collision with that of the plaintiff was actionable in trespass. In trespass the defendant's state of mind is irrelevant: the law looks only to the results of his conduct. Wilfulness is not necessary to constitute trespass. But if it is sought to make a master vicariously liable for the acts of his servant, case and not trespass is, the proper form of remedy—unless, indeed, the particular act complained of is done by the command of the principal.[46]

"*Damage*"

In case, damage is the gist of the action, and the plaintiff will fail if he cannot prove it. But in trespass it is not necessary to prove actual damage.

[40] *Hutchins* v. *Maugham* [1947] V.L.R. 131, 133.
[41] By Fortescue J. in *Reynolds* v. *Clarke* (1725) 1 Str. 634, 636.
[42] *Leame* v. *Bray* (1803) 3 East 593, 602, *per* Le Blanc J.
[43] *Reynolds* v. *Clarke* (1725) 1 Str. 634.
[44] *Nicholls* v. *Ely Beet Sugar Factory* [1931] 2 Ch. 84.
[45] (1803) 3 East 593. Even today intentional trespass is not equivalent to negligence; *Long* v. *Hepworth* [1968] 1 W.L.R. 1299, 1302.
[46] *Esso Petroleum Co. Ltd.* v. *Southport Corporation* [1956] A.C. 218, 244.

Trespass is actionable per se. This may be important when a remedy is sought for the infringement of personal liberty.[47]

Is trespass preferable to case?

At the present day trespass has been somewhat eclipsed by the growth of the action on the case for negligence, and it has even been suggested in the Court of Appeal that the time has come to abolish the difference between them.[48] This is partly because most actions for personal injuries are brought against an employer vicariously liable for the torts of his servant, and partly because of the growth of the rule that the plaintiff must prove negligence when damage has been caused to his person or chattels as a result of the defendant's conduct on the highway, or where his property adjacent to the highway has been injured in consequence of the defendant's conduct on the highway.[49] Further, it has been held that in an action for personal injuries, whether on or off the highway, the onus is always on the plaintiff to prove intention or negligence[50] in the defendant.[51] But the authority of this decision is doubtful, and many lawyers think that there is still a difference between trespass and case,[52] and that that difference has important practical consequences—for example, in relation to the burden of proof,[53] or inevitable accident,[54] or the limitation of actions,[55] or the place where the tort was committed, when an action is brought upon a foreign tort,[56] or remoteness of damage,[57] or the granting of an injunction to restrain the commission of an act which does not cause actual damage.[58] In Australia it has been asserted that "The two causes of action are not the same now and they never were,"[59] and "Despite many attacks by judges and scholars, the trespass action has survived in Canada."[60] Modern English statutes have also recognised the continued existence of trespass as a distinct concept. So the Theft Act 1968, s. 9 (1) refers to entry "as a trespasser," and the Family Law Reform Act 1969, s. 8 permits a minor to give a valid consent to acts which would otherwise "constitute a trespass to his person."[61] The action of trespass still has certain procedural advantages, and in an appropriate case will afford a wider degree of protection to the integrity of the subject's person[62] or property than many other systems of law.[63]

---

[47] See below, § 46.
[48] *Berry* v. *British Transport Commission* [1962] 1 Q.B. 307, 339; *Letang* v. *Cooper* [1965] 1 Q.B. 232, 238.
[49] See below, § 187.
[50] It is uncertain whether the term negligence here means any more than carelessness. Are the complexities of duty, breach and damage (see below, § 72) to be imported into another area of the law?
[51] *Fowler* v. *Lanning* [1959] 1 Q.B. 426; see below, § 46.
[52] See Buckley L.J., in *S.C.M. Ltd.* v. *Whittall Ltd.* [1971] 1 Q.B. 337, 357.
[53] See below, § 84.
[54] See below, § 8.
[55] See below, § 220.
[56] See below, § 225.
[57] See below, § 203.
[58] *Woollerton and Wilson Ltd.* v. *Richard Costain Ltd.* [1970] 1 W.L.R. 411.
[59] *Williams* v. *Milotin* (1957) 97 C.L.R. 465, 474 *per curiam.*
[60] *Bell Canada Ltd.* v. *Cope (Sarnia) Ltd.* (1980) 11 C.C.L.T. 170, at 180, *per* Linden J.
[61] See below, § 187.
[62] See below, § 43.
[63] Lawson, *Rational Strength of English Law,* Chap. 2.

CHAPTER 2

GENERAL PRINCIPLES OF LIABILITY

§ 3. THE NATURE OF A TORT

(1) Tort and crime[1]

A tort is a species of civil injury or wrong. The distinction between civil and criminal wrongs depends on the nature of the appropriate remedy provided by law. A civil wrong is one which gives rise to civil proceedings—proceedings, that is to say, which have as their purpose the enforcement of some right claimed by the plaintiff as against the defendant. Criminal proceedings, on the other hand, are those which have for their object the punishment of the defendant for some act of which he is accused. It is often the case that the same wrong is both civil and criminal—capable of being made the subject of proceedings of both kinds. Assault, libel, theft and malicious injury to property, for example, are wrongs of this kind. Speaking generally, in all such cases the civil and criminal remedies are not alternative but concurrent, each being independent of the other. The wrongdoer may be punished criminally by imprisonment or otherwise, and also compelled in a civil action to make compensation or restitution to the injured person.[2]

Damages essential mark of tort

Although a tort is a civil injury, not all civil injuries are torts, for no civil injury is to be classed as a tort unless the appropriate remedy for it is an action for damages. Such an action is an essential characteristic of every true tort. Thus a public nuisance is not a tort merely because the civil remedy of injunction may be obtained at the suit of the Attorney-General, but only in those exceptional instances in which a private person may recover damages for loss sustained by him in consequence thereof.[3] Again, the infringement of a statutory right to hold a fair on a common is not a tort, for it is remediable only by a declaratory judgment and an injunction when action is brought by the minority of the inhabitants of a parish.[4] Nor is any wrong a tort if the appropriate remedy is an action, not for unliquidated damages but for a liquidated sum of money—*e.g.* an action for money paid by mistake, or due under a judgment, or paid to the use of another without contract.[5] Such claims are classed by our law as quasi-contractual, but in

---

[1] See Winfield, *Province*, Chap. 8; Williams, "The Definition of Crime" [1955] C.L.P. 107; Brett, *An Inquiry into Criminal Guilt* (1963), Chap. 2; Hadden, "Contract, Tort and Crime: the Forms of Legal Thought" (1971) 87 L.Q.R. 240; Linden, "Tort Law as Ombudsman" (1973) 51 Can. Bar Rev. 150.

[2] In certain cases a criminal court may order a convicted person to pay a sum of money to the injured party by way of compensation: see the Powers of Criminal Courts Act 1973, ss. 35–38, as amended by the Criminal Law Act 1977, s. 60. These compensatory sums are unliquidated, but (unlike damages in tort) are not claimable in the first instance, but only in addition to some punishment.

[3] See below, § 25.

[4] *Wyld* v. *Silver* [1963] Ch. 243.

[5] *Att.-Gen.* v. *Canter* [1939] 1 K.B. 318.

truth they belong neither to contract nor tort, but to the distinct category entitled restitution.

The fact that damages are small does not necessarily mean that the case is unimportant, as it might in an action of contract, for the action may have been brought to establish a point of principle,[6] or to vindicate wounded feelings or character.[7] An unsolved problem is whether there can be a tort without damages being available to the party injured. It is usual to say that a person is liable in tort irrespective of whether or not a judgment for damages has been given against him.[8] He is liable from the moment he commits the tort.[9] But sometimes a party is under a duty but has some peculiar immunity from suit—e.g. the immunity from suit possessed by a spouse before 1962.[10] It has been said that in such a case the immunity is purely procedural[11]—there is a tort but the defendant cannot be sued for it. But this view has been strongly denied[12] and it may therefore be said that the existence of a sanction by way of damages is an essential mark of a tort.

But other remedies are important

Although an action for damages is the essential mark of and the characteristic remedy for a tort, there may be and often are other remedies also. An injunction is often the first remedy which the practitioner thinks of in a case of nuisance or wrongful dispossession, and the only one which is of any real value to the plaintiff.[13] So, despite the large number of statutory controls, the riparian owner's action in nuisance is still the most effective means of stopping pollution.[14] Again, in the emergent wrong of breach of confidence,[15] an injunction is the main remedy to prevent the disclosure of confidential information.[16] Although an injunction is a discretionary remedy, the House of Lords has held that the plaintiff need only show that there is a serious issue to be tried,[17] not that he has a prima facie case, as was once thought.

In an action for the detention of a chattel an order for specific restitution may be obtained in certain cases instead of judgment for its value.[18] In an action by a plaintiff dispossessed of his land he recovers the land itself in addition to damages if he has suffered any during the period of his dispossession.[19] But in all such cases it is solely by virtue of the right to damages that the wrong complained of is to be classed as a tort.

---

[6] A tort action may channel unfavourable publicity towards a powerful defendant—e.g. the actions by the thalidomide children against Distillers.

[7] Steljes v. Ingram (1903) 19 T.L.R. 534.

[8] Roberts v. Roberts [1962] P. 212, 217–218.

[9] Wah Tat Bank v. Kum [1975] A.C. 507, 518.

[10] See below, § 164.

[11] Broom v. Morgan [1953] 1 Q.B. 597.

[12] Tooth & Co. Ltd. v. Tillyer (1956) 95 C.L.R. 605, 615 ("metaphysical unreality"); Auten v. Rayner, The Times, March 15, 1960; Stratford & Son Ltd. v. Lindley [1965] A.C. 269, 304.

[13] Warder v. Cooper [1970] 1 Ch. 495, 501.

[14] See Newsom Q.C. in (1971) 2 Otago L.R. 383 ("I have never known a case of industrial pollution where the evil was not cured in consequence of the injunction").

[15] See below, § 10.

[16] Woodward v. Hutchins [1977] 1 W.L.R. 760.

[17] American Cyanamid Co. v. Ethicon Ltd. [1975] A.C. 396.

[18] See below, § 38.

[19] See below, § 208.

(2) Tort and contract [20]

The distinction between tort and contract is that the duties in the former are primarily fixed by the law, while in the latter they are fixed by the parties themselves. Further, in tort the duty is towards persons generally; in contract it is towards a specific person or persons.[21] Until the abolition of the forms of action confusion was often caused by the fact that it was possible to sue in tort for causes of action which were really contractual. It may still be of practical importance to determine whether an action is in substance contractual or for a tort—e.g. when the defendant is a minor,[22] or when it is sought to obtain leave to serve a defendant out of the jurisdiction,[23] or have a trial before a jury instead of a judge sitting alone,[24] or in relation to the running of time under the Limitation Acts 1939 to 1975[25]—in contract time runs from the breach of warranty, in tort from the occurrence of the damage,[26] or in relation to remoteness of damage.[27] If the plaintiff's claim can be said to be equally poised as between tort and contract he can at least rely upon that aspect which puts him in the more favourable position.[28]

Privity of contract and tortious liability[29]

At one time it seems to have been thought that if A undertook a contractual obligation towards B, and his non-performance or mis-performance of that obligation resulted in damage to C, then C could not sue A unless he could show that A had undertaken towards him the same obligation as he had assumed towards B. Thus in *Winterbottom* v. *Wright*[30] Lord Abinger C.B., speaking of a contract of repair, said: "Unless we confine the operation of such contracts as this to the parties who entered into them, the most absurd and outrageous consequences, to which I can see no limit, would ensue." Enlightenment came only when it was realised that the duty (if any) which A owed to C in such circumstances was not only referable to a legal origin distinct from that of the contractual obligation assumed towards B but also might well be framed in different terms. The "privity of contract fallacy" (as it has been conveniently called) was at last exploded by the House of Lords in *Donoghue* v. *Stevenson*,[31] in which it was held that a manufacturer of chattels was under a duty to the ultimate user or consumer even though there was no contractual relationship between them. This duty had its origin in the law of tort and not in the law of contract; nor did it amount to a warranty that care had been taken to see that the article was sound—an obligation appropriate only to the contractual relationship of vendor and purchaser: the duty was no more than to take reasonable care to protect the consumer. It has been more difficult to understand that a

---

[20] Guest, "Tort or Contract?" (1961) *University of Malaya Law Review* 191; Poulton, "Tort or Contract" (1966) 82 L.Q.R. 346; Fridman, "The Interaction of Tort and Contract" (1977) 93 L.Q.R. 422.
[21] Winfield, *Province*, p. 40.
[22] Below, § 162.
[23] *Matthews* v. *Kuwait Bechtel Corporation* [1959] 2 Q.B. 57.
[24] *Finlay* v. *Murtagh* [1979] I.R. 249.
[25] *Bagot* v. *Stevens Scanlan & Co. Ltd.* [1966] 1 Q.B. 197.
[26] See below, § 206.
[27] *Cook* v. *Swinfen* [1967] 1 W.L.R. 457. See below, § 200.
[28] *Chesworth* v. *Farrar* [1967] 1 Q.B. 407, 416.
[29] See also below, § 75.
[30] (1842) 10 M. & W. 109, 114.
[31] [1932] A.C. 562.

professional man such as an architect or banker might owe a duty of care to someone other than the other party to the contract. But even here liability has been imposed, whether the damage caused to the plaintiff has been physical,[32] or financial.[33] The duty is imposed not because he has made a contract, but because he has undertaken the work.[34] So the present position is that the "privity of contract fallacy" has disappeared.[35] The matter is open: the absence of a contract between the parties is but one of the factors to be considered in determining whether liability in tort exists. It is of course also necessary to avoid the converse fallacy of assuming that C will automatically have a good cause of action against A merely because A's failure to perform his contract with B has resulted in damage to C.

Concurrent liability

The former rule that an action by a client against a solicitor for damages for breach of his professional duty of care is necessarily and exclusively one in contract[36] is incompatible with modern developments in the law of torts, and has therefore been over-ruled in Ireland,[37] and in England.[38] It is the general proximity relationship, and not any particular manifestation in a contract which founds the duty. This falls short of saying that every breach of contract is a tort. Presumably other professional men who once claimed to be in the same position as solicitors—e.g. architects[39]—are now subject to the same duty to take reasonable care.

Some questions remain to be answered. One is whether a solicitor owes a similar duty to any person for whom he acts professionally without reward. According to *Hedley Byrne*[40] such a duty is owed unless there is disclaimer. This may put those who act for neighbourhood law centres and similar bodies in a difficult position, and the wisdom of thus suppressing charitable instincts and undermining professional responsibility may be doubted.[41]

Secondly, does this duty extend to anyone who may rely on the solicitor's skill, such as beneficiaries under a will or an intestacy? Again the *Hedley Byrne* principle points to liability, at least if the third party has changed his position in reliance on the defendant's professional skill—e.g. a home-purchaser who has relied on an architect's certificate.[42] But to hold a solicitor liable to one who has merely failed to obtain a benefit—e.g. a disappointed legatee, which would once have been regarded as quite novel, has now been done both in England[43] and in Ireland.[44] The solicitor in such cases knows that one specified person will suffer loss of a calculable

---

[32] *Clay* v. *A. J. Crump & Sons Ltd.* [1964] 1 Q.B. 533 (architect). But it is not easy to explain why an architect should be under a duty in tort towards third parties but not towards his client: see below, § 76.
[33] *Hedley Byrne & Co. Ltd.* v. *Heller and Partners Ltd.* [1964] A.C. 465. See below, § 76.
[34] *Voli* v. *Inglewood Shire Council* (1963) 110 C.L.R. 74, 85.
[35] *Candler* v. *Crane, Christmas & Co.* [1951] 2 K.B. 164, 177; *Greene* v. *Chelsea B.C.* [1954] 2 Q.B. 127, 138.
[36] Re-affirmed as recently as *Heywood* v. *Wellers* [1976] Q.B. 446.
[37] *Finlay* v. *Murtagh* [1979] I.R. 249.
[38] *Midland Bank* v. *Hett, Stubbs & Kemp* [1979] Ch. 384.
[39] *Bagot* v. *Stevens Scanlon & Co. Ltd.* [1966] 1 Q.B. 197.
[40] See below, § 76.
[41] Jolowicz, Noto, [1979] C.L.J. 54, 56.
[42] As in *Clay* v. *A. J. Crump & Sons Ltd.* [1964] 1 Q.B. 533.
[43] *Ross* v. *Caunters* [1980] Ch. 297.
[44] *Wall* v. *Hegarty* [June, 1980].

amount[45] if reasonable care is not taken in the drafting or execution of the document.

(3) Tort and Equity[46]

No civil injury is to be classed as a tort if it is only a breach of trust or some other merely equitable obligation.[47] The reason for this exclusion is historical only. The law of torts is in its origin a part of the common law, as distinguished from equity, and it was unknown to the Court of Chancery.

Tort defined[48]

Summing the matter up, we have seen that there are four classes of wrongs which stand outside the sphere of tort:
(1) Wrongs exclusively criminal;
(2) Civil wrongs which create no right of action for unliquidated damages, but give rise to some other form of civil remedy exclusively;
(3) Civil wrongs which are exclusively breaches of contract;
(4) Civil wrongs which are exclusively breaches of trust or of some other merely equitable obligation.

We may accordingly define a tort as *a civil wrong for which the remedy is a common law action for unliquidated damages, and which is not exclusively the breach of a contract or the breach of a trust or other merely equitable obligation.*[49]

§ 4. GENERAL CONDITIONS OF LIABILITY[50]

In general, a tort consists in some act done by the defendant whereby he has without just cause or excuse caused some form of harm to the plaintiff.[51] The law of torts exists for the purpose of preventing men from hurting one another, whether in respect of their property, their persons, their reputations, or anything else which is theirs.[52] The fundamental principle of this branch of the law is *alterum non laedere*—to hurt nobody by word or deed.

---

[45] There is thus no fear of liability in an indeterminate amount to an indeterminate class: see below, § 76.

[46] See the question discussed at length, Winfield, *Province*, Chap. 6.

[47] With the possible exception of damages awarded under Lord Cairns' Act: see below, § 219.

[48] The terms *tort* and *wrong* were originally synonymous. *Tort* is derived from the Latin *tortum*, while *wrong* is in its origin identical with *wrung*, both the English and the Latin terms meaning primarily, therefore, conduct which is crooked or twisted, as opposed to that which is straight or right (*rectum*). The first reported use of the word tort is in *Boulston* v. *Hardy* (1597) Cro.Eliz. 547, 548. *Tort*, however, has become specialised in its application, while *wrong* has remained generic. No satisfactory definition of a tort has yet been found. For criticisms of suggested definitions, see Prosser, *Torts*, pp. 1–7; Winfield, *Province*, Chap. 12, and Denning L.J. in (1947) 63 L.Q.R. 517. Landon (*Bell Yard*, Nov., 1931, 20, 32) defined a tort as "a breach of duty which would have been remediable before 1852 by one of the writs of trespass, case and detinue."

[49] This definition was approved in *Anglo-Saxon Petroleum Co. Ltd.* v. *Damant* [1947] K.B. 794, 796; *Philip Morris Ltd.* v. *Airley* [1975] V.R. 345, 347.

[50] See Williams and Hepple, *Foundations of the Law of Tort* (1976), Chap. 1.

[51] "Harm is the tort signature": Seavey, "Principles of Torts" (1942) 56 Harv.L.Rev. 72, 73. We shall see later (§ 9) that it is easier to explain the objects of the law of torts than to define a tort.

[52] *Lee Cooper Ltd.* v. *Jeakins (C. H.) & Sons Ltd.* [1967] 2 Q.B. 1, 8.

An action of tort, therefore, is usually a claim for pecuniary compensation in respect of damage suffered as the result of the invasion of a legally protected interest. An interest is a claim or demand or want or desire put forward by man in a civilised society. The task of the courts is first, to decide which interests should receive legal protection, and secondly, to hold the balance between interests which have received protection. It is obvious that not all objects of human desire can or should receive legal protection. The law began by affording protection against invasion of interests in bodily security, integrity of land or chattels, and freedom of reputation. In the course of time it has recognised other and less obvious (but perhaps equally valuable) interests. Thus interests in the security of domestic or contractual relationships have been protected, and in recent years considerable advances have been made in the direction of protecting interests in emotional security,[53] and in protecting financial or pecuniary interests against careless invasions.[54]

Damnum sine injuria

There are many forms of harm of which the law takes no account. Damage so done and suffered is called *damnum sine injuria*,[55] and the reasons for its permission by the law are various and not capable of exhaustive statement. For example, the harm done may be caused by some person who is merely exercising his own rights; as in the case of the loss inflicted on individual traders by competition in trade,[56] or where the damage is done by a man acting under necessity to prevent a greater evil.[57] Or the courts may hold, on balancing the respective interests of the parties, that sound policy requires that the interests of the defendant should prevail over those of the plaintiff. So the natural right to support of a landowner is subordinate to the natural right of his neighbour to exploit his property by the extraction of underground water not percolating through defined channels, whether the defendant has acted intentionally[58] or carelessly.[59] Other examples may be found in the law relating to damage caused by defamatory statements made on a privileged occasion.[60] Or the harm complained of may be too trivial, too indefinite, or too difficult of proof for the legal suppression of it to be expedient or effective. Thus no action will lie for mere mental suffering unaccompanied by physical harm, though caused by the wilful act or carelessness of the defendant.[61]

So also the harm done may be of such a nature that the law considers it inexpedient to confer any right of pecuniary redress upon the individual injured, but provides some other remedy, such as a criminal prosecution, as exclusively appropriate. Such is the case, for example, with the harm which an individual suffers in common with the public at large by reason of the

---

[53] See below, § 77.
[54] See below, § 76.
[55] The term *injuria* is here used in its original and proper sense of *wrong* (*in jus*, contrary to law). The modern use of "injury" as a synonym for damage is unfortunate but inveterate. See *Crofter Hand Woven Harris Tweed Co.* v. *Veitch* [1942] A.C. 435, 442.
[56] See below, Chap. 16.
[57] See below, § 185.
[58] *Bradford Corporation* v. *Pickles* [1895] A.C. 587.
[59] *Langbrook Properties Ltd.* v. *Surrey C.C.* [1970] 1 W.L.R. 161.
[60] Below, § 55.
[61] See below, § 77.

existence of a public nuisance.[62] Or pecuniary redress may be given some branch of the law other than the law of tort: so a landlord who cuts off his tenant's supply of gas and electricity without entering the premises is liable only for a breach of contract: there is no separate tort entitled "eviction,"[63] though there may be criminal as distinct from civil[64] liability under the Protection from Eviction Act 1977, s. 1. So too a landlord who serves a valid notice to quit cannot be held liable in tort because his motive was the vindictive one of punishing the tenant for having given evidence against him in other proceedings. There is no right of action for damages for contempt of court.[65]

Injuria sine damno

Just as there are cases in which damage is not actionable as a tort (*damnum sine injuria*), so conversely there are cases in which behaviour is actionable as a tort, although it has been the cause of no damage at all (*injuria sine damno*). Torts are of two kinds—namely, those which are actionable *per se*, and those which are actionable only on proof of actual damage resulting from them. Thus the act of trespassing upon another's land is actionable even though it has done the plaintiff not the slightest harm.[66] This is in essence the distinction between Trespass and Case which has already been considered.[67]

The importance which the law places upon the security of the plaintiff's interests in such a case can be seen from the fact that the onus lies on the defendant to justify his conduct—*e.g.* in an action of libel the defendant must show that the statement is true or privileged or protected by whatever other defence may be available. On the other hand, in torts such as negligence or malicious prosecution the onus lies on the plaintiff to show that the conduct of the defendant is legally unjustified.

Is there any general principle of liability?[68]

The basic question is: Does the law of torts consist of a fundamental general principle that it is wrongful to cause harm to other persons in the absence of some specific ground of justification or excuse, or does it consist of a number of specific rules prohibiting certain kinds of harmful activity, and leaving all the residue outside the sphere of legal responsibility? The first alternative is supported by a number of dicta[69] going back for a century,[70] which assert that an unlawful, intentional and positive act which inevitably causes damage to the plaintiff is prima facie actionable, at least if the

---

[62] See below, § 25.
[63] *Perera* v. *Vandiyar* [1953] 1 W.L.R. 672.
[64] *McCall* v. *Abelesz* [1976] Q.B. 585.
[65] *Chapman* v. *Honig* [1963] 2 Q.B. 502.
[66] *Nicholls* v. *Ely Beet Sugar Co.* [1936] Ch. 343, 350–351.
[67] See above, § 2.
[68] Williams, "The Foundation of Tortious Liability" (1939) 7 Camb.L.J. 111; Green, "Thrust and Torts" (1961) 64 W.Va.L.R. 1, 115, 441; Dworkin, "Intentionally Causing Economic Loss" 1974 1 Mon.L.R. 4.
[69] Also an emphatic Australian decision: *Beaudesert Shire Council* v. *Smith* (1969) 120 C.L.R. 145, 155–156, distd. in *Dunlop* v. *Woollahra Municipal Council* [1981] 2 W.L.R. 693.
[70] See, *e.g. Mogul Steamship Co.* v. *McGregor, Gow & Co.* (1889) 23 Q.B.D. 598, 613; *J. Bollinger* v. *Costa Brava Wine Co. Ltd.* [1960] Ch. 262, 283; *Rookes* v. *Barnard* [1964] A.C. 1129, 1216.

damage is to the plaintiff's person or tangible property as distinct from economic interests.[71]

Salmond's view

Salmond argued that the second of these alternatives was that which had been accepted by our law. "Just as the criminal law consists of a body of rules establishing specific offences, so," he said, "the law of torts consists of a body of rules establishing specific injuries. Neither in the one case nor in the other is there any general principle of liability. Whether I am prosecuted for an alleged offence, or sued for an alleged tort, it is for my adversary to prove that the case falls within some specific and established rule of liability, and not for me to defend myself by proving that it is within some specific and established rule of justification or excuse." For Salmond there was no English law of tort; there was merely an English law of torts, that is, a list of acts and omissions which, in certain conditions, were actionable. This book is entitled the *Law of Torts*, not the *Law of Tort*. "The forms of action," Salmond said elsewhere[72] "are dead, but their ghosts still haunt the precincts of the law. In their life they were powers of evil, and even in death they have not wholly ceased from troubling."

Invention of new torts

But it is very doubtful whether Salmond's theory is true now, or ever has been true.[73] There is not a single case[74] in the reports in which an action has been refused on the sole ground that it was new. It has been clearly established ever since the memorable judgment of Sir John Holt C.J. in *Ashby v. White*[75] that mere novelty is no bar to an action. 'I wish never to hear this objection again," said Sir Charles Pratt C.J. sixty years later.[76] "This action is for a tort: torts are infinitely various, not limited or confined, for there is nothing in nature but may be an instrument of mischief." Similar statements may be found in more modern cases.[77] The novelty of a claim may indeed raise a presumption against its validity. So a court may remark: "It is enough to say that the world has gone on very well without such actions as these; and I doubt whether it would continue to do so if such things were allowed,"[78] or "I would not exclude the possibility of such an

---

[71] *Home Office* v. *Dorset Yacht Co. Ltd.* [1970] A.C. 1004, 1027. So the 18th Report of the Law Reform Committee (Cmnd. 4774 (1971)), para. 25 recommended that an intentional act done without lawful justification involving interference with a chattel should be actionable as a new tort which will supersede conversion, detinue and trespass, but Parliament did not go as far as this when it enacted the Torts (Interference with Goods) Act 1977 (see below, Chap. 5).

[72] "Observations on Trover and Conversion" (1905) 21 L.Q.R. 43.

[73] Winfield, *Essays*, 3.

[74] Possible exceptions are *Barnardiston* v. *Soame* (1676) 6 St.Tr. 1063; *Hunt* v. *Damon* (1930) 46 T.L.R. 579.

[75] (1703) 2 Ld.Raym. 938; 14 St.Tr. 695. The question was whether an action lay against a returning officer for refusing to accept the vote of an elector. The Chief Justice, against the opinion of his three puisnes, held that it did, and his dissenting judgment was upheld in the H.L.

[76] *Chapman* v. *Pickersgill* (1762) 2 Wils. 145, 146.

[77] *Allen* v. *Flood* [1898] A.C. 1, 127–128; *Best* v. *Samuel Fox Ltd.* [1950] 2 All E.R. 798, 800; *Abbott* v. *Sullivan* [1952] 1 K.B. 189, 216.

[78] *Revis* v. *Smith* (1856) 18 C.B. 126, 141, *per* Cresswell J., cited with approval in *Marrinan* v. *Vibart* [1963] 1 Q.B. 234, 239. The "thing" was an action for damages in respect of perjured evidence.

action; but none as yet has ever appeared in the books. And this will not be the first."[79] But there is undoubtedly power to recognise a novel claim if justice so requires,[80] although the process may take time.[81]

We can trace back to particular decisions the origin of many torts which are recognised as such at the present day, of malicious prosecution,[82] of deceit in *Pasley* v. *Freeman*,[83] of inducement of breach of contract in *Lumley* v. *Gye*,[84] of the action for inducing a wife to leave her husband in *Winsmore* v. *Greenbank*,[85] of libel,[86] and of negligence.[87] Again, it was only in 1964 that the existence of the tort of intimidation was definitely established,[88] the House of Lords affirming that it had power to adapt the common law to changing social circumstances.[89] Again, although in 1888 a claim for damages for careless statement causing economic loss was dismissed as "an attempt to manufacture a new action which the court would not sanction,"[90] yet in 1963 the House of Lords recognised such a tort,[91] and in 1977 re-stated its boundaries.[92] In 1979 the House of Lords recognised a great expansion in the tort of passing-off.[93] But there are limits, difficult to state, but understood by most practitioners, "to what we can or should do. If we are to extend the law it must be by the development and application of fundamental principles. We cannot introduce arbitrary conditions or limitations: that must be left to legislation."[94] No English court would, or perhaps could, utter such a statement as "The law is what the law should be."[95]

---

[79] *Wheeler* v. *Somerfield* [1966] 2 Q.B. 94, 104, *per* Lord Denning M.R.
[80] So in *Brightside and Carbrook (Sheffield) Cooperative Society Ltd.* v. *Phillips* (1963) *The Times*, November 26, Sellers L.J. said: "I should be astounded if there was no cause of action in circumstances like these. It's high time there was one" (not reported in [1964] 1 W.L.R. 185).
[81] "The creation of a new tort is now very rare and takes a long time. It is rather like the process of canonisation. The cause is first of all fostered by academic well-wishers and then promoted in the lower courts. Eventually, if things prosper, the tort will be beatified by the Court of Appeal and then, probably after a long interval, it will achieve full sainthood in the House of Lords" (Lord Devlin in *The Listener*, December 12, 1968).
[82] Winfield, *History of Conspiracy*, Chap. 5.
[83] (1789) 3 T.R. 51.
[84] (1853) 2 E. & B. 216.
[85] (1745) Willes 577.
[86] Holdsworth, H.E.L., viii, 346–378. In the light of these cases, it is difficult to support the statement that by 1806 "practically the only tort that was known was the tort of trespass:" *Gardiner* v. *Moore (No. 2)* [1969] 1 Q.B. 55, 73 *per* Thesiger J.
[87] "If you read the great cases of *Ashby* v. *White, Pasley* v. *Freeman* and *Donoghue* v. *Stevenson* you will find that in each of them the judges were divided in opinion. On the one side there were the timorous souls who were fearful of allowing a new cause of action. On the other side there were the bold spirits who were ready to allow it if justice so required. It was fortunate for the common law that the progressive view prevailed": *Candler* v. *Crane, Christmas & Co.* [1951] 2 K.B. 164, 178 *per* Denning L.J. But it is worth recalling what Sir Francis North C.J. said in *Barnardiston* v. *Soame* (1676) 6 St.Tr. 1063, 1115: "My brother Atkyns said, the common law complied with the genius of the nation; I do not understand the argument. Does the common law change? Are we to judge of the changes of the genius of the nation? Whither may general notions carry us at this rate?"
[88] *Rookes* v. *Barnard* [1964] A.C. 1129.
[89] *Rookes* v. *Barnard* [1964] A.C. 1129,1169.
[90] *Priestley* v. *Stone* (1888) 4 T.L.R. 730, *per* Lord Esher M.R.
[91] *Hedley Byrne & Co. Ltd.* v. *Heller and Partners Ltd.* [1964] A.C. 465.
[92] *Anns* v. *Merton B.C.* [1978] A.C. 728.
[93] *Erven Warnink BV* v. *Townend & Sons Ltd.* [1979] A.C. 731. Note that Lord Diplock (at p. 744) expressly rejected the argument that to do so "would open the floodgates, or, more ominously, a Pandora's box of litigation".
[94] *Myers* v. *D.P.P.* [1965] A.C. 1001, 1021, *per* Lord Reid.
[95] *Williams* v. *State*, 260 N.Y.S. 2d 953, 955 (1965), *per curiam*, holding that a child born by A.I.D. can sue for "wrongful birth."

Conclusion

To some extent the critics seem to have misunderstood Salmond. He never committed himself to the proposition, certainly untenable now, and probably always so, that the law of torts is a closed and inexpansible system. "To say that the law can be collected into pigeon-holes does not mean that those pigeon-holes may not be capacious, nor does it mean that they are incapable of being added to."[96] Salmond merely contended that these changes were not exclusively referable to any single principle. In this he was probably right. The factors relevant to a decision to impose, or not to impose, liability are many and varied.[97]

§ 5. INTENTION AND MALICE[98]

The term malice, as used in law, is ambiguous, and possesses two distinct meanings which require to be carefully distinguished. It signifies either (1) the intentional doing of a wrongful act, without just cause or excuse; or (2) action determined by an improper motive. To act maliciously means sometimes to do the act intentionally, while at other times it means to do the act from some wrong and improper motive, some motive of which the law disapproves. This motive need not be that of spite or ill-will—that is to say, it need not amount to malice in the narrow and popular sense of the term. Any motive is malicious in the second sense which is not recognised by law as a sufficient and proper one for the act in question.

(1) Wilful and conscious wrongdoing

It is to malice in the first sense that the well-known definition in *Bromage* v. *Prosser*[99] is exclusively applicable: "Malice in common acceptation means ill-will against a person, but in its legal sense it means a wrongful act, done intentionally, without just cause or excuse." But the use of the term malice in this technical sense merely befogs the issue. It is true that sometimes the conservatism of pleaders has retained in statements of claim the allegation that the defendant "maliciously" or "falsely and maliciously" did the acts complained of;[1] but it was recognised as long ago as 1674 that these allegations were mere verbiage, which could not affect the legal characteristics of the act.[2]

(2) Improper motive

Clearly to be distinguished from the first sense of the term malice is the second sense, in which it signifies the existence of an improper motive. Thus,

---

[96] Williams (1939–41) 7 Camb.L.J. 111,114.
[97] See below, § 9.
[98] Gutteridge, "Abuse of Rights" (1935) 5 Camb.L.J. 22; Fridman, "Malice in the Law of Torts" (1958) 21 M.L.R. 484; Devine, "Some Comparative Aspects of the Doctrine of Abuse of Rights" (1964) *Acta Juridica* 48.
[99] (1825) 4 B. & C. 247, 255, *per* Bayley J., who was "a judge of outstanding quality" (Lord Edmund-Davies in *Hoskyn* v. *Metropolitan Police Commissioner* [1979] A.C. 474, 502.
[1] As in actions for defamation.
[2] "If we should make the words *falso et malitiose* support an action without a fit subject matter, all the actions of mankind would be liable to suit and vexation: they that have the cooking (as we call it) of declarations in actions of the case will be sure to put in the words, let the case be what it will; they are here pepper and vinegar in a cook's hand, that help to make sauce for any meat, but will not make a dish of themselves": *Barnardiston* v. *Soame* (1676) 6 St.Tr. 1063, 1114, *per* Sir Francis North C.J. See Sharwood, "*Barnardiston* v. *Soame*; A Restoration Drama" (1964) 4 *Melbourne University Law Review* 502.

malicious prosecution does not mean the intentional and wrongful prosecution of an innocent man; it means that prosecution inspired by an improper motive—a motive which the law does not allow and sanction; for example, the extortion of money.[3] A prosecution so inspired may be actionable even though there was an honest belief in the guilt of the accused. Nuisance, conspiracy, and injurious falsehood are other torts in which malice is on occasion relevant.[4] Similarly, defamation which (even though honestly and on reasonable grounds believed to be true in fact and therefore not actionable) is inspired by malice, *i.e.* an improper motive, loses the protection which the law normally affords to defamatory statements made on occasions of qualified privilege. An improper motive may also be relevant in the assessment of damages. The arrogant, wicked, or spiteful conduct of the defendant may inflame the damages awarded against him for an otherwise ordinary libel, assault, or trespass.[5]

Save in such exceptional cases malice in the sense of improper motive is entirely irrelevant in the law of torts. The law in general asks merely what the defendant has done, not why he did it. A good motive is no justification for an act otherwise illegal, and a bad motive does not make wrongful an act otherwise legal. The rule is based partly on the danger of allowing such a tribunal as a jury to determine the liability of a defendant by reference to their own opinions and prejudices as to the propriety of his motives, and partly on the difficulty of ascertaining what those motives really were.[6] So it has been held that a landlord who maliciously serves a valid notice to quit on a tenant, commits no civil wrong,[7] also that the inhabitants of a parish are entitled to exercise a long-defunct right to hold a fair solely to prevent another erecting buildings for which planning permission had been given.[8]

The leading case is *Bradford Corporation* v. *Pickles*,[9] in which the defendant was held not liable for intentionally intercepting, by means of excavations on his own land, the underground water that would otherwise have flowed into the adjoining reservoir of the plaintiffs, although his sole motive in so doing was to coerce the plaintiffs to buy this land at his own price. It was already settled law that the abstraction (as distinct from the pollution) of underground water not flowing in defined channels is not an actionable wrong, even though done intentionally,[10] but in this case an attempt was made to establish an exception to this rule when the damage was caused not merely intentionally but also maliciously. This contention, however, was rejected by the House of Lords. The same principle was affirmed in *Allen* v. *Flood*.[11] Yet the limits of the decision in *Bradford* v. *Pickles* should be noted. The respondent's conduct was not malicious in the sense of being actuated by spite or ill-will towards the appellants. His posi-

---

[3] *Mitchell* v. *Jenkins* (1833) 5 B. & Ad. 588, 595.
[4] See *Chapman* v. *Honig* [1963] 2 Q.B. 502, 520.
[5] Below, § 199.
[6] *Allen* v. *Flood* [1898] A.C. 1, 118–119, 153.
[7] *Chapman* v. *Honig* [1963] 2 Q.B. 502.
[8] *Wyld* v. *Silver* [1963] Ch. 243.
[9] [1895] A.C. 587.
[10] *Chasemore* v. *Richards* (1859) 7 H.L.C. 349, "which shows that if a man has the misfortune to lose his spring by his neighbour digging a well, he must dig his own well deeper": *Ibbetson* v. *Peat* (1865) 3 H. & C. 644, 650, *per* Bramwell B. Strangely enough, in *Bradford* v. *Pickles* the rights arising from the pollution of the water, though clearly established, were not discussed.
[11] [1898] A.C. 1.

tion was simple. He had something to sell and he did not see why the appellants should not pay the price he asked: it was an attitude with which they, as representatives of one of the great commercial communities of Yorkshire, must have been perfectly familiar.[12] In short, his motive was not an improper one in the eyes of the common law, which has never recognised as an illegal motive the instinct of self-advancement and self-protection, which is the very incentive to all trade.[13] Speaking generally, a man has never been required to use his property or conduct his trade under the pain of being obliged to pay damages to his neighbour if a judge and jury later think that what has been done is unreasonable.[14] The selfish and anti-social use of resources is a matter which may well be better regulated by some branch of public law than by the law of tort. Thus an indictment for public nuisance or conspiracy may lie against those who use their property or economic power to the detriment of the community;[15] or powers to inspect, regulate or license may be given to some administrative authority, as under the Town and Country Planning Acts and the Restrictive Practices Act. The doctrine of "Abuse of Rights" recognised by some Continental systems seems too vague to serve as a useful legal principle in the common law.

§ 6. FAULT

Arguments in Favour of Fault

Salmond said that a second condition usually demanded by the law for liability in an action of tort was the existence of either wrongful intention or culpable negligence on the part of the defendant. He wrote as follows: "Pecuniary compensation is not in itself the ultimate object or a sufficient justification of legal liability. It is simply the instrument by which the law fulfils its purpose of penal coercion. When one man does harm to another without any intent to do so and without any negligence, there is in general no reason why he should be compelled to make compensation. The damage done is not thereby in any degree diminished. It has been done, and cannot be undone. By compelling compensation the loss is merely shifted from the shoulders of one man to those of another, but it remains equally heavy. Reason demands that a loss shall lie where it falls, unless some good purpose is to be served by changing its incidence; and in general the only purpose so served is that of punishment for wrongful intent or negligence. There is no more reason why I should insure other persons against the harmful results of my own activities, in the absence of any *mens rea* on my part, than why I should insure them against the inevitable accidents which result to them from the forces of nature independent of human actions altogether."[16] More recently a Canadian author has reasserted the point.

[12] [1895] A.C. 587, 600, *per* Lord Macnaghten.
[13] *Mogul Steamship Co. Ltd.* v. *McGregor, Gow & Co.* (1889) 23 Q.B.D. 598, 615.
[14] Exceptions may be envisaged (*e.g.* the duties of those in a common calling, or cases where spite makes the defendant's acts unreasonable and a nuisance), but they are not relevant here.
[15] If Mr. Pickles had combined with another their conduct might have been indictable.
[16] 6th ed., pp. 12–13. It is odd that Salmond, who endeavoured to force the law of torts into the strait-jacket of "no liability without fault," should have denied the existence of a law of tort.

"One value at the heart of tort law is the notion of individual responsibility, something that is central to Western civilisation."[17]

Hence Salmond was logically compelled to say[18] of the decision in *Rylands* v. *Fletcher*,[19] which is founded upon a theory of strict liability: "No decision in the law of torts has done more to prevent the establishment of a simple, uniform, and intelligible system of civil responsibility."

Arguments Against Fault

Three objections may be raised to Salmond's powerful argument. They may be summarised briefly, if cynically, by saying that in England today "the real wrongdoer hardly ever pays for the damage he does. He is usually not worth suing. The payer is either his employer or an insurance company."[20] Not everyone approves of these developments. "One may regret the development away from some moral basis towards the arid and arbitrary solution of disputes by the mere adjustment of losses on the basis of ideas of social responsibility which may alter from generation to generation, or even from year to year."[21]

(1) Fault never essential

Fault has never been, and is not today, an essential element in tortious liability.[22] There are two main theories of the history in English law of the relations between blameworthiness and civil responsibility. According to Holmes,[23] the law began with liability based upon actual intent and actual personal culpability and tended, as it grew, to formulate external standards which might subject an individual to liability though there was no fault in him. According to Wigmore,[24] the law began by making a man act at his peril and gradually became more moralised until liability was connected with fault. Time out of mind there has been strict liability for innkeepers and common carriers—they are "quasi-insurers."[25] It was perhaps only natural that the beginning of the twentieth century should have found Salmond writing as he did in support of the school of Wigmore. For by that date the courts had largely abandoned the distinction between direct and indirect damage so familiar in the medieval common law. Instead the emphasis had shifted to the distinction between intentional and negligent conduct, which is now regarded as all-important.[26] In particular, the growing importance of the tort of negligence, with its familiar test of asking what a reasonable and prudent man would have done in the circumstances, had brought the ques-

---

[17] Linden, *Canadian Tort Law* (1978) p. 13.
[18] 6th ed., vii.
[19] See below, Chap. 13.
[20] Devlin, *Law and Morals* (Oxford, 1965), p. 39. See Jenkyn, Glass and Hughes, "Liability without Fault" (1963) A.L.J. 209 for the opposite view. The relationship of torts and insurance is discussed below, § 7.
[21] Lord Hunter (1967) 83 L.Q.R. 277, 282.
[22] "As an English lawyer, I can only say that we never heard of it here. Stated as a general proposition, it is contrary to the whole law of trespass, to much of the law of nuisance, to the whole law of defamation, and to the responsibility of principals for their agents": Pollock, "A Plea for Historical Interpretation" (1923) 39 L.Q.R. 164, 167.
[23] *Common Law*, Lects. III and IV.
[24] Wigmore, "Responsibility for Tortious Acts" (1893) 7 Harv.L.Rev. 315, 383, 441.
[25] *Fletcher* v. *Rylands* (1865) H. & C. 774, 793, *per* Martin B.
[26] *Long* v. *Hepworth* [1968] 1 W.L.R. 1299.

tion of fault to the forefront. But today we can say that neither view seems to be entirely correct.[27] The law has moved in cycles. A period of strict liability, an "unmoral" period, is succeeded by a period of fault liability, a "moral" period, and then the pendulum swings back again. So in 1953 Lord Goddard's Committee on Civil Liability for Animals[28] argued strongly in favour of replacing strict liability by negligence. But in 1967 the Law Commission,[29] after a further investigation, concluded that there were considerable advantages in retaining some forms of strict liability.

(2) Fault judged by an objective standard

It is clear that to Salmond, with his emphasis on *mens rea,* fault was a matter of personal shortcoming. But it has been well said "that the 'fault' upon which liability may rest is social fault, which may but does not necessarily coincide with personal immorality. The law finds 'fault' in a failure to live up to an ideal standard of conduct which may be beyond the knowledge or capacity of the individual."[30] Conversely, it is worth remembering that one who is under no legal liability for damage caused to another may yet think it right and proper to offer some measure of compensation.[31]

(3) Punishment not main object of law of torts

Since he held that wrongful intention or culpable negligence was a condition of civil liability in tort, it is natural that Salmond should have considered pecuniary compensation, not as in itself the ultimate object or a sufficient justification of legal liability, but as a means of punishment. But this was not the original conception of English law, nor is it generally considered to be the conception of English law today.[32] The object of a civil inquiry into cause and consequence is to fix liability on some responsible person and to give reparation for damage done, not to inflict punishment for duty disregarded.[33] So a series of decisions has emphasised that damages in actions for personal injuries are compensatory:[34] damages are to compensate the victim, not to reflect what the wrongdoer ought to pay.[35] On the

---

[27] In *Read* v. *Lyons* [1947] A.C. 156, 180, Lord Simonds, after referring to this "age-long conflict of theories which is to be found in every system of law," says that "It will not surprise the students of English law or of anything English to find that between these theories a middle way, a compromise, has been found. . . . For somewhere the line must be drawn unless full rein be given to the doctrine, that a man acts always at his peril, that 'coarse and impolitic idea' as Holmes J. somewhere [*Common Law*, p. 163] calls it."

[28] Cmd. 8746 (1953).

[29] Law Commission Published Working Paper No. 13 (H.M.S.O., 1967).

[30] Prosser, *Torts*, p. 18. See further on this topic, below, § 81, and *Workington Harbour and Dock Board* v. *SS. Towerfield (Owners)* [1951] A.C. 112, 160; *Gollins* v. *Gollins* [1964] A.C. 644, 664.

[31] As Pufendorf (*De Jure*, III, 1.6) remarked: "Should some poverty-stricken man, in a mere accident, be injured by a man of means, it will be seemly in a man of such station to confer some kindness upon the poor man." Contrast the attitude of the successful appellants in *Bolton* v. *Stone* [1951] A.C. 850 ("The cricket clubs of this country who supported the appeal to the House of Lords have done everything that they can to see that Miss Stone does not suffer financially": (1952) 68 L.Q.R. 3), and *Esso Petroleum Ltd.* v. *Southport Corporation* [1956] A.C. 218 (above, § 1).

[32] But if a plaintiff who has been deprived of all normal senses is entitled to substantial damages, although he can neither enjoy them in his lifetime nor bequeath them by will, as the House of Lords has affirmed in *Lim* v. *Camden Health Authority* [1980] A.C. 174, how can it be said that the aim of torts is compensation rather than punishment?

[33] *Weld-Blundell* v. *Stephens* [1920] A.C. 956, 986.

[34] See below, §§ 212–213.

[35] *Pickett* v. *British Rail Engineering Ltd.* [1980] A.C. 136.

other hand, the House of Lords has re-affirmed that punitive or exemplary damages, imposed to show a wrongdoer that tort does not pay, have a limited but definite place in the law.[36]

The main weakness of Salmond's theory lies in the fact that compensation payable in civil proceedings is often in no way commensurate either with the fault of the defendant or with his financial resources. A moment's inadvertence may result in personal injuries for which damages amounting to thousands of pounds can be recovered.[37] On the other hand, the grossest negligence may by good fortune produce only slight damage. It is worth noting that a different principle prevails in admiralty, whereby shipowners who have caused loss or damage to any other vessel by reason of improper navigation are entitled to limit their liability to one thousand gold francs[38] for each ton of their ship's tonnage.[39] This is very rough justice, for a small tug towing a large liner can do immense damage.[40]

Functions of damages

But although the present emphasis may be on compensation rather than punishment, this does not mean that the latter factor can be ignored entirely. It will always remain important so long as there is power to award aggravated or exemplary damages.[41] Again, although damages in libel are mainly compensatory, the sum awarded is not to be reduced by the fact that the judge has in his judgment excoriated the conduct of the defendant.[42] Compliments, even from the Bench, are no substitute for cash. Again, practitioners testify to the importance in popular morality of "making the defendant pay,"[43] and the courts would be unwise to ignore this feeling entirely.[44] For "a tort suit may provide some psychological satisfaction. Instead of demonstrating with a picket sign, an aggrieved individual may begin a law suit."[45] It should also be remembered that the law of torts aims not merely to provide compensation for losses which have occurred already, but also seeks to minimise or prevent entirely the occurrence of such losses in the future. Hence an award of damage may serve to compensate the plaintiff and also to deter the defendant and others from similar conduct in the future. So there is some evidence that the Press (but not, apparently, television) has been inhibited in its conduct by large damages in libel actions.[46] Another example is said to occur when an employer is held strictly responsible for breach of a statutory duty designed for the protection of his workmen, but some of the evidence available about employers' liability insurance policies does not support this belief. Some insurance companies take the view that accident prevention is not part of their function,

---

[36] *Cassell & Co. Ltd.* v. *Broome* [1972] A.C. 1027. Note the conflicting dicta by Lords Reid and Wilberforce on the function of compensation in torts. See below, § 199.
[37] As in *Winkworth* v. *Hubbard* [1960] 1 Lloyd's Rep. 150.
[38] £27·6396 is now the sterling equivalent: *The Abadesa* (No. 2) [1968] P. 656.
[39] Merchant Shipping Act 1894, s. 501.
[40] *The Bramley Moore* [1964] P. 200, 219.
[41] See below, § 199.
[42] *Associated Newspapers Ltd.* v. *Dingle* [1964] A.C. 371.
[43] So even supporters of insurance concede that "the social security system is less emotionally satisfying to the injured worker than the old Workmen's Compensation scheme was, since under the latter the employer was seen to pay the price of his wrongdoing": Barrett (1975) 2 Poly. Law Review 22, 25.
[44] Kelly, "The Inner Nature of the Tort Action" (1967) 2 *The Irish Jurist* (N.S.) 279.
[45] Linden, *Canadian Tort Law* (1978), p. 15.
[46] See below, § 212.

but should be left to the criminal law. Yet this is not very effective—in 1966 there were 296,610 reported accidents, but only 954 prosecutions, and the average fine was £40 14s. This is not an impressive sanction. The employer's liability insurance premium may be increased if his safety record is bad, but as the premium is a deductible expense for tax purposes, this too is not a serious sanction.[47] An increase in premiums may also result in attempts to avoid or defeat claims rather than to prevent accidents.

§ 7. TWO IMPORTANT INFLUENCES ON TRADITIONAL PRINCIPLES OF LIABILITY

(1) Insurance

The influence of insurance on the law of torts has been significant, both on a theoretical level and in practice. We shall examine first its influence at a theoretical level. Insurance has undermined one of the two purposes of an award of damages, and it has cast doubt on the value judgments made by the courts in determining which particular test of liability is appropriate in given circumstances.

Regardless of whether in the particular circumstances the appropriate principle of liability is intention, malice, fault, or strict liability, the purpose of common law damages remains the same. As has been said, the primary purpose of an award of damages is to compensate the victim for his loss, with a view to restoring him as near as possible to the position he would have been in but for the tort of the wrongdoer. But damages have another purpose: by making the *wrongdoer* responsible for meeting the award of damages, the courts are trying to deter others from committing similar tortious wrongs. Insurance[48] vitiates that secondary purpose of damages, at the same time incidentally ensuring that the primary purpose is more often achieved. It can scarcely be realistically asserted that insured defendants are deterred by the prospect of losing a no-claims bonus or by an increase of premium on renewal of their policies. Once it is conceded that insurance renders compensation the sole purpose of damages, then the tort action itself becomes more vulnerable to attack, for there are many ways—some perhaps fairer and administratively cheaper than tort—of compensating a victim for a loss he has suffered.

Prima facie, where a person suffers loss of a recognised kind as the result of another's act, then the latter should have to make good that loss. But, for valid reasons, the courts have held that, in certain circumstances, the actor will have to compensate his victim only if he (the actor) has been at fault. The victim's right to compensation is, therefore, curtailed in an attempt to be fair to both parties. The courts have made a policy decision that, in the circumstances, it is right to reward a defendant who has been careful by protecting him from liability for the consequences of his actions and that, as a corollary, the plaintiff must forgo his compensation. This policy decision is made on the supposition that the wrongdoer would himself have to pay the damages but for this protection; it by no means follows that the same deci-

---

[47] *The Times*, August 19, 1967
[48] It should be remembered that there are two principal kinds of insurance: liability or third party insurance, which provides compensation to a person injured by the insured if he can establish the insured's liability, and loss or first party insurance, which provides compensation for the insured in the event of certain insured contingencies occurring.

sion would be made if there were no risk of the wrongdoer's having to
provide the compensation.[49] It is difficult to judge why the victim's right to
compensation should be curtailed when that curtailment is not justified by a
corresponding benefit to the wrongdoer. The requirement of fault ceases to
play its role as the leveller between the victim's legitimate expectations and
the wrongdoer's legitimate expectations, and becomes instead simply a
hurdle in the victim's progress to compensation. At this theoretical level of
discussion, it is irrelevant whether the wrongdoer's relief from payment is
because of the intervention of the state or an insurance company[50];
whichever is involved, it turns upside-down any policy decisions made in its
absence. If it is accepted that one can insure against liability for harm
caused intentionally to another,[51] then similar arguments can be made about
the inappropriateness of the victim's having, in certain circumstances, to
prove an intention to do him harm, when it is irrelevant to the wrongdoer
whether he had such an intention or not. Again, the victim's right to compensation is being curtailed without any corresponding benefit to the
wrongdoer.

However, insurance has influenced the law of tort on a much more
practical level as well. While the fact of insurance is not of itself a reason for
imposing liability, or for refusing to permit a defendant to escape from
liability,[52] there can be no doubt that it does add "a little extra tensile
strength" to the chain which binds a wrongdoer to his responsibilities.[53] As
well, it has been given "a new horizon to damages"[54]; as Atiyah observed,
"It can hardly be supposed that judges would be habitually awarding
thousands of pounds in damages without a thought for the effect of such
awards on the defendant if they did not appreciate that the damages would
not be paid by the defendants themselves."[55] It is true that traditionally it
has been considered improper to inform the court that a defendant was

---

[49] For instance, if Parliament had decided from the start that all motorists should take out
liability insurance, then strict liability, rather than fault liability, might well have seemed
the fairer test for injuries caused on the highway.

[50] It is quite true that, at a practical level, liability insurance premiums would be higher if
society replaced fault liability with strict liability, although, to some extent, these higher
premiums would be offset by lower premiums for loss, or first party, insurance.

[51] It is well established that those guilty of manslaughter as a result of reckless and drunken
driving can still be indemnified by their insurance company: *Tinline* v. *White Cross
Insurance Association Ltd.* [1921] 3 K.B. 327; *James* v. *British General Insurance Co.
Ltd.* [1927] 2 K.B. 311, unless there is an appropriate exemption clause, as in *Marcel
Beller Ltd.* v. *Hayden* [1978] Q.B. 694, 703, but even then the victim will be able to claim
on his own policy. From the victim's point of view, it would be odd if his chances of
recovery were to be diminished the more reprehensible the injury upon him: Fleming,
"Insurance for the Criminal", (1971) 34 M.L.R. 176. Nor can it be realistically asserted
that crime would be encouraged if an intentional wrongdoer could rely on his insurers'
discharging his civil liability to his victim, because a person who is not deterred by the risk
of perhaps long imprisonment for his act is not going to be deterred by the fear of civil
liability to his victim: *Hardy* v. *Motor Insurers' Bureau* [1964] 2 Q.B. 745, 770, *per*
Diplock L.J.

[52] *White* v. *Blackmore* [1972] 2 Q.B. 651, 668.

[53] *Executor Trustee and Agency Co. Ltd.* v. *Hearse* [1961] S.A.S.R. 51, 54, *per* Chamberlain
J.

[54] *Skelton* v. *Collins* (1966) 39 A.L.J.R. 480, 494, *per* Windeyer J. Indeed, fears have been
expressed that damages might become excessively high with the result (a) that insurance
premiums would become so heavy that business would become impossible, and (b) that
small insurance companies would be ruined: *Heaps* v. *Perrite Ltd.* [1937] 2 All E.R. 60,
61, *per* Greer L.J.; *Fletcher* v. *Autocar and Transporters Ltd.* [1968] 2 Q.B. 322, 335, *per*
Lord Denning M.R.

[55] Atiyah, *Accidents, Compensation and the Law* (2nd ed.), p. 238.

insured,[56] but this is considered now an "old fashioned rule"[57] and it is frequently openly recognised that the defendant will be insured.[58]

Such a recognition is inevitable in certain areas because Parliament has decreed that insurance must be effected. For instance, the Employers' Liability (Compulsory Insurance) Act 1969 requires each employer to maintain an approved policy of insurance with an authorised insurer against liability for bodily injury or disease sustained by his employees and arising out of and in the course of their employment. Third party insurance cover is also compulsory in respect of nuclear installations, dangerous wild animals, riding establishments, and oil pollution from merchant ships. The most common instance of compulsory insurance is, of course, motorists' third party cover. The Road Traffic Act 1972, ss. 143 and 145, require every person who uses a vehicle on a road to take out a policy of insurance indemnifying him in respect of the death of or bodily injury to any person caused by, or arising out of, the use of a vehicle on a road. As well, a third person who suffers bodily injury as a result of the tortious act of the insured is, by section 207, given a direct right of action against the insurers, provided that the liability of the insured is first established.[58] Indeed, the real defendants in most tortious litigation are insurance companies, since 70 per cent. of the cases decided annually in the High Court are cases arising from personal injury caused by road accidents.

Insurance has also resulted in a reduction of litigation. As a matter of practice, English insurance companies contest in court only 1 per cent. of claims made against them; the rest they settle.[59] An uninsured defendant may well consider that he has little to lose by forcing the plaintiff to prove his case in court; even to settle may mean to him financial ruin, and so the risk of going to trial, with the possibility of staving off defeat by some means or other, is often worth running. Insurance companies almost invariably settle claims brought against their clients because any sum paid to plaintiffs can ultimately be recouped from the company's premium-paying no-policy-holders. As well, they have great experience in assessing what the outcome of a trial is likely to be.

So far, we have been talking principally of liability (or third party) insurance. Liability insurance provides compensation to a person injured by the insured if he can establish the insured's liability. Thus, such insurance is essentially parasitic; nothing is payable until the insured's legal liability in tort is proved. But there is another kind of insurance which is quite independent of tort and which is seen by some as the eventual successor of tort: this is loss insurance, sometimes called self-insurance or first party insurance. A person may take out a policy of insurance providing for benefits in the event of his death or personal injury. In short, liability insurance provides protection for tortfeasors; loss insurance provides

---

[56] *Davie* v. *New Merton Board Mills Ltd.* [1959] A.C. 604, 627.

[57] *Morey* v. *Woodfield* [1963] 3 All E.R. 533n.

[58] *Post Office* v. *Norwich Union Fire Insurance Society Ltd.* [1967] 2 Q.B. 363, 368; *Morgans* v. *Launchbury* [1973] A.C. 127.

[59] Report of the Royal Commission on Civil Liability and Compensation for Personal Injury, Cmnd. 7054 (1978) (hereinafter termed "Pearson Report"), para. 180. Because there is always some risk in any claim, the defendant's insurers often exploit this and make a discount in settlement offers: see Phillips and Hawkins, "Some Economic Aspects of the Settlement Process: A Study of Personal Injury Claims" (1976) 39 M.L.R. 497.

protection for those injured. Loss insurance is rarely compulsory. The main exception to that is the national insurance scheme, which provides benefits to those who suffer injuries at work. Each worker pays a contribution to this insurance; his employer and the state provide additional contributions.[60] In practice too, although not legally, householders with mortgages must insure against damage by fire: the effecting of such a policy is invariably stipulated by mortgagees. New Zealand's accident compensation scheme is in essence a system of compulsory loss insurance of a far-reaching kind. Because of that scheme's pervasiveness, a person's right to sue in tort if he suffers personal injury as the result of an accident was considered superfluous and has been abolished.[61]

The Royal Commission on Civil Liability and Compensation for Personal Injury (the Pearson Commission) thought that a scheme of general compulsory insurance would not be feasible. One real practical difficulty is the enforcement of compulsory insurance; all the present requirements for compulsory insurance are linked to a system of licensing or certification. Not all could afford the premiums for compulsory loss insurance; further, objection might justifiably be taken to a person's being compelled to insure against harm from risks caused by others. All-embracing compulsory liability insurance would seem irrational in that it would mean that the primary disadvantage of tort—namely, the enormous cost of operating the system—would remain, while its principal advantage—namely, that the wrongdoer pays for the consequences of his wrong—would disappear. The Pearson Commission did recommend, however, that, where compulsory insurance was now required, it should continue to be so required, and that consideration should be given to its imposition in respect of exceptional risks[62] and private aircraft.[63] Better the Commission thought to develop further the social security system and the relationship with tort than to expand by legislation the role of insurance, other than in certain defined areas posing special risks.

(2) Social security and other forms of state compensation

Of even greater significance than insurance has been the development this century of social security and other forms of state compensation. The breakaway from dependence on tort came in 1897, in the field of industrial accidents. The Workmen's Compensation Act of that year introduced the concept of liability without fault and the provision of cash benefits as of right and without a test of means. From that Act has developed the modern industrial injuries scheme, which provides various state benefits for those unable to work or disabled as a result of an accident "arising out of or in the course of" employment or because of a prescribed disease related to the nature of such employment.[64] Compensation under this scheme is paid each year in over 600,000 new cases of work injury and disease; the total annual cost is about £250 million. By comparison, only £70 million is paid each

---

[60] See below, § 180.
[61] See Pearson Report, where all the previous literature is collected; see too D.K. Allen (ed.) *Accident Compensation after Pearson* (1979), pp. 180–196.
[62] Pearson Report, para. 1668.
[63] *Ibid.* para. 1141.
[64] Annex 4 of the Pearson Report gives a useful summary of all the current social security benefits.

year in respect of work injuries to some 90,000 people through the tort system.[65]

In 1964 Great Britain[66] set up a non-statutory scheme[67] to provide compensation for those who suffer personal injuries[68] which are directly attributable to a crime of violence (including arson and poisoning), or to an arrest or attempted arrest of an offender or suspected offender, or to the prevention or attempted prevention of any offence. If the victim dies, his spouse or dependents may claim. There is no legal claim to a grant of compensation, but the Board[69] which administers the scheme makes awards within the framework laid down by the document establishing the scheme. Many awards are for comparatively small sums, but, to avoid trivial claims, no compensation is payable unless the injury was one for which damages of not less than £250 would be awarded. The award may be reduced because of the applicant's conduct, but any immunity of an offender attributable to his youth or insanity is left out of account. There is no right of appeal, but decisions of the Board are subject to *certiorari*.

On top of this, there is the vast network of social security benefits. Measures aiming at no more than the bare relief of extreme poverty have given place to a system in which cash benefits are provided as of right, together with comprehensive medical services and supporting social services to meet a wide variety of contingencies. At any one time, almost 20 million social security benefits, pensions and allowances are being paid in the United Kingdom. In the course of a year, about 11 million people receive sickness and injury benefit.[70]

The effect of this cornucopia of state compensation has been fully investigated by the Pearson Commission.[71] The Commission recommended that the tort system should be retained, despite widespread criticisms of its expensiveness,[72] because of its deterrent effect and because "[t]here is an elementary justice in the principle of the tort action that he who has by his fault injured his neighbour should make reparation".[73] Yet, at the same time, it acknowledged that "social security should be regarded as the primary

---

[65] Pearson Report, para. 772. The money paid under the tort system will nearly all come from insurance companies, of course, for there is now a statutory obligation on employers to insure against their liability for personal injury to their employees: Employer's Liability (Compulsory Insurance) Act 1969. The employer's liability is very wide; he is liable for not only his own negligence, but also the negligence of his employees towards one another, and even now for personal injury to employees caused by defects in equipment provided by him, even if the defect is attributable wholly or partly to the fault of a third party, for example a manufacturer or repairer: Employers' Liability (Defective Equipment) Act 1969.

[66] For Ireland, see Prl. 3658 (1974).

[67] See further, Atiyah, *Accidents, Compensation and the Law* (3rd ed.) Chap. 13.

[68] So damage to or loss of property is excluded.

[69] Its address is: 10 Russell Square, London WC1. In 1976–1977, there were 13,951 awards, with payments amounting to about £9.7 million.

[70] Pearson Report, Chap. 5.

[71] For some of the literature analysing the Commission's report, see Fleming, "The Pearson Report: Its Strategy" (1979) 42 M.L.R. 249; Marsh, "The Pearson Report on Civil Liability and Compensation for Death or Personal Injury" (1979) 95 L.Q.R. 513; Tunc, (1978) 30 *Revue International de Droit Comparé* 507; *Winfield & Jolowicz*, pp. 33–41; D. K. Allen (ed.), *Accident Compensation after Pearson* (1979).

[72] The operating costs of the tort system amount to about 86 per cent. of the value of tort compensation payments, or about 45 per cent. of the combined total of compensation and operating costs; by comparison, the cost of administering social security benefits for injured people is about 11 per cent. of the value of compensation payments, or 10 per cent. of the cost of payments and administration: Pearson Report, paras. 83, 121.

[73] Pearson Report, paras. 245–263.

method of providing compensation."[74] The Commission saw the need for an extension of the "no-fault" form of state compensation in certain select areas.[75] For injuries arising in the work-place, it advocated the continuance of the industrial injuries scheme, with higher benefits. It suggested a similar no-fault compensation scheme for injuries caused by motor vehicles; road injuries were singled out largely because they occur on a scale not matched by any other category of accidental injury within the Commission's terms of reference[76] and because they are particularly likely to be serious. At present, only about a quarter of those injured by motor vehicles recover tort compensation.[77] The Commission recommended the retention of the criminal injuries compensation scheme, although it thought it ought to be put on a statutory basis.[78]

The Commission's approach may be criticised on the ground that it is piecemeal and lacks any clear vision for the future course of compensation for accidents sickness. This is undoubtedly because the report is a compromise: there were three schools of thought within the Commission, one wanting a no-fault scheme covering all accidents, a second looking forward to the eventual disappearance of the tort system once it had been seen how the social security system could cope with the demands which the present recommendations if enacted would put upon it, and the third school hoping that there would always be a place for the tort system, whatever happened to no-fault provision.[79]

On the other hand, the report may be praised for coming to terms with the relationship of tort with social security and other forms of state compensation. For the first time, a clear guideline has been given as to how tort and state compensation should co-exist. At present, certain social security benefits are partially offset against any damages assessed for loss of income due to personal injury, but the general rule remains that benefits accruing to the plaintiff as a result of an accident are not to be deducted from his award of damages. As the Pearson Commission commented, "[t]he overall scope for the duplication of compensation is substantial".[80] Atiyah has noted that the principal beneficiaries of double compensation are those who are entitled to industrial injuries benefit, because of all the victims of accident and disease, they are treated most generously by both the tort system and the socal security system.[81] The reason for the overlap stems undoubtedly from the fact that tort and social security approach the problem of compensation from different perspectives, and neither has sufficiently taken into account the implications of the other. The Pearson Commission recommended that the full value of social security benefits payable to an injured person or his

[74] *Ibid.* para. 275.
[75] The Commission rejected a no-fault scheme covering all injuries as being outside its terms of reference (para. 239); this was perhaps an unnecessarily cautious construction of the terms of reference, as the Lord Chancellor had said, at the time of appointing the Commission, that it was within the terms of reference of the Royal Commission to consider the sort of all-embracing no-fault scheme adopted in New Zealand: Official Report (HL) December 19, 1972, Vol. 337, col. 976, cited in Pearson Report, Annex 1 (p. 391).
[76] Accidents in the home (which the Commission did not consider) account for injuries to about a million people in Britain each year.
[77] Pearson Report, para. 994.
[78] *Ibid.* para. 1591.
[79] *Ibid.* Chap. 33.
[80] *Ibid.* para. 172.
[81] Atiyah, *Accidents, Compensation and the Law* (3rd ed.), p. 464. Professor Atiyah's discussion of the "plethora of systems" (Chap. 18) is worthy of detailed reading.

dependants as a result of an injury for which damages are awarded should be deducted in the assessment of the damages.[82] By a majority, the Commission recommended that social security benefits should be divided into three categories—loss of earnings, expenses, and non-pecuniary loss; the benefits in each category should then be deducted in assessing the corresponding portion of the tort award.[83] As a further recognition of the influence of social security, the Commission recommended that damages for future pecuniary loss should no longer continue to be awarded on a lump sum basis, at least in cases where the accident has caused death or serious and lasting injury; instead, the compensation should be in the form of periodic payments.[84]

Thus, the Commission's Report acknowledged, not only that the social security system was already the main source of compensation, but also that it should play a greater role in the future. The tort system must at last recognise its new neighbour, and tortious damages should be awarded subject to social security benefits, so that duplication of compensation might be prevented. On the other hand, tort should be retained, if only in a reserve capacity as a means of preserving the common law principle of *restitutio in integrum*.[85] In the final analysis, it may be said that the report is a realistic document in the light of current political and economic circumstances,[86] and that all those in favour of change towards greater justice in compensating the injured should support it, even if on the basis that half a loaf is better than no bread at all. It seems unlikely, however, that there will be any early enactment of the major recommendations of the Commission.[87]

§ 8. LIABILITY WITHOUT FAULT

In certain cases, liability is independent of intention or negligence. Liability in libel does not depend on the intention of the defamer, but on the fact of defamation; so too there is strict liability for damage done by a wild animal, or by the escape of dangerous things accumulated for some non-natural purpose (the rule in *Rylands* v. *Fletcher*); again, liability is strict when one is vicariously responsible for the acts of another. In cases such as these the security of the particular interest of the plaintiff is predominant over the defendant's interest in freedom of action. It is a mistake, however, to think of the predominance as complete. In appropriate cases defences such as act

---

[82] Parliament has followed this recommendation when enacting the Vaccine Damage Payments Act 1979. Section 6 (4) provides that the receipt of the £10,000 lump sum payable under the Act does not prejudice the recipient's right to institute or carry on civil proceedings, but the Court must treat that payment as paid on account of any damages which the Court awards in respect of the disablement. But Parliament did not impose strict liability on the public authority which recommend the vaccination.

[83] Pearson Report, Chap. 13.

[84] *Ibid.* Chap. 14. The insurance industry has doubted its ability to provide such periodic payments: D. K. Allen (ed.), *Accident Compensation after Pearson*, p. 125.

[85] By preserving tort, the Commission thought that it would be assured that the injured received their just deserts, for there would be a separate body—"the independent courts of the realm"—to ensure that any statutory tariff was fair and sufficient in any particular case.

[86] The net cost of the Commission's proposals was estimated to be only £41 million a year, even though a new no-fault scheme for road accidents, improved benefits under the industrial injuries scheme, and a new benefit for severely handicapped children were recommended. This low figure is largely accounted for by savings in the administration of the tort system and by the avoidance of duplication of compensation.

[87] H. of C., November 17, 1978, cols. 771–875.

of God or act of a third party are available. Liability may be strict but it is never absolute.

Salmond also included under this heading two other matters: inevitable mistake and inevitable accident.

(1) Inevitable mistake

Inevitable or unavoidable mistake is commonly no defence against civil liability. Any act of wilful interference with the property, person, reputation, liberty, or other right of another on a supposed justification is done at the doer's peril; and if the justification does not in truth exist, a belief in its existence, however honest and reasonable, is no defence. Although the term inevitable mistake has been criticised,[88] it seems apt to cover cases in which the consequences of the actor's conduct were intended, but he did not appreciate that those consequences constituted an invasion of another's legally protected interest.[89] It makes no difference in such a case whether the mistake is one of fact or one of law. To this general principle of absolute liability for mistake the law recognises some exceptions, there being certain cases in which it would work such hardship or interfere so seriously with the exercise of lawful activities that it is necessary to relax it. Thus the mistaken prosecution of an innocent man is not in itself an actionable wrong; for such a rule would effectually impede the administration of the criminal law. A prosecutor incurs no liability unless he acted both maliciously and without reasonable cause.[90]

(2) Inevitable accident

Inevitable mistake must be distinguished from inevitable accident. The plea of inevitable mistake is that, although the act and its consequences were intended, the defendant acted under an erroneous belief, formed on reasonable grounds, that some circumstances existed which justified him. The plea of inevitable accident is that the consequences complained of as a wrong were not intended by the defendant and could not have been foreseen and avoided by the exercise of reasonable care and skill.[91]

An accident in its popular sense is any unexpected injury resulting from any unlooked-for mishap or occurrence.[92] In law a happening is only regarded as an accident if it is one out of the ordinary course of things, something so unusual as not to be looked for by a person of ordinary prudence.[93] So an ordinary fall of snow is not an accident, but only an incident which happens in the ordinary course of things.[94] One form of inevitable accident is that which is due to an act of God,[95] as when a car-driver has a sudden affliction, such as a stroke.[96] The driver will not be liable if his actions were wholly beyond his control.[97]

There is no general principle that inevitable accident is a good defence. In

---

[88] Landon found it "unintelligible": (1945) 61 L.Q.R. 205.
[89] As in *Consolidated Co.* v. *Curtis* [1892] 1 Q.B. 495, (see below, § 30).
[90] See below, § 155.
[91] *McBride* v. *Stitt* [1944] N.I. 7, 10.
[92] *Fenton* v. *Thorley & Co.* [1903] A.C. 443, 451.
[93] *Makin* v. *L. and N.E. Ry.* [1943] 1 All E.R. 362, 364–365.
[94] *Fenwick* v. *Schmalz* (1868) L.R. 3 C.P. 313, 316.
[95] *Makin* v. *L. and N.E. Ry.* [1943] K.B. 467, 475, 478.
[96] *Waugh* v. *Allan (J. K.) & Sons Ltd.*, 1964 S.C. 162.
[97] *Roberts* v. *Ramsbottom* [1980] 1 W.L.R. 823.

actions of trespass it is now settled (after some hesitation) that it may be pleaded as a defence; but it will probably succeed only if the defendant had in truth no control over the act which caused the damage.[98] In torts of strict liability (*e.g.* under the rule in *Rylands* v. *Fletcher*) only the special form of inevitable accident known as act of God (or possibly the uncontrollable act of a third party) affords a good defence. In actions in which negligence has to be proved by the plaintiff, the plea of inevitable accident may sometimes be tantamount to saying that the defendant has not failed to observe the standard of care required of him. Hence a court may well prefer to say that the defendant was not negligent rather than that he has affirmatively proved inevitable accident.[99] So in an action of negligence it is not necessary for the defendant to show that the accident was inevitable in the strictest sense—that is to say, incapable of being prevented at all, or only by the exercise of extraordinary care and skill. If a man drives a motor-car, and in spite of the exercise of all reasonable care on his part an accident happens, he may plead that it was due to inevitable accident; and it will be no answer to this plea to prove that if he had altogether refrained from those dangerous forms of activity it would not have ensued.[1]

Finally, a point of pleading should be noted—in an action of trespass, inevitable accident must be specifically pleaded; but in an action of negligence, evidence of inevitable accident, or the negligence of a third party, may be given when a general denial is pleaded.[2] It is then in substance not a separate defence but merely a denial of negligence.[3]

§ 9. PROVINCE AND FUNCTION OF TORTS[4]

The preceding discussion has enabled us to form some conclusions. First, the law of torts is not a static body of rules, but is capable of alteration to meet the needs of a changing society. One word of warning should be added. It is often rather hastily assumed that any desirable alteration in the law of torts must result in the expansion of the field of liability. But social needs may require contractions as well as expansion.[5] Thus it can hardly be doubted that the courts have been justified in refusing to introduce new heads of tortious liability to enable a witness to be sued for perjury,[6] or conspiracy to defame.[7] Equally Parliament was justified when it used three words ("Detinue is abolished") in section 5(2)(i) of the Torts (Interference with Goods) Act 1977 to abolish a tort which had existed for six centuries.[8] Again a tort may be invented or discovered only to have little use made of it. So for a century little has been heard of the action[9] for excluding the plaintiff from a public office to which he is legally entitled.

---

[98] See below, § 46.
[99] *McBride* v. *Stitt* [1944] N.I. 7, 14.
[1] *Cutler* v. *United Dairies* [1933] 2 K.B. 297, 305.
[2] *McKnight* v. *McLaughlin* [1963] N.I. 34. See an admirable note in (1963) 15 N.I.L.Q. 571.
[3] *Jockel* v. *Jockel* (1963) S.R. (N.S.W.) 230.
[4] See Fleming, *Introduction to the Law of Torts* (Oxford, 1967); Williams and Hepple, *Foundations of the Law of Tort* (1976).
[5] *Gallagher* v. *McDowell Ltd.* [1961] N.I. 26, 44.
[6] *Hargreaves* v. *Bretherton* [1959] 1 Q.B. 45.
[7] *Marrinan* v. *Vibart* [1963] 1 Q.B. 528.
[8] "It is not every day that the Lord Chancellor can have the pleasure of abolishing a tort": 378 H.L. col. 1060.
[9] Recognised in *Lawlor* v. *Alton* (1873) 8 Ir.Reb.C.L. 160.

Secondly, it is not possible to find a general formula or criterion which will at once explain all the cases in which liability has been imposed in the past and also furnish a guide for the decision of doubtful cases in the future. If reasonable foresight was ever believed to provide such a criterion, the belief has now been abandoned.[10] It is now recognised that the decision of a court to impose liability in tort may be influenced by a number of factors, of which one or more may be of decisive importance in the particular case, and that the most profitable inquiry is likely to be into the nature and significance of these factors. The Law Lords have shown themselves increasingly ready and willing to state and assess the various considerations of public policy which influence them in marginal cases.[11] Still, too much reliance should not be placed on isolated dicta[12]: the common law is shaped as much by the way it is practised as by dicta.[13] Thirdly, it should be remembered that other factors besides the value of the plaintiff's interest and the nature of the defendant's conduct may be relevant. We have already had examples of four such factors: (i) historical development; (ii) vengeance; (iii) deterrence; (iv) ability to bear the loss. A fifth factor is the economic and social background of the case. So the action by a master for the loss of the services of his servant was at one time regarded with increasing suspicion but is now felt to have some value.[14] "In the end one is left in the slack water of first principles."[15]

§ 10. EMERGENT TORTS

There are a number of cases in which the courts have displayed willingness to create new heads of liability. No more can be done here than to indicate the present state of development of four of these doubtful torts: (1) Invasion of privacy; (2) Abuse of statutory powers; (3) Infringement of status; (4) Intention and malice.

(1) Invasion of privacy[16]

English lawyers have always been sceptical about the effectiveness of general declarations for the protection of rights. So English law probably[17] does not, and in the view of the Younger Committee[18] should not, recognise any general right of privacy. But the right to privacy is recognised by the overwhelming majority of American courts, whose decisions have been analysed by Prosser under four different headings which are adopted here for the sake of convenience.

First, the tort covers cases in which there has been an intrusion upon the plaintiff's seclusion or solitude, or into his private affairs. This head of liability has obvious affinities with the present law governing trespass to the

---

[10] See below, § 74.
[11] See, *e.g. Mutual Life Co.* v. *Evatt* [1971] A.C. 793; *Dorset Yacht Co. Ltd.* v. *Home Office* [1970] A.C. 1004; *Anns* v. *Merton B.C.* [1978] A.C. 728.
[12] *West (Richard) and Partners Ltd.* v. *Dick* [1969] 2 Ch. 424, 431–432.
[13] *Jayasena* v. *R.* [1970] A.C. 618, 625.
[14] See below, §§ 128–129.
[15] *Gunton* v. *Richmond B.C.* [1980] 3 W.L.R. 714, at 722, *per* Shaw L.J.
[16] The Report of the Younger Committee on Privacy (Cmnd. 5012 (1972)) contains a full bibliography, to which add Wacks, "The Poverty of Privacy" (1980) 96 L.Q.R. 73.
[17] See the conflicting dicta in *Re X (A Minor)* [1975] Fam. 47, 58, and *Malone* v. *Metropolitan Police Commissioner* [1979] Ch. 344.
[18] Cmd. 5012 (1972), paras. 44 and 92.

person or property,[19] or nuisance,[20] or breach of copyright or infringement of patents or trade marks,[21] or the intentional infliction of emotional distress. English law gives an adequate remedy in these cases, usually civil but sometimes criminal,[22] subject to the qualification that the plaintiff must first bring his claim within the four corners of the recognised tort or crime. For example, it may be the tort of nuisance to telephone another unreasonably often,[23] or to subject him to constant aerial surveillance,[24] but as the plaintiff in nuisance must have a proprietary interest, this means that a guest in a house as distinct from the occupier could not complain of such conduct. A plaintiff may also obtain aggravated and, in a few cases, exemplary or vindictive damages if the conduct of the defendant has been outrageous or disgraceful[25] But the common law gives no remedy to one who complains that his neighbours have spied from their windows into his premises, or have cut off an attractive view from his house by erecting a spite-fence.[26] No recognised tort has been committed. Nor again is any remedy at present given to one who complains that his photograph (or other likeness) has been taken and reproduced without his permission[27] unless the publication is defamatory,[28] and it must be remembered that truth is a defence to an action for libel.[29] Nor does there seem to be any civil remedy for the interception of telephonic or other conversations,[30] or for industrial espionage.

On the other hand, the courts have borrowed features from property, equity, contracts, torts and bailments to create a jurisdiction to restrain by injunction the publication of confidential information, whether the source of the confidence is commercial, marital,[31] or even political,[32] if there has been a breach of good faith,[33] as distinct from a breach of contract,[34] unless it is in the public interest that the truth be known.[35] It has even been held that damages may be awarded independently of any claim for equitable relief,[36] or that "a search warrant in disguise" may be granted.[37]

There is clearly a need for some development if the right of individual freedom is to be safeguarded properly in the age of such scientific achieve-

---

[19] So in *Sheen* v. *Clegg, Daily Telegraph*, June 22 1961, damages for trespass were awarded against a defendant who had secretly installed a microphone over the plaintiff's marital bed. See below, § 11.
[20] See below, § 18.
[21] See below, § 151.
[22] *Kamara* v. *D.P.P.* [1974] A.C. 104.
[23] See below, § 18.
[24] *Bernstein* v. *Skyviews Ltd.* [1978] Q.B. 479, 489 ("monstrous invasion of privacy").
[25] *Cassell & Co. Ltd.* v. *Broome* [1972] A.C. 1027.
[26] See below, § 22.
[27] See Greer L.J. in *Tolley* v. *Fry* [1930] 1 K.B. 467, 478.
[28] *See* Pannam *"Unauthorised Use of Names or Photographs in Advertisements"* (1966) 40 Austr.L.J. 4.
[29] As it was in *Dunlop Rubber Co. Ltd.* v. *Dunlop* [1921] 1 A.C. 367. See below, § 54. *Funston* v. *Pearson, The Times*, March 12, 1915, was cited in previous editions of this book as an authority to the contrary, but Scrutton J. clearly rested his decision on the fact that it was defamatory to publish a photograph of a young lady without any teeth.
[30] *Malone* v. *Metropolitan Police Commissioner* [1979] Ch. 344. In Working Paper No. 63. the Law Commission refer to possible criminal offences.
[31] *Argyll* v. *Argyll* [1967] Ch. 302.
[32] *Att.-Gen.* v. *Jonathan Cape Ltd.* [1976] Q.B. 752.
[33] *Fraser* v. *Evans* [1969] 1 Q.B. 349.
[34] See the full discussion in Cmnd. 5012 (1972), Appendix 1, and Law Commission Working Papers Nos. 58 and 63.
[35] *Woodward* v. *Hutchins* [1977] 1 W.L.R. 760.
[36] *Seager* v. *Copydex Ltd.* (*No.* 2) [1969] 1 W.L.R. 809.
[37] *Anton Piller KG* v. *Manufacturing Processes Ltd.* [1976] Ch. 55.

ments as micro-miniature radio transmitters, subliminal and subaudial projection of images, truth drugs, the tape-recorder, telescopic cameras and television. Indeed the Superior Court of Quebec has awarded damages on the following facts. The plaintiff wrote to a television company to complain about the quality of one of their programmes. The announcer displayed the plaintiff's name and address on the screen and invited listeners to write or telephone to the plaintiff saying what they thought of his conduct. The resultant barrage of offensive letters and telephone calls was so great that the plaintiff was obliged to disconnect his telephone and suffered severe inconvenience and worry.[38]

Secondly, there are cases in which complaint is made about the public disclosure of embarrassing private facts about the plaintiff—for example, that he does not pay his debts. In the leading American case the defendant published to the world an account of the plaintiff's earlier career as a prostitute and the accused in a sensational murder trial. The plaintiff, who had quite left aside her earlier life of shame and now moved in reputable society, recovered damages.[39] Until the Rehabilitation of Offenders Act 1974 the defendants would have had the defence of justification if sued for libel in such a case in England.

Thirdly, there are cases relating to defendants who place the plaintiff in a false light in the public eye by publishing untrue statements about him. Here there will sometimes be a remedy under the law of defamation,[40] or copyright,[41] or passing off.[42]

Fourthly, there are cases in which the defendant has appropriated for his own purposes some attribute of the plaintiff's name or identity.[43] The law does not prevent any person from calling himself by the name of another, so long as he has no fraudulent purpose in doing so.[44] There is, however, some protection given in cases where a proprietary interest has been infringed, as we shall see later from the law governing the use of trade names and trade marks and copyright.[45]

(2) Abuse of statutory powers

There is a recognised tort of misfeasance in a public office.[46] Therefore damage caused by the excessive[47] or malicious[48] or negligent[49] exercise of

---

[38] *Robbins* v. *C.B.C.* (1958) 12 D.L.R. (2d) 35.
[39] *Melvin* v. *Reid* (1931) 112 Cal.App. 285, 297 Pac. 91.
[40] *Ridge* v. *The English Illustrated Magazine* (1913) 29 T.L.R. 592.
[41] Copyright Act 1956, s. 43, which specifically gives a cause of action for false attribution of authorship. The only reported case is *Moore* v. *News of the World Ltd.* [1972] 1 Q.B. 441.
[42] *Byron* v. *Johnston* (1816) 2 Mer. 29. As Pollock said (R.R. Vol. 16, Preface, v): "Lord Eldon has been often called hard names (unduly, as most lawyers think) for depriving Shelley of the custody of his truly begotten children: I am not aware that the world of letters has ever given him due credit for helping Byron to repudiate the spurious offspring which some pirate bookseller sought to father on him.".
[43] This may be on the verge of recognition as a distinct tort: *Athens* v. *Canadian Adventure Camps Ltd.* (1977) 80 D.L.R. 583.
[44] See below, § 150.
[45] See below, § 151.
[46] *Tampion* v. *Anderson* [1973] V.R. 715.
[47] *Warne* v. *Varley* (1795) 6 T.R. 443.
[48] *David* v. *Abdul Cader* [1963] 1 W.L.R. 834 does no more than suggest there may be a remedy. *Roncarelli* v. *Duplessis* [1952] 1 D.L.R. 680 definitely grants one, but as in *David* v. *Abdul Cader*, the court was applying the civil law, not the common law. On this ground the cases were distinguished in *Campbell* v. *Ramsay* [1966] 2 N.S.W.R. 431.
[49] The law is in a state of rapid development since *Anns* v. *Merton B.C.* [1978] A.C. 728. See below, § 191.

statutory powers by a public authority or public officer[50] is actionable. On the other hand, a statute may make the performance of a contract impossible. So a Minister who announces that it is government policy so to legislate cannot be sued for inducing a breach of contract.[51] This is an area of the law which may see some developments. In the present age it is of great importance that statutory powers of licensing and control should be exercised honestly and fairly. The public law remedies of the prerogative orders may need to be reinforced by an action for damages, and some constitutions provide for a claim for compensation in public law which is distinct from a tort.[52]

(3) Infringement of a status

In the modern world a person may suffer serious loss by reason of his expulsion from a trade union or trade association, or the revocation of a licence which is necessary to carry on his trade or profession. The courts in England[53] and in Ireland[54] are aware of the problem, and over the past few decades there has been a marked trend towards shielding the employee from undue hardships suffered at the hands of those who have power over his livelihood.[55] Therefore on occasion the remedies of damages or injunction or declaratory judgment are available[56] for an improper expulsion in breach of the principles of justice and fairness, even if the rules of the union purport to give an unfettered power of expulsion.[57] Yet no action is given for a refusal to admit to membership,[58] however unreasonable and however productive of loss to the plaintiff,[59] unless perhaps the refusal is by a self-appointed body with a monopoly in that trade or profession.[60] But there may be a remedy for discrimination on the grounds of race or sex under the Race Relations Act 1976 or the Sex Discrimination Act 1975.

(4) Intention and malice

It has already been noticed that there may be an emergent tort of causing loss by unlawful means.[61] An eminent judge has also suggested, both judicially[62] and extra-judicially,[63] that a tort of malicious interference with business or livelihood might be developed. The suggestion deserves more consideration. The jurisdiction to restrain breaches of confidence may be based on this notion.

---

[50] *Farrington* v. *Thomson* [1959] V.R. 286.
[51] *Roman Corporation Ltd.* v. *Hudson's Bay Oil and Gas Co. Ltd.* (1973) 36 D.L.R. (3d) 413.
[52] *Maharaj* v. *Att.-Gen of Trinidad and Tobago* [1979] A.C. 385.
[53] *McInnes* v. *Onslow Fare* [1978] 1 W.L.R. 1520.
[54] *Murphy* v. *Stewart* [1973] I.R. 97.
[55] *Hill* v. *Parsons (C. A.) & Co. Ltd.* [1972] Ch. 305.
[56] *Bonsor* v. *Musicians' Union* [1956] A.C. 105; *Vine* v. *National Dock Labour Board* [1957] A.C. 488.
[57] *Edwards* v. *Society of Graphical and Allied Trades* [1971] Ch. 354.
[58] As distinct from renewing membership: *McInnes* v. *Onslow Fare* [1978] 1 W.L.R. 1520.
[59] *Faramus* v. *Film Artistes' Association* [1964] A.C. 925.
[60] *Nagle* v. *Feilden* [1966] 2 Q.B. 633.
[61] *Rookes* v. *Barnard* [1964] A.C. 1129, 1216, *per* Lord Devlin.
[62] *Samples of Lawmaking* (Oxford, 1962), pp. 11–13.
[63] See above, § 4, and below, § 133.

(5) EEC Torts

Under Articles 85 and 86 of the Treaty of Rome conduct constituting undue restriction of competition and abuse of dominant position may be tort in England.[64]

---

[64] *Application des Gaz S.A.* v. *Falks Veritas Ltd.* [1974] Ch. 381.

CHAPTER 3

TRESPASS TO LAND

§ 11. The Nature of Trespass to Land

THE tort of trespass to land (trespass *quare clausum fregit*) consists in the act of (1) entering upon land in the possession of the plaintiff, or (2) remaining upon such land, or (3) placing or projecting any object upon it—in each case without lawful justification.

(1) Trespass by wrongful entry

The commonest form of trespass consists in a personal entry by the defendant, or by some other person through his procurement, into land or buildings occupied by the plaintiff. The slightest crossing of the boundary is sufficient—*e.g.* to put one's hand through a window, or to sit upon a fence. Nor, indeed, does it seem essential that there should be any crossing of the boundary at all, provided that there is some physical contact with the plaintiff's property.[1] There may be sufficient physical interference if matter is deliberately placed where natural forces will carry it to the land of the plaintiff—*e.g.* if oil is jettisoned in such circumstances that wind and wave must carry it to the foreshore of the plaintiff.[2] The courts have taken account of scientific developments, and the matter constituting a trespass probably need not be tangible—it may be a gas.[3] But depriving an occupier of facilities—*e.g.* gas and electricity—without interfering with his possession is not a trespass[4] or statutory tort, as distinct from a breach of contract.[5]

Trespass to land, like all other forms of trespass, is actionable *per se* without any proof of damage.[6] "Every invasion of property, be it ever so minute, is a trespass."[7] These principles have been part of English law for centuries. So the fundamental right of privacy of the home has been re-asserted by the House of Lords.[8] If the entry is intentional, it is actionable[9] even though made under an inevitable mistake of law or fact and even though the defendant honestly believed that the land was his own or that he had a right

---

[1] *Gregory* v. *Piper* (1829) 9 B. & C. 591. ("If a single stone had been put against the wall it would have been sufficient.").

[2] *Southport Corporation* v. *Esso Petroleum Ltd.* [1953] 3 W.L.R. 773, 776–777 (Devlin J.); [1954] 2 Q.B. 182, 204 (Morris L.J.); *contra*, [1954] 2 Q.B. 182, 195 (Denning L.J.); [1956] A.C. 242, 244 (Lords Radcliffe and Tucker). See Newark, Note (1953) 17 M.L.R. 580.

[3] *McDonald* v. *Associated Fuels* [1954] 3 D.L.R. 775.

[4] *Perera* v. *Vandiyar* [1953] 1 W.L.R. 672.

[5] *McCall* v. *Abelesz* [1976] Q.B. 585.

[6] *Ashby* v. *White* (1703) 2 Ld.Raym. 938. But in criminal law actual damage must be shown for a prosecution to succeed under the Criminal Damage Act 1971. Hence the notice "Trespassers will be Prosecuted" is "a wooden falsehood": Maitland, *Justice and Police* (1883), p. 13. But there may be a conviction under the Criminal Law Act 1977: see below, Chap. 25.

[7] *Entick* v. *Carrington* (1765) 19 St.Tr. 1029, 1066.

[8] *Morris* v. *Beardmore* [1980] 2 All E.R. 753.

[9] But not necessarily a criminal entry "as a trespasser" under the Theft Act 1968, s. 9 (1): *R.* v. *Collins* [1973] Q.B. 100.

[10] *Basely* v. *Clarkson* (1681) 3 Lev. 37 (in mowing his own land the defendant by mistake mowed grass on the plaintiff's adjoining land); *Hewlitt* v. *Bickerton* (1947) C.L.C. 10504 (no right to trespass on another's land to repair one's own buildings).

of entry on it.[10] There is no foundation for the assumption that a man cannot be a trespasser unless he knows he is one.[11] An action of trespass may also be used to determine a disputed title to land, though today a declaratory judgment may be preferred.

Accidental trespasses

Whether an accidental as opposed to a mistaken entry is actionable is open to doubt. The Statute of Limitations 1623, s. 5, enacts that in all actions of trespass *quare clausum fregit* the defendant may plead a disclaimer of any title or claim to the land, that the trespass was by negligence or involuntary, and a tender or offer of sufficient amends before action brought, in which case the plaintiff is barred of his action. This seems to imply that an involuntary trespass is actionable if no amends are tendered. The statute has been very strictly construed.[12] The ordinary rambler in the country trespasses by mistake, not involuntarily. But in *Beckwith* v. *Shordike*[13] it seems to have been the opinion of the court that it might be a good defence to prove that the trespass was accidental and involuntary, for example, trespass by one's dog. As it now seems settled that inevitable accident is a defence in actions of trespass to the person and to chattels[14] it would be strange if a different rule governed trespass to land.[15]

Statutory rights of entry

It must not be forgotten that many modern statutes confer a right of entry upon private property,[16] in addition to the older common law powers of entry.[17] Thus the National Parks and Access to the Countryside Act 1949, s. 60, provides that "where an access agreement or order is in force as respects any land a person who enters upon land comprised in the agreement or order for the purpose of open-air recreation without breaking or damaging any wall, fence, hedge or gate, or who is on such land for that purpose after having so entered thereon, shall not be treated as a trespasser on that land or incur any other liability by reason only of so entering or being on the land."[18] The Law Commission has recommended that landowners should have a statutory right of access to neighbouring land to do work on their own property.[18a]

Trespass by abuse of right of entry: highways

Even he who has a right of entry on the land of another for a specific purpose commits a trespass if he enters for any other purpose[19] or under any other claim or title apart from that under which he might lawfully

---

[11] *Conway* v. *Wimpey & Co.* (*No.* 2) [1951] 2 K.B. 266, 273.
[12] *Basely* v. *Clarkson* (1681) 3 Lev. 37; Williams, *Animals*, p. 196.
[13] (1767) 4 Burr. 2092.
[14] *National Coal Board* v. *Evans* (*J. E.*) & *Co. Ltd.* [1951] 2 K.B. 861, discussed below, § 46.
[15] *Mann* v. *Saulnier* (1959) 19 D.L.R. (2d) 130, 132.
[16] Below, § 97.
[17] For examples of these, see below, § 97.
[18] Such a person may, however, incur liability if he fails to observe any of the 15 restrictions on user set out in the Second Schedule to the Act, or any restriction contained in the access agreement or order itself.
[18a] See Working Paper No. 78 (1980).
[19] *Strong* v. *Russell* (1904) 24 N.Z.L.R. 916.

enter.[20] The chief application of this rule is the abuse of a right of way, public or private; but presumably the same principle applies to all rights of entry—for example, to one given by a contract or licence containing conditions[21]—e.g. that the entrant should not take photographs. So far as abuse of a right of way is concerned, a public highway is a piece of land vested either in some local authority or in the adjoining landowners and subject to a public right of way. The law vests in the highway authority the top spit, "or perhaps, I should say, the top two spits,"[22] of the road for a legal estate in fee simple determinable on its ceasing to be a highway. Any person who uses a highway for any purpose other than that of passage (including the subordinate purposes reasonably and ordinarily incident to passage, such as sitting down to rest[23] or perhaps even to sketch[24]) becomes a trespasser against the owner[25] of the subsoil.[26] Thus it is a trespass to depasture one's cattle on the highway,[27] or to go there for the purpose of interfering with the adjoining occupier's right of shooting,[28] or of persistently watching what is being done on the adjoining land,[29] or of picketing premises,[30] unless protected by the Trade Union and Labour Relations Act 1974, s. 15.[31]

So it is a trespass to put down permanent moorings in tidal waters.[32] Again it is a trespass against the Crown to use the foreshore for the purpose of bathing in the sea, for the only right of the public on the foreshore is the right to pass over it in boats when it is covered by water for the purposes of fishing[33] and navigating. The public have no general right of way along the foreshore.[34] It is not necessary that the thing so done in abuse of the right of entry should be the cause of any harm to the occupier of the land or to anyone else. It is enough that it falls outside the purpose for which the right is conferred. But if the act done on the land is within that purpose, it does not matter what ulterior object the defendant may have in exercising his right of entry. Thus it is not a trespass to walk along a highway with the object of committing a crime elsewhere.[35] Moreover, even a wrongful act done upon

---

[20] *Purtill* v. *Athlone U.D.C.* [1968] I.R. 205, 210.

[21] *Gross* v. *Wright* [1923] 2 D.L.R. 171, and the cases on trespass *ab initio*, below, § 15.

[22] *Tithe Redemption Commission* v. *Runcorn U.D.C.* [1954] Ch. 383, 407, *per* Denning L.J.

[23] Or parking a car for some temporary and limited purpose: *Rodgers* v. *Ministry of Transport* [1952] 1 T.L.R. 625; *Randall* v. *Tarrant* [1955] 1 W.L.R. 255.

[24] See *Liddle* v. *Yorkshire* (*North Riding*) *C.C.* [1934] 2 K.B. 101, 127.

[25] But it does not follow that other persons using the highway are thereby relieved of any duty to take reasonable care for the trespasser's safety: *Farrugia* v. *G.W. Ry.* [1947] 2 All E.R. 565. Yet see *Young* v. *Edward Box Ltd.* [1951] 1 T.L.R. 789, 793.

[26] *Hickman* v. *Maisey* [1900] 1 Q.B. 752. It is not clear how far this principle has survived; *Tithe Redemption Commission* v. *Runcorn U.D.C.* [1954] Ch. 383.

[27] *Dovaston* v. *Payne* (1795) 2 H.Bl. 527.

[28] *Harrison* v. *Rutland* (*Duke of*) [1893] 1 Q.B. 142.

[29] *Hickman* v. *Maisey* [1900] 1 Q.B. 752. It does not seem that the defendant in this case (unlike *Harrison* v. *Rutland*) owned the subsoil of the highway. *Cf. The Carlgarth* [1927] P. 93, 107–108, where Scrutton L.J. said: "There is no right to sit in the middle of a road and say one is exercising a right to use a public roadway."

[30] *Ferguson* v. *O'Gorman* [1937] I.R. 620; *Hubbard* v. *Pitt* [1976] Q.B. 142.

[31] For this, see below, § 134.

[32] *Fowley Marine Ltd.* v. *Gafford* [1967] 2 Q.B. 808, 823 (not challenged on appeal in [1968] 2 Q.B. 618).

[33] *Beckett Ltd.* v. *Lyons* [1967] Ch. 449.

[34] *Blundell* v. *Catterall* (1821) 5 B. & Ald. 268; *Brinckman* v. *Matley* [1904] 2 Ch. 313, 323 (in which Vaughan Williams L.J. observed that the judgment of Holroyd J. in *Blundell* v. *Catterall* "has come to be regarded as one of the finest examples we have of the way in which the judgment of an English judge ought to be expressed, and the reasons for it given").

[35] *Harrison* v. *Rutland* (*Duke of*) [1893] 1 Q.B. 142, 158.

the land itself does not make the defendant a trespasser within the present rule, unless it can be shown that he entered for that purpose. If he entered for a lawful purpose, he is no trespasser unless the case is one to which the doctrine of trespass *ab initio* applies.[36]

Ejectment

Any person wrongfully dispossessed of land may sue for the specific restitution of it in an action of ejectment. Originally this action was a special variety of trespass and available only to leaseholders. But in time and by the aid of the most elaborate fictions it came to be used by freeholders also.[37] All these fictions have now been swept away; in theory even the term ejectment has been replaced by the term action for the recovery of land. The older term is, however, retained in practice.

(2) Trespass by remaining on land

Even a person who has lawfully entered on land in the possession of another commits a trespass if he remains there after his right of entry has ceased. To refuse or omit to leave the plaintiff's land or vehicle[38] is as much a trespass as to enter originally without right. Thus any person who is present by the leave and licence of the occupier may, as a general rule, when the licence has been properly terminated, be sued or ejected as a trespasser, if after request and after the lapse of a reasonable time he fails to leave the premises.[39] A reasonable degree of force may be used to control the movements of a trespasser or to eject him.[40] This must be distinguished from the case of a person lawfully in possession of land who refuses or omits to give it up on the termination of his lease or other interest. A lessee holding over is no trespasser until demand made; for a trespass can be committed, as we shall see, only against the person in the present possession of the property.[39]

(3) Trespass by placing things on land

It is a trespass to place any thing upon the plaintiff's land,[42] or to cause any physical object or noxious substance[43] to cross the boundary of the plaintiff's land, or even simply to come into physical contact with the land, though there may be no crossing of the boundary: for example, to turn cattle upon the land, or to throw stones upon it, or to drive nails into a wall, to cause a Virginia creeper to grow upon it,[44] or to lean a ladder, planks or a shed, or to pile rubbish against it.[45]

Trespass and nuisance

In all such cases, in order to be actionable as a trespass, the injury must be direct, within the meaning of the distinction between direct and conse-

---

[36] *Hickman* v. *Maisey* [1900] 1 Q.B. 752, 757. See § 15.
[37] For details, see Holdsworth, H.E.L., iii, pp. 213–217; vii, pp. 4–23.
[38] *C.P.R.* v. *Gaud* [1949] 2 K.B. 239 (ship).
[39] *Cottreau* v. *Rodgerson* (1966) 53 D.L.R. (2d) 549, 557. See also § 23.
[40] See below, § 46.
[41] *Hey* v. *Moorhouse* (1839) 6 Bing.N.C. 52.
[42] *Turner* v. *Thorne* (1960) 21 D.L.R. (2d) 29 (parcels delivered in error).
[43] *McDonald* v. *Associated Fuels* [1954] 3 D.L.R. 775 (blowing carbon monoxide into a house a trespass).
[44] *Simpson* v. *Weber* (1925) 41 T.L.R. 302.
[45] *Westripp* v. *Baldock* [1939] 1 All E.R. 279.

quential injuries which has been already explained as determining the line between trespass and case.[46] It is a trespass, and therefore actionable *per se*, directly to place material objects upon another's land; it is not a trespass, but at the most a nuisance or other wrong actionable only on proof of damage, to do an act which consequentially results in the entry of such objects. To throw stones upon one's neighbour's premises is the wrong of trespass; to allow stones from a ruinous chimney to fall upon those premises is the wrong of nuisance.[47]

§ 12. CONTINUING TRESPASSES

That trespass by way of personal entry is a continuing injury, lasting as long as the personal presence of the wrongdoer, and giving rise to actions *de die in diem* so long as it lasts, is sufficiently obvious.[48] It is well settled, however, that the same characteristic belongs in law even to those trespasses which consist in placing things upon the plaintiff's land. Such a trespass continues until it has been abated by the removal of the thing which is thus trespassing; successive actions will lie from day to day until it is so removed: and in each action damages (unless awarded in lieu of an injunction)[49] are assessed only up to the date of the action.[50] Whether this doctrine is either logical or convenient may be a question, but it has been repeatedly decided to be the law.[51] It seems that, if things are placed on land under leave and licence and are not removed within a reasonable time after the licence is withdrawn, a continuing trespass is committed.[52] These cases of continuing trespass must be distinguished from cases of the continuing consequences of trespass which is over and done with. If I trespass on another's land, and make an excavation there without leaving any rubbish on the land, the trespass ceases as soon as I leave the land, and does not continue until I have filled the excavation up again. Consequently only one action will lie, and in it full damages are recoverable for both the past and the future.[53]

§ 13. TRESPASS BENEATH AND ABOVE THE SURFACE

In general he who owns or possesses the surface of land owns or possesses all the underlying *strata* also.[54] Any entry beneath the surface, therefore, at whatever depth, is an actionable trespass.[55] Where the possession of the surface has become separated from that of the subsoil (as by a conveyance of the subsoil for mining purposes, reserving the surface) any infringement of the horizontal boundary thus created is a trespass. It is also commonly said that the ownership and possession of land bring with them the ownership and possession of the column of space above the surface *ad infinitum*. *Cujus*

---

[46] See above, § 2.
[47] *Mann* v. *Saulnier* (1959) 19 D.L.R. (2d) 130, 132.
[48] *Winterbourne* v. *Morgan* (1809) 11 East 395, 405.
[49] *Masters* v. *Brent B.C.* [1978] Q.B. 841.
[50] Below, § 219.
[51] *Bowyer* v. *Cooke* (1847) 4 C.B. 236.
[52] *Konskier* v. *B. Goodman & Co. Ltd* [1928] 1 K.B. 421. Compare the case of persons entering under licence: below, § 23.
[53] *Clegg* v. *Dearden* (1848) 12 Q.B. 576.
[54] *Corbett* v. *Hill* (1870) L.R. 9 Eq. 671, 673.
[55] *Willcox* v. *Kettel* [1937] 1 All E.R. 222 (intrusion of concrete foundation by 20 inches a trespass).

est solum, ejus est usque ad coelum et usque ad inferos.[56] This is true to this extent, that the owner of the land has in private law the right to use for his own purposes, to the exclusion of all other persons, the air-space above it. He may build the Tower of Babel if he pleases, and may remove all things situated above the surface, even though they are the property of others, and though their presence there does him no harm and is no wrong for which he has any right of action against the owners. Thus he may cut the overhanging branches of a tree growing in his neighbour's land, whether they do him harm or not[57]; yet he has no right of action against the owner of the tree unless he can show actual damage.[58] So he may cut and remove an unauthorised telegraph or other electric wire stretched through the air above his land, at whatever height it may be, and whether he can show that he suffers any harm or inconvenience from it or not.[59]

All entries actionable

It ought not to follow from this that any entry above the surface is in itself an actionable trespass. Salmond thought[60] that such an extension of the rights of a landowner would be an unreasonable restriction of the right of the public to the use of the atmospheric space above the earth's surface. It would make it an actionable wrong to fly a kite, or send a message by a carrier pigeon, or ascend in an aeroplane, or fire a bullet across it,[61] even in cases where no actual or probable damage, danger, or inconvenience could be proved by the subjacent landowners. In his submission there could be no trespass without some physical contact with the land (including, of course, buildings, trees, and other things attached to the soil), and a mere entry into the air-space above the land was not an actionable wrong unless it caused some harm, danger, or inconvenience to the occupier of the surface, when there was a cause of action in the nature of nuisance.[62] But it has been held that a direct infringement of the air-space over another man's land is a trespass,[63] so that the owner of a one-storey shop was entitled to a mandatory injunction requiring the removal of an advertising sign protruding by no more than eight inches into the super-incumbent column of air-space. But in that case the sign was at a height at which it might have interfered with the owner's use of his land.

Aircraft, spacecraft and weather

In respect of aeroplanes and other aircraft this matter is now dealt with by statute. By section 40 of the Civil Aviation Act 1949 it is provided that "no action shall lie in respect of trespass or in respect of nuisance, by reason only of the flight of an aircraft over any property at a height above the

---

[56] Co.Litt. 4a; *Corbett* v. *Hill* (1870) L.R. 9 Eq. 671. "Law makes long spokes of the short stakes of men," was the comment of the poet William Empson: *Cambridge Poetry* (1929).
[57] *Lemmon* v. *Webb* [1895] A.C. 1.
[58] *Smith* v. *Giddy* [1904] 2 K.B. 448. Below, § 228.
[59] *Wandsworth Board of Works* v. *United Telephone Co.* (1884) 13 Q.B.D. 904, 927.
[60] 6th ed., p. 226.
[61] As in the Tasmanian cat case (*Davies* v. *Bennison* (1927) 22 Tas.L.R. 52) in which the defendant shot a cat on the plaintiff's roof. The plaintiff was held entitled to damages for trespass to land as well as for the value of the cat.
[62] Salmond's view was adopted by Griffiths J. in *Bernstein* v. *Skyviews Ltd.* [1978] Q.B. 479, 487, after a full review of the authorities.
[63] *Kelsen* v. *Imperial Tobacco Co. Ltd.* [1957] 2 Q.B. 334.

ground, which, having regard to wind, weather and all the circumstances of the case, is reasonable, or the ordinary incidents of such flight,[64] so long as" certain provisions of the Act[65] or any orders made thereunder are observed.[66] The Act does not expressly exclude the possibility of damages being recovered for such an invasion of privacy as aerial photography of one's house.[67] The same section of the same Act, however, makes the owner of aircraft liable for all material loss or damage caused by it, or by a person in, or by an article or person falling from it, while in flight, taking off,[68] or landing, whether to person or property, "without proof of negligence or intention or other cause of action, as if the loss or damage had been caused by the wilful act, neglect, or default of the owner of the aircraft," except where there is contributory negligence, and gives the owner a right of action over against the person whose negligence actually caused the damage.

Liability for damage done by spacecraft is governed by international law which recognises strict liability.[69]

§ 14. THE TITLE OF THE PLAINTIFF

A trespass is actionable only at the suit of him who is in possession of the land, using the word possession in its strict sense as including a person entitled to immediate and exclusive possession.[70] Actual entry by the true owner is not necessary to enable him to bring trespass, for as against a wrongdoer the slightest acts indicating an intention to regain or obtain possession,[71] by the person having title, or his predecessors, will be sufficient.[72] Where it is uncertain which of several claimants has possession, it will be adjudged to be in him who can prove title, *i.e.* the right to possess.[73] This may seem hard on a plaintiff who can show considerable actual use of the premises, but whose paper title is defective, unless the court can interpret the acts done by the party or parties not having the paper title as not amounting to the assertion of a possessory right.[74] This tort is essentially a violation of the right of possession, not of the right of property. Ownership unaccompanied by possession is protected by other remedies.[75] Thus a landlord cannot sue for a mere trespass to land in the occupation of his tenant; such an action can be brought only by the tenant.[76] The landlord has no right of action unless he can prove more than a mere trespass—*viz.* actual harm done to the property, of such sort as to affect the value of his reversionary interest in it.[77]

For the same reason the mere use of land, without the exclusive posses-

---

[64] In short, the Act gives legislative force to Salmond's view, but this implies that the common law did not adopt that view.
[65] In Ireland, the Air Navigation Act 1936, s. 55.
[66] By S.I. No. 289 of 1970 s. 40 has been applied to aircraft in the service of Her Majesty, "not being military aircraft".
[67] Cmnd. 5012 (1972), para. 396.
[68] See *Blankley* v. *Godley* [1952] 1 All E.R. 436n.
[69] See the 1972 Convention on Liability for Space Objects. Liability for damage caused by weather modification is fully discussed by Heilbronn in (1979) 6 Mon. L.R. 122.
[70] *Thompson* v. *Ward* [1953] 2 Q.B. 153, 158–159.
[71] *Ocean Estates Ltd.* v. *Pinder* [1969] 2 A.C. 19.
[72] *Portland Managements Ltd.* v. *Harte* [1977] Q.B. 306.
[73] *Hegan* v. *Carolan* [1916] 2 I.R. 27.
[74] *Fowley Marine (Emsworth) Ltd.* v. *Gafford* [1968] 2 Q.B. 618.
[75] *Wallis* v. *Hands* [1893] 2 Ch. 75.
[76] *Attersoll* v. *Stevens* (1808) 1 Taunt. 183, 190.
[77] See below, § 41.

sion of it, is not a sufficient title to found an action of trespass for the disturbance of that use. Thus, in general a lodger or boarder has no possession of the room in which he is lodged, and cannot sue in trespass for any disturbance of his use of it.[78] So with a guest at an inn or in a private house, or with a domestic servant or other member of a household. So also with the use of a seat in a theatre or a railway carriage[79] or the right to post advertisements on a wall or hoarding. Whether a person having thus the use of land without the possession of it has any remedy at all against a stranger who disturbs him is a question which we shall consider later.[80] In the meantime it is enough to note that he cannot sue as for a trespass to land, or exercise the rights of self-help available in the case of trespassers.[81] The purchaser, however, of a standing crop or of other things attached to land and removable by the purchaser acquires by his purchase a sufficient possession to enable him to bring an action of trespass for injury to the thing so purchased: as, for example, when damage is done by cattle straying from adjoining land through defective fences.[81]

Jus tertii no defence

The mere *de facto* and wrongful possession of land is a valid title of right against all persons who cannot show a better title in themselves, and is therefore sufficient to support an action of trespass against such persons. Just as a legal title to land without the possession of it is insufficient for this purpose, so conversely the possession of it without legal title is enough. In other words, no defendant in an action of trespass can plead the *jus tertii*—the right of possession outstanding in some third person—as against the fact of possession in the plaintiff.[83] It is otherwise, of course, if the defendant is himself the lawful owner[84] or has done the act complained of by the authority, precedent or subsequent, of him who is thus rightfully entitled.

The same rule holds good in an action of ejectment where the defendant has committed a trespass against the plaintiff. If, therefore, the plaintiff is in possession the *jus tertii* will afford the defendant no answer to the action.[85] But usually the plaintiff in an action of ejectment is not in possession: he relies upon his right to possession, unaccompanied by actual possession. In such a case, he must recover by the strength of his own title, without any regard to the weakness of the defendant's. The result, therefore, is that in an action of ejectment the *jus tertii* is in practice a good defence.[86] To the rule that it is in practice a good defence in ejectment there are two exceptions, or rather, applications of the general principle that the *jus tertii* is no defence: (1) Whenever a person has acquired possession through another whose title is defective, he cannot set up this defect against that other or anyone claiming through him,[87] although he may show that such title has since expired or

[78] *Allan* v. *Liverpool Overseers* (1874) L.R. 9 Q.B. 180, 191–192.
[79] *Lane* v. *Dixon* (1847) 3 C.B. 776, 784.
[80] Below, § 23.
[81] Below, § 56.
[82] *Wellaway* v. *Courtier* [1918] 1 K.B. 200.
[83] *Nicholls* v. *Ely Beet Sugar Factory* [1931] 2 Ch. 84.
[84] *Delaney* v. *T. P. Smith Ltd.* [1946] K.B. 393, 397.
[85] *Davison* v. *Gent* (1857) 1 H. & N. 744.
[86] *Doe* d. *Carter* v. *Barnard* (1849) 13 Q.B. 945.
[87] *Doe* d. *Johnson* v. *Baytup* (1835) 3 A. & E. 188.

been parted with.[88] This is an application of the principle of estoppel. The commonest instance is that the lessee is estopped from denying his lessor's title. (2) Probably, if the defendant's possession is wrongful as against the plaintiff, the plaintiff may succeed though he cannot himself show a good title.[89] For possession is prima facie evidence of title. If such prima facie evidence is not displaced by proof of title in a third person the plaintiff with prior possession will recover,[90] although this has been doubted.[91]

Trespass by relation

He who has a right to the immediate possession of land, and enters in the exercise of that right, is then deemed by a legal fiction to have been in possession ever since the accrual of his right of entry, and may accordingly sue for any trespass committed since that time. This is known as the doctrine of trespass by relation, because the plaintiff's possession relates back to the time when he first acquired a right to the possession. Thus a person wrongfully disseised of his land may after re-entry sue for any trespass committed on the land during the period of his dispossession. So a lessee may sue for a trespass done between the granting of the lease and his entry in pursuance of it. So a landlord entitled to re-enter after the termination of the lease may after re-entry sue for any trespass committed since the lease determined.[92] We shall see how the action for mesne profits in case of dispossesion is founded on the same rule of trespass by relation.[93]

Trespass as between co-owners

One tenant in common or joint tenant of land cannot sue his co-tenant in trespass or ejectment unless the act of the defendant amounts either to the total exclusion or ouster of the plaintiff or to destructive waste of the common property.[94] For each of the co-tenants is entitled to the possession of the land, to use it in a proper manner, and to take from it the fruits and profits of that user. If one of the owners receives from the common property a larger share of the profits than that to which he is entitled, this is no tort against the other owner, but the proper remedy is an action for an account.

§ 15. TRESPASS AB INITIO

In 1610 six carpenters entered the Queen's Head Inn, Cripplegate, and consumed a quart of wine (7d.) and some bread (1d.), for which they refused to pay. The question for the court was whether their non-payment made the entry tortious, so as to enable them to be sued in trespass *quare clausum*

---

[88] *Claridge* v. *MacKenzie* (1842) 4 M. & G. 142.

[89] *Davison* v. *Gent* (1857) 1 H. & N. 744.

[90] *Fowley Marine (Emsworth) Ltd.* v. *Gafford* [1968] 2 Q.B. 618.

[91] Wiren, "The plea of *jus tertii* in Ejectment" (1925) 41 L.Q.R. 139; Hargreaves, "Terminology and Title in Ejectment" (1940) 56 L.Q.R. 376; Holdsworth, (1940) 56 L.Q.R. 479.

[92] But only if the defendant is in possession wrongfully. Apparently for that reason the principle does not apply where a tenant is in possession under a lease after a breach of covenant until the landlord determines the lease by some such act as the issue of a writ: *Elliott* v. *Boynton* [1924] 1 Ch. 236. But see Denning, "Re-entry for Forfeiture" (1927) 43 L.Q.R. 53.

[93] Below, § 208.

[94] *Murray* v. *Hall* (1849) 7 C.B. 441.

fregit. The court held that[95]: "When entry, authority or licence is given to any one by the law, and he doth abuse it, he shall be a trespasser *ab initio*," but that the defendants were not liable as their non-payment did not constitute a trespass.

The rule is that the authority, having been abused by doing a wrongful act under cover of it, is cancelled retrospectively so that the exercise of it becomes actionable as a trespass. The rule is primarily one of procedure, the effect of it under the old practice being that a writ of trespass would lie for the entry or seizure itself, instead of a writ of trespass or of case for the subsequent abuse only. In this respect the rule has now lost its significance; but its secondary effect upon the substantive law still remains—*viz.* that it enables the plaintiff to recover damages for the entire transaction, and not merely for the wrongful portion of it.[96] The rule has been abolished by statute in the case of distress for rent[97] (but not for distress damage feasant) but otherwise it still exists,[98] though it is regarded with suspicion, the doctrine of relation back not being favoured.[99]

Limits of the rule

(1) The rule applies only to acts done in pursuance of an "entry, authority, or licence given to anyone by the law." "Where an entry, authority, or licence is given by the party, and he abuses it, there he must be punished for his abuse, but shall not be a trespasser *ab initio*. And the reason of this difference is, that in the case of a general authority or licence of law, the law adjudges by the subsequent act, *quo animo*, or to what intent, he entered; for *acta exteriora indicant interiora secreta*."[1] (2) The rule applies only when the subsequent abuse amounts to a positive wrongful act, as opposed to a mere omission or non-feasance. Thus in the *Six Carpenters' Case* itself it was resolved that the defendants were not trespassers *ab initio* merely because they refused to pay for the quart of wine and the pennyworth of bread which they bought and consumed in the plaintiff's inn.[2] (3) A lawful entry does not become by abuse a trespass *ab initio*, unless that abuse has reference to and so takes away the entire ground and reason of the entry. If there remains any independent ground or reason of entry, which is unaffected by the abuse, it will suffice to justify the entry and protect it from the rule of trespass *ab initio*.[3] Thus in *Elias* v. *Pasmore*[4] police constables lawfully entered premises to arrest one of the plaintiffs and whilst on the premises took possession of a large number of documents, some

---

[95] (1610) 8 Co.Rep. 146a. See Holdsworth, H.E.L., vii, pp. 498–501; Williams, "A Strange Offspring of Trespass ab initio" (1936) 52 L.Q.R. 106; Williams, *Animals*, pp. 97–100.

[96] *Oxley* v. *Watts* (1785) 1 T.R. 12.

[97] Distress for Rent Act 1737, s. 19 which creates a new statutory tort of irregular distress.

[98] *Cinnamond* v. *British Airports Authority* [1980] 1 W.L.R. 582, 588.

[99] *Chic Fashions (West Wales) Ltd.* v. *Jones* [1968] 2 Q.B. 299. But the rule was originally designed to provide a remedy against abuses of authority which might lead to the oppression of the subject: Holdsworth, H.E.L., vii, p. 500; and it might still be useful for this purpose: Denning, *Freedom under the Law*, p. 109.

[1] *Six Carpenters' Case* (1610) 8 Co.Rep. 146a.

[2] To work a horse which has been lawfully seized damage feasant is not in itself a trespass, but it makes the distrainor a trespasser *ab initio*: *Oxley* v. *Watts* (1785) 1 T.R. 12.

[3] *Chic Fashions (West Wales) Ltd.* v. *Jones* [1968] 2 Q.B. 299.

[4] [1934] 2 K.B. 164. If such cases are carried out to their logical consequences they cut down considerably the doctrine of trespass *ab initio* as it was understood in the time of the *Six Carpenters*.

rightfully, some wrongfully. It was held that they were trespassers only as to the documents which were wrongfully taken, and that they were not liable as trespassers *ab initio* for damage to the premises which they had lawfully entered for the purpose of the arrest.

CHAPTER 4

NUISANCE

§ 16. THREE KINDS OF NUISANCE[1]

(1) Statutory Nuisance

Every statutory nuisance is a criminal offence created by statute. Certain statutory nuisances are defined in the Public Health Act 1936,[2] which gives wide powers to local authorities, having obtained an order from a Magistrate's Court, to put an end to anti-social conduct amounting to a nuisance. Such enforcement orders may be very effective in practice, but they do not give rise to claims for damages, they are not considered here. Not every statutory nuisance is a public nuisance,[3] or, of course, a private nuisance.

(2) Public Nuisance

A public or common nuisance is a criminal offence. It is an act or omission which materially affects the reasonable comfort and convenience of life of a class of Her Majesty's subjects.[4] It is not necessary to establish that every member of the public, as distinct from a representative cross-section, has been affected.[5] The question whether the number of persons affected is sufficient to be described as a class is one of fact. One test is to ask whether the nuisance is so widespread in its range or indiscriminate in its effect that it would not be reasonable to expect one person to take proceedings to stop it as distinct from the community at large.[6] Examples of the crime of public nuisance are organising a festival of pop music which generates large-scale noise, traffic, and apprehension,[7] obstructing a highway,[8] or making it dangerous for traffic. Public nuisances are met by an indictment or by an action by the Attorney-General or a local authority[9] where an injunction is desired to put an end to the public nuisance.

Public and private nuisances are not in reality two species of the same genus at all. There is no generic conception which includes the crime of keeping a common gaming-house and the tort of allowing one's trees to overhang the land of a neighbour. A public nuisance falls within the law of torts only in so far as it may in the particular case constitute some form of

---

[1] See Holdsworth, H.E.L., iii, pp. 153–157; vii, pp. 324–342; viii, pp. 424–425; Newark, "The Boundaries of Nuisance", (1949) 65 L.Q.R. 480 (an article commended by Lord Simonds in *Jacobs* v. *L.C.C.* [1950] A.C. 361, 374); Eekelaar, "Nuisance and Strict Liability", (1973) 8 Ir.Jur. 191; Magnet, "Intentional Interference with Land", in *Studies in Canadian Tort Law* (1977), p. 287.
[2] See especially § 92.
[3] *Salford City Council* v. *McNally* [1976] A.C. 379, 390.
[4] *Att.-Gen.* v. *P.Y.A. Quarries Ltd.* [1957] 2 Q.B. 169, 184.
[5] *Att.-Gen. for Ontario* v. *Orange Productions Ltd.* (1971) 21 D.L.R. (3d) 257.
[6] *Att.-Gen.* v. *P.Y.A. Quarries Ltd.* [1957] 2 Q.B. 169, 191.
[7] *Att.-Gen. for Ontario* v. *Orange Productions Ltd.* (1971) 21 D.L.R. (3d) 257. For England, see the Second Report of the Working Group on Pop Festivals (H.M.S.O. 1978); a licensing system is recommended.
[8] This is considered in detail below, § 25.
[9] Local Government Act 1972, s. 222; and see *Solihull Metropolitan Borough Council* v. *Maxfern Ltd.* [1977] 1 W.L.R. 127.

tort also. Thus the obstruction of a highway is a public nuisance; but if it causes any special and peculiar damage to an individual, it is also a tort actionable at his suit. This tort has more in common with the tort based on breach of a statutory duty than with the tort of private nuisance.[10]

(3) Private nuisance

The generic conception involved in private nuisance[11] may really be found in the fact that liability in nuisance flows from an act or omission whereby a person is annoyed, prejudiced or disturbed in the enjoyment of land, whether by physical damage to the land or by other interference with the enjoyment of the land or with his exercise of an easement, profit or other similar right or with his health, comfort or convenience as occupier of such land.[12] Nuisance is really a field of tortious liability rather than a single type of tortious conduct: the feature which gives it unity is the interest invaded—that of the use and enjoyment of land. The tort emphasises the harm to the plaintiff rather than the conduct of the defendant.[13] Thus a judicial definition which has often been cited with approval is the following: "Private nuisances, at least in the vast majority of cases, are interferences for a substantial length of time by owners or occupiers of property with the use or enjoyment of the neighbouring property".[14]

It will be seen that "nuisance" even in the private nuisance context is an ambiguous word—sometimes it refers to the conduct of the defendant, sometimes to the results of that conduct, and sometimes to such results of that conduct as are actionable.[15] It is sometimes said that the basis of the law of nuisance is the maxim *sic utere tuo ut alienum non laedas*: a man must not make such use of his property as unreasonably and unnecessarily to cause inconvenience to his neighbour.[16] This maxim has also been called "mere verbiage"[17] and there is much in this criticism. It suggests, for instance, that any "use" of land is actionable if it results in harm to a neighbour's land, but that is inaccurate: if a "use" is ordinary and reasonable, there is no liability on the defendant for the harm caused to the plaintiff. But the maxim does encapsulate neatly the two principal features of the nuisance action, namely that liability springs from a condition on the

---

[10] The tort based on the crime of public nuisance will be discussed at the end of this chapter (§ 25) but that is not intended to imply any connection between public nuisance and private nuisance.

[11] The explanation of this threefold meaning of the nuisance is that in its origin it was merely a generic expression meaning wrongful harm, and that although it has now lost this wide signification it has failed to attain instead any specific application. The term is derived, through the French, from the late Latin *nocentia*: see Tertull Apol., Cap. 40—*Deus innocentiae magister nocentiae judex*. Chaucer used it in this generic sense. "Itelpe me for to weye ageyne the feende ... Keepe us from his nuisance.": (Mother of God, I, 21). Nuisance appears in the old Latin pleadings as *nocumentum*—*i.e.* harm. The terms trespass and tort, though similarly generic in their original use, have been more successful in the process of specification.

[12] *Hargrave* v. *Goldman* (1963) 110 C.L.R. 40, 62.

[13] *Gertsen* v. *Municipality of Toronto* (1973) 41 D.L.R. (3d) 646, 669.

[14] *Cunard* v. *Antifyre* [1933] 1 K.B. 551, 556–557; *Southport Corporation* v. *Esso Petroleum Co. Ltd.* [1956] A.C. 218, 224.

[15] See the (undelivered) judgment of Erle C.J. in *Brand* v. *Hammersmith Railway* (1867) L.R. 2 Q.B. 223, 247; Keeton, "Trespass, Nuisance and Strict Liability," (1959) 59 Col.L.Rev. 457, 464.

[16] *Aldred's Case* (1610) 9 Co. Rep. 57b, 59a; *Tenant* v. *Goldwin* (1704) 2 Ld.Raym. 1089, 1092; *Sedleigh-Denfield* v. *O'Callaghan* [1940] A.C. 880, 898.

[17] *Bonomi* v. *Backhouse* (1858) E.B. & E. 622, 643.

defendant's land and that protection is accorded to the plaintiff's enjoyment of his land.

§17. STATE OF AFFAIRS

As nuisance is a tort arising out of the duties owed by neighbouring occupiers, the plaintiff[18] cannot succeed if the act or omission complained of is on premises in his sole occupation. The nuisance must have arisen elsewhere than in or on the plaintiff's premises.[19] Liability in nuisance therefore usually arises from acts done on land in the occupation of the defendant, adjoining or in the neighbourhood of that of the plaintiff. The defendant need not necessarily be the owner or the occupier of that land; his liability will depend upon his degree of control in fact or in law for the state of affairs.

Nuisance is commonly a continuing wrong—that is to say, it consists in the establishment or maintenance of some state of affairs which continuously or repeatedly causes the escape of noxious things onto the plaintiff's land (e.g. a stream of foul water, or the constant noise or smell of a factory).[20] An escape of something on a single occasion would not ordinarily be termed a nuisance, although there is no reason in principle why it should not be.[21] If a neighbouring occupier's land or the buildings thereon are damaged by an errant cricket ball from a club ground on only a few occasions, the occupier may still maintain an action in nuisance.[22] The gist of the claim in nuisance is not the isolated act of hitting a ball on to the neighbouring land but the organising or carrying on of a game on property adjacent to the neighbouring land whereby the enjoyment of that land is rendered dangerous. The fact that balls reach that land only very occasionally is evidence that no dangerous state of affairs exists in the adjoining field. This approach enables us to explain cases of good authority in which the plaintiff has recovered for damage caused by a single escape of dangerous thing—water,[23] gas,[24] metal foil,[25] or fire.[26] So it has been rightly pointed out that "an intermittent noise, particularly when it does not come at stated intervals, is likely to be more disagreeable than if it were constant".[27] It has never been seriously suggested that the plaintiff whose house has been flooded or blown up as a result of the defendant's activities can recover only for the second or subsequent but not the first of such incidents.[28] The truth is that all wrongful escapes of deleterious things, whether continuous, intermittent, or isolated, are equally capable of being classed as nuisances. The type of harm caused by the escape[29]; the gravity

---

[18] For co-occupiers as plaintiffs, see *Hooper* v. *Rogers* [1975] Ch. 43, 53.
[19] But see *Clearlite Holdings* v. *Auckland City Corporation* [1976] 2 N.Z.L.R. 729, criticised by Chambers, "Nuisance—Judicial Attack on Orthodoxy," [1978] N.Z.L.J. 172.
[20] *Cunard* v. *Antifyre* [1933] 1 K.B. 551, 556.
[21] *S.C.M. (United Kingdom) Ltd.* v. *W.J. Whittall & Son Ltd.* [1970] 2 All E.R. 417, 430.
[22] *Matheson* v. *Northcote College Board of Governors* [1975] 2 N.Z.L.R. 106; *Lester Travers* v. *Frankston* [1970] V.R. 2; but cf. *Miller* v. *Jackson* [1977] Q.B. 966.
[23] *Rylands* v. *Fletcher* (1866) L.R. 1 Ex. 265 is of course the model of such a case.
[24] *Midwood & Co. Ltd.* v. *Manchester Corporation* [1905] 2 K.B. 597; *Northwestern Utilities Ltd.* v. *London Guarantee and Accident Co. Ltd.* [1936] A.C. 108.
[25] *British Celanese Ltd.* v. *A.H. Hunt (Capacitors) Ltd.* [1969] 1 W.L.R. 959.
[26] *Spicer* v. *Smee* [1946] 1 All E.R. 489.
[27] *Rapier* v. *London Tramways Co.* [1893] 2 Ch. 588, 591. per Kekewich J.
[28] Yet see *Att.-Gen.* v. *P.Y.A. Quarries Ltd.* [1957] 2 Q.B. 169, 192.
[29] The law of nuisance has always been readier to remedy damage to property than personal injuries.

of that harm, and the frequency of its occurrence are each relevant (but not conclusive) factors in determining whether the defendant has maintained on his premises a state of affairs which is a potential nuisance.[30] This balancing process is the hallmark of the nuisance action, and distinguishes it from trespass as well as negligence.

§ 18. THE RIGHT TO ENJOYMENT OF LAND

(1) "Harm"

Nuisance is designed to protect an occupiers's right to the enjoyment of his land[31]: a man has suffered "harm" if that enjoyment is impaired.

A man's enjoyment of his land will be affected adversely if the land is physically damaged. Damage to the land might be caused by sewage collecting on it[32] or by rainwater flowing on to it from overhanging eaves.[33] If an occupier's property is flooded as a result of wrongful acts on neighbouring land, his enjoyment is thereby impaired, for he cannot use the land in some ways (as a result of the flood) in which he has a legal right to use it.[34] His enjoyment will similarly be impaired if vibrations from powerful engines on land nearby cause structural damage to his house[35] and the threat of such damage may be grounds for the granting of an injuction.[36] If a man cannot grow crops or trees because of noxious fumes, his enjoyment is obviously impaired[37]; so too if he cannot use part of his land as he would like because of encroachment by the roots and branches of a neighbour's tree.[38]

Perhaps the most common way in which liability accrues is the occupier's suffering personal discomfort as a result of the defendant's activities on his land. If one runs a pig-farm, neighbours may be deprived of their full enjoyment because of smell,[39] and brick-burning may be similarly offensive.[40] Unreasonable noise may deprive one's neighbour of sleep.[41] These examples may seem to show injuries of a purely personal nature, but that is to misconceive them. The plaintiff in each case succeeded because he was unable to use and enjoy his land to the extent to which he was entitled by law. Newark expressed it thus: "A sulphurous chimney in a residential area is

[30] *Matheson* v. *Northcote College Board of Governors* [1975] 2 N.Z.L.R. 106, 111.
[31] *Read* v. *J. Lyons & Co. Ltd.* [1945] K.B. 216, 236, *per* Scott L.J.; *Howard* v. *Walker* [1947] 2 All E.R. 197, 199; *Southport Corporation* v. *Esso Petroleum Co. Ltd.* [1954] 2 Q.B. 182, 196; *Hargrave* v. *Goldman* (1963) 37 A.L.J.R. 277, 283, *per* Windeyer J.; Newark, 65 L.Q.R. 480, 482.
[32] *Jones* v. *Llanrwst Urban Council* [1911] 1 Ch. 393.
[33] *Tucker* v. *Newman* (1839) 11 Ad. & E. 39, 113 E.R. 327.
[34] *Sedleigh-Denfield* v. *O'Callaghan* [1940] A.C. 880; *Pemberton* v. *Bright* [1960] 1 W.L.R. 436.
[35] *Meux's Brewery Co.* v. *City of London Electric Lighting Co.* [1895] 1 Ch. 287; *Hoare & Co.* v. *McAlpine* [1923] 1 Ch. 167.
[36] *Colwell* v. *St. Pancras Borough Council* [1904] 1 Ch. 707.
[37] *St. Helen's Smelting Co.* v. *Tipping*, 11 H.L.C. 642; *Salvin* v. *North Brancepeth Coal Co.* (1874) L.R. 9 Ch. 705; *Manchester Corporation* v. *Farnworth* [1930] A.C. 171.
[38] *Woodnorth* v. *Holdgate* [1955] N.Z.L.R. 552; *Davey* v. *Harrow Corporation* [1958] 1 Q.B. 60.
[39] *Bone* v. *Seale* [1975] 1 All E.R. 787.
[40] *Bamford* v. *Turnley* (1860) 3 B. & S. 62. See too *Halsey* v. *Esso Petroleum Co. Ltd.* [1961] 2 All E.R. 145 (smell of oil "nauseating") *Adams* v. *Ursell* [1913] 1 Ch. 269 (fried fish shop).
[41] *Shelfer* v. *City of London Electric Lighting Co.* [1895] 1 Ch. 287 (engines); *Metropolitan Properties Ltd.* v. *Jones* [1939] 2 All E.R. 202, 204 (badly installed heating apparatus).

not a nuisance because it makes householders cough and splutter but because it prevents them taking their ease in their gardens".[42]

It has also been held that an occupier's right to enjoyment is affected if his land, in its natural state, is let down because of activities on neighbouring land.[43] A riparian proprietor will have an action in nuisance if his right of flow or right of purity is impaired.[44] But a landowner has no right to the use of the air space above his property to an unlimited height.[45]

The right to enjoyment of one's land is, in effect, a catch-all right which comprises a number of subsidiary rights—e.g. the right to pure air, the right not to have one's land flooded—which may be added to by judicial decision. It is predicted that Buckley J.'s view that "the ability to receive television free from occasional . . . electrical interference is [not] so important a part of an ordinary householder's enjoyment of his property" that it ought to be protected will not stand for long.[46] It may be too that ultimately the courts will recognise a limited right to prospect or view: so far, except in one dictum,[47] the English courts have not been prepared to acknowledge an impairment of enjoyment in these circumstances.[48] But the aesthetic sensibilities of the public are increasing and the law should keep pace.

(2) Sensible damage

Not every slight loss of enjoyment will be actionable: there must be sensible damage, damage which can in some way or other be measured. While most physical damage to land will be "sensible," that cannot be automatically assumed. For instance, where water flowed on to a plaintiff's property but he suffered only a "trivial injury" because the additional water was never "substantial in flow or frequent in occurrence," his claim in nuisance failed: he failed to establish "damage of a material kind."[49] Similarly, not every minor subsidence of a neighbour's land will give rise to liability in nuisance; the harm must be "appreciable".[50] A riparian proprietor must have suffered a "sensible diminution" of the natural flow of a stream as a result of the defendant's abstraction of the water before prima facie liability is established.[51] In *Swindon Waterworks Co. Ltd.* v. *Wilts. and Berks. Canal Navigation Co.,* the appellants drained water out of a

---

[42] 65 L.Q.R. 480, 488.
[43] *Dalton* v. *Angus* (1881) 6 App. Cas. 740, 791, *per* Lord Selborne L.C.; *Mitchell* v. *Darley Main Colliery Co.* (1884) 24 Q.B.D. 125, 137, *per* Bowen L.J.; *West Leigh Colliery Co. Ltd.* v. *Tunnicliffe & Hampson Ltd.* [1908] A.C. 27, 31.
[44] *Young* v. *Bankier Distillery* [1893] A.C. 691, 698.
[45] *Baron Bernstein of Leigh* v. *Skyviews & General Ltd.* [1978] Q.B. 479.
[46] *Bridlington Relay Ltd.* v. *Yorkshire Electricity Board* [1965] Ch. 436, 447.
[47] *Thompson-Schwab* v. *Costaki* [1956] 1 All E.R. 652, 654, where Lord Evershed M.R. held that the defendant's use of his house as a brothel forced itself "on the sense of sight" of the plaintiffs and as such interfered with the comfortable enjoyment of their land. If hesitating men, importuning women, and red lights can affect a neighbour's enjoyment, why not junk yards?
[48] A right to a view was acknowledged in *Lockwood* v. *Brentwood Park Investments Ltd.* (1970) 10 D.L.R. (3d) 143, 166; but cf. *Morris* v. *Dominion Foundries & Steel Ltd.* [1947] 2 D.L.R. 840, 845 (criticised by Silverstone, "Visual Pollution: Unaesthetic Use of Land as Nuisance," (1974) 12 Alta.L.Rev. 542, 545).
[49] *Nobilo* v. *Waitemata County* [1961] N.Z.L.R. 1064, 1067; see too *Bartlett* v. *Tottenham* [1932] 1 Ch. 114, 132; *Halsey* v. *Esso Petroleum Co.* [1961] 2 All E.R. 145, 151.
[50] *Mitchell* v. *Darnley Main Colliery Co.,* 24 Q.B.D. 125, 137.
[51] *Embrey* v. *Owen* (1851) 6 Ex. 353, 155 E.R. 579. The jury had found that there was no such diminution, and so Parke B. held that a verdict for the defendants was properly ordered (at 368, 585).

stream so as to provide water for an adjacent town, and thereby caused "sensible damage" to the respondents, lower riparian owners.[52]

Damage is, of course, quite easy to measure when it is physical: the plaintiff can point to his flooded land or his polluted stream. Harm to personal comfort by way of fumes, smoke, or noise, say, is not so easily measurable. But the courts have still used the test of sensible damage. In the *St. Helen's Smelting* case,[53] Lord Westbury L.C. spoke of "sensible personal discomfort," and in *Luscombe* v. *Steer*,[54] Rolt L.J. said that "a material injury" either to property or to the comfort of the existence of those who lived in the neighbourhood had to be established. A temporary annoyance will rarely constitute sensible harm.

In the *St. Helen's Smelting* case,[55] Lord Westbury said: "It is a very desirable thing to mark the difference between an action brought for a nuisance upon the ground that the alleged nuisance produces material injury to the property, and an action brought for a nuisance on the ground that the thing alleged to be a nuisance is productive of sensible personal discomfort. With regard to the latter ... whether that may or may not be denominated a nuisance must undoubtedly depend greatly on the circumstances of the place where the thing complained of actually occurs. ... " But that does not mean that there is a different test for "personal discomfort" cases: the "sensible damage" test is applicable to all cases of nuisance. All Lord Westbury was saying was that, when personal discomfort is the cause of the complaint, one cannot decide whether the discomfort is "sensible" until the locality is looked at. There is bound to be more smoke in the air in an industrial estate in Coventry than on the mountain-tops of Snowdonia: a man's enjoyment of his land in Coventry will be impaired only if he has suffered "sensible harm" in addition to that normally suffered by people living in Coventry, in the same way that an inhabitant of Rhyd-Ddu will succeed only if he can show that he has suffered "sensible harm" in excess of that harm normally suffered by people living in Snowdonia. A man living in Coventry cannot demand the same quality of air as his counterpart in Rhyd-Ddu. The standard is that "of the ordinary reasonable and responsible person" living in the particular area.[56] On the other hand, that same person never expects, no matter where he lives, to suffer physical damage to his property.

Thus, the locality is looked at in order to determine whether the plaintiff has suffered "sensible damage." In those cases where the harm is physical, there is no need for the court to investigate the character of the place where the plaintiff lives, because wherever one lives, one does not expect physical damage to one's land. But it would be wrong (and perhaps contrary to Lord Westbury's intention) to draw any sharp distinction between the two categories, for the actual test is the same in all cases of nuisance.

(3) Extraordinary or sensitive use of land by the plaintiff

If a plaintiff has suffered "sensible damage" only because he has put his land to an extraordinary or sensitive use—that is to say, he would not have suffered "sensible damage" had his use been normal—then the defendant will not be held liable. "A man cannot increase the liabilities of his neighbour by applying his own property to special uses, whether for business or pleasure."[57] Thus, the owners of a drive-in cinema could not complain if lights on an adjoining race-course prevented the cinema audience from being able to see the film,[58] and mink farmers could not expect their neighbours to give up all activities which created noise during the whelping season.[59] In short, the plaintiff must not be hypersensitive[60]—he has merely "a right to the ordinary enjoyment of his land."[61]

However, once it has been established that the right to the ordinary enjoyment has been infringed, the plaintiff can claim protection for his extraordinary or sensitive use. In *McKinnon Industries* v. *Walker*,[62] the plaintiff's enjoyment was impaired by the emission of fumes and sulphur dioxide gas from the defendant's works. The defendant argued that, even if an injunction were granted, it should be modified so as to exclude protection for the plaintiff's orchids, the growing of which is "from the horticultural point of view a particularly difficult and delicate operation." But the Privy Council rejected this argument: once the plaintiff's ordinary enjoyment was affected there was "no reason to treat damage to orchids differently from damage to any other flower plant or shrub."[63]

The principle relating to extraordinary or sensitive use is well justified both in terms of fairness and on economic grounds.[64] Why should the "normal" user and his consumers be penalised by the presence of an abnormal neighbour? If individuals require greater protection than is normal, they must procure it through statute or contract.

(4) Malice

The relevance of malice in nuisance may well be considered here. Where the plaintiff is using his land ordinarily, there is no difficulty: in that situation, if the defendant's activities cause sensible damage, then the defendant will be liable in nuisance, regardless of whether he has acted maliciously or not. He is liable because he has caused that sensible damage. That the defendant has been malicious may well deprive him of any reliance on the defence of ordinary and reasonable use, but it will not affect the establishment of *prima facie* liability one way or the other. If the defendant's activities are such that they would not interfere with an ordinary use of land (even if they interfere with this extraordinary use), then the defendant is not liable in nuisance. It does not make any difference if the defendant has acted maliciously for "it is certainly a general rule of our law that an act *prima*

---

[57] *Eastern and South African Telegraph Co.* v. *Cape Town Tramways Cos.* [1902] A.C. 381, 393.

[58] *Amphitheaters Inc.* v. *Portland Meadows* (1948) 198 P. 2d 847.

[59] *Grandel* v. *Mason* [1953] 3 D.L.R. 65, as explained in *Rattray* v. *Daniels* (1959) 17 D.L.R. (2d) 134, 138, where mink farming described as "delicate and sensitive" use of land.

[60] *Stretch* v. *Romford Football Club Ltd.* (1971) 115 S.J. 741.

[61] *Backhouse* v. *Bonomi* (1861) 9 H.L.C. 503, 512; 11 E.R. 825, 829; see too *Robinson* v. *Kilvert* (1889) 41 Ch.D. 88.

[62] [1951] 3 D.L.R. 577 (P.C.).

[63] *Ibid.* 581.

[64] Ogus and Richardson, "Economics and the Environment: A Study of Private Nuisance," [1977] C.L.J. 284, 303–304.

facie lawful is not unlawful and actionable on account of the motive which dictated it."[65]

Only one case conflicts with this proposition: *Hollywood Silver Fox Farm Ltd.* v. *Emmett.*[66] The plaintiff bred silver foxes. During the breeding season, their vixen are very nervous and are liable, if disturbed, to refuse to breed, to miscarry, or to kill their young. The defendant maliciously caused his son to discharge a gun on four consecutive nights within his boundary but as near as possible to the plaintiff's breeding pens. Counsel for the defendant referred to *Robinson* v. *Kilvert*[67] and *Eastern and South African Telegraph Co.* v. *Cape Town Tramways Cos.*[68] and said that a man could not increase his neighbour's liabilities by applying his property to special uses. But Macnaghten J. thought that, even though keeping a silver fox farm was not an ordinary use of land in Kent, it was nonetheless "perfectly lawful," and the fact that the shooting took place "intentionally" made it actionable.[69] But the fact that keeping a silver fox farm is "perfectly lawful" is beside the point: it may be lawful and yet extraordinary. The Eastern and South African Telegraph Co.'s activities were lawful too. The judge did not disagree with counsel's contention that there would have been no disturbance of the plaintiff's enjoyment had the use been ordinary (*e.g.* sheep or cattle farming)—that is to say, if the use had been ordinary, the defendant's act (although malicious) would have been lawful because no "sensible damage" would have been caused. And yet the judge said that because the shooting was malicious, that was enough to make this lawful act unlawful (*i.e.* 'actionable'). Such a conclusion is in direct conflict with *Allen* v. *Flood.*[70]

Christie v. *Davey*[71] is often thought to be in line with the Macnaghten approach, but is in fact quite different. The defendant played many kinds of instruments (rather badly), blew whistles, knocked on trays and boards, hammered, and shrieked and shouted so as to annoy the plaintiffs. Such behaviour, carried on as it was at all hours of the day and night, would clearly interfere with the plaintiff's ordinary enjoyment. The fact that the female plaintiff was also a music teacher and that this sometimes interfered with her lessons simply showed further harm on the lines of the *McKinnon Industries* decision.[72] The fact that the defendant acted maliciously prevented his relying on the defence of ordinary use, which North J. suggested (when giving judgment on the defendant's counterclaim) would be a good defence where the occupier was playing an instrument in his own home for a short time each week at reasonable hours.

But, although the Hollywood Silver Fox Farm ought not to have succeeded in nuisance, the plaintiff may have had a remedy in negligence. On similar facts in Canada,[73] it has been held that the defendant, having

---

[65] *Allen* v. *Flood* [1898] A.C. 1, 123, *per* Lord Herschell; to similar effect, 92, *per* Lord Watson.
[66] [1936] 2 K.B. 468, [1936] 1 All E.R. 825.
[67] 41 Ch.D. 88.
[68] [1902] A.C. 381.
[69] [1936] 1 All E.R. 825, 828—this is omitted from the Authorised Reports.
[70] [1898] A.C. 1.
[71] [1893] 1 Ch. 316. Note that this case was decided before *Allen* v. *Flood.*
[72] [1951] 3 D.L.R. 577.
[73] *Grandel* v. *Mason* [1953] 3 D.L.R. 65, 67; *MacGibbon* v. *Robinson* [1952] 4 D.L.R. 142, 144; cf. *Rattray* v. *Daniels* (1959) 17 D.L.R. (2d) 134 (action failed because no negligence proved).

committed without reasonable care certain acts which were foreseeably likely to injure his neighbour, was liable under the *Donoghue* v. *Stevenson*[74] principle. It has recently been held in England that an intentional act may amount to "a glaring breach" of a duty to take reasonable care—"and this is negligence."[75] Alternatively, perhaps this is further evidence of the need for a tort of malicious interference with business or livelihood.[76]

§ 19. WHO CAN SUE

It follows from what has been said above that the plaintiff must be able to show that he is entitled to the right to enjoyment of land which nuisance protects. That right normally vests in the person in possession of the land injuriously affected.[77] So a weekly tenant[78] or a tenant at will[79] may maintain an action for nuisance, though the duration of the tenancy may be relevant to the question whether and on what terms an injunction should be granted. Conversely, a reversioner has no cause of action unless he can prove a permanent injury to his proprietary right.[80] If the damage is of a continuing nature, such as encroaching roots, an occupier can recover for damage inflicted before as well as after he acquired his proprietary and possessory interest.[81]

A licensee with a right to possess land[82] may sue in nuisance, but licensees without exclusive possession cannot sue.[83] It has been suggested that members of the occupier's family should be able to sue, as long as they are resident on the land,[84] but there would seem little justification for that normally as, if the land is interfered with, the occupier himself should sue. However, the inchoate rights in land given to matrimonial partners under modern legislation would perhaps suggest that either spouse should be able to sue, regardless of his or her actual legal or equitable interest in the land.

De facto possession is sufficient[85]; indeed, it would be odd if it were otherwise because even in conversion which, unlike nuisance, necessarily involves a reflection on the plaintiff's title, actual possession is protected against all but the rightful owner.

That the plaintiff must be able to show an entitlement to use and enjoyment in land is not an anomaly but follows from the very nature of the action. The purpose of the action is to protect the right to use and enjoyment of land. Freeholders, licensors, licensees in exclusive occupation, and lessees can show such entitlement. Because a lessor has a definite right to

---

[74] [1932] A.C. 562.
[75] *Morris* v. *C.W. Martin & Sons Ltd.* [1966] 1 Q.B. 716, 738.
[76] See above § 10(4).
[77] *Read* v. *Lyons (J.) & Co. Ltd.* [1947] A.C. 156, 183.
[78] *Jones* v. *Chappell* (1875) L.R. 20 Eq. 539.
[79] *Burgess* v. *Woodstock* [1955] 4 D.L.R. 615.
[80] See, for a fuller discussion of the matter below, § 41.
[81] *Masters* v. *Brent L.B.C.* [1978] Q.B. 841.
[82] Although it is not necessary that he have any title in the land: *Newcastle-under-Lyme Corporation* v. *Wolstanton Ltd.* [1947] Ch. 92, 104, 108; on appeal, [1947] Ch. 427. The working of a coal and ironstone mine caused the surface land to move, with the result that the corporation's gas mains and pipes were damaged. Although the corporation had no title to the land, it did have exclusive possession of the area occupied by the pipes.
[83] *Malone* v. *Laskey* [1907] 2 K.B. 141; *Cunard* v. *Antifyre* [1933] 1 K.B. 551; *Masters* v. *Brent L.B.C.* [1978] Q.B. 841.
[84] McLaren, 10 Osgoode Hall L.J. 505, 517.
[85] *Foster* v. *Warblington U.D.C.* [1906] 1 K.B. 648; *Paxhaven Holdings Ltd.* v. *Att.-Gen.* [1974] 2 N.Z.L.R. 185, 189.

possession in the future, he can sue in nuisance if he can show that, unless something is done, he will suffer an impairment of enjoyment at the time when he does regain possession.

§ 20. WHO IS LIABLE: (1) OCCUPIER[86]

Speaking generally, the occupier of premises is liable for all nuisances which exist upon them during the period of his occupancy. His duty is not merely to refrain from positive acts of misfeasance which cause harm to his neighbours, but also to take care that such harm is not caused by his omission or by third parties or by nature, and to abate it if it does. "I have the control and management," said Sir Charles Abbott C.J.,[87] "of all that belongs to my land or my house, and it is my fault if I do not so exercise my authority as to prevent injury to another." Hence an occupier may be responsible for what is done, not only by his servants or (in some cases) independent contractors,[88] but also by his invitees or licensees.[89] The reason is that an owner of private property, if he likes to take the necessary measures, can prevent people coming on his land and causing harm, because he can shut everyone out if he so wishes.[90] Similarly, an occupier is liable even for a continuing nuisance which already existed on the premises when he first entered into possession of them.[91]

Nature of Liability

When the harm flows from a state of affairs which has been created by the defendant himself or by someone for whom he is responsible, it is usually no defence that all possible care and skill have been taken to prevent the operation becoming a nuisance.[92] But when the harm flows from the act of a trespasser, or otherwise without the act, authority, or permission of the occupier, the occupier is not responsible for that harm unless, with knowledge or means of knowledge of the existence of the state of affairs causing the harm, he suffers it to continue without taking reasonably prompt and efficient means for its abatement.[93]

Five Different Cases

The problems may arise in five different ways.

(i) *The harm may be due to the act of a trespasser or stranger, or to natural causes.*

In *Sedleigh-Denfield's* case[94] a trespasser laid a pipe and grating in the defendants' ditch in so inefficient a manner that the grating became choked

---

[86] See Blundell, "Liabilities of Landlord and Tenant in respect of Non-repair, Nuisance, and Dangerous Premises" (1941) 5 *The Conveyancer* 100, 163, 261; Friedmann, "The Incidence of Liability in Nuisance" (1943) 59 L.Q.R. 63.
[87] *Laugher* v. *Pointer* (1826) 5 B. & C. 547, 576.
[88] *Hughes* v. *Percival* (1883) 8 App. Cas. 443; *Spicer* v. *Smee* [1946] 1 All E.R. 489.
[89] *White* v. *Jameson* (1874) L.R. 18 Eq. 303.
[90] *Hall* v. *Beckenham Corporation* [1949] 1 K.B. 716, 724.
[91] *Broder* v. *Saillard* (1876) 2 Ch. D. 692.
[92] See below, § 22(3).
[93] *Sedleigh-Denfield* v. *O'Callaghan* [1940] A.C. 880, 893, 910; *Goldman* v. *Hargrave* [1967] 1 A.C. 645, 660; *Leakey* v. *National Trust* [1980] Q.B. 485.
[94] [1940] A.C. 880.

with leaves, and water overflowed onto the plaintiff's premises. The defendants knew of the existence of the pipe, which drained their own land, and ought to have recognised the possibility of a flood occurring, but (despite the lapse of nearly three years) did nothing to remedy the obstruction. "In my opinion," said Lord Maugham,[95] "an occupier of land 'continues' a nuisance if with knowledge or presumed knowledge of its existence he fails to take any reasonable steps to bring it to an end though with ample time to do so. He 'adopts' it if he makes any use of the erections, building, bank or artificial contrivance which constitutes the nuisance." The defendants were held liable because they had both continued and adopted the nuisance. It has since been held that there is no difference between such a hazard created by a human agency, such as a trespasser, and one arising from natural causes or act of God.[96] It is a logical extension of this reasoning to hold that an occupier who permits gypsies to act on his land in a way which offends all the senses may have adopted the nuisance.[97-98]

(ii) *The occupier may have taken over the nuisance when he acquired the property.*

Instances of this are the cases of the tenant of a house which obstructs the plaintiff's lights,[99] and the purchaser of land on which a nuisance exists.[1]

(iii) *The nuisance may be due to a latent defect.*

Here the occupier is not liable if he did not know and could not by the exercise of reasonable care have known of the existence of the nuisance.[2] It has been said that "the occupier or owner is not an insurer."[3] So in *Noble* v. *Harrison*[4] the occupier of land was held not liable when the branch of a beech tree growing on his land and overhanging a highway suddenly broke off owing to a latent defect not discoverable by any reasonable careful inspection and damaged the plaintiff's motor-coach which was passing along the highway.

(iv) *Things naturally on the land.*

It is now settled that there may be liability in nuisance for the escape of things naturally on the land, if the occupier has failed to take reasonable care.[5] So the Court of Appeal has held that an occupier was liable when a steep natural hill collapsed as a result of earth movements, as he was well aware of the hazard.[6] But the court, in assessing what is reasonable, cannot disregard the fact that the occupier has had the nuisance thrust upon him

---

[95] [1940] A.C. 880, 894.
[96] *Goldman* v. *Hargrave* [1967] 1 A.C. 645; *Leakey* v. *National Trust* [1980] Q.B. 485, 518.
[97-98] *Page Motors Ltd.* v. *Epsom & Ewell Borough Council* (1980) 78 L.G.R. 505.
[99] *Roswell* v. *Prior* (1701) 12 Mod. 635.
[1] *Penruddock's Case* (1597) 5 Co. Rep. 1006.
[2] *Wilkins* v. *Leighton* [1932] 2 Ch. 106.
[3] *Sedleigh-Denfield* v. *O'Callaghan* [1940] A.C. 880, 897 *per* Lord Atkin.
[4] [1926] 2 K.B. 332. "*Noble* v. *Harrison* saved the beautiful hedgerows of the English countryside:" Landon, (1940) 56 L.Q.R. 144. But the safety of the public must take precedence over the duty of the National Trust to safeguard amenities: *Quinn* v. *Scott* [1965] 1 W.L.R. 1004. See also *Caminer* v. *Northern and London Investment Trust* [1951] A.C. 88 (no duty to lop wellgrown elm near a highway in absence of anything which would signify danger to the prudent landowner).
[5] *Goldman* v. *Hargrave* [1967] 1 A.C. 645.
[6] *Leakey* v. *National Trust* [1980] Q.B. 485.

through no fault of his own, and must not expect an excessive expenditure of time or money.[7]

(v) *Premises on Highways.*

It has sometimes been said that the principle that knowledge of the defect must be proved has one exception. In *Wringe* v. *Cohen*[8] the Court of Appeal decided that where premises on a highway become dangerous and constitute a nuisance, so that they collapse and injure a passer-by or an adjoining owner, the occupier or owner of the premises, if he has undertaken the duty to repair, is answerable, whether he knew or ought to have known of the danger or not.[9] Damage due to want of repair was distinguished from damage due to the acts of trespassers or to a latent defect, *e.g.* a secret and unobservable operation of nature[10] such as a subsidence. "Positive act and neglect of duty are thus placed on the same footing."[11] "A duty to prevent his house from becoming dangerous from want of repair connotes a duty to inspect and examine, and if a landlord fails to do either, it is right that he should not be allowed to rely upon his want of knowledge. There is nothing latent in the premises becoming in such disrepair as to be in danger of collapse. That was the point in *Wringe* v. *Cohen*."[12] But this begs the question. Is there a duty in the absence of actual or presumed knowledge? The judgment in *Wringe* v. *Cohen* was delivered before the hearing in the House of Lords of *Sedleigh-Denfield's* case,[13] but it was not referred to either in the arguments of counsel or in any of the opinions delivered by the Law Lords.[14] It is not easy to reconcile with the assumptions underlying the opinions in the later case but has been regarded as binding in some later cases.[15] The judgment is certainly at variance with *Caminer* v. *Northern and London Investment Trust Ltd.*[16] where the House of Lords held the respondent not liable when his elm tree fell on the appellants' car because a prudent landowner would not have suspected the danger. The owner of a tree adjoining a highway should be in no different a position from the owner of a house adjoining the highway.

---

[7] *Goldman* v. *Hargrave* [1967] 1 A.C. 645, 661; *Leakey* v. *National Trust* [1980] Q.B. 485.

[8] [1940] 1 K.B. 229. Further discussion of this case: Friedmann, (1943) 59 L.Q.R. 305; Landon, (1940) 56 L.Q.R. 140, and in Pollock, p. 324; Blundell (1941) 5 *The Conveyancer* 100; Treitel, (1951) 14 M.L.R. 347.

[9] This is the essence of the decision as explained in *Jacobs* v. *L.C.C.* [1950] A.C. 361, 373 and *Mint* v. *Good* [1951] 1 K.B. 517, 524. Yet, as Lord Simonds said in the *Jacobs* case (at 373), "the dispute was between adjoining owners, the premises of one having been damaged by the defective condition and collapse of the other, and references to highway and passer-by were alike strictly unnecessary".

[10] This distinction has been drawn in Australia: *Cartwright* v. *McLaine & Long Ltd.* (1979) 53 A.L.J.R. 413.

[11] [1940] 1 K.B. 229, 248.

[12] *Spicer* v. *Smee* [1946] 1 All E.R. 489, 494, *per* Atkinson J. (who delivered the judgment of the Court of Appeal in *Wringe* v. *Cohen*).

[13] The Court failed to consider the Court of Appeal's judgment in *Sedleigh-Denfield's* case [1939] 1 All E.R. 725 and *Job Edwards Ltd.* v. *Birmingham Navigations* [1924] 1 K.B. 341, in which all three Lord Justices considered relevant the defendant's knowledge of the existence of the fire in the tip.

[14] Presumably because at the time notice of appeal had been given in *Wringe* v. *Cohen*, which was therefore *sub judice.*

[15] *Heap* v. *Ind Coope* [1940] 2 K.B. 476; *Cushing* v. *Walker & Son* [1941] 2 All E.R. 693. It was not followed in *O'Leary* v. *Meltitides* (1960) 20 D.L.R. (2d) 258, 266–268 and *Brewer* v. *Kayes* [1973] 2 O.R. 284.

[16] [1951] A.C. 88, 96, 110.

Liability after occupation ceases.

Does a person who is in occupation of premises on which there is a nuisance, and who is liable for that nuisance by virtue of his occupation, cease to be so liable when he ceases to occupy? Does a vendor of land, for example, put off his responsibility along with his ownership? Or does the liability of a tenant cease with the assignment, surrender, or determination of the lease? On this point there is little authority, but it is submitted that the better view is that liability lasts only so long as the occupation on which it is based. This follows from the fact that liability in nuisance stems from a state of affairs, and it must surely be in the power of the defendant to prevent or control that state of affairs. Once control is given up (as on a sale of the land or surrender of a lease), the liability ceases, or rather is passed to the person who assumes control (say, the purchaser or the new lessee).

§ 21. WHO IS LIABLE: (2) NON-OCCUPIERS

Prima facie, the person with the power to maintain a state of affairs on land is the occupier of that land. Lord Wright said in *Sedleigh-Denfield* v. *O'Callaghan* that "[t]he ground of responsibility is the possession and control of the land from which the nuisance proceeds."[17] It is submitted that this test is of general application,[18] although it must be recognised that "possession", "control" and "the land" must be given liberal interpretations. Although originally, under the assize of nuisance, the defendant had to be the freeholder of the servient tenement,[19] that has never been necessary under the action on the case which superseded it.

There is no difficulty in applying Lord Wright's test where the land is under the control of an owner in occupation. There is some difficulty where the land (or part of it) is leased, licensed, or under the control of an independent contractor.

(a) *Lessor-lessee.*

It is always wise to sue the tenant, because he has legal occupation of the premises and is thus in a position to maintain a state of affairs or use the land.[20] The position of the lessor is more difficult. His duty of care with regard to work done on or in relation to his premises and with regard to defects in the state of the premises has now been defined by statute,[21] but it is specifically provided that this duty of care in no way modifies his obligations under the law of nuisance.[22] It is true that the lessor does not have the right to immediate possession of the demised premises, but that is not to say he has no control over them. The position is best explained by considering some hypothetical examples.

Example 1. Landlord (L) demises the property excluding the roof and

---

[17] [1940] A.C. 880, 903.
[18] *Hall* v. *Beckenham Corporation* [1949] 1 K.B. 716, 724; *Smith* v. *Scott* [1973] Ch. 314, 321; *Hooper* v. *Rogers* [1975] Ch. 43, 50–51.
[19] Blackstone, 3 Bl.Com. 222.
[20] *Heap* v. *Ind Coope and Allsopp Ltd.* [1940] 2 K.B. 476, 480; *Wilchick* v. *Marks* [1934] 2 K.B. 56, 66, 68.
[21] Defective Premises Act 1972, ss. 3 and 4.
[22] *Ibid.* s. 6(2).

exterior walls to Tenant (T). A slate falls off the roof and damages the property of Neighbour (N).

T in this case will not be liable, because he had no control over the roof. That part of the property was not demised to him. L will be liable to N because he maintained a state of affairs on property he owned and retained control over, and harm was caused to N.

Example 2. L demises the property excluding the roof and guttering to T. Because of the defective design of the guttering, water overflows and floods part of the premises demised to T.

It is submitted that *prima facie* L will be liable to T in nuisance,[23] for the water has flowed from a place in L's control to a place in T's.[24] Of course, the landlord may often be able to rely on some defence, such as ordinary use or consent. But it is not true to say that strict liability is inapplicable between a lessee and his landlord: cases to that effect can all be traced to a dictum of Martin B. in *Carstairs* v. *Taylor*,[25] a dictum not assented to by the other three Barons sitting in that case.

Example 3. L demises the property excluding the roof and guttering to T. The gutters become blocked with leaves; as a consequence, water overflows and floods part of the premises demised to T.

In this case, the cause of the harm was not a structural defect but rather the failure to clear out the gutters. Some have concluded that T's cause of action in such cases is one in negligence. It may well be that L is liable to T in negligence, but it is submitted that an action in nuisance may also lie. T may have consented to run the risk of the guttering's failing because of defective design: by taking a lease of a house so constructed, he may be said to have consented to the risks embodied in its structure.[26] But it is most unlikely that the tenant consented to the risk of the defendant landlord's failing to exercise reasonable care in maintaining his part of the premises. The obligation is on the landlord to show either that he did exercise reasonable care or that the tenant consented to his failing to exercise such care. If he succeeds, then the action in nuisance fails; if he fails, then the plaintiff's action in nuisance succeeds, the defence not having been established. The importance of this distinction between negligence and nuisance is that, with the latter action, there is no onus on the plaintiff to establish that the defendant was negligent. It is for the defendant to prove that he did use reasonable care. To talk of a "modified doctrine of *Rylands* v. *Fletcher*"[27] merely obfuscates the issue.

Example 4. L demises the whole property to T, but covenants to keep the property in repair. A slate falls off the roof and damages N's property.

L will be liable in nuisance to N, for the fact that he has covenanted to

---

[23] Most of these cases have been decided on the basis of *Rylands* v. *Fletcher*, but the principle is the same whether under that doctrine or nuisance.
[24] *Reid* v. *Friendly Societies' Hall Co.* (1881) N.Z.L.R. 3 C.A. 238, 244; *Hart* v. *Rogers* [1916] 1 K.B. 646, 650–651; *Western Engraving Co.* v. *Film Laboratories Ltd.* [1936] 1 All E.R. 106; *A. Prosser and Son Ltd.* v. *Levy* [1955] 3 All E.R. 577.
[25] (1871) L.R. 6 Ex. 217, 222.
[26] *Peters* v. *Prince of Wales Theatre (Birmingham) Ltd.* [1943] K.B. 73, 78.
[27] *e.g. Cockburn* v. *Smith* [1924] 2 K.B. 119, 133; *Kiddle* v. *City Business Properties Ltd.* [1942] 1 K.B. 269, 274.

repair shows that he has control over the maintenance of the premises, which control is acknowledged and conceded by T.

Example 5. L demises the whole property to T. Nothing is said about the obligation to repair. A slate falls off the roof and damages N's property.

If the lease was weekly or short term, then "no term [is] more easily and more necessarily implied by law . . . than a right in the landlord to enter, or to re-enter, to examine the premises and to do necessary repairs."[28] That does not mean that the tenant will not be liable to the neighbour as well[29]: the tenant has after all possession of the demised premises and should effect the repairs himself if the landlord fails to honour the implied obligation of repair.

Even if the lease is long term, all the circumstances may show the parties intended that the landlord would undertake repairs. This is particularly likely where the landlord, while not covenanting to keep the property in repair, retains the right to enter the property and the power to effect repairs.[30] The reason why the landlord is liable in such circumstances is that, by reserving to himself this right over the premises, he has "to that extent, at any rate, exercised a measure of control over them".[31]

Example 6. L demises the whole property to T, and T covenants to repair. A slate falls off the roof and damages N's property.

It is submitted that, *prima facie,* L is not liable to N in nuisance[32]: only T is liable.[33] Such a rule is supported by good sense. The landlord has no right to enter the premises: he cannot effect the necessary repairs even if he so wanted. As well, he has accepted a lower rent because of the tenant's agreeing to bear the responsibilities of repair. It may well be true that "there is no reason why because the tenant has made a contract with his landlord that should alter the duty he owes to persons on the highway."[34] The tenant remains liable to third parties regardless of contractual duties and rights because of his occupation of the premises: he owes a duty to others by law and he cannot extinguish that duty by private agreement. But the converse is not necessarily true. A landlord's liability springs from the control over the premises given him by contract. If by contract he is given no control, then it follows that he cannot be liable in nuisance. It should be noted here that the courts are, of course, concerned with the reality of the situation, the actual degree of control exercised by the landlord. If the lessee is a "front man," "a man of straw" or "a penniless subsidiary," then the courts may conclude that the lessor had *in fact* retained control, regardless of the wording of any sham agreement.[35]

In *Brew Brothers* v. *Snax (Ross) Ltd.*[36] the Court of Appeal held the

---

[28] *Mint* v. *Good* [1951] 1 K.B. 517, 521.
[29] *Ibid.* 527.
[30] *Todd* v. *Flight* (1860) 9 C.B. (N.S.) 377; *Heap* v. *Ind Coope and Allsopp Ltd.* [1940] 2 K.B. 476, 483; *Spicer* v. *Smee* [1946] 1 All E.R. 489, 492.
[31] *Wilchick* v. *Marks* [1934] 2 K.B. 56, 63.
[32] Nor is he under the Defective Premises Act 1972, s. 4.
[33] *Pretty* v. *Bickmore* (1873) L.R. 8 C.P. 401, 404.
[34] *Wilchick* v. *Marks* [1934] 2 K.B. 56, 58; see too *Mint* v. *Good* [1951] 1 K.B. 517, 527.
[35] *Brew Brothers* v. *Snax (Ross) Ltd* [1970] 1 Q.B. 612, 638, *per* Sachs L.J.; 644, *per* Phillimore L.J.
[36] [1970] 1 Q.B. 612.

landlords liable, on facts falling within *Example 5*. The decision can be supported on the narrow ground that work required to make the wall safe was much more than "repairs" (which the tenants had covenanted to effect), and that in the circumstances this work was of a kind that the landlords were under an implied obligation to effect. But Sachs and Phillimore L.JJ. went further than that, largely because they thought it wrong that "liability should as regards third parties be shuffled off merely by signing a document which as between owner and tenant casts on the latter the burden of executing remedial work."[37] But it is hardly a case of the landlord "shuffling off" his liability. The *prima facie* position is that only the occupier, the tenant, is liable; it is this position which is often modified to provide that the landlord will exercise some control over the premises and hence will assume joint liability. The dissenting judgement of Harman L.J. is to be preferred, and is in line with earlier authority.[38]

However, although in the circumstances of this example, the landlord may not be liable in nuisance, he nonetheless is under certain statutory duties towards his neighbours.[39]

Example 7. L demises the whole property to T. T acts in such a way that N's enjoyment of his property is impaired.

Prime facie, L is not liable to N because he has no control over the state of affairs. Indeed, L may have even expressly forbidden T to act in such a way, as in *Smith* v. *Scott*,[40] where the tenants, a "problem family," committed physical damage to the plaintiffs' property and made so much noise that the plaintiffs' enjoyment of their property was diminished. Pennycuick V.-C. held the landlords not liable.

These seven examples, which cover the various ways in which a neighbour may be harmed, are all decided according to a common principle: the lessor's control of a state of affairs which causes harm. The relevance of any covenant between the landlord and the tenant is limited to showing the degree of control possessed by the landlord over the particular activity or condition which causes the harm.

(b) *Licensor-licensee.*

The licensor is a logical defendant in a nuisance action because he retains the right to some kind of possession and control over the land. But the distinction between leases and licences is a fine one, and there has been a growing tendency to label agreements where A has granted B exclusive possession of his land or part of his land as licences rather than leases.[41] In the analogous area of occupiers' liability, it has been held that both licensors and licensees can have sufficient control over a set of premises that both can be held liable for harm resulting to visitors[42]; so too may liability be found in

---

[37] *Ibid.* 638, *per* Sachs L.J.
[38] *Ibid.* 631; *Pretty* v. *Bickmore*, L.R. 8 C.P. 401, approved in *Wilchick* v. *Marks* [1934] 2 K.B. 56, 66.
[39] Defective Premises Act 1972, s. 3(1); see too Housing Act 1961, s. 32.
[40] s. 32 [1973] Ch. 314; see too *Rich* v. *Basterfield* (1847) 4 C.B. 783, 136 E.R. 715.
[41] See, *e.g.*, *Abbeyfield (Harpenden) Society Ltd.* v. *Woods* [1968] 1 W.L.R. 374; *Barnes* v. *Barratt* [1970] 2 Q.B. 657; *Shell-Mex and B.P. Ltd.* v. *Manchester Garages Ltd.* [1971] 1 W.L.R. 612.
[42] *Wheat* v. *E. Lacon & Co. Ltd.* [1966] A.C. 552; North, *Occupiers' Liability*, p. 18.

nuisance. The lack of precise guidelines is due to the diverse nature of licences. If A says to B, "You may walk across my land," B is a licensee; if C enters into an agreement with D whereby D is given exclusive possession over a room in C's house, D may well be a licensee. But the rights of B and D (and, for that matter, A and C) are vastly different, especially as to revocability of the licence.

This much can be said: it will be a rare case where the licensor cannot be held liable for a state of affairs existing on his land. This is because, in nearly all cases, he retains the right to possession of the land. At times too, depending on the nature of the licence, the licensee may be held to have sufficient control to justify his being held liable in nuisance. The clearest exposition of a licensee's liability is given in *Kraemers* v. *Attorney-General for Tasmania*.[43] Kraemers's neighbour granted the Public Works Department a licence to take gravel from his land. As a result of the Department's activities, the plaintiff's property was flooded. The court held that the respondent's control over the land "constituted sufficient management and control of the lands to found liability for nuisance emanating from it."[44] Obviously, a golfer does not have sufficient control, and thus cannot be held liable in nuisance if he drops a cigarette on the links and thereby starts a fire[45]; but a licensee with the right to excavate clay and make bricks or gypsies camping on a site and paying for the privilege do have sufficient control.[46] Many of the cases involving escapes of gas and water from pipes have involved licensees. In *Benning* v. *Wong*,[47] the defendants were licensees in occupation of the area of sub-soil containing their pipes under statutory authority, and "had control of the pipe up to the point of escape, to the complete exclusion of the plaintiff."[48]

(c) *Authoriser*

Under general tortious principle, "a person is liable for a tortious act committed by his *direction* subject to the qualification made above, that where knowledge of facts is an essential ingredient in the tort, the defendant must have had that knowledge."[49] Indeed, "even a mere permission may be sufficient to make a person liable where he has some control over the doing of the act so that his permission amounts to assistance in the commission of the tort."

This principle applies, of course, as much to the tort of nuisance as to any other tort. It is true that the authoriser may be liable in nuisance even though he does not have control over the state of affairs which causes the plaintiff harm. That does not mean that the principle of "control" is wrong, nor even that this is an exception to that principle. The principle of "control" is peculiar to the tort of nuisance; it is overlaid, however, by the principle of "authorisation" which is common to the law of tort in general. Of course,

---

[43] [1966] Tas.S.R. 113.
[44] *Ibid.* 118, *per* Burbury C.J., 135, *per* Gibson J.
[45] *Boulcott Golf Club Inc.* v. *Engelbrecht* [1945] N.Z.L.R. 556 (licensor held liable).
[46] *White* v. *Jameson* (1874) L.R. 18 Eq. 303, 305; *Att.-Gen.* v. *Stone* (1895) 60 J.P. 168, 169. See too *Hampstead and Suburban Properties Ltd.* v. *Diomedous* [1969] 1 Ch. 248.
[47] (1969) 43 A.L.J.R. 467.
[48] *Ibid.* 486; see too *Midwood* v. *Manchester Corporation* [1905] 2 K.B. 597; *Charing Cross Electricity Supply Co.* v. *Hydraulic Power Co.* [1914] 3 K.B. 772; *North-Western Utilities Ltd.* v. *London Guarantee and Accident Co.* [1936] A.C. 108.
[49] Atiyah, *Vicarious Liability*, pp. 291–292, 294; see too Williams, *Joint Torts*, p. 6.

the authorised agent must have maintained the harmful state of affairs on land within his control.

To be liable, the authoriser must have authorised a state of affairs from which harm was inevitable or "virtually certain" to result.[50] The most common way in which authority is given is "in the shape of a lease": where a field was "let for the very purpose and object of being worked as a lime quarry and for erecting lime kilns and burning lime," the authoriser (the lessor) was held liable in nuisance, as was, of course, the tenant who had possession of the field.[51] Harm was virtually certain to result from the activity authorised. But in *Rich* v. *Basterfield*,[52] the landlord neither had control over the defendant's activity nor had authorised it. In *Smith* v. *Scott*,[53] the corporation had clearly not authorised the tort; indeed, it had expressly prohibited the family from committing a nuisance. The decision of the Exchequer Chamber in *Brand* v. *Hammersmith Railway*[54] is best explained on the basis of authorisation. The plaintiff's house was affected by vibration, smoke, and noise from trains running on a line operated by the Great Western Railway Co. The defendant was the railway company which had constructed the line and which owned the land. The defendant authorised the Great Western to run the railway and it "is practically necessary . . . for the using of the line"[55] that vibrations would be caused.

§ 22. DEFENCES

We must consider six categories of defences[56]:

(1) Volenti non fit injuria and contributory negligence

It is now clear that it is no defence that the plaintiff himself came to the nuisance.[57] At one time, it was supposed that no one could complain of a nuisance if with full knowledge of its existence he chose to become the owner or occupier of the land affected by it, as if he knowingly took a house close to a noisy factory. But that, however, is not the law today. The *maxim volenti non fit injuria* is capable of no such application, at least when the conduct complained of is causing damage to property as distinct from damage to beneficial enjoyment.[58] It would be unreasonable to expect a person to refrain from buying land merely because the neighbouring occupier was abusing his rights.[59] Contributory negligence has never been successfully pleaded as a defence to a claim in nuisance, although it is available in cases of public nuisance.[60] It would seem that in such cases the standard of care to which the plaintiff is required to conform if he is not to be found guilty of contributory negligence is not necessarily as high as that

---

[50] *Smith* v. *Scott* [1973] Ch. 314, 321.
[51] *Harris* v. *James* (1876) 45 L.J.Q.B. 545, esp. at 546.
[52] (1847) 4 C.B. 783, 136 E.R. 715.
[53] [1973] Ch. 314.
[54] (1867) L.R. 2 Q.B. 223, reversed on appeal (1869) L.R. 4 H.L. 171, on the ground that s. 86 of the Railways Clauses Consolidation Act 1845 provided a good defence.
[55] *Ibid*. 230.
[56] For the defences of necessity and statutory authority, see below §§ 185, 191.
[57] *Miller* v. *Jackson* [1977] Q.B. 966. But the Court of Appeal thought the principle might be reviewed by the House of Lords. See too Ogus and Richardson, [1977] C.L.J. 284, 320.
[58] See above, § 18(2).
[59] *Sturges* v. *Bridgman* (1879) 11 Ch. D. 852.
[60] *Dymond* v. *Pearce* [1972] 1 Q.B. 496.

required of the defendant. So a person using a highway which he is entitled to expect will be free from nuisance is in much the same position as a workman in a factory: thoughtlessness or carelessness is not equivalent to contributory negligence.[61] The act of a third party is not necessarily a defence if it is the very kind of act which should have been foreseen when the defendant originally created the nuisance.[62]

(2) Public benefit

It is no defence that the nuisance, although injurious to the individual plaintiff, is beneficial to the public at large. A nuisance may be the inevitable result of some manufacture or other operation that is of undoubted public benefit—a benefit that far outweighs the loss inflicted upon the individual—but it is an actionable nuisance nonetheless.[63] No consideration of public utility can be suffered to deprive an individual of his legal rights without compensation.[64]

(3) Care and skill

In some cases dicta can be found which say that the tendency of modern law is to assimilate nuisance and negligence and to move away from strict liability.[65] The better view[66] is that nuisance is not yet, and perhaps never will be, a branch of the law of negligence.[67] So in 1979 plaintiff's counsel conceded before the Court of Appeal that a claim in negligence as distinct from nuisance would not be proceeded with because "it would give rise to much difficulty and expense."[68] "Herein lies the great merit of framing the case in nuisance as distinct from negligence. It greatly affects the burden of proof. It puts the legal burden where it ought to be, on the defendant, whereas in negligence it is on the plaintiff."[69] In nuisance the onus is on the defendant to exculpate himself.[70]

But many cases have confused nuisance and negligence, and much of the confusion seems to stem from an erroneous equation of "fault" (which is a prerequisite to liability in nuisance)[71] with "negligence" (which is not).

Where the defendant himself or someone for whom he is responsible has created the nuisance,[72] it is no defence that all possible care and skill are being used to prevent the operation complained of from amounting to a nuisance. If an operation cannot by any care and skill be prevented from causing harm, it cannot lawfully be undertaken at all, except with the consent of those injured by it or by the authority of a statute.[73]

---

[61] *Farrell* v. *John Mowlem & Co. Ltd.* [1954] 1 Lloyd's Rep. 437, 441.

[62] *Cunningham* v. *McGrath Bros.* [1964] I.R. 209. See below, § 204.

[63] *Shelfer* v. *City of London Electric Lighting Co.* [1895] 1 Ch. 287, 316; and below, § 219.

[64] *Bellew* v. *Cement Ltd.* [1948] I.R. 61.

[65] *British Road Services Ltd.* v. *Slater* [1964] 1 W.L.R. 498, 504.

[66] *Cunard* v. *Antifyre Ltd.* [1933] 1 K.B. 551, 558; *Sedleigh-Denfield* v. *O'Callaghan* [1940] A.C. 880, 904; *Spicer* v. *Smee* [1946] 1 All E.R. 489, 493; *Jacobs* v. *L.C.C.* [1950] A.C. 361, 374; *Farrell* v. *John Mowlem & Co. Ltd.* [1954] 1 Lloyd's Rep. 437, 440; *Paxhaven Holdings* v. *Att.-Gen.* [1974] 2 N.Z.L.R. 185.

[67] *Klimenko* v. *City of Winnipeg* (1966) 55 D.L.R. (2d) 573, 574.

[68] *Allen* v. *Gulf Oil Refining Co. Ltd.* [1980] Q.B. 156, 164.

[69] *Morton* v. *Wheeler, The Times*, February 1, 1956, *per* Denning L.J.

[70] *The Wagon Mound (No. 2)* [1963] 1 Lloyd's Rep. 402, 428.

[71] *The Wagon Mound (No. 2)* [1967] 1 A.C. 617, 639.

[72] *Gourock Ropework Co. Ltd.* v. *Greenock Corporation* 1966 S.L.T. 125, 128.

[73] *Powell* v. *Fall* (1880) 5 Q.B.D. 597. See also *Adams* v. *Ursell* [1913] 1 Ch. 269 (fried fish shop using "the most approved appliances"), and *Bone* v. *Seale* [1975] 1 W.L.R. 797, (defendant liable for smell, "though he really could not do any more about it").

(4) Contributory acts of others

Two or more persons may jointly create or continue a nuisance and then they will be joint tortfeasors.[74] But it is also no defence that the act of the defendant would not amount to a nuisance unless other persons acting independently of him did the same thing at the same time.[75] Thus if 20 factories pour out smoke and fumes into the atmosphere, the contribution of each may be so small and its detrimental effect so inappreciable that it does not *per se* amount to a nuisance. Yet the aggregate quantity may be the cause of serious harm or discomfort. In such a case each of the contributors is liable in nuisance and for his own proportion of the total damage.[76]

(5) Reasonable use of property

He who causes a nuisance cannot avail himself of the defence that he is merely making a reasonable use of his own property. Often a use has been held reasonable and yet the defendant has been held liable.[77] Yet it is none-theless clear that a defence of "reasonable use" or "ordinary use" is available, although the limits of the defence are by no means clear.

It is suggested that the defence is of two parts, both of which must be established by the defendant:

(a) The state of affairs must be, in all the circumstances, common and ordinary; and

(b) (i) Where the state of affairs is an activity, that activity must be reasonably undertaken;

(ii) Where the state of affairs is a condition on the land, the failure to prevent the condition's causing harm must be reasonable.[78]

In practice, this bi-partite test is relatively easy to apply. In *Bamford* v. *Turnley*,[79] the defendant failed the first limit of the test, for the burning of bricks in that locality was "not the common and ordinary use of land." In *Bayliss* v. *Lea*,[80] the finding of the trial judge that to introduce water for irrigation purposes on to a farming property in that sort of area was not a "non-natural use of land" was not challenged. But the plaintiff's prayer for an injunction nonetheless succeeded, because "the manner in which the defendants laid out their irrigation works and used them was not, in all the circumstances, in accordance with normal and proper practice, but on the contrary was an unreasonable and excessive user of the land." Thus, the defendant failed the second limb of the defence. In *Mihalchuk* v. *Ratke*,[81] the defendant was a crop farmer. The growth and production of crops is clearly a natural use of his land. Part of that use is the control of weeds. But

---

[74] *Brew Bros. Ltd.* v. *Snax (Ross) Ltd.* [1970] 1 Q.B. 612.

[75] *Lambton* v. *Mellish* [1894] 3 Ch. 163.

[76] *Pride of Derby and Derbyshire Angling Association Ltd.* v. *British Celanese Ltd.* [1952] 1 All E.R. 1326, 1342 (not considered at [1953] Ch. 149). There is no joint liability in such cases; each is severally liable for his own act.

[77] *Broder* v. *Saillard*, 2 Ch.D. 692, 701; *Vanderpant* v. *Mayfair Hotel Co. Ltd.* [1930] 1 Ch. 138, 166.

[78] *Bamford* v. *Turnley*, 3 B. & S. 62, 83; 122 E.R. 25, 33; *Bayliss* v. *Lea* [1962] S.R.(N.S.W.) 521, 540; *Kraemers* v. *Att.-Gen. for Tasmania* [1966] Tas.S.R. 113, 125.

[79] 3 B. & S. 62, 83; 122 E.R. 25, 33.

[80] [1962] S.R.(N.S.W.) 521, 525, 530.

[81] (1966) 57 D.L.R. (2d) 269.

when the defendant used an aircraft to spray the weeds, he adopted a method of control which was unreasonable and unusual in that area. The usual method was boom-spraying behind a tractor. The plaintiff's claim for damage to his crops by drift of the herbicide was, therefore, successful.

The defence is available in all nuisance cases, even where physical damage has been caused to the plaintiff.[82] The defence is in accordance with commonsense and justice. As only a defence, it preserves the basic principle that, if a person's enjoyment of his land is impaired, he is *prima facie* entitled to relief. But it is also just that a land owner should *prima facie* be exempted from liability for harm caused by normal and ordinary use of his land. If everyone is using his land in a particular way in a locality, then a principle of "mutual sufferance" would dictate that each should be willing to bear the cost of any harm caused to himself by another's ordinary and normal use. Such a principle is as much for the advantage of one owner as of another. An exemption from liability for ordinary use might, however, be abused: a defendant may not act "reasonably." It is, therefore, appropriate that the defendant should also have to prove that he has not acted negligently or improperly.

(a) The first limb

The state of affairs must be, in all the circumstances, common and ordinary. While the expression is "highly flexible,"[83] certain tests of "ordinariness" may be distilled from the cases and stated with some certainty:

(i) Dangerous state of affairs

The more dangerous the state of affairs, the less likely that the state of affairs will be termed ordinary. The Law Commission on one occasion thought that a working definition of a "dangerous activity" might be an activity which posed "a more than ordinary risk of accidents or a risk of more than ordinary damage if accidents in fact result."[84] Such a definition might be of use here. The reason why "dangerous" activities are not likely to be ordinary is that such activities are not likely to be part of the "give and take" of land occupation. Baron Bramwell's justification for the defence was that it was "as much for the advantage of one owner as of another": there is no equality of advantage if one of the parties is undertaking a dangerous activity.

It has been said that "the element of increased danger to others" is the "main criterion in deciding whether a land use is natural."[85] That the state of affairs is dangerous is not conclusive, however, as to ordinariness—the House of Lords' decision in *Read's* case[86] is proof of that.

---

[82] *Smith* v. *Kenrick*, 7 C.B. 515, 137 E.R. 205; *Rylands* v. *Fletcher*, L.R. 3 H.L. 330; *Blake* v. *Woolf* [1898] 2 Q.B. 426; *Wilkins* v. *Leighton* [1932] 2 Ch. 106; *Tilley* v. *Stevenson* [1939] 4 All E.R. 207; *Kara Pty Ltd.* v. *Rhodes* [1966] V.R. 77.

[83] Street, *Torts*, p. 252; Carroll, 8 Ir.Jur. 208, 218.

[84] Law Com. No. 32, para. 7(*b*).

[85] Williams, [1973] C.L.J. 310, 319; *Rickards* v. *Lothian* [1913] A.C. 263, 280. Lord Moulton made it clear that he saw no distinction between *Rylands* v. *Fletcher* and nuisance (at 275).

[86] [1947] A.C. 156.

(ii) Locality

It has already been shown that, where the harm caused is not physical damage but is discomfort to the senses, the plaintiff's locality is of relevance in determining whether he has suffered "sensible damage."[87] Locality (this time the *defendant's* locality) may also be of relevance in quite a different enquiry, namely whether the defendant's user of land is "ordinary." In this case, it is immaterial whether the plaintiff has suffered physical damage or discomfort to the senses. If a defendant is carrying on a particular trade or manufacture in locality devoted to that trade or manufacture, then that use is likely to be termed "ordinary."[88] Here clearly, the defence is "as much for the advantage of one owner as of another." Thus, to operate a printing press in Fleet Street or to erect a house in a new estate or to spin cotton in the industrial quarters of Bolton or Rochdale would be to maintain an ordinary state of affairs.[89] In determining the ordinary users of any locality, the Court may have regard to the zoning under modern planning legislation.[90]

(iii) Generality

The more widespread a use or state of affairs is, the more likely that it will be determined "ordinary." Virtually all premises today are equipped with fireplaces or apparatus for heating the premises and with a gas and water supply and a sewerage system.[91] However the "generality" principle cannot be carried too far: while the use of electricity, gas and water in one's home is ordinary, the handling of these agents "in bulk and in large quantities" is not.[92]

(iv) Nature

If the state of affairs has been brought about by nature, that state will be termed "ordinary." Natural conditions were specifically given as an example of ordinary use in *Rylands* v. *Fletcher*. It is normal and natural to have rocks on one's land[93] and weeds on one's station in the outback.[94]

(b) The second limb

Having proved that his user was ordinary, the defendant must then prove that the act causing the harm was reasonably done. This requirement is in effect a check against abuse. The test of reasonableness here is, to all intents,

---

[87] See above, § 18(2).
[88] *Sturges* v. *Bridgman* (1879) 11 Ch.D. 852, 865; *Rushmer* v. *Polsue & Alfieri Ltd.* [1906] 1 Ch. 234, 249; *Halsey* v. *Esso Petroleum Co. Ltd.* [1961] 1 W.L.R. 683, 692.
[89] Is the provision of parks and recreation grounds in residential areas "ordinary"? Perhaps yes—see *Miller* v. *Jackson* [1977] Q.B. 966.
[90] Williams, [1973] C.L.J. 310, 319. In *Bayliss* v. *Lea* (1959) 77 W.N.(N.S.W.) 272, 278, Hardie J. noted that the properties were situated in a proclaimed irrigation district.
[91] *Rickards* v. *Lothian* [1913] A.C. 263, 281–2 (water); *Sochacki Sas* [1947] 1 All E.R. 344, 344 (fireplace); *Brewer* v. *Kayes* [1973] 2 O.R. 284, 287 (fuel oil stored for domestic purposes).
[92] *Collingwood* v. *Home and Colonial Stores Ltd.* [1936] 3 All E.R. 200, 208; *Smeaton* v. *Ilford Corporation* [1954] Ch. 450, 471; cf. *Miller* v. *Robert Addie & Sons Collieries Ltd.* 1934 S.C. 150, but this is surely inconsistent with *Hanson* v. *Wearmouth Coal Co. Ltd.* [1939] 3 All E.R. 47 and *North-Western Utilities Ltd.* v. *London Guarantee & Accident Co.* [1936] A.C. 108.
[93] *Pontardawe Rural District Council* v. *Moore-Gwynn* [1929] 1 Ch. 656.
[94] *Sparke* v. *Osborne* (1908) 7 C.L.R. 51.

the same as the test pertaining in the law of negligence,[95] apart from the crucial distinction as to the onus of proof. It is not possible to lay down specific guidelines as to what is reasonable and what not. However, general principles may be distilled from the cases.

If the defendant has adopted the usual and expected means of proceeding, that will usually be reasonable.[96] An activity may be reasonable if undertaken at a certain time, but unreasonable if undertaken at another time.[97] An oil company's use of tankers in its yard throughout the night was unreasonable,[98] as was a builder's constant use of mechanical drills so as to make work during business hours almost impossible.[99] The more skill with which a defendant acts, the more likely it is that the court will find his act reasonable. If the defendant has acted maliciously, then his act is *ipso facto* unreasonable. This is made clear by *Christie* v. *Davey*[1] in which the defendant was held liable because his "musical" activities were undertaken maliciously, whereas the plaintiff (the defendant on the counterclaim) avoided liability because her piano playing was performed at reasonable hours for only a moderate length of time each week.

Finally, a particular activity is likely to be judged reasonable if to have acted otherwise would have involved the defendant in so much greater expense as to amount to an intolerable burden.[2] This test is likely to assume greater prominence in future owing to a gloss put upon it by the Privy Council in *Goldman* v. *Hargrave*[3] and by the Court of Appeal in *Leakey* v. *National Trust*.[4] In the former case, Lord Wilberforce suggested that the courts, when determining whether the cost of acting otherwise amounted to an "intolerable burden," ought to take into account the individual circumstances of the defendant: "less must be expected of the infirm than of the able-bodied." Normally the common law applied an objective test[5]: why should there be an exception in this case? Where the state of affairs has been created by a trespasser, the defendant occupier has not yet been able to plead a lack of resources.[6] Why should a distinction be made between that case and the situation where the state of affairs has been created by nature?[7] The subjective test has been applied in cases concerning an occupier's duty to trespassers. The rationale for that exception was provided by Lord Reid in *British Railways Board* v. *Herrington*: "An occupier does not voluntarily

---

[95] That does not mean, of course, that "unreasonableness of the defendant's conduct *vis-a-vis* the plaintiff is an ingredient in the action for nuisance as it is in the case of an action for negligence": *Kraemers* v. *Att.-Gen. for Tasmania* [1966] Tas.S.R. 113, 125.

[96] *e.g.* the mining cases: *Wilson* v. *Waddell*, 2 App. Cas. 95, 100 and *Hurdman* v. *The North Eastern Railway Co.*, 3 C.P.D. 168, 174—reasonable; *Baird* v. *Williamson*, 15 C.B.(N.S.) 376, 143 E.R. 831—unreasonable.

[97] *Gertsen* v. *Municipality of Metropolitan Toronto*, 41 D.L.R. (3d) 646, 665.

[98] *Halsey* v. *Esso Petroleum Co. Ltd.* [1961] 1 W.L.R. 683, 701.

[99] *Daily Telegraph Co. Ltd.* v. *Stuart* (1928) 28 S.R.(N.S.W.) 291, 294.

[1] [1893] 1 Ch. 316, 326–327.

[2] *Andreae* v. *Selfridge & Co.* [1938] Ch. 1, 9; *Hargrave* v. *Goldman*, 110 C.L.R. 40, 71, *per* Windeyer J.

[3] [1967] 1 A.C. 645, 663.

[4] [1980] Q.B. 485.

[5] *British Railways Board* v. *Herrington* [1972] A.C. 877, 898; *Glasgow Corporation* v. *Muir* [1943] A.C. 448, 457.

[6] *Att.-Gen.* v. *Tod Heatley* [1897] 1 Ch. 560, 573: the duty to abate arises as soon as the occupier has knowledge.

[7] Especially in view of the fact that it is now clearly established that there is no valid distinction "between a trespasser's act and an act of nature": *Leakey* v. *National Trust* [1980] Q.B. 485, 518, *per* Megaw L.J.

assume a relationship with trespassers. By trespassing they force a 'neighbour' relationship on him."[8] An occupier's neighbour does not "force a 'neighbour' relationship on him:" the occupier voluntarily assumes that when he purchases his property. O'Connor J. passed some doubt upon the subjective tests at first instance in *Leakey's* case,[9] finding it "more favourable" to the defendant than the approach in earlier cases, but the Court of Appeal considered the defendant's financial resources to be of relevance in determining the question of reasonableness.[10] Argument by counsel for the National Trust that the subjective test would result in delay in reaching decisions, increased complexity, the necessity for discovery of the defendant's bank account and a detailed examination of his financial resources was brushed aside by the Court of Appeal. It may be that the subjective test will be limited to cases where the hazard on the land has arisen exclusively through an act of nature.[11]

Thus, whether the defendant has acted reasonably or not would depend on the court's assessment of the method adopted, the time, the skill and care which he has shown, his motive, and the cost of acting otherwise. This assessment is, of course, necessary only when the defendant has already shown that the state of affairs he was maintaining was ordinary.

(6) Prescription

Although a person may be interfering with his neighbour's enjoyment of his land, he may be excused by reason of having acquired the right by prescription. In order to establish such a defence, the defendant must show that in doing the acts complained of he was acting openly and to the knowledge of the owner of the servient tenement.[12] Subject to these conditions, after the harm has been caused continuously for 20 years,[13] a prescriptive right to continue the harmful state of affairs is acquired as an easement appurtenant to the land on which it exists.[14] It is not sufficient, however, that the operations of the defendant which now cause the harm have been continued for the space of 20 years; they must have been actionable for that period. The time runs, not from the day when the state of affairs came into existence, but from the day when that state of affairs caused actionable harm. In *Sturges* v. *Bridgman*[15] the defendant had for more than 20 years used certain heavy machinery in his business as a confectioner. His premises in Wigmore Street adjoined the lower end of the garden of the plaintiff, a physician in Wimpole Street. Some short time before the action the plaintiff built a consulting room at the foot of his garden, and then found that in the use of it he was seriously inconvenienced by the noises of the defendant's machinery. The defendant pleaded a prescriptive right, but the defence was held insufficient, because there had been no actual nuisance until the erection of the plaintiff's consulting room, and until then he had had no right of action. It follows from the same principle that the nuisance must for 20 years have been a nuisance to

[8] [1972] A.C. 877, 898.
[9] [1978] Q.B. 849, 867–868.
[10] [1980] Q.B. 485.
[11] Although this is admittedly illogical. *Winfield & Jolowicz* favour such a narrow interpretation: see p. 87, footnote 66.
[12] *Liverpool Corporation* v. *Coghill (H.) & Son Ltd.* [1918] 1 Ch. 307.
[13] An arbitrary period, as to which see *Ogus and Richardson*, [1977] C.L.J. 284, 303.
[14] *Sturges* v. *Bridgman* (1879) 11 Ch.D. 852, 863.
[15] (1879) 11 Ch.D. 852.

the plaintiff or his predecessors in title, and that it is not enough that it has been for that period a nuisance to other people in the occupation of other property. The right can be acquired only against specific property, not against all the world.

§ 23. INJURIES TO SERVITUDES

We must now deal with those cases where there is a wrongful disturbance of an easement or other servitude appurtenant to land. Servitudes may be classified into easements, profits and licences. A profit entitles its owners to take away and appropriate some part of the produce or substance of the servient land, whereas an easement entitles him merely to the use or benefit of the land without any such appropriation, so that the owner of an easement cannot maintain trespass,[16] but must sue in nuisance. But the owner of a profit has been held entitled to sue in trespass for disturbance of his enjoyment of it, even though the defendant is the occupier of the land in question.[17] It is important to remember that the interest which is the subject-matter of an easement must be capable of forming the subject-matter of a grant. It is for this reason that there can be no easement consisting in a right to an uninterrupted view from the windows of a house,[18] nor can there be any right of privacy amounting to a legal easement—a right, for example, that the owner of a house shall not open windows in it so as to overlook the adjoining garden.[19] Hence, as we have seen,[20] an occupier of land is free to erect a wall or fence with the sole object of blocking his neighbour's view, or preventing him from acquiring an easement of light[21]—a "spite-fence" as it is sometimes called.[22] So it could be said that "English law had long recognised the duty of occupiers of land not to offend their neighbour's sense of smell or hearing, but had left them lamentably free to offend their neighbour's sense of sight."[23] Today, however, statutes such as the Public Health Act 1936 and the Town and Country Planning Act 1971, have provided wide powers for the protection of the amenities of residential neighbourhoods: the details do not belong to the law of tort.

Servitudes are either natural or acquired. Natural servitudes are those which are naturally appurtenant to land, and therefore require no special mode of acquisition, for example, the right of land, unencumbered by buildings, to the support of the adjoining land. But the right of a building to the support of adjoining land or buildings is an acquired easement. The chief recognised easements are (1) rights of way, (2) rights of entry for any

---

[16] *Paine & Co. v. St. Neots Gas Co.* [1939] 3 All E.R. 812, 823.
[17] *Mason v. Clarke* [1955] A.C. 778.
[18] "The law don't give an action for such things of delight": *Aldred's Case* (1610) 9 Co.Rep. 57b.
[19] *Turner v. Spooner* (1861) 30 L.J.Ch. 801. See also *Victoria Park Racing Co. v. Taylor* (1937) 58 C.L.R. 479 where the High Court of Australia held that it was *not* a nuisance to broadcast a description of horse races from adjoining land, and the Judicial Committee refused leave to appeal (*The Times*, January 20, 1938). See above, § 10.
[20] Above, § 10.
[21] The Rights of Light Act 1959 enables an occupier (if he wishes) to register a land charge which has the same effect as a "spite-fence."
[22] The largest "spite-fence" in Western Europe is probably to be found on the shores of Dublin Bay—a terrace of a dozen six-storey houses, which, although handsome in themselves, were erected with the object and effect of destroying the view from a nobleman's country house.
[23] *McVittie v. Bolton Corporation* [1945] K.B. 281, 283, *per* Scott L.J.

purpose relating to the dominant land, (3) rights in respect of the support of land and buildings, (4) rights of light and air, (5) rights in respect of water, (6) rights to do some act which would otherwise amount to a nuisance to the servient land, (7) rights of placing or keeping things on the servient land.

Any act done without lawful justification, either by the owner of the servient land or by a stranger, which interferes with the exercise or enjoyment of any easement or profit is a tort actionable at the suit of him who is in lawful possession of the dominant land or in whom the profit is legally vested in possession.

Possessory title to servitudes. The jus tertii

It is a difficult question to determine how far in the case of disturbance of servitudes mere *de facto* possession is a sufficiently good title against a wrongdoer. Such possession may be of two kinds: (1) The use and enjoyment without legal title of a legal servitude vested in some other person: as when I occupy without title land to which a right of ancient light or a right of way is legally appurtenant. (2) The use and enjoyment *de facto* of benefits of a kind capable of being the subject of a servitude: as when the owner of a house is *de facto* in the possession of support afforded to it by the adjoining land, or of the access of light to his windows, no legal right to such support or light having been acquired by grant, prescription, or otherwise.

(1) As to the first of these modes of possession a possessory title to land will bring with it a possessory title to all servitudes legally appurtenant to that land, and a stranger (*i.e.* any person other than the lawful owner or occupier of the servient land) can no more plead the *jus tertii* in an action for the disturbance of a right of way, light or support than in an action for trespass or nuisance. But can the servient owner himself plead the *jus tertii* of the true dominant owner? Probably in this case a distinction must be drawn between natural and acquired servitudes. In the case of natural servitudes a possessory title is valid even against the servient owner.[24] But in the case of acquired servitudes such a title is probably invalid, and the servient owner could plead that the person to whom the servitude had been granted was neither the plaintiff nor any person through whom he claimed. In such a case the plaintiff would have to plead and prove his title to an acquired easement.

(2) The use and enjoyment *de facto* of benefits capable of being the subject of a servitude has, of course, no protection as against the owner of the quasi-servient land; but the question which we have to consider is whether it is not protected *adversus extraneos*. If a trespasser on the adjoining land injures my house by interfering with its *de facto* support, or blocks up my modern windows, will he be permitted to plead that I have acquired no legal or equitable[25] servitude over the land entitling me to such support or light? The answer to this question is not clear. Some authorities hold that *de facto* enjoyment of an easement is protected against strangers,[26] but there are dicta in the Court of Appeal the other way.[27]

---

[24] *Nicholls* v. *Ely Beet Sugar Factory Ltd.* [1931] 2 Ch. 84. But Farwell J. was careful to limit his decision to pollution actions which are "not trespass, but very analogous to trespass."

[25] See *Mason* v. *Clarke* [1955] A.C. 778.

[26] See, *e.g. Keegan* v. *Young* [1963] N.Z.L.R. 770.

[27] *Paine & Co. Ltd.* v. *St. Neots Gas Co.* [1939] 3 All E.R. 812, 823.

§ 24. LICENCES[28]

A licence, in the sense of the term with which we are concerned in this chapter, is an agreement (not amounting to the grant of a lease or easement or *profit à prendre*) that it shall be lawful for the licensee to enter upon the land of the licensor or to do some other act in relation thereto which would otherwise be illegal.[29] The classical description of a licence was given by Sir John Vaughan C.J. in *Thomas* v. *Sorrell*[30]: "A dispensation or licence properly passeth no interest, nor alters or transfers property in anything, but only makes an action lawful which without it would have been unlawful. As a licence to go beyond the seas, to hunt in a man's park and carry away the deer killed to his own use, to cut down a tree in a man's ground, and to carry it away the next day after to his own use, are licences as to the acts of hunting and cutting down the tree, but as to carrying away the deer killed and the tree cut down, they are grants."

Lease and licence

Sometimes it is difficult to determine whether the transaction which has given rise to entry upon the premises of another is lease or a licence. If the transaction is a lease a proprietary interest passes to the lessee; the parties must comply with the conditions prescribed by the Law of Property Act 1925, s. 40; and the lessee may be able to take advantage of the protection afforded by the Rent Restriction Acts. It is quite clear that the difference between a lease and a licence does not depend on any label which the parties themselves have affixed to the transaction but upon the true interpretation in law of what they have done.[31] An important question is whether the entrant has obtained exclusive possession of the premises; if he has, it is probably a lease and not a licence. There may be cases in which a person with exclusive possession is rightly described as a licensee, but they are exceptional, *e.g.* where he has been let into possession as the result of a family arrangement.[32]

We must consider (1) the effect of the licence as between the parties to it, and (2) the extent to which it binds third parties.

(1) The effect of the licence as between the parties

The main distinction drawn here is between licences coupled with the grant of an interest and bare licences. Licences coupled with an interest (as they are often called) are irrevocable.[33] An injunction can be obtained to prevent the wrongful revocation of such a licence.[34] In such a case the licence and the proprietary interest thereby granted are distinct concepts.

It is uncertain whether the term "interest" is confined to interests in land or in goods on the land. It has been held to cover a right to attend a

---

[28] On this topic, see Dawson and Pearce, *Licences Relating to the Use of Occupation of Land* (1979).

[29] The term also means an agreement which authorises the licensee to use or enjoy any property of the licensor—*e.g.* the subject-matter of a patent: *Martin-Baker Aircraft Co. Ltd.* v. *Canadian Flight Equipment Ltd.* [1955] 2 Q.B. 556.

[30] (1673) Vaugh. 330, 351.

[31] *Shell-Mex and B.P. Ltd.* v. *Manchester Garages Ltd.* [1971] 1 W.L.R. 612.

[32] *Heslop* v. *Burns* [1974] 1 W.L.R. 1241.

[33] Some statutory licences are also irrevocable—*e.g.* those granted under the Domestic Violence Act 1976.

[34] *Frogley* v. *Lovelace* (1859) John. 333.

creditors' meeting[35] or a cinema performance,[36] but it is doubtful whether it covers a right to do specified works under a construction contract.[37]

Bare licence prima facie revocable at common law

Under a bare licence no interest in property passes: the licensee is simply not a trespasser. A licence of this kind may be either gratuitous or contained in a contract for valuable consideration: in either case at common law it was revocable at the will of the licensor and was therefore no justification for any act done in exercise of it after revocation. This was laid down in *Wood* v. *Leadbitter*,[38] and emphatically reaffirmed by the Court of Appeal in *Thompson* v. *Park*.[39]

In *Wood* v. *Leadbitter* the occupiers of Doncaster racecourse in breach of their agreement ordered the plaintiff, to whom they had sold a ticket for the races, to leave the premises while the races were going on, and on his refusal to leave they procured his forcible expulsion by their servant, the defendant. In an action for assault the defendant pleaded that the plaintiff was a trespasser. It was held by the Court of Exchequer that the action would not lie. Although the licence had been revoked improperly and in breach of contract its revocation was nonetheless effectual. The plaintiff was a trespasser. It will be noticed that the action was one of tort against the servant of the licensor and not one for breach of contract against the licensor himself. It is well settled[40] that an action for breach of contract will lie in such a case even at common law, and notwithstanding *Wood* v. *Leadbitter*. If, however, the licensee insists, notwithstanding the revocation of his licence (even though it is wrongful as being in breach of contract), in entering or remaining on the land or in otherwise exercising his licence, he becomes at common law a trespasser or other wrongdoer. The rule is an illustration of the difference between a legal *power* to do a thing effectively and a legal *right* or *liberty* to do it lawfully. A licensor has at common law the power to revoke the licence at any time, but he has no right to revoke it before the expiration of the term.[41]

Exceptions

There are two recognised qualifications to the rule in *Wood* v. *Leadbitter*:

(1) A licensee is entitled to a reasonable time in which to remove himself and his property after the licence has been revoked and he cannot be treated as a trespasser until the expiry of that time.[42] This packing-up period (as it

---

[35] *Vaughan* v. *Hampson* (1875) 33 L.T. 15.

[36] *Hurst* v. *Picture Theatres Ltd.* [1915] 1 K.B. 1.

[37] *Hounslow London Borough Council* v. *Twickenham Garden Developments Ltd.* [1971] Ch. 233.

[38] (1845) 13 M. & W. 838.

[39] [1944] K.B. 408. Other cases in which a licence was held to have been properly revoked are: *McBean* v. *Howey* [1958] N.Z.L.R. 25; *Stackman* v. *Delhi Court Ltd.* (1960) 24 D.L.R. (2d) 152.

[40] *Kerrison* v. *Smith* [1897] 2 Q.B. 445; *King* v. *David Allen & Sons Ltd.* [1916] 2 A.C. 54.

[41] *Thompson* v. *Park* [1944] K.B. 408, 410. But *Thompson* v. *Park* was said to have been decided "*quasi in furore*" in *Hounslow London Borough Council* v. *Twickenham Garden Developments Ltd.* [1971] Ch. 233, 249, and emphatically dissented from in *Verrall* v. *Great Yarmouth B.C.* [1980] 3 W.L.R. 258.

[42] *Tool Metal Manufacturing Co. Ltd.* v. *Tungsten Electric Co. Ltd.* [1955] 1 W.L.R. 761. And even a trespasser is not entirely without rights: below, § 98.

has been usefully called[43]) is available to gratuitous as well as to contractual licensees. It is unnecessary for the licensor in his notice of revocation to specify the period to which the licensee is entitled.[44] If the licensor gives insufficient, or no, notice of revocation, the licensee still cannot ignore the revocation and treat the licence as if it were still subsisting.[45] In some cases it seems that a licensee may be entitled to reasonable notice of the proposed revocation as well as to the packing-up period.[46]

(2) The premature revocation of a licence imposes no obligation upon the licensee to do any act for the purpose of preventing the continuing effect upon the servient land of any act which he may have lawfully done before the revocation.[47]

Wood v. *Leadbitter* doubted

Since the fusion of law and equity, according to the decision of the majority of the Court of Appeal in *Hurst* v. *Picture Theatres Ltd.*[48] the rule in *Wood* v. *Leadbitter* has to a very large extent become obsolete. In *Hurst's* case the majority held that the plaintiff, who had purchased from the defendants a ticket entitling him to occupy a seat at a cinema, had a good cause of action in *tort* for the act of the defendants in forcibly removing him from the building under the mistaken belief that he had wrongfully obtained admission without payment. Hence the plaintiff recovered substantial damages as for assault instead of the merely nominal damages which would have been recoverable in an action for breach of contract.[49] The majority of the court seem to have adopted the view that the decision in *Wood* v. *Leadbitter* turned on the absence of a seal and that since the Judicature Acts this ground of decision had become obsolete for all courts would now treat the plaintiff as being in the same position as if the licence had in fact been under seal. But a seal would have made no difference in *Hurst* v. *Picture Theatres*.[50] The essence of the matter is that the right to enter on premises to see a spectacle is not an interest in land in the ordinary use of legal language: it is not a proprietary interest capable of being the subject-matter of a grant, as is a lease, easement or a *profit à prendre*.[51] The law has always been reluctant to permit the number of proprietary interests in land to be

---

[43] *Winter Garden Theatre (London) Ltd.* v. *Millennium Productions Ltd.* [1948] A.C. 173, 206.
[44] *Isaac* v. *Hotel de Paris Ltd.* [1960] 1 W.L.R. 239.
[45] *Dorling* v. *Honnor Marine Ltd.* [1964] Ch. 560, 567 (reversed on another point [1965] Ch. 1).
[46] *Winter Garden Theatre (London) Ltd.* v. *Millennium Productions Ltd.* [1948] A.C. 173, 205.
[47] *Armstrong* v. *Sheppard and Short Ltd.* [1959] 2 Q.B. 384. But see above, § 12.
[48] [1915] 1 K.B. 1, followed by the Irish Supreme Court in *Whipp* v. *Mackey* [1927] I.R. 372, 387.
[49] It is generally believed that the damages obtainable by such a licensee in an action for breach of contract are limited to the value of his ticket, either because the assault and battery is too remote a consequence of the breach of contract, or because of the rule in *Addis* v. *Gramophone Co.* [1909] A.C. 488, which prohibits the award of aggravated damages in an action for breach of contract. If this belief should prove unfounded, as *Jackson* v. *Horizon Holidays Ltd.* [1975] 1 W.L.R. 1468 now indicates, many of the difficulties mentioned here might disappear.
[50] [1915] 1 K.B. 1, 18, *per* Phillimore L.J. (dissenting). As Alderson B. himself said: "It may further be observed, that a licence under seal (provided it be a mere licence) is as revocable as a licence by parol" ((1845) 13 M. & W. 838, 845).
[51] See above, § 23.

increased beyond the recognised categories of incorporeal hereditaments for fear lest purchasers should find themselves saddled with unknown and perhaps fanciful burdens.[52]

It has been said that the fallacy of this criticism of *Hurst's* case lies in its insistence upon discovering a proprietary right as a condition of affording protection to the licensee.[53] Contracts as well as grants may create irrevocable interests, and so the question whether any restrictions exist on the power of a licensor to determine a revocable licence must depend upon the circumstances of each case.[54] This view has received much support[55] since it was adopted by Lord Greene M.R. in the *Winter Garden Theatre* case[56] as a "rather simple way . . . to get round any difficulties which might be felt as to the reasoning in *Hurst* v. *Picture Theatres*."

The present law

It seems, therefore, that the former rule of law that a licence is revocable despite any contract has been converted into a rule of construction that a licence is *prima facie* revocable or variable[57] subject to the terms of any contract between the parties.[58] The extent to which the licensor has disabled himself from exercising his power of revocation will have to be ascertained according to the ordinary principles of construction. It may well be that an injunction could be obtained to restrain the revocation of a licence which is intended to extend over a substantial tract of time—*e.g.* a ticket entitling the holder to admission throughout the season at an open-air racecourse.[59] But the courts will also probably be ready to assume that a licence granted for valuable consideration for a limited time and for a limited purpose was intended to be irrevocable until that purpose has been accomplished in the manner contemplated.[60] If in such a case performance of the act or purpose licensed has actually begun the remedies of declaration or injunction will be available to the licensee to restrain the licensor from either revoking in breach of contract or acting on his purported revocation, as the case may require. So in a proper case a licence[61] or statutory right[62] to go upon or use land may be enforced by way of injunction. But it is still no easier than before to understand what the law is if the licence is not suitable to be

---

[52] It is not easy to find authority for this elementary proposition: "But to hold that one of the fundamental doctrines of real property can be called in question because it has not been in terms laid down by a judgment of the House of Lords is, in my opinion, to invest the judicial proceedings of this House with an authority to which they are not entitled. The ABC of the law is generally not questioned before your Lordships, just because it is the ABC"; *Johnston* v. *O'Neill* [1911] A.C. 552, 592, *per* Lord Dunedin.

[53] *Cowell* v. *Rosehill Racecourse Co.* (1937) 56 C.L.R. 605, 651, *per* Evatt J.

[54] *Minister of Health* v. *Bellotti* [1944] K.B. 298, 304; *Errington* v. *Errington* [1952] 1 K.B. 290, 298; *Bendall* v. *McWhirter* [1952] 2 Q.B. 466, 479; *Tool Metal Manufacturing Co. Ltd.* v. *Tungsten Electric Co. Ltd.* [1955] 1 W.L.R. 761.

[55] See, *e.g. Hounslow London Borough Council* v. *Twickenham Garden Developments Ltd.* [1971] Ch. 233, and *Verrall* v. *Great Yarmouth B.C.* [1980] 3 W.L.R. 258.

[56] [1946] 1 All E.R. 678, 685.

[57] *White* v. *Blackmore* [1972] 2 Q.B. 651.

[58] There is an implied condition in a licence to enter to see a spectacle that the licensee will behave in a reasonable manner: *Duffield* v. *Police* [1971] N.Z.L.R. 378.

[59] Evershed M.R. (1954) 70 L.Q.R. 339–340.

[60] *Duffield* v. *Police* N.Z.L.R. 378, 381.

[61] *Heidke* v. *Sydney City Council* (1952) S.R.(N.S.W.) 143.

[62] *Warder* v. *Cooper* [1970] Ch. 495.

specifically enforced by way of injunction (as in *Thompson* v. *Park*[63]), or if the licensee has been actually ejected (as in *Hurst's* case) before the aid of equity can be invoked,[64] or if he claims only damages and not an injunction. Still, as wrongful acts are no passport to favour in a court of equity, one wrongfully ejected may be put back in possession by a mandatory injunction.[65]

(2) Effects of the licence on third parties

Since a licence is not a legal servitude, it does not run with the servient land at law so as to bind all subsequent owners of it. At law, indeed, it is a mere agreement, which binds no one save the grantor himself. Such an agreement, however, if of such a nature as to be specifically enforceable, amounts to a good equitable servitude—that is to say, it binds and runs with the land in equity so as to be enforceable not merely against the grantor, but also against all subsequent owners and occupiers of the land except purchasers for value without notice of any such equitable right.[66] Thus it has been held that a licence to occupy premises is binding on the devisee of the licensor.[67]

Yet such an "equity" is enforceable against the third party only in the sense that he will be restrained by injunction from acting inconsistently with it. For although a licensee has an action for damages for breach of contract against the licensor for any disturbance of the licence committed by him, he has no remedy at law against any subsequent owner or occupier or any stranger for a disturbance of his right. This seems to follow logically from the fact that he has no legal estate or interest in the servient land, and it is against the policy of the law to create new proprietary interests.[68] Thus in *Hill* v. *Tupper*,[69] in which the plaintiff had acquired by grant under the seal of a canal company an exclusive right of keeping pleasure-boats for hire upon the canal, he unsuccessfully sued at law for damages a stranger who infringed this monopoly.

This absence of a remedy by way of damages available to a licensee against a stranger is an anomolous feature of our law. It seems curious that he who, by agreement with the occupier of a building, has expended money in painting advertisements upon one of its walls should have no civil remedy

---

[63] [1944] K.B. 408 (quarrelling schoolmasters: the courts cannot compel two men to be of one mind in a house). If the licence is not fit to be specifically enforced by way of injunction, neither is it fit to be exercised in defiance of the will of the licensor. Yet, until *Hurst's* case is overruled, this cannot be said to be the law.

[64] The suggestion that a judge who happened to pass by such an incident might have been persuaded to grant an *ex parte* injunction is no longer fanciful (as it once was: Megarry, 11 J.S.P.T.L. 181). Under Ord. 29, r. 1, an injunction may be granted in an urgent case before the writ or originating summons is issued: *Re N.* [1967] Ch. 512; and in *Allen* v. *Jambo Holdings Ltd.* [1980] 1 W.L.R. 1252, it would appear that the plaintiff's counsel successfully applied for a *Mareva* injunction by telephoning the judge. Still, "even the longest modern film would not have given Hurst time to get an injunction from a Chancery judge and return with his order to the cinema before the end of the showing": Evershed, (1954) 70 L.Q.R. 333.

[65] *Warder* v. *Cooper* [1970] 1 Ch. 495.

[66] *Bendall* v. *McWhirter* [1952] 2 Q.B. 466, 481. These rights are outside the scope of the Land Registration Act 1925, at any rate when the licensee is in actual possession or occupation of the land: *Binions* v. *Evans* [1972] Ch. 359.

[64] *Errington* v. *Errington* [1952] 1 K.B. 290.

[68] *National Provincial Bank Ltd.* v. *Ainsworth* [1965] A.C. 1175. See below, § 163.

[69] (1863) 2 H. & C. 121.

against a third person who wilfully defaces them.[70] There is, however, one important class of licences to which this rule has no application—namely, those in which the licence is of such a nature that it would, if created by deed or prescription, amount to a legal easement or profit. Thus in *Mason* v. *Clarke*[71] the appellant had the benefit of an oral agreement entitling him to catch rabbits on the Hothorpe estate (a *profit à prendre*); the House of Lords held that he could recover damages from the respondent for his interference with the exercise of those rights. The distinction between *Hill* v. *Tupper* and *Mason* v. *Clarke* is that in the former case what the plaintiff was trying to do was to set up, under the guise of an easement, a monopoly which had no normal connection with the ordinary use of his land, but which was merely an independent business enterprise.[72] It is also a question whether the power of courts of equity to grant an injunction to a licensee, taken in conjunction with their power to grant damages in lieu of injunction,[73] does not exclude the rule in *Hill* v. *Tupper* in all cases in which an injunction can be granted.

§ 25. RIGHTS OF WAY

Rights of way are either private or public. The former call for no special consideration, for they are governed by the ordinary principles already considered in relation to easements in general. Public rights of way, on the other hand, are not easements and demand more particular examination. They are of two kinds, for they exist either over highways or over navigable rivers.[74] The law as to these two is essentially the same.

A highway (including in that term any public way) is a piece of land over which the public at large possesses a right of way. A highway extends to the whole width of the space between the fences or hedges on either side, and is not confined to the metalled centre strip[75]—partly in order to admit light and air to it, and partly because "Macadam's system of road-making with broken stone was not introduced at the earliest until just before the end of the eighteenth century."[76] At common law the ownership of a highway is in the owner or owners of the land adjoining it on either side, the highway having been made such by an actual or presumed dedication of it to the use of the public by the proprietors of the land over which it runs. By statute certain kinds of highways are now vested in local authorities. These statutes, however, have been so interpreted as to vest in the local authorities not the whole of the land on which the highway lies *usque ad coelum et ad inferos*, but only so much of it above and below the surface as is reasonably necessary for the efficient construction, care, and use of the highway. The subsoil below and the space above the limits so defined remain as at common law in the owners of the adjoining lands.[77]

---

[70] *King* v. *David Allen & Sons, Billposting Ltd.* [1916] 2 A.C. 54. Perhaps this decision could be limited to cases in which the licence has not yet been acted on.
[71] [1955] A.C. 778.
[72] *Re Ellenborough Park* [1956] Ch. 131, 175.
[73] See below, § 219.
[74] *Esso Petroleum Co. Ltd.* v. *Southport Corporation* [1956] A.C. 218.
[75] *Holland* v. *Dublin County Council* (1967) 112 I.L.T.R. 1.
[76] *Harvey* v. *Truro R.D.C.* [1903] 2 Ch. 638, 643, *per* Joyce J.
[77] *Tithe Redemption Commission* v. *Runcorn U.D.C.* [1954] Ch. 383.

There are at least four distinct kinds of injury which may be committed in respect of a highway:

(1) Trespass and the highway

This has already been considered.[78]

(2) Nuisance to adjoining occupiers

This may arise in several ways—for example, keeping horses or vehicles standing constantly in front of a shop,[79] or watching or besetting premises with a view to compelling the occupier to do, or abstain from doing, what he is entitled to do, at any rate if there is intimidation, violence or obstruction. There is no general right to picket premises,[80] although some protection is given in trade disputes by Trade Union and Labour Relations Act 1974, s. 15.

(3) Disturbance of the rights of access to a highway[81]

Every person who occupies land immediately adjoining a highway has a private right of access to the highway from his land and vice versa; and any act done without lawful justification whereby the exercise of this private right is obstructed is an actionable wrong.[82] This right of access is a private right of property, and if what is complained of is sufficiently substantial to constitute an interference with that right, he may recover at least nominal damages, for it is an example of an action on the case succeeding without proof of special damage.[83] This right may indirectly protect the owner's interest in a view from or to his land, interference with which is not otherwise actionable.[84] Interference with a window display may be actionable if it deprives the plaintiff of his own right of access to that window.[85]

At common law a frontager had the right of entrance and exit from his land on to a highway at any point. But this common law right does not mean that the landowner can require that the highway should be in a condition or state, along his whole frontage, most convenient for the exercise of the right.[86] In any event, the common law right of access has been greatly cut down by statutes (see, for example, the Highways Act 1959, s. 155), especially since local authorities have had vested in them the surface of the highway.[87] Opening up a new access may also constitute development for which planning permission is required. This right of access to a highway by the occupier of land abutting upon it must be distinguished from the right of passing along the highway.[88] The former is a private and the latter a public right, and for any infringement of the former an action will lie; whereas, as we shall see in the next section, no action will lie for an infringement of the

---

[78] Above, § 11.
[79] *Benjamin* v. *Storr* (1874) L.R. 9 C.P. 400.
[80] *Hubbard* v. *Pitt* [1976] Q.B. 142. See below, Chap. 16.
[81] See Garner, "Rights in Highways" (1960) 24 *The Conveyancer* 454.
[82] *Barber* v. *Penley* [1893] 2 Ch. 447.
[83] *Walsh* v. *Ervin* [1952] V.L.R. 361.
[84] See above, § 23.
[85] *Hall* v. *Jamaica Omnibus Services Ltd.* (1966) 9 W.I.R. 344.
[86] *Holland* v. *Dublin County Council* (1967) 112 I.L.T.R. 1.
[87] Cork, "Right of Access to and from the Highway" [1952] J.P.L. 553.
[88] *Holland* v. *Dublin County Council* (1967) 112 I.L.T.R. 1.

public right of passing except on proof of some special or particular consequential damage suffered by the plaintiff. The private right of access thus
protected includes merely the right to get from the highway into the
plaintiff's land, and from his land into the highway; and does not include a
right to get to and from the plaintiff's land by going along the highway, for
this is merely the public right of passage.[89] A disturbance of this private
right of access may or may not be at the same time a disturbance of the
public right of passage. A man's doorway may be obstructed by an act
which in no way obstructs the use of the highway; and conversely the
highway may be obstructed, while the right of access remains unaffected.[90]

(4) Public nuisance to a highway

This consists in obstructing the highway or rendering it dangerous.[91]
These are two different categories of nuisance, and cases of dangers in the
highway are not necessarily authorities on obstruction.[92] For an obstruction, if unreasonable, is a public nuisance in itself, and it is not necessary
also to show that it is dangerous. The topic is fully considered in the following section.

§ 26. NUISANCE TO A HIGHWAY

The term nuisance is here used in the sense of public nuisance—*i.e.* an
indictable criminal wrong.[93] "In order to establish nuisance or obstruction
in a public highway something which is indictable—a punishable
offence—must be established."[94] No such nuisance can be legalised by
prescription.[95] On the other hand, the plaintiff must prove that the nuisance
was a cause of his injuries. So contributory negligence is a defence.[96]

(1) Obstructions to highway

Examples of this are stopping or narrowing a highway by erecting a
fence, scaffolding or hoarding,[97] or building[98] which projects beyond the
boundary line; leaving[99] horses and carts,[1] or motor-vehicles,[2] standing in it
for an unreasonable time or in unreasonable number[3] collecting a crowd of

---

[89] This established principle was re-affirmed in *R. (McCreash)* v. *Armagh County Court Judge*
    [1978] N.I. 164.
[90] *Walsh* v. *Ervin* [1952] V.L.R. 361.
[91] *Trevett* v. *Lee* [1955] 1 W.L.R. 113, 117; *Dymond* v. *Pearce* [1972] 1 Q.B. 496, 501.
[92] *Dymond* v. *Pearce* [1972] 1 Q.B. 496, 502.
[93] The Highways Act 1959, ss. 117–150, creates numerous criminal offences in relation to
    the obstruction of or damage to highways.
[94] *The Carlgarth* [1927] P. 93, 102, *per* Bankes L.J.
[95] *Hubbard* v. *Pitt* [1976] Q.B. 142.
[96] *Dymond* v. *Pearce* [1972] 1 Q.B. 496.
[97] *Harper* v. *Haden & Sons* [1933] Ch. 298.
[98] *Black* v. *Mitchell* [1951] N.I. 145 (projecting sunblind).
[99] This term connotes some degree of permanence: *Dymond* v. *Pearce* [1972] 1 Q.B. 496.
[1] *Fritz* v. *Hobson* (1880) 14 Ch.D. 542.
[2] *Chesterfield Corporation* v. *Arthur Robinson (Transport) Ltd.* (1955) 106 L.J.(News.) 61 is
    a good modern example. A main road was obstructed for 76 hours as a result of the
    defendants' negligent mode of conveying an outsize load of 83 tons. The plaintiffs
    recovered for the special damage which they had suffered through the diversion of their
    omnibus service.
[3] "No one can make a stableyard of the King's highway": *R.* v. *Cross* (1812) 3 Camp. 224,
    227 *per* Lord Ellenborough C.J.

people in it, as at the door of a theatre[4] or shop,[5] or holding a picket,
demonstration or procession.[6] But the procession must be an unreasonable
use of the highway[7]—it cannot be a nuisance for a number of people to use
the highway jointly and contemporaneously, for that is just what the
highway is made for.[8]

(2) Dangers to highway

This may be caused either by something done in the highway itself or by
something done on the land which adjoins it. It is now clear that the fact
that a vehicle has broken down on the highway in the dark and its lights
have gone out without any negligence on the part of the driver does not constitute nuisance (or negligence[9]) immediately and automatically. The driver
may, however, be liable if he allows the unlighted vehicle to obstruct the
highway without taking reasonable steps to light it or remove it or give warning of its existence,[10] for "any unlighted obstacle on a fast motor-road is a
danger to traffic. That is a proposition, not of law, but of common sense."[11]
Other examples are keeping in the highway defective and dangerous
tramway-lines, coal-plates, or cellar gratings[12]; leaving on the highway or
adjacent thereto matter on which passengers are likely to slip[13]; allowing a
house, fence, or other structure immediately adjoining the highway to
become ruinous and dangerous[14]; keeping unfenced an excavation so close
to the highway as to be a danger in case of accidental deviation[15]; keeping at
a golf-club a hole where players are in the habit of slicing onto the
highway.[16] The plaintiff's property need not be immediately contiguous to
the highway: it is enough if it is sufficiently proximate to the highway to be
affected by the misuse of it.[17]

Existing dangers

When, however, a road is dedicated to the public, it is presumed to be so
dedicated on the terms that the public right of passage is to be subject to all
obstructions and dangers which exist at the time of dedication; and the
adjoining owners and occupiers are therefore under no liability for maintaining such obstructions or dangers or for any mischief that may result from
them.[18] Nor are they liable for a mere passive failure to prevent new dangers
from arising on the highway or to give warning of their existence. *A fortiori*

---

[4] *Barber* v. *Penley* [1893] 2 Ch. 447 (crowds at *Charley's Aunt*).
[5] *Dwyer* v. *Mansfield* [1946] K.B. 437.
[6] *Hubbard* v. *Pitt* [1976] Q.B. 142.
[7] *R.* v. *Clark* [1964] 2 Q.B. 315.
[8] *Johnson* v. *Kent* (1975) 132 C.L.R. 164, 176.
[9] *Moore* v. *Maxwells of Emsworth Ltd.* [1968] 1 W.L.R. 1077.
[10] *Maitland* v. *Raisbeck* [1944] K.B. 689. For failure to light or guard obstructions erected in
the highway under statutory powers, see below, § 191.
[11] *Hill-Venning* v. *Beszant* 66 T.L.R. (Pt. 2) 921, 927, *per* Denning L.J.
[12] *Pretty* v. *Bickmore* (1873) L.R. 8 C.P. 401. See generally the Highways Act 1959, Pt. VII.
[13] *McGowan* v. *Masterson* (1952) 87 I.L.T.R. 102.
[14] *Harrold* v. *Watney* [1898] 2 Q.B. 320. Contrast *Morton* v. *Wheeler, The Times*, February
1, 1956 (spikes on shop window not a nuisance).
[15] *Jacobs* v. *L.C.C.* [1950] A.C. 361.
[16] *Castle* v. *St. Augustine's Links* (1922) 38 T.L.R. 615.
[17] *Southport Corporation* v. *Esso Petroleum Co. Ltd.* [1953] 3 W.L.R. 773, 776; [1956]
A.C. 218, 225.
[18] *Fisher* v. *Prowse* (1862) 2 B. & S. 770.

when something has been done on the highway itself which makes it
dangerous, there is no obligation on the occupier of the adjoining land to do
away with the danger. Were it otherwise, an intolerable burden would be put
upon the occupiers of land adjoining highways.[19] In these respects the public
must look after itself.

Unreasonable obstructions

It must be realised that it is not every obstruction of or danger to the
highway which constitutes a public nuisance. The law has to hold an even
balance between the conflicting claims of those who have an interest in the
use of the highway. On the one hand, it has been settled for at least a
century that "traffic on the highways, whether by land or sea, cannot be
conducted without exposing those whose persons or property are near to it
to some inevitable risk; and that being so, those who go on the highway, or
have their property adjacent to it, may well be held to do so subject to their
taking on themselves the risk of injury from that inevitable danger."[20] Hence
although a permanent obstruction erected in a highway without lawful
authority necessarily constitutes a public nuisance, as it in fact operates as a
withdrawal of part of the highway from the public, a temporary obstruction
may be permissible if it is negligible in point of time or authorised by Parliament or occasioned in the reasonable and lawful user of the highway as a
highway.[21] The law relating to the user of highways is in truth the law of
give and take.[22] Thus a person has a right to obstruct a highway by the erection of scaffolding and hoardings for the purpose of repairing his house,[23] so
long as the inconvenience to the public is necessarily so caused and does not
offend either in *quantum* or duration; or he may temporarily obstruct the
highway by causing his motor-car to stop outside his house for the purpose
of discharging passengers or goods going into the house.[24] Again a
temporary excavation[25] or stoppage[26] may be permissible.

On the other hand, we shall see that any person who procures or
authorises the doing in any highway of any dangerous act other than the use
of the highway for ordinary purposes of passage has imposed upon him a
duty of care so strict that it cannot be discharged by the employment of an
independent contractor.[27]

Particular Damage

A nuisance to a highway is a criminal offence and may be made the
subject of an indictment at common law. It may also be restrained by
injunction at the suit of the Attorney-General acting *ex officio* or at the rela-

---

[19] *Nicholson* v. *Southern Ry.* [1935] 1 K.B. 558.
[20] *Fletcher* v. *Rylands* (1866) L.R. 1 Ex. 265, 286, *per* Blackburn J. See the same learned
     judge in *River Wear Commissioners* v. *Adamson* (1877) 2 App.Cas. 743, 767. For other
     illustrations of this principle, see above, § 6, and below, § 46.
[21] *Buck* v. *Briggs Motor Bodies Ltd.*, *The Times*, April 18, 1959 (gate across pavement).
[22] *Harper* v. *Haden* (*G. N.*) *& Sons Ltd.* [1933] Ch. 298, 316–317, 320.
[23] *Harper* v. *Haden* (*G. N.*) *& Sons Ltd.* [1933] Ch. 298 (in fact in this case the scaffolding
     was erected for the purpose of adding another storey); *Almeroth* v. *Chivers Ltd.* [1948] 1
     All E.R. 53 is on the other side of the line.
[24] *Trevett* v. *Lee* [1955] 1 W.L.R. 113, 118.
[25] *Wall* v. *Morrissey* [1969] I.R. 10.
[26] *Dymond* v. *Pearce* [1972] 1 Q.B. 496.
[27] *Wall* v. *Morrissey* [1969] I.R. 10, 14. See below, § 184.

tion of a local authority or any private person interested in the matter. But it is not *per se* actionable at the suit of a private person—a rule established for the purpose of preventing oppression by means of a multiplicity of civil actions for the same cause. No such action will lie save at the suit of a person who can show special and particular damage suffered by himself and distinct from the general inconvenience endured by him in common with the public at large.[28] So in this branch of the law it is plain that it is not enough for the plaintiff to show that the damage was reasonably forseeable.[29] The terms "special" and "particular" are used, apparently indiscriminately, in this field of the law, to describe the nature of the damage which the plaintiff must prove. The latter term is preferable: the plaintiff need not prove that the damage which he has suffered is extraordinary. Again, the particular damage for which an individual can sue in his own name, is not limited to special damage in the sense of actual pecuniary loss, but may consist of proved general damage—*e.g.* inconvenience and delay, provided that it is substantial, direct and appreciably greater in degree than any suffered by the general public.[30] The damage must be of a substantial character, not fleeting or evanescent.[31]

Nature of particular damage[32]

The special or particular damage which must be proved may include injury to the plaintiff's person or chattels, depreciation of actual value of property and loss of custom.[33]

(1) Injury to person

In *Castle* v. *St. Augustine's Links*[34] a taxicab driver[35] who lost his eye from a sliced golf-ball recovered damages from the golf-club whose hole was so near the highway as to be a public nuisance.[36]

(2) Injury to chattels

When oily smuts from the defendant's refinery damaged both the clothes drying in his garden and the paintwork of his car parked in the road outside, the plaintiff recovered for the former in private nuisance but for the latter in public nuisance.[37] The most striking example is *The Wagon Mound* (*No. 2*),[38] in which it was conceded that the destruction by fire of two ships was particular damage entitling their owners to sue in nuisance.[39]

---

[28] *Winterbottom* v. *Derby* (*Lord*) (1867) L.R. 2 Ex. 316, 320, 322.
[29] *The Wagon Mound* (*No. 2*) [1967] 1 A.C. 617.
[30] *Walsh* v. *Ervin* [1952] V.L.R. 361.
[31] *Vanderpant* v. *Mayfair Hotel Co.* [1930] 1 Ch. 138, 153; *Harper* v. *Haden* (*G. N.*) *& Sons* [1933] Ch. 298, 304, 308.
[32] Prosser, "Private Action for Public Nuisance" (1966) 52 Va.L.Rev. 997.
[33] *Walsh* v. *Ervin* [1952] V.L.R. 361, 368.
[34] (1922) 38 T.L.R. 615.
[35] [36] Who had been General Plumer's driver throughout the First World War without injury. It is submitted that he can, as the right to be free of the fear of personal injury is part of the general right of ordinary enjoyment of one's land: see above, § 18(1).
[37] *Halsey* v. *Esso Petroleum Co. Ltd.* [1961] 1 W.L.R. 683.
[38] [1967] 1 A.C. 617.
[39] But not to recover damages in nuisance, because the loss was unforeseeable: see below, § 202.

(3) Injury to pecuniary interests

This kind of damage may occur when the plaintiff has incurred expense or suffered pecuniary loss by being prevented from using the highway. Thus in *Rose* v. *Miles*[40] the plaintiff, who complained of the obstruction of a navigable canal, was held to have good cause of action on proving that he had been compelled to unload his goods from barges and carry them overland thereby incurring additional expense. If the requirement of particular damage were carried to its logical conclusion, it would seem to exclude a plaintiff who had merely suffered delay through the nuisance, for his damage would be no different from that of others.[41] But the courts have tended to say that "time is money," and permitted recovery for any delay which is different in degree, and not necessarily in kind, from that suffered by other members of the public.[42] So recovery was permitted when "a medical man in large practice whose time is of substantial value" was delayed for 20 minutes at a level-crossing.[43] An action will lie even if the only special damage proved is an injury to the plaintiff's business, due to the fact that the obstruction to the highway has hindered the public from resorting to his business premises,[44] or the conduct of the business had become more expensive.[45] In other words, it is said that the special damage may be suffered by the plaintiff not because he has been prevented from using the highway as beneficially as heretofore, but merely because other persons have been so hindered, so that the result of their hindrance is a loss suffered by himself.[46] It is submitted therefore that damage done to the plaintiff in his trade by the illegal obstruction of a highway is an actionable wrong.[47]

Criticism

These principles are as old as any in the common law[48] and can now be altered only by legislation.[49] [50] In theory the proper remedies for personal injuries caused by such obstructions of the highway as amount to a public nuisance should be the actions of trespass and negligence.[51] But in practice the same result is achieved by the courts requiring proof of negligence in an action for personal injuries caused by an obstruction of the highway.[52]

Plaintiff off highway

The particular damage required to support an action must have been suffered as a result of the use of the highway.[53] Thus in *Jacobs* v. *L.C.C.*[54]

---

[40] (1815) 4 M. & S. 101.
[41] *Winterbottom* v. *Derby* (*Lord*) (1867) L.R. 2 Ex. 316.
[42] *Smith* v. *Wilson* [1903] 2 I.R. 45 (farmer obstructed on way to market).
[43] *Boyd* v. *G.N.R.* [1895] 2 I.R. 555 (yet the damages were only 10s.).
[44] *Campbell* v. *Paddington Corporation* [1911] 1 K.B. 869.
[45] *Gravesham B.C.* v. *British Rail* [1978] Ch. 379, 398.
[46] *Amalgamated Theatres Ltd.* v. *Charles S. Luney Ltd.* [1962] N.Z.L.R. 226, 229.
[47] *Blundy, Clark & Co.* v. *L. and N.E. Ry.* [1931] 2 K.B. 334; *Harper* v. *Haden (G.N.) & Sons* [1933] Ch. 298. This particular point was not taken in *Lyons, Sons & Co.* v. *Gulliver* [1914] 1 Ch. 631 (theatre queue obstructing access).
[48] *Hardcastle* v. *South Yorkshire Ry.* (1859) 4 H. & N. 67.
[49] [50] *Mumford* v. *Naylor* [1951] 1 T.L.R. 1068, 1070 (reversed on another point in [1951] W.N. 579). Although the law on the matter is commonly traced back to a dictum of Fitzherbert J. in 1536 (Y.B. 27 Hen. VIII, Mich., pl. 10), there was a divergence of opinion even before that date: *Walsh* v. *Ervin* [1952] V.L.R. 361, 367.
[51] See Newark, "The Boundaries of Nuisance" (1949) 65 L.Q.R. 480.
[52] [53] *Dymond* v. *Pearce* [1972] 1 Q.B. 496.
[54] [1950] A.C. 361.

the plaintiff, in order to reach a shop, stepped from the highway on to a paved forecourt separating the shop from the public pavement, and tripped over a stopcock about two feet from the boundary line which protruded about an inch and a quarter above the surrounding paving stones. It was held that (even assuming that a stopcock protruding by so little was capable of being a nuisance) the plaintiff had not suffered injury while using the highway and was without remedy.[55] Lord Simonds said that the "House was referred to no case and my researches have led me to none where a plaintiff has deliberately left the highway to go elsewhere, and having left it and having suffered injury upon the adjoining land, has then been held entitled to recover upon a claim of public nuisance in respect of which he suffered special damage. Far as the law of nuisance has travelled beyond its original limits, this further extension appears to me to be justified neither by reason nor by authority."[56] So also if a person climbs upon a stationary vehicle, which is left upon the highway, to see a cricket match and falls off and injures himself, it is not relevant for him to complain that the van was an obstruction to the highway and a nuisance. The accident does not happen because the vehicle is an obstruction to the highway, but because the plaintiff has trespassed upon it.[57] A mere temporary departure from the boundaries of the highway will not always, however, disentitle the plaintiff to recover. He may still be regarded as a user of the highway if he has diverged from it accidentally[58] or by reason of necessity.[59]

§ 26A. Liability for the Non-Repair of Roads[60]

(1) The common law

The law governing the liability of highway authorities towards individual members of the public exercising the common right of passage over the highway had no similarity or even analogy to the duties of occupiers of property to those permitted or invited to enter the premises.[61] At common law no action lay against any authority entrusted with the care of highways for damage suffered in consequence of the omission of the defendants to perform their statutory duty of keeping the highways in repair. This exemption extended only to cases of pure nonfeasance, and the public authority was responsible for any active misfeasance by which the highway was rendered dangerous.

(2) The Highways (Miscellaneous Provisions) Act 1961

"I never thought when, at Oxford many years ago, I first learned about the non-feasance rule, that it would fall to my lot nearly a generation later to move a Bill which would have the effect of bringing to an end what I think

---

[55] A claim founded on the duty owed by an occupier of dangerous premises to those who enter on them also failed: see below, § 90.

[56] [1950] A.C. 361, 377.

[57] *Donovan* v. *Union Cartage Co.* [1933] 2 K.B. 71, 78.

[58] *Barnes* v. *Ward* (1850) 9 C.B. 392.

[59] *McKenna* v. *Lewis* [1945] I.R. 66.

[60] See Holdsworth, H.E.L., x, pp. 314–319; Denning (1939) 55 L.Q.R. 343; Sawer, "Non-Feasance Revisited" (1955) 18 M.L.R. 541.

[61] *Buckle* v. *Bayswater Road Board* (1936) 57 C.L.R. 259, 280.

has generally been regarded as an anomaly which has resulted in injustice to many people."[62] In these words Lord Molson[63] introduced a Bill which amended the law on this point in consequence of many criticisms.[64] Section 1(1) of the Act, which binds the Crown,[65] abrogates "the rule of law exempting the inhabitants at large and any other persons as their successors from liability for non-repair of highways."[66]

The Act applies whether the plaintiff is suing in negligence or nuisance or for breach of a statutory duty. But section 1(2) provides that in an action against a public authority for damage resulting from their failure to maintain[67] a highway it shall be a defence to prove that the authority has taken such care as is reasonable in the circumstances to secure that the part of the highway to which the action relates was not dangerous for traffic. Section 1(3) specifically provides that in assessing what is reasonable the court shall have regard to such factors as the character of the highway and the traffic which might reasonably be expected to use it; the standard of maintenance appropriate for a highway of that character and used by that traffic; the state of repair in which a reasonable person would have expected to find the highway; and the authority's knowledge of the danger.[68] Further, the default of an independent contractor is not in general a defence.[69]

It was once held[70] that these sections do not make negligence an essential element in a plaintiff's cause of action, but rather provide a defence to a statutory claim based on strict liability. But in later cases the courts have adopted an interpretation more favourable to highway authorities. So that if a pavement is in continual use, inspected reasonably often, and no complaint has been made by the local inhabitants, the plaintiff may fail to prove that the defendants have not discharged their duty.[71] There is not a cause of action whenever someone trips over an uneven pavement or falls as a result of a fractional difference in levels between flagstones,[72] as distinct from a metal plate which protrudes by 1/8".[73] Further, there is a distinction between a transient danger due to the elements, *e.g.* a pool of water or a patch of ice or snow,[74] and a permanent danger due to want of repair.[75] The plaintiff may fail to discharge the burden of proof in the former case.

---

[62] 232 H.L.Deb., col. 1423 (July 5, 1961).
[63] Lancing and New College; First Class in Honour School of Jurisprudence 1925.
[64] Notably from the General Council of the Bar.
[65] s. 1 (5). This is important, as an increasing number of roads are being vested in the Crown in right of the Minister of Transport.
[66] In Ireland, similar provision is made by the Civil Liability Act 1961, s. 60, but the necessary ministerial order to bring the section into force has not yet been made.
[67] A duty to maintain may be wider than a duty to repair: *Haydon* v. *Kent C.C.* [1978] Q.B. 343.
[68] Yet another example of the growing tendency, both legislative and judicial, to spell out the factors relevant to the standard of care required: see also below, §§ 80–81.
[69] See below, § 184.
[70] *Griffiths* v. *Liverpool Corporation* [1967] 1 Q.B. 374.
[71] *Pridham* v. *Hemel Hempstead Corporation* (1970) 69 L.G.R. 523.
[72] *Littler* v. *Liverpool Corporation* [1968] 2 All E.R. 343.
[73] *Pitman* v. *Southern Electricity Board* [1978] 3 All E.R. 901.
[74] *Haydon* v. *Kent C.C.* [1978] Q.B. 343.
[75] *Burnside* v. *Emerson* [1968] 1 W.L.R. 1490.

CHAPTER 5

INTERESTS IN CHATTELS

§ 27. INTRODUCTORY

The Torts (Interference with Goods) Act 1977[1] abolishes the tort of
detinue but otherwise neither replaces nor redefines the other relevant torts,
though it applies the term "wrongful interference with goods" to all torts
which involve lost or damaged goods. So the old law is still important. "In
the development of our law, two principles have struggled for mastery. The
first is the protection of property. No one can give a better title than he
himself possesses. The second is the protection of commercial transactions.
The person who takes in good faith and for value without notice should get
a good title."[2] In the course of centuries both common law and statute have
created exceptions to the principle that no one can give a better title than he
himself has.

The common law has always recognised that the title of the true owner
may be divested in favour of a bona fide purchaser for value in two cases.
One depends upon a peculiarity in the property (*i.e.* money or negotiable
instruments); the other upon a peculiarity in the place where the purchaser
buys it (*i.e.* markets overt). So every shop in the City of London is a market
overt for the sale between sunrise and sunset[3] of goods ordinarily sold in
that shop, and the purchaser in good faith will get a good title even though
the vendor[4] has none.[5] Parliament has also given further protection to the
security of commercial transactions by the Factors Act 1889, and the Sale
of Goods Act 1979[6] which should be construed as one single code.[7] Thus a
mercantile agent who has possession of goods in his capacity as mercantile
agent[8] has power to pass title under section 2 (1) of the Factors Act 1889.
Section 27 of the Hire Purchase Act 1964, has effected a considerable
change in the law by providing that, where a hirer of a motor-vehicle under
a hire-purchase agreement wrongfully disposes of that vehicle to a bona fide
private purchaser[9] for value who has no notice of any relevant hire-purchase
agreement,[10] then a good title to the vehicle is passed, although the hirer
may still be liable to the finance company. Further, the tendency of the
courts is to magnify the protection which those Acts give to purchasers at
the expense of the true owner—perhaps unnecessarily, for it is doubtful

---

[1] ss. 12–17 and Sched. 1 came into force on January 1, 1978, and the remainder of the Act
on June 1, 1978.
[2] *Bishopsgate Motor Finance Corporation* v. *Transport Brakes Ltd.* [1949] 1 K.B. 322, 336-
337, *per* Denning L.J.
[3] *Reid* v. *Metropolitan Police Commissioner* [1973] Q.B. 551.
[4] To argue that the vendor, who may be the agent of the thief, should be protected by the
doctrine of market overt as well as the purchaser "capsizes the intellect": *Ganlay* v.
Ledwidge (1876) I.R. 10 C.L. 33, 36.
[5] *Bishopsgate Motor Finance Co.* v. *Transport Brakes Ltd.* [1949] 1 K.B. 322.
[6] Which came into force on January 1, 1980.
[7] To avoid misconception, it may be noted, that the mere fact that the owner has thus been
compulsorily divested of his property does not mean that he must bear the loss. A takes
B's goods and sells them to C in market overt: C gets a good title but A is liable to B for
the value of the goods.
[8] *Astley Industrial Trust Ltd.* v. *Miller* [1968] 2 All E.R. 36.
[9] But a trade purchaser is still liable in conversion: *Moorgate Mercantile Co. Ltd.* v. *Twitchings* [1976] Q.B. 225.   [10] *Barker* v. *Bell* [1971] 1. W.L.R. 983.

whether in practice the innocent purchaser of consumer durables other than motor-cars suffered much hardship.[11] So the Factors Act 1889, s. 2 (1), provides that if a mercantile agent is, with the consent of the owner, in possession of goods or the documents of title to goods, any sale, pledge or other disposition made by him when acting in the ordinary course of business of a mercantile agent, shall be effective to pass a good title to a bona fide purchaser for value. It is well settled that consent obtained by fraud is still consent for the purposes of this section,[12] so that when a rogue obtains possession of a motor-car by false pretences and sells it for cash in the Warren Street used-car market the purchaser gets a good title.[13] Even if a purchaser does not get a good title he may have an action for breach of warranty against his vendor.

Some have denied or doubted the existence of a law of property in chattels on the ground that our law recognises no real or proprietary action for the recovery of chattels corresponding to the *vindicatio* of Roman law.[14] But, "as modern experience shows, a very true and intense ownership of goods can be pretty well protected by actions in which nothing but money can with any certainty be obtained."[15] The value of the thing is obtained because the plaintiff shows that it belongs to him. It seems irrelevant that an historical accident denies him recovery *in specie*. Indeed there is reason to believe that in some respects the common law is more favourable to the owner of goods than systems founded on the civil law.[16] For the action of conversion, which is our normal remedy for one deprived of his goods, has features characteristic of both property and tort.[17] In so far as it is a *vindicatio* there is no room for inquiry as to the defendant's state of mind: liability in conversion is strict. In so far as it is an action in tort it lies against anyone who has at any time committed an act which constitutes a denial of the plaintiff's title. "Where there have been successive conversions of the same goods, trover lies against all persons guilty of conversion and recovery of damages against one is no answer by the defendants in subsequent actions, though . . . as soon as full satisfaction has been obtained the plaintiff has exhausted his rights."[18]

The object of the 1977 Act is to create a more general remedy based as far as possible on the existing incidents of the tort of conversion.[19] So we

---

[11] Yet the 12th Report of the Law Reform Committee (Cmnd. 2958 (1966)) recommends a further change in favour of the bona fide purchaser. See Atiyah Note, (1966) 29 M.L.R. 541.

[12] *Du Jardin* v. *Beadman Bros.* [1952] 2 Q.B. 712.

[13] *Newtons of Wembley Ltd.* v. *Williams* [1965] 1 Q.B. 560.

[14] This has been a commonplace since the time of Bracton, although after the Common Law Procedure Act 1854, the courts have had a discretionary power to order the specific restitution of chattels. This statute has removed the original reason for which we call lands "real" and chattels "personal" property; but the terms were adopted long ago and are likely to endure: Maitland, *The Forms of Action at Common Law*, p. 365. For the power to order the plaintiff to accept restitution instead of damages, see below, § 38.

[15] P. & M. ii, 181–182.

[16] See Lawson, *The Rational Strength of English Law*, pp. 125-131.

[17] This has made for difficulty in the search for the basis of liability in tort: above, § 4.

[18] *Morris (B.O.) Ltd.* v. *Perrott* [1945] 1 All E.R. 567, 569, *per* Lord Goddard. This is not to say that there may not be claims for contribution or indemnity between the defendants, but the primary concern of the law is to compensate the plaintiff for his loss: he is entitled to sue that person in the chain of converters who seems the most likely to be able to pay, leaving him to collect what he can from anybody else in the chain.

[19] See Palmer, "The Application of the Torts (Interference with Goods) Act 1977 to Actions in Bailment" (1978) 41 M.L.R. 629.

must now consider the details of the four actions which protected property interests in chattels: trespass, conversion, detinue, and replevin.

Section 1 of the 1977 Act provides a comprehensive description ("wrongful interference") for the tort of conversion and the other torts affecting goods.

§ 28. TRESPASS TO GOODS

The tort of trespass consists in committing without lawful justification any act of direct physical interference with a chattel in the possession of another person—that is to say, it is such an act done with respect to a chattel as amounts to a direct forcible injury within the meaning of the distinction drawn in the old practice between the writ of trespass and that of trespass on the case.[20] Thus it is a trespass to take away a chattel or to do wilful damage to it. The tort of trespass is wider than conversion in that a mere act of interference is sufficient, special damage need not be proved, and it is not necessary to prove a denial of title; but it is narrower than conversion in that the act of interference must be direct.

The tort may be committed against an animal,[21] *e.g.* it is a trespass to beat a dog,[22] or to shoot racing pigeons.[23] Even negligent damage, provided that it is direct and not merely consequential, falls within the scope of trespass: as in the case of a negligent collision between two vehicles.[24] Physical interference usually consists in some form of physical contact—some application of force by which the chattel is moved from its place or otherwise affected. So in *Kirk* v. *Gregory*[25] the plaintiff was the executor of one who had died in his own house in a state of *delirium tremens*. The defendant, alarmed by the fact that the servants and others were feasting and drinking in the house, moved certain rings from one room to another, in the mistaken but genuine belief that it was necessary to do so. The defendant was held liable in trespass[26] for the loss of the rings. But it is also presumably a trespass wilfully to frighten a horse so that it runs away, or to drive cattle out of a field in which they lawfully are,[27] or to kill a dog by giving it poisoned meat.

Trespass actionable per se

A trespass to chattels is actionable per se without any proof of actual damage.[28] Any unauthorised touching[29] or moving of a chattel is actionable at the suit of the possessor of it, even though no harm ensues. So it is a trespass to erase a tape-recording[30] or show a private letter to an

---

[20] Above, § 2.
[21] Or by an animal, *e.g.* if I train (or perhaps knowingly permit) my dog to fetch another's golf balls: *Manton* v. *Brocklebank* [1923] 2 K.B. 212, 229.
[22] *Wright* v. *Ramscot* (1667) 1 Wms.Saund. 84.
[23] *Hamps* v. *Darby* [1948] 2 K.B. 311.
[24] *Leame* v. *Bray* (1803) 3 East 593.
[25] (1876) 1 Ex.D. 55.
[26] Nominal damages of one shilling were awarded.
[27] *R.* v. *Riley* (1853) 22 L.J.M.C. 48.
[28] *Leitch & Co.* v. *Leydon* [1931] A.C. 90, 106; *Penfolds Wines Pty. Ltd.* v. *Elliott* (1946) 74 C.L.R. 204, 214–215.
[29] "Scratching the panel of a carriage would be a trespass": *Fouldes* v. *Willoughby* (1841) 8 M. & W. 540, 549, *per* Alderson B. *Everitt* v. *Martin* [1953] N.Z.L.R. 298 suggests that a merely accidental contact without any damage or asportation is not actionable: *sed quaere.*
[30] *The Times*, October 1, 1966 (damages: £200).

unauthorised person,[31] as distinct from merely looking at the letter when it is in another's possession,[32] or over-hearing a conversation.[33] It may be very necessary for the protection of certain kinds of property, *e.g.* museum specimens, that this should be the law.[34] Hence the successful plaintiff will always be entitled to nominal damages at least,[35] and, if the defendants are persons in authority guilty of outrageous behaviour,[36] to exemplary damages as well.[37] In this way the common law gives an indirect remedy for invasions of privacy.[38]

It was once unnecessary for the plaintiff in an action of trespass to chattels to prove intention or negligence in the defendant. But the present position is doubtful in view of the fact that it now seems settled that in an action of trespass for personal injuries the plaintiff must prove intention or negligence,[39] and in practice the courts assume that in trespass to chattels intention or negligence must be proved.[40] In any event the general principle that liability in trespass is strict has been much weakened by two admitted exceptions.

(i) Highway accidents

A person whose property on or adjoining the highway (*e.g.* a motor-car or house) has been damaged accidentally as the result of the activities of a user of the highway can recover only if he establishes negligence. This rule has been established more by the dicta of eminent judges and the common understanding of the profession than by any particular decision,[41] but its authority appears now to be beyond question.[42]

(ii) Inevitable accident

In *National Coal Board* v. *Evans*[43] the Court of Appeal held that inevitable accident was a good defence to an action for trespass to chattels. The plaintiffs' predecessors in title laid an electric cable under the land of a county council without informing it or the defendant contractors, whom it employed to conduct the excavation in the course of which the cable was damaged. It was held that since the accident was mainly attributable to the act of the plaintiffs in wrongfully placing their cable in another's land the defendants were excused as being utterly without fault.

---

[31] *Thurston* v. *Charles* (1905) 21 T.L.R. 659 (damages: £400).
[32] "The eye cannot by the laws of England be guilty of a trespass": *Entick* v. *Carrington* (1765) 19 St.Tr. 1029, 1066, *per* Lord Camden C.J.
[33] *Malone* v. *Metropolitan Police Commissioner* [1979] Ch. 344, 374–76.
[34] See Pollock, *Torts*, p. 265.
[35] As in *Kirk* v. *Gregory* (1876) 1 Ex.D. 55.
[36] As in the General Warrant Cases in the 1760s, discussed in Heuston, *Essays in Constitutional Law* (2nd ed.), pp. 35–36.
[37] *Cassell & Co. Ltd.* v. *Broome* [1972] A.C. 1027.
[38] See above, § 10.
[39] See below, § 46.
[40] *Electricity Supply Board* v. *Hastings* [1965] Ir.Jur.Rep. 51.
[41] *Holmes* v. *Mather* (1875) L.R. 10 Ex. 261, 267 (Bramwell L.J.); *River Wear Commissioners* v. *Adamson* (1877) 2 App. Cas. 743, 767 (Lord Blackburn); *Gayler and Pope* v. *B. Davies & Son* [1924] 2 K.B. 75.
[42] See also above, § 11.
[43] [1951] 2 K.B. 861, followed in *Electricity Supply Board* v. *Hastings & Co. Ltd.* [1965] Ir.-Jur.Rep. 51.

Searches and seizures[44]

A magistrate has a statutory power to issue a search warrant for stolen goods and for some other, but by no means all,[45] offences. If property not covered by the warrant is seized, the police may be liable in trespass. But in the interest of repressing crime the courts have extended the protection given to the police.[46] So when a police officer enters a house by virtue of a search warrant for stolen goods, he may seize not only the goods which he believes on reasonable grounds to be covered by the warrant, but also any other goods which he reasonably believes to have been stolen and to be material evidence on a charge of receiving, or perhaps of any crime,[47] against the person in possession of them, or anyone associated with him.[48] The police may also be justified in seizing, and retaining temporarily, articles which are of evidential value if there is reasonable cause to believe a serious offence has been committed,[49] but not just to meet a possible order of the court for compensation.[50]

The title of the plaintiff

Trespass to chattels, like trespass to land, is essentially an injury to possession and not to ownership. The plaintiff, therefore, in an action of trespass must have been in actual possession at the time of the interference complained of.[51] So even an owner of goods may be liable in trespass if he seizes those goods from one who has lawful possession of them—e.g. as a bailee.[52] The former rule that a defendant could show that a third party had a better title than the plaintiff has been abolished by the 1977 Act.[53]

§ 29. CONVERSION : HISTORY[54]

The wrong of conversion is dependent for a due understanding of its true nature upon a knowledge of its origin and historical development. There are three distinct methods by which one man may deprive another of his property, and so be guilty of a conversion and liable in an action of trover—(1) by wrongly taking it, (2) by wrongly detaining it, and (3) by wrongly disposing of it.[55] The term conversion was originally limited to the third of these cases. To convert goods meant to dispose of them, to make away with them, to deal with them, in such a way that neither owner nor wrongdoer had any further possession of them: for example, by consuming them, or by destroying them, or by selling them, or otherwise delivering them to some third person. Merely to take another's goods, however

---

[44] Raeburn. "The Law of Search Warrants" (1970) 9 Univ.W.A.L.Rev. 242; Bridge, [1974] Crim.L.R. 218.
[45] e.g. not murder: Ghani v. Jones [1970] 1 Q.B. 693.
[46] I.R.C. v. Rossminster Ltd. [1980] A.C. 952.
[47] Jennings v. Quinn [1968] I.R. 305.
[48] Chic Fashions Ltd. v. Jones [1968] 2 Q.B. 299.
[49] Ghani v. Jones [1970] 1 Q.B. 693.
[50] Malone v. Metropolitan Police Commissioner [1979] Ch. 344.
[51] Ward v. Macauley (1791) 4 T.R. 489.
[52] Keenan Bros. Ltd. v. C.I.E. (1962) 97 I.L.T.R. 54.
[53] s. 8. See also below, § 34.
[54] Holdsworth, H.E.L., vii, pp. 402–447; Fifoot, History and Sources, Chap. 6; Milsom, "Not Doing is no Trespass" [1954] C.L.J. 105; Simpson, "The Introduction of the Action on the Case for Conversion" (1959) 75 L.Q.R. 364.
[55] Penfolds Wines Pty. Ltd. v. Elliott (1946) 74 C.L.R. 204, 240.

wrongfully, was not to convert them. Merely to detain them in defiance of the owner's title was not to convert them. The fact that conversion in its modern sense includes instances of all three modes in which a man may be wrongfully deprived of his goods, and not of one mode only, is the outcome of a process of historical development whereby, by means of legal fictions and other devices, the action of trover was enabled to extend its limits and appropriate the territories that rightly belonged to other and earlier forms of action.

§ 30. CONVERSION : DEFINITION

A conversion is an act, or complex series of acts,[56] of wilful interference, without lawful justification, with any chattel in a manner inconsistent with the right of another, whereby that other is deprived of the use and possession of it.[57] Two elements are combined in such interference: (1) a dealing with the chattel in a manner inconsistent with the right of the person entitled to it, and (2) an intention in so doing to deny that person's right or to assert a right which is in fact inconsistent with such right.[58] But the word "intention" refers only to the intentional commission of the act. For where the act done is necessarily a denial of the other's right or an assertion of a right inconsistent with it, the tort may have been committed,[59] though the doer may not know of or intend to challenge the property or possession of that other.[60] If a person, not being an agent or bailee,[61] deals with the goods of another as his own, his intention is irrelevant, for liability in conversion is strict.[62]

Dealing with the chattel

In order to amount to conversion the act done with respect to the chattel must have been one of wilful and wrongful interference. He who so interferes with a chattel acts at his own risk, and if the loss of the chattel does in fact (whether intended or not) result from his act, he is liable for the value of it in an action of trover. But the "dealing" need not, though it often will, take the form of an interference with possession. There may be "conversion at a distance," if the plaintiff's right to the chattel has been denied, even though the defendant has not taken possession of it as when a vehicle's log-book is deliberately not returned.[63] In the absence, however, of a wilful and wrongful interference there is no conversion, even if by the negligence of the defendant the chattel is lost or destroyed. Thus in *Ashby* v. *Tolhurst*[64] a car-park attendant allowed a stranger, who had neither the ticket nor the key for a car which had been left in the parking-ground under a contract, to take the car away. His employers were not liable to the owner of the car for conversion.[65] Formerly a bailee who by accident lost the

---

[56] *Douglas Valley Finance Co. Ltd.* v. *Hughes (Hirers) Ltd.* [1969] 1 Q.B. 738.
[57] 18th Report of the Law Reform Committee (Cmnd. 4774 (1971)), para. 38.
[58] *Caxton Publishing Co.* v. *Sutherland Publishing Co.* [1939] A.C. 178, 202. 189; *Penfolds Wines Pty. Ltd.* v. *Elliott* (1946) 74 C.L.R. 204, 229.
[59] See below, § 30.
[60] As in *Moorgate Mercantile Finance Co. Ltd.* v. *Finch* [1962] 1 Q.B. 701.
[61] See below, § 31.
[62] See below, § 33.
[63] As in *Bryanston Leasings Ltd.* v. *Principality Finance Ltd.* [1977] R.T.R. 45.
[64] [1937] 2 K.B. 242.
[65] In such a case there may be liability for breach of an occupier's duty to his visitors: see below, § 93.

goods entrusted to him was not liable in conversion but merely in detinue.[66]. But now section 2 (2) of the 1977 Act provides that an action lies in conversion for loss or destruction of goods which a bailee has allowed to happen in breach of his duty to his bailor (that is to say it lies in a case which is not otherwise conversion, but would have been detinue before detinue was abolished).[67] But if there has been no loss or destruction of the goods, but simply a detention, without more, it is doubtful if any tort has now been committed. If the plaintiff alleges the conversion of a number of chattels, it is not necessary to particularise them item by item: a general description of their nature and value is sufficient.[68]

(1) Conversion by taking

Every person is guilty of a conversion who, without lawful justification, takes a chattel out of the possession of anyone else with the intention of exercising a permanent or temporary dominion over it, because the owner is entitled to the use of it at all times.[69] It is no defence that restoration has become impossible, even though no permanent taking was intended and the impossibility has resulted from no act or default of the defendant but solely through the loss or destruction of the property by some inevitable accident or the wrongful act of some third person.[70] For he who wrongfully takes possession of another's goods has them at his own risk and must in all events either return them or pay for them.[71]

But a mere taking unaccompanied by an intention to exercise such a dominion is no conversion, though it is actionable as a trespass. So the mere act of wrongfully removing a chattel from one place to another, without intent to assume possession of it or to deprive the owner of possession, is not in itself a conversion, but is mere trespass. Thus in *Fouldes* v. *Willoughby*[72] the plaintiff went on board the defendant's ferry-boat to cross from Birkenhead to Liverpool, having with him two horses; the defendant wrongfully refused to carry the horses and told the plaintiff that he must take them ashore. The plaintiff refused to do so and the defendant took the horses from him and put them on shore. The plaintiff remained on board the ferry-boat and was conveyed across the river. It was held that the mere act of removing the horses from the boat, although wrongful, and actionable as a trespass, did not amount to the wrong of conversion.[73]

(2) Conversion by detention

The detention of a chattel amounts to a conversion only when it is adverse to the owner or other person entitled to possession—that is to say, the defendant must have shown an intention to keep the thing in defiance of

---

[66] *Williams* v. *Gesse* (1837) 3 Bing. N.C. 849. Liability in negligence was imposed in *Fairline Shipping Corporation* v. *Adamson* [1975] Q.B. 180, but the cases cited were not considered.
[67] This sub-section is "an excellent example of how parliamentary drafting may be both crystal clear and quite unintelligible": (1978) 75 *Guardian Gazette* 78.
[68] *Brightside Co-operative Society* v. *Phillips* [1964] 1 W.L.R. 185.
[69] *Fouldes* v. *Willoughby* (1841) 8 M. & W. 540, 548.
[70] *Wellington City* v. *Singh* [1971] N.Z.L.R. 1025, 1027.
[71] See below, § 33.
[72] (1841) 8 M. & W. 540.
[73] The principle in *Fouldes* v. *Willoughby* is fully accepted in modern law; *Leitch & Co.* v. *Leydon* [1931] A.C. 90, 103–109; *Beaman* v. *A.R.T.S. Ltd.* [1948] 2 All E.R. 89, 92.

the plaintiff.[74] Merely to be in possession of a chattel without title is not a conversion,[75] nor indeed is it a tort of any kind. It cannot be detinue since that tort was abolished by section 2 (1) of the 1977 Act, which is as terse as section 2 (2) is verbose. Thus if a bailee merely holds over after the end of the period for which the chattel was bailed to him, he may be liable for a breach of contract, but he is not guilty of conversion.[76] So he who finds a chattel lost cannot be sued for a conversion, however long he keeps it, unless by refusing to give it up or in some other way he shows an intention to detain it adversely to the owner. No one is bound, save by contract, to take a chattel to the owner of it; his only obligation is not to prevent the owner from getting it when he comes for it.[77] But a denial of possession does not cease to be a conversion because it is accompanied by some excuse — e.g. that delivery will cause "trade union difficulties."[78]

Demand and refusal

The usual method of proving that a detention is adverse within the meaning of this rule is to show that the plaintiff demanded the delivery of the chattel, and that the defendant refused or neglected to comply with the demand.[79] The demand must be unconditional in its terms,[80] specify the goods which the plaintiff requires[81] and be brought to the knowledge of the defendant.[82] Demand and refusal, however, is not the sole method in which an adverse detention may be proved. If wrongful detention can be established without proving a demand there is a good cause of action.[83] Presumably any conduct of the defendant which shows that he not merely possesses the goods, but intends to hold them in defiance of the plaintiff and to deprive him of the possession of them is sufficient to constitute a conversion, even though there has been no formal demand for restitution. Thus if a person is entrusted with a pipe of wine and bottles it there is some evidence of a conversion even though none of the wine be actually drunk.[84] A failure to deliver up goods on demand is not in itself a conversion if at the time of the demand they are no longer in the power or possession of the defendant: as when they are already destroyed or consumed or have already got into the possession of some other person. No one can convert a chattel by refusing to give it up when he no longer has it; this is so even if it is due to his own act or default that delivery is no longer possible,[85] though he may be liable for some prior act of conversion.

It is possible that in one case there is no conversion even though there is an adverse detention. If A's chattel comes on to B's land neither by accident nor by the act of B nor by the act of a felonious third party, it is probably the law that B is not guilty of a conversion, even though he will not either

---

[74] *Clayton* v. *Le Roy* [1911] 2 K.B. 1031, 1052.
[75] *Caxton Publishing Co.* v. *Sutherland Publishing Co.* [1939] A.C. 178, 202.
[76] It may be otherwise if the bailee acts in a manner totally repugnant to the terms of the bailment: see below, § 33.
[77] *Capital Finance Co. Ltd.* v. *Bray* [1964] 1 W.L.R. 323, 329.
[78] *Howard E. Perry Ltd.* v. *British Railways Board* [1980] 1 W.L.R. 1375, 1384.
[79] *Capital Finance Co. Ltd.* v. *Bray* [1964] 1 W.L.R. 323.
[80] *Rushworth* v. *Taylor* (1842) 3 Q.B. 699.
[81] *Abington* v. *Lipscomb* (1841) 1 Q.B. 776.
[82] *King* v. *Walsh* [1932] I.R. 178.
[83] *London Jewellers Ltd.* v. *Sutton* (1934) 50 T.L.R. 193.
[84] *Philpott* v. *Kelley* (1835) 3 A. & E. 106.
[85] *Williams* v. *Gesse* (1837) 3 Bing. N.C. 849.

allow A to retake his chattel or himself restore it, provided that no inference can be drawn from his attitude of an assertion of title or an exercise of dominion over the goods.[86]

(3) Conversion by wrongful delivery

Every person is guilty of a conversion who, without lawful justification, deprives a person of his goods by delivering them to someone else[87] so as to change the possession. The leading case is *Hollins* v. *Fowler*.[88] A rogue obtained Fowler's cotton, and offered it for sale to Hollins, a broker; Hollins sold and delivered it to Micholls & Co., who worked it into yarn. Hollins accounted for the proceeds to the rogue, who disappeared. Hollins was liable in conversion to Fowler, even though he had acted in good faith and obtained only a broker's commission from Micholls & Co. So an auctioneer who sells and delivers[89] stolen property or property subject to a bill of sale is liable to the true owner or to the bill of sale holder, even though ignorant of any such adverse title, and even though he has already paid over the proceeds to his own client.[90] But it is possible that a bailee of goods for safe custody is not liable if he, or his servant, honestly but mistakenly[91] delivers the goods to someone who is not entitled to them, at least if the contract of bailment so provides.[92]

(4) Conversion by wrongful disposition

Every person is guilty of a conversion who, without lawful justification, deprives a person of his goods by giving some other person a lawful title to them. There are certain cases in which a person in possession of goods to which he has no title can nevertheless effectively, though wrongfully, so dispose of them by sale, pledge, or otherwise that he confers a good title to them on someone else. Any such disposition amounts to a conversion as against the true and original owner, for by the creation of this adverse title he has been deprived of his property. This is the case, for example, with a sale in market overt, or with a wrongful disposition made by a vendor of goods who continues or retains possession of them,[93] in whatever capacity,[94] or by one who has a motor-vehicle on hire-purchase.[95] Another example arises where A hands over to B the goods of C in such circumstances as to create a lien or special property in B—"If a person take my horse to ride and leave him at an inn that is a conversion; for though I may have the horse on sending for him and paying for the keeping of him, yet it brings a charge on me."[96] But a bailee of goods may have the express or implied authority of the owner to create a repairer's lien; this is the position of one

---

[86] See below, § 227.
[87] But it is no conversion to give the custody of the goods to your own servant, for legally they still remain in your possession.
[88] (1875) L.R. 7 H.L. 757.
[89] Whether under the hammer or by private treaty: *Willis* v. *British Car Auctions Ltd.* [1978] 1 W.L.R. 438.
[90] *Consolidated Co.* v. *Curtis* [1892] 1 Q.B. 495.
[91] As distinct from dishonestly: *Morris* v. *Martin (C.W.) & Sons Ltd.* [1966] 1 Q.B. 716, see below, § 178.
[92] *B. & G. Entertainments Ltd.* v. *Charing Cross Garages Ltd.* (1969), unreported (Cooke J.)
[93] Sale of Goods Act 1893, ss. 22, 25.
[94] *Worcester Works Finance Ltd.* v. *Cooden Engineering Co. Ltd.* [1972] 1 Q.B. 210.
[95] Though the purchaser may get a good title under the Hire-Purchase Act 1964, s. 27.
[96] *Syeds* v. *Hay* (1791) 4 T.R. 260, 264, *per* Buller J.

who has a motor-car or other chattel under a hire-purchase agreement.[97] In most of such cases, indeed, the wrongful disposition is also a wrongful delivery and therefore is a conversion for that reason also, but this coincidence is not essential. It seems, however, that in order to give rise to civil liability it is not enough to attempt to sell another's goods,[98] or even to sell them without delivering them to the purchaser or to his order, for a mere sale or other attempted disposition unaccompanied by delivery and ineffectual to divest the plaintiff's title to the property is not a conversion.[99]

(5) Conversion by wrongful destruction

Every person is guilty of a conversion who, without lawful justification, wilfully consumes or otherwise destroys a chattel belonging to another person.[1] Mere damage, however, which falls short of actual destruction, is not in itself a conversion.[2] The test of destruction, as opposed to mere damage, is presumably the disappearance of the identity of the article. Grapes are presumably destroyed when they are turned into wine, cotton when it is woven into cloth, corn when it is ground into flour.[3]

(6) Conversion of documents and tokens

The difficulty here is that primarily conversion means conversion of chattels, and the relation of bank to customer is that of debtor and creditor. As no specific coins in a bank are the property of any specific customer, a bank which pays part of what it owes to its customer to some other person not authorised to receive it is not at first sight converting its customer's chattels. Again, a bank which collects a cheque borrows from its customers the proceeds when collected, and in collecting exhausts the operation of the cheque. "The difficulty has been surmounted by treating the conversion as of the chattel, the piece of paper, the cheque under which the money was collected, and the value of the chattel converted as the money received under it."[4] The law regards the substance of the transaction and gives an adequate remedy for the wrong.[5] This principle is not limited to documents which are, or are in the nature of, negotiable instruments: but it may include documents which are evidence of a chose in action—*e.g.* trading stamps.[6]

It may also be extended to cover the tokens which are such a feature of contemporary life—*e.g.* bank and other credit cards, book tokens, and gaming chips.[7] The measure of damages will usually be the value of the property represented by the token.[8]

---

[97] *Tappenden* v. *Artus* [1964] 2 Q.B. 185. *Aliter* if the agreement has been validly determined by the finance company.
[98] But there may be a criminal prosecution in such a case: *Rogers* v. *Arnott* [1960] 2 Q.B. 244.
[99] *Consolidated Co.* v. *Curtis* [1892] 1 Q.B. 495, 498. See below, § 31.
[1] *Hollins* v. *Fowler* (1875) L.R. 7 H.L. 757, 768.
[2] Where the chattel continues to exist as such, there may be trespass, but there is no conversion: *Simmons* v. *Lillystone* (1853) 8 Ex. 431.
[3] *Northern Ireland Master Butchers' Wholesale Supply Association* v. *Belfast Corporation* [1965] N.I. 30. See below, § 38.
[4] *Per* Scrutton L.J. in *Lloyds Bank* v. *Chartered Bank, etc.* [1929] 1 K.B. 40, 55–56.
[5] *Morison* v. *London County and Westminster Bank* [1914] 3 K.B. 40, 356, 365–366.
[6] *Building, etc. Holidays Scheme Ltd.* v. *Post Office* [1966] 1 Q.B. 247.
[7] 18th Report of the Law Reform Committee (Cmnd. 4774 (1971)), paras. 90–91.
[8] See *Loosemore* v. *Radford* (1842) 9 M. & W. 657 (title deeds).

If a cheque has been converted, and the collecting bank[9] has acted without negligence, it may be protected under the Cheques Act 1957, s. 4. The onus is on the bank to show that it has followed the ordinary practice of careful bankers.[10]

(7) Miscellaneous forms of conversion

Every person is guilty of a conversion who, in any other way than those mentioned in the preceding sections, causes the loss of a chattel by any act of wilful interference without lawful justification. It has even been held that the use of another's motor-car for smuggling, entailing its liability for forfeiture to the Crown, amounts to a conversion.[11] So an infringement of copyright may be a conversion, [12] and innocence is no defence.[13] In such a case the plaintiff, in addition to claiming damages and an injunction for the infringement of his copyright, is in effect claiming to be the owner of all the infringing copies of his work, and requiring that he be compensated for the loss of his property. So there may be conversion even though the defendant has never been in physical possession of the goods, if he has dealt with them in such a way as to amount to an absolute denial and repudiation of the plaintiff's rights,[14] as by stripping a commercial vehicle of its A licence, or refusing to return a log-book.[15] But it is now clear that even an absolute denial and repudiation of the plaintiff's right, if unaccompanied by circumstances which make such denial a "dealing" with the goods, does not constitute conversion,[16] although it may amount to injurious falsehood,[17] or else the plaintiff may obtain a declaration that the defendant has no right to the goods.[18]

§ 31. ACTS NOT AMOUNTING TO CONVERSION

(1) Mere receipt of chattels no conversion

We have already seen that the mere possession of goods without title is neither a conversion nor any other kind of tort.[19] The only detention that is actionable is adverse detention—a withholding of possession from the person entitled to it. It seems to follow logically from this that merely to receive goods in good faith by way of pledge, sale or otherwise from a person who has no title to them is not a conversion by the recipient, who commits no tort until he refuses to deliver them to the true owner or wrongfully disposes of them. This was once held to be the law in the case of a person taking goods by way of deposit.[20] But the 1977 Act has reversed

---

[9] *Westminster Bank* v. *Zang* [1966] A.C. 182.
[10] *Marfani & Co. Ltd.* v. *Midland Bank Ltd.* [1968] 1 W.L.R. 956.
[11] *Moorgate Mercantile Credit Co. Ltd.* v. *Finch* [1962] 1 Q.B. 701.
[12] *Caxton Publishing Co.* v. *Sutherland Publishing Co.* [1939] A.C. 178.
[13] *W.E.A. Records Ltd.* v. *King* [1975] 1 W.L.R. 44.
[14] *Douglas Valley Finance Co. Ltd.* v. *Hughes (Hirers) Ltd.* [1969] 1 Q.B.738, 751.
[15] *Bryanston Leasings Ltd.* v. *Principality Finance Ltd.* [1977] R.T.R. 45.
[16] See s. 11 (3) of the 1977 Act, giving effect to the 18th Report of the Law Reform Committee (Cmnd. 4774 (1971)), para. 45.
[17] Below, § 147.
[18] A procedure used in *Loudon* v. *Ryder* (No. 2) [1953] Ch. 423.
[19] Above, § 30.
[20] *Spackman* v. *Foster* (1883) 11 Q.B.D. 99.

this decision. Section 11 (2) provides, tersely but definitely, that "Receipt of goods by way of pledge is conversion if the delivery of the goods is conversion."

Except on a sale

But even the common law recognised that where there is a taking by sale the rule is different, and liability in conversion is imposed.[21] "Certainly a man is guilty of a conversion who takes my property by assignment from another who has no authority to dispose of it; for what is that but assisting that other in carrying his wrongful act into effect."[22] The rule is an illustration of the principle that persons deal with the property in chattels or exercise acts of ownership over them at their peril.[23] Hence one who innocently buys and takes delivery[24] of goods from another who has no authority to sell them is liable in conversion.[25] A familiar situation in which this rule applies is when a banker collects for a customer a cheque to which the customer has no title or a defective title; the banker is liable in conversion to the true owner of the cheque unless he can show that he is protected by the Cheques Act 1957, s. 4.[26] Since the 1977 Act it must be doubted whether the exception has not swallowed up the rule.

(2) Redelivery no conversion

It further follows that if he who innocently acquires possession of another's goods by way of deposit redelivers them to him from whom he got them, before he has received notice of the plaintiff's claim to them, he is free from responsibility. He has not deprived the plaintiff of his property, for that property is now in exactly the same position as if the defendant had never interfered with it at all. "A warehouseman," said Blackburn, J.[27] in *Hollins* v. *Fowler*,[28] "with whom goods have been deposited is guilty of no conversion by keeping them or restoring them to the person who deposited them with him, though that person turns out to have no authority from the true owner."[29]

Delivery to third party

What shall be said, however, if the innocent holder has delivered the goods not to the person from whom he received them but at his order to

---

[21] Rightly, in the opinion of the 18th Report of the Law Reform Committee (Cmnd. 4774 (1971)), para. 43.

[22] *McCombie* v. *Davies* (1805) 6 East 538, 540, *per* Lord Ellenborough C.J.

[23] Below, § 33.

[24] As the vendor in a contract of sale under which the goods have not been delivered is not liable in conversion the buyer must also escape liability: *Douglas Valley Finance Co. Ltd.* v. *Hughes (Hirers) Ltd.* [1969] 1 Q.B. 738.

[25] *Hilbery* v. *Hatton* (1864) 2 H. & C. 822.

[26] *Lloyds Bank* v. *Chartered Bank* [1929] 1 K.B. 40, 69; *Bute (Marquess of)* v. *Barclays Bank Ltd.* [1955] 1 Q.B. 202. These cases are an interesting illustration of how the usage or practice of a trade or profession can be influenced by judicial decisions, which themselves take account of changing banking practices: *Marfani & Co. Ltd.* v. *Midland Bank Ltd.* [1968] 1 W.L.R. 956.

[27] "A judge who knew more about these matters than anyone else": *Rogers* v. *Lambert* [1891] 1 Q.B. 318, 325, *per* Lord Esher M.R.

[28] (1875) L.R. 7 H.L. 757, 767.

[29] *Aliter* if he has notice of the claim of the true owner. He should interplead. If he does not, he delivers at his peril: *Winter* v. *Bancks* (1901) 84 L.T. 504.

some third person? As when a carrier receives stolen goods from a consignor, and delivers them to the consignee; or a warehouseman delivers such goods to him to whom the delivery warrant has been transferred by the depositor. If in such a case the defendant acts in good faith and without any knowledge that the delivery made by him is in pursuance of some sale or other disposition purporting to affect the title and not merely the possession of the goods, it is probable that he is under no liability. He is a mere conduit-pipe. In a sentence, the carrier is not liable because he merely changes the position of the goods and not the property in them.[30] "On principle, one who deals with goods at the request of the person who has actual custody of them in the bona fide belief that the custodier is the true owner, or has the authority of the true owner, should be excused for what he does if the act is of such nature as would be excused if done by the authority of the person in possession, if he was the finder of goods or entrusted with their custody."[31] Similarly, the solicitor of a bankrupt who receives after-acquired property on behalf of his client and transfers it to another agent (even with knowledge that that agent has been instructed to sell it) is not liable in conversion at the suit of the trustee in bankruptcy.[32]

A doubtful case

If, however, a carrier, warehouseman, agent, or bailee has actual knowledge that his delivery of the goods is part of a transaction affecting the title and not merely the possession, the question of his liability would seem to be still an unsettled point. If *National Mercantile Bank* v. *Rymill*[33] is well decided,[34] there is no liability even under these circumstances. In this case it was held by the Court of Appeal that an auctioneer with whom the goods of the plaintiff had been wrongfully deposited for sale was not liable for a conversion, although he had delivered them at the request of the vendor to a person to whom, as the auctioneer knew, the vendor had sold them by private contract. The defendant had not sold the goods, or authorised their sale, but he had received the purchase price, and passed it on to the plaintiff after deducting commission. It is difficult to reconcile this decision with earlier cases such as *Stephens* v. *Elwall*,[35] and it is contrary to the opinion of Blackburn J. in *Hollins* v. *Fowler*.[36] If well decided it is an authority for this principle: that a bailee commits no conversion merely by redelivering the goods to his bailor or to the order of his bailor, even with the knowledge that the transaction is a sale or other disposition of the title, provided that he has no notice of any adverse claim on the part of the plaintiff. It is clearly otherwise, however, if the bailee has not merely delivered with knowledge of

---

[30] *Barker* v. *Furlong* [1891] 2 Ch. 172, 182.
[31] *Hollins* v. *Fowler* (1875) L.R. 7 H.L. 757, 766, *per* Blackburn J. The 18th Report of the Law Reform Committee (Cmnd. 4774 (1971)), paras. 46-50, reached a substantially similar conclusion after a full review of the problem. The 1977 Act is silent on the matter.
[32] *Re Samuel* (*No.* 2) [1945] Ch. 408.
[33] (1881) 44 L.T. 767.
[34] It was doubted in *Willis* v. *British Car Auctions Ltd.* [1978] 1 W.L.R. 438, but approved in *Barker* v. *Furlong* [1891] 2 Ch. 173, and *Consolidated Co.* v. *Curtis* [1892] 1 Q.B. 495, and is quite consistent with *Re Samuel* (*No.* 2) [1945] Ch. 408.
[35] (1815) 4 M. & S. 259. But in this case the defendant had "set the goods afloat upon a sea of strangers" by sending them out of the jurisdiction to America, which might well be a conversion even today (18th Report of the Law Reform Committee (Cmnd. 4774 (1971)), para. 41).
[36] (1875) L.R. 7 H.L. 757, 767.

the sale, but has himself sold as well as delivered, even though he sells merely as an agent and without claiming any beneficial interest in the property for himself.[37]

§ 32. CONVERSION BY ESTOPPEL[38]

A defendant who has in truth committed no conversion may be held liable for one because he is estopped by his own act from alleging the fact which constitutes his defence: for example, that he has never had possession of the goods, or that he is no longer in possession of them, or that the plaintiff has no title to them.[39] Thus a bailee is estopped from denying the title of his bailor, and therefore a refusal to redeliver the property is a conversion, even though in fact the plaintiff has no title to it.[40] Nor does it make any difference whether the plaintiff has no title at the time of the bailment, or has lost his title since the bailment, e.g. by re-selling to a third party.[41] But the estoppel of a bailee no longer exists if he has already, on the demand of the true owner, given up possession to him, or if he defends the action on his behalf, and by his authority.[42] Conversely, an owner is not estopped by his own negligence from suing in conversion.[43]

§ 33. INEFFECTUAL DEFENCES

(1) Mistake

Although a conversion is necessarily an intentional wrong in the sense already explained, it need not be knowingly wrongful. A mistake of law or fact is no defence to anyone who intentionally interferes with a chattel in a manner inconsistent with the right of another.[44] He does so *suo periculo* and takes the risk of the existence of a sufficient lawful justification for the act; and if it turns out that there is no justification, he is just as responsible in an action of conversion as if he had fraudulently misappropriated the property. "Persons deal with the property in chattels or exercise acts of ownership over them at their peril."[45] Thus an auctioneer who honestly and ignorantly sells and delivers property on behalf of a customer who has no title to it is liable for its value to the true owner, even though he has already paid the proceeds of the sale to his own client.[46]

---

[37] *Consolidated Co.* v. *Curtis* [1892] 1 Q.B. 495.
[38] This is a convenient expression, though estoppel is in general only a rule of evidence and not a cause of action.
[39] *Seton, Laing & Co.* v. *Lafone* (1887) 19 Q.B.D. 68.
[40] *Biddle* v. *Bond* (1865) 6 B. & S. 225. See Paton, *Bailment in the Common Law*, s. 85.
[41] *Rogers, Sons & Co.* v. *Lambert & Co.* [1891] 1 Q.B. 318.
[42] *Kahler* v. *Midland Bank Ltd.* [1950] A.C. 24, 38. For pleading the *jus tertii*, see § 34. The remedy of a bailee against whom adverse claims are made is to take interpleader proceedings. The estoppel of a bailee is closely analogous to the rule that a possessory title is good against all but the true owner. It is possible, indeed, that the former rule is in truth merely a particular application of the latter. See below, § 35.
[43] *Moorgate Mercantile Co. Ltd.* v. *Twitchings* [1977] A.C. 890. See also below, § 33.
[44] Sometimes the defence of agency of necessity may be available: see below, § 185.
[45] *Hollins* v. *Fowler* (1872) L.R. 7 Q.B. 616, 639, *per* Cleasby B. The facts of this leading case (see above, § 30) well illustrate this principle, which has not been questioned for a century: *Union Finance Ltd.* v. *British Car Auctions Ltd.* [1978] 2 All E.R. 385, 387.
[46] *Consolidated Co.* v. *Curtis* [1892] 1 Q.B. 495. "That is one of the risks of their profession"; *Sachs* v. *Miklos* [1948] 2 K.B. 23, 37, *per* Lord Goddard C.J.

(2) Contributory negligence

At common law there were a number of statements to the effect that contributory negligence was no defence. The majority view[47] was that an owner of property was entitled to be as careless as he liked. As liability in conversion is strict, the strange result was that a person is not bound to look after his own property as carefully as other people are expected to look after it for him. Now in England the 1977 Act confirms the common law. Section 11 (1) provides that contributory negligence is no defence in proceedings founded on conversion,[48] or on intentional trespass to goods.[49] On the other hand, contributory negligence is a good defence in some other jurisdictions[50]—e.g. Ireland,[51] New Zealand[52] and Ontario.[53]

(3) Remoteness of damage

If the defendant has thus intentionally interfered with a chattel without lawful justification and loss of the chattel does in fact result from the interference, it is no defence that such a loss was not intended, or even that it was not the natural or probable result. In *Hiort* v. *Bott*[54] the plaintiffs, by a mistake fraudulently induced by their own agent, consigned certain barley to the defendant which he had not ordered. They also sent him a delivery order which made the barley deliverable "to the order of consignor or consignee" to enable him to obtain it from the carrier. The plaintiffs' agent thereupon informed the defendant that the consignment was a mistake and induced him to indorse and hand over the delivery order to him (the agent) in order that the goods might be obtained by him from the carrier and redelivered to the plaintiffs. The agent thus obtained possession of the barley, sold it, and absconded with the proceeds; and the defendant was held liable in conversion for its value. It will be noted that the defendant in this case, although he had never come into possession of the goods, had done an act which affected the title in them which he was not obliged to do at all—for if he had done nothing the terms of the delivery order would have ensured that the barley would have stood at the order of the plaintiff consignors. His position is thus clearly distinguishable from that of an involuntary bailee, who is in general liable only if the unauthorised act which has deprived the plaintiff of his property is also a negligent one.[55]

(4) Defendant acting for account of another

It is not necessary that the defendant should have acted on his own account, or have converted the goods to his own use. He is equally liable if

---

[47] See, *e.g. Moorgate Mercantile Co. Ltd.* v. *Twitchings* [1977] A. C. 890, 925, and the full review in *Day* v. *Bank of New South Wales* [1978] 19 A.L.R. 32.

[48] But in relation to a bank which is relying on s. 4 of the Cheques Act 1957, s. 47 of the Banking Act 1979 provides that "a defence of contributory negligence shall be available to the banker notwithstanding the provisions of s. 11 (1) of the Torts (Interference with Goods) Act 1977."

[49] See below, § 197. But perhaps this defence is available if the action is framed in negligence.

[50] See Goldring, "The Negligence of the Plaintiff in Conversion" (1977) 11 M.U.L.R. 91.

[51] Civil Liability Act 1961, s. 34.

[52] *Helson* v. *McKenzies Ltd.* [1950] N.Z.L.R. 878.

[53] *Houson* v. *Houson* (1966) 55 D.L.R. 582, 593.

[54] (1874) L.R. 9 Ex. 86.

[55] *Elvin & Powell Ltd.* v. *Plummer, Roddis Ltd.* (1933) 50 T.L.R. 158; Burnett, "Conversion by an Involuntary Bailee" (1960) 76 L.Q.R. 364. See also below, § 227.

he has acted on behalf and for the benefit of some other person as his agent or servant.[56] On the other hand, a merely ministerial dealing with the goods at the request of an apparent owner having the actual control of them is not a conversion.[57] Even when the act is done for the supposed benefit of the true owner and with the honest intention of preserving or restoring the property, it will amount to a conversion if done without lawful justification and if it results in fact in a loss of the property: as if I find A's goods which I wrongly believe to have been lost or mislaid by him, and hand them to B to take to A, and B misappropriates them.[58]

(5) Loss not permanent

The loss or deprivation of possession suffered by the plaintiff need not be permanent. The duration of the dispossession is relevant with respect to the measure of damages, but makes no difference to the nature of the wrong.[59]

§ 34. THE TITLE OF THE PLAINTIFF[60]

Whenever goods have been converted, an action will lie at the suit of any person in actual possession or entitled at the time of the conversion to the immediate possession of them.[61] It is not necessary for the plaintiff to show that he is the owner of the goods.[62] Hence not merely can a bailee at will sue,[63] but also his bailor,[64] and also one who has a lien over goods,[65] or has an equitable title to them, as distinct from a more contractual right.[66] Conversely a person not so entitled cannot sue in conversion, even though he is the owner of the property. So the buyer of goods which remained in the possession of the seller until his lien for the unpaid purchase price had been discharged could not sue a third party.[67] Usually the defect in the plaintiff's right to immediate possession arises from an adverse right of possession in a third party, but a defect arising from other causes may be equally fatal.[68] We shall deal later with the remedies for injuries to reversionary interests in chattels.[69]

In certain cases, however, a person who has a merely reversionary interest is remitted to the right of immediate possession by the very act of conversion itself, which causes in certain circumstances a forfeiture and determination of the particular interest in possession.[69a] "Any act or disposition which is wholly repugnant to or as it were an absolute disclaimer of the holding as bailee revests the bailor's right to possession, and therefore

---

[56] *International Factors Ltd.* v. *Rodriguez* [1979] Q.B. 351.
[57] See above, § 31.
[58] See *Consolidated Co.* v. *Curtis* [1892] 1 Q.B. 495.
[59] *Penfolds Wines Pty. Ltd.* v. *Elliott* (1946) 74 C.L.R. 204, 243.
[60] Warren, "Qualifying as Plaintiff in an Action for a Conversion" (1936) 49 Harv. L. Rev. 1084.
[61] *Winkworth* v. *Christie, Manson & Woods Ltd.* [1980] Ch. 496.
[62] *The Winkfield* [1902] P. 42; *Bute (Marquess of)* v. *Barclays Bank Ltd.* [1955] 1 Q.B. 202.
[63] *Burton* v. *Hughes* (1824) 2 Bing. 173, 175.
[64] *U.S.A.* v. *Dollfus Mieg et Cie* [1952] A.C. 582.
[65] *Rogers* v. *Kennay* (1846) 9 Q.B. 592.
[66] *International Factors Ltd.* v. *Rodriguez* [1979] Q.B. 351.
[67] *Lord* v. *Price* (1874) L.R. 9 Ex. 54.
[68] *Kahler* v. *Midland Bank Ltd.* [1950] A.C. 24, 38, 55.
[69] Below, § 42.
[69a] *Citicomp Australia Ltd.* v. *Stillwell Fund Ltd.* (1979) 215 A.S.R. 142, 144.

also his immediate right to maintain trover or detinue even where the bailment is for a term or is otherwise not recoverable at will, and so *a fortiori* in a bailment determinable at will."[70] Thus if the hirer under a contract of hire-purchase sells the article bailed to him, the lessor accordingly becomes entitled to immediate possession and can therefore sue either the hirer or the auctioneer who has effected the sale or the purchaser in conversion and not merely for an injury to his reversionary interest.[71]

Finders[72]

The true owner of a chattel, if discoverable, has a better title to that chattel than its finder of the occupier of the land where it is found.[73] The finder is in the position of a sub-bailee, and owes to the owner a duty to take reasonable care of the chattel and to return it to him, if it is possible to do so.[74] But if the true owner is not discoverable the finder has title as against all other persons, and it has been settled for over three centuries that the measure of damages is the same as if the plaintiff's title was indisputable. So a chimney sweeper's boy who had found a jewel recovered its full value in trover from a jeweller to whom he gave it to value but who refused to return it.[75] Although the report is silent on the point, it seems legitimate to assume that the jewel had been found in a chimney.[76] The principle has been followed ever since. Thus in *Bridges* v. *Hawkesworth*[77] the finder of some banknotes lying in the public part of a shop was held entitled to them as against the owner of the shop. In *Hannah* v. *Peel*,[78] the finder of a brooch lying loose in the crevice on top of a window-frame was held entitled to it as against the owner of the house, who had never in fact been in occupation of the house. But to these authorities an exception, easily stated but difficult to explain, has been developed. If the article found is attached to or lying under the surface of the land, the owner of the land is entitled to it in priority to the finder,[79] unless it is treasure trove, when it goes to the Crown. Thus in *London Corporation* v. *Appleyard*[80]; a safe containing banknotes was found by two workmen in the basement wall of a house which they were demolishing. The lessee of the premises was held to have priority over the workmen.[81] Yet it is hard to see why a trespasser who finds an article should

---

[70] Pollock and Wright, *Possession*, pp. 132-133. This passage was approved in *Penfolds Wines Pty. Ltd.* v. *Elliott* (1946) 74 C.L.R. 204, 227; in *North General Wagon and Finance Co. Ltd.* v. *Graham* [1950] 2 K.B. 7, 15; in *Alexander* v. *Railway Executive* [1951] 2 K.B. 882, 888, and in *Union Finance Ltd.* v. *British Car Auctions Ltd.* [1978] 2 All E.R. 385, 391.

[71] *North General Wagon and Finance Co. Ltd.* v. *Graham* [1950] 2 K.B. 7. The position may be different if the contract provides that the finance company may only terminate the hire in some particular way, *e.g.* by giving notice to the hirer.

[72] See Goodhart, *Essays*, Chap. 4; 18th Report of the Law Reform Committee (Cmnd. 4774 (1971)), (Annex 1).

[73] *Moffatt* v. *Kazana* [1969] 2 Q.B. 152.

[74] *Gilchrist Watt Ltd.* v. *York Products Pty. Ltd.* [1970] 1 W.L.R. 1262.

[75] *Armory* v. *Delamirie* (1722) 1 Str. 505.

[76] Note that the owner of the chinmey was not a party to the proceedings.

[77] (1851) 21 L.J.Q.B. 75.

[78] [1945] K.B. 509.

[79] *Elwes* v. *Brigg Gas Co.* (1886) 33 Ch. D. 562; *South Staffordshire Water Co.* v. *Sharman* [1896] 2 Q.B. 44. One who finds articles on vehicles of the London Transport Board is guilty of a petty offence if he does not hand them over to the Board, but this would not affect his title in a civil suit.

[80] [1963] 1 W.L.R. 982.

[81] The men were given rewards of £500 each by the London Corporation: *The Times*, April 5, 1963.

be in a better position as against the occupier merely because he can say "I did not dig it up—I picked it up,"[82] and it has been suggested that the finder of unattached articles should have priority over the occupier only when the premises are of a public character.[83] It is not clear whether it makes any difference in what mode the plaintiff obtained the possession on which he relies, but probably he must be an innocent finder.[84-85] It is not the policy of the law to encourage people to pry on other persons' property.

Possessory title : the jus tertii

At common law it was settled that mere *de facto* possession is, as against a stranger, a sufficient title to support an action for a conversion, for as against a wrongdoer possession is title, and the defendant cannot plead the *jus tertii* unless he defends on behalf and by the authority of the true owner, or has already made satisfaction to him.[86]

The *jus tertii* rule was much criticised. There was something unjust, and indeed absurd, about a legal system which refused to listen to a defendant's incontrovertible proof that the plaintiff has no title to the goods whose value he nevertheless claims from the defendant,[87] so section 8 of the 1977 Act abolishes the rule of law known as *jus tertii* and enables a defendant in an action for wrongful interference to defend the action on the grounds that a third party has a better right to the goods, or part of them, than the plaintiff. Rules of Court[88] prescribe a procedure whereby (a) the plaintiff must give particulars of his title to the goods and specify any other person with an interest in them; and (b) the defendant will be able to join any other such person in the proceedings.

This section does not abolish or alter the relative strength of the different titles. But it prevents a defendant being faced successively with a finder and an owner, and having to pay twice.

A charge consequential on the abolition of the *jus tertii* is made by section 7, which modifies the law whereby a person may be required to pay damages more than once in respect of the same act of wrongful interference and may thereafter have no recourse against anyone. This may arise, for example, where, having paid damages in full for loss of goods to a person whose title to them is merely possessory and then once again, in subsequent proceedings, to the true owner, the wrongdoer has no remedy against the first plaintiff. Under the Act, where both claimants are parties, subsection (2) will avoid double liability. Where one claimant only is a party, and receives more from the wrongdoer than he would have received had all claims been considered at once, he is, by subsection (3), made liable to account over to the other possible claimants; and, under subsection (4), the wrongdoer can recover any amount which he has overpaid.

For example, if a converter of goods pays damages first to a finder of the goods, and then to the true owner, the finder is unjustly enriched unless he

---

[82] *Byrne* v. *Hoare* [1965] Qd.R. 135, 168.
[83] 18th Report of the Law Reform Committee (Cmnd. 4774 (1971)), (Annex 1). The Act of 1977 is silent on the whole matter.
[84-85] *Buckley* v. *Gross* (1863) 3 B. & S. 566, 574.
[86] There is a full discussion of this difficult topic in the 18th Report of the Law Reform Committee (Cmnd. 4774 (1971)), paras. 51–78.
[87] See 378 H.L. Deb., col. 1062 (16 December 1976).
[88] See S. 1 1978 No. 579.

accounts over to the true owner under subsection (3); and then the true owner is unjustly enriched.

It is uncertain whether the rule in *The Winkfield*[89] has been abolished by these provisions.

§ 35. CONVERSION AS BETWEEN CO-OWNERS[90]

The 1977 Act, in section 10 (1) (*a*), restates the common law on this topic. The basic principle is that when a chattel is held in common ownership, one of the owners cannot sue another of them in conversion unless the act of the defendant amounts to the destruction of the chattel or otherwise per-manently destroys the right of the plaintiff to the possession thereof—*e.g.* a sale in market overt. Each of the co-owners is equally entitled to the posses-sion and use of the chattel, and neither therefore commits any wrong as against the other by taking or retaining possession of it and using it for the purposes for which it is designed, even if the other is thereby prevented from making the like use of it. But if one co-owner does an act which can be justified only by claiming a right to exclusive possession, then he commits an act of conversion.[91] If any co-owner acquires from the use of the com-mon property a greater share of the profits derived therefrom than that to which he is entitled, he does not thereby commit any tort against the other owner, whose proper remedy is an action of account.[92]

§ 36. CONVERSION AND THE LIMITATION OF ACTIONS

The Limitation Amendment Act 1980, s. 2 provides that theft and allied offences shall be "imprescriptible" so that the thief or any person claiming through him cannot set up sections 2 and 3 of the 1939 Act. It often happens that two or more successive acts of conversion are committed in respect of the same property, either by the same person or by different persons, and difficult questions formerly arose as to the date from which in such cases the period of limitation began to run. Section 3 of the Limitation Act 1939, which has not yet been replaced by any later statutory provision, deals with both cases. Before the 1939 Act the only effect of the expiry of the period of limitation was to bar the plaintiff's right of action. Now under section 3 (2) of the Act of 1939 not only his right of action but his title to the chattel converted is extinguished as it had previously been, and still is, in the case of land under the Real Property Limitations Act 1833.[93] The Act of 1939, s. 3 (1) further provides: "Where any cause of action in respect of the conversion or wrongful detention of a chattel has accrued to any person[94] and, before he recovers possession of the chattel, a further conversion or wrongful detention takes place, no action shall be brought in respect of the further conversion or detention after the expiration of six years from the

---

[89] [1902] P. 42. See below, § 209.
[90] Derham, "Conversion by Wrongful Disposal as between Co-owners" (1952) 68 L.Q.R. 507.
[91] *Baker* v. *Barclays Bank Ltd.* [1955] 1 W.L.R. 822, 827.
[92] See *Jacobs* v. *Seward* (1872) L.R. 5 H.L. 464.
[93] s. 34.
[94] A proposal to amend the law on this point was dropped on the committee stage of the Torts (Interference with Goods) Act 1977.

accrual of the cause of action in respect of the original conversion or detention." So (1) where there are successive acts of conversion by the same
person, as where, for example, the defendant wrongfully takes a chattel, and
on a subsequent date wrongfully consumes it, or refuses to restore it on
demand, or (2) where there are successive conversions by different persons,
as where, for example, A wrongfully disposes of the plaintiff's chattel to B
who subsequently refuses to deliver it up on demand, the cause of action is
extinguished after six years from the original conversion.[95] The result is that
the defendant who originally acquired possession unlawfully is in a better
position than the defendant whose original possession was lawful, *e.g.* a
finder. For if the defendant was lawfully in possession the time runs from the
demand and refusal, no matter how long the goods have been in his possession. This has been called a "peculiarly immoral doctrine,"[96] but the rule
must be read in the light of the general exception of concealed fraud.[97] If the
prior act of conversion is a fraudulent one, the period of limitation runs not
from the date of that conversion but from the date of its subsequent
discovery by the plaintiff, which may expose an innocent purchaser to
serious risks.[98] On the other hand, if the prior act of conversion was not
fraudulent, the period of limitation begins to run whether or not the owner
knows that a tort has been committed.[99] Protection is now given to the
purchaser in good faith by section 2 of the 1980 Act.

§ 37. DETINUE

The common law was that a claim in detinue lay at the suit of a person who
had an immediate right to the possession of the goods against another who
is in actual possession of them, and who, upon proper demand,[1] failed or
refused to deliver them up without lawful excuse.[2] But now section 2 (1) of
the 1977 Act provides tersely that "Detinue is abolished."[3] The action is
now framed as one for wrongful interference with goods.

Form of judgment

Section 3 of the 1977 Act re-enacts the common law.[4] It provides in effect
that if the plaintiff is successful he obtains a judgment which may take one

---

[95] *R.B. Policies at Lloyd's* v. *Butler* [1950] 1 K.B. 76; *cf.* Denning J. in *Beaman* v. *A.R.T.S.
Ltd.* [1948] 2 All E.R. 89 (the judgment on this point is unaffected by the decision of the
C.A. in [1949] 1 K.B. 550). As to (1) the Act overrules *Miller* v. *Dell* [1891] 1 Q.B. 468;
as to (2) it overrules *Wilkinson* v. *Verity* (1871) L.R. 6 C.P. 206, unless that case was
correctly explained by Salmond (6th ed., s. 108 (2)) as one of concealed fraud. It was still
treated as law in *Rosenthal* v. *Alderton* [1946] K.B. 374, and in *Beaman* v. *A.R.T.S. Ltd.*
[1948] 2 All E.R. 89, 93.
[96] Jenks, "A Blind Spot in English Law" (1933) 49 L.Q.R. 215, 224.
[97] Below, § 221.
[98] As in *Eddis* v. *Chichester Constable* [1969] 2 Ch. 345.
[99] See Cmnd. 4774 (1971), paras. 84–86.
[1] *Alicia Hosiery Ltd.* v. *Brown, Shipley Ltd.* [1970] 1 Q.B. 195, 207.
[2] *Garrett* v. *Arthur Churchill Ltd.* [1970] 1 Q.B. 92.
[3] This must be one of the shortest sections on the statute-book: see *Howard E. Perry Ltd.* v.
British Railways Board [1980] 1 W.L.R. 1375, 1378, and above, § 30.
[4] See the full discussion by Diplock L.J. in *General and Finance Facilities Ltd.* v. *Cooks Cars
(Romford) Ltd.* [1963] 1 W.L.R. 644, 648–652 and by the 18th Report of the Law Reform
Committee (Cmnd. 4774 (1971)), paras. 92–97.

of three different forms: (i) for the value of the chattel as assessed[4a] and also
for damages for its detention: (ii) for the return of the chattel or recovery of
its value as assessed, and also for damages for its detention; or (iii) for
return of the chattel and damages for its detention. Form (i) is appropriate
for ordinary articles of commerce, or for cases in which the plaintiff does
not, or cannot, claim the return of the goods[5]; in such a case the judgment
itself deprives both parties of the right to insist on a return of the chattel.
Forms (ii) and (iii) are appropriate where damages would not be a suitable
remedy and specific restitution is desirable.[6] If there is an order for return or
delivery up of the chattel, the defendant is not entitled to remain inert, but
should take positive steps to return it, or the plaintiff may levy execution.[7]

§ 38. SPECIFIC RESTITUTION

We have already seen that at common law the owner of chattels had no
absolute right to the specific recovery of them.[8] The form of the judgment in
detinue gave the defendant the choice whether he would deliver up the
chattels or pay their assessed value. Later the law was altered by empower-
ing the court after judgment in an action of detinue to make on the application of the plaintiff an order for specific delivery of the property, enforceable
by way of execution. This jurisdiction is preserved by the Torts (Interference
with Goods) Act 1977 and the Rules of the Supreme Court made under it.[9]
The power of the court to order the specific restitution of chattels is
discretionary[10] and not a matter of right on the part of the plaintiff. Such an
order, therefore, may be either refused altogether, or made only on such
terms as to the court seems necessary to do complete justice between the
parties.[11] This being so, it may be assumed that one or other of these courses
will be adopted in all cases in which the value of the chattel exceeds the
amount of damages to which the plaintiff is entitled. Again when the chattel
is an ordinary article of commerce of no special value or interest and not
alleged to be of any special value to the plaintiff,[12] and damages will fully
compensate, the court will not order specific restitution.[13] If the defendant
has, since taking the property, increased the value of it by his own labour or
expenditure, the plaintiff is entitled to recover as damages only its original
and not its present value.[14] This being so, it is clear that if the plaintiff seeks
specific restitution instead of damages the court must either refuse this
remedy altogether or grant it only on the terms that the plaintiff shall make

---

[4a] The value was assessed at the date of the judgment: *Malhotra* v. *Choudhury* [1980] Ch.
52, 79.
[5] *e.g.* because they have been sold to a third party *pendente lite*: *Gillette* v. *Glasford* (1964) 7
W.I.R. 1.
[6] For these circumstances, see § 38.
[7] *Metals & Ropes Co. Ltd.* v. *Tattersall* [1966] 1 W.L.R. 1500.
[8] Above, § 27.
[9] Ord. 45, r. 4.
[10] In 1966/67 only 19 Writs of Delivery were issued in Greater London—2 for Rolls-Royce
cars.
[11] See the various relevant factors considered in *Howard Perry & Co. Ltd.* v. *British
Railways Board* [1980] 1 W.L.R. 1375.
[12] As distinct from the MS of a play by Dylan Thomas: *Thomas* v. *Times Book Co. Ltd.*
[1966] 1 W.L.R. 911.
[13] *Whiteley Ltd.* v. *Hilt* [1918] 2 K.B. 808, 819.
[14] § 210.

to the defendant a fair allowance in respect of the increased value of the property.[15]

Accessio, specificatio, and confusio[16]

It is in this circumstance that specific restitution is a matter of judicial discretion and not of right that we must find the solution in English law of all those puzzles concerning *accessio*, *specificatio*, and *confusio* which we find discussed with such unsatisfactory results in Roman law and the Continental systems founded upon it. *Accessio* is the combination of two chattels belonging to different persons into a single article: as when A's cloth is used to patch B's coat, or a vehicle let on hire–purchase has new accessories fitted to it. *Specificatio* is the making of a new article out of the chattel of one person by the labour of another: as when A's corn is ground into flour by B, or his grapes are made into wine. *Confusio* or *commixtio* is the mixture of things of the same nature but belonging to different owners so that the identification of the things is no longer possible: as when motor–vehicles are "cannibalised," and their parts used to build a new machine. In all these cases there are two distinct questions to be asked. The first, which is of subordinate importance, is: In whom is the ownership of the new article so created? The second is: Who is entitled to the possession of the new article, and on what terms will he be permitted to retain or recover it? As to the first question unless there is a contract covering the situation,[17] some cases display a tendency to follow the conclusions of Roman law on this matter.[18] It is submitted, however, that the true principle is that a man's property in chattels is not divested by any such events.[19] If my corn is wrongfully taken from me and made into flour, the flour is mine; and if my tree is cut down and sawn into timber, the timber is mine.[20] If my sheep become mixed with another's, so that their identification is impossible, he and I are owners in common of the whole flock in the proportions of our respective contributions to it.[21]

Over and above the question of ownership, however, there arises the question of the right of possession. Here English law avoids all difficulties by making the matter one of judicial discretion unfettered by any general principles. It may be assumed that in all ordinary cases the court will be guided by the relative values of the interests of the rival claimants. Posses-

---

[15] *Peruvian Guano Co.* v. *Dreyfus Bros.* [1892] A.C. 166, 176.

[16] See Slater, "Accessio, Specificatio, and Confusio" (1957) 37 Can.Bar Rev. 597; Guest, "Accession and Confusion in the Law of Hire-Purchase" (1964) 27 M.L.R. 505.

[17] As there may well be under the reservation of title clause so familiar in modern commercial practice—see *Re Bond Worth Ltd.* [1980] Ch. 228.

[18] *Northern Ireland Master Butcher's Wholesale Supply Association* v. *Belfast Corporation* [1965] N.I. 30, 33 ("To clarify the concepts of trespass and conversion, and in default of illumination from the conventional legal lamps, the shadowy figures of the Roman jurists Gaius and Justinian with their torches still alight walked in the detention and condemnation rooms of the Corporation abattoir, no doubt much to the astonishment of those who work there—and the word on their lips was 'specificatio.' ")

[19] See *Thomas* v. *Robinson* [1977] 1 N.Z.L.R. 385.

[20] But Lindley L.J. thought that if I build a house with another's bricks he can recover from me neither them nor their value: *Gough* v. *Wood & Co.* [1894] 1 Q.B. 713, 719. So also Blackburn J. in *Appleby* v. *Myers* (1867) L.R. 2 C.P. 651, 659.

[21] *Gill & Duffus (Liverpool) Ltd.* v. *Scruttons Ltd.* [1953] 1 W.L.R. 1407. It is said in some cases that if the *confusio* is due to the wrongful act of one of the owners he forfeits his property to the other: *sed quaere*: see Guest, (1964) 27 M.L.R. 505, 520.

sion will be awarded to him whose interest is the more substantial, on the terms that he pays the value of the other's interest.

Power to order plaintiff to accept restitution instead of damages

When property has once been converted there is a vested right of action which is not divested by the fact that the owner subsequently accepts restitution of the property. Such a recovery of possession goes merely in mitigation of damages and not in bar of the action. Therefore the plaintiff may still commence or proceed with his action for the recovery of such damages as are due in respect of his temporary dispossession.[22] But is the plaintiff bound to accept such a restitution of converted property; or can he refuse a tender of it, and insist on his right to sue for its value? Under the old practice a tender of the goods was a good plea in an action of detinue, for this action was brought not for damages but for the recovery of the goods themselves.[23] In trespass and trover, on the contrary, the plaintiff had a good cause of action for the value of the goods and was not bound to accept the goods themselves; and the only remedy of a defendant who was able and willing to restore the property was to apply to the court to exercise its discretionary power of staying the action on delivery of the goods. After some hesitation the courts finally consented to exercise this power in cases in which it was just to the parties that the plaintiff should be thus compelled to accept the property.[24] In other words the courts do not give the plaintiff a right to enforce a sale and so recover the full value of his property. Were the rule otherwise, much hardship might be caused to innocent defendants who have converted in good faith and are entirely willing to restore the property.

§ 39. REPLEVIN[25]

Whenever chattels are taken by one person out of the possession[26] of another, whether by way of distress[27] or otherwise, the latter may by way of proceedings in replevin recover immediate and provisional possession of them, pending the result of an action brought by him to determine the rights of the parties. The right to replevy goods is a right to get them back at once and provisionally, on giving security to bring an action of replevin, instead of having first to establish one's title to them in an action of trover, detinue, or trespass. The plaintiff must prove that at the commencement of the action he was the owner or entitled to possession of the chattel in question and that it was at that time being unjustly detained from him.[28]

Replevin is allowable only when the chattels have been taken by a trespass by the defendant out of the plaintiff's possession. It is not available for a mere detention or for any other dispute as to the title or right of possession. The process is based on the presumption that the possessor of goods is the owner of them, and that a seizure of them is illegal, conferring therefore

---

[22] *Moon* v. *Raphael* (1835) 2 Bing. N.C. 310.
[23] *Crossfield* v. *Such* (1852) 8 Ex. 159.
[24] *U.S.A.* v. *Dollfus Mieg* [1952] A.C. 582, 619.
[25] See Sutton, *Personal Actions,* pp. 66–71, and Williams, "A strange Offspring of Trespass *ab initio*" (1936) 52 L.Q.R. 106.
[26] So that a bailee can claim: *Swaffer* v. *Mulcahy* [1934] 1 K.B. 608.
[27] The best short account is in Chapman, *Statutes,* pp. 318–320.
[28] *McKenzie* v. *Somers* [1954] 1 D.L.R. 421.

upon the possessor a right to their provisional restoration pending an inquiry into the title.[29] The right of replevin is usually exercised only in cases of distress, whether for rent, for rates,[30] damage feasant, or otherwise, though it is legally available for all forms of taking whether under colour of distress or not.[31] If the plaintiff succeeds in an action of replevin he keeps the property which has been thus provisionally restored to him and has judgment for all damage (for example, annoyance in his trade) resulting from the defendant's seizure of it.[32] If the defendant succeeds, he has judgment for the restitution of the property, or in the alternative (when his claim is one of distress for rent), if he so requests, for payment of the amount claimed by him or (where the claim is one of distress damage feasant), if the plaintiff so requests, for the amount of the damages sustained by him.[33] Under section 4 of the 1977 Act a procedure for interim custody pending trial has been provided. The relationship to replevin is obscure.

§ 40. RESCOUS AND POUND–BREACH

Rescous involves the rescue of distrained goods before they reach the pound; pound–breach arises after they have been impounded. Rescous and pound–breach are still criminal offences,[34] and also torts, and one who commits either tort is liable to a statutory action for treble damages.[35] Once goods are impounded they are *in custodia legis*, and if a pound has been created it must be respected not merely by the tenant but by strangers as well. It was no defence that the defendant did not know that the goods were impounded. Liability was therefore strict. With the increase in the practice of "walking possession" by bailiffs this caused difficulties, and the law has now been modified. A defendant is not liable unless he has a guilty mind, that is, unless he knows that the goods which he took had been impounded.[36] But it is uncertain whether goods have been impounded if they have not been the subject of a distinct act which makes it obvious that they are not to be taken away but are *in custodia legis*. For although it was asserted that "walking possession" was valid as against strangers as well as the tenant,[37] this has been doubted.[38]

---

[29] *Mennie* v. *Blake* (1856) 6 E. & B. 842.
[30] As when a tram-car was seized in *L.C.C.* v. *Hackney B.C.* [1928] 2 K.B. 588.
[31] *Shannon* v. *Shannon* (1804) 1 Sch. & Lef. 324.
[32] *Smith* v. *Enright* (1893) 69 L.T. 724.
[33] County Court Rules, 1936, Ord. 33, rr. 1–3.
[34] But the Law Commission may recommend their abolition: Law Com. No. 12, para. 93 (1967).
[35] Distress for Rent Act 1689, s. 3.
[36] *Abingdon R.D.C.* v. *O'Gorman* [1968] 2 Q.B. 811.
[37] *Lavell & Co.* v. *O'Leary* [1933] 2 K.B. 200.
[38] *Abingdon R.D.C.* v. *O'Gorman* [1968] 2 Q.B. 811.

CHAPTER 6

REVERSIONARY INTERESTS

§ 41. REVERSIONARY INTERESTS IN LAND

Trespass and nuisance are essentially injuries to the possession of land and not to the ownership of it. We will now, therefore, consider the position of a reversioner—using that term in a wide sense to include any person having a lawful interest in land but not the present possession of it—*e.g.* a landlord whose land is in the occupation of a tenant. Injuries to reversionary interests are of two kinds, according as they are committed (1) by the tenant or other person in possession of the land, or (2) by a stranger. Injuries of the first kind may be included under the generic title of waste, which may be defined as unlawful damage done or permitted by the occupier of land as against those having reversionary interests in it. An account of the law of waste does not pertain to the law of torts but is a branch of the law of property.[1] It is otherwise with the second class of injuries to reversionary interests—*viz.* those which are committed not by the occupier, but by strangers. These injuries are governed by general principles which properly pertain to the law of torts.

A reversioner may sue for any trespass or nuisance if, and only if, it actually affects his reversionary interest; and in general this is so only if the effects of the injuries so committed are permanent. Temporary consequences give a cause of action only to the occupier; permanent consequences give a cause of action both to him and to the reversioner. Consequences are permanent in this sense if they are of a nature that they will continue to affect the land even after the interest of the reversioner has become an interest in possession.[2] Accordingly a mere trespass, unaccompanied by any physical injury to the land, is not actionable at the suit of a reversioner, even though committed under a claim to a right of way[3]; neither is a temporary nuisance, such as noise or smoke, which causes no enduring physical harm to the property.[4] It is otherwise, however, if permanent physical harm is done, whether by way of trespass, nuisance, or otherwise.[5] In applying this rule we must be careful not to confound a permanent injury with a continuing one. A permanent injury is a completed wrong the consequences of which will endure until the interest of the reversioner has fallen into possession, and for which accordingly he has a present right of action—*e.g.* the destruction of a building on land in the possession of the plaintiff's tenant. A continuing injury, on the other hand, is one which is still in process of being committed—*e.g.* a nuisance caused by the smoke or noise of a factory. We shall see[6] that even the occupier himself cannot recover damages for the future continuance of such a continuing injury,

---

[1] As regards the reversioner, the law treats waste as breach of a contractual obligation, although voluntary waste is also the subject-matter of an action of tort.

[2] *Shelfer* v. *City of London Electric Lighting Co.* [1895] 1 Ch. 287, 318.

[3] *Cooper* v. *Crabtree* (1882) 20 Ch.D. 589.

[4] *Jones* v. *Chappell* (1875) L.R. 20 Eq. 539; *Mott* v. *Shoolbred* (1875) L.R. 20 Eq. 22.

[5] *Jones* v. *Llanrwst Urban Council* [1911] 1 Ch. 393, 404 ("the sewage of Llanrwst will continue to be turned into the Conway unless and until something is done to divert it elsewhere").

[6] Below, § 218.

howsoever probable that continuance may be.[7] He recovers damages only for the past; and if the wrong continues he may sue a second time on a new cause of action thus arising. So the reversioner *a fortiori* must wait until his interest falls into possession, and then, if the injury still continues, he will have his action. But a reversioner may sue for any continuing injury which, by virtue of the law relating to prescription, will by its continuance pre-judicially affect his reversionary interest in the land by creating or destroying a servitude in relation thereto. On this principle it has been repeatedly decided that a reversioner may sue for an obstruction to ancient lights or for interference with a right of way.[8]

§ 42. REVERSIONARY INTERESTS IN CHATTELS

We have already seen[9] that a person not in actual possession and not entitled to immediate possession could not sue in conversion, even though he was the owner of the property. Thus no action of conversion would lie at the suit of a bailor of goods for a fixed term,[10] as distinct from a bailor at will[11]; or at that of a purchaser of goods which were still held by the vendor under his lien.[12] A similar rule limited the application of the actions of detinue[13] and of trespass.[14] In all such cases the remedy of the plaintiff was not conversion but a special action on the case for the injury done to his reversionary interest. There seems to be no particular reason why this specific action on the case should be retained separate from the tort of conversion,[15] but the 1977 Act does not specifically abolish it, although it is now to be described, under section 1 (*d*), as an action for wrongful interference with goods.

---

[7] Save when damages are awarded in substitution for an injunction as the price of the legalisation of future continuance.
[8] *Metropolitan Association* v. *Petch* (1858) 5 C.B. (N.S.) 504.
[9] Above, § 34.
[10] *Gordon* v. *Harper* (1796) 7 T.R. 9.
[11] *Manders* v. *Williams* (1849) 4 Ex. 339.
[12] *Lord* v. *Price* (1874) L.R. 9 Ex. 54.
[13] *Nyberg* v. *Handelaar* [1892] 2 Q.B. 202.
[14] *Ward* v. *Macauley* (1791) 4 T.R. 489.
[15] 18th Report of the Law Reform Committee (Cmnd. 4774 (1971)), para. 34.

CHAPTER 7

TRESPASS TO THE PERSON

§ 43. Battery

The torts known as assault and battery are based on the ancient action of trespass.[1] So any direct and immediate interference with personal liberty is actionable without proof of damage.[2] "English law goes to great lengths to protect a person of full age and capacity from interference with his personal liberty. We have too often seen freedom disappear in other countries not only by coups d'état but by gradual erosion; and often it is the first step that counts. So it would be unwise to make even minor concessions."[3] Therefore the "breathalyser" legislation has been strictly construed.[4] So also a compulsory medical examination is tortious unless clearly justified by statute, as also, probably, is any form of therapy administered without real consent.[5]

The application of force to the person of another without lawful justification amounts to the wrong of battery.[6] This is so, however trivial the amount or nature of the force may be, and even though it neither does nor is intended nor is likely or able to do any manner of harm. Even to touch a person without his consent or some other lawful reason is actionable.[7] Nor is anger or hostility essential to liability: an unwanted kiss may be a battery.[8] For the interest that is protected by the law of assault and battery is not merely that of freedom from bodily harm, but also that of freedom from such forms of insult as may be due to interference with his person. In respect of his personal dignity, therefore, a man may recover substantial damages for battery which has done him no physical harm whatever,[9] as when a man's finger-prints are taken without observing the statutory[10] requirements,[11] e.g. that the prints be taken in the building which houses the court which made the order.[12]

There is a dubious exception when the act (e.g. touching on the shoulder) is so trivial an interference with the liberty of the subject that it cannot properly be described as outside the duties of a police officer.[13] It is certainly

---

[1] The criminal offences of false imprisonment and kidnapping are surprisingly obscure in comparison with "the steady well-documented development" of the torts: see Napier, "Detention Offences at Common Law," in *Reshaping the Criminal Law* (ed. Glazebrook, 1978), p. 190, and Lambert (1979) Cambrian L.Rev. 20.
[2] See above, § 2.
[3] *S.* v. *McC.* [1972] A.C. 24, 43, *per* Lord Reid.
[4] *Morris* v. *Beardmore* [1980] 2 All E.R. 753.
[5] *Baugh* v. *Delta Water Ltd.* [1971] 1 W.L.R. 1295, 1298. For reality of consent, see *Chatterton* v. *Gerson* [1980] 3 W.L.R. 1003, and below, §§ 46, 185, 187.
[6] *Eisener* v. *Maxwell* [1951] 1 D.L.R. 816, 823.
[7] *Cole* v. *Turner* (1704) 6 Mod. 149; but not for him to invite you to touch him in an indecent manner: *D.P.P.* v. *Rogers* [1953] 1 W.L.R. 1017 (though it may be a criminal offence: Indecency with Children Act 1960).
[8] *Fogg* v. *McKnight* [1968] N.Z.L.R. 330. Rape is, of course, a battery. But in practice claims for damages are rare, although the Criminal Injuries Compensation Board often makes awards (the average is £1,200).
[9] *Stewart* v. *Stonehouse* (1926) 2 D.L.R. 683, 684.
[10] Magistrates' Courts Act 1952, s. 40.
[11] But the evidence so obtained may still be admissible at his trial: *Callis* v. *Gunn* [1964] 1 Q.B. 495.
[12] *R.* v. *Jones* [1978] 3 All E.R. 1098.
[13] *Donnelly* v. *Jackman* [1970] 1 W.L.R. 562.

clear that consent is implied to such physical contacts as are a reasonably necessary consequence of social life. A defence is therefore available for "the jostler, the back-slapper, and the hand-shaker,"[14] or the person who swats a horsefly on a friend's thigh.[15] Consent may also be implied to harm suffered in the course of some lawful game.[16] But a footballer has been ordered to pay £5,400 damages for deliberately fouling an opponent.[17]

Assault and battery[18]

Intentionally to bring any material object into contact with another's person is a sufficient application of force to constitute a battery; for example, to throw water upon him,[19] or to pull a chair from under him whereby he falls to the ground[20] or to apply a "tone-rinse" to his scalp.[21] So it is a battery forcibly to take from him some object which he holds[22] or wears.[23] It is also probably a battery to project heat, light, noise, or vapours onto another person in such a manner as to cause physical injury or personal discomfort.

It is a disputed question how far the term "battery" was, or is now, confined to cases of wilful or intentional injuries.[24] As the line of division between trespass and case depended on whether the damage was direct or indirect and not on whether it was intentional or negligent,[25] a long series of cases affirmed that a battery did not necessarily involve intention.[26] It was also quite clear that a person could be guilty of an assault without being guilty of a battery.[27] Fear in the sense of alarm is not an essential ingredient of the tort of battery. Indeed, not even apprehension of the infliction of force is required: a blow from behind is a battery. The position is very different in assault, in which fear or apprehension must be proved. On the other hand, in popular speech "assault" includes a battery, and Salmond himself[28] thought that the legal and the popular terminology should coincide. His view has been greatly strengthened by *Fowler v. Lanning*,[29] in which it was held that in an action of trespass to the person intention or negligence must be shown. But the status of this decision is still somewhat doubtful, and until it has been definitely[30] approved on appeal it is better to adhere to the traditional common law.

---

[14] Lord Devlin, *Samples of Lawmaking* (1962), p. 85.
[15] Lucas, in *Law, Morality and Society* (ed. Hacker), p. 87.
[16] See below, § 187.
[17] *Lewis v. Brookshaw, The Times,* April 10, 1970.
[18] See Trindade, "Some Curiosities of Negligent Trespass to the Person" (1971) 20 I.C.L.Q. 706.
[19] *Pursell v. Horn* (1838) 8 A. & E. 602.
[20] *Hopper v. Reeve* (1817) 7 Taunt. 698.
[21] *Nash v. Sheen* [1953] C.L.Y. 3726.
[22] *Green v. Goddard* (1702) 2 Salk. 641.
[23] *Humphreys v. Connor* (1864) 17 Ir.C.L.R. 1 (Orange lily).
[24] *Long v. Hepworth* [1968] 1 W.L.R. 1299.
[25] See above, § 2.
[26] *Covell v. Laming* (1808) 1 Camp. 497; *Eisener v. Maxwell* [1951] 1 D.L.R. 816, 827 (approving the views of Stallybrass in earlier editions), reversed [1951] 3 D.L.R. 345; *Mantey v. Spanks* [1952] 3 D.L.R. 783.
[27] *Jones v. Sherwood* [1942] 1 K.B. 127.
[28] 6th ed., s. 117.
[29] [1959] 1 Q.B. 426. See below, § 46.
[30] It was approved, *obiter*, in *Letang v. Cooper* [1965] 1 Q.B. 232.

Assault

The act of putting another person in reasonable fear or apprehension of an immediate battery by means of an act amounting to an attempt or threat to commit a battery amounts to an actionable assault.[31] The tort is remarkable, for it "remains the only instance in English jurisprudence of a mere offensive sensation unaccompanied by any untoward psychosomatic symptoms, let alone external trauma, giving a cause of action for damages."[32] Probably mere words do not constitute an assault,[33] however insulting or even menacing[34]; the intent to do violence must be expressed in threatening acts, not merely in threatening speech.[35] But words accompanying an act may render harmless what might otherwise be an assault.[36] Even threatening acts do not constitute an assault unless they are of such a nature as to put the plaintiff in fear or apprehension of immediate violence. To shake one's fist in a man's face is an assault; to shake it at a man who by his distance from the scene of action is inaccessible to such violence is none.[37]

There need be no actual intention or power to use violence, for it is enough if the plaintiff on reasonable grounds believes that he is in danger of it.[38] Thus it is actionable to point a gun at a man in a threatening manner, even though to the knowledge of the defendant, but not to that of the plaintiff, it is unloaded.[39] But if there is no reasonable fear there is no assault: as, for example, when a gun is pointed at a man behind his back.[40] Mere passive obstruction does not constitute an assault,[41] although if the plaintiff is thereby hindered from going about his lawful occasions he may use reasonable force by way of self-help.[42]

Criminal law[43]

An assault is not merely a tort, but also a criminal offence, and the civil and criminal remedies are in general concurrent and cumulative. It is provided, however, by the Offences against the Person Act 1861, ss. 44 to 45, that summary criminal proceedings, whether they result in a conviction or an acquittal (after an actual hearing on the merits, as distinct from a plea of guilty[44]), are a bar to any subsequent civil proceedings for the same cause.

---

[31] *Stephens* v. *Myers* (1830) 4 C. & P. 349.
[32] Fleming, *Introduction to the Law of Torts*, p. 3.
[33] They may be actionable on other grounds: below, § 48.
[34] See the authoritative survey by Handford, "Tort Liability for Threatening or Insulting Words" (1976) 54 Can. Bar Rev. 563.
[35] *Meade's and Belt's Case* (1823) 1 Lew. 184. "For Meade's case proves, or my Report's in fault, that singing can't be reckoned an assault": Adolphus, "The Circuiteers" (1884) 1 L.Q.R. 232. *Contra*, Lord Goddard C.J. in *R.* v. *Wilson* [1955] 1 W.L.R. 493, 494. But the traditional view is impliedly supported by *Wilkinson* v. *Downton* [1897] 2 Q.B. 57, in which the defendant had only spoken, and not acted (see below, § 77).
[36] *Tuberville* v. *Savage* (1669) 1 Mod. 3.
[37] *Stephens* v. *Myers* (1830) 4 C. & P. 349.
[38] *Bruce* v. *Dyer* (1966) 58 D.L.R. (2d) 211, 216.
[39] *R.* v. *St. George* (1840) 9 C. & P. 483, 493.
[40] *Osborn* v. *Veitch* (1858) 1 F. & F. 317.
[41] *Innes* v. *Wylie* (1844) 1 C. & K. 257 (defendant "like a door or wall").
[42] See below, § 46.
[43] North, "Civil and Criminal Remedies for Assault" (1966) 29 M.L.R. 16.
[44] *Ellis* v. *Burton* [1975] 1 W.L.R. 386.

§ 44. FALSE IMPRISONMENT

The wrong[45] of false[46] imprisonment consists in the act of arresting or imprisoning any person without lawful justification, or otherwise preventing him without lawful justification from exercising his right of leaving the place in which he is.[47] It may also be committed by continuing a lawful imprisonment longer than is justifiable,[48] or by imprisoning a person in an unauthorised place.[49] As it is derived from the action of trespass there is no need to prove actual damage. In any event, when the liberty of the subject is at stake questions as to the damage sustained become of little importance.[50] Aggravated damages may be awarded in a proper case,[51] as when the imprisonment, although in itself of a nominal character, is offensive or hurtful to the plaintiff's feelings.[52] In some circumstances exemplary damages may also be awarded.[53] The wrong of false imprisonment is in most cases that of assault also, but not necessarily so[54]; locking a man up in a room in which he already is by his own act amounts to false imprisonment but is no assault. Even if the plaintiff fails to prove some of the ingredients of this tort he may have a special action on the case for the infringement of his liberty,[55] or an action for defamation, malicious prosecution, or the intentional infliction of mental distress. He can also recover his liberty by a writ of habeas corpus.

The imprisonment

To constitute the wrong in question there need be no actual imprisonment in the ordinary sense—*i.e.* incarceration. Unlawful detention may be either custodial or non-custodial.[56] It is enough that the plaintiff has been in any manner completely deprived of his personal liberty. A mere unlawful arrest, for example, amounts in itself to false imprisonment, and so does any act whereby a man is unlawfully prevented from leaving the place in which he is: for example, a house[57] or a motor-car,[58] or a ski-lift,[59] or the common travel area at a port by refusing to allow him to enter immigration control.[60] The taking possession or control of the person, even without actual contact, seems to be the governing factor.[61] Whether or not a person has been arrested depends not on the legality of the arrest but on whether he has been deprived of his liberty to go where he pleases.[62] Hence it is unnecessary that

---

[45] For the crime, see above, § 43, n. 1.
[46] The term false is here used not in the ordinary sense of mendacious or fallacious, but in the less common though well-established sense of erroneous or wrong; as in the phrases false quantity, false step, false taste, etc.
[47] There may be criminal as well as tortious liability: see above, § 43, n. 1.
[48] *Mee* v. *Cruikshank* (1902) 86 L.T. 708.
[49] *Cobbett* v. *Grey* (1849-50) 4 Ex. 729.
[50] *John Lewis & Co.* v. *Tims* [1952] A.C. 676, 680.
[51] See below, § 199.
[52] *Fogg* v. *McKnight* [1968] N.Z.L.R. 330.
[53] *Cassell & Co. Ltd.* v. *Broome* [1972] A.C. 1027.
[54] *McPherson* v. *Brown* [1975] 12 S.A.S.R. 184.
[55] *Wright* v. *Wilson* (1699) 1 Ld.Raym. 739; *Bird* v. *Jones* (1845) 7 Q.B. 742, 752.
[56] *Blundell* v. *Att.-Gen.* [1967] N.Z.L.R. 492.
[57] *Warner* v. *Riddiford* (1858) 4 C.B. (N.S.) 180.
[58] *Burton* v. *Davies*, 1953 St.R.Qd. 26.
[59] *The Times*, June 26, 1963.
[60] Williams (1974) 23 I.C.L.Q. 642.
[61] *Conn* v. *David Spencer Ltd.* [1930] 1 D.L.R. 805.
[62] *Spicer* v. *Holt* [1977] A.C. 987, 1000.

there should be any actual use of force.[63] A threat of force, whereby the submission of the person threatened is procured, is sufficient: for example, showing a man a warrant for his arrest and thereby obtaining his submission is itself an arrest if it amounts to a tacit threat to execute the warrant by force if necessary; otherwise it amounts merely to a request with no threat or intent to use force.[64] "In such cases . . . though little may be said, much is meant and perfectly understood."[65] It is enough if the plaintiff shows that he has submitted to restraint because of moral pressure exerted by the defendant, e.g. if the plaintiff goes to answer a charge in order to avoid an embarrassing scene in a public place.[66] What is the position if a police officer invites a suspect against whom no charge has yet been made to accompany him to the police station for an interview? The law draws a very sensible distinction between one who goes to the police station voluntarily in the first instance[67] and one who, having had a charge made against him, goes voluntarily to meet it.[68] The second person may be able to sue for false imprisonment, but the first cannot: his liberty has not been interfered with, as he can leave the police station at any time.[69] The common law has never encouraged notions such as "preventive custody," which are familiar elsewhere.[70]

It has even been said that a man may be imprisoned without knowing it. "A person can be imprisoned while he is asleep, while he is in a state of drunkenness, while he is unconscious, and while he is a lunatic. So a man might in fact, to my mind, be imprisoned by having the key of a door turned against him so that he is imprisoned in a room in fact although he does not know that the key has been turned."[71]

To constitute imprisonment the deprivation of the plaintiff's liberty must be complete—that is to say, there must be on every side of him a boundary drawn beyond which he cannot pass. That boundary may be very narrowly,[72] or quite broadly,[73] drawn, but it must be complete and definite. It is no imprisonment to prevent the plaintiff from going in some directions while he is left free to go as far as he pleases in others. Thus no action for false imprisonment[74] will lie for unlawfully preventing the plaintiff from going along one part of the highway and compelling him to go round or

---

[63] *Blundell* v. *Att.-Gen.* [1967] N.Z.L.R. 492.

[64] *Warner* v. *Riddiford* (1858) 4 C.B. (N.S.) 180. It is doubtful whether the signing of the charge-sheet is sufficient to constitute false imprisonment: *Clubb* v. *Wimpey* [1936] 3 All E.R. 148: see Kodilinye, 28 I.C.L.Q. 766.

[65] *Bird* v. *Jones* (1845) 7 Q.B. 742, 748, per Williams J.

[66] *Clayton* v. *London etc. Fashions Ltd.* (1961) 31 D.L.R. (2d) 527.

[67] This is not so unlikely as might appear at first sight; a man often prefers to answer police inquiries at the station rather than at home within sight of curious neighbours: Devlin, *The Criminal Prosecution in England* (1960), p. 68.

[68] *Peters* v. *Stanway* (1835) 6 C. & P. 737.

[69] *Dunne* v. *Clinton* [1930] I.R. 366, 372. See, further, below § 46.

[70] For the distinction between arrest and custody, see below, § 46.

[71] *Meering* v. *Grahame-White Aviation Co.* (1919) 122 L.T. 44, 53, *per* Atkin L.J., who made the point that the plaintiff's captors might be boasting elsewhere of the imprisonment: but would not this be defamation? This case has been criticised by Goodhart, 'Restatement of the Law of Torts" (1935) 83 U.Pa.L.Rev. 411, 418, and is inconsistent with *Herring* v. *Boyle* (1834) 1 C.M. & R. 377, but is supported by Prosser, "False Imprisonment: Consciousness of Confinement" (1955) 55 Col.L.Rev. 847.

[72] *e.g.* the cubicle in a public lavatory: *Sayers* v. *Harlow U.D.C.* [1958] 1 W.L.R. 623.

[73] *e.g.* the perimeter of certain airport buildings: *Kuchenmeister* v. *Home Office* [1958] 1 Q.B. 496.

[74] But an action may lie for assault or intimidation.

back.[75] But the means of escape available must be such as are reasonable in all the circumstances of the case. Probably the means of escape are unreasonable if they involve exposure of,[76] or danger to,[77] the person, or material harm to the clothing, or damage to the person (as distinct from a mere trespass against the property[78]) of another.

Failure to afford facilities for leaving premises[79]

One who has lawfully entered premises is therefore entitled to leave them; but it is not clear whether he is entitled to leave by the same gate or door as that by which he entered. Such a right might be very inconvenient if exercised at, say, a crowded sporting event. So an occupier is entitled to stipulate that a visitor shall leave by some gate or door other than that by which he entered the premises.[80] An occupier of premises (a term which includes a vehicle) may also be entitled to stipulate that a visitor shall not leave except after the expiry of a reasonable time: a passenger on an express train is not entitled to get out at an unscheduled stop.[81]

But there is no positive duty to assist another to obtain his liberty. Towards persons who are upon his premises and who are unable to leave them unless active measures are taken by him in that behalf, an occupier owes no duty to take such measures. If my neighbour falls down a pit upon my land I am under no obligation to pull him out. In *Herd v. Weardale Steel Coke and Coal Co.*[82] certain miners, having been lowered down the defendants' mine, wrongfully refused to continue their work, and demanded that they should at once be taken to the surface. The defendants, however, refused to do so, and stopped the working of the cage, by reason of which the miners were compelled to remain for some little time in the mine against their will. In an action for false imprisonment it was held by the House of Lords that it was a case of *volenti non fit injuria*. Even if the motive was to punish the plaintiffs,[83] there was no cause of action, though it might have been otherwise if it had been a case of sudden illness, or if the mining company had been in breach of contract.[84]

§ 45. FALSE IMPRISONMENT AND ABUSE OF PROCESS[85]

No action for false imprisonment will lie against a person who has procured the imprisonment of another by obtaining against him a judgment or other judicial order of a court of justice, even though that judgment or order is erroneous, irregular, or without jurisdiction. The proper remedy in such a

---

[75] *Bird* v. *Jones* (1845) 7 Q.B. 742.
[76] As where the plaintiff is bathing and the defendant removes his clothes.
[77] As in *Sayers* v. *Harlow U.D.C.* [1958] 1 W.L.R. 623.
[78] So ruled by Sir John Holt C.J. at Nisi Prius: *Wright* v. *Wilson* (1699) 1 Ld.Raym. 693.
[79] Amos, "Contractual Restraint of Liberty" (1928) 44 L.Q.R. 464: Williams, "Two Cases on False Imprisonment," in *Law, Justice and Equity* (ed. Holland and Schwarzenberger) (1967).
[80] This is perhaps the best explanation of the difficult case of *Robinson* v. *Balmain New Ferry Co. Ltd.* [1910] A.C. 295.
[81] *Herd* v. *Weardale Steel, Coke and Coal Co. Ltd.* [1915] A.C. 67, 71.
[82] [1915] A.C. 67.
[83] As in *Burns* v. *Johnston* [1917] 2 I.R. 137; (1916) 50 I.L.T.R. 224.
[84] Salmond suggested (6th ed., p. 442) that there were other cases than breach of contract in which the facts might impose on the defendant a positive legal obligation to take active measures for the plaintiff's release.
[85] See Kodilinye, "False Imprisonment through Ministerial Officers" (1979) 28 I.C.L.Q. 766.

case is an action for malicious prosecution or other malicious abuse of legal process.[86] In an action of that description that plaintiff can succeed only if he proves both malice and the absence of any reasonable and probable cause for the proceedings complained of; whereas in an action for false imprisonment, just as in all other cases of trespass to person or property, liability is created, in general, even by honest and inevitable mistake.[87] The rule, therefore, that no action for false imprisonment will lie against a litigant in respect of judicial imprisonment procured by him is a valuable protection against liability for error in the course of legal proceedings. "The distinction between false imprisonment and malicious prosecution is well illustrated by the case where, parties being before a magistrate, one makes a charge against another, whereupon a magistrate orders the person charged to be taken into custody and detained until the matter can be investigated. The party making the charge is not liable to an action for false imprisonment, because he does not set a ministerial officer in motion, but a judicial officer. The opinion and judgment of a judicial officer are interposed between the charge and the imprisonment."[88] Accordingly, if the plaintiff has been wrongly arrested without warrant and taken before a magistrate, who remands him in custody, he must sue in respect of his imprisonment before the remand in an action for false imprisonment, but in respect of that which is subsequent to the remand in an action for malicious prosecution.[89] The reason for this distinction is that a man cannot be sued in trespass (and so not for false imprisonment) unless he himself, whether personally or by his agent, has done the act complained of. A court of justice, however, is not the agent of the litigant but acts in the exercise of its own independent judicial discretion. The litigant can be charged only with having maliciously and without reasonable cause exercised his right of setting a court of justice in motion.[90] This exemption of the litigant from any liability for false imprisonment extends even to cases in which the court ordering the imprisonment has acted without jurisdiction. It is the right of every litigant to bring his case before the court, and it is for the court to know the limits of its own jurisdiction and to keep within them.[91]

Ministerial officers

If, however, the litigant, after procuring a judicial order of imprisonment, proceeds to execute it by means of some ministerial officer whom he thereby makes his agent, he may thereby make himself responsible in an action for false imprisonment if the order was one which ought not to have been made.[92] Whether he will be so responsible or not depends on whether the order is of such a nature as, even though wrongful, to be a protection to those who act in reliance on it. An action for false imprisonment will lie against any person who authorises or directs the unlawful arrest or detention of the plaintiff by a merely ministerial officer of the law. He who sets in motion a merely ministerial officer, such as a constable, has no protection

---

[86] See below, § 134.
[87] See Sutton, *Personal Actions*, p. 61.
[88] *Austin* v. *Dowling* (1870) L.R. 5 C.P. 534, 540, per Willes J.
[89] *Lock* v. *Ashton* (1848) 12 Q.B. 871.
[90] See *Brown* v. *Chapman* (1848) 6 C.B. 365; *Lea* v. *Charrington* (1889) 23 Q.B.D. 45.
[91] *Brown* v. *Chapman* (1848) 6 C.B. 365.
[92] *Painter* v. *Liverpool Gas Light Co.* (1836) 3 A. & E. 433.

similar to that which is extended to the litigant in a court of justice.[93] If he makes that ministerial officer his agent he is responsible for any arrest or detention so procured or authorised. It is necessary to prove actual direction or authorisation; mere information given to such an officer, on which he acts at his own discretion, is no ground of liability.[94]

§ 46. DEFENCES[95]

The following eight defences are available: (1) consent; (2) contributory negligence; (3) self-defence; (4) that the defendant was acting to prevent a trespass or ejecting a trespasser; (5) that the defendant was acting in support of the criminal law to secure the public peace; (6) that the defendant was exercising parental or other authority; (7) inevitable accident; (8) statutory authority.

(1) Consent

This is considered elsewhere, as is the allied defence of necessity.[96]

(2) Contributory negligence

Contributory negligence is generally assumed to be a defence to assault[97] or false imprisonment,[98] but there is only one clear decision on the point.[99]

(3) Self-defence

It is lawful for any person to use a reasonable degree of force for the protection of himself or any other person against any unlawful use of force. In the older books a distinction is drawn between the defence of oneself and of certain persons with whom one is closely connected (such as a wife, child, or master), and the defence of a mere stranger.[1] It may be safely assumed, however, that at the present day all such distinctions are obsolete and that every man has the right of defending any man by reasonable force against unlawful force,[2] even if he has made a genuine mistake about the perilous position of that other.[3] Still, the relationship of the parties may be relevant to the reasonableness of force used.

Force is not reasonable if it is either (i) unnecessary—*i.e.* greater than is requisite for the purpose—or (ii) disproportionate to the evil to be prevented. In order that it may be deemed reasonable within the meaning of this rule, it is not enough that the force was not more than was necessary for the purpose in hand. For even though not more than necessary it may be unreasonably disproportionate to the nature of the evil sought to be avoided.

---

[93] This sentence certainly represents the law, but it is doubtful whether it gives an accurate picture of present police practice. The modern constable exercises his own discretion before effecting an arrest.
[94] *Grinham* v. *Willey* (1859) 4 H. & N. 496.
[95] See Beale, "Justification for Injury" (1928) 41 Harv.L.Rev. 553.
[96] Below, §§ 185-189.
[97] *Lane* v. *Holloway* [1968] 1 Q.B. 379.
[98] *Sayers* v. *Harlow U.D.C.* [1958] 1 W.L.R. 623.
[99] *Hoeberger* v. *Koppens* [1974] 2 N.Z.L.R. 597.
[1] *Leward* v. *Baseley* (1695) 1 Ld.Raym. 62.
[2] *The People* v. *Keatley* [1954] I.R. 12, 17; *Goss* v. *Nicholas* [1960] Tas.S.R. 133.
[3] *R.* v. *Fennell* [1971] 1 Q.B. 428.

"A man cannot justify a maim for every assault; as if A strike B, B cannot justify the drawing his sword and cutting off his hand; but it must be such an assault whereby in probability the life may be in danger."[4] It must also be noted that the law changes with differing social conditions. Once it was held "that if an author is to go and give a beating to a publisher who has offended him, two or three blows with a horse-whip ought to be quite enough to satisfy his irritated feelings,"[5] but today those ideas no longer prevail.[6] Still, "If you are attacked with a deadly weapon you can defend yourself with a deadly weapon or with any other weapon which may protect your life. The law does not concern itself with niceties in such matters. If you are attacked by a prize-fighter you are not bound to adhere to the Queensberry rules in your defence."[7] He on whom an assault is threatened or committed is not bound to adopt an attitude of passive defence: "I am not bound to wait until the other has given a blow, for perhaps it will come too late afterwards," it was said in the *Chaplain of Gray's Inn's Case* in 1400.[8] The defendant will be justified so long as he does not go beyond what is reasonable as a measure of self-defence. Nor need he make any request or give any warning, but may forthwith reply to force by force.[9] Provocation by the plaintiff may wipe out the element of aggravated damages but cannot be used to reduce the real damages for the harm done.[10]

(4) Prevention of trespass or ejection of a trespasser

It is lawful for any occupier of land, or for any other person with the authority of the occupier, to use a reasonable degree of force in order to prevent a trespasser[11] from entering[12] or to control his movements[13] or to eject him after entry.[14] So reasonable force may be used to eject a trespasser taking part in a demonstration on private premises.[15] This right of using force against trespassers is conferred only on the occupier of the land (or his agents), for it is only the occupier who is entitled to complain of a trespass and to take legal proceedings in respect thereof.[16] This right must be distinguished from forcible re-entry upon land of which possession has been wrongfully taken or detained[17] and from the right of an occupier to justify his acts on the ground of necessity.[18] Presumably any person entitled to the

---

[4] *Cook* v. *Beal* (1697) 1 Ld.Raym. 176 , 177, *per curiam.*
[5] *Fraser* v. *Berkeley* (1836) 7 C. & P. 621, 626, *per* Lord Abinger C.B.
[6] *Lane* v. *Holloway* [1968] 1 Q.B. 379, 392.
[7] *Turner* v. *M.-G.-M. Pictures Ltd.* [1950] 1 All E.R. 449, 471, *per* Lord Oaksey.
[8] Y.B. 2 Hen. IV, fo. 8, pl. 40.
[9] *Cottreau* v. *Rodgerson* (1965) 53 D.L.R. (2d) 549, 554.
[10] *Lane* v. *Holloway* [1968] 1 Q.B. 379, which was criticised in *Love* v. *Egan* (1970) 65 Q.J.P.R. 102, 104.
[11] In 178 H.L.Deb., cols. 421-432 (July 29, 1952), there is a statement by Lord Simonds on the position of a householder in relation to a person who has a statutory right of entry but does not produce a search warrant.
[12] For the legality of such devices as barbed wire and broken glass, see below, § 98.
[13] *Harrison* v. *Rutland (Duke of)* [1893] 1 Q.B. 142 (trespasser on grouse-moor held down by keepers until the drive was over).
[14] *Green* v. *Goddard* (1702) 2 Salk. 641.
[15] In *Ball* v. *Manthorpe* (1970) 15 D.L.R. (3d) 99, 100, a demonstration was judicially defined as "a noisy mob scene of the sort which until recently occurred only in countries inhabited by excitable foreigners who live under bizarre constitutions."
[16] *Dean* v. *Hogg* (1834) 10 Bing. 345; *Holmes* v. *Bagge* (1853) 1 E. & B. 782. As against a mere wrongdoer, however, actual possession without title is doubtless sufficient, just as in an action of trespass: *Brett* v. *Mullarkey* (1873) Ir.Rep. 7 C.L. 120.
[17] Below, § 226.
[18] Below, § 185.

possession of a chattel may also defend his possession by the use of reasonable force.[19]

Previous request necessary

A trespasser cannot be forcibly repelled or ejected until he has been requested to leave the premises and a reasonable opportunity of doing so peaceably has been afforded to him.[20] But as against him who enters or seeks to enter by force, "I need not request him to be gone, but may lay hands on him immediately, for it is but returning violence with violence. So if one comes forcibly and takes away my goods, I may oppose him without any more ado, for there is no time to make a request."[21] As to the amount of force that may be used the general rule is that it must not exceed that which is indicated in the old forms of pleading by the phrase *molliter manus imposuit*. That is to say, it must amount to nothing more than forcible removal and must not include beating, wounding, or other physical injury. Thus in *Collins* v. *Renison*[22] the plaintiff sued for the assault of throwing him off a ladder. It was held a bad plea that the plaintiff was trespassing and refused after request to leave the premises, and that the defendant thereupon "gently shook the ladder, which was a low ladder, and gently overturned it, and gently threw the plaintiff from it upon the ground, thereby doing as little damage as possible to the plaintiff." Sir Dudley Ryder C.J. held that such force was not justifiable in defence of the possession of land. In any event, as he very sensibly observed, "The overturning of the ladder could not answer the purpose of removing the plaintiff out of the garden; since it only left him upon the ground at the bottom of the ladder, instead of being upon it." Nor may an occupier do indirectly what he is prohibited from doing directly: he cannot eject the trespasser if his removal from the premises would expose him to serious risk of physical injury.[23]

There are two exceptions to this rule:

(1) If the trespasser in the course of eviction makes or threatens to make an assault upon the person evicting him, the case becomes one of the defence of the person, and thereafter any force may be used which is reasonable within the rule as to self-defence already considered, even though it involves beating or physical harm.

(2) If the trespasser enters or seeks to enter by means of a forcible offence the case falls within the rule that any force is justifiable which is necessary to prevent the commission of such an offence.[24]

---

[19] For forcible recaption of chattels, see below, § 227.

[20] See above, § 23.

[21] *Green* v. *Goddard* (1702) 2 Salk. 641, *per curiam*.

[22] (1754) Sayer 138.

[23] *Depue* v. *Flateau* (1907) 100 Minn. 299 (sick trespasser turned out into snow).

[24] The criminal law on the matter is not as clear as might be wished. In Dicey, *Law of the Constitution* (8th ed.), p. 494 (the passage is not in the current edition), the following remarkable opinion of Willes J. is given as related by "an ear-witness." "The judge was asked: 'If I look into my drawing-room, and see a burglar packing up the clock, and he cannot see me, what ought I to do?' Willes replied, as nearly as may be: 'My advice to you, which I give as a man, as a lawyer, and as an English judge, is as follows: In the supposed circumstances this is what you have a right to do, and I am by no means sure that it is not your duty to do it. Take a double-barrelled gun, carefully load both barrels, and then, without attracting the burglar's attention, aim steadily at his heart and shoot him dead.' " It cannot be supposed that Sir James Shaw Willes meant this to be taken seriously: he may have been answering a fool according to his folly.

(5) Defendant acting in support of the law

Sometimes an assault or imprisonment may be justified on the ground that the defendant was acting in support of the law. But the courts are anxious to see that the liberty of the subject is not invaded except under due process of law and the onus of proving legal justification lies on the defendant.[25] The plea of public interest or act of state is not enough.[26] So one who relies upon a statutory power of entry for public health[27] or mental health[28] purposes must prove that all the statutory conditions precedent to entry have been complied with, or else an assault upon him may be justifiable. An arrest may be carried out under powers given either by the common law or statute.

(i) *Breach of the peace*

It is the right, and indeed the duty,[29] of every subject[30] to arrest without warrant any person for a breach of the peace continuing in his presence or if there is a well-founded apprehension of its renewal.[31] An arrest after the breach of the peace is over is in general unjustifiable: a warrant should be obtained. A breach of the peace takes place when either an assault is committed on an individual or public alarm and excitement is caused. Mere annoyance or insult is not enough[32]: thus at common law a householder could not give a man into custody for violently and persistently ringing his door-bell.[33] It is the particular duty of a magistrate or police officer to preserve the peace unbroken; hence if he has reasonable cause to believe that a breach of the peace is imminent he may be justified in committing an assault[34] or effecting an arrest.[35] But there is no power to arrest and detain a person merely because it is apprehended that he may be in danger at some time in the future.[36] "If that were so, the adventurous spirits that sought the North Pole, or the interior of Africa, or that conquered the Atlantic in flight, might have been locked up for their own good. Nor does the fact that the supposed danger arises from the designs of wicked men warrant interference with the wish of him who desires to brave it. If it were otherwise, every informer in Irish history could have been locked up for life."[37] At common law it was clear that if civil commotion of such a degree as to amount to the offences of unlawful assembly or riot should occur, there is a duty imposed upon all subjects of the Crown to use such force (amounting even to the taking of life) as may be proper and reasonable to

---

[25] *Christie* v. *Leachinsky* [1947] A.C. 573.
[26] See below, § 158.
[27] *Stroud* v. *Bradbury* [1952] 2 All E.R. 76.
[28] *Townley* v. *Rushworth* (1963) 62 L.G.R. 95.
[29] *R.* v. *Brown* (1841) C. & M. 314.
[30] There is no recent example of such a prosecution against a private person, but a constable was convicted in *R.* v. *Dytham* [1979] Q.B. 723.
[31] *Timothy* v. *Simpson* (1835) 1 Cr.M. & R. 757. On the whole subject see Williams, "Arrest for Breach of the Peace" [1954] Crim. L.R. 578.
[32] *Bryan* v. *Robinson* [1960] 1 W.L.R. 506 (smiling and beckoning by Soho hostesses).
[33] *Grant* v. *Moser* (1843) 5 M. & G. 123. This is now an offence under the Town Police Clauses Act 1847.
[34] *Humphreys* v. *Connor* (1864) 17 Ir.C.L.R. 1 (removal of Orange lily from Protestant lady); *Coyne* v. *Tweedy* [1898] 2 I.R. 167.
[35] *Duncan* v. *Jones* [1936] 1 K.B. 218. It has been said that even a private person may arrest in such circumstances: *R.* v. *Light* (1857) 27 L.J.M.C. 1, 3.
[36] *Connors* v. *Pearson* [1921] 2 I.R. 51.
[37] *Ibid.* 91, *per* O'Connor L.J.

restore order.[38] But these authorities must now be read in the light of the Criminal Law Act 1967, s. 3 (1), which provides that a person may use such force as is reasonable in the prevention of crime, or in effecting or assisting the arrest of offenders or suspected offenders, or of persons unlawfully at large.[39] By section 3 (2) the provisions of section 3 (1) shall replace the rules of the common law on the question of the use of justifiable force in such circumstances.

(ii) *Arrestable offences*

The law relating to arrest is complex and badly in need of reform. The need has been accentuated and not diminished by the Criminal Law Act 1967, ss. 1 and 2, which abolish the traditional distinction between felonies and misdemeanours and create a new category entitled "arrestable offence." This statutory distortion of the English language is defined to mean an offence for which the punishment is fixed by law or for which a statute authorises imprisonment for five years, and also attempts to commit such offences.

The statute does not provide a comprehensive code of arrest nor does it introduce any radical reforms. It provides only (s. 2 (2)) that any person may arrest without warrant any person who is, or whom he suspects with reasonable cause to be, in the act of committing an arrestable offence. It also provides (s. 2 (3)) that any person who has reasonable cause to believe that a particular person is guilty of an arrestable offence may arrest him without warrant if that arrestable offence has in fact been committed. It will be noted that this preserves the rule in *Walters* v. *W. H. Smith & Son Ltd.*[40]—one of the strangest of common law rules, and a dangerous trap for the public-spirited citizen. The rule draws a distinction between arrest by a private person and arrest by a constable or other peace officer. A private person justifying an arrest must prove that the offence has actually been committed, whether by the person arrested or someone else, and if in fact that offence has not been committed it is no defence that there was reasonable and probable cause for believing the person arrested to be guilty. On the other hand, it is enough for the constable to show that there was reasonable and probable cause for suspicion even though no offence had in fact been committed.[41] Further, reasonable suspicion is not the same as prima facie proof. Suspicion can take into account matters which could not be given in evidence at all—*e.g.* previous convictions.[42] There is an analogy with the power of a bailiff who enters the house of a stranger to execute civil process: if the goods or person sought be there, he is justified: if not, he is a trespasser.[43] It will be seen that the legality of the arrest is therefore made to

---

[38] *Lynch* v. *Fitzgerald* [1938] I.R. 382.
[39] This might include escapers from mental hospitals: *Townley* v. *Rushworth* (1963) 62 L.G.R. 95.
[40] [1914] 1 K.B. 595.
[41] *Walters* v. *W. H. Smith & Sons* [1914] 1 K.B. 595; *Christie* v. *Leachinsky* [1947] A.C. 573. As Lord du Parcq remarked in the latter case (at p. 602), this is one of the few privileges which the common law confers on the police constable, "who may be described as a private person paid to perform as a matter of duty acts which, if so minded, he might have done voluntarily"—Stephen, Hist.Cr.Law, i, 494. See the comment on this in Hart, *The British Police* (London, 1952), pp. 12–13.
[42] *Hussien* v. *Chong Fook Kam* [1970] A.C. 942, 948–949.
[43] *Southam* v. *Smout* [1964] 1 Q.B. 308.

depend not on the presence or absence of reasonable cause in the mind of the citizen at the moment when he effects the arrest, but on the outcome of the eventual prosecution—an event for which he is in no way responsible, and which he cannot control. A prosecution may break down for a variety of reasons, some creditable, some not, but on this may depend the liability of the honest arrestor to pay damages.

At the time of arrest. As the common law is always solicitous for the freedom of the individual, the subject who is arrested is entitled to know the reason for his arrest so that he may know at once whether he is bound to submit.[44] The constable is not entitled to keep the reason to himself or give a reason which is not the true one: if he does so he will in general be liable for false imprisonment.[45] These rules must be interpreted in a reasonable manner. Thus explanation is unnecessary "if the arrested man is caught red-handed and the crime is patent to high heaven."[46] Nor is it necessary for any precise or technical language to be used,[47] at least if the arrested person has acquiesced in the arrest.[48] It is enough if the substance of the matter is conveyed to the person arrested.[49] So if a person is told he is being arrested for handling stolen drugs he cannot complain if the charge ultimately brought is one of unauthorised possession of drugs.[50] The constable must do the best he can in the circumstances and if it is what a reasonable man would have done he will be protected: if he is arresting a deaf person he is not bound to use a speaking-trumpet,[51] and if he is arresting someone who cannot speak English he is not obliged to find an interpreter.[52] It is irrelevant that the offence is apparently trivial or the person arrested of doubtful character.[53]

After the arrest

There is no intermediate position between liberty and detention. The law does not recognise any such procedure as "holding for questioning."[54] An arrested person cannot be detained whilst investigations are carried out,[55] but must be brought with reasonable expedition before a court.[56] It is unfortunately uncertain whether a failure to comply with the latter condition renders unlawful an arrest which was originally lawful,[57] or whether it makes any difference that the arrested person is later acquitted as distinct

---

[44] But a statute may derogate from common law rights—see, *e.g.* the Northern Ireland (Emergency Provisions) Act 1978, s. 14 (2).
[45] *Christie* v. *Leachinsky* [1947] A.C. 573.
[46] [1947] A.C. 593, *per* Lord Simonds.
[47] Except, perhaps, for "breathalyser" offences: *Walker* v. *Lovell* [1975] 1 W.L.R. 1141.
[48] *D.P.P.* v. *Walsh* [1980] I.R. 123.
[49] *Gelberg* v. *Miller* [1961] 1 W.L.R. 153.
[50] *R.* v. *Kulyncz* [1971] 1 Q.B. 367.
[51] *Tims* v. *John Lewis & Co.* [1951] 2 K.B. 459, 467.
[52] *Wheatley* v. *Lodge* [1971] 1 W.L.R. 29.
[53] *Leachinsky* v. *Christie* [1946] K.B. 124, 150-152, *per* Uthwatt J., followed in *The People* v. *White* [1947] I.R. 247, *McElduff* v. *Att.-Gen.* [1972] N.I. 1, and *R.* v. *Purdy* [1975] Q.B. 288. These rules apply to arrest by a private person as well as by a constable: [1947] A.C. 573, 588.
[54] "You may sometimes read in novels and detective stories, perhaps written by people not familiar with police procedure, that persons are sometimes taken into custody for questioning. There is no such power in this country. A man cannot be detained unless he is arrested": *R.* v. *Roberts* (unreported), *Manchester Guardian*, March 25, 1953, *per* Devlin J. The same point is made in Devlin, *The Criminal Prosecution in England* (1960), p. 68.
[55] *Blundell* v. *Att.-Gen.* [1968] N.Z.L.R. 341.
[56] *Dunne* v. *Clinton* [1930] I.R. 366, 372; *R.* v. *Brown (Michael)* (1976) 64 Cr. App. R. 231.
[57] See the division of opinion in *D.P.P.* v. *Walsh* [1980] I.R. 123.

from being convicted.[58] The law requires that a person arrested whether at common law or under a warrant should be brought before a magistrate or possibly handed over to a police officer[59] not necessarily immediately or by the most direct route but within a reasonable time. Thus in *John Lewis & Co.* v. *Tims*[60] a regulation of the appellants' department store provided that only a managing director or general manager was authorised to institute a prosecution. The respondent, having been arrested by the appellants' servants on suspicion of larceny, was accordingly brought back to the office and detained there for a short time while the necessary authority was obtained. The House of Lords refused to accept the contention that the defendants were guilty of false imprisonment because the plaintiff had not been taken before a magistrate or to the police station forthwith. "There are advantages in refusing to give private detectives a free hand and leaving the determination of whether to prosecute or not to a superior official."[61] Moreover, a police officer has been held to be justified in taking the arrested person elsewhere (*e.g.* to his home or place of work) for the purpose of obtaining further evidence, whether incriminatory or exculpatory.[62] This is probably justifiable on the ground that what is reasonable for a police officer may not be reasonable for a private person.

(iii) *Statutory powers of arrest*

Except in the case of a breach of the peace there is no power at common law to arrest without warrant on suspicion of an offence other than an arrestable offence (formerly a misdemeanour).[63] But statutes have given very extensive powers of arrest in such circumstances.[64] What is the position if the constable honestly and on reasonable grounds believed that the person he has arrested has committed such an offence when in fact he has not? In *Barnard* v. *Gorman*[65] the House of Lords refused to lay down any general principle, stating that the matter depended on the construction of the particular statute, but probably an honest suspicion founded on reasonable grounds is a defence.[66] It should be noted that the police are not required to have a prima facie case against the arrested person: it is enough to show reasonable suspicion.[67] Such a degree of executive discretion is not really a danger to individual liberty, for the discretion is subject to judicial control.

(6) Parental and other authority

A parent is not guilty of an assault if he physically interferes with his child by way of reasonable restraint or chastisement, or for therapeutic reasons—*e.g.* to take a blood test.[68] If the child is sent away to school, the schoolmaster is entitled to administer reasonable chastisement to the child,[69]

---

[58] See *R.* v. *Brown (Michael)* (1976) 64 Cr. App. R. 231.
[59] Unless he has simply been released from custody: *Wiltshire* v. *Barrett* [1966] 1 Q.B. 312.
[60] [1952] A.C. 676.
[61] [1952] A.C. 676, 691, *per* Lord Porter.
[62] *Dallison* v. *Caffery* [1965] 1 Q.B. 349.
[63] *Wershof* v. *Metropolitan Police Commissioner* [1978] 3 All E.R. 540.
[64] Details in *Index to the Statutes in Force, s.v.* "Arrest."
[65] [1941] A.C. 378.
[66] *Walker* v. *Lovell* [1975] 1 W.L.R. 1141.
[67] *Hussien* v. *Chong Fook Kam* [1970] A.C. 942.
[68] *S.* v. *McC.* [1972] A.C. 24. The right is recognised by s. 1 (7) of the Children and Young Persons Act 1933.
[69] *Ryan* v. *Fildes* [1938] 3 All E.R. 517.

or to expel him for reasonable cause.[70] According to the older authorities, the schoolmaster's power arose from a delegation to him of the parental authority; but the modern view is that the schoolmaster has his own independent authority to act for the welfare of the child.[71] Hence an education authority which has removed a child from its parents' care for the purposes of instruction is entitled to punish it. The schoolmaster's authority is not confined to the four walls of the school: it has been held that a schoolmaster was justified in administering five strokes of a cane to a boy under 16 who had, contrary to the rules, been smoking in the street during term after having returned home.[72]

Similarly the master of a ship has statutory[73] and common law[74] powers of arrest to preserve good order and discipline on board. The commander of an aircraft has similar powers.[75] There is one decision, much criticised, that it is not an assault for prison officials to take reasonable steps to preserve the health of those in custody—*e.g.* by forcible feeding.[76]

(7) Inevitable accident[77]

Inevitable accident provides a good excuse for a prima facie trespass which is otherwise actionable. An inevitable accident has been defined as an event over which the defendant had no control, and the effects of which could not have been avoided by the exercise of the greatest care and skill.[78] This may be said to be the generally accepted view since *Stanley* v. *Powell*.[79] In that case the defendant whilst firing at a pheasant accidentally and without negligence shot the plaintiff, who was employed to carry cartridges for a shooting party, with a pellet which ricochetted from a tree at a considerable angle. *Stanley* v. *Powell* might have been decided on the ground that the plaintiff had voluntarily accepted the risk by joining the party,[80] but Denman J.[81] based his decision on the ground that even if the action was in

---

[70] *Fitzgerald* v. *Northcote* (1865) 4 F. & F. 656 (in which the successfull plaintiff was the son of Fitzgerald J. of the Irish Queen's Bench).
[71] *Ramsay* v. *Larsen* [1965] A.L.R. 121.
[72] *R.* v. *Newport (Salop) J.J.* [1929] 2 K.B. 416.
[73] Merchant Shipping Act 1970, s. 79.
[74] *Hook* v. *Cunard Steamship Co. Ltd.* [1953] 1 W.L.R. 682.
[75] Tokyo Convention Act 1967, s. 3.
[76] *Leigh* v. *Gladstone* (1909) 26 T.L.R. 139. See below, § § 185-187.
[77] See Fridman, "Trespass or Negligence" (1971) 9 Alberta L.Rev. 250; Trindade, "Some Curiosities of Negligent Trespass" (1971) 20 I.C.L.Q. 706; Bates, "Accident, Trespass and Burden of Proof." (1976) 11 Ir. Jur. (N.S.) 88.
[78] *The Albano* [1892] P. 419, 429.
[79] [1891] 1 Q.B. 86. For criticisms on this case, see Landon's vigorous onslaught in Pollock, *Torts*, pp. 128-134 (of *National Coal Board* v. *Evans* he says: "all one can do is to wring one's hands and to note this recent case as a striking illustration of the old maxim *communis error facit jus*. And the point is still an open one for the House of Lords"); Gold in 21 *Bell Yard*, 25-28; Beven, *Negligence*, Vol. i, 568-570.
[80] Winfield (1939) 55 L.Q.R. 451, makes the point that in such a case it would be unnecessary for the defendant to disprove negligence. But surely the plaintiff takes upon himself the risk of careful, not of careless, shooting. And, even if that is not so, the difference in no way invalidates the suggestion that the case might have been decided on that ground.
[81] Landon (Pollock, *Torts*, p. 133) went too far in describing Denman J. as "an undistinguished puisne judge" who had obtained his position on the bench "*per stirpes* and not *per capita.*" He was indeed one of the sons (for another, see § 158) of Lord Denman C.J. (and as the son of a peer was one of the few High Court judges permitted to decline the customary knighthood), but in his youth he "had been Senior Classic and a Fellow of Trinity, but had other and perhaps greater titles to fame: he had been Captain of the

trespass, not case, the injury being accidental the defendant could not be liable. In *National Coal Board* v. *Evans*[82] the Court on Appeal, holding inevitable accident to be a good defence in an action of trespass to chattels, approved the reasoning in *Stanley* v. *Powell*.

Intention or negligence must now be shown

In so far as *Stanley* v. *Powell* decided that inevitable accident was a good defence to an action of trespass it probably cannot now be questioned. But in recent years a series of decisions by puisne judges in England,[83] the West Indies,[84] British Columbia,[85] and New Zealand[86] have extended *Stanley* v. *Powell* so far as to hold that a plaintiff in an action of trespass for injuries to the person must always prove intention or negligence on the part of the the defendant. It is submitted that these decisions are open to review in an appellate court[87] on the ground that they confuse the distinction between trespass and case which has been part of the common law "from time whereof the memory of man runneth not to the contrary." In this context the distinction has, or until very recently had, six important consequences. First, it has always been the understanding of the profession[88] that in trespass the defendant has to prove affirmatively that he was not negligent; in case for injuries to the person the plaintiff had to prove affirmatively intent or negligence in the defendant.[89] Hence when the plaintiff was injured by force applied directly to him by the defendant, his case was made by this fact and the onus then lay on the defendant to prove that the trespass was utterly without his fault.[90] This distinction may have great practical importance when the defendant is a young child,[91] against whom it will be difficult to establish intent or negligence,[92] or one who, having denied fault in the pleadings, fails to appear at the trial.[93] "The trespass action, though somewhat anomalous, may thus help to smoke out evidence possessed by defendants."[94] Secondly, there is a difference in relation to the proper test for remoteness of damage: in trespass it is probably directness,

---

Trinity Boat Club, not the Sculls, and had 'polished off a college porter at his gate.' Thus he was emphatically an all-round man and a popular character:" Winstanley, *Early Victorian Cambridge* (1955), p. 419.

[82] [1951] 2 K.B. 861.

[83] *Fowler* v. *Lanning* [1959] 1 Q.B. 426. In effect, this converted the exception into the general rule. The exception was the rule as to proof of negligence in actions arising out of highway accidents, which had become established in the nineteenth century (see below, § 187).

[84] *Robley* v. *Placide* (1966) 11 W.I.R. 58.

[85] *Walmsley* v. *Humenick* [1954] 2 D.L.R. 232. But not Ontario: *Bell Canada Ltd.* v. *Cope (Sarnia) Ltd.* (1980) 11 C.C.L.T. 170, or Novia Scotia: *Larin* v. *Goshen* (1975) 56 D.L.R. (3d) 719.

[86] *Beals* v. *Hayward* [1960] N.Z.L.R. 131; Davis, Note, (1965) 28 M.L.R. 674.

[87] The High Court of Australia avoided ruling on the point in *Chinning* v. *Venn* (1975) 49 A.L.J.R. 378.

[88] See the vivid illustration in Sutton, *Personal Actions*, pp. 56-63.

[89] *Exchange Hotel Ltd.* v. *Murphy* [1947] S.A.S.R. 112, 117.

[90] Amongst the many cases which support this are: *Hall* v. *Fearnley* (1842) 3 Q.B. 919; *Sadler* v. *South Staffs. Steam Tramways Co.* (1889) 23 Q.B.D. 17; *Blacker* v. *Waters* (1928) 28 S.R.(N.S.W.) 406; *Cook* v. *Lewis* [1952] 1 D.L.R. 1, 15; *Southport Corporation* v. *Esso Petroleum, Ltd.* [1953] 3 W.L.R. 773, 781; *Joyce* v. *Bartlett* [1955] 1 D.L.R. 615; *O'Brien* v. *McNamee* [1953] I.R. 86; *McHale* v. *Watson* (1964) 111 C.L.R. 384; *Dahlberg* v. *Naydink* (1968) 67 D.L.R. (2d) 31.

[91] See below, § 162.

[92] *Tillander* v. *Gosselin* (1966) 60 D.L.R. (2d) 18, 25.

[93] *Tsouvalla* v. *Bini* [1966] S.A.S.R. 157.

[94] *Bell Canada* v. *Cope (Sarnia) Ltd.* (1980) 11 C.C.L.T. 170, 180.

in negligence it is foreseeability.[95] Thirdly, until recently,[96] there was a difference in relation to the running of time under the Limitation Act 1939. Fourthly, there may still be a difference as to the date of the accrual of the cause of action.[97] Fifthly, trespass is actionable per se; in case, actual damage must be shown.[98] Sixthly, it is uncertain whether contributory negligence is a defence[99] to an action for a negligent trespass.[1]

(8) Statutory authority

Apart from statutory powers of arrest, Parliament has authorised medical examinations or tests which would otherwise constitute a serious battery—*e.g.* breath tests under the Road Safety Act 1967, ss. 2 and 3, or blood tests under sections 20 to 23 of the Family Law Reform Act 1969.

---

[95] See below, § 202.
[96] *Long* v. *Hepworth* [1968] 1 W.L.R. 1299. See below, § 220.
[97] See below, § 221.
[98] See above, § 2.
[99] See below, § 197.
[1] *Hollebone* v. *Barnard* [1954] 2 D.L.R. 278.

CHAPTER 8

DEFAMATION[1]

§ 47. DEFAMATION DEFINED

The wrong of defamation consists in the publication of a false and defamatory statement concerning another person without lawful justification. That person must be in being. So if an entity has no legal personality it cannot sue for defamation.[2] Hence not only does an action of defamation not survive for or against the estate of a deceased person,[3] but a statement about a deceased or unborn person is not actionable at the suit of his relatives, however great their pain and distress, unless the statement is in some way defamatory of them.[4]

Libel and slander[5]

A defamatory statement is not necessarily made in words, either written or spoken. A man may defame another by his acts no less than by his words. To exhibit an insulting picture[6] or effigy[7] holding up the plaintiff to ridicule or contempt is an actionable libel.

The wrong of defamation is of two kinds—namely, libel and slander.[8] In libel the defamatory statement is made in some permanent and visible form, such as writing, printing, pictures, or effigies.[9] In slander it is made in spoken words or in some other transitory form, whether visible or audible, such as gestures or inarticulate but significant sounds. It is not always easy to determine whether in a particular case the proper cause of action is libel or slander. Is the true difference between the two that slander is addressed to the ear, libel to the eye?[10] Or is it that libel is defamation crystallised into some permanent form, while slander is conveyed by some transient method of expression? The Court of Appeal in *Youssoupoff* v. *Metro-Goldwyn-Mayer Pictures*[11] did not have much difficulty in holding that defamation in a "talking" film was libel. But there is no authority as to whether

---

[1] See Lloyd, "Reform of the Law of Defamation" (1976) 29 C.L.P. 183. The report of the Committee on the Law of Defamation (Cmd. 7536 (1948)), of whom Lord Porter was chairman, is invaluable, as is that presided over by Faulks J. (Cmnd. 5909, 1975).The Report of the Porter Committee was followed by the Defamation Act 1952, but "well-nigh total apathy has reigned" since the Faulks Committe reported: see *Gleaves* v. *Deakin* [1979] 2 W.L.R. 665, 667.

[2] *EETPU* v. *Times Newspapers Ltd.* [1980] Q.B. 585.

[3] See below, § 166.

[4] Report of the Faulks Committee, para. 421. For the interesting steps taken by the relatives of Mr. Gladstone to defend his honour against the disgraceful aspersions of Captain Wright, see Dean, *Hatred, Ridicule or Contempt* (London, 1953); Walton, "Libel upon the Dead and the Bath Club Case" (1927) 9 J.C.L. 1.

[5] See Kaye, "Libel and Slander—Two Torts or One" (1975) 91 L.Q.R. 524.

[6] *Du Bost* v. *Beresford* (1810) 2 Camp. 511; *Garbett* v. *Hazell, Watson and Viney Ltd.* [1943] 2 All E.R. 359 (juxtaposition of pictures with captions). One may "Convey a libel in a frown, And wink a reputation down": Swift, *Journal of a Modern Lady.*

[7] *Monson* v. *Tussauds Ltd.* [1894] 1 Q.B. 671.

[8] Libel and slander give rise to distinct causes of action even if the nature of the defamation is the same in both: libel is one genus, slander a different genus: *Weber* v. *Birkett* [1925] 2 K.B. 152.

[9] *Monson* v. *Tussauds Ltd.* [1894] 1 Q.B. 671, 692.

[10] So held in *Mitchell* v. *Australian Broadcasting Commission* (1958) 60 W.A.L.R. 38.

[11] (1934) 50 T.L.R. 581.

defamatory matter recorded on a gramophone disc (unaccompanied by any pictorial or other matter) is libel or slander. It is addressed to the ear, not to the eye, but it is in permanent, not in transient form. It is submitted that the correct answer is that to utter defamatory words with the intention that they shall be recorded is slander only, but that when the record has been made, if it is published, the manufacturer is responsible for libel. In such a case the person whose voice is recorded might be responsible on the ordinary principles of vicarious liability, and presumably those who distribute or play the record to third persons are in the same position as the disseminators of a written libel. The Defamation Act 1952, apparently[12] settles a disputed point by providing[13] that the broadcasting of words[14] by means of wireless telegraphy[15] shall be treated as publication in permanent form. The Theatres Act 1968, s. 4, makes a similar provision for words published during the public performance of a play.

Although libel and slander are for the most part governed by the same principles, there are two important differences:

(1) Libel is not merely an actionable tort, but also a criminal offence; whereas slander is a civil injury only. It was once thought that the likelihood of a breach of the peace was a vital factor in criminal libel, but apparently this is now only one relevant factor.[16]

(2) Libel is in all cases actionable *per se*; but slander is, save in special cases, actionable only on proof of actual damage. This distinction has been severely criticised. It is indeed odd that the maker of a deliberately false and malicious public speech may not be liable in damages, but that a journalist who innocently reports it may be.[17] It was recognised by the Porter Committee to be "arbitrary and illogical,"[18] but a majority of the Committee[19] was not willing to recommend, or Parliament to enact, that libel and slander should be assimilated.

The different rules applicable to the wrongs of libel and slander are due to the different historical origin of the two actions.[20] The rules relating to slander derive from the common law action on the case, the rules relating to libel from criminal proceedings in the Star Chamber.

§ 48. NATURE OF A DEFAMATORY STATEMENT

A defamatory statement is one which has a tendency to injure the reputation of the person to whom it refers; which tends, that is to say, to lower him in the estimation of right-thinking members of society generally[21] and in particular to cause him to be regarded with feelings of hatred, contempt,

---

[12] *Church of Scientology* v. *Anderson* [1980] W.A.R. 71.
[13] s. 1.
[14] Defined by s. 16 (1) to include pictures, visual images, gestures and other methods of signifying meaning.
[15] As defined by s. 16 (3), means publication for general reception by means of wireless telegraphy within the meaning of the Wireless Telegraphy Act 1949.
[16] *Gleaves* v. *Deakin* [1979] 2 W.L.R. 665.
[17] See the Faulks Report, § 81.
[18] Cmd. 7536 (1948), para. 38.
[19] The Faulks Committee (§ 91) recommends the assimilation of libel and slander.
[20] See O'Sullivan, "Evolution of the Law of Libel" [1950] C.L.P. 84.
[21] *Sim* v. *Stretch* (1936) 52 T.L.R. 669, 671, *per* Lord Atkin.

ridicule, fear, dislike, or disesteem.[22] The statement is judged by the standard of an ordinary, right-thinking member of society. Hence the test is an objective one, and it is no defence to say that the statement was not intended to be defamatory, or uttered by way of a joke.[23] A tendency to injure or lower the reputation of the plaintiff suffices, for "If words are used which impute discreditable conduct to my friend, he has been defamed to me, although I do not believe the imputation, and may even know that it is untrue."[24] Hence it is settled[25] that a statement may be defamatory although no one to whom it is published believes it to be true.[26]

Injurious falsehood[27]

A defamatory statement must be distinguished from one which is merely injurious. Both are falsehoods told by one man to the prejudice of another, and both are on certain conditions actionable; but they are to a large extent governed by different rules. An injurious statement is a falsehood told about another which in no way affects his reputation, but nevertheless in some other manner causes loss to him. Thus it is not defamatory to state that a certain tradesman has ceased to carry on business; yet if this statement is wilfully false, an action will lie for it. Similarly, to say falsely of a shopkeeper that his goods are of a quality inferior to those of another trader is not the wrong of defamation, but that of injurious falsehood; but to say of him that he fraudulently sells inferior goods as of superior quality is an attack, not merely upon his business, but upon his reputation, and is therefore defamatory. There are many cases on the question whether defamation of goods involves defamation of the trader who sells those goods, but no clear test has yet emerged.[28]

Abuse

Mere insult or vulgar abuse does not amount to defamation,[29] whether it be spoken or written. Defamation is a false statement or suggestion of fact to the prejudice of a man's reputation; insult consists in words or conduct offensive to a man's dignity. Insult in itself seems to be no cause of action by the law of England, though particular forms of insult may be actionable if accompanied by other facts which confer a right of action. Assault, false imprisonment, and certain kinds of wilful and wanton trespasses to property amount to insults, as being attacks upon the dignity of the plaintiff as well as upon his person or property; and aggravated damages may accordingly be obtained for them.[30] Insulting threats not amounting to assault are apparently not actionable at all,[31] unless they fall under the rubric of intentional infliction of emotional distress.[32] But persons given to using abusive language may be required to enter into sureties to be of good behaviour

---

[22] *Capital and Counties Bank* v. *Henty* (1882) 7 App. Cas. 741.
[23] *Capital and Counties Bank* v. *Henty* (1882) 7 App. Cas. 741, 772.
[24] *Hough* v. *London Express* [1940] 2 K.B. 507, 515, *per* Goddard L.J.
[25] *Morgan* v. *Odhams Press Ltd.* [1971] 1 W.L.R. 1239.
[26] As in *Theaker* v. *Richardson* [1962] 1 W.L.R. 151.
[27] See Chap. 18 for a fuller discussion of this tort (sometimes called malicious falsehood).
[28] *Drummond-Jackson* v. *British Medical Association* [1970] 1 W.L.R. 688.
[29] *Parkins* v. *Scott* (1862) 1 H. & C. 153 ("You have been a whore from your cradle").
[30] Below, § 199.
[31] *Lane* v. *Holloway* [1968] 1 Q.B. 379 ("Shut up, you monkey-faced tart").
[32] Below, § 77.

under the Justices of the Peace Act 1361, or prosecuted under the Public Order Act 1936,[33] or the Race Relations Act 1976.

Hatred, ridicule, and contempt

The test of the defamatory nature of a statement is its tendency to excite against the plaintiff the adverse opinions or feelings of other persons. The typical form of defamation is an attack upon the moral character of the plaintiff, attributing to him any form of disgraceful conduct, such as crime, dishonesty, untruthfulness, ingratitude, or cruelty. But a statement may be defamatory if it tends to bring the plaintiff into ridicule or contempt even though there is no suggestion of any form of misconduct.[34] An action will lie, therefore, for the publication of a humorous story which exhibits the plaintiff in a ridiculous light, or for a caricature of his personal appearance or manners.[35] In some circumstances it might even be defamatory to say of a man that his acts were legally justified. Rightminded men sometimes think the less of one who has successfully pleaded a technical defence—*e.g.* the Gaming Acts or the Statute of Limitations. Successful litigants have in the past been booed on leaving the court.[36] Again a statement is defamatory if it amounts to a reflection upon the fitness or capacity of the plaintiff in his profession or trade, or in any other undertaking assumed by him.[37] So a novelist recovered damages against the publishers of a magazine for publishing under his name a story of which he was not the writer, on the ground that anyone reading the story would think him a mere commonplace scribbler.[38] So also a statement is defamatory if it attributes insanity to the plaintiff, though insanity is a misfortune, not a fault,[39] or if it imputes insolvency to a trader, even though there is no suggestion of discreditable conduct or incapacity,[40] or if it contains an allegation that a woman has been raped.[41] But a statement is not defamatory if it merely alleges a breach of conventional etiquette[42]—presumably because that does not lower the plaintiff in the estimation of right-minded people—as distinct from an allegation that a business man was "not conversant with ordinary business ethics."[43] Still, what is not defamatory today may be defamatory tomorrow, or vice-versa, for the political and social ideas of the reasonable man alter with the times.[44] Thus the appellations German,[45] Czech,[46] "Jewish inter-

---

[33] *Ward* v. *Holman* [1964] 2 Q.B. 580.
[34] *Cook* v. *Ward* (1830) 6 Bing. 409.
[35] *Dunlop Rubber Co.* v. *Dunlop* [1921] 1 A.C. 367. (Mr. Dunlop, the inventor of the pneumatic tyre and "a plain and ordinary citizen of Dublin," depicted in advertisements as a foppish old gentleman.)
[36] *Clarke* v. *Associated Newspapers Ltd.*, 1955 C.A. 158 (unrep.).
[37] *Capital and Counties Bank* v. *Henty* (1882) 7 App. Cas. 741.
[38] *Ridge* v. *The English Illustrated Magazine* (1913) 29 T.L.R. 592. *Cf. Archbold* v. *Sweet* (1832) 5 C. & P. 219, where the defendants published a third edition of the plaintiff's work on criminal law (with "many errors and mistakes") without stating that it had not been edited by the plaintiff.
[39] *Morgan* v. *Lingen* (1863) 8 L.T. (N.S.) 800.
[40] *Read* v. *Hudson* (1700) 1 Lord Raym. 610.
[41] *Youssoupoff* v. *Metro-Goldwyn-Mayer Pictures* (1934) 50 T.L.R. 581.
[42] *Sim* v. *Stretch* (1936) 52 T.L.R. 669, 672.
[43] *Angel* v. *Bushell & Co. Ltd.* [1968] 1 Q.B. 813.
[44] But even today an allegation of homosexuality is probably defamatory: *R.* v. *Bishop* [1975] Q.B. 274.
[45] *Slazengers Ltd.* v. *C. Gibbs & Co.* (1916) 33 T.L.R. 35.
[46] *Linklater* v. *Daily Telegraph Ltd., The Times,* November 11, 1964.

national financier,"[47] "Stonehouse"[48] and Communist[49] have all at different times been held capable of a defamatory meaning.

A statement is not defamatory merely because it excites hatred, contempt, ridicule, or other adverse feelings in some particular class of the community whose standard of opinion is such that the law cannot approve of it. Words are only defamatory if they impute conduct to the plaintiff which would tend to lower him in the eyes of a considerable and respectable class of the community though not in the eyes of the community as a whole.[50] Thus in *Byrne* v. *Deane*[51] the plaintiff complained of a typewritten piece of doggerel on the notice-board of a golf club which suggested that he had been guilty of disloyalty to his fellow-members by reporting to the police that there were some "diddler" (gambling) machines kept on the premises.[52] Although it is clear that any such charge would lower the plaintiff in the estimation of most of his fellow-members it was held that it cannot be defamatory to say of a man that he has put in motion the proper machinery for suppressing crime, whether in his own country or another.[53] So no ordinary person would, it is said, think the less of a student who is alleged to do espionage work in his or her university on behalf of the police.[54]

§ 49. PROOF OF REFERENCE TO THE PLAINTIFF[55]

It is essential in every action for defamation that the defamatory statement should be shown to refer to the plaintiff. A court has power in interlocutory proceedings[56] to dismiss the action on the ground that no reasonable person could conclude that the plaintiff should be identified with the person named in the matter complained of as defamatory.[57] At the trial the judge may also withdraw the case from the jury.[58] It is never necessary, however, that the reference to the plaintiff should be express. It may be latent; and it is sufficient in such a case that it should have been understood even by one person, although it remained hidden from all others. Thus in *Le Fanu* v. *Malcolmson*[59] the defendants published in a newspaper a statement that in some of the Irish factories cruelties were practised upon the workpeople, and they were held liable on a finding by the jury that the statement was understood to refer specially to the plaintiff's factory at Portlaw in County Waterford.

But the defendant must himself have published the statement complained of by the plaintiff.[60] A defendant is not responsible for statements made by

---

[47] *Camrose* v. *Action Press Ltd.* (1937) *The Times*, October 14 (damages: £12,500, Hilbery J. emphatically refusing a stay of execution). The report in the *Daily Telegraph* makes it quite clear that it was not alleged that the appellation "Jew" alone was defamatory. The innuendo was that the plaintiff was unscrupulous and unpatriotic.

[48] *Hinderer* v. *Cole*, *The Daily Telegraph*, March 11, 1977 (the plaintiff was an accountant).

[49] *Braddock* v. *Bevins* [1948] 1 K.B. 580; *Lewis* v. *Smith* (1959) *The Times*, July 10; *Brannigan* v. *Seafarers' International Union of Canada* (1963) 42 D.L.R. (2d) 249.

[50] *Quigley* v. *Creation Press Ltd.* [1971] I.R. 269, 272.

[51] [1937] 1 K.B. 818. See also *Fraser* v. *Kemsley Newspapers Ltd.* (1959) *The Times*, June 2.

[52] The words were: "But he who gave the game away May he byrnn in hell and rue the day."

[53] *Berry* v. *Irish Times Ltd.* [1973] I.R. 368.

[54] *Prinsloo* v. *S.A. Associated Newspapers Ltd.* 1959 (2) S.A. 693.

[55] See Symmons, "Proof of Reference to the Plaintiff" (1974) Anglo-Am. L. Rev. 98.

[56] See R.S.C., Ord. 18, r. 19.

[57] *Morgan* v. *Odhams Press Ltd.* [1971] 1 W.L.R. 1239.

[58] See below, § 50.

[59] (1848) 1 H.L.C. 637. For the innuendo, see § 51.

[60] For publication, see § 53.

third parties unless he has expressly or impliedly adopted them as his own.[61] So a speaker at a meeting is not responsible merely because he knows that reporters are present.[62] Nor is a defendant responsible to the plaintiff for statements made about third parties, unless those statements are also in themselves defamatory of the plaintiff.[63]

Innocence no defence

At common law[64] it was not necessary that the defendant should have intended the defamatory statement to refer to the plaintiff. The question was not whether the defendant intended any such reference, but whether any person[65] to whom the statement was published might reasonably think that the plaintiff was the person referred to. Nor was it any defence that the defendant had no reason to suppose that any such reference would be attributed to his words, or even did not know that any such person as the plaintiff existed. This application or extension of the doctrine that a man publishes defamatory statements at his peril was established by the House of Lords in *Hulton & Co, v. Jones.*[66] A newspaper published an article descriptive of life in Dieppe, in which one Artemus Jones, described as a churchwarden at Peckham, was accused of living with a mistress in France. The writer of the article was ignorant of the existence of any person of the name of Artemus Jones and invented the name as that of the fictitious character in his narrative. Unfortunately, however, the name so chosen was that of a real person, a barrister and journalist, and those who knew him supposed the newspaper article to refer to him. It was held by a majority of the Court of Appeal that the newspaper was responsible for a libel and the decision was unanimously affirmed (in an unreserved judgment[67]) by the House of Lords.[68]

It has also been held by the House of Lords[69] that there is no rule that before the publisher of a defamatory statement which identifies no definite person can be held liable, there must be found in the statement some key or pointer or peg which refers to the plaintiff. Extrinsic evidence[70] is admissible

---

[61] *Astaire* v. *Campling* [1966] 1 W.L.R. 34.
[62] Duncan and Neill, *Defamation*, § 8.19.
[63] *Wheeler* v. *Somerfield* [1966] 2 Q.B. 94.
[64] The Defamation Act 1952, s. 4 may now provide a defence. See § 52, below.
[65] It need not be a reasonable person: a hasty but sensible reader is the norm since *Morgan* v. *Odhams Press Ltd.* [1971] 1 W.L.R. 1239.
[66] [1910] A.C. 20.
[67] Lord Uthwatt told the present editor that after *Hulton* v. *Jones* the House of Lords had made it a rule of practice never to deliver an unreserved judgment—though there is at least one reported exception to this: see below, § 98.
[68] There is some evidence that the decision may have been based on the recklessness or even spite of the defendants. Stallybrass always said that this was the opinion of Lord Hewart, who was counsel for the plaintiff at all three stages of the action. The plaintiff had been a contributor to the defendants' paper for 12 years and his name was well known in their office, although not to the actual writer of the article. The managing director admitted in cross-examination that he had read the article in proof and thought at first reading that it referred to the plaintiff. See 10th ed., p. 377, n. (x) and letters to *The Spectator* of November 5 and 12, 1948, from Lady Artemus-Jones and C.K. Allen. The point is still important, for if the actual facts in *Hulton* v. *Jones* recurred today, the defendants might be held to have failed to establish reasonable care under s. 4 of the Defamation Act 1952: see below, § 52.
[69] *Morgan* v. *Odhams Press Ltd.* [1971] 1 W.L.R. 1239.
[70] See below, § 51.

to show that some people, perhaps with knowledge of special facts, thought the statement referred to the plaintiff.

Even if the defamatory words are true of some other person it was not impossible for them to be at the same time defamatory of the plaintiff, for they might be understood by reasonable persons to refer to him.[71] Thus in *Newstead* v. *London Express Newspaper Ltd.*[72] the defendants published an account of a trial for bigamy of "Harold Newstead, thirty-year-old Camberwell man." It was a true account of the trial of one Harold Newstead, a Camberwell barman, but not of Harold Newstead, a Camberwell hairdresser, of about the same age. The Court of Appeal held that the jury would have been justified in finding that reasonable persons would have understood the words complained of to refer to the latter. Where the words complained of are *ex facie* defamatory the hardship is not so serious as might appear. Writers who publish such statements may not unreasonably be expected to identify the person described so closely that the words cannot reasonably be capable of referring to someone else.[73]

Defamation of a class of persons

In every case where the plaintiff is not named the test whether the words used refer to him is the question whether the words are such as would reasonably lead persons acquainted with the plaintiff to believe that he was the person referred to. If the words can be regarded as capable of referring to the plaintiff, the jury still have to decide the question of fact—Do they lead reasonable people, who know him, to the conclusion that they do refer to him?[74] "The reason why a libel published of a large or indeterminate number of persons described by some general name generally fails to be actionable is the difficulty of establishing that the plaintiff was, in fact, included in the defamatory statement, for the habit of making unfounded generalisations is ingrained in ill-educated or vulgar minds, or the words are occasionally intended to be facetious exaggeration."[75] Thus no action would lie at the suit of anyone for saying that all mankind is vicious and depraved, or even for alleging that all clergymen are hypocrites or all lawyers dishonest.[76] For charges so general in their nature are merely vulgar generalisations.

But if the class is so small or so completely ascertainable that what is said of the class is necessarily said of every member of it, then a member of the class can sue.[77] Again, although the words purport to refer to a class, if in fact in the particular circumstances of the case they point to one or more

---

[71] Mr. Robert Graves had taken the point in 1936: see his admirable novel, *Antigua, Penny Puce*, p. 252.
[72] [1940] 1 K.B. 377. A similar case is *Lee* v. *Wilson* (1934) 51 C.L.R. 276.
[73] See the caustic judgment of MacKinnon L.J. [1940] 1 K.B. 377, 391–393. It is significant that the Faulks Committee recommend no change (see § 123).
[74] *Knupffer* v. *London Express Newspaper* [1944] A.C. 116, 121.
[75] *Knupffer* v. *London Express Newspaper* [1944] A.C. 116, 122, per Lord Atkin.
[76] *E.E.J.P.U.* v. *Times Newspapers Ltd.* [1980] Q.B. 585, 595–596. No doubt the criminal law of seditious libel might be invoked in serious cases. Neither the Porter Committee nor (after much discussion) Parliament could find a suitable remedy for "group defamation." For a curious unreported case in which a newspaper thought it prudent to settle an action brought by the 134 valuers employed by the L.C.C. see 682 H.C.Deb. 5, s., cols. 456–463, and 776 H.C.Deb., col. 1764.
[77] *Browne* v. *D.C. Thomson & Co.*, 1912 S.C. 359.

individual persons, those persons will have an action.[78] In deciding the question, the size of the class, the generality of the charge and the extravagance of the accusation may all be elements to be taken into consideration.[79] Similarly, an imputation may be defamatory and actionable at the suit of the plaintiff if it is made against some unspecified members of a class to which he belongs even though it is impossible to show that the defendant meant or was understood to mean the plaintiff individually. Thus if the defendant says in writing that his horse has been stolen either by A or B, he knows not which, then both A and B will have an action against him, for both are thereby brought under suspicion and defamed.[80] But here also the class must not be so large that the charge ceases to affect the reputation of any individual member of it.

§ 50. PROOF OF DEFAMATORY MEANING

Although the proper interpretation of a statement alleged to be defamatory may give rise to difficult questions of construction, there is one point which is perfectly clear and unquestioned: a statement is none the less defamatory because the defendant did not intend to bring the plaintiff into hatred, ridicule or contempt. The meaning to be attached to it is not necessarily the meaning with which the defendant published it but that which is, or may be presumed to be, reasonably given to it by the person to whom it is published. A defamatory purpose will not render the defendant liable if the statement has for others no libellous significance[81]; conversely, an innocent intention will be no defence for a person who makes a statement which has a defamatory meaning for those to whom he makes it,[82] though the fact that his intention was innocent may be given in evidence in mitigation of damages.[83] Something may depend on the nature of the publication. The ordinary sensible man reading an article in a popular newspaper is not expected to analyse it like a Fellow of All Souls. The general impression on such a reader is what counts.[84]

Functions of judge and jury

The interpretation of a defamatory statement is a question of fact for a jury or for a judge if sitting without a jury.[85] Since the Libel Act 1792 (usually called Fox's Act), "libel or no libel" has always been essentially a question for the jury.[86] It is true that the Act of 1792 is in terms limited to criminal proceedings, but it has always been regarded as merely declaratory of the common law.[87] The right of the jury in this matter is subject, however,

---

[78] *Le Fanu* v. *Malcolmson* (1848) 1 H.L.C. 637.
[79] *Knupffer's Case* [1944] A.C. 116, 124.
[80] *Harrison* v. *Thornborough* (1713) 10 Mod. 196. A verbal statement to this effect, however, would presumably fall within the rule that in the case of the imputation of a criminal offence words of mere *suspicion* are not actionable without proof of special damage: below, § 70.
[81] *Sadgrove* v. *Hole* [1901] 2 K.B. 1.
[82] *Hulton & Co. Ltd.* v. *Jones* [1910] A.C. 20, 23. For the innuendo, see below, § 51.
[83] *Morgan* v. *Odhams Press Ltd.* [1971] 1 W.L.R. 1239, 1246, 1254, 1264.
[84] See below, § 212.
[85] *Slim* v. *Daily Telegraph Ltd.* [1968] 2 Q.B. 157.
[86] *Broome* v. *Agar* (1928) 138 L.T. 698.
[87] *Truth (N.Z.) Ltd.* v. *Holloway* [1960] N.Z.L.R. 69, 92.

to one limitation. The judge must first be satisfied that there is sufficient evidence to go to the jury—that is to say, he must be satisfied that the statement is reasonably capable of the meaning which the plaintiff alleges and complains of, and if he considers that it is not so capable, the case must be withdrawn from the jury altogether.[88] In a clear and obvious case the plaintiff's statement of claim may also be struck out under R.S.C., Ord. 18, r. 19.[89] If more than one defamatory meaning is alleged, then the judge must rule whether the words are capable of bearing each, and if so, which, of those meanings.[90] It is not certain whether the plaintiff is confined to the defamatory meanings or inferences alleged in his statement of claim.[91]

In *Capital and Counties Bank* v. *Henty*[92] the defendants, having had a dispute with one of the branch managers of the plaintiff bank, sent a circular notice to their own customers[93] in these words: "Henty and Sons hereby give notice that they will not receive in payment cheques drawn on any of the branches of the Capital and Counties Bank." An action for libel was thereupon brought by the bank, alleging that the notice was defamatory, inasmuch as it amounted to an imputation of insolvency. It was held, however, by the House of Lords that the statement was not reasonably capable of such a meaning, and that there was no case fit to be left to a jury, although the notice resulted in a run of a quarter of a million pounds on the bank immediately it was issued, and the bank's customers were presumably ordinary men who believed the statement had the meaning alleged.[94] *Henty's* case has often been cited by defendants seeking to contend that if one non-defamatory meaning can be found the plaintiff cannot succeed, but it does not mean that.[95] It is more difficult to say positively what it does mean, for there are a large number of different judicial interpretations, particularly in cases involving innuendoes.[96] The most simple test[97] is that in deciding whether the words are capable of a defamatory meaning the court will reject those meanings which can emerge only as the product of some strained or forced or utterly unreasonable interpretation.

On the other hand, the words may be so plainly and necessarily defamatory that the judges should instruct the jury that they are calculated to bring the plaintiff into hatred or contempt, and should forthwith proceed

---

[88] *Lewis* v. *Daily Telegraph Ltd.* [1964] A.C. 234.
[89] *Drummond-Jackson* v. *British Medical Association* [1970] 1 W.L.R. 688.
[90] *Lewis* v. *Daily Telegraph Ltd.* [1964] A.C. 234, 286.
[91] *Slim* v. *Daily Telegraph Ltd.* [1968] 2 Q.B. 157. The conflicting dicta are assessed in the Faulks Report, § 112.
[92] (1882) 7 App.Cas. 741.
[93] This was an important point: see *Tolley* v. *Fry* [1931] A.C. 333, 342; *Lewis* v. *Daily Telegraph Ltd.* [1964] A.C. 234, 246.
[94] There are several statements to the effect that the law and the facts got pretty far apart from each other in *Henty's* case: *Youssoupoff* v. *M.-G.-M. Pictures Ltd.* (1934) 50 T.L.R. 581, 584; *Slim* v. *Daily Telegraph Ltd.* [1968] 2 Q.B. 157, 187. But in *Sim* v. *Stretch* [1936] 2 All E.R. 1237 the H.L. held the words in question incapable of a defamatory meaning, though three judges below had held they were so capable, and a jury that they were in fact defamatory.
[95] *Lewis* v. *Daily Telegraph Ltd.* [1964] A.C. 234, 246. It was held that the words "R.D." (or their equivalent) on the cheque of a non-trader were incapable of a defamatory meaning: *Plunkett* v. *Barclays Bank Ltd.* [1936] 2 K.B. 107, but now it is a question for the jury in each case: *Jayson* v. *Midland Bank Ltd.* [1968] 1 Lloyd's Rep. 409. The Irish Supreme Court was equally divided on the question in *Pyke* v. *Hibernian Bank Ltd.* [1950] I.R. 195; and "Present Again" has been held capable of a defamatory meaning: *Baker* v. *Australia and N.Z. Bank Ltd.* [1958] N.Z.L.R. 907.
[96] For these, see below, § 51.
[97] *Jones* v. *Skelton* [1963] 1 W.L.R. 1362, 1370.

to direct their attention to the question of damages. If a jury find a plain and obvious defamation, incapable of any innocent explanation, to be non-libellous, their verdict may be set aside.[98] But in England[99] and in Ireland[1] the circumstances must be very exceptional to justify such a course. There appear to be only two reported cases in which a verdict of a jury in favour of a defendant,[2] and none in which such a finding of a judge sitting alone,[3] has been reversed on appeal.

§ 51. THE INNUENDO

It is clear then that no statement is necessarily and in all circumstances defamatory. There is no charge or imputation, however serious on the face of it, which may not be explained away by evidence that in the special circumstances of the case it was not made or understood in a defamatory sense. It may be shown to have been made in jest, or by way of irony, or in some metaphorical or secondary innocent sense,[4] and that it was or ought to have been understood in that sense by those as to whom it was made.[5] Conversely, no statement is necessarily and in all circumstances innocent. An allegation which on the face of it contains no imputation whatever against the plaintiff may be proved from the circumstances to have contained a latent and secondary defamatory sense. It may suggest an imputation which it does not express. Thus even the language of praise may be sued on as defamatory, on proof that it was used in the way of irony.[6] So the plaintiff must bring evidence to establish a slang or cant meaning which he attaches to an apparently innocent word such as "pansy."[7] Although no statements are necessarily defamatory or necessarily innocent, yet all statements are divisible into two classes, according as they are (1) prima facie defamatory, or (2) prima facie innocent.

(1) Statements prima facie defamatory

A statement is prima facie defamatory when its natural, obvious, and primary sense is defamatory: such a statement is actionable unless its defamatory significance is successfully explained away; and the burden of such an explanation rests upon the defendant. In determining whether the words in their natural and ordinary meaning are defamatory the jury may have regard to the mode and occasion of the publication,[8] for example, that

---

[98] *Lockhart* v. *Harrison* (1928) 139 L.T. 521, 523, 524 (see the amusing explanation of this case given by Norman Birkett, K.C., the plaintiff's counsel, in 76 L.J. (News.) 366).

[99] *Lockhart* v. *Harrison* (1928) 139 L.T. 521, 524, where Lord Dunedin regretted the result: "I think the letter in question the mean letter of a coward ... That it was a libel has been the opinion of every judge who has had the case before him; but, of course, that is not the question. The question is whether it is a verdict at which twelve reasonable men could possibly have arrived."

[1] *Berry* v. *Irish Times Ltd.* [1973] I.R. 368.

[2] *Lockhart* v. *Harrison* (1928) 139 L.T. 521, 523.

[3] *Dingle* v. *Associated Newspapers Ltd.* [1964] A.C. 371, 376.

[4] *Grubb* v. *Bristol United Press Ltd.* [1963] 1 Q.B. 309, 328, 339.

[5] *Australian Newspaper Co.* v. *Bennett* [1894] A.C. 284.

[6] *Boydell* v. *Jones* (1838) 4 M. & W. 446.

[7] *Thaarup* v. *Hulton Press* (1943) 169 L.T. 309. ("I personally was not alive to the slang meaning of the word, nor, I think, was my brother MacKinnon, but my brother Goddard fortunately was quite alive to it, having had judicial experience as a result of which he had come to know about it": *per* Scott, L.J., 169 L.T. 310.)

[8] *Capital and Counties Bank* v. *Henty* (1882) 7 App.Cas. 741, 744.

they were published in large italicised block type in a popular newspaper.[9]
Sometimes a derogatory imputation can be found not so much in what one
says as in the way one says it; for example, in a telegram instead of a
letter.[10]

(2) Statements prima facie innocent

When a statement is prima facie innocent, the plaintiff must expressly and
explicitly[11] set forth in his pleadings the defamatory meaning which he
attributes to it.[12] That defamatory meaning may not be the ordinary meaning, or it may one of two or more ordinary meanings. In the first case the
plaintiff must,[13] and in the second case the plaintiff should,[14] set out the
meaning which he says the words bear. Such an explanatory statement is
called an innuendo.[15] It is not a true innuendo to repeat the obvious meaning
of defamatory words in other langauage, or in an embroidered or
exaggerated way.[16] Otherwise an ingenious pleader could perplex the judge
and jury and harry the defendant[17] by ringing the changes on the same
words,[18] creating numerous different causes of action, each requiring a
separate verdict. A true innuendo relies on a conjunction of the words used
and some extrinsic fact or facts.[19] Thus the statement "X is a good
advertiser" is innocent in itself, but carries a libellous innuendo if published
to persons who know the extrinsic fact that X is an eminent member of the
Bar.[20]

Although each innuendo gives rise to a distinct cause of action, the court
can look at the substance of the matter, and ask the jury to give one verdict
and make one award of damages, or permit the defendant to pay one single
sum into court.[21] The plaintiff is probably bound by his own innuendo and
must prove the meaning as so alleged by him.[22] He cannot at the trial fall
back upon some other secondary and latent sense, instead of that which he
himself alleged in his pleadings, although he may fall back on the primary
defamatory sense of the statement[23] if it is not worse than the meaning
alleged.[24]

A striking example of an innuendo being successfully pleaded can be

---

[9] *English and Scottish. Co-op. Society* v. *Odhams Press* [1940] 1 K.B. 440, 452–453.
[10] Goodhart, Note (1968) 52 L.Q.R. 454.
[11] *S. & K. Holdings Ltd.* v. *Throgmorton Publications Ltd.* [1972] 1 W.L.R. 1036.
[12] The plaintiff must also "give particulars of the facts and matters on which he relies in
support of such sense": Ord. 82, r. 3 (1). See *Fullam* v. *Newcastle Chronicle* [1977] 1
W.L.R. 651.
[13] *Lewis* v. *Daily Telegraph Ltd.* [1964] A.C. 234.
[14] *Allsop* v. *Church of England Newspapers Ltd.* [1972] 2 Q.B. 161.
[15] This term is also sometimes used of the identification of the plaintiff as the person referred
to: above, § 49.
[16] *Lewis* v. *Daily Telegraph Ltd.* [1964] A.C. 234.
[17] In particular, by preventing him from obtaining particulars under Ord. 82, r. 3 (1) of the
extrinsic facts necessary to support a true innuendo. *Loughans* v. *Odhams Press Ltd.*
[1963] 1 Q.B. 299, which seemed to permit such ingenuity, did not really do so: *Lewis* v.
Daily Telegraph Ltd. [1964] A.C. 234, 273, 280.
[18] As in *Grubb* v. *Bristol United Press Ltd.* [1963] 1 Q.B. 309.
[19] *Lewis* v. *Daily Telegraph Ltd.* [1963] 1 Q.B. 340, 364.
[20] See Faulks Report, § 98.
[21] *Pedley* v. *Cambridge Newspapers Ltd.* [1964] 1 W.L.R. 988.
[22] *"Truth" (N.Z.) Ltd.* v. *Holloway* [1960] 1 W.L.R. 997.
[23] *Sim* v. *Stretch* (1936) 52 T.L.R. 669, 671.
[24] *Slim* v. *Daily Telegraph Ltd.* [1968] 2 Q.B. 157.

found in *Tolley* v. *J. S. Fry & Sons Ltd.*[25] In that case an amateur golf champion sued the defendants, a firm of chocolate manufacturers, who had published an advertisement in the middle of which "there appeared a caricature of Mr. Tolley hitting one of his most vigorous drives, with a carton of Fry's chocolate sticking prominently out of his pocket and a comic caddy dancing with another carton of Fry's chocolate in his hand, and comparing in doggerel verse the excellence of the drive with the excellence of the chocolate. Mr. Tolley was, as most people would be, much annoyed at this piece of offensive vulgarity, which reflects very little credit on the good taste of those who control the advertising of Messrs. Fry. He does not eat Fry's chocolate, and his permission for the appearance of the cartoon had not been asked."[26] The innuendo alleged was in effect that he had consented to the use of his portrait as an advertisement for reward and had prostituted his reputation as an amateur golfer. The House of Lords held that there was evidence on which a jury would be entitled to find the advertisement to be defamatory of the plaintiff,[27] but ordered a new trial on the issue of damages.[28]

Cassidy's case

When the law relating to proof of an innuendo is combined with the rule that the test of the defamatory nature of a statement is objective and not subjective, it may well be asked whether it is not a necessary conclusion that a person is responsible for a statement which he believes to be innocent, but which is in fact defamatory by reason of facts unknown to him but known to the persons to whom he makes it. To this question the majority of the Court of Appeal gave an affirmative answer in *Cassidy* v. *Daily Mirror Newspapers Ltd.*[29] "The facts in this case are simple. A man named Cassidy, who for some reason also called himself Corrigan and described himself as a General in the Mexican Army, was married to a lady who also called herself Cassidy or Mrs. Corrigan. Her husband occasionally came and stayed with her at her flat, and her acquaintances met him. Cassidy achieved some notoriety in racing circles and in indiscriminate relations with women, and at a race meeting he posed, in company with a lady, to a racing photographer, to whom he said he was engaged to marry the lady and the photographer might announce it."[30] The defendants accordingly published the photograph with he following words underneath: "Mr. M. Corrigan, the racehorse owner, and Miss 'X', whose engagement has been announced." The innuendo placed upon these words by the plaintiff was that she was an immoral woman who had cohabited with Corrigan without being married to him, and some female acquaintances of the plaintiff gave evidence that they had formed a bad opinion of her on that ground as a result of the publica-

---

[25] [1931] A.C. 333.

[26] [1930] 1 K.B. 467, 472, *per* Scrutton L.J.

[27] Lord Blanesburgh dissenting on the ground that it was just because the publication was so offensive that no reasonable man could be assumed to have taken it seriously: to him, it was ([1931] A.C. 333, 347) "only another instance of the toll levied on distinction for the delectation of vulgarity." We have already seen (above, § 10) that the infringement of privacy is not yet a recognised tort.

[28] A common jury had awarded the plaintiff £1,000.

[29] [1929] 2 K.B. 331.

[30] [1929] 2 K.B. 331, 337, *per* Scrutton L.J. In 1946 Corrigan, aged 49, was found hanged in his cell in Brixton Prison where he was awaiting trial for obtaining money by false pretences.

tion. The jury found that the words did reasonably bear a defamatory meaning, and awarded the plaintiff £500 damages. A majority of the Court of
Appeal held that their verdict could not be disturbed. Further, it has since
been laid down[31] that where words are capable of being understood in a
defamatory sense by persons to whom special facts are known, it is
unnecessary to prove more than that there are people who knew those
special facts and so might reasonably[32] understand the words in a
defamatory sense. One way of proving this proposition is to call witnesses
with such knowledge and such understanding, but to say it is the only way
would be to fall into the elementary error of confusing the proposition to be
proved with the means of proving that proposition.

§ 52. THE DEFAMATION ACT 1952

Hulton v. *Jones* added "a terror to authorship."[33] That terror was intensified
by the decisions of the Court of Appeal in *Cassidy's* case, *Newstead's* case
and *Hough's* case.[34] "Liability for libel," said Russell L.J.,[35] "does not
depend on the intention of the defamer; but on the fact of defamation."
Hence there was much complaint by authors, printers and publishers. On
the other hand writers who publish statements which are *ex facie*
defamatory may not unreasonably be expected to identify the party
described so closely that the words cannot reasonably be interpreted as capable of referring to anyone else. If there is a risk of coincidence why should
it not be borne by the party who puts the mischievous statement in circulation rather than by the innocent person to whom the words are taken to
refer?[36] So after full consideration the Porter Committee decided to retain
the principle in *Hulton* v. *Jones*, subject to a major qualification.[37] The
Faulks Committee came to a similar conclusion.[38] The major qualification is
a new defence of Unintentional Defamation.

Unintentional defamation

The Act of 1952, s. 4, provides that a person who has published words[39]
alleged to be defamatory of another person may, if he claims that the words
were published by him innocently in relation to that other person, make an
offer of amends. Such an offer must be expressed to be made for the
purposes of this section, and must be accompanied by an affidavit specifying
the facts relied upon by the person making it to show that the words in question were published by him innocently in relation to the party aggrieved. An

[31] *Hough* v. *London Express Newspaper Ltd.* [1940] 2 K.B. 507.
[32] *Morgan* v. *Odhams Press Ltd.* [1971] 1 W.L.R. 1239.
[33] *Knupffer* v. *London Express Newspaper Ltd.* [1943] K.B. 80, 89.
[34] Yet it is easy to exaggerate the hardships; a jury is quick to detect a "gold-digging" action.
It is sometimes forgotten that the jury in *Newstead's* case gave the plaintiff one farthing
damages and the C.A. refused to interfere with its verdict. See, too, *Blenner-hassett* v.
Novelty Sales Services Ltd. (1933) 175 L.T.J. 393 (*The Yo-yo* case) and *Progress Bars
Ltd.* v. *Associated Newspapers Ltd., The Times*, June 9, 1950 (*The Moo-Cow Milk Bar*
case), each a case where plaintiffs theoretically within the protection of *Hulton* v. *Jones*
were laughed out of court.
[35] *Cassidy's* case [1929] 2 K.B. 331, 354.
[36] *Newstead's* case [1940] 1 K.B. 377, 388.
[37] Paras. 55, 73.
[38] Faulks Committee Report (Cmnd. 5909, §§ 121, 281).
[39] This includes pictures, visual images, gestures and other methods of signifying meaning:
s. 16 (1).

offer of amends shall be understood to mean an offer (i) in any case, to publish or join in the publication of a suitable correction of the words complained of, and a sufficient apology to the party aggrieved in respect of those words,[40] and (ii) where copies of a document or record containing the said words have been distributed by or with the knowledge of the person making the offer, to take such steps as are reasonably practicable on his part for notifying persons to whom copies have been so distributed that the words are alleged to be defamatory of the party aggrieved.

Such an offer may be either accepted or rejected. We shall indicate the statutory solution for either alternative.

(1) If the offer of amends is accepted

If the offer is accepted and duly performed, no proceedings for libel or slander shall be taken or continued by the party aggrieved against the person making the offer. This, however, is without prejudice to any cause of action against any other person jointly responsible for that publication. Any question as to the steps to be taken in fulfilment of the offer as so accepted shall in default of agreement be determined by the High Court, whose decision shall be final. Whether or not such proceedings are taken, the High Court has power, on the application of the party aggrieved, to order the person making the offer to pay to the party aggrieved costs "on an indemnity basis[41] and any expenses reasonably incurred or to be incurred by that party in consequence of the publication in question."

(2) If the offer of amends is rejected

If the offer is not accepted by the party aggrieved, then it shall be a defence, in any proceedings for libel or slander by him against the person making the offer, to prove that the words were published by the defendant innocently in relation to the plaintiff and that the offer was made as soon as practicable after the defendant received notice that they were or might be defamatory of the plaintiff,[42] and has not been withdrawn. But this provision does not apply in relation to the publication by any person of words of which he is not the author unless he proves that the words were written by the author without malice. This preserves (and indeed extends) the common law rule that the malice of one defendant infects his co-defendants.[43] It seems that if the editor of a newspaper publishes an anonymous letter containing statements *ex facie* innocent, but in fact not so by reason of the fact that the writer is secretly actuated by malice, the editor cannot make use of this statutory defence.

In the normal case the vital question will be whether the words have been published innocently. The Act provides that words shall be treated as having

---

[40] Note (1) that the apology need not apparently be brought to the notice of any person to whom the words complained of were published, and (2) that there must be an offer of such an apology in the offer of amends even though there has been an apology in earlier correspondence.

[41] For the intended meaning of these words, see Report of Proceedings in H.C. Sel. Cttee. B, March 4, 1952.

[42] See *Ross* v. *Hopkinson* [1956] C.L.Y. 5011 (six weeks may be too long).

[43] See below, § 64.

been published innocently only if either of the following conditions is satisfied:

> (i) that the publisher[44] did not intend to publish them of and concerning the party aggrieved, and did not know of circumstances by virtue of which they might be understood to refer to him[45]; or
>
> (ii) that the words were not defamatory on the face of them and the publisher did not know of circumstances by virtue of which they might be understood to be defamatory of the party aggrieved,[46]

and in either case that the publisher exercised all reasonable care in relation to the publication.[47]

Finally, it must be noticed that the facts which the publisher may adduce as evidence that the words were published innocently by him are restricted to those which he had set out in the affidavit accompanying his original offer of amends. It is therefore clear that a person who wishes to claim the protection of the Defamation Act 1952, s. 4, must ensure that the affidavit is drafted with care. For if the party aggrieved should refuse to accept the offer of amends the defendant will be severely hampered at the trial if some of the facts upon which he relies to establish his innocence have been omitted from the affidavit. In practice these pit-falls are such that little use is made of the statutory defence.

§ 53. PUBLICATION

(1) Mode of publication

Publication of the defamatory statement is an essential element of the cause of action.[48] It is the publication, not the composition, of a libel which is the actionable wrong. Often the person sued for publishing is not the writer. The injury done by a libel arises from the effect produced upon its readers.[49] Publication means the act of making the defamatory statement known to any person or persons other than the plaintiff himself.[50] It is not necessary that there should be any publication in the popular sense of making the statement public. A private and confidential communication to a single individual is sufficient. Nor need it be published in the sense of being written or printed; for we have seen that actions as well as words may be defamatory.[51] A communication to the person defamed himself,[52] however, is not a sufficient publication on which to found civil proceedings[53]; though it is otherwise in the case of a criminal prosecution, because such a com-

---

[44] This includes "any servant or agent of his who was concerned with the contents of the publication"—not, be it noted, "with the publication."
[45] This meets the problem of statements not intended to refer to the plaintiff at all, as in *Hulton* v. *Jones* and the *Newstead* case.
[46] This meets the problem of statements which are intended to refer to an existing person and are *ex facie* harmless, but by reason of facts unknown to the author or publisher are defamatory, either of the person intended to be referred to, or of some other person, as in *Cassidy's* case.
[47] See *Ross* v. *Hopkinson* [1956] C.L.Y. 5011. It is by no means clear that the defendants in *Hulton* and *Cassidy* would be held to have taken all reasonable care: see above, § 49.
[48] *Powell* v. *Gelston* [1916] 2 K.B. 615, 619.
[49] *Lee* v. *Wilson* (1934) 51 C.L.R. 276, 287.
[50] *Pullman* v. *Hill* [1891] 1 Q.B. 524, 527.
[51] Above, § 48.
[52] As when a credit agency gives a customer a copy of his file under the Consumer Credit Act 1974, s. 158.
[53] *Powell* v. *Gelston* [1916] 2 K.B. 615.

munication may provoke a breach of the peace.[54] Nor does a communication between husband and wife amount to publication[55]; domestic intercourse of this kind is exempt from the restrictions of the law of libel and slander.[56] But a statement by the defendant to the wife or husband of the plaintiff is a ground of action.[57] It may even be reasonable to foresee that the spouse of the plaintiff will open a letter addressed to the plaintiff.[58]

The contents of a written document may be published either by allowing someone to read the document for himself or by reading it out to him. It is submitted, however, that this latter mode of communication amounts to slander only, and not to libel. A defamatory statement may be published by being dictated to a secretary, typist, or other reporter who reduces it to writing, but it is submitted in this case also that such a publication amounts to slander only. There are dicta to the contrary, indeed, in certain cases[59] in which dictation to a secretary is said to be the publication of libel to the secretary; but it is difficult to see how A can publish to B a document which is written by B himself.[60] It is in any case clear that he who has been employed to print defamatory matter does not publish it merely by returning it to the author in its printed form.[61]

Publication need not consist of a positive or overt act. If a man deliberately refrains from removing or obliterating defamatory matter on premises under his control, he may make himself responsible for its continued presence in the place where it was put. If removal or obliteration was reasonably easy he will be held to have published it. But he will not be responsible if a stranger has made it impossible or very difficult for him to put an end to the libel, as where the objectionable words have been carved deep into the stone-work of his house.[62]

Every publication a new libel

When there are several publications of the same libel a separate action lies for each publication.[63] The actions may, however, be consolidated.[64] If they are not consolidated, but tried separately, there may be difficulties about the assessment of damages.[65] This power of consolidation extends to actions for slander and for slander of title and other forms of injurious falsehood.[66]

(2) Persons to whom published

A publication is not sufficient unless it is made to a person who understands the defamatory significance of the statement, and who also

---

[54] *R. v. Adams* (1888) 22 Q.B.D. 66.
[55] *Wennhak v. Morgan* (1888) 20 Q.B.D. 635. See below, § 61.
[56] Lord Denning would give a similar protection to inter-departmental memoranda: *Riddick v. T.B.M. Ltd.* [1977] Q.B. 881, 907.
[57] *Wenman v. Ash* (1853) 13 C.B. 836.
[58] *Theaker v. Richardson* [1962] 1 W.L.R. 151.
[59] *Pullman v. Hill* [1891] 1 Q.B. 524, 527, 529, *Boxsius v. Goblet Frères* [1894] 1 Q.B. 842, 844; *Marbé v. George Edwardes (Daly's Theatre) Ltd.* [1928] 1 K.B. 269, 277.
[60] *Osborn v. Thomas Boulter & Sons* [1930] 2 K.B. 226, 237.
[61] *Eglantine Inn Ltd. v. Smith* [1948] N.I. 29.
[62] *Byrne v. Deane* [1937] 1 K.B. 818, 838.
[63] *Brunswick (Duke of) v. Harmer* (1849) 14 Q.B. 185; *"Truth" (N.Z.) Ltd. v. Holloway* [1960] 1 W.L.R. 997. For the "single-publication" rule, see the Faulks Report (Cmnd. 5909, § 289).
[64] Law of Libel Amendment Act 1888, s. 5.
[65] See below, § 212.
[66] Defamation Act 1952, s. 13.

understands that it refers to the plaintiff. Thus in *Sadgrove* v. *Hole*[67] the defendant sent to a third person a postcard containing a defamatory statement relating to the plaintiff. The plaintiff's name, however, was not mentioned in it, and no stranger unacquainted with the circumstances would have known to whom it referred. It was held that there was no sufficient publication to the postman or other persons through whose hands the postcard passed.[68] Publication will be presumed and the burden of disproving it lies upon the defendant, in all cases in which the document is so put in the way of being read and understood by someone that it is probable that he actually read and understood it. Thus it is a sufficient proof of publication to prove that a letter was posted and therefore probably read by the person to whom it was addressed or by his clerks,[69] or his wife,[70] but not his butler[71]; or that a postcard was posted and therefore probably read by the post office officials or by the family or servants of him to whom it was sent[72]; or that a telegram was dispatched and therefore read by the telegraph operators.[73]

(3) Who is liable for publication

"Where defamatory matter is contained in a book, periodical, or newspaper, there are normally a series of publications each of which constitutes a separate tort. First, there is a publication by the author to the publisher, for which the author is solely liable. Secondly, there is the publication by the author and publisher jointly to the printer, for which the author and publisher are jointly liable. Thirdly, there is the publication of the printed work to the trade and the public, for which the author, publisher, and printer are jointly liable. It is normally in respect of this last publication that proceedings for libel are brought, although it is open to the plaintiff to sue in respect of the separate publications set out above."[74] Everyone is responsible for the publication of a defamatory statement by another with his authority: hence a speaker who knows that his words are being reported for the public press and who expressly or implicitly authorises such a publication can be sued for libel and not merely for slander.[75] Thus a publication to the wrong person by mistake is a ground of action: as when a document is meant to be sent to the plaintiff himself, or to some person privileged to receive it and it is sent to someone else,[76] or when a man making charges against the plaintiff to his very face or whilst talking scandal to his wife negligently allows what he says[77] to be overheard by a third person; or when he posts to the plaintiff himself or to a privileged person a defamatory message written on a postcard, instead of in a closed letter.

---

[67] [1901] 2 K.B. 1.
[68] No action lay for the publication to the person to whom the card was addressed, since, so far as he was concerned, the communication was privileged.
[69] *Warren* v. *Warren* (1834) 1 C.M. & R. 250.
[70] *Theaker* v. *Richardson* [1962] 1 W.L.R. 151.
[71] *Huth* v. *Huth* [1915] 3 K.B. 32.
[72] *Robinson* v. *Jones* (1879) 4 L.R.Ir. 391. *Aliter* in the case of a letter in an unclosed envelope: *Huth* v. *Huth* [1915] 3 K.B. 32.
[73] *Williamson* v. *Freer* (1874) L.R. 9 C.P. 393.
[74] Porter Committee Report, s. 116.
[75] *Douglas* v. *Tucker* [1952] 1 D.L.R. 657.
[76] *Hebditch* v. *MacIlwaine* [1894] 2 Q.B. 54, 64.
[77] *White* v. *Stone Ltd.* [1939] 2 K.B. 827, 836. But it seems that if he has no reason to suspect that his words will be overheard there is no publication.

(4) Innocent dissemination

The law adopts a more lenient attitude, however, towards him who is not the printer or the first or main publisher of a libel, but has taken only a sub-ordinate part in its dissemination—for example, a newspaper distributor or librarian or a bookseller.[78] Such a person, sometimes called "a mechanical distributor," may be held not to have published the work if he can prove that (1) he disseminated the work without knowing that it contained a libel; (2) there was nothing in the work or in the circumstances in which it came to him or was disseminated by him which ought to have led him to suppose that it contained a libel; (3) when the work was disseminated by him, it was not by any negligence on his part that he did not know that it contained a libel.[79] It is not very easy to see the difference between the second and the third of these questions, and Scrutton L.J. expressed the opinion[80] that in order to avoid confusing the jury, "the safest course for a trial judge is to follow Bowen L.J.,[81] who is a very good man to follow," and ask the jury simply: (i) whether the defendant knew, and (ii) whether he would have known if he had carried on his business properly.[82]

Defences and Remedies

We shall consider in detail the following six defences: (1) Justification; (2) Absolute Privilege; (3) Qualified Privilege; (4) Fair Comment; (5) Consent; (6) Apology. We have already considered the defence provided by the Defamation Act 1952, s. 4 for cases of "unintentional defamation." The question of what may be given in evidence in mitigation of damages will be considered later.[83] The remedies of damages and an injunction are con-sidered later.[84] These defences are of crucial importance in the law of defamation because of the low level of the threshold which a statement must pass in order to be defamatory.

§ 54. JUSTIFICATION

No action will lie for the publication of a defamatory statement if the defendant pleads and proves that it is true. "For the law will not permit a man to recover damages in respect of an injury to a character which he either does not, or ought not, to possess."[85] This is so even though the defendant is proved to have been actuated by malicious and improper motives. In this part of the law the interest in free speech prevails completely

---

[78] There is a striking contrast between the recognition of negligence in this part of the law of libel and its non-recognition in *Hulton* v. *Jones* (above, § 48).

[79] *Bottomley* v. *Woolworth & Co.* (1932) 48 T.L.R. 521 (American magazines sold by mul-tiple store). The defence, although commonly called "innocent dissemination," is strictly a defence of "never published": Porter Committee Report, s. 112. The defence is also avail-able in proceedings for contempt of court: Administration of Justice Act 1960, s. 11.

[80] In *Sun Life Assurance Co.* v. *W. H. Smith & Son Ltd.* (1933) 150 L.T. 211, 214.

[81] In *Emmens* v. *Pottle* (1885) 16 Q.B.D. 354, 358.

[82] In *Goldsmith* v. *Sperrings Ltd.* [1977] 1 W.L.R. 478 a majority of the C.A. (Lord Denning M.R. dissenting) seem to have thought that the liability of a subordinate distribution was strict, and the H.L. refused the defendants leave to appeal.

[83] See below, §§ 212, 219.

[84] See below, § 212.

[85] *McPherson* v. *Daniels* (1829) 10 B. & C. 263, 272, *per* Littledale J.

over the interest in security of reputation. The common law affords no
protection to the man who has led a blameless and worthy life for many
years but finds his youthful follies published to the world at large in gloating
and accurate detail by some malicious enemy.[86] The only exception is that
under the Rehabilitation of Offenders Act 1974, s. 8, a plaintiff who proves
that the defendant has maliciously published details of a spent conviction[87]
may recover damages.[88] But this section does not affect the defences of
absolute[89] or qualified privilege and fair comment. So that an employer will
(in the absence of malice) still be protected if he writes a reference which
mentions a spent conviction. The policy of this complex Act is open to question. It is strange that those who have been convicted should be better
protected by Parliament than those who have been acquitted.

In a criminal prosecution for libel the rule is different. At common law the
truth was no defence at all on an indictment[90]; but by the Libel Act 1843,
s. 6, the publication of the truth, however defamatory, is no longer a criminal
offence if the jury is of opinion that the publication of it was for the public
benefit. It has often been suggested that this requirement of public interest
should be extended to civil proceedings, but the Faulks Report did not
recommend such a change.[91]

The defence that the statement is true is termed a plea of justification, the
defendant being said to justify the publication. The burden of proof rests
upon the defendant; it is for him to prove that the statement is true, not for
the plaintiff to prove that it is false.[92] So the hallowed phrase in the statement of claim that the words were published "falsely and maliciously" is
illogical and bad pleading.[93] The defence is a dangerous one, for an
unsuccessful attempt to establish it may be treated as an aggravation of the
original injury. For if the statement is in fact false, it is no defence at all that
the defendant honestly and on reasonable grounds believed it to be true. He
who attacks the reputation of another does so at his peril; and mistake, however inevitable, is no excuse.

Literal truth unnecessary

On the plea of justification it is not necessary to prove that the statement
is literally true; it is sufficient if it is true in substance, if the essence of the
imputation is true and if the erroneous details in no way aggravate the
defamatory character of the statement or alter its nature.[94] Thus in
Alexander v. *N.E. Ry.*,[95] a statement that the plaintiff had been convicted of

---

[86] For the suggested tort of infringement of privacy, see above, § 10.

[87] In short, one imposed more than 10 years ago which resulted in a non-custodial sentence
or a custodial sentence of not more than 30 months.

[88] Note that the defendant need not show that the publication was in the public interest, as the
Bill originally provided, but that the onus is on the plaintiff to prove malice.

[89] For an exception, see § 56 below.

[90] "Dost know that old Mansfield Who writes like the Bible, Says the more 'tis a truth, sir,
The more 'tis a libel" (Burns, *The Reproof*). This familiar maxim is usually explained on
the ground that the more truthful the statement the more likely is the person defamed to
commit a breach of the peace.

[91] Cmnd. 5909, § 144.

[92] *Beevis* v. *Dawson* [1957] 1 Q.B. 195 (which see also for the practice when the plaintiff
intends to give evidence in rebuttal of the plea of justification).

[93] Faulks Report, § 143.

[94] *Sutherland* v. *Stopes* [1925] A.C. 47, 78–81.

[95] (1865) 6 B. & S. 340.

travelling in a train without a ticket, and had been fined one pound with *three weeks'* imprisonment in default of payment, was held capable of being sufficiently justified by proof that he had been fined one pound for that offence with a *fortnight's* imprisonment in default of payment. Today, the defamation Act 1952, s. 5, provides that in an action for libel or slander in respect of words[96] containing two or more distinct charges against the plaintiff, a defence of justification shall not fail by reason only that the truth of every charge is not proved, if the words not proved to be true do not materially injure the plaintiff's reputation having regard to the truth of the remaining charges.[97] But the defendant will be in a difficult position if the plaintiff disregards some of the charges and sues in respect only of those which are most favourable to his case.[98]

Rumours

When the defamatory statement is put forward by way of rumour or report only, it is not sufficient justification to prove that the rumour or report really existed; it is necessary to prove that it was true. For to give to it further currency is to suggest that it may be well founded, and it is this suggestion that must be justified. Were it not for this rule every man could escape the consequences of publishing libels and slanders by adopting the simple precaution of stating them as matters of rumour or suspicion, instead of as matters of fact.[99] On the other hand, a statement that the Fraud Squad of the police were inquiring into the affairs of the plaintiff has been held incapable of supporting the meaning that he was guilty of fraud,[1] as distinct from being suspected of it, but the statement in this case was not put forward by way of rumour.

Convictions and expulsions

It is not certain whether it is sufficient to justify a statement that a man has been warned off the turf or a boy expelled from school to prove that he has been so warned off or expelled. It has been said that "It would be an extraordinary result . . . that if you said that a properly constituted tribunal had found a man guilty of some wrongful act you could be sued for libel unless you could prove that the properly constituted tribunal had rightly decided that he was guilty."[2] But persons may be warned off or expelled for a variety of reasons, and it seems possible to place an actionable innuendo upon such a statement—*e.g.* that he has been rightly expelled for disgraceful conduct.[3] It is in any event clear that to say a man has been rightly convicted is quite different from saying simply that he has been convicted: so

---

[96] As defined by s. 16 (1); see above, § 48.
[97] For a successful invocation of this defence, see *Redgrave* v. *The Observer* (1978).
[98] As in *Speidel* v. *Plato Films Ltd.* [1961] A.C. 1090. The Faulks committee recommended a change (Cmnd. 5909, § 134).
[99] *Watkin* v. *Hall* (1868) L.R. 3 Q.B. 396.
[1] *Lewis* v. *Daily Telegraph Ltd.* [1964] A.C. 234. Awards of damages amounting to £217,000 were set aside by the House of Lords as being out of all proportion, and a new trial ordered. The defendants later paid £22,000 in settlement: *The Times*, December 18, 1964.
[2] *Cookson* v. *Harewood* [1932] 2 K.B. 478, 485, *per* Greer L.J.
[3] *Lewis* v. *Daily Telegraph Ltd.* [1963] 1 Q.B. 340, 372-373 (not considered in H.L.).

until the law was changed by the Civil Evidence Act 1968, s. 13, someone who published the former statement found himself under the heavy burden of fighting a criminal trial over again.[4]

§ 55. PRIVILEGE[5]

We have seen that in general he who publishes a defamatory statement does so at his peril, and is liable if this statement turns out not to be true, however honestly and carefully he may have acted, and however inevitable his mistake. This rule is subject to a number of important exceptions which are grouped together under the title of Privilege. A privileged statement[6] may be defined as one which is made in such circumstances as to be exempt from the rule that a man attacks the reputation of another at his own risk. In other words, privilege includes those exceptional cases in which it is not enough, in order to create liability, to prove that the defendant has published a false and defamatory statement. The defendant, being privileged,[6] is not responsible for this alone, but is either wholly free from responsibility or is liable only on proof that he was animated by a malicious motive and not by any genuine intention to use his privilege for the purpose for which the law gave it to him. It is common to speak of the statement as being privileged, but the better view[6] is that it is the occasion and not the statement which is privileged.[7]

The cases in which privilege exists are, speaking generally, those in which there is some just occasion for publishing defamatory matter in the public interest or in the furtherance or protection of the rights or lawful interests of individuals. In such cases the exigency of the occasion amounts to a lawful excuse for the attack so made upon the plaintiff's reputation. The right of free speech is allowed wholly or partially to prevail over the right of reputation. If the defamatory statement can be shown to be true, the defence of privilege is not required; for it is allowable to publish the truth on all occasions, privileged or not, and from all motives, good or bad. It is only when the statement is false, or cannot be proved to be true, that it is necessary to fall back upon the plea of privilege, and to prove that the occasion of the publication was such as to exempt the defendant from the consequences of his error. It has been held that a defendant may plead that the occasion on which he published the words was privileged, even though he also denies that he ever published the words in question.[8] Whenever privilege exists, however, it is wise to plead it instead of or along with a plea of justification; for the latter is a dangerous weapon, which often fails and even injures him who uses it.

---

[4] See *Hinds* v. *Sparks, The Times*, July 27, 1964. For a curious converse case, see *Loughans* v. *Odhams Press Ltd., The Times*, February 14, 1963. The Civil Evidence Act 1968, s. 13 now provides that if it is relevant in defamation proceedings whether a person committed a criminal offence, proof of conviction is conclusive evidence that he did commit that offence. But note that proof of an acquittal is not conclusive of innocence.

[5] The argument of Holmes, K.C., in *Perera (M.G.)* v. *Peiris* [1949] A.C. 1 reviews the history of the defence.

[6] *Minter* v. *Priest* [1930] A.C. 558, 571–572.

[7] *Angel* v. *Bushell Ltd.* [1968] 1 Q.B. 813.

[8] *Kirkwood Hackett* v. *Tierney* [1952] I.R. 185.

§ 56. ABSOLUTE PRIVILEGE

Privilege is of two kinds, distinguished as absolute and qualified. A statement is said to be absolutely privileged when it is of such a nature that no action will lie for it, however false and defamatory it may be, and even though it is made maliciously—that is to say, from some improper motive. The right of free speech is allowed to prevail wholly over the right of reputation. These cases are at the opposite extreme from the ordinary cases of unprivileged defamation. When a statement is not privileged, it is actionable, however honest its publication may have been; but if it is absolutely privileged, it is not actionable, however dishonest its publication may have been. As may be expected, the cases in which the right of free speech can be placed at so high a level are few in number and quite exceptional in character.

They are the following:

(1) Any statement made in the course of and with reference to judicial proceedings by any judge, juryman, party, witness, or advocate;

(2) Fair, accurate, and contemporaneous reports of public judicial proceedings published in a newspaper;

(3) Any statement made in Parliament by a member of either House;

(4) Parliamentary papers published by the direction of either House, and any republication thereof by any person in full;

(5) Any statement made by one officer of State to another in the course of his official duty;

(6) Communications between husband and wife;

(7) Certain publications by and to the Parliamentary Commissioner are protected,[9] as also are certain reports and other communications between a Local Commissioner and a local government authority.[10]

(1) Judicial privilege

"The authorities establish beyond all question this: that neither party, witness, counsel, jury, nor judge can be put to answer civilly or criminally for words spoken in office; that no action of libel or slander lies, whether against judges, counsel, witnesses, or parties, for words written or spoken in the course of any proceeding before any court recognised by law, and this though the words written or spoken were written or spoken maliciously without any justification or excuse, and from personal ill-will and anger against the person defamed. This absolute privilege has been conceded on the grounds of public policy to ensure freedom of speech where it is essential that freedom of speech should exist, and with the knowledge that courts of justice are presided over by those who from their high character are not likely to abuse the privilege, and who have the power and ought to have the will to check any abuse of it by those who appear before them."[11]

The privilege extends to all courts, superior and inferior, civil and military.[12] If the privilege is abused the remedy is removal from office rather

[9] Parliamentary Commissioner Act 1967, s. 10 (5).
[10] Local Government Act 1974, s. 32.
[11] *Royal Aquarium and Summer and Winter Garden Society Ltd.* v. *Parkinson* [1892] 1 Q.B. 431, 451, *per* Lopes L.J.
[12] *Scott* v. *Stansfield* (1868) L.R. 3 Ex. 220 (county court); *Thomas* v. *Churton* (1862) 2 B. & S. 475 (coroner); *Dawkins* v. *Rokeby (Lord)* (1873) L.R. 8 Q.B. 255 (court-martial); *Law* v. *Llewellyn* [1906] 1 K.B. 487 (magistrate); *Bottomely* v. *Brougham* [1908] 1 K.B. 584 (official receiver).

than the harassment of an action. But if the court is an inferior one privilege probably attaches only when the court has acted within jurisdiction.[13] The privilege also extends to tribunals acting in a manner similar to courts of justice,[14] so that Jasper Addis unsuccessfully argued that an order of the Disciplinary Committee of the solicitors' profession was not absolutely privileged.[15] The privilege even extends to purely domestic tribunals not established by statute,[16] but the privilege does not extend to officials possessing merely administrative as opposed to genuine judicial functions. Thus a meeting of a local authority engaged in hearing applications for music and dancing licences is not a court within the meaning of the rule, and statements made by a member of that body are not absolutely privileged.[17]

The privilege extends not merely to judges[18] but witnesses,[19] parties,[20] and advocates.[21] It includes not merely statements made by a witness in court but also statements made by him to a party, or to the party's solicitor, in the course of preparation for trial.[22] For it would not be of much use to grant absolute privilege to what is said in court, if a plaintiff could say: "I cannot sue you for what you said in the witness-box, but I am going to sue you for what you told your solicitor you were going to say in it."

The statement, in order to be privileged, need not be relevant, in the sense of having a material bearing upon the matter in issue in the case. Thus the statement of a witness is privileged, even though inadmissible as evidence, and even though so immaterial that no prosecution for perjury would be possible in respect of it. Nevertheless the statement, though it need not be relevant in this sense, must, it would seem, be made in the course of and with reference to the case in hand. A judge who from the Bench made a defamatory observation in respect of some entirely extraneous matter would no longer be speaking in his capacity as a judge, and would have no privilege.[23]

(2) Privileged reports

By the Law of Libel Amendment Act 1888, s. 3, it is provided that "A fair and accurate[24] report in any newspaper[25] of proceedings publicly heard before any court exercising judicial authority[26] shall, if published con-

---

[13] See below, § 153.
[14] *Trapp* v. *Mackie* [1979] 1 W.L.R. 377.
[15] *Addis* v. *Crocker* [1961] 1 Q.B. 11. But a complaint to the Bar Council (as distinct from the Benchers of an Inn) has only qualified privilege: *Lincoln* v. *Daniels* [1962] 1 Q.B. 237.
[16] *Trapp* v. *Mackie* [1979] 1 W.L.R. 377.
[17] *Royal Aquarium Society* v. *Parkinson* [1892] 1 Q.B. 431.
[18] *Scott* v. *Stansfield* (1868) L.R. 3 Ex. 220. In the case of judges, however, this is simply a special instance of a much more general rule of exemption from civil liability for judicial acts. As to this, see below, § 152.
[19] *Seaman* v. *Netherclift* (1876) 2 C.P.D. 53. Nor will an action for perjury lie against a witness: *Hargreaves* v. *Bretherton* [1959] 1 Q.B. 45. See above, § 4.
[20] *Kennedy* v. *Hilliard* (1859) 10 Ir.C.L.R. 195.
[21] *Munster* v. *Lamb* (1883) 11 Q.B.D. 588.
[22] *Watson* v. *M'Ewan* [1905] A.C. 480.
[23] *More* v. *Weaver* [1928] 2 K.B. 520, 525.
[24] It is no defence that the omission of a material statement during the proceedings was due to its not being heard by the reporter owing to inattention: *Mitchell* v. *Hirst, Kidd and Rennie Ltd.* [1936] 3 All E.R. 872. Lawrence J. there suggested during argument that it would have been otherwise if the omitted statemet *could* not have been heard.
[25] As defined in s. 1. A broadcast report is also protected: the Defamation Act 1952, s. 9 (2).
[26] Within the United Kingdom only: the Defamation Act 1952, s. 8. Reports of proceedings before foreign and Commonwealth tribunals may be the subject of qualified privilege: see below, § 60.

temporaneously with such proceedings, be privileged: provided that nothing in this section shall authorise the publication of any blasphemous or indecent matter." The report need not be a verbatim one; it is enough if it is in substance a fair account of what took place; a few slight omissions or inaccuracies are immaterial.[27] Nor is a newspaper obliged to verify whether what counsel or a solicitor or a witness has said is accurate; a fair and accurate report of counsel's opening address in (say) a fashionable libel action is just as much entitled to privilege as such a report of the judge's summing-up.[28] "Proceedings" covers anything done in the course of the proceedings which is in any way related to them,[29] but not an intervention in court which is wholly irrelevant to anything before the tribunal,[30] or evidence about a spent conviction which a court has ruled to be inadmissible under section 4 (1) of the Rehabilitation of Offenders Act 1974.[31]

It is generally understood that the word *privileged* in section 3 of the Act of 1888 means absolutely privileged.[32] If one of the statutory conditions has not been fulfilled it may be that the report has qualified privilege at common law.[33]

(3) Parliamentary privilege

It is clear that statements made by members of either House of Parliament in their places in the House, though they might be untrue to their knowledge, could not be made the foundation of civil or criminal proceedings, however injurious they might be to the interest of a third person.[34] The privilege is based on the Bill of Rights 1688, s. 1. The privilege also prevents the examination of proceedings in the House for the purpose of finding malice to support a cause of action which arises outside the House.[35]

(4) Parliamentary papers

By the Parliamentary Papers Act 1840, s. 1, absolute privilege is conferred upon the publication[36] by order of either House of Parliament of the reports, papers, votes, or proceedings of either House, and also upon the republication in full of any documents of this nature which have been already published by such authority. The publication of extracts or abstracts of a parliamentary paper is the subject of qualified privilege[37] under

---

[27] *Kimber* v. *Press Association* [1893] 1 Q.B. 65.
[28] *Burnett and Hallamshire Fuel Ltd.* v. *Sheffield Telegraph & Star Ltd.* [1960] 1 W.L.R. 502.
[29] *Farmer* v. *Hyde* [1937] 1 K.B. 728.
[30] *Lynam* v. *Gowing* (1880) 6 L.R.Ir. 259.
[31] Unless, according to s. 8 (7), the report in question is in a bona fide series of law reports, or has been published for bona fide educational purposes. Lecturers and students who refer to spent convictions in other ways—*e.g.* in seminars—may find themselves paying damages to rehabilitated persons.
[32] See *McCarey* v. *Associated Newspapers Ltd.* [1964] 1 W.L.R. 855 (not discussed on appeal in [1965] 2 Q.B. 86) and Spencer Bower, *Actionable Defamation*, pp. 406–408 ("anything more unjust or pernicious or inimical to public welfare cannot well be imagined"). This seems to be the assumption of the Defamation Act 1952, s. 8, although it was probably not what Parliament intended in 1888 (Faulks Report, § 189).
[33] *Thom* v. *John Fairfax & Sons Pty. Ltd.* [1964] N.S.W.R. 396.
[34] *Ex p. Wason* (1869) L.R. 4 Q.B. 573, 576; Davis, "Parliamentary Broadcasting and the Law of Defamation" (1948) 7 Univ. of Toronto L.J. 385.
[35] *Church of Scientology* v. *Johnson-Smith* [1972] 1 Q.B. 522.
[36] A term which now includes broadcasting: Defamation Act 1952, s. 9 (1).
[37] *Associated Newspapers Ltd.* v. *Dingle* [1964] A.C. 371, 407.

section 3 of the 1840 Act. At common law the protection accorded to statements made in Parliament did not extend to the publication of defamatory documents elsewhere, even by order of one of the Houses,[38] for one House cannot by its own resolution alter the law of the land. For that a statute is required.

(5) Official privilege

No action will lie against an officer of State for any defamatory statement made by him to another officer of State in the course of his duty.[39] It has not been established clearly what classes of public servants are officers of State. Protection has been extended to official reports made by a military officer to his superior,[40] by a Minster to a subordinate official,[41] and by the High Commissioner of a Commonwealth country to his Prime Minister,[42] but it is doubtful whether it extends to a report made by a police-inspector to his superior officer,[43] or to reports made by the security service of a foreign Power.[44] Probably this absolute immunity is given only where upon clear grounds of public policy a remedy must be denied to private injury because complete freedom from suit appears indispensable to the effective performance of judicial, legislative, or official functions. The presumption is against such a privilege and its extension is not favoured.[45] The fact that a communication relates to commercial matters does not preclude it from also relating to state matters.[46] The question has arisen whether privilege would attach to statements made in this country by the officials of a foreign government.[47] It would seem that if such protection were accorded it would be on the grounds of diplomatic privilege, whereas the rule attaching privilege to the communications of our own officials is based on public policy. It is doubtful whether such statements would ever be protected by absolute (as distinct from qualified) privilege, unless the sender of the document and the foreign government were both resident in England.[48]

(6) Statements between husband and wife

A defamatory statement made by one spouse to the other, as distinct from a statement made to the spouse of the plaintiff, cannot be the subject of an action. The older authorities put this upon the ground that there has been

---

[38] *Stockdale* v. *Hansard* (1839) 9 A. & E. 1. Lord Denman's was an "admirable judgment than which a finer never was delivered within these walls, and in which the spirit of Holt is combined with the luminous reasoning of a Mansfield": *Wason* v. *Walter* (1868) L.R. 4 Q.B. 73, 91, *per* Cockburn C.J.
[39] *Chatterton* v. *Secretary of State for India* [1895] 2 Q.B. 189.
[40] *Dawkins* v. *Lord F. Paulet* (1869) L.R. 5 Q.B. 94. The authority of the case is weakened by Cockburn C.J.'s powerful dissenting judgment.
[41] *Peerless Bakery Ltd.* v. *Watt* [1955] N.Z.L.R. 339. But see *Szalatnay-Stacho* v. *Fink* [1946] 1 All E.R. 303, 305 (the point was not discussed in the C.A.).
[42] *Isaacs & Sons Ltd.* v. *Cook* [1925] 2 K.B. 391.
[43] *Merricks* v. *Nott-Bower* [1965] 1 Q.B. 57.
[44] *Richards* v. *Naum* [1967] 1 Q.B. 620.
[45] *Gibbons* v. *Duffell* (1932) 47 C.L.R. 520. This privilege must be distinguished from the evidentiary privilege which enables a Minster to refuse to produce a document if it would be contrary to the public interest to do so.
[46] *Isaacs & Sons Ltd.* v. *Cook* [1925] 2 K.B. 391; *Peerless Bakery Ltd.* v. *Watt* [1955] N.Z.L.R. 339.
[45] *Richards* v. *Naum* [1967] 1 Q.B. 620.
[48] *Szalatnay-Stacho* v. *Fink* [1947] K.B. 1.

no publication; but it seems preferable today, when the fiction of the unity of husband and wife has been discarded, to say that it is an instance of absolute privilege, the reason for which is the highly confidential character of the relationship.[49]

If the occasion be covered by absolute privilege then consequential communications also are privileged in the same way. So, in *Isaacs & Sons Ltd.* v. *Cook*,[50] the publication of the report to the clerks and servants through whom the production and issue of the report were arranged was privileged along with the report itself.[51]

§ 57. QUALIFIED PRIVILEGE

When an occasion of qualified privilege exists a person (provided he is not actuated by malice) is entitled to make defamatory statements about another. The right of freedom of speech prevails over the right of reputation, but only to a limited extent. The statement must be made honestly and without any indirect or improper motive. Qualified privilege, therefore, is an intermediate case between total absence of privilege and the presence of absolute privilege. The principle is that the statement is protected if it is fairly made by a person in the discharge of some public or private duty, whether legal or moral, or in the conduct of his own affairs, in matters where his interest is concerned.[52] No complete list of such occasions is possible or desirable,[53] but it is generally agreed that the chief instances are the following:

(1) Statements made in the performance of a duty;
(2) Statements made in the protection of an interest;
(3) Reports of parliamentary, judicial, and certain other public proceedings;
(4) Professional communications between solicitor and client.

We shall now consider each in turn.

§ 58. (1) STATEMENTS IN PERFORMANCE OF A DUTY

A statement is conditionally privileged if it is made in the performance of any legal or moral duty imposed upon the person making it.[54] The privilege is that of the publisher; the person to whom the statement is published needs no privilege, because he commits no tort.[55] Nevertheless it is essential[56] that the person to whom the statement is made has a corresponding interest or duty to receive it. This is not to say that both parties must have a duty or both an interest: one may have an interest and the other a duty, as in the common case of a servant's character.[57] The duty need not be, and indeed

---

[49] Prosser, *Torts*, p. 785.
[50] [1925] 2 K.B. 391.
[51] As in cases of qualified privilege, below, § 63.
[52] *Toogood* v. *Spyring* (1834) 1 C. M. & R. 181, 193.
[53] *London Association for Protection of Trade* v. *Greenlands* [1916] 2 A.C. 15, 23.
[54] *Stuart* v. *Bell* [1891] 2 Q.B. 341.
[55] *Bryanston Finance Ltd.* v. *de Vries* [1975] 1 Q.B. 703, 726.
[56] *Watt* v. *Longsdon* [1930] 1 K.B. 130.
[57] *Phelps* v. *Kemsley* (1942) 168 L.T. 18, 21.

seldom is, one enforceable at law[58] it is sufficient that by the moral standard of right conduct prevalent in the community the defendant lay under an obligation to say what he did. It is not enough that he believed himself to be under such an obligation.[59] It is for the judge, and not for the jury, to decide whether on the facts as proved such a duty existed.[60] The judge will have to estimate the value of and make a choice between the various interests—of life, family, reputation, or property—involved in the case. It is plain that no universally valid criterion is possible. "Would the great mass of right-minded men in the position of the defendant have considered it their duty, under the circumstances, to make the communication?"[61] is one test often cited. One important kind of duty which will give privilege to a defamatory statement is the duty of answering inquiries made by some person having a lawful interest in the matter. Thus an employer may answer questions as to the character of a former servant made by any person proposing to engage that servant.[62] So an accusation of crime is privileged if made in reply to questions put by the police with a view to detecting an offender.[63]

Voluntary communications

A communication which is volunteered, without any inquiry on the part of anyone possessing a lawful interest, is unprivileged, unless there is some such confidential or other relation between the parties as creates a duty to speak without being asked. Thus the relationship of master and servant will justify the servant in telling his master facts which concern his interest in relation to the matters entrusted to the servant.[64] For the same reason a father or other near relative may warn a lady as to the character of the man whom she proposes to marry.[65] It would seem that there may even be circumstances in which a duty lies upon a third party to communicate to one spouse the delinquencies of the other, but in such cases the judge would be "much influenced by the consideration that as a general rule it is not desirable for anyone, even a mother-in-law, to interfere in the affairs of man and wife."[66] Again, a host owes a duty to his guest which will justify him in warning his guest against a servant suspected of dishonesty.[67] So the members of borough councils and other public bodies and officials of trading companies are privileged in respect of communications made to one another in the honest fulfilment of their functions.[68] On the same principle, in the case of a trade protection association which makes on behalf of its members inquiries into the financial position of persons with whom they propose to deal, communications made by the association or its agents to a member who has requested this information, and who has a lawful interest in obtain-

---

[58] There is a legal duty to make certain entries in a ship's log book under the Merchant Shipping Act 1970, s. 68.
[59] *Phelps* v. *Kemsley* (1942) 168 L.T. 18.
[60] *Watt* v. *Longsdon* [1930] 1 K.B. 130.
[61] *Watt* v. *Longsdon* [1930] 1 K.B. 130, 153, *per* Greer L.J.
[62] *Jackson* v. *Hopperton* (1864) 16 C.B. (N.S.) 829.
[63] *Kine* v. *Sewell* (1838) 3 M. & W. 297.
[64] *Lawless* v. *Anglo-Egyptian Cotton Co.* (1869) L.R. 4 Q.B. 262.
[65] *Todd* v. *Hawkins* (1837) 8 C. & P. 88.
[66] *Watt* v. *Longsdon* [1930] 1 K.B. 130, 150, *per* Scrutton L.J.
[67] *Stuart* v. *Bell* [1891] 2 Q.B. 341.
[68] *Andrews* v. *Nott Bower* [1895] 1 Q.B. 888; *Watt* v. *Longsdon* [1930] 1 K.B. 130.

ing it, are privileged,[69] at least if the association has not been created solely for the purposes of gain.[70]

§ 59. (2) STATEMENTS IN PROTECTION OF AN INTEREST

Even when there is no duty to make the statement, it is nevertheless privileged if it is made in the protection of some lawful interest of the person making it: for example, if it is made in the defence of his own property or reputation.[71] But here also there must be reciprocity. There must be an interest to be protected on the one side and a duty to protect it on the other.[72] Thus in *Adam* v. *Ward*[73] the plaintiff, in the House of Commons, had made against General Scobell charges of the most wounding character. General Scobell, as he was compelled to do by King's Regulations, referred the matter to the Army Council, which after investigation found that the attack was unjustifiable. It ordered the defendant, its secretary, to publish in the newspapers a letter to General Scobell vindicating him and also containing statements defamatory of the plaintiff. The House of Lords held that the occasion of this publication was privileged,[74] and that the privilege was not destroyed either by the number of people whom the publication might reach,[75] or by reason of the fact that it contained matter defamatory of the plaintiff, for where the defendant's character has been publicly attacked by the plaintiff, the courts will not be over-nice in their scrutiny of the language which he uses in his defence, although a counter-attack which makes irrelevant and spiteful allegations will not be privileged.[76] But no privilege attaches when the sender of the document makes a mistake, however genuine, about the nature of the occasion[77] or the interest of the recipient.[78]

There may sometimes be a common interest and a reciprocal duty in respect of the subject-matter of the communication.[79] Thus a master has a sufficient interest in the honesty of his servants to be privileged in warning them against the character of their associates.[80] So a tenant may make a complaint to his landlord of the conduct of persons engaged by the latter to effect repairs to the premises.[81] Conversely, a landlord may complain to his tenant of the conduct of the latter's lodgers at the windows of the house as having a tendency to bring the house into disrepute.[82] So shareholders[83] or

---

[69] *London Association for Protection of Trade* v. *Greenlands Ltd.* [1916] 2 A.C. 15.
[70] See the comments of the Younger Committee on Privacy, (Cmnd. 5012 (1972)) paras. 273–275.
[71] *Turner* v. *M.-G.-M. Pictures Ltd.* [1950] 1 All E.R. 449, 470.
[72] *White* v. *Stone Ltd.* [1939] 2 K.B. 827, 835.
[73] [1917] A.C. 309.
[74] "Every subject of the Crown, whatever portion of our far-flung Empire he may inhabit, has, and must have, an interest in the British Army, its courage, the confidence of its men in their officers, its discipline and efficiency ... It would be a disgrace and injury to the service if a man, publicly accused of the shameful breach of duty of which General Scobell was accused, was allowed to continue in command of a brigade in the Army unless and until he had been cleared of the accusation made against him. Every subject, therefore, who had an interest in the Army had an interest in being by a public communication informed of General Scobell's acquittal": *per* Lord Atkinson, [1917] A.C. 309, 343.
[75] See below, § 63.
[76] *News Media Ownership* v. *Finlay* [1970] N.Z.L.R. 1089.
[77] *Pyke* v. *Hibernian Bank Ltd.* [1950] I.R. 195.
[78] *Beach* v. *Freeson* [1972] 1 Q.B. 14, 24.
[79] *Watt* v. *Longsdon* [1930] 1 K.B. 130, 147.
[80] *Hunt* v. *G.N. Ry.* [1891] 2 Q.B. 189.
[81] *Toogood* v. *Spyring* (1834) 1 C.M. & R. 181.
[82] *Knight* v. *Gibbs* (1834) 1 Ad. & E. 43.
[83] *Lawless* v. *Anglo-Egyptian Cotton Co.* (1869) L.R. 4 Q.B. 262.

employees[84] in the same company may make privileged communications to each other in defence and furtherance of their common interests.

Charges against public persons

The same principle is applicable even when the interest of the defendant is merely the general interest which he possesses in common with all others in the honest and efficient exercise by public officials of the duties entrusted to them. Thus any member of the public may make charges of misconduct against any public servant and the communication will be privileged[85] but the charge must be made to the proper persons—that is to say, to those who have a corresponding interest. Otherwise there would be a startling licence to defame on a grand scale.[86] So a constituent may write to his Member of Parliament asking for his assistance to bring to the notice of the appropriate Minister or other person a complaint of improper conduct on the part of a public officer, for example, a police officer or a justice of the peace, acting in his constituency in relation to his office.[87] If this were not the law, a Member of Parliament would act at his peril if he extended his activities beyond the Palace of Westminster.[88] But a communication to the wrong person,[89] and *a fortiori* a publication of the complaint to the world at large in a newspaper or otherwise, is an excess of privilege, and the privilege will be thereby forfeited.[90] On the other hand, the Defamation Act 1952, provides[91] that a defamatory statement published by or on behalf of a candidate in any election to a local government authority[92] or to Parliament shall not be deemed to be published on a privileged occasion on the ground that it is material to a question in issue in the election, whether or not the person by whom it is published is qualified to vote at the election.

Privilege distinguished from fair comment

This privilege of making complaints against public persons must not be confounded with the right to make fair comments on matters of public interest, which will be discussed in a later section.[93] Privilege deals with false and defamatory statements of fact, not with defamatory comment on proved or admitted facts. A comment may be published to all the world; a specific charge of misconduct may be published only to the persons in authority over the offender.

§ 60. (3) PRIVILEGED REPORTS

Fair and accurate reports, whether in a newspaper or elsewhere, of the public proceedings of any municipal court of justice are conditionally

---

[84] *Bryanston Finance Ltd.* v. *de Vries* [1975] 1 Q.B. 703, 728.
[85] *Harrison* v. *Bush* (1855) 5 E. & B. 344.
[86] *London Artists Ltd.* v. *Littler* [1968] 1 W.L.R. 607, 615.
[87] *Beach* v. *Freeson* [1972] 1 Q.B. 14.
[88] *Beach* v. *Freeson* [1972] 1 Q.B. 14, 22.
[89] *De Buse* v. *McCarthy* [1942] 1 K.B. 156.
[90] *Truth (N.Z.) Ltd.* v. *Holloway* [1960] N.Z.L.R. 69 (not discussed on appeal, [1960] 1 W.L.R. 997).
[91] s. 10.
[92] *Plummer* v. *Charman* [1962] 1 W.L.R. 1469.
[93] Below, § 66.

privileged by the common law. The privilege extends to all courts, whether superior or inferior, and whether courts of record or not.[94] It makes no difference whether the proceedings are preliminary or final,[95] or whether they are taken *ex parte* or otherwise. The privilege is not excluded by the fact that the matter is one over which the court had no jurisdiction, provided that it has jurisdiction to inquire whether the matter is one which it could properly entertain[96]; A fair and accurate contemporaneous report of judicial proceedings before a foreign tribunal is also privileged (by judicial decision[97] in England, by statute[98] in Ireland), at least if the matter is of legitimate and proper interest to the public.[99] It seems, however, that no privilege attaches if the proceedings take place in a court to which the public are not admitted,[1] or in a domestic tribunal, *e.g.* the Stewards of the Jockey Club,[2] nor where the subject-matter of the publication is an obscene or blasphemous libel.[3] As has been already indicated,[4] a *newspaper* report of judicial proceedings is the subject of a statutory privilege, probably absolute, if it fulfils the requirements of section 3 of the Law of Libel Amendment Act 1888. If any of those requirements are not satisfied, the report is subject to the common law rule of qualified privilege only.[5] Fair and accurate reports of parliamentary debates are covered by qualified privilege at common law,[6] whilst the publication of extracts from or abstracts of reports or papers ordered by Parliament to be published is the subject of qualified privilege by statute.[7]

Reports of public meetings

At common law the reports, whether in a newspaper or elsewhere, of the proceedings of public meetings possessed no privilege.[8] Then the Law of Libel Amendment Act 1888, s. 4, gave a limited measure of protection to newspapers which published fair and accurate reports of certain meetings. The Porter Committee recommended,[9] that the defence should be extended, both by widening the definition of "newspaper" to include monthly journals as well as those published at shorter intervals and by extending the categories of reports entitled to such privilege so as to give effect to the changes in social, economic, and political conditions which had occurred during the preceding 60 years.

---

[94] *e.g.* a coroner's court: *McCarey* v. *Associated Newspapers Ltd.* [1964] 1 W.L.R. 855.
[95] *Kimber* v. *Press Association* [1893] 1 Q.B. 65.
[96] *Allbutt* v. *General Council of Medical Education* (1889) 23 Q.B.D. 400.
[97] *Webb* v. *Times Publishing Co. Ltd.* [1960] 2 Q.B. 535. See the interesting Note on this case in (1964) 64 Col.L.Rev. 1102.
[98] Defamation Act 1961, Sched. 2.
[99] Would not this always be true of judicial proceedings in another EEC country?
[1] *Kimber* v. *Press Association* [1893] 1 Q.B. 65.
[2] *Chapman* v. *Ellesmere (Lord)* [1932] 2 K.B. 431, 475. But privilege attaches to the publication of a decision of such a tribunal, in the terms in which the tribunal bona fide embodied it, in the publication chosen by the parties as the means of communication between the tribunal and the section of the public interested. This is merely an application of the rule *volenti non fit injuria*. In such a case the plaintiff cannot rely upon an innuendo: *ibid.* [1932] 2 K.B. 431.
[3] *R.* v. *Carlile* (1819) 3 B. & Ald. 167.
[4] Above, § 56.
[5] *Contra, Thom* v. *John Fairfax & Sons Pty. Ltd.* [1964] N.S.W.R. 396.
[6] *Wason* v. *Walter* (1868) L.R. 4 Q.B. 73.
[7] Parliamentary Papers Act 1840, s. 3. Above § 56.
[8] *Purcell* v. *Sowler* (1877) 2 C.P.D. 215.
[9] Paras. 95–111.

Two classes of reports

Accordingly the Defamation Act 1952, s. 7, provides that the publication in a newspaper[10] of the reports[11] or other matters about to be mentioned shall be the subject of qualified privilege. The reports and matters concerned fall into two categories:

(1) *Statements privileged without any explanation or contradiction.*

(2) *Statements privileged subject to explanation or contradiction.*

The defence of qualified privilege is not available to an action brought in respect of the publication of any of the statements mentioned in this second category if it is proved that the defendant had been requested by the plaintiff to publish in the newspaper in which,[12] or, in the case of a broadcast statement, in the manner in which,[13] the original publication was made a reasonable letter or statement by way of explanation or contradiction,[14] and has refused or neglected to do so, or has done so in a manner not adequate or reasonable having regard to all the circumstances.[15] The Act does not protect the publication of any matter the publication of which is prohibited by law, or of any matter which is not of public concern and the publication of which is not for the public benefit.[16] This limitation is important: the legislature never intended to extend protection to reports of defamatory remarks which have no relevance to the objects of the meeting.[17] Although the report must be fair and accurate it need not be verbatim; nor, provided it is substantially accurate, will minor errors deprive it of protection.[18]

(1) *Statements privileged without any explanation or contradiction*

(i) A fair and accurate report of any proceedings in public of the legislature[19] of any part of Her Majesty's dominions[20] outside Great Britain.

(ii) A fair and accurate report of any proceedings in public of an international organisation of which the United Kingdom or Her Majesty's Government in the United Kingdom is a member, or of

---

[10] Means any paper containing public news or observations thereon, or consisting wholly or mainly of advertisements, which is printed for sale and is published in the U.K. either periodically or in parts or numbers at intervals not exceeding 36 days. Broadcast statements are also protected: s. 9 (2).

[11] Note that it is the report which is protected, as distinct from the original statement.

[12] This must mean an issue of the newspaper subsequent to that in which the original publication was made.

[13] If the libel was contained in a variety sketch, or interview, it would hardly be necessary to reassemble the original cast: Chapman, *Statutes*, p. 295.

[14] A general demand by the plaintiff for an apology is not a request within the meaning of this section: *Khan* v. *Ahmed* [1957] 2 Q.B. 149.

[15] The reason for the distinction has been explained by E. C. S. Wade ((1950) 66 L.Q.R. 35): "It is surely not appropriate to require of editors when reporting overseas news ... that they should throw their columns open to overseas statesmen or litigants, say in Australia or the United States, who may claim the right to refute or explain derogatory statements made in the English press. On the other hand, in the case of statements falling into the second category, especially reports of proceedings of domestic tribunals and meetings of local authorities, a correction or explanation may go a long way towards meeting any slur which may have been cast upon the plaintiff." See *Khan* v. *Ahmed* [1957] 2 Q.B. 149.

[16] s. 7 (3). But most crimes are of public concern: *Boston* v. *Bagshaw & Sons Ltd.* [1966] 1 W.L.R. 1126.

[17] *Pankhurst* v. *Sowler* (1887) 3 T.L.R. 193.

[18] *Nowlan* v. *Moncton Publishing Co.* [1952] 4 D.L.R. 808.

[19] In relation to any territory comprised in Her Majesty's dominions which is subject to a central and a local legislature, means either of those legislatures.

[20] Means the whole of any territory within those dominions which is subject to a separate legislature.

any international conference to which that Government sends a representative.

(iii) A fair and accurate report of any proceedings in public of an international court.[21]

(iv) A fair and accurate report of any proceedings before any court exercising jurisdiction throughout any part of Her Majesty's dominions outside the United Kingdom or of any proceedings before a court-martial held outside the United Kingdom under the Naval Discipline Act, the Army Act, or the Air Force Act.

(v) A fair and accurate report of any proceedings in public of a body or person appointed to hold a public inquiry by the government or legislature of any part of Her Majesty's dominions outside the United Kingdom.

(vi) A fair and accurate copy of or extract from any register kept in pursuance of any Act of Parliament which is open to inspection by the public, or of any document which is required by the law of any part of the United Kingdom to be open to inspection by the public.

(vii) A notice or advertisement published by or on the authority of any court within the United Kingdom or any judge or officer of such a court.

(2) *Statements privileged subject to explanation or contradiction*

(i) A fair and accurate report of the findings or decision of any of the following associations, or any committee or governing body thereof, that is to say—

    (a) an association formed in the United Kingdom for the purpose of promoting or encouraging the exercise of or interest in any art, science, religion or learning, and empowered by its constitution to exercise control over or adjudicate upon matters of interest or concern to the association or the actions or conduct of any persons subject to such control or adjudication;

    (b) an association formed in the United Kingdom for the purpose of promoting or safeguarding the interests of any trade, business, industry or profession, or of the persons carrying on or engaged in any trade, business, industry or profession, and empowered by its constitution to exercise control over or adjudicate upon matters connected with the trade, industry, business or profession, or the actions or conduct of those persons;

    (c) an association formed in the United Kingdom for the purpose of promoting or safeguarding the interests of any game, sport or pastime to the playing or exercise of which members of the public are invited or admitted, and empowered by its constitution to exercise control over or adjudicate upon persons connected with or taking part in the game, sport or pastime,

being a finding or decision relating to a person who is a member or is subject by virtue of any contract to the control of the association.

---

[21] Means the International Court of Justice or any other judicial or arbitral tribunal deciding matters in dispute between states. Judicial proceedings in a foreign court may have qualified privilege at common law: above. n. 97.

(ii) A fair and accurate report of the proceedings at any public meeting held in the United Kingdom, that is to say, a meeting bona fide and lawfully held for a lawful purpose and for the furtherance or discussion of any matter of public concern, whether the admission to the meeting is general or restricted.[22]

(iii) A fair and accurate report of the proceedings at any meeting or sitting in any part of the United Kingdom of—

    (a) any local authority[23] or committee of a local authority or local authorities;

    (b) any justice or justices of the peace acting otherwise than as a court exercising judicial authority;

    (c) any commission, tribunal, committee or person appointed for the purpose of any inquiry by Act of Parliament, by Her Majesty or by a Minister of the Crown;

    (d) any person appointed by a local authority to hold a local inquiry in pursuance of any Act of Parliament;

    (e) any other tribunal, board, committee or body constituted by or under, and exercising functions under, an Act of Parliament,

not being a meeting or sitting admission to which is denied to representatives of newspapers and other members of the public.

(iv) A fair and accurate report of the proceedings at a general meeting of any company or association constituted, registered or certified by or under any Act of Parliament or incorporated by Royal Charter, not being a private company within the meaning of the Companies Act 1948.

(v) A copy or fair and accurate report or summary of any notice or other matter[24] issued for the information of the public by or on behalf of any Government Department, officer of state, local authority or chief officer of police.[25] This privilege protects only the newspaper publishing the notice and does not cover the source from which the newspaper obtained its information.[26]

§ 61. (4) PROFESSIONAL COMMUNICATIONS

Confidential communications between solicitor and client are privileged. The foundation of the privilege is the importance in the interests of justice that such communications should be free and unfettered by any fear of the consequences. The privilege is limited to the legal profession and covers all professional communications passing for the purpose of getting or giving professional advice,[27] and exists even if the solicitor does not accept the retainer.[28] The communication must be such as, within a very wide and generous ambit of interpretation, is fairly referable to the relationship of

---

[22] See *Khan* v. *Ahmed* [1957] 2 Q.B. 149.
[23] Means any authority or body to which the Public Bodies (Admission to Meetings) Act 1960, applies. Note that this Act confers qualified privilege on the communication of agenda to committee members.
[24] The notice may be oral: *Loveday* v. *Sun Newspapers* (1938) 59 C.L.R. 503 ("Hand-out").
[25] As in *Boston* v. *Bagshaw & Sons Ltd.* [1966] 1 W.L.R. 1126 ("wanted" notice on T V).
[26] *Foster* v. *Watson* (1944) 44 S.R. (N.S.W.) 399.
[27] *Minter* v. *Priest* [1930] A.C. 558, 581.
[28] *Minter* v. *Priest* [1930] A.C. 558, 584.

solicitor and client.[29] Thus the privilege is not confined to litigation: even conversations between a solicitor and client relating to the business of obtaining a loan for the deposit on the purchase of property are protected, as the business is professional business within the ordinary scope of a solicitor's employment.[28] It is probable that this is an instance of qualified, not absolute, privilege, though in *More* v. *Weaver*,[30] where the plaintiff was not represented by counsel, the Court of Appeal held it to be absolute. But in *Minter* v. *Priest*[31] the House of Lords expressly reserved opinion upon the point. This privilege must be distinguished from the privilege in the law of evidence which entitles a litigant, or a party to impending litigation, to object to an order for the production on discovery of a document on the ground that it is a professional communication.[32]

§ 62. MALICE[33]

The defence of qualified privilege is not available if the defendant was actuated by malice.[34] Malice means the presence of an improper motive, or even gross and unreasoning prejudice[35]; it does not necessarily mean personal spite or ill-will, though a desire to injure the plaintiff will usually be present. A statement is malicious when it is made for some purpose other than the purpose for which the law confers the privilege of making it. If the occasion is privileged it is for some reason, and the defendant is only entitled to the protection of the privilege if he uses the occasion for that reason. He is not entitled to the protection if he uses the occasion for some indirect and wrong motive.[36] It is neither necessary nor sufficient to constitute liability that the statement was made without reasonable and probable cause. Not necessary—for if the statement is made maliciously, and is in fact false, the defendant is liable for it although he had good grounds for believing it to be true; malice destroys the privilege, and leaves the defendant subject to the ordinary law by which a mistake, however reasonable, is no defence. Neither is the absence of reasonable and probable cause sufficient in itself to constitute liability. The law requires that a privilege shall be used honestly but not that it shall be used carefully. Negligence in making defamatory statements on a privileged occasion is not actionable.[37] The absence of any positive or honest belief in the truth of the statement is conclusive proof of malice, for the defendant cannot have had a proper motive in saying what he did not believe to be true.[38] On the other hand, a genuine belief in the truth of the statement is quite consistent with the existence of malice. If he uses the occasion for an improper motive he will be liable, even though he said

[29] *Minter* v. *Priest* [1930] A.C. 558, 568.
[30] [1928] 2 K.B. 520. In *Groom* v. *Crocker* [1939] 1 K.B. 194, the C.A. treated the privilege as qualified.
[31] [1930] A.C. 558.
[32] As in *Schneider* v. *Leigh* [1955] 2 Q.B. 195.
[33] See Duncan and Neill, *Defamation*, Chap. 17.
[34] *Horrocks* v. *Lowe* [1975] A.C. 135, 138.
[35] *Horrocks* v. *Lowe* [1975] A.C. 135.
[36] *Horrocks* v. *Lowe* [1975] A.C. 135, 149.
[37] *Clark* v. *Molyneux* (1877) 3 Q.B.D. 237; *Moore* v. *Canadian Pacific S.S. Co.* [1945] 1 All E.R. 128, 133.
[38] *Stewart* v. *Biggs* [1928] N.Z.L.R. 673. Save, indeed, in those exceptional cases in which a man may be under a duty to make some statement or communication, irrespective of whether he personally believes it to be true or not. His duty may make the truth of the matter no concern of his: *British Railway Traffic Co.* v. *The C.R.C. Co.* [1922] 2 K.B. 260, 271.

what he believed to be true: to avoid liability he must have said it for the purpose for which the law allows such a statement to be made.[39] But a court should be slow to draw such an inference.[40]

Onus of proof

The burden of proof lies upon the plaintiff, and the judge has to be satisfied that there is some reasonable evidence of malice to go to the jury.[41] "If, however, the plaintiff can show any example of spite or indirect motive, whether before or after the publication, he will establish his case provided that the examples given are so connected with the state of mind of the defendant as to lead to the conclusion that he was malicious at the date when the libel was published ... each piece of evidence must be regarded separately, and, even if there are a number of instances where a favourable attitude is shown, one case tending to establish malice would be sufficient evidence on which a jury could find for the plaintiff. Nevertheless, each particular instance of alleged malice must be carefully analysed, and if the result is to leave the mind in doubt, then that piece of evidence is valueless as an instance of malice whether it stands alone or is combined with a number of similar instances."[42] But the judge may be entitled to leave the issue of malice generally to the jury.[43]

Evidence of malice

This may be either intrinsic or extrinsic. Intrinsic evidence consists in the contents of the statement itself. Its language, for example, may be so violent or insulting—it may go so far beyond the just requirements of the occasion—as to amount in itself to sufficient evidence of malice.[44] But when considering whether the actual expressions used can be held as evidence of express malice no nice scales should be used.[45] The defendant will be protected even though his language should be violent or excessively strong or prejudiced,[46] if, having regard to all the circumstances of the case, he might honestly and on reasonable grounds have believed that what he wrote or said was true and necessary for his purpose, even though in fact it was not so.[47] Otherwise the protection which the law throws over a privileged occasion would be largely defeated. For the fact that the defendant has been unreasonable does not mean that he has been malicious.[48]

Extrinsic evidence consists in the circumstances under which the state-

---

[39] *Horrocks v. Lowe* [1975] A.C. 138, 146, 149.

[40] *Horrocks v. Lowe* [1975] A.C. 138, 150.

[41] *Horrocks v. Lowe* [1975] A.C. 138, 149. The plaintiff may find the task of proving malice a difficult one since R.S.C., Ord. 82, r. 6, abolished (on the recommendation of the Porter Committee) the power to administer interrogatories as to the sources of the defendant's information or belief. See below, § 66.

[42] *Turner v. M.-G.-M. Pictures Ltd.* [1950] 1 All E.R. 449, 455, *per* Lord Porter. If the case is tried with a jury the judge has a discretion to entertain and rule on a submission made by the defendant at the close of the plaintiff's case that there is no evidence to go to the jury without putting him to his election whether he will or will not call evidence: *Young v. Rank* [1950] 2 K.B. 510.

[43] *Boston v. Bagshaw & Sons Ltd.* [1966] 1 W.L.R. 1126.

[44] *Laughton v. Bishop of Sodor and Man* (1872) L.R. 4 P.C. 495, 505.

[45] *Turner v. M.-G.-M. Pictures Ltd.* [1950] 1 All E.R. 449, 470.

[46] *Horrocks v. Lowe* [1975] A.C. 138.

[47] *Adam v. Ward* [1917] A.C. 309, 339.

[48] *Turner v. M.-G.-M. Pictures Ltd.* [1950] 1 All E.R. 449, 463. See the similar rule in Fair Comment, below, § 66.

ment was made—circumstances which go to show that the statement, even though moderate and justifiable in its language, was in reality animated by some improper motive. It is not necessary that the plaintiff should prove affirmatively what this improper motive really was; it is sufficient to disprove the existence of a proper motive: for example, by showing that the defendant had no genuine belief in the truth of the statement.[49] Again, the behaviour of the defendant or his witnesses at the trial may be some evidence of malice, but the judge should tell the jury whether they would be justified in coming to such a conclusion.[50] A failure to apologise combined with a persistence in a plea of justification is not necessarily evidence of malice.[51]

§ 63. Excess of Privilege

Privilege is forfeited if it is exceeded—that is to say, if the publication of the defamatory statement is more extensive than the occasion of the privilege requires and justifies. The question whether privilege has been exceeded seems to be distinct from the question of whether there is evidence of malice.[52] It is also a question of law for the court and not of fact for the jury.[53] Certain forms of privilege, indeed, permit of publication to the whole world: for example, the reports of judicial proceedings. Privilege such as this cannot be exceeded in the sense now under consideration. So "where a man, through the medium of Hansard's reports of the proceedings in Parliament, publishes to the world vile slanders of a civil, naval, or military servant of the Crown in relation to the discharge by that servant of the duties of his office, he selects the world as his audience, and it is the duty of the heads of the service to which the servant belongs . . . to publish his vindication to the same audience to which his traducer has addressed himself."[54] "Do what you will, the stern chase after a lie that has got the start is apt to be a long one."[55] But in other cases the privilege is limited to publication to certain persons only; and any disregard, whether intentional or negligent, of the limits thus imposed is termed an excess of privilege, and deprives the defendant of the benefit of it.[56] Thus a message which would have been privileged had it been sent in a closed letter was unprivileged because sent by telegraph, for it was thereby published to the telegraph operator.[57]

Newspapers in no special position

This question often arises in relation to charges made in newspapers against public men. If such a charge is solely an assertion of fact, so that the defence of fair comment is not open,[58] a defendant newspaper which is

---

[49] *Clark* v. *Molyneux* (1877) 3 Q.B.D. 237, 245; *Watt* v. *Longsdon* [1930] 1 K.B. 130.

[50] *Turner* v. *M.-G.-M. Pictures Ltd.* [1950] 1 All E.R. 449, 469.

[51] *Broadway Approvals* v. *Odhams Press Ltd.* [1965] 1 W.L.R. 805, which also see on proof of malice if defendant is a corporation.

[52] *Horrocks* v. *Lowe* [1975] A.C. 138, 151.

[53] *Adam* v. *Ward* [1917] A.C. 309, 318, 320-321, 327, 348.

[54] *Adam* v. *Ward* [1917] A.C. 309, 343, *per* Lord Atkinson.

[55] *Adam* v. *Ward* [1917] A.C. 309, 324, *per* Lord Dunedin.

[56] There is another use sometimes made of the phrase "excess of privilege" in which it means, not an excessive publication of a privileged statement, but the improper and malicious use of that privilege. In this latter sense evidence of excess means merely evidence of malice: see Lord Porter in *Turner* v. *M.-G.-M. Pictures Ltd.* [1950] 1 All E.R. 449, 462.

[57] *Williamson* v. *Freer* (1874) L.R. 9 C.P. 393.

[58] If fair comment can be pleaded, the widest latitude is given to the critic: *Slim* v. *Daily Telegraph Ltd.* [1968] 2 Q.B. 157.

unable or unwilling to justify its allegations sometimes pleads privilege. The privilege is said to be created by the interest which the public at large have in hearing the details of such a charge against such a person. But the common law does not recognise any special privilege as attaching to the profession of journalism.[59] A journalist, like everyone else, is subject to the ordinary law: even a lady film critic may have her criticisms commented on by her victims.[60] A journalist who obtains information reflecting on a public man has no more right than any other private citizen to publish his assertions to the world at large[61]; such assertions are not privileged merely because the general topic developed in the article is of public interest.[62] It will be otherwise, of course, if the assertion is contained in a fair and accurate report of a public meeting or a judicial proceeding.[63] "It may be true in one sense to say that [newspapers] owe a duty to their readers to publish any and every item of news that may interest them. But this is not such a duty as makes every communication in their paper relating to a matter of public interest a privileged one. If it were, the power of the press to libel public men with impunity would in the absence of malice be almost unlimited."[64] So in *Chapman* v. *Lord Ellesmere*[65] it was held that, as the law then stood,[66] *The Times* newspaper (as distinct from the Racing Calendar) was not protected by privilege when it published a decision of the Stewards of the Jockey Club, although it was an accurate report of the decision.

It is not necessarily in the public interest to publish what interests the public.[67] A laxer view is taken in the United States, where public officials,[68] or even persons in the public eye,[69] must prove actual malice in an action for a libel on their public life. In England a Report published by Justice,[70] and written by a sub-committee of lawyers and journalists,[71] proposed that the Press should be given a new qualified privilege for statements based upon information which might reasonably be believed to be true, provided that the defendant published a reasonable statement from the plaintiff by way of explanation if so requested, and, if necessary, an apology. Outside Fleet Street the Report has not been well received whether in Parliament,[72] or in academic publications,[73] or by the Faulks Committee,[74] but the legislature of New South Wales has introduced such a defence.[75]

---

[59] *Truth (N.Z.) Ltd.* v. *Holloway* [1960] N.Z.L.R. 69, 83.
[60] *Turner* v. *M.-G.-M. Pictures Ltd.* [1950] 1 All E.R. 449. See also R. Churchill, *What I Said About the Press* (London, 1957).
[61] *Loveday* v. *Sun Newspapers Ltd.* (1938) 59 C.L.R. 503, 513.
[62] *Truth (N.Z.) Ltd.* v. *Holloway* [1960] N.Z.L.R. 69. (The ruling was not challenged on appeal to the J.C: [1960] 1 W.L.R. 997.)
[63] See *Russell* v. *Norfolk (Duke of)* [1949] 1 All E.R. 109; *Green* v. *Blake* [1948] I.R. 242; Lloyd, "The Disciplinary Powers of Professional Bodies" (1950) 13 M.L.R. 281, 297–299.
[64] *Chapman* v. *Ellesmere (Lord)* [1932] 2 K.B. 431, 474–475, *per* Romer L.J.
[65] [1932] 2 K.B. 431.
[66] The report would now be privileged under the Defamation Act 1952; see above, § 52.
[67] *London Artists Ltd.* v. *Littler* [1968] 1 W.L.R. 607, 615.
[68] *New York Times* v. *Sullivan*, 376 U.S. 245 (1964).
[69] *Curtis Publishing Co.* v. *Butts*, 87 S.Ct. 1975 (1967).
[70] *The Law and the Press* (London, 1965).
[71] One of whom has since changed his mind.
[72] 274 H.L.Deb., col. 1371. Lord Goodman has said that "the frequent assertion that newspapers have in their archives hundreds of files which would reveal dreadful goings-on has never been established to the satisfaction of any conscientious witness."
[73] Lord Lloyd of Hampstead, "The Law and the Press" [1966] C.L.P. 43; Heuston, "Recent Developments in the Law of Defamation" (1966) *The Irish Jurist*, Vol. i, p. 247.
[74] Cmnd. 5909, § 211.
[75] *Gorton* v. *A.B.C.* (1973) 1 A.C.T.R. 6.

Presence of uninterested persons

No publication, however, which is reasonably necessary for the effective use of the defendant's privilege amounts to an excess of it. Another way of putting this point is to say that there is an ancillary privilege for such incidental but necessary publications.[76] So as under current business practice the reasonable and ordinary way of getting a document written and despatched to its addressee is to dictate it to a typist, the publication of its defamatory contents to the typist attracts the same privilege as its subsequent publication to the addressee.[77] But in a business communication containing a very serious allegation against a man's character more care ought to be taken in limiting the communication to the higher officials of a firm than in writing an ordinary business letter.[78] Again, in *Toogood* v. *Spyring*,[79] in which Parke B, gave his classic exposition of the nature of a privileged occasion, the court held that, when the defendant charged the plaintiff (who was employed by him) in the presence of a third person with having broken open a cellar door when drunk, the occasion was privileged. The business of life could not well be carried on if unnecessary restraints were imposed on these communications. As the plaintiff has an interest in hearing the charges made against him there can be no doubt that the occasion is privileged, even though the statement is made to the plaintiff himself and so could not by itself have given him a cause of action.[80]

§ 64. JOINT LIABILITY

It is clear that the agents through whom a person properly publishes a privileged communication are themselves covered by the like privilege: for example, a printer who prints a privileged document, the printing of which is not an excess of privilege, or a solicitor who in the course of his duty towards his client publishes a statement which that client is privileged to publish.[81] It is not so clear what the position is if one (or more) of the co-defendants is inspired by malice. Does this defeat the privilege of his co-defendants? The earlier case of *Smith* v. *Streatfield*,[82] in which it was held that it did, was overruled by *Egger* v. *Chelmsford (Viscount)*,[83] in which four of the eleven defendants to a libel action against whom malice had not been found appealed successfully against a judgment that they were infected by the malice of the other seven defendants. Three of the four successful appellants each had an original privilege of his own, distinct from that of the others, and so far the decision can hardly be criticised. But the fourth

---

[76] *Bryanston Finance Ltd.* v. *de Vries* [1975] 1 Q.B. 703.
[77] *Bryanston Finance Ltd.* v. *de Vries* [1975] 1 Q.B. 703, 727.
[78] *Roff* v. *British and French Chemical Co.* [1918] 2 K.B. 677, 684.
[79] (1834) 1 C.M. & R. 181.
[80] It is submitted that the decision of the Court of Appeal to the contrary in *White* v. *Stone (J. & F.) Ltd.* [1939] 2 K.B. 827, is based upon a mistaken view of the authorities: see Goodhart, "Defamatory Statements and Privileged Occasions" (1940) 56 L.Q.R. 262.
[81] *Baker* v. *Carrick* [1894] 1 Q.B. 838.
[82] [1913] 3 K.B. 764.
[83] [1965] 1 Q.B. 248. Yet it is worth noting that the House of Commons specifically refused to accept the recommendation of the Porter Committee (paras. 127-132) to abolish the rule in *Smith* v. *Streatfield*: see H.C.Deb. Stdg. Cttee. B., March 6, 1952. But "we have come after several years to find that the law is as Lord Porter's Committee recommended it should be": [1965] 1 Q.B. 248, 265, *per* Lord Denning M.R., although the Porter Committee (para. 132) (unlike Lord Denning) insisted that there must not be negligence in failing to know of the other's malice.

appellant was the secretary of the defendants' committee. He too was successful, either on the narrow ground that such a person has an independent privilege, which arises whenever the official mouthpiece of a quasi-judicial body communicates its decisions, or on the wider ground that no man ought to be responsible for the malice of another except in cases of vicarious liability.[84] It is not easy to reconcile this broad ground with the view that it is the *occasion*, rather than the *person*, which is the subject of privilege,[85] but *Egger* v. *Chelmsford* has been followed.[86] It is uncertain whether the principle in *Egger* v. *Chelmsford* extends to Fair Comment as well as Privilege, but probably it does.[87]

§ 65. FAIR COMMENT[88]

A fair comment on a matter which is of public interest or is submitted to public criticism is not actionable. This right is one of the aspects of the fundamental principle of freedom of expression, and the courts are zealous to preserve it unimpaired.[89] "It must not be whittled down by legal refinements."[90] The jury are the guardians of the freedom of public comment as well as of private character. It is only on the strongest grounds that a court will set aside a verdict for a defendant when fair comment is pleaded.[91]

Comment or criticism must be carefully distinguished from a statement of fact. The former is not actionable if it relates to a matter which is of public interest; the latter is actionable, even though the facts so stated would, if true, have possessed the greatest public interest and importance. Comment or criticism is essentially a statement of opinion as to the estimate to be formed of a man's writings or actions. Being therefore a mere matter of opinion, and so incapable of definite proof, he who expresses it is not called upon by the law to justify it as being true, but is allowed to express it, even though others disagree with it, provided that it is honest.[92]

Nature of defence

Salmond held the view that fair comment is simply an instance of qualified privilege.[93] Although this view has the support of Willes J.,[94] there is considerable authority in favour of another view, which may be expressed as follows: The defence of fair comment is a denial of the libel, a traverse of the allegation in the statement of claim[95]; the defence of privilege is an admission of the libel, but a claim that it was published in such

---

[84] The view favoured by Lord Denning and Harman L.J. (but not Davies L.J.) in *Egger* v. *Chelmsford* [1965] 1 Q.B. 248, 263.

[85] See above, § 55.

[86] *Riddick* v. *TBM* [1977] Q.B. 881.

[87] Faulks Report, § 261.

[88] Johnston, "Uncertainties in the Defence of Fair Comment" (1978) 8 N.Z.U.L.R. 359 (one of the few academic articles on this topic).

[89] *Kemsley* v. *Foot* [1951] 2 K.B. 34, 46-47. See the history of the defence discussed by Diplock, K.C., in [1952] A.C. 345, 349.

[90] *Slim* v. *Daily Telegraph Ltd.* [1968] 2 Q.B. 157, 170, *per* Lord Denning M.R.

[91] *Odger* v. *Mortimer* (1873) 23 L.T. 472.

[92] *Cherneskey* v. *Armadale Publishers Ltd.* (1978) 79 D.L.R. (3d.) 180.

[93] 6th ed., s. 145 (9).

[94] *Henwood* v. *Harrison* (1872) L.R. 7 C.P. 606, 625.

[95] *Peter Walker & Son Ltd.* v. *Hodgson* [1909] 1 K.B. 239, 250.

circumstances as afford the defendant an immunity from the ordinary consequences of publishing a libel, a plea in confession and avoidance. "A privileged occasion is one on which the privileged person is entitled to do something which no one who is not within the privilege is entitled to do on that occasion. A person in such a position may say or write about another person things which no other person in the kingdom can be allowed to say or write. But, in the case of a criticism upon a published work, every person is entitled to do and is forbidden to do exactly the same things, and therefore the occasion is not privileged."[96] Therefore, the question to be put to the jury is, not whether the article is privileged, but whether it is or is not a libel.

Fair comment sui generis

It is true that in *Merivale* v. *Carson*, Bowen L.J. thought the question "rather academical than practical,"[97] but that must be taken merely to refer to the case then before the court. For if fair comment is no libel, the absence of malice should afford no defence if the comment is unfair; conversely the presence of malice should raise no liability if the comment is fair.[97] There is much to be said in favour of that opinion. If there are two criticisms of a book by different writers, both couched in similar terms, and each being on its face fair comment, it seems difficult to say that one exceeds the limit of fair comment because the writer of it is actuated by malice against the author, whereas the other does not exceed those limits because the writer is not so actuated. But such is now the law.[98] The Court of Appeal held in *Thomas* v. *Bradbury, Agnew & Co. Ltd.*,[99] and it has since been accepted in the House of Lords,[1] that express malice will destroy a plea of fair comment. It does not, however, follow that fair comment is merely one branch of qualified privilege. Round what is the privilege thrown, comment or only fair comment? If all comment be privileged, then honest belief would be a good defence to an action in respect of a comment prima facie unfair. No one has yet suggested that this is the law. It would be manifestly absurd. But if the privilege is thrown only round fair comments, and the presence of malice prevents a comment from being fair, there is no need to talk of privilege at all; or, if we needs must, the privilege is absolute, not qualified. In any event there are two admitted differences between the defence of fair comment and the defence of qualified privilege. If the publication was upon a privileged occasion, the burden is upon the plaintiff to prove express malice; the defendant, on the other hand, has first the burden of showing that a comment is fair before the burden of proving malice is cast back upon the plaintiff. On the other hand, the plaintiff who has submitted his work or his acts to public criticism bears the onus of proving that a prima facie protected occasion is not in fact protected, whereas the defendant who relies upon a qualified privilege has affirmatively to prove the existence of the privilege.[2] Again, some instances of abuse of privilege (*e.g.* excessive

---

[96] *Merivale* v. *Carson* (1887) 20 Q.B.D. 275, 280, *per* Lord Esher.

[97] 20 Q.B.D., 275, 283.

[98] See Duncan and Neill, *Defamation* (1978) § 12.36.

[99] [1906] 2 K.B. 627. This was the only successful libel action ever brought against the publishers of *Punch*. See the interesting account of the case by the defendants' counsel, A. Birrell, *Things Past Redress* (1937), pp. 161–162.

[1] *Sutherland* v. *Stopes* [1925] A.C. 47, 63–64.

[2] *Thomas* v. *Bradbury, Agnew & Co.* [1906] 2 K.B. 627, 640.

publication) can have no application to the defence of fair comment. The analogy between the defences of qualified privilege and fair comment is indeed far from close. It seems, contrary to the opinion of Salmond,[3] that the defence of fair comment is *sui generis*, and not merely a particular instance of qualified privilege.

§ 66. ELEMENTS OF FAIR COMMENT

The defence has three elements. It must be shown that the words complained of are (1) comment, (2) fair comment, and (3) fair comment on a matter of public interest.

(1) Comment and fact

It is essential to the plea of fair comment that the defamatory matter must appear on the face of it to be a comment and not a statement of fact. To come within a plea of fair comment the facts on which the comment is based must be stated or referred to and the imputation must appear as an expression of the defendant's opinion on those facts. It is a question for the jury (subject to the direction of the judge) whether the words, on their true construction in their context, amount to a positive statement of fact or an expression of opinion or inference. If they are the former they must be justified. If the defendant cannot justify them, then the only issue for the jury is the amount of damages.[4] Sometimes it is difficult to distinguish fact from comment or to decide how far the facts upon which comment is made have been set out or referred to in the alleged libel. In *Kemsley* v. *Foot*[5] the respondents had published an attack upon the conduct of one of Lord Beaverbrook's newspapers, with which the appellant, also a newspaper proprietor, had no connection, under the heading "Lower than Kemsley." It was argued that the plea of fair comment (as distinct from justification) was not open to the respondents because the subject-matter on which the comment "Lower than Kemsley"[6] was made was not indicated with sufficient particularity. But the House of Lords held that a sufficient substratum of fact could be found or indicated in the words complained of, namely, that Lord Kemsley was the active proprietor of and responsible for the Kemsley Press, which had a wide public circulation.[7]

The task of the critic in such a case would be impossible if he had to set out in detail the facts upon which his criticism was based. It is true that not all of those to whom the libel has been published will have read for themselves the issues of the periodical in question, but "its contents and con-

---

[3] So also F. R. Y. Radcliffe, "The Defence of Fair Comment" (1907) 23 L.Q.R. 97, and Collins M.R. in *Thomas* v. *Bradbury, Agnew* [1906] 2 K.B. 627, 641. The judgment of Collins M.R. does not really face the difficulty. He seems to assume that the presence of malice has "distorted" (p. 638) or "warped" (p. 642) the defendant's judgment, although he admits that it is "possible for a person to have a spite against another and yet to bring a perfectly dispassionate judgment to bear upon his literary merits." It is this latter case which really raises the problem.

[4] As in *London Artists Ltd.* v. *Littler* [1969] 2 Q.B. 375.

[5] [1952] A.C. 345.

[6] "It is not in my opinion a statement of fact that a newspaper is low: it is a comment. It may be a statement of fact to say that a man is fraudulent, for there is a legal sanction for fraud, but there is no legal sanction for publishing low newspapers": [1952] A.C. 345, 361, *per* Lord Oaksey.

[7] The proceedings were eventually compromised: *The Times*, June 26, 1952.

duct are open to comment on the ground that the public have at least the opportunity of ascertaining for themselves the subject-matter on which the comment is founded."[8] A similar principle applies to literary and artistic works submitted to the public: a critic is not shut out from the defence of fair comment because he has confined his remarks on, say, the first night of a new play to the words "This is a disgraceful production."[9] Although it is therefore not necessary for the defendant to have all the facts at the forefront of his mind, no man can comment upon future facts. The facts which form the basis of the comment must be in existence when the comment is made.[10]

(2) Fair comment on facts truly stated

Here there are three points to be considered: (i) the facts must be truly stated; (ii) the comment must be honest; (iii) imputations of corrupt or dishonourable motives must be warranted by the facts.

(i) *The facts must be truly stated*

The comment must not misstate facts: no comment can be fair which is built upon facts which are invented or misstated.[11] As Sir Alexander Cockburn C.J. once said: "To say that you may first libel a man, and then comment upon him is obviously absurd."[12] So when in a review of a play the defendant stated falsely that it contained an incident of adultery, his plea of fair comment failed.[13] Originally it was necessary to show that every statement of fact in the words complained of (however minor or unimportant) was true. But now the Defamation Act 1952, s. 6, provides that in an action for libel or slander in respect of words[14] consisting partly of allegations of fact and partly of expressions of opinion, a defence of fair comment shall not fail by reason only that the truth of every allegation of fact is not proved if the expression of opinion is fair comment having regard to such of the facts alleged or referred to in the words complained of as are proved. So now it is enough for the commentator to get his basic facts right.[15] It has been argued that this section has made a radical change in the law by conferring immunity in respect of unproved allegations of fact if the allegations of fact which are proved are sufficient to support the comment.[16] This was certainly not what the Porter Committee intended,[17] but it may well be what Parliament intended,[18] although whether it has succeeded in carrying that intention into effect is another matter. It is submitted that it has not,[19] and

---

[8] [1952] A.C. 345, 355-356, *per* Lord Porter.
[9] *McQuire* v. *Western Morning News* [1903] 2 K.B. 100 is a good illustration of this. The defendant will of course have to supply particulars of the facts on which he relies before trial; but he is not required to justify them all: see below, n. 24.
[10] *Cohen* v. *Daily Telegraph Ltd.* [1968] 1 W.L.R. 916.
[11] *Hunt* v. *Star Newspaper Ltd.* [1908] 2 K.B. 309, 317, 320; *Kemsley* v. *Foot* [1952] A.C. 345.
[12] *R.* v. *Carden* (1879) 5 Q.B.D. 1, 8.
[13] *Merivale* v. *Carson* (1887) 20 Q.B.D. 275.
[14] As defined in s. 16 (1): see above, § 52.
[15] *London Artists Ltd.* v. *Littler* [1969] 2 Q.B. 375, 391.
[16] Gatley, *Libel*, p. 332.
[17] See para. 89 of the Report.
[18] See Standing Committee B., H.C.Deb., March 6, 1952, cols. 846-855, and 500 H.C.Deb., col. 794.
[19] *London Artists Ltd.* v. *Littler* [1969] 2 Q.B. 375, 391.

the defence of fair comment still protects only the comment, and not unjustified statements of fact.

The rolled-up plea. In view of the distinction thus drawn between comment and matter of fact, and in view of the circumstances that comment and fact are so frequently combined in the same statement, the plea of fair comment used to be formulated as to justify at the same time the statements of fact thus included in the allegations complained of. The usual form of such a plea was that "in so far as the statements complained of are statements of fact they are true in substance and in fact, and in so far as they consist of comment they are fair comment on a matter of public interest." Such a plea, known as the "rolled-up plea," was a plea of fair comment only, and not of justification coupled with a plea of fair comment.[20] Although this plea was not regarded by the courts with favour it was much used, for the defendant could not be compelled to give particulars of the facts which he proposed to prove at the trial in support of his plea.[21] But now the defendant may be required to furnish "particulars stating which of the words complained of he alleges are statements of fact and of the facts and matters he relies on in support of the allegation that the words are true."[22] But the plaintiff is not entitled to such particulars if the defendant does not plead the "rolled-up plea" but only the general plea of fair comment.[23] Then the defendant is only obliged to give particulars of the basic facts on which he relies in support of his plea.[24]

Comment and privileged statements of fact. If a statement of fact is itself privileged, and the subject-matter is one which is open to comment, the plea of fair comment is not excluded by the circumstance that the statement of fact on which the comment proceeds is erroneous. For example, he who comments on the statements contained in the judgment of a court of justice, or made by a witness in the box,[25] or contained in a parliamentary paper,[26] may plead fair comment, although the statements are mistaken.

(ii) *The comment must be honest*

The comment must be honestly believed to be true, and not inspired by any malicious motive. It is now settled since the decision of the Court of Appeal in *Thomas* v. *Bradbury, Agnew & Co.*[27] that a comment which is objectively and prima facie fair may become unfair if made with a malicious motive. The absence of any genuine belief in the truth of the comment is conclusive proof of malice, for no man can have a proper motive for making defamatory statements which he does not believe to be justified. Even a

[20] *Sutherland* v. *Stopes* [1925] A.C. 47, 62–63.
[21] For this would have been an indirect way of compelling him to specify which of the statements complained of were statements of fact and which expressions of opinion, and this is a question to be decided by the jury.
[22] R.S.C., Ord. 82, r. 3.
[23] *Lord* v. *Sunday Telegraph Ltd.* [1971] 1 Q.B. 235.
[24] The defendant is not required to prove the truth of every fact so adduced; it is enough if he can establish sufficient facts to support the comment to the satisfaction of the jury: *Kemsley* v. *Foot* [1952] A.C. 345. "It is one thing to publish a defamatory statement of fact; it is quite another to allege a defamatory statement of fact in a pleading in order to show that a public comment was fair": *Kemsley* v. *Foot* [1952] A.C. 345, 361, *per* Lord Oaksey.
[25] *Grech* v. *Odhams Press Ltd.* [1958] 2 Q.B. 275, 285.
[26] *Cook* v. *Alexander* [1974] 1 Q.B. 279.
[27] [1906] 2 K.B. 627. See above, § 65.

comment genuinely believed to be true, however, will be actionable as unfair if it is inspired by any improper and malicious motive, though a court should be slow to draw such an inference.[28] It is sometimes said that comment is also to be classed as unfair, even in the absence of any dishonesty or malice, if the critic fails to show a certain degree of moderation, judgment and competence.[29] It is said that there is a certain measure of violence or perverseness on the part of a critic which will itself condemn his criticism as unfair and actionable. But this is not so. To apply any such test would mean that any jury would be at liberty to find a comment unfair simply because they did not agree with it and thought it unduly severe: it is of the highest importance to the community that the critic of literary or artistic matters should not have his work judged by the standard of "the man on the Clapham omnibus."[30] The violence, exaggeration or perverseness of a critic has not in itself any operation in making his criticism unfair, but is merely evidence that his criticism is not honest or that it is inspired by malice. "The question which the jury must consider is this: would any fair man, however prejudiced he may be, however exaggerated or obstinate his views, have said that which this criticism has said of the work which is criticised?"[31] In *Turner* v. *M.-G.-M. Pictures Ltd.*[32] Lord Porter said he would adopt these words, "except that I would substitute 'honest' for 'fair' lest some suggestion of reasonableness instead of honesty should be read in." It would be better if the defence was simply called Comment.[33]

(iii) *Imputations of corrupt motives*

A man's moral character is not a permissible subject of adverse comment, and this is so even though the person attacked occupies some public position which makes his character a matter of public interest. He who says or suggests that a person is dishonest, corrupt, immoral, untruthful, inspired by base and sordid motives, must either justify his accusation by proving it to be true, or show that the imputation is a correct inference from the facts commented on. It may be fair comment mistakenly to accuse an author of folly, but not to accuse him of vice; of want of dignity, but not of want of honesty; of incapacity, but not of corruption; of bad taste, but not of mendacity.[34] This important limitation upon the right of criticism was

---

[28] *Horrocks* v. *Lowe* [1975] A.C. 135, 150.

[29] *Wason* v. *Walter* (1868) L.R. 4 Q.B. 73, 96.

[30] *McQuire* v. *Western Morning News* [1903] 2 K.B. 100, 109; *Turner* v. *M.-G.-M. Pictures Ltd.* [1950] 1 All E.R. 449, 475.

[31] *Merivale* v. *Carson* (1887) 20 Q.B.D. 275, 281, *per* Lord Esher. See also *Silkin* v. *Beaverbrook Newspapers Ltd.* [1958] 1 W.L.R. 743; and the Faulks Report, § 177.

[32] [1950] 1 All E.R. 449, 461. In *Lea* v. *Justice of the Peace Ltd.* (*sub nom. Privacy and the Press*, Butterworths, 1947) there is a valuable discussion between Hilbery J. and Sir Valentine Holmes, K.C., on the scope of the defences of justification and fair comment. "*Holmes*: I have always thought that it is a tremendous misfortune, especially when you are trying to deal with lay clients, that a plea of fair comment is called fair comment, because it is so difficult to make a person understand that a comment which they think is grossly unfair may nevertheless be perfectly fair comment for the purpose of establishing a defence. *Hilbery*: It is easy for the lay mind to think that by 'fair comment' you mean 'moderate comment.' *Holmes*: Quite, my Lord."

[33] Faulks Report, § 177.

[34] But the "private life of a Member of Parliament may be material to his fitness to occupy his public office": *Lyle-Samuel* v. *Odhams Ltd.* [1920] 1 K.B. 135, 146, *per* Scrutton L.J. And literary productions can be criticised for their treatment of life and morals as freely as for bad writing: *Kemsley* v. *Foot* [1952] A.C. 345, 356.

established in *Campbell* v. *Spottiswoode*,[35] in which it was held actionable to suggest, however honestly, that the editor of a religious magazine, in advocating a scheme for missions to the heathen, was in reality an impostor inspired by motives of pecuniary gain. Such comment goes outside the realm of criticism of the plaintiff in relation to the book, its subject-matter, or the plaintiff as an author.[36] "A writer in a public paper," said Sir Alexander Cockburn C.J.,[37] *arguendo*, "may comment on the conduct of public men in the strongest terms; but if he imputes dishonesty, he must be prepared to justify."[38] In his judgment he reasserted the point. "It seems to me that a line must be drawn between hostile criticism on a man's public conduct and the motives by which that conduct may be supposed to be influenced; and that you have no right to impute to a man in his conduct as a citizen—even though it be open to ridicule or disapprobation—base, sordid, dishonest and wicked motives, unless there is so much ground for the imputation that a jury shall be of opinion, not only that you may have honestly entertained some mistaken belief upon the subject, but that your belief is well founded and not without cause."[39] Such a personal attack, therefore, is to be regarded as a defamatory statement of fact, and not as a mere comment. It is true that there is some authority for the view that it is enough for the defendant to prove that the attack was a reasonable inference from the proved facts,[40] but such a view runs counter to the whole nature of the defence.[41] If reasonableness is irrelevant in assessing the fairness of the comment, it should also be irrelevant here.

(3) What matters may be commented on

The right of comment is universal; there is full liberty to criticise all men and things of public interest, provided that the criticism is honest. Further, everyone is entitled to comment. A newspaper reporter or editor has the same rights as a private citizen, neither more nor less, so it does not matter whether the comment appears in a Sunday newspaper with an enormous circulation or in a private letter.[42] But it is only in a limited class of cases that there is any right to express one's own opinion honestly and fearlessly regardless of whether others can be induced to agree with it or not. The cases in which this right exists may be divided into two classes—namely, (i) matters of public interest or concern[43]; and (ii) matters which, although of no public interest, have been submitted to criticism by the persons concerned. In all other cases the defendant will be liable unless he can prove that the alleged libel is true not only in its allegations of fact but also in any comments made thereon.[44] He must justify both the facts and the comment.

---

[35] (1863) 3 B. & S. 769; 32 L.J.Q.B. 185.
[36] *Wilson* v. *Manawatu Daily Times Co. Ltd.* [1957] N.Z.L.R. 735, 742.
[37] *Campbell* v. *Spottiswoode* (1863) 32 L.J.Q.B. 185, 196.
[38] Approved in *Greville* v. *Wiseman* [1967] N.Z.L.R. 795, 800.
[39] (1863) 32 L.J.Q.B. 185, 199. The report in 3 B. & S. 769, 776 is slightly different.
[40] *Porter* v. *Mercury Newspapers Ltd.* [1964] Tas.S.R. 279.
[41] *Dakhyl* v. *Labouchère* [1908] 2 K.B. 325n., 329. See Duncan and Neill, *Defamation*, §§ 12, 25.
[42] *Silkin* v. *Beaverbrook Newspapers Ltd.* [1958] 1 W.L.R. 743, 746. See also above, § 57.
[43] *London Artists Ltd.* v. *Littler* [1969] 2 Q.B. 375.
[44] *Sutherland* v. *Stopes* [1925] A.C. 47, 62. "But that is not very good English, because I do not think a comment can ever be said to be true. It can only be said to be justified": Holmes, K.C., *arguendo* in *Lea* v. *Justice of the Peace Ltd.* (1947), *sub nom. Privacy and the Press*, 165. "True comment" presumably means comment which in the opinion of the court is warranted by the facts and well founded.

(i) *Matters of public interest or concern*

For example, the administration of justice,[45] the conduct of the government and of public servants,[46] the mode in which local authorities and other public bodies perform their functions,[47] the management of public institutions,[48] or of a private business of large extent,[49] the conduct of public worship in the Church of England.[50] It makes no difference that the public interest in the matter in question is limited to a particular locality, instead of extending throughout the realm. That which is primarily of public interest to the citizens of Manchester is indirectly of public interest to all England.[51]

(ii) *Matters submitted to public criticism by the persons concerned*

He who voluntarily gives up his right of privacy by submitting himself or his deeds to public scrutiny and judgment must submit to the exercise of a right of public comment. This right, therefore, extends to books and every form of published literature, works of art publicly exhibited, and public musical or dramatic performances.[52] It should be noted that works of criticism are themselves submitted to public scrutiny and their subject-matter and style may thus in turn be criticised.[53]

Burden of proof

The burden of proving that a comment is fair is on the defendant. He must establish that the facts upon which the comment is based are true, and that the comment thereupon is warranted in the sense that it is such as might be made by an honest man. Once the defendant has established that in this sense the comment is fair, the onus is shifted to the plaintiff if he wishes to prove that the prima facie protection is displaced by the presence of malice in the defendant.[54] In other words, there is a two-stage test, the first being objective and the second subjective. When the publisher is not the writer, as when a newspaper publishes a letter to the editor, it may be vital to keep them separate.[55]

It is a question for the jury whether the words are statements of fact or expressions of opinion, and, if the latter, whether they are fair or not. But it is for the judge to decide in the first place (1) whether the words are capable of being statements of fact, (2) whether the subject is one which is in law open to comment, and (3) whether there is any reasonable evidence to go to the jury that the comment is unfair.[56]

---

[45] *Hibbins* v. *Lee* (1864) 4 F. & F. 243 (conduct of magistrates). The law relating to contempt of court should here be borne in mind.
[46] *Henwood* v. *Harrison* (1872) L.R. 7 C.P. 606.
[47] *Purcell* v. *Sowler* (1877) 2 C.P.D. 215.
[48] *Cox* v. *Feeney* (1863) 4 F. & F. 13, 20.
[49] *London Artists Ltd.* v. *Littler* [1969] 2 Q.B. 375 (four West End theatres).
[50] *Kelly* v. *Tinling* (1865) L.R. 1 Q.B. 699.
[51] *Purcell* v. *Sowler* (1877) 2 C.P.D. 215, 218.
[52] *Turner* v. *M.-G.-M. Pictures Ltd.* [1950] 1 All E.R. 449 (insensitive but honest comment on broadcast by film critic).
[53] *Turner* v. *M.-G.-M. Pictures Ltd.* [1950] 1 All E.R. 449.
[54] *Jones* v. *Skelton* [1963] 1 W.L.R. 1362, 1378.
[55] *Cherneskey* v. *Armadale Publishers Ltd.* (1978) 79 D.L.R. 180.
[56] *London Artists Ltd.* v. *Littler* [1969] 2 Q.B. 375.

Effect of malice of writer on printer

We have seen that the printer of a privileged document may not be protected if the writer was actuated by malice.[57] The same rule applies to one who prints comment on a matter of public interest. Hence the editor of a literary journal who publishes a contributed article containing criticisms of the works of a living writer which he honestly agrees with may yet be liable for the malice which, unknown to him, has actuated the author of the article.[58] In practice, however, since 1949 this will probably only occur when the plaintiff is aware of the identity of the contributor. For in that year an amendment to the Rules of Court,[59] made on the recommendation of the Porter Committee,[60] provided that where a defendant, whether a newspaper or an ordinary person, pleads fair comment or qualified privilege no interrogatories as to the defendant's source of information or grounds of belief shall be allowed.[61] This "newspaper rule," as it has been called, is limited to interlocutory proceedings in actions for defamation, and does not extend to actions for breach of confidence.[62]

§ 67. CONSENT[63]

It is a defence that the plaintiff has expressly or impliedly consented to the publication complained of[64]—for example, in cases of slander the aggrieved party sometimes, perhaps rashly, invites the speaker "to repeat that before witnesses."

§ 68. APOLOGY[65]

The offer or the making of an apology is in general no defence to an action for libel, although it may be given in evidence in mitigation of damages.[66] But by section 2 of the Libel Act 1843, in actions for a libel contained in a public newspaper or periodical the defendant may plead that it was inserted without actual malice and without gross negligence and that before the commencement of the action or at the earliest opportunity afterwards he inserted in the newspaper or periodical a full apology, or, if the periodical is ordinarily published at intervals exceeding one week, had offered to publish such apology in any newspaper or periodical selected by the plaintiff. Every such defence must be accompanied by a payment of money into court by way of amends.[67] Although neither the fact nor the amount of the payment

---

[57] Above, § 63.
[58] See the example given by the Porter Committee, s. 130, and *Lyon* v. *Daily Telegraph* [1943] K.B. 746.
[59] R.S.C., Ord. 82, r. 6. But note that a journalist has no general evidential privilege entitling him not to answer questions: *Att.-Gen.* v. *Mulholland* [1963] 2 Q.B. 477.
[60] Cmnd. 7536 (1948) ss. 182–184.
[61] This also prohibits interrogatories as to the defendant's actual information and knowledge: *Adams* v. *Sunday Pictorial Newspapers* (1920) *Ltd.* [1951] 1 K.B. 354.
[62] *British Steel Corporation* v. *Granada Television* [1980] 3 W.L.R.774.
[63] See Boberg, "Defence of Consent in a Defamation Action" (1961) 78 S.A.L.J. 54.
[64] *Collerton* v. *Maclean* [1962] N.Z.L.R. 1045.
[65] See Fleming, "Retraction and Reply" (1978) 12 U.B.C. Law Rev. 15.
[66] See below, § 212.
[67] Libel Act 1845, s. 2.

into court must be disclosed to the jury,[68] it seems to be the practice to disclose both in the pleadings. But in practice little use is made of this defence, for if any branch of the defence fails the plaintiff must succeed in the action, damages are assessed without regard to the payment into court and the defendant is liable for the whole costs of the action.[69] In any event, the provisions of section 4 of the Defamation Act 1952, now afford wider protection in appropriate cases.

§ 69. SLANDER ACTIONABLE PER SE[70]

In the following cases slander is actionable *per se* without proof of special damage:–
  (1) An imputation that the plaintiff has committed a criminal offence;
  (2) An imputation that the plaintiff suffers from an existing contagious or infectious disease;
  (3) An imputation of unchastity against a woman;
  (4) An imputation against the plaintiff in the way of his business or office.

(1) Imputation of criminal offence

An imputation of a criminal offence to be actionable *per se* must amount to a direct charge, and must not be a mere suggestion or statement of suspicion.[71] The crime charged need not be indictable; but it must amount to an offence punishable with imprisonment in the first instance and not be an offence punishable by fine merely, even though there is power to imprison in default of payment of the fine.[72] It seems[73] that the basis of this rule is not that the words put the person defamed in jeopardy of a criminal prosecution, but that other people are likely to shun and avoid a person guilty of the conduct alleged.[74] So it is actionable *per se* to say of a man that he is "a convicted person," even though such an allegation does not put him in jeopardy of a prosecution.[75] It would seem to follow that a slander imputing to a corporation the commission of a criminal offence which in the case of a natural person would be punishable with imprisonment is actionable *per se*.[76]

(2) An imputation that the plaintiff suffers from an existing contagious or infectious disease

Here again the basis of the rule is that the imputation is likely to cause other persons to shun the plaintiff. The diseases included are venereal

---

[68] *Joyce* v. *Beaverbrook Newspapers Ltd.* [1959] Ir.Jur.Rep. 20.
[69] See *Bell* v. *Northern Constitution* [1943] N.I. 108 and note in 6 N.I.L.Q. 18. The better procedure is to pay a sum of money into court and plead the apology in mitigation of damages: Chapman, *Statutes*, p. 276; Duncan and Neill, *Defamation*, § 16.09.
[70] See above, § 47.
[71] *Simmons* v. *Mitchell* (1880) 6 App.Cas. 156.
[72] *Ormiston* v. *G. W. Ry.* [1917] 1 K.B. 598, 601. ("You have been travelling First Class with a Third Class ticket.")
[73] *Gray* v. *Jones* [1939] 1 All E.R. 798.
[74] Gatley, *Libel*, p. 84.
[75] *Gray* v. *Jones* [1939] 1 All E.R. 798.
[76] The point was left open by the C.A. in *D. & L. Caterers Ltd.* v. *D'Ajou* [1945] K.B. 364.

disease,[77] leprosy or plague,[78] and probably any contagious skin complaint caused by personal uncleanliness.[79]

(3) Accusation of unchastity

At common law a verbal imputation of unchastity was not actionable *per se*, but it is now provided by the Slander of Women Act 1891 that words spoken and published which impute unchastity or adultery to any women or girl shall not require special damage to render them actionable.[80] The plaintiff cannot recover more costs than damages unless the judge certifies at the end of, or after,[81] the trial that there was reasonable ground for bringing the action.

(4) Imputations in respect of profession, business, or office

Any defamatory imputation upon a man in the way of his profession, business, or office is actionable *per se*: for example, a charge of insolvency against a trader,[82] of incompetence against a surgeon, of ignorance against a lawyer. This is so however humble the profession or calling. A defamatory charge, however, against a man in respect of a business in which he is no longer engaged, or in respect of an office which he no longer holds, is not actionable *per se*.[83] At common law a charge was not actionable *per se* merely because it tended to injure the plaintiff in the way of his business or office; it must have amounted to a charge against him in relation to his business or office. Thus, it was not actionable *per se* to impute dishonesty to a solicitor, unless he was alleged to be dishonest towards his clients.[84] Nor was it actionable *per se* to impute immoral conduct to a schoolmaster except in the way of his business.[85] These cases show that the common law was capable of giving rise to serious injustice.[86] But now the Defamation Act 1952, s. 2, in accordance with the recommendation of the Porter Committee, provides that in an action for slander in respect of words[87] calculated to disparage the plaintiff[88] in any office, profession, calling, trade or business held or carried on by him at the time of the publication,[89] it shall not be necessary to allege or prove special damage, whether or not the words are spoken of the plaintiff in the way of his office, profession, calling, trade or

---

[77] *Houseman* v. *Coulson* [1948] 2 D.L.R. 62.

[78] See the old cases cited in Gatley, *Libel*, p. 90.

[79] Porter Committee's Report, para. 45.

[80] In *Youssoupoff* v. *Metro-Goldwyn-Mayer Pictures* (1934) *The Times*, March 6, p. 5, Avory J. said *obiter* that it was an attack upon a woman's chastity to say that she had been raped. And in the C.A. Scrutton L.J. seems to have been of the same opinion, but Slesser L.J. expressed no opinion: (1934) 50 T.L.R. 581, 584, 587. Unchastity includes lesbianism: *Kerr* v. *Kennedy* [1942] 1 K.B. 409.

[81] *Russo* v. *Cole* [1966] 1 W.L.R. 248.

[82] *Brown* v. *Smith* (1853) 13 C.B. 596.

[83] *Hopwood* v. *Thorn* (1849) 8 C.B. 293. A man may conduct several professions simultaneously: *Bull* v. *Vazquez* [1947] 1 All E.R. 334.

[84] *Hopwood* v. *Muirson* [1945] K.B. 313.

[85] *Jones* v. *Jones* [1916] 2 A.C. 481.

[86] See also the examples given by Earl Jowitt in 177 H.L.Deb. 5s., col. 1103.

[87] As defined in s. 16 (1): see above, § 47.

[88] This will include a corporation (*D. & L. Caterers Ltd.* v. *D'Ajou* [1945] K.B. 210, 364).

[89] These words seem wide enough to include offices of honour as well as offices of profit. Before 1952 words imputing unfitness for (as distinct from lack of integrity in) an office of honour were not actionable *per se* unless, if true, they would be a ground for removal from the office. This distinction still exists: Gatley, *Libel*, p. 94.

business. It was once thought not[90] actionable *per se* to say of a workmen that he is not a member of a trade union, but today a different view might be held.

§ 70. SLANDER: SPECIAL DAMAGE

In all other cases of slander the plaintiff must plead and prove that he has suffered special damage as the natural and probable result of the publication of the defamatory matter. This is so, however disgraceful the imputation and however certain it may be that it will damage the reputation of the plaintiff.[91] The special damage required in actions for slander must be the loss of some definite material advantage; it must not consist merely in the loss of reputation itself.[92] Actual damage might be a more accurate term. A loss of the voluntary hospitality of friends is sufficient, however,[93] and so also in all probability is a resulting separation between husband and wife.[94] Further, when special damage is proved, damages can be recovered not merely for it but for the injury to the plaintiff's reputation generally—*i.e.* compensation is not limited to the amount of actual loss proved, although proof of some actual loss is an essential foundation for a claim for general damages.

Special damage must not be too remote. But the law of causation in defamation does not differ from that in other torts.[95] It was once thought that damage immediately caused by the illegal act of a third party—*e.g.* his dismissal of the plaintiff from his employment was too remote. But it is submitted that today the test is whether the consequences in question is the natural and reasonable result of the defendant's words,[96] so that the dismissal of the plaintiff may in an appropriate case constitute special damage, whether it be wrongful or not.[97] Again, although it was once held[98] that illness resulting from mental trouble produced by slander was too remote, now the decision is questionable in view of modern developments in the law relating to nervous shock.[99]

Yet there is a well established rule that special damage is too remote if it is due not to the original slander, but to a repetition of it by other persons.[1] Therefore it is in ordinary cases insufficient for the plaintiff to prove that since the publication of the slander his business has fallen away; because such a result must have been due not to the original slander, but to the subsequent propagation of it by means of repetition.[2] But it is otherwise if the original slander is published to so many persons that the diminution of the

---

[90] *McMullan* v. *Mulhall* [1929] I.R. 470.
[91] *Jones* v. *Jones* [1916] 2 A.C. 481 (immoral conduct in a schoolmaster). But an allegation of cheating at cards imputes a criminal offence: hence the plaintiff in the Baccarat case did not have to show special damage: *Gordon-Cumming* v. *Green* (1891) 7 T.L.R. 408.
[92] *Roberts* v. *Roberts* (1864) 5 B. & S. 384.
[93] *Davies* v. *Solomon* (1871) L.R. 7 Q.B. 112. But not loss merely of the society of one's friends: *Palmer* v. *Solmes* (1880) 30 U.C.C.P. 481.
[94] *Best* v. *Samuel Fox & Co. Ltd.* [1952] A.C. 716, 732; *Lampert* v. *Eastern National Omnibus Co. Ltd.* [1954] 1 W.L.R. 1047. See below, § 131.
[95] *Rigby* v. *Mirror Newspapers Ltd.* [1964] S.R. (N.S.W.) 34. See below, § 200.
[96] *Chamberlain* v. *Boyd* (1883) 11 Q.B.D. 407.
[97] *Speake* v. *Hughes* [1904] 1 K.B. 138; *Longdon-Griffiths* v. *Smith* [1950] 2 All E.R. 662, 678 (not in [1951] 1 K.B. 295).
[98] *Allsop* v. *Allsop* (1860) 5 H. & N. 534.
[99] *Rigby* v. *Mirror Newspapers Ltd.* [1964] S.R. (N.S.W.) 34.
[1] *Ward* v. *Weeks* (1830) 7 Bing. 211; *Weld-Blundell* v. *Stephens* [1920] A.C. 956.
[2] *Dixon* v. *Smith* (1860) 5 H. & N. 450.

plaintiff's business may be reasonably attributed to it rather than to subsequent repetition.[3]

There are in any event two exceptions to the rule that damage caused by the repetition of a slander is too remote—(1) when the original statement is made to a person who is under a legal or moral duty to repeat it[4]; (2) when the repetition has been authorised or intended or perhaps foreseen by the defendant.[5]

[3] *Ratcliffe* v. *Evans* [1892] 2 Q.B. 524; *Cutler* v. *McPhail* [1962] 2 Q.B. 292.
[4] *Deny* v. *Handley* (1867) 16 L.T. (N.S.) 263.
[5] *Weld-Blundell* v. *Stephens* [1920] A.C. 956, 999; *Ward* v. *Lewis* [1955] 1 W.L.R. 9.

CHAPTER 9

NEGLIGENCE[1]

§ 71. INTRODUCTORY

Intention and negligence

In the law of torts negligence has two meanings: (1) an independent tort, with which we shall deal in the succeeding sections of this chapter; (2) a mode of committing certain other torts—*e.g.* trespass or nuisance. In this latter sense negligence is carelessness. In some cases either negligence or wrongful intent is required by law as a condition of liability. Each involves a certain mental attitude of the defendant towards the consequences of his act. He intends those consequences when he foresees and desires them, has a reasonable prospect of being able to bring them about through his own volition, and therefore does the act in order that they may happen.[2] He is guilty of negligence, on the other hand, when he does not desire the consequences, and does not act in order to produce them, but is nevertheless indifferent or careless whether they happen or not, and therefore does not refrain from the act notwithstanding the risk that they may happen.[3] The wilful wrongdoer is he who desires to do harm; the negligent wrongdoer is he who does not sufficiently desire to avoid doing it. Negligence and wrongful intent are inconsistent and mutually exclusive states of mind. He who causes a result intentionally cannot also have caused it negligently, and vice versa.[4]

The difficulty of this topic is due to some extent to the reluctance of English lawyers to generalise about their basic conceptions. There is no General Part in the common law as in the civil law. Three other factors have increased the confusion. First, the action of trespass today lies only if either intention or negligence is shown.[5] But secondly, the action of negligence lies not only for careless but also for intentional conduct: it would be no defence to such an action to plead that the conduct causing the harm amounted to a serious crime.[6] Thirdly, there is the constant citation of the misleading maxim, "a man must be taken to intend the natural and probable consequences of his act." The maxim is misleading because it confuses the proposition to be proved with the means of proving that proposition. "In fact people often intend something quite different from what they know to be the natural and probable result of what they are doing. To take a trivial example, if I say I intend to reach the green, people will believe me although we all know that the odds are ten to one against my succeeding; and no one

---

[1] The leading works for practitioners are Charlesworth, *Negligence*, and Bingham, *The Modern Cases on Negligence*. The voluminous periodical literature is cited later in appropriate places.

[2] *Betty's Cafés Ltd.* v. *Phillips Furnishing Stores Ltd.* [1959] A.C. 20, 34.

[3] *Grill* v. *General Iron Screw Collier Co.* (1860) L.R. 1 C.P. 600.

[4] *Re Armstrong and State Rivers and Water Supply Commission* [1952] V.L.R. 187, 197. The judgment further explains that a man may intend consequences without desiring them, and contrariwise.

[5] See above § 46.

[6] The facts of *Hardy* v. *Motor Insurers' Bureau* [1964] 2 Q.B. 745 are a good example. The habit of using "negligence" to describe a deliberate act is well established, but inaccurate: *I.C.I. Ltd.* v. *Shatwell* [1965] A.C. 656, 672.

but a lawyer would say that I must be presumed to have intended to put my ball in the bunker because that was the natural and probable result of my shot."[7]

Inadvertence

Negligence is usually accompanied by inadvertence, but it is not the same thing, and this coincidence is not invariable.[8] Carelessness as to possible consequences very often results in a failure to bring those consequences to mind—*i.e.* inadvertence.[9] Commonly, therefore, the careless person not only does not intend the consequence but does not even advert to it; its possibility or probability does not occur to his mind. But it is not always so, for there is such a thing as wilful—*i.e.* conscious and advertent— negligence. The wrongdoer may not desire or intend the consequence but may yet be perfectly conscious of the risk of it. He does not intentionally cause the harm but he intentionally and consciously exposes others to the risk of it. This has been described[10] as "an attitude of mental indifference to obvious risks."

Recklessness

The ordinary meaning of the word in the law of torts is a high degree of carelessness. It is the doing of something which in fact involves a grave risk to others, whether the doer realises it or not.[11] The test is therefore objective and not subjective. In the criminal law a full survey by the Law Commission[12] suggests that recklessness is a mental state which, although falling short of intention, requires some advertence as to the results of the risk created but the House of Lords has taken a different view.[12a]

§ 72. THE TORT OF NEGLIGENCE[13]

The decision of the House of Lords in *Donoghue* v. *Stevenson*[14] treats negligence, where there is a duty to take care, as a specific tort in itself,[15] and not simply as an element in some more complex relationship or in some specialised breach of duty.[16] Actions do not lie for a state of mind. Negligence is conduct, not a state of mind—conduct which involves an unreasonably great risk of causing damage. There is no necessary element of "fault" in the sense of moral blameworthiness involved in a finding that a

---

[7] *Gollins* v. *Gollins* [1964] A.C. 644, 664, *per* Lord Reid.
[8] *Hicks* v. *British Transport Commission* [1958] 1 W.L.R. 493, 503.
[9] *Sungravure Ltd.* v. *Meanie* (1964) 110 C.L.R. 24, 32.
[10] *Hudston* v. *Viney* [1921] 1 Ch. 98, 104, *per* Eve J. The attitude of the defendant in *Vaughan* v. *Menlove* (1837) 3 Bing. N.C. 468 (see below, § 80), is a very good example of this.
[11] *Shawinigan* v. *Vokins* [1961] 1 W.L.R. 1206, 1214 ("the best and most realistic test"); *Donovan* v. *Landy's Ltd.* [1963] I.R. 441, 461. *Contra, Herrington* v. *British Railways Board* [1971] 2 Q.B. 107.
[12] Law Com. No. 89 (1978), ss. 49–64, approved in *R.* v. *Stephenson* [1979] 2 All E.R. 1199.
[12a] *R.* v. *Lawrence* [1981] 2 W.L.R. 524.
[13] The best historical account is in Baker, *An Introduction to English Legal History*, Chap. 17.
[14] [1932] A.C. 562.
[15] See also Pritchard, "*Scott* v. *Shepherd* and the Emergence of the Tort of Negligence" (Selden Society, 1976). It may be asked why Intention is not a tort if Negligence is one. The answer is that some forms of intentional harm have already been given specific names—*e.g.* trespass, deceit, conspiracy. But the possibility of general liability for Intention has been suggested: above, § 10.
[16] *Grant* v. *Australian Knitting Mills* [1936] A.C. 85, 103.

defendant has been negligent.[17] It is negligence in the objective sense that is referred to in the well-known definition of Alderson B.[18] "Negligence is the omission to do something which a reasonable man, guided upon those considerations which ordinarily regulate the conduct of human affairs, would do, or doing something which a prudent and reasonable man would not do."[19] So also Lord Wright said[20]: "In strict legal analysis, negligence means more than heedless or careless conduct, whether in omission or commission: it properly connotes the complex concept of duty, breach and damage thereby suffered by the person to whom the duty was owing." It is worth noting that it is erroneous, although usual, to speak of injuries being caused by negligence: injuries do not result from legal concepts, but from acts or omissions which may involve or constitute negligence.[21]

§ 73. THE CONCEPT OF DUTY OF CARE[22]

(1) Carelessness and negligence

We proceed now to a discussion of the first of the three component parts—duty, breach, and damage—of the modern tort of negligence. This analysis is logically correct, but it does not avoid the need for looking at the tort of negligence as a whole: the three elements of duty, breach and damage may penetrate each other.[23] But it is clear that it is not enough for the plaintiff to establish that the defendant has been careless: he must establish that the defendant has been careless in breach of a specific legal duty to take care. "In most situations it is better to be careful than careless, but it is quite another thing to elevate all carelessness into a tort."[24] It is "a most vicious and elliptical habit,"[25] but one which it is only too easy to acquire, "by transposing the word 'careless' into 'negligent' to dismiss from one's mind the essential problem—namely, whether or not there was in any particular case a failure of duty."[26]

(2) Duty a question of law

It is a question of law whether in any particular circumstances a duty of care exists. Before 1932 there was no general principle.[27] The law had been

[17] *Workington Harbour and Dock Board* v. *SS. Towerfield (Owners)* [1951] A.C. 112, 160. See also above, § 6.
[18] *Blyth* v. *Birmingham Waterworks Co.* (1856) 11 Exch. 781, 784.
[19] "The avalanche of cases since then has not buried that simple statement: and nothing that has been said in them has bettered it": *Munnings* v. *Hydro-Electric Commission* [1971] A.L.R. 609, 622, *per* Windeyer J.
[20] *Lochgelly Iron and Coal Co.* v. *M'Mullan* [1934] A.C. 1, 25.
[21] *Central Asbestos Co. Ltd.* v. *Dodd* [1973] A.C. 518, 532, 546–547.
[22] See Harari, *The Place of Negligence in the Law of Torts* (Sydney, 1962); Millner, *Negligence in Modern Law* (1967), and Heuston, "*Donoghue* v. *Stevenson* in Retrospect" (1957) 20 M.L.R. 1 and "*Donoghue* v. *Stevenson*: A Fresh Appraisal" [1971] C.L.P. 37; Williams, "The Risk Principle" (1961) 77 L.Q.R. 179; Symmons, "The Duty of Care in Negligence" (1971) 34 M.L.R. 394.
[23] *Dorset Yacht Co. Ltd.* v. *Home Office* [1970] A.C. 1004, 1052.
[24] *Moorgate Mercantile Co. Ltd.* v. *Twitchings* [1977] A.C. 890, 919, *per* Lord Edmund-Davies.
[25] *Jones* v. *Vauxhall Motors* [1955] 1 Lloyd's Rep. 152, 153, *per* Stable J.
[26] *Sharp* v. *Avery* [1938] 4 All E.R. 85, 88, *per* Slesser L.J.
[27] "Few can go back 50 years as I can. Few can appreciate the law as to negligence as it then stood." Lord Denning, *The Discipline of Law* (1979), p. 229.

built up in disconnected slabs exhibiting no organic unity of structure.[28] In 1932 an attempt was made in the House of Lords in *Donoghue* v. *Stevenson*[29] to formulate some general criterion for the existence of the proximity which would give rise to a duty of care. The pursuer averred that she had suffered injury as a result of seeing and drinking the contaminated contents of a bottle of ginger beer manufactured by the respondent and bought from him by the owner of a café, from whom in turn it had been bought by a friend of the pursuer. The House of Lords, by a bare majority, held that if the pursuer could prove that which she averred she would have a good cause of action. We have already seen that the decision is an authority for two distinct propositions—(1) that negligence is a distinct tort[30]; and (2) that the absence of privity of contract between plaintiff and defendant does not preclude liability in tort.[31] It is also of course an indisputable authority for the proposition that manufacturers of products owe a duty of care to the ultimate consumer or user.[32] Although it was sometimes said that the *ratio decidendi* of the case was limited to this proposition,[33] it is now clear[34] that the case is authority for something more than the proposition that a duty of care is owed to consumers of snails in ginger-beer bottles.[35] By the beginning of the 1970s it was said that *Donoghue* v. *Stevenson* was an authority for opening up new categories of liability,[36] with caution,[37] but not disregarding existing categories,[38] or treating the law of negligence as entirely "open-ended."[39]

But by the end of that decade the Law Lords had moved so far as to hold that public policy primarily required the imposition of liability unless there was some other and secondary policy demanding an immunity from suit.[40] In *Anns* v. *Merton London Borough Council* this two-tier approach was clearly expounded by Lord Wilberforce.[41] The neighbour principle entitled the plaintiff to obtain judgment unless the defendant could point to some consideration which reduced or negatived the prima facie duty. Such a con-

---

[28] *Candler* v. *Crane, Christmas & Co.* [1951] 2 K.B. 164, 188, *per* Asquith L.J. The passage continues: "These categories attracting the duty had been added to and subtracted from from time to time. But no attempt had been made in the past to rationalise them; to find a common denominator between road users, bailees, surgeons, occupiers, and so on, which would explain why they should be bound to a duty of care and some other classes who might be expected equally to be so bound should be exempt—no attempt, that is, save that of Lord Esher M.R. (from which his colleagues dissociated themselves) in *Heaven* v. *Pender* (1883) 11 Q.B.D. 503, 510." Green, *Traffic Victims*, pp. 52–53, says that the statement by Lord Esher (Sir Baliol Brett at the date of the judgment) was "a brilliant generalisation" which "comes close to generalising English tort law for the first time."
[29] [1932] A.C. 562.
[30] See above, § 71.
[31] See above, § 3.
[32] This aspect of the case is considered fully below, § 105.
[33] This was apparently the view of the experienced reporter who framed the "somewhat conservatively worded headnote" (as Asquith L.J. described it in [1951] 2 K.B. at 189) and seems to be supported by *Grant* v. *Australian Knitting Mills* [1936] A.C. 85, 102; *Howard* v. *Walker* [1947] K.B. 860, 863; *Marshall* v. *Cellactite and British Uralite Ltd.* (1947) 63 T.L.R. 456, 457; *Travers* v. *Gloucester Corporation* [1947] K.B. 71; *Grossman* v. *The King* [1952] 2 D.L.R. 241, 255-256; *McPhail* v. *Lanarkshire C.C.*, 1951 S.C. 301; *Hindustan S.S. Co. Ltd.* v. *Siemens Bros. & Co. Ltd.* [1955] 1 Lloyd's Rep. 167, 176.
[34] *London Graving Dock Co.* v. *Horton* [1951] A.C. 737, 757.
[35] *Central Asbestos Co. Ltd.* v. *Dodd* [1973] A.C. 518, 550.
[36] *Hedley Byrne & Co. Ltd.* v. *Heller and Partners Ltd.* [1964] A.C. 465, 482, 524.
[37] *Weller* v. *Foot and Mouth Disease Research Institute Ltd.* [1966] 1 Q.B. 569, 577.
[38] See below, § 76.
[39] *Dorset Yacht Co. Ltd.* v. *Home Office* [1970] A.C. 1004, 1011.
[40] *Arenson* v. *Casson, Beckman, Rutley & Co.* [1977] A.C. 405, 419.
[41] [1978] A.C. 728, 751–752.

sideration would be that the defendant was an advocate,[42] or that the loss which the plaintiff had suffered was purely economic and so not recoverable.[43] The dicta in pre-*Anns* judgments supporting or criticising the neighbour principle are now only of historical interest.[44] The analysis in *Anns* is logical and compelling and has been accepted in New Zealand[45] and in British Columbia.[46]

(3) The neighbour principle

We must, therefore, refer at some length to the famous passage in which Lord Atkin formulated the proposition which has come to be generally known as "the neighbour principle,"[47] or the notion of proximity. Having referred to examples of specific situations or relations in which a duty had been held to exist, Lord Atkin continued[48]:

> "In this way it can be ascertained at any time whether the law recognises a duty, but only where the case can be referred to some particular species which has been examined and classified. And yet the duty which is common to all the cases where liability is established must logically be based upon some element common to the cases where it is found to exist. To seek a complete logical definition of the general principle is probably to go beyond the function of the judge. ... There must be, and is, some general conception of relations giving rise to a duty of care, of which the particular cases found in the books are but instances. ... The liability for negligence, whether you style it such or treat it as in other systems as a species of *culpa*, is no doubt based upon a general public sentiment of moral wrongdoing for which the offender must pay. But acts or omissions which any moral code would censure cannot in a practical world be treated so as to give a right to every person injured by them to demand relief. In this way rules of law arise which limit the range of complainants and the extent of their remedy. The rule that you are to love your neighbour becomes in law, you must not injure your neighbour; and the lawyer's question, Who is my neighbour?[49] receives a restricted reply. You must take reasonable care to avoid acts or omissions which you can reasonably foresee would be likely to injure your neighbour. Who, then, in law is my neighbour? The answer seems to be—persons who are so closely and directly affected by my act that I ought reasonably to have them

---

[42] *Saif Ali* v. *Mitchell & Co.* [1980] A.C. 198.

[43] See below, § 76.

[44] They are collected in the 17th edition of this work, § 73.

[45] *Takaro Properties Ltd.* v. *Rouling* [1978] 2 N.Z.L.R. 318, 323.

[46] *Tuews* v. *MacKenzie* (1980) 109 D.L.R. (3d) 473, 489.

[47] Lord Atkin's daughter wrote: "I remember his asking us whom we thought was our 'neighbour,' and he listened to us before he gave his opinion, which eventually became part of his judgment in *Donoghue* v. *Stevenson*. He was very interested in that case and told us he was altering the present law by his judgment": E. Cockburn Millar, "Some Memories of Lord Atkin" (1957) 23 *Glim* 13, 15.

[48] [1932] A.C. 562, 579.

[49] The lawyer who asked this famous question received as an answer the Parable of the Good Samaritan: St. Luke, x. 25–35. It is worth noting that the Christian obligation is (see Prammer, *Manuale Theologiae Moralis*, i, pp. 418–420) to love one's neighbour as oneself, not better than oneself. A trial judge who directed a jury that the test of "duty" was that laid down in the Book of Common Prayer was reversed on appeal: *Di Paolo* v. *Kila* (1960) 23 D.L.R. (2d) 362.

in contemplation as being so affected when I am directing my mind to the acts or omissions which are called in question."

This statement of principle gave rise to considerable discussion. At first some displayed uneasiness at the very wide and flexible terms in which it was propounded,[50] but as the years went by it became increasingly welcome and its place in the law is now assured.[51] It should be noted that although the neighbour principle forms part of the *ratio decidendi* of Lord Atkin's own judgment it is difficult to say that it forms part of the *ratio decidendi* of the decision itself. For although both Lord Thankerton and Lord Macmillan contemplated the addition of new duties to the law of negligence, neither of them attempted to formulate the principle or principles upon which this might be done.[52]

Neighbour principle and other duties

The decision in *Donoghue* v. *Stevenson* "stands on the frontiers of actionable negligence,"[53] and does not purport to give guidance on the obligations arising from already recognised duties or relationships—*e.g.* that of occupier and visitor.[54] Although in a general way the Atkinian principle describes the duty of an occupier to his neighbour,[55] or to his visitors[56] that principle does not exhaustively define the relationship. So a plaintiff must show that the defendant was an *occupier* within the technical meaning of that term.[57] Sometimes the particular duty can subsist contemporaneously with the Atkinian duty,[58] but sometimes it displaces it.[59] No clear principle has emerged. Nor is the generalising approach of the neighbour principle appropriate to the criminal law, where precision and certainty are all-important.[60]

§ 74. FORESIGHT AS A CRITERION OF LIABILITY

Although the neighbour principle is now an accepted part of English law there is still some uncertainty as to how far precisely it does extend. If Lord Atkin's statement were "read literally and without regard to the qualifying effect of its context or the *subjecta materies*" it would comprehend "conduct

---

[50] See *Farr* v. *Butters* [1932] 2 K.B. 606, 613–614; *Barnett* v. *Packer* [1940] 3 All E.R. 575, 577; and the strange outbursts by Glyn-Jones J. in *Cairns* v. *St. Marylebone B.C. The Times*, December 8, 1954 and Professor A. W. B. Simpson (1975) 91 L.Q.R. 247, 278.

[51] *Anns* v. *Merton London Borough Council* [1978] A.C. 728.

[52] Lord Macmillan's speech, in some respects more cautiously phrased than Lord Atkin's, is equally important. A much-cited passage ([1932] A.C. 562, 619) reads: "The grounds of action may be as various and manifold as human errancy; and the conception of legal responsibility may develop in adaptation to altering social conditions and standards. The criterion of judgment must adjust and adapt itself to the changing circumstances of life. The categories of negligence are never closed." On the last sentence, Lord Salmon has commented, "and there are now a great many of them": *Anns* v. *Merton B.C.* [1978] A.C. 728, 769.

[53] *Smith* v. *Howdens Ltd.* [1953] N.I. 131, 137, *per* Lord MacDermott C.J.

[54] *Smith* v. *Scott* [1973] Ch. 314.

[55] *Brew Bros. Ltd.* v. *Snax (Ross) Ltd.* [1970] 1 Q.B. 612, 620.

[56] *London Graving Dock Co. Ltd.* v. *Horton* [1951] A.C. 737, 766.

[57] See *McAuliffe* v. *Moloney* [1971] I.R. 200.

[58] *Commissioner for Railways* v. *McDermott* [1967] 1 A.C. 169, 187.

[59] *Commissioner for Railways* v. *Quinlan* [1964] A.C. 1054.

[60] *D.P.P.* v. *Withers* [1975] A.C. 842, 868.

of any kind, through any means (including negligent misstatement) causing damage of any kind recognised by the law, whether physical or not, to anyone who could bring himself within" the definition of a neighbour.[61] But to do this would be to fall into the error "of assuming that Lord Atkin was intending to formulate a *complete* criterion—almost like a definition in the prolegomena to a new theory of philosophy."[62] As Lord Wilberforce has said,[63] there may be considerations which negative or reduce the application of the neighbour principle.

Foresight not sole criterion

At the outset, it should be noticed that there are many torts to which the neighbour principle can, in the nature of things, have no application—for example, defamation, inducement of breach of contract, conspiracy. The interests of the individual are here protected in other ways. Nobody has seriously suggested that the whole law of tort should be reduced to a question of what the defendant ought reasonably to have foreseen in the circumstances of the particular case. The foresight of the reasonable man, or reasonable foreseeability, to use the customary but inelegant phrase, is not the necessary and sufficient condition of liability in tort—not necessary, because it has no place in torts of strict liability; not sufficient, because even within the field of what is commonly thought of as negligence, there are cases in which the defendant will escape liability although it is clear that he must have foreseen the likelihood of harm to the plaintiff.

Negations of neighbour principle

Some of these exceptions were established in the law before 1932, and their existence reaffirmed since on the express ground that they had not been affected by *Donoghue* v. *Stevenson*. Obvious examples of this class are the absence of any duty to prevent the subsidence of one's neighbour's premises by the abstraction of underground water in undefined channels,[64] and the law relating to trade competition.[65] Others have been established since that date. Examples are the refusal of the English courts to hold that a finance company is under a duty to a later purchaser to register a hire-purchase agreement[66]; or that a university or its examiners owe any duty to its students in respect of examinations[67]; or that a master is under any duty to protect his servant's property from the

---

[61] *Candler* v. *Crane, Christmas & Co.* [1951] 2 K.B. 164, 189, *per* Asquith L.J. See also *Deyong* v. *Shenburn* [1946] K.B. 227, 233. It is doubtful whether Lord Atkin intended his statement to comprehend pecuniary damage: below, § 76.

[62] *Haseldine* v. *Daw* [1941] 2 K.B. 343, 362, *per* Scott L.J. See also the same learned L.J. in *Anglo-Saxon Petroleum Co. Ltd.* v. *Damant* [1947] 2 All E.R. 465, 467 (not reported in [1947] K.B. 794).

[63] *Anns* v. *Merton B.C.* [1978] A.C. 728, 752.

[64] *Langbrook Properties Ltd.* v. *Surrey C.C.* [1970] 1 W.L.R. 161. *Contra, Bognuda* v. *Upton* [1972] N.Z.L.R. 741.

[65] See § 133. A shop keeper finds that a shop has been erected next door to him, the second shopkeeper selling the same class of goods at half the price charged by the first. The second man intends to injure the first, but the latter has no cause of action, though the two are physically neighbours.

[66] *Moorgate Mercantile Co.* v. *Twitchings* [1977] A.C. 890.

[67] *Thorne* v. *University of London* [1966] 2 Q.B. 237.

felonious act of a third party,[68] or that forwarding agents are under any duty
to the owners of goods to prevent fraudulent or other criminal acts by third
parties,[69] or that a judge owes any duty to the litigants before him,[70] or that
those taking part in a joint criminal venture are neighbours.[71] In the Commonwealth similar decisions can be found. Thus there are examples in the
reluctance of the High Court of Australia to impose liability on the Crown
for the acts of its servants engaged in active operations against its enemies[72];
and of the Supreme Court of Nova Scotia to hold that the pilot of an
aeroplane on a regular route was under any duty to avoid a ranch containing "noise-conscious mink"[73]; or of the Supreme Court of New Zealand to
hold that there is a duty of care to relatives of a deceased person.[74]

Conclusion

The courts are still free to hold that the plaintiff's interests are not in all
the circumstances of the case entitled to be protected against the defendant's
conduct. For reasons of policy there are limits to the actions of negligence.[75]
So Lord Denning has said that "It is, I think, at bottom a matter of public
policy which we, as judges, must resolve. This talk of 'duty' or 'no duty' is
simply a way of limiting the range of liability for negligence."[76] The courts
are now ready to isolate and discuss the various issues of public policy
which arise in a difficult case.[77]

§ 75. FORESIGHT FURTHER CONSIDERED

(1) Duty of care and standard of care

The concept of reasonable foresight is used in seeking the answer to at
least two distinct questions: was the defendant under any duty of care at all,
and, if so, did he observe the standard required in the circumstances of the
case? It is not surprising, therefore, to find some confusion in the language
of the cases—one judgment describing as breach of a duty the identical conduct which another judgment describes as breach of the requisite standard
of care.[78] Sometimes this can be explained by a difference of approach.[79] On
the whole it seems preferable to reserve the term "duty" for the relation
between parties which imposes on one a legal obligation for the benefit of

---

[68] *Edwards* v. *West Herts Group Hospital Management Committee* [1957] 1 W.L.R. 415
(see Goodhart, (1957) 73 L.Q.R. 313). Yet servants are under such a duty to protect their
master's property: *Stansbie* v. *Troman* [1948] 2 K.B. 48, below, §§ 176–177.
[69] *Pringle of Scotland Ltd.* v. *Continental Express Ltd.* [1962] 2 Lloyd's Rep. 80, 89.
Contra, Lee Cooper Ltd. v. *C. H. Jeakins & Sons Ltd.* [1967] 2 Q.B. 1.
[70] *Arenson* v. *Casson Beckman Rutley & Co.* [1977] A.C. 405. See below, §§ 75, 152.
[71] *Ashton* v. *Turner* [1980] 3 W.L.R. 736, 744.
[72] *Shaw, Savill & Co.* v. *Commonwealth* (1940) 66 C.L.R. 344.
[73] *Nova-Mink Ltd.* v. *Trans-Canada Airlines* [1951] 2 D.L.R. 241.
[74] *Marx* v. *Att.-Gen.* [1974] 1 N.Z.L.R. 164.
[75] *Ashton* v. *Turner* [1980] 3 W.L.R. 736, 743.
[76] *Dorset Yacht Co. Ltd.* v. *Home Office* [1969] 2 Q.B. 412, 426.
[77] As in *Spartan Steel and Alloys Ltd.* v. *Martin & Co. (Contractors) Ltd.* [1973] 1 Q.B. 27.
[78] As Holmes long ago pointed out (*Common Law*, p. 111) "the featureless generality, that
the defendant was bound to use such care as a prudent man would do under the
circumstances, ought to be continually giving place to the specific one, that he was bound
to use this or that precaution." Hence the temptation to say that he is under a duty to take
such a precaution. The Occupiers' Liability Act 1957 (below, § 93) imposes a "common
duty of care" which is really a standard.
[79] *Insurance Commissioner* v. *Joyce* (1948) 77 C.L.R. 39, 57, *per* Dixon J.

the other and to deal with particular conduct in terms of a legal standard of what is required to meet the obligation.[80] Confusion has also been caused by semantic refinements of the concept of foreseeability—("very likely," "not improbable" etc).

(2) Duty of care and remoteness of damage

Confusion has also arisen from the fact that the concept of reasonable foresight is relevant not only in testing the existence of a duty, *i.e.* to the question of culpability and not of compensation, but also in cases of admitted negligence (when the duty and its breach are admitted) to the question of remoteness of damage, *i.e.* of compensation and not of culpability. This source of confusion was particularly prevalent when the test of remoteness was directness and the test of duty was reasonable foresight.[81] But it is now settled that foresight is the test both for duty and for remoteness.[82] There may be difficulty in deciding whether the events which have occurred differ in kind or only in degree from those which ought reasonably to have been foreseen and guarded against,[83] but this is a question of fact and not of law.

(3) "Proximity"[84]

This term, apparently invented by Lord Esher,[85] was used by Lord Atkin himself to describe the nature of the neighbour principle, and has since been generally adopted in England,[86] and in Ireland.[87] Unless the sense in which it was used is understood it may be misleading. On the one hand it is clear that geographical proximity between the parties is not of itself sufficient to establish liability,[88] although it may be an important factor.[89] On the other hand it is also clear that the absence of proximity in time or space will not prevent the establishment of liability: the manufacturer of poisonous tinned food is liable although his product has been shipped to the other side of the world and consumed months later.[90] It is worth noting once again that the difficulties raised by terms like "reasonable foreseeability" and "proximity" really arise only within the field of negligence. For many other torts have, in a useful phrase,[91] "built-in" proximity rules—*e.g.* in trespass the damage must be *direct*, and in deceit the statement must have been known to be *relied upon*. The concept of proximity does not require that the identity

---

[80] Prosser, *Torts* (4th ed.), p. 334.
[81] See *Woods* v. *Duncan* [1946] A.C. 401.
[82] *The Wagon Mound (No. 1)* [1961] A.C. 388; *The Wagon Mound (No. 2)* [1967] 1 A.C. 617.
[83] The contrast between *Hughes* v. *Lord Advocate* [1963] A.C. 837 and *Doughty* v. *Turner Manufacturing Co. Ltd.* [1964] 1 Q.B. 518 is a good example: see below, § 81.
[84] See also above, § 3.
[85] *Thomas* v. *Quartermaine* (1887) 18 Q.B.D. 685, 688.
[86] *Clay* v. *A. J. Crump & Sons Ltd.* [1964] 1 Q.B. 533, 558; *Hedley Byrne & Co. Ltd.* v. *Heller & Partners Ltd.* [1964] A.C. 465.
[87] *Kearney* v. *E.S.B.* [1980] I.R. 45.
[88] As the facts of *Bourhill* v. *Young* [1943] A.C. 92 (below, § 77) clearly show.
[89] So in *Dorset Yacht Co. Ltd.* v. *Home Office* [1970] A.C. 1004 it was thought significant that the property damaged was in the vicinity of the place of detention of the Borstal boys.
[90] See below, § 105.
[91] See James, "The Fallacies of *Simpson* v. *Thomson*" (1971) 34 M.L.R. 149, 159.

should be known at the time of the negligent act,[92] at least when the damage is physical and not financial.[93]

(4) Two functions of reasonable foreseeability

Some confusion has also arisen from a failure to distinguish clearly between two very different functions of the concept of reasonable foreseeability. First, it may be used as a test of whether a new duty should be added to the existing list of admitted duties; secondly, it may be used as a test of the scope or extent of an admitted duty.[94] It is particularly important to make this distinction as it does not follow that because the neighbour principle is adopted in admitting a new duty into the law that the duty itself must be phrased in terms of reasonable foreseeability. The simplest illustration of this point is Lord Atkin's own judgment in *Donoghue* v. *Stevenson*: he created a new duty and adduced the neighbour principle as his authority for doing so; but the duty itself is, as we shall see,[95] formulated in language chosen with the greatest precision. It would be a strange reasonable man who could comprehend all its implications without instruction from a lawyer.[96] In comparatively straightforward cases of negligence,[97] however, the scope or extent of the duty of care which the defendant admittedly owes to the plaintiff is often formulated simply in terms of reasonable foreseeability. This is the duty owed, for example, by those who operate motor-vehicles on the highway.[98]

(5) Nature of the interest infringed

It is a characteristic of the definition of the tort of negligence that it does not refer to the scope of the protection it affords to the plaintiff but rather to the qualities of blameworthiness or fault to be attributed to the conduct of the defendant. The position is precisely the reverse in torts such as defamation or conversion: the mere enunciation of the name at once indicates the nature of the interest which the plaintiff claims to have been invaded by the defendant's conduct. A failure to remember that the nature of the plaintiff's interest is a relevant factor has been responsible for some confusion, as we shall see when we consider liability for pecuniary or financial loss, and for nervous shock. Yet a moment's reflection shows how vital this factor is in a legal system which retains the concept of duty of care. For a duty is a notional pattern of conduct,[99] and such a pattern can take shape in the mind only after a consideration of the person on whom the obligation is imposed, the mode of its performance, the person to whom it is owed, and the nature of the interest protected.[1]

---

[92] The defendants in *Anns* v. *Merton L.B.C.* [1978] A.C. 728 did not know who the purchasers would be when the foundations of the flats were carelessly inspected.

[93] For this, see below, § 76.

[94] See *McPhail* v. *Lanarkshire C.C.*, 1951 S.C. 301, 319.

[95] Below, § 105.

[96] So Denning L.J. in his well-known dissenting judgment in *Candler* v. *Crane, Christmas & Co.* [1951] 2 K.B. 164 (see below, § 76), invoked the neighbour principle for the purpose of showing that the court should admit a new duty into the law—but he was careful to formulate the duty itself in terms which owe little or nothing to reasonable foreseeability.

[97] *British Railways Board* v. *Herrington* [1972] A.C. 877, 910.

[98] See below, § 82.

[99] Dias [1955] C.L.J. 198, 202.

[1] It should be noted that a negligent act may infringe two distinct interests of the one plaintiff, as in *Brunsden* v. *Humphrey* (1884) 14 Q.B.D. 141 (see below, § 218).

§ 76. PECUNIARY OR FINANCIAL LOSS[2]

The general rule is that the common law duty to take care to avoid causing injury to others is restricted to physical injury either to person or to property.[3] This does not mean that the law refuses to protect a man's financial or pecuniary interests. The existence of the whole law of contract and of such torts as intimidation, deceit, injurious falsehood, inducement of breach of contract and conspiracy sufficiently demonstrates the wide degree of protection afforded—and a man can always protect those interests still further by making an express contract.[4] But the reluctance to grant a remedy for the careless invasion of financial or pecuniary interests is long-standing, deep-rooted and not unreasonable.[5] Even Parliament silently assumes that personal injury is more important than property damage.[6] So one who suffers pecuniary loss as the result of an inaccurate or false statement made either to himself (deceit) or to others (injurious falsehood) may have a remedy—but in each case the law requires that he should prove dishonesty and not merely carelessness. Although the tort of negligence has now been widened to bring economic loss within its scope, the mere fact that loss of that kind is foreseeable will not give rise to a duty of care. Something more than foreseeability is required.[7] "There comes a point where the logical extension of the boundaries of duty and damage is halted by the barrier of commercial sense and practical convenience."[8] Some modifiers of reasonable foresight must be found—e.g. that the existence of this very plaintiff was known to the defendant.

The problem may be considered under two heads—(1) careless acts, and (2) careless statements.

(1) Careless acts[9]

The careless act of the defendant may cause economic loss to the plaintiff either directly or indirectly. If it is caused directly, the principle now established in England[10] and in Ireland[11] is that there is no liability for economic loss unless there is also proved loss to the plaintiff's person or property. Thus in the *Spartan Steel* case,[12] when the defendants negligently cut a cable carrying electric power to the plaintiffs' factory, thus interrupting the supply for fourteen and a half hours, the plaintiffs were held entitled to damages for physical damage to the metal in their furnace (£368), and also for the loss of profit on the sale of that melt (£400), but could not recover for the loss of profit on four further melts (£1,767), which could have been com-

---

[2] See Cane, "Physical and Economic Loss" (1979) 95 L.Q.R. 117; Bishop, "Negligent Misrepresentation through Economists' Eyes" (1980) 96 L.Q.R. 360.
[3] *Levi* v. *Colgate-Palmolive* [1941] S.R. (N.S.W.) 48, 50.
[4] *Furniss* v. *Fitchett* [1958] N.Z.L.R. 396, 402.
[5] *Furniss* v. *Fitchett* [1958] N.Z.L.R. 396, 401; *Spartan Steel and Alloys Ltd.* v. *Martin & Co. (Contractors) Ltd.* [1973] 1 Q.B. 27, 42.
[6] See the Unfair Contracts Act 1977, discussed below, § 186.
[7] *Caltex Oil Ltd.* v. *The Dredge "Willemstad"* (1976) 136 C.L.R. 529, in which five different reasons were given for allowing the plaintiff to recover.
[8] *Lambert* v. *Lewis* [1980] 1 All E.R. 978, 1006.
[9] See *Ross* v. *Caunters* [1980] Ch. 297.
[10] *Spartan Steel and Alloys Ltd.* v. *Martin & Co. (Contractors) Ltd.* [1973] 1 Q.B. 27.
[11] *Irish Paper Sacks Ltd.* v. *Sisk & Sons Ltd.* (1972, High Court, unreported).
[12] *Spartan Steel and Alloys Ltd.* v. *Martin & Co. (Contractors) Ltd.* [1973] 1 Q.B. 27.

pleted but for the power cut.[13] The requirement of the interposition of physical damage between the negligent act and the plaintiff's economic loss has been criticised as an illogical and capricious exception to the principle of reasonable foreseeability,[14] but it is defensible on grounds of policy. It prevents the defendant's insurers being overwhelmed by claims arising of an open-ended catastrophic risk, for example, a national power cut.[15] But the limits of this principle have not yet been fixed. If the defendant carelessly damages the plaintiff's piece of paper, is there to be liability up to £100,000 because it is a pools ticket?[16]

If the loss has been caused indirectly, it will usually have been through the act or omission of a third party. There are undoubtedly many situations in which the negligent act or omission of A causing injury to B may deprive C of valuable economic benefits. Thus B may have been made incapable of furnishing the contractual benefit which (unknown to A[17];) he is bound to render to C,[18] or C may have insured B against the event which has happened,[19] or may be the charterer of B's ship which has been damaged by A's negligence,[20] or the prospective purchaser of part of the damaged cargo in that ship,[21] or C may be the wife or child or servant of B and obliged in consequence to nurse an irritable invalid or to seek new employment.[22] But in none of these cases is C, the third party, thereby invested with any right of action against the wrongdoer. The only exception to this general principle is to be found in the right of a master or husband to recover damages for the loss of the services rendered by his servant or wife. The exception is a deep-rooted historical anomaly and will not be extended.[23]

(2) Careless statements[24]

In 1951 the Court of Appeal had held[25] that the law distinguished between the negligent circulation of chattels and the issue of negligent misrepresentations. There was liability in the former case but not in the latter, and the distinction had not been affected by *Donoghue* v. *Stevenson*. But in 1963 a unanimous House of Lords in *Hedley Byrne & Co. Ltd.* v. *Heller & Partners Ltd.*[26] held that in principle there was no difference between

---

[13] So economic loss resulting from the interruption of the telephone service is not recoverable: *Elliott* v. *Sir Robert McAlphine & Sons Ltd.* [1966] 2 Lloyd's Rep. 482.

[14] See, *e.g.* the dissenting judgment of Edmund Davies L.J. in the *Spartan Steel* case.

[15] See the interesting remarks of an insurance broker in (1972) 12 J.S.P.T.L. 119.

[16] *Bart* v. *B.W.I.A.* [1967] 1 Lloyd's Rep. 239, 267; *Yumerovski* v. *Dani* (1977) 83 D.L.R. 588 (APEX ticket) is in favour of liability.

[17] If A does know, he may be liable for inducment of breach of contract.

[18] *La Société Anonyme de Remorquage à Helice* v. *Bennetts* [1911] 1 K.B. 243 (loss of profit on a towage contract). But see the conflicting dicta in *Morrison Steamship Co.* v. *Greystoke Castle (Cargo Owners)* [1947] A.C. 265, and *Seaway Hotels* v. *Spragg* (1959) 17 D.L.R. (2d) 292.

[19] *Simpson* v. *Thomson* (1877) 3 App.Cas. 279.

[20] *The World Harmony* [1967] P. 341.

[21] *Margarine Union* v. *Cambay Prince Steamship Co. Ltd.* [1967] 2 Lloyd's Rep. 315.

[22] *Best* v. *Samuel Fox & Co. Ltd.* [1952] A.C. 716, 731, 734. See below, § 131.

[23] See below, § 131.

[24] See note 2 above, and Wilson, "Chattels and Certificates in the Law of Negligence" (1952) 15 M.L.R. 160; Stevens, "*Hedley Byrne* v. *Heller*: Judicial Creativity and Doctrinal Possibility" (1964) 27 M.L.R. 121; Gordon, "*Hedley Byrne* v. *Heller* in the House of Lords" (1964) 38 Austr. L.J. 39, 79; Honoré, "*Hedley Byrne* v. *Heller*" (1965) 8 J.S.P.T.L. 284.

[25] *Candler* v. *Crane, Christmas & Co.* (*A Firm*) [1951] 2 K.B. 164, Denning L.J. dissenting.

[26] [1964] A.C. 465.

physical loss and financial loss,[27] and that a duty to take care in making statements existed whenever there was a special relationship and there had not been a disclaimer of responsibility. Although there has never been much difficulty in holding that there is liability for careless statements causing physical loss,[28] it was novel to impose liability when such statements caused economic loss.

The facts in *Hedley Byrne* were that the appellants, advertising agents, were anxious to discover the creditworthiness of Easipower Ltd., who had instructed the appellants to arrange substantial advertising contracts. Hedley Byrne asked their bank, the National Provincial, to make inquiries. National Provincial on two separate occasions made these inquiries of Hellers, a firm of merchant bankers, who were financing Easipower as well as being their bankers. The first inquiry was specifically stated by National Provincial to be "without responsibility" on the part of Hellers, and the second inquiry, asking whether Easipower was "trustworthy, in the way of business, to the extent of £100,000 per annum" was answered by Hellers stating, "without responsibility on the part of the bank or its officials," that Easipower was a "respectably constituted company, considered good for its ordinary business engagements. Your figures are larger than we are accustomed to see."[29] This reference was passed on to Hedley Byrne, who relied upon it, and suffered loss to the extent of £17,000 when, as *del credere* agents, they had to pay the sums due on the advertising contracts when Easipower went into liquidation.

The House of Lords did not decide whether Hellers had been negligent, for they held that the disclaimers were sufficient to negative any duty of care which might have existed on the assumption that there was a special relationship between the parties.[30]

The decision. Some have said[31] that the judgments are no more than *obiter dicta* in that the ultimate decision was against liability.[32] But this is too narrow an interpretation of the distinction between *ratio decidendi* and *obiter dictum*.[33] "To take only the qualification, which covered the actual facts, as being the ratio to the exclusion of the ruling as a whole, which gives it its meaning, would seem absurd."[34] It would be pedantic and unreal to dismiss as *obiter dicta* the fully considered judgments of five Law Lords delivered after hearing eight days of argument.[35]

---

[27] A point also emphasised in *Rookes* v. *Barnard* [1964] A.C. 1129. See below, § 135.

[28] *Clayton* v. *Woodman & Sons (Builders) Ltd.* [1962] 2 Q.B. 533.

[29] Bankers normally and naturally use careful terms when giving these references, but Heller's language was so guarded that only a very suspicious inquirer might have appreciated he was being warned not to give credit to the extent of £100,000. One week after the reference was given Heller began to press Easipower to reduce their overdraft.

[30] One of the many difficulties in stating the effect of the decision is that apparently Lords Morris and Hodson thought that a banker giving a general reference only owed a duty to be honest as distinct from being careful: see [1964] A.C. 465, 504, 513.

[31] See *Rondel* v. *Worsley* [1967] 1 Q.B. 443, 509.

[32] An argument in favour of regarding the judgments in the H.L. as *obiter* is to ask: what would have happened if those judgments had been given in the C.A. and not the H.L., and the defendants had wished to appeal in order to question the validity of the general principle that a bank would be liable in the absence of a disclaimer? They could not have done so, as there would have been no order against which to appeal: see *Penn-Texas Corporation* v. *Murat Anstalt* [1964] 2 Q.B. 647.

[33] *Saif Ali* v. *Mitchell & Co. Ltd.* [1980] A.C. 198, 212.

[34] Dias, Note [1963] C.L.J. 221. See also below, § 95.

[35] *Smith* v. *Auckland Hospital Board* [1965] N.Z.L.R. 191, 219.

Special relationships

Hedley Byrne affirms and extends the principle that a duty to be careful (as distinct from a duty to be honest) may exist in situations other than those in which there is a contract between the parties. It affirms that this duty may exist where there is a fiduciary relationship.[36] It extends that principle by suggesting that the duty extends to all relationships where the inquirer was trusting the other to exercise a reasonable degree of care, and when the other knew or ought to have known that the inquirer was relying on him.[37] There is no magic in the phrase "special relationship,"[38] but two views have emerged as to when such a relationship arises. A narrow view of the decision is that a special relationship exists only when, but for the absence of consideration, there would have been a contract.[39] On this view it is important to consider such factors as the gravity of the inquiry and the considered seriousness of the response by someone whose business it is to give such advice.[40] It might be desirable to ask for the advice in writing. A broad view is that liability exists wherever one party has been injured in reliance on a statement made by the other, so that a special relationship may even exist when the defendant is under a statutory duty to supply the certificate or other information in question,[41] at any rate if that statutory duty is executive rather than judicial or legislative in character.[42]

In this state of uncertainty, a helpful guide can be found in the famous dissenting judgment of Denning L.J. in *Candler*.[43] That judgment recognises that at bottom the problem is one of exclusion: negligence in word cannot in all respects be treated like negligence in act, for that would open up too wide an arc of liability.[44] Reasonable foresight as the only criterion of liability would bring in persons who, it is generally agreed, should be excluded—*e.g.* the solicitor giving casual advice during a railway journey,[45] or the marine hydrographer whose misplaced rock on a chart causes an ocean liner to go aground.[46] It is important to avoid "liability in an indeterminate amount for an indeterminate time to an indeterminate class."[47] One solution is to limit

---

[36] As was held in *Nocton* v. *Ashburton* [1914] A.C. 932. See below, § 145.

[37] See [1964] A.C. 465, 486, 502, 514, 529, 539, for the various formulae used by the five Law Lords, and Heevey (1968) 42 A.L.J. 3.

[38] *Esso Petroleum Co. Ltd.* v. *Mardon* [1976] Q.B. 801, 827.

[39] Perhaps this is what Hewson J. meant when he said that *Hedley Byrne* was nearer to contract than to tort: *The World Harmony* [1967] P. 341, 362.

[40] See the majority judgment of the Privy Council in *Mutual Life and Citizens' Assurance Co.* v. *Evatt* [1971] A.C. 793. But a distinct preference has developed for the dissenting judgment in the *M.L.A.* case—see *Howard Marine Ltd.* v. *Ogden & Sons Ltd.* [1978] Q.B. 574, 600.

[41] As in *Ministry of Housing* v. *Sharp* [1970] 2 Q.B. 223.

[42] *Welbridge Holdings Ltd.* v. *Greater Winnipeg Corporation* (1970) 22 D.L.R. (3d) 470.

[43] [1951] 2 K.B. 164. Lords Hodson, Devlin and Pearce approved it with varying degrees of emphasis: see [1964] A.C. 465, 503, 530, 539. "I was invited to sit in the Lords on the appeal, but I knew that my dissenting judgment in *Candler* would come under review. So I declined" (Lord Denning, *The Discipline of Law* (1979), p. 245.

[44] See this point very well developed by R. G. Wilson (1952) 15 M.L.R. 160, 166. The Lords conceded it: [1964] A.C. 465, 482-483, 494, 510, 534.

[45] Which worried Byles J. as long ago as *Fish* v. *Kelly* (1864) 17 C.B. (N.S.) 194.

[46] The possible misfortunes of this possible defendant have been much discussed. It has been rightly pointed out that most cartographers are Admiralty officials for whom the Crown would be vicariously liable: Grunfeld, "Reform in the Law of Contract" (1961) 24 M.L.R. 62, 82. But private chart producers still exist: see the definitive work by A. H. W. Robinson, *Marine Cartography in Britain* (Leicester, 1962), Chap. 7.

[47] *Ultramares Corporation* v. *Touche*, 255 N.Y. 170, 179; 174 N.E. 441, 450 (1931), *per* Cardozo C.J.

liability to cases where the information or advice is given in response to an inquiry for the guidance of the very person in the very transaction in question,[48] or perhaps the very class of whom the plaintiff is known to be one.[49] So the need for an identified plaintiff would render liable one who gave another a misleading reference as to the honesty of a prospective employee,[50] or a doctor who gave a misleading answer in response to an inquiry from a patient about a serious operation.[51] The fact that the parties are in a pre-contractual situation will not necessarily prevent a special relationship from arising.[52] The *Hedley Byrne* principle covers statements made to induce one to enter into a contract with the maker of the statement, or with a third party,[53] although it has been held that a manufacturer was not responsible to a supplier who relied on the former's inaccurate literature.[54]

But in the absence of circumstances bringing possible purchasers of shares into his reasonable contemplation,[55] an accountant preparing the balance sheet of a company is under no duty of care to such persons.[56]

It has also been held[57] that the defendant should be a person whose profession or trade it is to make statements or give information or advice; or who has a financial interest in the transaction in question.[58] It may be conceded that it would hardly be desirable to impose liability on a bystander who carelessly misdirected one on his way to an important appointment,[59] or a mere agent who misrepresents his authority[60]; but it is very difficult to see how a company can authorise the giving of such advice except as part of its business activities, so that it seems hard to hold that an insurance company is not liable for misleading advice about investments given to a policy-holder.[61] It is also hard to see how the defendant's financial interest can cause the plaintiff to trust the statement made to him.

Advocates.[62] It has been settled for a century that a barrister cannot be sued by his client for breach of contract.[63] The fees which he receives are an

---

[48] *Candler* v. *Crane, Christmas & Co.* [1951] 2 K.B. 164, 177–178. But it is worth noting that in *Hedley Byrne* it was immaterial that Hellers did not know that National Provincial required the information specifically for the appellants—and indeed National Provincial, when transmitting the reference, did not tell the appellants the name of the respondents: [1964] A.C. 465, 482, 503.

[49] *Scott Group Ltd.* v. *McFarlane* [1978] N.Z.L.R. 553.

[50] *Technovision Ltd.* v. *Reed, The Times,* April 14, 1964.

[51] *Smith* v. *Auckland Hospital Board* [1965] N.Z.L.R. 191.

[52] *Esso Ltd* v. *Mardon* [1976] Q.B. 801; *Howard Marine Ltd.* v. *Ogden & Son Ltd.* [1978] Q.B. 574.

[53] *McInerney* v. *Lloyds Bank Ltd.* [1974] 1 Lloyd's Rep. 246.

[54] *Lambert* v. *Lewis* [1980] 1 All E.R. 978 (which also shows that there may be liability if the statement is volunteered).

[55] Such circumstances existed in *Candler* itself.

[56] *Dimond Manufacturing Co. Ltd.* v. *Hamilton* [1969] N.Z.L.R. 609.

[57] *Mutual Life and Citizens' Assurance Co.* v. *Evatt* [1971] A.C. 793. The force of the decision is much weakened by the powerful dissenting judgments of Lords Reid and Morris, who had themselves sat in *Hedley Byrne.*

[58] As in *Anderson (W.B.) & Sons Ltd.* v. *Rhodes* [1967] 2 All E.R. 850, when one businessman carelessly misstated the creditworthiness of another.

[59] [1964] A.C. 465, 495, 502, 510, 539. *Contra,* Lord Devlin in [1964] A.C. 465, 529.

[60] *Jones* v. *Still* [1965] N.Z.L.R. 1071.

[61] As was done in *Mutual Life and Citizens' Assurance Co.* v. *Evatt* [1971] A.C. 793, 811. The decision may not be followed: *Howard Marine Case* [1978] Q.B. 574, 600.

[62] See Sir Ronald Roxburgh, "*Rondel* v. *Worsley*: the Historical Background" (1968) 84 L.Q.R. 178, and 513; Dunlop, "Lawyer's Negligence" (1971) 65 *Gazette of the Incorporated Law Society of Ireland* 71 (a useful comparative survey).

[63] *Kennedy* v. *Broun* (1863) 13 C.B. (N.S.) 677.

honorarium. But there was doubt as to the barrister's liability in negligence as a result of *Hedley Byrne*. These doubts were nearly all quietened when in *Rondel* v. *Worsley*[64] the House of Lords unanimously held that an advocate could not be sued by his client in respect of alleged negligence in the conduct of a criminal trial. It should be noted that *Rondel* v. *Worsley* does not lay down the rule that a barrister cannot be sued in negligence by his client. In fact *Rondel* v. *Worsley* lays down that as between barrister and client there is a special relationship giving rise to a duty of care, unless the barrister can bring himself within the exceptional immunity of an advocate. This immunity is quite distinct from the rule that there is no contractual relationship between barrister and client and is justifiable for a number of reasons on grounds of public policy—because there is a general public interest in a free and independent Bar and a barrister, who owes a duty to the court for the true administration of justice, cannot pick and choose his clients as a solicitor can,[65] or because an action for negligence against a barrister would inevitably involve the re-trial of the original proceedings, or because the barrister shares in the general immunity which is given to all those taking part in the judicial process. But the Law Lords in *Saif Ali* v. *Mitchell & Co.*[66] cut down the extent of the immunity, holding that a barrister was liable when he carelessly failed to advise re-settling the plaintiff's claim so as to add another defendant. So there might well be liability for an opinion given in chambers on a point of law, or for "paperwork" which was unconnected with litigation.[67] So a barrister voluntarily giving his services under a "Legal Aid" scheme may be liable in tort. Time would run from the date when the client sustained damage as a result of the negligence.[68] It has been left uncertain when the immunity of an advocate begins (perhaps with the letter before action), or to which tribunals it applies.[69]

Solicitors. A solicitor is in contractual relationship with his client, but is now liable in tort as well as in contract.[70] The claim accrues at the time of the breach of contract, and not at the time damage is suffered as a result of that breach.[71] It is probable, but not certain, that in his capacity as advocate the solicitor is entitled to the same immunity as the barrister.[72] It is now clear that a solicitor's duty of care extends to all those whom he knows rely on his professional skill.[73]

Arbitrators and valuers. An arbitrator is generally thought to enjoy the same immunity as a judge,[74] at any rate when he is exercising the judicial function of deciding a dispute rather than of answering a question. A valuer may also, if the parties who appoint him so agree, enjoy the same immunity:

---

[64] [1969] 1 A.C. 191.
[65] For the "cab-rank" rule, see W. W. Boulton, *Conduct and Etiquette at the Bar* (4th ed.), p. 17.
[66] [1980] A.C. 198. Yet it by no means follows that there is liability in negligence if an error takes place outside the area of immunity. A barrister must be careful: he need not be right.
[67] But the result of *Saif Ali* seems to be that advice *not* to sue is unprotected, yet it can hardly be in the public interest to protect barristers who launch unnecessary litigation.
[68] See below, § 220.
[69] See the speech of Lord Upjohn in [1969] 1 A.C. 191, 285.
[70] *Clark* v. *Kirby Smith* [1964] Ch. 506. See below, § 206.
[71] See above, § 3.
[72] Divergent views were expressed in *Rondel* v. *Worsley* [1969] 1 A.C. 191.
[73] *Ross* v. *Caunters* [1980] Ch. 297; *Finlay* v. *Murtagh* [1979] I.R. 249.
[74] *Sutcliffe* v. *Thackrah* [1974] A.C. 727.

otherwise he is liable in negligence.[75] Judicial immunity is an exception which is not to be extended.

The disclaimer[76]

The true analysis of *Hedley Byrne* is that the bank was not exempting itself from a duty which already lay upon it, but rather not undertaking any duty at all, for such a duty only arose upon a voluntary assumption of responsibility.[77] It should be noted that one who makes a prediction is not necessarily disclaiming responsibility singly because he indicates that the final decision lies with his superior in the organisation.[78] In practice bankers have always disclaimed responsibility, and so have some other persons or bodies—*e.g.* the Land Registry has for many years had notices in its waiting-rooms disclaiming responsibility for advice given in answer to inquiries. It is said that the decision is not very revoluntionary if it only compels professional men to take out insurance[79] or buy a rubber-stamp on which is "without responsibility,"[80] but many professional men might think such an automatic disclaimer would have a bad effect on their reputation,[81] and in any event the stamp might be omitted by mistake. The duty may also be a statutory one which cannot be disclaimed.[82] It might also be held that the disclaimer was inoperative because it fell within the terms of the Unfair Contract Terms Act 1977, which appear to apply to disclaimers as well as to exemption clauses.[83] Another difficulty is that the House of Lords has emphatically reaffirmed the rule that no third party can take a benefit under an exemption clause: there is no doctrine of vicarious immunity.[84] This would mean that the clerk might be sued when his principal could not[85]—hardly a satisfactory conclusion.

Conclusion

Hedley Byrne is the most striking decision in the field of negligence, perhaps in torts in general,[86] in the years between *Donoghue* v. *Stevenson* and *Anns* v. *Merton B.C.* All have recognised the judicial valour[87] shown in bringing economic loss caused by careless statements within the field of liability. Critics have pointed, with some justification, to the vagueness and imprecision of the language used.[88] Many further decisions will be required to elucidate its significance. But it seems harsh to complain of the

---

[75] *Arenson* v. *Casson, Beckman, Rutley & Co.* [1977] A.C. 405.
[76] For disclaimers in general, see below, § 186.
[77] So a disclaimer is irrelevant if the action is not in negligence but in deceit: *Commercial Banking Co. of Sydney Ltd.* v. *Brown & Co.* (1972) 46 A.L.J.R. 297.
[78] *Box* v. *Midland Bank* [1979] 2 Lloyd's Rep. 391.
[79] See Madge, *Professional Indemnity Insurance* (1968) for full details.
[80] Stevens (1964) 27 M.L.R. 121, 151.
[81] *e.g.* many accountants say that the use of a disclaimer would be inconsistent with their professional standards.
[82] *Ministry of Housing* v. *Sharp* [1970] 2 Q.B. 223.
[83] See below, § 186.
[84] *Scruttons Ltd.* v. *Midland Silicones Ltd.* [1962] A.C. 446.
[85] So held in *Dodds* v. *Milman* (1964) 45 D.L.R. (2d) 472. Note that the second disclaimer in *Hedley Byrne* purported to exempt the officials as well as the bank.
[86] *Contra, Arenson* v. *Arenson* [1972] 1 W.L.R. 1196, 1205.
[87] Pollock's phrase: see (1929) 45 L.Q.R. 293.
[88] Stevens (1964) 27 M.L.R. 121, 141, compares the House of Lords to Carlyle, who "led people out into the wilderness and left them there."

"Americanisation of English law," or to say that the decision gives the public "substantial benefits at the expense of the professional classes."[89] The Law Lords in *Hedley Byrne* were not laying down rules but were developing a principle.[90]

§ 77. EMOTIONAL DISTRESS[91]

The confusion between the three related but distinct concepts of duty, standard of care, and remoteness of damage can be clearly seen in the law relating to emotional disturbance (or nervous shock). This confusion has made the scope and basis of liability somewhat uncertain and the following analysis of the case-law is therefore necessarily of a tentative character.

First, it is probable, that no action lies for mere mental suffering.[92] It was once thought that the defendant was immune even if (as would usually be the case) the mental suffering had resulted in physical lesion or disturbance.[93] But "The crude view that the law takes cognisance only of physical injury resulting from actual impact has been discarded, and it is now well recognised that an action will lie for injury by shock sustained through the medium of the eye or the ear[94] without direct contact. The distinction between mental shock and bodily injury was never a scientific one, for mental shock is presumably in all cases the result of, or at least accompanied by, some physical disturbance in the sufferer's system."[95] Proof of physical disturbance prevents the courts from having to deal with frivolous or fanciful claims. In one case it was argued that the plaintiff was exceptionally susceptible to shock, and so outside the law's protection,[96] but the plea was rejected.[97]

Secondly, one who by extreme and outrageous conduct intentionally or recklessly causes severe emotional distress to another is liable for such emotional distress, provided that bodily harm results from it.[98] In *Wilkinson* v. *Downton*[99] the defendant, a licensed victualler, after going to the races, by way of a perverted practical joke had told the plaintiff that her husband was lying injured at a public-house in Leytonstone as the result of an accident, and that she was to go at once in a cab with two pillows to fetch him home.

---

[89] As does Gordon, 38 Austr. L.J. 79, 87–88.

[90] *Mutual Life and Citizens' Assurance Co.* v. *Evatt* [1971] A.C. 793, 813.

[91] See Goodhart, "The Shock Cases and Area of Risk" (1953) 16 M.L.R. 14; "Emotional Shock and the Unimaginative Taxicab Driver" (1953) 69 L.Q.R. 347; Havard, "Reasonable Foresight of Nervous Shock" (1956) 19 M.L.R. 478; Prosser, "Insult and Outrage" (1956) 44 Calif.L.Rev. 40.

[92] This interest is not given independent protection: it is "parasitic" upon the violation of some other legally recognised interest: see below, § 199.

[93] *Victorian Railways Commissioners* v. *Coultas* (1888) 13 App.Cas. 222. This case is now completely discredited: see *Chester* v. *Municipal Council of Waverley* (1939) 62 C.L.R. 1, 46–48.

[94] *Boardman* v. *Sanderson (Keel and Block Third Party)* (1961) [1964] 1 W.L.R. 1317.

[95] *Bourhill* v. *Young* [1943] A.C. 92, 103, *per* Lord Macmillan. Prosser, 44 Calif.L.Rev. 40, 43, says that emotional distress "includes all highly unpleasant mental reactions, such as fright, horror, grief, shame, humiliation, anger, embarrassment, chagrin, disappointment, worry and nausea."

[96] See below, § 82.

[97] *Chadwick* v. *British Railways Board* [1967] 1 W.L.R. 912. The plaintiff had led the "normal busy life" of a modern Englishman. "Indeed, the evidence showed that during those 16 years he had on one occasion been attacked by a gang of youths armed with bicycle chains."

[98] Restatement, Second, Torts. § 46.

[99] [1897] 2 Q.B. 57. *Janvier* v. *Sweeney* [1919] 2 K.B. 316 is a similar case.

The resultant shock to the plaintiff's nervous system produced severe and permanent physical consequences for which the defendant was held liable in damages[1] by R.S. Wright J.[2] The defendant is also probably liable if his conduct, though directed at some third party, causes emotional distress to another, who is known to be present and might reasonably have been foreseen as likely to be affected by it.[3]

Thirdly, an action lies for shock resulting in physical injury when the plaintiff has been placed in reasonable fear of immediate injury to himself as the result of the negligence of the defendant. The principle is that if the plaintiff has been put in peril of physical impact, it is immaterial that the impact did not materialise if physical injury is in fact caused by shock arising from the peril. "There seems to me to be no magic in actual personal contact. A threatened contact producing physical results should be an equivalent. The principle on which a threatened battery may justify damages for assault is in my view strictly analogous."[4] In such a case shock is in truth reasonably foreseeable. So in *Dulieu* v. *White & Sons*,[5] the defendants were held liable when their servant negligently drove a pair-horse van into the front of a public-house, with resultant shock and illness to the plaintiff, who was standing behind the bar.

Fourthly, an action lies for shock caused by the apprehension or the actual sight or sound of immediate physical injury to a relative or friend or (possibly) any person or object,[6] and in a proper case the damages may be substantial.[7] In *Dulieu* v. *White & Sons*[8] Kennedy J. expressed the view that "the shock, where it operates through the mind, must be a shock which arises from a reasonable fear of immediate personal injury to oneself." But the Court of Appeal has taken a different view on at least two occasions,[9] and it now seems settled that shock, if reasonably foreseeable, may give rise to a claim, even though it is not caused by fear for oneself or one's children,[10] at any rate if the injured party is within what might be broadly described as "the disaster area."[11] In *Hambrook* v. *Stokes Bros.*[12] the defendants had left their lorry with its engine running at the top of a steep hill in Folkestone. It began to run away down the hill. The plaintiff's wife, who had just left her children round a corner, received a severe nervous

---

[1] In all the plaintiff recovered £100 1s. 10½d.—£100 for emotional distress, and 1s. 10½d., the cost of a railway ticket to Leytonstone, for the distinct tort of deceit (see below, § 140). A false statement had been made with the object and effect that she should act on it to her detriment.

[2] "The most learned and accurate lawyer": *Peters* v. *Prince of Wales Theatre Ltd.* [1943] K.B. 73, 77, *per* Goddard L.J.

[3] See *Stevenson* v. *Basham* [1922] N.Z.L.R. 225 (threat to husband and resultant shock to wife).

[4] *Hambrook* v. *Stokes Bros.* [1925] 1 K.B. 141, 162, *per* Sargant L.J.

[5] [1901] 2 K.B. 669.

[6] *Boardman* v. *Sanderson* (1961) [1964] 1 W.L.R. 1317.

[7] *Hinz* v. *Berry* [1970] 2 Q.B. 40 (£4,000 to wife who saw husband killed and children injured).

[8] [1901] 2 K.B. 669, 675.

[9] *Hambrook* v. *Stokes Bros.* [1925] 1 K.B. 141; *Boardman* v. *Sanderson* (1961) [1964] 1 W.L.R. 1317.

[10] *Chadwick* v. *British Railways Board* [1967] 1 W.L.R. 912.

[11] *Pratt & Goldsmith* v. *Pratt* [1975] V.R. 378.

[12] [1925] 1 K.B. 141. The status of this decision is a little doubtful since the conflicting dicta of the H.L. in *Bourhill* v. *Young* [1943] A.C. 92; see Paton and Sawer,. "Ratio Decidendi and Obiter Dictum in Appellate Courts" (1947) 63 L.Q.R. 477. Some have thought it important that a breach of duty was admitted by the defendant: *King* v. *Phillips* [1953] 1 Q.B. 429.

shock which eventually caused her death as the result of fear for her children's safety. It was held that if these facts were proved, the plaintiff had a good cause of action under the Fatal Accidents Acts,[13] but that it would be otherwise had the shock been caused, not by what the deceased had seen with her own eyes, but by what she had been told by bystanders of her children's peril. There is a real distinction between witnessing an accident, which results in shock, and being told about it by a third party, which results in grief, as the Court of Appeal emphasised in 1981.[14]

But it must be noted that Kennedy J. in *Dulieu* v. *White* did not say that the only sense which the law would recognise as the medium for conveying the impression of fear to the mind was the sense of sight. "I cannot imagine that Kennedy J. would ever have said anything so foolish."[15] So the Court of Appeal[16] held the defendant liable when he ran over an infant while negligently backing a car belonging to the infant's father out of a garage, knowing that the father was in earshot in another part of the garage, and the father suffered nervous shock as a result of hearing his son's screams. There had been a direct perception of the accident as an entire event. Indeed, once a breach of duty is established, the difference between seeing and hearing is immaterial,[17] so that a plaintiff who had herself been rendered unconscious by the defendant's negligence was able to recover also for the shock caused by hearing of her husband's death from a third party after she had recovered consciousness. Such a decision is not inconsistent with the requirement of reasonable foreseeability, for if the plaintiff could have recovered if she had seen her husband killed, the deferment of her awareness of the disaster cannot put the shock outside the area of foresight.[18]

An action lies if the injury apprehended or actually seen or heard is to any relative other than a spouse or a child,[19] or to a friend,[20] or fellow-workman,[21] or even to any third party,[22] but the court ruled against liability when the plaintiff suffered shock from seeing her pet cat killed in front of her eyes.[23] No case seems to require knowledge or foresight of the relationship between the plaintiff and the injured party,[24] as distinct from knowledge or foresight of the plaintiff's presence. Protection may even be extended to one who has witnessed some unnerving or ghastly spectacle, though neither the life nor limb of any third party has been imperilled.[25]

The result of the cases is that it is unnecessary for the plaintiff to show

---

[13] Note that the plaintiff in an action under the Fatal Accidents Acts, as distinct from the deceased, need not have been within the disaster area.

[14] *McLoughlin* v. *O'Brian* [1981] 1 All E.R. 809.

[15] *Bourhill* v. *Young*, 1941 S.L.T. 364, 385, *per* Lord Justice-Clerk Aitchinson.

[16] *Boardman* v. *Sanderson* (1961) [1964] 1 W.L.R. 1317.

[17] *Schneider* v. *Eisovitch* [1960] 2 Q.B. 430, 441; approved in *Andrews* v. *Williams* [1967] V.R. 831.

[18] *Andrews* v. *Williams* [1967] V.R. 831.

[19] *Currie* v. *Wardrop*, 1927 S.C. 538 (fiancé); *Turbyfield* v. *G. W. Ry.* (1938) 54 T.L.R. 221 (sister).

[20] *Bourhill* v. *Young* [1943] A.C. 92, 117; *Dooley* v. *Cammell Laird Ltd.* [1951] 1 Lloyd's Rep. 271.

[21] *Mount Isa Mines Ltd.* v. *Pusey* [1971] A.L.R. 253.

[22] *Chadwick* v. *British Railways Board* [1967] 1 W.L.R. 912 (railway accident).

[23] *Davies* v. *Bennison* (1927) 22 Tas.Law Rep. 52. For another aspect of the Tasmanian Cat Case, see above, § 13.

[24] Except, perhaps, a dictum in *Fenn* v. *Peterborough* (1977) 73 D.L.R. (3d) 177, 208.

[25] *Owens* v. *Liverpool Corporation* [1939] 2 K.B. 394 (hearse containing relative's coffin overturned). But this decision was doubted by Lords Thankerton, Wright and Porter in *Bourhill* v. *Young*.

that he was himself in danger of physical impact. Foreseeability of injury from shock is what the law requires[26] as a necessary and sufficient condition of liability.[27] It is not required that the defendant should have foreseen the particular kind of mental illness (*e.g.* schizophrenia) which follows from his negligence.[28] It is true that in *Bourhill* v. *Young*[29] the House of Lords denied recovery to a plaintiff outside the area of physical impact who had suffered shock as a result of hearing a highway accident. The plaintiff was a fishwife who had heard the accident (which was caused by the admitted negligence of the deceased motor-cyclist) while she was getting her basket off the far side of a stationary tramcar some 50 feet away from the accident.[30] The House of Lords held that the motor-cyclist owed no duty to the plaintiff: he could not reasonably have anticipated that anyone in her position would be affected by his negligence. But this decision is no more than an application of the principle of reasonable foresight to the facts of the particular case.[31] The position of the plaintiff is a relevant (but not decisive) factor in determining whether the defendant ought reasonably to have foreseen the risk of emotional distress.[32]

Conclusion

The final result is not unsatisfactory: yet the mass of confusing dicta which the cases contain is in truth due to a failure to appreciate the fundamental fact that the question cannot be answered solely by logic and that an issue of policy is involved for which the concept of reasonable foreseeability is by itself incapable of providing a solution.[33] For whether a person outside the area of physical impact has a legally protected right to be free from the emotional distress occasioned by the sight of the peril in which others have been placed by the defendant's negligence is really a question which each legal system must decide for itself after due consideration of the various social interests involved.[34]

§ 78. Scope of the Duty

(1) Unforeseeable plaintiffs

There is no liability for negligence unless there is in the particular case a legal duty to take care, and this duty must be one which is owed to the plaintiff himself and not merely to others.[35] This duty of carefulness is not universal; it does not extend to all occasions, and all persons, and all modes of activity. So Lord Esher M.R. once uttered the characteristic remark that: "If a man is driving on Salisbury Plain, and no other person is near him, he

---

[26] *The Wagon Mound* [1961] A.C. 388, 426.
[27] *Chadwick* v. *British Railways Board* [1967] 1 W.L.R. 912.
[28] *Mount Isa Mines Ltd.* v. *Pusey* [1971] A.L.R. 253.
[29] [1943] A.C. 92.
[30] It is not too clear whether the plaintiff also saw the results of the collision. The truth seems to be that, after the custom of her kind, she returned to look at the blood on the road after she had delivered some of her fish: 1941 S.L.T. 364, 373.
[31] *Boardman* v. *Sanderson* [1964] 1 W.L.R. 1317.
[32] *Dooley* v. *Cammell Laird Ltd.* [1951] 1 Lloyd's Rep. 271; *King* v. *Phillips* [1953] 1 Q.B. 429; Goodhart (1953) 69 L.Q.R. 374.
[33] *Mount Isa Mines Ltd.* v. *Pusey* [1971] A.L.R. 253, 260.
[34] *Marx* v. *Att.-Gen.* [1974] 1 N.Z.L.R. 164, 176.
[35] *Palsgraf* v. *Long Island R.R.Co.* (1928) 284 N.Y. 339; 162 N.E. 99.

is at liberty to drive as fast and as recklessly as he pleases."[36] So a man may be under a duty of care towards one person, and yet in the same matter and on the same occasion under no duty of care towards another.[37] Two well-known cases illustrate the point. In *Palsgraf* v. *Long Island Railroad Co.*[38] two servants of the defendants, while helping a passenger to board a train, negligently dislodged a parcel carried by the passenger: the parcel fell and its contents (assumed to be fireworks) exploded. The shock of the explosion knocked over some scales about 25 feet away, which in turn struck and injured the plaintiff. A majority of the New York Court of Appeals held that she could not recover. Cardozo C.J. said: "The conduct of the defendants' guard, if a wrong in its relation to the holder of the package, was not a wrong in its relation to the plaintiff standing far away. Relative to her it was not negligence at all. Nothing in the situation gave notice that the falling package had in it the potency of peril to persons thus removed. . . . The law of causation, remote or proximate, is thus foreign to the case before us." The English equivalent of the *Palsgraf* case is *Bourhill* v. *Young*,[39] the facts of which have already been given,[40] in which the House of Lords held that the question was one of liability and not of remoteness and that in the circumstances the respondent owed no duty to the appellant: he could not reasonably have anticipated that anyone in her position would have been affected by his negligent act. In the light of these cases it would seem that in some of the older cases[41] facts which have in reality raised a problem as to the existence of a duty have been treated on the basis that the question involved was the remoteness of the damage.[42]

(2) Scope of the risk or hazard

The harm to the plaintiff's interest which has in fact occurred must be of a kind against which it was the duty of the defendant to take precautions. So, although a peculiar duty to take care is imposed on those who send firearms out into the world, nobody would contend that an action would lie if A lent a loaded gun to B, who dropped it onto C's toes.[43]

(3) Affirmative obligations[44]

In the absence of some existing duty the general principle is that there is no liability for a mere omission to act.[45] The fundamental notion appears to be that the imposition of an obligation to take positive steps for the benefit of another requires that that other should furnish something by way of

---

[36] *Le Lievre* v. *Gould* [1893] 1 Q.B. 491, 497. Lord Esher was not considering *criminal* liability.
[37] See also above, §§ 74–76.
[38] (1928) 284, N.Y. 339; 162 N.E. 99.
[39] [1943] A.C. 92.
[40] See above, § 77.
[41] *e.g. Smith* v. *L. & S.W. Ry.* (1870) L.R. 6 C.P. 14, 21.
[42] *Merrington* v. *Ironbridge Metal Works Ltd.* [1952] 2 All E.R. 1101, 1105.
[43] The well-known case of *Gorris* v. *Scott* (1874) L.R. 9 Ex. 125 (see below, § 85) is perhaps the best example of this point. See also *Jones* v. *Livox Quarries Ltd.* [1952] 2 Q.B. 608 (below, § 196).
[44] Lücke, "Towards a General Theory of Negligence" (1960) 2 M.U.L.R. 472; Gray and Sharpe, "Doctors, Samaritans and the Accident Victims" (1973) 11 Osgoode Hall L.J. 1.
[45] *The Ogopogo* [1970] 1 Lloyd's Rep. 257.

consideration.[46] So there is no legal obligation to warn one who is about to walk into a trap or to rescue him from his perilous situation when he has done so.[47] But there may be liability if the defendant is in the position of a master or invitor, or the risk has resulted from the use of some instrumentality under his control,[48] or land occupied by him,[49] or he has voluntarily intervened to render help. "The result of all this is that the good Samaritan who tries to help may find himself mulcted in damages, while the priest and the Levite who pass by on the other side go on their cheerful way rejoicing."[50] So a doctor who gives first aid to the victim of a traffic accident, although he has a statutory right to recover the cost of his treatment from the person using the vehicle at the time of the event out of which the bodily injury arose,[51] may find himself sued for negligence by the victim.[52] It is clear that one who has already entered into some relationship with another may be liable to that other for omissions as well as for acts.[53] An employer who fails to call in medical aid for an employee who has been injured in the course of his work may in certain circumstances be liable.[54] But it should be remembered that the burden of proof lies heavy on a plaintiff who alleges that the negligence complained of consists in an omission.[55]

(4) Volunteers

It is well established that in general one who has full knowledge of the nature and extent of the risk and is entirely free to avoid it, but nevertheless voluntarily goes on and is injured, cannot recover.[56] This may either be because the defences of *volenti non fit injuria* or contributory negligence have been raised successfully or because the defendant's duty in the particular relationship under consideration is held to have been discharged. The latter view has been adopted in cases dealing with the liability of drunken drivers of vehicles to their passengers.[57] This has been said to be a more satisfactory manner of ascertaining their respective rights than by opposing to a fixed measure of duty exculpatory considerations, such as the voluntary assumption of risk or contributory negligence,[58] but it is open to the serious objection that it infringes the general principle[59] that the standard of care is an objective one.[60]

---

[46] As in the former immunity of highway authorities for non-feasance: above, § 26. See also the contrast between the duties of invitors and licensors, below, §§ 95-96.
[47] *Quinn* v. *Hill* [1957] V.L.R. 439.
[48] *Vanvalkenburg* v. *Northern Navigation Co.* (1913) 19 D.L.R. 649.
[49] *Goldman* v. *Hargrave* [1967] 1 A.C. 645.
[50] Prosser, *Torts* (4th ed.), p. 344.
[51] Road Traffic Act 1972, ss.155–156.
[52] See also below, § 185.
[53] *Kelly* v. *Metropolitan Ry.* [1895] 1 Q.B. 944.
[54] *Kasapis* v. *Laimos Bros. Ltd.* [1959] 2 Lloyd's Rep. 378, 381.
[55] See below, § 83. Many of the cases of omission may be regarded as cases of comission: "A medical man who diagnoses a case of measles as a case of scarlet fever may be said to have omitted to make a correct diagnosis: he may equally be said to have made an incorrect diagnosis": *Harnett* v. *Bond* [1924] 2 K.B. 517, 541, *per* Bankes L.J. See also Denning L.J. in *Hawkins* v. *Coulsdon and Purley U.D.C.* [1954] 1 Q.B. 319.
[56] Below, §§ 187–189.
[57] *Insurance Commissioners* v. *Joyce* (1948) 77 C.L.R. 39.
[58] *Ibid.* p. 59, *per* Dixon J.
[59] See below, § 80.
[60] *Nettleship* v. *Weston* [1971] 2 Q.B. 691.

(5) Abnormal plaintiffs

Once a breach of duty has been established, the defendant must take his victim as he finds him.[61] In determining whether a duty exists, however, the law will not take account of abnormal susceptibilities or infirmities in the person[62] or property[63] of the plaintiff which the defendant neither knew nor could reasonably be taken to have foreseen. But if the defendant knows that the plaintiff has some characteristic or incapacity which will increase the risk of harm, the court may hold that the defendant owes a proportionately higher degree of care. So the House of Lords has held[64] that persons carrying out excavations in a London street ought to foresee the presence of blind persons (of whom there are some 7,000 in London) and protect them by some better device than a punner hammer[65] with a handle sloping at a height of two feet. This does not place an undue burden on defendants, for they are entitled to assume that there are places to which the blind will not go unaccompanied, and that they will take reasonable care for their own safety—e.g. by using a white stick.[66]

(6) Acts of third parties

In general there is no duty to control third parties. But there are special relations or situations when a defendant may owe a duty even though the immediate cause of the plaintiff's damage is the act or omission of a third party, and even though the defendant and the third party are not in the relationship of employer and employee or otherwise joint tortfeasors. The increasing incidence of violence has shown the courts ready to expand this area of liability. For example,[67] liability has been imposed on the Home Office for the escapes of Borstal inmates,[68] on a local authority for the escape of a known arsonist from a community home,[69] on railway companies for assaults by drunken passengers,[70] on innkeepers for harm done by, or even to[71] drunken customers, on a householder for negligence by one guest towards another,[72] and on a football club for vandalism by fans.[73]

§ 79. VALUE OF THE CONCEPT OF DUTY OF CARE

The concept is peculiar to the common law of England, and it has sometimes been criticised.[74] Reference has been made to "The fantastic edifice of doctrine . . . which now rivals in incomprehensibility the wilder doctrines of

---

[61] See below, § 202.
[62] *McLaughlin* v. *Trimmer* (1946) 79 L1.L.R. 649 (decayed tooth).
[63] *Nova-Mink Ltd.* v. *Trans-Canada Airlines* [1951] 2 D.L.R. 241 (extra-sensitive mink).
[64] *Haley* v. *London Electricty Board* [1965] A.C. 778.
[65] A hammer for beating down earth.
[66] *Haley* v. *London Electricity Board* [1965] A.C. 778, 795. A similar principle obtains in assessing the standard of care owed to children: see below, § 196.
[67] See also below, § 95.
[68] *Dorset Yacht Co. Ltd.* v. *Home Office* [1970] A.C. 1004. These cases may also be treated as raising problems in remoteness of damage: below, §§ 203-204.
[69] *Potter* v. *Essex County Council, Daily Telegraph,* 3 April, 1979. See also *Dunton* v. *Dover D.C. The Times,* 31 March, 1977 (gypsies).
[70] *Adderley* v. *Great Northern Ry.* [1905] 2 I.R. 378.
[71] *Menon* v. *Honsberger* (1973) 38 D.L.R. (3d) 105.
[72] *Moynihan* v. *Moynihan* [1975] I.R. 192.
[73] *Evans* v. *Glasgow D.C.* 1978 S.L.T. 17; *Hosie* v. *Arbroath F.C.,* 1978, S.L.T. 122.
[74] "An unnecessary abstraction which adds nothing to the substance of the law": Aityah, *Accidents and the Law* (3rd ed., 1980), p. 67.

the old law of property."[75] Indeed, it has been said that every case could be just as well decided on some ground not depending on duty at all—sufficiency of evidence for the jury, contributory negligence, remoteness of damage, inevitable accident, *volenti non fit injuria.* But the better view is that there are and must be limits to the action of negligence which have nothing to do with these factors. No doubt they "are relevant once one is in the field of negligence, but they do not explain why a person who fails in a prosecution cannot be made liable in tort without proof of malice. That is a matter of pure policy, and the technical way in which English law expresses it is by saying that a person is under no duty of care when instituting a prosecution."[76]

Another criticism which has sometimes been made of the concept of duty of care is that it is a formula which is expressed in terms of results rather than reasons.[77] It cannot be denied that there is much truth in this. Indeed the nature of negligence is such that there will always be much room for the exercise of a creative choice by a court confronted with a difficult problem,[78] and the concept of a duty (unlike the concepts of standard of care and remoteness) does at least bring this problem to the fore.[79] "The real effect of the foregoing is that categories become the servants and not the masters of the law of negligence. It may be a common tendency to attempt classification of the various human relationships which may give rise to a breach of duty. But the more modern decisions to which I have referred indicate that such classifications cannot be final. They cannot be set up as inflexible yardsticks, but must be regarded rather as convenient sensitive instruments fashioned and refashioned from time to time in the judicial workshops, to record and harmonise the relation between the law and altering social and business outlooks."[80]

§ 80. STANDARD OF CARE: (1) THE REASONABLE MAN

(1) Standard is objective

The standard of conduct required by the common law is that of the reasonable man. This has been settled ever since *Vaughan* v. *Menlove.*[81] The plaintiff had an interest in certain cottages on land adjoining that on which the defendant had erected a haystack which was not properly ventilated.

---

[75] Simpson, *History of the Common Law of Contract* (1975), p. 234n.
[76] Lawson, "The Duty of Care in Negligence: a Comparative Survey" (1947) 22 Tulane L.R. 111, 113. His conclusion is: "The concept of a duty of care, to be established as a matter of law to the satisfaction of the court, provides an admirable instance of cautious advance congenial to the English temperament and wholly appropriate to the genius of the common law."
[77] *Nova-Mink Ltd.* v. *Trans-Canada Airlines* [1951] 2 D.L.R. 241, 255.
[78] "The courts make what academics now like to call 'a value judgment' ": *McCarthy* v. *Wellington City* [1966] N.Z.L.R. 481, 519, *per* McCarthy J.
[79] See Dixon C.J. and Williams J. in *Thompson* v. *Bankstown Corporation* (1953) 87 C.L.R. 619, 623: "The difficulty in deciding this appeal arises from the possibility and perhaps the necessity of choosing between two competing categories of the law of torts and applying one of them to the facts to the exclusion of the other."
[80] *Crewe* v. *Star Publishing Co. Ltd.* (1942) 58 B.C.C.R. 103, 127, *per* O'Halloran J.A. (Wetter, *The Styles of Appellate Judicial Opinions* (1960), p. 313, is very severe about this case: "an exercise in legal barbarism.")
[81] (1837) 3 Bing. N.C. 468; 4 Scott 244.

The plaintiff's cottages were damaged by a fire which had spontaneously ignited in the haystack, which was insured. "When the condition of the stack, and the probable and almost inevitable consequence of permitting it to remain in its then state were pointed out to him, he abstained from the exercise of the precautionary measures that common prudence and foresight would naturally suggest, and very coolly observed that 'he would chance it'; it was manifest that he adverted to his interest in the insurance office."[82] The argument for the defendant that it was enough if he had acted bona fide to the best of his judgment was rejected.[83] A modern example is *The Lady Gwendolen*.[84] The directors of Guinness's brewery sent stout from Dublin to Liverpool in a ship whose captain relied entirely on radar when going up the Mersey at full speed. The directors were held guilty of "actual fault" under the Merchant Shipping Act 1894, s. 503, in failing properly to supervise the captain. "The law must apply a standard which is not relaxed to cater for their factual ignorance of all activities outside brewing: having become owners of ships, they must behave as reasonable shipowners."[85]

"The standard of foresight of the reasonable man," said Lord Macmillan,[86] "eliminates the personal equation and is independent of the idiosyncrasies of the particular person whose conduct is in question. Some persons are by nature unduly timorous and imagine every path beset with lions. Others, of more robust temperament, fail to foresee or nonchalantly disregard even the most obvious dangers. The reasonable man is presumed to be free both from over-apprehension and from over-confidence." "A reasonable man does not mean a paragon of circumspection."[87] So the judges recognise that even a housewife with young children cannot be in two places at once.[88] But the reasonable man (or woman) is also cool and collected and remembers to take precautions for his own safety even in an emergency.[89] So, while on the one hand an error of judgment may not amount to negligence,[90] on the other hand the fact that "it might happen to anyone" is not necessarily a defence[91]—even the most careful are sometimes careless. So the case for wearing seat belts is so strong that forgetfulness will not be accepted as an excuse.[92] A number of judicial metaphors or analogies are now firmly embedded in the law. "The person concerned is sometimes described as 'the man in the street,' 'the man on the Clapham omnibus,' or, as I recently read in an American author, 'the man who takes the magazines at home and in the evening pushes the lawn mower in his shirt sleeves.' "[93]

---

[82] (1837) 4 Scott 244, 254, *per* Vaughan J. This must be the earliest, and one of the most interesting, judicial references to the impact of insurance on torts: see above, § 7.
[83] (1837) 3 Bing. N.C. 468, 475.
[84] [1965] P. 294.
[85] [1965] P. 294, 305, *per* Winn L.J.
[86] *Glasgow Corporation* v. *Muir* [1943] A.C. 448, 457.
[87] *Billings & Son.* v. *Riden* [1958] A.C. 240, 255, *per* Lord Reid.
[88] *Carmarthenshire County Council* v. *Lewis* [1955] A.C. 549, 566.
[89] *Ghannan* v. *Glasgow Corporation*, 1950, S.C. 23.
[90] *Latimer* v. *A.E.C. Ltd.* [1953] A.C. 643, 656.
[91] *Lewis* v. *Carmarthenshire County Council* [1953] 1 All E.R. 1025, 1028.
[92] *Froom* v. *Butcher* [1976] Q.B. 286, 295.
[93] *Hall* v. *Brooklands Auto-Racing Club* [1933] 1 K.B. 205, 224, *per* Greer L.J. yet "God forbid that the standard of manners should be taken from the man on the Clapham omnibus": *Lea* v. *Justice of the Peace Ltd.* (reported *sub nom. Privacy and the Press*, London, 1947), p. 156, *per* Hilbery J.

(2) Different degrees of negligence not recognised

The law of torts[94] does not recognise different standards of care or different degrees of negligence in different classes of cases. The sole standard is the care that would be shown in the circumstances by a reasonably careful man, and the sole form of negligence is a failure to use this amount of care. It is true, indeed, that this amount will be different in different cases, for a reasonable man will not show the same anxious care when handling an umbrella as when handling a loaded gun.[95] Thus a manufacturer of carcinogens must take such a high degree of care as to be almost under strict liability.[96] On the other hand, there is a growing tendency in the field of occupiers' liability to expect more of a wealthy company or public authority than of a private individual,[97] and even in the case of a private occupier "the humane person" has made his appearance.[98]

Again a man may hold himself out as having a special skill which he does not in fact possess and then the maxim *imperitia culpae adnumeratur* applies. It is commonly a negligent act voluntarily to undertake the doing of any act which can be safely done only through the possession of special skill, unless the doer possesses, or believes on reasonable grounds that he possesses, the requisite skill.[99] The negligence does not consist in the lack of skill but in undertaking the work without skill. Thus a surgeon, though he is not an insurer against every accidental slip, must exercise such care as a normally skilful member of the profession may reasonably be expected to exercise.[1] Again, it may be quite reasonable for a householder to do his own carpentry or plumbing or painting, but this does not of itself protect him.[2] So a high standard of skill and care is demanded of the driver of a motor-car—since the motor-car has become a lethal weapon.[3] So in some circumstances the reasonable driver will take all possible care.[4] But this is a different thing from recognising different legal standards of care; the test of negligence is the same in all cases.[5] So a learner driver must comply with the same objective and impersonal standard as any other driver.[6] So also must a driver who is old or infirm, as distinct from totally unconscious.[7] But, perhaps illogically, it has been held that an unusually expert rally-driver must display towards a passenger in his car the skill of such a driver,[8] and it

---

[94] *Pentecost* v. *London District Auditor* [1951] 2 K.B. 759, 764. *Aliter* in other branches of law, *e.g.* trusts and criminal law.

[95] *Beckett* v. *Newalls Insulation Co. Ltd.* [1953] 1 W.L.R. 8, 17.

[96] *Wright* v. *Dunlop Rubber Co. Ltd.* (1972) 13 K.I.R. 255, 273.

[97] *British Railways Board* v. *Herrington* [1972] A.C. 877.

[98] *Southern Portland Cement Ltd.* v. *Cooper* [1974] A.C. 623, 644.

[99] See *The Lady Gwendolen* [1965] P. 294.

[1] *Whiteford* v. *Hunter* [1950] W.N. 533. See below, § 83.

[2] *Wells* v. *Cooper* [1958] 2 Q.B. 265.

[3] *Daly* v. *Liverpool Corporation* [1939] 2 All E.R. 142, 144.

[4] *Randall* v. *Tarrant* [1955] 1 W.L.R. 255, 259.

[5] Nevertheless, in *Coggs* v. *Bernard* (1703) 2 Ld. Raym. 909, an unfortunate attempt was made to introduce into English law the Roman doctrine. According to this doctrine there are three different kinds or degrees of negligence—ordinary, gross and slight. There are no authorities which compel us to admit that distinctions so vague and impracticable in their nature, so unfounded in principle, and so clearly rooted in historical error as to the rules of Roman law, form any genuine part of the law of England, particularly as the judges have often said they do not understand the expression "gross negligence": *Houghland* v. *R. R. Low (Luxury Coaches) Ltd.* [1962] 1 Q.B. 694, 697-698. But a spectator at a game can recover only for reckless acts (§ 187).

[6] *Nettleship* v. *Weston* [1971] 2 Q.B. 691.

[7] *Roberts* v. *Ramsbottom* [1980] 1 All E.R. 7.

[8] *McComiskey* v. *McDermott* [1974] I.R. 75.

has been suggested that a client who employs a solicitor of high standing and great experience is entitled to expect more than ordinary competence.[9]

(3) Defendant's incapacity irrelevant

The same principle applies to the lack of any other qualification for the safe conduct of an operation, such as knowledge, sound judgment, sound health, physical strength, or the possession of any other requisite mental or bodily faculty. The law "does not attempt to see men as God sees them, for more than one sufficient reason. . . . If, for instance, a man is born hasty and awkward, is always having accidents and hurting himself or his neighbours, no doubt his congenital defects will be allowed for in the courts of Heaven, but his slips are no less troublesome to his neighbours than if they sprang from guilty neglect."[10] The foolish and the forgetful are judged by the same external standard as other defendants. So if an occupier of property is aware of the existence on his premises of physical facts which would constitute a trap to a licensee, he will not be permitted to say that he did not appreciate that those facts constituted a trap.[11] An apparent exception to this principle may be found in the case of a minor: it is accepted that the standard of care required is only that which would reasonably be expected of a child of the defendant's age.[12] But the exception is apparent only, for the true question is, what is normal conduct in a child of this age, not this child?

If, however, a person thus deficient in some attribute of the ordinary and average man is placed without his own choice in some situation where the possession of that attribute is requisite for the avoidance of harm, he is not responsible for negligence merely because the ordinary man could have avoided the accident. He must be judged with reference to his own capacities of mind and body, and if he does his best, he does enough, even though a man better endowed would have been bound to do much more. A blind man must not voluntarily do an act which can be safely done only by those who have eyes to see, but if he has such action thrust upon him through no choice of his, he will not be judged as though he could see.

(4) Difficulties of reasonable foresight

The advantage of the test of reasonable foresight is that it keeps the law in touch with the needs of the ordinary man. The disadvantage is that in a complex society ordinary men may have little knowledge or experience of the activity under considerations so as to entitle them to set the appropriate standard of care. The result may be confused and contradictory decisions which lay down no clear guide for conduct. The best example is the *Wagon Mound* litigation. The facts were that the steamship *Wagon Mound* was taking in bunkering-oil some 600 feet away from a wharf in the harbour of Sydney. As a result of the carelessness of the seamen, a large quantity of oil spilt into the bay. Some sixty hours later that oil ignited and a fire spread rapidly and did considerable damage to the wharf and also to ships adjoining that

---

[9] *Argyll* v. *Beuselinck* [1972] 2 Lloyd's Rep. 172.
[10] Holmes, *The Common Law*, p. 108. See also *McGrath* v. *National Coal Board* (unreported), H.L., May 4, 1954, *per* Lord Reid.
[11] *Hawkins* v. *Coulsdon and Purley U.D.C.* [1954] 1 Q.B. 319.
[12] Below, § 196.

wharf. The outbreak of fire was due to the fact that wind and tide had together carried under the wharf some inflammable debris, on top of which lay some cotton waste which was then set alight by molten metal falling from the wharf as a result of welding operations being carried out on it. These flames in turn set the floating oil afire. The Judicial Committee in an action brought by the owners of the wharf held that the damage in question was not reasonably foreseeable at all.[13] In *The Wagon Mound* (*No.* 2) a different action was launched by different plaintiffs, the owners of the ships adjoining the wharf which had been damaged in the fire. The trial judge held that the plaintiffs were not entitled to recover in negligence, for although the damage was foreseeable, the risk was so remote that it could be disregarded and was therefore not *reasonably* foreseeable. A reasonable ship's officer would have appreciated, it was said, that there was some possibility of fire from floating oil on the sea water, but that possibility was so remote that he would be justified in disregarding it under the principles set out in *Bolton* v. *Stone*.[14] On appeal the Judicial Committee held[15] that on the facts the defendants ought reasonably to have foreseen damage by fire against which precautions should have been taken, and so they were liable in negligence. Nobody has yet produced a satisfactory reconciliation of the two decisions.

§ 81. STANDARD OF CARE: (2) THE CONCEPT OF RISK

There is now a marked tendency[16] to expound the standard of care required in any particular case more in terms of risk than in terms of reasonable foreseeability. A risk is a chance of harm to others which the party whose conduct has been called in question should have recognised. Hence negligence is conduct which falls below the standard established by the law for the protection of others against unreasonable risk of harm. (The risk or hazard in question must, as we have already seen, be to a legally protected interest of the plaintiff.[17]) There are three factors for consideration: (1) the magnitude of the risk to which the defendant exposes other persons by his action; (2) the importance of the object to be attained by the dangerous form of activity; (3) the burden of adequate precautions.[18] We shall consider each separately.

(1) The magnitude of the risk to which others are exposed

The law in all cases exacts a degree of care commensurate with the risk created.[19] There are two factors in determining the magnitude of a risk—the

---

[13] [1961] A.C. 388.
[14] [1951] A.C. 850.
[15] [1967] 1 A.C. 617.
[16] Legislative as well as judicial: see the Oil in Navigable Waters Act 1971, Sched. 2, para. 1.
[17] See above, § 74.
[18] *Hicks* v. *British Transport Commission* [1958] 1 W.L.R. 493, 505. This approach has been adopted in many other English cases: see *McCarthy* v. *Coldair Ltd.* [1951] 2 T.L.R. 1226; *Watt* v. *Hertfordshire C.C.* [1954] 1 W.L.R. 835; *Jones* v. *Vauxhall Motors* [1955] 1 Lloyd's Rep. 152; *Morris* v. *West Hartlepool S.N.Co.* [1956] A.C. 552; *Videan* v. *B.T.C.* [1963] 2 Q.B. 650.
[19] *Read* v. *J. Lyons & Co.* [1947] A.C. 156, 173; *Lloyds Bank* v. *Railway Executive* [1952] 1 All E.R. 1248, 1253. For a similar approach in the criminal law, see *The People* v. *Dunleavy* [1948] I.R. 95 (manslaughter).

seriousness of the injury risked, and the likelihood of the injury being in fact caused.[20]

(i) *Gravity of the injury*

In *Paris* v. *Stepney Borough Council*[21] the plaintiff, who had only one good eye, was blinded in the course of his employment. He contended successfully that his employers, by omitting to provide him with goggles, were in breach of their duty to take reasonable care of his safety because, though it was not the practice to provide goggles for that class of work, they must have known that the consequences of an accident to his good eye would be peculiarly disastrous. In the Court of Appeal Asquith L.J.[22] had said[23] that "A greater risk of injury is not the same thing as a risk of greater injury; the first alone is relevant to liability." This neatly phrased apophthegm was disapproved in the House of Lords. The duty of an employer to take reasonable care to protect his servant is owed to each individual workman and a reasonable and prudent employer would be influenced not only by the greater or less probability of an accident occurring to the workman in question but also by the gravity of the consequences to him if an accident did occur.[24] Protection in the way of goggles should be provided for two-eyed men as well as for one-eyed men if the risk if sufficiently great.[25]

But if an employee has some special susceptibility to harm it does not follow that his employers are guilty of negligence merely because they know of this and yet permit him to continue with the only work which they can offer him.[26]

(ii) *Likelihood of injury*

The general principle is that before negligence can be established it must be shown not only that the event was foreseeable but also that there is a reasonable likelihood of injury. To base liability upon foreseeability alone would be too severe, for "foreseeability does not include any idea of likelihood at all."[27] It is clear that "People must guard against reasonable probabilties, but they are not bound to guard against fantastic possibilities."[28] Thus in *Blyth* v. *Birmingham Water Works Co.*[29] the defendants were held not guilty of negligence "because their precautions

---

[20] *Paris* v. *Stepney B.C.* [1951] A.C. 367, 381. A vivid summary has been given by Judge Learned Hand: "The duty ... is a function of three variables: (1) the probability that she [defendant's ship] will break away; (2) the gravity of the resulting injury, if she does; (3) the burden of the adequate precautions. Possibly it serves to bring this notion into relief to state it in algebraic terms: if the probability be called P; the injury L; and the burden B; liability depends upon whether B is less than L multiplied by P; *i.e.* whether B $<$ PL": *United States* v. *Carroll Towing Co.* (1947) 159 F. (2d) 169, 173.
[21] [1951] A.C. 367.
[22] "Than whom there have been few greater masters of the English language in judicial interpretation or exposition": *Betty's Cafés Ltd.* v. *Phillips Furnishing Stores Ltd.* [1959] A.C. 20, 34, *per* Viscount Simonds.
[23] [1950] 1 K.B. 320, 324.
[24] *Smith* v. *Howdens Ltd.* [1953] N.I. 131. The difficulty of these cases is shown by the fact that although all the members of the House agreed on the law, two (Lord Simonds and Lord Morton of Henryton) dissented on its application to the facts.
[25] *Nolan* v. *Dental Manufacturing Co. Ltd.* [1958] 1 W.L.R. 936.
[26] *Withers* v. *Perry Chain Co. Ltd.* [1961] 1 W.L.R. 1314.
[27] *Chapman* v. *Hearse* (1961) 106 C.L.R. 112, 155, *per* Dixon C.J.
[28] *Fardon* v. *Harcourt-Rivington* (1932) 146 L.T. 391, 392, *per* Lord Dunedin.
[29] (1856) 11 Ex. 781.

proved insufficient against the effect of the extreme severity of the frost of 1855, which penetrated to a greater depth[30] than any which ordinarily occurs south of the polar regions." Again, in *Bolton* v. *Stone*,[31] the plaintiff, while standing in the quiet suburban highway outside her house, was struck by a cricket ball[32] from the defendant's ground, the batsman "having received the right kind of ball and dealt with it in the right kind of way."[33] The plaintiff was 100 yards from the batsman and the ball had cleared a 17-foot fence 78 yards from the batsman. Similar hits had occurred only about six times in the previous 30 years. The House of Lords held that the plaintiff had not established such a likelihood of injury as to convict the defendants of negligence in failing to take precautions against it. It was improbable that the ball would be hit out of the ground or would cause personal injuries if it was.[34]

The decision in *Bolton* v. *Stone* has been accepted in Australia[35] and in Ireland.[36] The case may be said to have established that, if an event is foreseeable, the antithesis of its being reasonably probable is that the possibility of its happening involves a risk so small that a reasonable man would feel justified in disregarding it.[37] No doubt if cricket cannot be played on a ground without creating a substantial risk it must not be played there at all,[38] but in this case the facts showed no substantial risk.[39] So again defendants who did nothing were held to be justified in their attitude when a man was electrocuted in a way which was "most unexpected" in that particular trade[40]; or when every witness said that "he had never heard of an accident of this kind before."[41] But it is not always justifiable to neglect a risk of small magnitude simply because it is small—the difficulty, expense and advantages of eliminating the risk must also be considered,[42] as well as the general practice in such cases.[43] It may well be that defendants are in a stronger position if the risk was so small that they had never thought about it but merely followed the usual practice than if they had considered it and decided that the risks were very small, and so could be disregarded.[44]

Unlikely hazards

On the other hand, it is not necessary that the chances that damage will result should be greater than the chances that no damage will occur.[45] So the

---

[30] Unstated, but the mains were laid more than 18 in. down.
[31] [1951] A.C. 850. See Goodhart (1951) 67 L.Q.R. 461; Lloyd (1951) 14 M.L.R. 499.
[32] Preserved in the museum at Lord's.
[33] *Booker* v. *Wenborn* [1962] 1 W.L.R. 162, 168, *per* Lord Evershed M.R.
[34] A claim in nuisance also failed; above, § 17. If the batsman had been sued in trespass, would the plaintiff have succeeded?
[35] *Chapman* v. *Hearse* (1961) 106 C.L.R. 112.
[36] *Healy* v. *Bray U.D.C.* [1962–63] Ir.Jur.Rep. 9, 17.
[37] *Carmarthenshire County Council* v. *Lewis* [1955] A.C. 549, 565.
[38] *Stone* v. *Bolton* [1950] 1 K.B. 201, 212; [1951] A.C. 850, 867.
[39] "It seems to me that a reasonable man, taking account of the chances against an accident happening, would not have felt himself called upon either to abandon the use of the ground for cricket or to increase the height of his surrounding fences. He would have done what the appellants did: in other words, he would have done nothing": [1951] A.C. 850, 869, *per* Lord Radcliffe.
[40] *Cilia* v. *James (H.M.) & Sons (A Firm)* [1954] 1 W.L.R. 721, 728.
[41] *Cuttress* v. *Scaffolding (G.B.) Ltd.* [1953] 1 W.L.R. 1311, 1316.
[42] *Goldman* v. *Hargrave* [1967] 1 A.C. 645.
[43] Below, § 82.
[44] *Morris* v. *West Hartlepool SN. Co. Ltd.* [1956] A.C. 552, 568.
[45] The Wagon Mound (*No.* 2) [1967] 1 A.C. 617.

fire in *The Wagon Mound (No. 2)*[46] was "extremely unlikely" but yet a real
danger which should have been reasonably foreseeable. An occurrence may
be unusual in the sense of infrequent and yet not unlikely.[47] Or a danger
may be likely to arise and yet an accident unlikely to happen.[48] So the fact
that the injury which has occurred is unique in character, or has happened
previously on a minimal number of occasions, or to a very few people, does
not necessarily prove that the defendant is under no duty to take precautions against it. Thus the fact that five million similar objects have been put
in circulation without complaint is not conclusive[49]; nor is the fact that
thousands of persons have safely passed over the premises in question.[50]
But, as we have just seen, *Bolton* v. *Stone*[51] holds that such a foreseeable
risk may sometimes be disregarded by a reasonable man. In this way justice
is done.[52]

The judges have used a bewildering variety of metaphors and analogies to
summarise the position. Perhaps the best phrase is "not unlikely to occur,"
because on the one hand it denies the proposition that the event or damage
should be apprehended as more likely than not to occur, and on the other
hand, by its negative form, it excludes possibilities which are negative and
unreal.[53]

What exactly must be foreseen?

It is not necessary to show that the particular accident which has
happened was foreseeable, any more than it is necessary to show that the
particular damage was foreseeable[54] or that the particular plaintiff was
foreseeable.[55] It is enough if it was reasonable in a general way to foresee the
kind of thing that occurred.[56] If it were necessary for the plaintiff to prove
that the defendant ought to have foreseen the particular harm which in the
event occurred, few actions for negligence would be successful. "The history
of negligence is the history of the unexpected. The books are full of odd
occurrences, strange conjunctions, and unpredictable contingencies."[57]

Thus in *Hughes* v. *Lord Advocate*[58] a small boy interfered with a paraffin
lamp marking a manhole cover in a street, and was severely burned when
the lamp exploded. It was argued for the defendants that they were not
responsible for a fire caused by explosion as distinct from conflagration, but
the House of Lords held that on the facts this was too fine a distinction. The
cause of the accident was a known source of danger behaving in an

---

[46] [1967] 1 A.C. 617. See below, § 202.
[47] *Green* v. *Perry* [1955] A.L.R. 761.
[48] *Cade* v. *British Transport Commission* [1959] A.C. 256; Goodhart (1958) 74 L.Q.R. 466.
[49] *Grant* v. *Australian Knitting Mills* [1936] A.C. 85.
[50] *Protheroe* v. *Railway Executive* [1951] 1 K.B. 376, 379; *Caminer* v. *Northern and London
    Investment Trust* [1951] A.C. 88, 111.
[51] [1951] A.C. 850.
[52] *Wyong Shire Council* v. *Shirt* (1980) 29 A.L.R. 217.
[53] *Caterson* v. *Commssioner for Railways* (1973) 47 A.L.J.R. 249, 251.
[54] *Draper* v. *Hodder* [1972] 2 Q.B. 556, 573.
[55] It is not necessary that there should be a specific person to whom the duty is owed at the
    time of the negligence: the duty may be potential or contingent or owed to a class—*e.g.*
    new customers as distinct from *this* new customer: *Grant* v. *Australian Knitting Mills*
    [1936] A.C. 85, 104; *Watson* v. *Fram Reinforced Concrete Co. Ltd., and Winget Ltd.*
    1960 S.C. 100, 116; *Chapman* v. *Hearse* (1961) 106 C.L.R. 112, 120.
[56] *Stewart* v. *West African Terminals Ltd.* [1964] 2 Lloyd's Rep. 371, 375.
[57] *Bourhill* v. *Young*, 1941 S.L.T. 364, 387, *per* Lord Justice-Clerk Aitchison. See also below
    § 196.
[58] [1963] A.C. 837.

unpredictable way. *Hughes* v. *Lord Advocate* was distinguished in *Doughty* v. *Turner Manufacturing Co. Ltd.*[59] An asbestos cover was inadvertently knocked into a cauldron containing molten liquid at a temperature of 800°C. The asbestos suffered a chemical change causing the eruption of liquid which burned the plaintiff workman. This was an unforeseeable risk, and not a variant of the perils from splashing—a foreseeable risk. All earlier cases must now be read in the light of *Hughes* and *Doughty*.[60]

Again, although damage from frostbite is unusual in England, the defendant was held liable because he ought to have foreseen the type, kind or order of harm in question—namely, damage from exceptionally cold weather. It was not required that he should foresee the degree of damage which in fact occurred.[61] So if a road accident is of a type which one would expect on a sub-standard road in bad weather, that ends the matter.[62] But when the plaintiff, a farm-worker, contracted a very rare disease as a result of contact with the urine of rats, as distinct from being bitten by those rats, the defendant escaped liability.[63]

(2) The importance of the object to be attained

The reasonableness of the defendant's conduct will also depend upon the proportion which the risk bears to the object to be attained. To expose others to a risk of harm for a disproportionate object is unreasonable, whereas an equal risk for a better cause may be lawfully run without negligence. By running trains at the rate of 50 miles an hour railway companies have caused many fatal accidents which could quite easily have been avoided by running at 10 miles an hour. But this additional safety would be attained at too great a cost of public convenience, and therefore, in neglecting this precaution, the companies do not fall below the standard of reasonable care and are not guilty of negligence.[64] Similarly, when it was suggested that a bank, which is under a duty to pay on demand a cheque which is in proper form, owed a duty to its customer to investigate all the indorsements, Lord Macnaghten said, "A banker so very careful to avoid risk would soon have no risk to avoid."[65] A different approach may be required if the object in view is of importance only to the defendant himself and not to the public. The saving of life or limb justifies taking risks which would not be permissible in the case of an ordinary commercial enterprise.[66]

(3) The burden of adequate precautions

The general principle is that the risk has to be weighed against the measures necessary to eliminate it. So the occupier of a small property on

[59] [1964] 1 Q.B. 518. Note that the leading judgment was given by Lord Pearce, who had been a member of the H.L. in *Hughes* v. *Lord Advocate*.
[60] *The Wagon Mound (No.* 2) [1967] 1 A.C. 617, 636.
[61] *Bradford* v. *Robinson Rentals Ltd.* [1967] 1 W.L.R. 337. See below, § 202.
[62] *Levine* v. *Morris* [1970] 1 W.L.R. 71.
[63] *Tremain* v. *Pike* [1969] 1 W.L.R. 1556.
[64] *Daborn* v. *Bath Tramways Motor Co.* [1946] 2 All E.R. 333, 336. No doubt it was a relevant (if unexpressed) consideration in *Bolton* v. *Stone* that the activity promoted by the defendants was the English national game of cricket. As Dr. Goodhart observed ((1951) 67 L.Q.R. 463), if a man reading in his chambers at midnight were to throw his book—or a cricket ball—out of the window in a fit of irritation he could hardly defend himself against an injured passer-by by alleging that such an injury was extremely unlikely.
[65] *Bank of England* v. *Vagliano Bros.* [1891] A.C. 107, 157.
[66] *Watt* v. *Hertfordshire County Council* [1954] 1 W.L.R. 835 (fireman).

which a hazard arises which threatens a neighbour with substantial interests should not have to do as much as one with larger interests of his own at stake and greater resources to protect them.[67] If the risk is very remote, it is material to consider the degree of security which the suggested measures would afford: if in such a case the suggested measures are of an elaborate nature and would result only in a possibility that the accident would have been prevented or its consequences mitigated, then the defendants may be justified in doing nothing.[68] It is also relevant to consider the degree of risk (if any) which taking the precautionary measures may involve.[69] But the greater the risk the less should be the weight given to questions of the cost of precautionary measures in time, trouble or money.[70] If the risk to life or property is really substantial, and no precautions would avail against it, it may be the duty of the defendants to cease to carry on the particular activity in question.[71]

If the defendant is held to be under a duty to take certain precautions for the safety of the plaintiff he may be permitted to excuse his failure to take those precautions by alleging that the accident would have happened even if he had fulfilled his duty. For even if he had taken the necessary precautions (*e.g.* provided a safety belt in the case of an industrial accident) the plaintiff might have refused to co-operate with his employer and failed to wear the belt. In such a case the plaintiff has in truth failed to prove that the defendant's breach of duty is causally relevant to the accident.[72]

§ 82. PARTICULAR CASES OF NEGLIGENCE

At one time it was regarded as well established that the only use of cases was for the propositions of law which they contained, and that it was no use to compare the facts of one case with those of another to see what decision should be arrived at in the latter. But this simple view became obscured as the law of negligence grew increasingly complicated. In particular, the disappearance of the civil jury meant that trials before a judge sitting alone became longer and more elaborate, and the judgments themselves correspondingly lengthier. A judge sitting alone feels obliged, unlike a jury, to explain why he is accepting or rejecting each of the arguments of counsel. Hence there was a natural but erroneous tendency to think that when a judge gave reasons for his decision he was laying down rules of law.[73] But the House of Lords has called a welcome halt to this process. In *Qualcast Ltd.* v. *Haynes*[74] it was emphatically reaffirmed that reasons given for deci-

---

[67] *Goldman* v. *Hargrave* [1967] 1 A.C. 645.
[68] *Marshall* v. *Gotham Co. Ltd.* [1954] A.C. 360, 376.
[69] *Morris* v. *West Hartlepool S.N. Co. Ltd.* [1956] A.C. 552, 574, 579; *Hicks* v. *British Transport Commission* [1958] 1 W.L.R. 493, 505.
[70] *Morris* v. *Luton Corporation* [1946] 1 All E.R. 1, 4; *Edwards* v. *National Coal Board* [1949] 1 K.B. 704, 710; *Marshall* v. *Gotham Co. Ltd.* [1954] A.C. 360.
[71] *Stone* v. *Bolton* [1950] 1 K.B. 201, 212; [1951] A.C. 850, 867; *Latimer* v. *A.E.C. Ltd.* [1953] A.C. 643.
[72] *McWilliams* v. *Sir William Arrol & Co. Ltd.* [1962] 1 W.L.R. 295. See also below, §§ 83, 181.
[73] It is instructive to compare the judgments on torts of a century ago with those of today. It is not only that Erle or Blackburn or Willes were right in the result—but their reasons were expressed with a clarity, simplicity and brevity rarely found today. Yet these judges had been trained under a system of pleading notorious for its verbosity and complexity.
[74] [1959] A.C. 743.

sions on questions of fact are not binding on future judges. The reports should not, therefore, be ransacked to discover isolated sentences with which to support an argument,[75] for owing to the great number of cases on negligence the "tests have been examined, discussed, and described in language either sober or picturesque."[76]

With these warnings in mind, we may consider some of the cases in which the courts have considered the duies owed by those engaged in particular professions, trades, or activities. We may take as examples professional men, schoolmasters, and users of the highway.

(1) Professional men

When the exercise of some special skill or competence, such as that of an architect, or doctor,[77] is in question, the test of the man on the Clapham omnibus is somewhat unreal. Instead the standard is that of the ordinary skilled man exercising and professing to have that special skill.[78] It is expected of such a professional man that he should show a fair, reasonable and competent degree of skill; it is not required that he should use the highest degree of skill, for there may be persons who have higher education and greater advantages than he has, nor will he be held to have guaranteed a cure.[79] So a barrister is not expected to be right: it is enough that he exercises reasonable care.[80] So a medical practitioner should not be found negligent simply because one of the risks inherent in an operation of that kind occurs, or because in a matter of opinion he made an error of judgment,[81] or because he has failed to warn the patient of every risk involved in a proposed course of treatment.[82] There is no rule that a doctor must tell a patient what is the matter with him.[83] A leading case is *Roe* v. *Minister of Health*.[84] In 1947 the plaintiff had been injected with nupercaine, a spinal anaesthetic, by a specialist anaesthetist in order to undergo a minor operation. The nupercaine was contained in glass ampoules, which were in turn kept in a jar of phenol. Some of the phenol percolated through cracks in the ampoules and contaminated the nupercaine. As a result the plaintiff was permanently paralysed below the waist. The cracks in the ampoules were not detectable by ordinary visual or tactile examination. This was a risk which was first drawn to the attention of the profession in 1951: it would not have been appreciated by an ordinary anaesthetist in 1947. "Nowadays it would be negligence not to realise the danger, but it was not then."[85]

---

[75] *Teubner* v. *Humble* (1963) 108 C.L.R. 491, 503.
[76] *Booker* v. *Wenborn* [1962] 1 W.L.R. 162, 172, *per* Danckwerts L.J.
[77] The duty is also owed by an unqualified person who undertakes to cure another: *Brogan* v. *Bennett* [1955] I.R. 119.
[78] *Greaves & Co. Ltd.* v. *Baynham Meikle & Partners* [1975] 1 W.L.R. 1095.
[79] *Challard* v. *Bell* (1959) 18 D.L.R. (2d) 150, 152.
[80] *Saif Ali* [1980] A.C. 198, 231.
[81] Emphatically re-affirmed by the House of Lords in *Whitehouse* v. *Jordan* [1981] 1 W.L.R. 246.
[82] *Smith* v. *Auckland Hospital Board* [1964] N.Z.L.R. 241.
[83] *Daniels* v. *Heskin* [1954] I.R. 73, 87.
[84] [1954] 2 Q.B. 66.
[85] *Per* Denning L.J. [1954] 2 Q.B. 66, 86. See the thought-provoking article by Sir Robert Macintosh (who first drew attention to this danger), "Deaths under Anaesthetics" (1949) 21 *British Journal of Anaesthesia* 107. For the defence of general practice, see below, p. 218.

(2) Parents and Schoolmasters

A schoolmaster is bound to take such care of his boys as a careful father would take care of his sons.[86] This is generally known as the "careful parent test,"[87] but in the same family one parent might be so prudent as to be criticised for fussiness whereas the other might be too anxious to encourage self-reliance in the child.[88] A schoolmaster may also have more opportunities of taking care than a parent.[89] The "careful parent test" is also hardly appropriate in some circumstances—*e.g.* very large schools[90] —and it is simpler to say that the duty of a schoolmaster is to take such care as is reasonable in the circumstances. The duty of a schoolmaster is somewhat higher than the common duty of care under the Occupiers' Liability Act 1957.[91] It is necessary to strike a balance between the meticulous supervision of children every moment of the time they are under the care of their schoolmaster and the very desirable object of encouraging the sturdy independence of children as they grow up.[92] It is not practicable to require constant supervision of children; only such supervision as is reasonable in the circumstances is required.[93] So the defendants were held liable when they failed to provide a guard for a gas stove at a cookery school attended by a girl of 11.[94] But when the plaintiff, a schoolboy of 14 years, was injured by a clod of earth thrown by another boy whilst they are "ragging" when helping a local farmer on a half-holiday, the defendant escaped liability.[95] "If every master is to take precautions to see that there is never ragging or horseplay among his pupils, his school would indeed be too awful a place to contemplate."[96] So there is no obligation to supervise children running races in playgrounds: that is what playgrounds are for.[97] A prudent master should also take precautions against his boys causing injury to persons unconnected with the school.[98]

(3) Users of the highway[99]

The operation of vehicles on the highway does not give rise to strict liability: the plaintiff must prove negligence,[1] although in some cases a high

---

[86] *Rich* v. *L.C.C.* [1953] 1 W.L.R. 895, 900, 902.
[87] *Durham* v. *Public School Board of North Oxford* (1960) 23 D.L.R. (2d) 711, 717.
[88] *Peters* v. *Hill, The Times*, March 29, 1957.
[89] *Rogers* v. *Rawlings* [1969] Qd. R. 262.
[90] *Beaumont* v. *Surrey C.C.* (1968) 66 L.G.R. 580, 585.
[91] *Reffell* v. *Surrey C.C.* [1964] 1 W.L.R. 358. This case also establishes that an action lies for breach of the statutory duty of care under s. 10 of the Education Act 1944. See below, § 85.
[92] *Jeffery* v. *L.C.C.* (1954) 52 L.G.R. 521.
[93] *Clark* v. *Monmouthshire C.C.* (1954) 118, J.P. 244 (knives in playground). It may be otherwise if the child is very young: *Carmarthenshire C.C.* v. *Lewis* [1955] A.C. 549.
[94] *Fryer* v. *Salford Corporation* [1937] 1 All E.R. 617.
[95] *Camkin* v. *Bishop* [1941] 2 All E.R. 713.
[96] [1941] 2 All E.R. 713, 716, *per* Goddard L.J. This case well illustrates the tendency to run together the questions of duty and standard of care. The Court of Appeal held that the defendant was under no duty to see that the boys whilst engaged upon such work were under supervision. It might as well or better have been held that the defendant was under a duty to take reasonable precautions for the safety of his pupils but that there was no evidence of failure to perform that duty.
[97] *Ward* v. *Hertfordshire C.C.* [1969] 1 W.L.R. 790.
[98] *Carmarthenshire C.C.* v. *Lewis* [1955] A.C. 549.
[99] Further information: Bingham, *Motor Claims Cases.*
[1] *Wing* v. *London General Omnibus Co.* [1909] 2 K.B. 652. The Pearson Report (§ 1075) recommended that there should be no formal reversal of the burden of proof in actions for motor vehicle injury.

standard of care is exacted.[2] An underlying principle is that all those using it, or land adjacent to it, must show mutual respect and forbearance.[3] The duty of a driver of a vehicle is to use proper care not to cause injury to persons on the highway or in premises adjoining the highway.[4] Proper care connotes avoidance of excessive speed, keeping a good look-out, observing traffic rules and signals and so on.[5] But there is no duty to foresee the driving of an insane person.[6] Highway authorities also owe to motorists a duty of reasonable care.[7] The duty is owed to persons so placed that they may reasonably expect to be injured by the omission to take such care.[8] In actions for personal injuries arising out of highway accidents it is particularly important to remember that the decision in every case turns upon its own facts—e.g. there is no rule of law that a person driving in the dark is negligent if he cannot stop within the limit of his lights,[9] or that the vehicle which has the other on its right-hand side is the one to give way,[10] or that a driver is entitled to emerge blind from a minor road onto a major road provided he does so very slowly.[11] The presence of an unlighted vehicle on a highway after dark is evidence of negligence, especially if that vehicle is large and dark-coloured,[12] as also is the presence of a vehicle which has been badly parked.[13] But the defendant may be able to rebut the presumption of negligence which arises in such a case.[14] Further, the standard expected may alter from time to time. In 1964 it was not negligence to fail to wear a safety-belt, but today it is held to be negligent for drivers and front-seat passengers to fail to do so, save in such exceptional cases as pregnant women. It is not an exception that the journey was not one which involved a high degree of risk.[15] Finally, there is no absolute right to enter a road junction merely because the lights are green[16]; another vehicle may be lawfully on the intersection.[17]

A failure on the part of any person to observe any provision of the Highway Code may in any civil proceedings be relied upon by any party to the proceedings as tending to establish or to negative any liability which is in question in those proceedings.[18] A failure to observe the provisions of the Road Vehicles Lighting Regulations 1955 will not of itself give a civil remedy to the injured party[19]; nor will a breach of the Motor Vehicles (Construction and Use) Regulations 1955,[20] or of the Various Trunk Roads (Prohibition of Waiting) (Clearways) Order 1963[21]; although in each case

[2] *Worsfold* v. *Howe* [1980] 1 W.L.R. 1175, 1178.
[3] *Searle* v. *Wallbank* [1947] A.C. 341, 361.
[4] *Bourhill* v. *Young* [1943] A.C. 92.
[5] [1943] A.C. 92, 104.
[6] *Challoner* v. *Williams & Croney* [1975] 1 Lloyd's Rep. 124, 128.
[7] *Levine* v. *Morris* [1970] 1 W.L.R. 71.
[8] *Bourhill* v. *Young* [1943] A.C. 92. Each user of the highway is owed a distinct duty: *Randolph* v. *Tuck* [1962] 1 Q.B. 175.
[9] *Morris* v. *Luton Corporation* [1946] K.B. 114.
[10] *MacIntyre* v. *Coles* [1966] 1 W.L.R. 831.
[11] *Worsfold* v. *Howe* [1980] 1 W.L.R. 1175.
[12] *O'Reilly* v. *Garvey* [1973] I.R. 89.
[13] *Chop Seng Heng* v. *Thevannasan* [1975] 3 All E.R. 572.
[14] *Moore* v. *Maxwells of Emsworth Ltd.* [1968] 2 All E.R. 779.
[15] *Froom* v. *Butcher* [1976] Q.B. 286.
[16] *Radburn* v. *Kemp* [1971] 1 W.L.R. 1502.
[17] *Ramoo* v. *Gan Soo Swee* [1971] 1 W.L.R. 1014.
[18] Road Traffic Act 1972, s. 37 (5); *Croston* v. *Vaughan* [1938] 1 K.B. 540.
[19] *Clarke* v. *Brims* [1947] K.B. 497.
[20] *Barkway* v. *South Wales Transport Co. Ltd.* [1950] 1 All E.R. 392.
[21] *Coote* v. *Stone* [1971] 1 W.L.R. 279.

breach of the regulations may be relied upon as evidence of negligence. But an action lies against a party in breach of the Pedestrian Crossings Regulations 1954,[22] which impose an absolute statutory duty on the motorist to be able to stop in the event of any conceivable use of a crossing by any conceivable pedestrian, other than a suicide.[23] The Road Traffic Act 1960, s. 25, provides that the speed limit on motor-vehicles shall not apply to any vehicle used for police purposes: but this does not exempt the driver of such a vehicle from civil liability for negligence.[24] Finally, it should be remembered that a pedestrian owes a duty of care to other users of the highway,[25] such as the driver of a motor-scooter[26]; and a passenger in a vehicle, although no longer identified with the contributory negligence of his driver,[27] may himself be guilty of negligence—e.g. by opening a door which knocks over a pedestrian.[28]

General Practice

The general rule is that a defendant charged with negligence can clear himself if he shows that he has acted in accordance with the general and approved practice.[29] So a man whose calling in life involves him in creating situations of danger will usually be justified in following the practice which his trade or profession has adopted or approved for dealing with such situations,[30] and he will not be convicted of negligence merely because he has failed to make use of every precaution which ingenuity might suggest.[31] But when there is developing knowledge of new risks he must make reasonable efforts to keep abreast of it.[32] Yet in malpraxis cases it should be remembered that the mere fact that the defendant has deviated from the normal practice is not enough: many advances in medical science have been due to such deviations.[33] So it is probably not necessary for the defendant to show that the circumstances of his own case are precisely similar to those of the general practice.[34] The common law has been approved by Parliament. The Congenital Disabilities (Civil Liabiliy) Act 1976, s. 1 (5) provides that a defendant is not liable "if he took reasonable care having due regard to then received professional opinion."

Faults of omission

When the negligence complained of consists of what may be called a fault of omission,[35] the governing principle was stated by Lord Dunedin in a

---

[22] *London Passenger Transport Board* v. *Upson* |1949| A.C. 155.
[23] *Kozimor* v. *Adey* (1962) 106, S.J. 431.
[24] *Gaynor* v. *Allen* [1959] 2 Q.B. 403.
[25] *Nance* v. *British Columbia Electric Ry.* [1951] A.C. 601, 611.
[26] *Barry* v. *McDonald* (1966) 110 S.J. 56.
[27] See below, § 196.
[28] *Curley* v. *Mannion* |1965| I.R. 543.
[29] *Vancouver General Hospital* v. *McDaniel* (1934) 152 L.T. 56, 57.
[30] Unless the common practice is inherently defective: *O'Donovan* v. *Cork County Council* |1967| I.R. 173.
[31] *Woods* v. *Duncan* [1946] A.C. 401 (naval officer); *Whiteford* v. *Hunter* |1950| W.N. 553 (surgeon).
[32] *Stokes* v. *Guest, Keen and Nettlefold Ltd.* [1968] 1 W.L.R. 1776, 1783.
[33] *Hunter* v. *Hanley*, 1955 S.C. 200, 206.
[34] *Cavanagh* v. *Ulster Weaving Co. Ltd.* [1960] A.C. 145, 158, 167.
[35] The distinction between acts of commission and acts of omission may be a fine one: *Cavanagh* v. *Ulster Weaving Co. Ltd.* [1960] A.C. 145, 165.

passage which has often been cited. "I think it is absolutely necessary that the proof of that fault of omission should be one of two kinds, either to show that the thing which he did not do was a thing which was commonly done by other persons in like circumstances, or to show that it was a thing which was so obviously wanted that it would be folly in anyone to neglect to provide it."[36] "The rule is stated with all the Lord President's trenchant lucidity. It contains an emphatic warning against a facile finding that a precaution is necessary when there is no proof that it is one taken by other persons in like circumstances. But it does not detract from the test of the conduct and judgment of the reasonable and prudent man. If there is proof that a precaution is usually observed by other persons, a reasonable and prudent man will follow the usual practice in the like circumstances. Failing such proof the test is whether the precaution is one which the reasonable and prudent man would think so obvious that it was folly to omit it."[37] The formulation of the law by Lord Dunedin has been applied for many years in scores of cases against employers in England, Scotland[38] and Ireland.[39] It should not be discarded in favour of some milder version,[38] as there might be a temptation to do if the word "folly" is thought to be equivalent to "ridiculous." But really it means no more than "imprudent" or "unreasonable."[40] Lord Dunedin was in truth laying down no new principle of law but simply stating the factual framework within which the law must be applied[41]—and the law is contained in the proposition that a master must take reasonable care for the safety of his servant.[42] The oft-cited formula does not mean that if a plaintiff calls no evidence of practice he must establish folly in order to make out a prima facie case.[43] Neither does it mean that if a practice is averred and proved which might have averted the accident, this is necessarily conclusive of negligence on the part of an employer who has not followed the practice.[44]

Wisdom after the event

But the general practice itself may not conform to the standard of care required of a reasonably prudent man. In such a case it is not a good defence that the defendant acted in accordance with the general practice.[45] Neglect of duty does not cease by repetition to be neglect of duty.[46] It does not follow that one must wait for an accident or series of accidents before a system can be condemned as unsafe.[47] On the other hand, the fact that experience subsequent to the alleged negligence proves that some additional precaution was necessary does not in itself prove negligence at the earlier

---

[36] *Morton* v. *William Dixon Ltd.,* 1909 S.C. 807, 809.
[37] *Paris* v. *Stepney Borough Council* [1951] A.C. 367, 382, *per* Lord Normand. Some judgments state that Lord Normand did not intend in any way to qualify Lord Dunedin's formula: *Cavanagh* v. *Ulster Weaving Co. Ltd.* [1960] A.C. 145, 165–166. Others assume that some gloss or qualification was intended: *Bradley* v. *C.I.E.* [1976] I.R. 217, 221.
[38] *Gallagher* v. *Balfour Beatty & Co. Ltd.,* 1951 S.C. 712, 717.
[39] *Bradley* v. *C.I.E.* [1976] I.R. 217.
[40] *Morris* v. *West Hartlepool S.N. Co. Ltd.* [1956] A.C. 552; *Cavanagh* v. *Ulster Weaving Co. Ltd.* [1960] A.C. 145, 162.
[41] *Cavanagh* v. *Ulster Weaving Co. Ltd.* [1960] A.C. 145, 166.
[42] See below, § 181.
[43] *Cavanagh* v. *Ulster Weaving Co. Ltd.* [1960] A.C. 145, 162.
[44] *Brown* v. *Rolls Royce Ltd.* [1960] 1 W.L.R. 210, 214.
[45] *Donovan* v. *Cork County Council* [1967] I.R. 173
[46] *Carpenters Co.* v. *British Mutual Banking Co.* [1937] 3 All E.R. 811, 820.
[47] *Atkinson* v. *Tyne-Tees Steam Shipping Co. Ltd.* [1956] 1 Lloyd's Rep. 244.

date.[48] "People do not furnish evidence against themselves simply by adopting a new plan in order to prevent the recurrence of an accident. I think that a proposition to the contrary would be barbarous. It would be, as I have often had occasion to tell juries, to hold that, because the world gets wiser as it gets older, therefore it was foolish before."[49] For it is easy to be wise after the event,[50] and nothing is so perfect that it cannot be improved.[51]

§ 83. THE PROOF OF NEGLIGENCE

The burden of proving negligence is on the plaintiff who alleges it. When accidential harm is done, if the action is case not trespass, it is not for the doer to excuse himself by proving that the accident was inevitable and due to no negligence on his part; it is for the person who suffers the harm to prove affirmatively that it was due to the negligence of him who caused it.[52] Unless the plaintiff produces reasonable evidence that the accident was caused by the defendant's negligence, there is no case to go to the jury, and it is the duty of the judge to enter judgment for the defendant.

Judge and jury

In withdrawing the case from the jury the judge does not substitute his own opinion as to the proof of negligence for their opinion; he decides, not that negligence has not been proved, but that no reasonable man or jury could think that it had been proved.[53] It is not necessary for the plaintiff to show that the defendant must be found guilty of negligence, or to eliminate every conceivable possibility by which the accident may have been caused without negligence on the defendant's part.[54] This rule is particularly important when the injured person has either been killed in the accident or has no recollection of it. But the plaintiff's evidence must pass beyond the region of pure conjecture into that of legal inference.[55] The dividing line between conjecture and inference is often a very difficult one to draw. A conjecture may be plausible, but it is of no legal value, for its essence is that it is a mere guess. An inference in the legal sense, on the other hand, is a deduction from the evidence, and if it is a reasonable deduction it may have the validity of legal proof.[56] It follows that there can be no inference unless there are objective facts from which to infer the other facts which it is sought to establish.[57] On such matters as the likelihood of injury and the practicality of safeguards evidence is essential.[58] It is to be noticed that this question is to be decided not by weighing the evidence of the plaintiff against the defendant but by disregarding altogether the evidence of the defendant, and by asking whether that of the plaintiff is, *per se* and apart from any con-

[48] *Philpott* v. *British Railways Board* [1968] 2 Lloyd's Rep. 495, 502.
[49] *Hart* v. *L. & Y. Ry.* (1869) 21 L.T. 261, 263, *per* Bramwell B.
[50] *The Wagon Mound* [1961] A.C. 388, 424.
[51] *Pipe* v. *Chambers Wharf and Cold Stores Ltd.* [1952] 1 Lloyd's Rep. 194, 195.
[52] *Jones* v. *G.W. Ry.* (1930) 144 L.T. 194.
[53] *Bridges* v. *North London Ry.* (1874) L.R. 7 H.L. 213, 233–236.
[54] *Horabin* v. *B.O.A.C.* [1952] 2 All E.R. 1016.
[55] *Jones* v. *G.W. Ry.* (1930) 144 L.T. 194.
[56] *Union Steamship Co. of N.Z. Ltd.* v. *Wenlock* [1958] N.Z.L.R. 173, 177.
[57] *Caswell* v. *Powell Duffryn Collieries* [1940] A.C. 152, 169.
[58] *Maloney* v. *Commissioner for Railways* (1978) 52 A.L.J.R. 292.

tradiction, sufficient or insufficient to bring conviction to a reasonable mind.[59]

Omissions[60]

It is difficult to prove causation when the breach of duty alleged consists in the failure to take some precaution prescribed by statute—*e.g.* under the Health and Safety at Work Act 1974. At one time the courts required the plaintiff to prove that the precaution in question would have been effective if it had been taken,[61] but now it is said to be enough for the plaintiff to prove that the defendants' omission materially increased the risk of the harm occurring.[62]

Submission of no case to answer

In cases which are tried by a judge sitting alone the judge is bound to put counsel who has submitted that there is no case to answer to his election whether he wants to stand on the submission or call his evidence before a ruling on the submission is given.[63] If the judge rules in favour of the defendant, but on appeal the plaintiff establishes that there was a case to answer, he is entitled to judgment and the court has no power to order a new trial. "That follows logically from the principle that the defendant, having elected to call no evidence, is bound by that election, and therefore cannot be given a new trial at which to call evidence that he ought to have called at the hearing."[64] Conversely, if the judge rules against the defendant, but the latter elects to give evidence and has judgment given against him, he cannot ask the Court of Appeal to disregard the evidence so given.[65] But in a jury action the judge probably has a discretion whether he will put counsel to his election, which he need not exercise until all the evidence is concluded.[66]

Onus of proof when several defendants[67]

The rule that the plaintiff must prove that the defendant's negligence was the cause of the accident may cause difficulties if the acts of two or more defendants are involved. While it is plain that the trial judge is entitled to dismiss the claim if there is no evidence from which negligence can be inferred on the part of one or the other or both of the defendants, it has also been held that if A has been injured in circumstances which must have been due to the negligence of B or C, but he is unable to establish which of them is responsible, then the onus of proof is on the defendant to exculpate himself. If he fails to do so, the plaintiff may recover against both defendants.[68] But this principle might cause great hardship to an innocent

---

[59] *Bill* v. *Short Bros. and Harland Ltd.* [1963] N.I. 1.

[60] See also above, § 81.

[61] *McWilliams* v. *Sir William Arrol & Co. Ltd.* [1962] 1 W.L.R. 295.

[62] *McGhee* v. *National Coal Board* [1973] 1 W.L.R. 1.

[63] *Young* v. *Rank* [1950] 2 K.B. 510; *Storey* v. *Storey* [1961] P. 63.

[64] *Goulding* v. *Ministry of Works* (unreported) 1955 C.A. 175A, *per* Jenkins L.J. But in *Portland Management Ltd.* v. *Harte* [1977] 1 Q.B. 306 an exception is suggested.

[65] *Payne* v. *Harrison* [1961] 2 Q.B. 403.

[66] *Payne* v. *Harrison* [1961] 2 Q.B. 403.

[67] See Hogan, "Cook v. Lewis Re-examined" (1961) 24 M.L.R. 331.

[68] *Cook* v. *Lewis* [1952] 1 D.L.R. 1. The parties in this case were "on what Canadians are pleased to call a 'hunting' trip, though we should perhaps call it a shooting holiday": *Re. T. (Infants)* [1968] 1 Ch. 704, 713, *per* Harman L.J.

defendant in a case in which the damage must have been caused by one or other of the defendants, but could not possibly have been caused by both.[69] Hence it may apply[70] only when the defendants are joint tortfeasors, either as being engaged on a concerted common design,[70] or as persons of whom one is vicariously liable for the acts of the other.[71] Thus when the plaintiff has suffered harm as a result of a negligent system of manufacture, inspection or repair adopted by the defendant, he is not required to lay his finger on the exact person in the whole chain who is responsible.[72]

Traffic accidents

The Court of Appeal constantly reminds trial judges that decisions on questions of fact do not lay down legal propositions.[73] When there is a highway collision between two motor-cars in circumstances which give rise to a prima facie case of negligence against each (*e.g.* a head-on collision in broad daylight), in the absence of any evidence enabling the court to distinguish between them, the proper course is for the court to say: both to blame and equally to blame.[74] But it is not easy to see the logic, as distinct from the utility, of this rule, for if a judge does not feel able to give judgment against one of the parties, he should hardly feel able to do the opposite and give judgment against both of them.[75]

Appeals

The powers of the Court of Appeal are wider in the case of an appeal from a judge of the High Court sitting alone than in the case of an appeal from the verdict of a jury. It must be noted that the vast majority of civil actions are today tried by a judge alone.[76] It has been held that in a personal injuries claim a jury should be ordered only in exceptional circumstances,[77] even if the injury is serious.[78] In *Benmax* v. *Austin Motor Co. Ltd.*[79] the House of Lords pointed out that on an appeal it is necessary to distinguish between the finding of a specific fact and a finding of fact which is really an inference from facts specifically found or, as has sometimes been said, between the perception and evaluation of facts. Thus an appellate court will be reluctant to reject a finding of specific fact which may be founded on the

---

[69] *Power* v. *Bedford Motor Co. Ltd.* [1959] I.R. 391, 418–420.
[70] No such limitation appears in the Irish Civil Liability Act 1961, s. 11 (3).
[71] *Cassidy* v. *Ministry of Health* [1951] 2 K.B. 343, 359; *Roe* v. *Minister of Health* [1954] 2 Q.B. 66, 80, 82, 88; *Walsh* v. *Holst & Sons Ltd.* [1958] 1 W.L.R. 800, 804.
[72] *Grant* v. *Australian Knitting Mills* [1936] A.C. 85, 101.
[73] *Worsford* v. *Howe* [1980] 1 All E.R. 1028 is one in a long series of such decisions.
[74] *Baker* v. *Market Harborough Co-operative Society Ltd.* [1953] 1 W.L.R. 1472; *Shiner* v. *Webster* (unreported), 1955 C.A. 140, *per* Denning L.J. The drivers are not, of course, joint tortfeasors.
[75] *Nesterczuk* v. *Mortimore* [1966] A.L.R. 163.
[76] The Civil Judicial Statistics, published annually by H.M.S.O., show that during the past decade less than 50 cases per annum were heard with a jury in the Q.B.D. In five of the Australian states jury trial in motor cases has been abolished. It still prevails in North America.
[77] *Ward* v. *James* [1966] 1 Q.B. 273. The Pearson Report (§ 734) recommended that jury trial should not be reintroduced for personal injury litigation.
[78] *Watts* v. *Manning* [1964] 1 W.L.R. 623.
[79] [1955] A.C. 370. See also *Northern Bank Finance Ltd.* v. *Charlton* [1979] I.R. 149, 180, 189.

credibility[80] of a witness[81]; but in cases where the point in dispute is the proper inference to be drawn from proved facts, an appeal court is generally in as good a position to evaluate the evidence as the trial judge, and ought not to shrink from the task,[82] though it ought, of course, to give weight to his opinion.[83] While it is useful to have such clear and authoritative guidance, it may perhaps be regretted that the law should have been laid down in such very wide terms. The reports contain many cases in which judges of the greatest eminence have differed as to the evaluation of admitted facts[84] and if appellate tribunals are to make full use of the powers given to them by *Benmax* v. *Austin Motor Co. Ltd.* the uncertainty of the law will greatly increase. But when the trial has been before a jury, then provided that there was evidence to go to the jury in the sense explained above, and no misdirection by the judge, the verdict can be set aside only if it is one which no reasonable men might have found on those facts.[85]

§ 84. RES IPSA LOQUITUR[86]

The rule that it is for the plaintiff to prove negligence, and not for the defendant to disprove it, is in some cases one of considerable hardship to the plaintiff, because it may be that the true cause of the accident lies solely within the knowledge of the defendant who caused it. The plaintiff can prove the accident, but he cannot prove how it happened so as to show its origin in the negligence of the defendant. This hardship is avoided to a considerable extent by the principle of *res ipsa loquitur.* "There must be reasonable evidence of negligence," said Sir William Erle C.J., delivering the judgment of the Court of Exchequer Chamber[87] in the leading case of *Scott* v. *London and St. Katherine Docks Co.,*[88] "but where the thing is shown to be under the management of the defendant or his servants, and the accident is such as in the ordinary course of things does not happen if those who have the management use proper care, it affords reasonable evidence, in the absence of explanation by the defendant, that the accident arose from want of care."[89] It is characteristic of the great Victorian masters of the common law who framed these limpid sentences (which constitute the whole of the relevant part of the court's judgment) that they should have avoided both lengthy elaboration of the obvious and the use of the Latin maxim *res ipsa*

---

[80] Is there a distinction between veracity and reliability? Lord Tucker said there was in *Wilts and Dorset Motor Services Ltd.* v. *Kitto* (1961) H.L. unreported.

[81] Although "If it could be shown that the course of events affirmed by the learned judge could not have occurred, that would be an excellent reason for reversing his view—in these mundane happenings there is no more conclusive argument than *non est credendum quia impossible*": *The Eurymedon* (1942) 73 L1.L.R. 217, 219, *per* Viscount Simon L.C.

[82] *Davies* v. *Tenby B.C.* [1974] 2 Lloyd's Rep. 469.

[83] *Benmax* v. *Austin Motor Co. Ltd.* [1955] A.C. 370, 376.

[84] *e.g. Carmarthenshire C.C.* v. *Lewis* [1955] A.C. 549; *Morris* v. *West Hartlepool Steam Navigation Co. Ltd.* [1956] A.C. 552; *Ross* v. *Associated Portland Cement Manufacturers Ltd.* [1964] 1 W.L.R. 768.

[85] *Metropolitan Ry.* v. *Wright* (1886) 11 App.Cas. 152.

[86] See Ellis Lewis, "A Ramble with *res ipsa loquitur*" (1951) 11 Camb.L.J. 74; O'Connell, "*Res Ipsa Loquitur*" [1954] C.L.J. 118; Aityah, "*Res Ipsa Loquitur* in England and Australia" (1972) 35 M.L.R. 337.

[87] Erle C.J. Crompton, Byles, Blackburn, Keating and Mellor JJ.

[88] (1865) 3 H. & C. 596, 601 (six bags of sugar falling from warehouse onto passer-by).

[89] See *Moorgate Mercantile Co. Ltd.* v. *Twitchings* [1977] A.C. 890, 900.

loquitur.[90] These temptations have not always been resisted by their successors, with the result that the law on this topic is still curiously complex and open to review in the House of Lords.[91] First, it should be observed that when all the facts are known there is no room for the application of the maxim: in such a case the only question is whether an inference of negligence becomes practically certain or practically impossible.[92] Secondly, when all the facts are not known the maxim helps the plaintiff to discharge the onus which lies upon him of proving negligence. So two distinct questions arise: (1) what are the conditions for the operation of the principle contained in the maxim? and (2) what is the effect of the operation of the principle, once it has been properly invoked?

(1) Conditions for operation of principle

The court in *Scott* v. *London and St. Katherine Docks Co.* stipulated (i) that "the thing is shown to be under the management of the defendant or his servants," and (ii) that "the accident is such as in the ordinary course of things does not happen if those who have the management use proper care." As to (i), it is sufficient here to note that the driver of a motor-vehicle is now held to have sufficient control over his vehicle and its surrounding circumstances to attract the operation of the principle in a suitable case.[93] So an unexplained and violent skid is evidence of negligence.[94] But if an object or operation is under the control of two (or more) persons not legally responsible for the acts of each other it is probable that the principle does not apply.[95] As to (ii), it is part of the common experience of mankind that if those who have control are exercising reasonable care, it is not usual for bags of flour to fall from warehouse windows[96] or for stones to be found in a bun[97] or for slippery matter to be left lying on the floor of a shop[98]—to mention only a few of the many cases in which the doctrine has been held to apply. On the other hand, "Everybody knows fires occur through accidents which happen without negligence on anybody's part,"[99] so there was no liability when an ordinary domestic fire was left burning in a grate and the room was set on fire in some unexplained way. Finally, it is not necessary that the doctrine should be pleaded. If the accident is proved to have happened in such a way that prima facie it could not have happened without negligence on the part of the defendants, then it is for the defendants to explain how the accident could have happened without negligence.[1]

A difficulty has arisen where negligence is alleged against surgeons or

---

[90] "If it had not been in Latin nobody would have called it a principle": *Ballard* v. *N.B. Ry.*, 1923, S.C. 43, 56, *per* Lord Shaw.
[91] *Colvilles Ltd.* v. *Devine* [1969] 1 W.L.R. 475, 478.
[92] *Barkway* v. *South Wales Transport Co.* [1950] 1 All E.R. 392, 395; *Bolton* v. *Stone* [1951] A.C. 850, 859.
[93] *Halliwell* v. *Venables* (1930) 99 L.J.K.B. 353.
[94] *Richley* v. *Faull* [1965] 1 W.L.R. 1454.
[95] See above, § 83.
[96] *Byrne* v. *Boadle* (1863) 2 H. & C. 722 (perhaps the first case in which the phrase *res ipsa loquitur* occurs). From a practical point of view, the importance of such a decision is that it dispenses the plaintiff from the necessity of calling witnesses from inside the warehouse to prove negligence.
[97] *Chaproniére* v. *Mason* (1905) 21 T.L.R. 633.
[98] *Ward* v. *Tesco Stores Ltd.* [1976] 1 W.L.R. 810.
[99] *Sochacki* v. *Sas* [1947] 1 All E.R. 344, 345, *per* Lord Goddard C.J.
[1] *Bennett* v. *Chemical Construction (G.B.) Ltd.* [1971] 1 W.L.R. 1571, 1575.

doctors, for it has been said that as a judge can have no personal knowledge of "the ordinary course of things" in, *e.g.* a complex abdominal operation, the maxim cannot apply in such cases.[2] But the better view is that, properly understood, the maxim may be of help even when the exercise of professional skill is under consideration.[3]

(2) Effect of operation of the principle

In a case in which the operation of the principle contained in the maxim *res ipsa loquitur* has been properly invoked the primary and fundamental effect is that the plaintiff is entitled to have his case left to the jury, so that if he has been non-suited by the trial judge a new trial will be ordered on appeal.[4] The secondary effect is that once the case has been properly left to the jury, the mere happening of the accident affords "reasonable evidence, in the absence of explanation by the defendant," that it was due to the defendant's negligence. Hence if the defendant gives no evidence a verdict for the plaintiff will stand. So clearly a prudent defendant will feel obliged to offer an "explanation." Opinions have differed as to the nature of the onus which rests upon him.

In the first place, it is well settled that the defendant is entitled to succeed even though he cannot explain exactly how the accident happened if he establishes that there was no lack of reasonable care on his part.[5] But it may be difficult for him to show that he took reasonable care if the disaster was caused by a latent defect.[6]

Difficulty arises when the defendant is still unable to explain the accident and his conduct is open to more than one interpretation. It is submitted that there is not, even where *res ipsa loquitur*, any legal presumption of negligence, so that the legal burden of disproving negligence lies on the defendant. Therefore if the defendant produces a reasonable explanation, equally consistent with negligence and no negligence, the burden of proving the affirmative, that the defendant was negligent and that his negligence caused the accident, still remains with the plaintiff.[7] For the scales which have been tipped in the plaintiff's favour by the doctrine of *res ipsa loquitur* would be once more in balance, and the plaintiff would have to begin again and prove negligence in the usual way.[8] So that on this view, if a motor-car leaves the road, and the defendant's explanation of this occurrence is that the steering failed, the onus of proof has not been discharged by the plaintiff, for the steering may have failed for a reason which is as consistent with the absence of negligence as its presence.[9] It would be different if the defendant had never adopted or followed any reasonable system of examination of the steering.

---

[2] *Mahon* v. *Osborne* [1939] 2 K.B. 14, 23.
[3] *Cassidy* v. *Ministry of Health* [1951] 2 K.B. 343.
[4] *Davies* v. *Bunn* (1936) 56 C.L.R. 246, 268-269. This was precisely the course of events in both *Byrne* v. *Boadle* and *Scott* v. *London, etc. Docks Co.*—though the difficulty of these matters is shown by the fact that in the latter case Erle C.J. dissented from his brethren on the application of the principle to the facts. In fact, when the case was re-tried, the verdict was for the defendants (13 L.T. (N.S.) 148)—which shows very clearly that when the maxim applies the plaintiff is entitled to have a trial, but is not entitled to win it.
[5] *Ludgate* v. *Lovett* [1969] 1 W.L.R. 1016.
[6] *Henderson* v. *Jenkins & Sons* [1970] A.C. 282.
[7] *Government Insurance Office* v. *Fredrichberg* (1968) 118 C.L.R. 403.
[8] *Colvilles Ltd.* v. *Devine* [1969] 1 W.L.R. 475.
[9] *Piening* v. *Wanless* (1968) 117 C.L.R. 498.

On the other hand, it has been held by the Court of Appeal,[10] and also, apparently, by the Privy Council,[11] and the House of Lords,[12] that the onus of disproving negligence lies on the defendant, at least in the sense that it is not sufficient for him to show that there were several hypothetical causes consistent with an absence of negligence, but he must go further and show either that the accident was due to a specific cause which does not connote his negligence, or that he had used all reasonable care in the matter. But this would mean that a plaintiff who establishes a prima facie case by invoking the maxim would be in a stronger position than one who made out a prima facie case in another way.[13]

Much of the confusion is due to a failure to appreciate that cases where *res ipsa loquitur* applies may vary enormously in the strength, significance and cogency of the *res* proved. There are many cases in which the most eminent judges have been divided on the question whether an inference of negligence could properly be drawn from the facts proved or admitted. Looked at in this light, it is not easy to see why the maxim should be treated as a special part of the law of evidence.[14]

---

[10] *Moore* v. *Fox (R.) & Son Ltd.* [1956] 1Q.B. 596. In New Zealand the balance of authority seems to favour this view: *Heywood & Co. Ltd.* v. *Att.-Gen.* [1956] N.Z.L.R. 668, which is also approved by Chapman (1957) 73 L.Q.R. 408, but not by Braybrooke (1959) 4 Univ. W.A. Ann.L.Rev. 209.

[11] *Swan* v. *Salisbury Construction Co. Ltd.* [1966] 1 W.L.R. 204.

[12] *Henderson* v. *Jenkins & Sons* [1970] A.C. 282.

[13] It would really put the plaintiff in the same position as if the action were one of trespass, in which the defendant would have to plead and prove inevitable accident, whereas the general rule in negligence is that the plaintiff must establish his case and the defendant need do no more than plead a general denial: see Devlin L. in *Southport Corporation* v. *Esso Petroleum Co. Ltd.* [1953] 3 W.L.R. 773, 781 (the point is not discussed in the H.L.).

[14] *Lloyde* v. *West Midlands Gas Board* [1971] 1 W.L.R. 749.

CHAPTER 10

STATUTORY DUTIES

§ 85. General Principles[1]

The common law was once willing to adopt the simple principle that the breach of a duty created by statute, if it results in damage to an individual, is a tort for which an action for damages will lie at his suit, if no, or no adequate, remedy is provided by the statute itself.[2] "It would be a fine thing," said Sir John Holt C.J., "to make a law by which one has a right but no remedy but in equity."[3] But this principle has not been followed since[4] in England,[5] although it is still the law that anyone who wilfully disobeys any statute is guilty of a common law misdemeanour.[6] Breach of statutory duty is a tort in itself,[7] and it is irrelevant that damage is not alleged. The question now in every case is one as to the intention of the legislature in creating the duty, and no action for damages will lie if, on the true construction of the statute, the intention is that some other remedy, civil or criminal, shall be the only one available. One of the means of determining the intention of the statute is to ascertain whether the duty is owed primarily to the State or community and only incidentally to the individual, or primarily to the individual or class of individuals and only incidentally to the State or community.[8] So there is no civil remedy if a statute merely makes conduct criminal without imposing a duty to a specific class.[9] But if the statute imposes a duty for the protection of particular citizens or a particular class of citizen, it prima facie creates at the same time a correlative right vested in those citizens and prima facie, therefore, they will have the ordinary civil remedy for the enforcement of that right—namely, an action for damages in respect of any loss occasioned by the violation of it.[10] Thus in *Groves* v. *Wimborne (Lord)*[11] the defendant, a manufacturer, was held liable in damages to one of his employees, who had sustained personal injuries through failure of the defendant to perform his statutory duty of fencing dangerous machinery. "The statutes say nothing about civil remedies for breaches of their provisions. The judgments of the courts say all."[12] Still it is not self-evident that the logical basis for the compensation of an injured workman should be the commission of a criminal offence by his employer.[13] In any event, this test is not conclusive. "The duty may be of such paramount importance that it is owed to all the public. It would be strange if

---

[1] See Fricke, "The Juridical Nature of the Action upon the Statute" (1960) 76 L.Q.R. 240; Williams, "The Effect of Penal Legislation in the Law of Tort" (1960) 23 M.L.R. 233.
[2] *Reffell* v. *Surrey C.C.* [1964] 1 W.L.R. 358.
[3] *Anon.* (1704) 6 Mod. 32.
[4] *Solomons* v. *Gertzenstein (R.) Ltd.* [1954] 2 Q.B. 243, 254.
[5] *Aliter* in Ireland: *Meskell* v. *C.I.E.* [1973] I.R. 121, 138.
[6] Law Commission Working Paper No. 63 (1975).
[7] *Gouriet* v. *Union of Post Office Workers* [1978] A.C. 435, 499.
[8] *Solomons* v. *Gertzenstein (R.) Ltd.* [1954] 2 Q.B. 243, 265.
[9] *Ex p. Island Records* [1978] Ch. 122.
[10] *East Suffolk Catchment Board* v. *Kent* [1941] A.C. 74, 88.
[11] [1898] 2 Q.B. 402. This was one of the important decisions for the protection of workmen given by the late nineteenth-century courts. For other examples, see §§ 187–188.
[12] *Boyle* v. *Kodak Ltd.* [1969] 1 W.L.R. 661, 672, *per* Lord Diplock.
[13] *F.E. Callow (Engineers) Ltd.* v. *Johnson* [1971] A.C. 335, 342.

a less important duty, which is owed to a section of the public, may be enforced by an action, while a more important duty owed to the public at large cannot."[14] It is doubtful, indeed, if any general principle can be found to explain all the cases on the subject. Thus the courts lean in favour of conferring on workmen a right to claim damages for breach of statutory duty imposed on their employers or the occupiers of factories in which they work[15]; but purchasers from vendors on whom statutory obligations have been imposed were in the past less favoured by the courts.[16] But this attitude may change in view of the fact that the Consumer Safety Act 1978, s. 6, has given to such purchasers a right of action for breach of the duties which that Act imposes.

In determining the intention of the legislature, the courts consider three different factors:

(i) *No private interest infringed*

The intention may be that there shall be no civil remedy available for an injured individual at all. The statutory duty is then a duty towards the public at large, and not towards individuals, and the correlative right is vested in the public and not in private persons, even though they may suffer special damage. The duty in such a case is to be enforced by way of mandamus on a criminal prosecution, or by way of injunction at the suit of the Attorney-General. But the Land Charges Act 1925 was passed for the benefit of incumbrancers and purchasers and intending purchasers, and these are a definite class distinct from the public generally.[17] Equally the parents of children deprived of education by a conspiracy between a trade union and a local authority can sue both the union and the authority for breach of statutory duty.[18] Homeless persons are also a distinct class.[19]

(ii) *Private interest protected only by special remedy*

The legislature, even while recognising a private right vested in the injured individual, may intend that it shall be maintained solely by some special remedy provided for the particular case, and not by the ordinary method of an action for damages. Thus, in *Atkinson* v. *Newcastle and Gateshead Waterworks Co.*[20] it was held by the Court of Appeal that the defendant company was not liable in damages for the destruction of the plaintiff's house by fire, although its destruction was directly due to the failure of the defendants to perform the duty laid upon them under the Waterworks Clauses Act 1847[21] to maintain a certain pressure of water in their water-pipes for the purpose of extinguishing fires. The statute in question provided that any breach of this duty should be an offence punishable by a fine of

---

[14] *Phillips* v. *Britannia Hygienic Laundry* [1923] 2 K.B. 832, 841, *per* Atkin L.J.
[15] *Groves* v. *Wimborne (Lord)* [1898] 2 Q.B. 402.
[16] *Solomons* v. *Gertzenstein (R.) Ltd.* [1954] 2 Q.B. 243, 255.
[17] *Ministry of Housing* v. *Sharp* [1970] 2 Q.B. 223.
[18] *Meade* v. *Haringey B.C.* [1979] 1 W.L.R. 637.
[19] See *Thornton* v. *Kirklees B.C.* [1979] Q.B. 626.
[20] (1877) 2 Ex.D. 441.
[21] s. 42. But a breach of the duty under s. 35 of the same Act to provide a supply of pure and wholesome water gives a right of action for damages to a ratepayer injuriously affected: *Read* v. *Croydon Corporation* [1938] 4 All E.R. 631. See now the Water Act 1945, s. 28; and for provisions corresponding to s. 42 of the 1847 Act, see Sched. 3, Pt. VIII to the 1945 Act.

£10, and the court came to the conclusion that on the true interpretation of the statute this was the sole remedy available, and that there was no intention of imposing on the waterworks company any such heavy civil liability as the opposite interpretations would have subjected them to.

On the other hand, it has been settled ever since *Monk* v. *Warbey*[22] that when a person uninsured against third party risks is permitted by the owner to use his car, and injury is caused by the borrower's negligent driving, the injured third party may, if the borrower is without means,[23] sue the owner of the car directly for breach of his statutory duty,[24] without first suing the uninsured driver. Otherwise the express object of the Act, namely, to give a remedy to third persons who might suffer injury by the negligence of the impecunious driver of a car, would have been defeated. The decision in *Monk* v. *Warbey* is a striking one. It is almost the sole exception to the general bias of the courts against the construction of penal statutes to create torts. Thus, although it is a criminal offence[25] to sell a motor-vehicle for delivery in such condition that its use on the road in that condition would be unlawful, the vendor of such a vehicle is not liable in damages for breach of statutory duty to one who has been injured as a result of the car's condition.[26] So, too, one who is injured as the result of the defendant's failure to comply with the statutory duties[27] relating to the construction of vehicles[28] has no right of action merely by reason of that fact.[29] When this principle was laid down in 1923 there was no compulsory obligation to insure,[30] but the decision has at all times been judicially accepted without comment,[31] and has been affirmed by the Privy Council.

(iii) *Damage suffered not of kind to be guarded against*

An action for damages will not lie at the suit of an injured person if the damage suffered by him is not of the kind intended to be guarded against. In *Gorris* v. *Scott*[32] the plaintiff sued the defendant, a shipowner, for the loss of sheep which had been swept overboard in consequence of the failure of the defendant to supply certain pens and other structures on the deck of his ship for the accommodation of sheep, as required by Act of Parliament. It was held, however, that the defendant was not liable, because the purpose of the statute in question was to make provision against the spread of contagious disease among the animals, and not to prevent such accidents as the plaintiff complained of.[33] The principle in *Gorris* v. *Scott*[32] has since been approved by the House of Lords, although the decision went the other way on the

---

[22] [1935] 1 K.B. 75.
[23] *Martin* v. *Dean* [1971] 2 Q.B. 208.
[24] Now s. 201 of the Road Traffic Act 1960. But there is no statutory duty to insure against the third party liability of passengers in, but not controlling the use of, the car: *Brown* v. *Roberts* [1965] 1 Q.B. 1.
[25] Road Traffic Act 1972, s. 60 (1).
[26] *Badham* v. *Lambs Ltd.* [1946] K.B. 45.
[27] Now the Motor Vehicles (Construction and Use) Regulations 1966 (S.I. No. 1228).
[28] *Phillips* v. *Britannia Hygienic Laundry Co.* [1923] 2 K.B. 832.
[29] So no action lay in *Coote* v. *Stone* [1971] 1 W.L.R. 279 (stopping on clearway). Nor is an emmployer under any duty to his employee to insure against third party risks a vehicle driven by the employee: *Semtex Ltd.* v. *Gladstone* [1954] 1 W.L.R. 945.
[30] First introduced by the Road Traffic Act 1930: see above, § 7.
[31] *Tan Chye Choo* v. *Chong Kew Moi* [1970] 1 W.L.R. 147, 152.
[32] (1874) L.R. 9 Ex. 125.
[33] *Sparrow* v. *Fairey Aviation Co. Ltd.* [1962] 1 Q.B. 161, 174.

interpretation of the relevant statute.[34] Again, when the object of a statutory regulation was to prevent men working on a roof from falling to the ground, it was immaterial that the plaintiff was injured by falling through a hole in the roof rather than by falling through fragile roofing material.[35] The distinction is clear and simple: if the damage which in fact occurs is within the risk, it is immaterial that it did not happen in precisely the way contemplated when the duty was imposed. It is the same distinction which caused the decision in *The Wagon Mound (No.1)*[36] to go one way, and the decision in *Hughes* v. *Lord Advocate*[37] to go the other way.

Finally it should be noted that even when the breach of the statute does not in itself give a right of action to an individual damnified thereby the right of action for breach of any common law duty to conduct oneself with reasonable care so as not to injure those persons likely to be affected by want of care is not excluded.[38] The statutory duty does not extinguish the common law duty unless there is an express provision or necessary implication to that effect.[39] There is no need to strain the statute if the common law can deal with the matter.[40]

Need for reform

It will now be apparent how difficult it is to lay down any definite principle. The law depends on the interpretation which the courts (with or without the aid of the principles of construction which are now falling into some disfavour) may place on any particular statute. "To a person unversed in the science, or art, of legislation it may well seem strange that Parliament has not by now made it a rule to state explicity what its intention is in a matter which is often of no little importance instead of leaving it to the courts to discover, by a careful examination and analysis of what is expressly said, what that intention may be supposed probably to be."[41] But Parliament has begun to attend to this complaint, and some statutes now state explicitly that a breach of duty thereby created is actionable. So the Sex Discrimination Act 1975, s. 66 (1), and the Race Relations Act 1976, s. 57 (1), provide that discriminatory acts "may be made the subject of civil proceedings in like manner as any other claim in tort . . . for breach of statutory duty."[42] Conversely, a statute may expressly provide that breach of a duty which it creates is not actionable.[43] Sometimes a court will evade the whole issue by granting another remedy, such as an injunction.[44]

---

[34] *Grant* v. *National Coal Board* [1956] A.C. 649. See also above, §§ 74-75.
[35] *Donaghey* v. *Boulton and Paul Ltd.* [1968] A.C. 1.
[36] [1961] A.C. 388.
[37] [1963] A.C. 837. See above, § 81.
[38] *East Suffolk Catchment Board* v. *Kent* [1941] A.C. 74, 89.
[39] *Read* v. *Croydon Corporation* [1938] 4 All E.R. 631, 654.
[40] *Smith* v. *N.C.B.* [1967] 1 W.L.R. 871, 875.
[41] *Cutler* v. *Wandsworth Stadium Ltd.* [1949] A.C. 398, 410, *per* Lord du Parcq. It should be noted that the neighbour principle expounded in *Donoghue* v. *Stevenson* [1932] A.C. 562 (see above, § 72) has not affected the established rules on this matter: *Commerford* v. *Board of School Commissioners of Halifax* [1950] 2 D.L.R. 207.
[42] See also the Copyright Act 1956, s. 43, the Deposit of Poisonous Waste Act 1972, s. 2, the Resale Prices Act 1976, s. 25 (3), the Health and Safety at Work Act 1974, s. 72, the Petroleum and Submarine Pipelines Act 1975, s. 30: the Consumer Safety Act 1978, s. 6.
[43] As with the Safety of Sports Grounds Act 1975, s. 13, or the Guard Dogs Act 1975, s. 5 (1).
[44] As in *ex p. Island Records* [1978] Ch. 122.

§ 86. ABSOLUTE STATUTORY DUTIES

When a duty is created by statute, the breach of which is an actionable tort, it is a question of construction whether the liability is absolute, or depends on wrongful intent or negligence on the part of the defendant. In other words, when a statute provides that a certain thing must be done, it is a question of interpretation whether this means that the thing is to be done in all events, or merely that the person upon whom the duty is imposed is to use due care and diligence in the endeavour to perform it, and that if he fails to perform it through no fault of his he shall be free from liability.[45] The reports contain many cases where actions have been brought for breach of the absolute duty to fence dangerous machinery imposed by the Factories Act 1961.[46] It may be wrong to describe the nature of the duty in these cases as "absolute," for that is a term which signifies a duty which exists independently of fault, and in these cases there has often been an intentional or negligent failure to comply with the statutory duty.[47]

Statutory negligence

The standard of care (or duty[48]) prescribed by the statute may be set out in minute detail (as under the Factories Act), or else merely phrased in general terms (as under the Occupiers' Liability Act). It seems that the decision of the House of Lords in *Lochgelly Iron and Coal Co.* v. *M'Mullan*[49] has settled that an action for breach of a statutory duty which involves the notion of taking care not to injure[50] is for the purposes of an action for damages equivalent to negligence.[51] Lord Wright said[52] that breach of such a duty had been "correctly described as statutory negligence." But in a later case[53] the same Law Lord expressed a contrary view. It is submitted that here second thoughts are best. There are obvious differences between the two claims: in one the standard of care is fixed by the legislature, in the other by the court[54]; in one the defence of *volenti non fit injuria* is applicable, in the other it is not.[55] Again negligence and breach of statutory duty are usually treated as two separate causes of action from a pleading point of view.[56] Further, a breach of statutory duty does not automatically throw on the defendant the onus of proving he was not in breach of his common law duty.[57] But although the causes of action are separate there is really only one head of damage for which redress is sought, so that satisfaction of one cause of action ends the whole claim.[58]

---

[45] *Greenwood* v. *Central Service Co.* [1940] 2 K.B. 447, 461.
[46] See below, § 87.
[47] Williams (1960) 23 M.L.R. 233, 238.
[48] See above, § 75.
[49] [1934] A.C. 1.
[50] In some cases (*e.g. Monk* v. *Warbey* [1935] 1 K.B. 75) the statutory duty in issue has nothing to do with negligence.
[51] So the statutory precautions must be carried out, even though some other precaution might be equally effective: *Stein & Co. Ltd.* v. *O'Hanlon* [1965] A.C. 890.
[52] [1934] A.C. 1, 23.
[53] *London Passenger Transport Board* v. *Upson* [1949] A.C. 155, 168.
[54] See above, §§ 71–72.
[55] See below, § 187.
[56] *Murfin* v. *United Steel Companies Ltd.* [1957] 1 W.L.R. 104.
[57] *Davis* v. *Everard (F.T.) & Sons, Ltd.* [1960] 1 Lloyd's Rep. 59.
[58] *Graham* v. *C. E. Heinke & Co. Ltd.* [1958] 1 Q.B. 432.

§ 87. STATUTORY DUTIES IN FACTORIES, MINES AND SHOPS

Although this book is concerned mainly with the common law duties of an employer to his employees, some indication must be given of the nature of the statutory duties which have been created for the protection of workmen, for claims for damages incurred through the breach of these duties are commonly joined with a claim for negligence at common law.[59] It has been settled for many years that a civil action for damages can be brought by a workman injured as a result of a breach of the safety provisions of the Factories Act and Mines and Quarries Act.[60] Breach of the duties imposed renders the occupier liable to criminal proceedings. But "The real incentive for the observance by employers of their statutory duties under Railway Acts, Factory Acts, Dock Acts, and similar legislation is not their liability to substantial fines, but the possibility of heavy claims for damages."[61]

The principal statute is the Factories Act 1961, consolidating the previous legislation. Its provisions will be replaced by regulations issued under the Health and Safety at Work Act 1974. This Act lays down the general legal obligations relating to employed persons, and provides for enforcement through a Health and Safety Commission. The general duties contained in sections 2 to 9 of the Act will be supplemented by Regulations and Codes of Practice. By section 47 the breach of these general statutory duties is not *per se* actionable. Meanwhile the law is based upon the Act of 1961, which imposes duties of which the following are the most important.

(1) Duty to fence

This is imposed by sections 12 to 16, and is the outstanding example of an absolute statutory obligation. By section 12 all prime movers (*i.e.* the machines where power originates) must with few exceptions be securely fenced whether they are safe or not, and whatever their position or construction. By section 13 every part of the transmission machinery must be securely fenced unless it is in such a position or of such construction as to be as safe to every person working on the premises as it would be if securely fenced. By section 14, every dangerous part of any machinery, other than prime movers and transmission machinery must be securely fenced unless it is in such a position or of such construction as to be as safe to every person employed or working on the premises as it would be if securely fenced. Hence under section 14 (as distinct from s.13) part[62] of the machinery must be proved to be dangerous before the duty to fence comes into existence. By sections 15 and 16 the fencing provided must be of sound construction and kept in position while the parts required to be fenced or safeguarded are in motion or in use,[63] unless the machinery is being examined, lubricated or adjusted.[64]

---

[59] The imposition of a statutory duty (other than by the Occupiers' Liability Act 1957) does not free the occupier of premises from his common law obligations; but if he complies with the statutory code of conduct it may be difficult to convict him of negligence: *Chipchase* v. *British Titan Products Co. Ltd.* [1956] 1 Q.B. 545.

[60] It does not follow that the person injured can sue every person in breach of those provisions: *Biddle* v. *Truvox Engineering Co. Ltd.* [1952] 1 K.B. 101 (supplier of defective machinery, as distinct from occupier of factory, not liable under the statute).

[61] *Hutchinson* v. *L.&N.E. Ry.* [1942] 1 K.B. 481, 488, *per* Goddard L.J.

[62] So it is not the machine as a whole which must be fenced, but a dangerous part of machinery: *British Railways Board* v. *Liptrot* [1969] 1 A.C. 136.

[63] *Stanbrook* v. *Waterlow & Sons Ltd.* [1964] 1 W.L.R. 825.

[64] *Richard Thomas and Baldwins Ltd.* v. *Cummings* [1955] A.C. 321.

Some of the points which have arisen in the many cases on these sections may be noted.

(i) Machinery is dangerous if it is a possible cause of injury to anybody acting in a way in which a human being may be reasonably expected to act in circumstances which may be reasonably expected to occur. Foreseeability is the test,[65] but once it is established by the plaintiff on the balance of probabilities that there was a breach of section 14 and that the accident occurred as a result of that breach, it does not matter that he cannot prove exactly how the accident happened.[66] Therefore careless or indolent conduct must be taken into account,[67] so that an act of folly outside the scope of the employment is relevant rather to contributory negligence or causation, than to breach of statutory duty.[68]

(ii) The obligation to fence securely is an absolute one, not to be qualified by any words such as "so far as practicable." Hence if dangerous machinery cannot be fenced securely it cannot lawfully be used at all.[69]

(iii) The duty is owed not only to the actual operator but to all persons employed or working on the premises.[70] Hence the employee of an independent contractor may be protected.

(iv) The obligation is imposed in order to guard against contact with any dangerous part of a machine and not to guard against articles ejected from it. "The fence is intended to keep the worker out, not to keep the machine or its product in."[71] But there may be liability if the juxtaposition of a stationary part of machinery with a moving workpiece renders the relevant part of the machinery dangerous, notwithstanding that in isolation or when the machine was not in use it would not be dangerous.[72] On the other hand, the duty does not in general require fencing against a tool which a man is holding coming into contact with the dangerous part of machinery,[73] as distinct from the clothing on his body, which can be regarded as part of himself.[74] It has also been held[75] that this duty does not require the dangerous part to be fenced for the purpose of preventing fragments of it, if shattered, from flying out of the machine. In other words, the courts have so interpreted section 14 as to deprive the workman of protection against a foreseeable danger—a gap in the law which neither logic nor common sense can justify, but which cannot now be closed by the courts as distinct from the legislature.[76]

---

[65] *Close* v. *Steel Co. of Wales Ltd.* [1962] A.C. 367.
[66] *F. E. Callow (Engineers) Ltd.* v. *Johnson* [1971] A.C. 335, 347.
[67] *John Summers & Sons Ltd.* v. *Frost* [1955] A.C. 740.
[68] *Allen* v. *Aeroplane Castings Ltd.* [1965] 1 W.L.R. 1244.
[69] *John Summers & Sons Ltd.* v. *Frost* [1955] A.C. 740. But the Act gives the Minister power to modify this obligation as regards any particular class of factory or type of machine.
[70] *John Summers & Sons Ltd.* v. *Frost* [1955] A.C. 740.
[71] *Nicholls* v. *F. Austin (Leyton)* [1946] A.C. 493, 505, *per* Lord Simonds.
[72] *F. E. Callow (Engineers) Ltd.* v. *Johnson* [1971] A.C. 335.
[73] *Sparrow* v. *Fairey Aviation Co. Ltd.* [1964] A.C. 1019.
[74] [1964] A.C. 1019, 1033, 1051-1053.
[75] *Close* v. *Steel Co. of Wales Ltd.* [1962] A.C. 367.
[76] *F. E. Callow (Engineers) Ltd.* v. *Johnson* [1971] A.C. 335, 343. See the interesting debate in 248 H.L.Deb. 5s., col. 1321-1358. The predominant opinion of the Lords (extrajudicially) was that it was really an engineering problem, and that there was no need to amend the Act.

(2) Duties in relation to lifting tackle and machines

Every hoist or lift must be of good mechanical construction, sound material and adequate strength, and maintained in an efficient state, in efficient working order, and in good repair. The duty is absolute, so that the occupiers were held liable where a workman was killed as a result of the inexplicable failure of the braking mechanism of a lift.[77] Chains, ropes and lifting tackle must also be of good construction.

(3) Duties concerning condition of premises

By section 25 all floors, steps, stairs, passages, gangways, and ladders must be soundly constructed and properly maintained.[78] There are also duties in relation to lighting, rails for staircases, and openings in floors. Although the duty is an absolute one, the obligation to maintain in an efficient state introduces a question of degree as to what is efficient: so a floor is not necessarily in an inefficient state because of some transient and exceptional condition.[79] The Factories Act 1961, s. 28 (1), provides that all floors, passages and stairs shall, so far as is reasonably practicable,[80] be kept free from any obstruction and from any substance likely to cause persons to slip. The slippery substance need not itself be in contact with the floor.[81] By section 29 (1) there must, so far as is reasonably practicable, be provided and maintained[78] safe means of access to every place at which any person has at any time to work, and every such work place shall, so far as is reasonably practicable, be made and kept safe for any person working there. So the duty extends to the work place and also to the means of access thereto. "Any person" means any person who is to work for the purposes of the factory.[82] This includes independent contractors and their employees,[83] but would exclude (say) trespassers, or police officers pursuing trespassers, or firemen.[84] It will be noted that the obligation of the occupier is only to do what is reasonably practicable.[85] There is a similar obligation to protect employed persons against inhalation of dust (s.31).[86]

(4) Duties relating to particular trades

Finally, Part IV of the Act gives power to make regulations for the conduct of dangerous trades or processes, and the Docks, Woodworking Machinery, Building, and Shipbuilding Regulations accordingly contain detailed rules for the protection of persons employed in those trades. It has

---

[77] *Galashiels Gas Co.* v. *Millar* [1949] A.C. 275.
[78] "Maintained" is defined by s. 152 to mean "maintained in an efficient state, in efficient working order, and in good repair." This duty is absolute: *Hamilton* v. *National Coal Board* [1960] A.C. 633.
[79] *Latimer* v. *A.E.C. Ltd.* [1953] A.C. 643. See § 201.
[80] *Jenkins* v. *Allied Ironfounders Ltd.* [1970] 1 W.L.R. 304.
[81] *Dorman Long (Steel) Ltd.* v. *Bell* [1964] 1 W.L.R. 333.
[82] *Wigley* v. *British Vinegars Ltd.* [1964] A.C. 307,324.
[83] *Wigley* v. *British Vinegars Ltd.* [1964] A.C. 307.
[84] *Wigley's Case* [1964] A.C. 307, 313, 324.
[85] *Levesley* v. *Thomas Firth & John Brown Ltd.* [1953] 1 W.L.R. 1206, 1210.
[86] *Adsett* v. *K. & L. Steelfounders and Engineers Ltd.* [1953] 1 W.L.R. 773 (the unsuccessful plaintiff in this case was ordered to pay costs amounting to £970 by monthly instalments of five shillings: *Manchester Guardian*, October 23, 1954); *Richards* v. *Highways Ironfounders (West Bromwich) Ltd.* [1955] 1 W.L.R. 1049.

been held that these regulations do not afford protection to one who is only a visitor to the factory.[87]

Farms

The Agriculture (Safety, Health and Welfare Provisions) Act 1956, and the very detailed Regulations made thereunder, impose duties on the occupiers of "agricultural units" and the employers of agricultural workers. A farm is now in the same position as a factory.

Offices and shops

The Offices, Shops and Railway Premises Act 1963, imposes a wide range of duties to protect the health, safety and welfare of employees. Breach of these duties is certainly a criminal offence, and probably gives rise to civil liability in tort.

Mines and quarries

The Mines and Quarries Acts 1954 to 1971, and Regulations made thereunder, provide a complete code with respect to the management of mines and quarries. Certain duties are imposed on the owners[88] and managers[89] of mines. For example, by section 48 there is a duty to take such steps as may be necessary for keeping the road or working place secure.[90] This is not an absolute duty to ensure that a road is at all times secure, but is rather a duty to exercise care and skill in the light of the best engineering knowledge then obtainable.[91] This is a less onerous obligation than that imposed by the Act of 1911. Unfortunately it is not clear just how onerous the duty now is: all that can be said, rather unhelpfully, is that it is higher than the common law duty.[92] There is also a duty under section 81 to ensure that all parts and working gear are properly maintained.[93] All the duties have to be read subject to the terms of section 157, which provides that it shall be a defence to prove that it was impracticable to avoid or prevent the contravention which is the subject of the proceedings. This, however, is a heavy burden to discharge.

Building and engineering

Operations of this kind are governed by the Construction (Working Place) Regulations 1966, and similar statutory schemes. Employers are responsible to their own men for breaches of the Regulations. Contractors and users of plant or equipment also owe certain duties. Persons employed, and self-employed persons,[94] are also required to comply with the Regula-

---

[87] *Hartley* v. *Mayoh & Co.* [1954] 1 Q.B. 383 (fireman).
[88] By s. 159 an owner is civilly liable for breach of a statutory duty by his employee, even though Parliament has imposed the duty directly upon the employee and not the owner. This disposes of one of the problems raised in *National Coal Board* v. *England* [1954] A.C. 403. See below, § 157.
[89] The object of imposing duties on the manager personally is to ensure that some definite person is responsible: otherwise, in a large colliery, "what is everybody's business is nobody's business": *Brown* v. *N.C.B.* [1962] A.C. 574, 597.
[90] The coal face itself must be made secure: *Gough* v. *N.C.B.* [1959] A.C. 698.
[91] *Brown* v. *National Coal Board* [1962] A.C. 574.
[92] *Tomlinson* v. *Beckermet Mining Co. Ltd.* [1964] 1 W.L.R. 1043.
[93] *Hamilton* v. *N.C.B.* [1960] A.C. 633.
[94] *Bunker* v. *Charles Brand & Sons Ltd.* [1969] 2 Q.B. 480.

tions. But a head contractor is not in general liable to the employees of a sub-contractor.[95] The liability of the head contractor will depend on whether the terms of the sub-contract permit him to supervise the sub-contractor's operations from the point of view of safety.[96]

Repair of a neon-lighting installation on the front of a building is not the repair or maintenance of the building itself so as to attract the operation of the Regulations.[97]

§ 88. NATURE OF STATUTORY DUTIES

(1) Absolute

We have seen that some of these duties are absolute in the sense that the obligation, whatever its meaning and effect, must be actually fulfilled and not merely that the occupier of the factory must do his best to fulfil them.[98] The code of conduct required is conclusively fixed by the statute. In such a case there is not so much a duty to perform as responsibility for circumstances.[99] At first sight, therefore, it might seem that these duties have little or nothing in common with the common law obligation to take reasonable care, which is in general measured by what is reasonably foreseeable in the circumstances. But the tendency of the decisions has been to introduce the notion of reasonable foreseeability in determining the true construction of the statutory obligation. So that whether part of a machine is "dangerous" so as to require it to be "securely" fenced, or placed in a "safe" position, or whether a floor is "maintained in an efficient state," involves a consideration of what ought reasonably to be foreseen.[1] But it is well settled that careless as well as careful conduct may have to be foreseen.[2]

(2) "Practicable"

Other duties are not absolute, in the sense that the statute only requires what is "practicable" or "reasonably practicable" to be done. This is often treated as closely analogous to the common law obligation of an employer to his employee,[3] but something more than reasonable care is required,[4] and what is "practicable" may require a higher standard than what is "reasonably practicable," although not as high a standard as "possible."[5] In general it may be said that the risk has to be balanced against the time, cost, efficiency, and trouble of remedial measures,[6] but, under "practicable,"

---

[95] *Smith* v. *Wimpey & Co. Ltd.* [1972] 2 Q.B. 329.
[96] *Donaghey* v. *Boulton and Paul Ltd.* [1968] A.C. 1.
[97] *Price* v. *Claudgen Ltd.* [1967] 1 W.L.R. 575.
[98] *Carroll* v. *Andrew Barclay & Sons Ltd.* [1948] A.C. 477, 487. It was suggested by the Monckton Committee on Alternative Remedies (Cmd. 6860 (1945–46), para. 82) that in an action for breach of statutory duty designed for the protection of workmen it should be a defence for an employer to prove that he had done everything reasonably practicable to prevent the breach. A clause to this effect was inserted in the Law Reform (Personal Injuries) Bill, but dropped by the Government on second reading: 449 H.C. Debates, cols. 2161–2166. Amongst other reasons, it was said the imposition of absolute duty led to a high standard of care on the part of employers.
[99] *Brown* v. *National Coal Board* [1962] A.C. 574, 592.
[1] *John Summers & Sons Ltd.* v. *Frost* [1955] A.C. 740.
[2] *John Summers & Sons Ltd.* v. *Frost* [1955] A.C. 740.
[3] See below, § 181.
[4] *Edwards* v. *National Coal Board* [1949] 1 K.B. 704, 709.
[5] *Jayne* v. *National Coal Board* [1963] 2 All E.R. 220.
[6] *Jenkins* v. *Allied Ironfounders Ltd.* [1970] 1 W.L.R. 304.

questions of cost may be eliminated, though what is done must still be possible in the light of the relevant knowledge and resources at the time of the breach.[7]

Onus of proof

The plaintiff must prove (i) breach of duty, and (ii) that such breach caused the injury complained of. The ordinary standard of proof in civil actions applies: the plaintiff must make it appear that at least on a balance of probabilities the breach of duty caused or materially contributed to his injury.[8] The House of Lords has emphasised the need for the plaintiff to prove causation,[9] but it has also said that this must not impose too severe a burden on him,[10] especially if the fault complained of is one of omission rather than commission.[11] But probably the onus of proving that safety measures were not reasonably practicable rests on the defendant, as the facts are peculiarly within his knowledge,[12] at any rate if the duty is qualified as distinct from absolute.[13]

§ 89. DEFENCES

(1) Volenti non fit injuria

Consent is no defence when the defendant is an employer who is himself under a statutory duty to the plaintiff.[14] The reason for this rule is that it is contrary to public policy that where there is a statutory obligation on the employer the workman should contract out of it.[15] Hence to give statutory force to a common law obligation is by no means an otiose procedure.[16]

But consent is a defence to an employer when two workmen, each of whom is under a particular statutory duty, embark upon a joint enterprise in breach of that duty and then seek to hold the employer vicariously responsible for the resulting damage.[17] In such a case public policy requires that a workman in breach of his statutory duty should not be entitled to recover damages by luring a fellow-workman to join him[18] in the breach.[19]

(2) Contributory negligence

In *Caswell* v. *Powell Duffryn Collieries, Ltd.*[20] the House of Lords unanimously, though *obiter*, held that the contributory negligence of the

---

[7] *Adsett* v. *K. and L. Steelfounders and Engineers Ltd.* [1953] 1 W.L.R. 137, 773; *Richards* v. *Highways Ironfounders (West Bromwich) Ltd.* [1955] 1 W.L.R. 1049; [1957] 1 W.L.R. 781.

[8] *Bonnington Castings Ltd.* v. *Wardlaw* [1956] A.C. 613.

[9] *McWilliams* v. *Arrol (Sir William) & Co. Ltd.* [1962] 1 W.L.R. 295.

[10] *Nicholson* v. *Atlas Steel Ltd.* [1957] 1 W.L.R. 613.

[11] *McGhee* v. *National Coal Board* [1973] 1 W.L.R. 1.

[12] *Quinn* v. *Cameron & Roberton Ltd.* [1958] A.C. 9.

[13] *Jenkins* v. *Allied Ironfounders Ltd.* [1970] 1 W.L.R. 304.

[14] *Wheeler* v. *New Merton Board Mills* [1933] 2 K.B. 669.

[15] *I.C.I. Ltd.* v. *Shatwell* [1965] A.C. 656.

[16] *Alford* v. *National Coal Board* [1952] 1 All E.R. 754, 757. The person on whom the obligation is laid will also usually be liable to criminal proceedings.

[17] *I.C.I. Ltd.* v. *Shatwell* [1965] A.C. 656.

[18] If he acted alone, he would be met by the defence of delegation.

[19] [1965] A.C. 656.

[20] [1940] A.C. 152. For this purpose there is not any difference between the duty imposed by one statute and another: *Sparks* v. *Edward Ash* [1943] K.B. 223, 239, 240.

plaintiff provides a good defence to the employer. Today the damages may be apportioned under the Law Reform (Contributory Negligence) Act 1945. But in the case of breach of provisions designed for the protection of workmen, too high a standard of care must not be demanded.[21] The standard to be applied is that of the ordinary prudent workman, and the court must "take into account all the circumstances of work in a factory, and that it is not for every risky thing which a workman in a factory may do in his familiarity with the machinery that a plaintiff ought to be held guilty of contributory negligence."[22] Again, a workman may be entitled to assume that statutory duties have been complied with.[23] This seems to mean that the same act may have different consequences when the injured man is the plaintiff suing his employers and where the employer is being sued by a third party (including another employee) in respect of the same act or omission.[24] But the distinction is justifiable on the ground that an employer put in breach of a statute solely by an employee's default is entitled to say that the accident, and consequent breach of duty, has been caused by the employee.[25] Sometimes, especially if the claim is for breach of the common law duty to take reasonable care, a competent and experienced man may safely be left to look after himself.[26]

Although on the whole the courts thus favour the injured workman, when the plaintiff began to repair a scaffolding in a way described as "fantastically wrong," he was held solely responsible for his consequent injuries.[27] The employer is not relieved of liability merely because the workman at the time of the accident was also guilty of a breach of his own duty under the statute, although the workman's breach may be such as to provide evidence of his negligence.[28] Finally, if it has been established that the injury would not have been caused if the employer's statutory duty had been performed, the onus is on the defendant to prove that the plaintiff's contributory negligence was a substantial or material co-operating cause.[29] It is not for the plaintiff to show exactly how the accident happened.[30]

(3) Delegation or co-terminous fault

In some cases it may be a defence to an action for breach of statutory duty that the employer has delegated the performance of that duty to the

[21] *Lewis* v. *Denye* [1940] A.C. 921, 931. "The Factories Act is there not merely to protect the careful, the vigilant and the conscientious workman, but, human nature being what it is, also the careless, the indolent, the inadvertent, the weary, and even, perhaps, in some cases, the disobedient": *Carr* v. *Mercantile Produce Co.* [1949] 2 K.B. 601, 608, *per* Stable J. In *Harrison* v. *Metropolitan-Vickers Electrical Co. Ltd.* [1954] 1 W.L.R. 324, 328, the same learned judge said that to attribute to such acts "the rather grim description of contributory negligence is like using an elephant rifle to shoot a rabbit."

[22] *Flower* v. *Ebbw Vale Steel Co.* [1934] 2 K.B. 132, 140, *per* Lawrence J.; approved in *John Summers & Sons Ltd.* v. *Frost* [1955] A.C. 740. This lenient standard, however, does not necessarily apply to simple cases of common law negligence: *Staveley Iron and Chemical Co. Ltd.* v. *Jones* [1956] A.C. 627; *Smith* v. *National Coal Board* [1967] 1 W.L.R. 871.

[23] *Westwood* v. *Post Office* [1974] A.C. 1.

[24] *Ross* v. *Associated Portland Cement Manufacturers Ltd.* [1964] 1 W.L.R. 768.

[25] *Leach* v. *Standard Telephones and Cables Ltd.* [1966] 1 W.L.R. 1392.

[26] *Richardson* v. *Stephenson Clarke Ltd.* [1969] 1 W.L.R. 1695.

[27] *Norris* v. *W. Moss & Sons Ltd.* [1954] 1 W.L.R. 346; *Rushton* v. *Turner Bros. Asbestos Co. Ltd.* [1960] 1 W.L.R. 96 ("a crazy thing to do").

[28] *Ross* v. *Associated Portland Cement Manufacturers Ltd.* [1964] 1 W.L.R. 768. *A fortiori* where the employee in breach is acting under the employer's orders: *Laszczyk* v. *National Coal Board* [1954] 1 W.L.R. 1426 (plaintiff held 5 per cent. responsible).

[29] *Caswell's case* [1940] A.C. 152, 172.

[30] *Smithwick* v. *National Coal Board* [1950] 2 K.B. 335.

plaintiff himself, who is then without remedy if he is injured, for he is held to be the author of his own misfortune.[31] The doctrine appears to have been invented in order to enable an employer to escape liability to an employee if the sole reason for the breach of statutory duty was the employee's own disobedience.[32] For it must be conceded that the doctrine of absolute liability could lead to absurd results when combined with the doctrine of vicarious liability.[33] But the principle of delegation fell into disfavour and now is probably obsolete.[34] It has been abolished by statute in Ireland.[35] The proper approach to the problem is to combine the rule that the plaintiff must prove causation[36] with the principles of contributory negligence.[37] The question is whether there has been some fault on the part of the employer which goes beyond or is independent of the fault on the part of the employee which as a result of the doctrine of vicarious liability constitutes a breach of statutory duty by the employer.[38] Were the faults of the employer and the employee simply co-extensive or co-terminous? If so, the plaintiff is without remedy,[39] at any rate if the statutory duty is imposed on him alone and not on his employer as well. In short, the fundamental question is: Whose fault was it?[40]

---

[31] *Smith* v. *Baveystock & Co.* [1945] 1 All E.R. 531.
[32] For the position when two (or more) employees are jointly disobedient, see *I.C.I. Ltd.* v. *Shatwell* [1965] A.C. 656.
[33] *Boyle* v. *Kodak Ltd.* [1969] 1 W.L.R. 661.
[34] *Ross* v. *Associated Portland Cement Manufacturers Ltd.* [1964] 1 W.L.R. 768.
[35] Civil Liability Act 1961, s. 57 (2).
[36] See above, § 83.
[37] See below, § 196.
[38] *Quinn* v. *Green* [1966] 1 Q.B. 509.
[39] *Leach* v. *Standard Telephones and Cables Ltd.* [1966] 1 W.L.R. 1392.
[40] *Ross* v. *Associated Portland Cement Manufacturers Ltd.* [1964] 1 W.L.R. 768.

CHAPTER 11

DANGEROUS PREMISES

§ 90. Introduction[1]

The principles discussed in sections 90 to 100 of this chapter apply only to persons who suffer injury while on another's[2] premises. Injuries suffered as a result of the dangerous state of another's premises by persons who have not entered thereon fall within the tort of nuisance[3] and are governed by different principles. It is essential to keep in mind where the accident takes place and why the plaintiff is in that place, because the duty of the occupier of dangerous premises to the plaintiff who is injured on the highway or on adjoining land may differ materially from his duty to the plaintiff who suffers damage from the defective state of the premises after having entered upon them. "It does not escape me," Lord Simonds said,[4] "that in the result a distinction which may appear capricious will exist between two cases... But, my Lords, such distinctions must exist in the law so long at least as a distinction exists between public and private property, and it is ultimately upon that distinction, perhaps, that the different fates of my hypothetical victims depend." But this does not mean that an unlawful entrant is completely without protection: occupation of property is now increasingly regarded as a ground of liability, not of exemption, both in England[5] and in Ireland.[6]

What are premises[7]

The principles which follow apply not only to real property but also to appliances or objects upon it of which the plaintiff has been invited or allowed to make use—for example, grandstands,[8] stagings,[9] diving-boards,[10] ships in dry dock,[11] ladders,[12] and electricity pylons.[13] These principles may[14] also apply to movables such as ships,[15] lifts,[16] and aeroplanes,[17] in so far as the injury complained of has arisen from the

---

[1] The main work is North, *Occupiers' Liability* (1971). See also Report of the Law Reform Committee (Cmd. 9305 (1954)); Odgers, "Occupiers' Liability" [1955] C.L.J. 1; Odgers, "Occupiers' Liability: a Further Comment" [1957] C.L.J. 39; Report of the Pearson Commission (Cmnd 7054, 1978), Chap. 28.

[2] Accidents in one's own home constantly occur. Usually there is no remedy, but it may be possible to sue a builder or decorator (see § 100), or the manufacturer of a dangerous chattel (see § 105).

[3] For one exception; see the detonator case: below, § 96.

[4] *Jacobs* v. *L.C.C.* [1950] A.C. 361, 377.

[5] *British Railways Board* v. *Herrington* [1972] A.C. 877, 913.

[6] *McNamara* v. *E.S.B.* [1975] I.R.I.

[7] See North, *Occupiers' Liability*, Chap. 4.

[8] *Francis* v. *Cockrell* (1870) L.R. 5 Q.B. 501.

[9] *Heaven* v. *Pender* (1883) 11 Q.B.D. 503.

[10] *Perkowski* v. *Wellington Corporation* [1959] A.C. 53.

[11] *London Graving Dock Co. Ltd.* v. *Horton* [1951] A.C. 737.

[12] *Woodman* v. *Richardson* [1937] 3 All E.R. 866.

[13] *McLaughlin* v. *Antrim Electricity Supply Co.* [1941] N.I. 23.

[14] See Davis, "What are Premises" [1965] N.Z.L.J. 135.

[15] *Duncan* v. *Cammell Laird* [1946] A.C. 401, 420, 439, 446; *London Graving Dock Co.* v. *Horton* [1951] A.C. 737; 750.

[16] *Haseldine* v. *Daw* [1941] 2 K.B. 343, 358.

[17] *Fosbroke-Hobbes* v. *Airwork Ltd.* [1937] 1 All E.R. 108.

dangerous structural condition of the conveyance. But they do not govern an act of negligence by the driver of it in the course of transit,[18] for it has been settled that the driver of a vehicle owes his passengers the same duty to take reasonable care for their safety whether they are gratuitous or fare-paying,[19] while the common law duty of an occupier of premises was elaborately graduated according to the character of the entrant.

These principles have been confirmed by the Occupiers' Liability Act 1957, s. 1(3), which provides that the rules thereby enacted[20] in relation to an occupier of premises and his visitors shall also apply, in like manner and to the like extent as the principles applicable to an occupier of premises and his invitees and licensees would apply, to regulate the obligations of a person occupying or having control over any fixed or movable structure,[21] including any vessel, vehicle or aircraft. But an occupier of premises does not necessarily occupy a chattel on them so as to render him liable for the use made of it by a contractor, *e.g.* a ladder not integrated into a scaffolding[22] as distinct from a large digging machine in a tunnel.[23]

Who is responsible

In dealing with dangerous premises it is necessary to distinguish between the responsibilities of the owner, those of the occupier or possessor, and those of third parties on the premises. Generally speaking, liability in such cases is based on occupancy or control, not on ownership. The person responsible for the condition of the premises is he who is in actual occupation or possession of them for the time being, whether he is the owner of them or not. For it is he who has the immediate supervision and control and the power of permitting or prohibiting the entry of other persons.[24] It is a question of fact in each case whether the defendant has such control, but the courts look at the matter broadly. So a local authority which has served both a notice to treat and a notice of entry before making a compulsory purchase order may be an occupier,[25] as also indeed may be a tenant who has left the premises but has retained the keys.[26] To this general principle there are two qualifications. First, there may be more than one occupier of property at the same time liable in respect of the same damage,[27] as when an occupier engages a head contractor to do repairs,[28] or when an employer remains in occupation through his employee or other licensee,[29] as he must if a corporate entity. In such a case each occupier owes, or may owe, a different duty to the visitor.[30] Secondly, it may be that if A invites B onto the

---

[18] *Haseldine* v. *Daw & Sons Ltd.* [1941] 2 K.B. 343, 373; Law Reform Committee (Third Report), para. 42; Occupiers' Liability Act 1957, s. 5(3).
[19] Kahn-Freund, *The Law of Inland Transport* (4th ed. 1965), p. 503.
[20] See § 93.
[21] *Kearney* v. *Eric Waller Ltd.* [1967] 1 Q.B. 29 (scaffolding).
[22] *O'Malley* v. *Sheppard & Son Ltd.* [1962] 2 Lloyd's Rep. 221.
[23] *Bunker* v. *Charles Brand & Son Ltd.* [1969] 2 Q.B. 480.
[24] *Hartwell* v. *Grayson, Rollo and Clover Docks* [1947] K.B. 901, 917; *Napier* v. *Ryan* [1954] N.Z.L.R. 1234, 1242; *Nicholls* v. *Lyons* [1955] N.Z.L.R. 1097, 1106; *Wheat* v. *Lacon & Co. Ltd.* [1966] A.C. 552, 574, 578.
[25] *Harris* v. *Birkenhead Corporation* [1976] 1 All E.R. 341.
[26] *Morrison Holdings Ltd.* v *Manders Property Ltd.* [1976] 1 W.L.R. 533, 542.
[27] *Fisher* v. *C.H.T. Ltd.* [1965] 1 W.L.R. 1093, *Harris* v. *Birkenhead Corporation* [1976] 1 All E.R. 341, 347.
[28] Such a head contractor may then be at once both an occupier and a visitor.
[29] *Wheat* v. *Lacon & Co. Ltd.* [1966] A.C. 552.
[30] [1966] A.C. 552, 581, 585, 587. Yet the Act (s. 1(1) and (2)) in three places refers to "an occupier."

premises of C in pursuance of some common material interest, he must either take reasonable care to ensure that C's premises are reasonably safe for the purpose in view or else warn B that he has not done so.[31]

There may be difficulty in distinguishing between a lease, under which exclusive possession passes to the lessee,[32] and a licence, under which it does not,[33] but the courts have been reluctant to permit an occupier to divest himself of his responsibilities by creating a lease for an artificially short period. So the occupiers were held liable when they had "hired" out premises for a dance for four hours, but had retained the right to supply refreshments.[34] "Dancing is hungry and thirsty work. A dance without refreshments would be what Lord Bowen called 'a melancholy spree.' The restaurant keepers were to supply the necessary restoratives in what had been, at all events up to 8 p.m., their own restaurant."[35] So a licensor may, like a lessor, be regarded as still in occupation if the terms of the licence permit or require such a conclusion.[36] Primarily, then, liability rests on the occupier, or the occupiers, and we will postpone until later, consideration of the liabilities of the owner not in occupation[37] and of third parties.[38]

Who may claim

The position at common law was concisely summarised as follows: "Where a question arises, not between parties who are both present in the exercise of equal rights *inter se*, but between parties of whom one is the owner or occupier of the place and the other, the party injured, is not there as of right,[39] but must justify his presence there if he can, the law has long recognised three categories of obligation."[40] Such a person may go to the premises (i) by the invitation, express or implied, of the occupier; (ii) with the leave and licence of the occupier; (iii) as a trespasser. These three categories were held to be exhaustive; the temptation to introduce further sub-divisions (*e.g.* a category of persons who enter as of right) was resisted.[41]

§ 91. NATURE AND VALUE OF COMMON LAW RULES

It was settled[42] that the rules on this topic were a special subhead of the general doctrine of negligence as expounded in *Donoghue* v. *Stevenson*.[43]

---

[31] *Hartwell* v. *Grayson, Rollo and Clover Docks Ltd.* [1947] K.B. 901, 913
[32] Although the lessor may also have duties imposed on him by the Defective Premises Act 1972, s. 4
[33] See above, § 23
[34] *Kelly* v. *Woolworth & Co.* [1922] 2 I.R. 5.
[35] [1922] 2 I.R. 5; 8; *per* Ronan L.J.
[36] *Wheat* v. *Lacon & Co. Ltd.* [1966] A.C. 552.
[37] See below, § 101.
[38] See below, § 100.
[39] *i.e.* either a right arising under a contract (for which, see § 94), or a right conferred by some rule of statute or common law (for which, see § 97).
[40] *Latham* v. *Johnson (R.) & Nephew Ltd.* [1913] 1 K.B. 398, 410, *per* Hamilton L.J. (An "exceedingly comprehensive and able judgment": *Robert Addie & Sons (Collieries) Ltd.* v. *Dumbreck* [1929] A.C. 358, 370, *per* Lord Dunedin.)
[41] *London Graving Dock Co.* v. *Horton* [1951] A.C. 737, 764.
[42] *London Graving Dock Co.* v. *Horton* [1951] A.C. 737, 766; *British Railways Board* v. *Herrington* [1972] A.C. 877, 912.
[43] See above, §§ 73–74.

But it is a subhead with some very special rules of its own, which should not be forgotten or confused.[44] Thus the plaintiff must establish that the defendant was an occupier,[45] and not just a licensee who might reasonably have had the plaintiff in contemplation.[46] Although there is proximity between the occupier and his visitors, the Atkinian neighbour principle does not exclusively define or describe that relationship.[47] It may be that if it had been earlier and more generally recognised that the topic was only one branch of the law of negligence it might have been seen that the occupier's duties could not conveniently be put into strait-jackets to fit the character in which the plaintiff came on the premises, and the law would then have been freed of some needless refinements and profitless distinctions.[48] Yet even if this method of approach had been adopted some distinctions between the various classes of entrants would have been necessary, for they correspond to real differences in the nature of the user of property and in the reasonable claims to protection of those who are permitted such use.

Need for reform

Various reasons may be assigned for the state of confusion into which the law fell. One significant reason may be found in the rule which before 1966 prohibited the House of Lords from reversing one of its own previous decisions. It was thus necessary for the legislature in the Occupiers' Liability Act 1957 to reverse at least three decisions of the House of Lords,[49] although this is a task which many feel that the Law Lords themselves would be better fitted to perform.[50] The Pearson Commission concluded that a no-fault scheme would not be appropriate for this area of the law. It should continue to be based on negligence.[51]

§ 92. CURRENT OPERATIONS[52]

Apart altogether from the Occupiers' Liability Act, the strictness of the common law was mitigated by cases in which the courts held that an entrant who is injured as a result of current operations conducted on the premises

---

[44] *Watson* v. *George* (1953) 89 C.L.R. 409, 418.

[45] See above, § 90.

[46] *McAuliffe* v. *Moloney* [1971] I.R. 200.

[47] *Commissioner for Railways* v. *McDermott* [1967] 1 A.C. 169, 186.

[48] See the Third Report of the Law Reform Committee (Cmd. 9305 (1954), s. 44).

[49] *Cavalier* v. *Pope* [1906] A.C. 428; *London Graving Dock Co.* v. *Horton* [1951] A.C. 737, *Thomson* v. *Cremin* [1956] W.L.R. 103n.

[50] See the remarks of Lord Reid on the Second Reading of the Occupiers' Liability Bill: 203 H.L.Deb. 5s., col. 262. Scottish lawyers always felt aggrieved by the decision in *Robert Addie & Sons (Collieries)* v. *Dumbreck* [1929] A.C. 358, which replaced the primitive simplicity of the law of delict by the more elaborate English doctrine. "That even greater inconveniences have arisen in the country of the doctrine's birth has not unnaturally been observed in Scotland with a certain smugness combined with a measure of admiration for the heroic, but hitherto unavailing, efforts of English lawyers to extricate themselves from what one of them has described as a morass": *Plank* v. *Stirling Magistrates*, 1956 S.C. 92, 104, *per* Lord Thomson. But as the Court of Session also felt itself unable to escape from "the doctrine of the categories" by accepting an invitation to hold that it had been impliedly overruled by *Donoghue* v. *Stevenson* [1932] A.C. 562 (see *Stewart* v. *Glasgow Corporation*, 1958 S.C. 28), it was necessary to enact the Occupiers' Liability (Scotland) Act 1960, which should be studied for its significant differences from the English statute.

[51] Cmnd. 7054, 1978, § 1550.

[52] See North, *Occupiers' Liability*, Chap. 6.

by the occupier need not bring his claim within the established invitee-licensee-trespasser categories but might have a remedy on the simple ground that the defendant has not fulfilled his duty to take reasonable care for the safety of the plaintiff.[53] In one of the most authoritative of these cases the court stated that its task was to choose between competing categories of the law of torts and to select one of them to the exclusion of the other.[54] In this case, in which a child had been electrocuted while climbing on the defendants' pylon (and so committing a technical trespass), the High Court of Australia selected as the basis of its decision the rule which imposes a high standard of care on those who carry on a dangerous activity (*i.e.* the supply of high-voltage electricity) in preference to the rule which exempts an occupier from any duty of care to a trespasser.[55] Again, in relation to a licensee, in *Slater* v. *Clay Cross Co. Ltd.*[56] the Court of Appeal held the defendants liable to the plaintiff (subject to a reduction of damages on the ground of her contributory negligence) when she had been knocked down by a train on the defendants' narrow gauge railway line.[57]

The distinction between the occupier's "activity duty" and his "occupancy duty" has been abolished by the Occupiers' Liability Act.[58] For section 1(1) provides that the rules enacted by the Act shall have effect, *in place of the rules of the common law*, to regulate the duty which an occupier of premises owes to his visitors in respect of dangers due to the state of the premises *or* to things done or omitted to be done on them.[59] The only duty which the occupier today owes to his lawful visitors is the common duty of care. *Obiter dicta* in the House of Lords also deny that the distinction

---

[53] *Miller* v. *South of Scotland Electricity Board*, 1958 S.C.(H.L.) 20, 37–38. The distinction is between the occupier's "activity duty" and his "occupancy duty": Newark, "Twine v. Bean's Express Ltd." (1954) 17 M.L.R. 102, 109. But note that the occupier has been held entitlted to exclude even his "activity duty" by a notice in adequate terms which have been sufficiently brought to the attention of the visitor: *White* v. *Blackmore* [1972] 2 Q.B. 651. See below, § 93.

[54] *Thompson* v. *Municipality of Bankstown* (1952) 87 C.L.R. 619, 623. The doctrine can be traced back to *Gallagher* v. *Humphrey* (1862) 6 L.T.(N.S.) 684, but the more recent decisions pray in aid of the neighbour principle in *Donoghue* v. *Stevenson* [1932] A.C. 562. See *Kennedy* v. *Union Estates Ltd.* [1940] 1 D.L.R. 662; *Merrington* v. *Ironbridge Metal Works Ltd.* [1952] 2 All E.R. 1101; *Burton* v. *Melbourne Harbour Trust* [1954] V.L.R. 645.

[55] The decision in *Thompson* v. *Bankstown* was expressly approved in *Commissioner for Railways* v. *Quinlan* [1964] A.C. 1054, and in *Munnings* v. *Hydro-Electric Commission* [1971] A.L.R. 609.

[56] [1956] 2 Q.B. 264.

[57] The Judicial Committee seem to have approved this view in *Perkowski* v. *Wellington Corporation* [1959] A.C. 53, 67, and *Commissioner for Railways* v. *McDermott* [1967] 1 A.C. 169, 186–187, but to have disapproved it in *Commissioner for Railways* v. *Quinlan* [1964] A.C. 1054, and *Cooper* v. *Southern Portland Cement Ltd* [1974] A.C. 623. The Court of Appeal has recognised that the distinction may be a fine one: *Videan* v. *British Transport Commission* [1963] 2 Q.B. 650, 664–665.

[58] The editor adheres to this view, (which is supported in the Report (1969) of the Alberta Law Reform Institute, p. 48), despite the contrary opinioins expressed by Odgers, [1957] C.L.J. 39–40; Winfield and Jolowicz, *Tort*, p. 196; Street, *Torts*, p. 184; Macintyre, [1959] J.P.L. 12, and North, *Occupiers' Liability* pp. 80–82. Those authors argue that the "activity duty" is not imposed in consequence of a person's occupation or control of premises. Even if this argument be true it overlooks the long title of the Act, which is expressed "to amend the law as to the liability of occupiers *and others*." This point may be important in a case where the statutory duty has been varied "by agreement or otherwise," for the statutory duty can be excluded by a warning notice, whereas the common law duty cannot be so excluded unless the entrant is *volens* (see § 187).

[59] The Act does not require that the premises should have become unsafe as a result of the occupiers' conduct, as the court suggested in *N.Z. Insurance Co. Ltd.* v. *Prudential Assurance Co. Ltd.* [1976] 1 N.Z.L.R. 84.

between the activity duty and the occupancy duty is relevant to the relationship of occupier and trespasser.[60]

§ 93. THE OCCUPIERS' LIABILITY ACT 1957

The degree of criticism to which the state of the common law relating to the liability of occupiers of premises to their visitors had given rise induced the Lord Chancellor to refer the matter to the Law Reform Committee. The Report of the Committee,[61] which contains a full and valuable survey of the common law, made a number of recommendations which were in substance adopted by Parliament in the Occupiers' Liability Act 1957, which came into force on January 1, 1958. The first and main change effected by the Act is that the rules which it contains replace the rules of the common law under which the duty of an occupier differs according as the visitor is an invitee or a licensee. Section 2(1) provides that an occupier of premises[62] owes the same duty, "the common duty of care," to all his lawful visitors, except in so far as he is free to and does extend, restrict, modify or exclude his duty to any visitor or visitors by agreement or otherwise. The common duty of care is not owed to trespassers.[63]

Common duty of care

The common duty of care is defined (section 2(2)) as a duty to take such care as in all the circumstances of the case is reasonable to see that the visitor will be reasonably safe in using the premises for the purpose for which he is permitted or invited to be there.[64] At common law it was not settled whether it is the particular visitor or the class to which he belongs who must be made safe,[65] but the Act's reference to "the visitor" makes it plain that the law is now concerned with the particular plaintiff. In any event, it will be noticed that it is the visitor who has to be made safe and not the premises.[66] So it would be unreasonable to impose on an occupier the same duty towards firemen as is owed towards his own workmen.[67] But it is important to note that the Act (section 1(2)) does not alter the common law as to the person on whom such a duty is imposed[68] or to whom it is owed; accordingly the persons who are to be treated as an occupier and as his visitors are the same[69] as the persons who would at common law be treated

---

[60] *British Railways Board* v. *Herrington* [1972] A.C. 877, 929, 942.
[61] Cmd. 9305 (1954). See Odgers [1955] C.L.J. 1; [1957] C.L.J. 39; Heuston (1955) 18 M.L.R. 271; Newark, "The Occupiers' Liability (Northern Ireland) Act" (1958) 12 N.I.L.Q. 203; Macintyre, The Occupiers' Liability Act 1957" [1958] J.P.L. 10, 93; Payne, "The Occupiers' Liability Act" (1958) 21 M.L.R. 359; Hutton, "Mechanics of Law Reform" (1961) 24 M.L.R. 18.
[62] Which includes any fixed or movable structure, including any vessel, vehicle or aircraft: s. 1(3).
[63] *British Railways Board* v. *Herrington* [1972] A.C. 877, 909, 922.
[64] s. 2 proceeds to deal in greater detail with some of the circumstances which may be relevant in any particular case—*e.g.* that the plantiff is a child, or has knowledge of the danger, or that the occupier has employed an independent contractor to repair the premises. These points are considered fully later.
[65] *O'Donoghue* v. *Greene* [1967] I.R. 40, 48.
[66] *Roles* v. *Nathan* [1963] 1 W.L.R. 1117, 1122.
[67] *Bermingham* v. *Sher Bros.* [1980] C.L. 274.
[68] The Act binds the Crown: s. 6.
[69] But a person entering any premises in exercise of rights conferred by virtue of an access agreement or order under the National Parks and Access to the Countryside Act 1949, is not, for the purposes of the Act, a visitor of the occupier of those premises: s. 1(4).

as an occupier and as his invitees or licensees.[70] The common duty of care is also owed to persons visiting the premises under a contractual right (section 5), or in exercise of a right conferred by law[71] (section 2(6)). In short, the effect of the Act is to reduce the number of categories of visitors to two—lawful visitors and trespassers—and to provide that only one duty is owed to all lawful visitors.

Area of lawful visit. The common duty of care is owed only to a visitor who is "using the premises for the purposes for which he is invited or permitted to be there." If a visitor exceeds the area of invitation or permission he becomes a trespasser, and is owed a lesser duty.[72] It is a question of fact whether in all the circumstances of the case the occupier has taken reasonable steps to warn his visitor of the existence and scope of the prohibited area.[73] For if a person has entered on an area to which he was clearly invited, and if he has strayed from that area, the question is not so much whether he has been invited to stray but whether there was anything to delimit the area of invitation.[74] The cases on delimitation of the area by the occupier apply also to delimitation of the invitation by time.[75]

Nature of common duty of care

As the duty is imposed by a statute it is arguable[76] that this branch of the law is now no longer part of the law of negligence, but should be considered under the heading of actions for breach of statutory duty.[77] Even if this is so, the duty in question differs considerably from the ordinary statutory duty as it is phrased in such wide and general terms.[78] "It is in effect hoping to replace a principle of the common law with a new principle *of the common law*: instead of having the judgment of Willes J. being construed as if it were a statute, one is to have a statute which can be construed as if it were a judgment of Willes J."[79]

Nature of damage recoverable[80]

At common law the better view was that the invitor's duty was to prevent damage not only to the person but also to the goods of an invitee.[81] The

---

[70] This is contrary to the recommendation of the Law Reform Committee, which was that the distinction between invitees and licensees should be abolished. The recommendation was not accepted because this part of the law is not sufficiently settled for codification: so Hylton-Foster, S.-G., on the Committee Stage of the Bill (Standing Committee A, March 26, 1957, col. 5).

[71] This does not include persons exercising a right of way: below, § 97.

[72] "When you invite a person into your house to use the staircase, you do not invite him to slide down the banisters": *The Carlgarth* [1927] P. 93, 110, *per* Scrutton L.J.

[73] So in the banisters case (previous note), the host in not obliged to put up a notice: the layout of the premises speaks for itself: *O'Keefe* v. *Irish Motor Inns Ltd.* [1978] I.R. 83, 101.

[74] *Reaney* v. *Thomas Lydon & Son Ltd.* [1957] Ir. Jur. Rep. 1, 3.

[75] *Stone* v. *Taffe* [1974] 1 W.L.R. 1575, 1580.

[76] See *British Railways Board* v. *Herrington* [1972] A.C. 877, 941.

[77] See above, § 85.

[78] A large number of cases have been reported in *Lloyd's Reports*, but they all seem to be on questions of fact. See North, *Occupiers' Liability*, pp. 55–58.

[79] So the chief parliamentary draftsman: (1961) 24 M.L.R. 18, 28–29. (The reference is to the judgment of Willes J. in *Indermaur* v. *Dames* (1866) L.R. 1 C.P. 274 (below, § 95).)

[80] North, *Occupiers' Liability*, Chap. 7.

[81] *The Cawood III* [1951] P. 270; *Workington Harbour and Dock Board* v. *Towerfield (Owners)* [1951] A.C. 112; *Drive-Yourself Lessey's Pty. Ltd.* v. *Burnside* (1959) S.R.(N.S.W.) 390. Contra, *Edwards* v. *West Herts Group Hospital Management Committee* [1957] 1 W.L.R. 415, 417, 422; Goodhart (1957) 73 L.Q.R. 313.

Occupiers' Liability Act 1957, s.1(3)(*b*), affirms[82] and extends the common law by enacting that the common duty of care which an occupier owes to his lawful visitors covers the obligations of a person occupying or having control over any premises or structure in respect of damage to[83] property, including the property of persons who are not themselves his visitors.[84] The words "damage to property" are not limited to damages in respect of physical damage but cover damages in respect of subsequent financial loss,[85] provided that the normal rules of remoteness of damage[86] are satisfied.

Can common duty of care be excluded or modified?[87]

It is necessary first to see how the law stood before the Occupiers' Liability Act 1957. If the visitor had entered under contract there was no doubt that the occupier could modify or exclude the duty which he would otherwise have owed by the insertion of appropriate terms in the contract. But if the visitor had entered by the invitation or licence of the occupier the position was not so clear. It was only on the eve of the passing of the Act that the Court of Appeal in *Ashdown* v. *Samuel Williams & Sons Ltd.*[88] approved the view that it is competent to an occupier of land to restrict or exclude any liability he might otherwise be under to any licensee of his, including his liability for his own or his employee's negligence, by conditions framed and adequately made known to the licensee.[89]

Section 2(1) of the 1957 Act provides, as we have seen, that an occupier of premises owes the same duty, the "common duty of care," to all his lawful visitors, except in so far as he is free to[90] and does extend, restrict, modify or exclude his duty to any visitor or visitors by agreement or otherwise.[91] It is difficult to resist the conclusion that Parliament authorised

---

[82] But see the doubts in Chapman, *Statutes*, pp. 50–51.

[83] It is still uncertain whether these words cover loss of property due to theft, or some other wrongful act of a third party: *AMF International Ltd.* v. *Magnet Bowling Ltd.* [1968] 1 W.L.R. 1028.

[84] This would protect the interest of, say, a company which hired out a motor-vehicle which was lawfully brought on to the occupier's premises by the hirer: *Drive-Yourself Lessey's Pty. Ltd.* v. *Burnside* (1959) S.R.(N.S.W.) 390. So an entity which is physically incapable of entering, and does not in fact enter, is yet protected by the Occupiers' Liability Act.

[85] *AMF International Ltd.* v. *Magnet Bowling Ltd.* [1968] 1 W.L.R. 1028.

[86] See below, § 202.

[87] See Symmons, "How Free is the Freedom of the Occupier?" (1974) *The Conveyancer* 253.

[88] [1957] 1 Q.B. 409. The decision was followed in *Mayor* v. *Ribble Motor Services, Ltd.*, unreported (1958) C.A. 261. See Gower (1956) 19 M.L.R. 532; (1957) 20 M.L.R. 181; Odgers, "Occupiers' Liability" [1957] C.L.J. 39; and below, § 186–187, for exemption clauses and disclaimers in general.

[89] [1957] 1 Q.B. 409, 421, *per* Jenkins L.J. See also Parker L.J. p. 427. (It should be noted that both these L.JJ. were members of the Law Reform Committee which produced the Report on Occupiers' Liability.)

[90] The occupier is not free in respect to visitors entering in pursuance of a contract between the occupier and a third party (see below, § 94), but in view of the decision in *Ashdown* v. *Samuel Williams & Sons Ltd.* [1957] 1 Q.B. 409 it is difficult to think of any other case in which the occupier is not so free. Perhaps the courts will not permit an occupier to exempt himself from liability to one who enters as of right, or perhaps s. 2(4)(*a*) could be invoked so as to require the warning to make the visitor reasonably safe: *White* v. *Blackmore* [1972] 2 Q.B. 651, 665.

[91] When the Bill was in Committee a proposal to delete the words "or otherwise" was defeated on the advice of Hylton-Foster, S.-G.: H.C. Standing Committee A, March 26, 1957, col. 30.

occupiers of premises to exempt themselves fom the duty which they would normally owe to their lawful visitors[92] by the simple device of exhibiting a notice which contains terms suitably framed for this purpose.[93] In other words, Parliament approved the decision in *Ashdown*.[94] But in the Unfair Contract Terms Act 1977, s. 1 (*c*), Parliament limited the scope of the *Ashdown* rule to trespassers and non-business visitors.[95]

Contributory negligence. Although the Act does not specifically deal with the point, it is generally understood[96] that the defence of contributory negligence is available.[97]

Effect of knowledge of danger. Even if the occupier has not exempted himself from liability by means of "agreement or otherwise" under section 2(1) of the Act, he may still be exonerated from liability in whole or in part by reason of the visitor's knowledge of the danger. This may happen in three ways.

(1) Section 2(5) of the Act provides that the common duty of care does not impose on an occupier any obligation to a visitor in respect of risks willingly accepted as his by the visitor, as when rugby football is played on a ground which complies with the appropriate by-laws.[98] The question whether a risk was so accepted is to be decided on the same principles[99] as in other cases in which one person owes a duty of care to another.[1] Knowledge by the plaintiff is not to be treated without more as absolving the occupier from liability unless in all the circumstances it was enough to enable the visitor to be reasonably safe.[2]

(2) The Act recognises the common law principle that a danger may cease to be a danger to those who know of it. But in each case it is to be a question of fact whether the visitor's knowledge of the danger relieves the occupier from liability, for section 2(4) provides that in determining whether the occupier of premises has discharged the common duty of care to a visitor, regard is to be had to all the circumstances, so that (for example), where damage is caused to a visitor by a danger[3] of which he has been warned by the occupier, the warning is not to be treated without more as absolving the occupier[4] unless in all the circumstances[5] it was enough[6] to enable the visitor to be reasonably safe.[7]

---

[92] Could the common humanity duty which is owed to trespassers be excluded? Probably not: see Law Com. No. 75, § 60.

[93] But observe the significant difference in the wording of s. 2(1) of the Occupiers' Liability (Scotland) Act 1960, which makes it plain that Parliament has given no such freedom to the Scottish occupier.

[94] *White* v. *Blackmore* [1972] 2 Q.B. 651, 674.

[95] See below, §§ 186–187.

[96] So in *Roles* v. *Nathan* [1963] 1 W.L.R. 1117 the C.A. apportioned the loss.

[97] North, *Occupiers' Liability*, p. 115.

[98] *Simms* v. *Leigh Rugby Football Club Ltd.* [1969] 2 All E.R. 923.

[99] For these principles, see below, §§ 187–188.

[1] See *White* v. *Blackmore* [1972] 2 Q.B. 651.

[2] *Bunker* v. *Charles Brand & Son Ltd.* [1969] 2 Q.B. 480, 489.

[3] Does this mean the peril itself or the facts or events which have created that peril?

[4] What is the effect of a warning given by a stranger?

[5] See the cogent example given in *Horton* v. *London Graving Dock Co. Ltd.* [1950] 1 K.B. 421, 428–429.

[6] As it was in *Roles* v. *Nathan* [1963] 1 W.L.R. 1117.

[7] Distinguish the warning which discharges the common duty of care (s. 2 (4)(*a*)) from the warning which excludes it (s. 2(1)). A warning may be sufficient for the latter purpose but not for the former, which is certainly an odd result: see *White* v. *Blackmore* [1972] 2 Q.B. 651.

(3) Knowledge of a danger may be evidence of contributory negligence on the part of a person injured by it.

§ 94. Lawful Visitors: (1) Under Contract

At common law there was much dispute about the scope and nature of the term to be implied in a contract relating to entry upon premises in favour of the entrant. But now Parliament has considerably simplified the law: it has provided that visitors under contract[8] shall be entitled to the common duty of care in the absence of any express provision in the contract governing the matter. Such a visitor may sue in contract or in tort at his option. The choice may be important if his contributory negligence is likely to be an issue, as in contract as distinct from tort his damages are not likely to be reduced.[9]

Section 5(1) of the Act provides that when persons enter or use, or bring, or send goods[10] to, any premises[11] in exercise of a right conferred by contract with a person occupying or having control of the premises, the duty he owes them in respect of dangers due to the state of the premises or to things done or omitted to be done on them, in so far as the duty depends on a term to be implied in the contract by reason of its conferring that right, shall be the common duty of care.[12] The section does not affect the obligations imposed on a person by or by virtue of any contract for the hire of, or for the carriage for reward of person or goods in, any vehicle, vessel, aircraft or other means of transport, or by virtue of any contract of bailment.

Effect of contract on occupier's liability to third party. The Occupiers' Liability Act, s.3(1), provides that where an occupier of premises is bound by contract to permit persons who are strangers to the contract[13] to enter or use the premises, the duty of care which he owes to them as his visitors cannot be restricted or excluded by that[14] contract,[15] but (subject to any provision of the contract to the contrary) shall include the duty to perform his obligations under the contract,[16] whether undertaken for their protection or not, in so far as those obligations go beyond the obligations otherwise involved in that duty. So a visitor to a tenant will always be entitled at the least to the benefits of the common duty of care; he will also be entitled to the benefit of any additional obligation undertaken by the lessor towards the lessee, unless the former has expressly excluded such an obligation. Section 3(4) also provides that the same principles shall apply when by the terms or

---

[8] Although the statute (s. 1 (1)) expressly abolishes the common law rules only in relation to invitees and licensees, it is inconceivable that Parliament intended them to subsist in relation to contractual visitors.

[9] *Sole* v. *Hallt Ltd.* [1973] 1 Q.B. 574. See also below, § 195.

[10] For damage to property, see § 93 above.

[11] A term which includes fixed and movable structures: s. 5(2). See above, § 90.

[12] As this duty is imposed or implied by the law and not by the parties it would seem that a claim for its breach should properly be regarded as a claim in tort. But s. 5 of the Act is preceded by the cross-heading "Liability in contract."

[13] Defined by s. 3(3) to mean persons not for the time being entitled to the benefit of the contract as parties to it or as the successors by assignment or otherwise of a party to it.

[14] But presumably could be by another contract.

[15] Such a lawful visitor is therefore in a peculiarly favourable condition, for normally (see above, § 93) the common duty of care can be restricted or excluded.

[16] Note that an occupier who has taken all reasonable care is not responsible for the defaults of an independent contractor unless the contract expressly provides otherwise: s. 3(2).

conditions governing any tenancy (including a statutory tenancy) either the landlord or the tenant is bound, though not by contract, to permit persons to enter or use premises of which he is the occupier.

§ 95. Lawful Visitors: (2) Invitees

(1) Who is an invitee

At common law entry by permission of the occupier is of two kinds. The permission amounts either to an invitation or to a mere licence. A person invited to enter is commonly referred to as an invitee,[17] or a licensee with an interest, while he who is merely licensed to enter is distinguished as a licensee, or bare licensee. The leading case is *Indermaur* v. *Dames*,[18] in which the occupier of a factory was held liable to the plaintiff, who was the employee of a gasfitter who had contracted to do certain work for the defendant, and who, while testing certain gas-fittings on the defendant's premises, fell through an unfenced opening in one of the upper floors. Willes J.[19] said:

> "The class to which the customer belongs includes persons who go not as mere volunteers, or licensees, or guests, or servants, or persons whose employment is such that danger may be considered as bargained for, but who go upon business which concerns the occupier and upon his invitation, express or implied."

Common interest required

The law then, rather paradoxically, requires something more than an express or implied invitation to enter upon premises to constitute the entrant an invitee. What that something more may be has been disputed. Salmond thought it sufficient if the occupier had a material interest in the visitor's presence. He defined an invitee as a person who enters on the premises by the permission of the occupier granted in a matter in which the occupier himself has some pecuniary or material interest.[20] He is a person who receives permission from the occupier as a matter of business and not as a matter of grace. An invitation is a request to enter for the purpose of the occupier; a licence is a permission to enter for the purposes of the entrant himself. The invitor says: "I ask you to enter upon my business." The licensor says: "I permit you to enter upon your own business."[21] But in *Pearson* v. *Lambeth*

---

[17] "To use a non-English word made common, if not invented, by our judges": *Haseldine* v. *Daw (C.A.) & Son Ltd.* [1941] 2 K.B. 343, 350, *per* Scott L.J. But, as Lord Eldon once said, it is "an expression which, though it should never have come into this court, cannot now be thrown out of it.": *Davis* v. *Marlborough (Duke of)* [1814–23] All E.R.Rep. 13, 17.

[18] (1866) L.R. 1 C.P. 274; 2 C.P. 311. The case was decided on February 26, 1866, and the judgment appeared in the part of the *Law Reports* published on April 1—"a speed of reporting which would these days fill us with amazement": *Wanless* v. *Piening* (1967) 68 S.R.(N.S.W.) 249, 256, *per* Jacobs J.A.

[19] "One of the greatest jurists of this or any other time": *Bowen* v. *Hall* (1881) 6 Q.B.D. 333, 342, *per* Lord Coleridge C.J.

[20] This economic benefit theory is generally adopted in England and in Ireland, but not in the U.S.A.: *O'Keeffe* v. *Irish Motor Inns Ltd.* [1978] I.R. 83, 99.

[21] This passage was cited with approval in *Ellis* v. *Fulham Borough Council* [1938] 1 K.B. 212, 234, *per* Mackinnon L.J. ("the best definition"), and in *Slade* v. *Battersea Hospital Committee* [1955] 1 W.L.R. 207, 210, *per* Finnemore J.

B.C.[22] Asquith L.J. thought that it is more exact to say that an invitee is a person who comes on the occupier's premises with his consent on business in which the occupier and he have a common interest. This requirement of community of interest is to be found in many of the cases,[23] and was approved in *Jacobs* v. *L.C.C.*[24] Lord Simonds, whose judgment was concurred in by the other members of the House, held that the plaintiff was a licensee because three of the Law Lords in the rather similar case of *Fairman* v. *Perpetual Investment Building Society*[25] had expressed the view that such was the status of a person in those circumstances. On this approach it was, of course, unnecessary to consider the principles on which a distinction may be drawn between an invitee and a licensee, and the problem still awaits an authoritative review. On the authorities the following have been classified as invitees: customers in a shop,[26] persons visiting sick relatives in hospital,[27] persons visiting sick strangers at their home,[28] persons meeting relatives arriving by train,[29] workmen employed by sub-contractors,[30] and firemen.[31] But the invitee of the tenant of a dwelling-house[32] or a shop[33] is only a licensee of the landlord. A person visiting a ship in dock is sometimes an invitee,[34] and sometimes not.[35]

Who is an invitor

We have seen that normally the duties of an invitor attach to the person in occupation or possession or control, and also considered the meaning of occupation.[36]

---

[22] |1950| 2 K.B. 353, 366. He was less critical in *Sutton* v. *Bootle Corporation* |1947| K.B. 359, 366.

[23] See Law Reform Committee (3rd Report), para. 7.

[24] |1950| A.C. 361. See Goodhart, "The 'I Think' Doctrine of Precedent: Invitor and Licensors" (1950) 66 L.Q.R. 374.

[25] |1923| A.C. 74. The plaintiff, a lodger of one of the tenants in a block of flats, caught her heel in a depression on the common staircase, which was in the occupation of the landlords. It had been suggested that under modern conditions a landlord clearly had a material interest in providing proper means of access to his flats or offices (at any rate for business visitors of his tenants, for their presence might enable the tenant to pay his rent more easily) and that the *Fairman* case laid down no general rule as to the status of the tenant's visitors *vis-à-vis* the landlord: *Haseldine* v. *Daw* |1941| 2 K.B. 343, 371; *Jacobs* v. *L.C.C.* |1949| 1 K.B. 685, 700. In any case it was arguable that the statements in the *Fairman* case were *obiter dicta*: *Pearson* v. *Lambeth B.C.* |1950| 2 K.B. 353, 361; Heuston (1950) 66 L.Q.R. 33. But in the *Jacobs* case the H.L. held that these statements were not *obiter dicta*. This seems a correct deduction from the principles governing the distinction between *ratio decidendi* and *obiter dicta*. "Before the court |in *Fairman*| could decide whether on the facts there was a failure in duty it had to have before it very clearly the legal duties owed, and that seems to me to be an inherent consideration for the determination of the case": *Stewart* v. *Glasgow Corporation*, 1958 S.C. 28, 33, *per* Lord Wheatley.

[26] *Indermaur* v. *Dames* (1866) L.R. 1 C.P. 274.

[27] *Slade* v. *Battersea Hospital Management Committee* |1955| 1 W.L.R. 207.

[28] *Jennings* v. *Cole* |1949| 2 All E.R. 191.

[29] *Bloomstein* v. *Railway Executive* |1952| 2 All E.R. 418.

[30] *London Graving Dock Co. Ltd.* v. *Horton* |1951| A.C. 737.

[31] *Hartley* v. *Mayoh & Co. Ltd.* |1954| 1 W.L.R. 355—a decision which has been said to be unaffected by the Occupiers' Liability Act: see *Bermingham* v. *Sher Bros.* |1980| C.L. 274.

[32] *Fairman* v. *Perpetual Investment Building Society* |1923| A.C. 74.

[33] *Jacobs* v. *L.C.C.* |1950| A.C. 361; *Percival* v. *Hope Gibbons Ltd.* |1959| N.Z.L.R. 642.

[34] *Smith* v. *London Graving Dock Co.* (1868) L.R. 3 C.P. 326.

[35] *Kininmonth* v. *France, Fenwick & Co. Ltd.* (1949) 82 Ll.L.R. 768.

[36] See above, §90.

(2) Common law duty

The scope of the duty owed at common law by an invitor to an invitee was laid down by Willes J. in *Indermaur* v. *Dames*.[37] This judgment was discussed in scores of cases and the law became subtle and confused in many respects before the Occupiers' Liability Act. As the Act specifically provides, in section 1 (1), that the rules which it enacts shall have effect "in place of the rules of the common law," those rules are now only of historical interest. It is enough to say that the leading distinction between an invitor and a licensor was that the former was liable not only for dangers of which he knew but also for those which he ought to have known.

(3) Statutory duty

The duty which an occupier now owes to an invitee is, under the Occupiers' Liability Act, s. 2 (2), the common duty of care—*i.e.* a duty to take such care as in all the circumstances of the case is reasonable to see that the invitee will be reasonably safe in using the premises for the purposes for which he is invited to be there. The Occupiers' Liability Act, s. 2 (3), by way of affirming the common law, also provides that the circumstances relevant to an assessment of the common duty of care owed in any particular case include the degree of care, and of want of care, which would ordinarily be looked for in such a visitor, so that (for example) in proper cases an occupier (1) must be prepared for children to be less careful than adults,[38] and (2) may expect that a person, in the exercise of his calling, will appreciate and guard against any special risks ordinarily incident to it, so far as the occupier leaves him free to do so. "For example, if a window-cleaner (not being an employee of the occupier) sustains injury through the insecurity of some part of the exterior of the premises which he uses as a foothold or handhold for the purpose of cleaning the outside of the windows, the occupier merely as such should not be liable. *Aliter*, if the window-cleaner is injured through some defect in the staircase when going upstairs in the ordinary way to reach the windows on an upper floor."[39] An occupier is entitled to assume that a chimney-sweep will guard against dangers from or in the flues which he is employed to sweep.[40]

An invitee is, however, entitled to assume that the premises are in a fit state for his reception: he need not adopt the wary attitude which a prudent licensee will assume in self-protection—unless, indeed, the nature of the premises would warn a prudent man to do so.[41] So as it is usual to descend a ladder feet first the opportunities for seeing a defective rung are almost nil.[42] On the other hand, the House of Lords has held that one using unlit back stairs in a public-house must proceed with great caution.[43] The courts are

[37] (1866) L.R. 1 C.P. 274, 287.
[38] For illustrative case, see below, § 99.
[39] Third Report of the Law Reform Committee, para. 77. See *Bates* v. *Parker* [1953] 2 Q.B. 231. If the window-cleaner were the employee of a contractor he might have an action against his employer: see below, § 181.
[40] *Roles* v. *Nathan* [1963] 1 W.L.R. 117. This is one of the few reported cases on the Act which raises a point of law.
[41] *Reaney* v. *Thomas, Lydon & Sons Ltd.* [1957] Ir.Jur.Rep. 1, 3.
[42] *O'Krane* v. *Alcyon Shipping Co. Ltd.* (1960) 24 D.L.R. (2d) 119, 123.
[43] *Wheat* v. *Lacon & Co. Ltd.* [1966] A.C. 552. See the criticism of this decision in [1966] A.S.C.L. 251. There is much to be said for the argument that "The greatest danger to which a publican can submit his customers is that of darkness. Any and every danger awaits the unwary in darkness": *Ryan* v. *Cullen* [1957] Ir.Jur.Rep. 65, 66.

readier today than in the past to find that the plaintiff was not taking reasonable care for his own safety since they now have the power to apportion the loss in cases of contributory negligence. If the invitee is aware of the danger he may be defeated for other reasons,[44] but the knowledge is no more than evidence of contributory negligence.

Effect of knowledge

The duty under *Indemaur* v. *Dames* was really founded, not on the existence of the danger but on the failure of the occupier to prevent damage from it. In some cases such damage might be prevented by giving notice of the danger to the invitee; in other cases the notice or knowledge might not enable the invitee to avoid the danger if he was effectively to accomplish the purpose for which he had entered the premises. In the latter case the better view[45] was that the invitor's duty was not discharged by the mere fact that the invitee knew as much (or more) about the danger as the invitor did. It was a question of fact whether in all the circumstances he had taken reasonable care for the safety of the entrant.[46] It is true that in *Horton's* case[47] a bare majority of the House of Lords held that the invitor's duty was discharged or at an end if he could show that the invitee encountered the danger with full knowledge and appreciation of the risk involved. The fact that the invitee was not really a free agent in accepting the risk because he was under a contract of service with a third party was held to be irrelevant in an action against the occupier.[48] But the decision was criticised by the Law Reform Committee,[49] which reported in favour of a change in the law. So the Occupiers' Liability Act, s. 2 (4), now provides, as we have seen,[50] that where damage is caused to a visitor by a danger of which he has been warned by the occupier, the warning is not to be treated without more as absolving the occupier from liability, unless in all the circumstances it was enough to enable the visitor to be reasonably safe.

Liability for third parties[51]

The invitor's duty most commonly has reference to the structural condition of the premises, but it may also be extended to include the use which he (or whoever has control so far as is material) permits a third party to make of the premises.[52] The occupier has the power of immediate supervision and control and the power of permitting or prohibiting the entry of other persons

---

[44] *e.g.* because of *volenti non fit injuria,* or because the invitor's duty is discharged.
[45] *Long* v. *Saorstat and Continental Steamship Co. Ltd.* (1953) 93 I.L.T.R. 137.
[46] *O'Donoghue* v. *Greene* [1967] I.R. 40.
[47] [1951] A.C. 737.
[48] See also above, § 93. It should be remembered that an invitee who was defeated at common law by reason of his knowledge of the risk might have a claim under the Factories Act 1961—*e.g.* for failure to provide safe means of access so far as is reasonably practicable (s. 29)—and such a claim is not defeated by knowledge of the risk.
[49] Cmd. 9305, ss. 77–78. The decision in *Horton's* case was criticised more severely than almost any other decision of the House of Lords in modern times: see Wright, (1951) 67 L.Q.R. 532; Goodhart, *ibid.* 428; Chapman (1957) 73 L.Q.R. 406. It was not followed in Ireland: *O'Donoghue* v. *Greene* [1967] I.R. 40.
[50] Above, § 93.
[51] North, *Occupiers' Liability,* pp. 82–84.
[52] *Glasgow Corporation* v. *Muir* [1943] A.C. 448, 463.

and he is under a duty to take reasonable care to prevent damage, at least from unusual danger, arising from such acts of third parties as could reasonably be foreseen.[53] So the occupier of a theatre has been held liable for a dangerous show put on by an independent contractor,[54] and the occupiers of a vehicle, club or restaurant for assaults committed by intoxicated passengers [55] or guests.[56] But the occupier of a camp-site was not liable when one visitor injured another in the course of giving a driving lesson.[57] Nor was the occupier of a public-house liable when an unknown third party removed an electric bulb over a dark staircase, although experience shows that this kind of behaviour is not uncommon.[58]

Independent contractors [59]

In *Thomson* v. *Cremin* in 1941[60] it was said in the House of Lords by Lord Wright that an invitor's duty to his invitee was personal in the sense that it could not be discharged merely by entrusting its performance to an independent contractor, however competent he appeared to be and however technical the nature of the work which he was employed to do. This was generally thought to interpret the occupier's duty to take reasonable care of his invitee's safety in too severe a sense and the courts interpreted *Thomson* v. *Cremin* restrictively.[61] Now in accordance with the recommendation of the Law Reform Committee [62] the Occupiers' Liability Act, s. 2 (4) (*b*), provides that where damage is caused to a visitor by a danger due to the faulty execution of any work of construction, maintenance or repair[63] by an independent contractor employed by the occupier, the occupier is not to be treated without more as answerable for the danger if in all the circumstances he had acted reasonably by entrusting the work to him and had taken such steps (if any) as he reasonably ought in order to satisfy himself that the contractor was competent and that the work had been properly done. So sometimes the law requires an occupier to exercise reasonable supervision over the work done by his independent contractors, as when he constructs a substantial building or a ship. Then he should call in a properly qualified professional man to supervise the contractor. But in other cases, as when a domestic building is re-wired, the occupier is entitled to trust the contractor: otherwise there would be "an almost endless retrogression."[64] The con-

---

[53] *Simons* v. *Winslade* [1938] 3 All E.R. 774 (vomit in yard of public-house); *Hobson* v. *Bartrams Ltd.* [1950] 1 All E.R. 412 (Argentine sailors leaving hatch-covers off).
[54] *Cox* v. *Coulson* [1916] 2 K.B. 177.
[55] *Cf. Adderley* v. *Great Northern Ry.* [1905] 2 I.R. 378 (assault by drunken fellow-passenger).
[56] *Jordan House Ltd.* v. *Menon* (1974) 38 D.L.R. (3d) 105.
[57] *Crickmar* v. *Cleavers, The Times*, October 8, 1964.
[58] *Wheat* v. *Lacon & Co. Ltd.* [1966] A.C. 552.
[59] See also below, § 184.
[60] [1953] 2 All E.R. 1185; [1956] 1 W.L.R. 103n.; *sub nom. Cremin* v. *Thomson* (1941) 71 L1.L.R. 1.
[61] *Davie* v. *New Merton Board Mills Ltd.* [1959] A.C. 604, 644.
[62] Cmd. 9305, p. 34.
[63] Would this phrase cover (say) demolition? It has been held not to cover careless stowage by stevedores: *Gaffney* v. *Aviation and Shipping Co. Ltd.* [1966] 1 Lloyd's Rep. 249. It would be paradoxical if *Thomson* v. *Cremin* itself (a stowage case) had not been affected by the Act.
[64] *AMF International Ltd* v. *Magnet Bowling Ltd.* [1968] 1 W.L.R. 1028, 1045.

tractor may himself be liable to the plaintiff, either if he is regarded as himself an occupier,[65] or under the general principles of negligence.[66]

§ 96. Lawful Visitors: (3) Licensees

(1) Who is a licensee

A licensee is one who enters on the premises by the permission of the occupier, granted gratuitously in a matter in which the occupier has no interest.[67] Often the occupier neither knows nor cares whether the licensee is making use of the permission granted to him, and at least until recent years, he was entitled to withdraw the permission at any time.[68] The typical example is a gratuitous licence to use a way across the occupier's land for purposes which exclusively concern the licensee himself. Another example is a guest receiving hospitality in a private house,[69] for "The law does not take account of the worldly advantage which the host may remotely have in view."[70] After considerable controversy it was settled that persons visiting a tenant or his family are licensees so far as any part of the premises which remains in the landlord's occupation is concerned.[71] It is also settled that persons visiting public parks or recreation grounds are licensees.[72]

Implied licences

A licence may be granted either expressly or impliedly, but one who claims that he is an implied licensee must show that the occupier has permitted his presence and not merely tolerated it. This is a question which most often arises in relation to children,[73] but the principles apply also to adult visitors. An occupier who resigns himself to the occasional and perhaps inevitable presence of trespassers on his property does not thereby take upon himself the obligations of a licensor.[74] "Permission must be proved, not tolerance, though tolerance in some circumstances may be so pronounced as to lead to a conclusion that it was really tantamount to permission," e.g. "a mere putting up of a notice 'No Trespassers Allowed' or 'Strictly Private,' followed, when people often come, by no further steps, would, I think, leave it open for a judge or jury to hold implied permission."[75] But it is not sufficient to make the plaintiff a licensee merely to prove that the occupier has not taken such measures as effectually to stop

---

[65] See above, § 90.
[66] See North, *Occupiers' Liability*, pp. 28–31.
[67] Above, § 23.
[68] Above, § 23.
[69] *Pitt* v. *Jackson* |1939| 1 All E.R. 129, 132.
[70] *Latham* v. *Johnson* |1913| 1 K.B. 398, 410, *per* Hamilton L.J.
[71] *Jacobs* v. *L.C.C.* |1950| A.C. 361.
[72] See below, § 97.
[73] See further below, § 99.
[74] *Phipps* v. *Rochester Corporation* |1955| 1 Q.B. 450, 455; *Koehler* v. *Pentecostal Assemblies* (1957) 7 D.L.R. (2d) 616, 621.
[75] *Addie & Sons* v. *Dumbreck* |1929| A.C. 358, 372, *per* Lord Dunedin. But "an open gate or an unfenced field does not amount to an invitation or licence *urbi et orbi* to enter upon private property": *Kenny* v. *Electricity Supply Board* |1932| I.R. 73, 84, *per* FitzGibbon J.

trespass.[76] There is no duty on a proprietor to fence his land against the world under sanction that, if he does not, those who come over it become licensees.[77] An unauthorised invitation by an employee of the occupier, acting outside the scope of his authority, to enter upon the premises will not prevent the person who accepts the invitation from being a trespasser.[78] For this reason it is submitted that a plaintiff who is on premises in breach of some by-law imposing penalties can never plead that he is there by leave and licence[79]: it is against the policy of the law to permit anyone to license another to commit a crime.[80] For a man (or a child) is none the less a trespasser because he does not realise that he is a trespasser.[81]

Test objective

It is not clear how far the state of mind of a visitor who relies upon an implied licence is relevant. Is it enough for such a visitor to show that the occupier has sufficiently expressed his consent for the entry of a class of persons, of whom the plaintiff is one, or must he show that he has personal knowledge of the acts of the occupier which are alleged to constitute a licence? A dictum favours the latter view,[82] but the former view seems more consistent with the objective test of knowledge which is applied when it is the state of mind of the licensor [83] or invitor [84] which is in issue.

(2) Common law duty

The occupier of premises is under no obligation to a licensee to make them safe for use by him. A mere licensee must be content to take the premises as they are.[85] This rule, however, is subject to three important qualifications.

First, although the occupier is not bound to use any care to make the premises safe for the use of a mere licensee, he is under an obligation to give warning to such a licensee of the existence of any concealed danger which exists on the premises and is known to the occupier. He is not entitled knowingly to lead even a bare licensee into a trap.[86] A trap involves the idea of concealment and surprise: there must be something like fraud before the

---

[76] See *Edwards* v. *Railway Executive* [1952] A.C. 737, 746, *per* Lord Goddard C.J.: "But repeated trespass of itself confers no licence; the owner of a park in the neighbourhood of a town knows probably only too well that it will be raided by young and old to gather flowers, nuts or mushrooms whever they get an opportunity. But because he does not cover hs park wall with a *chevaux de frise* or post a number of keepers to chase away intruders how is it to be said that he has licensed what he cannot prevent?"
[77] *British Railways Board* v. *Herrington* [1972] A.C. 877, 914.
[78] *Hillen* v. *I.C.I. (Alkali)* [1936] A.C. 65; *Conway* v. *Wimpey Ltd.* [1951] 2 K.B. 266.
[79] *Rich* v. *Commissioner for Railways (N.S.W.)* (1959) 101 C.L.R. 135, 143.
[80] See below, § 190.
[81] *Conway* v. *Wimpey Ltd.* [1951] 2 K.B. 266, 273. But involuntary trespassers sometimes have a right of action where voluntary trespassers have not (*Deane* v. *Clayton* (1817) 7 Taunt. 489, 519; *Braithwaite* v. *South Durham Steel Co. Ltd.* [1958] 1 W.L.R. 986) and an occupier may be liable in nuisance to those who accidentally deviate from a highway when he would not be liable to one who did so intentionally: *Barnes* v. *Ward* (1850) 9 C.B. 392.
[82] *Edwards* v. *Railway Executive* [1952] A.C. 737, 748.
[83] *British Railways Board* v. *Herrington* [1972] A.C. 877, 938.
[84] *O'Donoghue* v. *Greene* [1967] I.R. 40.
[85] *Perkowski* v. *Wellington Corporation* [1959] A.C. 53.
[86] *Baker* v. *Bethnal Green B.C.* [1944] 2 All E.R. 301, 305.

occupier can be responsible; he is in a position analogous to that of a donor.[87] The licensee cannot saddle the occupier with any more onerous obligation merely because the latter has made changes in the condition of the land after he has gone into occupation.[88] The question is simply whether the defect in question amounts to a trap. Nor does it make any difference that the concealed danger is of risk of injury outside the licensed area, for example, by falling over a cliff into the sea.[89]

Secondly, the occupier is liable if he or his employees do any positive act of negligent misfeasance by which the licensee suffers harm, as by negligently driving over a person who has been permitted to use a private way. The licence is granted subject to existing dangers, but no further act must be done by the grantor or his employees to endanger the safety of the person to whom it was given.[90] But if injury has been caused by the act of an independent third party which has no reference to the state of the premises the occupier is not liable,[91] although the third party himself may be on the ordinary principles of negligence.[92]

Thirdly, the position of a licensee must be distinguished from that of a person for whom the occupier has undertaken, even though gratuitously, to perform some service: for example, a gratuitous contract of carriage.[93] Such a contract imposes a duty of reasonable care in the performance of it, and this duty extends to ascertaining the safe condition of the premises on which the contract is to be performed.[94] So he who lends his motorcar to a friend is not bound to ascertain its safe condition[95]; but he who takes his friend for a drive apparently is so bound.[96]

Test of knowledge is objective

The licensor is only bound to warn the licensee of traps of which he actually knows. So if the licensee knows as much as the licensor, he cannot sue unless there is some other relationship displacing or co-existing with the former relationship—for example, the duty which arises out of the inherently dangerous activity of running trains over level-crossings.[97] The plaintiff is not, however, required to undertake the burden of showing that the occupier realised that facts of whose existence he was fully aware constituted a danger, for this would indeed be to favour the stupid or incompetent occupier at the expense of his more prudent and civilised neighbour. If the licensor does know of the physical facts which constitute the danger, which are sometimes called the primary facts,[98] and a reason-

---

[87] *Perkowski* v. *Wellington Corporation* [1959] A.C. 53, 66.
[88] *Perkowski* v. *Wellington Corporation* [1959] A.C. 53.
[89] *Perkowski* v. *Wellington Corporation* [1959] A.C. 53 (diving-board over shallow water).
[90] *Ashdown* v. *Williams (Samuel) & Sons Ltd.* [1957] 1 Q.B. 409, 421. Liability for "current operations" is further considered above, § 92.
[91] *Waring* v. *East Anglian Flying Services Ltd.* [1951] W.N. 55.
[92] As in *Billings* v. *A.C. Riden & Co. Ltd.* (1958) A.C. 240. In such a case it is irrelevant to consider the plaintiff's status with respect to the occupier: see further, below, § 100.
[93] *Heard* v. *N.Z. Forest Products Ltd.* [1960] N.Z.L.R. 329.
[94] *Heard* v. *N.Z. Forest Products Ltd.* [1960] N.Z.L.R. 329, 363. See also *Haseldine* v. *C.A. Daw & Sons Ltd.* [1941] 2 K.B. 343, 373; Paton, *Bailment*, pp. 140–143.
[95] See below, § 104.
[96] See above, § 82.
[97] *Commissioner for Railways* v. *McDermott* [1967] 1 A.C. 169.
[98] *Harris* v. *Birkenhead Corporation* [1976] 1 All E.R. 341, 352.

able man, having that knowledge, would appreciate the risk involved, the licensor is not excused by his own failure to appreciate the risk involved.[99]

(3) Duty under the Occupiers' Liability Act

An occupier of premises[1] owes the common duty of care to a visitor who would at common law have been treated as his licensee—*i.e.* he must take such care as in all the circumstances of the case is reasonable to see that the visitor will be reasonably safe in using the premises for the purpose for which he is permitted by the occupier to be there. It follows that the provisions of the statute relating to the visitor's knowledge of the danger, of the employment by the occupier of an independent contractor,[2] are applicable here also. It should be remembered that the occupier may extend, restrict, modify or exclude his duty by agreement or otherwise, in so far as he is free to do so.[3]

§ 97. LAWFUL VISITORS: (4) PERSONS ENTERING AS OF RIGHT[4]

Persons entering as of right but not in pursuance of any contract between the parties are not a separate category: they are either invitees or licensees, and so classified as lawful visitors since 1957. But it may be convenient, for the purpose of assessing the common duty of care, to distinguish between at least two distinct classes of such persons: (1) officials or others who in the exercise of a legal power or duty enter premises; (2) members of the public, who, as such, exercise their rights of using land or premises dedicated to public use such as highways, recreation grounds, lavatories, libraries, museums, and so forth.

It is possible that wives constitute a third class. A wife is on the matrimonial premises as of right, by virtue of her status,[5] but the possibility of a wife suing her husband for breach of the common duty of care has not been explored in England.[6]

(1) Persons entering in exercise of a power or duty

Modern statutes have vastly increased the numbers of those authorised to enter premises (whether public or private) for some official purpose: thus, to take only a few examples, there are powers of entry and inspection under the Factories Act 1961, the Rights of Entry (Gas and Electricity Boards) Act 1954, and the Atomic Energy and Radioactive Substances Acts 1946 to

---

[99] *Hawkins* v. *Coulsdon and Purley U.D.C.* [1953] 1 W.L.R. 882, 893; affirmed, [1954] 1 Q.B. 319. (The plaintiff in this case was the wife of Master Hawkins of the Ch. Div., himself a former member of the defendant U.D.C.) See, too, *British Railways Board* v. *Herrington* [1972] A.C. 877, 938.

[1] As defined above, § 90.

[2] See above, § 93.

[3] See above, § 93.

[4] See Paton, "The Liability of an Occupier to Those Who Enter as of Right," (1941) 19 Can. Bar Rev. 1; Prosser, "Business Visitors and Invitees," *Topics* Chap. 5; Wallis-Jones, "Liability of Public Authorities as Occupiers of Dangerous Premises," (1949) 65 L.Q.R. 367; Waters, "Public Rights of Entry" [1958] C.L.P. 132.

[5] *National Provincial Bank* v. *Ainsworth* [1965] A.C. 1175.

[6] See below; § 131.

1959.[7] The position of such persons at common law was not entirely clear, but the balance of opinion was in favour of treating them as invitees and not as licensees,[8] even though their right to enter by no means depended on any invitation issued by the occupier.[9] But now section 2 (6) of the Occupiers' Liability Act provides that persons who enter premises for any purpose in the exercise of a right conferred by law[10] are to be treated as permitted by the occupier to be there for that purpose, whether they in fact have his permission or not. They will, therefore, be entitled to the benefits of the common duty of care which the occupier now owes to all lawful visitors—namely, to take reasonable care to see that the premises are reasonably safe for the purpose in hand.[11]

(2) Persons entering on public premises

Those who make use of premises such as public libraries, churches [12] and recreation grounds appear to be in a different category, for the occupier in such a case is normally a public authority empowered but not obliged by statute to devote its premises to the purpose in question for the general benefit of society, whose members in turn are entitled but not in general specifically empowered or obliged to use the premises. At common law the balance of authority was in favour of treating such persons as licensees,[13] although there were weighty arguments in favour of regarding them as invitees.[14] The terms of section 2 (6) of the Occupiers' Liability Act, which have been set out in the previous paragraph, appear to place persons entering on public premises into the category of licensees. As such they are owed the common duty of care, the nature of which has already been explained.[15]

Passengers on a highway

Passengers on a highway across land in private ownership stand in a class apart. Apart from statutory modifications of the common law, a highway is merely a public right of way over land which remains in the occupation of the owner of that land. It is well established that such an occupier is under no responsibility as such towards users of the highway for its safety and is not liable for dangers thereon whether they exist at the time of dedication or

---

[7] For a table of the titles, duties, and responsible ministers of 3,887 persons entitled to enter private premises without a specific search warrant, see 178 H.L.Deb. 5s, col. 176 (July 23, 1952). In *An Inspector at the Door* (London, 1980) it is stated that there are at least 252 different "authorities" granting powers of entry to inspectors, as distinct from the police. A person who exceeds his statutory or common law power of entry is a trespasser and may be dealt with accordingly: *Darling* v. *Att.-Gen.* [1950] 2 All E.R. 793; *Stroud* v. *Bradbury* [1952] 2 All E.R. 76.

[8] *Fryer* v. *Salford Corporation* [1937] 1 All E.R. 617, 622; *Read* v. *J. Lyons & Co. Ltd.* [1947] A.C. 156 (factory inspector); *Hartley* v. *Mayoh & Co. Ltd.* [1954] 1 Q.B. 383 (fireman). This was the opinion of the Law Reform Committee: 3rd Report, ss. 37–38.

[9] *Aiken* v. *Kingborough Corporation* (1939) 62 C.L.R. 179, 190.

[10] With the exception of those entering by virtue of an access agreement or order under the National Parks and Access to the Countryside Act 1949, who are not to be treated as trespassers (s. 60 (1)): they may be called "uninvited entrants", according to Law Com. No. 75, § 49. Also excluded from the category of visitors are users of a private right of way: *Greenhalgh* v. *British Railways Board* [1969] 2 Q.B. 286, because the right is conferred by dedication and not by law.

[11] See above, § 93.

[12] *Kirwan* v. *Representative Church Body* [1959] I.R. 215.

[13] *Pearson* v. *Lambeth B.C.* [1950] 2 K.B. 353, 367.

[14] *Plank* v. *Stirling Magistrates*, 1956 S.C. 92.

[15] See above, § 93.

come into existence later.[16] The occupier is liable, of course, for acts of positive misfeasance whereby he obstructs the highway or renders it dangerous, and he is also liable for maintaining his adjoining premises in such a dangerous condition as to constitute a nuisance to the highway.[17] The liability in the case of a private right of way as between the grantor and the grantee is similar. The words of section 2 (6) of the Occupiers' Liability Act are not wide enough to convert such users of a public or private right of way into lawful visitors.[18]

§ 98. TRESPASSERS[19]

Hitherto we have confined our attention to the rights of persons who lawfully enter on dangerous premises and there come to harm. We have now to deal with the position of mere trespassers. The judge-made law on this point has not been affected by the Occupiers' Liability Act, probably because Parliament in 1957 could not make up its mind what to do, and not because Parliament impliedly approved of that law.[20]

(1) Who are trespassers

In several statutes, *e.g.* the Theft Act 1968 and the Animal Act 1971, Parliament has used the common law term "trespasser" as if it had a clear meaning. This is not so. While it is clear that a trespasser is not a visitor within the meaning of the Occupiers' Liability Act,[21] no generally accepted judicial definition has emerged, although one which has often been cited is "one who goes on the land without invitation of any sort and whose presence is either unknown to the proprietor, or, if known, is practically objected to."[22] It might be better to describe such persons as "uninvited entrants."[23]

The word "trespasser" has an ugly sound, but it covers the wicked and the innocent. The burglar and the arrogant squatter are trespassers, but so are all sorts of comparatively innocent and respectable persons[24] such as a walker in the countryside who unhindered strolls across an open field.[25] Perhaps much of the trouble in this area has arisen from "the simplistic stereotype" of the definition.[26] The courts are therefore beginning to recognise that the duty of the occupier may vary according to the nature of the trespasser. It is sometimes difficult to distinguish between a trespasser and a person entering lawfully by the tacit permission of the occupier.[27] Thus the

---

[16] *Greenhalgh* v. *British Railways Boards* [1969] 2 Q.B. 286, 294.

[17] *Wringe* v. *Cohen* [1940] 1 K.B. 229, 241.

[18] *Greenhalgh* v. *British Railways Board* [1969] 2 Q.B. 286. The Law Reform Committee (para. 33) expressly refused to recommend any change; and Hylton-Foster, S.-G., assured Standing Committee A of the House of Commons that in this respect the Act carried out the recommendations of the Law Reform Committee (March 26, 1957, col. 5).

[19] North, *Occupiers' Liability*, Chap. 11 Law Com. No. 75 (Cmnd. 6428, 1976).

[20] *British Railways Board* v. *Herrington* [1972] A.C. 877; 897.

[21] *British Railways Board* v. *Herrington* [1972] A.C. 877, 904.

[22] *Robert Addie & Sons (Collieries) Ltd.* v. *Dumbreck* [1929] A.C. 358, 371, *per* Lord Dunedin.

[23] See Law Com. No. 75, § 22.

[24] *Ilott* v. *Wilkes* (1820) 3 B. & Ald. 304, 312.

[25] *British Railways Board* v. *Herrington* [1972] A.C. 877, 904.

[26] *McNamara* v. *E.S.B.* [1975] I.R. 1, 22.

[27] Yet MacKinnon L.J. said in *Ellis* v. *Fulham B.C.* [1938] 1 K.B. 212, 233, "We all know what trespassers are, and that category is clear."

occupier tacitly invites and permits any member of the public coming on lawful business to enter his garden gate and come to the door.[28] If his dog bites a person so entering, liability will depend on whether that person falls within the class of persons so tacitly invited; for otherwise he is a mere trespasser to whom no duty is owing. Who, then, are thus entitled to enter, and to complain of injuries received? What shall be said, for example, of hawkers, beggars, tract distributors, canvassers,[29] or persons in a shop who are not genuine purchasers but "hostile or at any rate competitive observers"?[30] There is even some authority for the proposition that an entrant may be a trespasser if the ostensible purpose for his being on the premises is not his real purpose, which was unlawful.[31] The acceptable conclusion would seem to be that no person is to be accounted a trespasser who enters in order to hold any manner of communication with the occupier or any other person on the premises, unless he knows or ought to know that his entry is prohibited.[32] So police officers, like any member of the public, have implied licence to open the garden gate and walk up to the front door of a private house. But an implied licence to approach the front door does not give a right to enter the house itself.[33] Still, it should be remembered that the acquiescence of the occupier in habitual trespasses may be evidence of tacit leave and licence,[34] so as to transform the trespasser into licensee.[35]

(2) Scope of the duty

Unfortunately there are conflicting decisions of the appellate tribunals. It is necessary to consider separately the law in different jurisdictions, and, so far as the United Kingdom (except Scotland) is concerned, the position both before and after the important decision of the House of Lords in *British Railways Board* v. *Herrington*.[36]

(A) *The law before Herrington*

The authoritative, though often criticised, decision of the House of Lords in *Robert Addie & Sons (Collieries) Ltd.* v. *Dumbreck*[37] laid it down that he who enters wrongfully enters at his own risk. The occupier of property owes no duty[38] to a trespasser other than that of not inflicting damage intentionally or recklessly on a trespasser known to be present.

---

[28] *Robson* v. *Hallett* [1967] 2 Q.B. 939 (police officers).
[29] See *Dunster* v. *Abbott* [1954] 1 W.L.R. 58.
[30] *Chaytor* v. *London, etc., Fashion Ltd.* (1961) 30 D.L.R. (2d) 527, 534.
[31] *Purtill* v. *Athlone U.D.C.* [1968] I.R. 205, 210–211.
[32] *Christian* v. *Johannesson* [1956] N.Z.L.R. 664, 666. See also *R.* v. *Jones* [1976] 1 W.L.R. 672.
[33] *Robson* v. *Hallett* [1967] 2 Q.B. 393.
[34] Above, § 96.
[35] *Rich* v. *Commissioner for Railways* (*N.S.W.*) (1959) 101 C.L.R. 135; 143; *Commissioner for Railways* v. *Quinlan* [1964] A.C. 1054; 1082.
[36] [1972] A.C. 877.
[37] [1929] A.C. 358.
[38] It was, however, actionable to have on one's premises any excavation or other danger so close to the adjoining highway as to interfere with the safety of passengers, even though mischief cannot happen to them except by accidental deviation from the highway and resulting trespass on the defendant's land: *Jacobs* v. *L.C.C.* [1950] A.C. 361, 376. It was also an actionable wrong to place anything on one's land *for the purpose* of attracting and injuring the animals of the adjoining occupier: *Townsend* v. *Wathen* (1808) 9 East 277.

Now we must consider the undoubted exception which the House of Lords did recognise—that of intentional or reckless harm to a trespasser known to be present.

(i) *Intentional harm to trespassers*

An occupier who intentionally harms a trespasser known to be present by creating on his premises a source of danger for that purpose is liable for the harm so done, unless the danger so created by him can be justified as being nothing more than a reasonable and therefore lawful measure of self-defence.[39] "A trespasser is liable to an action for the injury which he does; but he does not forfeit his right of action for an injury sustained."[40] An occupier must not run a trespasser down with a roto-scythe,[41] or set a spring gun, "for that is just to arrange to shoot him without personally firing the shot."[42] Thus in *Bird* v. *Holbrook*[43] the defendant placed a spring gun in his garden to protect it from the depredations of trespassers. The plaintiff was a boy who, in ignorance of the fact that any such danger existed, trespassed in the garden in order to recapture a fowl which had strayed there. While so trespassing he was injured by the discharge of the gun, and he was held to have a good cause of action. In the earlier case of *Ilott* v. *Wilkes*[44] the facts were identical, except that the plaintiff knew of the existence of the danger, and it was held that this knowledge prevented him from having any remedy.

But deterrence permissible. If, however, the source of danger intentionally created on the defendant's property is nothing more than a reasonably necessary means of protecting that property from trespass, he is under no liability for injury so suffered by a trespasser. "That you may set traps for trespassers is obvious."[45] Although it is not lawful to defend one's land by means of a spring gun or a mine of dynamite, it is lawful to protect it by means of spikes or broken glass upon the top of a wall,[46] or by a barbed-wire fence. These have been called "deterrent" dangers. But he is not entitled to create "retributive" dangers, *i.e.* dangers created for the purpose of injuring trespassers, which are not obvious but concealed, especially if hidden within the boundaries of his property. Only that amount of injury produced by a retributive danger is lawful, which could be justified by the occupier had he done it personally and directly to the trespasser.[47]

---

[39] See Bohlen and Burns, "The Privilege to Protect Property by Dangerous Barriers and Mechanical Devices" (1926) 35 Yale L.J. 527.
[40] *Barnes* v. *Ward* (1850) 9 C.B. 392, 420, *per* Maule J. *Cf. Young* v. *Edward Box Ltd.* [1951] 1 T.L.R. 789, 793.
[41] *Westwood* v. *Hardy, The Times,* June 26, 1964.
[42] *Addie* v. *Dumbreck* [1929] A.C. 358, 376, *per* Lord Dunedin.
[43] (1820) 4 Bing. 628. At the date when the cause of action arose it was not a criminal offence to set a spring gun, as it is now under the Offences against the Person Act 1861, s. 31, re-enacting the Spring Guns Act 1826.
[44] (1820) 3 B. & Ald. 304, "a case which excited great attention both in Westminster Hall and beyond it": *Lynch* v. *Nurdin* (1841) 1 Q.B. 29, 36, *per* Denman C.J. The decision was accepted as correct by Pollock (*Torts,* p. 116), Holdsworth (H.E.L., xiii, p. 526), and Asquith J. (*Dann* v. *Hamilton* [1939] 1 K.B. 509, 516). See also Palmer, "The Iowa Spring Gun Case" (1971) 56 Iowa L. Rev. 1219.
[45] *The Carlgarth* [1927] P. 93, 109, *per* Scrutton L.J.
[46] *Deane* v. *Clayton* (1817) 7 Taunt. 489, 521.
[47] See Hart, "Injuries to Trespassers" (1931) 47 L.Q.R. 92. But see the criticism of Holdsworth, H.E.L., xiii, p. 526.

(ii) *Reckless disregard of trespassers*

A second qualification is that the occupier is liable even to a trespasser for positive acts of negligent misfeasance done by himself with knowledge of the trespasser's presence.[48] Thus in *Mourton* v. *Poulter*[49] the defendant was a nurseryman[50] who was felling an elm tree for the occupier of the land. Knowing that when the last root was cut the tree would fall within two minutes, he did not repeat the warnings which he had previously given to children to go away, and the tree fell and injured the plaintiff aged 10. It was held that though the plaintiff was a trespasser he could recover damages from the defendant. The principle just expounded provides the explanation of two decisions of the House of Lords which are not at first sight easily reconcilable—namely *Robert Addie & Sons (Collieries) Ltd.* v. *Dumbreck*[51] and *Excelsior Wire Rope Co.* v. *Callan*.[52]

Videan's Case

A new chapter opened with the decision of the Court of Appeal in *Videan* v. *British Transport Commission*.[53] "That new chapter contains many pages, but we are now, I hope, getting to the end of it."[54] In brief, the *Videan* case adopted the test of reasonable foresight. But this view, although expressly disapproved of by the Judicial Committee in the following year,[55] was in effect adopted by the House of Lords in *Herrington* v. *British Railways Board*,[56] and so is now the governing principle.

(B) *The law after Herrington*

There are two steps in *Herrington*—the first is the refusal to follow *Addie*, and the second is the substitution of a different test. The first step is clearly traceable in the different judgments—*Addie* is said to have been rendered obsolete and anomalous by changing social conditions. There are more children, they are less well controlled by their parents, they have fewer places in which to play, and the advance of technology has created greater dangers for them.[57] The decision should therefore not be followed today, at least on its facts.[58]

The second step is more difficult. All the Law Lords agreed that it will not do simply to adopt a test of reasonable forseeability[59] as in Scotland.[60] The

---

[48] In *Commissioner for Railways* v. *Cardy* (1961) 104 C.L.R. 274, 296, Fullagar J. cited this sentence and said that "so far as it goes, it is, I think sound, but it does not, in my opinion, go far enough." The learned judge held that an occupier owes a duty even to a trespasser for an omission to take a reasonable precaution required by all the circumstances of the case. But the editor's caution appears to have been justified by the decision in *Quinlan*.

[49] [1930] 2 K.B. 183, approved in *Commissioner for Railways* v. *Quinlan* [1964] A.C. 1054, 1076.

[50] Note that the defendant was not the occupier.

[51] [1929] A.C. 358.

[52] [1930] A.C. 404. (An unreserved judgment delivered without hearing counsel for the respondent.) The cases are considered more fully in the 17th edition of this work, § 98.

[53] [1963] 2 Q.B. 650.

[54] *Pannett* v. *McGuinness & Co. Ltd.* [1972] 2 Q.B. 599, 605, *per* Lord Denning M.R.

[55] *Commissioner for Railways* v. *Quinlan* [1964] A.C. 1054.

[56] [1972] A.C. 877.

[57] [1972] A.C. 877, 929.

[58] [1972] A.C. 877, 898, 941.

[59] Also the Law Commission: see Law Com. No. 75, §§ 16–18.

[60] [1972] A.C. 877, 898, 919.

trespasser has no right to be on the premises and so cannot force a neighbour relationship on the occupier.[61] So liability will still arise only in exceptional circumstances. The occupier is entitled to neglect a bare possibility that trespassers will appear.[62] The clue to the new approach is to be found in a sentence of Lord Reid.[63] The trespasser must take the occupier, rather than the land, as he finds him.

This implies a subjective test rather than the objective test which is so familiar in the tort of negligence. This new approach will enable due weight to be given to such factors as the occupier's wealth and resources. Less is to be expected of the impecunious suburban householder than of a large industrial concern or a public or local corporation. It is also important to consider whether the occupier has himself created the danger: if he has, more may be expected of him.[64] Other relevant factors are the gravity of the danger and the degree of likelihood of the trespasser's presence. In general there is no duty to do anything before the trespasser arrives. After he has arrived, his characteristics may also be relevant. The squatter who falls down the defective staircase may still be without a remedy, as distinct from a child with nowhere else to play.[65] The result is that the term "reckless" should only be used in the subjective sense of culpable or wilful harm[66] rather than in the objective sense of gross carelessness, as has hitherto been customary.[67] Another way of phrasing the new duty is that the occupier is expected to act with ordinary humanity,[68] or in accordance with common sense and common civilised behaviour,[69] "or whatever you like to call it."[70] Some guide-lines have been laid down in later cases,[71] but although the law has been restated it is still unsatisfactory,[72] because it does not provide clear principles which prevent litigation from arising, as distinct from providing a just solution for litigation which has arisen.

Scotland. Since the Occupiers' Liability (Scotland) Act 1960, s. 2, the duty owed to a trespasser in Scotland is the common duty of care. The decision in *Addie* (a Scottish appeal) therefore ceased to have effect in Scotland.[73] "The Scots are hardly noted for being impractical or unduly swayed by emotion. They have incorporated into their law the concept that a duty of care may be owed in some circumstances even to trespassers. The experience over the last ten years has proved that the catastrophes that have

---

[61] [1972] A.C. 877, 899, 920.
[62] *Southern Portland Cement Ltd.* v. *Cooper* [1974] A.C. 623.
[63] [1972] A.C. 877, 899.
[64] [1974] A.C. 623, 644.
[65] *McNamara* v. *E.S.B.* [1975] I.R. 1, 24.
[66] [1972] A.C. 877, 898, 909, 928. Yet it is hard to see how the Railways Board were reckless in this sense.
[67] See Edmund-Davies and Cross L.JJ. in [1971] 2 Q.B. 107, 133–134, 137.
[68] In *Penny* v. *Northampton B.C.* (1974) 72 L.G.R. 733, the defendants were not lacking in humanity or common sense towards a 9-year-old trespasser.
[69] [1972] A.C. 877, 898, 907, 939–941.
[70] *Pannett* v. *McGuinness & Co. Ltd.* [1972] 2 Q.B. 599, 607, *per* Lord Denning M.R. In this case the C.A. held that occupier/contractors were not absolved by previous warnings to a trespassing child.
[71] *Harris* v. *Birkenhead Corporation* [1975] 1 All E.R. 1001, 1004; *Penny* v. *Railways Commissioner* (1977) 137 C.L.R. 107.
[72] The term used in Law Com. No. 75, § 39, which recommended the creation of a statutory duty of reasonable care towards uninvited entrants (a proposal approved by the Pearson Report, § 169).
[73] *McGlone* v. *British Railways Board,* 1966 S.C. 1; 11.

been supposed to be inseparable from such a course are entirely illusory."[74] Indeed the House of Lords has held that an occupier who has taken reasonable steps to fence an artificial danger on his premises will not be liable to a trespasser who, being old enough to know what he is doing, insists on forcing his way through the protective barriers.[75]

Ireland. Formerly the decision in *Addie* was followed with some qualifications.[76] But in *Purtill* v. *Athlone U.D.C.*[77] the Supreme Court unanimously[78] restated the law on the basis of reasonable foresight. The plaintiff was a trespassing child who had removed some detonators from the defendant's premises and blown himself up with them elsewhere. The defendants were held liable for a failure to exercise the care required of the custodian of a dangerous article towards one whose presence was reasonably foreseeable. The court expressly stated that it would have reached the same conclusion if the accident had occurred on the defendant's premises, thereby committing itself to the view that the occupation of premises should not be regarded as a basis of exemption from liability even in the case of trespassers. The logical conclusion was *McNamara* v. *E.S.B.*[79] in which the court held the defendants, occupiers of a defectively insulated transformer sub-station, liable on the basis of reasonable foresight to a child trespasser from a housing estate. The same basis of liability governs the position of an adult trespasser.[80] But the court seems to prefer the tradional objective standard of care to the subjective approach favoured in *Herrington.*[81] It has since emphasised that the occupier is not an insurer: he is only obliged to take reasonable care.[82]

Other jurisdictions. Courts from which appeal still lies to the Privy Council are bound by the decision in *Commissioner for Railways* v. *Quinlan*[83] that the occupier of premises owes no duty to a trespasser other than that of not inflicting damage intentionally or recklessly on a trespasser known to be present.[84] The decision emphasised that actual personal knowledge of the trespasser's presence is a condition precedent to liability, unless it can be found that the occupier "as good as" knows of that presence because it is "extremely likely."[85] The only qualification admitted by the Judicial Committee is that the relationship of occupier and trespasser might be displaced by some other relationship in a proper case.[86] There are cases in which the occupier, in addition to being an occupier, stands in some other relation to a trespasser, so that the latter is not only a trespasser but is also

---

[74] *Herrington* v. *British Railways Board* [1971] 2 Q.B. 107, 123–124, *per* Salmon L.J.
[75] *McGlone* v. *British Railways Board,* 1966 S.C. 1.
[76] *Donovan* v. *Landy's Ltd.* [1963] I.R. 441.
[77] [1968] I.R. 205.
[78] In a judgment prepared by Walsh J. which is an interesting example of a novel judicial technique in a common law jurisdiction. The relevant principles are surveyed and the various arguments considered without citing a single case. In *Herrington* the H.L. considered 86 cases in 50 pages of the law reports, but did not leave the law in a markedly clearer state.
[79] [1975] I.R. 1.
[80] *O'Keeffe* v. *Irish Motor Ins. Ltd.* [1978] I.R. 83. (note that the plaintiff failed).
[81] See McMahon (1975) 91 L.Q.R. 323.
[82] *Kearney* v. *E.S.B.* [1980] I.R. 323.
[83] [1964] A.C. 1054.
[84] But not the Supreme Court of Canada: *Veinot* v. *Kerr-Addison Ltd.* (1975) 51 D.L.R. 533.
[85] [1964] A.C. 1054, 1077.
[86] [1964] A.C. 1054, 1081–1084.

the occupier's neighbour within the familiar principle expounded by Lord Atkin.[87]

In *Quinlan* the Judicial Committee did not itself offer any description or definition of the circumstances in which the occupier/trespasser relationship might be displaced by some other relationship, but in one later case[88] it held that the occupier/licensee relationship had been displaced or superseded by the duty to take all reasonable precautions which arises from the operation of express trains. This avenue of escape from the strict *Quinlan* principle has been followed by appellate tribunals in Australia[89] and New Zealand[90] in cases in which the defendant controlled some unusually dangerous thing or activity.

§ 99. DUTY TO CHILDREN

We now have to consider how far, if at all, the foregoing principles are subject to modification in their application to young children.

(1) Infant trespassers

Is an occupier of dangerous premises bound to take precautions against children trespassing thereon and coming to harm? There has been "some conflict both in the United States and in England between a view which may be called the 'humanitarian' view, that a child which has no knowledge or discretion to make it capable of contributory negligence must be guarded by the landowner on whose ground it is allowed or tempted to enter, and the 'hard' or 'Draconian' view, that a child must trespass at its own risk and, if it is so young as not to appreciate what it is doing, it is for its parents, and not for the landowner on whose land it enters without invitation, to protect it."[91] The distinction between the "hard" and the "humanitarian" views is perhaps unfortunate, for this does not mean that the judges who adopted the "hard" view are harsh or inhuman.[92] The American courts recognise that there may be situations in which the interest of society as a whole in the welfare of its children should prevail over its interest that landowners should within reasonable limits be free to use their property as they please.[93] In England it could be once said with some confidence that no such doctrine was recognised.[94] The Court of Appeal once thought that the duty of preventing babies from trespassing upon a railway line should lie upon their parents and not upon the railway company.[95] Yet this general principle was felt to be too harsh when the child trespasser has been injured as a result of a dangerous activity maintained for profit by the defendants, and the law has been restated so as to impose liability in such a case.[96]

---

[87] *Commissioner for Railways* v. *Cardy* (1961) 104 C.L.R. 274, 297.
[88] *Commissioner for Railways* v. *McDermott* [1967] 1 A.C. 169.
[89] *Penny* v. *Railways Commissioner* (1977) 137 C.L.R. 107.
[90] *McCarthy* v. *Wellington City* [1966] N.Z.L.R. 481.
[91] *Per* Scrutton L.J. in *Liddle* v. *Yorkshire C.C.* [1934] 2 K.B. 101, 110. But see the criticism in *Adams* v. *Naylor* [1944] K.B. 750, 755.
[92] *Commissioner for Railways* v. *Quinlan* [1964] A.C. 1054, 1078.
[93] Prosser, *Torts* (4th ed.), § 59, where all the authorities are reviewed.
[94] *Addie* v. *Dumbreck* [1929] A.C. 358, 376.
[95] *Liddle* v. *Yorkshire C.C.* [1934] 2 K.B. 101, 110.
[96] *British Railways Board* v. *Herrington* [1972] A.C. 877. For details, see above, § 98.

(2) Infant licensees

Where, however, an occupier habitually and knowingly acquiesces in the trespasses of children, these children cease to be trespassers and become licensees, and the occupier owes to them a certain duty of care and protection accordingly.[97] In *Cooke* v. *Midland Great Western Railway of Ireland*[98] the plaintiff was a child between four and five years of age who was injured while playing with his companions on a turntable on the defendant company's railway premises. The turntable was kept unlocked and was close to a public road. The company's employees knew that children were in the habit of entering on the premises from the road for the purpose of playing with the turntable but no precautions were taken by the company, either to exclude the children or to lock the turntable,[99] so as to prevent it from being an instrument of mischief. It was held by the House of Lords that there was evidence for a jury of negligence on the part of the railway company—not on the ground that there is any duty of care towards trespassing children, but on the ground that the habitual acquiescence of the company was sufficient evidence to entitle the jury to find that the plaintiff was not a trespasser, but was on the railway premises with the leave and licence of the company.[1] But in these cases the onus is on the plaintiff to establish his licence, and "to find a licence there must be evidence either of express permission or that the landowner has so conducted himself that he cannot be heard to say that he did not give it."[2] Real acquiescence or permission must be shown: tolerance is not acquiescence though it may be evidence of it.[3] The most recent dicta in the House of Lords are hostile to the concept of an imputed or implied or fictitious licence.[4] It may be predicted that the courts will now be less ready to accept the concept. In any event it is clear that a licence ought not to be inferred merely because every possible step to keep out intruders has not been taken: a landowner is under no obligation at common law[5] to fence his property against trespassers or to put up warning notices, however attractive his premises may be to

---

[97] *Adams* v. *Naylor* [1944] K.B. 750, 761.

[98] [1909] A.C. 229.

[99] Which was still in existence in 1953, when the present editor saw at least half a dozen children playing on it.

[1] See the explanation of *Cooke's* case in *Corporation of Glasgow* v. *Taylor* [1922] 1 A.C. 44; *Liddle* v. *Yorkshire C.C.* [1934] 2 K.B. 101; *Edwards* v. *Railway Executive* [1952] A.C. 737. Beven attacked the decision in *Cooke's* case with great vigour: his description of the infant plaintiff as one of "a rabble of Irish ragamuffin raiders" moved Mr. Byrne, the editor of the 4th edition of his work to protest that "the child—whom the editor chanced to see while the case was in the Irish courts—was the quite presentable little son of a respectable chemist" (*Negligence*, vol. i, p. 216). Some criticism of *Cooke's* case has ignored the fact that while the H.L. held there was sufficient evidence to go to the jury they did not indicate that they would have reached the same conclusion as the jury did. This point was made in *Smyth* v. *Keys* (1912) 46 I.L.T.R. 68, 69, the court emphasising that it would "not be guilty of the bad taste of criticising a decision of the House of Lords."

[2] *Edwards* v. *Railway Executive* [1952] A.C. 737, 747, *per* Lord Goddard C.J. If a statute makes it a criminal offence to trespass on premises it may be that such permission can never be lawfully given *Reardon* v. *Att.-Gen.* [1954] N.Z.L.R. 978; see also above, § 96. For how far knowledge of responsible subordinates can be imputed to the landowner himself, see *Matheson Att.-Gen.* [1956] N.Z.L.R. 849.

[3] Above, § 96.

[4] *British Railways Board* v. *Herrington* [1972] A.C. 877, 899, 934.

[5] Even if there is a statutory duty to fence (as under the Railways Clauses Consolidation Act 1845, s. 68) the duty is no more than to keep the premises shut off by a fence which is duly repaired when broken and obviously intended to keep intruders out: *Edwards* v. *Railways Executive* [1952] A.C. 737, 744.

trespassers.[6] Our law does not recognise the existence of a class of persons who, though not licensees, must be effectively prevented from becoming trespassers.[7]

"Traps" and "allurements"

(i) *Children naturally less careful than adults.* The Occupiers' Liability Act, s.2(3), provides that in assessing the common duty of care an occupier must be prepared for children to be less careful than adults. This probably does no more than re-enact the common law.[8] So a small child was able to claim when he fell through a gap in some railings which would not have been dangerous to an adult.[9] Many dangers which would be open and obvious to the adult may be concealed and secret traps for the child.[10] "In the case of an infant, there are moral as well a physcial traps. There may accordingly be a duty towards infants not merely not to dig pitfalls for them, but not to lead them into temptation."[11] Although an occupier is not bound to make his premises as safe as a nursery, most of the articles on which children come to grief are not such as are commonly found in nurseries, and this is to be borne in mind in considering whether they amount to a trap.[12] "While it is very plain that temptation is not invitation, it may be held that knowingly to establish and expose, unfenced, to children of an age when they follow a bait as mechanically as a fish, something that is certain to attract them, has the legal effect of an invitation to them although not to an adult."[13] It is a question of law whether a given object can be a trap in the double sense of being fascinating and fatal[14]: the mere fact that a child has been lured or tempted into disaster is not enough, for a child can hurt itself on anything. No exhaustive catalogue of "allurements" has been established. "Turntables, escalators and paddling pools have been held to 'allure.' Rivers, ponds and piles of paving stones have been held 'insufficiently seductive.' "[15] The tendency appears to be against extending the category. So chutes in recreation grounds[16] and low-loaders[17] have been

---

[6] *British Railways Board* v. *Herrington* [1972] A.C. 877, 920.

[7] *Adams* v. *Naylor* [1944] K.B. 750, 765. This is particularly important if the plaintiff is a child: for "children, small boys especially, resemble burglars; if they want to get in they will, take what precautions you may": *Edwards'* case [1952] A.C. 737, 747, *per* Lord Goddard C.J.

[8] *Martin* v. *Middlesbrough Corporation* (1965) 63 L.G.R. 385, 386.

[9] *Moloney* v. *Lambeth B.C.* (1966) 64 L.G.R. 440; see also above, § 96.

[10] *Williams* v. *Cardiff Corpn.* [1950] 1 K.B. 514 (a grassy slope with tins and broken glass at the bottom is a trap to a child of $4\frac{1}{2}$ years).

[11] *Latham* v. *Johnson* [1913] K.B. 398, 415, *per* Hamilton L.J.

[12] It is better not to use "allurement" to signify the circumstances under which a child enters premises: it remains a trespasser, however natural it may have been for it to enter. But once it has entered with permission it may find on the premises some attractive object which tempts it to meddle when it ought to abstain. This is an "allurement": a "trap" is something defective in the state of the premises themselves: see *Latham* v. *Johnson (R.) & Nephew Ltd.* [1913] 1 K.B. 398, 415–416; *Addie (R.) & Sons (Collieries)* v. *Dumbreck* [1929] A.C. 358, 376; *Williams* v. *Cardiff Corporation* [1950] 1 K.B. 514; *Edwards* v. *Railway Executive* [1952] A.C. 747, *Commissioner for Railways* v. *Cardy* (1961) 104 C.L.R. 274, 321.

[13] *Per* Holmes J. in *United Zinc and Chemical Co.* v. *Britt* (1922) 258 U.S. 268, 275, quoted by Scrutton L.J. in [1934] 2 K.B. 101, 110.

[14] *Latham* v. *Johnson (R.) and Nephew Ltd.* [1913] 1 K.B. 398, 411.

[15] *Sutton* v. *Bootle Corporation* [1947] K.B. 359, 368, *per* Asquith L.J.

[16] *Dyer* v. *Ilfracombe U.D.C.* [1956] W.L.R. 218.

[17] *O'Leary* v. *Wood* [1964] I.R. 269.

held to be unalluring. So for obvious dangers, such as unguarded fire[18] or water (natural or artificial), an occupier will not be liable[19] "If a landowner permits children to pick sticks or flowers in his woods, he is not bound to provide keepers to protect them against the 'allurements' of wasps' nests or poisonous toadstools."[20]

(ii) *Very young children.* The statement that an occupier is not liable for obvious dangers must be read subject to some qualification if the infant licensee is so young that it cannot really take care of itself at all. There is nothing upon which a toddler cannot hurt itself: the danger may be obvious to its eyes but concealed from its understanding.[21] In *Phipps* v. *Rochester Corporation*[22] Devlin J. was able to formulate a "duty so as to compromise between the robustness that would make children take the world as they found it and the tenderness which would give them nurseries wherever they go."[23] One October evening Ian Phipps, aged five, went out blackberrying with his sister, Yvonne, aged seven. They crossed over an open space on a building site of the defendants and there Ian fell into an open trench and broke his leg. He fell because he was not old enough to negotiate such an obstacle without assistance and Yvonne was not old enough to give it to him. The children had an implied licence to be where they were. Devlin J. held that although a licensor who tacitly permits the public to use his land without discriminating between its members must assume that the public will include little children, as a general rule he will have discharged his duty towards them if the dangers which they encounter are only those which are obvious to a guardian or of which he has given a warning comprehensible by a guardian.[24] In this case the defendants succeeded because in all the circumstances there was no reason to suppose that Ian's parents would allow him to wander unaccompanied by a proper guardian. But when a four-year-old child injured itself on the common staircase of the block of flats in which it lived the court held that the defendants ought to have foreseen that in those circumstances the child would be unaccompanied.[25]

(iii) *Technical trespasses may be disregarded.* If a child has a licence, express or implied, to enter upon the premises of the defendant, he does not necessarily become a trespasser merely because he moves to a place or onto an object outside the strict limits of the licence,[26] especially if the object is

---

[18] *Bohane* v. *Driscoll* [1929] I.R. 428, 436. But to a child aged 5 years a blazing fire is a danger: *Boughton* v. *Bray U.D.C.* [1964] Ir.Jur.Rep. 57.

[19] *Liddle* v. *Yorkshire (North Riding) County Council* [1934] 2 K.B. 101, 112; *Perry* v. *Thomas Wrigley Ltd.* [1955] 1 W.L.R. 1164, 1168.

[20] *Bohane* v. *Driscoll* [1929] I.R. 428, 436, *per* FitzGibbon J.

[21] *Phipps* v. *Rochester Corporation* [1955] 1 Q.B. 450.

[22] [1955] 1 Q.B. 450, approved by the Court of Appeal in *M'Gullie* v. *Butler*, unreported, (1959) C.A. 64A.

[23] [1955] 1 Q.B. 450, 459.

[24] [1955] 1 Q.B. 450, 472. This general rule would not apply to a place where, to the knowledge of the licensor, little children are permitted by their parents to go unaccompanied in the reasonable belief that they will be safe, *e.g.* a recognised playground. An alternative approach was rejected by Devlin J., *viz.* that a licence to a young child is conditional on its being accompanied by a competent guardian. This approach was adopted in some cases (*e.g. Bates* v. *Stone Parish Council* [1954] 1 W.L.R. 1249), but Devlin J.'s reasons for rejecting it seem conclusive.

[25] *Moloney* v. *Lambeth Borough Council* (1966) 64 L.G.R. 440.

[26] *Glasgow Corporation* v. *Taylor* [1922] 1 A.C. 44 (child of seven eating poisonous berry in botanic garden).

known to be an allurement.[27] A similar principle governs the liability of those who leave close to or in some public street or place an object which is likely to be attractive and dangerous to children. In such a case the facts attract some category of the law of torts and some concept of duty transcending the special rules concerning the duties of occupiers to entrants.[28] So in *Lynch* v. *Nurdin*[29] (the origin of all the law on this topic), the defendant was held liable when his employee left a horse and cart unattended in Compton Street, Soho, for half-an-hour and the plaintiff (aged under seven years) "indulged the natural instincts of a child" by playing on the vehicle, from which he fell and was injured. So if a four-year-old child sticks its head between iron railings alongside the highway, that is only what might be expected to happen.[30] A rotten fence,[31] a defective high-tension wire,[32] and a trailer,[33] have been held to be within this category, but not a pile of lime mortar.[34]

§ 100. LIABILITY OF NON-OCCUPIERS

It must not be supposed that the occupier of dangerous premises is the only person who can be responsible for dangers which there exist. Whoever actually creates a source of danger, even on premises not in his own occupation, is bound to use reasonable care by guiding, warning or otherwise to preserve from resulting harm persons who enter thereon. The status which the entrant enjoys *vis-à-vis* the occupier is not conclusive of any issue which may arise as between the entrant and some other party whose activities on the premises have created a source of danger, although it may well be relevant in an assessment of the standard of care appropriate to the circumstances.[35] An employee of the occupier is not necessarily a non-occupier.[36] Many cases may be found in which the fact that the injury has occurred on premises occupied by a third party has been treated as irrelevant. Thus in *Billings (A.C.) & Sons Ltd.* v. *Riden*[37] the House of Lords held that a contractor working on premises owes a duty to take reasonable care to prevent damage to persons whom he may reasonably expect to be affected by his work. The case is also a leading authority on the question how far the plaintiff's knowledge of the danger so created will bar his claim entirely or merely be a ground for reduction of his damages under the Law Reform (Contributory Negligence) Act 1945.[38] A non-occupier does not necessarily discharge this duty simply by warning the visitor: he may be under a duty to make the premises reasonably safe.[39] So an invitee may

---

[27] *Gough* v. *National Coal Board* [1954] 1 Q.B. 191 (railway trucks).
[28] *Commissioner for Railways* v. *Cardy* (1961) 104 C.L.R. 274, 321.
[29] (1841) 1 Q.B. 29.
[30] *Smyth* v. *Keys* (1912) 46 I.L.T.R. 68.
[31] *Harrold* v. *Watney* [1898] 2 Q.B. 320.
[32] *Thompson* v. *Bankstown Corporation* (1953) 87 C.L.R. 619.
[33] *Creed* v. *McGeoch & Sons Ltd.* [1955] 1 W.L.R. 1005.
[34] *Prince* v. *Gregory* [1959] 1 W.L.R. 177.
[35] *Miller* v. *South of Scotland Electricity Board*, 1958 S.C. 20, 37.
[36] Fleming, Note (1966) 82 L.Q.R. 25.
[37] [1958] A.C. 240.
[38] See below, § 188.
[39] *Johnson* v. *Rea Ltd.* [1962] 1 Q.B. 373.

recover against another invitee,[40] or a licensee against another licensee[41] on the broad ground that the defendant has failed to take such care as was reasonable in the circumstances. This simple principle was formerly subject to the anomalous exception that if the defendant subsequently sold or let the premises his potential liability for breach of duty come to an end. The transaction of sale or letting alone conferred the immunity. But the law has now been changed by the Defective Premises Act 1972, s. 2.[42]

Trespasser may sue

Even a trespasser may have a successful claim against a non-occupier who is not entitled to the protection of the occupier's immunity.[43] In *Buckland* v. *Guildford Gas Light and Coke Co.*[44] an active schoolgirl of thirteen years who climbed an attractive oak tree was electrocuted when she came into contact with the defendant's high-voltage electric wires, which were hidden in the foliage at the top. The defendants were held liable because they were in breach of their duty to take reasonable care for the safety of someone who might reasonably have been contemplated as likely to be affected by their want of care.[45] Normally a non-occupier will be entitled to assume that the premises will be free from trespassers, but on the facts of this case the defendant ought to have foreseen their presence. The fact that the girl might have been a trespasser *vis-à-vis* the owner of the tree did not automatically exclude the liability of the defendant, for the plaintiff was able[46] to point to some source of obligation other than the relation which the trespass itself created.[47] But if repeated warnings are given which are clearly understood by the trespasser the defendant is probably not obliged to suspend his operations.[48]

§ 101. LIABILITY OF LESSORS OR VENDORS AT COMMON LAW [49]

It is necessary to deal separately with the law before and after January 1, 1974, the date on which the Defective Premises Act 1972 came into force.

---

[40] *Canter* v. *Gardner & Co. Ltd.* [1940] 1 All E.R. 325 (servant of the sub-contractor injured by another sub-contractor). So in *Cleghorn* v. *Oldham* (1927) 43 T.L.R. 465 the plaintiff was on a golf-links with her brother and the defendant ("as a chaperone" the report says) when she was struck by a club owing to the defendant's negligence. The plaintiff recovered on the broad ground of negligence. Similar decisions are *Keegan* v. *Owens* [1953] I.R. 267; *Whitehorn* v. *Port of London Authority* [1955] 1 Lloyd's Rep. 54. Note that an invitee may owe a duty of reasonable care to his invitor: *Lomas* v. *Jones & Son* [1944] K.B. 4.
[41] *Corby* v. *Hill* (1858) C.B. (N.S.) 556; *Waring* v. *East Anglian Flying Services Ltd.* [1951] W.N. 55.
[42] See below, § 101.
[43] As was the contractor in *Mourton* v. *Poulter* [1930] 2 K.B. 183. See above, § 98.
[44] [1948] 2 All E.R. 1086.
[45] Although this doctrine (in so far as it affords protection to a trespasser) may perhaps be traced back to *Latham* v. *Johnson (R.) and Nephew Ltd.* [1913] 1 K.B. 398, the more recent cases are founded directly upon the neighbour principle of *Donoghue* v. *Stevenson*. They appear to represent the law, although critical dicta may be found in *Kenny* v. *Electricity Supply Board* [1932] I.R. 73, 92; *Creed* v. *McGeoch & Sons Ltd.* [1955] 1 W.L.R. 1005, 1008; *Miller* v. *South of Scotland Electricity Board,* 1958 S.C. 20, 36, and (most importantly) in *British Railways Board* v. *Herrington* [1972] A.C. 877, 914, 929, 942.
[46] As also in *Farrugia* v. *G.W. Ry.* [1947] 2 All E.R. 565.
[47] See also above, §§ 92, 98.
[48] *Deyo* v. *Kingston Speedway Ltd.* [1955] 1 D.L.R. 718.
[49] See North, *Occupiers' Liability,* Chap. 12; *Civil Liability of Vendors and Lessors for Defective Premises* (Law Com. No. 40, 1970) and, for Ireland, Law Reform Commission *Working Paper No. 1* (1977).

The Act cannot be understood without reference to its background, and in any case the common law will continue to govern claims arising out of incidents before that date,[50] or in other jurisdictions.

(1) Liability of landlord to tenant and others

Who is a lessor

It is important to distinguish between an occupier and lessor: the former owes many duties, the latter very few. A lessor is usually one who transfers to another the exclusive occupation of premises for a definite period. If that other does not obtain exclusive possession, he is only a licensee.[51] Hence the question has arisen whether an owner of premises can avoid his responsibilities by creating a lease of a few days, or even a few hours. There has naturally been a reluctance to permit him to do so, particularly if he is the owner of premises continually used for public purposes at a profit to himself. This has been the approach in two Irish cases, in which the premises were "let" for a dance[52] and whist drive.[53] These cases have been followed in Australia, although "there are some, not inconsiderable, differences between a whist drive and dance in Dublin and a meeting of tobacco growers in Texas, Queensland."[54]

Duty of lessor

Apart from any express or implied contract[55] to that effect, a landlord owes no duty, either towards his tenant or towards any other person who enters on the premises during the tenancy, to take care that the premises are safe either at the commencement of the tenancy or during its continuance.[56] The rule was so laid down in *Robbins* v. *Jones*.[57] Sir William Erle C.J., in a judgment prepared by Willes J., said: "A landlord who lets a house in a dangerous state is not liable to the tenant's customers or guests for accidents arising during the term; for, fraud apart, there is no law against letting a tumbledown house; and the tenant's remedy is upon his contract, if any." The rule was for long regarded as "beyond question,"[58] and not to have been affected by the general liberalisation of the law of negligence in recent decades.[59] But on the eve of the enactment of the Defective Premises Act 1972, it was doubted by the Court of Appeal,[60] and the House of Lords has since confirmed those doubts.[61] One exception to the general rule has been the decision that a covenant to keep the common parts of the premises in repair could be implied into a lease of a high-rise block of flats.[62] Even if the

---

[50] *Alexander* v. *Mercouris* [1979] 3 All E.R. 305.
[51] See above, § 23.
[52] *Kelly* v. *Woolworth Ltd.* [1922] 2 I.R. 5.
[53] *Boylan* v. *Dublin Corporation* [1949] I.R. 60.
[54] *Voli* v. *Inglewood Shire Council* (1963) 110 C.L.R. 74, 91, *per* Windeyer J.
[55] See *Sleafer* v. *Lambeth B.C.* [1960] 1 Q.B. 43 (an *obligation* to repair will not be implied merely because the lessor has a *right* to enter to effect repairs).
[56] *MacDonald* v. *Goderich* [1949] 3 D.L.R. 788, 793; *Collins* v. *Torresan* [1956] 3 D.L.R. 740, 743; *Titus* v. *Duke* (1963) 6 W.I.R. 135, 137.
[57] (1863) 15 C.B.(N.S.) 221, 240.
[58] *Cavalier* v. *Pope* [1906] A.C. 428, 430.
[59] *Auto Scooters (Newcastle) Ltd.* v. *Chambers* (1966) 197 E.G.D. 457.
[60] *Dutton* v. *Bognor Regis Building Co. Ltd.* [1972] 1 Q.B. 373. See above, § 78.
[61] *Anns* v. *Merton London Borough Council* [1978] A.C. 728. See below, § 101.
[62] *Liverpool C.C.* v. *Irwin* [1977] A.C. 399.

lessor has entered into an express covenant to repair there has to be read into such a covenant an implied condition that the lessor must have notice of the want of repair before his obligation arises.[63-64] Although this principle normally applies to the physical fitness of the premises it is equally applicable where the premises are, so to speak, legally unfit for the purpose required.

exception to the general rule. Such an agreement contains an implied warranty that the premises and the furniture are at the commencement of the tenancy fit for immediate occupation or use. If they are not so fit, the tenant may determine the tenancy or sue for damages in respect of any injury suffered.[65] On the other hand, there is no implied undertaking by the tenant that he or his family are in a fit state to occupy the premises.[66] But the letting of an unfurnished flat probably[67] falls within the general rule and not the exception.[68]

(2) Liability of landlord to third parties

The landlord's exemption from liability for dangers existing on premises in the occupation of his tenant extends not merely to injuries suffered by the tenant himself but to those suffered by other persons entering on the premises during the tenancy.[69] At common law the lease transfers all obligations towards such persons from the landlord to the tenant. This was so even if the landlord has by contract with the tenant taken upon himself the duty of keeping the premises in repair. Such a contract was *res inter alios acta*, and conferred upon strangers no rights against the landlord which they would not have had without it.[70] This was clearly established in *Cavalier* v. *Pope*.[71] The landlord of a defective house contracted with the plaintiff's husband to repair it. Nothing was done and one day the plaintiff fell through the floor and was injured. A common jury awarded her £75 damages and her husband £25. The House of Lords set aside the award in favour of the plaintiff. "There was but one contract and that was made with the husband. The wife cannot sue upon it."[72] But this principle was much criticised, and the actual decision in *Cavalier* v. *Pope* was reversed by the Occupiers'

[63-64] *Torrens* v. *Walker* [1906] 2 Ch. 166. *Quaere*, whether the lessor would be liable if he actually knew of the defect at the date when the term began: *Uniproducts (Manchester) Ltd.* v. *Rose Furnishers Ltd* [1956] 1 W.L.R. 45. But if the plaintiff is injured, not on the premises, but on the adjoining highway, he need not prove that the lessor had notice of the want of repair: see above, § 20. there has been said to be no illogicality in this *Mint* v. *Good* [1951] 1 K.B. 517, 525.

[65] *Collins* v. *Hopkins* [1923] 2 K.B. 617 (house recently occupied by person suffering from pulmonary tuberculosis). This warranty does not extend to defects arising after the commencement of the tenancy: *Sarson* v. *Roberts* [1895] 2 Q.B. 395. Another exception is the implied warranties relating to houses of low rateable value established by s. 6 of the Housing Act 1957, and s. 32 of the Housing Act 1961. But the lessor must have knowledge of the defect: *O'Brien* v. *Robinson* [1973] A.C. 912. In Ireland a similar warranty may be implied in lettings under the Housing Act 1966. A lessor of defective premises may also be required to repair them by the local authority under the Housing Act 1957, s. 9. On these statutory warranties, see Robinson, "Social Legislation and the Judges" (1976) 39 M.L.R. 43.

[66] *Humphreys* v. *Miller* [1917] 2 K.B. 122.

[67] See North, (1965) 29 *The Conveyancer* 207, 219.

[68] *Cruse* v. *Mount* [1933] Ch. 278; *Davis* v. *Foots* [1940] 1 K.B. 116.

[69] *Bromley* v. *Mercer* [1922] 2 K.B. 126; *Travers* v. *Gloucester Corporation* [1947] K.B. 71.

[70] *MacDonald* v. *Goderich* [1949] 3 D.L.R. 788, 793; *Collins* v. *Torresan* [1956] 3 D.L.R. 740, 743.

[71] [1906] A.C. 428.

[72] *Per* Lord James of Hereford.

Liability Act 1957, s. 4 (1). Now the Defective Premises Act 1972, s. 4 has repealed section 4 of the 1957 Act and substituted provisions of even wider scope.[73]

(3) Liability for landlord's own premises

In all these cases the plaintiff suffered damage while on the premises demised as a result of some defect in the condition of those premises. We have also already considered the position when the plaintiff suffers damage while on premises retained by the lessor in his own occupation (*e.g.* a common stairway).[74] Here there is a liability under the 1957 Act.[75] But what is the position when, as a result of the defective condition of the portion of the premises retained in the landlord's occupation, the tenant or one of the tenant's invitees or licensees is injured while on the portion of the premises demised? In *Cheater* v. *Cater*[76] the Court of Appeal held that a landlord who let a part of his land overhung by yew trees growing upon the land retained by him was not responsible to his tenant[77] for the loss of cattle which were poisoned by eating the overhanging branches. This was carried further in *Shirvell* v. *Hackwood Estate Ltd.*,[78] in which a branch fell from a beech tree which the occupying owner of the land knew to be in a defective condition upon the employee of a tenant to whom he had leased the adjoining land. It was said that even if the defendant was negligent there was no liability: but it is probable that those statements were only *obiter dicta*.[79] In any case it seems clear that the principle laid down in these cases is confined to situations where the danger existed and was apparent at the date of the demise.[80]

But although it may be assumed that the lessee takes his land subject to the inconvenience and detriment of an overhanging projection, such as a branch, or roof, or cornice (*e.g.* he could not complain if the shade of a tree prevents crops from growing or water from a roof drips onto his land), is he really presumed to agree that he will accept the risk of the projection falling on his premises? There is very persuasive authority to the contrary. In *Cunard* v. *Antifyre Ltd.*[81] the plaintiffs were tenants in the defendants' block of flats. The defendants retained the possession and control of the roof, from which a piece of guttering fell through the glass roof of a kitchen and injured the plaintiff's wife. A Divisional Court held the defendants liable. Talbot J. said[82]: "The plaintiffs' true cause of action (if they have one) if for

---

[73] See below, § 102.
[74] See above, §§ 95–96.
[75] *Wheat* v. *Lacon & Co. Ltd.* [1966] 1 Q.B. 335, 366.
[76] [1918] 1 K.B. 247.
[77] If the parties in *Cheater* v. *Cater* had been adjoining owners the defendant would have been liable: *Crowhurst* v. *Amersham Burial Board* (1879) 4 Ex. D. 5.
[78] [1938] 2 K.B. 577. See Hamson in (1938) 2 M.L.R. 215.
[79] *Taylor* v. *Lverpool Corporation* [1939] 3 All E.R. 329, 339.
[80] In *Shirvell* v. *Hackwood Estates* the risk of the branches of the dying tree falling had not become substantially greater after the date of the lease: [1938] 2 K.B. 577, 595, 602.
[81] [1933] 1 K.B. 551.
[82] [1933] 1 K.B. 551, 557, 562. Of whom Sir Frank MacKinnon wrote: "On the bench he displayed every quality of the ideal judge. He had learning, dignity, industry, patience, and courtesy: his decisions were invariably right, and on most occasions were thought to be so by the Court of Appeal": *Dictionary of National Biography*, 1931–1940, p. 846. Sir George Talbot was directly descended from Littleton J. (1422–1481), Bromley L.C. (1530–1587), and Talbot L.C. (1685–1737).

negligence, for failure by an occupier of property to take reasonable care that his property does not get into such a state as to be dangerous to adjoining property or persons lawfully thereon[83] ... it is in our opinion immaterial whether in such a case the plaintiff is in the place where he is injured as one of the King's subjects entitled to use the highway, or in the exercise of any other legal right.[84]

(4) Misfeasance after commencement of demise

It should be observed that the foregoing rules as to the exemption of a landlord from liability for the dangerous condition of the demised premises related solely to his acts of omission or nonfeasance. He was not bound to make the premises safe or to ascertain whether they were dangerous in the absence of an express covenant to do so, yet if by a positive act of negligent misfeasance after the commencement of the lease he actually created a source of danger he was responsible for any accident which was the direct result of his negligence. As we have seen,[85] even a stranger would be so responsible, and the liability of the owner of the premises was held[86] not to be less than that of a stranger.

(5) Liability of vendors, builders and others

It was well established[87] that the immunity of a lessor extended to a vendor, and that this immunity had escaped the flood-tide of liability released by *Donoghue* v. *Stevenson*,[88] so that at common law the vendor of a completed house[89] which turns out to be defective is under no liability to the purchaser in the absence of an express or implied warranty that the house is reasonably sound and fit for habitation.[90] If the purchaser has been fortunate or prudent enough to secure an express warranty no question will arise except whether on its true construction it covers the events which have in fact occurred.[91] Exemption clauses will be construed against the builder.[92] If there has been no express warranty it sometimes seems to have assumed that there can never be an implied one. This is true only in the sense that the law does not automatically imply such a warranty in the absence of a stipulation to the contrary, as it does in the case of the sale of an article to which section 14 of the Sale of Goods Act 1979 applies: *caveat emptor* is the general principle governing the sale of completed houses. It is clear, however, that such a warranty may be implied if the court should decide

---

[83] The fact that the defendant is in occupation distinguishes this from the line of cases based on *Cavalier* v. *Pope* [1906] A.C. 428.

[84] See also *Bishop* v. *Consolidated London Properties* (1933) 102 L.J.K.B. 257.

[85] See above, § 100.

[86] *Billings (A.C.) & Sons Ltd.* v. *Riden* [1958] A.C. 240.

[87] *Bottomley* v. *Bannister* [1932] 1 K.B. 458.

[88] [1932] A.C. 562.

[89] Or perhaps even an uncompleted house, when the structure stands at the time of the sale: *Perry* v. *Sharon Development Co. Ltd.* [1937] 4 All E.R. 390, 394.

[90] *Perry* v. *Sharon Dvelopment Co. Ltd.* [1937] 4 All E.R. 390. When, however, the contract is for the sale of a house *when completed*, there is an implied contract that the house shall be completed in such a way that it is fit for human habitation: *Lynch* v. *Thorne* [1956] 1 W.L.R. 303.

[91] In *Otto and Otto* v. *Bolton and Norris* [1936] 2 K.B. 46 the first plaintiff succeeded on her claim only because she had obtained such a warranty from one of the defendants.

[92] *Billyack* v. *Leyland Construction Co. Ltd.* [1968] 1 W.L.R. 471.

that in all the circumstances of the case it is proper to do so.[93] The courts began to favour the purchaser. It was therefore held that in every contract to build a house there was to be implied (in the absence of express words to the contrary[94]) a threefold undertaking by the builder: (i) that he will do his work in a good and workmanlike manner; (ii) that he will supply good and proper materials; and (iii) that the house, built or to be built,[95] will be reasonably fit for human habitation.[96] In any event, the vendor was not liable to the purchaser's visitors.[97] It was difficult for the law to place them in any better position than the purchaser himself.

§ 101A. ANNS v. MERTON LONDON BOROUGH COUNCIL[98]

This decision has made necessary a fundamental review of the law relating to the liability of vendors, builders and others.

The facts. Each of the plaintiffs had bought a long lease of a flat from the first defendants, Walcroft Property Co. Ltd., who owned and built the whole structure, the plans for which had been approved by the second defendants in February 1962. In February 1970, cracks and subsidence in the flats became manifest. It was alleged that these were due to the fact that Walcroft had not carried the foundations down to the depth required by regulations made by Merton under the Public Health Act 1936. It was also alleged that these defects should have been revealed by inspections made by Merton in the exercise of their statutory discretions or powers. Writs were issued against both defendants on February 21, 1972.[99] But Walcroft did not enter an appearance then or at any later stage in the proceedings.[1]

The issues

On these facts, it had to be decided whether the claims were statute-barred as having accrued to the plaintiffs before February 23, 1966.[2] All the respondents save one had bought their leases before that date. The Official Referee, His Honour Judge E. Fay, Q.C., held that they were so barred, because (he thought) the cause of action accrued at the date of the first con-

---

[93] See the authorities fully reviewed in *Brown* v. *Norton* [1954] I.R. 34.

[94] As there were in *Lynch* v. *Thorne* [1956] 1 W.L.R. 303.

[95] *McGeary* v. *Campbell* [1975] N.I.7.

[96] *Billyack* v. *Leyland Construction Co. Ltd.* [1968] 1 W.L.R. 471.

[97] *Otto and Otto* v. *Bolton and Norris* [1936] 2 K.B. 46.

[98] [1978] A.C. 728. For relevant literature, see N. Seddon, *The Negligence Liability of Statutory Bodies* (1978) 9 Fed.L.Rev. 326, P. P. Craig, "Negligence in the Exercise of a Statutory Power" (1978) 94 L.Q.R. 428; I N. D. Wallace, "Tort Demolishes Contract in New Construction" (1978) 94 L.Q.R. 60; J. A. Smillie, "Liability of Builders, Manufacturers and Vendors for Negligence" (1978) 8 N.Z.U.L.R. 109. See also J. Wylie, *Conveyancing*, (1979), pp. 162–64. The title of the case in the Appeal Cases is slightly misleading in that it does not reveal that there were eight plaintiffs (of whom Anns was the first alphabetically but not chronologically having acquired his lease by assignment), and two defendants. In the Court of Appeal the case is reported as *Anns* v. *Walcroft Property Ltd.* [1976] Q.B. 882, which identifies the first defendants, who seem to have been what the Court of Appeal has called "speculative builders": *Dutton* v. *Bognor Regis U.D.C.* [1972] 1 Q.B. 373, 393.

[99] Or 22 February, according to Lord Salmon. [1978] A.C. 728, 770.

[1] Nevertheless the House of Lords made an important judicial statement about the legal posi-.. tion of builders. Is that statement part of the *ratio decidendi* of the case? In an adversary system of litigation, is it possible or desirable to change the law judicially without hearing argument from the party affected by the change?

[2] For the computation of time, see below, § 220.

veyance of each of the properties, the latest such date being November 5, 1965. This decision was unanimously reversed by the Court of Appeal, which in turn was unanimously upheld by the House of Lords. These tribunals are generally understood to have held that the relevant date was that on which the defect first emerged or became reasonably discoverable,[3] or that on which the state of the property constituted imminent danger to the occupier[4]. So that on the assumption that either of these tests were satisfied in 1970,[5] it was clear that the writs were issued in time. The actions then proceeded against Merton.[6]

The Law Lords also expressed at length their views on the duties owed at common law and under statute by the defendants.

The common law problem

It is now settled that the neighbour principle applies unless there is some reason to reduce or negative that principle.[7] On the facts of *Anns* no such reason appeared. So the plaintiffs were owed a duty. A number of questions arise.

(a) Who owes the duty?

First, the local authority owes it if the statutory framework within which it operates permits the imposition of such a duty.[8]

Secondly, the inspector or other official employed by the local authority is liable—at least in theory.[9]

Thirdly, the architect is liable. This has been settled in England,[10] Ireland,[11] Australia[12] and New Zealand[13] for some years.

Fourthly, all five Law Lords in *Anns* agreed that the builder would be liable, whether or not he owned the building (as Walcroft Property did).[14] Lord MacDermott's judgment 20 years ago[15] imposing liability on a builder has thus been triumphantly vindicated. Whether this statement is part of the

---

[3] These dates will normally, but not necessarily, coincide. See below, § 220, for further consideration of this point.

[4] The view of Lord Wilberforce and three other Law Lords.

[5] This assumption may not have been true in the case of Mr. and Mrs. O'Shea, who had acquired their lease in 1962: *see* Lord Salmon in [1978] A.C. 728, 770. As Lord Salmon had a large practice in building cases when at the Bar, his opinion on these points is of particular value.

[6] Every local authority, architect, builder and inspector was anxious to learn the result. But in March 1979 (nearly 18 years after the building had been erected) the parties arrived at a settlement. Its terms are confidential, and so may never be known.

[7] See above, § 73.

[8] See further, below, § 191.

[9] The whereabouts of Bateman, the Council's Building Inspector in 1962, were not known ten years later. It is also worth remembering that the reports at least twice record that a potential defendant had "gone to Australia": see *Castle* v. *St. Augustine's Links Ltd.* (1922) 38 T.L.R. 615; *Dutton* v. *Bognor Regis Building Co. Ltd.* [1972] 1 Q.B. 373, 390. In another leading case the party most to blame had chosen New Zealand: *Candler* v. *Crane, Christmas & Co. (A Firm)* [1951] 2 K.B. 164.

[10] *Clayton* v. *Woodman & Son (Builders) Ltd.* [1962] 2 Q.B. 533.

[11] *Buckley* v. *Lynch* [1978] I.R. 6.

[12] *Voli* v. *Inglewood Shire Council* (1963) 110 C.L.R. 85.

[13] *Bowen* v. *Paramount Builders Ltd.* [1977] 1 N.Z.L.R. 394.

[14] So a speculative builder/vendor was held liable in *Hone* v. *Benson* [1978] C.L.Y. 2062.

[15] *Gallagher* v. *N. McDowell Ltd.* [1961] N.I. 26.

ratio decidendi of the case is doubtful, but it will certainly be followed.[16] Whether it is desirable to provide potential plaintiffs with so many defendants, some of doubtful financial standing, must also be doubtful.[17] It might be better policy for the law to channel liability on to one defendant of good financial standing.[18] This would at least avoid the necessity for each of several potential defendants taking out a separate insurance policy.

But *Anns* does not definitely hold that a vendor who is not a builder is liable. *Anns* does not clearly over-rule *Bottomley* v. *Bannister*,[19] although Lord Denning was ready to take this step,[20] and his reasoning was approved by Lord Wilberforce.[21]

(b) To whom is the duty owed?

Lord Wilberforce stated clearly[22] that it is owed to the owner or occupier *who is such when the damage occurs*. This neat formula avoids the possibility of open-ended liability to an indeterminate number of persons. It has the advantage that it covers subsequent purchasers: a building is intended to last, and is normally transferred to a subsequent owner who is therefore entitled to sue.[23] (His cause of action cannot arise before he becomes the owner[24]—although it is possible that by that date he will have lost his claim.)

The italicised words in Lord Wilberforce's statement have caused problems. "Suppose the damage occurs in 01's time; he dies, leaving the property by will to his wife, 02; why should she not be able to sue?"[25] It also seems that a mere user of the premises, such as a guest or member of the family, cannot sue. Such a person must bring his claim under the distinct sub-head of occupiers' liability.

It is also unclear how the new rule relates to the provisions concerning concealed fraud or mistake in section 26 of the 1939 Act, which assume that time normally begins to run from the date of the infliction of the damage, but should be postponed until the fraud or mistake is discovered. The relationship of the new rule to the Defective Premises Act 1972, s.1(5) is also unclear. That statutory cause of action arises when the building has been completed.[26]

(c) In respect of what is the new duty owed?

It is not clear whether it includes products which are part of buildings—*e.g.* high-alumina cement or structures which are assembled rather than built, as with pre-fabricated buildings. Perhaps these are governed by the law on products liability.

---

[16] As in the Irish High Court in *Colgan* v. *Connolly Construction Co. Ltd.* (29 February 1980).
[17] In *Young* v. *Tomlinson* [1979] 2 N.Z.L.R. 441 there were four defendants.
[18] See also above §§ 7–9.
[19] [1932] 1 K.B. 458.
[20] See *Dutton* v. *Bognor Regis U.D.C.* [1972] 1 Q.B. 373, 393.
[21] See [1978] A.C. 728, 759.
[22] [1978] A.C. 728, 760.
[23] As in *Colgan* v. *Connolly Construction Co. Ltd.* (Irish High Court, 29 February 1980).
[24] *Buckley* v. *Lynch* [1976] I.R. 6, 10.
[25] See Bennett, (1978) N.L.J. 25, 26.
[26] See below, § 102.

(d) In respect of what kinds or heads of damage is the duty owed

On this important point the judgment in *Anns* need to be supplemented by those in *Bowen* v. *Paramount Building Co. Ltd.*[27] and *Batty* v. *Metropolitan Properties Ltd.*[28] The following propositions can be put forward:
  (i) the cost of repairing a defective structure is certainly recoverable;
  (ii) probably, the cost of preventive repairs (or timeous loss) is also recoverable.[29] In some cases—*e.g.* high-alumina cement—this may be very costly. It is a novelty to award such damages in tort as distinct from contract, but perhaps it can be justified on the ground that the cost of such repairs is the true measure of the damage to the structure;
  (iii) the cost of damage to other property of the plaintiff, movable or immovable, is recoverable;
  (iv) probably, the diminution in value of the building, when repaired, is also recoverable, for the depreciation in value is a consequence of the physical malformation of the premises;
  (v) personal injuries caused by the defect are recoverable.
But defects which do not affect the health or safety of the occupiers or the disability of the dwelling itself are not recoverable. The principle of *Donoghue* v. *Stevenson* does not extend to defects in the quality of the product itself.[30]

§ 102. LIABILITY OF LESSORS OR VENDORS UNDER STATUTE[31]

The Defective Premises Act 1972, which came into force on January 1, 1974, was passed as a result of recommendations made by the Law Commission.[32] The Act has four main effects. First, the creation of a statutory duty to build dwellings properly, which is to be owed to any person who acquires an interest in the dwelling. Secondly, the abolition of the *caveat emptor* rule. Thirdly, the imposition on a landlord of a wider statutory duty of care in virtue of his obligation or right to repair the premises demised. Fourthly, the exclusion or restriction of any of the duties imposed by the Act is expressly prohibited.

(1) Duty to build dwellings properly

Section 1(1) provides that,
    A person taking on work[33] for or in connection with the provision of a dwelling (whether the dwelling is provided by the erection or by the conversion or enlargement of a building) owes a duty—
      (a) if the dwelling is provided to the order of any person, to that person; and

---

[27] [1977] 1 N.Z.L.R. 394.
[28] [1978] Q.B. 554.
[29] If such an expenditure constitutes damage, even though it has not occurred in fact, the relationship of the *Anns* rule to the general structure of the Limitation Acts is even more obscure. Perhaps such expenditure is properly recoverable as being reasonably incurred by the plaintiff in mitigation of his loss.
[30] See below, § 106.
[31] See Spencer, "The Defective Premises Act" [1974] C.L.J. 307; [1975] C.L.J. 48.
[32] *Civil Liability of Vendors and Lessors for Defective Premises* (Law Com. No. 40, 1970).
[33] For the meaning of this curious phrase, see *Alexander* v. *Mercouris* [1979] 3 All E.R. 305.

(b) without prejudice to paragraph (a) above, to every person who acquires an interest (whether legal or equitable) in the dwelling;

to see that work which he takes on is done in a workmanlike or, as the case may be, professional manner, with proper materials and so that as regards that work the dwelling will be fit for habitation when completed. The reference to the dwelling being " fit for habitation when completed" is not part of the duty itself. Rather it refers to the intended consequence of the proper performance of the duty, so that relief can be claimed before the dwelling is completed.[34]

But subsection (2) safeguards the position of those persons who take on work of the nature described on terms that shall be done in accordance with instructions. It provides that a person who takes on any such work for another on terms that he is to do it in accordance with instructions given by or on behalf of that other shall, to the extent to which he does it in accordance with those instructions, be treated for the purposes of this section as discharging the duty imposed on him by subsection (1) above, except where he owes a duty to that other to warn him of any defects in the instructions and fails to discharge that duty.

On the other hand, by subsection (3) a person shall not be treated as having given instructions for the doing of work merely because he has agreed to the work being done in a specified manner, with specified materials or to a specified design. So a builder or developer who offers plans or specifications on a "take it or leave it" basis to a prospective purchaser will continue to be liable.[35]

Subsection (4) extends the statutory duty imposed by subsection (1) on builders and the like to others, such as developers and local authorities who, in the course of a business or in the exercise of statutory powers, provide or arrange for the provision of dwellings, and who accordingly arrange for others to take on such work.

Subsection (5) provides that the period fixed by the Limitation Acts[36] runs from the completion of the building. This date might well be months, or even years, before the completion of the purchase, whereas at common law time runs from the date when the purchaser knew, or ought to have known, of the defect.[37]

It should be noted that although the statutory duty cannot be excluded or restricted by any term of an agreement (s.6(3)), it does not, by section 2, apply at all when the dwelling is constructed or first sold with the benefit of a scheme approved by the Secretary of State. The approved scheme is that of the National House-Builders Registration Council (N.H.B.R.C.).[38]

(2) Abolition of caveat emptor rule

This is done in a complex way. The Act does not state in a positive way what are the responsibilities of the vendor or lessor. Instead, it assumes that the immunity of the lessor or vendor is due, not to his status as such as had hitherto been thought, but to the transaction of sale or letting. It is therefore,

---

[34] *Alexander* v. *Mercouris* [1979] 3 All E.R. 305.
[35] But a careless valuer is not liable under the Act: he does not provide a dwelling.
[36] See below, §§ 220–221.
[37] See above, § 101a, and below, §§ 220–222.
[38] See S.I. 1973 No. 1843.

in effect, provided that such a transaction shall not have such an effect, so that the general principles of negligence will apply to work done before the transaction. Therefore section 3 provides that:

(1) Where work of construction, repair, maintenance or demolition or any other work[39] is done on or in relation to premises, any duty of care owed, because of the doing of the work, to persons who might reasonably be expected to be affected by defects in the state of the premises created by the doing of the work shall not be abated by the subsequent disposal[40] of the premises by the person who owed the duty.

(2) This section does not apply—

    (a) in the case of premises which are let, where the relevant tenancy[41] of the premises commenced, or the relevant tenancy agreement of the premises was entered into, before the commencement of this Act;

    (b) in the case of premises disposed of in any other way, when the disposal of the premises was completed, or a contract for their disposal was entered into, before the commencement of this Act; or

    (c) in either case, where the relevant transaction disposing of the premises is entered into in pursuance of an enforceable option by which the consideration for the disposal was fixed before the commencement of this Act.

In a case which is not covered by these complex provisions it is possible that there will be a remedy under the common law as re-interpreted in *Anns* v. *Merton London Borough Council*.[42]

(3) Landlord's duty of care

It has already been noted[43] that the severity of the rule in *Cavalier* v. *Pope*[44] had been mitigated by section 4(4) of the Occupiers' Liability Act 1957. That section has now been repealed and replaced by wider provision in section 4 of the 1972 Act, which in effect gives a remedy for an omission to carry out repairs, as distinct from the liability for careless repairs imposed by section 3.

(1) Where premises[45] are let under a tenancy[46] which puts on the landlord an obligation to the tenant for the maintenance or repair of the premises, the landlord owes to all persons who might reasonably be expected to be affected by defects in the state of the premises a duty to take such care as is reasonable in all the circumstances to see that they are reasonably safe from personal injury[47] or from damage to their property caused by a relevant defect.

(2) The duty is owed if the landlord knows (whether as the result of

---

[39] Would this cover mere omissions?
[40] As defined in s. 6(1).
[41] As defined in s. 6(1).
[42] [1978] A.C. 728. See above, § 101a.
[43] See above, § 101.
[44] [1906] A.C. 428.
[45] See *Hopwood* v. *Cannock Chase D.C.* [1975] 1 W.L.R. 373.
[46] As defined in ss. 4 (6) and 6(1).
[47] As defined in s. 6(1).

being notified by the tenant or otherwise) or if he ought in all the circumstances to have known of the relevant defect.[48]

The section applies to tenancies existing at the commencement of the Act as well as to future tenancies, and the duty which it imposes cannot be excluded or restricted by any agreement.

The section changes the previous law in three respects, namely:

(i) The duty of care imposed in replacement of the similar duty imposed by section 4 of the 1957 Act is to be owed not merely to visitors to the premises but to all those who might reasonably be expected to be affected by defects in the state of the premises, *e.g.* a passer-by on the highway or a neighbour in his garden, or perhaps even a trespasser.

(ii) Liability for breach of the duty of care imposed will no longer depend upon whether or not the landlord has been notified of the relevant defect in the premises, for subsection (2) provides that he owes the duty not only when he knows, but also when he ought to have known of the defect.

(iii) The duty thus imposed on the landlord is to be extended, by virtue of subsection (4), to apply in cases where the landlord has a right (expressed or implied) to enter the premises to carry out any description of maintenance or repair but no obligation to do so.

But it should be noted that this section has not been adopted by the Defective Premises (Northern Ireland) Order 1975, which in other respects changed the law in that jurisdiction to correspond with the English law. It was thought unfair to impose such a burden on landlords in view of the amount of bomb damaged property in Northern Ireland.

---

[48] As defined in s. 4(3).

CHAPTER 12

DEFECTIVE PRODUCTS[1]

Consumer protection

(1) *By statute*

Defective products may fall under the Sale of Goods Act 1979, the Trade Descriptions Acts 1968 and 1972, the Fair Trading Act 1973 or the Unfair Contract Terms Act 1977. Products which are unsafe as distinct from defective are governed by the Consumer Safety Act 1978. The duties imposed by this Act are enforced by criminal rather than civil proceedings brought by the Trading Standards Departments of local authorities. Although the Consumer Safety Act, s.6, specifically provides that a civil action lies for breach of the duties thereby imposed, little use seems to have been made of this.

(2) *At common law*

Fault is still the basis of liability. But there have been a number of proposals for a régime of strict liability. The most important of these are the Strasbourg Convention on Products Liability, prepared by the Council of Europe, and the Third Draft Directive of the EEC,[2] and the Report of the English and Scottish Law Commissions on Liability for Defective Products.[3] These in turn were discussed by the Pearson Commission, whose Report[4] preferred the form of strict liability favoured by the Strasbourg Convention rather than the EEC.[5] The Pearson Report recommended no exceptions for any particular type of product, no special defence for development risks, and no financial limits on liability.

The present position at common law will be considered under three headings:

(1) The liability of the possessor of an object to persons permitted or invited to make use of it or to enter upon it;

(2) The liability of him who delivers an object for damage suffered by the recipient of it;

(3) The liability of him who delivers an object for damage suffered by persons other than the recipient.

---

[1] See the full survey in Miller, *Product Liability and Safety Encyclopaedia* (1979).
[2] Approved by the Commission on September 26, 1979 after considering criticisms of earlier drafts. The European material is reprinted in Miller, *Product Liability and Safety Encyclopaedia* (1979), Sect. 5.
[3] Law Com. No. 82 (Cmnd. 6831, 1977).
[4] Cmnd. 7054, 1978, Chap. 22.
[5] The House of Lords Select Committee on the European Communities has also favoured the Convention instead of the Directive, stigmatising some provisions of the latter as "incomprehensible and unworkable" (H.L. 236, 1980). See also H.L. Debates for November 12, 1980.

§ 103. DUTY TO PERSONS PERMITTED OR INVITED TO USE OBJECT

We have already considered this aspect of the law and seen that it is governed by principles similar to those which regulate the position of those who enter on dangerous premises.[6]

§ 104. DUTY TO IMMEDIATE TRANSFEREE[7]

(1) Transfer under contract

Where a dangerous product is delivered by the defendant to the plaintiff, the liability of the defendant depends on the terms, express or implied, of the contract between them. The extent of responsibility varies in different classes of contract.[8] Thus in a contract of sale there is in many cases an implied condition that the goods are fit for the purpose for which they are bought.[9] In such cases the seller is responsible in damages for any injury caused by a dangerous imperfection in the goods, apart altogether from any negligence.[10] A similar warranty may be implied in cases of transactions closely analogous to a contract of sale—*e.g.* where a dealer supplies a motor-car through a finance company on hire-purchase terms.[11]

The fact that liability under the Sale of Goods Act does not depend on proof of fault on the part of the defendant vendor is not appreciated either by the normal retailer or by his customers, each of whom normally expects the manufacturer to settle any claim.[12] Yet the liability of the manufacturer in tort, as distinct from contract, is dependent on proof of fault.[13]

In general it is an implied fundamental term of an agreement between a hirer and a finance company that the vehicle hired shall correspond with the description of the vehicle to be hired.[14] Under the Hire-Purchase Act 1964, s.10, any representations made by a dealer with respect to goods the subject of a hire-purchase agreement shall be deemed to have been made by him as agent for the owner or seller. Further, in contracts to which the Hire-Purchase Act 1964 applies, there are certain implied conditions as to merchantability and description. In a contract for the hiring of goods there is also an implied[15] warranty of fitness and safety, and a similar liability for dangerous defects.[16] So also under a contract for work and materials the contractor impliedly warrants that the materials will be of good quality and reasonably fit for the purpose, unless the circumstances show that such an

---

[6] Above, § 90.
[7] Whincup, "Reasonable Fitness of Cars" (1975) 38 M.L.R. 660.
[8] *Taylor & Sons* v. *Union-Castle SS. Co.* (1932) 48 T.L.R. 249, 250.
[9] Sale of Goods Act 1979. s. 14.
[10] As *Grant* v. *Australian Knitting Mills* [1936] A.C. 85 clearly shows.
[11] *Andrews* v. *Hopkinson* [1957] 1 Q.B. 229.
[12] So *Which?* (September, 1971) refers to "the advice we have given before: if you're in trouble with a product and the shop won't help, write directly to the manufacturer."
[13] See below, § 106.
[14] *Astley Industrial Trust Ltd.* v. *Grimley* [1963] 1 W.L.R. 584.
[15] Note that the warranty is only an implied one, and may be excluded by the express terms of the contract of hire, as in *Hadley* v. *Droitwich Construction Co. Ltd.* [1968] 1 W.L.R. 37.
[16] *Reed* v. *Dean* [1949] 1 K.B. 188. The warranty in contracts of hiring does not extend to latent defects which are not discoverable by reasonable care on the part of anyone.

implied warranty is excluded.[17] In a contract for the carriage of goods by a person under a statutory duty to carry, there is an implied warranty by the consignor that the goods may be safely carried and are not dangerous,[18] and if the goods are dangerous the consignor must give notice to such a carrier, unless the means of knowledge that the goods are dangerous are equally open to both parties.[19]

In any event the recipient of an article may expressly agree to run all risks and in this case there is no duty even to disclose concealed dangers actually known.[20]

(2) Transfer by way of gift

Story noticed[21] that gifts "have furnished very little occasion for the interposition of judicial tribunals, for reasons equally honourable to the parties and to the liberal spirit of polished society." It was once thought to be settled that in the case of a gratuitous loan or gift of a thing, there is not even the duty of reasonable care. The donor or lender owes no duty except to give warning of any dangers actually known to him.[22] In short, the transferee cannot complain if he knows as much about the state of the article as does the transferor himself.[23] The only exception to this principle arises when the article belongs to the category of things dangerous *per se*: liability in such a case does not depend on the donor's knowledge of the defect. In recent years, however, the validity of the principle itself has been questioned on the ground that the decision in *Donoghue* v. *Stevenson* makes the earlier cases on gifts quite out of date,[24] but it is not clear whether this change in the law is to be ascribed to the principle governing the liability of the manufacturers of goods or to the wider neighbour principle.[25] So there may now be a duty to take reasonable care in the case of a gratuitous bailment, as when a ladder or a lawn-mower is lent to a neighbour, at least if the object is used for the purpose contemplated.[26]

§ 105. DUTY TO ULTIMATE TRANSFEREE

It remains to consider the liability of him who delivers a dangerous article for damage suffered, not by the recipient himself, but by some third person. When A, for example, sells or gives a defective gun to B, who gives or sells it

---

[17] *Gloucester County Council* v. *Richardson* [1969] 1 A.C. 480. The customer should disclose to the contractor any known relevant abnormal circumstance: *Ingham* v. *Emes* [1955] 2 Q.B. 366 (plaintiff allergic to hair-dye).

[18] The consignor is probably liable if he does not warn the carrier that the goods are of a dangerous nature, whether he is himself ignorant of the fact or not: *Burley* v. *Stepney Corporation* [1947] 1 All E.R. 507.

[19] *Transoceanica Societa* v. *Shipton* [1923] 1 K.B. 31.

[20] (1878) 4 App.Cas. 13. On the other hand, a sale expressly excluding all warranties leaves subsisting a duty to disclose known dangers: *Clarke* v. *Army and Navy Co-operative Society* [1903] 1 K.B. 155.

[21] *Commentaries on the Law of Bailments*, s. 285.

[22] *Coughlin* v. *Gillison* [1899] 1 Q.B. 145, 147.

[23] *Fraser* v. *Jenkins* [1968] N.Z.L.R. 816, 824.

[24] *Hawkins* v. *Coulsdon and Purley U.D.C.* [1954] 2 Q.B. 319, 333. Marsh, "The Liability of the Gratuitous Transferor: a Comparative Survey" (1950) 66 L.Q.R. 39, also supports this new view.

[25] *Gledhill* v. *Liverpool Abattoir Utility Co. Ltd.* [1957] 1 W.L.R. 1028 could be cited to support either view.

[26] *Campbell* v. *O'Donnell* [1967] I.R. 226.

to C, who is injured by the bursting of it, is A under any liability to C? Although there is no liability in such cases merely on the ground of the defendant's breach of contract with the immediate recipient of the dangerous thing,[27] there are certain other circumstances which will create a good cause of action. Such liability exists in the following cases:

(1) Fraud

The defendant is responsible if he fraudulently represents the article to be safe, and so misleads the recipient into causing damage to the plaintiff. Thus in *Langridge* v. *Levy*,[28] the defendant sold to the plaintiff's father for the use of the plaintiff a gun which he fraudulently stated to be of good construction, and the plaintiff, having been injured by the bursting of the weapon, was held entitled to sue the seller for damages although there was no contract between them.

(2) Negligence

The defendant is liable if he has been guilty of a breach of a duty of care owed to the plaintiff. Such a duty of care will arise in three cases.

(i) Things dangerous in themselves[29]

A distinction has been drawn between things classed as dangerous in themselves and things dangerous in the particular case or *sub modo*. "It has, however, again and again been held that in the case of articles dangerous in themselves, such as loaded firearms, poisons, explosives, and other things *ejusdem generis*, there is a peculiar duty to take precaution imposed upon those who send forth or install such articles when it is necessarily the case that other parties will come within their proximity. The duty being to take precaution, it is no excuse to say the accident would not have happened unless some other agency than that of the defendant had intermeddled with the matter. A loaded gun will not go off unless someone pulls the trigger, a poison is innocuous unless someone takes it, gas will not explode unless it is mixed with air and then a light is set to it. Yet the cases of *Dixon* v. *Bell* (1816) 5 M. & S. 198, *Thomas* v. *Winchester* (1852) 6 N.Y. 397, and *Parry* v. *Smith* (1879) 4 C.P.D. 325, are all illustrations of liability enforced. On the other hand, if the proximate cause of the danger is not the negligence of the defendant, but the conscious act of another volition, then he will not be liable."[30] It is a question of law whether a particular object is capable of coming within the category of things dangerous *per se* and a question of fact whether it is dangerous in all the circumstances of the case.[31] The following

---

[27] See above, § 3.
[28] (1837) 2 M. & W. 519.
[29] Stallybrass, "Dangerous Things and the Non-Natural User of Land" (1929) 3 Camb. L.J. 376; Goodhart, "Dangerous Things and the Sedan Chair" (1949) 65 L.Q.R. 518; Mathieson, "The Detonator Case" (1966) N.Z.L.J. 261, 297; Waddams, "The Strict Liability of Suppliers of Goods" (1974) 37 M.L.R. 154.
[30] *Dominion Natural Gas Co.* v. *Collins* [1909] A.C. 640, 646, *per* Lord Dunedin. In *Donoghue* v. *Stevenson* [1932] A.C. 562, 596, Lord Atkin said this statement "exactly summed up the position."
[31] *Blacker* v. *Lake and Elliot Ltd.* (1912) 106 L.T. 533.

objects, amongst others, have been held to be dangerous: loaded guns,[32] petrol,[33] explosives,[34] an electric space-heater,[35] noxious hair-dye,[36] and earthenware jars containing sulphuric acid.[37] On the other hand, the following are not dangerous *per se*: an oil-can,[38] a domestic boiler,[39] a catapult[40] and an air-gun.[41]

The distinction doubted

There is, however, also a remarkable number of judicial statements casting doubt upon the validity of the distinction between things dangerous *per se* and things dangerous *sub modo*. The distinction is certainly difficult to support in principle. There is nothing which is at all times and in all circumstances dangerous; there is an element of danger in every object.[42] The following passage from the argument of Sir Hartley Shawcross, Att.-Gen., in *Read* v. *J. Lyons & Co.*[43] summarises the present law neatly and accurately[44]: "The true question is not whether a thing is dangerous in itself but whether, by reason of some extraneous circumstances, it may become dangerous. There is really no category of dangerous things; there are only some things which require more and some which require less care." In other words, the measure of care increases in proportion with the danger involved in the custody or control of an agency potentially harmful, that is to say, the danger should the safeguards employed, if any, prove insufficient or unsuccessful.[45] In such a case not only the degree of care but also the range of persons to whom a duty is owed may be extended.[46] So the duty owed by those who store explosives is not limited to those who enter the premises but extends to all who have been foreseeably injured by them—*e.g.* children to whom they have been distributed by those who have entered.[47] Even if the category of things dangerous *per se* does exist, the liability of the owner of such an object is not absolute: he is not an insurer.[48] The case of dangerous things is really "a special instance of negligence where the law exacts a degree of diligence so stringent as to amount practically to a guarantee of safety."[49] In truth, the time has surely come[50] to recognise clearly that since the decision in *Donoghue* v. *Stevenson* the category of things dangerous *per se* has become unnecessary: the sole question is now whether the degree of care appropriate to the circumstances has been exercised. The fact that

---

[32] *Sullivan* v. *Creed* [1904] 2 I.R. 317, 340.
[33] *Jefferson* v. *Derbyshire Farmers Ltd.* [1921] 2 K.B. 281, 290.
[34] *Rainham Chemical Works* v. *Belvedere Fish Guano Co.* [1921] 2 A.C. 465.
[35] *Robinson* v. *Technico Ltd.* (1953) (unreported) (see Delany, (1954) 70 L.Q.R. 170).
[36] *Watson* v. *Buckley* [1940] 1 All E.R. 174.
[37] *Adelaide Chemical Co. Ltd.* v. *Carlyle* (1940) 64 C.L.R. 514.
[38] *Wray* v. *Essex C.C.* [1936] 3 All E.R. 97.
[39] *Ball* v. *L.C.C.* [1949] 2 K.B. 159.
[40] *Smith* v. *Leurs* (1945) 70 C.L.R. 256.
[41] *Donaldson* v. *McNiven* [1952] 2 All E.R. 691.
[42] *Oliver* v. *Saddler* [1929] A.C. 584, 599.
[43] [1947] A.C. 156, 161.
[44] *Beckett* v. *Newalls Insulation Co. Ltd.* [1953] 1 W.L.R. 8, 15.
[45] *Swinton* v. *The China Mutual Steam Navigation Co. Ltd.* (1951) 83 C.L.R. 553, 566–567.
[46] *Donoghue* v. *Stevenson* [1932] A.C. 562, 596.
[47] *McCarthy* v. *Wellington City* [1966] N.Z.L.R. 481.
[48] *Adelaide Chemical Co.* v. *Carlyle* (1940) 64 C.L.R. 514.
[49] *Donoghue* v. *Stevenson* [1932] A.C. 562, 611–612.
[50] As Goddard L.J. affirmed as long ago as *Paine* v. *Colne Valley Electricity Supply Co. Ltd.* [1938] 4 All E.R. 803, 808.

there is a special duty to take precautions does not mean that there is a special category in which alone the duty exists.[51]

(ii) Non-disclosure of known dangers

If the defendant has actual knowledge of the dangerous nature of the thing delivered by him, and gives no warning of it to the recipient, he may be liable for resulting injury to third persons even though the thing is not within the category of things dangerous *per se*.[52] In other words, a thing not dangerous in itself is brought into the category of dangerous things if there is knowledge of a dangerous defect,[53] as where a valve was reassembled with the bridge upside down so that steam escaped and scalded the plaintiff.[54]

Scope of the duty. If A places in the hands of B a thing which belongs to the category of things dangerous *per se*, or if A actually knows of some dangerous defect, a duty of care rests upon A, not only towards the recipient, but also towards all such persons as may reasonably be contemplated as likely to be endangered.[55] Thus in *Farrant* v. *Barnes*[56] the defendant delivered to a carrier a carboy of nitric acid without informing him of the dangerous nature of its contents, and was held liable in damages to the carrier's servant who was injured by the bursting of the carboy while he was carrying it on his shoulders. "The duty has never been stated to rest on knowledge. If A chooses to sell things of a class dangerous in themselves he cannot be heard to say he did not know of or appreciate the danger."[57]

Effect of warning. In certain cases the duty of the transferor may be discharged if he delivers the article to a competent person who knows of the danger already or is given an adequate warning about it.[58] It is a question of fact whether the warning is adequate: the transferor need not take the transferee by the hand or the ear, and show or tell him exactly what is wrong.[59] The transferor may be entitled to assume that the recipient will pass on the warning to the ultimate transferee, or will so act as to minimise or nullify the danger. So in *Holmes* v. *Ashford*[60] the manufacturer of hair-dye was held not liable to one who had contracted dermatitis after the dye had been applied by a hairdresser, for it was shown that the dye had been delivered to the hairdresser by the manufacturer with an adequate warning of its potential dangers. Yet a warning is not a sufficient discharge of the

---

[51] *Rae* v. *Eaton & Co. Ltd.* (1958) 28 D.L.R. (2d) 522, 529–530; *Tanner* v. *Atlantic Bridge Co. Ltd.* (1966) 56 D.L.R. (2d) 162, 163.

[52] *Barnes* v. *Irwell Valley Water Board* [1939] 1 K.B. 21, 44, 46.

[53] As with the doctrine of *scienter* in the case of animals.

[54] *Howard* v. *Furness Houlder Ltd.* [1936] 2 All E.R. 781, 792.

[55] *Anglo-Celtic Shipping Co. Ltd.* v. *Elliott* (1926) 42 T.L.R. 297; *Adelaide Chemical and Fertiliser Co. Ltd.* v. *Carlyle* (1940) 64 C.L.R. 514; *Robinson* v. *Technico Ltd.* (1953) (unreported) (see (1954) 70 L.Q.R. 170).

[56] (1862) 11 C.B. (N.S.) 553.

[57] *Burfitt* v. *Kille* [1939] 2 K.B. 743, 749, *per* Atkinson J.

[58] It may even be that neither the warning nor the knowledge need be of the exact amount of the danger: *Bottomley* v. *Bannister* [1932] 1 K.B. 458, 473.

[59] *Hurley* v. *Dyke* [1979] R.T.R. 265.

[60] [1950] 2 All E.R. 76. Yet it may be asked why a person who has created a dangerous situation should be held not liable on the ground that it has not been abated by another whose duty it was to do so: Goodhart (1941) 57 L.Q.R. 163, and see cases cited below, § 106.

duty if the person to whom the thing is delivered is not a competent person—*e.g.* a child to whom a defective "safety-pistol"[61] or petrol[62] is sold.

(iii) Negligence with respect to unknown dangers

Before 1932 it was extremely doubtful whether there was any liability on the part of a manufacturer of goods to the ultimate consumer or user with whom there was no contractual relationship, when there was no fraud, when he did not know the article to be dangerous, and when it did not belong to the category of things dangerous *per se.* But in that year the decision of a majority of the House of Lords in *Donoghue* v. *Stevenson,*[63] an appeal from the Court of Session, established that in such circumstances the manufacturer might owe a duty to the ultimate consumer. We shall proceed to discuss this great case in fuller detail.

§ 106. DONOGHUE *v.* STEVENSON[64]

The question for the House of Lords in this appeal was whether the averments made by the pursuer in her pleadings, if true, disclosed a good cause of action. The pursuer's averments were that in August 1928 she had entered a cafe in Paisley occupied by one Minchella, and that a friend[65] who accompanied her had bought from Minchella some refreshment for both of them. The refreshment consisted of two slabs of ice-cream, each of which was placed in a tumbler, and over which was then poured part of the contents of a bottle of ginger-beer. The ginger-beer had been manufactured by the defender Stevenson, and bought from him by Minchella. It was contained in a stoppered bottle made of dark opaque glass. When the pursuer had partly finished the confection, her friend attempted to replenish her glass by pouring into it the remains of the contents of the bottle. As she was doing this the remains of a decomposed snail floated out. The appellant averred that as a result of the nauseating sight of the snail and the impurities in the ginger-beer which she had already consumed, she had suffered from shock and severe gastroenteritis. A majority of the House of Lords (Lords Atkin, Macmillan, and Thankerton) held that if the pursuer could prove that which she averred she would have a good cause of action.[66]

> "If your Lordships," said Lord Atkin,[67] "accept the view that this pleading discloses a relevant cause of action you will be affirming the proposition that by Scots and English law alike a manufacturer of products, which he sells in such a form as to show that he intends them

---

[61] *Burfitt* v. *Kille* [1939] 2 K.B. 743, 748.

[62] *Yachuk* v. *Oliver Blais Co.* [1949] A.C. 386.

[63] [1932] A.C. 562.

[64] See Heuston, "*Donoghue* v. *Stevenson* in Retrospect" (1957) 20 M.L.R. 1; Heuston, "*Donoghue* v. *Stevenson*: A Fresh Appraisal" [1971] C.L.P. 37 and above, § 72.

[65] Who seems to have been female and not male: see Lord Macmillan's speech.

[66] There has been a persistent rumour (which has found support in the Court of Appeal: *Adler* v. *Dickson* [1954] 1 W.L.R. 1482, 1483) (and in the House of Commons (958, H.C.Deb., col 820, November 17, 1978)) that when the case was tried it was discovered that there never had been a snail in the bottle at all. This is not so. The truth is that the issue of fact was never decided: the defender died before proof and the pursuer in consequence compromised the action and received £100 in settlement of her claim: see Heuston (1957) 20 M.L.R. 2, n. 5.

[67] [1932] A.C. 562, 599.

to reach the ultimate consumer in the form in which they left him with no reasonable possibility of intermediate examination and with the knowledge that the absence of reasonable care in the preparation or putting up of the products will result in an injury to the consumer's life or property, owes a duty to the consumer to take that reasonable care. It is a proposition which I venture to say no one in Scotland or England who was not a lawyer would for one moment doubt. It will be an advantage to make it clear that the law in this matter, as in most others, is in accordance with sound common sense."

Whatever hesitations may have been felt about Lord Atkin's attempt to formulate a general criterion of the duty of care[68] this exposition of the obligation owed by a manufacturer of chattels in the circumstances mentioned has never been questioned. Indeed, in the years since 1932 it has been adopted and expanded in over one hundred reported cases throughout the common law world.[69] It will be convenient to discuss briefly some of the more significant phrases in this passage.[70]

(1) "A manufacturer"

The principle has been extended to include repairers,[71] assemblers,[72] erectors[73] and builders.[74] Inspectors and certifiers are also included.[75] Those who let out goods on hire are probably also included.[76] So it might be better to refer to producers rather than to manufacturers. It was once argued that the principle should not include vendors, bailors, or donors of articles not dangerous *per se*, who know nothing of the defect, have not created it, and do not fraudulently or carelessly[77] represent that the article is harmless on the ground that they have done nothing to create the danger. To hold such persons responsible would come very near to imposing liability for mere omissions on persons who are simply distributors and not producers.[78] But liability has been imposed[79] upon a dealer in second-hand motor-cars who supplied the plaintiff[80] with a vehicle containing a latent defect, and upon a

---

[68] See above, § 72.

[69] See 36 *English and Empire Digest* 458, and add to the cases there cited *Kirby* v. *Burke* [1944] I.R. 207, and *Campbell* v. *O'Donnell* [1967] I.R. 226.

[70] This mode of exposition is adopted simply for the sake of clarity and simplicity: no countenance is intended to be given to the heresy of treating the word of a famous judgment as if they were a passage in statute.

[71] *Malfroot* v. *Noxal* (1935) 51 T.L.R. 551; *Stennett* v. *Hancock* [1939] 2 All E.R. 578; *Herschtal* v. *Stewart and Ardern* [1940] 1 K.B. 155; *Haseldine* v. *Daw* [1941] 2 K.B. 343; *Power* v. *Bedford Motor Co. Ltd.* [1959] I.R. 391.

[72] *Howard* v. *Furness Houlder Ltd.* [1936] 2 All E.R. 781.

[73] *Brown* v. *Cotterill* (1934) 51 T.L.R. 21.

[74] *Sharpe* v. *E.T. Sweeting & Sons Ltd.* [1963] 1 W.L.R. 665.

[75] *Anns* v. *Merton London Borough Council* [1978] A.C. 728.

[76] *White* v. *Steadman* [1913] 3 K.B. 340; *Astley Industrial Trust Ltd.* v. *Grimley* [1963] 1 W.L.R. 584.

[77] The distributors in *Watson* v. *Buckley and Osborne, Garrett & Co. Ltd.* [1940] 1 All E.R. 174 were liable on this ground: they had distributed to the hairdressing trade with laudatory advertisements a dye which they had not tested at all and which had been made by "a gentleman who had emerged quite unexpectedly from Spain."

[78] See the Pearson Report, § 1238. The liability of donors or gratuitous bailors is also considered above, § 105.

[79] *Andrews* v. *Hopkinson* [1957] 1 Q.B. 229.

[80] By way of a hire-purchase transaction—*i.e.* the dealer sold the car to a finance company, who in turn leased it to the plaintiff under a hire-purchase agreement. In strict legal analysis, therefore, the relationship of vendor and purchaser did not exist between the plaintiff and the dealer.

store which sold defective cleaning fluid to the plaintiff's husband.[81] The defect would have been discoverable by a reasonable examination, but the defendants neither carried out such an examination nor warned the plaintiff that it had not done so.

(2) "Of products"

This term is no longer limited to articles of food or drink. It includes, for example, underwear,[82] tombstones,[83] motor-cars,[84] lifts,[85] hair-dye[86] and ships' telegraphs.[87] It also covers cases in which the injurious element is not a foreign body but something intrinsically part of the commodity itself.[88] It may cover cases in which there is no allegation that the product has been carelessly made, but it is dangerous to use in the absence of proper warnings or directions.[89] The principle has also been extended, after earlier doubts, to cover land,[90] although the vendor or lessor of premises may still enjoy certain immunities.[91] Careless statements were once also excluded, but there may now be liability for them under a distinct head of negligence.[92] Under the Draft European Convention (1979) liability does not extend to primary agricultural and artistic products, but is limited to movables which have been industrially produced.

(3) "Which he sells in such a form as to show that he intends them to reach the ultimate consumer in the form in which they left him"

First, it should be noted that "consumer" has been extended[93] to include the ultimate user of the article,[94] or, indeed, anyone through whose hands the article may pass,[95] and perhaps even anyone who is in physical proximity to it.[96] Equally, liability is no longer limited to one who sells, but extends to any distributor, including donors.[97]

Secondly, it is not of the essence of this principle that the article should reach the consumer or user in the same sealed package or container in which it left the manufacturer: it is enough to show that it reached him subject to the same defect. This was made clear in *Grant* v. *Australian Knitting*

---

[81] *Fisher* v. *Harrods Ltd.* [1966] 1 Lloyd's Rep, 500.
[82] *Grant* v. *Australian Knitting Mills* [1936] A.C. 85.
[83] *Brown* v. *Cotterill* (1934) 51 T.L.R. 21.
[84] *Herschtal* v. *Stewart and Ardern* [1940] 1 K.B. 155.
[85] *Haseldine* v. *Daw* [1941] 2 K.B. 343.
[86] *Watson* v. *Buckley* [1940] 1 All E.R. 174.
[87] *Hindustan SS. Co. Ltd.* v. *Siemens Bros. & Co. Ltd.* [1955] 1 Lloyd's Rep. 167. (In this case the article was defective because of its design.)
[88] *Tarling* v. *Noble* [1966] A.L.R. 189 (bone in chicken sandwich).
[89] *Distillers Co. (Biochemicals) Ltd.* v. *Thompson* [1971] A.C. 458.
[90] *Anns* v. *Merton B.C.* [1978] A.C. 728, 758-759. As Lord Atkin himself spoke of "products," without any restriction, it is not clear why anyone should have had doubts.
[91] See above, § 101.
[92] See above, § 76.
[93] Paradoxically, the definition in the Malony Report on Consumer Protection (Cmnd. 1781 (1962), para.2) is narrower.
[94] *Grant* v. *Australian Knitting Mills* [1936] A.C. 85.
[95] *Barnett* v. *Packer* [1940] 3 All E.R. 575 (shop-assistant laying out chocolates for display injured by protruding wire).
[96] *Brown* v. *Cotterill* (1934) 51 T.L.R. 21 (child on tombstone); *Stennett* v. *Hancock* [1939] 2 All E.R. 578 (pedestrian hit by lorry-wheel). Yet see the doubts of Lord Goddard C.J. in *Shave* v. *Rosner* [1954] 2 All E.R. 280, 282 (a passage not reported in [1954] 2 Q.B. 113).
[97] See above § 105.

Mills.[98] In this case the plaintiff contracted dermatitis as a result of wearing woollen underwear containing an excess of sulphites. The underwear had been sent out by the defendant manufacturers in paper packets containing six sets of which two were sold by retailers to the plaintiff: yet the manufacturers were held liable.

Thirdly, the use of the article for a purpose materially different from that which the maker designed it or which he might reasonably be taken to have contemplated may afford an answer to a claim[99] based on the article's defective condition.[1] In short, the type of accident must not be of a kind entirely different from anything reasonably foreseeable.[2] Further, it may well be that after the article has left the manufacturer's hands it has been exposed to vicissitudes which render it defective and for which the manufacturer is in no way to blame: in such a case the plaintiff will have failed to prove that the cause of the damage was the negligence of the manufacturer.[3] Fourthly, and conversely, the mere fact that the damage is foreseeable will not make for liability. The purpose of making cigarettes is that they should be smoked: but that does not automatically give one who develops lung-cancer a remedy.

(4) "With no reasonable possibility of intermediate examination"

Here three different situations have given rise to difficulty. First, there may have been an opportunity for examination, but that opportunity has not been taken; secondly, such an opportunity may have been taken, but without success, so that the defect is still unrevealed; thirdly, the opportunity may have been taken successfully, and the defect revealed, but the plaintiff has nevertheless used the article in its defective condition.

(i) *Opportunity not used*

Does the mere existence of an opportunity for intermediate examination, even if it is not used, or indeed expected by anyone that it could or would be used, suffice to exonerate the defendant? In *Donoghue* v. *Stevenson* itself it was of course unnecessary for Lord Atkin to consider anything else than a "reasonable possibility," for the facts were of a nature which not merely precluded examination by any person interposed between the manufacturer and the consumer but also made it unlikely in the extreme that the consumer would discover the defect for himself. After an initial period of uncertainty,[4]

---

[98] [1936] A.C. 85.

[99] As when a step-ladder is used as a working platform (*Campbell* v. *O'Donnell* [1967] I.R. 226), or a fishing vessel as an excursion boat for children (*Conole* v. *Red Bank Oyster Co. Ltd.* [1976] I.R. 191).

[1] *Davie* v. *New Merton Board Mills Ltd.* [1957] 2 Q.B. 368 (Ashworth J.—the point was not considered on appeal in either the C.A. or the H.L.).

[2] *O'Dwyer* v. *Leo Buring Pty. Ltd.* [1966] W.A.R. 67.

[3] In *Donoghue* v. *Stevenson* [1932] A.C. 562, 622, Lord Macmillan suggested that "it may be a good general rule to regard responsibility as ceasing when control ceases," but in *Grant's* case [1936] A.C. 85, 104, Lord Wright showed that this test might sometimes prove unhelpful. This is important, because Lord Macmillan was a member of the Judicial Committee in *Grant's* case and would hardly have accepted an incorrect interpretation of his judgment in *Donoghue* v. *Stevenson*.

[4] *Dransfield* v. *British Insulated Cables Ltd.* [1937] 4 All E.R. 382. See Goodhart, "*Dransfield* v. *British Insulated Cables Ltd.*" (1938) 54 L.Q.R. 59.

it is now fairly[5] plain[6] that the mere existence of such an opportunity will not exonerate the defendant[7]: the proper question is whether he should reasonably have expected that the plaintiff would use the opportunity for inspection in such a way as to give him warning of the risk.[8] In short, the decision in *Donoghue* v. *Stevenson* did not depend on the bottle being stoppered and sealed.[9] Thus in *Grant* v. *Australian Knitting Mills*[10] the manufacturers' contention that the purchaser could have protected himself by washing the underwear before use[11] was answered by Lord Wright in one sentence: "It was not contemplated that they should be first washed." "If there was any doubt about the governing principle of *Donoghue* v. *Stevenson*, Lord Wright has dissipated it."[12]

Warning notices. One way in which the manufacturer could show that he reasonably expected intermediate examination would be by showing that he had attached to the article a warning notice which was adequate in all the circumstances of the case to give effective protection.[13] In such an event, it would be the retailer and not the manufacturer who would in general be responsible to the ultimate user. It should be noticed that it is not necessary for the defendant to prove that the plaintiff consumed or used the article with full knowledge of the risk; it is enough if examination and consequent knowledge are to be expected.[14] More recent cases seem to require a manufacturer to warn consumers of subsequently discovered defects.[15]

(ii) *Opportunity used, but unsuccessfully*

What is the position if an intermediate examination has been carried out, but so carelessly that it fails to reveal the defect? It was once held that the manufacturer is exonerated in such circumstances,[16] but the prevalent view now is that the manufacturer is not in general excused[17] by the fact that an intermediary has failed to perform his duties properly.[18] Thus an architect

[5] *Taylor* v. *Rover Co. Ltd.* [1966] 1 W.L.R. 1491 adopts the older view.
[6] *Shields* v. *Hobbs, etc. Co.* (1962) 34 D.L.R. (2d) 307; *Cathcart* v. *Hull* [1963] N.Z.L.R. 333.
[7] So in *Paine* v. *Colne Valley Electricity Co.* [1938] 4 All E.R. 803, 808, Goddard L.J. suggested that Lord Atkin meant "possibility in a business sense," for a "person who buys 100 cases of tinned salmon from the packers has a physical opportunity of examining each tin. Commercially speaking it would be impossible for him to do so." As Finnemore J. remarked, many reputable manufacturers would be insulted at the suggestion that inspection of their products was necessary before use: *Mason* v. *Williams and Williams Ltd.* [1955] 1 W.L.R. 549, 551.
[8] This sentence was approved in *Cathcart* v. *Hull* [1963] N.Z.L.R. 333, 346, and, with reservations in *Jull* v. *Wilson and Horton* [1968] N.Z.L.R. 88, 92, and in *Bowen* v. *Paramount Builders Ltd.* [1977] 1 N.Z.L.R. 394, 412, and in *Griffiths* v. *Arch Engineering Co. Ltd.* [1968] 3 All E.R. 217, 222. The same principle is stated in slightly different language in s.34 (2)(*f*) of the Irish Civil Liability Act 1961, which also puts the burden of proof on the defendant.
[9] *Clay* v. *Crump & Co. Ltd.* [1964] 1 Q.B. 533, 558.
[10] [1936] A.C. 85, 105.
[11] A practice adopted by "some rather particular people": [1941] 2 K.B. 377.
[12] *Haseldine* v. *Daw & Son Ltd.* [1941] 2 K.B. 343, 377, *per* Goddard L.J. See the full review of authorities in *Herschtal* v. *Stewart and Ardern Ltd.* [1940] 1 K.B. 155.
[13] *Kubach* v. *Hollands* [1937] 3 All E.R. 907; *Holmes* v. *Ashford* [1950] 2 All E.R. 76.
[14] *London Graving Dock Co.* v. *Horton* [1951] A.C. 737, 750.
[15] *Rivtow Marine Ltd.* v. *Washington Iron Works Ltd.* (1973) 40 D.L.R. (3d) 530.
[16] *Buckner* v. *Ashby and Horner Ltd.* [1941] 1 K.B. 321; *Holmes* v. *Ashford* [1950] 2 All E.R. 76.
[17] He was in *Taylor* v. *Rover Co. Ltd.* [1966] 1 W.L.R. 1491.
[18] *Power* v. *Bedford Motor Co.* [1959] I.R. 391; *Clay* v. *A. J. Crump & Sons Ltd.* [1964] 1 Q.B. 533.

who carelessly plans a building or supervises a demolition operation may be liable to any lawful visitor to the premises, and is not entirely exempt[19] from liability merely because the builders or demolition contractors[20] or a public authority[21] have inspected the plans or the site.

(iii) *Successful intermediate examination*

The general principle is that if the plaintiff has discovered the defect for himself he is without remedy, because in such a case he has in truth failed to prove that the defendant caused the damage.[22] This is the explanation of *Farr* v. *Butters Bros.*,[23] a case which seems to have caused some difficulty. The defendant crane-manufacturers sent out a crane in parts to be assembled by the buyers. Their foreman, an experienced man, realised that it was defective but nevertheless assembled and worked it and was killed. The defendants were held not liable; the plaintiff had deliberately incurred the risk. This interpretation of *Donoghue* v. *Stevenson* has not in theory been affected by the Contributory Negligence Act: if there is a probability of intermediate examination the defendant owes no duty, and so there are no damages to be reduced.[24] In practice the courts look at the matter broadly and seem to be ready to reduce the damages.[25] But it is clear that the general principle does not apply when it could reasonably be contemplated that the plaintiff, despite his knowledge of the defect, might yet reasonably incur the risk. Thus in *Denny* v. *Supplies and Transport Co.*[26] the defendants sent out a barge loaded with timber so badly stowed that the plaintiff, who realised the danger, was injured while unloading it in the course of his employment. There was no practicable alternative course of action open to him for it was shown that there is no safe way of unloading badly stowed timber.[27] It was held that the plaintiff's opportunity of inspection did not break the chain of causation. There is no magic in a warning, and a danger is not removed by the mere process of the plaintiff gazing at it.[28]

(5) "And with the knowledge that the absence of reasonable care in the preparation or putting up of the products"

Reasonable care must be taken to ensure not only that the product itself is safe but also that any container or package in which it is sent out is suitable for its purpose.[29] Reasonable care must also be taken to ensure that any

---

[19] There may be claims for contribution or indemnity; see § 168.
[20] *Clay* v. *A. J. Crump & Sons Ltd.* [1964] 1 Q.B. 533.
[21] *Voli* v. *Inglewood Shire Council* (1963) 110 C.L.R. 74.
[22] *Grant* v. *Australian Knitting Mills* [1936] A.C. 85, 105; *Conole* v. *Red Bank Oyster Co. Ltd.* [1976] I.R. 191, 196.
[23] [1932] 2 K.B. 606.
[24] *Cathcart* v. *Hull* [1963] N.Z.L.R. 333.
[25] *Jull* v. *Wilson and Horton* [1968] N.Z.L.R. 88.
[26] [1950] 2 K.B. 374.
[27] This clearly distinguishes the case from *Farr* v. *Butters Bros.*, where there was no evidence of any legal or economic obligation on the plaintiff to work the crane until the defect had been remedied: see (1950) 66 L.Q.R. 427, and *Gledhill* v. *Liverpool Abattoir Utility Co. Ltd.* [1957] 1 W.L.R. 1028.
[28] *A. C. Billings & Sons Ltd.* v. *Riden* [1958] A.C. 240. Compare the law governing visitors to premises, above, § 93.
[29] *Donoghue* v. *Stevenson* [1932] A.C. 562, 595, 616, which must be taken to have overruled *Bates* v. *Batey & Co.* [1913] 3 K.B. 351, though Horridge J. (who had decided it) thought not in *Pattendon* v. *Beney* (1933) 50 T.L.R. 10. Pollock ((1934) 50 L.Q.R. 28) said that the opinions of the Law Lords had brought *Bates* v. *Batey & Co.* "well within the classical precept, 'Put that case out of your books, for it is not law.' "

labels or instructions which accompany the article and are necessary for its proper use are so worded as to ensure that the article can be used with safety.[30] For sometimes an article of the highest standard of construction may be rendered dangerous by some misrepresentation which accompanies it—*e.g.* a steam boiler when the figures on the pressure gauge have been misplaced.[31]

(6) "Will result in injury to the consumer's life or property"

The principle enunciated by Lord Atkin was once limited to cases where physical injury to person or property has been caused. But it has been held in England,[32] and in Canada,[33] that the cost of repairing a defective product is recoverable before it has actually injured anyone, as well as the loss of profit on the re-sale of the product. Such economic loss is reasonably foreseeable, but the result is equivalent to saying that there is a warranty in tort as well as in contract that the article is reasonably fit for its purpose.[34] Some still believe that a claim in respect of unsuitable, as distinct from dangerous, products should be brought only in contract and not in tort.[35]

(7) "Owes a duty to take that reasonable care"

The onus of proving negligence rests on the plaintiff. There has been some dispute whether he can pray in aid the maxim *res ipsa loquitur*. In principle there seems to be no reason why he should not be permitted to do so.[36] Thus in *Grant* v. *Australian Knitting Mills* (in which the defendants showed that their factory was the most up to date possible and that they had sold over a million similar garments without complaint) the Judicial Committee said: "If excess sulphites were left in the garment, that could only be because someone was at fault. The appellant is not required to lay his finger on the exact person in all the chain who was responsible, or to specify what he did wrong. Negligence is found as a matter of inference from the existence of the defects taken in conjunction with all the known circumstances."[37] It is submitted that this is the better opinion, having been followed in a number of cases,[38] and supported by the Law Commission.[39]

---

[30] *Blacker* v. *Lake and Elliot* (1912) 106 L.T. 533, 541; *Kubach* v. *Hollands* |1937| 3 All E.R. 907; *Watson* v. *Buckley* |1940| 1 All E.R. 174; *Holmes* v. *Ashford* |1950| 2 All E.R. 76.

[31] *Hindustan SS. Co. Ltd.* v. *Siemens Bros. & Co. Ltd.* |1955| 1 Lloyd's Rep. 167.

[32] *Batty* v. *Metropolitan Realisations Ltd.* |1978| Q.B. 554 (loss of profit on house). But the Law Commission recommended that pure economic loss should be excluded because it could be covered by first-party insurance.

[33] *Rivtow Marine Ltd.* v. *Washington Iron Works* (1973) 40 D.L.R. 530. See Law Com. No. 64, §§ 94–114.

[34] Neither the Draft European Convention on Products Liability nor the Draft EEC Directive imposes liability for design defects or development defects.

[35] *Colgan* v. *Connolly Construction Co. Ltd.* (Irish High Court, February 29, 1980).

[36] *Contra*, Lord Macmillan in |1932| A.C. 562, 622.

[37] |1936| A.C. 85, 101. It will be recalled that Lord Macmillan was a member of the Board.

[38] *Cassidy* v. *Ministry of Health* |1951| 2 K.B. 343, 359; *Mason* v. *Williams and Williams Ltd.* |1955| 1 W.L.R. 549; *Lockhart* v. *Barr*, 1943 S.C. 1, *Hill* v. *Crowe Ltd.* |1978| 1 All E.R. 812 and *Martin* v. *Thorn Ltd.* |1978| W.A.R. 10; *Daniels* v. *White & Sons* |1938| 4 All E.R. 258 (manufacturers of lemonade containing carbolic acid excused when they proved "a fool-proof method" of cleaning and filling the bottles and adequate supervision) is not now followed in England.

[39] See Law Com. No. 64, §§ 39–45.

Date at which duty arises

For the purposes of the law relating to limitation of actions, it may be necessary to ascertain the moment of time at which the duty arises. It seems that the duty arises at the stage of manufacture and is a continuing duty, although the plaintiff's cause of action does not accrue until he has suffered damage[40] which is more than minimal.[41] The manufacturer's duty is a continuing one in the sense that if later research discloses a defect hitherto unknown, he should do what is reasonable to cure that defect, or even perhaps cease to market the product.[42] If there is indeed a duty to issue warning notices, or to recall the product, then this may be an exception to the general rule that there is no liability for omissions.

---

[40] *Watson* v. *Winget Ltd.*, 1960 S.C. 100, and below, § 221.
[41] *Cartledge* v. *Jopling & Sons Ltd.* [1963] A.C. 758. For undiscoverable damage, see below, § 221.
[42] *Wright* v. *Dunlop Rubber Co. Ltd.* (1973) 13 K.I.R. 250.

CHAPTER 13

THE RULE IN RYLANDS *v.* FLETCHER
AND LIABILITY FOR FIRE

§ 107. RULE IN RYLANDS *v.* FLETCHER[1]

The hazards arising from a highly developed technological society are often regulated by statute—*e.g.* the Nuclear Installations Act 1965 and 1967, the Control of Pollution Act 1974. The Pearson Commission[2] recommended that strict liability should be imposed by statute on controllers of unusually hazardous things (*e.g.* explosives) or of operations carrying a risk of serious casualties (*e.g.* dams and bridges). As new things and operations displayed extraordinarily dangerous[3] characteristics, they could be brought under the statute by statutory instrument. But at common law the judiciary have attempted to solve the problem by the development of the doctrine, principle or rule first clearly established in *Rylands* v. *Fletcher*.[4] This principle is one of the most important examples of absolute or strict[5] liability recognised by our law—one of the chief instances in which a man acts at his peril and is responsible for accidental harm, independently of the existence of either wrongful intent or negligence. The rule may be formulated thus:

The occupier of land who brings and keeps upon it anything likely to do damage if it escapes is bound at his peril to prevent its escape, and is liable for all the direct consequences of its escape, even if he has been guilty of no negligence.[6]

In *Rylands* v. *Fletcher* the two defendants[7] constructed a reservoir upon their land,[8] in order to supply water to their mill, and upon the site chosen for this purpose there was a disused and filled-up shaft of an old coal mine, the passages of which communicated with the adjoining mine of the plaintiff. Through the negligence of the contractors or engineers by whom the work was done (and who were not the employees of the defendants) this fact was not discovered, and the danger caused by it was not guarded against. When the reservoir was filled, the water escaped down the shaft and thence into the plaintiff's mine, which it flooded, causing damage estimated at £937.

In a judgment which has always been recognised as one of the masterpieces of the Law Reports, Blackburn J., for the Court of Exchequer

---

[1] See Prosser, *Topics*, Chap.III; Newark, "Non-Natural User and *Rylands* v. *Fletcher*" (1961) 24 M.L.R. 557; West, "Nuisance or *Rylands* v. *Fletcher*" (1966) 30 *The Conveyancer* 95; *Civil Liability for Dangerous Things and Activities* (Law Com. No. 32, 1970).

[2] Cmnd. 7054, Chap. 31.

[3] Since 1977 this is the term preferred by the *Restatement of Torts, Second*, instead of the former "ultra-hazardous."

[4] (1868) L.R. 3 H.L. 330.

[5] Winfield suggested ("The Myth of Absolute Liability" (1926) 42 L.Q.R. 37, 51) that "strict" was a better term than "absolute" in view of the admitted exceptions to the rule, and this is now recognised as the appropriate term in English law: *Read* v. *J. Lyons & Co.* [1945] K.B. 216, 226.

[6] *St. Anne's Well Brewery Co.* v. *Roberts* (1928) 140 L.T. 1, 6; *Hale* v. *Jennings Bros.* [1938] 1 All E.R. 579, 582, 584; *Read* v. *J. Lyons & Co. Ltd.* [1945] K.B. 216, 247; *Vaughn* v. *Halifax-Dartmouth Bridge Commission* (1961) 29 D.L.R. (2d) 523, 525.

[7] John Rylands and Jehu Horrocks.

[8] They seem to have been in occupation as lessees.

Chamber, held the defendants liable, and the House of Lords dismissed their appeal. Blackburn J. said[9]:

> "The question of law therefore arises, What is the obligation which the law casts on a person who, like the defendants, lawfully brings on his land something which, though harmless while it remains there, will naturally do mischief if it escapes out of his land? It is agreed on all hands that he must take care to keep in that which he has brought on the land and keeps there, in order that it may not escape and damage his neighbours: but the question arises whether the duty which the law casts upon him under such circumstances is an absolute duty to keep it at his peril or is, as the majority of the Court of Exchequer have thought, merely a duty to take all reasonable and prudent precautions in order to keep it in, but no more . . .
>
> We think that the true rule of law is that the person who for his own purposes brings on his lands and collects and keeps there anything likely to do mischief if it escapes, must keep it in at his peril, and if he does not do so is prima facie answerable for all the damage which is the natural consequence of its escape. He can excuse himself by showing that the escape was owing to the plaintiff's default; or, perhaps, that the escape was the consequence of *vis major* or the act of God; but as nothing of the sort exists here, it is unnecessary to inquire what excuse would be sufficient."[10]

§ 108. ORIGIN AND NATURE OF RULE[11]

It is important to distinguish between the immediate and the more remote origins of the Rule in *Rylands* v. *Fletcher*.

Immediate origins. The fundamental phrase in Sir Colin Blackburn's judgment is that which runs: "the person who for his own purposes brings on his lands and collects and keeps there anything likely to do mischief if it escapes." The basis of liability is the artificial accumulation of things not in or on the land by the ordinary course of nature. This can be clearly seen if we distinguish three cases of damage done by water:

(i) rain falls on the defendant's land, and the resultant water passes off by natural gravitation on to the plaintiff's premises. The defendant is not responsible, as there is no liability under *Rylands* v. *Fletcher* for things naturally on the land[12];

(ii) water accumulates itself on the defendant's land in the ordinary course of nature, and is released on to the plaintiff's land by the defendant carrying on his normal operations in a reasonable way. Thus in *Smith* v. *Kenrick*[13] it

---

[9] *Fletcher* v. *Rylands* (1866) L.R. 1 Ex. 265, 279.

[10] This sentence is significant: it shows that Blackburn J. himself recognised the possibility of exceptions to his general rule, so that liability may be strict but not absolute: see note 5, above.

[11] See Molloy, "*Fletcher* v. *Rylands*—A Re-Examination of Juristic Origins" (1941) 9 U.Chi.L.Rev. 266; Newark, "Non-Natural User and *Rylands* v. *Fletcher*" (1961) 24 M.L.R. 557; Prosser, *Topics*, Chap. III; Linden, "Whatever Happened to *Rylands* v. *Fletcher*?" in Klar (ed.), *Studies in Canadian Tort Law* (1978), p. 287.

[12] This always used to be considered indisputable, but the law appears to be changing with regard to a defendant's liability for things naturally on his land: see below, § 112.

[13] (1849) 7 C.B. 515.

was held that the plaintiff had no cause of action when water which had accumulated itself in a natural pool or reservoir flowed into the plaintiff's mine as a result of the ordinary mining operations of the defendant; and

(iii) water is accumulated artificially by the defendant for his own purposes and then flows on to the plaintiff's land. Here the defendant is liable. The distinction between the *Smith* v. *Kenrick* type of case and the *Rylands* v. *Fletcher* type of case is that between the escape of water naturally present on the defendant's land and the escape of water artificially accumulated there. The reasons of policy for such a distinction were clearly stated by Blackburn J.:

> "It seems but reasonable and just that the neighbour, who has brought something on his own property which was not naturally there, harmless to others so long as it is confined to his own property, but which he knows to be mischievous if it gets on his neighbour's, should be obliged to make good the damage which ensues if he does not succeed in confining it to his own property. But for his act in bringing it there no mischief could have occurred, and it seems but just that he should at his peril keep it there so that no mischief may accrue, or answer for the natural and anticipated consequences. And upon authority, this we think is established to be the law whether the things so brought be beasts, or water, or filth, or stenches."

Remoter origins of the rule

(i) *Historical*

The historical background of the rule in *Rylands* v. *Fletcher* was four-fold. In early law a landowner had four remedies against his neighbour whose use of his land injuriously affected him in the exclusive enjoyment of his property; the action of trespass where the injury was direct, the assize of nuisance in which the primary object of the proceedings was abatement, the action upon the case "upon the custom of the realm" for harm done by the spread of fire, and the action of cattle-trespass. To none of these actions (except perhaps that for the escape of fire[14]) was it a good defence to prove that the defendant was without fault. Blackburn J. did not intend to make new law[15] in *Rylands* v. *Fletcher*; he made a generalisation which covered the cases of absolute liability which had survived the general "moralisation" of the law in the eighteenth and nineteenth centuries. In the language of Wigmore, these cases of liability without fault "wandered about, unhoused and unshepherded, except for a casual attention, in the pathless fields of jurisprudence, until they were met by the master-mind of Mr. Justice Blackburn, who guided them to the safe fold where they have since rested. In a sentence epochal in its consequences this judge co-ordinated them all in their true category."[16]

---

[14] See below, § 117.

[15] This was Blackburn J.'s own opinion: "I wasted much time in the preparation of the judgment in *Rylands* v. *Fletcher* if I did not succeed in showing that the law held to govern it had been law for at least 300 years"; *Ross* v. *Fedden* (1872) 26 L.T. 966, 968.

[16] "Responsibility for Tortious Acts" (1894) 7 Harv. L. Rev. 441, 454. But Lord Simon has said that "it appears to me logically unnecessary and historically incorrect to refer to all these instances as deduced from one common principle." *Read* v. *Lyons* [1947] A.C. 156, 167.

(ii) Social

Some attention has also been given to the social or economic background of the case. No doubt the decision (like all decisions) is to some extent rooted in the society which gave it birth,[17] but there seems no foundation for the belief that Sir Colin Blackburn and the ten other judges who took part in the three stages of the case were influenced, consciously or unconsciously, by a desire to propitiate the dominant landed gentry of the time, who, it is alleged, regarded the right of exclusive dominion over land as paramount to its commercial exploitation.[18] The decision has also been attributed to the growth of collectivism,[19] but there is no real evidence for this hypothesis either.

The Future

Today, as the Law Commission has said,[20] strict liability is justified in respect of certain things and certain activities which involve special danger, *i.e.* a more than ordinary risk of accident or a risk of more than ordinary damage if accidents in fact result. The Pearson Commission has recommended[21] that there should be a statutory scheme of strict liability with power to add by statutory instrument new things or processes to the list.

Relationship to other torts

(i) Nuisance

A strong case can be made for the view that the rule in *Rylands* v. *Fletcher* is but an application or instance of liability in nuisance. Certainly Manisty Q.C.,[22] counsel for the plaintiffs, argued that the case fell to be decided on the *sic utere* (*i.e.* nuisance) principle,[23] and the authority he cited was almost entirely nuisance law.[24] Bramwell B., dissenting in the Court of

---

[17] "This basis of the English rule is to be found in the metereological conditions which obtain there. England is a pluvial country, where constant streams and abundant rains make the storage of water unnecessary for ordinary or general purposes ... In Texas we have conditions very different from those which obtain in England ... The country is almost without streams; and without the storage of water from rainfall in basins constructed for the purpose, or to hold waters pumped from the earth, the great livestock industry of West Texas must perish." *Turner* v. *Big Lake Oil Co.* (1936) 128 Tex. 155, 96 S.W. (2d) 221, 225–226, *per* Cureton J.

[18] This was the view put forward by Bohlen (*Studies*, pp. 368–369), but effectively criticised by Molloy, "*Fletcher* v. *Rylands*—A Re-Examination of Juristic Origins" (1941) 9 U. Chi. L.. Rev. 266 and Pound, "The Economic Interpretation and The Law of Torts," (1940) 53 Harv. L. Rev. 365, 383. It might be added that Rylands and Horrocks had developed their mill and reservoir with the consent of their lessor, the Earl of Wilton—a member of the family of Grosvenor, famous not only for the extent of their acres but also for the efficient commercial development of them.

[19] Dicey, *Law and Public Opinion in England* (2nd. ed.), p. 259 *et seq.*; see criticism by Buxton, "The Negligent Nuisance" (1966) 8 Malaya L.R. 1, 7.

[20] Law Com. No. 32, para. 7.

[21] Cmnd. 7054, Chap. 31.

[22] The case appears to have advanced the careers of those who argued it as well as the reputation of Blackburn J. for by the time the case reached the Exchequer Chamber, Manisty and Mellish (for the defendants) had both taken silk.

[23] 3 H. & C. 774, 781.

[24] *Smith* v. *Kenrick* (1849) 7 C.B. 515; *Aldred's Case* (1610) 9 Co. Rep. 576; *Tenant* v. *Goldwin* (1704) 2 Ld. Raym. 1089; *Williams* v. *Groucott* (1863) 4 B. & S. 149, 157; 122 E.R. 416, 419.

Exchequer, thought that the defendants could be held liable in nuisance,[25] and his judgment was effectively adopted by Blackburn J. on appeal. His Lordship could see no distinction between the man "whose mine is flooded by the water from his neighbour's reservoir" and the man "whose cellar is invaded by the filth of his neighbour's privy, or habitation is made unhealthy by the fumes and noisome vapours of his neighbour's alkali works": each "is damnified without any fault of his own."[26] He proceeded to compare the present case with several actions which had been brought "against the occupiers of some alkali works at Liverpool for the damage alleged to be caused by the chlorine fumes of their works"—clearly actions in nuisance. Those occupiers had been held liable. "There is no difference in this respect between chlorine and water; both will, if they escape, do damage, the one by scorching, the other by drowning."[27]

In the House of Lords, Lord Cairns L.C. fully accepted Blackburn J.'s judgment in the Exchequer Chamber and held that the case was indistinguishable from *Baird* v. *Williamson*,[28] a nuisance case. The case was to be distinguished from *Smith* v. *Kenrick*,[29] another nuisance case in which the defendants had avoided liability because of a defence of "ordinary use." To construct a reservoir was not an ordinary use, just as pumping up water was not an ordinary use in *Baird's* case[30]; consequently, the ordinary principles of nuisance applied, and the defendants were liable for allowing the water "to pass off into the close of the plaintiff."[31] Lord Cranworth's judgment was expressly founded on the *sic utere* principle.

The view that the rule in *Rylands* v. *Fletcher* was and is but an example of a nuisance action is receiving increasing judicial support. The fullest analysis to date has been that of Windeyer J. in the High Court of Australia in *Benning* v. *Wong*.[32] He saw the doctrine as merely "a special form of the ancient cause of action for nuisance" and said further that the distinctions tabulated for students of law by the writers of textbooks "between actionable nuisances of traditional kinds and *Rylands* v. *Fletcher* actions" were not fundamental.[32] Sir John Salmond, in his judicial capacity, held that "the actual or apprehended escape into [the plaintiff's] land from that of the defendant of a dangerous thing kept by the defendant—namely an artificial heap of soil" gave rise to an action in nuisance.[33] In *Read* v. *J. Lyons & Co. Ltd.*, the doctrine of *Rylands* v. *Fletcher* was said to derive "from a conception of mutual duties of adjoining or neighbouring land-owners" and as "in harmony with a strictly analogous branch of the law, the law of nuisance."[34] There are now many other cases to like effect[35] so that one can say that,

[25] 3 H. & C. 774, 789.
[26] (1866) L.R. 1 Ex. 265, 280.
[27] *Ibid.* 285–286.
[28] 15 C.B. (N.S.) 376; 143 E.R. 831.
[29] (1849) 7. C.B. 515.
[30] 15 C.B. (N.S.) 376; 143 E.R. 831.
[31] L.R. 3 H.L. 330, 339.
[32] (1969) 43 A.L.J.R. 467, 484; see too the judgment of Barwick, C.J. especially at p.471.
[33] *Knight* v. *Bolton* [1924] N.Z.L.R. 806, 808. "A heap of earth" was one of the very instances of liability cited by Blackburn J. And see the 6th. ed. of this book, pp.257 *et seq.*, where *Rylands* v. *Fletcher* was clearly seen as coming within the law of nuisance.
[34] [1947] A.C. 156, 173, 182.
[35] *Rickards* v. *Lothian* [1913] A.C. 263, 275; *Eastern and South African Telegraph Co.* v. *Cape Town Tramways Cos.* [1902] A.C. 381, 394; *Musgrove* v. *Pandelis* [1919] 2 K.B. 43, 47, 49, 51; *J. P. Porter Co. Ltd.* v. *Bell* [1955] 1 D.L.R. 62, 64; *Shell-Mex & B.P. Ltd.* v. *Belfast Corporation* [1952] N.I. 72, 75.

although most authority takes the view that *Rylands* v. *Fletcher* is distinct from nuisance, there is authority—indeed, sound authority from the House of Lords, the Privy Council and the High Court of Australia—to the contrary.

(ii) *Trespass*

Some judges, *e.g.* Stirling L.J.,[36] Parker J.[37] and Astbury J.,[38] have regarded the action under the rule in *Rylands* v. *Fletcher* as in the nature of trespass, the underlying idea being that a man releases some force brought by him onto his own property, which gets beyond his control and injures his neighbour. But clearly in most cases under the rule the injury done to the plaintiff is consequential and not direct.

(iii) *Negligence*

Other writers[39] have regarded the rule in *Rylands* v. *Fletcher* as a branch of the law of negligence. But it is perfectly clear that a man may be liable under the rule even though neither he nor anyone else has been guilty of any negligence in allowing the escape.[40] It is equally clear that he may be liable though he has done no unlawful act in introducing the dangerous thing onto his land. In practice the importance of the distinction can be seen from the fact that if the plaintiff states his claim on the principle of *Rylands* v. *Fletcher* he need plead only the escape, whereas if he states his claim in negligence he must plead and prove negligence. It has been suggested that these cases can be regarded as a special instance of negligence, where the law exacts a degree of diligence so high as to amount practically to a guarantee of safety.[41] But, if the concept of "duty of care" is to be meaningful, the defendant must always have the opportunity of meeting the standard required; it must never be the case that, because damage has occurred, one *automatically* assumes that the duty has been breached. By contrast, in *Rylands* v. *Fletcher*, care or the lack of it continues to be an irrelevant factor.[42]

§ 109. THE PLAINTIFF

Who may sue

This problem was much discussed by the House of Lords in *Read* v. *J. Lyons & Co. Ltd.*[43] The appellant was injured by an explosion in the respondents' munitions factory while performing her duties as an inspector

---

[36] *Foster* v. *Warblington U.C.* [1906] 1 K.B. 648, 672.
[37] *Jones* v. *Llanwrst U.C.* [1911] 1 Ch. 393, 403.
[38] *Hoare & Co.* v. *McAlpine* [1923] 1 Ch. 167, 175.
[39] Thayer, "Liability Without Fault" (1916) 29 Harv. L. Rev. 801.
[40] *Att.-Gen.* v. *Cory Bros.* [1921] A.C. 521, 539, 544. It is no defence that the defendant did not know of the dangerous character of that which he was keeping: it is no defence that there was no reason why he should know: *West* v. *Bristol Tramways* [1908] 2 K.B. 14, 16.
[41] *Donoghue* v. *Stevenson* [1932] A.C. 562, 611–612; *Haseldine* v. *Daw & Sons Ltd.* [1941] 2 K.B. 343, 355–356.
[42] *West* v. *Bristol Tramways* [1908] 2 K.B. 14, 16; *Att.-Gen.* v. *Cory Brothers* [1921] 1 A.C. 521, 539, 544; *Benning* v. *Wong*, 43 A.L.J.R. 467, 487.
[43] [1947] A.C. 156, 170. "Nothing could be simpler than the facts in this appeal; nothing more far-reaching than the discussion of fundamental legal principles to which it has given rise": Lord Macmillan.

of the Ministry of Supply. She neither alleged nor proved negligence on the respondents' part. "Boldly she averred and by her counsel maintained the averment before this House, that he who lawfully carries on the business of manufacturing high-explosive shells upon his premises, is, without proof of negligence, liable to any person lawfully upon those premises who suffers damage by reason of an explosion. For, she said, high-explosive shells are 'dangerous things' and the respondents knew it."[44] Her contention was unanimously repudiated. That high-explosive shells are "dangerous things" was admitted, but "the strict liability recognised by this House to exist in *Rylands* v. *Fletcher* is conditioned by two elements which I may call the condition of 'escape' from the land of something likely to do mischief if it escapes, and the condition of 'non-natural use' of the land."[45] The House reserved its opinion on the question of non-natural use,[46] for the case could be disposed of by denying that there had been an escape. It was stressed that "[t] he duty is to refrain from injuring not *alium* but *alienum*" and the principle was said to be no more than "a principle applicable between occupiers in respect of their land."[47] Lord Simonds held that the position was exactly analogous with the law of nuisance, where only he who had suffered an invasion of some proprietary or other interest in land had a lawful claim.[48]

It is not suggested that the action in *Rylands* v. *Fletcher* is limited to adjacent freeholders; the action in nuisance is not so limited. An "occupier" has been defined as one who has "some right or interest in land beyond that of a mere gratuitous licensee."[49] Thus, lessees[50] and licensees in exclusive occupation, including occupation of the sub-soil,[51] can maintain an action in *Rylands* v. *Fletcher* as in nuisance. Although there are dicta contrary to this view in some recent English decisions,[52] it has been stated explicitly in a

---

[44] [1947] A.C. 156, 179, *per* Lord Simonds. In the Court of Appeal her case was based not only on the rule in *Rylands* v. *Fletcher* but also on absolute liability for the "miscarriage of ultra-hazardous activities carefully carried on" formulated in 3 *Restatement of the Law of Torts*, s. 519. The Court held that English law did not recognise this doctrine "Ultra-hazardous" has now been replaced by the phrase "extraordinarily dangerous" in the *Restatement*.

[45] [1947] A.C. 156, 167, *per* Lord Simon. The need for an "escape" was re-emphasised in *J. Doltis Ltd.* v. *Isaac Braithwaite & Sons Ltd.* [1957] 1 Lloyd's Rep. 522.

[46] For this, see below § 110.

[47] *Ibid*. 173, *per* Lord Macmillan, 186, per Lord Uthwatt.

[48] *Ibid.* 182. Weak *obiter dicta* to the contrary in earlier cases must be considered overruled by these unequivocal speeches from their Lordships: *Miles* v. *Forest Rock Granite Co. (Leicestershire) Ltd.* (1918) 34 T.L.R. 500; *Shiffman* v. *The Grand Priory in the British Realm of the Venerable Order of the Hospital of St John of Jerusalem* [1936] 1 All E.R. 557 (both actually decided in negligence). Certainly neither case is binding on any court now: *cf. Halsey* v. *Esso Petroleum Co. Ltd.* [1961] 2 All E.R. 145, 152.

[49] *Benning* v. *Wong*, 43 A.L.J.R. 467, 494, *per* Windeyer J. The plaintiff was an occupier, and the remarks of Barwick C.J. and Menzies J. were carefully so confined (*ibid*. 467, 477). Wider *obiter dicta* to the effect that, even had the plaintiff not been an occupier, he would still have been able to sue (*ibid*. 494) were not assented to by the other members of the High Court.

[50] *Farrer* v. *Nelson* (1885) 15 Q.B.D. 258; *Federic* v. *Perpetual Investments Ltd.* (1968) 2 D.L.R. (3d) 50, 52.

[51] *Hale* v. *Jennings Brothers* [1938] 1 All E.R. 579; *Charing Cross Electricity Supply Co.* v. *Hydraulic Power Co.* [1914] 3 K.B. 772; *Eastern and South African Telegraph Co.* v. *Cape Town Tramways Cos.* [1902] A.C. 381; *Vaughn* v. *Halifax-Dartmouth Bridge Commission* (1961) 29 D.L.R. (2d) 523, 525 (licensee not in exclusive possession, therefore no action).

[52] *Perry* v. *Kendricks Transport Ltd.* [1956] 1 W.L.R. 85 (*obiter dicta* on this point, as case turned on defence of "act of a stranger"); *British Celanese Ltd* v. *A.H. Hunt (Capacitors) Ltd.* [1969] 2 All E.R. 1252, 1258, *per* Lawton J. (again *obiter dicta*, as plaintiff was in fact occupier).

recent New Zealand case that "liability under *Rylands* v. *Fletcher* requires proof of interference with the use of the land of another."[53] It is, of course, conceded that it is illogical to insist on the plaintiff's having an interest in land if *Rylands* v. *Fletcher* is seen as a form of liability for harm caused by dangerous things, or as an action to redress harm caused by extra-hazardous activities; for various reasons, it is submitted that *Rylands* v. *Fletcher* is neither.[54] However, that has undoubtedly influenced those who assert that the plaintiff need not be an occupier and that *Rylands* v. *Fletcher* is merely an action arising *from* occupation to land.[55]

Personal injuries

The analogy with nuisance provides the clue to the problem whether damages for personal injuries may be recovered under the rule in *Rylands* v. *Fletcher*. Some observations of Lord Macmillan in *Read* v. *Lyons*[56] have sometimes been interpreted to mean that damages for personal injuries can never be recovered unless negligence is proved. This is not so. Those observations must (like all other judicial statements) be read in the light of the facts of the particular case and mean no more than this: that a non-occupier must prove negligence before he can recover for personal injuries.[57]

The distinction turns on the character of the claimant and not on the character of his injuries. Blackburn J. himself allowed an occupier to recover for damage to his chattels under the rule in *Rylands* v. *Fletcher*,[58] although he was equally clear that a non-occupier had no such claim.[59] Both on principle and on authority the same conclusion follows in the case of personal injuries. On principle, for it would be absurd to suppose that the law did not give a remedy to an occupier who had been submerged under thousands of gallons of escaping water or oil. On authority, the Court of Appeal has held in *Hale* v. *Jennings Bros.*[60] and *Dunne* v. *North Western Gas Board*[61] that occupiers can recover in *Rylands* v. *Fletcher* for personal injuries. The High Court of Australia has similarly held that an occupier may recover for personal injuries.[62]

§ 110. NON-NATURAL USE OF LAND

The concept of "non-natural use" of land has caused more difficulty than any other aspect of the rule in *Rylands* v. *Fletcher*. Much of the difficulty stems from the fact that the concept finds no mention in Blackburn J.'s decision in the Exchequer Chamber, but appears for the first time in Lord

---

[53] *N.Z. Forest Products Ltd.* v. *O'Sullivan* [1974] N.Z.L.R. 80, 83.
[54] See s. 108.
[55] *e.g.* West, "Nuisance or *Rylands* v. *Fletcher*" (1966) 30 *The Conveyancer* 95, 101.
[56] [1947] A.C. 156, 173. *Cf.* Lord Simon at 168–169.
[57] See above, § 17.
[58] *Jones* v. *Festiniog Ry. Co.* (1868) L.R. 3 Q.B. 733. A similar decision is *Halsey* v. *Esso Petroleum Co. Ltd.* [1961] 1 W.L.R. 683. See also *Vaughn* v. *Halifax-Dartmouth Bridge Commission* (1961) 29 D.L.R. (2d) 523 and *British Celanese Ltd.* v. *A. H. Hunt (Capacitors) Ltd.* [1969] 2 All E.R. 1252.
[59] *Cattle* v. *Stockton Waterworks Co.* (1875) L.R. 10 Q. B. 453; approved by Widgery J. in *Weller* v. *Foot and Mouth Disease Research Institute* [1966] 1 Q.B. 569.
[60] [1938] 1 All E.R. 579.
[61] [1964] 2 Q.B. 806. But in *Aldridge* v. *Van Patter* [1952] 4 D.L.R. 93, non-occupiers were permitted to recover for personal injuries.
[62] *Benning* v. *Wong* (1969) 43 A.L.J.R. 467.

Cairns's judgment in the House of Lords. Some have therefore concluded that Lord Cairns's judgment is in some way at variance with Blackburn J.'s or that Lord Cairns added a further refinement to the rule or that there are "two rules."[63] But it is submitted that the explanation is clear if one examines carefully the arguments put forward by counsel. When the action first came before the Liverpool Assizes, Fletcher secured a verdict, subject to the award of an arbitrator, who was afterwards empowered by a judge's order to state a special case instead of making an award. There was a finding that the defendants had not been personally negligent, but that the contractors had been. This was a crucial finding of fact. It meant that, if the defendants were to succeed, they had to establish that the proper cause of action was negligence, for it had been held in *Quarman* v. *Burnett*[64] that an employer was liable for the negligence of his servants, but not for the negligence of his independent contractors. The only negligence found in this case was the contractors'. The defendants were doomed if nuisance were held to be the appropriate cause of action, for in nuisance an employer (*qua* occupier) remains liable notwithstanding the fact that the specific act causing the harm is perpetrated by a contractor: there was clear authority before 1865 to that effect.[65] Thus, the defendants did not even acknowledge that nuisance was the appropriate cause of action, and certainly did not attempt to rely on the defence of ordinary or natural use, which had recently been authoritatively established as a defence to a claim in nuisance.[66] It would be most irregular for a judge to raise a defence in his judgment which had not been argued before him.

When the case came on appeal before the House of Lords, tactics changed. Battle on nuisance was joined. All the leading cases on ordinary and reasonable use were cited. Manisty Q.C. strongly submitted that the case was indistinguishable from *Baird* v. *Williamson*[67] and discussed "the proper and ordinary way of working mining property."[68] In his judgment, Lord Cairns dealt at length with this argument; for the rest, he was content to adopt Blackburn J.'s judgment, but this point had not been argued in the Exchequer Chamber. Lord Cairns acknowledged that use "in the ordinary course of the enjoyment of land"—almost Baron Bramwell's very words in *Bamford* v. *Turnley*[69]—was lawful, and this sort of use he termed "natural user." "Natural" obviously must be equated with "ordinary."[70]

Lord Cairns then turned from that example, which was illustrated by *Smith* v. *Kenrick*,[71] to another example, which was illustrated by *Baird* v. *Williamson*.[72] Where the defendant did not stop at the natural or ordinary use of his land but used it for a purpose termed "non-natural" the defendant

---

[63] *Porter (J.P.) Co. Ltd.* v. *Bell* [1955] 1 D.L.R. 62, 66.
[64] (1840) 6 M. & W. 499.
[65] *Laugher* v. *Pointer* (1826) 5 B. & C. 547, 108 E.R. 204; *Reedie* v. *London and North Western Railway* (1849) 4 Ex. 244, 154 E.R. 1201; *Knight* v. *Fox* (1850) 5 Ex. 721, 155 E.R. 316; *Overton* v. *Freeman* (1852) 11 C.B. 867, 138 E.R. 717.
[66] *Bamford* v. *Turnley*, 3 B. & S. 62, 122 E.R. 25; *St. Helen's Smelting* v. *Tipping*, 11 H.L.C. 642; 11 E.R. 1483.
[67] 15 C.B. (N.S.) 376; 143 E.R. 831.
[68] L.R. 3 H.L. 330, 336.
[69] 3 B. & S. 62, 83; 122 E.R. 25, 33.
[70] Stallybrass, "Dangerous Things and the Non-Natural User of Land," (1929) 3 C.L.J. 376, 390–1.
[71] 7 C.B. 515, 137 E.R. 205.
[72] 15 C.B. (N.S.) 376; 143 E.R. 831.

was liable for any damage caused to a neighbour. Natural or ordinary use was thus contrasted with non-natural or extraordinary use. Later cases support this interpretation.[73] Thus, the defence of reasonable use in nuisance[74] and the defence of natural use in *Rylands* v. *Fletcher* both have a common origin and have developed similarly. The requirements of the defence are discussed in detail above.[75]

§ 111. DANGEROUS THINGS

To what "things" does the rule in *Rylands* v. *Fletcher* apply? Blackburn J.'s language is very wide—"anything likely to do mischief if it escapes." He did not restrict the rule to things likely to escape; or to cases in which the defendant is making use of his land in a way which is fraught with exceptional peril to others. Most things are likely to do mischief if they escape, and it seems that notwithstanding the breadth of Blackburn J.'s language, we must treat the rule as subject to both limitations.[76] So subsequent decisions have equated the expression with "dangerous things."[77] We have seen[78] that it is difficult to find a test by which to distinguish those things which are dangerous in themselves. It is not much easier to discover what are the things which are likely to do mischief if they escape. An examination of all the cases in which the rule in *Rylands* v. *Fletcher* has been held to apply does not carry us very far. Chemicals, fire and electricity are always treated as falling under the rule; water, trees, chimney stacks, motor-cars and unloaded guns sometimes do and sometimes do not come under it.

It would seem that it is necessary for the defendant to have knowledge of the danger. In *Rylands* v. *Fletcher* itself, Blackburn J. said that liability arose only if the thing brought on to the property was *known to be mischievous*.[79] In later cases based on the principle, the courts have held that knowledge of the harm was a prerequisite of liability[80] and have used as a guide "the common experience of mankind."[81]

Indeed, it may be that the whole concept of "dangerousness" is but another way of saying that harm must be foreseeable. That a thing is

---

[73] Although Newark did not in his article in 24 M.L.R. 557. Newark himself concedes, however, that this was the accepted interpretation after about 1885 (although Newark asserts that the later cases are in error). But *cf.* Stallybrass, 3 C.L.J. 376, 396, and Goodhart, "Liability for Things Naturally on the Land," (1930) 4 C.L.J. 13, 24. Cases supporting this interpretation are *Nichols* v. *Marsland* (1875) L.R. 10 Ex. 255, 260, *per* Bramwell B.; *Wilson* v. *Waddell* (1876) 2 App. Cas. 95, 99–100, *per* Lord Blackburn: *Farrer* v. *Nelson*, 15 Q.B.D. 258, 260; *National Telephone Co.* v. *Baker* [1893] 2 Ch. 186; *West* v. *Bristol Tramways Co.* [1908] 2 K.B. 14.

[74] "Reasonable use" is a deceptive term to the extent that it suggests that the defendant must prove only that his use was reasonable—but it is a convenient expression and less ambiguous than "natural use."

[75] See above, § 22(5).

[76] L.R. 1 Ex. 265, 279. In *Jones* v. *Festiniog Ry. Co.* (1868) L.R. 3 Q.B. 733, 736, 738, a railway engine was described by Blackburn J. as "a thing of a dangerous nature."

[77] See Stallybrass (1929) 3 Camb. L.J. 378; *Northwestern Utilities Ltd.* v. *London Guarantee Co.* [1936] A.C. 108, 118 and *Hale* v. *Jennings Bros.* [1938] 1 All E.R. 579.

[78] Above § 104.

[79] L.R. 1 Ex. 265, 280.

[80] *Ball* v. *Nye* (1868) 99 Mass, 582, 584. *Imperial Furniture Pty. Ltd.* v. *Automatic Fire Sprinklers Ltd.* [1967] 1 N.S.W.R. 29, 38.

[81] *Crowhurst* v. *Amersham Burial Board* (1878) 4 Ex. D. 5, 12; *Sullivan* v. *Creed* [1904] 2 Ir. R. 317, 325; *West* v. *Bristol Tramways Co.* [1908] 2 K.B. 14, 21.

"dangerous" simply means that it is "likely to cause damage,"[82] and that is neither more nor less than a finding that harm is foreseeably likely to result. There is no reason in principle why a tort of strict liability (in the sense that negligence need not be established) is incompatible with a concept of foreseeability.[83] Certainly, in *Benning* v. *Wong*,[84] Windeyer J. thought that foreseeability of harm was now applicable to *Rylands* v. *Fletcher* cases, just as it is now applicable in nuisance.[85]

§ 112. THINGS NATURALLY ON LAND

It was once thought that a defendant could not be liable under the rule in *Rylands* v. *Fletcher* if the thing which escaped was the product of natural forces or had accumulated itself on the defendant's land. Thus in *Giles* v. *Walker*[86] it was held that the occupier of land was not liable when he ploughed up forest land and in consequence a large crop of thistles sprang up and the thistledown was blown onto the neighbouring land.[87] But in *Leakey* v. *National Trust*[88] it was held that developments in negligence and nuisance have eroded the decision in *Giles* v. *Walker*. Such a defendant may now be held liable in negligence[89] or in nuisance.[90]

This is the position today under *Rylands* v. *Fletcher* as well. It must be remembered, however, that to have things naturally on land will *prima facie* constitute an ordinary and reasonable use of land, but a defendant will be liable for their escape unless his failure to prevent their escape is reasonable in all the circumstances.[91]

§ 113. CONSENT OF THE PLAINTIFF

The rule in *Rylands* v. *Fletcher* is subject to a number of important exceptions, there being particular classes of cases in which the occupier is either not liable at all, or not liable in the absence of negligence. When stated without the exceptions, it is a rule of absolute liability, but there are so many exceptions to it that it has been said to be doubtful whether there is much of the rule left.[92] The rule is not applicable to the escape of things brought or kept upon his premises by the defendant with the consent of the plaintiff. In such cases the defendant is not liable except for negligence.[93] Although not so limited,[94] this principle finds its chief application in those cases in which the different storeys of a building are in the occupation of different persons, and the occupant of a lower storey complains of the damage done by the

---

[82] *Mulholland & Tedd Ltd.* v. *Baker* [1939] 3 All E.R. 253, 256.
[83] Carroll, 8 Ir. Jur. 208, 222–223.
[84] 43 A.L.J.R. 467, 494.
[85] See above, § 20.
[86] (1890) 24 Q.B.D. 656.
[87] "It may be that the court was disinclined to regard thistledown as sufficiently noxious to be dignified as a nuisance, and in 1890 agriculture was perhaps the least regarded of British industries.": *Davey* v. *Harrow Corporation* [1958] 1 Q.B. 60, 72, *per curiam*.
[88] [1980] Q.B. 485.
[89] *French* v. *Auckland City Corporation* [1974] 1 N.Z.L.R. 340 (decision same whether in nuisance or negligence).
[90] *Morgan* v. *Khyatt* [1964] 1 W.L.R. 475: (In the course of the argument, Viscount Simonds said *Davey* v. *Harrow Corporation* had been rightly decided).
[91] See above, § 22(5).
[92] *St. Anne's Well Brewery Co.* v. *Roberts* (1928) 140 L.T. 1, 6.
[93] *Att.-Gen.* v. *Cory Bros. & Co.* [1921] 1 A.C. 521, 539.
[94] *Kiddle* v. *City Business Properties Ltd.* [1942] 1 K.B. 269, 274.

escape of water from an upper storey. The water has been collected or brought there for the mutual benefit and with the express or implied consent of both parties; there is therefore no sufficient reason why the risk of accident should lie upon the upper rather than upon the lower occupant, and the only duty is one of reasonable care.[95] The same principle would doubtless apply to an escape of gas or any other deleterious substance[96] which is there with the consent and for the mutual benefit of the occupants. In most of these cases the benefit of the water or other thing is common to both parties, but the mutual benefit, though an important element in showing that there was consent, is not decisive. It has been said that the exception really depends upon the fact that the defendant has taken the premises as they are and must put up with the consequences.[97] But it is hard to reconcile this assertion with the established rule that it is no defence that the plaintiff came to the nuisance.[98]

§ 114. THE ACT OF A STRANGER

The rule in *Rylands* v. *Fletcher* is not applicable to damage done by the act of a stranger. Thus if a trespasser lights a fire on my land I am not liable if it burns my neighbour's property,[99] unless with knowledge or presumed knowledge of its existence I have failed to extinguish it within a reasonable time.[1] So in *Box* v. *Jubb*[2] the defendants were held not responsible for damage done through an overflow from their reservoir, when that overflow was caused by an act of a third person who emptied his own reservoir into the stream which fed that of the defendant. So in *Rickards* v. *Lothian*[3] it was held by the Judicial Committee on this ground that the occupier of an upper storey of a block of flats was not liable for damage done to the occupier of a lower storey by the escape of water from a lavatory, when the escape was caused by the malicious act of a third person. In this context malicious means a conscious or deliberate[4] act which could not reasonably have been foreseen. It has been held that sky-larking at a fair is "just the kind of behaviour that ought to have been anticipated. People go there in a spirit of fun."[5] The onus is on the defendant to show affirmatively that the escape was due to the deliberate or conscious act of a stranger over whom he had no control and against whose acts he could not reasonably be expected to have taken precautions.[6]

But it should be noted that an occupier may be liable in negligence for the

---

[95] *Akerib* v. *Booth Ltd.* [1960] 1 W.L.R. 454, 458 (reversed on another ground [1961] 1 W.L.R. 367).
[96] *Collingwood* v. *Home and Colonial Stores* [1936] 3 All E.R. 200 (domestic electric wiring).
[97] *Prosser (A.) & Son Ltd.* v. *Levy* [1955] 1 W.L.R. 1224.
[98] See above § 18.
[99] *Balfour* v. *Barty-King* [1957] 1 Q.B. 496, 504.
[1] *Goldman* v. *Hargrave* [1967] 1 A.C. 645.
[2] (1879) 4 Ex. D. 76.
[3] [1913] A.C. 263.
[4] *Northwestern Utilities* v. *London Guarantee Co.* [1936] A.C. 108, 119. *Cf. Dominion Natural Gas Co.* v. *Collins* [1909] A.C. 640, 647 ("the conscious act of another volition": Lord Dunedin); *Smith* v. *G.W. Ry.* (1926) 42 T.L.R. 391; *Philco Radio Ltd.* v. *Spurling* [1949] 2 All E.R. 882; *Perry* v. *Kendricks Transport Ltd.* [1956] 1 W.L.R. 85, 90.
[5] *Hale* v. *Jennings Bros.* [1938] 1 All E.R. 579, 585.
[6] *Northwestern Utilities* v. *London Guarantee Co.* [1936] A.C. 108, 120; *Prosser (A.) & Sons Ltd.* v. *Levy* [1955] 1 W.L.R. 1224.

acts of strangers even though he escapes liability under the rule in *Rylands* v. *Fletcher*. When the stranger's act is of a kind which ought to have been anticipated and guarded against the occupier will be liable for a failure to take reasonable care. Thus in *Northwestern Utilities* v. *London Guarantee and Accident Co.*[7] the appellants, who were carrying gas at high pressure under the streets of Edmonton, Alberta, were held liable when an hotel insured by the respondents was destroyed owing to the escape of gas due to a leak caused by the operations of third persons, since those operations were conspicuous and ought to have been foreseen and guarded against. But "They left it all to chance,"[8] and were thereby guilty of negligence.[9]

It does not clearly appear, however, who is a stranger within the meaning of this rule. The term certainly includes a trespasser, and also any person who, without entering on the defendant's premises at all, wrongfully and without the defendant's authority causes the escape of dangerous things from those premises.[10] It is equally clear that the term stranger does not include any person employed or authorised by the defendant to deal in any way with dangerous things on his land; for the acts of such a person, even though he is an independent contractor, and even though he acts in excess or disregard of his authority, the occupier is liable.[11] But what shall be said of persons lawfully upon the defendant's land with his permission, but without authority to bring upon it, or to deal with, dangerous things—for example, the members of his family, his employees, his guests, or licensees permitted to use the land? It is submitted that the occupier is liable for the acts of all such persons in bringing or keeping dangerous things on the premises, or in meddling with such things already on the premises[12] unless it can be said that in all the circumstances the occupier had no control over the activities of the person in question.[13]

§ 115. ACT OF GOD

Much printers' ink has been used (and wasted) over the years in learned commentaries upon the "defence" of Act of God—and yet it is believed that the defence has been successfully raised only once. That was in *Nichols* v. *Marsland*.[14] The defendant was in possession of certain artificial pools formed by damming a natural stream. The embankments and weirs were well and carefully constructed and were adequate for all ordinary occasions. A very violent storm, however—described by witnesses as the heaviest within

---

[7] [1936] A.C. 108. See the article by Lord Wright (who delivered the judgment of the Judicial Committee) in his *Legal Essays*, Chap. 5, and Goodhart, "The Third Man" [1951] C.L.P. 177.

[8] [1936] A.C. 108, 127.

[9] *Shell-Mex and B.P. Ltd.* v. *Belfast Corporation* [1952] N.I. 72 is a similar case.

[10] *Box* v. *Jubb* (1879) 4 Ex. D. 76. It also includes an employee acting in a place to which he is forbidden access: *Stevens* v. *Woodward* (1881) 6 Q.B.D. 318, 321.

[11] *Hale* v. *Jennings Bros.* [1938] 1 All E.R. 579, 583; *Balfour* v. *Barty-King* [1957] 1 Q.B. 496, 504.

[12] This may be inferred by analogy from such cases as *Beaulieu* v. *Finglam* (1401) Y.B. 2 Hen. IV, f. 18, pl. 6, and *Lawrence* v. *Jenkins* (1873) L.R. 8 Q.B. 274. But see *Whitmores Ltd.* v. *Stanford* [1909] 1 Ch. 427, 438.

[13] *Perry* v. *Kendricks Transport Ltd.* [1956] 1 W.L.R. 85, 90; *Behrens* v. *Bertram Mills Circus Ltd.* [1957] 2 Q.B. 1, 22.

[14] (1876) 2 Ex. D. 1. See the criticism of this case by Goodhart, "The Third Man" [1951] C.L.P. 177, 178–182.

human memory—broke down the embankments, and the rush of water down the stream carried away certain bridges, in respect of which damage the action was brought. It was held, notwithstanding *Rylands* v. *Fletcher*, that the defendant was not liable, inasmuch as the jury had found that there was no negligence on the part of anyone and that the accident was due directly to the Act of God.

In *Greenock Corporation* v. *Caledonian Railway Co.*,[15] on the other hand, a case with very similar facts, the defence was unsuccessful, even though rain fell in "a heavy, it may be an extraordinary and it may be an unprecedented, spate."[16] The two decisions cannot stand together[17] and their Lordships in effect said that the earlier case was wrong.[18] The *Greenock Corporation* case[19] has since been followed by the House of Lords in the *Sedleigh-Denfield* case.[20]

It is submitted that the defence should be relegated to the pages of legal history[21] as its purpose has been taken over by the concept of foreseeability of harm. If the wall of a house collapses solely because of an earthquake, then the owner of the house may not be liable for the damage because harm was not foreseeable, not because earthquakes are Acts of God.

§ 116. STATUTORY AUTHORITY

Sometimes a statute imposes strict liability for the escape of dangerous things, *e.g.* the Reservoirs Act 1975, in respect of accumulated water, or the Nuclear Installations Act 1965 and 1969, in respect of the escape of ionising radiations.[22] Again an International Convention has attempted to regulate responsibility for oil pollution on the high seas.[23] The problem of toxic waste is a real one today. The Litter Acts 1958 to 1971 have been reinforced by the Control of Pollution Act 1974. More often a statute authorises or requires the performance of a dangerous activity but is silent about the application of the rule in *Rylands* v. *Fletcher*. It has sometimes been said that a local authority exercising statutory duties (*e.g.* of sewage disposal) is altogether outside the rule in *Rylands* v. *Fletcher*.[24] It seems, however, that the better view is that a local authority or other body exercising statutory powers or duties is within the scope of the rule unless the statute expressly or impliedly exempts it from the liability to which it would otherwise be subject. Some judges have asserted that it may well be right to construe the statute in a manner favourable to the defendant.[25] Thus in *Green* v. *Chelsea*

---

[15] [1917] A.C. 556.
[16] *Ibid.* 580.
[17] "[T]here is [no] difference on this topic between the law of England and that of Scotland": *Greenock Corporation* v. *Caledonian Railway Co.* [1917] A.C. 556, 579.
[18] [1917] A.C. 556, 575, 580–581. Lord Wrenbury (at 584) distinguished *Nichols* v. *Marsland* on the ground that the facts were different, but he seems to have misunderstood the facts of the earlier case—in both cases, the pools were formed by daming a stream.
[19] [1917] A.C. 556.
[20] [1940] A.C. 880, 886; *Nichols* v. *Marsland* was not cited.
[21] Jolowicz, [1968] C.L.J. 50, 62. The defence is not recognised in the American *Restatement* (s.522).
[22] Note that s.12 channels liability on to the licensee of the site: no other person can be sued.
[23] See Ingram, "Oil Pollution and *Rylands* v. *Fletcher*" (1971) 121 N.L.J. 183.
[24] See Denning L.J. in *Pride of Derby and Derbyshire Angling Association* v. *British Celanese* [1953] Ch. 149, 189. *Contra* Evershed M.R. at 176.
[25] *Northwestern Utilities Ltd.* v. *London Guarantee and Accident Co.* [1936] A.C. 108; *Smeaton* v. *Ilford Corporation* [1954] Ch. 450.

Waterworks Co.[26] a main belonging to the defendant company burst, and the water flooded the plaintiff's premises. It was held by the Court of Appeal that the company, being authorised by Act of Parliament to lay the main, and having a statutory duty to maintain a continuous supply of water, and having been guilty of no negligence, was not liable in damages to the plaintiff. The governing principle is that statutory powers are meant to be exercised. The defence of statutory authority is further considered below.[27]

§ 117. LIABILITY FOR FIRE[28]

At common law

Liability for damage done by the spread of fire was established many centuries before the rule in *Rylands* v. *Fletcher* was formulated. The usual remedy was trespass upon the case for negligently allowing one's fire to escape in contravention of the general custom of the realm. The allegation was that the defendant *tam negligenter custodivit ignem suum* that the plaintiff's property was burnt. Difficulty has arisen over both parts of this phrase.

Tam negligenter. Whatever this meant, it was not negligence in the modern sense.[29] There is some authority[30] that the common law held an occupier absolutely liable for damage done by fire, but also some authority the other way.[31] It is unlikely that the matter will ever need to be settled. The Act of 1774 clearly assumes that liability was not, but ought to be, based on fault.

Ignis suus. As there must also be an escape of the fire from the defendant's premises to some place or thing outside those premises,[32] the courts seem to be anxious to equate this form of liability with nuisance and *Rylands* v. *Fletcher*. So it has even been held that the defendant is liable in his capacity as occupier of premises, and not on the ground of ordinary negligence.[33] It must be remembered that more than one person may be the occupier of premises.[34] The occupier is liable for fires negligently started or spread by his servants, contractors or lawful visitors.[35] But he is not liable for a fire started by an act of God[36] or a stranger whose activities cannot be controlled, although they may have been foreseen[37]—such a fire is not *ignis suus*.

[26] (1894) 70 L.T. 547.
[27] See below, § 191.
[28] See Newark, "The Accidental Fires Act (Northern Ireland)" (1945) 6 N.I.L.Q. 134 (the scope of which is wider than the title of the article suggests); Ogus, "Vagaries in Liability for the Escape of Fire" [1969] C.L.J. 104.
[29] *Hargrave* v. *Goldman* (1964) 110 C.L.R. 24, 56.
[30] *Collingwood* v. *Home and Colonial Stores Ltd.* [1936] 3 All E.R. 200, 203; *Mulholland and Tedd Ltd.* v. *Baker* [1939] 3 All E.R. 253, 255; and above, § 108.
[31] *Turberville* v. *Stampe* (1697) 1 Ld. Raym. 264 (in which Holt C.J. clearly assumed that liability was based on negligence); *Commissioner for Railways* v. *Wise Bros. Pty.* (1947) 75 C.L.R. 59.
[32] *Doltis Ltd.* v. *Braithwaite Ltd.* [1957] 1 Lloyd's Rep. 522; and above, § 109.
[33] *Sturge* v. *Hackett* [1962] 1 W.L.R. 1257.
[34] *H. & N. Emanuel Ltd.* v. *Greater London Council* [1971] 2 All E.R. 835.
[35] *H. & N. Emanuel Ltd.* v. *Greater London Council* [1971] 2 All E.R. 835.
[36] *Hargrave* v. *Goldman* (1964) 110 C.L.R. 24, 56.
[37] *Holderness* v. *Goslin* [1975] 2 N.Z.L.R. 46.

Under statute

The Fires Prevention (Metropolis) Act 1774,[38] which substantially re-enacted an Act of 1706 (6 Anne c. 31), provides "that no action, suit, or process whatever shall be had, maintained, or prosecuted against any person in whose house, chamber, stable, barn, or other building, or on whose estate any fire shall . . . accidentally begin, nor shall any recompense be made by such person for any damage suffered thereby, any law, usage or custom to the contrary notwithstanding." Some of the difficulties which have arisen may be noted.

"in whose house . . . or on whose estate." The Act's protection will not, therefore, apply when a steam-engine is used on the highway.[39]

"any fire." It is almost certain that the Act is not limited to fires caused by lightning or spontaneous combustion, but extends to fires intentionally lit which then spread accidentally from the defendant's premises. Otherwise the scope of the Act would be so limited as to be almost useless.[40]

"shall . . . accidentally begin." One possible interpretation of this phrase is that it abolished all liability for accidental fires, whether they are due to negligence or not.[41] But it was held in *Filliter* v. *Phippard*,[42] which has been approved in the Judicial Committee,[43] that the statute extends only to fires caused by mere chance, or incapable of being traced to any cause,[44] and that fires due to negligence are still a source of liability.[45] So are fires due to a nuisance created by the landlord or those for whom he is responsible.[46]

"begin." In *Musgrove* v. *Pandelis*[47] it was further held that the statute confers no protection even if the fire begins without negligence, provided that the spread of it which did the mischief complained of was due to negligence. The fire which accidentally begins, within the meaning of the statute, is the fire which actually does the mischief and not the fire in its initial and harmless stage.[48] Hence, since the statute there can be no liability for accidental fire only if there is no negligence on the part of anyone concerned. The present law is a rule of vicarious liability for the negligent acts of all persons except mere strangers—not a rule of absolute liability for accidents for which no one is to blame. Thus there was no liability when, in the absence of any evidence of negligence, such as the fire being too large for

---

[38] s. 86. This Act despite its title is not limited to London: *Filliter* v. *Phippard* (1847) 11 Q.B. 347. In Ireland, similar provisions are contained in the Accidental Fires Act 1943.
[39] *Mansel* v. *Webb* (1919) 88 L.J.K.B. 323.
[40] Holdsworth, H.E.L., Vol. xi, p. 608.
[41] The opinion of Blackstone: Bl. Comm., Vol. i, p. 431.
[42] (1847) 11 Q.B. 347.
[43] *Goldman* v. *Hargrave* [1967] 1 A.C. 645.
[44] As in *Collingwood* v. *Home and Colonial Stores* [1936] 3 All E.R. 200.
[45] The onus is on the plaintiff to prove negligence: *Mason* v. *Levy Auto Parts of England Ltd.* [1967] 2 Q.B. 530.
[46] *Spicer* v. *Smee* [1946] 1 All E.R. 489; *Williams* v. *Owen* [1955] 1 W.L.R. 1293.
[47] [1919] 2 K.B. 43.
[48] *Sturge* v. *Hackett* [1962] 1 W.L.R. 1257; *Goldman* v. *Hargrave* [1967] 1 A.C. 645, 665.

the grate, the ordinary domestic fire of a lodger spread from the fireplace and damaged the house.[49]

"nor shall any recompense be made by such person." At common law it was well established that an occupier was liable for his employees[50] acting within the scope of their employment,[51] or guests,[52] or those who had entered his house by his leave or knowledge,[53] and in this respect the statute of 1774 as interpreted by *Filliter* v. *Phippard* is probably merely declaratory of the common law. It is also settled that an occupier is responsible for an escape of fire caused by the negligence of his independent contractor.[54] Although an occupier has no right to control the mode in which a contractor performs his task,[55] he yet has control over him in the sense that he has invited him onto the premises and can require him to leave.[56] An occupier will not, however, be responsible for the acts of a mere stranger over whom he has no control, such as a trespasser[57]—unless with knowledge of the fire started by the stranger, he has failed to extinguish it within a reasonable time.[58]

"any law, usage or custom ... notwithstanding." It follows from this phrase that an innkeeper is entitled to the protection of the Act, and is not under his strict common law liability.[59] But in *Musgrove* v. *Pandelis*[60] it was held that the statute did not afford a good defence when the rule in *Rylands* v. *Fletcher* applied. Such a fire did not "accidentally begin." In so holding the Court of Appeal went very far.[61] In *Musgrove* v. *Pandelis* the defendant's motor-car caught fire in his garage, over which the plaintiff occupied rooms which were burnt out. It was held that a motor-car with its tank full of petrol was a mischievous thing within the rule in *Rylands* v. *Fletcher* and that therefore the defendant must make good the loss. Although it may be doubted whether the rule in *Rylands* v. *Fletcher* was correctly applied to the facts of this case,[62] the decision has, however, been followed.[63] But the *Musgrove* v. *Pandelis* principle has been restated so as to impose liability only when (i) the defendant brought onto his land things likely to catch fire, and kept them there in such conditions that, if they did ignite, the fire would be likely to spread to the plaintiff's land, and (ii) he did these things in the course of some non-natural use of the land.[64]

---

[49] *Sochacki* v. *Sas* [1947] 1 All E.R. 344.
[50] *Beaulieu* v. *Finglam* (1401) Y.B. 2 Hen. IV, f. 18, pl. 6. Yet note that the Act 6 Anne c. 31, imposed on the employee by whose negligence the fire began a fine of £100, to be distributed amongst the victims. This is very unlike the modern notion of vicarious liability.
[51] *Eriksen* v. *Clifton* [1963] N.Z.L.R. 705.
[52] *Boulcott Golf Club Inc.* v. *Engelbrecht* [1945] N.Z.L.R. 556.
[53] *Turberville* v. *Stampe* (1697) 1 Ld. Raym. 264; *Balfour* v. *Barty-King* [1957] 1 Q.B. 496.
[54] *H. & N. Emanuel Ltd.* v. *Greater London Council* [1971] 2 All E.R. 835.
[55] See below, § 184.
[56] *Balfour* v. *Barty-King* [1957] 1 Q.B. 496.
[57] *Balfour* v. *Barty-King* [1957] 1 Q.B. 496, 504.
[58] *Goldman* v. *Hargrave* [1967] 1 A.C. 645. See above, § 20.
[59] *Williams* v. *Owen* [1955] 1 W.L.R. 1293. In Ireland it is otherwise: see the Hotel Proprietors Act 1963, s. 11.
[60] [1919] 2 K.B. 43. See too *Mulholland & Tedd Ltd.* v. *Baker* [1939] 3 All E.R. 253, 256; *MacKenzie* v. *Sloss* [1959] N.Z.L.R. 533.
[61] *Mason* v. *Levy Auto Parts of England Ltd.* [1967] 2 Q.B. 530, 541.
[62] See above, § 110.
[63] *Mulholland and Tedd Ltd.* v. *Baker* [1939] 3 All E.R. 253; *Balfour* v. *Barty-King* [1956] 1 W.L.R. 779.
[64] *Mason* v. *Levy Auto Parts of England Ltd.* [1967] 2 Q.B. 530.

Who may sue

The right of action is not limited to the adjoining occupier. "If I happen to be on somebody else's land at a time when a fire spreads to that land and my motor-car or property is destroyed, I have just as much right against the person who improperly allows the fire to escape from his land as the owner of the land on which I happen to be."[65]

Who may be sued

Primarily liability rests upon occupancy or control of premises, rather than on the fact that the defendant has failed to control "his fire" (*ignis suus*).[66]

Reform

It will be observed that the protection conferred by section 86 is very limited—at least as the section has been interpreted—and it may well be that the time is fast approaching when section 86 should be repealed. There is no justification today for fire being treated any differently from any other dangerous thing on one's land, and social conditions have changed dramatically in two important respects since 1774: an occupier can now insure himself (and nearly always does) against damage to others and to himself caused by the spread of fire, and modern fire fighting techniques and equipment make it relatively easy to confine a fire within a limited area. There is now little risk of an "accidental" fire destroying streets of houses, and the occupier of the house from which the fire spreads being liable to dozens of occupiers.

---

[65] *Sochacki* v. *Sas* [1947] 1 All E.R. 344, 345, *per* Lord Goddard C.J.

[66] *Sturge* v. *Hackett* [1962] 1 W.L.R. 1257. If the Court of Appeal in this case had adopted the latter view, the liability of the defendant's insurers would have been limited to £10,000, and not extended to £100,000. Liability for fires caused by the escape of sparks or cinders from locomotives is now governed by the Railway Fires Acts 1905 and 1923, which provide that railway companies shall be liable, notwithstanding their statutory authority, to the extent of £200 at the most, for the damage done to agricultural land or crops by the escape of sparks or cinders from locomotive engines.

CHAPTER 14

LIABILITY FOR ANIMALS

§ 118. Different Forms of Liability[1]

"The law of torts has grown up historically in separate compartments, and ... beasts have travelled in a compartment of their own."[2] At common law the responsibility of the owners of animals for damage done by them has developed along two main lines, one a branch of the law of trespass, and the other a branch of the law which imposes upon the owner of a dangerous animal or thing a duty to take measures to prevent it from doing damage.[3] In addition, a man may be involved in liability for damage caused by his animals under the general principles of negligence or nuisance. Finally, the Animals Act 1971 has made major changes in England,[4] but the concepts of the common law relating to trespass and the *scienter* action have been simplified rather than abandoned.

§ 119. Strict Liability for Dangerous Animals

From the fourteenth century an action on the case provided a remedy for harm done by savage or dangerous animals. The action was commonly known by the convenient although inelegant title of "the *scienter* action."[5] For liability was dependent upon proof that the defendant knew or ought to have known of the animal's dangerous character.[6] But the law at an early date decided that certain animals were in their nature so dangerous to mankind that the keeper of them could not be suffered to say that he did not know of their character. *Scienter* was in such a case to be conclusively presumed. Hence under this branch of the law there are two classes of animals: (1) animals *ferae naturae*, *e.g.* a tiger or a gorilla, which are obviously of a dangerous nature, although individual animals may be more or less tamed; (2) animals *mansuetae naturae*, *e.g.* a dog, a cow, or a horse, which have in individual cases given indications of the development of a vicious or dangerous disposition. The Law Commission, upon whose Report the Animals Act 1971 is founded, approved the basic distinction between dangerous and non-dangerous animals. Accordingly the Act reformulates the principles of strict liability for the keeping of dangerous animals. First,

---

[1] See Williams, *Liability for Animals* (Cambridge, 1939); Report of the Committee on the Law of Civil Liability for Damage done by Animals (Cmd. 8746 (1953)); Law Commission Working Paper No. 13 (H.M.S.O., 1967); North, *The Modern Law of Animals* (1971). It is worth noting that no English court is entitled to look at Law Commission No. 13 to interpret an ambiguous provision of the Act of 1971. A clause in the Bill, supported by three Law Lords, which would have given such power, was deleted by the House of Commons on the ground that its effect would be to reduce the authority of Parliament and inflate that of the Law Commission.

[2] *Read* v. *Lyons* [1947] A.C. 156, 182, *per* Lord Simonds.

[3] *Buckle* v. *Holmes* [1926] 2 K.B. 125, 128.

[4] In Northern Ireland similar changes are made by the Animals (Northern Ireland) Order 1976. For the Irish Republic, see the Law Reform Commission's Working Paper No. 3 (1977).

[5] See Jackson, "On the Origins of Scienter" (1978) 94 L.Q.R. 85.

[6] *Quod defendens quendam canem ad mordendum oves consuetum scienter retinuit*: so ran the form of the old writ (1 Roll. Abr. 4).

section 1 of the Act provides that the sections which follow replace "the rules of the common law imposing a strict liability in tort for damage done by an animal on the ground that the animal is regarded as *ferae naturae* or that its vicious or mischievous propensities are known or presumed to be known." Secondly, section 2 then replaces the rules of the *scienter* action by the following provisions:

(1) Where any damage is caused by an animal which belongs to a dangerous species, any person who is a keeper of the animal is liable for the damage, except as otherwise provided by this Act.

(2) Where damage is caused by an animal which does not belong to a dangerous species, a keeper of the animal is liable for the damage, except as otherwise provided by this Act, if—

(*a*) the damage is of a kind which the animal, unless restrained, was likely to cause or which, if caused by the animal, was likely to be severe; and

(*b*) the likelihood of the damage or of its being severe was due to characteristics of the animal which are not normally found in animals of the same species or are not normally so found except at particular times or in particular circumstances; and

(*c*) those characteristics were known to that keeper or were at any time known to a person who at that time had charge of the animal as that keeper's servant or, where that keeper is the head of a household, were known to another keeper of the animal who is a member of that household and under the age of sixteen.

Some of the problems raised by these provisions will now be considered.

(1) What animals are included

The Act does not define "animal" (as distinct from "livestock"), but probably the term includes birds, reptiles and insects, but not bacteria.[7] The Act distinguishes between animals of a dangerous species[8] and other animals. This distinction is not to be found in nature, but is of crucial importance to the lawyer, for upon it depends the question whether the relevant provision is section 2 (1) or section 2 (2). Under section 2 (2) there will only be liability if the keeper of the animal has knowledge of its dangerous characteristics, whereas such knowledge is not necessary under section 2 (1). It is a question of law whether a particular species of animal is dangerous, and it is irrelevant what the characteristics of the particular animal are. "The reason why this is a question of law and not a question of fact is because it is a matter of which judicial notice has to be taken. The doctrine has from its formulation proceeded upon the supposition that the knowledge of what kinds of animals are tame and what savage is common knowledge. Evidence is receivable, if at all, only on the basis that the judge may wish to inform himself."[9] Thus it is a rule of law, and not a mere proposition of fact, that it is not natural for a dog to bite mankind. "The

---

[7] North, *Animals*, p. 22, n. 5.
[8] Which s. 6 defines to include subspecies and variety.
[9] *Behrens* v. *Bertram Mills Circus Ltd.* [1957] 2 Q.B. 1, 15, *per* Devlin J. Yet Scrutton L.J. thought that "a judge should not rely on his general knowledge about such matters, even though some judges know a good deal about horses": *Glanville* v. *Sutton* [1928] 1 K.B. 571, 575.

law," said Sir John Holt C.J.,[10] "takes notice that a dog is not of a fierce nature, but rather the contrary."

The Act in section 6 (2) defines a dangerous species as follows:

A dangerous species is a species—

(a) which is not commonly domesticated in the British Islands[11]; and

(b) whose fully grown animals normally have such characteristics that they are likely, unless restrained, to cause severe damage or that any damage they may cause is likely to be severe. It may be predicted that such general phrases as "commonly domesticated" and "severe damage" will give rise to many difficulties of interpretation.

(2) Nature of liability

At common law the principle was that he who keeps a dangerous animal keeps it at his peril.[12] This rule was probably not so much a vestigial relic of otherwise discarded doctrine as a special rule of practical good sense. At any rate, it was too well established to be challenged.[13]

Similarly liability under section 2 (1) of the Act is strict.[14] The liability is for "any damage" caused by an animal of a dangerous species: it is irrelevant that the particular animal is in fact tame, or was acting out of fright rather than viciously.[15] It would seem to follow that the test of remoteness of damage is not reasonable foreseeability but directness of consequence.

(3) Liability for non-dangerous species

When damage is done by a dangerous animal its keeper is liable without proof that the animal had a tendency to do such damage, or (if the animal had such a tendency) that the defendant knew of it. But when damage is done by an animal of a non-dangerous species, section 2 (2) of the 1971 Act requires (in effect) that the plaintiff must show that the animal had certain abnormal characteristics, and that its keeper had knowledge, actual or constructive, of those characterisitics.

(i) Abnormal characteristics

At common law it was uncertain whether it must be proved that the animal's vicious tendency was contrary to the nature of animals of that class. In the past liability has been imposed for bulls charging, horses kicking, and dogs chasing pheasants. But the need for proof of an unnatural tendency was emphatically affirmed by the Court of Appeal in *Fitzgerald* v. *E. D. and A. D. Cooke Bourne (Farms) Ltd.*,[16] in which it was held that there was no liability in *scienter* for personal injuries inflicted by a young filly which was following its own natural propensities, which were also those of fillies as a class, by galloping up to and prancing round lawful visitors to a

---

[10] *Mason* v. *Keeling* (1699) 12 Mod. 332, 335.
[11] *e.g.* a camel: *Tutin* v. *Mary Chipperfield Promotions Ltd.* N.L.J., September 4, 1980.
[12] *Gould* v. *M'Auliffe* [1941] 1 All E.R. 515, 519, affirmed [1941] 2 All E.R. 527.
[13] *May* v. *Burdett* (1846) 9 Q.B. 101.
[14] But not absolute: the defences are discussed below, § 120.
[15] A point already settled by *Behrens* v. *Bertram Mills Circus* [1957] 2 Q.B. 1, 17.
[16] [1964] 1 Q.B. 249.

field. In short, the animal must have a vicious tendency to injure people or animals by attacking them. The court may well have been unduly tender to owners of horses,[17] and much of its reasoning seems to be based on an anthropomorphic conception of animals. For a dog cannot reason like a human being, and there is something bizarre in seeking the *mens rea* of a pony. It is therefore to be hoped that the 1971 Act will be so interpreted as to impose liability in such a case.

(ii) *Knowledge*

Three different situations are covered by section 2 (2)—the knowledge of the keeper himself, or of his servant,[18] or of a member of his household under the age of 16 who is also a keeper of the animal.[19] The Act does not define "knowledge," so presumably the common law is still relevant. If so, it is not necessary to prove that the animal has on any previous occasion actually done the kind of harm complained of; it is enough that it has sufficiently manifested a tendency to do such harm, and that the defendant was aware of the fact.[20] But it is necessary to prove knowledge that the animal is prone to do or has done the particular kind of damage complained of. If a horse bites a man the keeper's knowledge is not established by proving that the horse was known to bite other horses.[21] On the other hand, if the animal is known to have a propensity to attack people (in the sense explained above) it is immaterial that it does so from non-vicious motives—*e.g.* an over-friendly large dog which hugs the plaintiff.[22]

(4) Who is liable[23]

Liability under either subsection of section 2 of the 1971 Act is placed on a "keeper" of the animal. Section 6 (3) of the Act provides that: a person is a keeper of an animal if—
> (*a*) he owns the animal or has it in his possession; or
> (*b*) he is the head of a household of which a member under the age of
> 16 owns the animal or has it in his possession;
> and if at any time an animal ceases to be owned by or to be in the
> possession of a person, any person who immediately before that time
> was a keeper thereof by virtue of the preceding provisions of this sub-
> section continues to be a keeper of the animal until another person
> becomes a keeper thereof by virtue of those provisions.

But where an animal is taken into and kept in possession for the purpose of preventing it from causing damage or of restoring it to its owner, a person is not a keeper of it by virtue only of that possession.

---

[17] Diplock L.J. said that it would be "an intolerable burden" on horse-owners to impose liability.

[18] The servant must be in charge of the animal as the keeper's servant. Notice to the servant is not necessarily notice to the master: *Maclean* v. *The Forestry Commission*, 1970 S.L.T. 265.

[19] So the knowledge of a minor who occasionally takes the household pet for a run will not necessarily be ascribed to the head of the household.

[20] *Barnes* v. *Lucille Ltd.* (1907) 96 L.T. 680. So the common maxim "Every dog is entitled to its bite" is no more accurate law than "Trespassers will be prosecuted."

[21] *Glanville* v. *Sutton & Co. Ltd.* [1928] 1 K.B. 571.

[22] *Fitzgerald* v. *Cooke (E.D. and A.D.) Bourne (Farms) Ltd.* [1964] 1 Q.B. 249, 259.

[23] The many problems are fully considered in North, *Animals*, pp. 23–34.

§ 120. DEFENCES TO ACTION UNDER SECTION 2 OF ANIMALS ACT

The following defences are available:—

(1) Contributory negligence and fault of the plaintiff

Section 5 (1) provides that there is no liability under section 2 for damage which is due wholly to the fault of the person suffering it. If the damage is due partly, as distinct from wholly, to the fault of the plaintiff, then sections 10 and 11 enable the apportionment provisions of the Law Reform (Contributory Negligence) Act 1945 to be applied. The law was the same before the Act.

(2) Plaintiff a trespasser

It was formerly a good defence that the plaintiff, when injured by the animal, was trespassing upon the defendant's premises where the animal was kept, unless it was kept there with the deliberate purpose of injuring him.[24] The Act in section 5 (3) now provides that a person is not liable for any damage caused by an animal kept on any premises or structure[25] to a person trespassing there, "if it is proved either—
  (a) that the animal was not kept there for the protection of persons or property[26]; or
  (b) (if the animal was kept there for the protection of persons or property) that keeping it there for that purpose was not unreasonable."

It has been held not to be unreasonable to keep a savage dog in a built-up area to protect scrap metal,[27] but the events in the case occurred before the passage of the Guard Dogs Act 1975, which imposed certain restrictions on the keeping of such animals.

If for any reason the claim is not brought under section 2—e.g. because the defendant is not the occupier of the premises trespassed upon—the ordinary principles of negligence will apply.[28]

(3) Volenti non fit injuria

The maxim *volenti non fit injuria* was no less applicable to dangerous animals than to other dangerous things of which the plaintiff has agreed to run the risk.[29] So a person who intervened in a dog-fight might be met with this defence.[30] Section 5 (2) of the Act now specifically provides that a person is not liable under section 2 for any damage suffered by a person who has voluntarily accepted the risk thereof. So, in accordance with the settled rules on the matter,[31] it has been held that the defendant must prove more than the fact that the plaintiff knew there was a dangerous dog loose.[32]

---

[24] *Sarch* v. *Blackburn* (1830) 4 C. & P. 297; above, § 98.
[25] This probably includes an aircraft or motor-car: see above, § 90.
[26] But some animals—*e.g.* dogs—are kept both for companionship and for protection.
[27] *Cummings* v. *Grainger* [1977] 1 Q.B. 397.
[28] See below, § 125.
[29] *Behrens* v. *Bertram Mills Circus Ltd.* [1957] 2 Q.B. 1.
[30] *Smith* v. *Shields* (1964) 108 S.J. 501.
[31] See below, §§ 187-189.
[32] *Cummings* v. *Grainger* [1976] 1 Q.B. 397 (followed in *Tutin* v. *Chipperfield Ltd.* 1980, N.L.J. September 4, (camel).

Further, by section 6 (5) when a person employed as a servant by a keeper of an animal incurs a risk incidental to his employment he shall not be treated as accepting it voluntarily.[33]

(4) Act of third person

How far, if at all, it was a good defence that the immediate cause of the damage complained of was the unlawful act of a third person in letting the animal loose or inciting it to mischief cannot be regarded as being definitely decided before the Act. In *Baker* v. *Snell*[34] the question was much discussed by a Divisional Court and by the Court of Appeal, but there was such a conflict of judicial opinion that it is difficult to determine what the case decided or to regard it as authority.[35] But in *Behrens* v. *Bertram Mills Circus Ltd.*[36] Devlin J. held that the judgments of Sir Herbert Cozens-Hardy M.R. and Farwell L.J. in *Baker* v. *Snell* were authority for the proposition that the wrongful act of a third party is no defence, and the Law Commission[37] was of the same opinion for the reason that the act of a third party is one of the circumstances against which the person creating the risk should take precautions. As the Act does not mention this defence in section 5, it must be assumed to have disappeared. The possible defence of act of God[38] must also have gone.

§ 121. LIABILITY FOR DOGS

Section 3 provides that "where a dog causes damage by killing or injuring livestock, any person who is a keeper[39] of the dog is liable for the damage, except as otherwise provided by this Act."

This section replaces the provisions of the Dogs Acts 1906 to 1928. By section 11 "livestock" means "cattle, horses, asses, mules, hinnies, sheep, pigs, goats and poultry, and also deer not in the wild state and, while in captivity, pheasants, partridges and grouse."

It will be noted that liability under this section is quite independent of the proof of knowledge or negligence on the part of the keeper of the dog. It is peculiarly revealing of the Englishman's scale of values, or else of the influence of the farmers' lobby on Parliament, that sheep should be better protected from dogs than human beings.[40] Finally, section 9 of the Act provides a statutory defence to an action for killing or causing injury to a dog if the defendant was acting, or had reasonable grounds for believing he was acting, for the protection of livestock. The Guard Dogs Act 1975 displays a different legislative policy. The Act (s.1) provides that a person

---

[33] *Rands* v. *McNeil* [1955] 1 Q.B. 253 is accordingly reversed.
[34] [1908] 2 K.B. 352, 825. For a remarkably outspoken criticism, see Beven, "Responsibility at Common Law for the Keeping of Animals" (1909) 22 Harv.L.Rev. 465; Pollock, "The Dog and the Potman: or 'Go it, Bob!' " (1909) 25 L.Q.R. 317.
[35] But Dr. Goodhart, "The Third Man" [1951] C.L.P. 177, 185, while admitting that the judgments "are, perhaps, not as clearly expressed as one might have wished," says that "it has never been suggested that the authority of a precedent depends on the force of the arguments advanced in its support," and that a conflict of judicial opinion "gives it added force because it makes it clear what the particular point in issue was."
[36] [1957] 2 Q.B. 1.
[37] Report, § 24.
[38] See *Nichols* v. *Marsland* (1875) L.R. 10 Ex. 255, 260.
[39] Not the owner, as under the previous Dogs Act.
[40] *Hughes* v. *Williams* [1943] K.B. 574, 580.

shall not use, or permit the use of, a guard dog[41] on any premises unless a competent handler is present and a warning notice is exhibited at the entrance. But although breach of section 1 is a criminal offence, section 5 (1) specifically provides that it shall not confer a civil right of action.[42] Finally, in practice it may be the best course to apply to a magistrates' court under the Dogs Act 1871, s. 2 for an order for the destruction of a dangerous dog.

§ 122. LIABILITY FOR STRAYING LIVESTOCK

We now pass to the second branch of the law relating to liability for harm done by animals. Cattle-trespass was one of the oldest grounds of liability in English law.[43] It has now been abolished by section 1 (1) of the Act, and replaced by the following provisions in section 4 (1). Where livestock belonging[44] to any person strays[45] on to land in the ownership or occupation of another[46] and—

(a) damage is done by the livestock to the land or to any property on it which is in the ownership or possession of the other person[47]; or

(b) any expenses are reasonably incurred by that other person in keeping the livestock while it cannot be restored to the person to whom it belongs or while it is detained in pursuance of section 7 of this Act, or in ascertaining to whom it belongs;

the person to whom the livestock belongs is liable for the damage or expenses, except as otherwise provided by this Act.

§ 123. DEFENCES TO ACTION FOR STRAYING LIVESTOCK

As section 4 (1) provides that the person in possession of straying livestock is liable for them "except as provided by this Act," it follows that the common law defences to cattle-trespass have been abolished. Thus the act of a third party, which was a defence both in England[48] and in Ireland,[49] is now inapplicable to a claim under section 4. The only defences recognised by the 1971 Act are the following.

(1) Plaintiff's own default

In section 5 (1) it is specifically provided that a person is not liable under section 4 for any damage which is wholly due to the fault of the person suffering it. But section 5 (6) provides that "the damage shall not be treated as due to the fault of the person suffering it by reason only that he could have prevented it by fencing; but a person is not liable under that section

---

[41] The breed of such a dog is irrelevant: the Act concentrates on its function.
[42] Still, an occupier in breach of the Act would hardly be acting reasonably for the purpose of s. 5 (3) of the Animals Act 1971.
[43] See Williams, *Animals*, pp. 127–135, and Holdsworth, H.E.L., Vol. viii, pp. 470–471.
[44] Under s. 4(2) livestock belongs to the person in whose possession it is: so the owner out of possession cannot be sued.
[45] Note that the Act does not require a trespass: so it is doubtful whether *Ellis* v. *Loftus Iron Co.* (1874) L.R. 10 C.P. 10 is still law.
[46] But not from the highway on to that land (s.5(5)). As at common law, negligence must be shown: *Tillett* v. *Ward* (1882) 10 Q.B.D. 17. See below, § 123.
[47] So there is no liability for personal injuries, and *Wormald* v. *Cole* [1954] 1 Q.B. 614 has been overruled.
[48] *Sutcliffe* v. *Holmes* [1947] K.B. 147.
[49] *Moloney* v. *Stephen* [1945] Ir.Jur.Rep. 37.

where it is proved that the straying of the livestock on to the land would not have occurred but for a breach by any other person, being a person having an interest in the land, of a duty to fence."

(2) Contributory negligence

If the plaintiff's damage is due partly, as distinct from wholly, to his own negligence, the apportionment provisions of the Law Reform (Contributory Negligence) Act 1945 seem to apply by virtue of sections 10 and 11 of the 1971 Act.

(3) Straying from the highway

The Act in section 5 (5) specifically recognises the well-established rule[50] that the occupier of premises adjoining a highway is presumed to have accepted the risks incidental to the passage of ordinary traffic along that highway.

§ 124. DETENTION AND SALE OF TRESPASSING LIVESTOCK

The common law remedy of distress damage feasant[51] is expressly abolished by section 7 (1). In its place section 7 (2) to (6) provides a right to detain the livestock and to sell it at the end of 14 days. The animal must be adequately fed and watered. The right of detention ceases after 48 hours unless within that time notice of the detention is given to the police, and to the person to whom the livestock belongs, if he is known, or if there is a tender of amends. The Act provides in section 7 (5) for the disposition of the proceeds of the sale, which must be at a market or public auction, in order to obtain a fair price. The grant of a power of sale, which did not exist in distress damage feasant, is to be welcomed, but there is something odd about giving the occupier of a suburban house the right to detain and feed a trespassing pony. It might be simpler to drive it away.

§ 125. LIABILITY IN NEGLIGENCE

Apart altogether from the doctrines of cattle-trespass and *scienter* there was at common law the ordinary liability in negligence for the keeping of animals.[52] This was confirmed by the Court of Appeal in *Draper* v. *Hodder*,[53] decided after the Animals Act 1971 became law, but on events which had occurred in 1968. The infant plaintiff had been savaged by a pack of Jack Russell terriers which had escaped from the defendant's land. There was no evidence that any of these terriers had ever attacked a human being, so there could not be liability under the *scienter* action. But in view of evidence that Jack Russell terriers are dangerous when in a pack and

---

[50] *Tillett* v. *Ward* (1882) 10 Q.B.D. 17.
[51] See below, § 229.
[52] *Fardon* v. *Harcourt-Rivington* (1932) 146 L.T. 391, 392, *per* Lord Atkin. "One can perhaps with hindsight deduce from the language of the speeches in *Fardon* v. *Harcourt-Rivington* how *Donoghue* v. *Stevenson* was likely to be decided": *Draper* v. *Hodder* [1972] 2 Q.B. 556, 578, *per* Roskill L.J.
[53] [1972] 2 Q.B. 556. The H.L. refused leave to appeal.

allowed to roam free, the defendant was held liable in negligence for failing to take precautions against a foreseeable risk. Liability based on negligence is quite distinct from the statutory strict liability under the Animals Act 1971—the defendant may be different, the duty is different, and so is the test of remoteness of damage. But before the Act of 1971 there was one important common law exception to the general principle of liability in negligence.

Fences. In *Searle* v. *Wallbank*[54] the House of Lords affirmed the long-standing rule that the owner or occupier of land adjoining the highway is under no duty to users of the highway to prevent his domestic animals not known to be dangerous from straying on to the highway.[55] This rule was founded upon our ancient social conditions and was in no way related to, or liable to be qualified by, such matters as the relative levels of fields and highway, the nature of the highway, or the amount of traffic upon it.[56] Such an occupier might incur criminal liability under the Highways Act 1959, s. 135 (1),[57] but there is no civil liability for breach of that statutory duty.[58] In particular there was no ground for a distinction[59] between town and country.[60] It also followed that since there was no duty to maintain a fence at all, it could not be a breach of duty to maintain one which was imperfect.[61] Although protests against this rule may be found in the reports from 1699[62] to the present day,[63] a number of private members' Bills to change the law failed to secure enactment.[64] Finally section 8 of the Animals Act 1971 put an end to the privileged position of the farmer and imposed a duty to take care to prevent damage from animals straying on to the highway. This duty was created, not by imposing a statutory duty of care on the land-owner, but by abolishing the rule in *Searle* v. *Wallbank*. In section 8 (1) the Act provides that "so much of the rules of the common law relating to liability for negligence as excludes or restricts the duty which a person might owe to others to take such care as is reasonable to see that damage is not caused by animals straying on to a highway is hereby abolished." So it will be for the tribunal of fact to give due weight to such circumstances on the nature of the land and of the adjoining highway, and of the type of animal. But Parliament recognised that it might be unreasonable to subject

---

[54] [1947] A.C. 341.
[55] The H.L. correctly stated what had been the common law of England and is still that of South Australia: *State Government Insurance Commission* v. *Trigwell* (1979) 53 A.L.J.R. 656.
[56] *Brock* v. *Richards* [1951] 1 K.B. 529, 534.
[57] But the penalty is only 25p a head (with a maximum of 150p) and Sir Carleton Allen knew "of one offender—a serious menace to his neighbourhood—with eighty-four convictions, punishable each time with 5s. only": *Law in the Making* (7th ed.), p. 301. His activities were stopped only when he was bound to keep the peace in the sum of £25: (1961) 77 L.Q.R. 27.
[58] *Davies* v. *Davies* [1975] Q.B. 172.
[59] As was once thought: *Deen* v. *Davies* [1935] 2 K.B. 282.
[60] *Gomberg* v. *Smith* [1963] 1 Q.B. 25, 40; *Ellis* v. *Johnstone* [1963] 2 Q.B. 8, 26.
[61] *Searle* v. *Wallbank* [1947] A.C. 341, 361; *Brock* v. *Richards* [1951] 1 K.B. 529, 535.
[62] *Mason* v. *Keeling*, 1 Ld. Raym. 606. In (1699) 12 Mod. 332, 333 counsel is reported as saying "It is hard that one should have a remedy for the least trespass done in his land, and none for a trespass done thus to the person by wounding or maiming."
[63] *Ellis* v. *Johnstone* [1963] 2 Q.B. 8, 27.
[64] The Supreme Court of Canada had refused to follow *Searle* v. *Wallbank* in *Fleming* v. *Atkinson* (1959) 18 D.L.R. (2d) 81, 113, but the High Court of Australia has held that such a change is a matter for the legislature: *State Government Insurance Commission* v. *Trigwell* (1979) 53 A.L.J.R. 656.

the occupiers of unfenced land, such as is usual in the north of England, to ordinary liability in negligence. So section 8 (2) of the Act provides that

> where damage[65] is caused by animals[66] straying from unfenced[67] land to a highway a person who placed them on the land shall not be regarded as having committed a breach of the duty to take care by reason only of placing them there if—
>
> (a) the land is common land, or is land situated in an area where fencing is not customary, or is a town or village green[68]; and
> (b) he had a right to place the animals on that land.[69]

§ 126. Liability for Nuisance

Actions for nuisance caused by animals do not require lengthy consideration.[70] It might well have been held that obstruction of a highway by an animal was a nuisance but the cases have almost all been decided on the basis of negligence.[71] But a dog with a long loose lead running about by itself in the streets of London is a nuisance.[72] If animals escape on to a highway in such numbers as to amount to an obstruction there also may be liability in nuisance. It is a question of fact in each case: 24 cows on an Irish country road have been held to be a nuisance,[73] but not two sheep on a country road in South Australia.[74] It is necessary to rely upon nuisance when there is no escape or no negligence, or when the animal is not livestock within the definition in section 11 of the Animals Act 1971—e.g. it is a cat or a dog. The stench of pigs,[75] the barking of dogs,[76] and the crowing of cockerels[77] have each been held to constitute a nuisance.

In general, there is no liability for the escape of noxious animals naturally on the defendant's land, such as rats,[78] rabbits[79] or deer.[80] These decisions may be open to review in the light of the tendency to impose liability for the escape of things naturally on the land if the defendant has behaved unreasonably.[81] In any event, if for the purposes of sport or otherwise, a man purposely accumulates rabbits or game upon his land, he is probably

---

[65] As defined in section 11, includes the death of or injury to, any person (including any disease and any impairment of physical or mental condition).

[66] There is no statutory definition of animals, as distinct from livestock, so there is now a duty to prevent dogs, cats, and even poultry, from straying.

[67] "Fencing" includes the construction of any obstacle designed to prevent animals from straying.

[68] "Common land," and "town or village green" have the same meanings as in the Commons Registration Act 1965.

[69] See *Davies* v. *Davies* [1975] Q.B. 172.

[70] See Williams, *Animals*, pp. 235–262.

[71] See above, § 125.

[72] *Pitcher* v. *Martin* [1937] 3 All E.R. 918.

[73] *Cunningham* v. *Whelan* (1917) 52 I.L.T.R. 67.

[74] *State Government Insurance Commission* v. *Trigwell* (1979) 53 A.L.J.R. 656.

[75] *Aldred's Case* (1610) 9 Co. 57b.

[76] The cases are collected in Williams, *Animals*, pp. 236–237. There may also be criminal liability under a local by-law, as in *Morrissey* v. *Galer* [1955] 1 W.L.R. 110, or under the Public Health Act 1936, s. 92.

[77] *Leeman* v. *Montagu* [1936] 2 All E.R. 1677 (but the cockerels sounded like "a football crowd cheering a cup-tie").

[78] *Stearn* v. *Prentice Bros.* [1919] 1 K.B. 394.

[79] *Pratt* v. *Young* (1952) 69 W.N.(N.S.W.) 214.

[80] *Brady* v. *Warren* [1900] 2 I.R. 632.

[81] See above, § 110.

liable for all damage done by them to neighbouring proprietors.[82] So if he keeps bees[83] in an unreasonable number[84] or manure in such unreasonable quantities as to attract flies[85] or, it seems, rats[86] he will be liable for a nuisance. It has been held that rooks may be a nuisance to the neighbourhood where they are.[87]

§ 127. LIABILITY IN OTHER TORTS[88]

As with negligence[89] and nuisance,[90] liability for other torts is unaffected by the 1971 Act. So it has long been settled that trespass to the person can be committed through the agency of an animal, as when the defendant sets his dog onto the plaintiff[91]; again trespass to chattels is committed if I train my dog to take another's golf balls.[92] Again a lawful visitor to premises may apparently base his claim on the rules relating to the liability of occupiers[93] rather than on the Animals Act, and so may a trespasser if the case is not covered by section 5 (3) of the Act. It is possible that there might be liability under the principle in *Rylands* v. *Fletcher*[94] for the escape of a tiger[95] or a fox.[96]

[82] *Farrer* v. *Nelson* (1885) 15 Q.B.D. 258, 260; *Seligman* v. *Docker* [1949] Ch. 53.
[83] Sir K. Swan, *A Receiver of Stolen Property* (Middle Temple, 1956), is a monograph on bees and the law.
[84] *O'Gorman* v. *O'Gorman* [1903] 2 I.R. 573.
[85] *Bland* v. *Yates* (1914) 58 S.J. 612. But see Williams, *Animals*, p. 260.
[86] *Stearn* v. *Prentice Bros.* [1919] 1 K.B. 394.
[87] *Hannam* v. *Mockett* (1824) 2 B. & C. 943.
[88] See North, *The Modern Law of Animals*, Chap. 6.
[89] See above, § 125.
[90] See above, § 126.
[91] *Scott* v. *Shepherd* (1773) 3 Wils. 403, 408.
[92] *Manton* v. *Brocklebank* [1923] 2 K.B. 212, 219.
[93] *Kavanagh* v. *Stokes* [1942] I.R. 596.
[94] See above, Chap. 13.
[95] *Behrens* v. *Bertram Mills Circus Ltd.* [1957] 2 Q.B. 1, 22.
[96] *Brady* v. *Warren* [1900] 2 I.R. 632, 651.

CHAPTER 15

DOMESTIC RELATIONS

§ 128. INTRODUCTORY

In this chapter we shall consider those tortious acts which are an injury neither to the person, nor reputation, nor physical property, but are based on a wrongful interference with a man's relations with others, for example, his wife, his children or those with whom he holds a contract. For a man may be damnified by the death of another person,[1] by the loss of his wife's consortium, by the seduction of his daughter, by the deprivation of the work of his servants or by the non-fulfilment of contractual obligations due to him from another. If the law had been developed on a rational basis without reference to the accidents of history it might have been expected that a fundamental distinction would have been taken between intentional and careless invasions of the security of existing domestic and contractual relations. On the one hand, it would have been natural to find a remedy given to one who had suffered loss from a wilful act done with the object and effect of depriving him of the benefits which he enjoyed from a relationship with another, at least whenever the deprivation was permanent, and whether the relationship was with a spouse, parent, child, employer, servant, partner, or contractor. For the general principle is that violation of a legal right committed knowingly gives a cause of action unless there is some reason to the contrary.[2] On the other hand, it would have been surprising to find a remedy given to one who had suffered such a loss as the result of an act not done with the object (although having the effect) of depriving him of the advantages of the continuance of the relationship in question. The only exception might have been the case of a family deprived of its bread-winner. For it is equally clear that the general principle is that the mere fact that an injury to A prevents a third party getting from A a benefit which he would otherwise have obtained does not invest the third party with a right of action against the wrongdoer.[3] This rational approach has not been adopted, either at common law or under the Law Reform (Miscellaneous Provisions) Act 1970.

The vagaries of English legal development have therefore produced a situation in which the interest which one person has in the continuance of his existing relationship (whether domestic or contractual) with another is protected by the law in a way which is at once surprisingly wide and surprisingly narrow. We shall consider in turn the relations of (1) master and servant, (2) parent and child, and (3) husband and wife, and in respect of each relationship we shall consider the actions for (1) loss of services, (2) enticement, and (3) harbouring.

---

[1] "Whenever a man dies, if he is a man of an active type, it has repercussions, great or small, on all those with whom he has been previously concerned": *Burgess* v. *Florence Nightingale Hospital for Gentlewomen* [1955] 1 Q.B. 349, 355, *per* Devlin J.

[2] See above, §§ 3–5.

[3] *Att.-Gen. for New South Wales* v. *Perpetual Trustee Co. Ltd.* [1955] A.C. 457, 484; *Commissioner for Railways (N.S.W.)* v. *Scott* (1959) 102 C.L.R. 392. See also above, § 76.

§ 129. MASTER AND SERVANT[4]

(1) Action per quod servitium amisit

It is a tort actionable at the suit of a master to take away, imprison, or cause bodily harm to his servant, if (i) the act is a tort as against the servant, and (ii) the master is thereby deprived of his servant's services.[5] Note that no action lies if the servant is killed by the defendant, as distinct from being injured[6]—one of the many anomalies which disfigure this area of the law. From the earliest days of the common law the master had an action of trespass against the wrongdoer whose battery or other wrongful act had brought about the loss of the services of his servant (*per quod servitium amisit*). It is significant that the action was originally in trespass and not in case: for although the act complained of must have been wrongful as against the servant himself,[7] it was also regarded as being a direct invasion of the interest of a proprietary nature which the master had either in the servant himself or in the services which were the fruit of the relationship between them.[8] Despite the great social and economic changes which have occurred in the relationship of master and servant this is still the basis of the action—which, however, is today best thought of as "innominate" rather than as one of trespass or case.[9] In truth, the doctrine is an historical relic of the days when a master had a proprietary interest in his servant[10] and seems anomalous in modern industrial conditions.[11]

On the other hand, it can be persuasively argued that the situation of the employer who has sustained loss by an injury to his servant may be of serious economic importance today for the first time since the years following the Black Death. This is partly because many employers are bound, either legally or morally, to pay their employees sick pay and medical expenses in the event of injury, and partly because it may be very difficult to replace a skilled man on whose training much money may have been spent. The courts may have acted too rapidly in confining the scope of the action.[12]

---

[4] See Cowen, "The Action Per Quod Servitium Amisit and the Police" [1953] 2 Univ. of W.A.Ann.L.Rev. 263; Brett, "Consortium and Servitium" (1955) 29 Aust.L.J. 321, 389, 428; Gareth Jones, "Per Quod Servitium Amisit" (1958) 74 L.Q.R. 39; Holdsworth, H.E.L., iv, pp. 383–385; viii, p. 448; 11th Report of the Law Reform Committee (Cmnd. 2017, 1963); Law Commission Working Paper No. 19 (1968).

[5] *Bermann* v. *Occhipinti* [1954] 1 D.L.R. 560, 563.

[6] *Admiralty Commissioners* v. *SS. Amerika* [1917] A.C. 38. For the reason, see below, § 217.

[7] In the action by a parent for the seduction of his child this would never (and in the actions for enticing and harbouring or procuring breach of contract not necessarily) have been the case. Hence, whatever the history of the matter, these causes of action (though related) are now distinct: *Perpetual Trustee Co. Case* [1955] A.C. 457, 486.

[8] *Inland Revenue Commissioners* v. *Hambrook* [1956] 2 Q.B. 641. See note 10 below.

[9] *Perpetual Trustee Co. Case* (1952) 85 C.L.R. 237, 248, *per* Dixon J.

[10] Or rather, perhaps, in the services which were the fruit of the relationship between them: *Commissioner for Railways (N.S.W.)* v. *Scott* (1959) 102 C.L.R. 392, 450.

[11] See the *Perpetual Trustee Co. Case* [1955] A.C. 457, 482, and the Law Reform Committee (11th Report, p. 3), and the Pearson Report (Cmnd. 7054), § 447.

[12] So the Law Reform Committee (Cmnd. 2017), although recommending the abolition of the action, also suggested that an employer who has incurred expense in consequence of the injury to his employee should be able to recover from the tortfeasor to the extent that the latter's liability to the employee has been reduced. The Law Commission, in its provisional conclusion (Working Paper No. 19), also favoured the abolition of the action, but Parliament did not accept this in the Law Reform (Miscellaneous Provisions) Act 1970. The Law Commission's second thoughts can be found in its Working Paper No. 41 (1971), paras. 191–196.

(i) *Who is a servant*

The fact that the basis of the action is the injury done to the master's proprietary interest means that its scope is at once surprisingly wide and surprisingly narrow. On the one hand, the plaintiff may be the head of a household who has been deprived of the services of his wife, child, apprentice, or servant. The action does not depend on any contract of service but on the single fact of service.[13] This is most clearly illustrated by the seduction cases.[14] Hence the question has arisen whether the scope of the action extends to anyone employed under a contract of service, no matter how specialised or skilful the nature of the services may be, as does the doctrine of vicarious liability. Indeed the Court of Appeal has held that the scope of the action must be restricted to those menial servants[15] who originally formed part of the *familia* or household.[16] But this decision has been the subject of damaging criticism on historical grounds.[17] and the action has been held to lie in respect of the loss of services of a "servant and traveller,"[18] an apprentice,[19] and a music-hall artiste.[20] There are conflicting dicta on the question whether the action might lie in respect of the loss of the services of the director or general manager[21] or other servant[22] of a modern trading company.

But as there is a fundamental difference between the domestic relation of master and servant and that of the holder of a public office and the state which he serves, the action does not lie for the loss of the services of a police officer,[23] a member of the armed forces,[24] or an established civil servant.[25] Moreover, if the relationship of master and servant exists it is irrelevant that at the time of the wrongful act the servant was off duty[26]: if the law were otherwise there would, as Lord Goddard remarked,[27] be a short and simple answer in most of the seduction cases.[28]

On the other hand the scope of the action is narrow in that "notice is only taken of the wrong done to the superior of the parties related . . . while the

---

[13] *Perpetual Trustee Co. Case* [1955] A.C. at 483; *Inland Revenue Commissioners* v. *Hambrook* [1956] 2 Q.B. 641, 666. So it is possible for two or more masters to sue in respect of the same wrong done to a servant: *Rist* v. *Faux* (1863) 4 B. & S. 409. But under the doctrine of vicarious liability only one master is liable for a wrong done by a servant: below, § 175.
[14] See below, § 130.
[15] So called from the obsolete Middle English term *meinie*, signifying family, household, or retinue. The derivation given in Blackstone (Comm.I, 425) is incorrect.
[16] *Inland Revenue Commissioners* v. *Hambrook* [1956] 2 Q.B. 641.
[17] *Commissioner for Railways (N.S.W.)* v. *Scott* (1959) 102 C.L.R. 392.
[18] *Martinez* v. *Gerber* (1841) 3 Man. & G. 88.
[19] *Hodsoll* v. *Stallebrass* (1840) 11 Ad. & E. 301. *Non constat* that the decision is wrong: "Perhaps he slept under the counter": [1956] 2 Q.B. 641, 664, *per* Denning L.J.
[20] *Mankin* v. *Scala Theodrome Co. Ltd.* [1947] K.B. 257. See the *Perpetual Trustee Co. Case* (1952) 85 C.L.R. 237, 286.
[21] *Perpetual Trustee Co. Case* (1952) 85 C.L.R. 237, 248; *Lee* v. *Sheard* [1956] 1 Q.B. 192; *I.R.C.* v. *Hambrook* [1956] 2 Q.B. 641, 666.
[22] *Schwartz* v. *Hotel Corporation of America* (1970) 15 D.L.R. (3d) 764; *Geneveux* v. *Peterson, Howell & Heather Ltd.* (1973) 34 D.L.R. (2d) 614.
[23] *Perpetual Trustee Co. Case* [1955] A.C. 457, 489.
[24] *The Commonwealth* v. *Quince* (1944) 68 C.L.R. 227.
[25] *I.R.C.* v. *Hambrook* [1956] 2 Q.B. 641. A restrictive interpretation has also been adopted in South Africa: *Union Government* v. *Ocean Accident Corpn.*, 1956 (1) S.A. 571 and in Ireland: *Att.-Gen.* v. *Ryan's Car Hire Ltd.* [1965] I.R. 642, but not in Canada: *The Queen* v. *Murray* (1967) 60 D.L.R. (2d) 647.
[26] As in *Pratt* v. *Pratt* [1975] V.R. 378.
[27] *I.R.C.* v. *Hambrook* [1956] 2 Q.B. 641, 657.
[28] See below, § 130.

loss of the inferior by such injuries is totally unregarded."[29] This language "falls a little strangely on modern ears"[30] but the conclusion is a perfectly logical deduction from the principle that he alone can sue who can show a proprietary interest in the services of another. The result is curious, for it means that the husband who was on the worst of terms with his wife can claim.[31] Further "If the injured man was engaged in a business, and the injury is a serious one, the business may have to be closed down and the employees be dismissed. A daughter of the injured man may have to give up work which she enjoys and stay at home to nurse a father who has been transformed into an irritable invalid."[32] But the wife, child, servant, partner, or insurer is without a remedy, either under this form of action or in negligence.[33]

(ii) *Nature of the wrongful act*

"It does not matter as regards the master's right to sue how the injury is caused to the person of his servant, whether by an assault, by battery,[34] by negligence,[35] or otherwise.[36]"[37] The defendant is responsible whether or not he knew that the relationship of master and servant existed, and even though the master may have been ten thousand miles away. Proximity is irrelevant. So it is also irrelevant that the servant has been guilty of contributory negligence.[38] Yet the Law Reform Committee[39] thought the employee's contributory negligence should be taken into account in assessing the expenses necessarily incurred in consequence of the injury to the servant. This is certainly illogical, although it may have the attraction of the justice commonly described as rough, for the employer's expenses are the same whether the employee has been guilty of contributory negligence or not.

(iii) *Damage*

It was settled at an early date that although the action was in trespass it had to be laid with a *per quod* showing consequential damage and was not actionable *per se*. What has to be assessed is the value of the services which the plaintiff has lost, and it seems to be assumed (perhaps with little justification) that the appropriate standard is in general provided by the payments made, or to be made, by way of wages to the injured man, though it might be more logical to measure the master's loss by the payments which he has had to make to a substitute by way of wages or overtime rates.[40] The value

[29] Bl. Comm., III, 142.
[30] *Best* v. *Samuel Fox & Co.* [1951] 2 K.B. 639, 666 *per* Birkett L.J.
[31] *Spaight* v. *Dundon* [1961] I.R. 201, 214.
[32] *Best* v. *Samuel Fox & Co.* [1952] A.C. 716, 734, *per* Lord Morton of Henryton.
[33] See above, § 77.
[34] Such an action lay as far back as Y.B. 19 Hen. 6. pl. 94.
[35] As in *Mankin* v. *Scala Theodrome Co.* [1947] K.B. 257.
[36] As in *Hodsoll* v. *Stallebrass* (1840) 11 Ad. & E. 301 (dog biting off thumb of watch-maker's apprentice).
[37] Dicey, *Parties in an Action*, p. 326.
[38] *I.R.C.* v. *Hambrook* [1956] 2 Q.B. 641, 657, 669, 673. But in Ireland the employee's contributory negligence can be taken into account: Civil Liability Act 1961, s. 35 (2)(*b*).
[39] 11th Report, p. 6.
[40] This difficult matter is discussed in Fleming (1959) 22 M.L.R. 685–686; Parsons, "Damages in Actions for Personal Injury" (1957) 30 A.L.J. 618.

of future loss of services is recoverable,[41] but on the other hand no claim can be made in respect of voluntary payments to the injured party.[42] Hence the value of voluntary or *ex gratia* payments by way of pensions[43] or sick pay[44] cannot be recovered, either in this action or in quasi-contract.[45] It would seem to follow that medical expenses which have not been incurred in pursuance of some legal duty are not recoverable, but in practice claims for such expenses, if incurred reasonably and naturally, are not challenged.[46]

The difficulty of the problem is increased by the fact that there is still some uncertainty as to the measure of damages which the servant himself is entitled to in his own action against the tortfeasor.[47] At present English law relieves the tortfeasor of part of his burden by insisting that the injured party shall give credit for wages and other collateral benefits which he has received. Various solutions have been proposed,[48] but none has found general acceptance.

(2) Enticement of a servant

At an early date a remedy by way of an action on the case was developed when a stranger had deprived a master of his servant not by force, but by persuasion. In the absence of lawful justification it is a tort actionable at the suit of a master to induce his servant to leave his employment wrongfully[49] or to induce him by illegal means, such a fraud or intimidation, to leave his employment even rightfully, or to conspire to do so.[50] When no illegal means of inducement or coercion are used by the defendant, it is not a tort to induce a servant to leave his master's service, unless the act of the servant in doing so is wrongful. Therefore, to persuade a servant to leave a merely *de facto* service[51] or to terminate a contractual service by due notice is not actionable.

Lumley v. *Gye*

The action is available even though employer and employed do not stand in the strict relation of master and servant. This has been established ever since *Lumley* v. *Gye*.[52] The plaintiff was the lessee and manager of a theatre. Miss Johanna Wagner, an artiste of some distinction, had agreed with the plaintiff to sing in his theatre for a definite term and during that term not to sing elsewhere. The defendant, "knowing the premises, and maliciously intending to injure the plaintiff," before the expiration of the term enticed

---

[41] *Hodsoll* v. *Stallebrass* (1840) 11 Ad. & E. 301. *Cf.* the approach in *Mankin* v. *Scala Theodrome Co. Ltd.* [1947] K.B. 257.

[42] *Admiralty Commissioners* v. *S.S. Amerika* [1917] A.C. 38, 42, 61.

[43] *Admiralty Commissioners* v. *S.S. Amerika* [1917] A.C. 38, 42, 61.

[44] *Inland Revenue Commissioners* v. *Hambrook* [1956] 2 Q.B. 641.

[45] *Receiver for the Metropolitan Police District* v. *Croydon Corporation* [1957] 2 Q.B. 154.

[46] They were permitted in *Barnes* v. *Pooley* (1935) 51 T.L.R. 391.

[47] See below, § 215.

[48] By the Law Commission in its Report on Personal Injury Litigation (Law Com. No. 56, 1973). The Report (§ 161) also recommends the abolition of the actions for enticement and harbouring of a servant.

[49] *Lumley* v. *Gye* (1853) 2 E. & B. 216; *Bowen* v. *Hall* (1881) 6 Q.B.D. 333.

[50] *Conway* v. *Wade* [1909] A.C. 506, 510; *Sorrell* v. *Smith* [1925] A.C. 700, 747.

[51] *De Francesco* v. *Barnum* (1890) 45 Ch.D. 430. This limitation is perhaps implied in the judgments in *Evans* v. *Walton* (1867) L.R. 2 C.P. 615. But an action lay for enticing from *de facto* service under a voidable contract in *Keane* v. *Boycott* (1795) 2 H.Bl. 512; and see *Sykes* v. *Dixon* (1839) 9 A. & E. 693, and *Dixon* v. *Dixon* [1904] 1 Ch. 161.

[52] (1853) 2 E. & B. 216.

and procured Miss Wagner to refuse to perform. A majority of the Court of
Queen's Bench held that the defendant was liable in damages to the plaintiff.
The action for enticement was not limited to such menial servants as were
comprehended by the Statute of Labourers.[53]

(3) Harbouring a servant

It is still[54] actionable knowingly to continue to employ the servant of
another, though the person so continuing to employ the servant did not
procure him to leave his master or know when he engaged him that he was
the servant of another.[55] The action lies even when the relationship is not
strictly one of master and servant.[56] As the action is one of case, damage
flowing from the new employment as distinct from the old breach of contract must be proved. Hence it is a defence to show that the servant would
not in any event have returned to the first employer.[57]

§ 130. PARENT AND CHILD

No parent has, as such, any right in respect of his child of such sort that an
action for damages will lie against any other person for a violation of that
right.[58] The only right which a parent has as such is a right to the possession
and custody of his child during minority. The remedy for the infringement of
this right is not an action for damages against the person who deprives him
of his child but the recovery of possession either by means of a writ of
habeas corpus or by an application to the Family Division to exercise its
power in respect of the guardianship of infants.[59] Nor, conversely, has a
child any action for any loss which he may have suffered from interference
with his relationship with his parents (apart from that provided by the Fatal
Accidents Act, 1976).[60] The law has, however, given to a parent in his
capacity as employer the following remedy in respect of the loss of his child.

(1) Action for loss of services[61]

It is a tort actionable at the suit of a father (or other person in *loco
parentis*) to take away, imprison, or cause bodily harm to his child (male or
female), if (i) the relation of master and servant existed between them, (ii) the

---

[53] As Coleridge J. in his powerful dissenting judgment had suggested. Note that it was not by
reason of any wrong done to Miss Wagner that the plaintiff suffered damage. The decision
is also the basis of the rule that it is a tort maliciously to procure a breach of contract: see
below, § 136.
[54] The action has not been affected by the Law Reform (Miscellaneous Provisions) Act 1970:
see below, §§ 130–131.
[55] *Jones Bros. (Hunstanton) Ltd.* v. *Stevens* [1955] 1 Q.B. 275.
[56] *De Francesco* v. *Barnum* (1890) 63 L.T. 514 (a different action from that reported in
(1890) 45 Ch.D. 430).
[57] *Jones Bros. (Hunstanton) Ltd.* v. *Stevens* [1955] 1 Q.B. 275. It is hard to see how a
plaintiff could ever rebut this, especially in a state of full employment.
[58] *Hall* v. *Hollander* (1825) 4 B. & C. 660.
[59] It is true, indeed, that an action of trespass would formerly lie at the suit of the father for
the taking away of his son and heir, but this remedy did not extend to the taking away of
his other children, and the ground of the action even in the case of the son and heir was the
valuable interest which the father had in the marriage of the child under the old system of
tenure in chivalry.
[60] Some American jurisdictions give a child a cause of action in such circumstances: see
Prosser, *Torts*, § 124.
[61] The Pearson Report (Cmnd. 7054), § 447, recommended the abolition of this action.

act is a tort as against the child, other than a tort founded upon the rape, seduction or enticement of that child,[62] and (iii) the parent is thereby deprived of his child's services.

As to (i), all rights of action vested in a parent in respect of his child are vested in him not in his capacity as a parent but in his capacity as the master of his child and are therefore dependent on the existence in the particular case of the relation of master and servant. If this relation does not exist, either because the child is too young to give any services,[63] or because he is in the service of some other person, or for any other reason, the father has no remedy for any wrong done to him in respect of his child.[64] The service may be contractual, *de facto*, or constructive. As to (ii), it is irrelevant whether the wrongful act be intentional[65] or negligent,[66] provided it does not constitute rape, seduction, or enticement,[67] or that the defendant did not know the injured person was a child of the plaintiff. As to (iii), the parent must prove damage resulting from the loss of services. Hence no damages can be recovered for injuries to a child too young to perform any services.[68] Nor can the plaintiff recover damages for the injury to his feelings, as he can in the action for seduction.

(2) Actions for enticement, harbouring and seduction

It was once actionable in England[69] to induce a child under age but capable of service to leave his or her parent against the latter's will, or not to return home, having so left, unless there was some justification.[70] But this cause of action has been abolished by the Law Reform (Miscellaneous Provisions) Act 1970, section 5. This section also abolished the action in tort given to a parent (or person standing in place of a parent) for the loss of services caused by the rape or seduction of his child, although it is possible that an ordinary employer, as distinct from a parent, still has the action: a curious situation.

§ 131. HUSBAND AND WIFE[71]

Injuries to the husband

For many years the interest which a husband has in the companionship and services of his wife was protected against the interference of strangers in

---

[62] A restriction introduced by the Law Reform (Miscellaneous Provisions) Act 1970, s.5. Yet the husband can still sue if his wife is raped and he loses her services: see § 131.

[63] *Hall* v. *Hollander* (1825) 4 B. & C. 660.

[64] *Lough* v. *Ward* [1945] 2 All E.R. 338, 346.

[65] *Jones* v. *Brown* (1794) 1 Peake 306 (assault).

[66] As in *Barnes* v. *Pooley* (1935) 51 T.L.R. 391 (road accident).

[67] Law Reform (Miscellaneous Provisions) Act 1970, s.5. It is an oddity of English law that a father should be able to sue if a neighbour's dog has bitten his daughter, but not if he has raped her.

[68] *Hall* v. *Hollander* (1825) 4 B. & C. 660. But the court left it open whether medical expenses necessarily incurred by the parent will be recovered. In insurance practice such claims are not challenged: *Metroplitan Police District Receiver* v. *Tatum* [1948] 2 K.B. 68, 73; *Kirkham* v. *Boughey* [1958] 2 Q.B. 338.

[69] And still is in Ireland: see the full survey of the law in Working Paper No. 6 of the Law Reform Commission (1979).

[70] *Evans* v. *Walton* (1867) L.R. 2 C.P. 615; *Lough* v. *Ward* [1945] 2 All E.R. 338.

[71] See Parsons, "Torts Affecting Domestic Relations" (1953) 2 Univ. of W.A.Ann.L.Rev. 591; Fridman, "Consortium as an Interest in Torts" (1954) 32 Can. Bar Rev. 1065; Brett, "Consortium and Servitium" (1955) 29 A.L.J. 321, 389, 428.

four distinct ways, but three of these were abolished by the Law Reform (Miscellaneous Provisions) Act 1970, ss. 4 and 5.[72]

(i) *Action for loss of services*

It is still a tort actionable at the suit of a husband to take away, imprison, or do physical harm to his wife, if (i) the act is wrongful as against the wife,[73] and (ii) the husband is thereby deprived of her society or services. A husband has a right as against third persons to the *consortium et servitium* of his wife, just as a master has a similar right to the *servitium* of his servant. Any tortious act, therefore, committed against the wife is actionable at the suit of her husband, if he can prove that he was thereby deprived for any period of her society or services (*per quod consortium amisit* or *servitium amisit*).[74]

Distinct from enticement. It will be noted that the husband's remedy is not limited to cases where he has been deprived of his wife's *consortium* by reason of the defendant's enticement, although the tort is often called by that name. This action depends on entirely different principles from those on which the action of enticement is founded. The latter was founded (or at any rate justifiable) on the principle that the violation of a legal right committed knowingly is a cause of action[75]; the former is a relic of the proprietary rights a husband was once thought to possess in his wife.[76] If the matter had arisen for decision in this century the courts would almost certainly have refused to give an action to the husband merely for loss of *consortium* due to the negligence of a third party, but it is too late now for the courts to deny an action which has existed for hundreds of years.[77]

Distinct from wife's own claim. The two causes of action thus vested in a wife and her husband respectively are concurrent and cumulative. Thus if a married woman suffers physical harm in a railway accident, the company is liable in two actions—one at the suit of the wife for the damage so sustained by herself, and another at the suit of the husband alone for the injury done to him. These two actions may be brought separately or together.[78] The husband's action is quite distinct from any claim which his wife may have.[79] He is not affected by her contributory negligence (if any) and he recovers his

---

[72] As a result of recommendations made by the Law Reform Committee (11th Report, pp. 8–10), and the Law Commission (Working Paper No. 19).

[73] On the assumption that A.I.D. does not constitute adultery, the conduct of the donor and the doctor is not wrongful towards the wife, as she is a consenting party: *Scott* v. *Marshall* (1965) 55 D.L.R. (2d) 58.

[74] *Smee* v. *Tibbetts* (1953) 53 S.R.(N.S.W.) 391, 392.

[75] *Best* v. *Samuel Fox Ltd.* [1952] A.C. 716, 729.

[76] Petruchio's remarks in *The Taming of the Shrew*, III, ii, vividly express the attitude of the common law:

> "I will be master of what is mine own:
> She is my goods, my chattels; she is my house,
> My household stuff, my field, my barn,
> My horse, my ox, my ass, my any thing;
> And here she stands, touch her whoever dare;
> I'll bring mine action on the proudest he
> That stops my way in Padua."

[77] *Best* v. *Samuel Fox Ltd.* [1952] A.C. 716, 733.

[78] *Brockbank* v. *Whitehaven Ry.* (1862) 7 H. & N. 834.

[79] *Mallett* v. *Dunn* [1949] 2 K.B. 180. See below, § 196.

damages in full.[80] The proprietary basis of the action is prominent here, for the husband recovers even if he is ten thousand miles away at the date of the accident: proximity has nothing to do with it. On the other hand, the result of the decision in *Baker* v. *Bolton*[81] is that if the wife is not merely injured but killed, the husband's claim for loss of *consortium et servitium* is limited to the interval between her injury and her death. But he may have a claim to compensation for her death under the Fatal Accidents Acts, or even at common law if the cause of her death was a breach of contract as between himself and the defendant.[82] The action for loss of *consortium* should also be distinguished from any claim which the husband may have in respect of a tort committed against him as a direct result of which his wife leaves him.[83]

Damage. Although the action *per quod consortium et servitium amisit* is one of trespass and not case, damage to the husband is the gist of the action.[84] Hence when there is no loss of *consortium et servitium* the husband will recover no, or no more than nominal, damages, as when he was at the time of the act complained of permanently separated from his wife.[85] After a period of uncertainty, it is now settled in England[86] and Australia[87] that an action lies for partial impairment, as distinct from total loss,[88] of *consortium*, at least when the plaintiff proves some consequential material loss. Hence if a husband can prove that he has suffered definite loss he is entitled to damages, even though his wife's injuries have not deprived him entirely of her physical presence and society.[89] In a proper case such damages may be substantial, but the present English tendency is to award low sums.[90] The husband is certainly also entitled to recover damages for the cost of employing a housekeeper,[91] and for earnings lost as a result of being with his wife during her illness,[92] as well as medical expenses incurred on her behalf,[93] and the cost of visiting her in hospital, at any rate if the visits help her to recover and so mitigate the damage flowing from the loss of *consortium*.[94] The victim himself may now recover such expenses incurred by his family.[95] But neither husband nor wife can recover for the fact that the wife has had to

---

[80] *Curran* v. *Young* (1965) 112 C.L.R. 99. In Ireland the law is different: see the Civil Liability (Amendment) Act 1964, s.4.

[81] (1808) 1 Camp. 493. See below, § 217.

[82] *Jackson* v. *Watson & Sons* [1909] 2 K.B. 193.

[83] *Cameron* v. *Nottingham Insurance Co. Ltd.* [1958] S.A.S.R. 174.

[84] *Toohey* v. *Hollier* (1955) 92 C.L.R. 618.

[85] *Izard* v. *Izard* (1889) 14 P.D. 45.

[86] *Cutts* v. *Chumley* [1967] 1 W.L.R. 742, C.A. (the H.L. refused leave to appeal: [1968] 1 W.L.R. 668).

[87] *Toohey* v. *Hollier* (1955) 92 C.L.R. 618.

[88] In Ireland a total loss is required—see *Spaight* v. *Dundon* [1961] I.R. 201—but the effect of this is lessened by a later decision that the loss may be total even though it is for a limited period, and even though there is a limited measure of communication between the spouses: *O'Horan* v. *Divine* (1964) 100 I.L.T.R. 53.

[89] *Toohey* v. *Hollier* (1955) 92 C.L.R. 618.

[90] *Cutts* v. *Chumley* [1967] 1 W.L.R. 742 (£200 for loss of society, £5,000 for loss of services). The Law Commission (Working Paper No. 19, para. 46) are quite definite in their approval of the decision: "We think it would be generally agreed that it would have been outrageous if he had not been compensated in respect of the latter item at least and that the award was not over-generous."

[91] *Cutts* v. *Chumley* [1967] 1 W.L.R. 742.

[92] *Kirkham* v. *Boughey* [1958] 2 Q.B. 338; *McNeill* v. *Johnstone* [1958] 1 W.L.R. 888.

[93] *Best* v. *Samuel Fox Ltd.* [1952] A.C. 716.

[94] *McNeill* v. *Johnstone* [1958] 1 W.L.R. 888.

[95] *Donnelly* v. *Joyce* [1974] Q.B. 454.

work harder in the house as a result of the accident. It is possible that if the husband's loss is of a temporal kind (*e.g.* absolute deprivation of sexual intercourse), he can recover for it even though he has not been obliged to incur expenditure in consequence.[96]

(ii) *Harbouring a wife*

It was actionable to harbour the wife of another, after a request by the husband to deliver her up,[97] although the defendant did not procure her to leave her husband or know when he took her in that she was the wife of another,[98] provided that loss of *consortium* is proved.[99] It was held "on principles of humanity" to be a defence that owing to the husband's conduct the wife is justified or (perhaps) is honestly believed by the defendant to be justified in leaving her husband.[1] But the tort was abolished by the Law Reform (Miscellaneous Provisions) Act 1970, s. 5.

(iii) *Enticement*

The same Act has also abolished the tort of enticement in England,[2] which was committed when the defendant, without lawful justification, induced the plaintiff's wife to leave him or to remain away from him against his will.[3]

(iv) *The action for "criminal conversation"*

An action (whether of trespass or case is uncertain,[4] but probably trespass[5]) formerly lay against one who had committed adultery[6] with the wife of the plaintiff. It was known as an action for criminal conversation.[7] The wife's consent was irrelevant. The action was distinct from that of enticement: one may commit adultery without enticing a wife away from her husband. The action was no doubt a necessity when divorce could only be obtained by Act of Parliament: as Parliament was not a tribunal suitable for trying allegations of adultery it was reasonable to require the petitioner to establish the truth of his allegations before a court of law. The action might also have been justified on the ground that the plaintiff is in substance com-

---

[96] *Birch* v. *Taubmans Ltd.* (1957) 57 S.R.(N.S.W.) 93.

[97] *Spencer* v. *Relph* [1969] N.Z.L.R. 713.

[98] *Winsmore* v. *Greenbank* (1745) Willes 577.

[99] *Winchester* v. *Fleming* [1958] 1 Q.B. 259. So if the wife would not have returned to her husband in any event the plaintiff cannot recover: *Spencer* v. *Relph* [1969] N.Z.L.R. 713.

[1] *Place* v. *Searle* [1932] 2 K.B. 497, 513, 517. Even under the old writ of ravishment the defendant was not liable if he conducted the wife on a pilgrimage or took her into his house when she was "in danger of being lost in the night or of being drowned with water": Brooke, abridg. *s.v. Trespass*, pll. 207, 213.

[2] It still exists in New Zealand: see *Shelbourne* v. *Watt* [1979] N.Z.L.R. 50, which holds that the plaintiff must prove some real inducement: the defendant is under no duty "to get out of the way."

[3] *Smith* v. *Kaye* (1904) 20 T.L.R. 261.

[4] *Jones Bros. (Hunstanton) Ltd.* v. *Stevens* [1955] 1 Q.B. 275.

[5] *Pritchard* v. *Pritchard and Sims* [1967] P. 195.

[6] A.I.D. is probably not adultery: *Maclennan* v. *Maclennan* 1958 S.C. 105.

[7] *Norfolk (Duke of)* v. *Germaine* (1692) 12 St. Tr. 929 is the first reported action of this kind. The plaintiff alleged that the defendant had "by lascivious conversation" committed adultery with the duchess, and claimed £100,000 damages. The jury were severely reprimanded by Holt C.J. for awarding £66 13s. 4d.

plaining of the invasion of the privacy of his marriage, and the insult thereby caused to his honour as a husband.[8] But when the Divorce Court was established in 1857 the reason for the action disappeared and it was accordingly abolished in England. (But it may still exist in some Canadian provinces,[9] and in Ireland[10]). After 1857 a husband's claim for damages for adultery was made by way of petition in matrimonial proceedings, whether accompanied by a petition for divorce or not. However, this procedure in its turn became unpopular, but as the common people of England saw no reason why a wealthy seducer of a poor man's wife should not pay for what he had done[11] the Law Commission felt it could not recommend its abolition,[12] although Parliament finally effected this by the Law Reform (Miscellaneous Provisions) Act 1970, s. 4.

Injuries to the wife

(i) *Enticement and harbouring*

No action will lie against another woman by a wife for adultery committed with her husband.[13] But at common law she could sue for enticement,[14] although not for harbouring.[15] But the 1970 Act has also abolished these claims.

(ii) *Loss of consortium*

A married woman has no right of action against a person who by a negligent act or omission has deprived her of her husband's society or services. This claim was put forward (apparently for the first time) in *Best* v. *Samuel Fox Ltd.*,[16] in which the plaintiff's husband had, by reason of the defendant's negligence, suffered injuries the effect of which was to deprive the plaintiff of the opportunity of having normal marital relations. It was argued that in modern conditions it was anomalous to grant such an action to the husband and refuse it to the wife. But the House of Lords held that the real anomaly today was the husband's right of action for loss of his wife's *consortium* and that there was no reason for extending such an anomaly.[17] The decision in *Best* v. *Fox* cannot be evaded by suing in negligence.[18] On the other hand, for the death of her husband a wife, if dependent, may claim compensation under the Fatal Accidents Act.[19]

---

[8] *Maher* v. *Collins* [1975] I.R. 232.
[9] *Skinner* v. *Allen* (1977) 81 D.L.R. 592.
[10] *Maher* v. *Collins* [1975] I.R. 232.
[11] So one Labour M.P. opposed the abolition of the action as being "an open sesame to some rich philanderer, who would be able to cruise past the factory gates in his leather upholstered Rolls-Royce and importune away the prettiest wife at the works": Standing Committee C, February 11, 1970, col. 38.
[12] Law Com. No. 19, paras. 91–92.
[13] *Newton* v. *Hardy* (1933) 149 L.T. 165.
[14] *Best* v. *Samuel Fox Ltd.* [1952] A.C. 716, 729–730.
[15] *Winchester* v. *Fleming* [1958] 1 Q.B. 259.
[16] [1952] A.C. 716.
[17] Most American jurisdictions now give the wife a cause of action: Prosser, *Torts*, § 125.
[18] *Marx* v. *Att.-Gen.* [1974] 1 N.Z.L.R. 164.
[19] See below, § 217.

§ 132. DEATH OF RELATIVES[20]

At common law it was not a civil wrong to cause the death of a human being.[21] So although a husband could sue at common law for any wilful or negligent harm done to his wife whereby he was temporarily deprived of her society or services, he could not sue in respect of that permanent deprivation which he suffered by reason of her death. A father's rights in respect of his children were similarly limited. Thus in *Osborn* v. *Gillett*[22] a father sued at common law[23] for the death of his daughter, who had been negligently run over and killed by the defendant. The defendant pleaded that the deceased had been killed on the spot and therefore that the plaintiff had not been deprived of the services of his daughter otherwise than by her death; and it was held that the plea was good. Had the death ensued after an interval only, the plaintiff would have had a good cause of action for loss of service during that interval,[24] but none in respect of the death. In *Jackson* v. *Watson and Sons Ltd.*,[25] however, it was decided that this rule does not apply in an action for breach of contract, but is limited to cases of pure tort. But when the breach of a contract made with the plaintiff results in the death of some third person in whose life the plaintiff has an interest, the damages recoverable in an action of contract will, it seems, include any pecuniary loss resulting, not too remotely, from that death. Thus in *Jackson* v. *Watson* itself, a husband, in an action for breach of warranty in a contract of sale, recovered damages (independently of the Fatal Accidents Act) for the death of his wife caused by eating certain poisonous food sold to him by the defendants. In other words, the killing of a human being, although not itself a cause of action, may be taken into account in assessing damages for an independent cause of action in contract.

We shall see[26] that the Law Reform (Miscellaneous Provisions) Act 1934, abolished the effect of the maxim *actio personalis moritur cum persona*. But that rule is entirely distinct from the rule in *Baker* v. *Bolton*, which deprives other persons than the deceased of any remedy where they have suffered damage as the result of the death. The latter rule seems to be based, in so far as it refers to inability to recover for the loss of services by the infliction of death, on the principle that a trespass is merged in a felony, a reason inadequate in Lord Ellenborough's time, and now obsolete.[27] It is probable that it was introduced into the law owing to a confusion of the *actio personalis*

---

[20] See Holdsworth, "The Origin of the Rule in *Baker* v. *Bolton*" (1916) 32 L.Q.R. 431; (1917) 33 L.Q.R. 107–109; Holdsworth, H.E.L., 3rd ed., iii, pp. 331–336, 576–583; Report of Law Revision Committee (Cmd. 4540 (1934)).

[21] *Baker* v. *Bolton* (1808) 1 Camp. 493. The reporter of Lord Ellenborough's decisions at Nisi Prius was the future Lord Campbell, who in his *Life* (ii, p. 215), after paying tribute to the high judicial qualities of the Chief Justice, said: "When I arrived at the end of my fourth and last volume, I had a whole drawer full of 'bad Ellenborough law.'" If Lord Campbell had put *Baker* v. *Bolton* into that drawer he would have earned the gratitude of later generations—though then he would not have given his name to a statute.

[22] (1873) L.R. 8 Ex. 88.

[23] It does not appear from the report why the action was not brought under the Fatal Accidents Act. Under this Act damages could in such a case be recovered to the extent of the value of the daughter's gratuitous services to her father: *Berry* v. *Humm & Co.* [1915] 1 K.B. 627.

[24] As in *Baker* v. *Bolton* itself.

[25] [1909] 2 K.B. 193.

[26] Below, § 166.

[27] In any event the civil remedy is only suspended, not extinguished: *Rose* v. *Ford* [1937] A.C. 826, 846.

maxim with the former rule[28] that no action will lie for a tort which is also a felony until the felon has been prosecuted, a rule which will not support the doctrine in its present wide form. But although the rule may be both unjust and technically unsound, it is the present law of England, for it was affirmed by the House of Lords in *Admiralty Commissioners* v. *SS. Amerika.*[29] "We can only regard the decision as perhaps the strongest illustration which we have in our books of the manner in which *communis* error sometimes *facit jus.*"[30] Although its abolition was recommended by the Law Revision Committee[31] the Government felt it would be difficult to allow an employer to recover for the death of his servant without also making provision for the converse situation.[32] We shall deal later with the statutory exceptions to the rule in *Baker* v. *Bolton* created by the Fatal Accidents Acts 1846 to 1959,[33] now consolidated in the Fatal Accidents Act 1976.

[28] See below, § 166.
[29] [1917] A.C. 38.
[30] Holdsworth, H.E.L., Vol. iii, pp. 336, 667.
[31] Cmd. 4540 (1934) s. 15(e).
[32] Hutton, "Mechanics of Law Reform" (1961) 24 M.L.R. 18, 23.
[33] See below, § 217.

CHAPTER 16

ECONOMIC RELATIONS

§ 133. Introductory[1]

The fundamental case is *Allen* v. *Flood*.[2] Flood and Taylor were shipwrights employed "for the job" (*i.e.* by the day) by the Glengall Iron Company. Some iron men who also worked for the company objected to the employment of shipwrights, and Allen, a trade union official acting on their behalf, informed the company's manager that unless Flood and Taylor were dismissed the men would "knock off work," or "be called out." (It was uncertain exactly which phrase he used.) Flood and Taylor thereupon were lawfully dismissed by the Glengall Company at the end of the day. Kennedy J. awarded the plaintiffs damages and his judgment was upheld by the Court of Appeal, which held that it was a tort (1) maliciously to procure the lawful dismissal of another, and (2) maliciously to procure another to abstain from making a contract. A majority of the House of Lords held that the Court of Appeal was wrong on both points, and that Flood and Taylor had no cause of action against Allen. No unlawful act had been committed by him: he had not induced or procured the breach of any contract. Nor had he entered into any conspiracy. The fact that his motives might have been malicious made no difference. "At the end of the day all that *Allen* v. *Flood* decides is that where there is no element of combination so far as the individual is concerned what he does is either lawful or unlawful; if it is unlawful it is not saved by good intentions, and if it is lawful it is not made unlawful by reason of malice on his part."[3]

It was also settled in *Allen* v. *Flood* that so far as a single defendant is concerned there is a chasm between inducing a breach of contract and inducing a person not to enter into a contract.[4] The common law does not protect mere expectancies as distinct from promised advantages. Perhaps the clearest illustration of the conduct which might be actionable if such a tort existed is to be found in the American case of *Tuttle* v. *Buck*,[5] in which the plaintiff, who had carried on his hairdressing business in a small town for many years, incurred the enmity of the defendant, a wealthy man, who deliberately set up a rival establishment in the same town with the object and effect of driving the plaintiff out of business by under-cutting his rates. The court held that an action lay.

In other words, what the plaintiff is trying to establish in a case like *Tuttle* v. *Buck* is "*Quinn* v. *Leathem* without the conspiracy."[6] Sir John Holt in

---

[1] See Heydon, *The Economic Torts* (2nd ed., 1978); Burns, "Tort Injury to Economic Interests" (1980) 50 Can. Bar Rev. 103.
[2] [1898] A.C. 1.
[3] Lord Gardiner Q.C., *arguendo*, in *Rookes* v. *Barnard* [1963] 1 Q.B. 623, 645.
[4] *Rookes* v. *Barnard* [1964] A.C. 1129, 1168, 1234.
[5] (1909) 107 Minn. 145; 119 N.W. 946.
[6] Lord Devlin's memorable phrase in *Rookes* v. *Barnard* [1964] A.C. 1129, 1216. In North America this is sometimes called the prima facie tort doctrine.

1705 and Sir William Erle in 1869 suggested that such an action might lie[7] and the following Law Lords have at various times and in various words contemplated the likelihood of such an action: Lord Lindley in *Quinn* v. *Leathem*[8]; Lord Loreburn in *Conway* v. *Wade*[9]; Lords Cave, Atkinson and Sumner in *Sorrell* v. *Smith*[10]; and Lord Devlin in *Rookes* v. *Barnard*.[11] On the other hand Lord Dunedin described this view as "the leading heresy,"[12] and Lord Donovan in *Stratford and Son Ltd.* v. *Lindley*[13] also opposed it. But the draftsman of the second limb of section 3 of the Trade Disputes Act 1906,[14] clearly assumed that deliberate interference with trade, business or employment without lawful justification might be held to be a tort.[15] If it be said that this view is untenable since section 13 (2) of the Trade Union and Labour Relations Acts 1974 and 1976, the reply[16] is that the position was uncertain in 1906 and Parliament was putting in a provision which would be necessary if the law as interpreted by the courts went one way[17] but unnecessary if it went the other way.

There is much to be said for the view that if *Allen* v. *Flood* had gone the other way the courts would have had a useful weapon against intolerable conduct. Also much of the complex legislation on race relations would have been unnecessary.[18]

But it is really irrelevant to discuss the possibility of the courts distinguishing *Allen* v. *Flood*, because Parliament[19] has made it plain that even if the decision were reversed, the defendant in an industrial dispute would still be protected from an action in tort, and outside the area of industrial disputes *Allen* v. *Flood* is only of academic interest.[20]

So far as is possible to find a common element in all the cases on trade competition it seems to be that the defendant has used a third person to harm the plaintiff.[21] "Pressure is at the heart of this branch of tort."[22] "This is not surprising. One can bloody one's neighbour's nose unaided, but to ruin him usually requires assistance; the defendant in the economic torts is commonly Iago, not Jehu."[23] It is important to note that the defendant has

---

[7] *Keeble* v. *Hickeringhall* (1706) 11 East 573n. 575; Erle, *Trade Unions* (1869), p. 12. This was also the view of 6 of the 8 High Court judges summoned to advise in *Allen* v. *Flood* |1898| A.C. 1. It is worth remembering that of the 21 judges before whom *Allen* v. *Flood* was argued, only 8 were in favour of the trade union official who was the successful defendant, but 6 of those 8 were Lords of Appeal.

[8] |1901| A.C. 495, 537. See also below, § 137.

[9] |1909| A.C. 506, 511.

[10] |1925| A.C. 700, 713, 739.

[11] |1964| A.C. 1129, 1215.

[12] *Sorrell* v. *Smith* |1925| A.C. 700, 719.

[13] |1965| A.C. 269, 340.

[14] See below, § 139.

[15] See |1964| A.C. 1129, 1177, 1216, and Hoffmann in (1965) 81 L.Q.R. 116 on the parliamentary history of the section.

[16] *Rookes* v. *Barnard* |1964| A.C. 1129, 1216.

[17] *i.e.* by recognising "*Quinn* v. *Leathem* without the conspiracy."

[18] See Heydon, *Economic Torts*, p. 28.

[19] In s. 13 (2) of the Trade Union and Labour Relations Act 1974. See below, § 139.

[20] In any event, the decision may be justifiable from the standpoint of policy. So Pollock though it was correct "for a world of people who mostly get muddled over subtle distinctions, and think them unjust whenever they can't understand" (Pollock-Holmes) *Letters*, Vol. I, pp. 84–85).

[21] See Silkin *arguendo* |1963| 1 Q.B. 623, 652.

[22] *Morgan* v. *Fry* |1968| 2 Q.B. 710, 738, per Russell L.J. So in *Rookes* v. *Barnard* the defendant Fistal said in evidence "We secured our desires by pressure" (Printed Case, p. 39).

[23] Weir, Note |1964| C.L.J. 225, 227.

not procured the third party to commit any tort: if he had done this, there would be no problem, for the defendant and the third party would be joint tortfeasors. The difficulties arise partly because the act of the third party is lawful, and partly because the common law is better adapted to deal with force than with cunning.

§ 134. STRIKES AND THE LAW

At the outset attention should be directed to two difficult questions of terminology—"the right to strike" and "threats."

"The right to strike"

This is a loose phrase, for there is no right in the strict sense of the term—*i.e.* a claim to which there is opposed a duty. The phrase really means immunity from the ordinary criminal and civil processes.[24] Since the Conspiracy and Protection of Property Act 1875, a strike has been in general lawful from the standpoint of the criminal courts. Whether a strike is lawful from the point of view of the Law of Torts or Contracts is a different question.

"A strike"

A man is always entitled to terminate his employment by giving lawful notice. This is fundamental in a free society—unless Parliament for sufficient reasons (*e.g.* wartime, or the creation of a status such as that of a dock labourer under the Dock Labour Scheme) has deprived the workman of the right, or he has himself bargained it away by entering into a non-strike agreement, as happened in *Rookes* v. *Barnard*.[25]

A strike more usually and properly means the concerted and unlawful withdrawal of all or some part of labour by the men.[26] But it may be possible to imply a term in the contract of service that the workmen might lawfully strike after due notice, that notice being not less than the notice required to terminate the contract.[27] But this is a novel view which gives rise to many difficulties,[28] and has not been followed.[29]

"Threats"

Another difficulty arises from the word "threat." A threat is a preintimation of proposed action of some kind, and that everything depends upon whether the action proposed (with, it is understood, the object and effect of injuring the plaintiff) is lawful. At one time there was a tendency to distinguish between a threat on the one hand and a notice or warning on the other hand, so that if a trade union official says "all my members have decided to embark upon this course of action," it would be a question whether he was just acting as a messenger or uttering a threat. But it is now

---

[24] *Stratford (J.T.) & Son Ltd.* v. *Lindley* [1965] A.C. 269, 304; Donovan Report (Cmnd. 3623, paras. 928–935).
[25] [1964] A.C. 1129.
[26] *Rookes* v. *Barnard* [1964] A.C. 1129 (Lords Devlin and Hodson).
[27] *Morgan* v. *Fry* [1968] 2 Q.B. 710; *Becton, Dickinson & Co. Ltd.* v. *Lee* [1973] I.R. 1, 37.
[28] Cmnd. 3623, paras. 942–945.
[29] *Simmons* v. *Hoover Ltd.* [1977] Q.B. 284.

generally agreed that this distinction is unhelpful.[30] A threat is not *per se* unlawful. The distinction between unlawful and lawful threats is drawn according to the nature of the act threatened and not according to the nature of the threat. One might give proper notice of termination of a contract in the most violent language: conversely, an announcement of an intention to call out all the workers in a vital industry may be couched in subdued tones. The conclusion is that if one may do something, one may threaten to do it.

It has been said that the threat must be a coercive one—*i.e.* coupled with some demand, so that if my gardener tells me he is not going to dig my potatoes that is only an announcement and not a threat unless he couples it with, say, a demand for higher wages.[31] But this view seems to rest upon the now outmoded difference between a threat and an announcement or warning. It is certainly clear that the threat may be either an "if" threat or an "unless" one. There is no difference between saying that one will break one's contract if an employer does something, and saying that one will break one's contract unless he does something.[32] A threat is usually made by, or on behalf of, a number of people, but a threat by one important employee may be very effective.

The Employment Act 1980

This statute imposes further restrictions on the right to strike. It is best considered after a detailed consideration of the torts of inducement of breach of contract, conspiracy and intimidation.

§ 135. INDUCEMENT OF BREACH OF CONTRACT[33]

Intentionally and without lawful justification to induce or procure anyone to break a contract made by him with another is a tort actionable at the suit of that other, if damage has resulted to him.[34] In practice today the courts seem to be more willing to grant injunctions in such cases than they were in the past.[35] The tort had its origin in the action for enticing away the servant of another. In *Lumley* v. *Gye*[36] it was held that such an action lay even when the contract, breach of which had been procured, was not one of service in the strict sense of the term. It was, however, for some time believed that the principle so established was confined to cases where (i) the defendant's action was malicious, and (ii) the contract in question was one to render exclusive personal services for a fixed period.[37] But now it is perfectly well established that the scope of the action is not limited in either of these ways.

---

[30] *Hodges* v. *Webb* [1920] 2 Ch. 70. But see Lords Reid, Evershed and Hodson in *Rookes* v. *Barnard* [1964] A.C. 1129, and Lord Reid *arguendo* in *Stratford (J.T.) & Son Ltd.* v. *Lindley, The Times,* July 2, 1964.

[31] Lord Denning M.R. in *Stratford (J.T.) & Son Ltd.* v. *Lindley* [1965] A.C. 269, 287.

[32] [1965] A.C. 269, 292.

[33] See Lauterpacht, "Contracts to break a Contract" (1936) 52 L.Q.R. 494; Hughes, "Liability for Loss Caused by Industrial Action" (1970) 86 L.Q.R. 181; Smith, "The Economic Torts" (1977) 41 *The Conveyancer* 318.

[34] *James McMahon Ltd.* v. *Dunne* (1965) 99 I.L.T.R. 45, 49; *Becton, Dickinson Ltd.* v. *Lee* [1973] I.R. 1, 45.

[35] *Swiss Bank Corporation* v. *Lloyd's Bank Ltd.* [1979] 2 All E.R. 853, 871.

[36] (1853) 2 E. & B. 216. See above, § 129.

[37] *Bowen* v. *Hall* (1881) 6 Q.B.D. 333.

Indeed, the modern cases indicate that the tort has become so broad as to be better described as unlawful interference with contractual relations.

(1) The unlawful intention

Proof of malice in the sense of spite or ill-will is unnecessary.[38] "I think," said Lord Macnaghten,[39] "the decision [in *Lumley* v. *Gye*] was right, not on the ground of malicious intention—that was not, I think, the gist of the action—but on the ground that a violation of legal right committed knowingly is a cause of action, and that it is a violation of legal right to interfere with contractual relations recognised by law, if there be not sufficient justification for the interference." It is no justification for the defendant to say that he had an honest doubt whether he was interfering with the plaintiff's contract,[40] or without malice,[41] or in good faith,[42] or that the breach was really for the plaintiff's benefit, if he had only properly understood the position.[43] It is enough to show that the defendant did an act which must damage the plaintiff: it need not be proved that he intended it to do so.[44]

(2) The contracts protected

The principle in *Lumley* v. *Gye* protects contracts which involve a continuous course of dealing as well as those to do a particular act.[45] Nor is the principle any longer confined to inducements to break contracts of service. Thus in *Temperton* v. *Russell*[46] certain builders had contracted with the plaintiff to purchase from him their building materials. The defendants, officials of a trade union which wished to bring pressure to bear upon the plaintiff, procured the builders to break these contracts by threatening them with labour trouble if they refused to do so. The Court of Appeal held the defendants liable.

The court was also of the opinion that it was actionable to induce persons not to enter into contracts with the plaintiff, but in this it was wrong. "So far from thinking it a small step from one decision to the other, I think there is a chasm between them."[47] In short, the principle in *Lumley* v. *Gye* protects promised advantages and not mere expectancies.[48] But to this proposition there is a qualification: if the plaintiff's contract has been breached by the defendant, the court can, by way of injunction,[49] restrain interference not only with that contract but also with any other similar contract which he may make in the future.[50] This is justifiable because what is restrained is a

---

[38] *Dirassar* v. *Kelly, Douglas & Co. Ltd.* (1966) 59 D.L.R. (2d) 452.
[39] *Quinn* v. *Leathem* [1901] A.C. 495, 510.
[40] *Swiss Bank Corporation* v. *Lloyd's Bank* [1979] 2 All E.R. 853.
[41] *Greig* v. *Insole* [1978] 1 W.L.R. 302, 332.
[42] *Pratt* v. *British Medical Association* [1919] 1 K.B. 244, 265–266.
[43] *South Wales Miners' Federation* v. *Glamorgan Coal Co. Ltd.* [1905] A.C. 239, 246.
[44] *National Phonograph Co. Ltd.* v. *Edison-Bell Phonograph Co. Ltd.* [1908] 1 Ch. 335, 357.
[45] *National Phonograph Co. Ltd.* v. *Edison-Bell Phonograph Co. Ltd.* [1908] 1 Ch. 335, 367–368.
[46] [1893] 1 Q.B. 715.
[47] *Allen* v. *Flood* [1898] A.C. 1, 121, *per* Lord Herschell. Trade competition, however ruthless, is not in itself wrongful: see above, § 133.
[48] But one whose customers (as distinct from prospective customers) have been driven away by threats of violence or other illegal acts may have a remedy for intimidation: see above, § 138.
[49] *Acrow Ltd.* v. *Rex Chainbelt Inc.* [1971] 1 W.L.R. 1676.
[50] *Torquay Hotel Co. Ltd.* v. *Cousins* [1969] 2 Ch. 106.

breach of contract, whether to take place now or in the future, which is not the same as ordering a person not to make a contract.[51]

(3) The breach procured

It has been held that no action will lie for the inducement of the breach of a contract which is void, *e.g.* a wagering contract,[52] or one which is in restraint of trade.[53] Probably no action lies for breach of a contract which is not void but only unenforceable—*e.g.* one covered by the Law of Property Act 1925, s. 40.[54] It has been suggested that no action will lie for the inducement of the breach of a contract which is determinable at pleasure, for (unless illegal means have been used) in such a case there has been in truth no breach at all,[55] but as the gist of the action is the intentional violation of contractual rights this view may be too simple. For if a union official induces a supplier not to fulfil his contract with an employer, the official may be liable to the employer in tort, even though the supplier is protected as against the employer by a *force majeure* clause,[56] or the contract is regarded by the parties to it as suspended rather than broken.[57] It has been said that the breach procured must be one which goes to the root of the contract in question,[58] but this is now doubtful,[59] especially since the law has moved so far as to hold that a direct and deliberate interference with a contract may be tortious even though no breach has been caused.[60]

Interference without breach

A deliberate interference with contractual relations is actionable if it prevents or hinders one of the parties to that contract from performing his obligations under it[61]; even though he is not thereby in breach of it.[62] To that extent a direct and deliberate interference with the trade or business of another is a tort.[63] On the other hand, it can also be asserted that (apart from cases of conspiracy to injure) acts of a third party lawful in themselves do not constitute an actionable interference with contractual rights merely because they bring about a breach of contract, even if they were done with the object and intention of bringing about such a breach.[64] Indirect interference is unlawful only if unlawful means are used.[65] So no tort is committed if A buys up all the goods in the market ahead of B with the object

---

[51] *Midland Cold Storage Ltd.* v. *Steer* [1972] Ch. 630.
[52] *Joe Lee Ltd.* v. *Dalmeny* (Lord) [1927] 1 Ch. 300.
[53] *Greig* v. *Insole* [1978] 1 W.L.R. 302.
[54] *Smith* v. *Morrison* [1974] 1 W.L.R. 659.
[55] *McManus* v. *Bowes* [1938] 1 K.B. 98, 127.
[56] *Torquay Hotel Co. Ltd.* v. *Cousins* [1969] 2 Ch. 106.
[57] *Daily Mirror Newspapers Ltd.* v. *Gardner* [1968] 2 Q.B. 762.
[58] *De Jetley Marks* v. *Greenwood* (Lord) [1936] 1 All E.R. 863, 872.
[59] *D.C. Thomson & Co. Ltd.* v. *Deakin* [1952] Ch. 646, 664, 689–690.
[60] *Torquay Hotel Co. Ltd.* v. *Cousins* [1969] 2 Ch. 106.
[61] *e.g.* if the defendant increases the plaintiff's costs of performing a contract to keep a highway in repair by dumping rubbish upon it.
[62] *Torquay Hotel Ltd.* v. *Cousins* [1969] 2 Ch. 106.
[63] *Acrow Ltd.* v. *Rex Chainbelt Inc.* [1971] 1 W.L.R. 1676.
[64] *D.C.Thomson & Co. Ltd.* v. *Deakin* [1952] Ch. 646, 693.
[65] *Torquay Hotel Co. Ltd.* v. *Cousins* [1969] 2 Ch. 106, 139; *Acrow Ltd.* v. *Rex Chainbelt Inc.* [1971] 1 W.L.R. 1676, 1682; *Brekkes* v. *Cattel* [1972] 1 Ch. 105; *Midland Cold Storage Ltd.* v. *Steer* [1972] Ch. 630.

and effect of preventing B from fulfilling his contract with C.[66] Nor does it make any difference that such acts were done out of spite or ill-will.

But the plaintiff is favoured in that he is not obliged to prove that the defendant knew the precise terms of the contract breached: it is enough if the defendant's knowledge is sufficient to entitle the court to say that he has knowingly or recklessly[67] procured a breach.[68] The result is to hold that it is enough for the plaintiff to prove an intent on the defendant's part to bring the contract to an end.[69] So constructive knowledge of the term of the contract breached may suffice, in the sense that it may be enough to show common knowledge of the way in which business is conducted,[70] at least when the plaintiff's application is for an interlocutory injunction.[71]

(4) The inducement or procurement

Subject to the important immunities given by section 13 of the Trade Union and Labour Relations Act 1974, as amended by the Employment Act 1980, the necessary ingredients of an actionable interference with contractual rights will exist in the following cases:

(1) When a third party, with knowledge of the contract and the intent to procure its breach, directly persuades or procures or induces one of the parties to that contract to break it. This is the most obvious form of actionable interference and is well illustrated by *Lumley* v. *Gye* itself,[72] or by the cases in which there is unlawful picketing.[73]

(2) When a third party, instead of acting on the mind of the contract-breaker, physically detains him[74] or otherwise renders it impossible for him to perform his contract, *e.g.* by breaking his essential tools or machinery.[75] On such facts the contract-breaker will himself have an action for assault or intimidation. These acts must, of course, be done with knowledge of the contract and intent to bring about its breach. If this knowledge is not proved, an action for loss of services may lie, but not one for procurement of breach of contract. In these cases of direct disablement the means used need not be intrinsically unlawful,[76] as they must be when the inducement is indirect.[77]

(3) When a third party and the contract-breaker deal together in a manner which the third party knows to be inconsistent with the contract, *e.g.* when A pays for and takes delivery of a new car from B, knowing that it is offered to him in breach of a covenant against the resale of new cars.[78] (In this case the tort of conspiracy will probably also

---

[66] But it might be different if A was acting in breach of a statute or by-law: *Emms* v. *Brad Lovett Ltd.* [1973] 1 N.Z.L.R. 282.

[67] *Emerald Construction Co. Ltd.* v. *Lowthian* [1966] 1 W.L.R. 691, 701.

[68] *Stratford (J.T.) & Son Ltd.* v. *Lindley* [1965] A.C. 269, 332.

[69] *Greig* v. *Insole* [1978] 1 W.L.R. 302.

[70] *James McMahon Ltd.* v. *Dunne* (1965) 99 I.L.T.R. 45 ("timber does not enter the Port of Dublin like manna from Heaven").

[71] *Daily Mirror Newspapers Ltd.* v. *Gardner* [1968] 2 Q.B. 762.

[72] See above, § 129.

[73] *Becton, Dickinson Ltd.* v. *Lee* [1973] I.R. 1, 35–36.

[74] As if Gye had kidnapped Johanna Wagner: Weir [1964] C.L.J. 225, 228.

[75] *D.C.Thomson Ltd.* v. *Deakin* [1952] Ch. 646, 678, 695–696.

[76] *Esso Petroleum Ltd.* v. *Kingswood Motors Ltd.* [1974] 1 Q.B. 142.

[77] See the distinction drawn between direct and indirect interference in *Greig* v. *Insole* [1978] 1 W.L.R. 302, 334.

[78] *B.M.T.A.* v. *Salvadori* [1949] Ch. 556.

have been committed.) The contract-breaker may himself be a willing party to the breach: it is the interference with existing contractual relations which is the essence of the tort, not the inducement to break them.[79] The tort is only committed if the inconsistent dealing is begun, or continued, after the third party has notice of the contract.[80]

(4) Again, so far from persuading or inducing or procuring one of the parties to the contract to break it, the third party may commit an actionable interference with the contract, against the will of both and without the knowledge of either, if, with knowledge of the contract, he does an act which, if done by one of the parties to it, would have been a breach. Of this type of interference the case of *G.W.K. Ltd.* v. *Dunlop Rubber Co. Ltd.*[81] affords a striking example.[82]

(5) When a third party, with knowledge of the contract and intent to secure its breach, definitely and unequivocally persuades, induces or procures the servant of one of the parties to break his contract of employment, provided that the breach of the commercial contract forming the alleged subject of interference in fact ensues as a necessary consequence of the breach of the contract of employment.[83] It must be clearly shown that the effect of the withdrawal of the services of the particular servant concerned was to render it quite impracticable for the contract-breaker to perform his contract.[84] So "general exhortations issued in the course of a trade dispute, such as 'Stop supplies to X,' 'Refuse to handle X's goods,' 'Treat X as "black,"'' and the like,"[85] will not usually constitute a sufficient inducement to be actionable (even if the other requisites are present), for the persons moved by such advocacy might well respond in a perfectly lawful way. So if the interference or disablement is indirect, it must be distinctly shown that unlawful means were advocated with the intent of interfering with the performance of a particular contract.[86] But in *Stratford (J.T.) & Son Ltd.* v. *Lindley*[87] the House of Lords clearly recognised that inducing breaches of employment contracts could be unlawful means in relation to inducing breaches of commercial contracts.

Advice distinguished from inducement

It will be noticed that the tort is variously described as "procuring" or "inducing" a breach of contract or "interfering with contractual relations." Do these expressions cover mere advice? In the first place it is clear that the advice or inducement to be actionable must have been acted upon.[88]

---

[79] *Sefton (Earl)* v. *Tophams Ltd.* [1964] 1 W.L.R. 1408; [1965] Ch. 1140. The appeal to the H.L. was on another point: [1967] 1 A.C. 50.
[80] *De Francesco* v. *Barnum* (1890) 63 L.T. 514, 515; *D.C.Thomson Ltd.* v. *Deakin* [1952] Ch. 646.
[81] (1926) 42 T.L.R. 376 and 593 (removal of rival's tyres from the car at motor show).
[82] *D.C.Thomson Ltd.* v. *Deakin* [1952] Ch. 646, 694, *per* Jenkins L.J.
[83] *Stratford & Son Ltd.* v. *Lindley* [1965] A.C. 269, 333, which is the leading case on indirect or secondary boycotts.
[84] *D.C.Thomson Ltd.* v. *Deakin* [1952] Ch. 646, 682, 696.
[85] *D.C.Thomson Ltd.* v. *Deakin* [1952] Ch. 646, 696, *per* Jenkins L.J.
[86] *Acrow Ltd.* v. *Rex Chainbelt Inc.* [1971] 1 W.L.R. 1676, 1681.
[87] [1965] A.C. 269.
[88] *Read* v. *Friendly Society of Stonemasons* [1902] 2 K.B. 732, 737.

Secondly, the better view is that merely to give advice or information[89] is not inducement.[90] So there is no liability when a trade union official advises a customer of the employer in dispute that he should consider his business relations with that employer in the light of the dispute, or a physician advises a patient to break a contract of service for his health's sake. This advice will not consitute an inducement even if it calls attention to the possible dangers of continuing the contract in question—*e.g.* that a supplier's men may be called out if he maintains his contract with the employer in dispute. There must be an inducement in the strict sense—that is to say, the intentional creation of some inducing cause or reason for the breach of contract: for example, to induce a servant to leave his employment by an offer of higher wages, or by a threat to inflict some harm upon him, legal or illegal, if he continues in it. To induce a breach of contract means to create a reason for breaking it; to advise a breach of contract is to point out the reasons which already exist. The former is certainly actionable: the latter is probably innocent.[91]

(5) The defence of justification

To induce a breach of contract is not actionable if there is in the circumstances of the case a legal justification for the inducement.[92] What amounts to a justification is a question to which no precise answer can be given,[93] It was said by (Sir Robert) Romer L.J.,[94] in a passage often approved,[95] that most attempts to give a complete and satisfactory definition would probably be mischievous and that it must be left to the good sense of the tribunal to analyse the circumstances of the particular case. In so doing regard might be had to the nature of the contract broken; the position of the parties to the contract; the grounds for the breach; the means employed to procure the breach; the relation of the person procuring the breach to the person who breaks the contract; and to the object of the person in procuring the breach.[96] Presumably it would be a good justification if, in inducing a breach of contract made by A with the plaintiff, the defendant was doing nothing more than insisting on the performance of another and inconsistent contract previously made between himself and A.[97] But the breach by B of his contract with A cannot properly be held to justify or excuse A in procuring C to break an independent contract with B.[98]

[89] *Torquay Hotel Co. Ltd.* v. *Cousins* [1969] 2 Ch. 106, 125.
[90] This was the opinion of the Royal Commission on Trade Unions (Donovan Commission), 1968, Cmnd. 3623, para. 891.
[91] The question was discussed obiter in *South Wales Miners' Federation* v. *Glamorgan Coal Co.* [1905] A.C. 239, and in *D.C.Thomson Ltd.* v. *Deakin* [1952] Ch. 646. See also *De Stempel* v. *Dunkels* [1938] Ch. 352, 366, in which Simonds J. expressed an opinion opposed to that in the text.
[92] *South Wales Miners' Federation* v. *Glamorgan Coal Co.* [1905] A.C. 239; *Quinn* v. *Leathem* [1901] A.C. 510; *Smithies* v. *National Association of the Operative Plasterers* [1909] 1 K.B. 310.
[93] There is a full review of the cases in *Pete's Towing Services Ltd.* v. *Northern Industrial Union* [1970] N.Z.L.R. 32, 49, and in *Posluns* v. *Toronto Stock Exchange* (1964) 46 D.L.R. (2d) 210.
[94] *Glamorgan Coal Co.* v. *South Wales Miners' Federation* [1903] 2 K.B. 545, 574–575.
[95] *Greig* v. *Insole* [1978] 1 W.L.R. 302, 340.
[96] *Dirassar* v. *Kelly, Douglas Ltd.* (1966) 59 D.L.R. (2d) 452, 481–482.
[97] *Smithies* v. *National Association of Operative Plasterers* [1909] 1 K.B. 310, 337; *Pratt* v. *British Medical Association* [1919] 1 K.B. 244, 265.
[98] *Smithies* v. *National Association of Operative Plasterers* [1909] 1 K.B. 310, 341.

Moral duty

There are dicta[99] which suggest that where the defendant is acting under the pressure of moral duty he may possibly be justified, as, for example, when the claims of family relationship or guardianship demand an interference amounting to protection.[1] But it is significant that there are apparently only two reported cases in which a breach has been so justified. In one, *Brimelow* v. *Casson*,[2] the conduct of the plaintiff had been "utterly disgraceful,"[3] in that he had paid the chorus girls in his theatrical company such low wages that they had been driven to prostitution. In the other case, a defendant was justified[4] in procuring a breach in order to expose the "absolutely nonsensical mumbo-jumbo" of the plaintiff scientologists which was capable of injuring the public's health. Lord Denning has suggested[5] that union officials taking industrial action against members of a break-away union would be justified if those persons "were really trouble-makers who fomented discord." But other dicta assert that it is no sufficient justification that the defendant was acting as an altruist, seeking only the good of another and careless of his own advantage[6] or that he was performing a public service.[7] It has been held that it is no justification that an association has a duty cast upon it to protect the interests of its members and has acted in pursuance of that duty[8] otherwise every official of a trade union who procured a breach of contract in the course of a trade dispute would be protected independently of the Trade Union and Labour Relations Act 1974, s. 13 (2).[9]

Inducement by servant

Notwithstanding the general rule, a servant or agent acting on behalf of his employer or principal within the scope of his employment or authority is not liable in tort for inducing or procuring a breach of contract by his employer or principal. For in such a case the servant is not really an intervener or interferer in the contractual relationship but only the *alter ego* of one of the parties to it. If, for example, a company acting by its directors breaks its contract, the only remedy of the other party is to sue the company for breach of contract; he cannot sue the directors for the tort of inducing that breach.[10] But the possibility of procuring an injunction against a servant to restrain him from procuring his employer to break his contract with his own customer has certainly been considered.[11]

---

[99] *South Wales Miners' Federation* v. *Glamorgan Coal Co.* [1905] A.C. 239, 249; *Camden Nominees* v. *Forcey* [1940] Ch. 352, 366.
[1] *Midland Bank Trust Co. Ltd.* v. *Green* [1979] 3 All E.R. 28, 42. But this may perhaps be better explained as an instance of advice as distinct from inducement.
[2] [1924] 1 Ch. 302.
[3] *Pritchard* v. *Briggs* [1980] Ch. 338, at 416, *per* Goff L.J.
[4] *Church of Scientology* v. *Kaufman* [1973] R.P.C. 627, 635.
[5] *Morgan* v. *Fry* [1968] 2 Q.B. 710, 729.
[6] *Read* v. *Friendly Society of Stonemasons* [1902] 2 K.B. 88, 97.
[7] *Camden Nominees* v. *Forcey* [1940] Ch. 352, 366.
[8] *South Wales Miners' Federation* v. *Glamorgan Coal Co.* [1905] A.C. 239. But since 1942 the House of Lords has recognised that trade union objects are legitimate: see below, § 136.
[9] See below, § 139.
[10] *D.C.Thomson Ltd.* v. *Deakin* [1952] Ch. 646, 680–681; *Rutherford* v. *Poole* [1953] V.L.R. 130. See, however, *de Jetley Marks* v. *Greenwood* (Lord) [1936] 1 All E.R. 863, 872.
[11] *Bowles & Son* v. *Lindley* [1965] 1 Lloyd's Rep. 207.

(6) Remedies

This is a tort in which the swift and peremptory remedy of an injunction may be more valuable than damages.[12] But now the Trade Union and Labour Relations Act 1974, s. 17, provides that an *ex parte* injunction shall not be granted in respect of acts connected with a trade dispute unless all reasonable steps have been taken to ensure that the party to be enjoined has been notified of the application. In 1975 a further provision was introduced by the Employment Protection Act for, as the Act states, the avoidance of doubt.[13] Thus subsection (2) of section 17 provides that where an application is made to a court for an interlocutory injunction and the other party claims that he acted in contemplation or furtherance of a trade dispute, the court[14] shall, in exercising its discretion whether or not to grant the injunction, have regard to the likelihood of that party succeeding at the trial of the action in establishing a defence under sections 13–15 of the 1974 Act. The phrase "have regard to" has caused difficulties. A High Court judge who refused an injunction because there was "a high degree of probability that the defence will succeed" was held by the House of Lords to have exercised his discretion correctly.[15] But there are dicta of the Law Lords which indicate that the court has a residual discretion to grant an injunction despite the fact that the defence may succeed at the trial, so that the conduct enjoined is ultimately held to have been lawful. But it would require an altogether exceptional case before such an injunction could be granted—*e.g.* where the consequences to the employer or to third parties or to the public or the nation might be disastrous if it were refused.[16] If the case is a suitable one for the grant of an interim injunction to preserve the *status quo* until trial, then the defendant may be restrained from interfering with future contracts as well as existing ones, for the plaintiff is entitled to carry on business in the usual way until trial of the action.[17]

§ 136. CONSPIRACY[18]

Although both the crime and the tort of conspiracy have a common root in the reign of Edward I, the tort did not achieve prominence until the industrial disputes of the nineteenth century. Salmond even doubted whether the tort existed,[19] and said that the cases of conspiracy were in reality only instances of the tort of intimidation. But Lord Dunedin described this as

---

[12] The Donovan Commission (Cmnd. 3623, para. 848) noted that because violation of an injunction might be followed by imprisonment for contempt of court, it was as serious a penalty as that likely to follow from a criminal prosecution. See above, § 3.

[13] The doubt appears to have arisen from the decision in *American Cyanamid Co.* v. *Ethicon* [1975] A.C. 396 (see below, § 219) which lessened the burden of proof on an applicant for an injunction.

[14] The discretion is that of the trial judge, and so cannot be reviewed on appeal unless he has misdirected himself in law: *Duport Steels Ltd.* v. *Sirs* [1980] 1 W.L.R. 142, 163, 171.

[15] *Duport Steels Ltd.* v. *Sirs* [1980] 1 W.L.R. 142.

[16] *Duport Steels Ltd.* v. *Sirs* [1980] 1 W.L.R. 142, 166, 171.

[17] *Torquay Hotel Co. Ltd.* v. *Cousins* [1969] 2 Ch. 106.

[18] See Citrine, *Trade Union Law*, Chap. 3; Haslam, *Trade Combinations*, Chaps. ii and iii; Report of the Royal Commission on Trade Unions (Cmnd. 3623, 1968); Heydon, *The Economic Torts* (2nd ed., 1978).

[19] See 6th ed., pp. 576–578, and his view still has judicial support in New Zealand: *P.T.Y. Homes Ltd.* v. *Shand* [1968] N.Z.L.R. 93, 109.

"the leading heresy,"[20] and it is now well established[21] that conspiracy is the gist of the wrong and that it is in the fact of the combination that the unlawfulness resides, though damage must be proved. In such cases conspiracy is an independent tort.[22] The confusion which prevailed was largely due to the difficulty of explaining and reconciling the speeches in three cases in the House of Lords, *Mogul Steamship Co.* v. *McGregor, Gow & Co.,*[23] *Allen* v. *Flood*[24]; and *Quinn* v. *Leathem.*[25] Though these cases have ceased from troubling it is still desirable for a true understanding of the law to advert to them briefly, accepting the interpretation of the *ratio decidendi* given in the *Crofter Company's*[26] case as canonical.

(1) The Mogul case

The plaintiff alleged (*inter alia*) that the defendants, who were an associated body of traders in China tea, had wilfully caused loss to him, a rival trader, by compelling certain merchants in China to cease to act as his agents by means of a threat that if they continued to do so the agency of the defendant association would be withdrawn from them. This was held by the House of Lords not to be actionable, it being a justifiable measure of self-protection on the part of the association to prevent the same persons from occupying the inconsistent position of agents both for the association and for the plaintiff. The defendants in Mogul escaped liability because in a capitalist economy what they did was regarded as justifiable. It is notable that today the remedy for such abuse of power is to be found before the Monopolies Commission or the Restrictive Practices Court.

(2) Allen v. Flood

The facts and decision in this case have already been given.[27] The case is clear authority that, where the element of combination is absent, the motive of the defendant is immaterial, and that damage done intentionally and even malevolently to another gives no cause of action so long as no legal right of the other is infringed. In short, competition in labour must be equated with competition in trade.

(3) Quinn v. Leathem

A few years later the pendulum swung sharply back. In *Quinn* v. *Leathem,* an appeal from Ireland, the plaintiff was a butcher who had a dispute with the trade union of which the defendants were officials, with respect to the employment of certain workmen who did not belong to the union. The defendants requested the plaintiff to discharge these men, but he

---

[20] *Sorrell* v. *Smith* [1925] A.C. 700, 719. See above, § 133.
[21] *Crofter Company's Case* [1942] A.C. 435, 489.
[22] When a tort has been committed an allegation of conspiracy adds nothing to the plaintiff's case. Although such an allegation is often put in the statement of claim to widen the scope of a possible order for discovery of documents it should not be encouraged. *Hesperides Hotels Ltd.* v. *Aegean Hotels Ltd.* [1979] A.C. 508. Equally, if a joint tort has been committed, there is no need to have recourse to the tort of conspiracy; *Galland* v. *Mineral Underwriters Ltd.* [1977] W.A.R. 116, 121.
[23] [1892] A.C. 25.
[24] [1898] A.C. 1.
[25] [1901] A.C. 495.
[26] [1942] A.C. 435.
[27] See above, § 136.

refused. Whereupon, with a view to compelling him to do so, the defendants compelled the plaintiff's chief customer to cease to deal with him, by threatening that otherwise they would call out that customer's workmen. The jury found that the defendants had maliciously conspired to induce the plaintiff's customers not to deal with the plaintiff.[28] It was held that the plaintiff was entitled to sue the defendants for damages[29] for the loss which he had sustained through the withdrawal of his customer. It is doubtful if a similar decision on these facts would be arrived at today, for neither the judges[30] nor a Belfast jury at the end of the nineteenth century could be expected to appreciate the importance of the "closed shop" in trade union organisation. But the effect of *Quinn* v. *Leathem* was almost immediately neutralised by the Trade Disputes Act 1906, s. 1,[31] which provided that conduct by two should only be actionable if it would have been wrongful if done by one—and *Allen* v. *Flood* was accepted as establishing that one person could do these acts with impunity.

(4) The Crofter Company's case

The law was completely re-stated in the light of modern industrial conditions in *Crofter Hand Woven Harris Tweed Co.* v. *Veitch*[32] in the House of Lords in 1941. Harris tweed originally was not only woven by hand looms in the island of Lewis by the crofters but was woven out of yarn which had been hand spun in the island. Later the spinning and finishing were done by mills in the island but the yarn was still woven by the crofters. Ninety per cent. of the spinners in those mills, and all the dockers at the island port of Stornoway, were members of the Transport and General Workers' Union, of which the defendants were officials. The union officials were anxious that only members of the union should be employed as weavers by the mill-owners and that the spinners' wages should be increased, but the mill-owners refused to agree to this on the ground that it was impossible in view of the cut-throat competition of the plaintiffs and others, seven small producers, who also produced Harris tweed and employed the crofters to weave by hand yarn which they imported from the mainland at a cheaper price than that spun in the island. It was to the interest of the union to have 100 per cent. membership and to the interest of the mill-owners to eliminate competition and for these reasons the defendants bona fide believed their action to be in the general interest of the Harris tweed industry.[33] The defendants instructed the dockers not to handle the plaintiff's yarn or to export the cloth made from it, and the dockers, without any breach of

---

[28] The malice was apparently to be found in the fact that the defendants had refused a reasonable compromise, and stipulated that the men "must walk the streets" for a year. But today it might be realised that from a union point of view it would be harmful to its bargaining power to give the impression that non-members could regain the advantages of membership simply by paying back-dues and fines.

[29] All the Law Lords assumed that there was also a criminal conspiracy.

[30] Lord Lindley thought that if one defendant had done the acts in question he would have been liable—in other words, he refused to accept *Allen* v. *Flood*, and thought that liability rested on interference with the plaintiff's liberty to trade. This view has some support (above, § 133), but cannot be regarded as the *ratio decidendi* of the case.

[31] See now the Trade Union and Labour Relations Act 1974, s. 13 (below, § 139).

[32] [1942] A.C. 435.

[33] Note that in effect a progressive manufacturer using modern methods was driven out of business by an alliance between an old-fashioned producer and a trade union.

contract,[34] acted on their instructions. It was held that, even if there was a combination between the defendants and the mill-owners, the plaintiffs had no cause of action since the predominant purpose of the combination was the legitimate promotion of the interests of the persons combining. In other words, the *Crofter* case in effect reversed *Quinn* v. *Leathem* by recognising that the "closed shop" was a legitimate object of union activity.[35] The result in practice is that the defence of justifiable self-interest has severely limited the application of the tort of conspiracy.[36]

§ 137. ACTIONABLE COMBINATIONS

(i) *Unlawful objects*

A combination[37] wilfully to do an act causing damage to a man in his trade or other interests is unlawful and if damage in fact is caused is actionable as a conspiracy,[38] even if no unlawful means are used. Further there is liability if the conspirators know all the facts, even if they do not know that they are acting unlawfully.[39] To this there is an exception where the defendants' real and predominant purpose is to advance their own lawful interests in a matter in which they honestly believe that those interests would directly[40] suffer if the action against the plaintiff was not taken.[41]

It had previously been thought by some[42] that a combination to damage a man was not actionable unless it was inspired by malice or "disinterested malevolence." The true proposition seems to be that it is actionable unless there is some justification. Such justification will be found if it is inspired by self-interest. The pursuit of selfish ends provides in law, whatever may be the case in morals, its own justification.[43] Even the fact that the damage inflicted to secure such a legitimate selfish purpose is disproportionately severe, though it may throw doubts on the bona fides of the avowed purpose, does not necessarily involve liability.[44] On the other hand, it seems that, though not inspired by malevolence, a combination would be actionable if its object was to demonstrate the power of those combining to dictate policy or to prove themselves masters in a given situation, or if it were inspired by a dislike of the religious views or the politics or the race or the colour[45] of the plaintiff or by mere wantonness, as by vindictively punishing dissidents for the sake of punishment,[46] or continuing a boycott after a trade dispute has ended,[47] for none of these are legitimate objects.

---

[34] This was an important point: *Thomson* v. *Deakin* |1952| Ch. 646, 675.
[35] See the Donovan Report (Cmnd. 3623 (1968), para. 853).
[36] *Pete's Towing Services Ltd.* v. *Northern Industrial Union* |1970| N.Z.L.R. 32, 56.
[37] It is preferable to speak of a "combination" rather than of an "agreement," which might imply (wrongly) that a contract was necessary: *Belmont Finance Ltd.* v. *Williams Furniture (No.* 2) |1980| 1 All E.R. 393.
[38] |1942| A.C. 435, 446, 451, 464.
[39] *Pritchard* v. *Briggs* |1980| Ch. 388.
[40] |1942| A.C. 435, 447.
[41] |1942| A.C. 435, 446, 450, 464, 469.
[42] *e.g.* Lord Sumner in *Sorrell* v. *Smith* |1925| A.C. 700, 737; Evatt J. in *McKernan* v. *Fraser* (1931) 46 C.L.R. 343, 398.
[43] *Crofter Company's Case* |1942| A.C. 435, 450, 469–471, 496.
[44] |1942| A.C. 435, 447.
[45] *Scala Ballroom (Wolverhampton) Ltd.* v. *Ratcliffe* |1958| 1 W.L.R. 1057.
[46] As in *Huntley* v. *Thornton* |1957| 1 W.L.R. 321 ("ruffled dignity" of trade union leaders).
[47] As in *Hutchison* v. *Aitchison* (1970) 9 K.I.R. 69.

It remains to be seen what objects other than self-interest will be recognised as providing a justification. The objects or purposes for which combinations may be formed are clearly of great variety, and it is probably as profitless to attempt to define them as it is to attempt to define the justification for inducing a breach of contract.[48] In determining the existence of a justification regard must be had to the circumstances of each case as it arises.[49] Clearly self-interest is not to be interpreted too strictly, and acts done for the protection of trade interests, such as limiting competition, increasing profits or raising wages are within the protection, as are other acts done in the genuine belief that the prosperity of the defendant's industry is jeopardised,[50] and it would seem that for this end it may be legitimate to punish a man in order to deter others from similarly offending.[51] It also seems that the interests which can be lawfully protected are not confined to those which can be exchanged for cash, so that it was permissible for union officials to organise a boycott of a dance-hall which operated a colour-bar.[52]

Mixed motives

Yet motives are often mixed.[53] In the case of conspiracy this may be true in two respects. The same individual may be inspired by more than one motive, or different parties to the combination may be inspired by different motives. In the former case liability will depend upon ascertaining which is the predominant object or the true motive or the real purpose of the defendant,[54] and that must be judged broadly as a jury would judge.[55] It is less easy to determine how a difference in the object of different parties to the combination affects liability.[56] It seems clear that there need not be a complete identity of interest between all the parties. It is sufficient if all the various combining parties have their own legitimate trade or business interests to gain, even though these interests may be of differing kinds,[57] as in the *Crofter Company*'s case itself. But it would seem that if the interest of one of the parties is merely separate and mercenary or if one of the parties is actuated merely by hate or vindictive spite that party can have no lawful excuse,[58] and if the other knew of and countenanced his purpose by giving assistance to his malicious acts, he also would be a participant in the wrong.[59]

(ii) *Unlawful means*

A second form of actionable conspiracy exists when two or more combine to injure a third person by unlawful means—*e.g.* the commission of a crime or tort,[60] or the infringement of a guaranteed constitutional right.[61] An

[48] See above, § 135.
[49] [1942] A.C. 435, 496.
[50] [1942] A.C. 435, 477.
[51] [1942] A.C. 435, 475.
[52] *Scala Ballroom (Wolverhampton) Ltd.* v. *Ratcliffe* [1958] 1 W.L.R. 1057.
[53] See Lord Sumner in *Sorrell* v. *Smith* [1925] A.C. 700, 739, 742.
[54] [1942] A.C. 435, 445, 452, 478.
[55] [1942] A.C. 435, 490.
[56] See Evatt J. in *McKernan* v. *Fraser* (1931) 46 C.L.R. 343.
[57] [1942] A.C. 435, 453.
[58] [1942] A.C. 435, 453, 480.
[59] [1942] A.C. 435, 495.
[60] *National Phonograph Co. Ltd.* v. *Edison-Bell Phonograph Co. Ltd.* [1908] 1 Ch. 335.
[61] *Meskell* v. *C.I.E.* [1973] I.R. 121.

agreement to commit a tort may also be a criminal conspiracy if it involves an invasion of the public domain.[62] In such a case it is irrelevant that the object of the conspirators in using those means may be legitimate.[63] If all the facts which make the transaction unlawful were known to the parties, ignorance of the law is no excuse.[64] Combinations of this kind must be contrasted with what might be called "*Quinn* v. *Leathem* conspiracies," where the means are legitimate but the object is not. Conspiracies of this kind are not protected by section 13 (4) of the Trade Union and Labour Relations Act 1974, which is limited to cases where the act is not actionable if done by one person.[65] Hence a conspiracy may be actionable if either the end or the means, or both, are unlawful. But a plaintiff must make up his mind whether he is going to rely on one or other or both of these allegations, and if he has put his case in one of these ways he cannot thereafter bring the same transactions before the court and say that he is relying on a new cause of action.[66]

(iii) *Limits of conspiracy*

The *Crofter Company*'s case has settled some other points in the law of conspiracy. The action is not limited to trade competition and labour disputes nor is the justification limited to the protection of business interests.[67] Nor is the tort limited to those cases in which the combination is to bring pressure on third persons to cease to deal with or otherwise damnify the plaintiff. If, with the intention of causing damage to A and B, A's servants combine and threaten to leave him unless he ceases to deal with B, and in consequence of this threat he ceases to deal with him, with resulting loss both to himself and to B, both A and B will have a good cause of action.[68] And it would appear that this is also the case even though the defendants had no knowledge that their acts were likely to cause damage to A.[69]

(iv) *Terminology*

More precision is desirable here, as it is in the use of phrases like "the right to strike."[70] The expressions commonly employed in these cases[71] are "conspiracy to injure" and "intent to injure." But such expressions really beg the question at issue. "Injury" is strictly limited to an actionable wrong, in contrast to "damage," which means loss or harm occurring in fact, whether actionable as an injury or not.[72] Again in some of the judgments[73] in these cases there is a confusion between "motive" and "intention." It is better to use the words "purpose" or "object."[74]

---

[62] *R.* v. *Kamara* [1974] A.C. 104.
[63] [1942] A.C. 435, 460.
[64] *Belmont Finance Ltd.* v. *Williams Furniture Ltd.* (*No.* 2) [1980] 1 All E.R. 393.
[65] See below, § 139.
[66] *Greenhalgh* v. *Mallard* [1947] 2 All E.R. 255, 257.
[67] [1942] A.C. 435, 446–447, 462, 478, 492.
[68] *Reynolds* v. *Shipping Federation* [1924] 1 Ch. 28, 40.
[69] This seems to be implicit in *Sorrell* v. *Smith* [1925] A.C. 700.
[70] See above, § 133.
[71] *Crofter Company's Case* [1942] A.C. 435, 468–471.
[72] [1942] A.C. 435, 442.
[73] *e.g.* in Lord Dunedin's speech in *Sorrell* v. *Smith* [1925] A.C. 700, 724.
[74] *Crofter Company's Case* [1942] A.C. 435, 444, *per* Viscount Simon L.C.

(v) *Burden of proof*

There is authority that the burden of proving absence of justification is on the plaintiff,[75] but also that it is on the defendant.[76] The former view is consistent with the analogy between the crime and the tort of conspiracy (the plaintiff must prove *mens rea*), but the latter is more consistent with the general principle that harm intentionally inflicted is wrongful unless justification is shown, as well as with the general reluctance of the law to require a plaintiff to prove a negative.

(vi) *Conclusion*

The tort is unusual because it emphasises the purposes of the defendants rather than the results of their conduct.[77] The common law may have taken the view that there is always the danger that any combination may be oppressive, and may have thought that a general rule against injurious combinations was desirable on broad grounds of policy.[78] But, though there is a very serious difference between the oppressive power of a single person and that of a trade union having ten thousand members, there is no material difference between the power of one person and that of two. Moreover, it is clear that a single person may by reason of great wealth or influence be able to exercise coercive power over others in a degree exceeding that which is possible even to a large combination of smaller men.[79] Why should the combination be liable, while the single individual of even greater wealth and power goes free?[80] One answer is that the action for conspiracy was derived from the crime of conspiracy developed in the Star Chamber. The essence of conspiracy on which a civil action is founded is a criminal conspiracy, though unless actual damage has followed no civil action will lie. The moment that fact is recognised, the spirit of the criminal law, where motive or intention—the *mens rea*—is everything, is introduced.[81]

§ 138. INTIMIDATION[82]

The wrong of intimidation includes all those cases in which harm is inflicted by the use of unlawful threats whereby the lawful liberty of others to do as they please is interfered with.[83] This wrong is of two distinct kinds, for the liberty of action so interfered with may be either that of the plaintiff himself or that of other persons with resulting damage to the plaintiff. In other words, the defendant may either intimidate the plaintiff himself, and so compel him to act to his own hurt, or he may intimidate other persons, and so compel them to act to the hurt of the plaintiff. There is an analogy with

---

[75] [1942] A.C. 435, 471, 488, 495; *Stratford & Son Ltd.* v. *Lindley* [1965] A.C. 269.
[76] [1942] A.C. 435, 447–457.
[77] But in *Midland Bank Trust Co. Ltd.* v. *Green* (No. 3) [1980] Ch. 590, Oliver J. thought that the law emphasised the combined or concerted action as distinct from the agreement.
[78] *Crofter Company's Case* [1942] A.C. 435, 468.
[79] *Crofter Company's Case* [1942] A.C. 435, 443.
[80] *Sorrell* v. *Smith* [1925] A.C. 700, 739–741.
[81] *Crofter Company's Case* [1942] A.C. 435, 443–444; *Sorrell* v. *Smith* [1925] A.C. 700, 724–726; *R.* v. *Kamara* [1974] A.C. 104, 129.
[82] See Hughes, "Liability for Loss Caused by Industrial Action" (1970) 86 L.Q.R. 181; Burns, "Tort Injury to Economic Interests" (1980) 50 Can. Bar. Rev. 103.
[83] See the similar definition in *Pete's Towing Services Ltd.* v. *Northern Industrial Union* [1970] N.Z.L.R. 32, 41.

fraud and injurious falsehood, in the former of which the defendant may deceive the plaintiff himself, but in the latter deceive other persons to the plaintiff's injury.

(1) Intimidation of the plaintiff himself

(A) *By illegal acts*

It is an actionable wrong intentionally to compel a person, by means of a threat of an illegal act, to do some act whereby loss accrues to him.[84] For example, an action will lie at the suit of a trader who has been compelled to discontinue his business by means of threats of personal violence made against him by the defendant with that intention,[85] or by a creditor who has been threatened by his debtor that the latter will pay nothing unless the former accepts a lesser sum in full settlement.[86] So where A uses force to prevent B from carrying out his contract with C, A can be sued for intimidation by B and for procurement of breach of contract by C.[87]

(B) *By legal acts*

But it is clear that the threat complained of must be a threat to do an act which is in itself illegal. No threat to exercise one's legal rights can amount to a cause of action, even if made for the purpose of intimidation or coercion, and even if inspired by malicious motives. So if one party to a contract asserts what he reasonably considers to be his contractual rights, the other party should contest that assertion by suing for breach of contract.[87a] To decide otherwise would mean overruling a clear decision of the House of Lords,[88] or at least distinguishing it on some ground which is not obvious. This has many consequences. English law permits a wealthy company to drive its competitors out of the field by under-cutting prices to an uneconomic level,[89] or an essential servant to threaten to leave unless his wages are substantially increased, or another servant, whom he dislikes, is lawfully dismissed.[90] In such cases it makes no difference that the threat is couched in menacing and disagreeable language: for if one may lawfully do a thing, one may threaten to do it.[91] But, as we have seen, it may be different if two or more are involved.

(2) Intimidation of other persons to the injury of the plaintiff

In certain cases it is an actionable wrong to intimidate other persons with the intent and effect of compelling them to act in a manner or to do acts which they themselves have a legal right to do which cause loss to the

---

[84] *Allen* v. *Flood* [1898] A.C. 1, 17; *The Tubantia* [1924] P. 78; *Cory Lighterage Ltd.* v. *T.G.W.U.* [1973] 1 W.L.R. 792, 814; *Huglich* v. *Hale* [1973] 2 N.Z.L.R. 279, 285.
[85] *Rookes* v. *Barnard* [1964] A.C. 1129, 1205.
[86] *D. & C. Builders Ltd.* v. *Rees* [1966] 2 Q.B. 617.
[87] *Williams* v. *Hursey* (1959) 103 C.L.R. 30, 77.
[87a] *Central Canada Potash Co. Ltd.* v. *Government of Saskatchewan* (1978) 88 D.L.R. (3d) 609, 639–640.
[88] *Allen* v. *Flood* [1898] A.C. 1. See above, § 133.
[89] See below, § 137.
[90] See the example given in *Allen* v. *Flood* [1898] A.C. 1, 138–139. But the other servant might have an action for intimidation.
[91] See above, § 137.

plaintiff: for example, the intimidation of the plaintiff's customers whereby they are compelled to withdraw their custom from him,[92] or the intimidation of an employer whereby he is compelled to discharge his servant, the plaintiff. There are at least two cases in which such intimidation may constitute a cause of action:

(i) When the intimidation consists in a threat to do or procure an illegal act;

(ii) When the intimidation is the act, not of a single person, but of two or more persons acting together in pursuance of a common intention.[93]

Intimidation by threats of illegal act

Any person is guilty of an actionable wrong who, with the intention and effect of intimidating any other person into acting in a certain manner to the harm of the plaintiff, threatens to commit or procure an illegal act. Illegal acts now include breaches, or threatened breaches, of contract, as well as those which are criminal or tortious.[94] But a "strike notice" of proper length is not unlawful.[95] The existence of this form of intimidation was emphatically affirmed by the House of Lords in *Rookes* v. *Barnard.*[96]

The threat in *Rookes* v. *Barnard* was that strike action on the part of all A.E.S.D. men employed by B.O.A.C. would occur within three days unless the plaintiff was withdrawn from the design department.[97] The plaintiff was a non-unionist and the defendants Barnard and Fistal were two employees of B.O.A.C., union members of the A.E.S.D., and Silverthorne, the local trade union official, who was not himself under a contract of employment with B.O.A.C. The threat made by the defendants was a wrongful act, being in breach of the no-strike agreement made between B.O.A.C. and the union. This was a breach of "a flagrant kind."[98] So there were threats of wrongful acts aimed and directed at the plaintiff's employment with the object and result of causing its termination, for B.O.A.C. were so impressed by the threat that they responded to it by giving Rookes one week's notice of dismissal. At the trial the jury[99] found for the plaintiff, and awarded him £7,500 damages. The magnitude of this award showed how seriously the plaintiff's fellow-citizens regarded the interference with his right to work. On appeal, the House of Lords ordered a new trial on the issue of damages,[1] but otherwise upheld the verdict.

The House of Lords held that the defendants' threats constituted the tort of intimidation and that the defendants were not protected by section 3 of the Trade Disputes Act 1906,[2] for the acts of the defendants were not

---

[92] "Picketing" in a trade dispute is considered in detail below, § 139.

[93] *Rookes* v. *Barnard* [1964] A.C. 1129, 1205.

[94] *Cory Lighterage Ltd.* v. *T.G.W.U.* [1973] 1 W.L.R. 792.

[95] See above, § 134.

[96] [1964] A.C. 1129. The plaintiff has published his own account of the case: Rookes, *Conspiracy* (London, 1966). His leading counsel has also recorded his memories: "I don't care for bearded pacifists, and I told him I didn't think an English jury would, either, and I forecast much lower damages than he was later awarded. But the enemy were so unattractive in the witness box that we easily beat the £1,500 paid into court": Sir Neville Faulks, *A Law unto Myself* (1978), p.96.

[97] See [1964] A.C. 1129, 1182.

[98] *Morgan* v. *Fry* [1968] 2 Q.B. 710, 724.

[99] The jury panel was drawn from those living near London Airport: Printed Case, p. 24.

[1] The proceedings were eventually settled for £4,000.

[2] See now below, § 139.

immune from action "on the ground only that they interfered with the trade, business or employment of the plaintiff," since they also constituted the tort of intimidation.[3] If the party intimidated does not respond to the threat, then the plaintiff cannot sue,[4] for the plain reason that he has not been damaged. The damage to the plaintiff must be linked to the coercion of the threatened party. This meets the case where the threat is whimsical—for example, the office boy who threatens to leave unless the chairman of the company is removed,[5] or the case where the person threatened is brave enough to stand up to the threat, as was Mr. Stratford in *Stratford & Sons Ltd.* v. *Lindley*.[6] The decision certainly shows the willingness of the courts to treat economic loss in the same way as physical loss and is in general justifiable on the ground that intimidation of any kind is highly objectionable and that there is no reason to limit the unlawful acts which constitute the wrong to those which are criminal or tortious as distinct from those which are breaches of contract.[7]

Actionable threats are not limited to cases of trade disputes though doubtless they are its most common illustration. For a lessor who threatened breaches of, say, the covenant for quiet enjoyment in a lease with the object of damaging one of the tenant's friends or relations would be liable.[8]

The defence of justification

It is uncertain what kinds of acts beside those which are criminal or tortious or threatened breaches of contracts are sufficiently unlawful to be comprehended within the tort of intimidation, or what justification, if any, might be held a defence.[9] If the defendants' conduct is unlawful as against the party intimidated it is hard to see how it can ever be justifiable as regards the plaintiff.[10] It has certainly been assumed in at least one House of Lords case[11] that an actual breach of statutory duty was actionable. The unlawful means which constitute the tort may also extend to cover threats of breaches of statutory duty,[12] or threats of vexatious litigation,[13] or the entry into an agreement which is contrary to the public interest.[14]

---

[3] It is not too clear why Silverthorne was held liable; he had no contract to threaten to break. Perhaps it was because he was a party to a conspiracy: *Morgan* v. *Fry* [1968] 2 Q.B. 710, 729.
[4] *Morgan* v. *Fry* [1968] 2 Q.B. 710, 724.
[5] *Rookes* v. *Barnard* [1963] 1 Q.B. 623, 666–667.
[6] [1965] A.C. 269.
[7] [1964] A.C. 1129, 1219.
[8] [1964] A.C. 1129, 1187.
[9] Lord Devlin alone mentioned this defence in [1964] A.C. 1129, 1206.
[10] *Morgan* v. *Fry* [1968] 1 Q.B. 521, 548.
[11] *Smith* v. *London Transport Executive* [1951] A.C. 555. Such a breach may be illegal means for conspiracy: *Williams* v. *Hursey* (1959) 103 C.L.R. 30.
[12] Wedderburn (1964) 27 M.L.R. 257, 260; (1968) 31 M.L.R. 440.
[13] *Allen* v. *Flood* [1898] A.C. 1, 105.
[14] *Brekkes* v. *Cattel* [1972] 1 Ch. 105.

CHAPTER 17

TRADE DISPUTES[1]

§ 139. THE TRADE UNION AND LABOUR RELATIONS ACTS 1974 AND 1976

The 1974 Act repealed the Industrial Relations Act 1971, which had given rise to much political controversy. The 1971 Act had repealed the Trade Disputes Act 1906, but the 1974 Act to some extent revived the immunities from actions in tort given by the 1906 Act. The cases decided on the Acts of 1906 and 1971 are a helpful guide to the interpretation of the 1974 Act, which in turn has been amended in important respects by the Act of 1976 and the Employment Act 1980. The official mode of citation, according to section 4 of the 1976 Act, is the Trade Union and Labour Relations Acts 1974 and 1976, but for convenience they will be cited as T.U.L.R.A.

The immunity or protection given to a union must be carefully distinguished from that given to its members or officials. So far as the union itself is concerned, section 14 protects it (subject to one exception)[2] from any action in tort. So far as the members or officials are concerned, the statute gives certain immunities or protections to those who do certain acts in the contemplation or furtherance of a trade dispute. The immunities or protections in question are given by section 13, which must be reproduced in full.

> (1) An act done by a person in contemplation or furtherance of a trade dispute shall not be actionable in tort on the ground only—
>
> (a) that it induces another person to break a contract or interferes or induces another person to interfere with its performance; or
>
> (b) that it consists in his threatening that a contract (whether one to which he is a party or not) will be broken or its performance interfered with or that he will induce another person to break a contract or to interfere with its performance.
>
> (2) For the avoidance of doubt it is hereby declared that an act done by a person in contemplation or furtherance of a trade dispute is not actionable in tort on the ground only that it is an interference with the trade, business or employment of another person, or with the right of another person to dispose of his capital or his labour as he wills.
>
> (3) [This sub-section has been repealed by section 17(8) of the Act of 1980.]
>
> (4) An agreement or combination by two or more persons to do or procure the doing of any act in contemplation or furtherance of a trade dispute shall not be actionable in tort if the act in question is one which, if done without any such agreement or combination, would not be actionable in tort.

It will be observed that the draftsman was set the task of reversing or nullifying the effect of three well-known decisions, namely *Lumley* v. *Gye*,[3]

---

[1] Simpson, "Trade Dispute and Industrial Dispute in British Labour Law" (1977) 40 M.L.R. 16; Kerr, "Contemplation or Furtherance" (1979–80) D.U.L.J. 59.

[2] See below, § 161.

[3] (1853) 2 E. & B. 216. See above, § 135.

Rookes v. *Barnard*[4] and *Quinn* v. *Leathem*,[5] and of quietening certain doubts which had arisen from dicta in a fourth, *Allen* v. *Flood*.[6] In addition, section 15 reverses *Lyons & Sons* v. *Wilkins*.[7] Each of these problems will now be considered.

(1) The Reversal of Lumley v. Gye and Rookes v. Barnard

A detailed analysis of section 13(1) is required.

"An act done by a person"

The protection is not limited to trade unions[8] or their members. On the other hand, trade unions no longer have the total immunity from any action in tort, whether or not connected with a trade dispute,[9] which they were held to possess under section 4 of the Trade Disputes Act 1906, which is now repealed.

"In contemplation or furtherance"

Until the decision of the House of Lords in *Express Newspapers Ltd.* v. *McShane*[10] there was much division of opinion about the meaning of these words. But in *McShane* it was laid down by a majority of the Law Lords that the test was subjective and not objective, as the Court of Appeal had thought.[11] It was the policy of the Act to exclude industrial disputes from judicial review.[12] It followed that, if there was a trade dispute within the section, and that was an issue over which the courts still retained some control, then an act done as against a customer or a supplier of the party in dispute with the union might be protected, if the doer of the act honestly believed that it would further the cause of the union. So secondary blacking or secondary boycott was legitimised in a trade dispute. In *Duport Steels Ltd.* v. *Sirs*[13] the House of Lords again emphatically reaffirmed the subjective interpretation established in *McShane* in preference to the objective interpretation favoured by the Court of Appeal in a series of decisions.[14] But section 17 (1) of the 1980 Act removes the statutory protection when the contract in question is not a contract of employment and the acts done involve secondary action which goes beyond the complex provisions of the Act. According to section 17 (3) there are some kinds of secondary action which continue to be protected. This may occur when the principal purpose of such action was directly to prevent or disrupt the supply during the

---

[4] |1964| A.C. 1129. See above, § 138.
[5] |1901| A.C. 495. See above, § 136.
[6] |1898| A.C. 1. See above, § 133.
[7] |1899| 1 Ch. 11. See above, § 24.
[8] As defined in s. 28 (1).
[9] See below, § 161.
[10] |1980| A.C. 672.
[11] "Subsequent events and subsequent comments have shown convincingly that the four in the majority in the House of Lords made the wrong choice. Yet, as they had the last word, no one can gainsay it": *R.* v. *Crown Court (Sheffield)* |1980| Q.B. 530 at 539, *per* Lord Denning M.R. But Parliament has now set limits to secondary industrial action in the Employment Act 1980 s. 17.
[12] *N.W.L. Ltd.* v. *Woods* |1979| 1 W.L.R. 1294.
[13] |1980| 1 W.L.R. 142.
[14] No less than nine distinct limitations on union immunities can be traced in the cases before *McShane*: see Kerr, (1979–80) D.U.L.J. 59, 68.

dispute of goods or services between an employer who is a party to the dispute and the employer under the contract of employment to which the secondary action relates.

"Of a trade dispute"

Although the scope of judicial review has been limited by the House of Lords in *McShane* and *Sirs* it has not been entirely excluded. There must be some objective event or situation before there can be a statutory trade dispute. So if the dispute has in truth ceased to exist months[15] or years[16] ago it cannot be revived simply by asserting that it still exists.

T.U.L.R.A. provides an elaborate definition of "trade dispute." By section 29 (1) it means a dispute between employers and workers, or workers and workers, which is "connected with one or more" of seven different matters, *e.g.* terms and conditions of employment, matters of discipline, or the membership of a union. So that the courts are entitled to inquire whether there is a genuine connection between the dispute and the matters listed.[17] By section 29 (2) disputes between workers and a Minister of the Crown are to be treated as a trade dispute, and so also, by section 29 (3), are disputes as to matters occurring outside Great Britain.

"Shall not be actionable in tort"

The words "in tort" were not included in the corresponding section of the 1906 Act, under which it was held[18] that the court was precluded from granting an injunction as well as awarding damages. An employee who breaks his contract of service may still be sued *in contract* by his employer, but a strike after due notice is no longer a breach of contract.[19]

Under the 1906 Act it was uncertain whether the words "shall not be actionable" meant that the act in question was not actionable at the suit of anyone who is affected by it,[20] or whether it meant only that it was not actionable at the suit of the other party to the contract the breach of which is induced or procured, while remaining actionable at the suit of any third party who was able to build a cause of action upon it.[21] Section 13(3) of T.U.L.R.A. made it plain that the former interpretation is that preferred by Parliament, but that sub-section was itself repealed by the Employment Act 1980, s. 17(8), so that the former law has been revived.[21a]

"On the ground only"

This phrase, which also appeared in the 1906 Act, is very difficult to construe.[22]

---

[15] *Hutchison* v. *Aitchison* (1970) 9 K.I.R. 69.
[16] *Esso Ltd.* v. *McGowan* [1974] I.R. 148.
[17] See *British Broadcasting Corporation* v. *Hearn* [1977] 1 W.L.R. 1004, which was approved in *Express Newspapers Ltd.* v. *McShane* [1980] A.C. 672.
[18] *Torquay Hotel Co. Ltd.* v. *Cousins* [1969] 2 Ch. 106. S. 17 of T.U.L.R.A. attempts to restrict a court's power to grant interlocutory injunctions: see below, § 219.
[19] See above, § 134.
[20] The view of Lord Denning M.R. in *Morgan* v. *Fry* [1968] 2 Q.B. 710, 729.
[21] The view of Lord Pearce in *Stratford (J.T.) & Son Ltd.* v. *Lindley* [1965] A.C. 269, 336.
[21a] *Hadmor Productions Ltd.* v. *Hamilton, The Times,* April 10, 1981.
[22] Lord Reid in *Rookes* v. *Barnard* [1964] A.C. 1129, 1172.

No responsible trade unionist has ever claimed the right to commit acts amounting to (say) arson, assault or libel, in the course of a trade dispute, but it was thought the section protected "the right to strike."[23] After much argument it was held in *Rookes* v. *Barnard*[24] that section 3 of the 1906 Act did not prevent actions if they were based on some ground other than inducement of breach of contract, or interference with business—*e.g.* slander, deceit or intimidation.[25] Although *Rookes* v. *Barnard* was reversed by the Trades Disputes Act 1965, whose provisions are re-enacted in section 13 (1) (*b*) of T.U.L.R.A., the interpretation which it gave to "on the ground only" seems to be correct.

"That it induces another person to break a contract or interferes or induces another person to interfere with its performance."

The wide meaning given to "induces" in modern cases has already been considered.[26]

"A contract" is a much wider term than that used in the Acts of 1906 and 1974, "a contract of employment." Parliament then clearly intended to protect breaches of commercial contracts procured in the course of an industrial dispute.[27] But the door thereby opened to secondary boycotts and secondary picketing has been partially closed by section 17 of the Act of 1980.

Protection is also extended to one who "interferes with the performance of a contract." This is a notable parliamentary recognition of the judicial broadening of the scope of the principle in *Lumley* v. *Gye* to cover not only inducing breach of contract but also preventing the performance of it.[28] Similarly, section 13 (1) (*h*) re-enacts section 1 (1) of the 1965 Act, with equally broad meanings given to the concepts of contract, threats, and prevention of performance.

(2) Allen v. Flood approved

The second subsection of section 13 of T.U.L.R.A. apparently gives the parliamentary death-blow to the residual tort of interference with business relations, which has had judicial support for two centuries.[29]

(3) The Reversal of Quinn v. Leathem

It will be seen that subsection (4) of section 13 of T.U.L.R.A., which substantially re-enacts section 1 of the 1906 Act, restricts the bringing of an action of conspiracy to cases in which the acts in question would also be actionable if done by one person instead of by two or more. But it will be recalled that the courts had largely evaded the strict logic of *Quinn* v. *Leathem* by conceding that the defendants' objects were not unlawful if their intention was to advance their own lawful interests.[30]

---

[23] See above, § 133.
[24] [1964] A.C. 1129.
[25] See above, § 135.
[26] See above, § 136.
[27] *Stratford* v. *Lindley* [1965] A.C. 269.
[28] See above, § 136.
[29] See above, § 133.
[30] See above, § 138.

Still the 1974 Act is valuable because it disposes of an awkward doubt which arose out of dicta in *Rookes* v. *Barnard*—namely, whether threats by employees to break their own contracts of employment might not be unlawful means sufficient to found a charge of conspiracy.[31]

(4) The Reversal of Lyons v. Wilkins

At common law the torts of nuisance[32] or intimidation[33] may[34] be committed by watching or besetting or obstructing the access to premises, at least if done in a violent or menacing way. There is, therefore, no general legal right to demonstrate or picket in support of a political or economic or social cause.[35] English law does not recognise "consumer picketing." But in the 1906 Act a certain degree of protection was given to peaceful picketing in the course or furtherance of a trade dispute. The 1971 Act made some changes, and then there were further changes in the Acts of 1974 and 1980.

The governing provisions are now contained in section 15 of the 1974 Act, which, as amended by section 16 of the 1980 Act, reads as follows:

15.—(1) It shall be lawful for a person[36] in contemplation or furtherance of a trade dispute[37] to attend—

(*a*) at or near his own place of work,[38] or

(*b*) if he is an official of a trade union, at or near the place of work of a member of that union whom he is accompanying and whom he represents,[39]

for the purpose only[40] of peacefully obtaining or communicating information, or peacefully persuading any person to work or abstain from working.[41]

(2) If a person works or normally works—

(*a*) otherwise than at any one place, or

(*b*) at a place the location of which is such that attendance there for a purpose mentioned in subsection (1) above is impracticable,

his place of work for the purposes of that subsection shall be any premises of his employer from which he works or from which his work is administered.

(3) In the case of a worker who is not in employment and whose last employment was terminated in connection with a trade dispute, subsection

---

[31] See the comments of the Donovan Commission in Cmnd. 3623 (1968), para. 854.

[32] *J. Lyons & Sons* v. *Wilkins* [1899] 1 Ch. 255. See above, § 24.

[33] *Bird* v. *O'Neal* [1960] A.C. 907.

[34] *Torquay Hotel Co. Ltd.* v. *Cousins* [1969] 2 Ch. 109, 120.

[35] *Hubbard* v. *Pitt* [1976] Q.B. 142.

[36] It is noteworthy that from 1906 to 1980 the statutory protection was given to "one or more persons."

[37] The meaning of this phrase is discussed above.

[38] The "attendance" may be "at or near" but not "*in*": so a "sit-in" is a trespass. The section in effect legalises the use of the highway for purposes which would otherwise be trespassory as against the owner of the sub-soil: *Ferguson* v. *O'Gorman* [1937] I.R. 620. Note that picketing of an employer's house, or even of another work-place of that employer (or an associated company) is not now protected.

[39] These words attempt to place some limits on the presence of extraneous elements on the picket-line—*e.g.* "flying pickets."

[40] Picketing which is neither informational nor persuasive may therefore be wrongful—*e.g.* as intimidation or battery. There is no right to stop a vehicle bringing in supplies or other workers: *Broome* v. *D.P.P.* [1974] A.C. 587.

[41] If the picketing really is peaceful in the sense explained above, then these words will protect conduct which might otherwise be actionable as an inducement of a breach of contract.

(1) above shall in relation to that dispute have effect as if any reference to his place of work were a reference to his former place of work.

(4) A person who is an official of a trade union by virtue only of having been elected or appointed to be a representative of some of the members of the union shall be regarded for the purposes of subsection (1) above as representing only those members; but otherwise an official of a trade union shall be regarded for those purposes as representing all its members. (2) Nothing in section 13 of the 1974 Act shall prevent an act done in the course of picketing from being actionable in tort unless it is done in the course of attendance declared lawful by section 15 of that Act.[42]

The main effect of the 1980 amendment is "to withdraw the present immunity from secondary picketing whenever it takes place, whoever undertakes it, and whatever the nature of the dispute," as the Secretary of State told the House of Commons on March 18, 1980.

---

[42] But the protection given by s. 15 (1) is limited to primary picketing. Secondary picketing may be actionable under this sub-section, or separately under s. 17 as being secondary industrial action, unless excusable under s. 15(2).

CHAPTER 18

DECEIT AND INJURIOUS FALSEHOOD

Wrongs of fraud or misrepresentations are of two kinds essentially distinct—first, the wrong of deceiving the plaintiff so that he causes harm to himself by his own mistaken act, and, secondly, the wrong of deceiving other persons so that they by their mistaken acts caused harm to the plaintiff. The first of these injuries may be called, in a narrow and specific sense of the term, the wrong of Fraud or Deceit; the second has no recognised distinctive title, and in default of a better designation it will here be called the wrong of Injurious Falsehood. We proceed to consider the former of these.

§ 140. ELEMENTS OF DECEIT

The tort of deceit consists in the act of making a wilfully false statement with intent that the plaintiff shall act in reliance on it, and with the result that he does so act and suffers harm in consequence.[1] As we have seen,[2] the origin of the tort can be clearly traced to the decision in *Pasley* v. *Freeman*.[3] There are four main elements in this tort[4]: (1) there must be a false representation of fact; (2) the representation must be made with knowledge of its falsity; (3) it must be made with the intention that it should be acted on by the plaintiff, or by a class of persons which includes the plaintiff, in the manner which resulted in damage to him; (4) it must be proved that the plaintiff has acted upon the false statement, and has sustained damage by so doing.[5]

§ 141. (1) THE FALSE REPRESENTATION OF FACT

Here three points are to be noted. First, the false statement may be made either by words or by conduct. Any conduct designed to deceive another by leading him to believe that a certain fact exists is equivalent in law, as in morals, to a statement in words that that fact does exist. Thus it is a fraud to obtain goods on credit in Oxford by wearing without right an undergraduate's cap and gown,[6] or to take measures for concealing the defects of an article sold.[7]

Secondly, the defendant must have made a positive false statement; a mere passive non-disclosure of the truth, however deceptive in fact, does not

---

[1] *Bradford Building Society* v. *Borders* [1941] 2 All E.R. 205, 211.
[2] Above, § 3.
[3] (1789) 3 T.R. 51. "I am old enough to remember when this species of action came into use," said Sir Vicary Gibbs C.J. (b. 1751) in *Ashlin* v. *White* (1816) Holt 387, 388, "It was dexterously intended to avoid the Statute of Frauds." Although this particular loophole was stopped by Lord Tenterden's Act 1828 (see below, § 146), the action of deceit flourished and is now of general application.
[4] *Bradford Building Society* v. *Borders* [1941] 2 All E.R. 205, 211.
[5] *Diamond* v. *Bank of London & Montreal Ltd.* [1979] Q.B. 333, 349.
[6] *R.* v. *Barnard* (1837) 7 C. & P. 784.
[7] *Horsfall* v. *Thomas* (1862) 1 H. & C. 90, 99.

amount to deceit in law.[8] This principle, however, is subject to four qualifications:

(1) The non-disclosure of a part of the truth may make the statement of the residue positively false. It is permissible to tell the whole truth, or to tell none of it, but it is not always possible to tell merely part of it without falling into positive falsehood.[9]

(2) Active concealment of a fact is equivalent to a positive statement that the fact does not exist. By active concealment is meant any act done with intent to prevent a fact from being discovered: for example, to cover over the defects of an article sold with intent that they shall not be discovered by the buyer has the same effect in law as a statement in words that those defects do not exist.[10]

(3) As it is an actionable fraud to leave uncorrected a false statement which is ultimately acted on by the plaintiff to his detriment,[11] it follows that if the defendant makes a statement which he believes to be true and he afterwards discovers that it is false before it has been acted on by the plaintiff, or if he makes a statement which is true when made but becomes false to his knowledge before it has been acted on,[12] it is his duty to disclose the truth.[13] In such a case a person who is not the maker of the statement may also be liable, either if he is vicariously responsible for the acts of the representor[14] or if he deliberately and knowingly uses the delusion created by the fraud in the injured party's mind in order to profit by it.[15]

(4) In certain cases there is a statutory duty of disclosure, the breach of which is apparently an actionable fraud. For example, there is a statutory duty to disclose certain matters in a company prospectus.[16]

Thirdly, the misrepresentation must be a false statement of fact, and not a mere broken promise. If the words of the defendant amount to a mere promise, they cannot be the basis of an action of tort, and impose no liability on him unless they conform to all the requirements of a valid contract. There is no such thing known to the law as a promise which is not good enough for a contract, but the breach of which is actionable as a tort.[17] The term fact, however, is used to include everything except a promise. Thus a statement of opinion, if wilfully false, is actionable as a tort.[18] So an expression of opinion concerning a present or future event may be a

---

[8] *Arkwright* v. *Newbold* (1881) 17 Ch.D. 301, 318; *Bradford Building Society* v. *Borders* [1941] 2 All E.R. 205.

[9] *Peek* v. *Gurney* (1873) L.R. 6 H.L. 377, 392; *Arkwright* v. *Newbold* (1881) 17 Ch.D. 301, 318.

[10] *Horsfall* v. *Thomas* (1862) 1 H. & C. 90.

[11] *Briess* v. *Woolley* [1954] A.C. 333.

[12] The tort becomes complete only when the misrepresentation—not having been corrected in the meantime—is acted upon by the misrepresentee: if false when made but true when acted upon there is no misrepresentation: *Briess* v. *Woolley* [1954] A.C. 333, 353. Although no action will lie until damage has been suffered (which may be after the act induced) the tort is complete in the sense that this is the moment relevant to an inquiry into its falsity: see *Diamond* v. *Bank of London & Montreal Ltd.* [1979] Q.B. 333.

[13] *Incledon* v. *Watson* (1862) 2 F. & F. 841; *Brownlie* v. *Campbell* (1880) 5 App.Cas. 925, 950. The question was left open by Lord Porter in *Bradford Building Society* v. *Borders* [1941] 2 All E.R. 205, 228, but the matter seems settled by *Briess* v. *Woolley* [1954] A.C. 333.

[14] *Briess* v. *Woolley* [1954] A.C. 333.

[15] *Bradford Building Society* v. *Borders* [1941] 2 All E.R. 205, 208.

[16] Companies Act 1948, s. 38. See also the Prevention of Fraud (Investments) Act 1958.

[17] *Jordan* v. *Money* (1854) 5 H.L.C. 185.

[18] *Anderson* v. *Pacific Insurance Co.* (1872) L.R. 7 C.P. 65, 69.

representation of fact if it implies that it is an opinion presently held.[19] "It may be that in the first instance the description of an object is a matter of opinion; but, if everyone's opinion about it is agreed, the description achieves sufficient certainty to become a fact."[20] Similarly there seems no real reason to doubt that an action will lie for a fraudulent misrepresentation of law.[21] So also an action of tort will lie for a false representation of intention.[22] An unfulfilled promise to do a thing is actionable as a contract or not at all; a false statement of intention to do a thing may be actionable as a tort. Thus in *Edgington* v. *Fitzmaurice*,[23] the directors of a company were held liable for fraud in borrowing money on behalf of the company on a false statement of the purpose to which the loan was to be applied. "The state of a man's mind," said Bowen L.J., "is as much a fact as the state of his digestion."[24]

§ 142. (2) KNOWLEDGE OF THE STATEMENT'S FALSITY

A false statement is not actionable in deceit, as distinct from in negligence,[25] unless it is wilfully false. This is established by the House of Lords in the leading case of *Derry* v. *Peek*.[26] The facts were that the directors of a tramway company which had authority to use steam power with the consent of the Board of Trade, believing, honestly but unreasonably, that this consent would be given as a matter of course, issued a prospectus in which it was stated that they had the right to use steam power without reference to any condition. In reliance on this statement the plaintiff took shares in the company. The promoters were held not liable in damages, on the ground that there was no proof that the error was fraudulent.

Dishonest belief essential

When, then, is a statement false within the meaning of the rule in *Derry* v. *Peek*? The test is the existence of a genuine belief in the truth of the statement. It is not necessary for liability that the defendant should have known it to be false; it is sufficient if he did not genuinely and honestly believe it to be true. Every statement is explicitly or implicitly a statement as to the belief of the speaker, and if that belief does not exist the statement is knowingly and wilfully false.[27]

Recklessness, in the sense of gross negligence, is no ground of liability.[28] Although an absence of reasonable grounds for believing a statement to be

---

[19] *Bisset* v. *Wilkinson* [1927] A.C. 177, 182; *Ballard* v. *Gaskill* [1954] 4 D.L.R. 427.
[20] *Armstrong* v. *Strain* [1951] 1 T.L.R. 856, 860, *per* Devlin J.
[21] *West London Commercial Bank* v. *Kitson* (1884) 13 Q.B.D. 360; *Eaglesfield* v. *Londonderry (Marquis of)* (1877) 4 Ch.D. 693.
[22] And also a criminal prosecution since the Theft Act 1968.
[23] (1885) 29 Ch.D. 459.
[24] 29 Ch.D. 459, 483. It is not actionable fraud, however, for a seller or buyer to obtain an advantageous bargain by falsely stating that he is not prepared to take less or give more for the property than a certain sum. In such a case the plaintiff can show no legal damage; he has lost a better bargain, indeed, but he has lost nothing to which he had any legal right: *Vernon* v. *Keys* (1810) 12 East 632.
[25] See above, § 76.
[26] (1889) 14 App.Cas. 337.
[27] *Smith* v. *Chadwick* (1884) 9 App.Cas. 187, 203.
[28] Yet in *Brown Jenkinson Ltd.* v. *Percy Dalton Ltd.* [1957] 2 Q.B. 621, the defendants were liable in deceit although they had unthinkingly followed normal commercial practice.

true is not in itself a ground for liability, it is important evidence that no such belief really exists and therefore that the defendant is guilty not of negligence but of fraud.[29]

If a statement is ambiguous, it must be taken in the sense in which the defendant himself meant it—that is to say, in the sense in which he intended that it should be understood by the plaintiff. It is not legitimate for the court to construe the statement as it thinks it ought to have been construed by a reasonable man.[30] If both the representor and the representee in fact intended and understood, respectively, the statement to bear a certain meaning, the representor cannot then say that a reasonable man would have understood it in another sense.[31] On the other hand, it is immaterial that the objective meaning is more natural, and that the plaintiff understood the statement in that sense and was deceived by it; for in such a case the defendant is guilty of negligence only, and not of fraud. This may be very hard on the plaintiff, particularly if the defendant "is not the sort of man who worries too much about what he wrote last week when writing a letter this week."[32]

§ 143. (3) INTENT THAT STATEMENT SHALL BE ACTED ON

A false statement is not actionable, whatever damage may result from acting in reliance on it, unless it was made with intent that the plaintiff should act in reliance on it in the manner in which he did act. He who tells lies is not responsible to the whole world for the consequences of them. The only person entitled to rely on a statement and to act accordingly is he who is intended to rely on it and to act upon it by the person making it. All others accept it at their own risk, and if they come to harm, must blame their own credulity only. Thus in *Peek* v. *Gurney*[33] it was held that a person who in reliance on a fraudulent prospectus issued by promoters bought shares in the market and so suffered loss had no cause of action against the promoters: for the purpose of a prospectus is to induce persons to apply to the company for shares, not to induce them to buy in the market shares already issued. The plaintiff, therefore, had acted in a manner not intended, and had relied on the false statement for a purpose that was foreign to it. On the other hand, it is not necessary that the false statement should be made directly to the plaintiff[34] with intent that any specific individual should be deceived and act in reliance on it.[35] Nor need there be an intention to cause loss to the plaintiff; the only necessary intent is that the plaintiff shall be deceived and shall act in a certain way; and if, as the natural and probable

---

[29] *Derry* v. *Peek* (1889) 14 App.Cas 337, 375. For the protection afforded by legal advice, see *Delaney* v. *Keogh* [1905] 2 I.R. 267, 290; and for the burden of proof to be discharged by the plaintiff, see *Hornal* v. *Neuberger Products Ltd.* [1957] 1 Q.B. 247.

[30] *Akerhielm* v. *De Mare* [1959] A.C. 789. There are, indeed, several dicta to the contrary, but they are prior to *Derry* v. *Peek* and must now be treated as unsound. See Williams in (1945) 61 L.Q.R. 384, 392; Devlin J. in *Armstrong* v. *Strain* [1951] 1 T.L.R. 856, 871, and the same learned judge in (1937) 53 L.Q.R. 344, 360–361.

[31] *Woodhouse Cocoa Ltd.* v. *Nigeria Produce Marketing Co. Ltd.* [1972] A.C. 741.

[32] *Gross* v. *Lewis Hillman Ltd.* [1970] 1 Ch. 445, 465.

[33] (1873) L.R. 6 H.L. 377. The relevance of *Peek* v. *Gurney* to current Stock Exchange practice has been doubted: Gower, *Principles of Modern Company Law*, pp. 316–317.

[34] *Commercial Banking Co. of Sydney Ltd.* v. *Brown & Co.* (1972) 46 A.L.J.R. 297.

[35] *Andrews* v. *Mockford* [1896] 1 Q.B. 372.

result of so acting, any damage is suffered by him, the defendant is responsible for it, whether he meant that damage to ensue or not.[36]

It is not enough, therefore, that it is the natural and probable consequence of the false statement that the plaintiff will rely and act on it, if this was not the intention of the defendant. It would seem on principle, however, that it is enough if the defendant's apparent intention was that the plaintiff should act on his statement, whatever his real and concealed intention may have been.[37] If the defendant makes a wilfully false statement, which the plaintiff naturally and reasonably believes to be made to him with intent that he shall act in reliance on it in a certain manner, and he does so act, it would seem right that the defendant should be estopped from alleging that his apparent intention was not his real intention.[38]

"Materiality"

If the statement is actually relied on, it is no defence that the plaintiff was negligent or foolish in doing so, or that he had a full opportunity of discovering the truth for himself. Consent is no defence. Every man has in law a right to believe and act on all lies told him by others with intent to deceive him.[39] Nor is it any defence to say that the representation is not "material," or would not have induced a reasonable man. The true question is whether the statement was a real inducement to the plaintiff: a representation may be material as between the parties, though not to a normal man.[40]

§ 144. (4) Damage to the Plaintiff

No action will lie for a false statement unless the plaintiff did in fact rely and act upon it, even if he acted in the way intended by the defendant and suffered harm in consequence.[41] A mere attempt to deceive is not actionable.[42] It is sufficient, however, that the false statement was one of the reasons which induced the plaintiff to act as he did.[43] Nevertheless, if the plaintiff, although he relied on the statement, would have acted as he did, even had the statement not been made, he will have no cause of action.[44] In such a case he has suffered no damage by the fraud. The plaintiff must also prove damage, and it is worth noting that the damage need not necessarily have been suffered at the moment at which the plaintiff acted on the

---

[36] *Edgington* v. *Fitzmaurice* (1885) 29 Ch.D. 459, 482.
[37] *Polhill* v. *Walter* (1832) 3 B. & Ad. 114.
[38] (1873) L.R. 9 Q.B. 34.
[39] *Pearson* v. *Dublin Corporation* [1907] A.C. 351. Nor is it any defence that the plaintiff's agent knew of the falsity of the statement, if the plaintiff himself did not: *Wells* v. *Smith* [1914] 3 K.B. 722.
[40] *Nicholas* v. *Thompson* [1924] V.L.R. 554, 566, 578.
[41] *Macleay* v. *Tait* [1906] A.C. 24.
[42] *Horsfall* v. *Thomas* (1862) 1 H. & C. 90. "It is common knowledge that the well-known case of *Peek* v. *Derry* very nearly never got beyond the court of first instance, because Sir Henry Peek could not be induced to say that he relied upon the statements in the prospectus. It was only by the most skilful management of counsel that he was ultimately got to say that he took the shares relying on the statements in the prospectus": *Horwood* v. *Statesman Publishing Co. Ltd.* (1929) 141 L.T. 54, 58, *per* Scrutton L.J.
[43] *Edgington* v. *Fitzmaurice* (1885) 29 Ch.D. 459, 485; *Paul and Vincent Ltd.* v. *O'Reilly* (1913) 49 I.L.T.R. 89.
[44] *Macleay* v. *Tait* [1906] A.C. 24. The question, however, seems mainly academic: for the wrongdoer has no right to institute a conjectural inquiry as to what would have happened if certain things had been said which were in fact not said, or had been said differently: *Smith* v. *Kay* (1859) 7 H.L.C. 750, 759.

statement.[45] In this tort the test of remoteness of damage is direction and not reasonable foresight.[46] In an action for fraudulent misrepresentation on a sale of land or goods the usual measure of damage is the difference between the price paid and the fair market value at the time of the contract, for to permit the plaintiff to recover for the loss of prospective gains would be to equate him with a buyer suing for breach of contract.[47] But in special circumstances other heads of damage may be recovered.[48]

§ 145. EXCEPTIONS TO RULE IN DERRY v. PEEK

The rule in *Derry* v. *Peek* is subject to nine exceptions or qualifications:

(1) Liability under Hedley Byrne v. Heller

The scope of liability in negligence for careless statements which cause financial loss has already been considered.[49]

(2) Physical harm

The rule in *Derry* v. *Peek* does not apply to cases in which physical harm to person or property is caused by dangerous chattels or premises negligently represented to be safe. Liability may or may not exist in these cases, but the question is governed by different considerations from those which relate to false representations in general. A distinct category of the law of torts is applicable.[50] There is also authority that an action will lie if physical harm results from careless statements made in other circumstances.[51]

(3) Contractual duty

When there is a contractual relation between the plaintiff and defendant which involves a contractual duty to use care in the making of statements, the rule in *Derry* v. *Peek* is excluded.[52] A person may take on himself by contract a duty which the common law does not impose upon him. It should be noticed, however, that even where there is a contractual duty of careful statement the rule in *Derry* v. *Peek* is excluded only in favour of the person with whom the contract is made and not in favour of third persons who are injured by negligent statements made in breach of it.[53]

(4) Fiduciary relationship

When there has been a breach of a special duty recognised in equity, whether arising from the fiduciary relationship of the parties or the special

[45] *Diamond* v. *Bank of London & Montreal Ltd.* [1979] Q.B. 333.
[46] See below, § 202.
[47] *Foster* v. *Public Trustee* [1975] N.Z.L.R. 24.
[48] *Hornal* v. *Neuberger Products Ltd.* [1957] 1 Q.B. 247; *Canavan* v. *Wright* [1957] N.Z.L.R. 790.
[49] See above, § 76.
[50] See above, § 76.
[51] See above, § 76.
[52] See, for example, *De la Bere* v. *Pearson Ltd.* [1908] 1 K.B. 280.
[53] *Dickson* v. *Reuter's Telegram Co.* (1877) 3 C.P.D. 1.

circumstances of the case, the defendant will be liable for "constructive fraud," even though he has no fraudulent intention. In such a case no damages can be given for tort, but the plaintiff will be given an indemnity for the loss he has suffered—an equitable remedy.[54] So in *Nocton* v. *Ashburton*[55] a mortgagee claimed to be indemnified against the loss which he had sustained by having been improperly advised and induced by the defendant, acting as his confidential solicitor, to release a part of a mortgage security, whereby the security had become insufficient. Although the solicitor had not been guilty of fraud the House of Lords held that that did not preclude the plaintiff from obtaining relief on the footing of a breach of duty arising from the fiduciary relationship. A similar relationship exists between a bank and its customers, whether actual or potential.[56]

(5) Warranty of authority

Every person who purports to act as the agent of another is deemed in law to have entered into an implied contract of warranty of authority with any person who contracts or otherwise deals with him in reliance on his authority. If, therefore, the agent misrepresents the existence or extent of his authority, he is liable in damages for any loss thereby suffered by those who have dealt with him; the rule in *Derry* v. *Peek* being excluded by the existence of a contract implied in law.[57]

(6) Estoppel

The rule as to estoppel by representation is not affected by *Derry* v. *Peek*, and may in certain cases so operate as to impose liability in damages for a false statement which is not fraudulent. A company, for example, which registers a forged transfer of shares is liable by way of estoppel to a purchaser who buys the shares in reliance on the share certificate so issued; for the company is estopped from denying the truth of that certificate, and therefore the title of the plaintiff.[58]

(7) Statutory duty

In certain cases a duty of giving correct information is imposed by statute. Immediately after the decision in *Derry* v. *Peek* Parliament passed the Directors' Liability Act 1890, which gave a right of action for damages

---

[54] See this stressed by Sealy, "Some Principles of Fiduciary Obligation" [1963] C.L.J. 119, 137–139.
[55] [1914] A.C. 932. On May 20, 1914, Pollock wrote to Holmes: "Haldane [L.C.] asked me last week to a tobacco talk of *Derry* v. *Peek* and the possibility of minimising its consequences. The Lords are going to hold that it does not apply to the situation created by a positive fiduciary duty such as a solicitor's, in other words, go as near as they dare to saying it was wrong, as all Lincoln's Inn thought at the time"; Pollock-Holmes, *Letters* (Ed. M. Howe), Cambridge University Press (1941), Vol. i, p. 215.
[56] *Woods* v. *Martins Bank Ltd.* [1959] 1 Q.B. 55, 72. See above, § 76.
[57] *Collen* v. *Wright* (1857) 8 E. & B. 647; *Starkey* v. *Bank of England* [1903] A.C. 114. "Seen in retrospect, *Collen* v. *Wright* looks like a curious island. If it had asserted liability for negligent, as well as fraudulent, misrepresentation of authority, it could hardly have escaped immersion by *Derry* v. *Peek*. But, because it placed the liability in the particular case on so high a ground, the flood swept past it and it escaped and grew": Mr. Justice Fullagar "Liability for Representations at Common Law" (1951) 25 Austr. L.J. 278, 283. Wedderburn, "Collateral Contracts" [1959] C.L.J. 58, 68, offers another explanation.
[58] *Re Bahia and San Francisco Ry.* (1868) L.R. 3 Q.B. 584.

to persons who had suffered damage as the result of acting upon incorrect statements negligently inserted in a prospectus issued by the promoters or directors of a company. This statute has now been repealed and its provisions re-enacted in section 43 of the Companies Act 1948.

(8) Principal's liability for fraud of agent

The judgments of the Court of Appeal in *London County Freehold Properties Ltd.* v. *Berkeley Property Co. Ltd.*[59] suggest that there may be yet another exception to the rule in *Derry* v. *Peek*. In order to understand the problem it is necessary to see how far a principal is liable for the frauds of his agent. The principal is clearly liable if he expressly authorises an agent to make a statement which the agent believes to be true but which the principal knows to be false,[60] or if he purposely employs an agent who is ignorant of the true facts hoping that he will give false information. He may also be liable if he deliberately stands by and allows his innocent agent to make deceitful statements.[61] Nor can it be doubted that the principal is liable if the agent knowingly makes a false statement in the course of his employment. This is so even though the false statement reaches the third party who acts on it to his detriment either through the principal himself[62] or through the agency of a fellow servant,[63] and even though either of them honestly believes the statement to be true. For in such a case the false representation is made by the agent just as truly as if it had been sent through the post or by the hand of a messenger.[64]

But what is the position if one agent innocently makes a false representation and the principal (or another agent) knows facts which make the representation false but does not know or have any reason to believe that the agent will make the representation? The language used in the *London County Freehold Properties* case was wide enough to suggest liability even in such a case, but in the following year Atkinson J. said[65] that the decision had been based on a finding of fraud against the defendant's property manager, Jasper Addis, who had supplied the information which was conveyed to the plaintiff by another agent of the company, one De Rees, who honestly believed it to be true. In 1951 the point came before Devlin J. in *Armstrong* v. *Strain*.[66] He found himself unable to adopt the interpretation of Atkinson J. and preferred to follow the apparently inconsistent decision

---

[59] [1936] 2 All E.R. 1039.
[60] *Ludgater* v. *Love* (1881) 44 L.T. 694. If the agent also knows it is false, then they are joint tortfeasors.
[61] *Gordon Hill Trust Ltd.* v. *Segall* [1941] 2 All E.R. 379, 390.
[62] *Pearson & Son Ltd.* v. *Dublin Corporation* [1907] A.C. 351, as explained in *Anglo-Scottish Beet Sugar Corporation Ltd.* v. *Spalding U.D.C.* [1937] 2 K.B. 607, 619–621.
[63] *London County Properties* case, as explained by Atkinson J. in the *Anglo-Scottish Beet Sugar Corporation* case in a judgment described by Singleton L.J. as "a masterly analysis of it, and of the authorities on the subject": *Armstrong* v. *Strain* [1952] 1 K.B. 232, 243.
[64] *Pearson* v. *Dublin Corporation* [1907] A.C. 351, 367.
[65] *Anglo-Scottish Beet Sugar Corporation Case* [1937] 2 K.B. 607, 624.
[66] [1951] 1 T.L.R. 856. By a strange coincidence, Sir Patrick Devlin, when a junior at the common law Bar, had written an article ("Fraudulent Representation" (1937) 53 L.Q.R. 344) containing penetrating criticism of the *London County Freehold* case (in which he had been of counsel for the unsuccessful defendants: see 155 L.T. 190 (not in [1936] 2 All E.R. 1039)). Much of the reasoning in this article (to which "I was not unnaturally referred") finds a place in his judgment.

of the Court of Appeal in *Gordon Hill Trust Ltd.* v. *Segall.*[67] Devlin J. pointed out that ever since *Derry* v. *Peek* it had been necessary to find actual fraud or dishonesty—conscious knowledge of the falsity of the statement—on the part of the defendant, and it was precisely this finding of conscious knowledge which it was impossible to make in the case of an innocent division of ingredients.[68] But in the Court of Appeal the view of Atkinson J. was preferred, Singleton L.J. saying[69] that the *London County Freehold* case "should not be treated as an authority except and in so far as the decision was based on the fraud of Addis." Although the court would thus seem to have denied that there was any inconsistency between its own previous decisions,[70] and so absolved itself from considering in detail the criticisms of the doctrine that the elements of fraud may be collected from the various agents of the defendant, it is clear from the whole tenor of the judgments that that doctrine is no longer supported by any convincing reasoning.[71]

(9) The Misrepresentation Act 1967[72]

One of the objects of this Act is to remove certain bars to rescission for innocent misrepresentation in the law of contract. But another object is to extend the tort of deceit by enabling a person who has entered into a contract as a result of a misrepresentation made to him by another party to that contract to recover damages for his loss if the party making the misrepresentation would have been liable in damages if that misrepresentation had been made fraudulently. In effect there is now a statutory duty not to state matters of the kind in question. Further, the statutory duty is one of strict liability.[73] The Act has been unpopular with conveyancers. Thus the Law Society's Conditions of Sale, and also the National Conditions, attempt to exclude its operation[74] in various ways. The clauses in question do not attempt to exclude liabilities or remedies; rather they attempt to prevent some or all pre-contract statements obtaining, or retaining, the status of representations. Finally, the Act in no way affects the decision in *Hedley*

---

[67] [1941] 2 All E.R. 379. "I find it impossible to believe that the Court of Appeal would convict of fraud a man whom the trial judge had acquitted without making it plain that they were doing so"—[1951] 1 T.L.R. 856, 862. But on appeal Singleton L.J. said that Devlin J. had been misled by "the somewhat nebulous way in which the judgments in the case are expressed"—[1952] 1 K.B. 232, 243.

[68] [1951] 1 T.L.R. 856, 872.

[69] [1952] 1 K.B. 232, 244.

[70] "Is a decision of the Court of Appeal that two previous decisions of its own are reconcilable, less or more binding on it, than a decision of the Court of Appeal that two previous decisions of its own are irreconcilable?" This was a question which Asquith L.J. invited the Public Teachers of Law to solve: [1950] 1 J.S.P.T.L. 350, 362.

[71] See in particular the explanation of the judgment of (Sir Mark) Romer L.J. in the *London County Properties* case given by (Sir Charles) Romer L.J. in *Armstrong* v. *Strain* [1952] 1 K.B. 232, 248. It is true that there is some authority for the proposition that a master may be liable even though his servant has not committed any actionable tort (below, § 173), and that the decision in *Armstrong* v. *Strain* may cause serious difficulty to a plaintiff who wishes to hold a corporation responsible for the statements of two or more of its employees. See *Woyka & Co.* v. *London and Northern Co.* (1922) 10 Ll.L.Rep. 110; *Howse* v. *Quinnell Motors Ltd.* [1952] 2 D.L.R. 425; *Smith and Youngson (Pvt.) Ltd.* v. *Dubie Bros.*, 1959 (1) R. & N. 351.

[72] See the elaborate and highly critical analysis by Treitel and Atiyah, "The Misrepresentation Act 1967" (1967) 30 M.L.R. 369.

[73] *Diamond* v. *Bank of London & Montreal Ltd.* [1979] Q.B. 333.

[74] For exclusion clauses in general, see below, § 186.

Byrne—the plaintiff in that case had not "entered into a contract after a misrepresentation had been made to him by another party thereto" (s. 2 (1)).

§ 146. REPRESENTATIONS AS TO CREDIT

There is one kind of false statement which is no ground of action unless made in writing—namely, a representation as to the credit of a third person. This exception is established by the Statute of Frauds Amendment Act 1828, s. 6, commonly known as Lord Tenterden's Act, by which it is provided that "No action shall be brought whereby to charge any person upon or by reason of any representation or assurance made or given concerning or relating to the character, conduct, credit, ability, trade, or dealings of any other person, to the intent or purpose that such other person may obtain credit, money, or goods upon [*sic*],[75] unless such representation or assurance be made in writing signed by the party to be charged therewith." The purpose of this enactment was to prevent the evasion of the fourth section of the Statute of Frauds 1677 (which requires a guarantee to be in writing), by suing on a verbal guarantee in an action of tort instead of contract, and alleging that the defendant had made a false and fraudulent representation as to the credit or financial ability of the debtor.[76] A writing, therefore has been made essential for the tort as well as for the contract.[77] But Lord Tenterden's Act applies only to actions of tort based on fraudulent misrepresentation; not to actions for breach of contract,[78] or for the breach of some other duty of care in making representations,[79] such as the duty of care established by the decision in *Hedley Byrne* v. *Heller*.[80]

The signature of an agent is not sufficient for the Act requires the personal signature of the defendant himself.[81] This is so even when the defendant is a body corporate—although in such a case no signature except that of an agent is possible. Thus an incorporated bank is not responsible for a fraudulent representation as to credit made by a manager of one of its branches.[82]

Lord Tenterden's Act is not to be read literally in accordance with the vague and unrestricted generality of its terms, but is on the contrary to be restrictively construed by reference to the known object of the legislature and the known mischief which it was intended to prevent.[83] This has produced some curious distinctions. So the Act applies only to those cases in which the defendant's representations have been made for the purpose of inducing the plaintiff to give credit to the third person.[84] Where, on the other hand, the plaintiff is induced by the defendant's representations to act in

---

[75] The word "upon" is nonsensical, and evidently represents some clerical error in the Act. It has been suggested that the word "credit" has been accidentally transposed, and should follow the word "upon" so that the phrase would read "may obtain money or goods upon credit." Other suggestions are that "upon" is a mistake for "thereupon" or that "it" should be inserted after "upon." However this may be, the word as it stands is meaningless, and must be disregarded in construing the section: *Lyde* v. *Barnard* (1836) 1 M. & W. 101.
[76] See above, § 140.
[77] *Lyde* v. *Barnard* (1836) 1 M. & W. 101, 114.
[78] *Banbury* v. *Bank of Montreal* [1918] A.C. 626.
[79] *Anderson (W.B.) & Sons Ltd.* v. *Rhodes Ltd.* [1967] 2 All E.R. 850.
[80] [1964] A.C. 465. See above, § 76, for the scope of this principle.
[81] *Swift* v. *Jewsbury* (1874) L.R. 9 Q.B. 301.
[82] *Hirst* v. *West Riding Union Banking Co. Ltd.* [1901] 2 K.B. 560.
[83] *Banbury* v. *Bank of Montreal* [1918] A.C. 626, 691.
[84] *Diamond* v. *Bank of London & Montreal Ltd.* [1979] Q.B. 333.

some other way than that of giving credit to a third person. Lord Tenterden's Act is not applicable, even though those representations may fall within the letter of the Act as relating to the character, conduct, ability, trade or dealings of that third person. Thus, if the defendant has induced the plaintiff to buy the goodwill of A's business by fraudulent statements as to the nature, prosperity and prospects of that business, the defendant will plead in vain that those statements were not in writing signed by him. Again, since *Hedley Byrne* v. *Heller* it is clear that a fraudulent oral representation is not actionable in tort, while a negligent representation is so actionable.[85] But Lord Tenterden's Act is a good defence even though the intent of the defendant in inducing the plaintiff to give credit to the third person was thereby to obtain a pecuniary advantage for himself, as for example the payment of a debt owing to him by that third person. The statute looks to the immediate intent with which the false representation was made, not to the ulterior motive of the person who makes it.[86]

§ 147. INJURIOUS FALSEHOOD: SLANDER OF TITLE AND SLANDER OF GOODS[87]

We proceed now to the consideration of the second form of actionable misrepresentation—namely, Injurious Falsehood.[88] The wrong of deceit consists, as we have seen, in false statements made to the plaintiff himself whereby he is induced to act to his own loss. The wrong of injurious falsehood, on the other hand, consists in false statements made to other persons concerning the plaintiff whereby he suffers loss through the action of those others. The one consists in misrepresentations made to the plaintiff, the other in misrepresentations made concerning him.

It may be stated as a general rule that it is an actionable wrong maliciously to make a false statement respecting any person or his property with the result that other persons deceived thereby are induced to act in a manner which causes loss to him.[89] This wrong of injurious falsehood is to be distinguished not only from the wrong of deceit, but also from that of defamation, to which it is analogous, but from which it is distinct. Both in defamation and in injurious falsehood the defendant is liable because he has made a false and hurtful statement respecting the plaintiff; but in one case the statement is an attack upon his reputation, and in the other it is not. The distinction is clearly made in the following quotation[90]: "Thus the malicious publication in a newspaper to the effect that Y, the famous pop-singer, had commenced his novitiate with a closed order of monks would not lower him in the esteem of right-thinking people—quite the reverse possibly—but would lose him engagements and therefore money, and therefore be actionable at his suit." It should be noted that no action lies for such a statement unless it has been made maliciously: here, as in some other branches of the

---

[85] *Anderson (W.B.) & Sons Ltd.* v. *Rhodes (Liverpool) Ltd.* [1967] 2 All E.R. 850.
[86] *Clydesdale Bank Ltd.* v. *Paton* [1896] A.C. 381.
[87] See Wood, "Disparagement of Title and Quality" (1942) 20 Can. Bar Rev. 296, 430; Prosser, "Injurious Falsehood: the Basis of Liability" (1959) 59 Col.L.Rev. 425.
[88] Salmond's term has been generally accepted, although the draftsman of the Defamation Act 1952, s. 3, described the tort as Malicious Falsehood.
[89] *Ratcliffe* v. *Evans* [1892] 2 Q.B. 524, 527.
[90] From the Report of the Younger Committee on Privacy (Cmnd. 5012, 1972), App. 1, para. 8.

law of torts, carelessness alone, however gross, does not suffice to establish liability.[91] Thus one who has his application for employment refused as the result of an inaccurate (but not dishonest) medical report has no remedy against the careless doctor.[92]

Examples of injurious falsehood

The earliest cases concern oral aspersions on the plaintiff's title to land. Later the law was extended to cover written aspersions and the title to property other than land, and then to cover disparagement of quality as distinct from title.[93] An example of "slander of title" in the narrow sense occurs when a sale by auction is defeated or prejudiced by an adverse claim made to the property by the defendant, or when the plaintiff's trade is affected by a false charge that the goods offered by him for sale are an infringement of a patent or copyright.[94] Another example of the wrong of injurious falsehood is a false and malicious depreciation of the quality of the merchandise manufactured and sold by the plaintiff.[95] No action, however, will lie for any statement, however false or malicious, which is nothing more than a statement by one trader that his goods are better than those of a rival. This is a special exception to the general rule of liability for injurious falsehood—an exception established to prevent traders from using litigation as a means of advertisement.[96] It is otherwise, however, with a specific allegation of some defect in the plaintiff's goods, even though made by a rival with the view of promoting the sale of his own.[97] But an action for injurious falsehood lies not only in cases of slander of title, slander of goods and passing off, but in analogous cases where damage has been wilfully done without just cause or excuse. So in *Ratcliffe* v. *Evans*[98] the defendant was held liable in damages for having falsely and maliciously published in a newspaper a statement that the plaintiff had ceased to carry on business, in consequence of which statement the plaintiff's trade fell off.

Remedies

It should be remembered that the tort of injurious falsehood is one of those in which the remedies of injunction and declaratory judgment may be more appropriate than an action for damages. In particular, the court has power to make a declaration as to the defendant's title in an action for slander of title or goods, even though such slander has not been proved, when the court thinks it appropriate to state its conclusion upon the title of the plaintiff which the defendant has challenged.[99]

---

[91] See below, § 149.
[92] *Chissel* v. *Chapman* (1954) 56 Ceylon N.L.R. 121. Liability for careless statements made to the plaintiff himself is another matter: above, § 76.
[93] Prosser, 59 Col.L.Rev. 425–426.
[94] *Malachy* v. *Soper* (1836) 3 Bing. N.C. 371; *Royal Baking Powder Co.* v. *Wright, Crossley & Co.* (1901) 18 R.P.C. 95.
[95] *White* v. *Mellin* [1895] A.C. 154. Note that words which merely disparage a man's goods without in any way casting reflections on his personal or trading character do not give rise to an action for libel: *Alcott* v. *Millar's Karri Forests Ltd.* (1905) 91 L.T. 722.
[96] *White* v. *Mellin* [1895] A.C. 154.
[97] *Alcott* v. *Millar's Forests Ltd.* (1905) 91 L.T. 722.
[98] [1892] 2 Q.B. 524.
[99] *Reuter (R.J.) Co. Ltd.* v. *Muhlens* [1954] Ch. 50.

§ 148. CONDITIONS OF LIABILITY

"To support such an action it is necessary for the plaintiffs to prove (1) that the statements complained of were untrue; (2) that they were made maliciously—*i.e.* without just cause or excuse; (3) that the plaintiffs have suffered special damage thereby."[1]

(1) Falsity

The statement must be untrue. This requirement is considered more fully in the next section.

(2) Malice[2]

Lord Davey, in the passage already cited, defined malice as the absence of just cause or excuse. Notwithstanding Lord Davey's dictum, it is now apparently settled that malice in the law of slander of title and other forms of injurious falsehood means some dishonest or otherwise improper motive. The onus of proof is on the plaintiff.[3] A bona fide assertion of title, however, even though mistaken, if made for the protection of one's own interest or for some other proper purpose, is not malicious.[4]

(3) Damage

The common law required the plaintiff to prove special damage as the action was case and not trespass. In 1948 the Porter Committee on the Law of Defamation[5] said: "The necessity of furnishing proof of special damage has rendered this type of action rare in the extreme: but statements of these kinds may cause very serious damage which, owing to technical rules of evidence, it is impossible to prove strictly as special damage. In the result, the injured person is left without any remedy for the loss which he has suffered." Thus when the plaintiff proved that the *Daily Mail* had published a statement that his house was haunted ("by a little old man creeping about the house") he failed because he was unable to prove special damage.[6] This defect has now been remedied by the Defamation Act 1952. Section 3 provides that it shall not be necessary to allege or prove special damage if the words[7] upon which the action is founded are calculated to cause

---

[1] *Royal Baking Powder Co.* v. *Wright Crossley & Co.* (1901) 18 R.P.C. 95, 99, *per* Lord Davey.
[2] See *Balden* v. *Shorter* [1933] Ch. 427, 430; *London Ferro-Concrete Co. Ltd.* v. *Justicz* (1951) 68 R.P.C. 261, 265, *Loudon* v. *Ryder* (No. 2) [1953] Ch. 423, 428.
[3] *London Ferro-Concrete Co. Ltd.* v. *Justicz* (1951) 68 R.P.C. 261.
[4] *Greer's Ltd.* v. *Pearman & Corder Ltd.* (1922) 39 R.P.C. 406, 417; see also *British Ry. Traffic Co.* v. *The C.R.C. Co.* [1922] 2 K.B. 260; *Shapiro* v. *La Morta* (1923) 130 L.T. 622; *Joyce* v. *Motor Surveys Ltd.* [1948] Ch. 252; *Serville* v. *Constance* [1954] 1 W.L.R. 487, (1954) 71 R.P.C. 146 (better report). Newark, "Malice in Actions on the Case for Words" (1944) 60 L.Q.R. 366, came to the conclusion that the plaintiff need prove no more than that the words were spoken with intent to disparage, and that malice need only be proved if the defendant raises a privilege, *e.g.* by claiming a title in himself. But Newark did not consider the equity cases and his conclusion is not justified by the modern authorities, which clearly distinguish this tort from defamation.
[5] Cmd. 7536 (1948), para. 51.
[6] *Barrett* v. *Associated Newspapers Ltd.* (1907) 23 T.L.R. 666. By a strange coincidence, the Supreme Court of Canada dealt with a similar allegation in the same year: *Manitoba Free Press Co.* v. *Nagy* (1907) 39 S.C.R. 340.
[7] This includes broadcast statements.

pecuniary damage to the plaintiff and are published in writing or other permanent form,[8] or if they are calculated to cause pecuniary damage to the plaintiff in respect of any office, profession, calling, trade or business held or carried on by him at the time of publication.

§ 149. INJURIOUS FALSEHOOD: PASSING OFF[9]

To sell merchandise or carry on business under such a name, mark, description, or otherwise in such a manner as to mislead the public into believing that the merchandise or business is that of another person is a wrong actionable at the suit of that other person. This form of injury is commonly, though awkwardly, termed that of *passing off* one's goods or business as the goods or business of another and is the most important example of the wrong of injurious falsehood, though it is so far governed by special rules of its own that it is advisable to treat it separately.[10] The gist of the conception of passing off is that the goods are in effect telling a falsehood about themselves, are saying something about themselves which is calculated to mislead.[11] The law on this matter is designed to protect traders against that form of unfair competition which consists in acquiring for oneself, by means of false or misleading devices, the benefit of the reputation already achieved by rival traders. Normally the defendant seeks to acquire this benefit by passing off his goods as and for the goods of the plaintiff in one or more of the modes specified later. But in the *Champagne* case[12] it was held that the law governing trade competition is wide enough to prevent a person attaching to his product a name or description with which it has no natural connection in order to make use of the reputation and goodwill gained by a product genuinely indicated by that name and description. This principle was approved by the House of Lords in the *Dutch Advocaat* case[13] so that the scope of the tort has been widened.

The wrong of passing off is not confined to cases of the sale of goods but assumes many forms, of which the following are the most important:

(1) A direct statement that the merchandise or business of the defendant is that of the plaintiff

Thus it is an actionable wrong to seek to sell a publication by falsely putting the name of a well-known author on the title-page.[14]

---

[8] The Faulks Committee (Cmnd. 5909, § 594) recommends the abolition of the distinction between written and spoken words.

[9] Morison, "Unfair Competition and 'Passing-off'" (1956) 2 Sydney L.Rev. 50; Cornish, "Unfair Competition" (1972) 12 J.S.P.T.L. 126.

[10] Under the Patents Act 1949, s. 65, it is a tort to cause loss to anyone by making threats of legal proceedings in respect of alleged infringements of patent rights, unless the allegations of infringement are true or the proceedings so threatened are commenced and prosecuted with due diligence. Many of the cases cited above are "threats actions" under the Patents Act.

[11] *Draper* v. *Trist* [1939] 3 All E.R. 513, 517–518.

[12] *J. Bollinger* v. *Costa Brava Wine Co. Ltd.* [1960] Ch. 262. The result of this decision has been said to be the creation of "a new-fangled tort called 'unfair competition'": *Vine Products Ltd.* v. *Mackenzie & Co. Ltd.* [1969] R.P.C. 1, 28.

[13] *Erwen Warnink BV* v. *Townend (J.) & Sons Ltd.* [1979] A.C. 731.

[14] *Byron (Lord)* v. *Johnston* (1816) 2 Mer. 29. But the bare unauthorised use of another's name without more (*e.g.* that it is a libel) is not actionable: *Tolley* v. *Fry* [1930] 1 K.B. 467, 478. See above, § 48.

(2) Trading under a name so closely resembling that of the plaintiff as to be mistaken for it by the public

Thus in *Hendriks* v. *Montagu*[15] the Universal Life Assurance Society obtained an injunction preventing a company subsequently incorporated from carrying on business under the name of the Universe Life Assurance Association. In these days of international trade it is not necessary for the plaintiff company to prove it has obtained its goodwill by trading within the jurisdiction.[16]

(3) Selling goods under a trade name already appropriated for goods of that kind by the plaintiff, or under any name so similar thereto as to be mistaken for it

A trade name means a name under which goods are sold or made by a certain person and which by established usage has become known to the public as indicating that those goods are the goods of that person. A trade name is opposed to a merely descriptive name—namely, one under which the goods are sold, but which indicates merely their nature, and not that they are the merchandise of any particular person.[17] The principle is not confined to purely commercial matters, for "if a man, be he musician, portrait painter or writer of articles in newspapers, gets to be known under a particular name, that name becomes inevitably part of his stock-in-trade, and apart from some special contract or anything of that kind, he is entitled to say that it is his name, and that anyone who adopts or causes the adoption of that name by some other person is inflicting on him an injury."[18] But "It is established beyond argument that under the law of England a man is not entitled to exclusive proprietary rights in a fancy name *in vacuo*."[19] The activities of the defendant must have misled the public into confusing his profession, business or goods with those of the plaintiff.[20] It may be that misappropriation of personality is on the verge of recognition as a distinct tort.[21]

(4) Selling goods with the trade mark of the plaintiff or any deceptive imitation attached thereto

A trade mark is at common law any mark habitually attached by a trader to goods manufactured or sold by him in order to indicate that they are his merchandise, and by established usage known to the public as possessing that significance. Under the Trade Marks Act 1938[22] no damages can be recovered for the infringement of an unregistered trade mark, but the rights of action for passing off goods as the goods of another person are not

---

[15] (1881) 17 Ch.D. 638.
[16] *C. & A. Modes* v. *C. & A. (Waterford) Ltd.* [1976] I.R. 198; *Maxims Ltd.* v. *Dye* [1977] 1 W.L.R. 1155.
[17] *British Vacuum Cleaner Co.* v. *New Vacuum Cleaner Co.* [1907] 2 Ch. 312 ("Vacuum Cleaner").
[18] *Hines* v. *Winnick* [1947] Ch. 708, 713, *per* Vaisey J.
[19] *McCulloch* v. *May Ltd.* [1947] 2 All E.R. 845, 849, *per* Wynn-Parry J. (The plaintiff, who was well known as "Uncle Mac" of the BBC Children's Hour had no common field of activity with the defendants, who distributed "Uncle Mac's Puffed Wheat.")
[20] *Sim* v. *J. Heinz & Co. Ltd.* [1959] 1 W.L.R. 313.
[21] *Athens* v. *Canadian Adventure Camps Ltd.* (1977) 80 D.L.R. 583. See above, § 10.
[22] s. 2.

affected by the Act. The statute law as to the infringement of registered trade marks does not exclude or supersede this common law protection.

(5) Imitating the get-up or appearance of the plaintiff's goods so as to deceive the public

When there is anything so characteristic in the get-up or appearance of the plaintiff's goods that it identifies those goods as the merchandise of the plaintiff, any deceptive adoption or imitation of that get-up or appearance is subject to the same rules as the deceptive adoption or imitation of his trade name or trade mark.[23] The tort is also committed when second-hand goods are sold as new.[24] A tort (perhaps a form of misrepresentation analogous to passing off) is also committed where the defendant knowingly uses unauthorised articles in the performance of some service or process which has acquired a brand or fancy name by reason of the use in it of the plaintiff's branded articles—e.g. a "Jamal hair wave" means not a particular style but a process performed with certain materials.[25] The *Champagne* case[26] extended the tort beyond cases in which the defendant claims that his goods or services are identical with those of the plaintiff. Champagne properly means French champagne, which is associated with being "drunk at the gayest parties and in distinguished circles"[27]: it was therefore wrong for the defendant to market his product under the name "Spanish champagne." The principle has been further extended to cover cases in which the name by which the genuine product is known has no geographical connotation, but has a definite and distinctive meaning.[28]

Basis of passing-off action

The courts have wavered between two conceptions of a passing-off action—as a remedy for the invasion of a quasi-proprietary right in a trade name or trade mark, and as a remedy, analogous to the action on the case for deceit, for invasion of the personal right not to be injured by fraudulent competition. The true basis of the action is that the passing off injures the right of property in the plaintiff, that right of property being his right to the goodwill of his business.[29] In general the violation of a right to property is actionable, even though it is innocent and though no damage has been proved. At common law it was necessary to prove an actual fraudulent intention, but a different view was taken in equity, and now it is generally accepted[30] that it is not necessary in an action for passing off to prove an intent to deceive. Indeed, talk about deceit tends to obscure the essential fact that the plaintiff himself has not been deceived: his complaint is that the defendant has deceived other persons and that that deception is injuring the

[23] *Illustrated Newspapers* v. *Publicity Services* [1938] Ch. 414.
[24] *Morris Motors Ltd.* v. *Lilley* [1959] 1 W.L.R. 1184.
[25] *Sales Affiliates Ltd.* v. *Le Jean Ltd.* [1947] Ch. 295.
[26] *J. Bollinger* v. *Costa Brava Wine Co. Ltd.* [1960] Ch. 262.
[27] [1961] R.P.C. 116, 125.
[28] *Erwen Warnink BV* v. *Townend (J.) & Sons Ltd.* [1979] A.C. 731 ("Dutch Advocaat").
[29] *Cadbury-Schweppes Pty. Ltd.* v. *Pub Squash Pty. Ltd.* [1981] 1 W.L.R. 193, 204.
[30] *Erwen Warnink BV* v. *Townend* [1979] A.C. 731.

plaintiff's trade.[31] It is sufficient in all cases to prove that the practice complained of is calculated (that is to say, likely) to deceive.[32]

The remedies of the plaintiff in an action for passing off are (1) an injunction, and (2) either damages or an account of profits, at the plaintiff's option. The uncertainty as to the conception underlying the action has led to uncertainty as to the requirement of proof of damage. Damage or likelihood of damage to property is the gist of all such actions according to many authorities,[33] but the contrary has also been stated.[34] Probably it is sufficient to prove that the practice complained of is of such a nature that it is likely in the ordinary course of business to deceive the public.[35] Indeed, it seems that the essence of the tort lies in the misrepresentation that the goods in question are those of another; an offer to sell, as distinct from an actual sale, may be enough to constitute an actionable wrong.[36] This is sufficient for an injunction in equity and even for nominal damages at common law. In considering whether deception is probable, account is to be taken, not of the expert purchaser, but of the ordinary ignorant and unwary member of the public.[37] On the other hand, it is not enough that a thoughtless person may unwarrantably jump to a false conclusion. In cases of fraud the onus of proving likelihood of damage is not heavy; the court will readily assume that the defendant will succeed in accomplishing that which he has set himself to accomplish; but where there is no fraud the onus is a very heavy one.[38] Indeed, it may be that nothing more than nominal damages, if even those, can be given for an innocent passing off.[39] In one respect it seems agreed that the protection given by the action differs from the protection given to a full right of property. No damages or account of profits will be granted in respect of innocent user before actual notice of the plaintiff's right. In this respect the right of a trader to be protected against deceptive competition is not like a right of property, an infringement of which, however innocent, will give rise to an action for damages.

§ 150. CONFUSION THROUGH USE OF SIMILAR NAMES

A name originally merely descriptive, and therefore *publici juris*, may by exclusive use in connection with the plaintiff's goods acquire a secondary sense as the trade name of those goods, and will then become subject to the ordinary rule as to trade names; so that the use of it by other persons ceases to be *publici juris*, and is actionable unless they take sufficient precautions to prevent deception. So in *Reddaway* v. *Banham*[40] it was found by a jury that the term "camel-hair belting" had by long and exclusive association with the plaintiffs' manufacture come to mean, not merely belting made

---

[31] *J. Bollinger* v. *Costa Brava Wine Co. Ltd.* |1960| Ch. 262, 275.
[32] *Cellular Clothing Co.* v. *Maxton* |1899| A.C. 326, 334; *Spalding* v. *A. W. Gamage Ltd.* (1915) 84 L.J.Ch. 449; *Draper* v. *Trist* |1939| 3 All E.R. 513, 517.
[33] *Society of Motor, etc., Traders* v. *Motor Manufacturers', etc., Insurance Co.* |1925| Ch. 675, 686; *Sturtevant Engineering Co.* v. *Sturtevant Mill Co.* |1936| 3 All E.R. 137, 145.
[34] *Draper* v. *Trist* |1939| 3 All E.R. 513, 518.
[35] *Reddaway* v. *Bentham Hemp Spinning Co.* |1892| 2 Q.B. 639, 644.
[36] *Spalding & Bros.* v. *A. W. Gamage Ltd.* (1915) 32 R.P.C. 273; (1918) 35 R.P.C. 101.
[37] *Singer Manufacturing Co.* v. *Loog* (1882) 8 App.Cas. 15, 18.
[38] *Society of Motor Manufacturers and Traders* v. *Motor Manufacturers', etc., Insurance Co.* |1925| Ch. 675, 686, 689.
[39] *Draper* v. *Trist* |1939| 3 All E.R. 513, 518, 525, 528.
[40] |1896| A.C. 199.

from camel hair, but belting made by the plaintiffs. "The whole merit of that description, its one virtue for Banham's purposes, lies in its duplicity. It means two things. At Banham's works, where it cannot mean Reddaway's belting, it may be construed to mean belting made of camel's hair; abroad, to the German manufacturer, to the Bombay mill-owner, to the up-country native, it must mean Reddaway's belting; it can mean nothing else. I venture to think that a statement which is literally true, but which is intended to convey a false impression, has something of a faulty ring about it; it is not sterling coin; it has no right to the genuine stamp and impress of truth."[41] Hence it was held that the term could not be used by other persons, unless they took adequate precautions against deceiving the public by means of it. The burden, however, of proving this secondary sense is not a light one. The courts will not be easily persuaded to sanction such appropriation of words which belong to the common stock of our language. But even in these cases it seems, though suggestions have been made to the contrary,[42] that fraud is not essential any more than in the case of a name which is primarily a trade name and not descriptive at all.

A name which is originally a trade name may through general use cease to indicate specifically the merchandise of any particular person and may so become merely descriptive and *publici juris*. Thus Liebig's Extract of Meat no longer means a material prepared by Liebig or his assigns,[43] nor does Harvey's Sauce mean a sauce sold by the original maker of the article so called.[44] In such a case the onus is reversed: it is for the defendant to show that the word-mark has entirely lost its original meaning and that no purchaser can be deceived by its use.[45]

Use of own name

The application of the rule as to passing off to cases in which the instrument of deception is the use by the defendant of his own personal name is obscure. It would appear, however, that subject to certain qualifications an individual is entitled to trade under his own name regardless of the fact that his business may be thereby confused with a business of some other person bearing the same or a similar name. Nor does it make any difference in such a case that a trader using his own name is well aware of the fact that his business will be confused with that of a rival trader, and intends to take the advantage which such confusion will confer upon him.[46] This can be very inconvenient, but not necessarily wrongful. "There is a great deal to be said in favour of a man who engages in any pursuit using therein his own name. If the accomplished but rather disreputable Lord Chancellor of King James was the author of the tragedy of *Hamlet*, as some misguided people think, he would have saved the world much discussion if he had published it under the name of Bacon, or St. Albans, or Verulam, instead of allowing it to

---

[41] |1896| A.C. 199, 218–219, *per* Lord Macnaghten.
[42] *Cellular Clothing Co.* v. *Maxton* [1899] A.C. 326, 339.
[43] *Liebig's Extract of Meat Co.* v. *Hanbury* (1867) 17 L.T.(N.S.) 298.
[44] *Lazenby* v. *White* (1871) 41 L.J.Ch. 354n.
[45] *Havana Cigar and Tobacco Factories Ltd.* v. *Oddenino* |1924| 1 Ch. 179.
[46] *Burgess* v. *Burgess* (1853) 3 De G.M. & G. 896 (on which Lord Macnaghten once remarked that "The judgment of Turner L.J. though eclipsed in public favour by the brilliancy and point of his colleague's language is an accurate and masterly summary of the law": *Reddaway* v. *Banham* |1896| A.C. 199, 220).

appear in the name of one of the best-known men in London of the time."[47]
It is different if he intends to deceive and not merely to confuse.[48]

A surname is not a man's legal property, and if a man is called by some
other than his real name he may acquire his second name by reputation.[49] In
such a case also he will not be restrained from using it honestly. So in *Jay's
Ltd.* v. *Jacobi*[50] the defendant, who was manageress of a ladies' outfitters'
shop, had been known to everyone for fifteen years as Miss Jay, and it was
held that she had acquired that name by reputation and was entitled to trade
under it so long as she acted honestly, even though the similarity of the
name to that of the plaintiffs might occasionally lead to the goods of the one
being mistaken for those of the other.

But a man is not entitled to use his own name dishonestly in order that his
goods may be passed off as and for the goods of another.[51] But in order to
deprive him of the right there must be evidence of dishonesty outside the
mere use of the name, for example, a resemblance in the manner of the
display of the name, or the concealment of that part of the name which
differs from the plaintiff's by the use of smaller characters.[52] Again, if a
defendant pleads that, although deception of the public is proved, the instrument of such deception is nothing more than the lawful exercise by him of
his right to use his own name, he must show that the deception complained
of is due exclusively to the use of his own name *simpliciter*, and that it is not
due to the fact that he has abbreviated his name, or altered it, or added
something to it, or used it in some special manner producing confusion not
normally or necessarily incident to the mere exercise of his right to trade
under his own name.[53] Although an individual trader is entitled to trade
under his own name, even though he thereby gets the benefit of the reputation of a rival trader of the same name, an incorporated company has not
the same right to use the names of its shareholders. By the Companies Act
1948, s. 17, a company is prevented from being registered with a name
which in the opinion of the Board of Trade is undesirable. Independently of
this statutory provision, a company must select a name which is not
calculated to deceive, and it is no excuse for choosing a deceptive name that
a shareholder to whom that name belongs might lawfully use it in his own
business.[54] The rule as to passing off is not to be extended to cases in which
there is no appropriation by one man of the trade reputation or custom of
another, but merely some other form of loss or inconvenience caused by the
deception of the public. In the absence of actual fraud no action will lie in
such a case. Thus, in *Day* v. *Brownrigg*[55] the plaintiff and defendant
occupied adjoining villas, and the defendant changed the name of his
residence, and gave it the same name as that of the plaintiff. An injunction to
prevent this was refused, although it was proved that inconvenience would

[47] *Dickson* v. *Dickson* [1909] 1 I.R. 185, 202, *per* Holmes L.J.
[48] *Parker-Knoll Ltd.* v. *Knoll International Ltd.* [1962] R.P.C. 265.
[49] *Massam* v. *Thorley's Cattle Food Co.* (1880) 14 Ch.D. 748, 760. No specific formality
seems to be required to change one's surname, but a Christian name may (apart from
statute) be changed only at confirmation and, possibly, on adoption: *Re Parrott* [1946]
Ch. 183. *Cf. Re Lewis's Will Trusts* [1951] 2 T.L.R. 1032.
[50] [1933] Ch. 411.
[51] *Sykes* v. *Sykes* (1824) 3 B. & C. 341; *Croft* v. *Day* (1843) 7 Beav. 84.
[52] *Brinsmead's Case* (1913) 29 T.L.R. 237, 238.
[53] *Shorts Ltd.* v. *Short* (1914) 31 R.P.C. 294.
[54] *Tussaud* v. *Tussaud* (1890) 44 Ch.D. 678.
[55] (1878) 10 Ch.D. 294.

result to the plaintiff through the confusion thus caused. Had the parties been rival traders the result might have been different.

§ 151. IMMATERIAL PROPERTY: TRADE MARKS

The forms of immaterial property known to our law are patents, copyright, registered trade marks, and the various franchises which may be vested in private persons, such as markets and ferries. A violation of any of these rights of property is an actionable tort. The law as to these matters is, however, too special in its nature to call for examination here. It belongs rather to the law of property. It is advisable, however, to point out here the true relation of the law as to trade marks to the common law of passing off.

The law as to trade marks is now contained in the consolidating Trade Marks Act 1938.[56] A trade mark validly registered under the Act of 1938 becomes thereby a species of incorporeal property analogous to a patent or copyright, and conferring upon the proprietor an exclusive right to the use of it in respect of the classes of goods in relation to which it is registered (s. 4 (1)). The use of it or of any deceptive imitation of it by any other person is *per se* an actionable infringement of the statutory monopoly so created. Marks registered in Part A of the register are protected to a greater degree than those registered in Part B. Several differences between the protection given by common law and by statute may be mentioned. First, the common law recognises no monopoly or right of property in the use of any name, mark or other trade description. The cause of action in a common law action for passing off is probably not the infringement of any monopoly or right of property vested in the plaintiff but damage done to the plaintiff in his business by the deceptive mode in which the defendant carries on his own.[57] In other words, at common law the use of the plaintiff's trade mark is never in itself any cause of action, but is merely one of several means by which the wrong of deceiving the public to the plaintiff's prejudice may be committed. Secondly, passing off can occur in cases which have nothing to do with trade marks, *e.g.* imitating the get-up or appearance of the plaintiff's goods. Thirdly, the law relating to passing off will protect established lines of goods or businesses from imitation, but will not protect a new business while goodwill is being built up. It is otherwise with the protection given by the Trade Marks Act. Fourthly, an action for infringement of a trade mark may be simpler and less costly than an action for passing off. In particular it avoids the difficulty (often great in practice) of proving that the defendant's mode of conducting business is bound to cause confusion.

---

[56] The law and its history are surveyed in *General Electric Co.* v. *The General Electric Co. Ltd.* [1972] 1 W.L.R. 729.

[57] See above, § 150.

CHAPTER 19

WRONGFUL PROCESS OF LAW

In the case of legal proceedings which are erroneous, malicious, or otherwise wrongful it is necessary to consider the liability of the judges, magistrates, or other judicial officers, and the liability of the parties. We must also distinguish between the liability of the superior courts, *e.g.* the Supreme Court of Judicature, with unlimited jurisdiction, and that of inferior courts with limited jurisdiction, and again between that of courts of record and that of courts not of record. Courts of record include the Supreme Court as well as various inferior courts. The essential feature of such courts is that their proceedings can be proved only by their own official record, and that their judges possess the power to punish for contempt of court.

§ 152. LIABILITY OF THE OFFICERS OF SUPERIOR COURTS

A judge of one of the superior courts is absolutely exempt from all civil liability for acts done by him in the execution of his judicial functions.[1] His exemption from civil liability[2] is absolute, extending not merely to errors of law and fact, but to the malicious, corrupt, or oppressive exercise of his judicial powers.[3] For it is better that occasional injustice should be done and remain unredressed under the cover of this immunity than that the independence of the judicature and the strength of the administration of justice should be weakened by the liability of judges to unfounded and vexatious charges of error, malice, or incompetence brought against them by disappointed litigants—"otherwise no man but a beggar, or a fool, would be a judge."[4] The remedy for judicial errors is some form of appeal to a higher court, and the remedy for judicial oppression or corruption is a criminal prosecution or the removal of the offending judge; but in neither case can he be called on to defend his judgment in an action for damages brought against him by an injured litigant. Nor is the Crown vicariously liable for his acts,[5] as judicial error is not a tort.[4] It is possible that there is liability under the European Convention on Human Rights.[6]

Acts beyond jurisdiction

When, however, the illegal act complained of is beyond the limits of the defendant's jurisdiction, it is not definitely settled whether a superior judge is free from liability; or whether, as in the case of inferior judges, he is civilly

---

[1] Immunity from actions for defamation has already been considered: above, § 56. In this section we consider actions of trespass for invasions of personal or proprietary interests as the result of an unauthorised or erroneous decision. The history is in Holdsworth, H.E.L., vol. vi, pp. 234–240.

[2] It will be recalled that the Habeas Corpus Act 1679 provides that a High Court judge who unlawfully refuses to issue a writ of habeas corpus during the vacation is liable to pay a penalty of £500 to the person detained.

[3] *Anderson* v. *Gorrie* [1895] 1 Q.B. 668; *Tughan* v. *Craig* [1918] 1 I.R. 245.

[4] *Arenson* v. *Casson, Beckman Rutley & Co.* [1977] A.C. 405, at p. 440, *per* Lord Fraser.

[5] *Maharaj* v. *Att.-Gen. of Trinidad* [1979] A.C. 385.

[6] A Belgian criminal who was criticised by a judge obtained substantial compensation for remarks which were such "as to disturb the serenity of the atmosphere during the proceedings": *Boeckmans* v. *Belgium* (No. 1727/62).

responsible for such an excess of jurisdiction. This much is clear: in order to establish exemption as regards proceedings in an inferior court the judge must prove that he had jurisdiction,[7] whereas the plaintiff must prove want of jurisdiction in the case of proceedings in a superior court.[8] Probably, however, the exemption is absolute even in this case. An appellate court may reverse his decision but there is no court of first instance which has any authority to entertain an action against him and give judgment against him for damages merely because its opinion on the point decided differs from his. So in *Taafe* v. *Downes*[9] an action was brought in the Irish Court of Common Pleas against the Chief Justice of the Irish Court of King's Bench for issuing a warrant ordering the arrest of the plaintiff, but a majority of the court held that no such action lay against a judge of one of the superior courts. This is justifiable not merely on grounds of public policy but also as a deduction from the principle that a superior court always has power to determine the limits of its own jurisdiction: it follows that an erroneous conclusion as to the ambit of its jurisdiction is merely an abuse of its jurisdiction and not an act outside its jurisdiction.[10] Protection is also extended to the acts of one whose appointment as a judge is in fact a nullity: the principle appears to be that the acts of a person holding the office of judge *de facto* and with colour of right are unimpeachable in any way.[11] But it is well settled that the protection accorded to judicial acts is not extended to ministerial acts of a judicial officer.[12]

§ 153. LIABILITY OF OFFICERS OF INFERIOR COURTS

Judges of an inferior court possess the same immunity as judges of the superior courts so long as they do not exceed their jurisdiction.[13] There are many dicta, however, to the effect that justices of the peace (and therefore, presumably, other judicial officers whose courts are not of record) are liable for the malicious exercise of their judicial powers even within the limits of their jurisdiction.[14] The Justices of the Peace Act 1979, s. 44 seems to assume that this is the law; for it provides that any action against a justice of the peace for an act done within the limits of his jurisdiction shall be an action on the case as for a tort, and that it shall be necessary to prove malice and the absence of reasonable and probable cause. There is, however, no case in which any such action has been maintained, and it is difficult to justify any such distinction between different classes of magistrates. The trend of recent opinion is against any such distinction.[15]

---

[7] *Carratt* v. *Morley* (1841) 1 Q.B. 18.
[8] *Peacock* v. *Bell* (1667) 1 Saund. 73.
[9] (1812) 3 Moore P.C. 36n. See also *Anderson* v. *Gorrie* [1895] 1 Q.B. 668; *Tughan* v. *Craig* [1918] 1 I.R. 245; *New Zealand Waterside Workers' Federation* v. *Fraser* [1924] N.Z.L.R. 689, 706–707 (judgment of Sir John Salmond); Cooke, "*Venire de Novo*" (1955) 71 L.Q.R. 100, 117.
[10] *Sirros* v. *Moore* [1975] 1 Q.B. 118, 139.
[11] *Re Aldridge* (1893) 15 N.Z.L.R. 361.
[12] *Ferguson* v. *Kinnoull (Earl of)* (1842) 9 Cl. & F. 311, 312.
[13] *Sirros* v. *Moore* [1975] 1 Q.B. 118.
[14] *Cave* v. *Mountain* (1840) 1 M. & G. 257, 263; *Linford* v. *Fitzroy* (1849) 13 Q.B. 240, 247; *Taylor* v. *Nesfield* (1854) 3 El. & Bl. 724, 730.
[15] See Sheridan, "Protection of Justices" (1951) 14 M.L.R. 267; Thompson, "Judicial Immunity and the Protection of Justices" (1958) 21 M.L.R. 517.

Liability for excess of jurisdiction

A judge of an inferior court is civilly liable for any act done by him in excess of his jurisdiction and in the nature of a trespass against the person or property of the plaintiff or otherwise a cause of damage to him.[16] Such a judge determines the limits of his own jurisdiction at his own peril, and (speaking generally) he will answer for any mistake; nor is it necessary for the plaintiff to prove any malice or want of reasonable or probable cause. A superior court, on the other hand, is entrusted with the power of determining its own jurisdiction, and is no more answerable for a judicial error on this point than for a judicial error on any other.[17] It should be noted that it is not the mere making of the order in excess of or without jurisdiction which gives rise to the cause of action in trespass, but the acts done against the plaintiff in consequence of that order, *e.g.* his committal to prison or the levying of a distress against his goods.[18] One who is aggrieved by an invalid order is not permitted to have the option either of appealing it or of obeying it and then suing the judge for damages.[19] Justices and their clerks who have acted reasonably may be indemnified out of local funds.[20]

The distinction thus drawn between an excess of jurisdiction and a wrongful act within the limits of jurisdiction is one which it is easier to state in general terms than to define with accuracy or apply with precision.[21] It may probably be said, however, that a judge may exceed his jurisdiction in three ways:

(i) When he has no power to deal with the kind of matter brought before him: as when a county court judge tries an action of libel other than an action remitted to him by the High Court or an action in which jurisdiction has been given by consent.

(ii) When he has no power to deal with the particular person concerned: for example, because that person has not been properly summoned before him, or is not resident within the local jurisdiction of the court.

(iii) When, although there is jurisdiction over the matter and the person, the judgment or order given or made in the matter is of a kind which he has no power to give or make: as if he imprisons instead of fining, or imprisons for a longer period than the law permits.[22]

In all these cases the judge is liable as for an excess of jurisdiction. When, on the other hand, he has power to give the kind of judgment which he has given, against the person complaining of it, he is not liable merely because his judgment is erroneous in law or in fact, or because there has been some

---

[16] *Abbott* v. *Sullivan* [1952] 1 K.B. 189, 202. The majority of the court held that no action in tort lay against a domestic tribunal which had acted *ultra vires* but without malice in expelling the plaintiff from a voluntary association. The position may be different if the tribunal is a statutory one. Today domestic tribunals wield great powers over the members of trades or professions, but it is difficult to say how far they will be controlled by the ordinary courts: see Lloyd, "The Disciplinary Powers of Professional Bodies" (1959) 13 M.L.R. 281; Morris, "The Courts and Domestic Tribunals" (1953) 69 L.Q.R. 318.

[17] *Wilkinson* v. *Barking Corporation* [1948] 1 K.B. 721, 725.

[18] *O'Connor* v. *Issacs* [1956] 2 Q.B. 288.

[19] [1956] 2 Q.B. 288, 302.

[20] Justices of the Peace Act 1979, s. 53.

[21] See on the whole of this topic the exhaustive articles by Gordon: "The Relation of Facts to Jurisdiction" (1929) 45 L.Q.R. 459; "The Observance of Law as a Condition of Jurisdiction" (1931) 47 L.Q.R. 386, 557; "*Tithe Redemption Commissioner* v. *Wynne*" (1944) 60 L.Q.R. 250.

[22] *O'Connor* v. *Isaacs* [1956] 2 Q.B. 288.

irregularity of procedure. Such an error or irregularity is merely a wrongful exercise of jurisdiction, not an excess of it.[23]

When a judge exceeds his jurisdiction by reason of a mistake of law, his liability is absolute, being independent of any malice or negligence. He is bound at his peril to know the law as to his own powers.[24] When, on the other hand, his mistake is one of fact, he is not liable unless he either knew or ought to have known the facts which deprived him of jurisdiction. There must, in other words, be either knowledge[25] of the want of jurisdiction or an absence of any reasonable and probable cause for believing that jurisdiction existed.[26] Thus if a judge imprisons a person who by reason of his residence outside the district of the court is not subject to his jurisdiction, he is liable if the mistake is one of law, but not liable if it is an excusable mistake of fact.[27]

§ 154. LIABILITY OF PARTIES

Having considered the liability of magistrates and judges in the case of wrongful legal proceedings, it remains to deal with the liabilities of the parties to these proceedings. This matter must be considered under two heads—(1) proceedings instituted maliciously; (2) proceedings instituted erroneously and irregularly. Formerly there was a third head—proceedings maintained by parties with no interest, or maintained for a share of the fruits of the action. But the torts of maintenance and champerty have been abolished by the Criminal Law Act 1967, s. 14 (1).

Proceedings Instituted Maliciously[28]

It is an actionable wrong to institute certain kinds of legal proceedings against another person maliciously and without reasonable and probable cause. The tort clearly has some affinities with defamation and false imprisonment, but there are also differences. There is an obvious analogy between this tort and actionable slander.[29] It differs from defamation not only in having an earlier and distinct historical origin but also in affording protection to the plaintiff's interest in the security of his person and property as well as his reputation. The tort differs from false imprisonment, as we have seen,[30] in that the acts of a court of justice cannot be imputed to the litigant at whose suit they have been done: the litigant can be charged only with having maliciously and without reasonable cause exercised his right of setting a court of justice in motion. The tort is commonly called malicious prosecution, but the word "prosecution" has a wider meaning than in the criminal law and, conversely, not all proceedings which are technically prosecutions are capable of founding an action for malicious prosecution.[31] The chief classes of proceedings to which this rule applies are the following:

---

[23] *Cave* v. *Mountain* (1840) 1 M. & G. 257.
[24] *Houlden* v. *Smith* (1850) 14 Q.B. 841.
[25] *Palmer* v. *Crone* [1927] 1 K.B. 804, 810.
[26] *Abbott* v. *Sullivan* [1952] 1 K.B. 189, 217.
[27] *Houlden* v. *Smith* (1850) 14 Q.B. 841.
[28] For the history of this action, see Winfield, *History of Conspiracy*, pp. 118–130; Holdsworth, H.E.L., viii, pp. 385–391; Winfield, *Present Law*, pp. 174–204; Harper, "Malicious Prosecution, False Imprisonment, and Defamation" (1937) 15 Tex.L.Rev. 157; Fridman, "Compensation of the Innocent" (1963) 26 M.L.R. 481.
[29] *Reid* v. *Webster* (1966) 59 D.L.R. (2d) 189, 201.
[30] Above, § 44.
[31] See below, § 155.

(1) Malicious criminal prosecutions

It is the wrong known as malicious prosecution to institute criminal proceedings against anyone if the prosecution is inspired by malice and is destitute of any reasonable cause. The offence charged need not be an indictable one. So a prosecution under a municipal by-law may form the basis for an action if the by-law provides for imprisonment in default of payment of a fine, and the prosecution touches the accused in his trade.[32]

As it is an action on the case damage must be proved. Unfortunately there is doubt about the definition of damage. As far back as 1701 Sir John Holt C.J. said[33] that there were three sorts of damage which would maintain the action: (1) "The damage to a man's fame, as if the matter whereof he is accused be scandalous"; (2) damage to the person; (3) damage to property, "as where he is forced to expend his money in necessary charges, to quit himself of the crime of which he is accused." As to (1), it has been held by the Court of Appeal[34] that the test is whether the charge is necessarily and naturally defamatory of the plaintiff, or, in other words, whether the statement that the plaintiff was charged with the offence in question is capable of a non-defamatory meaning. This is a very severe test. It has been held[35] that a conviction for pulling a communication cord on a train without reasonable cause does not damage the "fair fame" of the person charged, because he might have done so for a number of reasons—*e.g.* because he had left valuable property behind on the platform. Paradoxically, a charge of failing to pay a tram-car fare has been held such an offence,[36] apparently because it necessarily involves fraud.[37] The decisions are open to review on the ground that they misunderstand Sir John Holt's test: what he really meant was whether an oral imputation of the crime would have amounted to a slander actionable *per se*.[38]

As to (2), damage to the person, the courts have in this instance interpreted *Savile* v. *Roberts* in an unexpectedly wide way, by holding that it covers any crime punishable with imprisonment in the first instance, even though the plaintiff has not in fact been imprisoned.[39]

As to (3), damage to property, it has now been held that the difference between party and party costs and solicitor and client costs is sufficient damage to found an action.[40]

(2) Malicious bankruptcy and liquidation proceedings

A similar liability attaches to him who maliciously and without reasonable cause petitions to have another person adjudicated a bankrupt,[41] or to have a company wound up as insolvent.[42]

---

[32] *Reid* v. *Webster* (1966) 59 D.L.R. (2d) 189.
[33] *Savile* v. *Roberts* (1698) 1 Ld.Ryam. 374.
[34] *Wiffen* v. *Bailey* [1915] 1 K.B. 600.
[35] *Berry* v. *British Transport Commission* [1962] 1 Q.B. 306.
[36] *Rayson* v. *South London Tramways Co.* [1893] 2 Q.B. 304.
[37] *Nimmo* v. *Lanarkshire Tramways*, 1912 S.C. 23; *Wiffen* v. *Bailey* [1915] 1 K.B. 600.
[38] See Diplock J. in *Berry* v. *British Transport Commission* [1961] 1 Q.B. 149, 166 (not disapproved in C.A. [1962] 1 Q.B. 306).
[39] *Wiffen* v. *Bailey* [1915] 1 K.B. 600. Note the analogy with slander actionable *per se.*
[40] *Berry* v. *British Transport Commission* [1962] 1 Q.B. 306. See Dworkin, Note (1962) 25 M.L.R. 89.
[41] *Johnson* v. *Emerson* (1871) L.R. 6 Ex. 329.
[42] *Quartz Hill Gold Mining Co.* v. *Eyre* (1883) 11 Q.B.D. 674.

(3) Malicious arrest

Similarly it is an actionable injury to procure the arrest and imprisonment of the plaintiff by means of judicial process, whether civil or criminal, which is instituted maliciously and without reasonable cause.[43] Although no action lies against a witness for giving false evidence,[44] the plaintiff is not debarred from bringing an action for wrongful arrest by reason only of the fact that a step in procuring the arrest consisted of evidence given in court in the course of another person's trial.[45] This species of wrong is to be distinguished from false imprisonment. False imprisonment is the act of the defendant himself or of a merely ministerial officer put in motion by him.[46]

(4) Malicious execution against property

On the same principle it is an actionable wrong maliciously and without reasonable and probable cause to issue execution against the property of a judgment debtor.[47] Both malice and want of reasonable and probable cause must be proved: the former relates to motive, the latter to intention.[48]

The bringing of an ordinary civil action (not extending to any arrest or seizure of property) is not a good cause of action, however unfounded, vexatious and malicious it may be.[49] The reason alleged for this rule is that an unfounded and unsuccessful civil action is not the cause of any damage of which the law can take notice. Even for the injury whicn baseless accusations made in a civil action may inflict upon the reputation of the defendant it would seem that no action lies. It seems that a litigant may maliciously and without any reasonable ground make the gravest charges of fraud or other disgraceful conduct without incurring any other liability than that of paying the costs of the proceedings. To what classes of civil proceedings this exemption applies is far from clear. Will an action lie at the suit of a person maliciously joined as a co-respondent in a divorce suit,[50] or at the suit of a person against whom affiliation proceedings have been maliciously taken, or at the suit of a solicitor whom the defendant has maliciously endeavoured to have struck off the roll? If malicious proceedings in bankruptcy are, as we have seen, a good cause of action, there seems no reason why a similar conclusion should not be drawn with respect to the proceedings mentioned.[51] Again, there seems to be no reason why an action should not lie for the institution of unfounded and malicious proceedings before a court-martial,[52]

---

[43] *Foth* v. *O'Hara* (1959) 15 D.L.R. (2d) 332, 336.

[44] *Hargreaves* v. *Bretherton* |1959| 1 Q.B. 45.

[45] *Roy* v. *Prior* |1971| A.C. 470.

[46] See above, § 45.

[47] *Clissold* v. *Cratchley* |1910| 2 K.B. 244.

[48] *Horner* v. *Irwin & Son Ltd.* |1972| N.I. 202, 205.

[49] *Quartz Hill Gold Mining Co.* v. *Eyre* (1883) 11 Q.B.D. 674, 689. It has also been held that no action lies for conspiracy to give perjured evidence: *Cabassi* v. *Vila* (1940) 64 C.L.R. 130; *Hargreaves* v. *Bretherton* |1959| 1 Q.B. 45. *Cf. Roberts* v. *Stone (J.F.) Ltd.* (1945) 172 L.T. 240 (action lies for none-appearance of witness summoned *subpoena*).

[50] No, according to *Fenn* v. *Paul* (1932) 32 S.R.(N.S.W.) 315.

[51] As a matter of history there is no reason why such an action should not lie: *Fenn* v. *Paul* (1932) 32 S.R.(N.S.W.) 315. An action will lie for procuring a search warrant to be issued maliciously and without reasonable and probable cause: *Everett* v. *Ribbands* |1952| 2 Q.B. 198, 205.

[52] In *Fraser* v. *Balfour* (1918) 87 L.J.K.B. 1116 the H.L. held that the question was still open. The question is fully discussed by McCardie J. in *Heddon* v. *Evans* (1919) 35 T.L.R. 642 (fuller report in R. O'Sullivan, *Military Law and the Supremacy of the Civil Courts*, 1921).

or some administrative or domestic tribunal. The adverse decision of such a body may cause serious damage to the reputation or livelihood of the party accused.

§ 155. ESSENTIALS OF MALICIOUS PROSECUTION

In order that an action shall lie for malicious prosecution or the other forms of abusive process which have been referred to, the following conditions must be fulfilled:

(1) The proceedings must have been instituted or continued by the defendant;

(2) He must have acted without reasonable and probable cause;

(3) He must have acted maliciously;

(4) The proceedings must have been unsuccessful—that is to say, must have terminated in favour of the plaintiff now suing.

We shall deal with these requirements in their order.

(1) Institution of proceedings

The proceedings complained of by the plaintiff must have been instituted by the defendant—that is to say, he must be the person who put the law in motion against the plaintiff. It is not necessary, however, that he should be a party to the proceedings. Thus an action for malicious abuse of process will lie against the solicitor who in his client's name has set the law in motion against the plaintiff.[53] So in the case of malicious prosecution by way of indictment in the name of the Queen, the person liable is the prosecutor to whose instigation the proceedings are due. Laying an information before a magistrate is sufficient to found an action, even though the infomation is withdrawn before a summons or a warrant has been issued.[54] One who has been bound over to prosecute when magistrates have decided to send the case forward for trial on indictment probably cannot deny that he has instituted the prosecution if the action of the magistrates is the natural and reasonable result of his accusation.[55]

(2) Want of reasonable and probable cause

No action lies for the institution of legal proceedings, however malicious, unless they have been instituted without reasonable and probable cause.[56] This is a difficult part of the law and two points may be noted at the outset. First, the burden of proving absence of reasonable and probable cause is on the plaintiff, who thus undertakes the notoriously difficult task of proving a negative.[57] Further, if the defendant denies it, it is not the practice to require

---

[53] *Johnson* v. *Emerson* (1871) L.R. 6 Ex. 329.

[54] *Casey* v. *Automobiles Renault of Canada Ltd.* (1965) 54 D.L.R. (2d) 600.

[55] *Fitzjohn* v. *Mackinder* (1860) 8 C.B. (N.S.) 78. The proceedings need not have reached a stage when they can be accurately described as a prosecution: it is enough if damage to the plaintiff may result: *Mohammed Amin* v. *Bannerjee* [1947] A.C. 322.

[56] *Williams* v. *Taylor* (1829) 6 Bing. 183, 186, *per* Tindal C.J.: "Malice alone is not sufficient, because a person actuated by the plainest malice may none the less have a justifiable reason for prosecution."

[57] *Abrath* v. *N.E. Ry.* (1883) 11 Q.B.D. 440. Otherwise in false imprisonment: *Hicks* v. *Faulkner* (1878) 8 Q.B.D. 167, 170.

him to give particulars of his denial.[58] Secondly, the existence of reasonable and probable cause is a question for the judge and not for the jury.[59] This anomalous rule was established as a precaution against erroneous verdicts for the plaintiff—*per doubt del lay gents.* The question was withdrawn from the jury under the pretence that it was a question of law. Still, the rule is subject to the qualification that all preliminary questions of fact on which this issue depends are for the jury. Thus if the defendant alleges that he prosecuted the plaintiff because of information received from a third person, it is for the jury to say whether that information was really received by the defendant and (if the question is relevant) whether it was really believed by him, and it is for the judge to decide whether, if it was so received and believed, it constituted a reasonable ground for the prosecution.[60] This division of functions between judge and jury may be effected at the discretion of the judge in one of two ways. He may either direct the jury to find the facts specially and then decide for himself on the facts so found whether there was reasonable and probable cause, or he may tell the jury that if they find the facts to be such and such then there is reasonable and probable cause, and if they find the facts to be otherwise then there is none, thus leaving the jury to find a general verdict on this hypothetical direction.[61]

Reasonable and probable cause means a genuine belief, based on reasonable grounds, that the proceedings are justified. The terms reasonable and probable are synonyms. *Probabilis causa* was an expression which was not unknown in classical Latin and became familiar in medieval usage.[62] *Probabilis* means primarily provable—hence capable of being put to the test—hence reliable, approved, right, good, justifiable. *Probabilis causa* means a good reason—a ground of action which commends itself to reasonable men.[63] The defendant is not required to believe that the accused is guilty: it is enough if he believes there is reasonable and probable cause for prosecution.[64] He need only be satisfied that there is a proper case to lay before the court.[65] In *Hicks* v. *Faulkner*[66] Hawkins J. said, "I should define reasonable and probable cause to be an honest belief in the guilt of the accused, based upon a full conviction, founded on reasonable grounds, of the existence of a state of circumstances which, assuming them to be true,

---

[58] *Stapeley* v. *Annetts* [1970] 1 W.L.R. 70.

[59] *Lister* v. *Perryman* (1870) L.R. 4 H.L. 521. So also in false imprisonment: *Hailes* v. *Marks* (1861) 7 H. & N. 56.

[60] *Herniman* v. *Smith* [1938] A.C. 305, 317–317. Since this is an inference of fact, the judge necessarily has to determine it without any guidance from precedent, for each case depends on its own facts, and his task might therefore be thought to be a difficult one. Yet Lord du Parcq said: "A judge is frequently set the task of deciding whether there was 'reasonable and probable cause' for an action and I have heard no complaint that the question is too vague to be answered with accuracy"—*Tyne Improvement Commissioners* v. *Armement Anversois S/A* [1949] A.C. 326, 353.

[61] *Abrath* v. *N.E. Ry.* (1883) 11 Q.B.D. 440, 458. In some cases the question has been left to the jury whether the defendant took reasonable care to ascertain the facts, but to ask such a question is to take the decision of the issue out of the hands of the judge to whom in the interests of prosecutor and accused alike it has been confided. It is impossible to distinguish the question whether the defendant showed reasonable care and judgment in ascertaining the facts from the question whether he showed reasonable care and judgment in estimating the significance of facts known to him, and both questions are equally for the judge: *Herniman* v. *Smith* [1938] A.C. 305, 316–317.

[62] See references in 6th edition of this work, p. 590.

[63] *Robinson* v. *Keith*, 1936 S.C. 25, 48.

[64] *Tempest* v. *Snowden* [1952] 1 K.B. 130, 135.

[65] *Glinski* v. *McIver* [1962] A.C. 726, 758.

[66] (1878) 8 Q.B.D. 167, 171.

would reasonably lead any ordinary prudent and cautious man, placed in the position of the accused, to the conclusion that the person charged was probably guilty of the crime imputed."[67] It is a degree of presumption which is hard to define in words, but in practice is quite comprehensible.[68] The prosecutor must himself honestly believe in the case which he is making: it may not be enough that he is acting (if a police officer) on the instructions of his superiors,[69] or in blind reliance on the opinion of counsel.[70] But if a private person honestly states his complaint to a responsible police officer, who advises him to prosecute, he will be protected.[71]

The question whether the defendant possessed such an honest belief should not be left to the jury in every case, but only if it is in dispute and the plaintiff leads some evidence of its absence.[72] If it were asked in every case it would put every police officer at the mercy of an accused who happened to be acquitted.[73] The plaintiff must give some evidence from which the actual belief of the defendant can be inferred: merely to prove that the defendant had before him information which might or might not have led a reasonable man to form an opinion that the plaintiff was guilty supplies no evidence that the defendant did not believe him to be guilty.[74] When honest belief is in issue the question left to the jury should be in the form "Did the defendant honestly believe in the charges he was making?"[75] The question should not contain any reference to reasonable grounds for belief. For to ask the jury whether the defendant had an honest belief that he had reasonable and probable grounds for prosecuting is to ask them a question (albeit one of fact) which it is for the judge alone to answer.[76]

Grounds for belief

Further, even if the defendant honestly believed the proceedings to be justified there is no reasonable and probable cause unless this belief was based on reasonable grounds. This question is to be determined by the facts actually known to the defendant at the time when he laid the information and subsequently proceeded with the prosecution, not to the facts as they actually existed.[77] So facts unknown to the prosecutor do not prevent the facts which were known to him from constituting reasonable and probable cause.[78] When a person embarks upon a prosecution without any evidence

---

[67] Lord Atkin, in a judgment concurred in by other members of the House, said he knew of no better statement than this: *Herniman* v. *Smith* [1938] A.C. 305, 316. But Sir Raymond Evershed M.R. remarked that "If that is the meaning of the question 'Was there reasonable and probable cause,' it is no wonder that it is a question not to be left to a jury": *Tempest* v. *Snowden* [1952] 1 K.B. 130, 135.

[68] *R.* v. *Brixton Prison Governor, ex p. Armah* [1968] A.C. 192, 252.

[69] *Glinski* v. *McIver* [1962] A.C. 726, 756, 769.

[70] *Abbott* v. *Refuge Assurance Co. Ltd.* [1962] 1 Q.B. 432, 456; *Glinski* v. *McIver* [1962] A.C. 727, 745.

[71] *Malz* v. *Rosen* [1966] 1 W.L.R. 1008.

[72] *Glinski* v. *McIver* [1962] A.C. 726, 744, 768.

[73] *Dallison* v. *Caffery* [1965] 1 Q.B. 348, 368.

[74] *Mitchell* v. *Heine (John) & Sons Ltd.* (1938) 38 S.R.(N.S.W.) 466.

[75] *Glinski* v. *McIver* [1962] A.C. 726, 761, 767.

[76] *Tempest* v. *Snowden* [1952] 1 K.B. 130.

[77] *Herniman* v. *Smith* [1938] A.C. 305, 315. The question of reasonable and probable cause is one which the court has to determine objectively on the evidence before it: *Tims* v. *John Lewis & Co. Ltd.* [1951] 2 K.B. 459, 472. But the prosecutor need not test every fact: "His duty is not to ascertain whether there is a defence but whether there is reasonable and probable cause for a prosecution"—[1938] A.C. 305, 319, *per* Lord Atkin.

[78] *Herniman* v. *Smith* [1938] A.C. 305; *Wright* v. *Sharp* (1947) 176 L.T. 308.

at all or with evidence on which no reasonable jury would convict, then (whatever his state of mind) there is strong evidence that he had no reasonable and probable cause.[79] Further, one who continues a prosecution, which has been instituted with reasonable and probable cause, after he has discovered facts which indicate that it is groundless may well be held to have no reasonable and probable cause for continuing unless he at least informs the court of the facts which have been discovered. Having regard, however, to the facts known to the defendant, he must show a reasonably sound judgment and use reasonable care in determining whether there are sufficient grounds for the proceedings instituted by him, and any failure to exhibit such judgment or care will be imputed to him as a want of reasonable and probable cause.[80] It may be inferred from *Herniman* v. *Smith*,[81] in which the point was allowed to go by default, that it is not enough in itself to establish a reasonable or probable cause that the plaintiff was committed for trial or even that he was convicted by a court at first instance and subsequently acquitted on appeal. This seems good sense, for, though these facts would be weighty evidence of a reasonable and probable cause, they should not be conclusive. The original conviction might have been obtained as a result of the prosecutor's own fraud or of evidence of which he was unaware.

(3) Malice

No action will lie for the institution of legal proceedings, however destitute of reasonable and probable cause, unless they are instituted maliciously—that is to say, from some wrongful motive.[82] Malice and absence of reasonable and probable cause must unite in order to produce liability. So long as legal process is honestly used for its proper purpose, mere negligence or want of sound judgment in the use of it creates no liability; and, conversely, if there are reasonable grounds for the proceedings (for example, the probable guilt of an accused person) no impropriety of motive on the part of the person instituting these proceedings is in itself any ground of liability. Therefore it is necessary to distinguish between honesty of belief and honesty of motive; the former is relevant to the question of reasonable and probable cause, the latter to the question of malice.[83]

Malice means the presence of some improper and wrongful motive—that is to say, an intent to use the legal process in question for some other than its legally appointed and appropriate purpose.[84] It can be proved either by showing what the motive was and that it was wrong, or by showing that the circumstances were such that the prosecution can only be accounted for by imputing some wrong or indirect motive to the prosecutor[85]: for example, prosecuting a person for theft in order to deter others from committing similar depredations,[86] the levying of blackmail, or the coercion of the

---

[79] *Tims* v. *John Lewis & Co. Ltd.* [1951] 2 K.B. 459, 472–474 (reversed on another point [1952] A.C. 676).

[80] The circumstances that the mistake of the defendant is one of law and not of fact does not necessarily amount to proof of want of reasonable and probable cause. The duty of a prosecutor is merely to show due judgment, care and discretion as to the guilt of the accused in law no less than in fact: *Phillips* v. *Naylor* (1859) 4 H. & N. 565.

[81] [1938] A.C. 305. See Winfield, Note (1937) 53 L.Q.R. 12.

[82] *Williams* v. *Taylor* (1829) 6 Bing. 183, 186.

[83] *Horner* v. *Irwin & Son Ltd.* [1972] N.I. 202, 204.

[84] *Pike* v. *Waldrum* [1952] 1 Lloyd's Rep. 431, 451.

[85] *Brown* v. *Hawkes* [1891] 2 Q.B. 718, 722.

[86] *Stevens* v. *Midland Counties Ry.* (1854) 10 Ex. 352, 356.

accused in respect of some unconnected matter, such as the obtaining of compensation or restitution from the accused (the civil law, not the criminal, being the appropriate instrument for this purpose). Again, a prosecution is not malicious merely because inspired by anger for the injury suffered,[87] for this is one of the motives on which the law relies to secure the prosecution of offenders against the criminal law.[88]

Burden of proof

The burden of proving malice lies on the plaintiff; and, subject to two qualifications, the question is one for the jury and not, like that of reasonable and probable cause, one for the judge.[89] The first of these qualifications is that the question whether any particular motive is a proper or improper motive for the proceeding in question is a matter of law for the determination of the judge. Malice is any motive of which the law disapproves, not any motive which is displeasing to a jury. The jury has merely to decide whether the motive exists. The second qualification is that there must be some reasonable evidence of malice, otherwise the case will be withdrawn from the jury.[90] Want of reasonable and probable cause is itself in certain cases sufficient evidence of malice to go to a jury.[91] Nevertheless, a jury is not at liberty in all cases to infer malice from want of reasonable cause. Want of reasonable cause is sufficient evidence of malice in those cases only in which it is sufficient evidence that there was no genuine belief in the accusation made. If it appears that there was such a belief, the plaintiff must produce some independent evidence of malice, and cannot rely on the absence of reasonable cause. On the other hand, malice is in general never evidence of want of reasonable cause,[92] unless the same fact supplies evidence both of malice and of absence of reasonable and probable cause, as where it is established that when the defendant instituted the prosecution he knew that the plaintiff was innocent.[93] For a prosecutor may be inspired by malice and yet have a genuine and reasonable belief in the truth of his accusation.[94]

(4) Termination of the proceedings in favour of the plaintiff

No action for a malicious prosecution, or for any other malicious proceeding which involves a judicial decision of any question at issue between the parties, will lie until or unless the prosecution or other proceeding has terminated in favour of the person complaining of it. No person, for example, who has been convicted on a criminal charge can sue the prosecutor for malicious prosecution even though he can prove that he is an innocent man and that the accusation was a malicious and unfounded one.[95] Even if the prosecution or other proceeding is still pending, the same rule

---

[87] As distinct from anger at some other activity of the accused—*e.g.* his perjured evidence in other proceedings: *Glinski* v. *McIver* [1962] A.C. 726.
[88] *Brown* v. *Hawkes* [1891] 2 Q.B. 718, 722.
[89] *Mitchell* v. *Jenkins* (1833) 5 B. & Ad. 588.
[90] *Brown* v. *Hawkes* [1891] 2 Q.B. 718.
[91] [1891] 2 Q.B. 718, 723.
[92] *Johnstone* v. *Sutton* (1786) 1 T.R. 510, 544.
[93] *Mitchell* v. *John Heine & Sons Ltd.* (1938) 38 S.R.(N.S.W.) 466.
[94] *Glinski* v. *McIver* [1962] A.C. 726, 782.
[95] *Basebé* v. *Matthews* (1867) L.R. 2 C.P. 684.

applies. "It is a rule of law that no one shall be allowed to allege of a still depending suit that it is unjust."[96] If the prosecution had actually determined in any manner in favour of the plaintiff it matters nothing in what way this has taken place. There need not have been any acquittal on the merits. What the plaintiff requires for his action is not a judicial determination of his innocence but merely the absence of any judicial determination of his guilt. Thus it is enough if the prosecution has been discontinued,[97] or if the accused has been acquitted by reason of some formal defect in the indictment,[98] or if a conviction has been quashed,[99] even if for some technical defect in the proceedings.[1] Conversely, if the proceedings have actually determined against the plaintiff it is immaterial that the judgment cannot be attacked by way of appeal.[2] This rule applies not only to malicious prosecution but to all malicious proceedings which involve the judicial determination of any question at issue. Thus no action will lie for maliciously procuring the plaintiff to be adjudicated a bankrupt, until and unless the adjudication has been set aside.[3] But the rule does not apply to proceedings which involve no such judicial decision.[4]

§ 156. ERRONEOUS AND IRREGULAR PROCEEDINGS

Having considered the liability of litigants for the malicious abuse of legal process, it remains to consider how far they are responsible for mere errors and irregularities of procedure in the absence of any malice. The rule is that no action will lie against any person for procuring an erroneous decision of a court of justice. This is so even though the court has no jurisdiction in the matter and although its judgment or order is for that or any other reason invalid. A court of justice is not the agent or servant of the litigant who sets it in motion so as to make that litigant responsible for the errors of law or fact which the court commits.[5] Every party is entitled to rely absolutely on the presumption that the court will observe the limits of its own jurisdiction and decide correctly on the facts and the law.[6] But a party who has actually misled the tribunal by his fraud or malice may be liable, and there is even authority for saying that one who prefers a charge to a magistrate (even though in vague language and by way of suspicion) is liable for the ulterior consequences and may not say they were due to the mistake or indiscretion of the tribunal he has set in motion.[7]

No action will lie against any person for issuing execution or otherwise acting in pursuance of a valid judgment or order of a court of justice even though it is erroneous and even though it is afterwards reversed or set aside for error.[8] A valid judgment, however erroneous in law or fact, is a sufficient

---

[96] *Gilding* v. *Eyre* (1861) 10 C.B.(N.S.) 592, 604, *per curiam.*
[97] *Casey* v. *Automobiles Renault of Canada* (1965) 54 D.L.R. (2d) 600.
[98] *Wicks* v. *Fentham* (1791) 4 T.R. 247.
[99] *Herniman* v. *Smith* [1938] A.C. 305, 315.
[1] *Romegialli* v. *Marceau* (1963) 42 D.L.R. (2d) 481, 483; *Casey* v. *Automobiles Renault of Canada* (1965) 54 D.L.R. (2d) 600, 605–606.
[2] *Metropolitan Bank* v. *Pooley* (1885) 10 App.Cas 210.
[3] *Everett* v. *Ribbands* [1952] 2 Q.B. 198.
[4] *Gilding* v. *Eyre* (1861) 10 C.B. (N.S.) 592.
[5] See above, § 45.
[6] (1848) 12 Q.B. 871.
[7] *Fitzjohn* v. *Mackinder* (1860) 8 C.B. (N.S.) 78.
[8] *Williams* v. *Williams* [1937] 2 All E.R. 559.

justification for any act done in pursuance of it. The remedy of an aggrieved litigant is some form of appeal whereby the judgment may be reversed or set aside and not an action for damages against those who enforce or act on the judgment while it stands. If, however, any litigant executes any form of legal process which is invalid for want of jurisdiction, irregularity, or any other reason, and in so doing he commits any act in the nature of a trespass to person or property he is liable therefor in an action of trespass and it is not necessary to prove any malice or want of reasonable or probable cause. This is an application of the fundamental principle that mistake, however honest or inevitable, is no defence for him who intentionally interferes with the person or property of another.[9] But a distinction is to be drawn between process which is wholly void and process which is merely voidable. Process which is void is no defence at all and an action will lie without taking any steps to set it aside.[10] But when process is merely voidable it is a sufficient justification until it has been set aside; though when it has been set aside it becomes void *ab initio* and an action will thereupon lie for acts done in pursuance of it.

[9] *Painter* v. *Liverpool Oil Gas Light Co.* (1836) 3 Ad. & E. 433.
[10] *Brooks* v. *Hodgkinson* (1859) 4 H. & N. 712.

CHAPTER 20

PARTIES

§ 157. THE CROWN

The law on this topic was greatly changed by the Crown Proceedings Act 1947.[1] At common law the procedure by way of petition of right generally provided a remedy against the Crown in cases of breach of contract and possibly also enabled real or personal property to be recovered. But it was impossible to sue the Crown in tort, either for wrongs which it had expressly authorised or for wrongs committed by its servants in the course of their employment. Nor was it possible to sue the head of the department or other official superior of the wrongdoer, for all the servants of the Crown were and are fellow-servants and do not stand to each other in the relationship of master and servant.[2] The individual wrongdoer was, of course, liable and could not plead the commands of the king or state necessity as a defence.[3] These rules became highly unsatisfactory when the Crown became one of the largest employers of labour and occupiers of property in the country. Various devices were available to ensure that substantial justice was done. Thus the Treasury might, as a matter of grace, undertake to satisfy any judgment awarded against the individual Crown servant who had committed a tort in the course of his employment. These makeshifts became unnecessary when the Crown Proceedings Act 1947 was passed.[4]

Section 2 (1) of the Act provides as follows:

"Subject to the provisions of this Act, the Crown shall be subject to all those liabilities in tort to which, if it were a private person of full age and capacity, it would be subject:—

    (*a*) in respect of torts committed by its servants or agents;

    (*b*) in respect of any breach of those duties which a person owes to his servants or agents at common law by reason of being their employer[5]; and

    (*c*) in respect of any breach of the duties attaching at common law to the ownership, occupation, possession or control of property."[6]

Proceedings are instituted against the appropriate Government Department (to be selected from a list published by the Treasury), or, if there is doubt about this, against the Attorney-General.

---

[1] See Bickford Smith, *The Crown Proceedings Act 1947*; Glanville Williams, *Crown Proceedings*; Treitel, "Crown Proceedings" [1957] *Public Law* 321.

[2] *Bainbridge* v. *P.-M.-G.* [1906] 1 K.B. 178. Superior servants of the Crown were in no special position in this respect; it is a general principle of the common law: see below, § 175.

[3] *Entick* v. *Carrington* (1765) 19 St.Tr. 1029. This is still the law. For the defences of act of State and statutory authority, see §§ 158, 191. It has, however, been held that neither the Crown nor its individual servants are liable in negligence for acts or omissions done by H.M. Forces in active operation against the enemy: *Nisbet Shipping Co.* v. *The King* (1951) 4 D.L.R. 636.

[4] For proceedings against the State in Ireland, see the Civil Liability Act 1961, s. 57, and *Byrne* v. *Ireland* [1972] I.R. 241.

[5] See below, § 181.

[6] The Crown is bound by the Occupiers' Liability Act 1957 (see s. 6).

Although the Act appears to have given rise to very few difficulties there are a few points which may be mentioned in detail.

(1) Torts committed by servants or agents

First, it is notable that the proviso to section 2 (1) states that the Crown is not liable unless the act or omission of the servant or agent would (apart from the provisions of the Act) have given rise to a cause of action against him. The object of this proviso may have been to ensure that the Crown could avail itself of any defence open to the primary wrongdoer.[7] Secondly, the liability of the Crown for the torts of its officers (a term which includes any servant or Minister of the Crown) is restricted to cases where the officer is appointed by it directly or indirectly and was at the material time paid in respect of his duties as an officer of the Crown wholly out of the Consolidated Fund, moneys provided by Parliament,[8] or a fund certified by the Treasury as equivalent. The main effect of this is to exclude liability for the police, for the funds out of which they are paid are not (even in the case of the Metropolitan Police) provided wholly by Parliament.[9] In any case a constable is not a servant of the Crown in such a sense that the ordinary law of master and servant determines the relationship of the parties.[10] But although a constable is a servant neither of the Crown, nor of the police authority, nor of the chief constable, the Police Act 1964, s. 48, provides that the chief officer of police of any area shall be liable in respect of torts committed by constables under his control in the performance of their functions in like manner as a master is liable in respect of torts committed by his servants in the course of their employment. The chief constable is a joint tortfeasor with the delinquent constable, but the police fund is automatically charged with the payment of any damages or costs awarded against a chief constable. Thirdly, the 1947 Act provides[11] that the Crown is not liable for anything done by any person while discharging responsibilities of a judicial nature vested in him, or any responsibilities which he has in connection with the execution of judicial process. Fourthly, there may be difficulty in ascertaining which of the numerous persons, organs and institutions necessary for the government of the United Kingdom today are Crown servants, in the absence of a clear provision in the enabling statute.[12] In particular, questions have arisen as to the status of the public corporations. In *Tamlin* v. *Hannaford*[13] the Court of Appeal held that the British Transport Commission was not a servant or agent of the Crown. The court suggested that in general the proper inference, at any rate in the case of commercial corporations,[14] would be that the corporation acted on its own behalf even

---

[7] See *Grossman* v. *The King* (1952) 2 D.L.R. 241.

[8] This means moneys paid out of the Consolidated Fund on the authority of the annual Consolidated Fund Acts or Appropriation Acts instead of on the authority of permanent legislation.

[9] Nor are they the servants of the police authority which appoints, pays and dismisses them (*Fisher* v. *Oldham Corporation* [1930] 2 K.B. 364): for the reasons for this, see below, § 172.

[10] *Att.-Gen. for N.S.W.* v. *Perpetual Trustee Co.* [1955] A.C. 457.

[11] s. 2 (5). The judicial officer himself has certain immunities: above, § 152.

[12] It has, however, been settled since *Mersey Docks Trustees* v. *Gibbs* (1866) L.R. 1 H.L. 93 that the mere fact that a body has been created by statute for public purposes does not mean that it is a servant or agent of the Crown.

[13] [1950] 1 K.B. 18.

[14] *e.g.* the Gas Boards and Airways Corporations.

though controlled by a Government Department. The better view is that hospital authorities are not servants of the Crown.[15]

(2) Breach of statutory duty

Section 2 (2) imposes on the Crown liability for breach of statutory duty[16] when the duty is binding both on persons other than the Crown and on the Crown itself. If the statute expressly states that it binds the Crown (*e.g.* the Factories Act 1961, s. 173) no problem arises. If the statute is silent there may be difficulty, for the Act preserves the common law principle of construction that the Crown is not bound by a statute in the absence of express words or necessary implication.[17]

(3) Her Majesty's Forces and the Post Office

Although the general object of the Act is to place the Crown in the same position as a private subject it is plain that the Crown cannot in all respects be treated in exactly the same way as a private employer. Hence H.M. Forces and the Post Office occupy a special status.

(i) *H.M. Forces*

By section 10 (1) the Crown is exempt from liability in tort for death or personal injury[18] caused by a member of the armed forces when on duty to another member of the armed forces, provided that the latter is either on duty or is on any land, premises, ship or vehicle being used for the purposes of the armed forces of the Crown, and the Minister of Pensions certifies that the death or injury will be treated as attributable to service for pension purposes.[19] It should be noted that the exemption from liability is extended to the actual wrongdoer himself unless the court is satisfied that the act or omission complained of was not connected with the performance of his duties.[20] By section 10 (2) the Crown is also exempted from liability in tort for death or personal injury suffered by a member of the armed forces in consequence of the nature or condition of any land, premises, ship, aircraft or vehicle being used for the purpose of the armed forces or in consequence of the nature or condition of any equipment or supplies used for that purpose if the Minister of Pensions certifies that the death or injury will be attributable to service for pension purposes. Any individual officer of the Crown at fault is also exempted.[20]

---

[15] Marshall, "Hospitals and Health Services Act" [1952] C.L.P. 81, 93; *Bullard* v. *Croydon Hospital Committee* [1953] 1 Q.B. 511, 514. See below, § 174.

[16] See above, § 85.

[17] The Crown is generally regarded as bound by the Fatal Accidents Acts 1846 to 1908 and the Law Reform (Miscellaneous Provisions) Act 1934, s. 1.

[18] Liability for other torts remains.

[19] See *Adams* v. *War Office* [1955] 1 W.L.R. 1116.

[20] The exemption of the actual wrongdoer has been criticised on the ground that it is contrary to general principles. But if this had not been done there would probably have been a revival of the practice of suing the individual wrongdoer in the hope that the Crown would stand behind him. Injustice may, however, arise in the not unlikely case of a member of the armed forces being killed or injured by the combined negligence of a fellow-member of the armed forces and a civilian in circumstances covered by s. 10 (1). In such a case the civilian will be liable for the whole of the plaintiff's damage without any right of contribution or indemnity from the service tortfeasor. We shall see that this is not the only example of such a situation: below, § 168.

(ii) *The Post Office*

Under the Post Office Act 1969 the Post Office is no longer to be regarded as a servant or agent of the Crown, but is constituted a separate public authority. Nevertheless the Act of 1969 retains some of the privileges which the former law conferred on the Post Office. Thus section 29 (1) provides that no proceedings shall lie in tort[21] against the Post Office in respect of any loss or damage suffered by an person in respect of acts or omissions in the postal or telecommunications services. Further, section 29 (2) provides that no officer or servant of the Post Office shall be subject to any civil liability, except at the suit of the Post Office, for any act for which the Post Office itself is not liable.[22] On the other hand, by section 30 the Post Office is under a certain measure of liability for the loss of or damage to[23] registered inland packets.

§ 158. ACTS OF STATE[24]

It is a fundamental principle of our law that the Crown or its servants must be prepared to justify before the ordinary courts the legality of any act which interferes with the person or property of the subject. The justification must be found in some distinct rule of common law or statute: there is in our law no principle which permits the Crown in time of peace to act for the public good as it thinks best. This was established in *Entick* v. *Carrington*.[25] The action was one of trespass for breaking and entering the plaintiff's house and seizing his papers.[26] The defendants pleaded that they had acted in obedience to warrants issued by the Secretary of State. The Court of Common Pleas held that there was no legal justification for such warrants. "And with respect to the argument of state necessity," said Sir Charles Pratt C.J. in his famous judgment, "the common law does not understand that kind of reasoning." But the defence of act of State is available when the plaintiff is a non-resident and the wrong complained of is suffered elsewhere than in British territory,[27] and done by the authority, precedent or subsequent, of the Crown. A British subject owes allegiance to the Crown in whatever part of the world he may be; it seems therefore that the Crown cannot plead act of State as against him,[28] wherever the wrong may have been committed.[29] On the other hand, those who owe no allegiance to the Crown may, save in British territory, be dealt with by the Crown as it

---

[21] This prohibition cannot be evaded by suing in bailment: *Stephen & Co. Ltd.* v. *The Post Office* [1977] 1 W.L.R. 1172.

[22] It is less easy to see why the individual wrongdoer has been rendered exempt in this case. It seems that if a postmaster tore up a customer's unregistered letter before his eyes the customer would be without remedy.

[23] This covers financial loss or damage: *Building and Civil Engineering Holidays Scheme Management Ltd.* v. *Post Office* [1966] 1 Q.B. 247.

[24] See de Smith, *Constitutional and Administrative Law*, Chap. 4.

[25] (1765) 19 St.Tr. 1029.

[26] It is characteristic of our failure to distinguish clearly between public and private law that an important constitutional principle should be established in an ordinary action of tort.

[27] *Buron* v. *Denman* (1848) 2 Ex. 167.

[28] *Walker* v. *Baird* [1892] A.C. 491. Note that in this case the plaintiff was within British territory.

[29] The preceding sentence was approved by Lord Denning M.R. and Winn L.J. in the C.A., and by Lord Pearce in the H.L., in *Att.-Gen.* v. *Nissan* [1968] 1 Q.B. 286, 339, 347; [1970] A.C. 179, 225, but Lords Morris of Borth-y-Gest, Wilberforce and Pearson hinted that in some circumstances act of State might be pleaded against British subjects.

pleases. Thus in *Buron* v. *Denman*[30] the defendant, the commander of a British man-of-war, had destroyed certain property of an alien slave-trader on the coast of Africa in circumstances that would have given a good cause of action to a British subject. It was held, however, that inasmuch as the act of the defendant had been ratified by the British Government, it was an act of State for which no action would lie at the suit of an alien. In such cases if redress is to be obtained it must be through diplomatic channels. The Crown or its servant is really contending not that the act is innocent but that the plaintiff has chosen to proceed before a tribunal which has no jurisdiction to inquire into the matter.

The rule in *Buron* v. *Denman* has no application in time of peace to injuries inflicted within the Queen's dominions. An alien friend resident within those dominions owes temporary allegiance to the Queen and has the same legal protection as a British subject against acts committed by or on the authority of the Crown. Thus in *Johnstone* v. *Pedlar*[31] the respondent was an American citizen who resided in Dublin (before the establishment of the Irish Free State) and sympathised actively with Irish nationalism. After serving a sentence of imprisonment for illegal drilling he successfully sued the appellant, the Chief Commissioner of Police, to recover a sum of money which had been found on him at the time of his arrest and the seizure of which had been subsequently adopted as an act of State by the Chief Secretary for Ireland. The decision might have been different if the Crown had actually withdrawn its protection on the ground of his treasonable activities. Similarly, if an alien friend, though resident abroad, owns property in England his title thereto will have the same protection, even against the Crown, as if it belonged to a British subject.[32] An alien enemy, on the other hand, possesses no rights against the Crown. His residence within the realm by the express or tacit licence of the Crown gives him legal protection against private persons,[33] and the courts are open to him, but probably he remains none the less at the mercy of the Crown, which may do with him and with his property as is thought fit. Thus, he may be interned or expelled at pleasure.[34]

§ 159. FOREIGN SOVEREIGNS, AMBASSADORS AND PUBLIC OFFICIALS

A foreign sovereign is not personally liable in the English courts for any tort committed by him, unless he has waived his immunity.[35] The only remedy for injuries done by him is by way of diplomatic action on the part of the British Government. It makes no difference that the wrongful act is committed in England. A foreign sovereign does not by residing in British territory waive his privilege or submit himself to the jurisdiction of the local courts. Nor does it make any difference that the wrongful act is done by the sovereign in his private capacity. The exemption extends to all the acts of the sovereign and not merely to acts of State.[36] But the sovereign's immunity

---

[30] (1848) 2 Ex. 167. The defendant in this case was a younger son of Lord Denman, at that time C.J.Q.B., who was himself an ardent opponent of the slave trade.
[31] [1921] 2 A.C. 262.
[32] *Commercial and Estates Co. of Egypt* v. *Board of Trade* [1925] 1 K.B. 271, 290, 297.
[33] *Johnstone* v. *Pedlar* [1921] 2 A.C. 262, 283.
[34] *R.* v. *Bottrill* [1947] K.B. 41.
[35] *The Cristina* [1938] A.C. 485, 490.
[36] *Mighell* v. *Sultan of Johore* [1894] 1 Q.B. 149.

ceases (except possibly for acts of State) upon the termination of his sovereign status, *e.g.* abdication.[37] The only exception to this broad principle of immunity is that trading transactions are not protected since the State Immunity Act 1978.

Diplomatic immunity

The object of the Diplomatic Privileges Act 1964 is to replace the old law on the privileges and immunities of diplomatic representatives in the United Kingdom. The old law granted a wider degree of immunity to more people than is common in many other countries. Once a person had been accepted as a diplomatic representative by the Foreign Office he was totally immune from the criminal and civil jurisdiction of the English courts during the period of his term of office. The new law is mainly contained in the Schedule to the 1964 Act, which gives the force of law to the relevant provisions of the Vienna Convention on Diplomatic Relations 1961.

The main change made by the Act is to adopt the continental practice of dividing the members of a diplomatic mission into three classes:

(1) Members of the diplomatic staff, who will have full personal immunity, civil and criminal, with three exceptions:

    (*a*) a real action relating to private immovable property situated in the territory of the receiving state, unless he holds it on behalf of the sending state for the purpose of the mission;

    (*b*) an action relating to succession in which the diplomatic agent is involved as executor, administrator, heir or legatee as a private person and not on behalf of the sending state;

    (*c*) an action relating to any professional or commercial activity exercised by the diplomatic agent in the receiving state outside his official functions;

(2) members of the administrative and technical staff, who enjoy full immunity for official acts, but who are liable civilly (but not criminally) for acts performed outside the course of their duties;

(3) members of the service staff, who enjoy immunity for official acts, but are liable civilly and criminally for acts performed outside the course of their duties.

It can thus be seen that for the first time the courts will have power to determine whether an act committed by a member of a diplomatic mission was performed in the course of his duties. An important practical result is that an embassy chauffeur who is involved in a traffic accident will no longer be entitled as of right to have the writ in any proceedings against him set aside, for the court will have power to determine whether he was acting within the scope of his employment.

Visiting forces

Under the Visiting Forces Act 1952, s. 9, the Minister of Defence has been authorised to make arrangements for the settlement of claims against members of visiting forces from the Commonwealth and States which are parties to the North Atlantic Treaty.[38] The scheme thus ensures that a claim

---

[37] *Munden* v. *Brunswick (Duke of)* (1847) 10 Q.B. 656.
[38] For details, see *Law Society's Gazette*, June 1954, p. 241.

against an individual member arising out of a tort committed in the performance of an official duty will be satisfied.

§ 160. CORPORATIONS[39]

(1) Capacity to be sued

Inasmuch as a corporation is an artificial person distinct in law from its members, it is not capable of acting *in propria persona*, but acts only through its agents or servants. All the acts, and therefore all the wrongful acts, of a body corporate are in fact the acts of its agents or servants, though imputed in law to the corporation itself. But this does not mean that the liability of a body corporate is therefore in all cases a vicarious liability for the acts of other persons. A distinction can be drawn between the personal and the vicarious liability of a corporation in much the same way as is done with the liability of natural persons.[40] So it has always been assumed that a corporation is personally liable for breach of the duties which an employer owes at common law to his servants.[41]

The existence and extent of the liability of a corporation in actions of tort were at one time a matter of doubt, due partly to technical difficulties of procedure and partly to the theoretical difficulty of imputing wrongful acts or intentions to fictitious persons.[42] It is now well settled, however, that the liability of a corporation for the torts committed by its agents or servants is governed by the same rules as those which determine the liability of any other principal or employer. This liability extends, moreover, to wrongs of malice or fraud, no less than to wrongs of other descriptions. Thus a corporation can be sued for malicious prosecution, or for malicious libel on a privileged occasion, or for fraudulent misrepresentation,[43] no less than for trespass, conversion, or negligence.[44]

Ultra vires torts

It is sometimes said that the liability of a corporation for the acts of its agents or servants exists only where the scope of the authority or employment of those agents or servants is within the statutory or other legal limits of the corporation's powers, and that if a corporation goes beyond the limits set by law for its activities, and enters upon any business or undertaking which is *ultra vires*, it cannot be made liable for torts committed by its agents or servants in the course of that business or undertaking.[45] There is, however, no sufficient authority for any such exemption of corporations from the consequences of their disregard of the limits of their powers.

In order to discover the law distinction must be drawn between the primary representatives of a corporation and its servants. "A corporation is

---

[39] Atiyah, *Vicarious Liability*, Chap. 34.
[40] See below, § 173.
[41] See below, § 181.
[42] *Abrath* v. *N.E. Ry* (1886) 11 App.Cas 247, 250–251.
[43] Usually actions of deceit are brought against one or more of the directors or other persons responsible for the misrepresentation; for their liability remains although the claim against the company may be barred by (*e.g.*) the fact that it has gone into liquidation.
[44] *Citizens' Life Assurance Co.* v. *Brown* [1904] A.C. 423.
[45] This rule has now been restricted by the European Communities Act 1972, s. 9 (1).

an abstraction. It has no mind of its own any more than it has a body of its own; its active and directing will must consequently be sought in the person of somebody who for some purposes may be called an agent, but who is really the directing mind and will of the corporation, the very ego and centre of the personality of the corporation. That person may be under the direction of the shareholders in general meeting; that person may be the board of directors itself,"[46] or it may be the managing director or general manager[47] or other person having authority from the board of directors to conduct the company's business.[48] So in *Campbell* v. *Paddington Corporation*[49] a metropolitan borough, in pursuance of a formal resolution of its council, erected a stand in a highway which was a public nuisance. It was held that the corporation was liable, although they had no legal right to erect the stand. Accordingly, the true principle is the following: Every act done, authorised, or ratified on behalf of a corporation by the supreme governing authority of that corporation, or by any person or body of persons to whom the general powers of the corporation are delegated, is for the purpose of the law of torts the act of the corporation itself, whether *intra vires* or *ultra vires* of the corporation, and the corporation is liable accordingly for that act or for any tort committed in respect of it by any agent or servant of the corporation within the scope of his authority or employment.[50]

Liability of members

The members of a corporation are not as such liable for torts committed by the corporation. For the purposes of the law of torts, no less than for those of the law of contracts or of property, a body corporate is a personality distinct from its members; and just as a member is not responsible for the debts contracted by a corporation, so also he is not responsible for torts committed by it. From this undoubted principle the very doubtful inference has sometimes been drawn that the members of a corporation are not liable for torts committed by it, even if they have themselves acted as the agents by whom the corporation has so acted.[51] But it is undoubted law that the servants or agents by whom a corporation commits a tort are themselves personally liable to the same extent as any other servants or agents who commit torts in the service or on behalf of their principals or employers. It is difficult, therefore, to understand why the

---

[46] *Lennard's Carrying Co.* v. *Asiatic Petroleum Co.* [1915] A.C. 705, 713, *per* Lord Haldane.

[47] *Fanton* v. *Denville* [1932] 2 K.B. 309, 329.

[48] *Rudd* v. *Elder Dempster & Co. Ltd.* [1933] 1 K.B. 566, 594. Welsh "The Criminal Liability of Corporations" (1946) 62 L.Q.R. 345 demonstrates that the criminal law has developed on similar lines.

[49] [1911] 1 K.B. 869.

[50] Goodhart criticised these views on the ground that an *ultra vires* contract is not binding on a corporation, and that to hold a company liable for an *ultra vires* tort, when it is not held bound by an *ultra vires* contract, would be contrary to established principles. A corporation, he said, is not liable for torts committed in the course of an *ultra vires* enterprise because it cannot employ a servant to do the act, even if it were done rightfully: 2 Camb.L.J. 350; *Essays*, p. 90. Goodhart was logical, but Holdsworth (H.E.L., Vol. ix, p. 52) said: "Practical convenience rather than theoretical considerations have [sic] from the days of the Year Books onwards, determined what activities are possible and what are impossible to a corporation." Another objection to Goodhart is that vicarious liability may exist without a contract: see § 173.

[51] *e.g.* by Kelly C.B. in *Mill* v. *Hawker* (1874) L.R. 9 Ex. 309, 321. On appeal to the Exchequer Chamber no opinion was expressed on this point, the court being apparently divided.

corporators themselves, if they act as the agents of the corporation, should not be equally liable for any wrongful acts so committed by them.

In any case, it is clear that a corporation is liable to its members for the torts of its agents to the same extent as it is liable to strangers. To this there is one anomalous exception: an action of deceit will not lie against a company at the suit of a shareholder until his allotment of shares has been rescinded.[52]

(2) Capacity to sue

In general a corporation may sue for any tort (*e.g.* malicious presentation of a winding-up petition)[53] in the same way as an individual. The only qualifications are (i) the tort must not be of a kind which it is impossible to commit against a corporation—*e.g.* assault or false imprisonment; (ii) in case of defamation, it must be shown that the defamatory matter reflects upon the corporation itself, and not merely on its officers or members,[54] and also that it is of such a nature that its tendency[55] is to cause actual damage to the corporation in respect of its property or business.[56] Actual loss need not be shown if the libel has a tendency to damage the trading reputation of the plaintiff corporation.[57] An action of libel will lie at the suit of a trading corporation charged with insolvency or with dishonest or incompetent management.[58] It was once held that a non-trading corporation, such as a local government authority, could not sue for libel charging it with corruption and bribery[59] but the modern view is that such a body is entitled to have its reputation[60] as well as its property protected.[61]

§ 161. UNINCORPORATED BODIES

Trade unions

Until 1901 it was generally agreed that a corporation and an individual or individuals were the only entities known to the common law who could sue or be sued. But in that year, in *Taff Vale Ry.* v. *Amalgamated Society of Railway Servants*[62] it was held by the House of Lords that a registered trade union, though not a corporate body, was a legal entity having sufficient of the characteristics of a juristic person to enable it to be sued in tort for the wrongful acts of its officials. The decision was in effect reversed by section 4 of the Trade Disputes Act 1906. But now the 1906 Act has itself been repealed[63] by the Trade Union and Labour Relations Act 1974. The present

---

[52] *Houldsworth* v. *City of Glasgow Bank* (1880) 5 App.Cas 317.
[53] *Quartz Hill Gold Mining Co.* v. *Eyre* (1883) 11 Q.B.D. 674.
[54] *Bognor Regis U.D.C.* v. *Campion* [1972] 2 Q.B. 169.
[55] *Irish People's Assurance Co.* v. *Dublin City Assurance Co.* [1929] I.R. 25.
[56] *D. & L. Caterers Ltd.* v. *D'Ajou* [1945] K.B. 364.
[57] *Company of Proprietors of Selby Bridge* v. *Sunday Telegraph Ltd.* [1966] C.L.Y. 6973.
[58] *Metropolitan Saloon Omnibus Co.* v. *Hawkins* (1859) 4 H. & N. 87.
[59] *Manchester (Mayor of)* v. *Williams* [1891] 1 Q.B. 94.
[60] *Church of Scientology* v. *Anderson* [1980] W.A.R. 71, 76.
[61] *Bognor Regis U.D.C.* v. *Campion* [1972] 2 Q.B. 169. The Faulks Report (Cmnd. 5909, § 342) recommends that such corporations should have to prove special damage.
[62] [1901] A.C. 426. Somewhat similar reasoning enabled liability to be imposed on an unregistered union for the wrongful acts of shop stewards in *Heatons Transport (St. Helens) Ltd.* v. *Transport & General Workers' Union* [1973] A.C. 15.
[63] For the United Kingdom: it is still in force in Ireland.

law relating to the immunity of trade unions (and employers' associations) is to be found in section 14 of the 1974 Act. Section 14 (1) provides that no action in tort shall lie in respect of any act done by or on behalf of a trade union, or so threatened or intended to be done.[64] But section 14 (2) removes the immunity from any negligence, nuisance or breach of duty resulting in personal injury to any person, or from breach of any duty imposed in connection with the ownership, occupation, possession, control or use of property, unless those breaches arose from acts done in contemplation or furtherance of a trade dispute.[65]

Formerly it was thought that as a trade union is a legal entity it has the correlative right to sue in its registered name.[66] But as the 1974 Act s. 2 (1) expressly provides that a trade union shall not be treated as a corporate body, it has been held that a union cannot be a plaintiff in a libel action.[67]

Other unincorporated entities

It is uncertain how far the principle in the *Taff Vale* case applies to the many heterogeneous bodies known to English law. It has been held to cover a registered Friendly Society,[68] and a Trustee Savings Bank,[69] but not an ordinary members' club which is neither incorporated nor proprietary. In some cases it may be possible to prove that the actual wrongdoer was the servant or agent of a particular member or members (*e.g.* the committee[70]); in other cases it may be possible to obtain a representation order under R.S.C., Ord. 15, r. 12, provided that the members whose names appear on the writ are persons who may fairly be taken to represent the body of club members, and that they and all the other club members have the same interest in the action.[71]

§ 162. MINORS[72]

(1) Capacity to be sued

A person under full age may now be described as a minor instead of as an infant,[73] as used to be customary before the age of majority was lowered from 21 to 18 years by the Family Law Reform Act 1969, s. 1. A minor[74] is in general liable for his torts in the same manner and to the same extent as an adult. In certain other branches of the law liability is excluded by the fact that the defendant is below a certain age. Thus a child under ten years of age

---

[64] So relief by way of injunction, as distinct from damages, is now clearly excluded.
[65] So the general immunity granted by s. 14 (1) is not limited to trade disputes. For the liability of members of a union, as distinct from the union itself, see above, § 139.
[66] *National Union of General and Municipal Workers* v. *Gillian* [1946] K.B. 81; *Willis* v. *Brooks* [1947] 1 All E.R. 191; *B.M.T.A.* v. *Salvadori* [1949] Ch. 556.
[67] *Electrical and Plumbing Union* v. *Times Newspapers* [1980] Q.B. 585.
[68] *Longdon-Griffiths* v. *Smith* [1951] 1 K.B. 295.
[69] *Knight and Searle* v. *Dove* [1964] 2 Q.B. 631.
[70] As in *Brown* v. *Lewis* (1896) 12 T.L.R. 455 (members of committee of Blackburn Rovers Football Club personally liable for defective stand).
[71] *Campbell* v. *Thompson* [1953] 1 Q.B. 445; Lloyd, Note (1953) 16 M.L.R. 359.
[72] See Bohlen, "Liability in Tort of Infants and Insane Persons" (1924) 23 Mich.L.Rev. 9; *Studies*, Chap. 11.
[73] Family Law Reform Act 1969, s. 12.
[74] A person in law reaches majority on the commencement of the 18th anniversary of his natal day: Family Law Reform Act 1969, s. 9.

is exempt from all responsibility for crimes committed by him. A child between the ages of 10 and 14 is presumed to be incapable of criminal intent, though this presumption may be rebutted by proof to the contrary. But the Children and Young Persons Act 1969 proposes that all criminal proceedings against children (those under 14) will be abolished (except for homicide), and those against young persons (14 to 17 years) severely restricted. A person under the age of 18 is in general free from all liability for breach of contract. In the law of torts, however, there are no similar rules of exemption. Thus a child of any age may be sued for trespass to land or goods,[75] or to the person,[76] at least if he is old enough to form an intention to do the necessary act,[77] and will be held liable in damages just as if he were an adult.[78] The youth of the defendant is not however in all cases wholly irrelevant. For it may be evidence of the absence of the particular mental state which is an essential element in the kind of tort in question. Thus, if an action is based on malice or on some special intent, the fact that the defendant is extremely young is relevant as tending to disprove the existence of any such malice or intent.[79] Similarly, in order to make a child liable for negligence, it must be proved that he failed to show the amount of care reasonably to be expected from a child of that age. It is not enough that an adult would have been guilty of negligence had he acted in the same circumstances. This, indeed, seems never to have been decided,[80] but it would seem implied in the decisions on the contributory negligence of children.[81] The precise age of the child may be of importance. "At some stages in life one year's difference in age matters nothing; but in youth and early manhood when knowledge is rapidly blossoming, a twelve-month is a very long time."[82] In general the principle is that a minor who is incapable of forming a culpable intention or of realising the probable consequences of his conduct is relieved from liability in those cases in which fault is essential to liability, but that wherever a liability is imposed irrespective of fault he is fully liable as a normal adult.[83]

It sometimes seems to be assumed that it is not worthwhile suing an infant in tort, because he may have no assets out of which to satisfy the judgment. Apart from the fact that this assumption may be untrue in the affluent society, it is worth remembering that a judgment debtor now without funds may acquire them later, and that he may be sued on the judgment, or execution may be issued on it, up to six years from its date, or even after that period with the leave of the court.[84] If judgment is given against an

---

[75] *O'Brien* v. *McNamee* [1953] I.R. 86 (child of seven liable in trespass for burning plaintiff's haystack).
[76] *McHale* v. *Watson* (1966) 115 C.L.R. 199.
[77] *Tillander* v. *Gosselin* (1966) 60 D.L.R. (2d) 18 (three-year-old child not liable).
[78] *Walmsley* v. *Humenick* [1954] 2 D.L.R. 232, 239.
[79] Note the cases holding that in trespass intention or negligence must be shown: above, § 46.
[80] Though in *Williams* v. *Humphrey* (*The Times*, February 20, 1975) it was held that a boy aged 15 years and 11 months was to be judged by the same standard as an adult, and the defendant was ordered to pay £13,352 damages for personal injuries suffered by the plaintiff as a result of being pushed into a swimming pool.
[81] *Lynch* v. *Nurdin* (1841) 1 Q.B. 29; *Harrold* v. *Watney* [1898] 2 Q.B. 320; *Yachuk* v. *Oliver Blais Ltd.* [1949] A.C. 386; *Liddle* v. *Yorkshire C.C.* [1934] 2 K.B. 101, 125. See also the law relating to infant entrants on premises, above, § 99.
[82] *Kerry* v. *Carter* [1969] 1 W.L.R. 1372, at 1377, *per* Edmund Davies L.J.
[83] *Walmsley* v. *Humenick* [1954] 2 D.L.R. 232, 239; *McHale* v. *Watson* (1966) 115 C.L.R. 199, 205, 233.
[84] R.S.C., Ord. 46, r. 2.

infant, and if, as is usual, it is made payable by instalments, it is an abuse of the process of the court for him to lodge his petition in bankruptcy.[85]

Tort and contract

When the act of a minor is both a tort and a breach of contract, is he liable for the tort, notwithstanding that the contract is not binding on him,[86] or does his exemption from an action for breach of contract protect him against an action for the tort also? Here the law has seen some development. By the middle of the seventeenth century it was settled that if an action against an infant was in truth founded on contract the plaintiff could not convert it into an action of tort lest "touts les infants in Angleterre serront ruine."[87] In the eighteenth century "Lord Mansfield, indeed, frequently said, that this protection was to be used as a shield, and not as a sword; therefore if an infant commit an assault, or utter slander, God forbid that he should not answer for it."[88] But the courts still would not permit the plaintiff to sue in tort for what was in truth a breach of contract. So in *Jennings* v. *Rundall*[89] the infant defendant was held not liable for riding too hard a mare which he had hired from the plaintiff. But in 1863 "a far stronger and more learned court"[90] made the distinction, which is now accepted law, between acts which were merely wrongful modes of performing the contract and acts which were outside the contract altogether. In *Burnard* v. *Haggis*[91] the defendant, an undergraduate of Trinity College, Cambridge, under the age of 21, hired a mare for riding, but in breach of an express term in his agreement he used her for jumping and so injured her. It was held that the defendant was liable in tort, notwithstanding the fact that it was at the same time the breach of a void contract. So if an infant bailee refuses to redeliver the chattel bailed, contrary to an express term of the contract of bailment, he can be sued for conversion.[92] In such a case the infant has gone outside the four corners of the contract, or to put it in another way, has committed a breach of a fundamental term of the contract which determines the bailment and constitutes an independent trespass.[93] But it is well settled that the courts will not allow a plaintiff to enforce a void contract in a roundabout way by framing his action in tort. So if a minor purchases goods, and retains them in his possession while refusing to pay for them, he cannot be sued in

---

[85] *Re A Debtor* [1967] Ch. 590.
[86] It will be recalled that the Infants Relief Act 1874, s. 1, provides that contracts with infants for goods supplied or to be supplied, other than necessaries, are "absolutely void."
[87] *Johnson* v. *Pye* (1665) 1 Sid. 258. The garbled Law-French of Restoration reports is a well-known oddity. In the collateral report in 1 Keb. 905 Sir John Keeling C.J. is reported to have said that if the action were allowed "the whole foundation of the common law will be shaken."
[88] *Jennings* v. *Rundall* (1799) 8 T.R. 335, 336–337, per Lord Kenyon C.J. ("Where Lord Mansfield led, Lord Kenyon C.J. followed, though he was not a judge who followed blindly": *Government of India* v. *Taylor* [1955] A.C. 491, 605, per Viscount Simonds.)
[89] (1799) 8 T.R. 335.
[90] Pollock, *Revised Reports*, iv, 5. Pollock thought *Jennings* v. *Rundall* "perhaps not adequately argued." But the decision on the facts seems quite correct. There was no express agreement not to override the mare.
[91] (1863) 14 C.B. (N.S.) 45 (Erle C.J., Willes, Byles and Keating JJ. "What Erle C.J. and Willes J. twice and Byles J. once stated to be the law in 1864 cannot be lightly disregarded in 1973": *Henriksens Rederi A/S* v. *Rolimpex* [1974] Q.B. 233, at 262, per Roskill L.J.
[92] *Ballet* v. *Mingay* [1943] K.B. 281.
[93] Compare the cases on exemption clauses, below, § 186.

detine. In such a case the property in the goods passes to the infant by delivery. The contract, though void, is sufficiently recognised at law to constitute a *causa* for the transfer of property just as *donatio* was one *causa* for the passing of property by *traditio* under Roman law,[94] so that the infant can give a good title to a third party to whom he sells the non-necessary goods which he has obtained under a void contract.[95]

There is, however, an important exception to the rule that a minor is liable for his torts. He is not liable in tort for procuring a contract by means of fraudulent representations either as to his age or as to any other matter. If a minor fraudulently pretends to be of full age, whereby the plaintiff is induced to contract with him, the contract is not for that reason binding on the minor, nor is he estopped from pleading his infancy.[96] Neither can the plaintiff sue in tort for the deceit. This was clearly established by the Court of Appeal in *R. Leslie Ltd.* v. *Sheill.*[97] "At the time of the transaction in question," said Lord Sumner,[98] "the appellant was an infant. He succeeded in deceiving some money-lenders by telling them a lie about his age, and so got them to lend him £400 on the faith of his being adult. Perhaps they were simpler than money-lenders usually are: perhaps the infant looked unusually mature. At any rate, when they awoke to the fact that they could not enforce their bargain and sought to recover the £400 paid, charging him with fraud, the jury found that the appellant had been guilty of fraud, and he does not now complain of the verdict. . . . It is not a pretty story to begin life with, and one might have expected that the appellant's chief anxiety would have been to live it down, but money is money, and I suppose that £400 is more than he cares to pay, or rather to repay, if he can avoid it." The court allowed the infant's appeal. Although a minor who procures a contract by fraudulent representation that he is of age is not liable either on the contract or in tort, he is nevertheless subject to an equitable obligation of somewhat undefined extent to restore any property or other advantage thereby obtained by him.[99]

Parents not responsible for their children's torts[1]

A father[2] is not as such liable for the torts of his children, even while they are under age and living in his house,[3] and even though he has control over them.[4] Nor is a father, as such, liable to a child: the blood relationship does not of itself impose a duty of care.[5] It is to be observed, however, that a child

---

[94] *R. Leslie Ltd.* v. *Sheill* [1914] 3 K.B. 607, 613, 627; *Stocks* v. *Wilson* [1913] 2 K.B. 235, 246.
[95] *Hall* v. *Wells* [1962] Tas.S.R. 122.
[96] *Levene* v. *Brougham* (1909) 25 T.L.R. 265.
[97] [1914] 3 K.B. 607.
[98] [1914] 3 K.B. 607, 611.
[99] *R. Leslie Ltd.* v. *Sheill* [1914] 3 K.B. 607. It seems impossible to reconcile with this decision some of the dicta of Lush J. in *Stocks* v. *Wilson* [1913] 2 K.B. 235. The decision on the facts in the latter case, however, seems to be correct.
[1] Waller, "Visiting the Sins of the Children" (1963) 4 M.U.L.R. 17.
[2] Presumably the same rule applies to a mother (or indeed any person *in loco parentis*) in the absence of a father.
[3] Although the law permits him to sue third parties for interference with such a relationship: see above, § 130.
[4] See below, § 174.
[5] *Hahn* v. *Conley* (1971) 126 C.L.R. 276.

may be his father's servant, so as to bring the father within the rule as to employers' liability. If a father sends his son on an errand with a motor-car, he will answer for his son's negligence in driving; but he will answer for him, not as being his father, but as being his employer.[6] Secondly, a father may be liable for his own personal negligence in affording or allowing his child an opportunity of doing mischief. So in *Newton* v. *Edgerley*[7] a father was held liable when he supplied his 12-year-old son (who was "young for his years") with a .410 rifle without giving him proper instructions for handling it and an accident occurred. On the other hand, in *Gorely* v. *Codd*[8] a father was held not liable when he entrusted a .22 rifle to his son aged 15 years with adequate instructions. The son (together with the 16-year-old plaintiff[9]) was at a special school, but the evidence showed that the son's "considerable retardation" related only to "book-learning" and not to his ability to handle a gun. Now the plaintiff in such a case would be in an even stronger position, for the Firearms Act 1968, s. 24, makes it a criminal offence to give an air weapon to a person under fourteen years, or for him to accept it. The Act also places severe restrictions upon the use or possession of air weapons by young persons except under supervision. Breach of these provisions might give rise to an action for breach of statutory duty,[10] and could always be relied upon as evidence of negligence.[11] In any event, it will not necessarily be a defence to plead that the child was warned to be careful, for everyone knows that even well-behaved children sometimes disobey their parents' warnings.[12] In some American cases[13] parents have been held liable for assaults committed by children known to have the habit of attacking people: this "vicious child" doctrine has not yet been applied in England, though a reasonably prudent parent may be personally, as distinct from vicariously, liable if he fails to take reasonable care to prevent small children escaping on to the highway, and injuring users of it,[14] or to control such children when they have been brought onto the highway,[15] or are passengers in a vehicle.[16]

Finally, it should be remembered that the Criminal Injuries Compensation Board may award to a victim of an infant's wrongdoing a sum sufficient to make an action in tort unnecessary. The Board assumes jurisdiction even if the child is under the age of ten, and so not criminally responsible.

(2) Capacity to sue

Apart from the procedural rule that he must sue by his next friend[17] an infant is in this respect no different from an adult. It has even been decided

---

[6] *Gibson* v. *O'Keeney* [1928] N.I. 66.
[7] [1959] 1 W.L.R. 1031.
[8] [1967] 1 W.L.R. 19.
[9] Who obtained judgment against the infant defendant personally for £1,000.
[10] See above, Chap. 10.
[11] *Hinds* v. *Direct Supply Co. Ltd.* [1966] C.L.Y. 5210.
[12] *Newton* v. *Edgerley* [1959] 1 W.L.R. 1031.
[13] Prosser, *Torts*, § 123.
[14] *Carmarthenshire County Council* v. *Lewis* [1955] A.C. 549.
[15] *McCallion* v. *Dodd* [1966] N.Z.L.R. 710.
[16] *Curley* v. *Mannion* [1965] I.R. 543 (children known to be in habit of opening off-side door).
[17] Usually his parent: Ord. 80, r. 2.

that an infant may sue its own parent for negligence.[18] But in one respect an infant plaintiff in tort may be in an unfavourable position: he may be held to be *volens* to the wrongful act of the defendant, even though a contract not to sue would not have been for his benefit, and so not binding on him.[19]

Pre-natal injuries[20]

In Ireland the Civil Liability Act 1961, s. 58 provides that the law relating to wrongs shall apply to an unborn child for his protection in like manner as if the child were born, providing the child is subsequently born alive. In England the commom law was uncertain,[21] but now the Congenital Disabilities (Civil Liability) Act 1976, s. 1 provides that a person responsible for an occurrence affecting the parent of a child, causing the child to be born disabled, will be liable to the child if he would have been liable in tort to the parent affected.[22] Liability is thus derivative. There are various exceptions and qualifications—*e.g.* there is no liability for a pre-conceptual occurrence if the parents accepted the particular risk.

§ 163. MENTAL DISORDER[23]

There is not much English authority as to the liability of mentally disordered or insane persons for their torts. On principle, however, we may say with some confidence that insanity is not in itself any ground of exemption. The object of the law of torts is compensation and not punishment,[24] so there is nothing illogical in holding an insane person civilly responsible. If insanity is no defence to a charge of cruelty in matrimonial proceedings,[25] there is no reason why it should be a defence in tort. Still insanity may be relevant, for, like infancy, it operates (if at all) as evidence that the mental state requisite to create liability is not present. It is probable that the M'Naughten Rules[26] do not provide the test of insanity for the civil as distinct from the criminal law.[27] In any event, it is necessary to distinguish between different species of wrongs:

(1) In wrongs based on malice or on some specific intent, like malicious prosecution, malicious libel on a privileged occasion, or deceit, insanity may be a good defence as disproving the existence of any such malice or intent.

(2) In wrongs of voluntary interference with the person, property, reputa-

---

[18] *McCallion* v. *Dodd* [1966] N.Z.L.R. 710; *Kuchel* v. *Corley* [1971] 1 S.A.S.R. 73. This is certainly the assumption behind the Congenital Disabilities (Civil Liability) Act 1976, ss. 1 and 2, which specifically provide that a mother is not liable to her own disabled child, except when she drives a motor-vehicle negligently.

[19] *Buckpitt* v. *Oates* [1968] 1 All E.R. 1145.

[20] See Lovell and Griffith-Jones, "The Sins of the Fathers" (1974) 90 L.Q.R. 531; Pace, "Civil Liability for Pre-Natal Injuries" (1977) 40 M.L.R. 141.

[21] Some thalidomide babies' claims were settled: *H.* v. *Distillers Co. (Biochemicals)* [1970] C.L.Y. 734.

[22] The Law Commission has made recommendations to this effect—see Cmnd. 5709, 1975 (Law Com. No. 60).

[23] The English authorities are fully surveyed in Fridman, "Mental Incompetency" (1963) 79 L.Q.R. 502, (1964) 80 L.Q.R. 84.

[24] *White* v. *White* [1950] P. 39, 58. See above, § 6.

[25] *Williams* v. *Williams* [1964] A.C. 698.

[26] (1843) 10 Cl. & F. 200.

[27] *Williams* v. *Williams* [1964] A.C. 698.

tion, or other rights of other persons, such as trespass, assault, conversion, or defamation, it is no defence that the defendant was under an insane delusion as to the existence of a sufficient legal justification. If he knew the nature and quality of his act it is no defence that he did not know that what he was doing was wrong, whatever the position may be in the criminal law.[28] An insane person, therefore, who converts another's property to his own use under the delusion that it is his own, or who publishes a defamatory statement under the belief that it is true, is just as liable as if he were sane.[29] If, however, the insanity of the defendant is of so extreme a type as to preclude any genuine intention to do the act complained of, there is no voluntary act at all, and therefore no liability.[30] Mischief done by an epileptic in one of his paroxysms, or by a fever patient in his delirium, or by a somnambulist in his sleep is presumably not actionable.[31]

(3) In wrongs of strict liability there is no reason why insanity should be any defence, unless it is of so extreme a nature as to deprive the act in question of its voluntary quality.

(4) In wrongs dependent upon negligence the conduct of the defendant must be judged by reference to his knowledge or means of knowledge. Insanity, therefore, may be relevant as evidence that the necessary knowledge or means of knowledge did not exist. It has been held that automatism is no defence to an action for negligence in operating a motor-vehicle, unless it is so extreme as to render the defendant's acts completely involuntary.[32]

§ 164. MARRIED PERSONS

(1) Actions between spouses

Since August 1, 1962 each of the parties to a marriage has had the like right of action in tort against the other as if they were not married. This change was effected by section 1 of the Law Reform (Husband and Wife) Act 1962, in consequence of the recommendations of the Law Reform Committee.[33] The only restriction is that when an action in tort is brought by one party to the marriage against the other party during the subsistence of the marriage the court may stay the action if (a) it appears that no sub-

---

[28] *Morriss* v. *Marsden* [1952] 1 All E.R. 925 (person of unsound mind liable for assault and battery), cited with apparent approval by Lord Pearce in *Williams* v. *Williams* [1964] A.C. 698, 751. Similar cases are *Donaghy* v. *Brennan* (1900) 19 N.Z.L.R. 289; *Phillips* v. *Soloway* (1957) 6 D.L.R. (2d) 570; *Adamson* v. *Motor Vehicle Trust* (1957) 58 W.A.L.R. 56.
[29] *Vaughan* v. *Ford*, 1953 (4) S.A. 486 (anonymous letters sent by a person with emotional age of child of 8).
[30] *Tindale* v. *Tindale* [1950] 4 D.L.R. 363.
[31] *Morriss* v. *Marsden* [1952] 1 All E.R. 925, 927.
[32] *Roberts* v. *Ramsbottom* [1980] 1 All E.R. 7.
[33] Ninth Report (Cmnd. 1268 (1961)). Actions between spouses were once thought to be unseemly and undesirable, but the modern practice of insurance (compulsory in some cases) has had its effect on some traditional ideas: "The growth of liability insurance has to a great extent changed the effect of a law-suit between relatives, or even friends, from the traditional friction to the closest sort of amicable co-operation. Nothing draws two people together like a mutual desire to get something out of one's insurance carrier": Larson, "A Problem in Contribution" (1940) 4 Wis.L.Rev. 467, 499.

stantial benefit[34] would accrue to either party from a continuance of the proceedings, or (b) the question could be more conveniently disposed of under section 17 of the Married Women's Property Act 1882, which provides for the settlement of disputes between husband and wife as to the ownership or possession of property. A judge of the High Court or of the county court is empowered, on application by summons, to make in such a case such an order as he thinks just. A husband may even be required to leave the matrimonial home.[35] Elaborate changes in this area were made by the Matrimonial Causes Act 1973, ss. 21–26.

(2) Liability of a wife to third persons

Since the Law Reform (Married Women and Tortfeasors) Act 1935, s. 1, a married woman may be sued for her torts, and is subject to the law relating to bankruptcy and to the enforcement of judgments and orders in all respects as if she were a *feme sole*. Before that Act any damages recovered against her could be levied only out of her separate property not restrained from anticipation and she could not be made bankrupt unless she was carrying on a separate trade.

(3) Liability of a husband for his wife's torts

The Act of 1935 made a still bigger change in the position of the husband. At common law a husband was liable to be joined with his wife in all actions for torts committed by her during the subsistence of the marriage and the House of Lords decided[36] that this liability had not been taken away by the Married Women's Property Act 1882. But as the Act of 1882 had deprived the husband of all his interest *jure mariti* in his wife's separate property and earnings out of which he might have satisfied a claim for his wife's wrongdoing it became his hard fate to continue to bear the burden of his wife's wrongdoings when he had been relieved of the means which would have assisted him to bear it.[37] This injustice has now been remedied. Under the Act of 1935[38] the husband of a married woman is not, by reason only of his being her husband,[39] liable in respect of any tort committed by her whether before or after the marriage, or to be sued or made a party to any proceeding brought in respect of any such tort. Section 4 (2) (c) also provides that nothing in the Act "prevents a husband and wife from rendering themselves, or being rendered, jointly liable in respect of any tort, contract, debt, or obligation, and of suing and being sued either in tort or in contract or otherwise, in like manner as if they were not married." It has been argued that this provision enables a husband and wife to be sued for conspiracy,[40]

---

[34] On second reading in the House of Lords the Government spokesman said this phrase was intended to mean benefit of financial value to the parties, and not that it should include ethical or moral values: 241 H.L.Deb., 5s., col. 1104 (Viscount Colville of Culross).
[35] *Bassett* v. *Bassett* [1975] Fam. 76.
[36] *Edwards* v. *Porter* [1925] A.C. 1.
[37] In *Newton* v. *Hardy* (1933) 149 L.T. 165 the plaintiff recovered damages for the enticement of her husband by the wife of the defendant, who was himself entirely innocent.
[38] s. 3.
[39] So he will be liable where he has authorised the tort on the general principle of liability for an agent: *Barber* v. *Pigden* [1937] 1 K.B. 664.
[40] *Auten* v. *Rayner, The Times*, March 15, 1960.

and it is now settled that a conspiracy between husband and wife is capable of giving rise to tortious liability.[41]

§ 165. PRISONERS AND BANKRUPTS

Criminals, even when undergoing imprisonment, have the same rights of action for torts as a man with a blameless life. Those who break the law remain the Queen's subjects—they are not her enemies.[42]

Bankrupts

(1) Liability

The Bankruptcy Act 1914[43] provides that demands in the nature of unliquidated damages arising otherwise than by reason of a contract, promise or breach of trust are not provable against the trustee in bankruptcy. This is generally taken to exclude claims for damages in tort.[44] But if the demand arises from a contract it is not the less provable against the trustee because it might also be framed in tort, as where a passenger on a tram was injured owing to the negligence of the driver.[45] And under the Law Reform (Miscellaneous Provisions) Act 1934[46] where the plaintiff has a right of action in tort against the estate of a deceased wrongdoer, and that estate is insolvent, he may prove in the administration of the estate for unliquidated damages.

(2) Power to sue

Where a right of action exists for a tort committed against the bankrupt a distinction is taken. A right of action in respect of a tort which results in injuries mainly to the person of the bankrupt does not pass to the trustee.[47] On the other hand, a right of action which results in injuries mainly to the estate of the bankrupt passes to the trustee. Where the tort results in injuries both to the estate and also to the person of the bankrupt, the right of action for the tort, in so far as it results in injuries[48] to the estate,[49] will pass to the trustee: in so far as it results in injuries to the person of the bankrupt, it will remain in him. In such a case the trustee and bankrupt can either bring separate actions or join as plaintiffs in one action in which case the damages will be assessed under two separate heads.[50]

---

[41] *Midland Bank Trust Co. Ltd.* v. *Green* (No. 3) [1979] Ch. 496, on appeal, see [1979] 3 All E.R. 28, 35.

[42] *Gibbons* v. *Duffell* (1932) 47 C.L.R. 520, 535.

[43] s. 30 (1).

[44] *Re Berkeley Securities (Property) Ltd.* [1980] 1 W.L.R. 1589, 1610.

[45] *Re Great Orme Tramways Co.* (1934) 50 T.L.R. 450. Such a distinction between contract and tort seems anomalous today: see above, § 3.

[46] s. 1 (6).

[47] *Beckham* v. *Drake* (1849) 2 H.L.C. 579. In such a case the bankrupt may spend the damages, if he recovers any, in the maintenance of himself and his family: *Ex p. Vine* (1878) 8 Ch.D. 364.

[48] *Rose* v. *Buckett* [1901] 2 K.B. 449.

[49] *Wenlock* v. *Moloney* [1965] 1 W.L.R. 1236.

[50] *Wilson* v. *United Counties Bank* [1920] A.C. 102.

§ 166. EXECUTORS AND ADMINISTRATORS

The question whether a cause of action survives the death of the person injured must be carefully distinguished from the question whether the act of causing the death of a person gives any right of action for damages to his relatives. The former question is that which is considered in this section: the latter will be dealt with later in connection with the provisions of the Fatal Accidents Acts.[51]

Actio personalis moritur cum persona

Until 1934, subject to important exceptions, no executor or administrator could sue or be sued for any tort committed against or by the deceased in his lifetime. This was the purport of the maxim of the common law *actio personalis moritur cum persona*—a personal action dies with the parties to the cause of action.[52] An action for a tort had to be begun in the joint lifetime of the wrongdoer and the person injured. But sweeping changes were made in the previous law by the Law Reform (Miscellaneous Provisions) Act 1934.[53] Before that Act it was often said to be cheaper to kill than to maim or cripple.[54] This defect in the law became particularly noticeable with the growth of motor traffic. A person injured in a collision due to the negligence of another might (even after the Road Traffic Act 1930 had made it compulsory to insure against third-party risks) find himself left without remedy because the negligent party had himself been killed in the accident. The Law Reform Act in section 1 (1) lays down the general rule that in future on the death[55] of any person all causes of action subsisting against or vested in him shall survive against, or, as the case may be, for the benefit of, his estate.[56] But there is no survival of causes of action for defamation.[57] The Act does not, however, abolish the common law rule that it is no tort to cause the death of another. It does not make the infliction of death into a new tort: death is only the event which is required to enable an existing cause of action to descend to the personal representatives. It is necessary to emphasise this, because in *Rose* v. *Ford*[58] the House of Lords held that a right of action for damages for loss of expectation of life survived to the personal representative. A living person can claim damages for such loss. The right is vested in him in life and on his death passes to his personal representative who stands in his shoes. The fact that the expectation is realised, *i.e.* that the death comes at the time anticipated or sooner, cannot make any difference. The cause of action is not the death but the negligence

---

[51] Below, § 217.
[52] See the Interim Report of the Law Revision Committee (Cmd. 4540 (1934)); Holdsworth, H.E.L., iii, pp. 576–583.
[53] See the interesting account of the genesis of the Act by the First Parliamentary Counsel (Sir Noël Hutton) in "Mechanics of Law Reform" (1961) 24 M.L.R. 18.
[54] But see *H. West & Son Ltd.* v. *Shephard* [1964] A.C. 307, 342.
[55] This includes suicide: *Pigney* v. *Pointers Transport Services* [1957] 1 W.L.R. 1121.
[56] For Ireland, see the Civil Liability Act 1961, ss. 6–10.
[57] s. 1 (1). It is not clear why this should be so. Defamation may cause much more harm to the next-of-kin than an assault, and it is hard to see why the death of the defamer should deprive the plaintiff of his damages. The reason given by the Law Revision Committee 1934 (Cmd. 4540, p. 7) that "the presence of the plaintiff or of the defendant may be of the greatest importance" is unconvincing, as the Faulks Committee thought (Cmnd. 5909, § 417).
[58] [1937] A.C. 826.

which caused it, and even if there is only a split second between that act of negligence and the death—and, it would seem, even if the death is instantaneous—the action will descend to the personal representative.[59] But in Ireland the decision in *Rose* v. *Ford* has been reversed by statute.[60]

§ 167. JOINT AND SEVERAL TORTFEASORS[61]

(1) Who are joint tortfeasors

Where the same damage is caused to a person by two or more wrongdoers those wrongdoers may be either joint or independent tortfeasors. Persons are to be deemed joint tortfeasors within the meaning of this rule whenever they are responsible for the same tort—that is to say, whenever the law for any reason imputes the commission of the same wrongful act to two or more persons at once. This happens in at least three classes of cases—namely, agency,[62] vicarious liability,[63] and common action, *i.e.* where a tort is committed in the course of a common action, a joint act done in pursuance of a concerted purpose.[64] In order to be joint tortfeasors there must be a concurrence in the act or acts causing damage, not merely a coincidence of separate acts which by their conjoined effect cause damage.[65] The *injuria* as well as the *damnum* must be the same.[66] So that if the presence of a particular mental intent is necessary to constitute liability each tortfeasor must be proved to have that intent.[67] This may give rise to special problems when qualified privilege is pleaded as a defence in libel.[68] But there are many cases in which the same damage is caused by independent and separate wrongful acts of several persons, as where a plaintiff sustains a single damage from the combined negligence of two motor-car drivers, who are not engaged in a common design (*e.g.* racing on the road).[69] A handler of stolen goods is not necessarily, therefore, a joint tortfeasor with the thief.[70]

(2) Nature of liability

"If a number of persons jointly participate in the commission of a tort, each is responsible, jointly with each and all of the others, and also severally, for the whole amount of the damage caused by the tort, irrespec-

---

[59] *Morgan* v. *Scoulding* [1938] 1 K.B. 786.
[60] Civil Liability Act 1961, s. 7 (2).
[61] The leading work is Williams, *Joint Torts and Contributory Negligence*. Many of the ideas expressed in this book were given legislative form in ss. 11–33 of the Irish Civil Liability Act 1961.
[62] See below, § 170.
[63] See below, § 172. A master is always treated as a joint tortfeasor with the servant for whom he is vicariously liable (*Jones* v. *Manchester Corporation* [1952] 2 Q.B. 852, 870), although it is difficult to see why this should be so: *Semtex Ltd.* v. *Gladstone* [1954] 1 W.L.R. 945, 949; *Treacy* v. *Robinson & Son* [1937] I.R. 255, 266.
[64] *Brooke* v. *Bool* [1928] 2 K.B. 578, 585.
[65] *The Koursk* [1924] P. 140, 159.
[66] *The Koursk* [1924] P. 140, 156.
[67] *Gardiner* v. *Moore* [1969] 1 Q.B. 55, 91.
[68] § 64.
[69] *The Koursk* [1924] P. 140; *Drinkwater* v. *Kimber* [1952] 2 Q.B. 281, 292.
[70] *Toome Eel Fishery (N.I.) Ltd.* v. *Cardwell* [1966] N.I. 1, 29.

tive of the extent of his participation."[71] That is to say, the person injured
may sue any one of them separately for the full amount of the loss; or he
may sue all of them jointly in the same action, and even in this latter case
the judgment so obtained against all of them may be executed in full against
any one of them. So when the court assesses the damages to be awarded
against joint tortfeasors sued in the same action, only one sum is to be
awarded.[72] But if the tortfeasors were independent or separate "the person
damnified might sue them one by one and recover from one alone or from
such as he chose to execute judgment against, provided that he did not
recover more than the greatest sum awarded or, against any defendant,
more than was awarded in the action against him."[73] In the next section we
shall consider how far there is any right of contribution or indemnity
between the tortfeasors.

(3) Effect of judgment

At common law a judgment obtained against one joint wrongdoer
released all the others, even though it was not satisfied, and even though the
defendant did not then know of the existence of the other tortfeasors. The
tort was merged in the judgment.[74] This rule was completely abolished[75] by
the Law Reform (Married Women and Tortfeasors) Act 1935.[76] This has
now been repealed and replaced by the Civil Liability (Contribution) Act
1978 s. 3. This provides that judgment recovered[77] against any person liable
in respect of any debt or damage shall not be a bar to an action, or to the
continuance of an action, against any other person jointly liable with him in
respect of the same debt or damage. The result is that an unsatisfied judgment against one tortfeasor is no longer a bar to recovery against another
tortfeasor, whether that unsatisfied judgment arose out of a single action
against the tortfeasors resulting in separate judgments,[78] or out of successive
separate actions against the tortfeasors.[79]

But section 4 provides that if successive actions are brought, the plaintiff
may not recover costs in any but the first action unless the court decides
there was reasonable ground for bringing the subsequent action. The Act of
1935, but not that of 1978, also provided[80] that if more than one action was
brought in respect of the same damage by or on behalf of the person by
whom it was suffered, against tortfeasors liable in respect of the damage
(whether as joint tortfeasors or otherwise) the sums recoverable under the
judgments given in those actions by way of damages should not in the
aggregate exceed the amount of the damages awarded by the judgment first
given. The effect of the disappearance of this rule is that a plaintiff in a

---

[71] *Dougherty* v. *Chandler* (1946) 46 S.R.(N.S.W.) 370, 375, *per* Jordan C.J.
[72] *Wah Tat Bank Ltd.* v. *Chan* [1975] A.C. 507.
[73] *Wimpey (George) & Co. Ltd.* v. *British Overseas Airways Corporation* [1955] A.C. 169,
   181, *per* Lord Porter.
[74] *Brinsmead* v. *Harrison* (1871) L.R. 7 C.P. 547. This rule never applied to independent
   tortfeasors.
[75] *Wah Tat Bank Ltd.* v. *Chan* [1975] A.C. 507, 518.
[76] s. 6 (1) (*a*).
[77] So that if there is a release of one tortfeasor there is apparently no right of action against
   the other or others. *Aliter* in cases of contribution between tortfeasors: below § 168.
[78] As in *Bryanston Finance Ltd.* v. *de Vries* [1975] 1 Q.B. 703.
[79] As in *Wah Tat Bank Ltd.* v. *Chan* [1975] A.C. 507.
[80] s. 6 (1) (*b*). Full discussion in Williams, *Joint Torts*, pp. 39–43.

second action can now recover more than he recovered in the first action—*e.g.* if he has under-estimated his damage at the time of the first action.[81] The sanction against abuse of this process is the power given by section 4 to deprive such a plaintiff of his costs.[82]

(4) Release

The release of one joint wrongdoer releases all the others, even though this was not the intention of the parties, the reason being that the cause of action, which is one and indivisible, having been released, all persons otherwise liable thereto are consequently released.[83] This rule is equally applicable to a release under seal and to a release by way of accord and satisfaction.[84]

A mere covenant or other agreement not to sue one of the joint wrongdoers must, however, be distinguished from an actual release given to him, whether by deed or by accord and satisfaction.[85] An agreement not to sue does not, like a release, destroy the cause of action, but merely prevents it from being enforced against the particular wrongdoer with whom the agreement was made.[86] A transaction which is in form an actual release, whether by deed or by accord and satisfaction, will be construed as being merely an agreement not to sue, if it contains an express or implied[87] reservation of the right to proceed against the other wrongdoers. For this reservation would otherwise be wholly ineffective.

§ 168. CONTRIBUTION[88]

"How some rules of law arose is not always known. For instance, except for the fact that in 1799 Lord Kenyon C.J. laid it down categorically in *Merryweather* v. *Nixan*[89] that there was no contribution between joint tortfeasors, no one has ever discovered whence the rule came, but it remained the law till abrogated by the Law Reform (Married Women and Tortfeasors) Act 1935."[90] That Act provided that where damage is suffered by any person as a result of a tort (whether a crime or not), any tortfeasor liable in respect of that damage may recover contribution from any other tortfeasor who is, or would if sued have been, liable in respect of the same damage, whether as a joint tortfeasor or otherwise. The 1935 Act did not

---

[81] This seems to undermine a rule generally thought to have been settled since 1701: see below, § 218.

[82] See Lord Scarman (extra-judicially) in (1978) 395 H.L. Deb. col. 252.

[83] *Duck* v. *Mayeu* [1892] 2 Q.B. 511, 513. It has been suggested (Foster, "Law Revision" (1938) 2 M.L.R. 14, 20) that the principle upon which this rule is founded having been repudiated by the abolition of the rule in *Brinsmead* v. *Harrison*, this rule should also go.

[84] *Thurman* v. *Wild* (1840) 11 A. & E. 453.

[85] "An arid and technical distinction without any merits," *per* Lord Denning M.R. in *Bryanston Finance Ltd.* v. *de Vries* [1975] Q.B. 703, 723. But the distinction has not been affected by the 1978 Act, and was expressly preserved by s. 17 (1) of the Irish Civil Liability Act 1981.

[86] *Duck* v. *Mayeu* [1892] 2 Q.B. 511.

[87] *Gardiner* v. *Moore* [1969] 1 Q.B. 55.

[88] See Williams, *Joint Torts and Contributory Negligence* (1951), Chap. 6; Law Commission Report on Contribution, Law Com. No. 79, 1977.

[89] (1799) 8 T.R. 186.

[90] *Carmarthenshire C.C.* v. *Lewis* [1955] A.C. 549, 560, *per* Lord Goddard C.J., "whose knowledge of the history of the common law was profound": *per* Lord Diplock in *Bremer Vulcan Schiffbau* v. *South Indian Shipping Ltd.* [1981] 2 W.L.R. 141,148.

cover a wrongdoer who was not a tortfeasor—*e.g.* one guilty of a breach of contract or trust—but this has now been done[91] by the Civil Liability (Contribution) Act 1978, s. 6 (1). So the legislation now provides for two cases—the normal one in which the plaintiff sues the two (or more) persons responsible for his damage in the same action,[92] and the exceptional one in which he decides to proceed against only one of them. If the latter course is followed, the defendant is entitled to claim against any other person not made a party to the action (the third party), and the third party then becomes a party to the action with the same rights in respect of his defence against any claim made against him, and otherwise, as if he had been sued by the defendant.[93]

Under the pre-1978 law there were two problems which caused great difficulties.[94] The first was whether a tortfeasor who had settled the claim made against him, with or without an admission of liability, was entitled to claim contribution. The second was whether contribution could be recovered from a defendant who had been sued to judgment and held not liable (either on the merits, or because of some procedural defence peculiar to him), even if he would have been held liable if he had been sued at some other time or in some other way. Since 1978 a person claiming contribution must be liable in an action, actual or hypothetical, brought in England or Wales (s. 1 (6)). But it is also clear from section 1 (4) of the new Act that a wrongdoer who enters into a bona fide settlement or compromise with the plaintiff may claim a contribution "without regard to whether or not he himself is or ever was liable in respect of the damage, provided, however, that he would have been liable assuming that the factual basis of the claim against him could be established." It is immaterial that the person claiming contribution has ceased to be liable (by virtue of a compromise) since the time when the damage occurred (s. 1 (2)). Furthermore, by section 1 (3), a person is liable to make contribution "notwithstanding that he has ceased to be liable in respect of the damage in question since the time when the damage occurred,[95] unless he ceased to be liable by virtue of the expiry of a period of limitation or prescription which extinguished the right on which the claim against him in respect of the damage was based."[96] Thus, where the plaintiff effects a bona fide compromise (not amounting to a release) with one of two or more wrongdoers and then brings an action against the other(s), the first is liable to make contribution to that other (and can himself claim contribution in respect of any payment made under the compromise) unless such liability has ceased through effluxion of time.

An important qualification to section 1 (3) is effected by section 1 (5), which provides that a judgment given[97] in any action brought by the person who suffered the damage in question against any person from whom con-

---

[91] It had already been done in Ireland by the Civil Liability Act 1961, s. 11 (2).
[92] Hence contribution may be ordered between several concurrent tortfeasors—*e.g.* two motorists, not engaged in a common design, whose combined negligence injures the plaintiff: *Pride of Derby and Derbyshire Angling Association Ltd.* v. *British Celanese Ltd.* [1952] 1 All E.R. 1326.
[93] See Ord. 16 for the machinery of contribution.
[94] See the 17th edition of this work, § 168.
[95] This reverses the decision in *George Wimpey & Co. Ltd.* v. *B.O.A.C.* [1955] A.C. 169.
[96] There may be difficulty here if a foreign limitation statute is involved: see Law Commission Working Paper No. 75 (1980).
[97] In any part of the United Kingdom.

tribution is sought shall be conclusive in the proceedings for contribution as to any issue determined by that judgment in favour of the person from whom contribution is sought.

Contracts of indemnity. Nothing in the 1978 Act affects any express or implied contractual or other right to indemnity which would be enforceable apart from the Act, or, conversely, renders enforceable any agreement for indemnity which would not be enforceable at common law.[98]

At common law an insured person cannot himself recover from his insurers if the contract purports to indemnify him against the consequences of his own intentional criminal act.[99] It was also apparently settled that a contract to indemnify another against the consequences of committing a tort is unlawful, unless either the act to be done is not obviously tortious, or the party to be indemnified has been induced to commit it by the fraudulent statement of the other.[1] The policy of protecting the victims of traffic accidents has also led to decisions whereby a contract of insurance is valid even though the circumstances of the accident gave rise to criminal liability (*e.g.* manslaughter) on the part of the insured motorist.[2] The Act of 1978, by section 2 (2), specifically gives the court power to order a complete indemnity. The result of the Act is "that if A considers he has against B a right of indemnity or contribution under a contract enforceable under the law as it was before the passing of the Bill, he can sue on that contract and in doing so will neither require nor receive any help from the Bill: if he considers that apart from the contract he has a right of contribution against B under the Bill, he can add an alternative claim for such contribution. In the event of his contract being held valid he will get what the contract provides for; in the event of its being held invalid, he will get under the Bill such amount, if any, as the court thinks he ought to have."[3]

Libel. Contracts of indemnity are common in actions for libel. The Law Reform Committee upon whose recommendations[4] the Act of 1935 was based gave as one instance of the hardship of the common law the case of *W. H. Smith & Son* v. *Clinton.*[5] In that case the plaintiffs agreed to publish a newspaper for the defendants, one of the terms being that the defendants should give the plaintiffs a letter of indemnity against claims arising out of the publication of libellous matter in the newspaper. A libel was published, and the plaintiffs were unsuccessful in their action on the letter of indemnity to recover the damages which they had paid to the person libelled, for they well knew that matter published was libellous. They might still be unable to recover on the letter of indemnity,[6] but they might take proceedings for such contribution as might be found to be just and equitable.

Implied indemnities—(1) A wrongdoer cannot recover contribution from

---

[98] See s. 7 (3) of the 1978 Act, which in substance reproduces part of s. 6 of the 1935 Act.
[99] *Hardy* v. *Motor Insurers' Bureau* [1964] 2 Q.B. 745.
[1] *W.H. Smith & Sons* v. *Clinton* (1908) 99 L.T. 840, 841.
[2] *Hardy* v. *Motor Insurers' Bureau* [1964] 2 Q.B. 745.
[3] An extract from an unpublished memorandum on the 1935 Bill by its draftsman, Sir Granville Ram, K.C.B., K.C.
[4] Cmd. 4637.
[5] (1908) 99 L.T. 840.
[6] The Defamation Act 1952, s. 11, provides only that agreements for indemnity in respect of liability for libel shall not be unlawful unless at the time of publication the person claiming to be indemnified knows that the matter is defamatory and does not reasonably believe there is a good defence to an action brought upon it.

an innocent person whom he has led into the commission of a tort. For a principal must indemnify his agent for all liability incurred by him in consequence of the act authorised being (without the knowledge of the agent) an illegal one. This principle is of the widest general application.[7] Thus an auctioneer is entitled to be indemnified by a client who has instructed him to sell goods to which, as it subsequently appeared, he had not title.[8] There are also many statutes which empower local authorities to indemnify their employees.[9]

(2) It is the converse of the former principle that a wrongdoing servant is obliged to indemnify his master who has been held vicariously responsible for the tort.[10] Hence a servant who has been sued in respect of some tort committed in the course of his employment cannot claim an indemnity from his innocent master.

Assessment of contribution

The framers of the Act of 1935 borrowed the principles of the Maritime Conventions Act 1911,[11] in determining the measure of contribution, and provided[12] that in proceedings against any person for contribution the amount of the contribution recoverable should be such as may be found by the court to be just and equitable having regard to the extent of that person's responsibility for the damage. The assessment must be made[13] having regard to the parties who are before the court: the negligence or contributory negligence of a party not before the court cannot be considered.[14] There has been some controversy whether the Act contemplates that damages should be apportioned on the basis of causation or on the basis of the respective degrees of fault or culpability of the parties,[15] or by combining the concepts of causation and blameworthiness. This third approach is in accord with the practice under the contributory negligence legislation,[16] though it may give rise to difficulties in cases involving breaches of totally different kinds of duties.[17]

Limitation. As the right of contribution is not a cause of action in tort but is a right *sui generis* the limitation period available in contribution proceedings was once held to be six years.[18] But now in England[19] the Limitation Act 1963, s. 4, provides that where a tortfeasor becomes entitled (after July 31, 1963) to a right to recover contribution in respect of any damages from another tortfeasor, no action to recover contribution shall be brought after

---

[7] *Secretary of State* v. *Bank of India Ltd.* [1938] 2 All E.R. 797, 801.
[8] *Adamson* v. *Jarvis* (1827) 4 Bing. 66.
[9] *e.g.* the Town and Country Planning Act 1971, s. 4 (6).
[10] *Lister* v. *Romford Ice and Cold Storage Co. Ltd.* [1957] A.C. 555. See below, § 183.
[11] See below, § 194.
[12] s. 6 (2).
[13] The trial judge should deal with the question of contribution at the end of the trial: *Calvert* v. *Pick* [1954] 1 W.L.R. 456. Only in very exceptional cases should an appeal court interfere with the judge's apportionment: *The MacGregor* [1943] A.C. 197.
[14] *Maxfield* v. *Llewellyn* [1961] 1 W.L.R. 1119.
[15] This view was adopted in *Weaver* v. *Commercial Process Co.* (1947) 63 T.L.R. 466 (*contra Collins* v. *Hertfordshire C.C.* [1947] K.B. 598) and is approved by Williams, *Joint Torts,* pp. 157–158; Chapman (1948) 64 L.Q.R. 26 ("Causation itself is difficult enough; degrees of causation would really be a nightmare").
[16] See below, § 198.
[17] See 129 N.L.J. 509.
[18] *Harvey* v. *O'Dell* [1958] 2 Q.B. 78.
[19] For Ireland, see *Buckley* v. *Lynch* [1978] I.R. 6.

the end of two years from the date on which that right accrued to the first tortfeasor. This may still be hard on a defendant called upon to defend contribution proceedings brought many years after the accident, but the Law Commission's Final Report on the Limitation of Actions[20] did not feel able to recommend any reform. There is a saving (s. 4 (3)) for cases of fraud, disability and mistake. Section 4 (2) provides that the date on which the right to recover contribution accrued shall be ascertained as follows:

(a) if the tortfeasor is held liable in respect of that damage by a judgment given in any civil proceedings, or an award made on any arbitration, the relevant date shall be the date on which the judgment is given, or the date of the award, as the case may be;

(b) if, in any case not falling within the preceding paragraph, the tortfeasor admits liability in favour of one or more persons in respect of that damage, the relevant date shall be the earliest date on which the amount to be paid by him in discharge of that liability is agreed by or on behalf of the tortfeasor and that person, or each of those persons, as the case may be;

and for the purposes of this subsection no account shall be taken of any judgment or award given or made on appeal in so far as it varies the amount of damages awarded against the tortfeasor.

§ 169. PERSONS JOINTLY INJURED

Where two or more persons possess a right of action in respect of one and the same injury—as, for example, a trespass or other wrong to the property of co-owners, or a libel on a firm of partners in the way of their business—is it necessary that those persons should all join in one and the same action, or can one of them sue without the others? The old rule of the common law on this point was that (with certain exceptions which need not be now considered) all persons so suffering a joint injury must join in one action. But now the non-joinder of persons jointly injured is no bar to an action by one or some of them. The only effect of such a non-joinder is that the court may, in its discretion, order the other persons so jointly injured to be joined as parties to the action, either as plaintiffs or (if they will not consent) as defendants. Where two or more persons have suffered a joint, but not a several, injury, a release granted by one of them will, in the absence of fraud, destroy the whole cause of action, and operate as a bar to an action by any of the others.[21]

§ 170. PRINCIPAL AND AGENT[22]

Usually an agent, as distinct from a servant, is engaged to perform a particular task, and has authority to do whatever is required for that purpose but has no general authority. But whether he is a servant or an agent the test of vicarious liability is the same: was he acting on behalf of, or within the scope of the authority conferred by, the master or principal?[23] There may also be liability under the doctrine of ratification

---

[20] Cmnd. 6923 (1977), para. 5.
[21] *Phillips* v. *Clagett* (1843) 11 M. & W. 84.
[22] See Atiyah, *Vicarious Liability*, Chaps. 27–28.
[23] *Heatons Transport (St. Helens) Ltd.* v. *Transport and General Workers' Union* [1973] A.C. 15, 99.

Any person who authorises or procures a tort to be committed by another is responsible for that tort as if he had committed it himself: *Qui facit per alium facit per se*. Principal and agent, therefore, are jointly and severally liable as joint wrongdoers for any tort authorised by the former and committed by the latter. This is one way in which the employer of an independent contractor can be held liable[24] for a tort committed by the contractor. It must be clearly shown that the principal gave to the agent express or implied authority to commit the acts complained of. So the Transport and General Workers' Union was finally held responsible for certain activities of certain shop stewards in the docks at Liverpool and Hull.[25] Those shop stewards were not the servants of the union but still had authority to take the industrial action complained of, which was in accordance with union policy.

Ratification

If one person commits a tort while acting on behalf of another, but without his authority, and that other subsequently ratifies and assents to the act so done, he thereby becomes responsible for it, just as if he had given a precedent authority for its commission.[26] When an illegal act done by one person on behalf of another but without his authority would have been legal had it been done with his authority, it becomes legal *ab initio* if he subsequently ratifies it.[27] An act may be thus justified by ratification, even after the commencement of an action against the agent; but the ratification must in all cases have taken place at a time when the principal still retained the power of lawfully authorising the act to be done.[28] The following conditions must be fulfilled:

(1) The wrongful act must have been done on behalf of the principal. No man can ratify an act which was done, not on his behalf, but on behalf of the doer himself.[29] In the case of contracts it has been decided[30] that there can be no ratification unless the agent not merely contracts on behalf of the principal, but also avows that intention at the time. Possibly the same rule applies to torts also.[31] But the necessary avowal need not be expressed in words, but may sufficiently appear from the conduct of the parties and the facts of the case. It cannot be necessary for a railway official who arrests a passenger for defrauding the railway company to state in terms that he does so on behalf of the company.

(2) The principal must know the nature of the act which has thus been done on his behalf, unless, indeed, he is content to dispense with any such knowledge and to approve and sanction the acts of the agent whatever they may be.[32] It is sufficient, however, if the principal has such knowledge of the nature of the act as would have sufficed to make him liable had he actually authorised it or done it himself. Mistake or ignorance is no greater defence

[24] *Jolliffe* v. *Willmet & Co.* (1970) 114 S.J. 619.
[25] *Heatons Transport (St. Helens) Ltd.* v. *Transport and General Workers' Union* [1973] A.C. 15.
[26] *Wilson* v. *Tumman* (1843) 6 M. & G. 236, 242.
[27] *Buron* v. *Denman* (1848) 2 Ex. 167.
[28] *Bird* v. *Brown* (1850) 4 Ex. 786.
[29] *Eastern Construction Co.* v. *National Trust Co.* [1914] A.C. 197, 213.
[30] *Keighley, Maxsted & Co.* v. *Durant* [1901] A.C. 240.
[31] *Keighley, Maxsted* v. *Durant* [1901] A.C. 240, 260.
[32] *Freeman* v. *Rosher* (1849) 13 Q.B. 780.

to a principal who gives an authority subsequent than to one who gives an authority precedent.[33]

§ 171. PARTNERS[34]

By the Partnership Act 1890, ss. 10 and 12, it is provided that partners are jointly and severally liable for each other's torts committed in the ordinary course of the business of the firm. Thus in *Hamlyn* v. *Houston & Co.*[35] a firm was held liable for the act of one of the partners who, on behalf of the firm, induced by bribery a servant of the plaintiff to commit a breach of his contract of service. Whether the act of a partner is one done in the course of the business of the firm is a question to be determined on the same considerations as those which determine the responsibility of a master for the acts of his servant. As liability is joint and several, it follows that there can be no judgment against the partnership or any one of the partners if the actual tortfeasor has some substantive defence peculiar to himself,[36] although the courts do not favour such a plea.[37]

§ 172. MASTER AND SERVANT[38]

A master is jointly and severally liable for any tort committed by his servant while acting in the course of his employment. This is by far the most important of the various cases in which vicarious responsibility or vicarious liability[39] is recognised by the law. Vicarious liability[40] means that one person takes or supplies the place of another so far as liability is concerned.[41] Although the doctrine has its roots in the earliest years of the common law, it was Sir John Holt (1642–1710) who began the task of adapting medieval rules to the needs of a modern society, and his work was continued by the great Victorian judges. By the beginning of the twentieth century it was firmly established that the master's liability was based, not on the fiction that he had impliedly commanded his servant to do what he did, but on the safer and simpler ground that it was done in the scope or course of his employment or authority. Today it has been developed so far "that it would be a good deal safer to keep lions or other wild animals in a park than to engage in a business involving the employment of labour."[42]

Some different theories

It will never be possible, or perhaps even desirable, to expound a theory which will at once explain and justify all aspects of the doctrine,[43] although

---

[33] *Hilbery* v. *Hatton* (1864) 2 H. & C. 822.
[34] Atiyah, *Vicarious Liability*, Chap. 11.
[35] [1903] 1 K.B. 81.
[36] *Kliendienst* v. *Kliendienst & Sons* (1959) S.R. (N.S.W.) 150. See further below, § 173.
[37] *Meekins* v. *Henson* [1964] 1 Q.B. 472.
[38] Atiyah, *Vicarious Liability* is the leading monograph. See also Munkman, *Employer's Liability*; Newark, "*Twine* v. *Bean's Express Ltd.*" (1954) 17 M.L.R. 102; Glanville Williams, "Vicarious Liability" (1956) 72 L.Q.R. 522; "Liability for Independent Contractors" [1956] C.L.J. 180.
[39] The ordinary speech of lawyers draws no distinction between these two phrases—perhaps mistakenly: see Hart, "Varieties of Responsibility" (1967) 83 L.Q.R. 346.
[40] A term which Pollock claimed he had invented: *Pollock-Holmes Letters*, vol. i, p. 233.
[41] *Launchbury* v. *Morgans* [1971] 2 Q.B. 245, 253.
[42] *Kay* v. *I.T.W. Ltd.* [1968] 1 Q.B. 140, 155, *per* Danckwerts L.J.
[43] Atiyah, *Vicarious Liability*, Chap. 2, considers nine theories.

it has long been accepted as necessary and beneficial.[44] The combined effect of all the reasons may be overwhelming, though one or more in isolation may be dubious. The maxim *respondeat superior* does not explain why the superior should answer: it does not enshrine a principle, but announces rather a result[45]—namely, that the employer ought to pay.[46] The maxim *qui facit per alium facit per se*, although often cited with approbation,[47] is similarly unhelpful.[48] The truth is that "a mixture of ideas has inspired many unconvincing judicial efforts to find a common basis for the maxim. What was once presented as a legal principle has degenerated into a rule of expediency, imperfectly defined, and changing its shape before our eyes under the impact of changing social and political conditions."[49] But there is one idea which is to be found in the judgments from the time of Sir John Holt[50] to the present day,[51] namely, public policy. As Lord Brougham[52] said: "The reason that I am liable is this, that by employing him I set the whole thing in motion; and what he does, being done for my benefit and under my direction, I am responsible for the consequences of doing it." In short, vicarious liability is based on "social convenience and rough justice."[53] This is an adequate explanation of the doctrine, subject to two qualifications. First, the master may be liable even though the act or default is not for his benefit, and even though he has expressly prohibited it.[54] Secondly, the master's right of control is the criterion of the existence of the relationship which gives rise to vicarious liability, and not in itself a justification of that liability. In all this there is no doubt that the courts have been much influenced by the fact that the master is usually more able than the servant to satisfy claims by injured persons and can pass on the burden of liability by way of insurance.[55] There is also some evidence to show that the imposition of strict liability on the master results in the prevention of accidents: the master takes more care than he would otherwise have done.[56]

§ 173. The Nature of Vicarious Liability

There has been some discussion about the nature of the doctrine of vicarious liability, as well as of the reason for it.[57] The orthodox view assumes that the master is vicariously liable for the servant only when the servant himself would be liable. "In every case . . . the first question is to see whether the

---

[44] Few dissenting voices have been raised, though Lord Bramwell (always a sturdy individualist) opposed it in 1877: C. 285, p. 46.
[45] *Kilboy* v. *South-Eastern Fire Area Joint Committee*, 1952 S.C. 280, 287. See also *Staveley Iron and Chemical Co. Ltd.* v. *Jones* [1956] A.C. 627, 643, and Maitland's explanation of the maxim's early history in P. & M., vol. ii, p. 533.
[46] *Morgans* v. *Launchbury* [1973] A.C. 127, 135.
[47] As by two Law Lords in *Morgans* v. *Launchbury* [1973] A.C. 127, 140.
[48] *Moynihan* v. *Moynihan* [1975] I.R. 192, 200.
[49] *Kilboy* v. *South-Eastern Fire Area Joint Committee*, 1952 S.C. 280, 285, *per* Lord Cooper.
[50] See his opinion cited below, § 178.
[51] *Nettleship* v. *Weston* [1971] 2 Q.B. 691, 700; *Rose* v. *Plenty* [1976] 1 W.L.R. 141, 147–148.
[52] *Duncan* v. *Finlater* (1839) 6 Cl. & F. 894 at 910.
[53] *I.C.I. Ltd.* v. *Shatwell* [1965] A.C. 656, 686, *per* Lord Pearce.
[54] See below, § 177.
[55] *Launchbury* v. *Morgans* [1971] 2 Q.B. 245, 254.
[56] See above, § 87.
[57] See literature cited above, § 172.

servant was liable. If the answer is yes, the second question is to see whether the employer must shoulder the servant's liability."[58] This is the view which was adopted in the Crown Proceedings Act 1947, s. 2 (1),[59] and which has been approved judicially.[60] So in the normal case there has been only one tort, but as it has been committed in the course of employment the master is jointly responsible for it.[61] But four exceptional cases have caused difficulties, and given rise to an unorthodox theory.

(1) There is some authority for the proposition that the employer may be liable even if the conduct of no single employee is tortious if the conduct of a number of the employees can be regarded as a composite tort.[62] But it is difficult to see how innocence can be added to innocence to produce guilt.[63]

(2) Sometimes the servant has not committed a tort (or at any rate an actionable tort) but the master is still responsible. Thus in *Broom* v. *Morgan*[64] the defendant, the licensee of the "Bird in Hand" public house, West End Lane, Hampstead, employed both the plaintiff and her husband. The plaintiff was injured as a result of her husband's negligent act committed in the course of his employment, and the Court of Appeal held that she was entitled to hold the defendant vicariously responsible for it, even though she could not have sued her husband as the law then stood.[65] It has been said that such a decision (and indeed all decisions on vicarious liability) can be explained on the ground that it is the acts or omissions and not the torts of the servant which the law attributes to the employer: the true question is said to be whether the employer himself has broken his own personal duty to the plaintiff.[66] But *Broom* v. *Morgan* itself is explicable on the simple ground preferred by the majority of the Court of Appeal—an immunity from suit conferred upon A cannot be taken advantage of by B.[67] It would be different if the servant was under no duty at all, as distinct from enjoying an immunity from suit in respect of an admitted duty: in such a case the master is entitled to share the servant's exemption.[68] In so far as the new theory purports to supply a general basis for the doctrine of vicarious liability it is open to the following objections. First, it would revive the notion (forgotten since the mid-nineteenth century) that the master is liable

[58] *Young* v. *Edward Box & Co.* [1951] 1 T.L.R. 789, 793, *per* Denning L.J. In later cases Denning L.J. departed from this simple view (below, note 66), but more recently has re-adopted it: *Rose* v. *Plenty* [1976] 1 W.L.R. 141, 143.

[59] See above, § 157.

[60] *Staveley Iron and Chemical Co. Ltd.* v. *Jones* [1956] A.C. 627; *I.C.I. Ltd.* v. *Shatwell* [1965] A.C. 656; *Byrne* v. *Ireland* [1972] I.R. 241, 280.

[61] Above, § 170.

[62] *W. B. Anderson & Sons Ltd.* v. *Rhodes (Liverpool) Ltd.* [1967] 2 All E.R. 850.

[63] See above, § 145.

[64] [1953] 1 Q.B. 597.

[65] See above, § 164.

[66] See Uthwatt J. in *Twine* v. *Bean's Express Ltd.* [1946] 1 All E.R. 202, and Denning L.J. in *Broom* v. *Morgan* [1953] 1 Q.B. 597 and *Jones* v. *Staveley Iron Co. Ltd.* [1955] 1 Q.B. 474: his views were not approved by the H.L. in [1956] A.C. 627, or by Fullagar J. (*contra*, Taylor and Kitto JJ.) in *Darling Island Stevedoring Co.* v. *Long* (1957) 97 C.L.R. 36, or Windeyer J. in *Parker* v. *Commonwealth* (1965) 112 C.L.R. 295, but were in *Nadaraja* v. *Att.-Gen.* (1957) 54 *Ceylon Law Weekly* 65.

[67] There are authorities analogous to *Broom* v. *Morgan*. Thus, before the Criminal Law Act 1967, s. 1, I was able to be sued if my servant converted another's goods in circumstances amounting to felony but had not yet been prosecuted, and again I was vicariously liable for an assault by my servant although he had procured a certificate of dismissal under the Offences against the Person Act 1861, s. 45. See *Osborn* v. *Gillett* (1873) L.R. 8 Ex. 88; *Dyer* v. *Munday* [1895] 1 Q.B. 742; *Corney* v. *Ministry of Labour* [1959] *Pubic Law* 170.

[68] *I.C.I. Ltd.* v. *Shatwell* [1965] A.C. 656, 686.

because he commanded (expressly or impliedly) his servant to do the act: the modern view is based on the fact that the act was done in the course of the employment. Secondly, it would mean that master and servant would never be joint tortfeasors: each would have committed a distinct tort. Thirdly, it would mean that the master would be free from liability in many cases in which he is now held responsible. For his duty could not (save in some rather exceptional cases) be a strict one: it could only be a duty to take reasonable care. Hence it would be a defence for him to show that he had taken reasonable care to select an apparently competent servant—a defence which has never been allowed within modern times.[69] There seems to be no reason to depart from the traditional theory.

(3) There is authority for saying that if the tort in question is solely the breach of a duty imposed directly upon the servant himself either by common law[70] or statute[71] the master is not vicariously liable for it: he will be liable, it is said, only if he has committed (as he may have) a breach of some duty laid upon him personally, or has intervened in the matter with express orders to the servant. These dicta seem to have introduced an unnecessary subtlety and refinement into the law. They seem to be based upon the obsolete and misleading notion that vicarious liability depends upon the existence of the master's power to control the way in which the work is done: the true theory, however, is that the relationship of master and servant of itself gives rise to the liability, and that the right of control is only one factor in determining whether the relationship exists.[72]

(4) Sometimes an injured person will be in the position of being able to allege that the defendant is liable to him on two distinct grounds—first, as vicariously responsible for the tort of his servant; secondly, as personally responsible for a breach of some obligation laid directly on him.[73] So it seems that a hospital authority is not only vicariously responsible for those in its service but also under a primary obligation to take reasonable care to provide proper treatment.[74] But these duties are distinct in their nature and origin, and serious confusion may arise from a failure to keep them separate.[75] So a plaintiff who pleads that the defendant is vicariously liable may not be permitted to amend his claim to one based on personal responsiblity.[76]

In order that the doctrine of vicarious liability may apply, there are two conditions which must co-exist:

(1) The relationship of master and servant must exist between the

---

[69] Nor could the decision in *Armstrong* v. *Strain* [1952] 1 K.B. 232 (above, § 145) be reconciled with the new view. *Contra*, Williams (1956) 72 L.Q.R. 531–532.

[70] As with a police officer's power of arrest: *Att.-Gen. for N.S.W.* v. *Perpetual Trustee Co.* [1955] A.C. 457.

[71] As with a sanitary inspector's power to seize diseased animals: *Stanbury* v. *Exeter Corporation* [1905] 2 K.B. 838. The similar point raised in *England* v. *National Coal Board* [1953] 1 Q.B. 724 has been settled by the Mines and Quarries Act 1954, s. 159. See also *Stapley* v. *Gypsum Mines Ltd.* [1953] A.C. 663, 685. There is no clear English decision, but the High Court of Australia has decided that the master is not liable: *Darling Island Stevedoring Co. Ltd.* v. *Long* (1957) 97 C.L.R. 36.

[72] So far as Crown servants are concerned, the point is provided for by the Crown Proceedings Act 1947, s. 2 (3): *The Truculent* [1952] P. 1.

[73] As in *Fairline Shipping Corporation* v. *Adamson* [1975] Q.B. 180 (managing director and his company).

[74] See below, § 174.

[75] See *Staveley Iron and Chemical Co. Ltd.* v. *Jones* [1956] A.C. 627.

[76] *Esso Petroleum Co. Ltd.* v. *Southport Corporation* [1956] A.C. 218. See above, § 1.

defendant and the person committing the wrong complained of;
(2) The servant must in committing the wrong have been acting in the course of his employment.

We shall consider each in turn.

§ 174. WHO IS A SERVANT?

Agents and servants

A servant may be defined as any person employed by another to do work for him on the terms that he, the servant, is to be subject to the control and directions of his employer in respect of the manner in which his work is to be done.[77] If we use the term agent to mean any person employed to do work for another, we may say that agents are of two kinds, distinguishable as servants and independent contractors. It is for the first kind of agent only that his employer is responsible under the rule which we are now considering. When the agent is an independent contractor, his employer is not, in general, answerable for the torts either of the contractor himself or of his servants. But when the agent is a servant, his employer will answer for all torts committed in the course of the employment, whether or not the employer has obtained any benefit thereby.[78]

It is sometimes said that there may be vicarious liability for the torts of agents, and the cases in which car-owners have been held liable for the negligence of drivers who could not be described as servants in any normal sense of that term[79] certainly support this view. But the main reason why this view cannot be accepted is that it would entail that every independent contractor was an agent.[80] In any event both the House of Lords[81] and the Court of Appeal[82] have asserted that the long-established difference between the liability for the acts of a servant and the liability for the acts of an agent has not been abrogated by social changes in the fields of car ownership and industrial relations. It is for Parliament and not for the courts to change the fundamental principles of the common law.

Servant distinguished from independent contractor

What, then, is the test of this distinction between a servant and an independent contractor? The distinction is important not only for the doctrine of vicarious liability but also in relation to the legislation governing tax and social security benefits and unfair dismissal.[83] The test is the existence of a right of control over the agent in respect of the manner in which his work is to be done. A servant is an agent who works under the

---

[77] This definition can "hardly be bettered," according to MacKinnon L.J. in *Hewitt* v. *Bonvin* [1940] 1 K.B. 188, 191.
[78] The preceding paragraph was cited by Rowell C.J. in *T. G. Bright & Co. Ltd.* v. *Kerr* [1937] 2 D.L.R. 153, 165, with the remark that "Greatly as I respect any statement of law contained in Salmond, this statement does not appear to me to be adequate or exhaustive." But on appeal ([1939] 1 D.L.R. 193), three judges said Rowell C.J. was wrong.
[79] As in *Morgans* v. *Launchbury* [1973] A.C. 127.
[80] Atiyah, *Vicarious Liability*, Chap. 9.
[81] *Morgans* v. *Launchbury* [1973] A.C. 127.
[82] *Heatons Transport* v. *T.G.W.U.* [1972] 3 W.L.R. 73 (not considered in H.L.).
[83] *Massey* v. *Crown Life Co. Ltd.* [1978] 1 W.L.R. 676.

supervision and direction of his employer; an independent contractor is one
who is his own master. A servant is a person engaged to obey his employer's
orders from time to time; an independent contractor is a person engaged to
do certain work, but to exercise his own discretion as to the mode and time
of doing it—he is bound by his contract, but not by his employer's orders.[84]
Thus my chauffeur is my servant; and if by negligent driving he runs over
someone in the street, I am responsible. But the cabman whom I engage for
a particular journey is not my servant; he is not under my orders; he has
made a contract with me, not that he will obey my directions, but that he
will drive me to a certain place: if an accident happens by his negligence, he
is responsible and not I.[85] So I am responsible for the domestic servants in
my house, but I am not responsible for a skilled man whom I engage to do a
certain job in my house—for example, to paint it, or to mend a window.
(Nor, as we shall see, am I responsible to him for the safety of my premises
to the same degree as I am to a servant.)[86]

This may be put in another way by drawing a distinction between one
employed under a contract of service (a servant) and one employed under a
contract for services (an independent contractor). "The distinction between
a contract for services and a contract of service can be summarised in this
way: In the one case the master can order or require what is to be done,
while in the other case he can not only order or require what is to be done
but how itself it shall be done."[87] This right of control has always been
accepted[88] as a necessary, but not sufficient,[89] mark of a contract of service.
Other marks of a contract of service are (i) the master's power of selection
of his servant, (ii) the payment of wages or other remuneration, (iii) the
master's right of suspension or dismissal. One should also consider who
owns the tools or equipment, and "what in modern parlance is called
economic reality."[90] On the servant's side there is an obligation to present
himself for work at the agreed time, to obey all reasonable directions, to
continue to work for the agreed period, and also to indemnify his master
against liability to third parties.[91]

Yet it cannot be doubted that a contract of service may exist although one
or more of these elements is absent altogether or present only in an unusual
form.[92] In particular it is now accepted that the degree of control exercised
by the employer over the servant is no longer the decisive factor.[93] Thus,
although the right of control is present, the contract may be some other kind
of contract (*e.g.* one of carriage) if its provisions, taken as a whole, are

[84] *Honeywill and Stein* v. *Larkin* [1934] 1 K.B. 191, 196.
[85] *Performing Right Society* case [1924] 1 K.B. 762, 768; *Hamelin* v. *Canada Egg Products Ltd.* (1966) 56 W.W.R. 14, 18. "The late Mr. Southmayd, of New York, though he possessed a fine carriage and horses, used always to drive in a hired conveyance for this reason": Baty, *Vicarious Liability*, p. 33n. Note that the proprietors of cabs are responsible for the negligence of the drivers to whom they are hired (in London, under the London Hackney Carriages Act 1843; elsewhere, under the Town Police Clauses Act 1847), even though the relationship is really that of bailor and bailee.
[86] See below, § 181.
[87] *Collins* v. *Hertfordshire C.C.* [1947] K.B. 598, 615, *per* Hilbery J.
[88] At least since *Yewens* v. *Noakes* (1880) 6 Q.B.D. 530, 532–533. See W. H. D. Winder, Note (1964) 80 L.Q.R. 160.
[89] *Ready Mixed Concrete (South East) Ltd.* v. *Minister of Pensions* [1968] 2 Q.B. 497.
[90] *Argent* v. *Minister of Social Security* [1968] 1 W.L.R. 1749, 1760, *per* Roskill J.
[91] See below, § 183.
[92] *Kilboy* v. *S.E. Fire Area Joint Committee*, 1952 S.C. 280, 285–286.
[93] *Global Plant Ltd.* v. *Secretary of State* [1972] 1 Q.B. 139, 150.

inconsistent with its being a contract of service.[94] The mere fact that A has control over B does not make B the servant of A—otherwise a parent would be responsible for his child,[95] and a superior servant for his subordinates.[96] The House of Lords[97] and the Privy Council[98] have reserved the right to restate the elements of a contract of service in the light of modern industrial conditions,[99] for the powers of the Government to control or direct entry into employment and the restrictive practices of trade associations and trade unions may affect materially the position of an employer as it was formerly understood.[1]

The right of control

One criticism of this distinction between a contract of service and a contract for services is that there are many contracts which are undoubtedly contracts of service but in which the master does not or cannot control the way in which the work is done: the captain of a ship and the house surgeon at a hospital are each under a contract of service but each would greet with some astonishment a direction from his employer stating how a particular task was to be performed. Indeed in many cases the employer lacks the technical skill necessary to give such a direction. Or, even though he may have the skill, he may not have the time, as would be the case in fast-moving modern traffic, even if the employer were the most skilled of drivers and was sitting beside his servant.[2] Or, as is so often the case in industrial accidents, the employer may be a limited company incapable of controlling anybody except through its own superior servants or agents.[3] The significant fact may be the employer's right to control his insurance rather than to control his agent.[4] But although the distinction may ultimately rest on economic theories no longer fashionable,[5] and even though it may be conceded that control is not as determinative as it was once thought,[6] the distinction is still real.[7] An employer may well be unable or unwilling to give specific orders to a skilled man, thinking it best to allow him to carry out the task in his own way,[8] but that will not necessarily relieve the employer from liability. It does

---

[94] *Ready Mixed Concrete (South East) Ltd.* v. *Minister of Pensions* [1968] 2 Q.B. 497.
[95] See above, § 162.
[96] See below, § 175.
[97] *Short* v. *Henderson (J.W.) Ltd.* (1946) 62 T.L.R. 427, 429.
[98] *Montreal* v. *Montreal Locomotive Works Ltd.* [1947] 1 D.L.R. 161, 169.
[99] See now *Ferguson* v. *Dawson Ltd.* [1976] 1 W.L.R. 1213.
[1] *Re Hughes* [1966] 1 W.L.R. 1369, 1374–1375.
[2] *Union S.S. Co.* v. *Colville* [1960] N.Z.L.R. 100, 109.
[3] For their position, see § 175.
[4] *Nottingham* v. *Aldridge* [1971] 2 Q.B. 739, 749.
[5] See this brought out by Professor Kahn-Freund (1951) 14 M.L.R. 504.
[6] *Whittaker* v. *Minister of Pensions* [1967] 1 Q.B. 156, 167.
[7] "It is often easy to recognise a contract of service when you see it, but difficult to say wherein the difference lies. A ship's master, a chauffeur, and a reporter on the staff of a newspaper are all employed under a contract of service; but a ship's pilot, a taxi-man, and a newspaper contributor are employed under a contract for services. One feature which seems to run through the instances is that, under a contract of service, a man is employed as part of the business, and his work is done as an integral part of the business; whereas, under a contract for services, his work, although done for the business, is not integrated into it but is only accessory to it": *Stevenson, Jordan and Harrison Ltd.* v. *Macdonald Evans* [1952] T.L.R. 101, 111, *per* Denning L.J.
[8] "A good leader of men (and an employer is a leader of men) leaves to his men as much discretion as he can, otherwise unforeseen circumstances will upset the best laid plan": *Winter* v. *Cardiff R.D.C.* [1950] 1 All E.R. 819, 823, *per* Lord Oaksey. See also below, § 175.

not follow that because in any particular case it has not been found necessary to exercise a paramount authority that that authority does not exist.[9] There may well be such an authority in relation to incidental or collateral features of the employment. As Lord Porter said in *Mersey Docks and Harbour Board* v. *Coggins and Griffith (Liverpool) Ltd.*,[10] "the ultimate question is not what specific orders, or whether any specific orders, were given but who is entitled to give the orders as to how the work should be done." Indeed, in this very case, where the issue was whether the general or special employer was vicariously liable for the negligence of a driver of a crane, the driver had said in evidence: "I take no orders from anybody." That, as Lord Simonds remarked, was "a sturdy answer which meant that he was a skilled man and knew his job and would carry it out in his own way. Yet ultimately he would decline to carry it out in the appellants' way at his peril, for in their hands lay the only sanction, the power of dismissal."[11] Perhaps it would be better to make the test of control depend on the master's right to control the servant's time rather than the manner of doing his job in that time[12]—what has been called the "when" and the "where," rather than the "how," of the work.[13]

Hospital cases. These principles have been much discussed in a series of cases dealing with the liability of hospital authorities for their staff. For many years uncertainty prevailed because of the opinion expressed in *Hillyer* v. *St. Bartholomew's Hospital*[14] that a hospital was not responsible for the negligence of its professional staff (including trained nurses) in matters involving professional care and skill as distinct from matters of a purely administrative nature. But in *Gold* v. *Essex C.C.*[15] the Court of Appeal repudiated this opinion and held a hospital authority liable for the negligence of a radiographer employed under a full-time contract of service. The position of the permanent medical staff was considered in *Collins* v. *Hertfordshire C.C.*,[16] where the defendants were held liable for the negligence of a resident house-surgeon employed under a contract of service, and by the Court of Appeal in *Cassidy* v. *Ministry of Health*.[17] In the latter case the plaintiff's hand was rendered useless by the negligent post-operational treatment afforded by the full-time employees (assistant medical officer, house-surgeon and nurses) of the hospital authority, each of whom was employed under a contract of service. The fact that these employees were exercising professional care and skill was held to be no defence. There can be no doubt that the principle of these cases applies to hospital authorities such as regional hospital boards and hospital manage-

---

[9] *Samson* v. *Aitchison* (1911) 30 N.Z.L.R. 160, 165.
[10] [1947] A.C. 1, 17.
[11] *Ibid.* 20.
[12] W. H. D. Winder, Note, (1964) 80 L.Q.R. 160.
[13] Atiyah, *Vicarious Liability*, p. 47.
[14] [1909] 2 K.B. 820, 829. The court may have been influenced by a reluctance to impose liability upon voluntary charitable bodies (as hospitals then were) although it has been settled since *Mersey Docks and Harbour Board Trustees* v. *Gibbs* (1866) L.R. 1 H.L. 93 that for the purpose of vicarious liability there is no difference between charitable bodies and others.
[15] [1942] 2 K.B. 293; Lord Denning was counsel for the plaintiff: see (1959) 5 J.S.P.T.L. 85.
[16] [1947] K.B. 598 (lethal cocaine injected instead of harmless procaine).
[17] [1951] 2 K.B. 343.

ment committees, and that they will accordingly be liable for any negligence established against their permanent medical staff.[18]

It is said to be uncertain whether there is liability for a visiting or consulting surgeon or physician (although in *Roe* v. *Minister of Health*[19] the Court of Appeal was prepared to impose liability for the acts of a part-time specialist anaesthetist), as such a person is not employed under a contract of service so as to attract the operation of the doctrine *respondeat superior*.[20] But it seems that there is no need to pray in aid of that doctrine. Under the National Health Service Act 1946, a hospital authority is itself under a duty to provide treatment and not merely to make arrangements for treatment by and at the sole risk of independent specialist contractors. This duty, the scope of which in any particular case is a question of fact, is one which cannot be delegated, and the professional man who performs it does so as the agent of the hospital authority (unless he has been selected and employed by the patient himself).[21] Hence the word "consultant" is now rather a title denoting the holder's place in the hospital staff than a term denoting his relationship with the hospital authority.[22] The courts today will hold that the hospital is also liable for the acts of its nurses done in the operating theatre on the orders of the surgeon.[23]

Gratuitous service[24]

One person may be the servant of another although employed not continuously, but for a single transaction only, and even if his service is gratuitous or *de facto* merely, provided that the element of control is present. The relationship of master and servant is commonly a continuing engagement in consideration of wages paid; but this is not essential. The service may be merely gratuitous,[25] as when a child acts *de facto* as the servant of his father. But this must not be taken too far. The owner of a dog is hardly liable if a friend takes it for a walk and a pedestrian trips over the lead carelessly held.[26] Nor is a householder liable if a guest, as distinct from a hired domestic help, carelessly pours hot tea over a fellow-guest.[27] For it must always be remembered that the mere existence of a right of control is not sufficient to found liability. Otherwise a parent would always be

---

[18] *Macdonald* v. *Glasgow Western Hospitals Board of Management*, 1954 S.C. 453. It is also generally accepted that the hospital authority and not the Minister of Health is the proper defendant even though the hospital authority is carrying on the services of the Crown: *Pfizer Corporation* v. *Minister of Health* [1965] A.C. 512. This is the assumption of circular H.M. (54) (issued by the Ministry of Health), which contains detailed provisions for the conduct of such actions, in so far as they may effect the various possible parties—doctors, hospital authorities, and medical defence societies.

[19] [1954] 2 Q.B. 66.

[20] *Gold's Case* [1942] 2 K.B. 293, 299, 305, 313; *Collins* v. *Hertfordshire C.C.* [1947] K.B. 598, 619; *Cassidy* v. *Ministry of Health* [1951] 2 K.B. 343, 351, 358.

[21] *Razzel* v. *Snowball* [1954] 1 W.L.R. 1382; *Macdonald* v. *Glasgow Western Hospitals Board of Management*, 1954 S.C. 453.

[22] *Razzel* v. *Snowball* [1954] 1 W.L.R. 1382, 1386.

[23] *Gold's Case* [1942] 2 K.B. 293, 299, 305, 313; *Cassidy's Case* [1951] 2 K.B. 343, 361–362; *Fox* v. *Glasgow South Western Hospitals*, 1955 S.L.T. 337.

[24] Atiyah, *Vicarious Liability*, Chap. 13; Osborough, "The Vicarious Liability of the Vehicle Owner" (1971) 6 *Irish Jurist* 77.

[25] *Johnson* v. *Lindsay* [1891] A.C. 371, 377. See the cases on volunteers below, § 189.

[26] *Nottingham* v. *Aldridge* [1971] 2 Q.B. 739, 749.

[27] *Contra, Moynihan* v. *Moynihan* [1975] I.R. 192.

responsible for the torts of his child,[28] or the Crown for the torts of its prisoners.[29] But the owner[30] of a motor-vehicle who asks or permits another to drive it may find that the fact of ownership very easily gives rise to an inference that the driver was his servant or agent.[31] The right of control which is the test of the existence of a contract of service may be deduced from the fact that the owner of the motor-car remains in it while allowing another to drive,[32] even though the speed of modern traffic or his own intoxicated state,[33] may render his right of control meaningless.

Vehicle owners

The social desirability of compensating persons injured in traffic accidents led to an extension of the concept of gratuitous service. Some courts even favoured the view that the owner of a family car should be held responsible for the negligent driving of any member of the household whom he permitted to drive it. So the Court of Appeal once held a wife, owner of a Jaguar, responsible for an accident when her husband used the car for a "night-out," and asked a friend to drive him home when he became intoxicated.[34] But this decision was unanimously reversed by the House of Lords.[35] Such a change in the basic concept of vicarious liability must be made by Parliament and not by the courts. Until the law has been so changed in England,[36] it is clear that in order to fix vicarious liability on the owner of a car in such a case it must be shown that the driver was using it for the owner's purposes, under delegation of a task or duty.[37] Mere permission to use the vehicle is not enough to establish vicarious liability. Nor is it enough to show, as was once thought,[38] that the owner had an interest or concern in the safe use of the vehicle, for every bailor can be said to have an interest in the safety of the article lent. Still, the fact that the journey is at the owner's request[39] is some evidence that the driver was acting as the owner's agent. It may be helpful to ask whether the proposal for the use of the car emanated from the owner or from the driver.[40] But it is not necessary for the plaintiff to prove a contract between the owner and the driver, as distinct from a casual social agreement.[41] Conversely, the mere fact that the car is being used for the owner's purposes, but without his consent, will not involve him in responsibility.[42] This conclusion is indeed implicit in the deci-

---

[28] See above, § 162.
[29] See above, § 157.
[30] In the economic, rather than the legal sense. Nobody has yet sought to make a finance company liable for its vehicles let on hire-purchase.
[31] *Rambarran* v. *Gurrucharran* [1970] 1 W.L.R. 556.
[32] *Samson* v. *Aitchison* [1912] A.C. 844; *The Trust Co.* v. *de Silva* [1956] 1 W.L.R. 376.
[33] As in *Morgans* v. *Launchbury* [1973] A.C. 127.
[34] *Launchbury* v. *Morgans* [1971] 2 Q.B. 245.
[35] [1973] A.C. 127.
[36] The Irish Parliament made the change as long ago as 1933: the governing provision now in that jurisdiction is the Road Traffic Act 1961, s. 118.
[37] [1973] A.C. 127, 135, 140.
[38] *e.g.* in *Ormrod* v. *Crosville Motor Services Ltd.* [1953] 1 W.L.R. 409.
[39] As in *Ormrod* v. *Crosville Motor Services Ltd.* [1953] 1 W.L.R. 409.
[40] *Carberry* v. *Davies* [1968] 1 W.L.R. 1103.
[41] *Morgans* v. *Launchbury* [1973] A.C. 127, 140.
[42] *Klein* v. *Caluori* [1971] 1 W.L.R. 619; *Nottingham* v. *Aldridge* [1971] 2 Q.B. 739.

sion in *Morgans* v. *Launchbury*,[43] which emphasises that the consent or permission of the owner is not enough to fix him with liability.

§ 175. Servant with Two Masters[44]

A servant may have two or more masters at the same time in respect of different employments. In particular a master may lend or hire his servant to another person for a certain transaction so that *quoad* that employment he becomes the servant of the person to whom he is so lent, though he remains for other purposes the servant of the lender. When a servant is sent by his employer to do work for another, it is a question depending on the construction of the contract between the general and the special employer, whose servant he may be.[45] If there is no contract, then it is a question of fact, depending on the nature of the arrangement and the degree of control exercised over the servant. When a servant has thus two masters, the responsibility for a tort committed by him lies exclusively upon the master for whom he was working when he did the act complained of. It must lie on one or the other; for the law does not recognise a several liability in two principals who are unconnected,[46] although it would certainly simplify the task of the plaintiff if it did,[47] and the normal law relating to joint tortfeasors applied. The question may be important in modern industrial conditions, when the servants of an employer and the servants of his contractors and sub-contractors often work together on the same task—for example, a large new building. As in general an employer is not liable for the torts of his contractor's servants (and never for their acts of collateral negligence[48]), a person injured by such a tortious act will be obliged, if he wishes to proceed against the main employer, to prove that he has become the temporary master of the delinquent servant of his own contractor.[49] This may be important for the injured party, as the main contractor may be as solvent as the sub-contractor is insolvent,[50] but it may not be easy to prove such a transfer[51] in view of the decision of the House of Lords in *Mersey Docks and Harbour Board* v. *Coggins and Griffith (Liverpool) Ltd.*,[52] which has been followed in the Irish Republic[53] and in Northern Ireland.[54]

The appellant board owned a number of mobile cranes, each driven by a skilled workman engaged and paid by them, which they were accustomed to let out on hire. The respondents, master stevedores, hired one of these cranes so driven to load a ship. The contract provided that the driver should be the servant of the hirers. In the course of the loading a third party was

---

[43] [1973] A.C. 127.
[44] Atiyah, *Vicarious Liability*, Chap. 18.
[45] See *Arthur White Ltd.* v. *Tarmac Civil Engineering Ltd.* [1967] 1 W.L.R. 1508 for a contract which did transfer liability from the general to the special employer.
[46] *Laugher* v. *Pointer* (1826) 5 B. & C. 547, 558; *Treacy* v. *Robinson & Son* [1937] I.R. 255, 266.
[47] Atiyah, *Vicarious Liability*, p. 156.
[48] See below, § 184.
[49] He may be able to frame his claim in another way—*e.g.* for breach of the duty owed by an occupier of premises.
[50] See above, § 7.
[51] See *McArdle* v. *Andmac Roofing Co. Ltd.* [1967] 1 W.L.R. 356.
[52] [1947] A.C. 1.
[53] *Lynch* v. *Palgrave Murphy Ltd.* [1964] I.R. 150.
[54] *Maguire* v. *Lagan Navigation Ltd.* [1976] N.I. 49.

injured through the driver's negligence. At the time of the accident the
stevedores had the immediate direction and control of the operations to be
executed by the crane-driver—*e.g.* the power to order him to pick up and
move a particular piece of cargo. But they had no power to direct the driver
how to manipulate the crane or its controls. It was held that the appellant
board as the driver's general employers were responsible for his negligence.

In such a case a heavy burden of proof rests on the general or permanent
employer to shift his prima facie responsibility for the negligence of servants
employed and paid by him onto the hirer who for the time being has the
advantage of the particular service rendered.[55] No universal test can be laid
down, although it may be helpful to ask whether the servant was transferred
or only the use and benefit of his work.[56] "Who is paymaster, who can
dismiss,[57] how long the alternative service lasts, what machinery is
employed,[58] have all to be kept in mind."[59] If an employer sends out a skilled
man to work for another, the general rule is that he remains the servant of
the general employer.[60] The question will often be answered by asking who
has the right to control the way in which the work is to be done.[61] The hirer
(as in the *Mersey Docks* case) may often have control over the task to be
performed but not over the way in which it is to be done.[62] The hirer may, of
course, intervene to give a specific order which is in fact obeyed by the
workman, and if damage then results he will in general be liable as a joint
tortfeasor with the workman, but this is not by reason of any relationship of
master and servant.[63] Nor is it conclusive as against the injured third party
that (again as in the *Mersey Docks* case) the two employers have made a
contract stating whose servant the employee is to be on the particular occasion: servants cannot be transferred from one service to another without
their consent.[64] Such a contract may determine the liability of the employers
inter se[65] but it has only an indirect bearing on the question which of them is
to be regarded as master of the workman on a particular occasion.[66] But it
may be easier to assume a transfer of employment when the plaintiff is not a
third party, but the workman himself, who is claiming that he has been

---

[55] Indeed the burden is so heavy that it has not been discharged in any reported case in this
century: *Bhoomidas* v. *Singapore Harbour Authority* [1978] 1 All E.R. 956.
[56] *Ready Mixed Concrete Ltd.* v. *Yorkshire Traffic Area Licensing Authority* [1970] 2 Q.B.
397, 405.
[57] This is not conclusive: *Garrard* v. *Southey & Co.* [1952] 2 Q.B. 174, 180.
[58] There may be a distinction between a case where a complicated piece of machinery and a
driver are lent and a case where labour only (and not necessarily of a skilled character) is
transferred. In the former case it may be more difficult to assume that the general employer
intended to allow the hirer to direct the manner in which a valuable piece of machinery
should be operated: *Garrard* v. *Southey & Co.* [1952] 2 Q.B. 174, 179; *Denham* v.
Midland Employers Mutual Assurance Ltd. [1955] 2 Q.B. 437.
[59] *Mersey Docks* case [1947] A.C. 1, 17, *per* Lord Porter.
[60] *Savory* v. *Holland and Hannen and Cubitts (Southern) Ltd.* [1964] 1 W.L.R. 1158.
[61] Yet see Lord Wright in *Century Insurance Co.* v. *Northern Ireland Road Transport Board*
[1942] A.C. 509, 517. The fact that he who has the right of control may not have the
requisite technical knowledge to give an order is irrelevant: see above, § 174.
[62] See *Lynch* v. *Palgrave, Murphy Ltd.* [1964] I.R. 150.
[63] *Mersey Docks* case [1947] A.C. 1, 12.
[64] *Mersey Docks* case [1947] A.C. 1, 14. Such a transfer may well involve difficult questions
of health and accident insurance benefits, and this increases the strength of the presumption against it: *Denham* v. *Midland Employers Mutual Assurance Ltd.* [1955] 2 Q.B. 437.
[65] *Arthur White Ltd.* v. *Tarmac Civil Engineering Ltd.* [1967] 1 W.L.R. 1508.
[66] *Herdman* v. *Walker (Tooting) Ltd.* [1956] 1 W.L.R. 209; *The Panther and the Ericbank*
[1957] P. 143.

injured by reason of the hirer's failure to fulfil some duty owed by an employer to his servants—*e.g.* the duty to provide a safe system of work.[67]

Superior servant not responsible for subordinates

A superior servant is not the master of the inferiors who are under his control, and he is not responsible for their torts. Thus strike pickets appointed by a trade union are not the servants of the executive committee or general secretary of the union.[68] Again, the directors of a company are not responsible for the torts committed by inferior servants of the company, although those servants are appointed and controlled by the directors, and even though the directors are the sole directors and sole shareholders in the company.[69] Any other decision would destroy the whole object of the Companies Act, which is that the limited liability of a company should be substituted for the unlimited liability of individuals, so that enterprise and adventure may be encouraged. But it should be noted that an officer of a company, such as a chairman or managing director, is capable of being a joint tortfeasor with the company itself if he procures or directs the commission of a tort.[70] The company might then also be vicariously responsible for his wrongful acts.[71] It has become increasingly common so to join individual servants in actions against their companies.[72]

§ 176. THE COURSE OF EMPLOYMENT

A master is not responsible for a wrongful act done by his servant unless it is done in the course of his employment. It is deemed to be so done if it is either (1) a wrongful act authorised by the master, or (2) a wrongful and unauthorised mode of doing some act authorised by the master.[73] It is clear that the master is responsible for acts actually authorised by him: for liability would exist in this case, even if the relation between the parties was merely one of agency, and not one of service at all.[74] But a master, as opposed to the employer of an independent contractor, is liable even for acts which he has not authorised, provided they are so connected with acts which he has authorised that they may rightly be regarded as modes—although improper modes—of doing them. In other words, a master is responsible not merely for what he authorises his servant to do, but also for the way in which he does it. If a servant does negligently that which he was authorised to do carefully, or if he does fraudulently that which he was authorised to do honestly, or if he does mistakenly that which he was authorised to do correctly, his master will answer for that negligence,

---

[67] *Johnson* v. *J. H. Beaumont Ltd.* [1953] 2 Q.B. 184; *Gibb* v. *United Steel Companies Ltd.* [1957] 1 W.L.R. 668.
[68] *Bird* v. *O'Neal* [1960] A.C. 907.
[69] *British Thomson-Houston Co.* v. *Sterling Accessories Ltd.* [1924] 2 Ch. 33; *Performing Right Society* v. *Ciryl Theatrical Syndicate* [1924] 1 K.B. 1, 14.
[70] *Wah Tat Bank Ltd.* v. *Chan* [1975] A.C. 507, 514–515.
[71] *Yuille* v. *B. & B. Fisheries (Leigh) Ltd. and Bates* [1958] 2 Lloyd's Rep. 596.
[72] See *Fairline Shipping Corpn.* v. *Adamson* [1975] 1 Q.B. 180.
[73] *Poland* v. *Parr (John) & Sons* [1927] 1 K.B. 236, 240; *Warren* v. *Henlys Ltd.* [1948] 2 All E.R. 935, 937; *Ilkiw* v. *Samuels* [1963] 1 W.L.R. 991, 997, 1002, 1004.
[74] See above, § 170.

fraud or mistake.[75] On the other hand, if the unauthorised and wrongful act of the servant is not so connected with the authorised act as to be a mode of doing it, but is an independent act, the master is not responsible: for in such a case the servant is not acting in the course of his employment, but has gone outside of it.[76]

As is often the case, the principle is easy to state but difficult to apply. All that can be done is to provide illustrations on either side of the line. In a border-line case the plaintiff may be helped by the onus of proof.[77] Once it is conceded that the servant was doing something in his working hours, on his employers' premises, and that his act had a close connection with the work which he was employed to do, then the onus[78] shifts to the employers to show that the act was one for which they were not responsible. It should also be noted that the courts today are reluctant to dissect the servant's employment into its component parts—e.g. loading, driving and unloading a vehicle. A broad approach is now preferred.[79]

(i) Outside the course of employment

In *Beard* v. *London General Omnibus Co.*[80] the defendant company was held not liable for a collision caused by the negligence of the conductor of an omnibus, who, at the end of a journey and in the temporary absence of the driver, took upon himself to drive the omnibus for the purpose of turning it round for the return journey. Driving an omnibus is not a mode, rightful or wrongful, of performing the duties of a conductor; and the accident happened, not because the conductor failed to perform his own duty, but because without authority he attempted to fulfil that of a driver. But today, when almost everyone can drive a motor-vehicle, there is a tendency to distinguish *Beard's* case.[81] So it has been held that a sevant who is authorised to drive a motor-vehicle, and who permits an unauthorised person to drive it in his place, may yet be acting within the scope of his employment.[82] The act of permitting another to drive may be a mode, albeit an improper one, of doing the authorised work. The master may even be responsible if the servant impliedly, and not expressly, permits an unauthorised person to

---

[75] *Barwick* v. *English Joint Stock Bank* (1867) L.R. 2 Ex. 259, 266. He will be liable in an action on the case, even if a trespass is an incident in the wrong done: *Goh Choon Seng* v. *Lee Kim Soo* [1925] A.C. 550.

[76] The preceding paragraph constitutes "the well-known passage in Salmond on Torts" (*Keppel Bus Co.* v. *Ahmad* [1974] 1 W.L.R. 1082, 1084), which has been approved by different courts on many occasions: *Canadian Pacific Ry.* v. *Lockhart* [1942] A.C. 591, 599; *Warren* v. *Henlys Ltd.* [1948] 2 All E.R. 935, 938; *London County Council* v. *Cattermoles (Garages) Ltd.* [1953] 1 W.L.R. 997, 998; *Hamilton* v. *Farmers' Ltd.* [1953] 3 D.L.R. 382, 386; *Kirby* v. *National Coal Board*, 1958 S.C. 514, 533, 540; *Daniels* v. *Whetstone Entertainments Ltd.* [1962] 2 Lloyd's Rep. 1, 5 ("cannot be bettered": *per* Davies L.J.); *Ilkiw* v. *Samuels* [1963] 1 W.L.R. 991; *Att.-Gen.* v. *Hartley* [1964] N.Z.L.R. 785, 801; *Kay* v. *I.T.W. Ltd.* [1968] 1 Q.B. 140, 153–154; *Stone* v. *Taffe* [1974] 1 W.L.R. 1575, 1582.

[77] This is doubted by Edmund Davies L.J. in *Chapman* v. *Oakleigh Animal Products Ltd.* (1970) 8 K.I.R. 1063, 1071.

[78] In the sense of the evidential burden, as distinct from the legal burden, which throughout rests on the plaintiff.

[79] *Rose* v. *Plenty* [1976] 1 W.L.R. 141.

[80] [1900] 2 Q.B. 530.

[81] *Kay* v. *I.T.W. Ltd.* [1968] 1 Q.B. 140.

[82] *Ilkiw* v. *Samuels* [1963] 1 W.L.R. 991.

drive the vehicle, as where he leaves it unattended in such a manner that it is reasonably foreseeable that the third party will attempt to drive it, at least if the driver retains notional control of the vehicle.[83]

A master is not responsible for the negligence or other wrongful act of his servant simply because it is committed at a time when the servant is engaged on his master's business. It must be committed in the course of that business, so as to form a part of it, and not be merely coincident in time with it. On this principle, in *Abrahams* v. *Deakin*,[84] the owner of a public-house in Holborn was held not liable for the act of his servant who, while in charge of the bar, gave the plaintiff, a solicitor, into custody on a mistaken charge of having attempted to pass bad money. This is further illustrated by cases in which a servant invites another to come onto his master's property,[85] or invites one who is already lawfully upon it to engage in some activity or to go to some place which is outside the area of the original invitation,[86] and that other, although knowing that the servant has no authority to extend such an invitation,[87] accepts it and is injured as a result of the defective condition of the property. The plaintiff's status as a trespasser is not altered by the servant's unauthorised invitation, for which the master is not responsible.[88]

(ii) *Within the course of employment*

We may contrast the decision of the House of Lords in *Century Insurance Co.* v. *Northern Ireland Road Transport Board*,[89] in which the driver of a petrol lorry, whilst transferring petrol from the lorry to an underground tank, struck a match to light a cigarette and threw it on the floor, and thereby caused a fire and an explosion which did great damage. It was held that his employers were liable. His negligence was negligence in the discharge of his duties. Though the act of lighting his cigarette was done for his own comfort and convenience and was in itself both innocent and harmless, it could not be regarded in abstraction from the circumstances and was a negligent method of conducting his work. A similar case in which the decision went the other way was *Hilton* v. *Thomas Burton (Rhodes) Ltd.*[90] Four workmen were permitted to use their employers' Bedford van to go to work on a demolition site in the country. After half a day's work they decided to knock off and go to a cafe seven miles away for tea. When they had almost reached the cafe they changed their minds and started back again. On that journey one of them was killed through the negligent driving of another. The employer was not vicariously responsible, as the men were

---

[83] *Fulwood House Ltd.* v. *Standard Bentwood Chair Ltd.* [1956] 1 Lloyd's Rep. 160.
[84] [1891] 1 Q.B. 516.
[85] As in *Twine* v. *Bean's Express* [1946] 1 All E.R. 202 (motor vehicle).
[86] As in *Hillen* v. *I.C.I. (Alkali) Ltd.* [1936] A.C. 65 where the crew of a barge invited stevedores to unload cargo in a dangerous and prohibited way. Lord Atkin said: "The owner of a barge does not clothe the crew with apparent authority to use it or any part of it for purposes which are known to be extraordinary and dangerous. The crew could not within the scope of their employment convert it into a dancing hall or drinking booth. They could not invite stevedores to work the engines or take part in the navigation."
[87] If he did not know this, he may still be without a remedy: see n. 9 below.
[88] But trespassers are now regarded more favourably: *Rose* v. *Plenty* [1976] 1 W.L.R. 141.
[89] [1942] A.C. 509.
[90] [1961] 1 W.L.R. 705.

"on a frolic of their own."[91] No term could be implied[92] that the employees were directly or indirectly discharging their duties to their employer.

Implied and ostensible authority[93]

There is a difference between implied authority and ostensible authority. The servant's act may be an authorised act for the purposes of vicarious liability even if it is done solely for his own purposes if in the circumstances the permission of the master can be implied. Ostensible authority may be held to exist if, whatever the true state of affairs, the stranger has been misled by appearances. So as a general rule a servant has an implied authority upon an emergency to endeavour to protect his master's property if he sees it in danger or has reasonable ground for thinking that he sees it in danger.[94] In an emergency a servant may be impliedly authorised to do an act different in kind from the class of acts which he is expressly authorised or employed to do.[95] So in *Poland* v. *John Parr & Sons*,[96] where a carter, whilst off duty, seeing his employers' wagon apparently being robbed by boys, in order to prevent the theft struck one of the boys, who in consequence was run over and lost his leg, the employers were held liable. The distinction between this case and *Abrahams* v. *Deakin*[97] is that the courts are more ready to infer that a servant has authority to act for the protection of his master's property than that he has authority to punish for a supposed infringement of the law.

In *Lloyd* v. *Grace, Smith & Co.*[98] the House of Lords in effect decided that the scope of an agent's employment is not limited to the rightful performance of his duties, but may be extended to his apparent or ostensible authority. So a modern company secretary is no longer a mere clerk but an officer with extensive duties and responsibilities, who can be regarded as having ostensible authority to hire cars to meet the company's customers.[99]

§ 177. EFFECT OF EXPRESS PROHIBITION

Even express prohibition of the wrongful act is no defence to the master at common law,[1] if that act was merely a mode of doing what the servant was employed to do.[2] Thus in *Limpus* v. *London General Omnibus Co.*[3] the defendant company was held liable for an accident caused by the act of one of its drivers in drawing across the road so as to obstruct a rival omnibus. It was held to be no defence that the company had issued specific instructions to its drivers not to race with or obstruct other vehicles: the driver whose

---

[91] This phrase, which goes back to Parke B. in *Joel* v. *Morison* (1834) 6 C. & P. 501, 503, is often used as a rough test of liability.
[92] As it was in *Elleanor* v. *Cavendish Woodhouse Ltd.* [1973] 1 Lloyd's Rep. 313.
[93] See Atiyah, *Vicarious Liability*, Chaps. 20–24.
[94] *D'Urso* v. *Sanson* [1939] 4 All E.R. 26. A similar rule applies to claims for industrial injury benefit under the Social Security Act 1975, s. 54.
[95] *Poland* v. *John Parr & Sons* [1927] 1 K.B. 236, 244.
[96] [1927] 1 K.B. 236.
[97] [1891] 1 Q.B. 516.
[98] [1912] A.C. 716. See Reynolds, Note (1967) 83 L.Q.R. 189; Atiyah, Chap. 23.
[99] *Panorama Developments (Guildford) Ltd.* v. *Fidelis Furnishing Fabrics Ltd.* [1971] 2 Q.B. 711.
[1] It may also be no defence to a claim for industrial injury benefit under the Social Security Act 1975, s. 52.
[2] *London County Council* v. *Cattermoles (Garages) Ltd.* [1953] 1 W.L.R. 997, 1005.
[3] (1862) 1 H. & C. 526.

conduct was in question was engaged to drive and the act which did the mischief was a negligent mode of driving for which his employers must answer,
irrespective of any authority or of any prohibition.[4] The question has often
arisen when the servant, in breach of an express prohibition, gives a lift in a
motor-vehicle which he is employed to drive, and the person to whom he
gives the lift[5] is injured as a result of his negligence. Thus in *Rose* v. *Plenty
and Co-operative Retail Services Ltd.*[6] the first defendant was a milkman
employed by the second defendants, who expressly prohibited him from
using children in the performance of his duties. Nevertheless the milkman
permitted the plaintiff, a 13-year-old boy, to ride on the milk float to assist
him in the delivery of milk—and, indeed, had paid him to do so. As these
acts were done for the purpose of the employers' business, they were held
vicariously responsible for the milkman's negligence in driving the float.[7]
There may also be liability in the case of a stray passenger, picked up by a
driver to whom no contrary instruction had been given,[8] or if the plaintiff
could show that the defendants had acquiesced in their servant's breaches of
his instructions.[9] The question also arises in cases in which the servant
deviates from the route prescribed by the master and an accident occurs
during the deviation. If the deviation constitutes an unauthorised *journey*,
then the servant is "on a frolic of his own."[10] But if the deviation is no more
than an unauthorised *route*, then it is a question of fact and degree whether
the deviation is sufficiently substantial to put it outside the course of
employment.[11] Further illustrations are unnecessary; for in every case it is a
question of fact whether a servant is acting within the scope of his
employment.[12]

§ 178. WHICH TORTS GIVE RISE TO LIABILITY

The liability of a master extends to assault,[13] or arson[14] or fraud and other
wilful wrongs, such as passing off or breach of copyright, no less than to
negligence. If his servant does fraudulently what he is employed to do
honestly, the master must answer for the fraud. Thus in *Barwick* v. *English
Joint Stock Bank*[15] the defendant bank was held liable for a fraudulent
representation made to the plaintiff by the manager of one of the bank's
branches in relation to the business under his control. It was long supposed

---

[4] "The law casts upon the master a liability for the act of his servant in the course of his
employment; and the law is not so futile as to allow a master, by giving secret instructions
to his servant, to discharge himself from liability": *per* Willes J. 539.
[5] In North America such a person is called a rider.
[6] [1976] 1 All E.R. 97.
[7] Note that the plaintiff also recovered judgment for £600 against the milkman personally.
[8] *Twine* v. *Bean's Express Ltd.* [1946] 1 All E.R. 202, 205.
[9] *Conway* v. *Wimpey (George) Ltd.* [1951] 2 K.B. 266, 274–275. *Cf. Young* v. *Box (Edward)
Ltd.* [1951] 1 T.L.R. 789; *Kearney* v. *Clare Line Co. Ltd.* [1966] I.R. 338, 344. These
cases show an alternative approach to the problem: the plaintiff in such a case is a
trespasser on the defendants' vehicle (and nonetheless so because the driver may have
induced him to believe he was not) and so unable to recover from the employers (as distinct
from the driver). But now that trespassers are more favoured these decisions have less
authority: *Rose* v. *Plenty* [1976] 1 W.L.R. 141.
[10] *Joel* v. *Morison* (1834) 6 C. & P. 501, 503, *per* Parke B.
[11] *A. & W. Hemphill Ltd.* v. *Williams* [1966] 2 Lloyd's Rep 101.
[12] *Marsh* v. *Moores* [1949] 2 K.B. 208, 215.
[13] See Rose, "Liability for an Employees' Assaults" (1977) 40 M.L.R. 420.
[14] *Photo Production Ltd.* v. *Securicor Ltd.* [1980] A.C. 827.
[15] (1867) L.R. 2 Ex. 259.

that where the fraud or other wilful wrongdoing of the servant was committed for his own benefit and not on his master's behalf, his master was not responsible. It was, however, decided by the House of Lords in *Lloyd* v. *Grace, Smith & Co.*,[16] distinguishing *Barwick* v. *English Joint Stock Bank*,[17] that this was not so. The facts, as recounted by Lord Macnaghten,[18] were that "in the office of Grace, Smith & Co., a firm of solicitors in Liverpool of long standing and good repute, the appellant, Emily Lloyd, a widow woman in humble circumstances, was robbed of her property. It was not much, just a mortgage for £450 bequeathed to her by her late husband, and two freehold cottages at Ellesmere Port which she had bought herself without legal assistance for £540 after her husband's death. But it was all she had; and after the order of the Court of Appeal reversing a decision in her favour pronounced by Scrutton J., who tried the case with a special jury, she was compelled to appeal to this House as a pauper."[19] The "robbery" was committed by the solicitor's managing clerk, who had induced Mrs. Lloyd, a client of the firm, to transfer a mortgage to him by fraudulently misrepresenting the nature of the deed of assignment, and thereupon obtained and misappropriated the mortgage moneys. The solicitor was held liable to his client for the fraud although it was committed solely for the benefit of the fraudulent servant himself. The House held that so long as a servant is acting within the scope of the employment entrusted to him, his employer is liable for all frauds committed by that servant, whether for the benefit of the employer or for his own profit. It has since been decided[20] that the employer is similarly liable even though the fraud involves a forgery and even though the victim of the fraud is not a client but a third person who is damnified by relying on the apparent or ostensible authority possessed by the clerk. Although the decision in *Lloyd* v. *Grace, Smith & Co.*[21] came as a surprise at the time it was given, these cases would seem to be covered by the principle enunciated by Sir John Holt C.J. in *Hern* v. *Nichols*,[22] and, despite its early date, often since approved: "Seeing somebody must be a loser by this deceit, it is more reason that he, that employs and puts a trust and confidence in the deceiver, should be a loser than a stranger."[23]

Malice of servant[24]

The mere fact that the servant has acted out of personal vengeance or malice or resentment or by way of a practical joke[25] will not necessarily exonerate the master provided that the act was within the scope of his employment. But this proviso is important, for the courts have shown a distinct reluctance to hold an employer liable for aggressive acts committed

---

[16] [1912] A.C. 716.
[17] On this see Cross, *Precedent in English Law* (2nd ed., 1968), 42–43.
[18] "To generations who have passed their lives in the law his is truly *clarum et venerabile nomen*": *Public Trustee* v. *I.R.C.* [1960] A.C. 398, 409, *per* Viscount Simonds.
[19] [1912] A.C. 716, 727.
[20] *Uxbridge Permanent Benefit Building Society* v. *Pickard* [1939] 2 K.B. 248.
[21] [1912] A.C. 716.
[22] (c. 1700), 1 Salk. 289.
[23] See *British Railway Traffic Co.* v. *Roper* (1939) 162 L.T. 217, 221; *Rose* v. *Plenty* [1976] 1 W.L.R. 141.
[24] See Rose, "Liability for an Employee's Assaults" (1977) 40 M.L.R. 420.
[25] *Hudson* v. *Ridge Manufacturing Co. Ltd.* [1957] 2 Q.B. 348.

by a servant even though they are generated by the latter's employment. So
there has been no liability for an assault committed by an ill-mannered bus
conductor.[26] So when a patron of a dance-hall was assaulted twice by a
steward[27] in the course of ejecting unruly persons, first inside the hall and
secondly outside it, it was held that the second assault, as distinct from the
first, was an act of private retribution for which the employers were not
liable.[28]

But although a principal is liable for the fraud or malice of his agent, an
innocent agent is not liable for the fraud or malice of his principal—there is
no doctrine of *respondeat inferior*.[29]

Bailments

The liability of a master for thefts committed by his servant of property
bailed to the master or otherwise committed to his charge was once a matter
of doubt. It used to be believed that a bailee was not responsible for the loss
of the property by theft, even though the thief was the bailee's own servant,
unless the bailee had given occasion for the theft by his own negligence or
by that of some other servant employed to take care of the property.[30] But
this belief is a heresy since the Court of Appeal held in *Morris* v. *Martin
(C.W.) & Sons Ltd.*[31] that the responsibility of the bailee must depend on
whether the servant by whom the theft is committed is one to whom the
charge or custody of the thing stolen has been entrusted by his master. If
such a servant[32] steals the thing entrusted to him, he is acting nevertheless in
the course of his employment—he is doing fraudulently what he is
employed to do honestly—and his employer is liable for the loss of the
goods.[33] So in *Morris* v. *Martin* a firm of cleaners to whom a furrier had
sent the plaintiff's mink stole were liable for the theft of the stole by an
employee[34] whose duty it was to clean it. It will be a question of fact whether
the employment merely provided an opportunity for the theft, or was part of
the task on which the servant was engaged.[35] But if the theft is committed by
a servant to whom the property has not been entrusted, the theft is outside
the scope of his employment, and the master is not responsible unless he has
been negligent in the selection of the servant or the theft has been induced by
his own negligence or by the negligence of some other servant to whom the
charge of the property has been committed.[36] The distinction between

---

[26] *Keppel Bus Co.* v. *Ahmad* [1974] 1 W.L.R. 1082.
[27] Aggression is to be expected from such a person, who is not employed "for his intelligence
or beauty": *Lehnert* v. *Nelson* [1947] 4 D.L.R. 473, 475.
[28] *Daniels* v. *Whetstone Entertainments Ltd.* [1962] 2 Lloyd's Rep. 1, 10.
[29] *Egger* v. *Chelmsford (Viscount)* [1965] 1 Q.B. 248.
[30] *Cheshire* v. *Bailey* [1905] 1 K.B. 237.
[31] [1966] 1 Q.B. 716.
[32] The employment of a known thief may prevent the employer from relying on an exemption
clause: *W. J. Lane* v. *Spratt* [1970] 2 Q.B. 480.
[33] There is no liability for pecuniary loss caused by delay in delivery of goods: *B.W.I.A.* v.
Bart (1966) 11 W.I.R. 378.
[34] The employee might himself have been sued in conversion: *Fairline Corporation* v.
Adamson [1975] Q.B. 180, 190.
[35] *Leesh River Tea Co. Ltd.* v. *British India S.N. Co. Ltd.* [1967] 2 Q.B. 250.
[36] *Morris* v. *C. W. Martin & Sons Ltd.* [1966] 1 Q.B. 716. The decision has been approved
both by the Privy Council (*Port Swettenham Authority* v. *T. W. Wu Ltd.* [1979] A.C. 580,
591.) and the House of Lords (*Photo Production Ltd.* v. *Securicor Transport Ltd.* [1980]
A.C. 827.)

personal and vicarious liability is one which may be helpful here as elsewhere.[37]

Improper use of master's property

The same principle applies when a servant makes unauthorised use not amounting to larceny of property which has been bailed to his employer—for example, a garage-hand who takes out for his own purpose a motor-car left with his employers for repair and damages it. In such a case, it will be no defence to an action by the bailor for the employer to plead that the servant was "on a frolic of his own"[38] if that servant was one whom the charge or custody of the car has been entrusted, for in such a case there will have been a breach of the implied term of the bailment to use reasonable care in the custody of the goods.[39] But there can be little doubt that such a plea would be a good defence if the plaintiff was a bystander or other person injured by the servant's careless driving; in such a case the bailment is irrelevant.[40] For a master is not responsible for the negligence of his servant in the unauthorised use of his master's property for the servant's own purposes. This rule has been applied on many occasions when harm has been done by the negligent driving of servants while using their masters' vehicle for their own ends.[41]

Permission is not authority

On the same principle, a master is not responsible for the negligence of his servant while engaged in doing something which he is permitted to do for his own purposes, but not employed to do for his master. I am liable only for what I employ my servant to do for me, not for what I allow him to do for himself.[42] If I permit my servant for his own ends to drive my car, I am not liable for his negligence in doing so.[43] In this respect he is not my servant, but a mere bailee to whom I have lent my property; and there is no more reason why I should answer for his conduct in such a matter than reason why I should answer for that of my friends or my children to whom, without personal negligence on my own part, I lend or entrust property that may be made the instrument of mischief.[44] In such a case, much may depend on whether the act was performed in the master's interests or supposed interests,[45] or was reasonably incidental to the servant's duties.[46]

§ 179. THE DOCTRINE OF COMMON EMPLOYMENT

Formerly a master was not responsible for negligent harm done by one of his servants to a fellow-servant engaged in a common employment with him.

---

[37] See below, § 181.
[38] *Joel* v. *Morison* (1834) 6 C. & P. 501, 503, *per* Parke B.
[39] *Morris* v. *C. W. Martin & Sons Ltd.* [1966] 1 Q.B. 716.
[40] *Adams (Durham) Ltd.* v. *Trust Houses Ltd.* [1960] 1 Lloyd's Rep. 380, 385–386.
[41] See, *e.g.* *Hilton* v. *Thomas Burton (Rhodes) Ltd.* [1961] 1 W.L.R. 705; *Jones* v. *McKie and Mersey Docks and Harbour Board* [1964] 1 W.L.R. 960.
[42] *Hilton* v. *Thomas Burton Ltd.* [1961] 1 W.L.R. 705.
[43] *Britt* v. *Galmoye* (1928) 44 T.L.R. 294.
[44] *Carter & Co. (Pty.) Ltd.* v. *McDonald*, 1955 (1) S.A. 202, 208.
[45] See above, § 176.
[46] See above, § 177.

This rule was abolished after many years of criticism[47] by the Law Reform (Personal Injuries) Act 1948, but some account of its history and nature is necessary. The rule is generally, but perhaps mistakenly,[48] traced back to *Priestley* v. *Fowler*.[49] The doctrine was based on a fictitious implied term in the contract of service to the effect that the servant agreed to run the risks naturally incident to his employment, and that one of these risks was that of harm due to the negligence of a fellow-servant. The doctrine became complex and subtle with the passing years. In particular, it could no longer be stated in the simple form that one servant could not claim damages from his master for the negligence of a fellow-servant. Two conditions had to be filled before the doctrine could apply: (1) The servant injured and the servant causing the injury must have been fellow-servants—*i.e.* they must be servants of the same master; (2) they must at the time of the accident have been engaged in a common work.[50]

Curtailment and abolition[51]

The story of how the doctrine of common employment was gradually limited in scope and eventually abolished is an interesting one. Legislation and judicial decision have combined with each other to complicate the story: the effect of neither can really be understood in isolation from the other. Still, it is convenient to deal first with the changes made by statute. In 1880 the Employers' Liability Act abrogated the defence in a limited number of strictly defined cases.[52] Next the important decision of the Court of Appeal in *Groves* v. *Wimborne (Lord)*[53] made it plain that common employment was no defence when the cause of action was based on the breach of a statutory duty imposed on the employer.[54] The doctrine was at last abolished by the Law Reform (Personal Injuries) Act 1948, with effect from July 5, 1948. Section 1 (3) of that Act provides that any provision contained in a contract of service or apprenticeship or agreement collateral thereto which would have the effect of excluding or limiting any liability of the employer in respect of personal injuries[55] caused to the person employed or apprenticed by the negligence of persons in common employment[56] with him shall be void.

---

[47] It was described by MacKinnon L.J. as "a doctrine which lawyers who are gentlemen have long disliked": *Speed* v. *Thomas Swift* [1943] K.B. 557, 569. Yet a nationalised industry did not disdain the defence: *Harrison* v. *National Coal Board* [1951] A.C. 639.

[48] Newark, "Bad Law" (1966) 17 N.I.L.Q. 469, 477.

[49] (1837) 3 M. & W.1.

[50] See *Lancaster* v. *L.P.T.B.* [1948] 2 All E.R. 796. It is appropriate that the *Lancaster* case should have been argued on the very day on which the Law Reform (Personal Injuries) Bill received the Royal Assent.

[51] Howells, "*Priestley* v. *Fowler* and the Factory Acts" (1963) 26 M.L.R. 367.

[52] If the respondents in *Smith* v. *Baker & Sons* [1891] A.C. 325 (see below, § 188) had been successful, workmen would have been deprived of even the limited protection given by the Act of 1880. As Lord Devlin observed (41 M.L.R. at 506), the English judges "outpaced Parliament" in the provision of remedies for workmen.

[53] [1898] 2 Q.B. 402.

[54] See the interesting (extra-judicial) remarks of Lord Reid in 248 H.L. Deb., 5s., col. 1338.

[55] The doctrine never seems to have applied in cases of other torts (*e.g.* assault, defamation), but there is no reason to suppose its revival would be encouraged: Chapman, *Statutes*, p. 27.

[56] See *Smith* v. *British European Airways* [1951] 2 K.B. 893. The phrase "common employment" appears in the section, and for that reason alone it is still necessary to know something of the old law.

The Act also provides a solution for the problem of how far the right of action for damages for personal injuries should be affected by the provision of benefits under the National Insurance (Industrial Injuries) Act 1946 (now the Social Security Act 1975). It had been suggested[57] that an injured person should not have the same need met twice over and the question was considered by a departmental committee on alternative remedies.[58] The committee recommended that the injured person should not be put to his election between damages and benefits, but was divided on the question how far the measure of damages should be affected by such benefits. The Act adopted a compromise solution. By section 2 (1), in an action for damages for personal injuries against an employer, there must in assessing the damages be taken into account,[59] against any loss of earnings or profits which has accrued or probably will accrue to the injured person from the injuries, one-half[60] of the value of any rights which have accrued or probably will accrue to him from the injuries in respect of industrial injury benefit, industrial disablement benefit, or sickness benefit for the five years from the accrual of the cause of action. The amount of the disablement benefit to be taken into account should be half of such proportion of the gratuity as the five-year period (or the unexpired period thereof) bears to the injured person's expectation of life, if the gratuity is for life, or to any less period specified for the duration of the gratuity.[61] Unemployment benefit,[62] but not national assistance,[63] must also be taken into account. The benefits to be taken into account are not restricted to those paid during the period of incapacity but include those paid after that period has ceased, even though paid as a result of a mistake on the part of the insurance officer.[64] This deduction is made from the total of the damages assessed before any deduction is made for contributory negligence, or, if the damages otherwise recoverable are limited by any Act or contract, from the damages as they would have been assessed apart from the limitation.

It is certainly odd that damages should be set off against benefits, and not vice versa: why should the wrongdoer be entitled to throw part of his burden on to the taxpayer?[65]

§ 180. THE NATIONAL INSURANCE ACTS

The Workmen's Compensation Act 1897 adopted a new approach. The Act provided compensation for a workman injured in the course of his employment even though no negligence on the part of his employer or anyone else

---

[57] In the Beveridge Report (Cmd. 6404 (1942)), which recommended the abolition of the right of action for personal injuries in these cases.

[58] Under Sir Walter Monckton (Cmd. 6860 (1945–46)). The relationship between tort and social security is considered further above, § 7.

[59] The court has no discretion in the matter, except in so far as it need not make an exact calculation but can take a round sum: *Flowers* v. *George Wimpey & Co. Ltd.* [1956] 1 Q.B. 73.

[60] In Ireland the whole value: Social Welfare Act 1966, s. 39.

[61] *Hultquist* v. *Universal Pattern and Precision Engineering Co. Ltd.* [1960] 2 Q.B. 467. The complex practical problems which may arise are carefully considered in (1960) 110 L.J.(N.) 649.

[62] *Parsons* v. *B.N.M. Laboratories Ltd.* [1964] 1 Q.B. 95.

[63] *Foxley* v. *Olton* [1965] 2 Q.B. 306.

[64] *Flowers* v. *George Wimpey & Co. Ltd.* [1956] 1 Q.B. 73.

[65] See the Pearson Report, Cmd. 7054, §§ 164–172.

could be shown. The basis of the workman's claim was not negligence or fault but accident. It was assumed that the employer would insure against this liability and pass on the premium to the public by way of increased prices.[66] The scope of the Act was widened by subsequent legislation which was consolidated in the Workmen's Compensation Act 1925.

This in turn was replaced by the National Insurance (Industrial Injuries) Act 1946 and later legislation. The National Insurance Acts have now been consolidated in the Social Security Act 1975, which establishes a basic scheme of contributions and benefits.

(1) Insurable employment

The Act covers all those employed in Great Britain under a contract of service or apprenticeship, written or oral, express or implied. There is not (as there was under the Workmen's Compensation Acts) any upward limit on the amount of earnings. This very large class is the main category of insured persons. Self-employed persons are also covered.

(2) Risks insured against

Work-related accidents continue to receive the preferential treatment to which they have been entitled since 1892. A person in insurable employment is entitled to benefit if he suffers personal injury by accident arising out of and in the course of his employment, and he is also insured against any pre-scribed disease or prescribed personal injury not so caused by accident but which is a disease or injury due to the nature of that employment. The terms "personal injury," "accident," and "arising out of and in the course of such employment" were taken over from the Workmen's Compensation Acts. They had been the subject of a vast number of judicial decisions, and it was thought "better to stick to the devil we know than to fly to the devils we know not of."[67] Once the insured person has shown that the accident arose in the course of the employment he is relieved (in the absence of evidence to the contrary) from proving that it arose out of the employment (s. 50). The Act (ss. 52–55) specifically brings within the employment four cases which would normally be outside it: (1) If the injured person at the time of the accident is acting in breach of any rules of his employment, statutory or otherwise, or is acting without his employer's instructions the accident is deemed to have arisen out of and in the course of his employment, provided (i) the accident would be deemed to have so arisen if there had not been any such breach, and (ii) the act is done for the purpose of and in connection with the employer's trade or business. (2) Where the insured person is injured while travelling to or from work in his employer's transport. (3) Where the insured person suffers an accident while in or about premises at

---

[66] It is worth noting that Lord Bramwell in his dissenting speech in *Smith* v. *Baker & Sons* [1891] A.C. 325, 340, said: "I am not certain it would not be a good thing to give a person injured as the plaintiff was a right to compensation, perhaps from the state, even where there was no blame in the master; even where there was blame in the servant. Men would not wilfully injure·themselves, and then compensation would be a part of the cost of the work." This point (made, incidentally, by one who was a sturdy exponent of Victorian individualism) has been developed at much greater length by some modern writers: see above, § 7.

[67] 414 H.C.Deb. (5th ser.), col. 270.

which he is employed for the purposes of his employer's business when aiding in an emergency (actual or supposed) at those premises persons who are (or are thought to be) imperilled, or is acting to avert or minimise serious damage to property.[68] (4) When the accident is caused by another person's "misconduct, skylarking or negligence."

(3) Contributions

A proportion is paid by the employer and another proportion by the workman. A further contribution is provided by Parliament. So in effect the state and not the employer is the insurer.

(4) Benefits

The term "compensation" is not used. The unemployment and industrial injury benefit and sickness benefit to which the claimant is entitled is not "compensation" or "damages" at common law but money payable under a statutory scheme of insurance.

(5) Administration

This has been taken away from the ordinary courts and vested in the Secretary of State. Claims to injury benefit are made in the first instance to the local insurance officer; from him an appeal may be taken to a local appeal tribunal and thence to the National Insurance Commissioner (a barrister of ten years' standing).

§ 181. MASTER'S COMMON LAW DUTIES TO SERVANTS[69]

Before the Employers' Liability Act 1880, the courts themselves intervened to mitigate the severity of the doctrine of common employment. The doctrine went no further than to imply in the contract of employment a term by which the servant agreed to bear the risks arising from the negligence of a fellow-servant who had been selected with due care by the master. The doctrine did not mean that the servant impliedly agreed to hold the master immune from liability for the consequences of the master's own personal negligence. The common law has always held the master to be under an obligation to take reasonable care for his servant's safety. The nature of the duty was expounded by Lord Herschell in *Smith* v. *Charles Baker & Sons*[70] in words which have been consistently cited with approval: "It is quite clear that the contract between employer and employed involves on the part of the former the duty of taking reasonable care to provide proper appliances, and to maintain them in a proper condition, and so to carry on his operations as not to subject those employed by him to unnecessary risk." Those words are important both in prescribing the positive obligation and in negativing by implication anything higher.[71]

Four points may be made about the scope and nature of the duty which

---

[68] See the rescue cases at common law, below, § 189.

[69] See Fleming, "Tort Liability for Work Injury," Vol. 15 of the *International Encyclopaedia of Comparative Law* (1975).

[70] [1891] A.C. 325, 362.

[71] *Davie* v. *New Merton Board Mills Ltd.* [1959] A.C. 604, 620. Though the duty is not absolute "a high standard is exacted": *Winter* v. *Cardiff R.D.C.* [1950] 1 All E.R. 819, 822, *per* Lord Porter.

they impose on the employer. First, there are several judicial warnings against interpreting the duty too strictly.[72] Secondly, the duty in question is apparently capable of being pleaded either in contract or in tort. There are conflicting judicial dicta on the matter.[73] In some cases it may be advantageous to sue in contract,[74] in others in tort.[75] The normal practice is to sue in tort. Thirdly, the duty is imposed upon the master himself, and if he entrusts the performance of it to another instead of performing it himself he is liable for the negligence of that other. The duty remains personal to the master even though he is obliged by statute to entrust to a duly qualified person the task of providing a safe system of work and is forbidden to interfere in the working himself.[76]

It was once held that an employer who buys from a reputable source a tool with a latent defect not discoverable by reasonable care which injures an employee had fulfilled his duty to take reasonable care for his safety.[77] But this decision was reversed by the Employer's Liability (Defective Equipment) Act 1969, s. 1, which imposes strict liability on an employer providing defective equipment[78] for the purposes of his business, and an employee[79] in consequence suffers personal injury.[80] In such a case, if the defect[81] is attributable wholly or partly to the fault of a third party (whether identified or not), the injury shall be deemed to be also attributable to negligence on the part of the employer. The employer may then recover from the manufacturer—who may still be sued directly by the employee. The employer is obliged to insure under the Employers' Liability (Compulsory Insurance) Act 1969.

Fourthly, it has been customary ever since *Wilsons and Clyde Coal Co.* v. *English*[82] to expound these duties under the threefold heading of the provision of a competent staff of men, adequate material, and a proper system of work. But there are not in truth three duties but only one duty.[83] It is only for convenience of exposition that the simple duty to take reasonable care is regarded as having three different facets.

(1) Competent staff of men

This duty still exists, though it is usually of little importance since the abolition of the defence of common employment has made an employer

---

[72] *Pease* v. *British India Steam Navigation Co. Ltd.* [1953] 1 Lloyd's Rep. 207; *Chattaway* v. *Maltby & Sons Ltd.* [1954] 2 Lloyd's Rep. 424; *Buckingham* v. *Daily News Ltd.* [1956] 2 Q.B. 534.

[73] So the House of Lords has said both that the duty is tortious (*Davie* v. *New Merton Board Mills Ltd.* [1959] A.C. 604) and that it is contractural (*Lister* v. *Romford Ice Co. Ltd.* [1957] A.C. 555). The various dicta are surveyed in *Matthews* v. *Kuwait Bechtel Corporation* [1959] 2 Q.B. 57.

[74] *e.g.* where the wrong has been committed out of the jurisdiction: *Matthews* v. *Kuwait Bechtel Corporation* [1959] 2 Q.B. 57. See above, § 3.

[75] *e.g.* where the claim is in a county court: see above, § 3.

[76] *Wilsons and Clyde Coal Co.* v. *English* [1938] A.C. 57, 81.

[77] *Davie* v. *New Merton Board Mills Ltd.* [1959] A.C. 604.

[78] As defined in s. 1 (3), includes any plant and machinery, vehicle aircraft and clothing. If vehicles had not been included, the Occupiers' Liability Act 1957, s. 1 (3) (see above, § 90) might have governed the matter.

[79] As defined in s. 1 (3). Note that a self-employed person is excluded.

[80] As defined in s. 1 (3), this includes loss of life, any impairment of a person's physical or mental condition, and any disease.

[81] It is the defect, and not the injury, which must be attributed to the third party's fault.

[82] [1938] A.C. 57.

[83] See below, § 182.

liable for the negligence of the plaintiff's fellow-servants. But an employer has been held personally liable for practical jokes[84] or bullying[85] by the plaintiff's fellow-servants.

(2) Proper plant, appliances and premises

"The providing of proper plant," said Sir Arthur Channell in *Toronto Power Co.* v. *Paskwan,*[86] "as distinguished from its subsequent care, is especially within the province of the master rather than of his servants. . . . It is true that the master does not warrant the plant, and if there is a latent defect which could not be detected on reasonable examination, or if in the course of working plant becomes defective and the defect is not brought to the master's knowledge and could not by reasonable diligence have been discovered by him, the master is not liable, and further, a master is not bound at once to adopt the latest improvements and appliances." Although the duty is not only to provide proper plant but also to maintain it, it is not broken by a merely temporary failure to keep in order or adjust the plant or appliances. The duty to provide proper appliances obliges the employer to make reasonable provision for avoiding or mitigating the foreseeable consequences of injury.[87]

The duty to provide and maintain safe premises is similar. It extends as well to the servant's working place as to the means whereby the servant has to reach it.[88] The duty is to make the place of work as safe as reasonable care and skill will permit[89]; it is probably not as high as the obligation under the Factories Act 1961, to provide safe premises and means of access.[90] Neither the statutory nor the common law duty is broken if the place of work becomes unsafe through some transient or exceptional condition.[91] The proper approach can be seen in *Latimer* v. *A.E.C. Ltd.*[92] The respondents employed more than four thousand persons in their fifteen-acre factory at Southall. One August day an exceptionally heavy rainstorm caused the floor to be flooded with water. The water eventually subsided but an oily film remained on the surface of the floor. The respondents did their best to get rid of the film before the plaintiff came on duty with the night-shift but he slipped and was injured. The House of Lords held that the respondents were not in breach of their duty. The degree of risk involved was not sufficiently great to justify the trial judge's finding that the works should have been closed down until the danger had disappeared.

(3) Safe system of work

The duty covers all acts which are normally and reasonably incidental to the day's work.[93] The most valuable analysis of the scope of the duty is to be

---

[84] *Hudson* v. *Ridge Manufacturing Co. Ltd.* [1957] 2 Q.B. 348.
[85] *Veness* v. *Dyson, Bell & Co.* [1965] C.L.Y. 2691.
[86] [1915] A.C. 734, 738. ("One of the most eminent judges before whom I ever had the good fortune to practise": *R.* v. *Kritz* [1950] 1 K.B. 82, 87, *per* Lord Goddard C.J.)
[87] *Smith* v. *Howdens Ltd.* [1953] N.I. 131.
[88] *Hurley* v. *Sanders & Co. Ltd.* [1955] 1 All E.R. 833, 835 (this point is not reported in [1955] 1 W.L.R. 470).
[89] *Naismith* v. *London Film Productions Ltd.* [1939] 1 All E.R. 794, 798.
[90] *Latimer* v. *A.E.C. Ltd.* [1953] A.C. 643, 658.
[91] *O'Reilly* v. *National Rail and Tramway Appliances Co.* [1966] 1 All E.R. 499.
[92] [1953] A.C. 643.
[93] *Davidson* v. *Handley Page Ltd.* [1945] 1 All E.R. 235 (washing teacups).

found in the judgment of Lord Justice-Clerk Aitchison in *Wilsons and Clyde Coal Co.* v. *English*[94]: "Broadly stated, the distinction is between the general and the particular, between the practice and method adopted in carrying on the master's business of which the master is presumed to be aware and the insufficiency of which he can guard against, and isolated or day-to-day acts of the servant of which the master is not presumed to be aware and which he cannot guard against; in short, it is the distinction between what is permanent or continuous on the one hand and what is merely casual and emerges in the day's work on the other hand." For such a casual departure from the system the employer is not liable. It has been made plain[95] that the duty to provide a safe system may arise in relation to an isolated task which may never have to be repeated in exactly the same way—*e.g.* the loading and unloading of ships. The duty owed is to men of ordinary phlegm and fortitude, not to those who are unreasonably apprehensive[96]; but it is also owed to each servant as an individual. So all the circumstances relevant to that servant must be considered by a prudent employer, including the gravity of the injury which he may suffer if an accident occurs.[97]

As the standard of care required is no higher than that to be expected of an ordinary prudent employer the defendant will usually succeed if he shows that his sytem of protection is in accordance with the general practice in that particular trade,[98] or with the relevant statute or statutory regulations.[99] One common difficulty arises from the fact that men often disregard a system which has been established for their own protection. Their folly may be due either to inexperience or over-confidence. The employer must then consider the situation and do what is reasonable to ensure that a suitable system of protection is kept in operation: he cannot expect his workmen to lay down and operate a system for themselves. "Workmen are not in the position of employers. Their duties are not performed in the calm atmosphere of a boardroom with the advice of experts. They have to make their decisions on narrow window sills and other places of danger, and in circumstances in which the dangers are obscured by repetition."[1] Thus in *General Cleaning Contractors Ltd.* v. *Christmas*[2] the House of Lords held that it was not a safe system to employ window-cleaners to work outside high self-locking windows on a sill $6\frac{1}{4}$ inches wide and 27 feet above the ground without giving them any orders to keep one sash open or any appliance to prevent both sashes closing. The case shows clearly that in cases where perils are involved, which thought or planning might avoid or lessen, it may not be enough for the employer to entrust that thought or planning to the skill and experience, however great, of the man who carried out the work.[3] But there certainly are cases in which an employer is entitled to rely on a skilled man being sensible enough to avoid a danger of which he has been warned.[4] The relationship between employer and skilled workman is not equivalent to that

[94] 1936 S.C. 883, 904.
[95] *Colfar* v. *Coggins and Griffith (Liverpool) Ltd.* [1945] A.C. 197, 202.
[96] *Lawrence* v. *Daily Mirror Newspapers Ltd.* (unreported), 1954 C.A. 344.
[97] *Paris* v. *Stepney Borough Council* [1951] A.C. 367.
[98] See above, § 83.
[99] See above, § 87.
[1] *General Cleaning Contractors Ltd.* v. *Christmas* [1953] A.C. 180, 189, *per* Lord Oaksey.
[2] [1953] A.C. 180.
[3] *Barcock* v. *Brighton Corporation* [1949] 1 K.B. 339, 343 ("A system of work is not devised by telling a man to read the regulations and not to break them.")
[4] See *Qualcast (Wolverhampton) Ltd.* v. *Haynes* [1959] A.C. 743.

of a nurse and imbecile child,[5] or matron and patient,[6] or school-master and pupil.[7] The common law does not require employers to refuse to employ people who are willing to work with them simply because they think it is not in that person's best interests to do the work.[8]

Proof

The plaintiff is not obliged in every case to plead and prove an alternative system of work which would have been safe; in some cases it may be prudent for him to do so,[9] but in others it may be enough for him to allege that the system provided was dangerous and that a prudent employer would have done better.[10] But the onus is on the plaintiff to prove causation,[11] and this may be difficult when the fault complained of is one of omission.[12]

Contributory negligence[13]

It must be remembered that a great deal of work which has to be done is dangerous, and if it is not really practicable for the master to diminish or eliminate the danger then the risk of it is a necessary incident of the employment and a risk which the servant is paid to take.[14] Again, a servant who is aware that the work is dangerous and knows of the precautions which should be taken to avert the danger but yet does nothing may be guilty of contributory negligence and have to bear some of the loss himself. In actions under the Factories Act the courts have adopted a lenient standard by which to judge whether the workman is guilty of contributory negligence: for as the purpose of imposing the absolute statutory obligation is to protect the workman against those very acts of inattention which may constitute contributory negligence, too strict a standard would defeat the object of the statute. But this doctrine cannot be used so as to require any modification in the standard of care required of a workman in a simple case of common law negligence, where there is no evidence of repetitive work being performed under strain or for long hours at dangerous machines.[15] Still, if a skilled man adopts a dangerous course of conduct not for the sake of saving himself trouble but primarily in order to get on with his employer's business the courts will be slow to put blame on him.[16]

Servant working on premises of third party

The protection afforded by the law to one who is directed by his employer to work on premises occupied by a third party is not as clear as might be wished. First, the servant may possibly have a claim against some other contractor working on the premises who by his misfeasance has created a

---

[5] *Smith* v. *Austin Lifts Ltd.* [1959] 1 W.L.R. 100, 105.
[6] *Haynes* v. *Qualcast Ltd.* [1958] 1 W.L.R. 225, 230.
[7] *Withers* v. *Perry Chain Co. Ltd.* [1961] 1 W.L.R. 1314, 1320.
[8] *Withers* v. *Perry Chain Co. Ltd.* [1961] 1 W.L.R. 1314.
[9] *Vickers* v. *B.T.C. Docks Board* [1964] 1 Lloyd's Rep. 275.
[10] *Dixon* v. *Cementation Co. Ltd.* [1960] 1 W.L.R. 746.
[11] *McWilliams* v. *Sir William Arrol Ltd.* [1962] 1 W.L.R. 295.
[12] See above, §§ 82–83.
[13] See below, § 196.
[14] *Hurley* v. *Sanders & Co. Ltd.* [1955] 1 All E.R. 833, 836.
[15] *Staveley Iron and Chemical Co. Ltd.* v. *Jones* [1956] A.C. 627.
[16] *Machray* v. *Stewarts and Lloyds Ltd.* [1964] 3 All E.R. 716.

source of danger.[17] Secondly, it may be possible for him to establish that the occupier is in such close control of the situation as to have become his temporary employer, so as to owe him the duty which we have already expounded.[18] But at present the courts do not favour such claims.[19] Thirdly, the servant will be a lawful visitor of the occupier and so will be entitled to the common duty of care under the Occupiers' Liability Act 1957.[20]

It should be noted that until the common law was altered by the Occupiers' Liability Act the rule was that an invitee who continued his work or activities with knowledge of the danger which ultimately caused him injury was without remedy against the occupier.[21] So in order to safeguard workmen, it was held that a master who sent his men out to work on another's premises was still subject to his common law obligation to take reasonable care for their safety by providing a safe system of work on those premises [22] as distinct from seeing that the premises themselves were safe.[23] But fine distinctions are now to be avoided: the three headings under which it is customary to consider the liability of a master to his servant are really only manifestations of the fundamental duty to take such care as is reasonable in the circumstances.[24] In some circumstances a warning of the danger may be enough[25]; in other cases the employer may be obliged to take positive steps to protect the employee, and in such cases the fact that the servant knowingly incurs the risk only goes to the question of his contributory negligence.[26] The cases have produced the rather curious result[27] that a skilled man working on the premises of a third party is not very well protected. For the more skilled he is the less likely is he to be the temporary servant of the occupier, and if the latter is sued for breach of the common duty of care he can plead that he is entitled to expect that a skilled man will guard against the normal risks of his calling.[28] It seems that if the person injured in such a case is a "labour-only" independent contractor and not a workman, he is not owed the *Smith* v. *Baker* duty.[29] A householder is entitled to expect that a self-employed window-cleaner will take his own precautions against risks customarily incidental to his work, such as ill-balanced weights or loose plywood.[30]

§ 182. SUMMARY OF MODERN LAW

What effect have these changes had on the legal relationship of master and servant? First, it is plain that though the benefits payable under the National

---

[17] See above, § 92.
[18] Above, § 175.
[19] Savory v. *Holland and Hannen and Cubitts (Southern) Ltd.* [1964] 1 W.L.R. 1158.
[20] See above, § 93.
[21] *London Graving Dock Co. Ltd.* v. *Horton* [1951] A.C. 737.
[22] *General Cleaning Contractors Ltd.* v. *Christmas* [1953] A.C. 180.
[23] *Cilia* v. *James (H.M.) & Sons (A Firm)* [1954] 1 W.L.R. 721.
[24] *Wilson* v. *Tyneside Window Cleaning Co. Ltd.* [1958] 2 Q.B. 110, 121.
[25] *Smith* v. *Austin Lifts Ltd.* [1959] 1 W.L.R. 100, 117.
[26] *A. C. Billings & Sons Ltd.* v. *Riden* [1958] A.C. 240; *Minto* v. *Great Northern Transport Co. Ltd.* [1959] N.Z.L.R. 749.
[27] See, *e.g. Savory* v. *Holland and Hannen and Cubitts (Southern) Ltd.* [1964] 1 W.L.R. 1158.
[28] See above, § 93.
[29] *Jones* v. *Minton Construction Co. Ltd.* (1973) 15 K.I.R. 309.
[30] *Bates* v. *Parker* [1953] 2 Q.B. 231; *Smith* v. *Austin Lifts Ltd.* [1959] 1 W.L.R. 100, 115. (Note that the employers in this case had on four different occasions warned the occupier that the premises were unsafe.)

Insurance Acts, are greatly superior to those provided by the Workmen's Compensation Acts, there are still very many cases where a servant injured in the course of his employment will wish to institute proceedings at common law. "Perhaps the most-quoted case in the courts today" is *Wilsons and Clyde Coal Co.* v. *English.*[31] For the damages awarded by the courts (even after the deductions described above have been made) will often exceed the benefits made available by the Ministry of Social Security. State compensation does little to promote safety in the workshop. But, on the other hand, common law liability arises from only a small proportion of accidents.[32] Secondly, it seems that the threefold obligation of *Wilsons'* case is now capable of being expressed more simply and truly as a duty to take reasonable care for the servant's safety.[33] The reason for drawing a distinction between a failure to take reasonable care to provide proper plant and a safe system of work (for which the master was personally responsible) and an isolated act of negligence by a fellow-servant (for which the master was not) has disappeared with the defence of common employment itself. The master is now vicariously liable for all negligent acts of his servants committed in the course of their employment and it seems irrelevant that the plaintiff is a fellow-servant and not a stranger.[34] This view has been adopted in Scotland[35] and in Australia[36] and it is suported by a dictum of Lord Simon.[37] But the distinction between the duty owed by a master personally and the vicarious liability which rests upon him as master may be important if the defendant is a corporation, for the responsibility for the proper discharge of its duties lies squarely on the board of directors in the light of the knowledge which it has or ought to have from the personnel of the company.[38]

§ 183. SERVANT'S DUTIES TO MASTER

One who is under a contract of service owes to his employer a number of different duties:

(1) Duty to take reasonable care[39]

There is an implied term in the contract of service that the servant will take reasonable care not only of his master's property entrusted to him but also generally in the performance of his duties.[40] It seems that this duty is to

[31] [1938] A.C. 57. The phrase is from Birkett, "Law and Social Change in Contemporary Britain" (1952) 15 M.L.R. 277, 279. See, too, the comments in *McLeod* v. *Bauer* (1951) 85 Ll.L.R. 125, 126; *Chattaway* v. *T. F. Maltby Ltd.* [1954] 2 Lloyd's Rep. 424; *Knight* v. *Glen Line Ltd.* [1954] 2 Lloyd's Rep. 392, and above, § 7.
[32] E. Young, *Industrial Injuries* (1964), pp. 162–165.
[33] See the remarks of Pearce L.J. in *Wilson* v. *Tyneside Window Cleaning Co. Ltd.* [1958] 2 Q.B. 110, 121, cited above, § 181.
[34] *Smallwood* v. *Lamport and Holt Lines Ltd.* [1959] 2 Lloyd's Rep. 213, 225.
[35] *Lindsay* v. *Connell & Co.*, 1951 S.C. 281, 285.
[36] *Katsilis* v. *B.H.P.* [1978] A.L.R. 181, 208.
[37] *Bristol Aeroplane Co.* v. *Franklin* [1948] W.N. 341. See also *Winter* v. *Cardiff R.D.C.* [1950] 1 All E.R. 819, 823. This may be the meaning of Lord Simonds' description of safe system of work as "the familiar though inapt phrase": *Paris* v. *Stepney B.C.* [1951] A.C. 367, 378. Lord Tucker objected to it on the ground that it "omits what is an essential element in the cause of action, *viz.* negligence": *General Cleaning Contractors Ltd.* v. *Christmas* [1953] A.C. 180, 195. It must be admitted that the phrase is still used, both in statute (Mines and Quarries Act 1954, s. 193), and in the cases.
[38] *Wright* v. *Dunlop Rubber Co. Ltd.* (1972) 13 K.I.R. 255.
[39] Atiyah, *Vicarious Liability*, Chap. 38.
[40] *Century Insurance Co. Ltd.* v. *N.I.R.T.B.* [1942] A.C. 509, 519.

be thought of as an implied contractual obligation rather than as a particular example of the tort of negligence.[41] Hence if the servant breaks this obligation his employer has a cause of action for breach of contract to recover damages for such loss as is not too remote a consequence of the breach. The damage which the master has suffered may be either physical[42] or financial—e.g. the sums which the master, as vicariously responsible for his servant's torts, has paid to third parties injured by such a tort committed in breach of the implied contractual obligation.[43] Thus in *Lister* v. *Romford Ice and Cold Storage Co. Ltd.*[44] the appellant and his father were employed by the respondents. One day Lister junior, in the course of his duties as a lorry driver, knocked down Lister senior, who was acting as his mate. Lister senior recovered damages for his personal injuries from the respondents, as being vicariously liable for the tort of Lister junior. The respondents' insurers, in virtue of their right of subrogation and of an express term in the policy of insurance, then instituted proceedings against the appellant (in the name but without the knowledge of the respondents) to recover the damages and costs which had been paid to his father. The House of Lords, by a bare majority, held that the respondents, whose rights were of course neither greater nor less than if they had not been insured, were entitled to succeed. The House refused to accept the appellant's argument that a term should be implied in his contract of service to the effect that he was entitled to the benefit of any insurance taken out by his employers.

There may be difficulty if a master who has himself been negligent pursues a claim for breach of implied contractual duty against his negligent servant.[45] Unless the servant can plead that the claim should be made under the 1935 Act,[46] it is hard to see how the damages can be less than 100 per cent.[47]

(2) Duty to indemnify at common law

The ancient rule of the common law (now abolished) that one wrongdoer could not seek indemnity or contribution from another[48] was confined to cases in which the person seeking redress must be presumed to have known that he was committing an illegal act. If he were personally free from any blame, it seems that he could sue the other for redress. So an agent would be entitled to indemnity if he reasonably believed that the act was one which his principle could authorise. It seems clear on principle, also, that in all cases of vicarious liability the person held vicariously liable for the tort of another must have a right of indemnity as against that other.[49] Thus a master who

---

[41] *Lister* v. *Romford Ice and Cold Storage Co. Ltd.* [1957] A.C. 555.

[42] In *Digby* v. *General Accident Fire and Life Assurance Corporation Ltd.* [1943] A.C. 121, Miss Merle Oberon, the film actress, recovered £5,000 damages from her own chauffeur for injuries caused by his negligent driving.

[43] The implied obligation extends no further than those acts which the servant is actually employed to do: *Harvey* v. *O'Dell Ltd.* [1958] 2 Q.B. 78.

[44] [1957] A.C. 555.

[45] As in *Jones* v. *Manchester Corporation* [1952] 2 Q.B. 852.

[46] See above, § 168.

[47] See Atiyah, *Vicarious Liability*, Chap. 38.

[48] See above, § 168.

[49] *Jones* v. *Manchester Corporation* [1952] 2 Q.B. 852, 865; *Semtex Ltd.* v. *Gladstone* [1954] 1 W.L.R. 945, 948; *Romford Ice Co.* v. *Lister* [1956] 2 Q.B. 180, 199 (on appeal see [1957] A.C. 555, 570); *Overmyr Co. of Canada Ltd.* v. *Transfer Ltd.* (1975) 65 D.L.R. (3d) 717, 721.

has paid for the negligence of his servant can doubtless sue that servant for indemnity, at least if it is just and equitable that he should do so.[50]

(3) Statutory duty to provide indemnity or contribution

It has now been settled that as master and servant are joint tortfeasors the former is entitled to claim contribution or indemnity from the latter to such extent as the court thinks just and equitable in accordance with the provisions of the Law Reform (Married Women and Tortfeasors) Act 1935.[51] Thus if the negligence of the employer himself (or one of his other servants) has contributed to the damage the employer will be able to recover only a contribution and not an indemnity.[52] Similar rules govern those cases in which a principal is liable for the torts of his independent contractors.[53] In practice an indemnity of 100 per cent. seems to be commonly given in the ordinary case of vicarious liability, even though the claim at common law fails for one reason or another.[54]

§ 184. INDEPENDENT CONTRACTORS[55]

The general rule is that although an employer is responsible for the negligence and other wrongdoing of his servant, he is not responsible for that of an agent who is not a servant but an independent contractor. There are, however, certain cases in which an employer is liable for the acts of an independent contractor.[56] Although the tendency of development is in the direction of extending rather than restricting this liability,[57] the advantages of departing from the traditional distinction are not very obvious.[58] It is worth noticing that many of the decisions come from the time before it was clearly established[59] that a careless contractor might himself be liable directly to the injured party, and that an employer today usually stipulates for an indemnity from the contractor.[60] On the other hand, "sub-contracting" in the building industry has given rise to great evils: financially

---

[50] *Morris* v. *Ford Motor Co. Ltd.* [1973] Q.B. 792.
[51] The relevant cases are those cited in note 39 and *Davenport* v. *Commissioner for Railways* [1953] 53 S.R.(N.S.W.) 552. See also Jolowicz, "Right to Indemnity between Master and Servant" [1956] C.L.J. 101; Jolowicz (1959) 22 M.L.R. 71, 189; Williams, "Vicarious Liability and Master's Indemnity" (1957) 20 M.L.R. 220. Some grave issues of policy raised by these decisions are discussed in the Report of an Inter-Departmental Committee (H.M.S.O., 1959; Gardiner, (1959) 22 M.L.R. 652), which discovered that there was "a gentleman's agreement" amongst insurance companies not to take advantage of the *Lister* case, unless the evidence clearly indicated collusion or wilful misconduct on the part of the employee. The medical profession (always a strongly organised body) has secured the consent of the Minister of Health to an agreement under which hospital authorities will invoke the Act against negligent doctor servants only when the doctor is not assisted by one of the professional medical defence societies: Circular H.M. 54 (32).
[52] As in *Jones* v. *Manchester Corporation* [1952] 2 Q.B. 852.
[53] *Burnham* v. *Boyer* [1936] 2 All E.R. 1165; *Daniel* v. *Rickett, Cockerell & Co. Ltd.* [1938] 2 K.B. 322.
[54] *Harvey* v. *O'Dell Ltd.* [1958] 2 Q.B. 78.
[55] Atiyah, *Vicarious Liability*, Chap. 8, 29: Chapman, "Liability for Contractors" (1934) 50 L.Q.R. 71; Williams, "Liability for Independant Contractors" [1956] C.L.J. 180.
[56] *Salsbury* v. *Woodland* [1970] 1 Q.B. 324, 347.
[57] *British Road Services Ltd.* v. *A. V. Crutchley & Co. Ltd.* [1967] 1 W.L.R. 835.
[58] This is clearly brought out by Atiyah, *Vicarious Liability*, Chap. 29.
[59] In *Donoghue* v. *Stevenson* [1932] A.C. 562. See above, § 72.
[60] See an example of an indemnity clause in *Hosking* v. *De Havilland Aircraft Co. Ltd.* [1949] 1 All E.R. 540, 542.

irresponsible contractors, and their employers, may leave an injured person without remedy.[61]

The liability of the employer of an independent contractor is not properly vicarious: the employer is not liable for the contractor's breach of duty; he is liable because he has himself broken his own duty.[62] He is under a primary liability and not a secondary one.[63] Hence it is misleading to think of the law on this point as a general rule of non-liability subject to a more or less lengthy list of exceptions. The real question is whether the defendant is, in the circumstances of the particular case, in breach of a duty which he owes to the plaintiff. If the plaintiff proves such a breach it is no defence to say that another has been asked to perform it. The performance of the duties, but not the responsibility for that performance, can be delegated to another. This seems to be all that is meant by talk of "non-delegable duties."[64]

When a duty exists

The main difficulty in this branch of the law is to discover when the law will impose such a duty. One thing can, however, be said with confidence: the mere fact that the work entrusted to the contractor is of a character which may cause damage to others unless precautions are taken is not sufficient to impose liability on the employer.[65] There are few operations entrusted to an agent which are not capable, if due precautions are not observed, of being sources of danger and mischief to others; and if the principal was responsible for this reason alone, the distinction between servants and independent contractors would be practically eliminated from the law.[66] If I employ a contractor to manufacture explosives for me, I am hardly responsible if an explosion happens because of the negligence of his servants in the course of manufacture.[67] So a head contractor on a building site is not necessarily responsible because a sub-contractor breaks his statutory duties.[68] Here, as elsewhere in the law of negligence, it is not enough to establish liability to show that a reasonable man could have foreseen damage as a result of the defendant's acts. It may be helpful if we draw a distinction between two classes of duties—(1) a duty to take reasonable care, and (2) a duty to see that care is taken.[69] In the former there is in general no liability for the default of an independent contractor, in the latter there is.

(1) Duty to take reasonable care

The normal duty imposed by the law of negligence is no higher than one of reasonable care. As always, it is a question of fact in each case whether reasonable care has been taken. But it is certainly material to consider

---

[61] See Clark, "Industrial Law and the Labour-Only Sub-Contract" (1967) 30 M.L.R. 6.
[62] *Daniel* v. *Rickett, Cockerell & Co. Ltd.* [1938] 2 K.B. 322, 325.
[63] It is hardly necessary to add that the contractor himself will normally be liable to the injured party.
[64] *Cassidy* v. *Ministry of Health* [1951] 2 K.B. 343, 363.
[65] *Hughes* v. *Percival* (1883) 8 App.Cas. 443, 446.
[66] *Cape Breton* v. *Chappells Ltd.* (1962) 36 D.L.R. (2d) 58, 73; *Salsbury* v. *Woodland* [1970] 1 Q.B. 324, 337.
[67] *Rainham Chemical Works Ltd.* v. *Belvedere Fish Guano Co.* [1921] 2 A.C. 465, 491.
[68] *Donaghey* v. *Boulton and Paul Ltd.* [1968] A.C. 1.
[69] See *The Pass of Ballater* [1942] P. 112, 117.

whether what has to be done is something which forms part of the obligor's ordinary trade or business. If the act or process in question is one which involves technical skill or knowledge, then the ordinary man will discharge his duty by entrusting its performance to an apparently competent contractor.[70] A good example is the duty owed by those who take motor-vehicles onto a highway. It is no more than a duty to take reasonable care to avoid injury to other users of the highway. So if the owner of such a vehicle entrusts its repair to an apparently competent contractor, he is not liable[71] if, as a result of the contractor's[72] careless work, a wheel comes off and injures a passer-by.

On the other hand the principal may be liable when due care is not taken to see that the agent is properly qualified for the performance of the task so committed to him, or where proper instructions are not given to him in order to enable him to avoid the dangers incidental to the work.[73] For it is important not to give an undue advantage to the ignorant employer who confides all his affairs to independent contractors.[74]

Exceptions

There are, however, two cases in which it was generally assumed until recently that an employer was liable for the defaults of his contractor, even though the obligation imposed on him belonged to the category of negligence rather than of strict liability.

(a) *Duty to invitees.* Before the Occupiers' Liability Act 1957, it seemed that an occupier was, in general, liable to his invitees under the rule in *Indermaur* v. *Dames* for the default of his independent contractor. The law was stated in these general terms by Lord Simon L.C. and Lord Wright in *Thomson* v. *Cremin.*[75] They were not given the opportunity of considering the earlier decision of the Court of Appeal in *Haseldine* v. *Daw & Sons Ltd.,*[76] which followed the orthodox principle in holding that an occupier is not liable when the performance of his duty requires technical skill or knowledge, and he has taken all reasonable care to select an expert having that skill or knowledge, and to follow his advice. In this case the occupier of property on which hydraulic lifts were in operation was held to have discharged his duty when he employed "a first-class firm of lift engineers" to inspect and report on them. But in *Woodward* v. *Mayor of Hastings*[77] the

---

[70] *Riverstone Meat Co. Pty. Ltd.* v. *Lancashire Shipping Co. Ltd.* [1960] 1 Q.B. 536, 580–582.

[71] *Stennett* v. *Hancock* [1939] 2 All E.R. 578, 581 (which also decides that he is not obliged to inquire whether the repairer has done his work properly).

[72] But the contractor himself may well be liable under the principles in *Donoghue* v. *Stevenson* [1932] A.C. 562; see above, § 72.

[73] *Robinson* v. *Beaconsfield R.D.C.* [1911] 2 Ch. 188.

[74] *Sumner* v. *William Henderson & Sons Ltd.* [1964] 1 Q.B. 450, 471.

[75] (1941) [1953] 2 All E.R. 1185, 1188, 1191–1192; [1956] 1 W.L.R. 103n. This case is also reported (*sub nom. Cremin* v. *Thomson*) in (1941) 71 Ll.L.R. 1.

[76] [1941] 1 K.B. 688. It is unfortunate but scarcely surprising that each case should have been decided in ignorance of the other: argument in the H.L. had concluded on July 24, and judgment was delivered on October 20: judgment in the C.A. in *Haseldine* v. *Daw* was delivered on July 31. A badly drafted sentence on p. 563 of the 12th edition of this book misled Oliver J. in *Thompson* v. *Anglo-Saxon Petroleum Co. Ltd.* [1955] 2 Lloyd's Rep 363 into saying that *Cremin* was decided before *Haseldine*.

[77] [1945] 1 K.B. 174. Similar cases are *Bloomstein* v. *Railway Executive* [1952] 2 All E.R. 418; *Hartley* v. *Mayoh & Co.* [1954] 1 Q.B. 383.

governors of a school were held liable when a contractor failed to brush snow away from the school steps and the plaintiff was in consequence injured. "The craft of a charwoman may have its mysteries, but there is no esoteric quality in the nature of the work which cleaning a snow-covered step demands."[78] As the question was not actually in issue in *Thomson* v. *Cremin*,[79] the courts displayed a certain preference for distinguishing *Thomson* v. *Cremin* and instead following the decision in *Haseldine* v. *Daw & Sons Ltd.*[80] Now the Occupiers' Liability Act 1957, s. 2 (4), puts the matter almost[81] beyond doubt. It provides that where damage is caused to a visitor by a danger due to the faulty execution of any work of construction, maintenance or repair[82] by an independent contractor employed by the occupier, the occupier is not to be treated "without more" as answerable for the danger if in all the circumstances he had acted reasonably in choosing and supervising the contractor.[83]

(b) *Master's duty to servants.* It has been said[84] that the duty which a master owes to his servants to take reasonable care of their safety cannot be avoided by entrusting its performance to a contractor, at least if the duty is to be performed on the master's own premises, and would normally be so performed by one of his own servants, and the negligent workmanship is discoverable by reasonable inspection.[85] There has been only one direct decision to this effect,[86] (and a number of conflicting dicta[87]), and it is submitted that it is of doubtful authority because the abolition of the doctrine of common employment changed the judicial approach in this branch of the law. The Employers' Liability (Defective Equipment) Act 1969, s. 1 imposes liability on an employer for breach of its provisions when the defect is attributable to the fault of a third party. But as those provisions are limited to cases in which injury has been caused by the supply of defective equipment, the common law will still govern cases in which an independent contractor has been entrusted by the employer with the performance of some task which injures the employee.

(2) *Duty to see that care is taken*

In some cases the law imposes a duty irrespective of negligence. Liability is strict or absolute. Where the act which the contractor is employed to do is one of the kind which the employer does at his own peril—so that the existence of negligence is immaterial—it is no defence that the cause of the

---

[78] [1945] 1 K.B. 174, 183, *per* du Parcq L.J.
[79] See *Davie* v. *New Merton Board Mills Ltd.* [1959] A.C. 604, 644–645, 648–649.
[80] See *Green* v. *Fibreglass Ltd.* [1958] 2 Q.B. 245; *Lyons* v. *Nicholls* [1958] N.Z.L.R. 409.
[81] See above, § 95.
[82] Note that the draftsman has omitted the words "or other like operation," which occur in the recommendation of the Law Reform Committee: Cmd. 9305, p. 34. See also above, § 93.
[83] *AMF International Ltd.* v. *Magnet Bowling Ltd.* [1968] 1 W.L.R. 1028.
[84] *Paine* v. *Colne Valley Electricity Supply Co. Ltd.* [1938] 4 All E.R. 803, 807; *Marshment* v. *Borgstrom* [1942] 4 D.L.R. 1.
[85] *Davie* v. *New Merton Board Mills Ltd.* [1959] A.C. 604, 646.
[86] *Sumner* v. *William Henderson Ltd.* [1964] 1 Q.B. 450 (revd. in C.A. on another point [1964] 1 Q.B. 472).
[87] In *Davie* v. *New Merton Board Mills Ltd.* [1959] A.C. 604, the decision in which has been reversed by the Employers' Liability (Defective Equipment) Act 1969, s. 1. See above, § 181.

mischief was the negligence of an independent contractor by whose agency the act was done.[88] If an employer is under a duty to a person or class of persons, he is liable if that duty is not performed and damage thereby results, and cannot evade that liability by delegating the performance of the duty to an independent contractor. Whether there is such a duty will depend upon whether the employer as a reasonable man ought to foresee that the persons who suffer damage are likely to be affected by the performance of the independent contractor's acts,[89] provided always that the case falls within one of the following recognised categories of duties.

(i) *Statutory duties and powers*

When an absolute duty is laid by statute upon an individual or class of individuals, the performance of it cannot be delegated to an independent contractor to enable liability to be evaded,[90] This principle applies whether the duty is owed to the public or only to a section of the public.[91] The carrier of goods by sea does not fulfil his statutory obligation to use due diligence even if he employs a competent ship repairer and has his work inspected by a Lloyd's surveyor in the usual way.[92] The duties imposed by the Factories Act 1961, to fence dangerous machinery[93] and to provide safe means of access[94] are of this kind, but not the duty to take safety precautions required by the Construction (Working Place) Regulations 1966, unless on the facts of a particular case it can be said that the sub-contract is of such a trivial kind that the head contractor is in truth in charge of the work.[95] The courts are moving in the direction of holding that the duties imposed on hospital authorities are also of this character.[96] It is possible that an employer who exercises statutory powers through the agency of a contractor is responsible for that contractor's defaults.[97]

(ii) *Common law duties*

(a) *Public nuisance.* Such a duty is imposed when a person employs a contractor to do in a highway (or perhaps in any place to which there is a public right of access or entry)[98] some dangerous act other than the ordinary use of the highway for the purposes of passage or traffic,[99] or when a person, having done such an act in the highway, delegates to a contractor the work of taking the precautions necessary to prevent mischievous consequences. Such employment or delegation is permissible only on the terms of warranting the public against the negligence of the contractor so entrusted with the work. The duty covers work done in the space above or below, but

---

[88] *Balfour* v. *Barty-King* [1956] 1 W.L.R. 779, 783.
[89] *Savage* v. *Wilby* [1954] 3 D.L.R. 204, 206–207.
[90] *The Pass of Ballater* [1942] P. 112, 117.
[91] *Mulready* v. *J. H. & W. Bell Ltd.* [1953] 2 Q.B. 117.
[92] *Riverstone Meat Co. Pty. Ltd.* v. *Lancashire Shipping Co. Ltd.* [1961] A.C. 807.
[93] *Groves* v. *Wimborne (Lord)* [1898] 2 Q.B. 402.
[94] *Hosking* v. *De Havilland Aircraft Co. Ltd.* [1949] 1 All E.R. 540.
[95] *Donaghey* v. *Boulton and Paul Ltd.* [1968] A.C. 1.
[96] See above, § 157.
[97] *Darling* v. *Att.-Gen.* [1950] 2 All E.R. 793.
[98] *Pickard* v. *Smith* (1861) 10 C.B.(N.S.) 470 (railway station platform).
[99] When there is liability only for personal negligence: above, § 174. This distinction has been severely criticised: Atiyah, *Vicarious Liability*, Chap. 30.

not near or alongside, the highway.[1] This duty, which was well established at common law,[2] is recognised by the Highways (Miscellaneous Provisions)Act 1961, s. 1 (3), which provides that in an action for damage arising from non-repair of highways or bridges it shall not be relevant to prove that the highway authority had arranged for a competent person to carry out or supervise the maintenance of the part of the highway to which the action relates, unless it is also proved that the authority had given proper instructions with regard to the maintenance of the highway and that he had carried out the instructions.

(b) *Hazardous operations*. There is liability under the rule in *Rylands* v. *Fletcher* for the acts of an independent contractor.[3] The principle is the same in the case of escape of fire,[4] or of damage done by a savage animal.[5] Again, in the case of extra-hazardous acts, that is, acts which, in their very nature, involve in the eyes of the law special danger to others, an obligation may be imposed upon the ultimate employers to take special precautions which they cannot delegate by having the work carried out by independent contractors. Thus in *Honeywill and Stein Ltd.* v. *Larkin Bros.*[6] it was held that the plaintiffs who employed the defendants to take flash-light photographs in a cinema were liable to the owners of the cinema for a fire caused by the defendants in carrying out the work.[7] But most later cases[8] go the other way, and it can hardly be regarded as in accordance with the views of the Law Lords in *Read* v. *J. Lyons & Co. Ltd.*,[9] which emphasise fault rather than strict liability.

(c) *Private Nuisance.* We have already seen that an occupier is responsible for the acts of his independent contractor which cause a nuisance to the highway or interfere with his neighbour's right of support.[10] A similar conclusion was arrived at in *Matania* v. *National Provincial Bank*,[11] in which the nuisance complained of was dust and noise caused by building operations on an extensive scale. It has been suggested that this decision covers the case of any nuisance caused by an independent contractor and incidental to the work which he is instructed to do.[12] But it is

---

[1] *Salsbury* v. *Woodland* [1970] 1 Q.B. 324.
[2] *Penny* v. *Wimbledon U.D.C.* [1899] 2 Q.B. 72; *Holliday* v. *National Telephone Co.* [1899] 2 Q.B. 392; *Clements* v. *Tyrone C.C.* [1905] 2 I.R. 415, 542 (survey of authorities by Palles C.B.).
[3] The best authority for this proposition is *Rylands* v. *Fletcher* itself. See above, § 107.
[4] *Spicer* v. *Smee* [1946] 1 All E.R. 489; *Balfour* v. *Barty-King* [1957] 1 Q.B. 496.
[5] See above, § 118.
[6] [1934] 1 K.B. 191.
[7] But "extra-hazardous," a phrase of American origin has now been replaced by "extraordinarily dangerous" in the U.S.A. itself: see above, § 107, n. 1 (b).
[8] To arrange for a journey by aeroplane was not even in 1937 to set in motion a thing dangerous in itself: *Fosbroke-Hobbes* v. *Airwork Ltd.* [1937] 1 All E.R. 108; nor is the employment of a plumber to repair a water system: *Torette House Pty. Ltd.* v. *Berkman* (1939) 62 C.L.R. 637, or a contractor to fell a tree: *Salsbury* v. *Woodland* [1970] 1 Q.B. 324, or a builder to demolish a wall: *Stoneman* v. *Lyons* (1975) 133 C.L.R. 550.
[9] [1947] A.C. 156. See above, § 109.
[10] Above, § 22.
[11] [1936] 2 All E.R. 633.
[12] Friedmann, (1943) 59 L.Q.R. 70. *Spicer* v. *Smee* [1946] 1 All E.R. 489, which might seem to support this, was a case of escape of fire.

submitted that this is not so: *Matania's* case was specifically stated to be "not a case of a mere ordinary building operation."[13]

(d) *Bailees.* A bailee for reward, such as a warehouseman, man have attributed to him the negligence of a contractor employed to guard the subject of the bailment.[14] If the bailment is of valuable goods for carriage, there is no implied right to sub-contract.[15]

Collateral negligence[16]

An employer is never liable for the collateral or casual negligence of his independent contractor. It is not always easy to decide whether the negligent act in a particular case is collateral or not. Thus in *Padbury* v. *Holliday and Greenwood Ltd.,*[17] where one of the sub-contractors' workmen placed a tool on a window-sill, not in the ordinary course of the work which the contractors were employed to do, and the casement having been blown to by the wind the tool fell and injured the plaintiff, it was held that this was collateral negligence and the ultimate employers were not liable. On the other hand, in *Holliday* v. *National Telephone Co.,*[18] where, owing to the negligence of a plumber employed as an independent contractor to do work in a public street, molten solder was scattered by the explosion of a benzoline lamp, judgment was given for the defendant in the court below on the express ground that the negligence of the plumber was merely collateral. Nevertheless the Court of Appeal disagreed with this view and gave judgment for the plaintiff, holding that the negligence was in the very act which the plumber was employed to perform.

Probably the rule as to collateral negligence means nothing more than that the negligence required to impose liability upon the employer of an independent contractor must be negligence committed in the doing of the act itself which he is employed to do, and that negligence in other operations which, though connected with that work, are not themselves part of the work which he has contracted to do is not sufficient.[19] The employer is exempt from liability, not so much because the act done cannot be foreseen or guarded against, but because it is outside the scope of the duty imposed on the employer. If this is all that "collateral negligence" means, it is only an obscure way of saying that an employer is only liable for acts which are within the scope of the contractor's authority—which is obvious, but unhelpful in any particular case.

---

[13] [1936] 2 All E.R. 633, 651, *per* Finlay J.
[14] *British Road Services Ltd.* v. *A. V. Crutchley & Co. Ltd.* [1967] 1 W.L.R. 835.
[15] *Garnham, Harris and Elton Ltd.* v. *Alfred W. Ellis (Transport) Ltd.* [1967] 2 All E.R. 940.
[16] Atiyah, *Vicarious Liability*, Chap. 33.
[17] (1912) 28 T.L.R. 492.
[18] [1899] 2 Q.B. 392. See also *Thompson* v. *Anglo-Saxon Petroleum Co. Ltd.* [1955] 2 Lloyd's Rep. 363—one of the few reported cases in which collateral negligence has been successful as a defence.
[19] *McDonald* v. *Associated Fuels* [1954] 3 D.L.R. 775, 779.

CHAPTER 21

MISCELLANEOUS DEFENCES

§ 185. NECESSITY[1]

In some cases even damage intentionally done may not involve the defendant in liability when he is acting under necessity to prevent a greater evil. The precise limits of the defence are not clear, for it has affinities with certain other defences, such as an act of God, self-help, duress, or inevitable accident. It is distinguishable from self-defence on the ground that this pre-supposes that the plaintiff is prima facie a wrongdoer: the defence of necessity contemplates the infliction of harm on an innocent plaintiff.[2] The defence, if it exists, enables a defendant to escape liability for the intentional[3] interference with the security of another's person[4] or property[5] on the ground that the acts complained of were necessary to prevent greater damage to the commonwealth or to another or to the defendant himself, or to their or his property. The use of the term necessity serves to conceal the fact that the defendant always has a choice between two evils. This is what distinguishes the defence of necessity from that of impossibility. Here, as elsewhere in the law of torts, a balance has to be struck between competing sets of values and no more can be done here than to indicate the factors relevant to such a choice. So there is some authority that the subject as well as the Crown has a right and a duty at common law to justify a trespass or other tort on the ground of necessity in the defence of the realm, but such a right has been said to be obsolescent. "No man now, without risking an action against him in the courts, could pull down his neighbour's house to prevent the fire spreading to his own; he would be told that he ought to have dialled 999 and summoned the local fire brigade."[6] But outside the United Kingdom a duty to prevent fire in such cases may be recognised.[7]

Again, it seems plain that "the safety of human lives belongs to a different scale of values from the safety of property. The two are beyond comparison and the necessity for saving life has at all times been considered a proper ground for inflicting such damage as may be necessary upon another's

---

[1] See Bohlen, "Incomplete Privilege to Inflict Intentional Invasions of Interests of Property and Personalty," (1926) 39 Harv.L.Rev. 307; Williams, "The Defence of Necessity" [1953] C.L.P. 216; Glazebrook, "The Necessity Plea in English Criminal Law" [1972A] Camb.L.J. 87; Bates, "Consenting to the Necessary" (1972) 46 A.L.J.R. 73; Zellick, "Forcible Feeding" [1976] *Public Law* 153.

[2] But if A so parks his car that B cannot move his, would not B be justified in breaking A's window to release the brake? See *Proudman* v. *Allen* [1954] S.A.S.R. 336.

[3] It is inconceivable that the careless invasion of another's interests should be defensible on the ground of necessity.

[4] Examples of this are rare: our law does not recognise "protective custody" or enforced therapy: see above, § 46, and below, § 187. But see *Leigh* v. *Gladstone* (1909) 29 T.L.R. 139 (forcible feeding of hunger-striker permissible: but perhaps the case, which has been much criticised, illustrates the proper use of discipline—see above § 46).

[5] *London Borough of Southwark* v. *Williams* [1971] Ch. 734.

[6] *Burmah Oil Co.* v. *Lord Advocate* [1965] A.C. 75, 165, *per* Lord Upjohn. Nor is it permissible for the driver of a fire-engine to ignore traffic signals: *Buckoke* v. *Greater London Council* [1971] Ch. 655. The Fire Services Act 1947, s.30(1) in effect gives the defence of necessity to a *criminal* charge of trespass.

[7] *Russell* v. *McCabe* [1962] N.Z.L.R. 392.

property."[8] So in the course of medical or surgical treatment to which the patient's consent has been obtained there may suddenly arise an emergency which puts the patient's life at risk. In such a case the degree of necessity may obviate the need to obtain consent to further treatment, at least if it is broadly of the same character.[9] When the defendant has acted in protection of a private rather than a public interest it seems that the law was once stricter than it now is. "For the rule that the property in question must be actually under attack has been substituted the more generous rule that it must be in real or imminent danger; and for the absolute criterion that the act of trespass must be shown—in the light of subsequent events—to have been necessary for the preservation of the property has been substituted the more relative standard of reasonable necessity, *viz.* that any reasonable man would, in the circumstances of the case, have concluded that there was no alternative to the act of trespass if the property endangered was to be preserved."[10] Thus in *Cope* v. *Sharp*[11] the defendant committed certain acts of trespass on the plaintiff's land in order to prevent the spread of heath-fire to land over which the defendant's master had shooting rights.[12] It was shown that the fire never in fact damaged the property of the defendant's master and would not have done so even if the preventive measures had not been taken. The Court of Appeal, however, held that the defendant was entitled to succeed: the risk to his master's property had been real and imminent, and a reasonable person, placed in the defendant's position, would have acted as he had done. It has since been laid down both by the courts[13] and by Parliament[14] that the principle in *Cope* v. *Sharp* affords a general justification for acts of trespass.

It is uncertain whether the defence of necessity is available if the defendant has acted in good faith otherwise than for the protection of property—*e.g.* if out of mercy he kills a dog which has been run over,[15] but on principle the defendant should be protected.

But the defence of necessity is not in general favoured by the courts.[16] "The good samaritan is a character unesteemed by the English law."[17] It is important that people should not interfere with the person or property of others without due sense of responsibility, particularly as the obligation to pay compensation for any damage done is uncertain. The obligation to compensate certainly binds the Crown acting under its prerogative,[18] but how

---

[8] *Southport Corporation* v. *Esso Petroleum Ltd.* [1953] 3 W.L.R. 773, 779, *per* Devlin J. On appeal, see [1956] A.C. 218, 235, 242.

[9] *Murray* v. *McMurchy* [1949] 2 D.L.R. 442. See also below, § 187.

[10] *Cresswell* v. *Sirl* [1948] 1 K.B. 241, 247, *per* Scott L.J. For criticism of the phrase "reasonably necessary" see *Re Naylor Benzon Mining Co.* [1950] Ch. 567, 575.

[11] [1912] 1 K.B. 496.

[12] Note that the defendant was not a mere volunteer, as he was in *Carter* v. *Thomas* [1893] 1 Q.B. 673 (well-intentioned entrant on another's premises to extinguish a fire at which firemen were already working held a trespasser).

[13] *Cresswell* v. *Sirl* [1948] 1 K.B. 241, 248.

[14] See the Animals Act 1971, (s.9), which gives protection, subject to numerous conditions, to one who kills or injures a dog which is worrying livestock.

[15] See *Workman* v. *Cowper* [1961] 2 Q.B. 143.

[16] *London Borough of Southwark* v. *Williams* [1971] Ch. 734. So that when it was attempted to defend a nuisance caused by noisy building operations on the ground that they were necessary to save time and money, Bennett J. said: "I cannot help being reminded of a line I remember in *Paradise Lost*: 'So spake the Fiend, and with necessity, the tyrant's plea, excused his devilish deeds.' " : *Andreae* v. *Selfridge & Co. Ltd.* [1936] 2 All E.R. 1413, 1422.

[17] Lord Devlin, *Samples of Lawmaking* (1962), p. 90.

[18] *Burmah Oil Co. Ltd.* v. *Lord Advocate* [1965] A.C. 75.

much further it extends is doubtful. There is some authority that any rescuer of life, as distinct from property, is entitled to be reimbursed his expenditure, particularly if he is a professional man. In any case, the defence is hardly available if the predicament in which the defendant found himself was brought about by his own negligence.[19-20]

§ 186. EXEMPTION CLAUSES AND DISCLAIMERS

Exemption clauses

Although parties to a contract are in general free to make what bargain they please, the courts lean against clauses which purport to exempt a party from the liability which would otherwise fall on him.[21] Parliament too disapproves of such clauses. Neither the operator of a public service vehicle[22] nor the Railways, Waterways and London Transport Boards[23] are able by contract to limit their liability in respect of the death of, or bodily injury to, any passenger[24] other than one travelling under a free pass. Formerly the owner of a private vehicle was entitled to exclude liability to a passenger by means of an aptly worded notice,[25] but the Road Traffic Act 1972, s.148(3), annuls all such notices or agreements. So too the duties owed under the Dangerous Premises Act 1972 are non-excludable. These trends were generalised by the Unfair Contract Terms Act 1977[26]; Section 2 provides that liability for death or personal injury resulting from negligence cannot be excluded, while such exclusion or restriction of liability for other loss or damage is subject to the test of reasonableness.

Even if an exemption clause has been validly inserted in a contract, the courts have held that general words in such a clause will not ordinarily exempt the party seeking to rely on them from liability for his own negligence or that of his servants, unless the only scope for the operation of the clause is the negligence of that party or his servants.[27] But it is generally accepted that the words "howsoever caused" are wide enough to exclude liability for negligence.[28] The question whether a party who has been guilty of a fundamental breach of contract can rely on an exemption clause was much discussed before the House of Lords held that there was no rule of law requiring any particular construction of the contract in issue.[29] Nor in general can such a clause be relied on by a negligent servant of the contractor: there is no doctrine of vicarious immunity.[30] But apparently if there is a valid contract not to sue the servant, then even though the servant could not take advantage of such a contract, an action against him may be stayed by the court as a fraud on the employer.[31] Where but for the contract there

---

[19-20] *Southport Corporation v. Esso Petroleum Ltd.* |1954| 2 Q.B. 182, 185, 199.
[21] *Spurling (J.) Ltd. v. Bradshaw* |1956| 1 W.L.R. 461.
[22] Road Traffic Act 1960, s.151.
[23] Transport Act 1962, s.43(7).
[24] As distinct from goods, which may be carried either at Board's Risk or at Owner's Risk.
[25] As in *Birch v. Thomas* |1972| 1 W.L.R. 294.
[26] The detailed provisions of this very complex Act must be sought in text-books on the law of contract.
[27] *White v. Warwick (John) & Co. Ltd.* |1953| 1 W.L.R. 1285.
[28] *White v. Blackmore* |1972| 2 Q.B. 651.
[29] *Photo Production Ltd. v. Securicor Transport Ltd.* |1980| A.C. 827.
[30] *Scruttons Ltd. v. Midland Silicones Ltd.* |1962| A.C. 446.
[31] *Gore v. Van der Lann* |1967| 2 Q.B. 31, on which see: F. J. Odgers, "The Strange Case of Mrs. Gore" (1970) 86 L.Q.R. 69.

would be a concurrent liability in tort and contract the contract may give express protection to what would otherwise be a tort. The plaintiff cannot then disregard any limitation of liability under the contract by alleging a wider liability in tort.[32]

Disclaimers

The common law does not usually permit one who is under a duty of care (*e.g.* a user of the highway) to disclaim responsibility for his actions regardless of the wishes of others.[33] So it is impossible to disclaim liability for a dishonest statement made with intent that another shall act on it.[34] Statutes—*e.g.* the Road Traffic Act 1972, s. 148(3)—also sometimes prohibit disclaimers of liability.[35] But the Occupiers' Liability Act 1957 gave statutory permission for an occupier to disclaim the common duty of care which he owes to lawful visitors, and the disclaimer was effective even though the defence of consent was inapplicable.[36] But now the Unfair Contract Terms Act 1977, s. 2 controls non-contractual exemption clauses and disclaimers as explained above.

§ 187. VOLENTI NON FIT INJURIA[37]

No injury is done to one who consents. This maxim had its origin in the process by which Roman Law validated the act of a free citizen selling himself into slavery. In the nineteenth century it somehow found its way into the law of torts, in which it applies both to intentional and accidental harms.[38] It might be helpful if a distinction was drawn between *consent* (as a defence to intentional harms) and *assumption of risk* (as a defence to negligent harms).[39]

(1) Intentional harms: consent[40]

No act is actionable as a tort at the suit of any person who has expressly or impliedly assented to it: *Volenti non fit injuria*. No man can enforce a right which he has voluntarily waived or abandoned.[41] The maxim applies to intentional acts which would otherwise be tortious: consent, for example, to an entry on land or goods[42] which would otherwise be a trespass, or consent to physical harm which would otherwise be an assault, as in the case of involuntary contacts in a crowded street.[43] The only exception appears to be

---

[32] *White* v. *Warwick (John) & Co. Ltd.* [1953] 1 W.L.R. 1285, 1294.
[33] Honoré, 8 J.S.P.T.L. 291–292.
[34] *Commercial Banking Co. of Sydney Ltd.* v. *Brown & Co.* (1972) 46 A.L.J.R. 297.
[35] See below, § 187.
[36] *White* v. *Blackmore* [1972] 2 Q.B. 651. See above, § 93.
[37] See Williams, *Joint Torts and Contributory Negligence*, Chap. 12; Atiyah "Causation, Contributory Negligence, and *Volenti Non Fit Injuria*" (1965) 43 Can. Bar. Rev. 609; Dias, "Consent of Parties and *Voluntas Legis*" [1966] Camb.L.J. 75.
[38] *O'Hanlon* v. *Electricity Supply Board* [1969] I.R. 75, 90.
[39] In Ireland, since the Civil Liability Act 1961, s.34(1), the correct phrase is not *volenti* but "the statutory defence that the plaintiff before the act complained of agreed to waive his legal rights in respect of it": *McComiskey* v. *McDermott* [1974] I.R. 75, 93.
[40] See Skegg, "A Justification for Medical Procedures Performed Without Consent" (1974) 90 L.Q.R. 512; Zellick, "Forcible Feeding" [1976] *Public Law* 153.
[41] *Chapman* v. *Ellesmere* [1932] 2 K.B. 431, 463; *Buckpitt* v. *Oates* [1968] 1 All E.R. 1145, 1148.
[42] *Leitch* v. *Leydon* [1931] A.C. 90, 109.
[43] See above, § 43.

the tort of deceit.[44] So the maxim affords a defence to a physician or surgeon for an act done in the proper course of medical or surgical treatment,[45] which is within the scope of the patient's real consent,[46] whether express or implied. The defendant must establish that the plaintiff's consent was fully and freely given.[47]

What is the position if a surgeon operates on a person who is unable, because of his condition, to give consent, but still in need of treatment? There is no clear English authority on the point,[48] but in practice the English medical profession extract written consents from parents or other relatives. In an emergency, such as a traffic accident, or when relatives are unavailable, the law should in principle allow the defence of necessity[49] or implied consent[50] to an action for battery brought by an ungrateful patient,[51] but there are difficulties in each of these defences, and the common law has always emphasised an individual's interest in the integrity of his body.[52] The law prefers self-determination to paternalism. If the person subjected to medical treatment is under the age of majority (now eighteen), the defendant may be protected by the Family Law Reform Act 1969, s. 8(1). This provides that the consent of a minor who has attained the age of sixteen to surgical, medical or dental treatment[53] which, in the absence of consent, would constitute a trespass to his person,[54] shall be as effective as it would be if he were of full age. The same Act, in section 8(3), provides that consents at common law retain whatever validity they have, but as the common law is not clear, this is hardly a helpful section.

(2) Accidental harms: assumption of risk

The maxim applies, in the second place, to consent to run the risk of accidental harm which would otherwise be actionable as due to the negligence of him who caused it. There is some authority for saying that the maxim means a waiver by the plaintiff of an admitted breach of duty, but the better view is that consent here means the agreement of the plaintiff, express or implied, to exempt the defendant from the duty of care which he would otherwise have owed.[55]

It follows that if the defendant owes to the plaintiff no duty of care at all, no question of *volenti non fit injuria* arises. The Court of Appeal has held

---

[44] See above, § 143.
[45] *Bravery* v. *Bravery* [1954] 1 W.L.R. 1169.
[46] *Chatterton* v. *Gerson* [1980] 3 W.L.R. 1003.
[47] *Lane* v. *Holloway* [1968] 1 Q.B. 379.
[48] But in *Banbury* v. *Bank of Montreal* [1918] A.C. 626, 689, Lord Atkinson thought it was settled that a doctor owed a duty of care in such a case.
[49] See above, § 185.
[50] Lord Devlin, *Samples of Lawmaking* (1962), pp. 83–94.
[51] For the doctor's right to recover expenses, see § 185.
[52] See above, § 43.
[53] As defined in s.8(2), is probably limited to therapeutic procedures. It is doubtful if a minor over 16 can validly consent to a transplant or to a blood donation.
[54] Note this interesting Parliamentary recognition of the difference between Trespass and Case: see above, §§ 2, 43.
[55] *Morrison* v. *Union Steamship Co. Ltd.* [1964] N.Z.L.R. 468, 478; *Buckpitt* v. *Oates* [1968] 1 All E.R. 1145, 1148. It is sometimes said that the law of negligence assumes the principle of *volenti* to be inapplicable: *Dann* v. *Hamilton* [1939] 1 K.B. 509, 517; *Wooldridge* v. *Sumner* [1963] 2 Q.B. 43, 69. This means no more than that the duty of care persists beyond the specific conduct or state of things which is the subject of consent (*Insurance Commissioner* v. *Joyce* (1948) 77 C.L.R. 39, 56), which is the very point at issue.

that spectators at games and sporting events assume the risk of any harm caused by the players unless it results from intentional or reckless conduct.[56] It would seem to follow that no participant in a game is owed the ordinary duty of care by any other participant. But the better view is that it is a question of fact in each case whether a duty exists, and that the rules of the game are a relevant but not a conclusive factor in deciding whether the defendant has taken reasonable care, or whether the plaintiff has consented to the risk.[57] So it would be relevant that the defendant was a competitor in a race in which he was expected to go "all out" to win.[58] But if the person sued is the occupier of the premises a duty of care to spectators and players may exist, although the defendant may find it easy to prove that the visitor willingly accepted the risk.[59]

If there is an express agreement to exempt the defendant from the consequences which would ordinarily follow from his negligent act no difficulty arises, except that it should be remembered that such contracts are construed strictly as against the party claiming the benefit of the exemption,[60] and that sometimes they are prohibited by statute. So Parliament has expressly provided that agreements shall be void which purport to exclude or restrict liability for death or personal injury resulting from negligence.[61] Exclusions or restrictions of liability for other heads of loss or damage must satisfy the test of reasonableness.[62] Conversely, Parliament may expressly provide that there is no liability for any particular damage suffered by a person who has voluntarily accepted the risk thereof.[63]

Otherwise it is in each case a question of fact whether a real consent to the assumption of the risk without compensation can be deduced from all the circumstances of the case.[64] The issue is whether the plaintiff has consented to run the risk, or consented to the lack of care which produces the risk, at his own expense.[65] For the issue is not whether the plaintiff voluntarily and rashly exposed himself to the risk of injury, but whether he agreed that if injury befell him, the loss should be on him and not on the defendant.[66] The true question in every case is: did the plaintiff give a real consent to the assumption of the risk without compensation; did the consent really absolve the defendant from the duty to take care?[67] It is not necessary that his consent should have been given in a *contract* under seal or supported by consideration[68]: any acts or statements from which free con-

---

[56] *Wooldridge* v. *Sumner* [1963] 2 Q.B. 43. All decisions on games must be reconsidered in the light of this case, but it is open to serious criticism both on the law and the facts (see Goodhart, Note (1962) 78 L.Q.R. 490), and has been distinguished in *Wilks* v. *Cheltenham Home Guard Motor Cycle Club* [1971] 1 W.L.R. 668.
[57] *Rootes* v. *Shelton* (1967) 41 A.L.J.R. 172.
[58] *Wilks* v. *Cheltenham Home Guard Motor Cycle Club* [1971] 1 W.L.R. 668.
[59] *Simms* v. *Leigh Rugby Football Club Ltd.* [1969] 2 All E.R. 923.
[60] See *Wooldridge* v. *Sumner* [1963] 2 Q.B. 43, 66.
[61] Unfair Contract Terms Act 1977 s.2(1).
[62] Unfair Contract Terms Act 1977 s.2(2) "Reasonableness" is dealt with in s. 11.
[63] As in the Animals Act 1971, s.5(2). So a plaintiff who trespasses knowing that a savage Alsatian dog is running loose has no remedy: *Cummings* v. *Grainger* [1977] Q.B. 397.
[64] *Merrington* v. *Ironbridge Metal Works Ltd.* [1952] 2 All E.R. 1101, 1103.
[65] *Kelly* v. *Farrans Ltd.* [1954] N.I. 41, 45.
[66] *Car and General Insurance Corporation Ltd.* v. *Seymour* [1956] 2 D.L.R. 369, 371–372; *Wilson* v. *Darling Island, etc. Co.* (1955) 95 C.L.R. 43, 82.
[67] *Seymour's case* [1956] 2 D.L.R. 369, 378; *Lehnert* v. *Stein* (1962) 36 D.L.R. (2d) 159, 164.
[68] *Bennett* v. *Tugwell* [1971] 2 Q.B. 267.

sent can be deduced will be sufficient for the purposes of the law of torts.[69] So if the plaintiff has in fact consented, it is irrelevant that he is a minor[70] or an alien.[71] Conversely, the defence of *volenti* cannot be raised if the plaintiff has clearly shown that he does not accept the legal risk of injury falling on him—*e.g.* by asking whether the defendant is insured,[72] or by treating a disclaimer as a joke.[73]

Four more points may be noticed. First, many of the cases in which the maxim has been considered have been cases of master and servant,[74] in which special considerations apply[75]—so much so that the defence has almost disappeared in such cases,[76] unless the claim is for breach of a statutory duty imposed directly on a fellow-workman.[77] The employer is entitled to the benefit of such an implied consent by the plaintiff workman.[78]

Secondly, the traditional form of the question (*i.e.* did the plaintiff assume the risk?) tends to disguise the fact that the defendant is setting up acceptance of the risk as a term of the undertaking, the burden of proof of which lies on him. The question really is: can the defendant reasonably be heard to say, as an inference from the facts,[79] that the risk of injury from his own misconduct was required by him to be, and was in fact, accepted by the plaintiff as such a term?[80]

Thirdly, the maxim may extend to a bargain to accept *future* negligent acts on the part of the defendant—a licence to commit a tort, in other words. Such a bargain or licence might be capable of arising in cases of passengers in vehicles accepting lifts from drunken drivers,[81] but the courts lean against such an interpretation,[82] for if the act relied upon to establish consent precedes the negligence, the plaintiff is unlikely to have acquired full knowledge of the extent as well as the nature of the risk.[83] Still, the defence is certainly available in such a case,[84] for the essence of it is not so much assent to the infliction of injury as assumption of the risk of it.[85]

Fourthly, it has long been established[86] that he who uses a highway consents to run the risk of pure accidents, but not the risk of injury due to other persons' carelessness. It is for this reason that although the injury is direct and forcible and therefore prima facie a trespass to the person the plaintiff has to prove negligence in order to succeed. This principle was laid down more by a series of dicta[87] and the tacit approval of the profession from the

---

[69] *Wilson* v. *Darling Island, etc. Co.* (1955) 95 C.L.R. 43, 82; *Morrison* v. *Union Steamship Co. Ltd.* [1964] N.Z.L.R. 468.
[70] *Buckpitt* v. *Oates* [1968] 1 All E.R. 1145.
[71] *Geier* v. *Kujawa* [1970] 1 Lloyd's Rep. 364.
[72] As in *Nettleship* v. *Weston* [1971] 2 Q.B. 691.
[73] As in *McComiskey* v. *McDermott* [1974] I.R. 75.
[74] Also considered below, § 188.
[75] *Merrington* v. *Ironbridge Metal Works Ltd.* [1952] 2 All E.R. 1101, 1103.
[76] *I.C.I. Ltd.* v. *Shatwell* [1965] A.C. 656, 680, 686.
[77] *O'Hanlon* v. *Electricity Supply Board* [1969] I.R. 75, 90.
[78] *I.C.I. Ltd.* v. *Shatwell* [1965] A.C. 656.
[79] The approach is objective, not subjective: *Bennett* v. *Tugwell* [1971] 2 Q.B. 267.
[80] *Car & General Insurance Corporation Ltd.* v. *Seymour* [1956] 2 D.L.R. 369, 371.
[81] *Dann* v. *Hamilton* [1939] 1 K.B. 509.
[82] *Turner* v. *Union Steamship Co. Ltd.* [1964] N.Z.L.R. 468, 477–479, 482.
[83] As in *White* v. *Blackmore* [1972] 2 Q.B. 651.
[84] As in *Buckpitt* v. *Oates* [1968] 1 All E.R. 1145 (notice on dashboard of car warning passengers they travelled at own risk).
[85] *Burnett* v. *British Waterways Board* [1973] 1 W.L.R. 700.
[86] *Holmes* v. *Mather* (1875) L.R. 10 Ex. 261. See also above, § 46.
[87] *Per* Lord Blackburn in *Fletcher* v. *Rylands* (1866) L.R. 1 Ex. 265, 286–287, and in *River Wear Commissioners* v. *Adamson* (1877) 12 App.Cas. 743, 767.

mid-nineteenth century onwards than by any definite decision.[88] The same principle is extended to those who own property adjoining a highway. They must submit to the dangers incident to the ordinary use of the highway for purposes of traffic, so long as they are not aggravated by the negligence of him whom they seek to make liable for them.[89] So in *Tillett* v. *Ward*[90] the defendant drove cattle along the highway, and was held not liable for damage done by the entrance of an ox through the open doorway of an iron-monger's shop.

Intoxicated drivers

One particular difficulty arises when injuries are suffered by a passenger in a motor-car driven by a person intoxicated by drink or drugs. A solution might have been found by holding that a special relationship exists whenever a passenger is aware of facts which show that the driver cannot be expected to drive other than dangerously.[91] But the courts have been reluctant to assert that an intoxicated driver owes no duty to his passenger, and have preferred to use the concepts of contributory negligence or *volenti* to defeat an unmeritorious claim. In *Dann* v. *Hamilton*.[92] the plaintiff, who voluntarily chose to travel by motor-car though she knew the driver was under the influence of drink and though she could have made her journey by omnibus, was injured in an accident caused by the driver's drunkenness.[93] The defence of *volenti* was held to be capable of arising out of the relationship of the parties, although the plaintiff succeeded on the facts. But today the courts lean against the defence of *volenti* when it is sought to deduce or infer a licence in advance to commit a tort, although defendants have occasionally succeeded in proving that the plaintiff had clearly assented to being carried at his own risk.[94] It is certainly clear that a passenger is not necessarily deprived of his remedy if he travels with a driver who is known to have driven negligently in the past.[95] From a practical viewpoint this favours the passenger: he is not *volens* merely because he refuses to leave the car. This is understandable if it is impracticable to leave

---

[88] The pre-1852 running-down cases are listed in Harari, *The Place of Negligence in the Law of Torts* (Sydney, 1962), Appendix A.

[89] *Esso Petroleum Co. Ltd.* v. *Southport Corporation* [1956] A.C. 218, 244.

[90] (1882) 10 Q.B.D. 17.

[91] *Nettleship* v. *Weston* [1971] 2 Q.B. 691. See also above, § 75.

[92] [1939] 1 K.B. 509, 517–518. Possibly the plaintiff could have succeeded on the ground that her consent to the criminal act of driving under the influence of drink was void, but Asquith J. was doubtful of this (at 519). The case has been much criticised (Goodhart, Note (1971) 87 L.Q.R. 444), and Lord Denning has said it is wrong: *Nettleship* v. *Weston* [1971] 2 Q.B. 691. But the decision is defended in *Car and General Insurance Corporation Ltd.* v. *Seymour* (1956) 2 D.L.R. (2d) 369. It may also be justified either on the ground that the consent of the plaintiff did not release the defendant completely from his duty to take care towards her, but only from the duty to take the care of a reasonable man (Burnett, Note, 38 Can.Bar Rev. 107), or on the ground that drunken driving is a grave social evil and passengers should be discouraged from aiding and abetting such conduct by depriving them of their civil rights.

[93] Although the defence of contributory negligence was not raised (in (1953) 69 L.Q.R. 317 Lord Asquith of Bishopstone explained why not), it might be available on such facts: *Owens* v. *Brimmell* [1976] 3 All E.R. 765. But it is difficult to see that in such a case the damage is caused partly by the fault of the plaintiff himself: the cause of the accident will be the same whether the plaintiff knew of the driver's drunkenness or not: *Bankhead* v. *McCarthy*, 1963 S.L.T. 144. *Contra, Dawrant* v. *Nutt* [1961] 1 W.L.R. 253, but as Pollock would have said, this case "cannot be law as reported."

[94] *Bennett* v. *Tugwell* [1971] 2 Q.B. 267.

[95] See *Walker* v. *Turton-Sainsbury* [1952] S.A.S.R. 159.

the car; but its justice in other cases is not so clear. If the risk is clearly known in advance, why should a plaintiff be entitled to say, "I didn't think it would happen to me"?[96]

§ 188. KNOWLEDGE NOT CONSENT

Mere knowledge of an impending wrongful act, or of the existence of a wrongfully caused danger, does not in itself amount to consent, even though no attempt is made by the plaintiff to prevent or avoid that act or danger. Consent involves an express or implied agreement that the act may be rightfully done or the danger rightfully caused. The maxim of the law is *volenti non fit injuria*, not *scienti non fit injuria*.[97] Thus in *Brunswick (Duke of)* v. *Harmer*[98] the plaintiff successfully sued for libel, although the only publication was the sale of a copy of the libellous paper to a person whom the plaintiff himself had instructed to buy it for the very purpose of enabling an action to be brought. The same principle applies to the other branch of the maxim *volenti non fit injuria*, relating to the consent to run the risk of accidental harm. Accordingly a servant who knowingly works on dangerous premises or with defective plant or tools is not for that reason *ipso facto* debarred from suing his employer when an accident happens.[99] The question is not whether he knew of the danger, but whether in fact he agreed to run the risk, in the sense that he exempted his employer from his duty not to create the danger, and agreed that if injury happened the loss should be on him and not on his employer. Knowledge of the danger may be evidence of such an agreement, but it is nothing more.[1] This principle was established by the House of Lords in the leading case of *Smith* v. *Charles Baker & Sons*,[2] and has never since been doubted.

It received express recognition in the Unfair Contract Terms Act 1977, s. 2(3), which states: "Where a contract term or notice purports to exclude or restrict liability from negligence, a person's agreement to or awareness of it is not of itself to be taken as indicating his voluntary acceptance of any risk".

Other effects of knowledge

But there may be cases in which knowledge of the danger, even if it does not prove an agreement to undertake the risk within the rule in *Smith* v. *Baker*, may nevertheless be relevant to the success of the plaintiff's action for two other reasons:

(1) It may negative the existence of any negligence on the part of the defendant in causing that danger;
(2) It may establish the existence of contributory negligence on the part of the plaintiff.

---

[96] Lord Donovan in [1965] A.C. 565, 692.
[97] *Thomas* v. *Quartemaine* (1887) 18 Q.B.D. 685, 696, *per* Bowen L.J.
[98] (1849) 14 Q.B. 185. For another aspect of this decision, see above, § 53.
[99] But "in these days of trade unions and shop stewards I very much doubt if there are many cases in which a workman would be placed in such a position": *Horton* v. *London Graving Dock Co.* [1949] 2 All E.R. 169, 171, *per* Lynskey J.
[1] *Neilsen* v. *Redel* [1955] 1 D.L.R. 125, 132. See also above, § 89.
[2] [1891] A.C. 325.

In the first place, there are certain cases in which he who causes a danger fulfils all his legal duty of care by giving notice of that danger to the persons whom it affects. Thus, he who lends a chattel gratuitously is probably not bound to do anything more than disclose the existence of any dangerous quality of which he actually knows and of which the borrower does not know.[3]

In the second place, there are cases in which the act of the plaintiff in knowingly running a risk created by the defendant's wrongful act amounts to contributory negligence on his own part. Since the Law Reform (Contributory Negligence) Act 1945, this is not a complete bar to recovery but the loss is apportioned between the parties according to their respective degrees of fault. The assessment will depend on whether the conduct of the plaintiff was reasonable, having regard to the magnitude of the risk and the urgency of the occasion. A certain amount of risk I am entitled to face, even with full knowledge, rather than submit to being deprived of my liberty of action by the wrongful act of another. In *Clayards* v. *Dethick*,[4] the plaintiff, a cab-driver, occupied certain stables in Gower Mews, Gower Street, and the defendant wrongfully dug a trench along the passage which afforded the only outlet from the mews to the street. The plaintiff attempted to lead out one of his horses along the passage and over the heaps of soil which the defendant had excavated, and while doing so the horse fell into the trench and was injured. It was held that the defendant was liable; for the plaintiff was not bound to submit to be thus deprived of the use of his stables. "The whole question was, whether the danger was so obvious that the plaintiff could not with common prudence make the attempt."[5] This principle was reaffirmed by the House of Lords in *A. C. Billings & Sons Ltd.* v. *Riden*.[6] In any event, no risk can be made the ground of a charge of contributory negligence if the defendant himself requested or ordered or authorised the act of the plaintiff[7] in running the risk.[8]

Summary

Before the Law Reform (Contributory Negligence) Act 1945, the courts did not often distinguish very clearly between the defences of *volenti non fit injuria* (or assumption of risk), remoteness of damage, and contributory negligence, for it was seldom necessary for them to do so. But today it is of great importance to keep them distinct, for while *volenti non fit injuria* and remoteness of damage still afford a complete defence there is now power to apportion the loss in cases of contributory negligence. In any event the various concepts are entirely distinct. For a plaintiff may be guilty of contributory negligence if he did not know but ought to have known of the danger which confronted him. But he can never be held to have been *volens* unless it is shown that he had full knowledge of the nature and extent of the risk.[9] Again, a plaintiff may be, and usually is, guilty of contributory

---

[3] See above, § 104.
[4] (1848) 12 Q.B. 439.
[5] (1848) 12 Q.B. 439, 466, *per* Patteson J. ("who, of course, was a judge of very great experience and learning" : *Davies* v. *Property Corporation Ltd.* [1929] 2 K.B. 222, 228, *per* Talbot J.).
[6] [1958] A.C. 240.
[7] As in *Bowater* v. *Rowley Regis Corporation* [1944] K.B. 476.
[8] *Meani* v. *Sungravure Ltd.* [1964] N.S.W.R. 11, 16.
[9] See Lord Reid in *I.C.I. Ltd.* v. *Shatwell* [1965] A.C. 656, 672.

negligence when he is careless for his own safety, but he may be truly *volens* even when he is exercising the utmost care for his own safety.[10]

§ 189. REALITY OF CONSENT

The consent must be a real consent.[11] It can hardly be doubted that consent obtained by duress (actual violence or threats of violence to the person of the plaintiff) is no real consent. But it is probably not enough for the plaintiff to show that his consent was given reluctantly, or under the mistaken belief that the defendant was legally entitled to act as he did.[12] If the mistake was induced by the fraud of the defendant, however, it vitiates the consent. It is true that in *Hegarty* v. *Shine*[13] the plaintiff was unsuccessful in an action for assault against her paramour, who had infected her with venereal disease, but the decision of the Irish Court of Appeal was based partly on the ground that the defendant's non-disclosure of his disease was not such a fraud as to vitiate consent, and partly on the ground that *ex turpi causa non oritur actio*.[14] Although there is no liability in criminal law in such a case unless the victim's mistake is as to the real nature of the whole transaction and not merely as to the consequences of the act done,[15] there is no reason to suppose that this distinction applies in the civil law. Again, a man cannot be said to give a real consent if he acts under the compulsion of a legal duty. Thus it is the duty of a servant to protect his master's premises from fire. If in so doing he runs risks he is not a volunteer, and, if he is injured, he will have a remedy against him whose negligence caused the fire.[16] A man cannot be said to be "willing" unless he is in a position to choose freely; and freedom of choice predicates the absence from his mind of any feeling of constraint interfering with the freedom of his will.[17]

Rescue Cases[18]

The "rescue cases" hold that the same principle applies if the plaintiff has acted under a moral duty. In *Haynes* v. *Harwood*[19] the Court of Appeal laid it down that, "the doctrine of the assumption of risk does not apply where the plaintiff has, under an exigency caused by the defendant's wrongful misconduct, consciously and deliberately faced a risk, even of death, to rescue another from imminent danger of personal injury or death, whether the person endangered is one to whom he owes a duty of protection, as a member of his family, or is a mere stranger to whom he owes no such special

---

[10] *Prior* v. *Kyle* (1965) 52 D.L.R. (2d) 272, 281.
[11] *Chatterton* v. *Gerson* [1980] 3 W.L.R. 1003.
[12] *Latter* v. *Braddell* (1881) 50 L.J.Q.B. 448.
[13] (1878) 4 L.R.Ir. 288.
[14] On this maxim, see below, § 190.
[15] *R.* v. *Clarence* (1888) 22 Q.B.D. 23; *R.* v. *Williams* [1923] 1 K.B. 340.
[16] *D'Urso* v. *Sanson* (1939) 4 All E.R. 26; *The Gusty* [1940] P. 159. He may also be entitled to benefit under the Social Security Act 1975, s. 54.
[17] *Bowater* v. *Rowley Regis Corporation* [1944] K.B. 476, 479; *Merrington* v. *Ironbridge Metal Works Ltd.* [1952] 2 All E.R. 1101.
[18] Mannie Brown, "A Study in Negligence" (1932) 10 Can.Bar Rev. 556; Linden, "Rescuers and Good Samaritans" (1971) 34 M.L.R. 241; Binchy, "The Good Samaritan" (1974) 25 N.I.L.Q. 147.
[19] [1935] 1 K.B. 146.

duty."[20] In that case the defendants' servant had left his van and horses unattended in a crowded street. The horses bolted when a boy threw a stone at them. The plaintiff was a police constable on duty inside a police station; he saw that if nothing was done a woman and children were in grave danger, and at great personal risk managed to stop both horses, but in so doing suffered serious personal injuries. He was entitled to damages. As the negligent act preceded the alleged consent, the case would have been a model one for the application of the maxim, had not the court been able to find an exception to it.

The principle is the same when the plaintiff is under no legal duty[21] to effect the rescue, for example, a passer-by who is injured while rescuing a little girl from the danger of being run over by a lorry,[22] or a doctor who descends a gas-filled well to attempt to rescue two workmen overcome by fumes.[23] The principle is that if one person by his negligence causes another to be in a position of danger, he should have regard to the probability that a third person, acting bravely and promptly and subjugating any timorous over-concern for his own well-being or comfort, may attempt a rescue.[24] No distinction appears to be drawn between the rescuer who acts instinctively and the one who takes time for reflection before he encounters the risk.[25] It has even been held that a first rescuer who bungles his attempt may be liable to a second rescuer.[26] In some cases it may be argued that a plaintiff who has shown supreme courage has been "unreasonably brave," but the courts do not favour such a plea.

The principle also covers cases where the risk has been incurred to save property belonging to the rescuer himself[27] or to a third party,[28] or even to the defendant.[29] It is material to consider in every case whether or not it is life or property which is in danger. It is material to consider the relationship of the plaintiff who intervenes in the matter to the property in peril or to the person in peril. It is relevant to consider the degree of danger and risk, and so forth.[30] It is possible that the rescuer of property owes a duty of care to its owner.[31] The rescuer also owes to the rescued a duty to effect the rescue with reasonable care.[32] So if a fire breaks out it is reasonable to foresee that volunteers may be injured while trying to rescue persons or property.[33]

The principle also covers cases where the person rescued, who is the defendant in the action brought by the rescuer, has been put in peril by his own negligence, and not by that of another.[34] The principle even extends to

---

[20] *Per* Greer L.J., 157, citing the language of Goodhart, "Rescue and Voluntary Assumption of Risk" (1935) 5 Camb.L.J. 192, 196
[21] The fact that the plaintiff is under a legal duty to act in the emergency which has arisen is sometimes treated as a point in his favour, as in *Haynes* v. *Harwood* [1935] 1 K.B. 146, and sometimes as a point against him, as in *Russell* v. *McCabe* [1962] N.Z.L.R. 392, 406.
[22] *Gregory* v. *Miller, The Times*, February 9, 1933; *Morgan* v. *Aylen* [1942] 1 All E.R. 489.
[23] *Baker* v. *T.E. Hopkins & Sons Ltd.* [1959] 1 W.L.R. 966.
[24] *Baker* v. *T.E. Hopkins & Sons Ltd.* [1959] 1 W.L.R. 966, 976, 977.
[25] *Haynes* v. *Harwood* [1935] 1 K.B. 146, 158–159, 164.
[26] *Horsley* v. *MacLaren* (1972) 22 D.L.R. (3d) 545.
[27] *Hutterley* v. *Imperial Oil Co. and Calder* (1956) 3 D.L.R. (2d) 719.
[28] *Russell* v. *McCabe* [1962] N.Z.L.R. 392.
[29] *Hyett* v. *G.W.Ry.* [1948] 1 K.B. 345.
[30] *Hyett* v. *G.W.Ry.* [1948] 1 K.B. 345, 347–348.
[31] *The Tojo Maru* [1972] A.C. 242.
[32] *The Ogopogo* [1970] 1 Lloyd's Rep. 257.
[33] *Russell* v. *McCabe* [1962] N.Z.L.R. 392.
[34] *Baker* v. *T.E. Hopkins & Sons Ltd.* [1958] 1 W.L.R. 993, 1004.

cases where the person rescued has himself no cause of action at all, for example, because he is a trespasser or has waived his rights by a contract.[35] For the duty of care owed to a rescuer is an original one; it is not derived from or secondary to any duty owed to the rescued person by another,[36] but is an example of the "neighbour principle" in *Donoghue* v. *Stevenson.*[37] So it is settled that the rescuer is not deprived of remedy merely because the risk which he runs is not the same as that run by the party rescued. Indeed, the very fact of rescue involves unexpected things happening.[38] But the defendant, whether the person rescued or another, must first be proved to have been at fault. There is no liability when the defendant's negligence has not imperilled the person whose rescue the plaintiff attempted.[39]

Sometimes the courts have preferred to treat the rescue cases as raising a problem in the law relating to remoteness of damage. Is the intervention of the rescuer an act which breaks the causal sequence of events set in motion by the defendant's initial act of negligence? But "If what is relied upon as *novus actus interveniens* is the very kind of thing which is likely to happen if the want of care which is alleged takes place, the principle embodied in the maxim is no defence. The whole question is whether . . . the accident can be said to be 'the natural and probable result' of the breach of duty."[40] It is a question of fact in each case whether the damage suffered by the rescuer is a natural and probable, or reasonably foreseeable, result of the defendant's negligence. Thus a person who rushes out to stop a horse bolting on a desolate country road and is injured is probably without remedy.[41]

Volunteers

It was once held that the doctrine of common employment applied to any person who, on his own initiative, or at the request of a servant or his master, gratuitously and temporarily assisted the servant in his work. By such assistance he put himself *quoad hoc* in the position of a fellow-servant of the servant assisted by him, and therefore precluded himself from suing the employer for any harm resulting. Today it seems best to free these cases as far as possible from the entanglement of the obsolete doctrine of common employment. It is suggested that the true principle should be that one who interferes wilfully and officiously in another's affairs takes the risk of all injuries which are not inflicted in deliberate disregard of his presence. Such a person is a mere volunteer with no claim to better treatment than a trespasser.[42] This principle, however, has no application where (1) the

---

[35] *Videan* v. *British Transport Commission* |1963| 2 Q.B. 650, 669. It is a little difficult to follow the reasoning whereby the Court of Appeal held that the defendants ought to have foreseen that a stationmaster would attempt to rescue an infant on the lines (the infant being the stationmaster's son), yet need not have foreseen the presence of that infant himself.

[36] *Videan* v. *British Transport Commission* |1963| 2 Q.B. 650.

[37] For this, see above, § 72.

[38] *Chadwick* v. *British Railways Board* |1967| 1 W.L.R. 912.

[39] *Horsley* v. *MacLaren* (1972) 22 D.L.R. (3d) 545.

[40] *Haynes* v. *Harwood* |1935| 1 K.B. 146, 156, *per* Greer L.J.

[41] |1935| 1 K.B. at 163. See also *Cutler* v. *United Dairies (London) Ltd.* |1933| 2 K.B. 297; *Sylvester* v. *Chapman Ltd.* (1935) 79 S.J. 777 (plaintiff mauled by leopard whilst inside barrier endeavouring to extinguish cigarette end lying on straw at circus: action failed).

[42] This would be in accord with the refusal of the law of contracts to recognise the *negotiorum gestor* of Roman law. In our law liabilities are not to be forced on people behind their backs.

relationship of master and servant is in fact established between the parties, or (2) the plaintiff had volunteered to save the property of another in an emergency,[43] or (3) the plaintiff had a common interest in the matter with the defendant,[44] or (4) where the defendant was in all the circumstances of the case under a duty to take reasonable care for the plaintiff's safety. Such a duty may be established when the defendant invites the plaintiff to assist him in some job of work, even though the plaintiff stands to gain nothing from it.[45]

§ 190. PLAINTIFF A WRONGDOER[46]

This is a rather obscure corner of the law. Confusion has been increased by the use of the maxim *ex turpi causa non oritur actio*, which has its proper field of application in the law of contract.[47] There is also an overlap with the defences of consent and contributory negligence. So in *Murphy* v. *Culhane*[48] the Court of Appeal held that the defendant, who had pleaded guilty to the manslaughter of the plaintiff's husband, was entitled to raise these three defences in a civil action because the deceased had initiated the affray which led to his death. Another approach is to say that no duty of care exists as between participants in a crime.[49] Meanwhile at common law it is settled that if an act is in itself a criminal act it does not cease to be criminal because the person to whose detriment it is done consents to it. "No person can license another to commit a crime."[50] Thus no person can lawfully consent to his own death, so that killing a man in a duel is murder. Nor can anyone lawfully consent to bodily harm, save for some reasonable purpose: for example, a proper surgical operation or manly sports.[51]

It is not so clear whether consent in such cases is a good defence to a civil action, although it is submitted that on principle it ought to be, provided that the wrongful act is a step in the execution of the common illegal purpose, and not totally unconnected with it. So no action for negligence lies by a passenger in a vehicle against the driver of it, if the parties were joint participants in a burglary.[52] It may be different if the driver has, to the passenger's knowledge, simply been disqualified from driving.[53] On the other hand, "if A and B are proceeding to the premises which they intend burglariously to enter, and before they enter them, B picks A's pocket and steals his watch, I cannot prevail on myself to believe that A could not sue in tort."[54] In such a case the appropriate principle is that the mere fact that the

---

[43] *Cutler* v. *United Dairies Ltd.* [1933] 2 K.B. 297, 306–307.
[44] *Hayward* v. *Drury Lane Theatre* [1917] 2 K.B. 899; *Lomas* v. *Jones* [1944] K.B. 4.
[45] *Fitzgerald* v. *G.N.R. (I.) Ltd.* [1947] N.I. 1—a full review of the cases by MacDermott, J.
[46] See Williams, "Vicarious Liability" (1956) 72 L.Q.R. 522, 537–539; Crago, "The Defence of Illegality in Negligence Actions" (1964) 4 M.U.L.R. 534; Fridman, "The Wrongdoing Plaintiff" (1972) 18 *McGill L.J.* 276.
[47] *Smith* v. *Jenkins* (1970) 44 A.L.J.R. 78, 83.
[48] [1977] Q.B. 94.
[49] *Ashton* v. *Turner* [1981] Q.B. 137.
[50] *R.* v. *Donovan* [1934] 2 K.B. 498, 507.
[51] *R.* v. *Donovan* [1934] 2 K.B. 498, 509; *Bravery* v. *Bravery* [1954] 1 W.L.R. 1169.
[52] *Ashton* v. *Turner* [1981] Q.B. 137.
[53] *Jackson* v. *Harrison* (1978) 138 C.L.R. 438.
[54] *National Coal Board* v. *England* [1954] A.C. 403, 428, *per* Lord Asquith of Bishopstone. If the plaintiff in *Donoghue* v. *Stevenson* (above, § 73) had stolen the bottle of ginger-beer, would she have been successful? It is suggested that she would, because historically, causally, and morally, there is no significant relationship between the theft and the damage.

plaintiff is a wrongdoer is no defence.[55] Some examples of this principle may be offered. One who is a trespasser on land cannot be maltreated with impunity by the occupier,[56] and one who is in breach of the obligations for ensuring safety imposed by the Road Traffic Acts, or the Factories Acts, or the Mines and Quarries Act, is not debarred from suing although his damages may be reduced on the ground of contributory negligence.[57] It has even been held that one induced by fraud to transfer money can sue in deceit, although the transfer was in breach of the Exchange Control Act 1947.[58] It would be helpful if a statute briefly provided that it shall not be a defence merely to show that the plaintiff is in breach of the civil or criminal law.[59]

§ 191. STATUTORY AUTHORITY[60]

When a statute specially authorises a certain act to be done by a certain person, which would otherwise by unlawful and actionable, no action will lie at the suit of any person for the doing of that act. For such a statutory authority is also a statutory indemnity, taking away all legal remedies provided by the law of torts for persons injuriously affected. No compensation is obtainable save that, if any, which is expressly provided by the statute itself. This defence of statutory authority has its most important application in actions of nuisance, but it is one of general application throughout the whole sphere of civil liability. This statutory authority and indemnity extends not merely to the act itself but also to all its necessary consequences. When the legislature has authorised an act, it must be deemed also to have authorised by implication all inevitable results of that act; for otherwise the authority to do the act would be nugatory.[61] The test of the necessity of a consequence is the impossibility of avoiding it by the exercise of due care and skill. "The onus of proving that the result is inevitable is on those who wish to escape liability for nuisance, but the criterion of inevitability is not what is theoretically possible but what is possible according to the state of scientific knowledge at the time, having also in view a certain common-sense appreciation, which cannot be rigidly defined, of practical feasibility in view of situation and of expense."[62] "For I take it, without citing cases, that it is now thoroughly well established, that no action will lie for doing that which the legislature has authorised, if it be done without negligence, although it does occasion damage to anyone; but an action does lie for doing that which the legislature has authorised, if it be done negligently. And I think that if by a reasonable exercise of the powers, either given by statute to the promoters, or which they have at common law, the damage could be prevented, it is, within this rule, negligence not to make such reasonable exercise of their powers."[63]

---

[55] *Green* v. *Carroll* [1961] N.Z.L.R. 1010.
[56] Above, § 98.
[57] *National Coal Board* v. *England* [1954] A.C. 403.
[58] *Shelley* v. *Paddock* [1980] Q.B. 348.
[59] As does the Irish Civil Liability Act 1961, s. 57(1).
[60] See Craig, "Compensation in Public Law" (1980) 90 L.Q.R. 413.
[61] *Allen* v. *Gulf Oil Refining Co. Ltd.* [1981] 2 W.L.R. 188.
[62] *Manchester Corporation* v. *Farnworth* [1930] A.C. 171, 183, *per* Lord Dunedin. See *Provender Millers* v. *Southampton C.C.* [1940] Ch. 131, 136–140, 150.
[63] *Geddis* v. *Proprietors of Bann Reservoir* (1878) 3 App.Cas. 430, 455, *per* Lord Blackburn. *Dunne* v. *North-Western Gas Board* [1964] 2 Q.B. 806 is one of the many cases in which this dictum has been approved.

Thus in *Pride of Derby and Derbyshire Angling Association Ltd.* v. *British Celanese Ltd.*[64] the second defendant, the Derby Corporation, admitted that it had polluted the plaintiff's fishery in the River Derwent by discharging into it insufficiently treated sewage, but claimed that by the Derby Corporation Act 1901, it was under a duty to provide a sewerage system, and that the system which had accordingly been provided had become inadequate solely from the increase in the population of Derby. The Court of Appeal held that it was not inevitable that the work constructed under the Act of 1901 should cause a nuisance, and that in any case the Act on its true construction did not authorise the commission of a nuisance.

Different Classes of Statutes

It is very necessary, however, in the application of the foregoing rule to distinguish between absolute and conditional statutory authority. Absolute authority is authority to do the act notwithstanding the fact that it necessarily causes a nuisance or other injurious consequence. Conditional authority is authority to do the act provided it can be done without causing a nuisance or other injurious consequence. This condition is sometimes expressed, but is more often left to be implied from the general provisions of the statute. Where the authority is imperative, and not merely permissive, it is necessarily absolute—that is to say, when the statute not merely authorises but also directs a thing to be done, then it may be done regardless of any nuisance that necessarily flows from it.[65] An authority which is merely permissive, on the other hand, is prima facie conditional only; for the legislature will not be deemed, even at the present day, in the absence of special reasons for so holding, to have intended to take away the rights of private persons without compensation.[66] The burden of proof lies upon those who seek to show that a statute is intended to have such an intention to take away the private rights of individuals without compensation.[67]

In considering this question, a distinction may be drawn between statutory powers to execute some particular work or carry on some particular undertaking (*e.g.* the erection of a smallpox hospital in *Metropolitan Asylum District* v. *Hill*[67a]), when the power will be held to be limited to the particular act authorised, and statutory powers to execute a variety of works of specified descriptions in a given area which will necessarily involve some interference with the rights of others whenever the body invested with the power deems it expedient to do so in furtherance of a general duty imposed on it by the statute. The court will be readier to conclude that the case falls within the latter class and the common law right of action taken away if the statute expressly provides a remedy by way of compensation for persons injured by the exercise of the powers conferred. But the authority upon whom such statutory powers are conferred must in any case be acting in good faith and within the scope of the powers conferred.[68]

---

[64] [1953] Ch. 149.
[65] *Metropolitan Asylum District* v. *Hill* (1881) 6 App.Cas. 193, 213.
[66] (1881) 6 App.Cas. 193, 213.
[67] But the fact that no compensation has been provided for does not mean that no interference with private rights was intended: *Allen* v. *Gulf Oil Refining Co. Ltd.* [1981] 2 W.L.R. 188.
[67a] (1881) 6 App.Cas. 193.
[68] *Marriage* v. *East Norfolk Catchment Board* [1950] 1 K.B. 284, 305–306.

But cases such as *Metropolitan Asylum District* v. *Hill* are rare, for unless the statute gives the right to interfere with private rights it is seldom of much value.

Powers and duties[69]

After *East Suffolk Rivers Catchment Board* v. *Kent*[70] a distinction was drawn between statutory duties and statutory powers. If the statute imposed a duty, then a breach of that duty might be actionable in tort at the suit of a private person, provided always that a court could hold that such was the intention of Parliament when the statute was enacted.[71] But if there was a statutory power or discretion, then there could be no complaint about its exercise until the plaintiff suffered more harm than if nothing at all had been done.

This distinction gave rise to increasing doubts, and in *Anns* v. *Merton London Borough Council*[72] the law was re-stated. There has been no change in the accepted principles governing actions for breach of statutory duties.[73] But if there is a statutory power, then a further distinction must be made between policy or planning decisions and operational decisions. Policy decisions are a matter for public law alone. But operational decisions may give rise to a common law duty of reasonable care. Whether the statutory framework permits the imposition of such a duty cannot be answered simply by an invocation of the neighbour principle. A closer analysis of the relevant statute will be required before the relevant degree of proximity can be discovered. This is a fast-moving area of the law.[74] So in *Anns* itself the question how many, if any, inspectors should be appointed was a matter of policy for which the council were responsible only to the electors. But the question whether there was carelessness in carrying out an inspection was an operational matter for which the Council would be vicariously responsible if the plaintiff could prove his case by interrogatories or otherwise.

§ 192. CONTRIBUTORY NEGLIGENCE: PRELIMINARY

Contributory negligence once comprised one of the most difficult branches of the law. Fortunately, however, the Law Reform (Contributory Negligence) Act 1945, and several decisions of the highest courts, have introduced a straightforward and comprehensive body of principles in place of a mass of subtle arguments and tedious refinements. The account which follows is intended to contain no more than is necessary for an understanding of the present law,[75] which is derived from more than one source. In particular it embodies two distinct principles which do not always har-

---

[69] See N. Seddon, *The Negligence Liability of Statutory Bodies* (1978) 9 F.L.R. 326, P.P. Craig, "Negligence in the Exercise of a Statutory Power" (1978) 94 L.Q.R. 428; D. Oliver, "*Anns Reconsidered*" (1980) C.L.P. 269.

[70] [1941] A.C. 74.

[71] See Chap. 10 above for the complex law on this matter.

[72] [1978] A.C. 728. See above, § 101A.

[73] The decision in *Anns* "is miles away" from these principles: *Haydon* v. *Kent County Council* [1978] Q.B. 343, 361, *per* Lord Denning M.R.

[74] *Takaro Properties Ltd.* v. *Rowling (No.* 2) [1978] 2 N.Z.L.R. 314, 316.

[75] Further information: Williams, *Joint Torts and Contributory Negligence*; Keeler, "Alford v. Magee and the Apportionment Legislation" (1967) 41 A.L.J. 148; Fleming, "Comparative Negligence At Last" (1976) 64 Calif.L.Rev. 239.

monise. The doctrine that if the plaintiff's act was the proximate cause of the damage the plaintiff could not recover was a well-established principle of medieval law. In the sixteenth and seventeenth centuries the conception of negligence as a ground of liability worked its way into the common law. Therefore a practice grew up of alleging that a plaintiff could not recover because he was debarred by his own negligence. So we find a penal theory of contributory negligence.[76] In the same way it is common to speak of a plaintiff as being "guilty" of contributory negligence. But the penal theory is inconsistent with the application of the law by the courts. A plaintiff may have been ever so negligent at some stage of the proceedings, but he will be able to recover if his negligence did not contribute to the accident, even if his negligence was criminal. On the other hand, the doctrine of contributory negligence is more than an application of the rule as to remoteness of damage. For if a third party is injured the negligence of each—both the plaintiff and the defendant—is treated as a cause of the accident: each is liable to the third party.[77] Nor is the defence of contributory negligence an application of the maxim *volenti non fit injuria*, although the two principles have often been confused.[78] The defence of contributory negligence confesses and avoids a prima facie liability, it excludes the idea of deliberation, and relies upon the failure of the plaintiff to exercise reasonable care. Of the defence that the plaintiff has consented to run the risk, none of these three statements is true.

§ 193. CONTRIBUTORY NEGLIGENCE: THE COMMON LAW

"The rule of law," said Lord Blackburn,[79] "is that if there is blame causing the accident on both sides, however small that blame may be on one side, the loss lies where it falls." Thus in *Butterfield* v. *Forrester*[80] the defendant wrongfully obstructed a street in Derby by placing a pole across it, and the plaintiff rode along the street "at eight o'clock in the evening of August, when they were just beginning to light candles," but while there was still sufficient light to notice the obstruction, and coming into collision with the pole he was thrown from his horse and injured. It was held that he had no cause of action, as he could, notwithstanding the defendant's negligence, have avoided the accident by the use of due care.

Principle in Davies v. Mann

It soon became apparent, however, that there were cases where there was so substantial a difference between the position of the two parties at the material time that, although the accident would not have occurred without

---

[76] See *Wakelin* v. *L.S.W.Ry.* (1886) 12 App.Cas. 41, 45.
[77] *M'Kenna* v. *Stephens and Hull* [1923] 2 I.R. 112; *Grant* v. *Sun Shipping Co.* [1948] A.C. 549, 563–564. See the cases on the doctrine of identification, below, § 194, and the valuable anonymous brochure published in Tasmania in 1936 and entitled *Contributory Negligence and Third Parties*.
[78] See also above, § 188.
[79] *Cayzer, Irvine & Co.* v. *Carron Co.* (1884) 9 App.Cas. 873, 881.
[80] (1809) 11 East 60. This case is commonly cited as the source of the doctrine but the term "contributory negligence" is not used in it and the conception can be traced further back.

the plaintiff's negligence, it would not be fair or reasonable to regard him as the author of his own wrong. This is the fundamental (though seldom openly expressed) idea behind a series of cases which begin with *Davies* v. *Mann*.[81] In this case the plaintiff negligently left his donkey, with its legs tied, in the highway. The defendant, driving his waggon and horses "at a smartish pace," crashed into the animal and killed it. It was held that the defendant was liable. "Although the ass may have been wrongfully there," said Parke B.,[82] "still the defendant was bound to go along the road at such a pace as would be likely to prevent mischief. Were this not so, a man might justify the driving over goods left on a public highway, or even over a man lying asleep there, or the purposely running against a carriage going on the wrong side of the road." In this case the expression "contributory negligence" was not used, nor is it clear whether the defendant did or did not see the ass; he probably did see it but too late.[83]

Salmond invents the last opportunity rule

The doctrine laid down in these cases with the object of mitigating the harshness of the original common law rules has often been called (although not in the cases themselves) the doctrine, or rule, of the "last opportunity," the "last clear opportunity," or the "last clear chance." Indeed, the first person to use the term appears to have been Salmond himself. Writing in 1912[84] he summarised the effect of the cases at that time in the following words[85]: "*Ex hypothesi* in all cases of contributory negligence the defendant has been guilty of negligence which caused the accident: therefore in all cases he could by the exercise of reasonable care have avoided the accident; and therefore . . . he is liable notwithstanding the contributory negligence of the plaintiff. Clearly, therefore, something more than a mere opportunity of avoiding the accident by reasonable care is required in order to bring the rule in *Davies* v. *Mann* into operation. . . . Subject to certain qualifications, it would seem that the true test is the existence of the *last* opportunity of avoiding the accident. . . . "[86]

This admirable passage is open to discussion on two points. First, it necessarily required modification in later editions in order to accommodate the strange case of *British Columbia Electric Ry.* v. *Loach*.[87] The facts of that case were as follows: An action was brought against a railway company by the administrator of a man who, while being driven in a waggon across a level crossing, was run down and killed by an electric car. The

[81] (1842) 10 M. & W. 546.
[82] *Ibid.* 549. ("Probably the most acute and accomplished lawyer this country ever saw": *Brinsmead* v. *Harrison* (1871) L.R. 7 C.P. 547, 554, *per* Blackburn J.).
[83] This is the accepted view. Rand J. thought he did not: *Bruce* v. *MacIntyre* [1955] 1 D.L.R. 785, 787. The collateral report in 6 Jur. 954 makes it clear that the defendant was some distance behind his horses (presumably on foot) at the moment of collision.
[84] 3rd ed., pp. 39–43; 6th ed., pp. 40–42.
[85] Which were cited with approval by the High Court of Australia in *Alford* v. *Magee* (1952) 84 C.L.R. 437, 456.
[86] "What the defendant has to avoid is, not the consequences of the plaintiff's negligence, but the accident, which is the consequence of the combined effect of his own and of the plaintiff's negligence, and without both of which it would not have happened": *Neenan* v. *Hosford* [1920] 2 I.R. 258, 291, *per* Ronan L.J. It is put thus in all the best authorities.
[87] [1916] 1 A.C. 719.

deceased was guilty of negligence in failing to look out for the car before entering upon the line.[88] The company was also guilty of negligence in running the car at an excessive speed and with a defective brake. The driver saw the horses as they came into view from behind a shed, when they were ten or twelve feet from the nearest rail, and he at once applied his brake. He was then 400 feet from the crossing, and if the brake had been in good order he could have stopped the car in 300 feet. In fact, however, the brake was out of order, and the car overran the crossing and ran the waggon down. The Judicial Committee held the railway company liable, notwithstanding the negligence of the deceased. From *Loach's* case it appears that a last opportunity which the defendant would have had but for his own negligence is equivalent in law to one which he actually had.[89]

Secondly, Salmond's use of the phrase "the last opportunity" was understood as suggesting that such an opportunity must have been always available to one or other of the parties, although "this is clearly remote from what the author meant."[90] The fallacy of the notion that the test of the last opportunity was a rule of law applicable over the whole field of contributory negligence can be demonstrated most readily by reference to the very common case of a highway collision between two modern fast-moving vehicles, for here the maximum period of time available to either party for avoiding the accident is seldom as much as a few seconds.[91] Yet it was in just such a case that the House of Lords was invited to say that Humphreys J. had misdirected a Cambridge special jury by refusing to leave to them the issue of the last opportunity and asking them instead to answer the simple question: Whose negligence was it that substantially caused the injury?[92] But the House held that in the circumstances of that case (a crossroads collision between a car and a motor-cycle) that was a sufficient direction.[93] Henceforward this interpretation of the rule of last opportunity became increasingly suspect and finally it was abandoned in *The Boy Andrew (Owners)* v. *St. Rognvald (Owners).*[94]

---

[88] The case, as Scrutton L.J. pointed out in *Compania Mexicana de Petroleo* v. *Essex Transport Co.* (1929) 141 L.T. 106, 112, is a "very odd" one, because it suggests that a passenger is bound to take extraordinary precautions to see that the road is clear. Yet a passenger is no longer identified with his driver. The fact that the deceased was a passenger escaped Lord Wright in his judgment in *McLean* v. *Bell* (1932) 147 L.T. 262, 264.

[89] Few decisions given by so eminent a tribunal (Lord Sumner delivered the judgment of a Board composed of himself, Lord Haldane and Lord Parker of Waddington) have given rise to so much criticism. "The truth is that no one knows precisely what it settled": Williams, *Contributory Negligence*, p. 234. See also Monteith, Note (1949) 65 L.Q.R. 318. *Loach's* case is no longer law: *Marvin Sigurdson* v. *British Columbia Electric Railway Co.* [1953] A.C. 291, 312.

[90] *Alford* v. *Magee* (1952) 85 C.L.R. 437, 457.

[91] See *Gomersall* v. *Yole* [1954] V.L.R. 269.

[92] *Swadling* v. *Cooper* [1931] A.C. 1.

[93] Yet it should be noticed that the jury returned to court and told the judge that they did not understand it. (This lends point to the remarks of du Parcq L.J. in *Gibby* v. *East Grinstead Gas Co.* [1944] 1 All E.R. 358, 363: "Unless the trial had taken place in a university city and it had happened that the jury was composed mainly of philosophers and logicians, I doubt if a discussion of theories of causation would have either assisted or interested them.") The jury's difficulty was no doubt caused by the fact that although the question was perfectly sensible they could not (as the law then stood) return a sensible answer to it. For if they replied: "They both caused it," as they would rightly wish to do, and did, the plaintiff would recover nothing—as in fact happened.

[94] [1948] A.C. 140, 148–149. (In [1947] 2 All E.R. 350, *sub nom.* (more correctly) *Admiralty Commissioners* v. *North of Scotland and Orkney and Shetland Steam Navigation Co.*).

Conclusion

A number of other judicial statements of high authority[95] have made it clear that the rule of last opportunity, in this incorrect sense of the term, suffered a demise quite independently of the Act of 1945.[96] Indeed, it may well be that in this sense the rule was never really law at all, for it seems to have been adopted in no case of good authority in any jurisdiction in the Commonwealth.[97] On the contrary, some judges always realised that the principle in *Davies* v. *Mann* was not entirely equivalent to the last opportunity rule.[98] As the High Court of Australia has said[99]: "It is a sound 'rule,' only if it is framed in the terms in which it was originally framed by Salmond, and if it is recognised that it does not cover the whole ground. If it is expanded in a hopeless attempt to meet cases to which it is inappropriate, and subjected to innumerable refinements, it becomes not merely unsound but unintelligible." The last opportunity rule no longer exists in England, according to judicial decision,[1] or in Ireland, according to statute.[2]

§ 194. CONTRIBUTORY NEGLIGENCE: IN ADMIRALTY

Before the Law Reform (Contributory Negligence) Act 1945 is discussed it may be helpful to indicate the rules of maritime law governing collisions at sea. For although by section 3 (1) of the Law Reform (Contributory Negligence) Act that Act does not apply to any claim to which section 1 of the Maritime Conventions Act 1911 applies, the principles to be applied at common law are now the same as those applied in admiralty. The Maritime Conventions Act enabled the court to apportion the loss according to the degree to which each party was in fault,[3] but the court had first to decide whether the fault of either vessel had contributed to the loss or damage suffered. This problem was in general solved by applying the principles familiar to the courts of common law: "The legal doctrine of causation in admiralty law was not different from the rule at common law—it merely differed in respect of the consequences."[4] In practice, this has been

---

[95] Speaking of the period after *Swadling* v. *Cooper*, Lord du Parcq said: "But the 'rule of the last opportunity' still haunted the courts. I well remember the pained expression which used to appear on the faces of some counsel when, as a comparatively young judge, I irreverently expressed doubts about its existence. I might have been Betsy Prig questioning the existence of Mrs. Harris, 'Have I know'd Mrs. Harris five-and-thirty year,' said Mrs. Gamp, 'to be told at last that there ain't no such person living?' Perhaps Betsy Prig was not the only unbeliever, certainly I was not, and now the daring statement of the Law Revision Committee that 'there is no such rule' has been adopted and authoritatively affirmed by Viscount Simon *ex cathedra* in the House of Lords. . . . How much has been swept away with the débris of the rule—what a mass of verbal refinements, of logic-chopping, of the results of pointless microscopical research!": *Aspects of the Law* (Holdsworth Club, 1948), p. 22. See also *Grant* v. *Sun Shipping Co.* [1948] A.C. 549, 563.
[96] *Davies* v. *Swan Motor Co.* [1949] 2 K.B. 291, 318, 321, *Jones* v. *Livox Quarries Ltd.* [1952] 2 Q.B. 608, 615.
[97] *Alford* v. *Magee* (1952) 85 C.L.R. 437, 457.
[98] *Davies* v. *Swan Motor Co. Ltd.* [1949] 2 K.B. 291, 318.
[99] *Alford* v. *Magee* (1952) 85 C.L.R. 437, 460.
[1] *Chisman* v. *Electromation (Export) Ltd.* (1969) 6 K.I.R. 456.
[2] Civil Liability Act 1961, (s.56).
[3] (s.1): "Where, by the fault of two or more vessels, damage or loss is caused to one or more of those vessels, to their cargoes or freight, or to any property on board, the liability to make good the damage or loss shall be in proportion to the degree in which each vessel was in fault: Provided that if, having regard to all the circumstances of the case, it is not possible to establish different degrees of fault, the liability shall be apportioned equally."
[4] *Davies* v. *Swan Motor Co.* [1949] 2 K.B. 291, 310, *per* Bucknill L.J.

interpreted, probably wrongly, against a background of pre-existing practice, to mean that the court should depart from a 50-50 per cent. allocation of loss only when there is clear evidence.[5]

The principle in The Volute

The "rule of last opportunity," in the erroneous sense which has already been explained, was, however, never accepted in admiralty. There was no place for it. It had been invented by the courts of common law as an exception to their general rule that the contributory negligence of the plaintiff defeated his claim, but since the Court of Admiralty did not recognise that rule there was no need for the exception. All this was made plain in the memorable speech of Viscount Birkenhead L.C. in *The Volute*,[6] which received the rare distinction of warm approval from the other members of the House.[7] Lord Birkenhead said:

> "Upon the whole I think that the question of contributory negligence must be dealt with somewhat broadly and upon commonsense principles as a jury would probably deal with it. And while no doubt, where a clear line can be drawn, the subsequent negligence is the only one to look to, there are cases in which the two acts come so closely together, and the second act of negligence is so much mixed up with the state of things brought about by the first act, that the party secondly negligent, while not held free from blame under the *Bywell Castle* rule,[8] might, on the other hand, invoke the prior negligence as being part of the cause of the collision so as to make it a case of contribution."

In this case a collision had occurred in the North Atlantic between the *Radstock*, a destroyer, and the *Volute*, a merchant ship under convoy. The collision was due to the fault of the *Volute* in changing her course without giving the proper whistle-signal, and to the immediately subsequent fault of the *Radstock* in increasing her speed with knowledge of the danger caused by the *Volute's* change of course. For the *Volute* it was argued that apportionment was possible only when the faults of the two ships were simultaneous or synchronous and never when (as was alleged against the *Radstock*) one ship had an opportunity of avoiding the accident which the other had not. Equally fallacious was the argument of the *Radstock* to the effect that whenever a collision was brought about by the faults of two vessels the loss must automatically be divided in some proportion, for it might be possible to find a clear dividing line so as to entitle the court to throw the entire loss on the party subsequently and severably negligent. A middle view was possible and desirable. It was held that both ships were to

---

[5] *The Lucile Bloomfield* [1967] 2 All E.R. 633 (this point is not reported in [1967] 1 W.L.R. 697).
[6] [1922] 1 A.C. 129, 144.
[7] "I regard the judgment to which we have just listened as a great and permanent contribution to our law on the subject of contributory negligence, and to the science of jurisprudence": Lord Finlay (with whom Lord Shaw concurred) at 145. But it has been said that the speech was really written by Lord Phillimore, and that Lord Finlay's effusive praise was in truth subtle denigration: Lord Wright (1950) 13 M.L.R. 17; Goodhart, 7 J.S.P.T.L. 181. The speech (whatever its source) has been consistently cited with approval.
[8] For this rule, see below, § 196.

blame and that both were responsible, although the last opportunity of avoiding the collision was with the *Radstock*.

§ 195. WHAT NEGLIGENCE IS CONTRIBUTORY

Such then are the main causes of the confusion which has prevailed in the law of contributory negligence. With them present to our minds we will endeavour to state the governing principles of this defence, leaving aside for the moment any question arising out of *Davies* v. *Mann*. The present law may be summarised in the following propositions.

(1) Plaintiff need not owe any duty to defendant

The question of contributory negligence does not depend upon any breach of duty as between the plaintiff and the defendant.[9] This is a significant exception to the general principle that the question whether the plaintiff's conduct amounts to contributory negligence is to be decided according to the same principles as the question whether the defendant's conduct amounts to negligence. To this extent contributory negligence is subjective, whereas primary negligence is objective.[10] All that the defendant is obliged to prove is that the plaintiff failed to take reasonable precautions for his own safety in respect of the particular danger which in fact occurred, so that he thereby contributed to his own injury.[11] So a plaintiff motor cyclist who fails to wear a crash helmet is not thereby in breach of any duty to the defendant, but yet he may be held guilty of contributory negligence.[12] The same is true of a passenger in a vehicle who fails to use a seat belt, for, in determining what is contributory negligence, the court is entitled to look to the cause of the damage as well as the cause of the negligence.[13] This, however, is not to say that in all cases the plaintiff who is guilty of contributory negligence owes to the defendant no duty to act carefully. Such a duty will normally be owed in most cases of highway collisions.[14]

(2) Inoperative negligence to be distinguished from contributory negligence

It may be useful to observe that these difficult problems never arise unless it is proved, not merely that both parties were negligent, but that the negligence of each of them was a contributory cause of the accident.[15] The defendant may have been negligent, but if the accident was caused exclusively by the negligence of the plaintiff, it is not a case of contributory negligence at all. Conversely, the plaintiff may have been negligent, but unless that negligence was an operative cause of the accident none of the problems connected with contributory negligence arise. He may have been drunk, but if the defendant would have equally run him down had he been

---

[9] *Nance* v. *British Columbia Electric Ry. Co.* [1951] A.C. 601. It is strange that this company should have been the unsuccessful party to an appeal in three of the leading cases on contributory negligence.
[10] *McHale* v. *Watson* (1964) 111 C.L.R. 384.
[11] *Moor* v. *Nolan* (1960) 94 I.L.T.R. 153.
[12] *O'Connell* v. *Jackson* [1972] 1 Q.B. 270.
[13] *Froom* v. *Butcher* [1976] Q.B. 286.
[14] *Nance* v. *British Columbia Electric Ry. Co.* [1951] A.C. 601, 611.
[15] See Lord Simon in the *Boy Andrew Case* [1948] A.C. 140, 148—where each ship admitted she was to blame but maintained her negligence was not even a cause of the collision.

sober there is no question of contributory negligence.[16] In such a case the
negligence of the plaintiff did no more than account for his being in a place
where the negligence of the defendant operated.[17] The governing principle is
that the plaintiff's failure to exercise reasonable care for his own protection
does not amount to contributory negligence in respect of damage unless that
damage results from the particular risk to which his conduct has exposed
him.[18] Therefore, no question of operative contributory negligence arises in
a case where the defendant proves only that the plaintiff has failed to take
precautions against a foreseeable danger which has not occurred and that
those precautions, if taken, would have been effective to protect him against
the unforeseeable danger which in fact occurred.[19] A motorist who drives
straight across a light-controlled crossing against the red light and knocks
down a pedestrian who has begun to cross in reliance on the lights but without looking over his right shoulder cannot be heard to say that the
pedestrian is thereby guilty of contributory negligence as against him,
though such conduct on the part of the pedestrian might attract that description if he had been knocked down by a motorist lawfully turning left with the
green light in his favour.[20] The statement that the plaintiff must be shown to
have failed to take proper precautions for his own safety against the
particular danger which in fact occurred does not mean that the particular
form in which the danger manifested itself should actually have occurred to
his mind. It is sufficient if it is a danger of a particular class whose
occurrence he should anticipate and take reasonable precautions to guard
against.[21]

(3) The plaintiff's right to rely on the care of others[22]

In many cases the plaintiff is entitled to assume that there is no danger. So
a workman is entitled to assume that his employer has complied with his
statutory duties.[23] If an accident happens in such a case, the defendant will
not be heard to say that the plaintiff might have avoided it by care, because
no such care was obligatory on him.[24] There is in general no duty to
anticipate that another will be negligent, and to avoid the effects of that
negligence by anticipation.[25] So both the pedestrian[26] and the motorist[27] is
entitled to proceed more or less upon the assumption that the drivers of all
the other vehicles will do what it is their duty to do, namely, observe the
rules regulating the traffic of the streets. But there is a distinction between
legal duties and the common courtesies of the road. So a driver who flashes
his lights at another who is waiting to come out of a side-road does not
thereby undertake any duty to that other: he merely means "Come forward,

[16] *Woods* v. *Davison* [1930]) N.I. 161 (H.L.).
[17] *Moor* v. *Nolan* (1960) 94 I.L.T.R. 153, 159.
[18] *Jones* v. *Livox Quarries Ltd.* [1952] 2 Q.B. 608. The law is so stated in the Irish Civil
     Liability Act 1961, s.34(2)(c).
[19] *Moor* v. *Nolan* (1960) 94 I.L.T.R. 153.
[20] *Eva (Joseph) Ltd.* v. *Reeves* [1938] 2 K.B. 393; *Moor* v. *Nolan* (1960) 94 I.L.T.R. 153.
[21] *Moor* v. *Nolan* (1960) 94 I.L.T.R. 153, 160-161.
[22] See also above, §§ 80–82.
[23] *Westwood* v. *Post Office* [1974] A.C. 1.
[24] *Grant* v. *Sun Shipping Co.* [1948] A.C. 549, 567.
[25] *Compania Mexicana* v. *Essex Transport Co.* (1929) 141 L.T. 106, 115.
[26] "The passenger is not bound to look out for mats on the highway. He may look at the stars
     if he likes": *De Teyron* v. *Waring* (1884) 1 T.L.R. 414, *per* Lord Coleridge C.J.
[27] *Toronto Railway Co.* v. *King* [1908] A.C. 260, 269.

I am waiting for you."[28] Yet there are some cases where a prudent man will guard against the possible negligence of others when experience shows such negligence to be common.[29] Experience shows this to be particularly common on the highway. A driver is not bound to anticipate folly in all its forms, but he is not entitled to put out of consideration the teachings of experience as to the form those follies commonly take.[30] So a driver entering a light-controlled crossing with the green light in his favour is not entitled to assume that no other driver will enter against the red light. He is still obliged to keep a reasonable look-out commensurate with the circumstances existing at the time, although his duty is not so onerous as if the crossing was uncontrolled.[31]

But although pedestrians are under a duty to guard against normal acts of careless driving they are not under a duty to guard against "monstrous driving."[32] Highway authorities must also have regard to foreseeable hazards—*e.g.* that motorists will leave the carriageway, whether through a fault of their own or not.[33]

(4) The doctrine of alternative danger: the "dilemma principle"

Where the plaintiff is perplexed or agitated or deceived by being exposed to danger by the wrongful act of the defendant, it is sufficient if he shows as much judgment and self-control in attempting to avoid that danger as may reasonably be expected of him in the circumstances. Although the reasonable man is cool and collected and remembers to take precautions for his own safety even in an emergency,[34] what is done or omitted to be done in "the agony of the moment" cannot fairly be treated as negligence,[35] unless the plaintiff's trade or calling is such that a certain degree of aptitude for dealing with dangerous situations may be expected of him.[36] The courts do not demand of the plaintiff the care of a superman,[37] but only that of a man of ordinary nerve and presence of mind. So in *Jones* v. *Boyce*,[38] in a coach accident, the plaintiff was placed by the negligence of the defendant in a perilous alternative—to jump or not to jump. He jumped and was injured. Had he kept his seat he would have escaped. But he was able to recover from the defendant, for he had acted reasonably and not from a rash apprehension of danger. So a lady locked in a public lavatory is entitled to make reasonable efforts to escape from her predicament.[39] The same rule is applied in cases of collisions at sea and is known as the rule in *The Bywell Castle*.[40] On the other hand, it must be remembered that such an emergency does not last for ever.[41]

---

[28] *Clarke* v. *Winchurch* [1969] 1 W.L.R. 69.
[29] *Grant* v. *Sun Shipping Co.* [1948] A.C. 549, 567.
[30] *L.P.T.B.* v. *Upson* [1949] A.C. 155, 173.
[31] *Doyle* v. *H.F. Murray Ltd.* [1967] I.R. 390.
[32] *Frank* v. *Cox, The Times,* May 11, 1967.
[33] *Levine* v. *Morris* [1970] 1 W.L.R. 71.
[34] *Ghannan* v. *Glasgow Corporation,* 1950 S.C. 23, 28 ("It will not do to equate the reasonable man to the young man in a hurry"—*per* Lord Cooper).
[35] *Jones* v. *G.W. Ry.* (1930) 144 L.T. 194, 201.
[36] *Brown* v. *Hunt,* 1953 (2) S.A. 540.
[37] *U.S. Shipping Board* v. *Laird Line Ltd.* [1924] A.C. 286, 292.
[38] (1816) 1 Starkie 493.
[39] *Sayers* v. *Harlow U.D.C.* [1958] 1 W.L.R. 623.
[40] (1879) 4 P.D. 219.
[41] *Rickman* v. *Railway Executive* (1950) 83 Ll.L.R. 409, 411.

So also a plaintiff is not necessarily guilty of contributory negligence simply because he has knowledge of a danger which the defendant has wrongfully created, but chooses to run the risk rather than to forgo the exercise of his liberty of action.[42] Similarly if the plaintiff is invited or ordered by the defendant to run the risk in question he cannot be held guilty of contributory negligence in doing so.[43] This doctrine has been further extended to cover the case of a plaintiff acting under the compulsion of a legal or moral duty.[44] This doctrine of alternative danger applies not only where one of the parties to an action has been negligent (and it should be remembered that it may apply in favour of the defendant as well as of the plaintiff),[45] but also when the emergency has been created by the negligence of a third party or by an act of God.[46] It also extends to cases where the property (as distinct from the person) of the plaintiff or another has been endangered.[47]

It may well be that since the courts have been given power to apportion the loss the doctrine of alternative danger (like the test of last opportunity) has lost its place in the law.[48] The question now is whether the party acted reasonably in all the circumstances of the case.

(5) Contributory negligence of children and persons under disability

The governing principles here are in theory the same as for the standard of care to be expected of a defendant.[49] But in practice a subjective approach is often adopted, which takes into account the deficiencies or idiosyncrasies of the plaintiff.[50] In the case of a child of tender years there must be some age up to which the child cannot be expected to take any pre-cautions for his own safety.[51] In cases where contributory negligence is alleged against a child, it is the duty of the trial judge to rule, in each particular case, whether the plaintiff, having regard to his age and mental development, may properly be expected to take some precautions for his own safety and consequently be capable of being guilty of contributory negligence. Having ruled in the affirmative, it becomes a question of fact for the jury, on the evidence, to determine whether he has fallen short of the standard which might reasonably be expected from him having regard to his age and development. In the case of an ordinary adult person the standard is what should be expected from a reasonable person. In the case of a child, the standard is what may reasonably be expected, having regard to the age and mental development of the child and the other circumstances of the

---

[42] *Billings (A.C.) & Sons Ltd.* v. *Riden* [1958] A.C. 240. See above, § 188.
[43] *Yarmouth* v. *France* (1887) 19 Q.B.D. 647.
[44] *Haynes* v. *Harwood* [1935] 1 K.B. 146. See above, § 189.
[45] *Swadling* v. *Cooper* [1931] A.C. 1, 9; *McLean* v. *Bell* (1932) 147 L.T. 262, 263.
[46] *Brown* v. *Hunt*, 1953 (2) S.A. 540.
[47] *Wilson* v. *United Counties Bank* [1920] A.C. 102, 125; *Sutherland* v. *Glasgow Corporation*, 1951 S.C. 1. *Contra*, Lord Sumner in *Singleton Abbey (Owners)* v. *Paludina (Owners)* [1927] A.C. 16, 28.
[48] Williams, (s. 91).
[49] See above, § 80.
[50] *Kingston* v. *Kingston* (1968) 102 I.L.T.R. 65.
[51] In *Donovan* v. *Landy's Ltd.* [1963] I.R. 441 a child of 6½ was held capable of contributory negligence.

case.[52] The phrase "age and mental development" may mean either the mental development of the particular child, or the mental development of the average child of that age,[53] but in practice the courts are not anxious to penalise a child who is unusually intelligent or well-informed. Certainly an ordinary thirteen-year-old girl is not necessarily guilty of contributory negligence if she crosses the road at the signal of a halted lorry-driver without pausing to see if a vehicle is wrongly overtaking the lorry on the far side.[54]

(6) Contributory negligence in factory cases[55]

It has been laid down in a series of cases arising out of claims made under the Factories Act that it is not every error of judgment or heedlessness or inadvertence which amounts to contributory negligence.[56] But when the defendant has been guilty of a flagrant and continuous breach of the regulations, and an accident happens which is of the nature intended to be guarded against by the regulations, then the court "must be careful not to emasculate that regulation by the side-wind of apportionment."[57]

(7) Contributory negligence of plaintiff's servants and agents[58]

The contributory negligence of a servant of the plaintiff is a good defence, in the same cases and to the same extent as that of the plaintiff himself, whenever the plaintiff would have been responsible for that negligence of his servant had harm ensued from it. In other words, the rule that the negligence of a servant in the course of his employment is imputed to his master is applicable when the master is a plaintiff no less than when he is a defendant.[59] It should be remembered that one spouse may be the servant or agent of the other. Hence if a husband is a passenger in a motor-car which is being driven by his wife as his servant or agent, and a collision occurs as a result of the combined negligence of the wife and a third party in which the husband is injured, the damages which may be awarded to him for his personal injuries may be reduced by the amount to which she is in fault.[60] Presumably the same principle applies to other forms of vicarious liability.[61]

---

[52] *Fleming* v. *Kerry County Council* [1955–56] Ir.Jur.Rep. 71, 72, *per* O'Byrne J., approved in *Macnamara* v. *E.S.B.* [1975] I.R. 1, 18.
[53] *Duffy* v. *Fahy* [1960] Ir.Jur.Rep. 69, 74.
[54] *Gough* v. *Thorne* [1966] 1 W.L.R. 1387. Most of the law on this topic goes back to *Lynch* v. *Nurdin* (1841) 1 Q.B. 30, which is considered above, § 99.
[55] See Fagelson, "The Last Bastion of Fault" (1979) 42 M.L.R. 646.
[56] *Mullard* v. *Ben Line Steamers Ltd.* [1970] 1 W.L.R. 1414. See also above, § 130.
[57] *Mullard* v. *Ben Line Steamers Ltd.* [1970] 1 W.L.R. 1414, 1418, *per* Sachs L.J.
[58] On this topic consult MacIntyre, "The Rationale of Imputed Negligence" (1944) 5 Univ. of Toronto L.J. 368; Williams, *Contributory Negligence*, (s. 115).
[59] The Law Reform (Contributory Negligence) Act 1945, does not expressly provide for this situation, but it cannot have been intended to alter the well-settled law on this point. In *Mallett* v. *Dunn* [1949] 2 K.B. 180, it was assumed that the Act applied in a case of imputed negligence.
[60] *Berrill* v. *Road Haulage Executive* [1952] 2 Lloyd's Rep. 490; *Lampert* v. *Eastern National Omnibus Co.* [1954] 1 W.L.R. 1047; *Rome* v. *Manawatu County* [1955] N.Z.L.R. 165. *Aliter* with his claim for loss of services, which is a distinct cause of action: *Mallett* v. *Dunn* [1949] 2 K.B. 180; Davis, "Contributory Negligence: the Second Plaintiff" (1950) 13 M.L.R. 213.
[61] *The Bernina* (1888) 13 App.Cas. 1, 16.

Exploded doctrine of identification

(i) Passengers

The contributory negligence of an independent contractor or other agent of the plaintiff for whom he is not responsible, on the other hand, is no bar to the plaintiff's action. If a taxi-cab hired by the plaintiff comes into collision with another vehicle by the negligence of both drivers, and the plaintiff is hurt, he can recover damages not only from his own driver but also from the other.[62] It was for some time, indeed, believed that this was not so, and that the negligence of the driver of a vehicle was imputed to the passenger with the result that the passenger lost his remedy against third persons. This unreasonable doctrine, sometimes known as "the doctrine of identification," was overruled by the House of Lords in *Mills* v. *Armstrong, The Bernina.*[63]

(ii) Children in the charge of adults

It was once thought that a child in the charge of an adult was so far "identified" with that adult as to disentitle it from suing for personal injuries caused by the negligence of the adult and a third party.[64] In *Oliver* v. *Birmingham and Midland Omnibus Co.,*[65] in which the plaintiff, aged four years, was injured due to the combined negligence of his grandfather (in whose care he was) and the defendants, it was held that since *The Bernina* this doctrine was no longer law. The fact that the child is in the charge of an adult may, however, in certain cases exempt the defendant from a duty which would otherwise exist of care towards the child—the defendant being entitled to assume that the child will be duly protected by its adult guardian, and therefore is not in danger.[66]

(8) Burden of proof

The burden of proving the negligence of the plaintiff and that it contributed to the damage in such a way as to exonerate the defendant wholly or partially lies upon the defendant.[67] The defendant must always establish such contributory negligence as will amount to a defence: it is not true that the onus of establishing that the defendant failed to take advantage of a last opportunity rests upon the plaintiff.[68]

§ 196. Principle in Davies v. Mann today

It has already been seen that "the rule of last opportunity," in the sense of an inflexible rule of law applicable over the whole field of contributory

---

[62] *France* v. *Parkinson* [1954] 1 W.L.R. 581.
[63] (1888) 13 App.Cas. 1. Nor is the bailor of a chattel precluded by the contributory negligence of his bailee from recovering damages from a third person by whose negligence the chattel has been injured or destroyed: *Wellwood* v. *King (Alexander) Ltd.* [1921] 2 I.R. 274; *Krahn* v. *Bell* [1930] 4 D.L.R. 480. The C.A. assumed this to be the law in *France* v. *Parkinson* [1954] 1 W.L.R. 581.
[64] *Waite* v. *North Eastern Ry.* (1858) E.B. & E. 719. See the full discussion of the case in Anon., *Contributory Negligence and Third Parties*, pp. 52-63 (Tasmania, 1936).
[65] [1933] 1 K.B. 35. The principle of this decision applies to other persons incapable of looking after themselves—*e.g.* the very old: [1933] 1 K.B. 35, 41.
[66] See above, § 99, for an example.
[67] *Heranger S.S. Co.* v. *Diamond S.S. Co.* [1939] A.C. 94, 104.
[68] *Alford* v. *Magee* (1952) 85 C.L.R. 437, 463.

negligence, had become obsolete even before the Act of 1945.[69] This does not mean that the plain and sensible principle expounded in *Davies* v. *Mann* has also become obsolete. Just as there is room for it in admiralty after the Act of 1911, so there is room for it at common law after the Act of 1945. For, as Lord Birkenhead went to such pains to emphasise in *The Volute*, the mere fact that a collision has occurred in consequence of the blameworthy conduct of two vessels does not necessarily imply that the loss must automatically be distributed between the parties in some proportion. It might be possible to find "a sufficient separation of time, place or circumstance" to enable "a clear line to be drawn" between the faults of the two parties. The same principle now applies at common law.[70] Hence it is still the law that sole liability may be imputed to one party even though the misdoings of both are relevant to the cause of the accident.[71] It will be convenient to examine the application of this principle to different situations of fact.

(1) Collisions between two moving objects

It has already been seen that in admiralty it is seldom possible to draw "a clear line" in cases of this kind.[72] The position is similar in the case of collisions on land between two modern fast-moving vehicles.[73] So in *France* v. *Parkinson*,[74] in which two motor-cars proceeding along cross-roads of equal status had come into collision at the centre of the crossing, it was said that there was a prima facie case of negligence against both drivers.

(2) Collisions between moving and stationary objects

The perennial temptation to turn decisions on facts into rules of law should be resisted here as elsewhere. In particular there is no rule that one who erects or maintains a danger in a public place must necessarily have attributed to him the greater share of fault for an accident than the person who collides with it.[75] Still it may be possible to draw a clear line between the respective faults in such a case. Time and knowledge are factors which are critical but not necessarily decisive.[76]

(3) Principle applies to non-highway cases

The fact that the cases which have so far been discussed have concerned actions for personal injuries arising out of traffic accidents does not mean that the principle in *Davies* v. *Mann* is limited to such cases. This is clearly shown by the decision of the House of Lords in *Stapley* v. *Gypsum Mines Ltd.*[77] Stapley and Dale were miners employed by the respondents. They were of equal status, neither being in charge of the other. The roof of their stope (or working place) in the mine became unsafe and likely to fall. It

---

[69] Above, § 193.
[70] *Stapley* v. *Gypsum Mines Ltd.* [1953] A.C. 663, 681.
[71] *Sigurdson* v. *B.C. Electric Ry.* [1953] A.C. 291, 304.
[72] Above, § 194.
[73] *Alford* v. *Magee* (1952) 85 C.L.R. 437, 465.
[74] [1954] 1 W.L.R. 581. Contrast the difficulties which arose on similar facts in *Swadling* v. *Cooper* [1931] A.C. 1 (above, § 193).
[75] *Carroll* v. *Clare County Council* [1975] I.R. 221, 228.
[76] *Sigurdson* v. *B.C. Electric Ry. Co.* [1953] A.C. 291.
[77] [1953] A.C. 663. (See Hamson [1954] C.L.J. 40; Denning [1955] C.L.J. 114.)

thereupon became their duty to take the roof down and not to work in the stope until this had been done. They were so instructed by their foreman. After they had tried unsuccessfully to take the roof down they jointly decided to abandon their attempts and to return to their ordinary work. So Dale went away from the stope and Stapley stayed on. Shortly afterwards Dale returned and found Stapley dead: he had been buried under a quantity of gypsum which had fallen from the roof and killed him. His widow, Mrs. Seagull Gladys Stapley, alleged that Dale's negligence had contributed to her husband's death and that the respondents were vicariously responsible for it. There was much division of judicial opinion. To some Stapley was entirely responsible for the disaster which befell him: "His resumption of work, in the circumstances, was the crossing of the legal Rubicon."[78] Others thought that, "looking at the matter broadly and upon common-sense principles," it was "impossible to say that the acts of Dale and Stapley did not 'come so closely together and were not so closely mixed up' that Dale's breach of duty could be regarded as not being part of the cause of Stapley's death."[79] In the event the House of Lords held (Lords Porter and Asquith of Bishopstone dissenting) that the default of Dale[80] contributed to a certain extent to Stapley's death.[81] To the latter was, however, ascribed 80 per cent. of the responsibility for his own death: hence his widow recovered only one-fifth of the damage which she had sustained through the death of her husband.

§ 197. CONTRIBUTORY NEGLIGENCE: THE ACT OF 1945[82]

The Law Reform (Contributory Negligence) Act 1945, by section 1 (1), provides as follows: "Where any person suffers damage[83] as the result partly of his own fault[84] and partly of the fault of any other person or persons, a claim in respect of that damage shall not be defeated by reason of the fault of the person suffering the damage, but the damages recoverable in respect thereof shall be reduced to such extent as the court thinks just and equitable having regard to the claimant's share in the responsibility for the damage: . . . " Although the statutory definition of fault seems to authorise a reduction of damages because the plaintiff has been guilty of a tort *or* of

---

[78] [1953] A.C. 663, 688, *per* Lord Asquith of Bishopstone.

[79] *Ibid.* 678, *per* Lord Oaksey.

[80] The exact nature of the duty which Dale owed to Stapley was not fully explored, nor was the defence of *volenti non fit injuria* pleaded: *Stapley's* case is a decision solely on causation: *I.C.I. Ltd.* v. *Shatwell* [1965] A.C. 656.

[81] Of the nine judges before whom the case came, five held that Dale's default did not contribute to the accident and four that it did, but three of these four were in the House of Lords. This division of opinion shows the difficulty of drawing that "clear line" which Lord Birkenhead mentioned in *The Volute*.

[82] See Taggart, "Contributory Negligence" (1977) 3 Auckland Univ.L.Rev. 140; Fagelson, "The Last Bastion of Fault?" (1979) 42 M.L.R. 646.

[83] "Includes loss of life and personal injury": s.4. The word has been held to cover a case in which the plaintiff's lack of care contributes to the extent of his injury rather than to the accident: *O'Connell* v. *Jackson* [1972] 1 Q.B. 270 (failure to wear crash helmet).

[84] "Means negligence, breach of statutory duty or other act or omission which gives rise to a liability in tort or would, apart from this Act, give rise to the defence of contributory negligence" s.4. The definition has been extended to liability for animals: see the Animals Act 1971, ss.10 and 11. As the Act expressly contemplates that a plaintiff in breach of some statutory duty imposed upon him may yet recover part of his damages, the defence of *ex turpi causa non oritur actio* cannot be raised in such a case: see above, § 190.

contributory negligence, in the great majority of cases it has been assumed that contributory negligence must be proved against the plaintiff, and not just (say) a breach of statutory duty.[85] The court cannot of its own motion reduce the plaintiff's damages: the defence of contributory negligence must be pleaded.[86]

It is probable that the provisions of the Act are not limited to those cases in which the defendant is charged with negligence, "as though the negligences belong to the same pack and one trumps the other."[87] This would seem to follow from the definition of "fault" in section 4.[88] The rules on contributory negligence therefore apply to actions for breach of statutory duty,[89] nuisance,[90] and also to actions for breach of the duties owed by occupiers of dangerous premises,[91] and even to a claim based on strict liability, such as the escape of fire.[92] Contributory negligence is probably not, however, a defence in an action of trespass to the person.[93] It is certainly not a defence to trespass to goods or conversion.[94] It is uncertain how far the defence[95] is available for breaches of contract. It seems that the defendant in an action for breach of a duty imposed solely by a contract cannot plead that the plaintiff is guilty of contributory negligence unless the contractual duty is co-terminous with a tortious one.[96] It is curious that a plaintiff in an action for personal injuries should be able to recover in full if he proves a breach of contract, but is liable to have his damages reduced if he proves a tort, especially as a plaintiff now has the option of suing either in contract or in tort.

Section 1 (3) of the 1945 Act incorporates the law relating to apportionment of liability between joint tortfeasors.[97] This means that when a collision has been caused by the fault of two parties, and a third party also suffers damage, partly as the result of his own fault and partly as the result of the faults of the first two parties, the responsibility of each party should be assessed separately.[98]

So the present position is that "the common law rule has been brought into line with that obtaining in admiralty and in each the problem should be approached broadly avoiding those fine distinctions which were apt to be drawn when some slight act of negligence on the part of the plaintiff might defeat his claim altogether."[99] Although the Act was intended to do no more than alter the legal consequences of negligence by both parties causing or contributing to the damage complained of and does not affect the rules for

---

[85] See *Westwood* v. *Post Office* [1974] A.C. 1.
[86] *Fookes* v. *Slaytor* [1978] 1 W.L.R. 1293.
[87] *Caswell* v. *Powell Duffryn Collieries Ltd.* [1940] A.C. 152, 165, *per* Lord Atkin.
[88] See note 84 above.
[89] As under the Animals Act 1971: see note 84 above.
[90] *Trevett* v. *Lee* [1955] 1 W.L.R. 113, 121.
[91] § 117.
[92] *McWhirter* v. *Emerson-Elliott (No. 2)* [1962] W.A.R. 162, 265.
[93] *Lane* v. *Holloway* [1968] 1 Q.B. 379; *Gray* v. *Barr* [1971] 2 Q.B. 554. See above, § 46.
[94] The Torts (Interference with Goods) Act 1977, s. 12(1) specifically so provides. See above, § 33.
[95] See the exhaustive survey by Palmer and Davies, "Contributory Negligence and Breach of Contract" (1980) 29 I.C.L.Q. 415.
[96] *Quinn* v. *Burch Bros. Ltd.* [1966] 2 Q.B. 370, *affd.* [1966] 2 Q.B. 381; *Sole* v. *Hallt Ltd.* [1973] Q.B. 574.
[97] See above, § 168.
[98] *The Miraflores and The Abadesa* [1967] 1 A.C. 826.
[99] *Boy Andrew (Owners)* v. *St. Rognvald (Owners)* [1948] A.C. 140, 155, *per* Lord Porter.

determining whether negligence has been established[1] the power to apportion the loss equitably between the parties has led in practice to a broader
approach.

§ 198. BASIS OF APPORTIONMENT

When a court has decided, according to the principles already discussed,
that the case is one in which it is proper to apportion the loss between the
parties, the result is that the claimant's damages are "reduced to such extent
as the court thinks just and equitable having regard to the claimant's share
in the responsibility for the damage."[2] There may be sub-apportionments in
respect of subsequent heads of damage properly traceable to the original
disaster.[3]

There has been some discussion whether the apportionment is to be made
on the basis of responsibility or of fault. It is significant that (unlike the
Maritime Conventions Act 1911) the Act of 1945 does not contain the word
"cause."[4] While responsibility (or fault) is not to be equated with causation,
it does flow from causation in the sense that it is settled[5] that if there is no
causation there is no tort.[6] But if there is causation, so that the plaintiff is
contributorily negligent, then his damages must be reduced by some proportion. The Act requires that the damages "shall be reduced," so the court
cannot refuse to make any reduction merely because it thinks it just and
equitable to do so.[7] Hence it is necessary in England[8] and in Ireland[9] to
consider not only the causative potency of a particular act but also its
blameworthiness. So if a pedestrian is struck by a motorist while crossing
the road, and both driver and pedestrian have a clear view of each other,
while the causative factors of the accident are in one sense equal,
nevertheless the motorist may be held much more to blame than the
pedestrian, who is going at perhaps three miles per hour and has to look
both sides as well as forwards.[10] But culpability here, as elsewhere in the law
of torts,[11] means not so much moral blameworthiness as a departure from
the standard of care of the reasonable man.[12] It is the blameworthiness by
reference to what a reasonable man or woman would have done in the
circumstances of the contributions of the plaintiff and defendant to the

---

[1] *Davies* v. *Swan Motor Co.* [1949] 2 K.B. 291, 310; *Stapley* v. *Gypsum Mines Ltd.* [1953]
A.C. 663, 677. Although not admissible evidence, it is interesting to note that this was
Lord Simon's own view. On June 14, 1945, he wrote to Winfield: "Of course the law as to
what constitutes contributory negligence is not altered by my Bill at all; it is the effect of it
upon the rights of the parties which is changed" (Simon papers).
[2] s. 1(1).
[3] *The Calliope* [1970] P. 172.
[4] "That Act, with which I had some slight connection as a member of the Law Revision
Committee, carefully avoided all references to the word 'causation.' While it was being
finally prepared by Lord Simon, the then Lord Chancellor, I discussed it with him, and he
emphasised that he was not going to allow any idea of causation to confuse the issue":
Goodhart, "Appeals on Questions of Fact" (1955) 71 L.Q.R. 402, 413–414.
[5] See above, § 73.
[6] *O'Sullivan* v. *Dwyer* [1971] I.R. 275. 284.
[7] *Boothman* v. *British Northrop Ltd.* (1972) 13 K.I.R. 112, 122.
[8] *The Miraflores and The Abadesa* [1967] 1 A.C. 826, 845; *Keaney* v. *British Railways
Board* [1968] 1 W.L.R. 879, 893; *Froom* v. *Butcher* [1976] Q.B. 286.
[9] *Carroll* v. *Clare County Council* [1975] I.R. 221.
[10] *Baker* v. *Willoughby* [1970] A.C. 467.
[11] See above, § 6.
[12] *O'Sullivan* v. *Dwyer* [1971] I.R. 275, 286.

happening of the accident which is to be the basis of the apportionment.[13] For it would be as misleading to place the whole emphasis on "fault" as it would be to place it on "causation."[14] The court must also consider a third factor—namely, what is "just and equitable."[15] Hence the precise percentage by which the award is reduced is a question of fact in each case. The respective faults are not to be assessed according to some mathematical computation, but by looking at the matter broadly.[16]

The following points should be noticed.

(1) By section 1 (2) the court should find and record the total damages which would have been awarded if the claimant had not been at fault.[17]

(2) The court cannot deal with minute percentages: the Act operates only when it has been determined that one of the parties is at least 10 per cent. responsible.[18] The combined percentages must be 100 per cent. and not some lesser figure.[19]

(3) An appellate court, in a case in which the findings of fact are not disputed,[20] will interfere with the apportionment made at the trial only when it is clearly wrong: it will not interfere merely because its members might themselves have made a different apportionment.[21] This principle is easy to state, but in practice its application varies from time to time. At one time the House of Lords was ready to alter apportionments even though one or more of the Law Lords agreed with the trial judge,[22] and this made the Court of Appeal less restrained.[23] Later that court emphatically rebutted the suggestion that it was ready to alter the trial judge's attribution. "If there is any widespread belief to that effect at the Bar, it should be discarded."[24] But more recently the Court has reverted to its earlier position, and stated that it has the same attitude to apportionment as it has to damages.[25] In Ireland the courts exercise a closer control over juries than those in England.[26]

(4) Costs may,[27] but need not necessarily, be[28] apportioned between the parties on the same basis as the loss.

[13] *Carroll* v. *Clare County Council* [1975] I.R. 221.
[14] See Lamb Q.C., *arguendo* in *Stapley's Case* [1953] A.C. 663, 670.
[15] *Turner* v. *Ford Motor Co. Ltd.* [1978] 1 W.L.R. 948, 953–954.
[16] *Gregory* v. *Kelly* [1978] R.T.R. 426.
[17] *Kelly* v. *Stockport Corporation* [1949] 1 All E.R. 893.
[18] *Johnson* v. *Tenant Bros.* (unreported) 1954 C.A. 229. In the light of this decision of the C.A. it is obvious that the apportionments in a number of cases (*e.g. Johnson* v. *Croggan & Co. Ltd.* [1954] 1 W.L.R. 195) were made *per incuriam.*
[19] *Black* v. *McCabe* [1964] N.I. 1.
[20] For the powers of an appellate court in this respect, see above, § 83.
[21] *British Fame (Owners)* v. *Macgregor (Owners)* [1943] A.C. 197; *Sigurdson* v. *British Columbia Electric Ry.* [1953] A.C. 291.
[22] *Stapley* v. *Gypsum Mines Ltd.* [1953] A.C. 663; *National Coal Board* v. *England* [1954] A.C. 403.
[23] *McArdle* v. *Andmac Ltd.* [1967] 1 W.L.R. 356.
[24] *Brown* v. *Thompson* [1968] 1 W.L.R. 1003, 1009, *per* Winn L.J.
[25] *Kerry* v. *Carter* [1969] 1 W.L.R. 1372, 1376.
[26] *Barnes* v. *Irish Fibres Ltd.* (1967) 101 I.L.T.R. 172.
[27] *Gillespie* v. *FitzPatrick* [1970] I.R. 102.
[28] *Smith* v. *Smith (W.H.) & Sons Ltd.* [1952] 1 All E.R. 528.

CHAPTER 22

DAMAGES: GENERAL PRINCIPLES

Remedies for torts are of two kinds, being either judicial or extra-judicial—remedies by way of an action at law, and remedies by way of self-help. The various forms of extra-judicial remedy, such as distress, the retaking of property, and the abatement of a nuisance, will be considered in another chapter, and we are here concerned with the other class alone. The remedies obtainable for a tort by means of an action are of three chief kinds—damages, injunction,[1] and specific restitution of property.[2] The first of these is the ordinary and characteristic remedy.

§ 199. DAMAGES

Damages are classified in several ways.

(1) Nominal, contemptuous or real

Nominal damages are a small sum of money—for example, one pound—awarded not by way of compensation for any actual loss suffered, but merely by way of recognition of the existence of some legal right vested in the plaintiff and violated by the defendant. Real damages, on the other hand, are those which are assessed and awarded as compensation for damage actually suffered by the plaintiff, and not simply by way of mere recognition of a legal right violated. Damages are not nominal merely because they are very small. If actual damage, however small, is proved, and damages, however small, are awarded in respect of it, such damages are real and not nominal. Nominal damages must also be distinguished from contemptuous damages: the former term is appropriate in a case where the plaintiff is not concerned with his actual loss (if any), but brings his action with the sole and proper object of establishing his right; the latter term indicates that in the opinion of the jury the action should not have been brought at all.[3]

When nominal damages recoverable

It follows accordingly that nominal damages are recoverable only in the case of torts which are actionable *per se*. If such a right is violated the law presumes damage and an action will lie even though no damage at all has in fact been suffered by the plaintiff. This is the case in all types of trespass, whether to land, goods or the person, and in some actions on the case, as in libel and in certain cases of slander. Thus in *Ashby* v. *White*,[4] Sir John Holt C.J. held that an elector had a right of action against a returning officer who wrongfully and maliciously rejected his vote at an election, even though the

---

[1] See § 219, below.

[2] See § 38, above.

[3] As in *Bloom* v. *News of the World* (1977) *Daily Telegraph*, 11 March (1/2p). But where loss of liberty is concerned there is no room for contemptuous damages: *Pike* v. *Waldrum* [1952] 1 Lloyd's Rep. 431, 455; *Hook* v. *Cunard Steamship Co. Ltd.* [1953] 1 All E.R. 1021.

[4] (1703) 2 Ld.Raym. 938. The principle of this case is unaffected by the protection given to returning officers by the Representation of the People Act 1949, s. 50.

candidate for whom he intended to vote was elected. "So if a man gives another a cuff on the ear, though it cost him nothing, no not so much as a little diachylon,[5] yet he shall have his action, for it is a personal injury. So a man shall have an action against another for riding over his ground, though it did him no damage: for it is an invasion of his property and the other has no right to come there."[6] So again in *Constantine* v. *Imperial London Hotels*[7] the plaintiff, the famous West Indian cricketer, was held entitled to nominal damages of five guineas because the defendants wrongfully refused to receive him into one of their hotels to which he wished to go, though they provided him with lodging in another of their hotels.

(2) Real damages

But in many cases the plaintiff's only right is not to be caused damage by the defendant, and in such a case he must prove actual damage. Damage then is the gist of the action. Thus, for example, damage must be proved in an action of negligence, and indeed in the great majority of actions on the case. Where the damages are real it becomes necessary to determine what is the measure of damages in each case.[8] The general English rule today is that damages are compensatory, whether in contract or in tort. The function of damages is therefore to put the person whose right has been invaded in the same position as if it had been respected.[9] It is well settled, at least in the economic torts, that the basic question is, what has the plaintiff lost, not what can the defendant pay.[9a]

It is sometimes said[10] that the general principle of assessment is *restitutio in integrum*. But this cannot always be applied to actions in tort. "If by somebody's fault I lose my leg and am paid damages, can anyone in his senses say that I have had *restitutio in integrum*?"[11] There are some kinds of damage for which no true compensation can be given in this world by any amount of money, no matter how elaborate an arithmetical computation is employed. This is particularly so with claims for loss of amenities and pain and suffering. Yet the courts are obliged to do the best they can. In such cases the plaintiff is entitled to fair and reasonable, as distinct from perfect, compensation, assessed in the light of previous rewards in respect of comparable damage.[12] It might be better to say that such sums are "an acknowledgement of regret for having caused a hurt that is imponderable rather than a compensation properly so called,"[13] or if the legislature fixed a definite sum to which the relatives would be entitled by way of *solatium*,[14] as it has done in Ireland by the Civil Liability Act 1961, s. 49.[15]

---

[5] Plaster.
[6] 2 Ld.Raym. 938, 955. (Yet note that in *Ashby* v. *White* itself the damages which the plaintiff recovered were real and not merely nominal.)
[7] [1944] K.B. 693.
[8] In the sense explained below, § 200.
[9] *The Albazero* [1977] A.C. 774, 841.
[9a] *General Tire and Rubber Co. Ltd.* v. *Firestone Tyre Co. Ltd.* [1975] 1 W.L.R. 819.
[10] *The Kate* [1899] P. 165.
[11] *Admiralty Commissioners* v. *S.S. Valeria* [1922] 2 A.C. 242, 248, *per* Lord Dunedin.
[12] *Fletcher* v. *Autocar and Transporters Ltd.* [1968] 2 Q.B. 322.
[13] *M'Leish* v. *Fulton & Sons*, 1955 S.C. 46, 49, *per* Lord Carmont.
[14] Lord Devlin in [1968] A.C. 529, 550.
[15] Knight, "Some Aspects of Damages under the Civil Liability Acts" (1966) *The Irish Jurist* (N.S.), Vol. ii.

(3) General or special

General damages are compensation for general damage; special damages for special damage. General damage is that kind of damage which the law presumes to follow from the wrong complained of and which, therefore, need not be expressly set out in the plaintiff's pleadings. Special damage, on the other hand, is damage of such a kind that it will not be presumed by the law and must therefore be expressly alleged in those pleadings so that the defendant may have due notice of the nature of the claim—otherwise the plaintiff will not be permitted to give evidence of it nor will the jury be at liberty to award compensation in respect of it. Thus in the case of a collision between two ships or motor-cars due to the negligence of the defendant, the plaintiff will be able to recover general damages for the loss of the use of his ship during the repairs,[16] even if it be not used for trading for profit,[17] or for the loss of the use of his motor-car even though it be used only for pleasure purposes. Nor will it avail the defendant to prove that even apart from the collision the plaintiff would not have in fact made use of the damaged vehicle. "What right," asked Lord Halsbury L.C., in *The Mediana*,[18] "has a wrongdoer to consider what use you are going to make of your vessel? . . . Supposing a person took away a chair out of my room and kept it for twelve months, could anybody say you had a right to diminish the damages by showing that I did not usually sit in that chair, or that there were plenty of other chairs in the room?"

(4) Compensatory, aggravated and exemplary

Compensatory damages are awarded as compensation for, and are measured by, the material loss suffered by the plaintiff. A distinct category is that of aggravated damages, which may be awarded when the motives and conduct of the defendant aggravate the injury to the plaintiff. Insult and injured feelings are a proper subject for compensation. So a substantial sum was awarded for an "insolent and high-handed trespass" by an inquiry agent.[19] In such a case damages are at large precisely because the "real" damage cannot be ascertained: it is not a matter of determining the "real" damage and adding to that a sum by way of aggravated damages.[20] Yet another category is that of punitive or exemplary damages, which reflect the jury's view of the defendant's outrageous conduct. Aggravated damages are given for conduct which shocks the plaintiff: exemplary damages for conduct which shocks the jury.[21]

There has been considerable dispute about both the nature of and the conditions for the award of exemplary damages. Sir John Salmond thought that exemplary damages were a sum of money awarded in excess of any material loss or by way of *solatium* for an insult or other outrage to the plaintiff's feelings that is involved in the injury complained of.[22] It seems clear that Salmond thought of exemplary damages as being part of

---

[16] *Carslogie Steamship Co.* v. *Royal Norwegian Government* [1952] A.C. 292.
[17] *The Hebridean Coast* [1961] A.C. 545.
[18] [1900] A.C. 113, 117. See also *Caxton Publishing Co.* v. *Sutherland Publishing Co.* [1939] A.C. 178, 192, 203.
[19] *Jolliffe* v. *Willmet & Co.* (1970) 114 S.J. 619.
[20] *McCarey* v. *Associated Newspapers Ltd.* [1965] 2 Q.B. 86. See below, § 212.
[21] *Whelan* v. *Madigan* [1980] I.R. —.
[22] See *Australian Consolidated Press Ltd.* v. *Uren* [1969] 1 A.C. 590, 636–637.

aggravated compensatory damages, or, conversely, as not being punitive or vindictive. Salmond also asserted that the sole condition for the award of such damages was a case of conscious wrongdoing in contumelious disregard of another's rights.[23]

Unfortunately it is no longer possible in England to uphold either branch of Salmond's statement. As a result of two cases in the House of Lords it is plain not only that exemplary damages are criminal, vindictive, or punitive in nature, but also that they are not to be awarded merely because of contumelious disregard of another's rights. The conclusion is that exemplary damages are to be awarded only in very restricted categories of cases. This was laid down in *Rookes* v. *Barnard*,[24] and re-asserted in *Cassell & Co. Ltd.* v. *Broome*.[25] Many have thought this considerable pruning operation was too severe.[26] Nevertheless there are strong logical arguments against exemplary damages—they bring a criminal element into the civil law without the safeguards of criminal procedure; they lead to excessive awards, and are an unmerited windfall for the plaintiff.[26a] It must also be remembered that an obligation to pay a large sum by way of compensatory damages has itself a punitive element in it, as has the English rule that costs follow the event.[27]

But even opponents recognised that exemplary damages showed a continued vitality,[28] perhaps because the ordinary man feels that a defendant ought to be made to pay for insolent or outrageous conduct.[29] So the Court of Appeal in *Cassell & Co.* v. *Broome* declared[30] that the decision in *Rookes* had been *per incuriam* and should not be followed by trial judges. This remarkable assertion was emphatically and unanimously repudiated in the House of Lords by the Lord Chancellor and six Law Lords.[31] Of these seven, only two[32] were prepared to say that the Court of Appeal were correct in preferring the substantive law laid down in *Ley* v. *Hamilton*[33] to that laid down in *Rookes* v. *Barnard*.[34] The result is that in *Cassell* v. *Broome* five Law Lords thought that the restrictive principles laid down in *Rookes* were in general correct.[35]

---

[23] His views on this point have the approval of the High Court of Australia: *Uren* v. *John Fairfax & Sons Pty. Ltd.* (1967) 117 C.L.R. 118, 150, 154.

[24] [1964] A.C. 1129.

[25] [1972] A.C. 1027.

[26] Appellate tribunals in Australia, Canada, New Zealand and Ireland have refused to follow *Rookes* v. *Barnard* and have insisted on retaining a wider power to award exemplary damages: see *Uren* v. *John Fairfax Pty. Ltd.* (1967) 117 C.L.R. 118, affid. by the P.C. in [1969] A.C. 590; *Fogg* v. *McKnight* [1968] N.Z.L.R. 330; *Dillon* v. *Dunnes' Stores* (*No. 2*) (1968) (Ireland, Unreported); *Paragon Ltd.* v. *Magna Ltd.* (1972) 24 D.L.R. (3d) 156.

[26a] So the Faulks Committee (Cmnd. 5909, § 360) recommended their abolition.

[27] [1972] A.C. 1027, 1095, 1114. The unsuccessful appellants in this case (who had not raised the issue) were required to pay damages of £40,000 (compensatory, £15,000; exemplary, £25,000), with costs calculated at more than £60,000. Eventually the H.L. ordered the costs of the appeal to be halved: [1972] A.C. 1136.

[28] Lord Wilberforce in [1972] A.C. 1027, 1114.

[29] Kelly, "The Inner Nature of the Tort Action" (1967) *Irish Jurist* (N.S.), Vol. ii, p. 279.

[30] [1971] 2 Q.B. 354. (A case in which there were "grave libels perpetrated quite deliberately and without regard to their truth by a young man and a firm of publishers interested solely in whether they would gain by the publication of this book.")

[31] [1972] A.C. 1027.

[32] Viscount Dilhorne, an ex-Lord Chancellor, and Lord Wilberforce.

[33] (1935) 153 L.T. 384.

[34] [1964] A.C. 1129.

[35] Although one, Lord Diplock, was in favour of allowing the appeal on the ground that the jury had not been properly directed in accordance with those principles.

The English principles relating to the award of exemplary damages[36] are now therefore as follows. First, exemplary damages are not to be awarded merely because the tort has been committed with a contumelious disregard of the plaintiff's rights.[37] Secondly, however, exemplary damages may be awarded in three categories of cases, provided always that both aggravated and compensatory damages are inadequate, and that a careful direction is given to the jury. Thirdly, when there are two or more defendants, the total sum awarded by way of exemplary damages must not exceed that to be awarded against the least blameworthy,[38] save that in a case of vicarious liability the plaintiff is entitled to get from the employer the same amount as he would have got from the servant.[39]

Finally, the Privy Council has held[40] that when exemplary damages are awarded they need not be specified separately from the amount of compensatory damages awarded. It is not easy to fit this decision into any coherent theory, or even with judicial practice in other cases on assessment.[41]

The categories

First. Oppressive, arbitrary or unconstitutional action by servants of the government may justify such an award.[42] Today a wide interpretation is to be given to the term "government,"[43] but outrageous action by the private bully is to be dealt with by the award of aggravated, rather than exemplary, damages.[44] It is noteworthy that what is decisive here is not the conduct of the defendant, or even the character of the plaintiff, but simply the defendant's status as a public official. A citizen with no reputation to lose who had been wrongly imprisoned might get only a small sum by way of compensatory damages: but the courts may also rightly award him a sum which will deter flagrant injustices.[45]

Second. Aggravated damages will not do justice when the defendant's conduct has been calculated by him to make a profit for himself which may well exceed the compensation payable to the plaintiff. The facts of *Cassell* v. *Broome* were such that it was "a forlorn hope" for the appellants to argue that they were not within this second category.[46] An arithmetical calculation is not required—the profit motive is a factor and not a condition.[47] So when a tenant has been unlawfully evicted in an outrageous way exemplary damages have been awarded in England[48] and in Ireland.[49]

[36] This term is to be preferred to "vindictive" or "punitive": [1972] A.C. 1027, 1073, 1124.
[37] [1972] A.C. 1027, 1080, 1082.
[38] See [1972] A.C. 1027, 1063, 1081, 1118.
[39] *Carrington* v. *Att.-Gen.* [1972] N.Z.L.R. 1106.
[40] *Att.-Gen. of St. Christopher* v. *Reynolds* [1980] A.C. 637, 662.
[41] See below, § 214.
[42] *Kelly* v. *Faulkner* [1973] N.I. 31.
[43] [1972] A.C. 1027, 1077, 1087–1088, 1130, 1134.
[44] [1972] A.C. 1027, 1078, 1134.
[45] [1972] A.C. 1027, 1134. So John Wilkes, a man of imperfect character, was awarded £4,000 against Lord Halifax in 1769 (19 St.Tr. 1466). Even then the sum was so much less than expected "that the jurymen were obliged to withdraw privately for fear of being insulted."
[46] See [1972] A.C. 1027, 1059. Of the 11 judges who heard this case, 10 agreed that, assuming the second category existed, and assuming that the jury had been properly directed on it, the facts justified an award within this category.
[47] [1972] A.C. 1027, 1079, 1130.
[48] *Drane* v. *Evangelou* [1978] 1 W.L.R. 455.
[49] *Whelan* v. *Madigan* [1980] I.R. —.

Third. A statute may occasionally permit such an award—*e.g.* the Reserve and Auxiliary Forces (Protection of Civil Interests) Act 1951, s.13(2).[50]

In cases outside these three categories, whether of libel, assault or trespass, aggravated damages should be able to do the work of exemplary damages.[51] Finally, these principles do not permit the award of exemplary or aggravated damages in respect of torts for which they had not previously been awarded, *e.g.* negligence[52] or nuisance.[53]

"Parasitic" damages

It sometimes happens that damage which is in itself *damnum sine injuria* is caused by an act which, by reason of some other kind of damage also caused by it to the same person, is wrongful and actionable at the suit of that person. For example, a building which wrongfully obstructs the ancient lights of an adjoining building may at the same time obstruct other windows in that building which have not yet acquired legal protection.[53a] In such cases the damages recoverable for the wrongful act include compensation for the whole loss so caused, even though part of that loss is in itself *damnum sine injuria.*[54] Again the protection of privacy, or redress for purely economic loss carelessly caused,[55] is often dependent on some other cause of action, such as trespass to land or chattels. This has been aptly called the "parasitic" element in damage.[56] But it must be admitted that the term has never been adopted in any judgment in England, as distinct from Ireland.[57] Indeed, it has been severely criticised by Lord Denning.[58]

§ 200. REMOTENESS OF DAMAGE: INTRODUCTION[59]

In a former chapter, under the head of *damnum sine injuria,* it has been pointed out in general terms that a person is not necessarily responsible in law for all the harm that he inflicts either wilfully, negligently or accidentally on other persons.[60] A plaintiff who has suffered damage in consequence of the act of the defendant may be disentitled to recover compensation:

(1) Because the defendant's act was not wrongful at all;

---

[50] But note Lord Kilbrandon's doubts in [1972] A.C. 1027, 1133–1134.
[51] [1972] A.C. 1027, 1076–1077.
[52] [1972] A.C. 1027, 1076, 1080, 1131.
[53] *Griffith* v. *Clay (Richard) & Sons Ltd.* [1912] 2 Ch. 291.
[53a] *Oldham* v. *Lawson* [1976] V.R. 208.
[54] See also *Campbell* v. *Paddington Corporation* [1911] 1 K.B. 869 (loss of a view).
[55] *S.C.M. Ltd.* v. *Whittall Ltd.* [1971] 1 Q.B. 337.
[56] Street, *Foundations of Legal Liability,* Vol. i, p. 461. At p. 470 he says: "The treatment of any element of damage as a parasitic factor belongs essentially to a transitory stage of legal evolution. A factor which is today recognised as parasitic will, forsooth, tomorrow be recognised as an independent basis of liability."
[57] *Scott* v. *Goulding's Fertilisers Ltd.* [1973] I.R. 200.
[58] *Spartan Steel and Alloys Ltd.* v. *Martin & Co. (Contractors) Ltd.* [1973] 1 Q.B. 27, 35.
[59] The leading monograph is Hart and Honoré, *Causation in the Law* (Oxford, 1959). See also Keeton, *Legal Cause in the Law of Torts* (Ohio, 1963). The periodical literature is vast, but pre-*Wagon Mound* publications are now only of historical interest. The more valuable post-1960 articles are: Dias, "Remoteness of Liability and Legal Policy" [1962] Camb.L.J. 178; *idem,* "Trouble on Oiled Waters" [1967] Camb.L.J. 62 (which has a useful bibliography); Cooke, "Remoteness of Damage and Judicial Discretion" [1978] C.L.J. 288.
[60] See above, §§ 3–4.

(2) Because the plaintiff is not the person to whom the defendant owed the duty which he has violated;

(3) Because the damage is not of a kind recognised by the law;

(4) Because the damage has been caused in a manner which the law does not recognise as a sufficient ground of liability.

These four cases will be considered in their order.

(1) Damnum sine injuria

The first class of case calls for no special consideration. This is the case of *damnum sine injuria* in the strictest sense of that term. There is *damnum* suffered by the plaintiff, but no *injuria* committed by the defendant, either against the plaintiff or against any other person. The plaintiff's interests are not protected against conduct of this kind. Illustrations from cases which have already been discussed are damage done by way of competition in trade[61]; or by the withdrawal of underground water.[62]

(2) Damnum suffered by one person and injuria by another

In the second class of case there is both *damnum* and *injuria*, but the *damnum* is suffered by one person and the *injuria* by another. A person who suffers *damnum* cannot recover compensation on the basis of *injuria* suffered by another. He who does a wrongful act is liable only to the person whose rights are thereby violated. He is not bound to make compensation to all persons who, in the result, suffer harm from his wrongdoing. The *damnum* and *injuria* must be united in the same person. So there is no remedy for economic loss which is the consequential result of damage to a chattel, unless the plaintiff has some proprietary or possessory right in that chattel.[63]

(3) Damnum of a kind not recognised by law

The third class of case is that in which, although the defendant's act is wrongful, and although the duty violated by him was a duty towards the plaintiff, nevertheless the damage resulting to the plaintiff is not recoverable, because it is not the kind of damage which it is the purpose of the law to prevent or to give redress for.[64] Thus at common law, before the Fatal Accidents Acts 1846 to 1959, no damages could be recovered for the death of a human being. The protection of human life was left to the criminal law.

It is often helpful to distinguish between remoteness (what items?) and measure of damages (what loss?). The former question is always prior to the latter.[65] The actual quantification of damage is always a matter of procedure and so governed by the *lex fori*. But differences in the heads of damage—*e.g.* general damages for pain and suffering as against special

---

[61] *Mogul Steamship Co.* v. *McGregor, Gow & Co.* [1892] A.C. 25.
[62] *Bradford (Mayor of)* v. *Pickles* [1895] A.C. 587.
[63] *Spartan Steel and Alloys Ltd.* v. *Martin & Co. (Contractors) Ltd.* [1973] 1 Q.B. 27. See also above, § 76.
[64] See above, § 85.
[65] *Wieland* v. *Cyril Lord Carpets Ltd.* [1969] 3 All E.R. 1006.

damages for pecuniary loss—are a matter of substantive law, according to the balance of English judicial opinion.[66]

(4) Damnum too remote

It remains to consider the fourth and last class of case in which damage is irrecoverable. In this class of case the plaintiff fails because the chain of causation connecting the defendant's act with the damage resulting from it is of such a nature that the law for some reason refuses to regard it as sufficiently continuous for liability. Damage of this kind is said to be too remote. It has its most common application in the field of negligence. The plaintiff in negligence must prove duty, breach and damage.[67] Thus when a casualty officer at a hospital failed to see and examine a patient who complained of vomiting, the doctor was said to be "negligent." Yet it was held that his negligence had not *caused* the death of the patient, which was due to arsenical poisoning which could not have been detected and cured in time in any event.[68] But there may be responsibility for another's tort under the doctrine of vicarious liability without the master (as distinct from the servant) having been proved to have caused the wrong.

Common sense and causation

This doctrine of remoteness of damage is one of very considerable obscurity and difficulty.[68a] "In the varied web of affairs, the law must abstract some consequences as relevant, not perhaps on grounds of pure logic but simply for practical reasons."[69] This statement is typical of many to be found in the reports. There are many judicial statements praising the value of "common-sense principles"[70] and stating that in any case the question at issue can be determined by applying common sense to the facts of the particular case.[71] There are also many judicial warnings against too ready a reliance on "philosophy,"[72] or the "grave danger of being led astray by scholastic theories of causation and their ugly and barely intelligible jargon."[73] Some judges and writers go so far as to say that it is impossible to characterise any principles on which common sense proceeds. "This seems a counsel of despair which we should hesitate to accept. . . . Common sense is not a matter of inexplicable or arbitrary assertions, and the causal notions which it employs, though flexible and complex and subtly influenced by context, can be shown to rest, at least in part, on stateable principles; though the

---

[66] Lords Hodson, Pearson, Wilberforce, Denning and Diplock L.J. in *Chaplin* v. *Boys* [1971] A.C. 356. *Contra*, Lords Guest, Donovan and Upjohn.

[67] See above, § 72.

[68] *Barnett* v. *Chelsea Hospital Management Committee* [1969] 1 Q.B. 428.

[68a] See Watkins L.J. in *Lamb* v. *Camden L.B.C., The Times,* March 14, 1981.

[69] *Liesbosch Dredger* v. *Edison* [1933] A.C. 449, 460, *per* Lord Wright. See also *Monarch Steamship Co.* v. *A/B Karlshamns Oljefabriker* [1949] A.C. 196, 226.

[70] *e.g.* in *Alphacell Ltd.* v. *Woodward* [1972] 1 Q.B. 127.

[71] *Barty-King* v. *Ministry of Defence* [1979] 2 All E.R. 80, 89.

[72] As in the following quotation: "The common law of this country has been built up, not by the writings of logicians or learned jurists, but by the summings-up of judges of experience to juries consisting of plain men, not usually students of logic, not accustomed to subtle reasoning, but endowed, so far as my experience goes, as a general rule, with great common sense, and if an argument has to be put in terms which only a school-man could understand, then I am always very doubtful whether it can possibly be expressing the common law": *Smith* v. *Harris* [1939] 3 All E.R. 960, 967, *per* du Parcq L.J.

[73] *Overseas Tankship (U.K.) Ltd.* v. *Morts Dock and Engineering Co. Ltd.* (*The Wagon Mound*) [1961] A.C. 388, 419.

ordinary man who uses them may not, without assistance, be able to make them explicit."[74] Nor should it be assumed (as it seems sometimes to have been done) that philosophy is equivalent to that department of it called metaphysics: much can be learnt from the empiricists of the past and their influential descendants of the present day.[75]

An attempt has been made to state more explicitly those common-sense principles of causation according to which the courts have consistently said that causal questions must be decided.[76] These principles cannot provide conclusive answers to the complex causal questions which the courts are sometimes obliged to answer, but serve rather as an organising framework within which a choice may be made according to whatever considerations of policy the law may consider to be relevant. At the outset it should be noted that a question as to the cause of an event may lead to answers which vary according to the context of the inquiry. "A car skids while cornering at a certain point, turns turtle, and bursts into flames. From the car-driver's point of view, the cause of the accident was cornering too fast, and the lesson is that one must drive more carefully. From the county surveyor's point of view, the cause was a defective road surface, and the lesson is that one must make skid-proof roads. From the motor-manufacturers' point of view, the cause was defective design, and the lesson is that one must place the centre of gravity lower."[77] The word "cause" can hardly be defined, but is one "to which converging limits can be assigned in its context as concrete cases come to be decided."[78]

This passage also helps us to understand the basic principle in the common-sense notion of cause that "*the cause*" is one condition selected from a complex set of conditions which, according to known generalisations, are together jointly sufficient for the occurrence of the consequence in question. For, even though the road surface is defective, a car will not skid unless certain other conditions are satisfied—*e.g.* the car must be of a certain weight and construction and be moving at a certain minimum speed.[79] Within this jointly sufficient set of conditions common sense (like the law) distinguishes mere conditions from causes, and the principal criterion for this distinction lies in the contrast between (1) a voluntary human action and other conditions, (2) an abnormal contingency (*e.g.* an act of God or a coincidence) and other conditions. The legal distinctions of *novus actus interveniens*, superseding cause, and proximate cause may be defined in terms of these contrasts. It should be noted that although either an abnor-

---

[74] Hart and Honoré, *Causation in the Law*, p. 24.

[75] Even a Law Lord has said that he used the term philosopher "in no disparaging sense, for what is a philosopher but who one, *inter alia*, reasons severely and with precision?": *Stapley* v. *Gypsum Mines Ltd.* [1953] A.C. 663, 687, *per* Lord Asquith of Bishopstone.

[76] Hart and Honoré, *Causation in the Law*, Chap. 2.

[77] Collingwood, "The Idea of Cause" (1938) Aristotelian Society Proceedings 85 (cited in (1953) 69 L.Q.R. 433). Note some words of Lord Porter, written before he became a judge (5 Camb.L.J. 189): "The fact is that judges like the rest of us are human and, where for a particular decision accuracy is not essential, will use several words in the same sense or one in several. It is not by pressing the meaning attributed to a word in one or two instances that its true meaning can be obtained."

[78] *Commissioner of Customs and Excise* v. *Top Ten Promotions Ltd.* [1969] 1 W.L.R. 1163 at 1178, *per* Lord Wilberforce.

[79] It should be remembered that the jointly sufficient set of conditions may include negative conditions—*e.g.* the failure to give the appropriate signal—as well as positive ones. The contrary view rests on the erroneous belief that "a cause" is analogous to a physical movement. See below, n. 92.

mal contingency or a voluntary human act may negative causal connection, there are differences between them. Thus an abnormal contingency only negatives causal connection if it intervenes in time between the wrongful act and the consequence; whereas a voluntary act may negative causal connection even though it precedes in time both the wrongful act and the harm.

Finally, it is worth noting that the broad open question "What is the cause of this event?" is more suited to those inquiries in which we are seeking to discover the explanation of how or why some contingency happened. But when an explanation has been provided (or when none is needed) the more circumscribed question "Given this wrongful act (or other designated event) and given this loss or harm, is the latter the consequence of the former?" is appropriate. To ask the question in this way makes it plain that we are not seeking to understand what has happened but to allocate responsibility. This form of question is also helpful when we are considering a case which raises the issue of *novus actus interveniens*, for it makes it plain that the real problem is whether some third factor (which may be the act or omission of a human being, or the act of an animal, or a natural event or state of affairs) prevents the attribution of a given harm to a given action or contingency as its consequence.

Some conclusions

Before investigating this difficult topic more fully, it may be convenient to summarise briefly some conclusions which both on principle and authority seem to be indisputable.

First, an event may be the consequence of several causes. Until the Law Reform (Contributory Negligence) Act 1945, altered the law, there was a tendency to believe that there could not have been more than one effective cause of any single event. This error has been exposed.[80] It is now a commonplace that one event may have several causes.[81] But it is still necessary to avoid the fallacy of assuming that because one cause might have brought about a certain event therefore more than one cause could not have done so.[82]

Secondly, the doctrine of remoteness of damage applies not merely to wrongs of negligence, but to wrongs of all kinds, whether wilful, negligent, or of strict liability. Even a wilful wrongdoer is not liable *ad infinitum* for all the consequences which in fact flow from his wrongful act.

Thirdly, on the other hand, a consequence cannot be held too remote if it was actually intended by the wrongdoer.[83] The defendant is held responsible for all those consequences which he actually desired and intended to inflict upon the plaintiff, however remote may be the chain of causation by which he effected his purpose.[84] In other words, an extraordinary conjunction of events, if intended, or designed, does not amount to such a coincidence as to negative causal connection.

Fourthly, the question as to remoteness of damage must always be carefully distinguished from the preliminary question whether the defendant has been guilty of any wrongful act at all. It is only if this latter question is

[80] *Cork* v. *Kirby MacLean Ltd.* [1952] 2 All E.R. 402, 406.
[81] *Baker* v. *Willoughby* [1970] A.C. 467, 492.
[82] *Stapley* v. *Gypsum Mines Ltd.* [1953] A.C. 663, 665.
[83] *Quinn* v. *Leathem* [1901] A.C. 495, 537.
[84] *Jones* v. *Fabbi* (1973) 37 D.L.R. (3d) 27, 35.

answered in the affirmative that the first question arises at all. Until recent years the two questions were answered by the application of different tests. In considering the authorities it is not always easy to trace this distinction and to keep it clearly in mind.[85]

Fifthly, it is for the judge to direct the jury whether there is any evidence that a particular consequence is in law capable of being "natural and direct" or "reasonably foreseeable," and it is then for the jury to find as a fact whether a particular head of damages is such a consequence.[86] In this sense the question of remoteness may be said to be one of fact.

§ 201. TESTS OF CAUSATION

A number of different tests of causation have been proposed. We shall now consider in detail the more important judicial and extra judicial suggestions.

(1) Different kinds of cause

Various qualifying adjectives have been attached to the word "cause" to determine whether the consequence is too remote. Thus it has been said by some that damage is too remote unless the act of the defendant is the real, by some the effective, by some the substantial cause of it,[87] whilst others have distinguished the *causa causans* from the *causa sine qua non*.[88] The question has been much, and fruitlessly, discussed in cases on the assessment of damages for personal injuries. Is the tort the *causa causans* of the payment of a pension[89] or an insurance benefit,[90] or the remarriage of a widow to a man who turns out to be a kind step-father.[91]

(2) The chain of causation

Others again have said that the test of remoteness is whether the chain of causation has been interrupted or broken by some independent intervening cause: that a defendant remains liable for all consequences until such an interruption or breach frees him from further liability. Such is, however, the language of metaphor,[92] and the metaphor is not completely satisfactory. It

---

[85] This is the point which is so well illustrated by *Palsgraf* v. *Long Island Railroad Co.* (1928) 248 N.Y. 339: see above, § 78.
[86] *Mehmet Dogan Bey* v. *Abdeni Ltd.* [1951] 2 K.B. 405.
[87] *Gray* v. *Barr* [1971] 2 Q.B. 554.
[88] *Weld-Blundell* v. *Stephens* [1920] A.C. 956, 984; *Holling* v. *Yorks Traction Co.* [1948] 2 All E.R. 662, 664. "Dominant," "immediate" and "precipitating" are other adjectives which have been judicially used: *Minister of Pensions* v. *Chennell* [1947] K.B. 250; *Howgate* v. *Bagnall* [1951] 1 K.B. 265.
[89] No, according to Cohen L.J. in *Payne* v. *Railway Executive* [1952] 1 K.B. 26, 36.
[90] No, according to *Bradburn* v. *G.W.Ry.* (1874) L.R. 10 Ex. 1.
[91] Yes, according to *Mead* v. *Clark, Chapman & Co. Ltd.* [1956] 1 W.L.R. 76.
[92] Other metaphors which have been judicially used refer to conduit pipes, transmission gears, nets, rivers and streams. "It was his hand that let the tiger out of the cage," said Oliver J. of an employee who switched on a dangerous machine to clean it: *Williams* v. *Sykes and Harrison Ltd.* [1955] 1 W.L.R. 1180, 1189. Geoffrey Lane J. preferred "he who first put a match to the blue touch-paper": *Electrochrome Ltd.* v. *Welsh Plastics Ltd.* [1968] 2 All E.R. 205, 208. The main objection to metaphors about causation is that they foster a confused conception of a cause as something which, like a human being or a moving thing, may exert more or less power at different times. Despite the many criticisms of metaphors they contine to be used. "The instrument most effective to move the mind seems to be the lucky metaphor. Perhaps the main business of the lawyer in this matter of causation is simply the finding of that metaphor which is capable of moving he mind to see in the event (which is probably neutral in itself) the pattern which he desires to be seen there": Hamson [1954] C.L.J. 41.

cannot mean that the chain of causation is broken or interrupted in fact; for in that case the damage would not be a consequence of the defendant's act at all. The meaning can only be that, though the chain of causation remains unbroken in fact, it is deemed in law to have been interrupted so as to save the defendant from further liability for ensuing damages. But this is the very question for determination.

(3) The test of proximate cause

Another test sometimes proposed is that of proximate cause. But this might suggest that only the cause which is latest in time is significant, whereas the proximate cause, in the sense of the dominant or efficient cause, is not necessarily the one which operates last.[93] "The old flint-lock musket required a flash in the pan to ignite the powder and drive out the bullet, but death due to penetration by the bullet would not naturally be described as death by fire."[94] It is a fallacy to suppose that the last cause is the sole cause.[95] There may even be two dominant or proximate causes.[96]

(4) The doctrine of equivalence of conditions

A number of writers have accepted the view that all the necessary conditions of an event are equally entitled to be called the causes of that event: every event is the result of a "cone of causation" stretching back to the beginning of the world. It follows that these writers are obliged not only to deny the existence of the distinction between causes and mere conditions (a distinction which is, as we have seen, embedded in the structure of common-sense thinking about causation) but also to assert that when a court selects one out of the multiplicity of necessary conditions as "the cause" of an event its decision is based upon some irrational and inexplicable ground of policy. But this doctrine has not been accepted by the courts.[97]

(5) The test of reasonable foreseeability

There was always some authority[98] for the proposition that a wrongdoer is liable only for damage which was intended by him or which, though not intended, was the natural and probable consequence[99] of his wrongful act. This test of reasonable foreseeability, having been decisively rejected by the

---

[93] *Gray* v. *Barr* [1971] 2 Q.B. 554, 566–567.

[94] *Boiler Inspection and Insurance Company of Canada* v. *Sherwin-Williams Company of Canada* [1951] A.C. 319, 337, *per* Lord Porter. Yet Prosser said: "I doubt that all the manifold theories of the professors really have improved at all upon the old words 'proximate' and 'remote,' with the idea they convey of some reasonable connection between the original negligence and its consequences": *Topics*, p. 242.

[95] *Miller* v. *South of Scotland Electricity Board*, 1958 S.C.(H.L.) 20, 39.

[96] *Wayne Tank and Pump Co. Ltd.* v. *Employers' Liability Assurance Corporation Ltd.* [1974] 1 Q.B. 57, 61, 67.

[97] "The argument in the old fable in which the loss of a kingdom is traced back to an originating and ultimate cause in the loss of a single nail from a horse's shoe does not commend itself to me as adaptable to this case": *Norris* v. *William Moss & Sons Ltd.* [1954] 1 W.L.R. 346, 351, *per* Vaisey J.

[98] It rested mainly upon dicta of Pollock C.B. in two cases decided upon the same day, May 8, 1850—*Rigby* v. *Hewitt*, 5 Ex. 240, 243, and *Greenland* v. *Chaplin*, 5 Ex. 243, 248. These dicta were of an extremely non-committal character, and were not agreed to by the other members of the court, but were accepted by Pollock's grandson in successive editions of his *Torts* and by Salmond as a correct statement of the law.

[99] For the meaning of this phrase, see above, § 155.

Court of Appeal in *Re Polemis*,[1] was as decisively accepted and restored to favour by the Judicial Committee in *Overseas Tankship (U.K.) Ltd.* v. *Morts Dock and Engineering Co. Ltd.*,[2] an appeal from the Full Court of the Supreme Court of New South Wales. (This case is generally known as *The Wagon Mound*, the name under which it is reported in the courts below.[3]) We shall consider first the decision in *Re Polemis* and then the decision in *The Wagon Mound*.

(6) The test of direct consequences

The Court of Appeal in *Re an Arbitration between Polemis and Furness, Withy & Co.*[4] rejected the supposed rule that a wrongdoer is only responsible for the natural and probable consequences of his act. The court held that the probability of evil consequences is a test of whether the defendant was negligent or not; but if he was negligent, he is liable for the direct physical consequences whether probable or not. In that case Messrs. Polemis and Boyazides, the owners of the Greek steamship *Thrasyvoulos*, chartered the ship to Furness, Withy and Company, who loaded in the hold a quantity of petrol[5] in tins. During the voyage the tins leaked, and in consequence there was a considerable quantity of petrol vapour in the hold. At Casablanca in Morocco it became necessary for the Arab stevedores, servants of the charterers, to shift some of the cases, and for this purpose they placed a number of heavy planks at the end of the hatchway for use as a platform. While a sling containing the cases was being hoisted, the rope was negligently allowed to come into contact with these planks and to displace one of them, which fell into the hold. The fall of the plank was immediately followed by an outbreak of fire in the hold caused by the ignition of the petrol vapour by a spark struck by the falling plank. The ship was totally destroyed by fire.

The shipowners then claimed the value of the ship from the charterers, who relied, by way of defence, on the excepted perils clause in the charterparty, which was in the customary form, "act of God, the King's enemies, loss or damage from fire on board . . . excepted." The reply to this was that an excepted perils clause has no effect if the peril in question has been brought about by the negligence of the charterers or their servants. This was the issue referred to arbitration, and at first sight it might seem that the claim had little or nothing to do with the tort of negligence. The claim was upon a contract (a charterparty), and the issue was the simple one whether the negligence (in the sense of carelessness), of the defendants disentitled them from relying on the exemption clause.[6] But the charterers expressly pleaded that the damage was too remote,[7] and the case was regarded as one of tort before Sankey J. and the Court of Appeal. The experienced

---

[1] [1921] 3 K.B. 560.

[2] [1961] A.C. 388.

[3] [1958] 1 Lloyd's Rep. 575 (Kinsella J.); [1959] 2 Lloyd's Rep. 697 (Full Court).

[4] [1921] 3 K.B. 560.

[5] Described in some reports as benzine—a foreign term for petrol.

[6] *The Wagon Mound* [1959] 2 Lloyd's Rep. 697, 706.

[7] See McNair, "This *Polemis* Business" (1931) 4 Camb.L.J. 125, where the pleadings and the judgment of Sankey J. are set out in full. (This point seems to have escaped Manning J. in *The Wagon Mound*.) The Judicial Committee ([1961] A.C. 388, 415) said the point might be relevant for a tribunal for which *Re Polemis* was a binding authority.

arbitrators[8] from whom the appeal was brought found as a fact that the causing of the spark could not reasonably have been anticipated from the falling of the plank, though some (unspecified) damage to the ship might reasonably have been anticipated[9] A strong Court of Appeal[10] unanimously held the charterers liable to the owners for the loss, which amounted to nearly £200,000.[11] For to allow the plank to fall into the hold was in itself an act of negligence, inasmuch as it would not improbably cause some damage to the ship or cargo. The charterers, therefore, being guilty of negligence, were held liable for the direct consequences of that negligence, though in nature and magnitude those consequences were such as no reasonable man would have anticipated.

Impecuniosity

Some light was later thrown upon the meaning of direct cause by the decision of the House of Lords in 1932 in *Liesbosch Dredger (Owners)* v. *Edison (Owners)*.[12] In that case a dredger was sunk owing to the negligence of the *Edison*. The owners of the dredger required it for the performance of a contract, delay in the completion of which exposed them to heavy penalties. Owing to want of funds they could not purchase a dredger to take the place of the *Liesbosch*, and were forced to hire one at an exorbitant rate. It was held that the increased loss which the plaintiffs suffered due to their impecuniosity could not be recovered. The decision has never been fully accepted.[13] In particular it is hard to reconcile it with the principle that it is the plaintiffs' duty to mitigate his loss.[14] The plaintiffs' impecuniosity was in no sense either a result of the tort or an independent cause: it merely affected their ability to mitigate their loss. It may be that the decision is an authority for the proposition that the principle of *Re Polemis* is limited to direct consequences to the particular interest of the plaintiff which has been invaded,[15] but in *The Wagon Mound*[16] the Judicial Committee said it was not easy to see why such a distinction should be drawn or where the line was to be drawn.

End of Polemis

The principle in *Re Polemis* could claim the support of some of the most eminent common lawyers: from Sir William De Grey C.J. in 1773,[17]

---

[8] W. Clifton, A.F. Wootten, and Stuart Bevan, K.C.

[9] Goodhart says that this finding "was obviously incorrect": *Essays*, p. 146n.

[10] Bankes, Scrutton and Warrington L.JJ. ("I always like, if I can, to find authority from Scrutton L.J., who was one of the greatest judges of my time": *Kemshead* v. *British Transport Commission* [1958] 1 W.L.R. 173, 174, *per* Lord Goddard C.J.).

[11] It is interesting that both counsel for the unsuccessful appellants, the future Lords Wright and Porter, later independently accepted the decision as correct: see Porter, 5 Camb. L.J. 176; Wright (1951) 14 M.L.R. 393.

[12] [1933] A.C. 449. Lord Wright, whose speech in this case was concurrred in by the other Law Lords, later published some further reflections on the case in *Legal Essays*, pp. 96-123.

[13] In *Muhammed Issa El Sheikh Ahmed* v. *Ali* [1947] A.C. 414 (an action in contract) the Judicial Committee without referring to the *Liesbosch* case permitted a plaintiff to recover for the increased loss due to his impecuniosity.

[14] *Dodd Properties (Kent) Ltd.* v. *Canterbury City Council* [1980] 1 W.L.R. 433.

[15] So Lord Wright himself in *Bourhill* v. *Young* [1943] A.C. 92, 110; (1951) 14 M.L.R. 398, and Tilley, 33 Mich. L.R. 829, 847–851.

[16] [1961] A.C. 388, 424.

[17] *Scott* v. *Shepherd* (1773) 2 W.Bl. 892, 899.

through Channell B, and Blackburn J. in 1871,[18] down to Lord Sumner in 1920,[19] there is clear authority to support the view that the defendant is liable for all the direct and immediate consequences of his wrongful act[20]—although, as we have seen,[21] there is also authority the other way. The decision in *Re Polemis* itself was strongly criticised,[22] but also strongly defended.[23] But in the years after 1922 it appeared as if the courts were try- ing to avoid a direct decision on the merits of *Re Polemis* by holding that there was no duty because the damage to this particular plaintiff was not reasonably foreseeable,[24] or that the defendant, although under a duty to take care, had observed the requisite standard in the particular case.[25]

But in 1960 the issue was squarely raised before the Judicial Committee of the Privy Council in *The Wagon Mound*[26] on appeal from New South Wales.

— § 202. THE WAGON MOUND: REASONABLE FORESEEABILITY[27] —

The facts of this case have already been set out.[28] The Judicial Committee considered whether the appellants, the charterers of the *SS. Wagon Mound*,[29] were liable for the consequential damage of the destruction of the wharf by fire, as the courts of New South Wales had (reluctantly) held them to be. The Judicial Committee reversed the courts below and found that the appellants were not responsible for the fire because the damage in question was not reasonably foreseeable. The Judicial Committee held that the deci- sion in *Re Polemis* should no longer be regarded as good law and that the test of direct consequences was therefore inappropriate. The Judicial Com- mittee stated that the decision in *Re Polemis* was objectionable on the ground that "it does not seem consonant with current ideas of justice or morality that for an act of negligence, however slight or venial, which results in some trivial foreseeable damage the actor should be liable for all conse- quences however unforeseeable and however grave, so long as they can be said to be 'direct.' It is a principle of civil liability, subject only to qualifica- tions which have no present relevance, that a man must be considered to be responsible for the probable consequences of his act. To demand more of him is too harsh a rule, to demand less is to ignore that civilised order requires the observance of a minimum standard of behaviour."[30] Yet it

---

[18] *Smith* v. *L. & S.W. Ry.* (1871) L.R. 6 C.P. 14, 21. Yet Pollock (*Torts*, p. 29n.) thought "Blackburn and Willes JJ. would have been shocked beyond measure by *Polemis'* case."
[19] *Weld-Blundell* v. *Stephens* [1920] A.C. 956, 984. It should be noted that Lord Sumner used the test of direct consequences to limit liability and not to extend it: he thought that what had happened was foreseeable but not direct.
[20] So Atkin L.J. said in *Hambrook* v. *Stokes Bros.* [1925] 1 K.B. 141, at 156 that *Re Polemis* "laid down no new law."
[21] Above, n. 98.
[22] Particularly by Goodhart: *Essays*, Chaps. 6–7; *ibid.*, "The Imaginary Necktie and the Rule in *Re Polemis*" (1952) 68 L.Q.R. 514.
[23] Landon in Pollock, *Torts*, pp. 43–45.
[24] As in *Bourhill* v. *Young* [1943] A.C. 92.
[25] As in *Woods* v. *Duncan* [1946] A.C. 401.
[26] [1961] A.C. 388.
[27] Dias, "Trouble on Oiled Waters" [1967] C.L.J. 62, and also above, § 200.
[28] See above, § 80.
[29] So called after a little known battle at Wagon Mound, New Mexico.
[30] [1961] A.C. 388, 422.

might be asked why it is "consonant with current ideas of justice or morality" that the innocent plaintiff should have to suffer without compensation the loss of his wharf.[31]

The authority of the decision

The present state of the law is not too clear. The decision in *The Wagon Mound*, according to the strict doctrine of precedent, is binding only upon all, or perhaps only some[32] tribunals in the Commonwealth, and is of only persuasive authority[33] in the final appellate tribunal in the United Kingdom. Yet in the House of Lords it has been assumed,[34] and in the Court of Appeal,[35] and in the High Court,[36] expressly stated, that *Polemis* is no longer law, and that *The Wagon Mound* is the governing authority. It may turn out that the controversy has little practical effect. For one interpretation of the *Wagon Mound* cases is that they establish a rule that the tortfeasor is liable for any damage which he can reasonably foresee, however unlikely it may be, unless it can be brushed aside as far fetched.[37] Such a test may not be so different from the rejected direct consequences rule of *Re Polemis*—a decision which was probably correct on its facts.[38]

There are a few factors which might, however, be taken into account by any court which feels that it has a free choice in the matter. First, it is not too clear why the Judicial Committee considered the facts of *The Wagon Mound* to raise the same issue as that in *Re Polemis*. If anything is clear about that decision, it is that the damage which resulted did flow directly from the negligence of the defendant's employees dealing with highly inflammable vapour in a confined space, without the intervention of third parties or extraneous physical causes. But in *The Wagon Mound* it was the conduct of the *plaintiff's* employees which triggered off the ignition of low-grade oil spread out on sea-water more than fifty hours after the defendant's ship had left the vicinity.[39] The Judicial Committee appeared to have considered the ignition as direct but unforeseeable, though their reference to the question is oblique and casual. Secondly, neither the justice nor the convenience of making foresight the criterion of liability is obvious to everyone.[40] In the areas of duty and standard of care it has produced much uncertainty.[41] The best example of this uncertainty is *The Wagon Mound* (*No.* 2), in which the Judicial Committee in effect reversed its previous decision by holding that the fire in question was reasonably foreseeable, and that the owners of ships adjoining the wharf, as distinct from the owners of the wharf, were entitled

---

[31] *Shulhan v. Peterson, Howell and Heather Ltd.* (1966) 57 D.L.R. (2d) 491.
[32] So it has not been followed in Saskatchewan: *Shulhan v. Peterson, Howell and Heather Ltd.* (1966) 57 D.L.R. (2d) 491.
[33] The judgment in *The Wagon Mound* is rather ambiguous. In one place it expressly recognises that there are tribunals for which *Re Polemis* is still binding authority: in another it talks about "overruling" that case: see [1961] A.C. 388, 415, 420.
[34] *Hughes v. Lord Advocate* [1963] A.C. 837.
[35] *Doughty v. Turner Manufacturing Co. Ltd.* [1964] 1 Q.B. 518, 528, 532.
[36] *Smith v. Leech Brain & Co Ltd.* [1962] 2 Q.B. 405.
[37] *Koufos v. Czarnikow* [1969] 1 A.C. 350, 422.
[38] See Mr. Justice Cooke, "Remoteness of Damage and Judicial Discretion" [1978] C.L.J. 288, 292.
[39] See Leon Green, "Foreseeability in Negligence Law" (1961) 61 Col.L.Rev. 1401, 1414.
[40] See Lord Denning M.R. in *Parsons v. Ingham* [1978] Q.B. 791, 802.
[41] See above, §§ 74–76.

to recover in negligence.[42] Many still feel that justice requires that the wrongdoer rather than his innocent victim should bear the loss.[43]

On the other hand, the advantage of *The Wagon Mound* is that it provides a readily comprehensible test which is the same for each of the three component parts of the tort of negligence—duty, breach, and damage.

In this state of uncertainty it may be helpful to indicate a number of situations in which it seems clear that the principle in *The Wagon Mound* does not operate. One can often best judge the significance of a decision by observing what is excluded from it. The principle that reasonable foreseeability is the test of remoteness does not apply:

(1) *When the tort is one of strict liability*

The Judicial Committee itself recognised this exception so far as the rule in *Rylands* v. *Fletcher* was concerned,[44] and so has a later decision.[45] Probably in liability for dangerous animals[46] the test of remoteness is directness and not foresight. It is possible that libel is another exception.[47]

(2) *When the claim is under the Fatal Accidents Act, or for loss of services*

It is obvious that the test of remoteness in these torts is not foresight. The question simply is whether the defendant has caused harm of a kind for which the law gives compensation. One who has deprived a family of its bread-winner, or a husband of the consortium of his wife, cannot plead that he reasonably supposed he injured a person of independent means or a spinster.[48]

(3) *When the claim is for breach of a strict statutory duty*

The cases clearly show that in actions for (say) the failure to fence dangerous machinery securely foresight of the consequences is irrelevant.[49]

(4) *When the claim is for fraud*

In an action for the tort of deceit the defendant must pay for all the actual damage of whatever character[49a] directly flowing from the fraudulent inducement.[50]

(5) *When the damage which has occurred, although foreseeable, is not damage of a kind against which it was the duty of the defendant to guard*

The leading case of *Gorris* v. *Scott*[51] is perhaps the clearest example of this exception.

---

[42] See above, § 80.
[43] See *Siwek* v. *Lambourn* [1964] V.R. 337, 339.
[44] [1961] A.C. 388, 426–427.
[45] *British Celanese Ltd.* v. *A.H. Hunt (Capacitors) Ltd.* [1969] 1 W.L.R. 959.
[46] See above, §§ 119, 122.
[47] *Morgan* v. *Odhams Press Ltd.* [1971] 1 W.L.R. 1239.
[48] *Haber* v. *Walker* [1953] V.R. 339. See below, § 217.
[49] See above, § 86.
[49a] *Shelley* v. *Paddock* [1980] Q.B. 348.
[50] *Doyle* v. *Olby Ltd.* [1969] 2 Q.B. 158. See also the similar decision of the Irish Supreme Court in *Northern Bank Finance Co. Ltd.* v. *Charlton* [1979] I.R. 149.
[51] (1874) L.R. 9 Ex.125. See above, § 85.

(6) *When the defendant cannot be said to have caused the damage, although that damage was in fact foreseeable, and a duty was owed to the particular plaintiff*[52]

The *Wagon Mound* cases have laid it down that the plaintiff must prove foreseeability as well as causation. So there has been a tendency to emphasise foreseeability and to forget causation. But causation must still be proved. Thus in *Performance Cars Ltd.* v. *Abraham*[53] the defendant was held not liable when his car negligently collided with the plaintiff's Rolls-Royce for which the plaintiff claimed the cost (£75) of a re-spray, for at the time of the accident the Rolls already needed such a re-spray as the result of a previous collision with a third party. Contrariwise, it is settled by *Baker* v. *Willoughby*[54] that a tortfeasor's liability remains unaffected by a later tortious[55] event causing the same or greater damage to the plaintiff so long as the original tort remains one cause of the damage. To put it in another way, a second accident to the plaintiff may be a foreseeable risk.[56]

(7) *When the damage which has been caused is damage of the same type or kind that might have been foreseen, but is greater in amount than could have been foreseen*

This is perhaps the most important exception to the *Wagon Mound* principle. That principle requires that the type of damage must have been reasonably foreseeable; it does not require that the amount of that damage must have been foreseeable.

(i) *Type of damage must be foreseen.* It has been made plain that the precise details of the accident, or the exact concatenation of circumstances, need not be foreseen. It is sufficient if the type, kind, degree, category or order of harm could have been foreseen in a general way.[57] The question is, was the accident a variant of the perils originally brought about by the defendant's negligence?[58] The law of negligence has not been fragmented into a number of distinct torts.[59]

(ii) *Amount of damage need not be foreseen.* If the damage which occurs is damage of the type or kind which ought to have been foreseen, in the sense explained in the preceding paragraph, then it is immaterial that the extent or amount of the damage was unforeseeable. As we have already seen,[60] there is a distinction between remoteness of damage and measure of damages, and the principle of foreseeability is applicable only to the former head. Indeed, once actionable injury has been established, compensation is

---

[52] See McGregor, "Variations on an Enigma" (1970) 33 M.L.R. 378.
[53] [1962] 1 Q.B. 33.
[54] [1970] A.C. 467.
[55] If the later event is non-tortious it may be held to have interrupted the wheels which were set in motion by the initial tort: *Hodgson* v. *G.E.C. Ltd.* [1978] 2 Lloyd's Rep. 210.
[56] *Wieland* v. *Cyril Lord Carpets Ltd.* [1969] 3 All E.R. 1006.
[57] *Hughes* v. *Lord Advocate* [1963] A.C. 837 (liability for fire caused by an explosion as distinct from a conflagration: see above, § 81).
[58] *Doughty* v. *Turner Manufacturing Co. Ltd.* [1964] 1 Q.B. 518 (eruption of liquid by chemical change not a variant of the perils from the foreseeable risk of splashing: see above, § 81).
[59] *Bradford* v. *Robinson Rentals Ltd.* [1967] 1 W.L.R. 337, 344–345 (frostbite unusual, but a foreseeable variant of the perils of the English winter).
[60] Above, § 199.

rarely, if ever, just a valuation of that injury, but is rather a valuation of the harm suffered as a result of that injury.[61]

The "egg-shell skull" rule

This seventh exception, to the effect that the amount of damage need not be foreseen, is illustrated by the well-established rule that, at least so far as the physical[62] condition of the victim is concerned, abnormal circumstances existing at the time of the wrongful act do not negative causal connection. So if the consequences of a slight personal injury are aggravated by the state of health of the person injured, the wrongdoer is nonetheless liable to the full extent,[63] though he had no knowledge of that state of health and no reason to suspect it.[64] So in the leading case of *Smith* v. *Leach Brain & Co. Ltd.*[65] it was held that if a victim of a negligent act suffers from a pre-cancerous condition which is activated by that act, the wrongdoer is responsible for all the disastrous consequences. This is always known as the "egg-shell skull" rule, although there appears to be only one case in which the plaintiff in fact suffered from this peculiar disability.[66] After a period of uncertainty, it has now been held in England,[67] Scotland,[68] Ireland,[69] New Zealand[70] and Canada[71] that *The Wagon Mound* did not affect the "egg-shell skull" rule. Although the rule is usually advantageous to the plaintiff, the facts of *Performance Cars Ltd.* v. *Abraham*[72] show that it may work to the advantage of the defendant.

The same rule applies when damage has been done to chattels. So we have it on the authority of Sir James Shaw Willes that a case was "tried before me at Newcastle spring assizes, 1859, in which a chemist who sold ointment to rub sheep with was held liable to pay to their owner the whole of their value, £2,000 and upwards, it having killed them; and yet it was hard that a man who could only make a profit of a few pence should be held responsible for so heavy a loss."[73] Again, if a chemical is supplied which is liable to explode on contact with water, and that hazard and consequent damage to property are reasonably foreseeable, then it matters not that the magnitude of the former and the extent of the latter were not so foreseeable.[74]

§ 203. Effect of an Intervening Act[75]

It remains to consider how far, if at all, the general principles of remoteness of damage are affected by the circumstance that the damage has been

---

[61] *Wieland* v. *Cyril Lord Carpets Ltd.* [1969] 3 All E.R. 1006, 1009.
[62] Or perhaps even financial (*The Despina R.* [1977] 1 Lloyd's Rep. 618, 620), or emotional (*Malcolm* v. *Broadhurst* [1970] 3 All E.R. 508, 511).
[63] *Dulieu* v. *White* [1901] 2 K.B. 669, 679.
[64] *Robinson* v. *Post Office* [1974] 1 W.L.R. 1176.
[65] [1962] 2 Q.B. 405.
[66] *Wilson* v. *Birt (Pty.), Ltd.*, 1963 (2) S.A. 508.
[67] *Smith* v. *Leech Brain & Co. Ltd.* [1962] 2 Q.B. 405.
[68] *McKillen* v. *Barclay Curle & Co. Ltd.*, 1967 S.L.T. 41.
[69] *Burke* v. *John Paul & Co. Ltd.* [1967] I.R. 277.
[70] *Stephenson* v. *Waite Tileman Ltd.* [1973] 1 N.Z.L.R. 152.
[71] *Winteringham* v. *Rae* (1965) 55 D.L.R. (2d) 108.
[72] [1962] 1 Q.B. 33, cited in previous sub-head.
[73] *Mullett* v. *Mason* (1866) L.R. 1 C.P. 559, 561.
[74] *Vacwell Engineering Co. Ltd.* v. *B.D.H. Chemicals Ltd.* [1971] 1 Q.B. 88, 110 (on appeal, [1971] 1 Q.B. 111n).
[75] Millner, "Novus Actus Interveniens" (1971) 22 N.I.L.Q. 168.

brought about by some overwhelming supervening event which is of such a character that it relegates into history matters which would otherwise be looked on as causative factors.[76] Such an event or act is often called a *novus actus interveniens*.[77] In discussing this difficult subject it will be helpful to recall that it is beyond question that human action does not *per se* sever the connected sequence of acts.[78] There are two main views as to the proper test of causation in such a case. The one is that of probability, the other is that of isolation. It is in dealing with the effect of a *novus actus interveniens* that the divergence between these two views is most marked.

(1) The probability test

This test involves two propositions: first, if a consequence which actually results from the defendant's tort is a probable or foreseeable consequence, then the defendant may be liable; secondly, if a consequence which actually results from the defendant's tort is an improbable or unforeseeable consequence, then the defendant is not liable. If the *novus actus interveniens* is unforeseeable, it is much easier to recognise it as entirely independent and so efficient in its own effects that it should properly be regarded as having relegated the original act to an event of merely historical significance.[79] But even if the *novus actus* is foreseeable, the defendant may not be responsible, for it is often easy to foresee unreasonable conduct.[80]

(2) The isolation test

The isolation test is best expressed in the words of Lord Sumner[81] in *Weld-Blundell* v. *Stephens*.[82] "In general (apart from special contracts and relations and the maxim *Respondeat superior*), even though A is in fault, he is not responsible for injury to C, which B, a stranger to him, deliberately chooses to do. Though A may have given the occasion for B's mischievous activity, B then becomes a new and independent cause. It is hard to steer clear of metaphors. Perhaps one may be forgiven for saying that B snaps the chain of causation; that he is no mere conduit pipe through which consequences flow from A to C, no mere moving part in a transmission gear set in motion by A; that in a word he insulates A from C." According to Lord Sumner[83] it is even immaterial that the intervening act is the probable consequence of the defendant's own wrongful act. This, undoubtedly, is a hard saying. Salmond was therefore reluctant to accept Lord Sumner's dictum as

---

[76] *R.* v. *Anderson and Morris* [1966] 2 Q.B. 110, 120.

[77] du Parcq L.J. thought that we could get on equally well without this phrase: *Ingram* v. *United Automobile Services* [1943] 2 All E.R. 71, 73, but, like the metaphor "chain of causation," it is a conveniently compendious expression and hallowed by long usage. "It has often been said that Latin phrases cannot help to solve problems of causation, but they are sometimes so convenient a label that the careful avoidance of them becomes an inverted kind of pedantry"; *Hogan* v. *Bentinck West Hartley Collieries (Owners) Ltd.* [1949] 1 All E.R. 588, 596, *per* Lord Normand.

[78] *The Oropesa* [1943] P. 32, 37; *Woods* v. *Duncan* [1946] A.C. 401, 442.

[79] *Iron and Steel Holdings and Realisation Agency* v. *Compensation Appeal Tribunal* [1966] 1 W.L.R. 480.

[80] *McKew* v. *Holland and Hannen and Cubitts (Scotland) Ltd.* [1969] 3 All E.R. 1621.

[81] "Lord Sumner was a reputed master of explicit language and clear thought. Few could say so precisely what they meant, and no one was less likely to say what he did not mean": *The People* v. *Kirwan* [1943] I.R. 279, 315, *per* Black J.

[82] [1920] A.C. 956, 986.

[83] *Weld-Blundell* v. *Stephens* [1920] A.C. 956, 988.

a correct statement of the law,[84] and in view of the severe criticisms passed upon the dictum by the Judicial Committee in *The Wagon Mound (No.* 1)[85] his reluctance would seem to have been fully justified. There are undoubtedly many decisions which are expressed to rest upon the principle that damage which is the natural and probable consequence of the defendant's wrongdoing is imputable to him notwithstanding an intervening act.[86]

§ 204. LIABILITY WHERE INTERVENING ACT FORESEEABLE

It must always be a question of fact in each case whether the intervening act or omission was foreseeable, but the cases fall into five categories.

(1) Novus actus intentionally procured by defendant

Clearly the defendant will be liable wherever he has actually authorised or instigated the intervening act,[87] or omission.[88] He will also be liable if he has intentionally induced or procured the intervening act by putting the necessary means, opportunity, or inducement in the way of him who does it. If A publishes a libel with intent that B shall repeat it, A is responsible for such repetition no less than if he had authorised it.[89]

(2) Where the novus actus is a natural and probable result of the breach of duty

In some cases the law imposes a duty to take care that harm shall not be caused by the act of a third party. So Greer L.J. in *Haynes* v. *Harwood*[90] said: "If what is relied upon as *novus actus interveniens* is the very kind of thing which is likely to happen if the want of care which is alleged takes place, the principle embodied in the maxim is no defence. The whole question is whether or not, to use the words of the leading case, *Hadley* v. *Baxendale*,[91] the accident can be said to be 'the natural and probable result' of the breach of duty." This statement has often been cited with approval. Thus in *Stansbie* v. *Troman*[92] a householder was obliged to leave a painter working alone in his house. The painter also left the house for about two hours to obtain some wallpaper and (although warned by the householder to shut the front door when he left the house) left the door unlocked. The painter was held liable for the loss of jewellery stolen by a third party who had entered the house in his absence, because this was just the kind of thing which was likely to happen.

It has also long been settled that if a person collects a crowd to the

---

[84] See 6th ed., (s.36). Yet it should not be forgotten that these statements of Lord Sumner followed a passage in which he had given at least half-a-dozen examples of cases where a defendant would be held responsible despite the intervening act of some third party.

[85] [1961] A.C. 388, 417.

[86] See the cases cited below, § 204.

[87] Above, § 167.

[88] It should be noted that a deliberate omission is just the same in quality as an act of commission. It is a voluntary act: *Harnett* v. *Bond* [1924] 2 K.B. 517.

[89] *Weld-Blundell* v. *Stephens* [1920] A.C. 956, 999.

[90] [1935] 1 K.B. 146, 156.

[91] (1854) 9 Ex. 341.

[92] [1948] 2 K.B. 48. *Cobb* v. *Great Western Ry.* [1894] A.C. 419 (no liability for pickpockets in overcrowded carriage) is not now treated as law.

annoyance of his neighbours that may constitute a nuisance, and that it is unnecessary to show that it was his object to create a nuisance, or that it was the inevitable result of his act. It is sufficient to show that the collecting together of the crowd was, according to the common experience of mankind, the probable consequence of his act. So liability has been imposed where a crowd has collected in consequence of an interesting shop-window,[93] a theatrical success,[94] and a racecourse.[95] Another example is the duty imposed on those who send out dangerous chattels. A chemist who sells a poisonous liquid in a bottle which has been carelessly labelled with the name of some innocuous substance will not be allowed to say that the cause of subsequent disaster was the voluntary act of the ignorant victim who drank it, for that is just what might be expected to happen in those circumstances. A similar principle governs the liability of those who give or lend firearms to young persons: everyone knows they are likely to be meddlesome and mischievous and to interfere with the trigger or safety-catch.[96] The plaintiff need not prove that the defendant ought to have foreseen every step in the chain of events leading to the accident.[97]

On the other hand, if the proximate cause of the danger is not the negligence of the defendant, but the conscious act of another's volition, then he will not be liable.[98] But it may not be easy to prove such an independent conscious act of volition.[99] Thus it was once held[1] that where the defendant is entitled to rely upon some other person to guard against the dangerous situation which he has created and that other person fails in his duty, his failure may negative the existence of negligence in the defendant. But the more recent cases hold that a defendant who has broken his duty is not entitled to rely on the failure of a third party to notice the breach and take precautions against it.[2]

(3) Where the intervening actor is not fully responsible

Again the chain of causation is not broken and the consequence is direct if the *novus actus interveniens* is the act of some person who is not fully responsible for his acts, and whose lack of responsibility should have been foreseen, such as a child,[3] a person in a state of excusable ignorance or one in a state of excusable alarm produced by the defendant's own wrongful act[4] or a workman in a factory whose senses have been dulled by routine work.[5] In maritime law the problem arises when there has been a collision caused

---

[93] *R.* v. *Carlile* (1834) 6 C. & P. 636, in which it was questioned whether the beautiful daughter of Mr. Very, a Regent Street confectioner, whose shop was daily beset by admiring crowds, might not have been an indictable nuisance.

[94] *Barber* v. *Penley* [1893] 2 Ch. 447 (*Charley's Aunt*).

[95] *Dewar* v. *City and Suburban Racecourse Co.* [1899] 1 I.R. 345.

[96] *Newton* v. *Edgerley* [1959] 1 W.L.R. 1031, 1035.

[97] *Wieland* v. *Cyril Lord Carpets Ltd.* [1969] 3 All E.R. 1006, 1009. See above, §§ 75, 202.

[98] *Dominion Natural Gas Co.* v. *Collins* [1909] A.C. 640, 646.

[99] *Philco Radio Ltd.* v. *J. Spurling Ltd.* [1949] 2 All E.R. 882. The defendants misdelivered some crates of highly inflammable material to the plaintiff's premises. A typist aged 19 set fire to it with a cigarette but the Court of Appeal held this was not such a conscious act of volition as would relieve the defendants from liability.

[1] *Buckner* v. *Ashby and Horner* [1941] 1 K.B. 321.

[2] *Clay* v. *A.J. Crump & Sons Ltd.* [1964] 1 Q.B. 533.

[3] *Latham* v. *Johnson* [1913] 1 K.B. 398, 413. See also above, § 196.

[4] *Weld-Blundell* v. *Stephens* [1920] A.C. 956, 985.

[5] See above, § 196.

by the negligence of the defendant's ship, and there then follow other collisions or groundings. Here again the courts have had recourse to metaphors,
and have asked, for example, if those on board the ship during the second
disaster "were still in the grip of the collision."[6]

The doctrine of "alternative danger"

One of the most familiar examples in this branch of the law is of a person
acting in a state of excusable alarm produced by the defendant's own
wrongful act.[7] Thus in *Scott* v. *Shepherd*[8] the defendant threw a lighted
squib into the market-house at Milborne Port on a fair-day. The squib fell
upon the stall of Yates, who sold ginger-bread; one Willis, in order to prevent injury to himself and the goods of Yates, instantly picked up the squib
and threw it across the market-place; it landed upon the stall of one Ryal,
who also sold ginger-bread, and who in his turn threw the squib to another
part of the market-house. On this occasion the squib burst in the plaintiff's
face and destroyed one of his eyes. A majority of the Court of Common
Pleas held that the defendant was responsible in trespass. "It has been urged
that the intervention of a free agent will make a difference; but I do not consider Willis and Ryal as free agents in the present case, but acting under a
compulsory necessity for their own safety and self-preservation."[9]

It has been said[10] to be desirable to limit the application of this principle
to those cases in which the danger is personal danger and the plaintiff or
third person has taken "instant action on the first alarm," where the choice
has been automatic and without reflection. But the better view is that the
doctrine extended to cases in which the plaintiff or third person had acted
reasonably and "not unnaturally" and to cases in which the danger was
danger to property.[11]

(4) Where the intervening act is done in pursuance of a duty

On the same principle the consequence is direct where the intervening act
is that of a person acting under the compulsion of a legal or even only a
moral duty. The commonest example is the rescue cases, which we have
already discussed.[12] The action of the rescuer follows naturally and properly
in the natural sequence of events from the act of the wrongdoer.[13]

(5) Where the intervening act is done in defence of rights

Again, the chain of causation is not treated as broken when the intervening act is that of a person acting in the exercise or defence of his rights and

[6] *The Calliope* [1970] P. 172, 185.
[7] The doctrine of "alternative danger," as it is sometimes called, is also important in the law
   relating to contributory negligence: see above, § 196.
[8] (1773) 2 W.Bl.892. The plaintiff in this leading case was the grandfather of C.P. Scott, the
   famous editor of the *Manchester Guardian*: J.L. Hammond, *Life of C.P. Scott* (London,
   1934), p. 1.
[9] (1773) 2 W.Bl. 892, 900, *per* De Grey C.J. The famous dissenting judgment of Blackstone
   J. was based on the view that the acts of Willis and Ryal were not such a direct and
   immediate consequence of Shepherd's original act as to render him liable in *trespass*, as
   distinct from *case*. Denning L.J. said he agreed with Blackstone J.: the *Esso Petroleum
   Case* [1954] 2 Q.B. 182, 196.
[10] *Singleton Abbey (Owners)* v. *Paludina (Owners)* [1927] A.C. 16, 28.
[11] *Sutherland* v. *Glasgow Corporation*, 1951 S.C. 1.
[12] Above, § 189.
[13] *The Gusty* [1940] P. 159, 165.

without intention to injure others.[14] So it is a foreseeable consequence of obstructing a highway that some passer-by may lawfully attempt to abate the nuisance and in so doing create a source of danger.[15]

Slander an exception. As the authorities stand[16] one exception must be admitted to the general rule that a foreseeable *novus actus* does not break the chain of causation. In *Ward* v. *Weeks*[17] it was decided that in an action for slander the defendant cannot be held responsible for damage caused not by the utterance of the defamatory words by the defendant himself but by their unauthorised and unintended repetition by other persons. In these cases the mere fact that it was antecedently probable that the intervening actor would act as he did—"for more than half of human kind are tale-bearers by nature"[18]—did not make the defendants liable.

Acts done to minimise damage

It is the duty of the plaintiff to minimise damage, so no act which he does reasonably with that object in view will break the chain of causation.[19] The duty to mitigate damage is really an application of the broad principle of contributory negligence, so that the plaintiff cannot recover damages for an aggravation or prolongation of his injuries which is due to his own neglect or wilful default.[20] "If a man suffering from a sprained leg wishes to win a prize in a high-jumping competition and proceeds to endeavour to win it and thereby makes his leg so much worse that it takes an additional six months to recover, he is only entitled to damages for such part of his suffering as was not due to such heedless conduct."[21] Conversely, any profits earned as a result of the mitigating acts must be brought into account against the loss caused by the wrongful act.[22]

Erroneous professional advice or treatment

So also a refusal by the plaintiff to accept medical advice or treatment (even when given by the defendant's doctors) may in all the circumstances be unreasonable and so damages should be assessed as if he had undergone the treatment and it had been successful.[23] Similarly, if the medical attention which the plaintiff receives aggravates his existing injury or causes a new injury, the defendant will probably not be liable if such injury is properly attributable to the actionable negligence of the surgeon or doctor, or some chemical or physical freak occurrence.[24] The erroneous advice of counsel does not break the chain of causation resulting from a solicitor's

---

[14] A good illustration of the principle is *Clayards* v. *Dethick* (1848) 12 Q.B. 439, the facts of which are given above, § 188.
[15] *Cunningham* v. *McGrath Bros.* [1964] I.R. 209.
[16] But see above, § 70.
[17] (1830) 7 Bing. 211.
[18] *Weld-Blundell* v. *Stephens* [1920] A.C. 956, 988, 991, *per* Lord Sumner.
[19] *McKew* v. *Holland and Hannen and Cubitts (Scotland) Ltd.* [1969] 3 All E.R. 1621.
[20] [1969] 3 All E.R. 1621, 1623.
[21] *Jones* v. *Watney, Combe, Reid & Co. Ltd.* (1912) 28 T.L.R. 399, 400.
[22] *The World Beauty* [1970] P. 145.
[23] *McAuley* v. *London Transport Executive* [1957] 2 Lloyd's Rep. 500.
[24] As in *Alston* v. *Marine and Trade Insurance Co. Ltd.* 1964 (4) S.A. 112, in which the plaintiff suffered a stroke after eating cheese following the administration of the drug parstellin.

negligence.[25] On the other hand, the defendant will be liable if the original injury still subsists, although in an aggravated form, after an operation prudently advised and properly carried out.[26] Again, if the owner of a damaged chattel (not being a unique object) insists on having it repaired at a cost greatly in excess of the market replacement value, he has not taken reasonable steps to mitigate the damage.[27] But in criminal law it has been held that the wrongdoer must take his victim as he finds him. So it does not lie in the mouth of the assailant to say that his victim's religious beliefs, which inhibited him from accepting certain kinds of treatment, were unreasonable.[28-30]

Novus actus where contractual duties

Liability for consequences caused by a *novus actus* in cases in which there is a contract depends upon the terms, express or implied, of that contract. Thus a bailee of goods is bound to use due care for their safety, and if for want of such care they are lost by theft, he cannot plead in defence that the immediate cause of their loss was an act of wilful wrongdoing on the part of the thief.[31] So in *London Joint Stock Bank* v. *MacMillan*[32] it was held that a customer of a bank owes to the bank a contractual duty of care so to draw his cheques as not to facilitate an increase of the amount thereof by forgery. Even if there is no contractual duty, the signer of a document may be estopped by his negligence if he signs it in blank and an innocent third party acts on it to his detriment.[33]

§ 205. CURRENCY OF AWARD[33a]

It is now possible for an English court to award damages in some currency other than sterling. In the case of tort, damages may be calculated in the currency in which the loss was effectively felt or borne by the plaintiff, having regard to the currency in which he generally operates.[33b] This is really no more than an application of the general principle of reasonable foreseeability.

§ 206. CONTRACT AND TORT

A large number of conflicting dicta exist on the relationship of the rules governing remoteness of damage in contract and in tort. All must now be read in the light both of the two *Wagon Mound* cases[34] and also of the decision of the House of Lords in *Czarnikow Ltd.* v. *Koufos*.[35] It is clear that the

---

[25] *Cook* v. *Swinfen* [1967] 1 W.L.R. 457.
[26] *Hogan* v. *Bentinck West Hartley Collieries (Owners) Ltd.* [1949] 1 All E.R. 588, 596, 607.
[27] *Darbishire* v. *Warran* [1963] 1 W.L.R. 1067.
[28-30] *R.* v. *Blaue* [1975] 1 W.L.R. 1411.
[31] *Coldman* v. *Hill* [1919] 1 K.B. 443.
[32] [1918] A.C. 777.
[33] *Gallie* v. *Lee* [1971] A.C. 1004.
[33a] See Knott, "Foreign Currency Judgments in Tort" (1980) 43 M.L.R. 18.
[33b] *The Despina R.* [1979] A.C. 685.
[34] Above, §§ 200–202.
[35] [1969] 1 A.C. 350. Note that the leading judgment was delivered by Lord Reid, who had also sat in both *Wagon Mound* appeals.

measure of damages in contract is not the same as in tort.[36] Beyond that, all is obscure, and there has been judicial complaint about a "sea of semantic exercises."[37] So the following analysis is tentative.

In contract the rule is that the plaintiff can recover for loss which the defendant, when he entered into the contract, ought to have contemplated as a reasonable man was of a very substantial degree of probability or was not unlikely to result from a breach. The plaintiff cannot recover, as he can in tort, for loss which is a serious, possibility or a real danger. The reason for this distinction between contract and tort is that in contract, if one party wishes to protect himself from a risk which to the other part would appear unusual, he can direct that other's attention to it before the contract is made. But in tort there is no such opportunity available to the injured party, and so the tortfeasor cannot complain if he has to pay for some very unusual but still foreseeable damage which results from his wrongdoing. Therefore liability in tort is normally wider than liability in contract—but not necessarily so, for the parties to a contract may expressly agree that there shall be liability for some remote and quite unforeseeable head of damage. So damages for the tort of deceit are quite different from damages for breach of warranty.[38] Thus in deceit it is settled that a plaintiff cannot recover damages for loss of his bargain: he is only entitled to be put in the position which he would have been in had the representation not been made. Yet in an action for breach of contract he is entitled to be put in the same position as if the representation had been true.[39]

---

[36] *Czarnikow Ltd.* v. *Koufos* |1969| 1 A.C. 350, 385, 411, 413, 422.
[37] *Parsons Ltd.* v. *Ingham Ltd.* |1978| Q.B. 791, 802, *per* Lord Denning M.R. See also the article by Cooke J. in |1978| C.L.J. 288.
[38] *Doyle* v. *Olby (Ironmongers) Ltd.* |1969| 2 Q.B. 158.
[39] *McGregor on Damages* (13th ed.), Chap. 39.

CHAPTER 23

MEASURE OF DAMAGES IN PARTICULAR TORTS

§ 207. Trespass

(1) Trespass to land

When a trespass has caused physical damage to the land, the measure of damages is the loss thereby caused to the plaintiff, which in all ordinary cases is measured by the resulting diminution in the value of the property. This measure of damages is necessarily not the cost of reinstatement—the cost of restoring the land to the condition in which it formerly was—for this is a cost which may greatly exceed the actual diminution in the value of the land.[1] Thus if an old building is pulled down, the plaintiff cannot recover the cost of putting up a new one, but merely the value of the old,[2] unless his house was unique, or the case is in some other way exceptional.[3] But prospective damages can be recovered.[4] When a trespass consists in some beneficial use wrongfully made of the plaintiff's land, even if it causes no damage, the plaintiff is entitled to claim by way of damages a reasonable remuneration for that use, as if it had been had under an agreement[5]; and in this remuneration compensation for any damage done to the land will be included.[6]

(2) Trespass to goods

If the plaintiff has been deprived of his goods the measure of damages is the value of the goods. If the plaintiff has a limited interest in the goods (*e.g.* as bailee) he may recover the full value of them, although he will have to account to the owner for what he recovers beyond his own interest.[7] Where the defendant has an interest in the goods the measure of damages is limited to the value of the plaintiff's interest.[8] If the plaintiff has not been deprived of the goods, it is the loss actually suffered as the direct consequence of the trespass, but if the trespass was accompanied by aggravating circumstances the court will not inquire too nicely into the jury's verdict.

Wrongful severance of goods

When part of the land has been wrongfully severed and turned into a chattel, the value of that chattel is sometimes greater and sometimes less than the resulting diminution in the value of the land. In such cases what is the measure of damages—the value of the chattels so taken away, or the resulting diminution in the value of the land? It depends on whether the wrongdoing has been wilful.

---

[1] *Nalder* v. *Ilford Corporation* [1951] K.B. 822.
[2] *Lodge Holes Colliery* v. *Wednesbury Corporation* [1908] A.C. 323.
[3] *Munnelly* v. *Calcon Ltd.* [1978] I.R. 397.
[4] *Townend* v. *Askery Coal Co.* [1934] Ch. 463.
[5] *Strand Electric Co.* v. *Brisford* [1952] 2 Q.B. 246.
[6] *Yakamia Dairy Pty Ltd.* v. *Wood* [1976] W.A.R. 57.
[7] *The Winkfield* [1902] P. 42. See also below; §§209–210.
[8] *Brierly* v. *Kendall* (1852) 17 Q.B. 937.

(i) *Wilful wrongdoing*

The rule is that the plaintiff may elect to claim either the one or the other, and he will of course claim the amount which is the larger in the particular case. The chattel, although it has been severed and made into a chattel by the labour and expenditure of the defendant, nevertheless belongs to the plaintiff, who may recover its full value without making any allowance for the fact that part of that value has been given to it by the defendant.[9]

(ii) *No wilful wrongdoing*

This penal rule[10] by which the plaintiff recovers more than his actual loss does not apply where there is no fraud or conscious wrongdoing on the part of the defendant. In such a case the plaintiff cannot recover the value of the chattel, and is entitled to nothing more than his actual loss—*viz.* the diminution of the value of the land. So that if the plaintiff's coal is severed and taken by mistake as to title or boundaries, the measure of damages is the value of the coal in the seam, as if it had been bought *in situ* by the defendant.[11] Whether the penal measure of damages applies in the case of negligence as well as in that of fraud is unsettled. There are certain dicta in favour of its application to such a case, but it is doubtful whether it would be followed today.[12]

(3) Trespass to the person

Aggravated damages are permissible if the assault or battery has occurred in humiliating or undignified circumstances.[13] Provocation by the plaintiff may wipe out the element of aggravated or exemplary damages, but cannot be used to reduce the appropriate figure of compensation for physical loss.[14]

§ 208. THE ACTION FOR MESNE PROFITS

Any person wrongfully dispossessed of land had, in addition to a right of action for the recovery of the land, a right of action for damages in respect of all loss suffered by him during the period of his dispossession. Such an action is termed an action for mesne profits. A claim for mesne profits is now usually joined with the action for recovery of the land.[15] Whether the dispossession had or had not been effected by way of trespass, the claim for mesne profits was always in form a claim for damages for a continuing trespass upon the land. Such a claim was based upon the doctrine of

---

[9] *Peruvian Guano Co.* v. *Dreyfus Bros.* [1892] A.C. 166, 173–177.
[10] It is an illustration of one of the categories in which an award of exemplary damages if permissible: *Cassell & Co. Ltd.* v. *Broome* [1972] A.C. 1027, 1130.
[11] *Townend* v. *Askern Coal Co.* [1934] Ch. 463.
[12] See McGregor on Damages, §§ 998–1004, on the whole subject. These principles were worked out by the courts with exclusive reference to the extraction of coal. The distinction between an innocent and fraudulent defendant is unknown to the law of conversion: *Caxton Publishing Co.* v. *Sutherland Publishing Co.* [1939] A.C. 178, 193. See also Gordon, "Anomalies in the Law of Conversion" (1955) 71 L.Q.R. 347; Law Reform Committee, 18th Report, paras. 89–90.
[13] See above, § 43.
[14] *Lane* v. *Holloway* [1968] 1 Q.B. 379. But later the Court of Appeal seems to have departed from this principle: *Murphy* v. *Culhane* [1977] Q.B. 94.
[15] R.S.C., Ord. 13, rr. 4, 5.

trespass by relation. It followed that the action would not lie until after the plaintiff had re-entered and recovered the possession of the land. But this requirement of re-entry as a condition precedent to an action for mesne profits is now abolished, to this extent only, that a claim for such profits may in all cases be joined with the action. The law, then, seems to be as follows: A person dispossessed of land may (1) sue for recovery and for mesne profits in one action; (2) sue for mesne profits, if he has already got back into possession; (3) sue for mesne profits without recovery of possession, if his interest in the land has already come to an end.[16] In an action for mesne profits (notwithstanding the name of the action) the plaintiff is not limited to a claim for the profits which the defendant has received from the land, or those which he himself has lost. The plaintiff recovers all the loss which has resulted from the dispossession.[17] Profits are assessable from the date of the writ, not from that of the breach of covenant or other wrongs.[18] It seems not to have been decided whether a defendant in an action for mesne profits can set off the value of improvements made by him to the property in good faith during the period of his possession.

§ 209. CONVERSION[19]

The Torts (Interference with Goods) Act 1977 abolishes detinue but otherwise only re-groups the existing torts (trespass, conversion and negligence) within a wider framework. The specific changes which it made in the scope of the remedies available are best understood as a gloss on the common law.

If a plaintiff relies upon a right of possession he can recover only according to the amount of his interest.[20] But a plaintiff who had actual possession of a chattel is entitled, in an action for the conversion of it, to recover its full value as damages, even although he is not the owner of it, but has merely a limited interest in it, such as that of a bailee, agent or pledgee. In other words, the plaintiff in conversion is entitled either to the property or to its pecuniary equivalent. The law seems to have assumed that the value of the chattel must always represent the plaintiff's actual loss. But there are cases in which this is far from being the truth, and to permit the plaintiff to recover more than his actual loss is a significant departure from the principle, which in general governs the award of damages, that compensation of the plaintiff is the object of the law. The leading case is *The Winkfeld*,[21] in which the Postmaster-General was held entitled as bailee to recover the whole value of certain mails which were lost through a collision at sea caused by the negligence of the defendants, although the Postmaster-General was, as the law then stood,[22] under no liability to the parties interested in the lost letters and parcels. The same principle applies in actions for conversion.[23]

---

[16] *Southport Tramways* v. *Gandy* [1897] 2 Q.B. 66.
[17] *Strand Electric Co.* v. *Brisford* [1952] 2 Q.B. 246.
[18] *Elliott* v. *Boynton* [1924] 1 Ch. 236.
[19] See Peden, "Measure of Damages in Conversion and Detinue" (1970) 44 Austr. L.J. 65; Law Reform Committee, 18th Report (Cmnd. 4774, 1971); parts 55–78; Palmer, *Bailment* (1979) Appendix I.
[20] *Bloxam* v. *Hubbard* (1804) 5 East 407.
[21] [1902] P. 42. See also *Morrison Steamship Co.* v. *Greystoke Castle (Cargo Owners)* [1947] A.C. 265, 298.
[22] For the present law, see above, § 157.
[23] *Swire* v. *Leach* (1865) 18 C.B. (N.S.) 479.

The damages so recovered by the plaintiff above the value of his own interest are recovered and held by him on account of the other persons interested in the property, and he is liable to those others in an action for money had and received to their use. So if the bailee insures the goods, he holds for the owner any excess recovered under the policy beyond his own indemnity.[24] The rule in *The Winkfield* has been cut down when the plaintiff is a finance company, whose right of action as a bailor would not have accrued but for the conversion. Therefore, if one who is the bailee of a motor-car under a contract of hire-purchase with a finance company sells or pledges it to a third party, the damages payable by that third party to the finance company for the conversion of its property are limited to the value of the plaintiff's interest, that is, the amount of the unpaid instalments, or the value of the car, whichever is the less.[25] There is no reason why the third party purchaser should be liable for the market value of the chattel if it is more than the total of the unpaid instalments. Similarly an unpaid vendor who wrongly disposes of the goods,[26] and is then sued in conversion by the purchaser, is entitled to deduct the price for which the purchaser is no longer liable.[27]

Although it has never been decided, it is presumably the law that a plaintiff entitled under the rule in *The Winkfield* to recover the whole value of the property on account of himself and all other persons interested can do so only if these others stand by and make no objection. Therefore if the bailor or principal has already received with or without an action the value of his interest from the defendant, it is impossible for the bailee to recover more than his own interest. It seems also to follow that, even though no such prior satisfaction has been made, it is a good defence to an action brought by a plaintiff with a limited interest that a claim has been already made on the defendant by another person interested in the property, and that the action is defended on that person's behalf and by his authority. It is settled that this is a good plea in an action brought by a plaintiff with a merely possessory interest,[28] and there seems no reason why it should be less effective in a claim by a plaintiff with a limited interest for damages in excess of that interest.

When a defendant has, in accordance with the rule in *The Winkfield*, paid the full value of the property to a claimant with a limited interest, he is probably thereby discharged from all liability to any other person interested in the property.[29] This rule was first put forward in 1374[30] and has never since been disputed, but the matter has been very little considered and involves serious difficulties.[31] The rule is clearly otherwise in the case of pay-

---

[24] *A. Tomlinson (Hauliers) Ltd.* v. *Hepburn* [1966] A.C. 451 in which *The Winkfield* was approved.
[25] *Wickham Holdings Ltd.* v. *Brooke House Motors Ltd.* [1967] 1 W.L.R. 295. If the hire-purchase agreement has been terminated by the company, the hirer will have no right to the goods unless he has paid one-third of the purchase price.
[26] As distinct from re-possessing them: *Healing Ltd.* v. *Inglis Electrix Ltd.* (1968) 42 A.J.L.R. 280.
[27] *Chinery* v. *Viall* (1860) 5 H. & N. 288.
[28] *Biddle* v. *Bond* (1865) 6 B. & S. 225.
[29] *The Winkfield* [1902] P. 42, 61. See Warren, "Qualifying as Plaintiff in an Action for a Conversion" (1936) 49 Harv.L.Rev. 1084, 1095; *Eastern Construction Co.* v. *National Trust Co.* [1914] A.C. 197, 210.
[30] Holdsworth, H.E.L., vii, pp. 461–462.
[31] *Morrison Steamship Co.* v. *Greystoke Castle (Cargo Owners)* [1947] A.C. 265, 278, 298.

ment to a wrongdoer having a merely possessory title; payment to him, even by compulsion of the law, is no defence against a subsequent claim by the true owner.[32]

§ 210. ASSESSMENT OF VALUE

In all actions for a conversion the plaintiff may recover, in addition to the value of the property or of his interest in it, any additional damage which he may have sustained by reason of the conversion which is not too remote.[33] Primarily the value of an article is its market price, or if there is no market in such goods, the cost of replacement.[34] Damages in conversion may be reduced by the return of the property converted[35] and sometimes the plaintiff may be compelled to accept the return of the property. Further, where the defendant is able to prove that the plaintiff has got back part of the proceeds of the property wrongfully converted he is *pro tanto* excused.[36] But mere receipt of moneys from the wrongdoer will not go in diminution of damages unless the plaintiff has received the benefit of the sum in question and has received it with knowledge of the conversion.[37] When there is a doubt about the value of a chattel which has been converted the defendant must either produce it or account for its non-production. If he does not do so, it will be assumed against him that it was of the highest possible value. *Omnia praesumuntur contra spoliatorem.*[38]

The foregoing rules as to the measure of damages for a conversion apply, *mutatis mutandis*, to actions for any wrongful destruction of or damage to chattels not amounting to conversion.[39]

Value assessed as at date of conversion

The value recoverable in an action for conversion is in general the value of the property at the date of the conversion, and not its value at any earlier or later date,[40] together with any consequential damage which is not too remote to be recoverable.[41] In detinue the critical date was that of the judgment, but as detinue has been abolished,[42] the conversion date is now the important one.[43]

Effect of rise or fall in value

If the property falls in value after the date of the conversion, as may happen with shares, even without any act or default of the defendant, he is nevertheless liable to account for its original value.[44] For *non constat* that

---

[32] *Attenborough* v. *London and St. Katherine's Dock Co.* (1878) 3 C.P.D. 450, 454. See above, § 34.
[33] *The Arpad* [1934] P. 189, 232–236; *Aitken* v. *Gardiner* (1956) 4 D.L.R. (2d) 119, 138.
[34] *J. E. Hall Ltd.* v. *Barclay* [1937] 3 All E.R. 620.
[35] *Solloway* v. *McLaughlin* [1938] A.C. 247; *U.S.A.* v. *Dollfus Mieg* [1952] A.C. 582, 619.
[36] *Liggett (Liverpool) Ltd.* v. *Barclays Bank* [1928] 1 K.B. 48.
[37] *Lloyds Bank* v. *Chartered Bank* [1929] 1 K.B. 40.
[38] *Armory* v. *Delamirie* (1721) 1 Stra. 505.
[39] *The Winkfield* [1902] P. 42.
[40] *Caxton Publishing Co.* v. *Sutherland Publishing Co.* [1939] A.C. 178, 192–193.
[41] *General and Finance Facilities Ltd.* v. *Cooks Cars (Romford) Ltd.* [1963] 1 W.L.R. 644, 649.
[42] By 5. 2(1) of the 1977 Act.
[43] [1948] 2 K.B. 23.
[44] *Solloway* v. *McLaughlin* [1938] A.C. 247, 258.

the plaintiff would not, before such a loss occurred, have sold the property and so obtained the value of it at the time of the sale. If, on the other hand, the property increases in value after the date of the conversion, a distinction has to be drawn. If the increase is due to the act of the defendant, the plaintiff has no title to it, and his claim is limited to the original value of the property.[45] So indirectly the improver is compensated for the value of his improvement.

The 1977 Act s. 6(1) specifically re-states this common law principle, although limiting its operation to cases in which the defendant improver has acted in the honest but mistaken belief that he had a good title to the goods. A purchaser from an improver is also protected. But it is doubtful whether the section covers one who has only maintained the goods without improving them.[45a]

If, however, the subsequent increase of value is not due to the act of the defendant, but would have occurred in any case, even had no conversion been committed, the plaintiff is entitled to recover it as special damage resulting from the conversion, in addition to the original value of the property converted: as when goods taken or detained have risen in value by reason of the fluctuation of the market.[46] But if the plaintiff knew or ought to have known of the conversion he cannot claim the benefit of the subsequent rise in value, for he is under a duty to mitigate his damages.[47]

§ 211. Effect of Judgment in Action of Conversion

A mere judgment for the value of the property without actual satisfaction does not in any way affect the plaintiff's title to the property.[48] Therefore he may exercise all his rights as owner notwithstanding the judgment, e.g. he may seize the chattel either from the defendant or from anyone else in whose hands it is. Yet in no case can he by the exercise of such concurrent remedies obtain a double satisfaction. If he actually recovers the property his judgment for its value becomes inoperative; and if he actually receives its value he cannot exercise his right of recaption or enforce his judgment for specific restitution. And if he receives its value from one defendant he cannot enforce his judgment against another.[49]

Although judgment without satisfaction has thus no effect upon the property or upon the rights of the owner of it, a defendant who satisfies a judgment in damages representing the value of goods detained or damages for their conversion acquires thereby such title to the goods as was vested in the plaintiff whose judgment has been satisfied.[50] It is in effect a compulsory purchase of the goods by the defendant. After such satisfaction, therefore, the former owner is deprived of all his rights of recaption and specific

---

[45] In trespass the result is otherwise: see above, § 207.
[45a] See *Munro* v. *Willmott* [1949] 1 K.B. 295, in which the defendants knew they had no title to the goods.
[46] *Aitken* v. *Gardiner* (1956) 4 D.L.R. (2nd) 119, 138.
[47] *Sachs* v. *Miklos* [1948] 2 K.B. 23.
[48] The judgment may be either for the value alone or for the value with an alternative provison for the return of the property. The rule is the same in either case: *Ellis* v. *John Stenning & Son* [1932] 2 Ch. 81, 90.
[49] *Ellis* v. *John Stenning & Son* [1932] 2 Ch. 81, 90.
[50] *U.S.A.* v. *Dollfus Mieg* [1952] A.C. 582, 622.

restitution. This principle has been affirmed by s. 5 of the 1977 Act, which in effect provides that full payment of damages (or of any agreed sum by way of settlement or compromise) as compensation for the claimant's whole interest extinguishes the claimant's title to that interest. Conversely, if the damages are for the impairment of an interest, the owner retains his title. Property so divested from the plaintiff by satisfaction made does not necessarily vest in the defendant. It may vest instead in some person who claims under him and therefore has a better title to the property than he has; for example, when A takes property from B and sells it to C, satisfaction made by A to B will vest the property in C.[51]

§ 212. LIBEL AND SLANDER[52]

(1) General principles of assessment

The spectrum of awards ranges from contemptuous damages of $1/2p$[53] to exemplary damages of scores thousands of pounds.[54] But some material injury to reputation must be proved: mere mental suffering is not an object of compensation.[55] Otherwise almost the only guidance is the vague principle that the award must be reasonable and moderate.[56] A jury is the constitutional tribunal for assessing the proper sum to be paid for an attack on the reputation of a fellow-citizen, particularly on one in a public position, such as a politican,[57] and within wide limits its award will not be interfered with by an appellate court.[58] All matters relating to the mode of publication, the circumstances of the parties, and the conduct of the defence (e.g. a failure to apologise, or bullying tactics by counsel[59]) can be considered. If the trial is before a judge without a jury, it was once thought that the award could be reduced by reason of the fact that the judge could use his tongue to exonerate the plaintiff or excoriate the defendant, but this is no longer the law.[60] The plaintiff is entitled to the sum which is appropriate compensation. Therefore the plaintiff may recover not only the estimated amount of his past and future losses but also, "in case the libel, driven underground, emerges from its lurking place at some future date, he must be able to point to a sum awarded by a jury sufficient to convince a bystander of the baselessness of the charge."[61]

If the defendant has been guilty of outrageous or disgraceful conduct

---

[51] See the detailed provisions of 5.5(4) of the 1977 Act for cases in which the claimant accounts over to a third party.
[52] Samuels, "Assessing Damages for Defamation" (1963) 79 L.Q.R. 63; Kuper, "Damages for Defamation" (1966) 83 S.A.L.J. 277.
[53] As in *Bloom* v. *News of the World* (1977), *Daily Telegraph*, 11 March.
[54] As in *Cassell & Co. Ltd.* v. *Broome* [1972] A.C. 1027.
[55] *Wheeler* v. *Somerfield* [1966] 2 Q.B. 94.
[56] *Lewis* v. *Daily Telegraph Ltd.* [1964] A.C. 234.
[57] *Snyder* v. *Montreal Gazette Ltd.* (1978) 87 D.L.R. 5 (which has 3 useful appendices, listing awards in different jurisdictions).
[58] *Youssoupoff* v. *M.-G.-M. Ltd.* (1934) 50 T.L.R. 581.
[59] See *Greenlands Ltd.* v. *Wilmhurst* [1913] 3 K.B. 507. All those who have practical experience, as distinct from academic critics, are in favour of retaining the jury: H.C. Deb. Vol. 776, col. 1774.
[60] *Associated Newspapers Ltd.* v. *Dingle* [1964] A.C. 371.
[61] *Cassell & Co. Ltd.* v. *Broome* [1972] A.C. 1027, 1071, *per* Lord Hailsham of St. Marylebone L.C.

there is power to award exemplary damages when the defendant has calculated that the publication of the libel will bring him in a profit which will exceed any damages which a court may order him to pay to the plaintiff.[62] This does not mean that a newspaper will be liable to have punitive damages awarded against it merely because its circulation increases after an attack on a public figure, but only if there is evidence of a wicked, callous,[63] cynical[64] or reckless[65] attempt to increase circulation at the expense of the plaintiff's reputation. But in practice the scope of compensatory damages is wide enough to permit them to be aggravated by the wounding, insulting or outrageous circumstances surrounding the publication of the libel.[66] In this way a remedy can be given for hurt feelings, although they are not a primary object of compensation.[67] There is, therefore, in England a distinction between conduct which shocks the plaintiff (aggravated damages) and conduct which shocks the jury (exemplary damages).[68] This is not an example of parasitic damages: the award if permissible simply because the real damages are at large.[69]

(2) Mitigation of damages

Several matters may be given in evidence in mitigation of damages.

1. Although an apology is no defence,[70] section 1 of the Libel Act 1843, provides that in any action for defamation the defendant may, provided he gives notice at the time of delivering his defence, give in evidence in mitigation of damages that he made or offered an apology before the commencement of the action or at the earliest opportunity afterwards if he had had no opportunity before.[71] No payment into court need be made.

2. The defendant, even though he does not plead justification, is entitled to adduce in mitigation of damages evidence of the plaintiff's general bad reputation prior to the publication of the libel. For since the plaintiff sues for an injury to his reputation, it is permissible for the defendant to prove in this way that such reputation was of little value. But the evidence is limited to general evidence as to the plaintiff's reputation, and to that reputation in the same sector of life; it does not include specific evidence of disreputable conduct or of rumours of such conduct, otherwise the position of the plaintiff would be intolerable. In other words, the defendant may prove that the plaintiff did have a bad reputation, not that he ought to have had one. The law is concerned with the plaintiff's reputation rather than with his disposition.[72] Yet the dividing line may be a fine one,[73] for sometimes a man's reputation rests upon specific incidents of some notoriety.[74] More often, however, a man's reputation is based upon the judgment of his fellows

---

[62] See above, § 199.
[63] *Broadway Approvals Ltd.* v. *Odhams Press Ltd.* [1965] 1 W.L.R. 805.
[64] *Manson* v. *Associated Newspapers Ltd.* [1965] 1 W.L.R. 1038.
[65] *Cassell & Co. Ltd.* v. *Broome* [1972] A.C. 1027, 1079.
[66] *Ley* v. *Hamilton* (1935) 153 L.T. 384, 386.
[67] *Wheeler* v. *Somerfield* [1966] 2 Q.B. 94. As Tennyson wrote in *Locksley Hall*, "But the jingling of the guinea helps the hurt that Honour feels."
[68] *Broadway Approvals Ltd.* v. *Odhams Press Ltd.* [1965] 1 W.L.R. 805, 822.
[69] See above, § 199.
[70] Above, § 68.
[71] See Chapman, *Statutes*, p. 274.
[72] *Plato Films Ltd.* v. *Speidel* [1961] A.C. 1090, 1131.
[73] See Faulks Report (Cmnd. 5909), § 365.
[74] *Waters* v. *Sunday Pictorial Newspapers Ltd.* [1961] 1 W.L.R. 967.

on his general life over a period of time before the publication of the libel in suit.[75] It also follows that a defendant cannot give in evidence in mitigation of damages the repetition of the same defamatory words by other persons contemporaneously with his publicaton.[76]

There is an exception to the general rule in the case of previous convictions, which are admissible provided that they are recent and relevant to the sector of the plaintiff's life which has been attacked. It would be outrageous if a person serving a sentence of 30 years' imprisonment for robbery should be able to sue for libel as if his character were unblemished.[77]

In the absence of any plea of justification, notice must be given to the plaintiff before trial of the defendant's intention to adduce such evidence in mitigation of damages and the particulars thereof.[78] If the plaintiff in a libel action gives evidence, he is, of course, subject to cross-examination as to credit like any other witness; but if he is cross-examined as to specific incidents, not mentioned in the particulars, and denies them, no further evidence can be called to rebut his denials, and the cross-examination is not admissible to mitigate damages.[79] Where the plaintiff's own evidence or answers elicited in cross-examination show him to have been guilty of malpractices which are completely unconnected with the defamatory statement, the damages will not be reduced on the ground that his reputation is not all that it might have been.[80]

3. It is provided by the Defamation Act 1952, s. 12, that in any action for libel or slander the defendant may give evidence in mitigation of damages that the plaintiff has recovered damages, or has brought actions for damages for libel or slander in respect of the publication of words to the same effect as the words on which the action is founded, or has received or agreed to receive compensation in respect of any such publication. But the defendant cannot get relief unless the plaintiff has chosen to sue more than one publisher: in this respect the ordinary law relating to joint tortfeasors[81] has not been followed.[82] The jury should be told to consider how far the plaintiff's loss can be attributed solely to the libel with which they are concerned, and how far to the joint result of the two libels. They must be reminded that the plaintiff is not to be compensated twice for the same loss.[83] But it is irrelevant that the libel has been published elsewhere on a privileged occasion.[84]

---

[75] *Associated Newspapers Ltd.* v. *Dingle* [1964] A.C. 371, 399, 406.
[76] *Associated Newspapers Ltd.* v. *Dingle* [1964] A.C. 371. But see the Defamation Act 1952, s.12, considered below.
[77] *Goody* v. *Odhams Press Ltd.* [1967] 1 Q.B. 333. See now Civil Evidence Act, 1968 s. 13.
[78] Ord. 82, r. 7.
[79] *Scott* v. *Sampson* (1882) 8 Q.B.D. 491; *Hobbs* v. *Tinling* [1929] 2 K.B. 1. "In the result, a libel action may resolve itself into a tactical battle in which the defendant adopts such manoeuvres as are likely to force the plaintiff into a position where he is compelled to go into the box and give some evidence—however little—in chief, so that there may be put to him in cross-examination as to credibility the very questions which are inadmissible in cross-examination on mitigation of damages under the rule in *Scott* v. *Sampson*": so the Porter Committee in para. 151, and also Earl Jowitt, 178 H.L.Deb. 5s., col. 340. Parliament, however, did not change the law, (see Faulks Report, § 368) though the judge at the trial may discourage cross-examination of this kind: see Lord Denning in [1961] A.C. 1090, 1143.
[80] *Hobbs* v. *Tinling* [1929] 2 K.B.1.
[81] See above, § 167.
[82] *Associated Newspapers Ltd.* v. *Dingle* [1964] A.C. 371.
[83] *Lewis* v. *Daily Telegraph Ltd.* [1964] A.C. 234, 261.
[84] *Associated Newspapers Ltd.* v. *Dingle* [1964] A.C. 371.

4. Facts which tend to disprove malice may also be given in evidence.[85] Thus, the defendant may prove any facts which show that he never intended to refer to the plaintiff or did not intend the words to be understood in a defamatory sense,[86] or honestly believed that the statement was true,[87] or (conversely) that the statement was vague and sensational and believed by few or none of its readers.[88]

§ 213. ACTIONS FOR INJURIES TO THE PERSON[89]

This is a topic of considerable complexity.[90] Some of the difficulty is due to the absence of any coherent philosophy behind the different sources of compensation to accident victims in the welfare state. Torts is not the only, nor the main, source of compensation today, for social security must be taken into account.[91] Within torts the cases on damages reveal a striking discordance of views on the most elementary matters. Because of the great mass of reported cases it is not possible to do more here than indicate the broad general principles governing the matter. In each case the proper computation is a question of fact.[92] Hence it is for the judge in his discretion to decide whether he will permit counsel to refer to decisions showing the amount awarded in similar cases, but in practice such citations are increasingly frequent.[93] It is often discussed whether the governing principle is that of *restitutio in integrum*, or whether the defendant is only obliged to give the plaintiff fair compensation. The truth appears to be that each of these principles of assessment has its own proper sphere of operation. There is no criterion which is universally valid over the whole field of damages.

One classification distinguishes pecuniary loss from non-pecuniary loss. Another classification is between special damages and general damages. Special damages can be defined as pecuniary loss actually suffered up to the date of the trial—*e.g.* loss of earnings, and general damages are then the other heads of loss—*e.g.* pain and suffering. Special damage must be pleaded and proved[94]; general damage is implied.[95] The principle of *restitutio in integrum* is appropriate to the first of these heads: so far as actual or prospective pecuniary loss is concerned the amount of compensation can be assessed with a degree of accuracy which will go far towards putting the injured person in the same position as he would have been in had

---

[85] Provided that the terms of Ord. 82, r. 7 (above, n. 78), are complied with.

[86] *Jones* v. *Hulton* [1909] 2 K.B. 444, 479.

[87] *Campbell* v. *Spottiswoode* (1863) 3 B. & S. 769, 781.

[88] *Morgan* v. *Odhams Press Ltd.* [1971] 1 W.L.R. 1239.

[89] This section deals with damages in actions of negligence as well as of trespass. For the principles of assessment under the Fatal Accidents Act, see below, § 217.

[90] The outstanding general survey is in Atiyah, *Accidents, Compensation and the Law* (3rd ed., 1980). See also Kemp and Kemp, *The Quantum of Damages in Personal Injury Claims*; (note that this is a different work from Kemp, *Damages for Personal Injury and Death*); Munkman, *Damages for Personal Injuries and Death; McGregor on Damages*, Chap. 33; the *Report on Personal Injury Litigation—Assessment of Damages* (Law Com. No. 56, 1973), and the Pearson Report (Cmnd. 7054), §§ 343–614.

[91] See the magisterial survey by Fleming, *International Encyclopaedia of Comparative Law*, vol. xi (1971).

[92] *Waldon* v. *War Office* [1956] 1 W.L.R. 51.

[93] *Waldon* v. *War Office* [1956] 1 W.L.R. 51. The proper course is for counsel to inquire whether the court wishes to have assistance. The practitioner is careful to avoid the trap into which the student so often falls—citing a mass of cases without being asked to do so.

[94] *Domsalla* v. *Barr* [1969] 1 W.L.R. 630.

[95] *British Transport Commission* v. *Gourley* [1956] A.C. 185, 206.

he not sustained the wrong. But the principle of fair and reasonable compensation is more appropriate to the second of these heads of damages.[96] Money cannot renew a shattered human frame.[97] Still, the law has said that this is a head of damage for which monetary compensation can be awarded and so the court must do the best it can in the light of such comparable cases as it may consider to be of assistance to it.[98]

Again, there is dispute whether the object of an award of damages is to compensate the plaintiff or punish the defendant.[99] In England the main object is compensation which is fair and adequate but not perfect.[1] So awards of exemplary damages have been cut down[2] and within the field of compensatory damages the plaintiff must bring into account some collateral benefits.[3]

§ 214. PECUNIARY LOSS

Pecuniary loss (sometimes called special damages) must be pleaded and proved.[4] In general there are two distinct heads—expenses and loss of earnings. They will be considered separately, and then it will be discussed how far the sum awarded must be reduced because of collateral benefits or liabilities.

(1) Expenses

The plaintiff is entitled to recover all expenses actually and reasonably incurred as a result of the accident before the date of the trial.[5] This will enable him to recover for such items as loss of, or damage to, clothing, medical expenses,[6] the cost of lost board and lodging,[7] nursing expenses,[8] and loss of a no-claims bonus.[9] A literal application of *Gourley*[9a] might seem to require the *deduction* of living expenses from the total award on the ground that the plaintiff would have had to maintain himself anyway. But it has been held that although it would be proper to take into account expenditure which would have been incurred in earning future wages it does not follow that general living expenses are deductible.[10] Deductions for expenses saved are not in practice a significant element in the calculation.

---

[96] *The Mediana* [1900] A.C. 113, 116.
[97] *West & Son Ltd.* v. *Shephard* [1964] AC. 326, 345.
[98] *Waldon* v. *War Office* [1956] 1 W.L.R. 51.
[99] See McGregor, "Compensation versus Punishment in Damages Awards" (1965) 28 M.L.R. 629.
[1] *West (H.) & Son Ltd.* v. *Shephard* [1964] A.C. 326, 346.
[2] See above, § 199.
[3] See below, § 214.
[4] *British Transport Commission* v. *Gourley* [1956] A.C. 185, 206.
[5] Expenses which may crystallise in the future should be claimed as general damages: *Shearman* v. *Folland* [1950] 2 K.B. 43, 51.
[6] Expenditure is not to be impeached on the ground that the plaintiff has not taken advantage of the facilities of the National Health Service: Law Reform (Personal Injuries) Act 1948, s. 2(4); *Lim* v. *Camden Health Authority* [1980] A.C. 174, 188. Sometimes the value of necessary services voluntarily furnished to the plaintiff can be recovered; *Gage* v. *King* [1961] 1 Q.B. 188 but it is no longer necessary for a kind relative to make a contract before nursing the plaintiff: see *Donnelly* v. *Joyce* [1974] Q.B. 454, for it is the plaintiff's loss of capacity which creates the need for those services, and that loss has been caused by the defendant.
[7] *Liffen* v. *Watson* [1940] 1 K.B. 556.
[8] *Shearman* v. *Folland* [1950] 2 K.B. 43.
[9] *Ironfield* v. *Eastern Gas Board* [1964] 1 W.L.R. 1125n.
[9a] See below, p. 534.
[10] *Daish* v. *Wauton* [1972] 2 Q.B. 262.

(2) Loss of earnings

It is settled that the plaintiff is entitled to damages for the loss of the earnings or profits which would normally have accrued to him up to the date of
the judgment.[11] But what he is entitled to claim is the loss of what would
have been in his pay-packet—*i.e.* the net amount after deduction of income
tax[12] and social security contributions,[13] or unemployment benefit.[14] Normally the amount can be calculated easily by multiplying the plaintiff's
weekly wage or salary by the number of weeks during which he was
incapacitated by his injuries.[15] The existence of inflation makes it important
to take into account any increases in remuneration.

(3) Future pecuniary loss

The main component of a claim for future pecuniary loss is, almost
invariably, loss of income or, in fatal cases, lost dependency. As these sums
can merely be estimated, being prospective, they are claimed as general
damages. The use of the multiplier is the ordinary and best method of
assessing the sum, and the actuarial method of calculation should not be
used except as a check or guide.[16]

Two special problems have arisen. First, should loss of earning capacity
be regarded by the courts as an item of damages separate from future loss of
income? The answer provided by *Moeliker* v. *A. Reyrolle & Co. Ltd.*[17] is in
the affirmative, but the view supported by the Pearson Commission[18] is that
loss of earning capacity should be regarded simply as a factor to be taken
into account when assessing damages for future loss of earnings.

Secondly, should a plaintiff be entitled to damages for his loss of earnings
in the years for which he would normally have lived but for his injuries? It
was held in *Oliver* v. *Ashman*[19] that damages for loss of income during the
"lost years" were to be regarded as part of the damages for loss of expectation of life. These damages had in effect been set at a small conventional
figure by the House of Lords in *Benham* v. *Gambling.*[20] Such a decision was
not in accordance with the principle that a plaintiff is entitled to be compensated for loss of anything having a money value, and has been over-ruled
by the House of Lords in *Pickett* v. *British Rail Engineering Ltd.*[21] The law
now is, as recommended both by the Law Commission and by the Pearson

---

[11] Subject to the deduction in respect of National Insurance benefits required by the Law
Reform (Personal Injuries) Act 1948, s. 2: see above, § 182.
[12] *British Transport Commission* v. *Gourley* [1956] A.C. 185.
[13] *Cooper* v. *Firth Brown Ltd.* [1963] 1 W.L.R. 418.
[14] *Parsons* v. *B.N.M. Laboratories Ltd.* [1964] 1 Q.B. 95.
[15] See the calculation in *Harris* v. *Bright's Asphalt Contractors Ltd.* [1953] 1 Q.B. 617. This
sum may have to be reduced if there is any possibility that, apart from his injuries, the
plaintiff might for some reason have been unable to earn the same wages: *Rouse* v. *Port of
London Authority* [1953] 2 Lloyd's Rep. 179, 184. But if the injured plaintiff is a person
legally entitled to be paid wages by his employer during the period of incapacity, he cannot
claim under this head, for he has not sustained any loss as a result of the defendant's
wrong: *Receiver for Metropolitan Police District* v. *Croydon Corporation* [1957] 2 Q.B.
154.
[16] *Taylor* v. *O'Connor* [1971] A.C. 115.
[17] [1977] 1 W.L.R. 132
[18] Report, §§ 337–338.
[19] [1962] 2 Q.B. 210.
[20] [1941] A.C. 157, see below § 215.
[21] [1980] A.C. 136.

Commission,[22] that the plaintiff should recover damages in respect of earnings in the "lost years", after deduction of an estimated sum to represent his living expenses during those years.[23] There may also be a deduction for the fact that the "lost years" may be a long way off.

Damages for future pecuniary loss are awarded at present as a lump sum. In assessing the damages, the court must make guesses about a number of factors, including the likely duration of the plaintiff's incapacity, his chances for promotion or increase in earnings, and the future rates of inflation, tax, and return on invested capital.[24] The court has to be wrong on only one of these guesses for the plaintiff to be extensively over-compensated or under-compensated. There is no opportunity for making a correction subsequently. To try to minimise the chances of under-compensation, plaintiff's counsel tend to postpone the trial of the action or settlement so that any possible deterioration in the plaintiff's health can be more accurately predicted; but this in turn has the undesirable consequences of delay and even "compensation neurosis."[25] The Pearson Commission acknowledged these drawbacks in lump sum awards for future pecuniary loss and recommended by a majority that, in cases of death or serious and lasting injury, the plaintiff ought to be able to take his damages in the form of periodic payments. These payments would be administered by the defendant's insurer (where he was insured), and would be revalued annually in line with the movement in average earnings. The awards would also be subject to review by the courts, but such a review would be confined to changes in the plaintiff's pecuniary loss brought about by changes in his medical condition.

Offsets

(i) *Taxation liabilities*[26]

In *British Transport Commission* v. *Gourley*[27] the House of Lords held that in assessing damages for loss of personal earnings in cases of personal injury the tax which the plaintiff would have had to pay had he continued to receive those earnings must be taken into account. On the facts of the *Gourley* case itself this meant that the plaintiff recovered £6,695 instead of £37,720. This decision at first seemed novel and inequitable to many: it was not easy to see why the courts should tax when the Revenue did not,[28] particularly when the beneficiary was not the Revenue but the defendant's insurance company. But the decision is no more than a logical application of the settled principle that damages are intended to put the plaintiff in the same position as he would have been in had he not received the injury. Damages are intended to compensate the plaintiff for that which he has lost, and in assessing the value of what has been lost to him it would be

---

[22] Law Com. No. 56, para. 87; Pearson Report, ss. 331–336. But why should disabled persons be maintained for the rest of their lives at the standard of living which they enjoyed before the disablement?

[23] But there are now serious difficulties as to the relationship between these damages and those awarded under the Fatal Accidents Act: see below, § 216.

[24] See Atiyah's analysis in *Accidents, Compensation and the Law*, (3rd ed.), chap. 7.

[25] See, e.g. *Lattimer* v. *Orient Steam Navigation Co.* [1953] 2 Lloyd's Rep. 168.

[26] The Law Commission's Report (Law Com. No. 56, 1973).

[27] [1956] A.C. 185.

[28] [1957] A.C. 403, 410.

unrealistic for the court to close its eyes to the incidence of taxation. It is true that the court may be called upon to make elaborate calculations, but the courts are not unfamiliar with complex arithmetical computations, and the estimate "will be none the worse if it is formed on broad lines, even though it may be described as rough and ready."[29] So *Gourley* has been followed in Ireland,[30] and in Australia,[31] but not in Canada.[32]

Various other criticisms have been made of the decision in *Gourley*.[33] One is that it is wrong that the defendant should profit from the fact that the plaintiff is in a high tax bracket. The answer to this is that the defendant can hardly be supposed to have selected on purpose a plaintiff who was a large taxpayer. Another criticism is that a person whose earning capacity is wholly or partially destroyed thereby loses a capital asset, and as it is[34] a fundamental principle of English revenue law that a capital asset is not taxable, it should follow that the compensation which replaces that asset is also tax-free. But while it is true that a man's skill and experience are in the nature of capital assets, all that was done in *Gourley* was to value those assets by the income which they are likely to produce, and that income was affected by the predictable factor of taxation. In short, the Law Lords in *Gourley* faced the realities of life and refused to be misled by maxims such as *res inter alios acta*.[35] There is no reason why someone who has lost a net sum should receive a gross sum.

The principle in the *Gourley* case also applies to actions for damages for wrongful dismissal,[36] for trespass and conversion,[37] for libel in so far as the damages compensate for loss of trade,[38] and for statutory compensation for compulsory acquisition.[39] A logical application of the principle that potential liabilities must be taken into account means that a plaintiff may be compelled to disclose particulars of his tax position,[40] and to give credit for a tax rebate.[41]

(ii) *Collateral Benefits*

If a plaintiff receives collateral benefits of any kind in compensation for an injury, it might be thought that his damages in tort ought to be correspondingly reduced; otherwise, he will be over-compensated, for the aim of the law is simply to restore him as near as possible to the position he would have been in but for the accident. But the law has not insisted on such

---

[29] [1956] A.C. 185, 203, *per* Earl Jowitt.
[30] *Glover* v. *B.L.N. Ltd.* [1973] I.R. 432.
[31] *Cullen* v. *Trappell* (1980) 29 A.L.R.1.
[32] *The Queen* v. *Jennings* (1966) 57 D.L.R. (2d)644.
[33] But it is significant that neither the Law Reform Committee (Seventh Report, Cmnd. 501 (1958)) nor the Law Commission (report, 1973 (Law Com. No. 56)) wished to recommend a reversal of *Gourley*.
[34] Or was until the introduction of the Capital Gains Tax, which, significantly, does not apply to awards for personal injuries.
[35] So Lord Reid (who had sat in *Gourley*) in *Parry* v. *Cleaver* [1970] A.C. 1, 15.
[36] *Parsons* v. *B.N.M. Laboratories Ltd.* [1964] 1 Q.B. 95. Aliter if the damages exceed £5,000, for then (exceptionally) they are taxable under the Finance Act 1960, ss. 37–38, which enabled the Revenue to share in "golden handshakes." The *Parsons* case means that the benefit of the tax is diverted to the employer who has broken his contract.
[37] *Hall & Co.* v. *Pearlberg* [1956] 1 W.L.R. 244.
[38] *Lewis* v. *Daily Telegraph Ltd.* [1964] A.C. 235, 262
[39] *West Suffolk C.C.* v. *Rought* [1957] A.C. 403
[40] *Phipps* v. *Orthodox Unit Trusts* [1958] 1 Q.B. 314.
[41] *Hartley* v. *Sandholme Iron Co. Ltd.* [1975] Q.B. 600.

a reduction in all cases, usually for overriding policy reasons. Various benefits will now be considered in turn.

(i) Loss insurance

Benefits received under a contract or insurance are not deducted from damages for personal injury.[42] The rationale is that the beneficiary has paid for this policy, and it would not be right to deprive him of his benefit under this contract.[43]

(ii) Payments by an employer

Occupational sick pay diminishes the plaintiff's loss, and so should be taken into account in assessing damages.[44] The Pearson Commission recommended that sick pay should not be taken into account where the plaintiff is by his contract of service under a contractual obligation to refund it from damages or where it was advanced by his employer as a loan on the express understanding that it would be repaid if damages were recovered.[45]

(iii) Occupational pensions

In *Parry* v. *Cleaver*,[46] the House of Lords held that a disability pension, whether or not discretionary and whether or not contributory, should be left out of account in assessing a plaintiff's lost earnings. The majority argued that a disability pension should be regarded as a form of loss insurance, which was in large measure paid for—either directly in the form of contributions, or indirectly in lieu of higher wages—by the beneficiary himself. The minority view was that an occupational disability pension should be regarded as a benefit provided by the employer, analogous to sick pay. The Pearson Commission thought neither view exactly reflected the realities of occupational pensions provision, but on balance thought it nearer the truth to regard such pensions as benefits provided by the employee.[47]

However, disability pensions should be taken into account in assessing damages for loss of a retirement pension—for example, where the plaintiff, after completing his service, would have received a full retirement pension rather than a lower disability pension.

(iv) Social security benefits

The law is in a muddled state as to whether social security benefits should be offset against the plaintiff's damages. Unemployment benefit has been taken into account.[48] Supplementary benefit, it has been said, should not be

---

[42] *Bradburn* v. *Great Western Railway Co.* (1874) L.R. 10 Ex 1. As regards damages following death, the Fatal Accidents Act 1976 s. 4(1) specifically provides that insurance money shall not be taken into account.
[43] The Law Commission and the Pearson Commission recommend no change in the Law: Law Com. No. 56, s. 151; Pearson Report, ss 513–516.
[44] *Metropolitan Police Receiver* v. *Croydon Corporation* [1957] 2 Q.B. 154.
[45] Pearson Report, s 505.
[46] [1970] A.C. 1.
[47] Pearson Report, ss 517–521; see too Law Com. No. 56, s 152.
[48] *Parsons* v. *B.N.M. Laboratories* [1964] 1 Q.B. 95. (This decision may soon be reviewed by the House of Lords: see *Nabi* v. *British Leyland Ltd.* [1980] 1 W.L.R. 529).

taken into account, even if unemployment benefit is,[49] although Lord Reid said that he found it difficult to draw a distinction between the two benefits.[50] A state retirement benefit payable by the Ministry of Social Security has been held non-deductible,[51] as also are attendance allowances and mobility allowances.[52] These decisions seem to be a correct purposive interpretation of the Social Security Act. Parliament did not intend these benefits to be an advantage to the wrongdoer. The legislature's own contribution to this question has been singularly unhelpful. By section 2(1) of the Law Reform (Personal Injuries) Act 1948, in assessing damages for loss of income due to personal injury, the court is obliged to take into account one half of the value of certain social security benefits[53] for five years. Such an odd provision was an attempted reconciliation of the majority and minority views of the Departmental Committee on Alternative Remedies.[54]

The Pearson Commission boldly called for a "full co-ordination of the compensation provided by tort and social security"; it recommended that the full value of social security benefits payable to an injured person or his dependants as a result of an injury for which damages are awarded should be deducted in the assessment of the damages. But this end should not be achieved simply by deducting the total value of the benefits from the total tort award: the functions of compensation for pecuniary loss and for non-pecuniary loss are distinct and these losses should be separately assessed. The Commission recommended that social security benefits payable in respect of personal injury should be divided into three main categories: those compensating for loss of income (e.g. sickness benefit); those compensating for expenses (e.g. attendance and mobility allowances); and those compensating for non-pecuniary loss (disablement benefit and hospital treatment allowance). The benefits in each category should then be deducted in assessing the corresponding portion of the tort award. There should be no carry over between categories.[55]

Interest

Interest is compensation for not getting the right amount of money at the right time. Since the Administration of Justice Act 1969 s.22, empowered a court to award interest on damages for which judgment was given, it has become usual for trial judges to itemise their awards, as interest has to be awarded, at different rates, upon the sums given for the different heads of damage. The decision of the Court of Appeal on this point in *Jefford* v. *Gee*[56] has since been modified by the House of Lords in *Pickett* v. *British Rail Engineering Ltd.*[57] and the following rules now apply[58]:

---

[49] *Foxley* v. *Olton* [1965] 2 Q.B. 306, 311.
[50] *Parry* v. *Cleaver* [1970] A.C. 1, 19.
[51] *Hewson* v. *Downs* [1970] 1 Q.B. 73. For policy under the Fatal Accidents Act 1976, see § 217.
[52] *Bowker* v. *Rose* (1978), Kemp and Kemp, vol. 1, p.151.
[53] *viz.*, sickness benefit, invalidity benefit, non-contributory invalidity pension, injury benefit, and disablement benefit.
[54] The Monckton Committee: Cmd. 6860 (1946).
[55] Pearson Report, ss 467–495.
[56] [1970] 2 Q.B. 130.
[57] [1980] A.C. 136.
[58] See Law Notes, 1979, p. 165. Interest may well add between 10% and 30% to the assumed damages, so "ticking up the interest is a powerful argument for serving a writ very quickly": *Kemp, Damages for Personal Injury*, p. 14.

Special damages - interest at half the appropriate rate from the date of accident to the date of trial. The appropriate rate is that which is payable on money in court which is placed on short-term investment account. As from March 1979 that rate is 12 1/2%.

Loss of future earnings - no interest should be awarded, as the money in question is neither ascertainable nor due until the date of the judgment. On the contrary, there must be a discount for the early receipt of a lump sum.

Pain suffering and loss of amenities - interest at the full rate from the date of service of the writ to the date of the trial. So issuing a writ but not serving it (as some solicitors like to do) merely loses interest.

Fatal Accidents Act Cases - interest at half rate on the pecuniary loss from the date of death to the date of trial. No interest on future loss.

These rules are of considerable practical importance because R.S.C. Ord. 22 r. 1 (8) provides that no payment into court is fully effective unless it includes interest.

§ 215. NON-PECUNIARY LOSS

By definition, money cannot make good a non-pecuniary loss. Yet damages are recoverable for it in almost all tort systems. Even under the New Zealand accident compensation scheme, lump sum compensation is payable for non-pecuniary loss. The Pearson Commission concluded that there is a place for damages for non-pecuniary loss, although it stressed that the main aim of any compensation system should be to make good pecuniary loss.

Non-pecuniary loss is of three kinds: pain and suffering; loss of amenities of life; and shortened expectation of life. Damages for loss under the first two heads are made in a single sum. The figure assessed[59] is arbitrary.[60] After an exhaustive review of this difficult subject, the Law Commission was unable to arrive at any conclusion, except to say that "the only helpful question that we think can be asked is not whether the damages awarded are 'right' but who ought to decide what these arbitrary amounts should be."[61] The Pearson Commision rejected the idea of a legislative tariff providing a scale of damages. The Commission, however recommended that no damages should be recoverable for non-pecuniary loss suffered during the first three months after the date of injury: the rationale was to eliminate the bulk of small claims, while continuing to allow damages to those suffering lasting pain and loss of amenity.[62] The Commission members were divided as to whether there should be a ceiling for non-pecuniary damages. The problem as to whether compensation and benefits from other sources should be deducted has been considered above.[63]

[59] 'Assessment' is the term more appropriate than 'calculation' for non-pecuniary loss, on general as distinct from special damages.
[60] Atiyah commented, "All such damage awards could be multiplied or divided by two overnight and they would be just as defensible or indefensible": *Accidents, Compensation and the Law* (3rd ed.), p. 213.
[61] Law Com. No. 56, s. 20.
[62] Pearson Report, paras. 373–389. The Commission estimated that this change would result in a saving of £44 million a year, almost one-fifth of all tort compensation for personal injury.
[63] See § 214.

(1) Pain and suffering

Contemporary English courts agree that damages may be awarded[64] for the pain and suffering[65] and nervous shock[66] which the plaintiff has undergone in the past and is likely to undergo in the future.[67] But in the absence of clear evidence of reasonably prolonged suffering there should be no reward under this head.[68]

(2) Loss of amenities of life[69]

The courts may award substantial damages for loss of amenity or loss of faculty.[70] This can be called loss of enjoyment, as distinct from loss of expectation, of life. But these damages can only be fair and adequate compensation: no sum could be perfect compensation for a grave injury. Here everything must depend upon the nature of the injury and the circumstances of the particular plaintiff. A young and active man who has been blinded or crippled might recover substantial damages under this head. "The joy of life will have gone from him. He cannot ride a bicycle, cannot kick a football."[71] So a plaintiff who, when aged sixteen-and-a-half, had been so severely injured that he would need constant attention and nursing for the rest of his life was awarded £25,000.[72] Equally a successful professional woman of 36 whose life had been totally transformed has been held entitled to at least £20,000.[73] The court will look at all the facts of the case, and endeavour to give fair compensation not only for the injury itself but also for all its unpleasant consequences.[74]

If the plaintiff has actually been deprived of the amenities of life, the fact that he cannot appreciate this loss, or that he cannot use or enjoy the damages awarded to him, is no ground for reducing the amount of the award. So in *West (H.) and Son, Ltd.* v. *Shephard*[75] the plaintiff had been rendered partially unconscious and totally paralysed as a result of the defendant's negligence. She needed full-time nursing, and her expectation of life was reduced to five years. The House of Lords refused to interfere with an award of £17,500 for loss of amenities and £500 for loss of expectation of life. Her "grave and sombre deprivation"[76] entitled her to substantial compensation: unconsciousness was relevant only in respect of those heads of damage which can be felt or appreciated—*e.g.* pain and suffering.[77] The

---

[64] It is not so in Marxist countries (except Poland), and was not always so in England: Pollock C.B. once said, "In my personal judgment, it is an unmanly thing to make such a claim": *Theobald* v. *Railway Passengers Assurance Co.* (1862) 15 Jur. 583, 586.

[65] Suffering is the subjective appreciation of objective pain: *Cutts* v. *Chumley* [1967] 1 W.L.R. 742.

[66] *Hinz* v. *Berry* [1970] 2 Q.B. 40.

[67] *Heaps* v. *Perrite Ltd.* [1937] 2 All E.R. 60.

[68] *Bishop* v. *Cunard White Star Ltd.* [1950] P. 242, 247.

[69] Ogus, "Damages for Lost Amenities" (1972) 35 M.L.R. 1.

[70] The latter term was preferred in *Andrews* v. *Freeborough* [1967] 1 Q.B. 1.

[71] *Heaps* v. *Perrite Ltd.* [1937] 2 All E.R. 60, *per* Greer L.J.

[72] *Povey* v. *Governors of Rydal School* [1970] 1 All E.R. 841. In all, the plaintiff was awarded £78,000, but an appeal was settled for £62,000.

[73] *Lim* v. *Camden Health Authority* [1980] A.C. 174.

[74] *West (H.) & Son Ltd.* v. *Shephard* [1964] A.C. 326, 349, 365.

[75] [1964] A.C. 326.

[76] [1964] A.C. 326, 351, *per* Lord Morris of Borth-y-Gest.

[77] There can be no award under the head of pain and suffering, as distinct from that of loss of amenity, in a case in which there was no evidence that the plaintiff appreciated his dreadful state, as in *Wise* v. *Kaye* [1962] 1 Q.B. 638. If the plaintiff does appreciate his position, the award may be substantial: *Cutts* v. *Chumley* [1967] 1 W.L.R. 742.

basis of the award is that an objective thing of value has been lost, not that the plaintiff has been deprived of his subjective happiness. Life is worth living quite apart from any happiness or pleasure it may bring. The decision was unanimously approved by the House of Lords in 1979[78] after full consideration of the various objections to it. In particular it was held that the conventional low award (in 1979 it was £1,250)[79] for loss of expectation of life has no application to damages for loss of amenity.

(3) Shortened expectation of life

In *Flint* v. *Lovell*[80] an exceptionally active gentleman of sixty-nine years was knocked down by the defendant's motor-car and the plaintiff's doctor said that he could now no longer look forward to more than a year of invalid life.[81] The Court of Appeal held that he might recover as an independent head of damage compensation for the shortening of his normal expectation of life. To many lawyers this seemed a novel head of damage: it has been settled for over a century that loss of life itself was not the subject of a claim, and it was thought that damages for shortened expectation of life had hitherto been only taken into account as a subjective element in awarding damages for pain and suffering.[82] But two years later in *Rose* v. *Ford*,[83] when the administrator of a girl of twenty-three, who died four days after a collision between two motor-vehicles, claimed such damages as part of her estate under the Law Reform (Miscellaneous Provisions) Act 1934, the House of Lords held that *Flint* v. *Lovell* was rightly decided.

The chaos which might have been anticipated prevailed in courts of first instance, not much relieved by a number of judgments in the Court of Appeal. In *Benham* v. *Gambling*[84] the opportunity of clarifying the law in this respect[85] was seized. The House of Lords reduced an award of £1,200 in respect of a child two-and-a-half years old to £200. The child, who had survived the accident by a few hours, but had been unconscious during that period, was described as living "in favourable circumstances." In a judgment concurred in by six other Law Lords[86] Viscount Simon L.C. approved a standard of measurement which has resulted in lower and more uniform awards being given. (1) The main rule is that, whether in the case of a child or an adult, very moderate figures should be chosen. So the starting-point, whatever sum it might be,[87] should also in general be the finishing-point,

---

[78] *Lim* v. *Camden Health Authority* [1980] A.C. 174.
[79] *Gammell* v. *Wilson* [1980] 2 All E.R. 557.
[80] [1935] 1 K.B. 354.
[81] In the event he was still alive 3 years later: *Rose* v. *Ford* [1937] A.C. 826, 833.
[82] The passage to this effect in the 9th edition of this book (at p. 363) was adopted as part of his argument by unsuccessful counsel in *Rose* v. *Ford* and, 40 years later, this was the conclusion of the Law Commission's *Report* (Law Com. No. 56, 1973), §§ 92–107, and also of the Pearson Commission (Report, §§ 363–372). The arguments for the abolition of this head of damages are overwhelming now that damages for "the lost years" are recoverable as future pecuniary loss.
[83] [1937] A.C. 826.
[84] [1941] A.C. 157, 168.
[85] The decision has not been interpreted as giving guidance on the different question of the assessment of damages for loss of the amenities of life: under this head much more generous awards are permissible: *West (H.) & Son Ltd.* v. *Shephard* [1964] A.C. 326.
[86] According to *Pickett* [1980] A.C. 136, 147, there were only five other Law Lords, and it would have been better if they had given separate judgments. Yet in *Lim* [1980] A.C. 174 seven months later, four Law Lords concurred in only one judgment.
[87] The conventional sum has been increased to £1,250: *Gammell* v. *Wilson* [1980] 3 W.L.R. 891.

though to a limited extent the court may have regard to inflation.[88] (2) The sum given is not to be determined by applying a statistical or actuarial test as to the number of days or years of life of which the individual has been deprived. For "the thing to be valued is not the prospect of length of days, but the prospect of a predominantly happy life."[89] The loss of a measure of prospective happiness was thereby in effect substituted for the shortening of life as the true head of damage in these cases, but in these cases alone.[90] Hence the prospect of a predominantly unhappy life may justify a lower award than usual.[91] But there is a presumption in favour of happiness.[92] (3) But, though the court must be satisfied that the circumstances of the individual life were calculated to lead on balance to a positive measure of happiness (based on the character or habits of the individual) the test is objective, and not subjective. It follows that it is also irrelevant that the plaintiff has suffered mental injuries which make it impossible for him to realise what he has lost.[93] (4) The adoption of a conventional or artificial figure means that the youth or age of the victim is not of primary signifi-cance, though normally in the case of a mature person there will be more material on which to build an expectation of happiness.[94] (5) The social posi-tion of the victim, his prospects of worldly possessions, the financial losses or gains of which he has been deprived are to be excluded from consideration.[95]

The principle laid down in *Benham* v. *Gambling* is logically applicable whether the victim has died before action brought or before judgment (as in *Pickett* v. *British Rail Engineering Ltd*[96]), or is alive and suing in his own right.[97] But if the victim is dead the plaintiff is often not concerned to argue strongly for a high figure, as the Law Reform Act damages will be deducted from a Fatal Accidents Act award.[98]

Inflation[99]

It is certain that public policy does not require an award to be reduced in order to contain inflation.[1] It is less certain how far an award should be increased to reflect the fall in the value of the pound. The controlling view is that inflation should not be taken into account because it can be off-set by prudent investment, so that the problem "is taken care of in a rough and

---

[88] *Yorkshire Electricity Board* v. *Naylor* [1968] A.C. 529.
[89] [1941] A.C. 157, 166.
[90] In *Wise* v. *Kaye* [1962] 1 Q.B. 638 Diplock L.J. (dissenting) made a striking attempt to restate the whole law under the general principle of loss of happiness. But a majority of the H.L. refused to accept this in *West (H.) & Son Ltd.* v. *Shephard* [1964] A.C. 326.
[91] *Burns* v. *Edman* [1970] 2 Q.B. 541 (professional criminals have unhappy lives).
[92] *West (H.) & Son Ltd.* v. *Shephard* [1964] A.C. 326, 363.
[93] *West (H.) & Son Ltd.* v. *Shephard* [1964] A.C. 326.
[94] *Yorkshire Electricity Board* v. *Naylor* [1968] A.C. 529.
[95] *Benham* v. *Gambling* [1941] A.C. 157, 167.
[96] [1980] A.C. 136.
[97] As in *Harris* v. *Bright's Asphalt Contractors Ltd.* [1953] 1 Q.B. 617, in which £500 was awarded to a plaintiff "who had an A1 prospect of life" reduced to two years by negligence of the defendant.
[98] See below, § 216. Yet in *Yorkshire Electricity Board* v. *Naylor* [1968] A.C. 529, the sole claim was under the Law Reform Act, no dependency being alleged.
[99] See Fleming, "The Impact of Inflation on Tort Compensation" (1978) 26 Am. Jo. of Comp. Law. 51.
[1] *Walker* v. *McLean (J.) & Sons Ltd.* [1979] 1 W.L.R. 760.

ready way."[2] It is conceded that in an exceptional case, where there is a high tax factor in the assumed annuity basis, it might be appropriate to increase the multiplier.[3] Otherwise there are several sound reasons for adhering to the present practice.[4] But Lord Scarman has also said that "in truth, of course, judicial awards of damages follow, but rarely keep pace with inflation."[5]

Functions of an appellate court

There is here an important but not very convincing[6] difference between trial by judge and jury and trial by a judge sitting alone. On an appeal from a judge the Court of Appeal rehears the case and has the power to correct erroneous judgments, but on an appeal from the verdict of a jury there is no power of correction but only of supervision.[7] When the verdict is that of a jury, it will only be set aside if the appellate court is satisfied that the amount of damages is such that it is out of all proportion to the circumstances of the case.[8] In such a case it is better not to apply epithets such as "scandalous" or "outrageous" to the award which is under appeal, but to say simply that there is no reasonable proportion between the award and the circumstances of the case.[9] For an award by a jury cannot be attacked simply on the ground that it is out of conformity with whatever pattern may have emerged from the decisions of judges in comparable cases.[10] One reason for this is that as the law prohibits the jury being informed about comparable cases it can hardly complain if their award diverges from them. Another reason is that the views of juries may form a valuable corrective to the views of judges.[11] A difficult situation would arise if another jury on a retrial independently awarded the same or a higher amount.[12] Still, "to say, as judges have come as near to saying as decorum permits, that juries must find a figure as best they can and escape criticism by being anonymous and dumb and accordingly proof against everything but 'perversity,' is a poor position in which to leave the matter."[13] So it has been held by the Court of Appeal that in order to achieve uniformity trial before a judge sitting alone should be ordered unless there are exceptional circumstances.[14] Uniformity has been thought to be desirable because it promotes justice as between different parties in different cases and also because it helps lawyers to predict awards.[15] So in England the jury is no longer a factor in the assessment of damages.

When the award is that of the judge alone, the appeal is by way of rehear-

---

[2] *Cookson* v. *Knowles* [1979] A.C. 556, 571, *per* Lord Diplock.
[3] *Cookson* v. *Knowles* [1979] A.C. 556.
[4] So said Lord Scarman and three other Law Lords in *Lim* v. *Camden Health Authority* [1980] A.C. 174.
[5] *Pickett* v. *British Rail Engineering Ltd.* [1980] A.C. 136, 173.
[6] *Warren* v. *King* [1964] 1 W.L.R. 1, 9.
[7] *Warren* v. *King* [1964] 1 W.L.R. 1.
[8] *Davies* v. *Powell Duffryn Associated Collieries Ltd.* [1942] A.C. 601, 616. But the C.A. has said that in future it will review such awards more readily: *Ward* v. *James* [1966] 1 Q.B. 273.
[9] *McGrath* v. *Bourne* (1876) 10 Ir. Rep.C.L. 160, 164.
[10] *Scott* v. *Musial* [1959] 2 Q.B. 429.
[11] *Scott* v. *Musial* [1959] 2 Q.B. 429, 434.
[12] *McCarey* v. *Associated Newspapers Ltd.* [1965] 2 Q.B. 86.
[13] *Admiralty Commissioners* v. *S.S. Chekiang (Owners)* [1926] A.C. 637, 643, *per* Lord Sumner.
[14] *Ward* v. *James* [1966] 1 Q.B. 273.
[15] See the Law Commission's Working Paper No. 41 (1971), §§ 209–216.

ing on damages as on all other issues, but generally there is so much room for legitimate difference of opinion that the appellate court will be slow to interfere. It must be satisfied either that the judge, in assessing the damages, applied a wrong principle of law (as by taking into account some irrelevant factor or leaving out of account some relevant one); or, short of this, that the amount awarded is either so inordinately low or so inordinately high that it must be a wholly erroneous estimate of the damage.[16] It has been said that the court would interfere if it said to itself "Good gracious me—as high as that."[17] In exceptional circumstances the Court of Appeal may take account of facts occurring after the date of the judgment.[18]

Reforms[19-20]

Many suggestions for reform have been made. It has been argued[21] that the court should have the assistance of an actuary in estimating the cost of an annuity to bring in the desired annual sum over the years which are left to the plaintiff, or in assessing the diminution of future earning capacity. But in England it is thought by the courts[22] that actuarial tables are imprecise[23] and so unhelpful in particular cases.[24] Another possibility is that there should be two trials (or a split trial[25])—one on liability soon after the accident, when the events are fresh in the minds of witnesses, and the other on damages at a later date, when the extent of the loss will be more clearly manifest. The proposal that damages should no longer be awarded in a lump sum, but an interim payment ordered which can be increased or decreased later as circumstances may require in order to prevent the plaintiff being over- or under-compensated, was carried into effect by the Administration of Justice Act 1969, s.20. The Pearson Report[26] makes further recommendations for provisional awards. But the desire for exact justice may lengthen litigation and lead to "compensation neurosis": it is significant that interim payments were discarded in 1946 by the Ministry of National Insurance.

§ 216. SURVIVAL ACTIONS: PERSONAL REPRESENTATIVE AS PLAINTIFF

In general, as the cause of action is that of the deceased, damages are recoverable under the same heads and assessable according to the same

---

[16] *Nance* v. *British Columbia Electric Ry.* [1951] A.C. 601, 613.

[17] *McCarthy* v. *Coldair Ltd.* [1951] 2 T.L.R. 1226, 1229, *per* Denning L.J. If it is said that the award is unreasonable, this means, not that the court below was unreasonable, but that having regard to the relevant principles of assessment, the court below has arrived at a result not reasonably in accord with those principles: *M'Leish* v. *Fulton & Sons*, 1955 S.C. 46, 50.

[18] *Mulholland* v. *Mitchell* [1971] A.C. 666.

[19-20] See the Report of the Winn Committee on Personal Injuries Litigation (Cmnd. 3691 (1968)), the Law Commission's Report on Personal Injury Litigation (Law Com. No. 56, 1973), the Pearson Report (Cmnd. 7054, 1978), Chaps. 12–14, and the Cantley Committee Report (Cmnd. 7476, 1979).

[21] *Hodges* v. *Harland and Wolff Ltd.* [1965] 1 W.L.R. 523, 526.

[22] *Taylor* v. *O'Connor* [1971] A.C. 115. The Irish Supreme Court insists on such evidence: *Arnott* v. *O'Keeffe* [1977] I.R.1.

[23] *Fletcher* v. *Autocar and Transporters* [1968] 2 Q.B. 322.

[24] But the Law Commission *Report* recommends legislation to promote the use of actuarial evidence.

[25] This is now provided for by R.S.C. Ord. 33, v. 3.

[26] Chap. 14. But in *Lim* v. *Camden Health Authority* [1980] A.C. 174, 183, the limited nature of this jurisdiction was stressed.

standards as if the deceased were still alive.[27] Thus damages may be recovered for loss of earnings,[28] pain and suffering,[29] medical and hospital expenses (if incurred), and loss of expectation of life.[30] Exceptions may be found in section 1 (2) of the Law Reform (Miscellaneous Provisions) Act 1934,[31] which provides that, when the executor or administrator is plaintiff, the damages recoverable for the benefit of the estate:

(1) shall not include exemplary damages,[32]

(2) where the death has been caused by the act or omission which gives rise to the cause of action, shall be calculated without reference to any loss or gain to the estate consequent on the death, except that a sum in respect of funeral expenses may be included.[33] Thus if the deceased's life was insured the receipt of the insurance moneys will be disregarded, as will death grants payable under the Social Security Acts, and repayments of taxes previously over-paid.[34]

Duplication of damages

The Act expressly provides by section 1 (5) that the rights for the benefit of the estates of deceased persons are in addition to and not in derogation of the rights conferred on dependants by the Fatal Accidents Act and the Carriage by Air Act 1961. What, then, is the position where those who benefit under the Fatal Accidents Act are the same persons as those who benefit under the will or on intestacy under the Law Reform Act?[35] It has been made clear that there can be no duplication of damages.[36] If the action under the Law Reform Act is brought first or at the same time as the action under the Fatal Accidents Act (as it normally is), the damages recovered under the latter Act will be *pro tanto* reduced, for the Law Reform Act damages will be a benefit accruing to dependants as a result of the deceased's death.[37] But damages for lost earnings are not regarded as such a benefit,[38] even though such damages in respect of "the lost years" are now recoverable[39]; and may amount to a substantial sum. Indeed, if such damages exceed the value of the dependency, there may be a nil award in the Fatal Accidents Act claim. On the other hand; if the action under the Fatal Accidents Act is brought first then the possibiliy of any Law Reform

---

[27] See above, § 215.
[28] Including the "lost years": *Gammell* v. *Wilson* [1981] 2 W.L.R. 248.
[29] But in the period 1936–66 such damages have been recovered by the estate in only one reported case: *Andrews* v. *Freeborough* [1967] 1 Q.B. 1, 28.
[30] But not in Ireland: the Civil Liability Act 1961, s. 7 prohibits the estate from recovering damages for pain and suffering, or loss of expectation of life or personal injury.
[31] The Act "has proved to be a singularly unsuccessful experiment in law reform": Munkman *Damages*, p. 137.
[32] See above, § 199.
[33] See *Gammell* v. *Wilson* [1981] 2 W.L.R. 248.
[34] *Gammell* v. *Wilson* [1981] 2 W.L.R. 248.
[35] If the deceased has left his estate away from his family, then the consequences for the tort feasor may be extremely serious, as he will have to pay substantial sums in two different actions.
[36] *Davies* v. *Powell Duffryn Collieries* [1942] A.C. 601, 623.
[37] *Rose* v. *Ford* [1937] A.C. 826, 835; *Davies* v. *Powell Duffryn Collieries* [1942] A.C. 601. But it is best to claim the whole of the damages under the Fatal Accidents Act: *Hutchinson* v. *L. & N.E. Ry.* [1942] 1 K.B. 481, 491. For damages recovered under the Law Reform Act are subject to the claims of creditors. Indeed, there is much to be said for the view that Law Reform Act damages are a needless complication and should be abolished.
[38] *Gammell* v. *Wilson* [1981] 2 W.L.R. 248.
[39] *Pickett* v. *British Rail Engineering Ltd.* [1980] A.C. 136.

Act damages coming to the plaintiff dependants must be taken into account.[40] But Law Reform Act damages themselves cannot be reduced by anything which the dependants may recover.[41]

§ 217. DEPENDENCY ACTIONS: THE FATAL ACCIDENTS ACT 1976[42]

The rule that no man has any legally protected interest in the life of another has been to a great extent derogated from by statute, but it still remains the general principle, the Fatal Accidents Acts 1846 to 1959, now consolidated in the Fatal Accident Act 1976, having merely established exceptions to it. Section 1 of the 1976 Act provides: "If death[43] is caused[44] by any wrongful act, neglect, or default, which is such as would (if death had not ensued) have entitled the person injured to maintain an action and recover damages in respect thereof, the person who would have been liable if death had not ensued shall be liable to an action for damages, notwithstanding the death of the person injured."[45] The Act came into force on September 1, 1976. The action is brought in the name of the executor or administrator for the benefit of certain near relatives of the deceased, if those relatives have suffered a pecuniary loss in consequence of his death. The following points on the interpretation of the Act should be noted:

(1) What relatives are covered

The relatives whose interests are thus protected are, by section 1 (2), the following: husband, wife,[46] children, grandchildren, step-children, father, mother, step-parents, and grandparents. The class of dependants also includes any person who is, or who is the issue of, a brother, sister, uncle, or aunt of the deceased person. By section 1 (4) illegitimate and adopted[47] children are for the purposes of the Acts to be deemed to be children, any relationship by affinity is to be treated as a relationship by consanguinity, and any relationship of the half-blood as of the whole blood. Posthumous children also come under the Act.[48] In Scotland, those entitled to claim under the corresponding Act, the Damages (Scotland) Act 1976, also include all ascendants and descendants, any person accepted by the deceased as a child of his family, whether or not legally adopted, and a divorced spouse. The Pearson Commission thought that English law should be brought into line with Scottish law on this point.[49]

---

[40] *Davies* v. *Powell Duffryn Collieries Ltd.* [1942] A.C. 601, 608.

[41] [1942] A.C. 601, 615.

[42] See *McGregor on Damages*, Chap. 34.

[43] There is no limitation as to the place of the wrong or of the death, or as to the nationality or domicile of the parties: *The Esso Malaysia* [1975] Q.B. 198.

[44] Foresight is irrelevant in an action under the Fatal Accidents Act: causation alone is the test: *Haber* v. *Walker* [1953] V.R. 339. See also above, § 202.

[45] It has been held that an action will lie if the deceased committed suicide as a result of insanity caused by the defendant's negligence: *Pigney* v. *Pointers Transport Services* [1957] 1 W.L.R. 1121.

[46] But not a divorced wife: *Payne-Collins* v. *Taylor Woodrow Ltd.* [1975] Q.B. 300, or the so-called common law wife (who is not a wife at common law): *K.* v. *J.M.P. Co. Ltd.* [1976] Q.B. 85.

[47] Legally, as distinct from *de facto*, adopted. Perhaps here the law should be changed to bring it into line with the Matrimonial Proceedings and Property Act 1970, s. 27(1). An unmarried mother is not a dependant: *K.* v. *J.M.P. Co. Ltd.* [1976] Q.B. 85.

[48] *The George and Richard* (1871) L.R. 3 A. & E. 466.

[49] Pearson Report, § 404.

(2) The action

Only one action is to be brought in the name of the deceased's personal representative,[50] giving full particulars of the person for whose benefit the action is brought.[51] The action must be brought within three years after the date of death, or the date of the knowledge of the person for whose benefit the action is brought, whichever is the later. The action is brought by the executor or administrator of the deceased on behalf of the relatives; but if there is no executor or administrator, or if he does not commence an action within six months, any relative entitled to the protection of the Act may sue in his own name on behalf of himself and the others.[52]

(3) Damages not part of the deceased's estate

The amount recovered is not part of the estate of the deceased so as to be liable for debts. The executor or administrator recovers it, not in his ordinary capacity as the personal representative of the deceased, but in a special capacity in right of the relatives.[53]

(4) Deceased himself must have been able to sue

There is no right of action unless the deceased himself could have sued had he been merely injured by the defendant's act and not killed. Therefore, if he has in his lifetime, in the interval between the accident and his death, accepted full compensation from the defendant and so extinguished his right of action, his relatives cannot sue in respect of his death, nor can they if he has obtained judgment against the defendant.[54] Compensation must be claimed within three years, but if it is claimed too soon the result may be disastrous for the deceased's family.[55] The same rule applies if the deceased agreed to take the risk of the accident on himself so as to exclude any right of action in accordance with the maxim *volenti non fit injuria*,[56] or if at the time of his death the Limitation Acts have already run against him.[57] If the deceased has been guilty of contributory negligence, the Fatal Accidents Act 1976, s.5, provides that the damages awarded under that Act may be reduced proportionately, and the same rule applies by analogy if a plaintiff dependant has been guilty of contributory negligence.[58] But the contributory negligence of one dependant does not affect the rights of another.[59]

(5) A new cause of action

Nevertheless the cause of action conferred upon the relatives of the deceased by the Act is a new cause of action and not merely a continuance

---

[50] Fatal Accidents Act 1976, s. 2(3).
[51] s. 2(4). See *Cooper* v. *Williams* [1963] 2 Q.B. 567.
[52] Limitation Act 1939, s. 2B(3), as amended by the Limitation Act 1975. The court has a discretionary power to allow a time-barred action to proceed.
[53] *Marginson* v. *Blackburn B.C.* [1939] 2 K.B. 426.
[54] At least before the right to recover damages for "the lost years" was held to survive for the benefit of the estate: See above, § 216.
[55] *Griffiths* v. *Dudley (Earl of)* (1882) 9 Q.B.D. 357.
[56] *British Columbia Electric Ry.* v. *Gentile* [1914] A.C. 1034, 1042.
[57] See Williams, *Joint Torts and Contributory Negligence*, pp. 440 *et seq.*
[58] *Mulholland* v. *McCrea* [1961] N.I. 135.
[59] *Dodds* v. *Dodds* [1978] Q.B. 543.

of that which was formerly vested in the deceased himself.[60] The measure of damages may be entirely different: the deceased, if alive, could only have recovered damages for his personal injuries; the relatives recover substantially for the loss of their bread-winner.[61] This is strikingly illustrated by the fact that if the period of limitation under the Limitation Act 1954, was not complete as against the deceased at the date of his death, it cannot be completed afterwards so as to bar the claim of the relatives under the Act. This claim is subject to its own period of limitation as fixed by the Act itself and commencing on the death of the deceased, and is not subject to the provision of the Limitation Acts affecting the claim of the deceased himself.[62]

(6) Method of assessing damages

In the difficult task of estimating the amount of damages to be awarded the courts often find help in the principles enunciated by Lord Wright in *Davies* v. *Powell Duffryn Associated Collieries Ltd.*[63]: "The starting point is the amount of wages which the deceased was earning, the ascertainment of which to some extent may depend upon the regularity of his employment. Then there is an estimate of how much was required or expended for his own personal and living expenses. The balance will give a datum or basic figure[64] which will generally be turned into a lump sum by taking a certain number of years' purchase. That sum, however, has to be taxed down by having due regard to uncertainities." In making the assessment the court can look at events since the accident to see whether contingencies have become certainities. "The court should never speculate where it knows."[65] But at the end of the day arithmetic may have to be mitigated by common sense, for it is an assessment and not a calculation which is being made.[66]

Some particular applications of these principles must be mentioned:

(1) *The multiplier*

The estimate of the probable length of the deceased's earning period should be the basis for the computation of the plaintiff's loss. This will serve to fix the upper and the lower limits of his claim, for it is impossible to compute the loss on a strictly arithmetical or actuarial basis.[67] The multiplier is not intended to reflect the number of years the dependency would have continued, for this might result in over-compensation for the dependants.[68] Hence no definite figure can be chosen as a multiplier which will give a correct result in all cases: the court has a discretion in the matter. But probably 16 years' purchase is near the upper limit.[69] Whatever figure is chosen ought not to be materially reduced by reason of the hazardous

---

[60] *The Vera Cruz* (1884) 10 App. Cas. 59, 70.
[61] Unless their bread was being won by criminal means: *Burns* v. *Edman* [1970] 2 Q.B. 541.
[62] *Venn* v. *Tedesco* [1926] 2 K.B. 227.
[63] [1942] A.C. 601, 617.
[64] Now generally called the multiplicand.
[65] *Curwen* v. *James* [1963] 1 W.L.R. 748, 753, *per* Harman L.J.
[66] *Daniel* v. *Jones* [1961] 1 W.L.R. 1103.
[67] *Nance* v. *British Columbia Electric Ry.* [1951] A.C. 601, 614–617.
[68] *Taylor* v. *O'Connor* [1971] A.C. 115.
[69] *Mallett* v. *McMonagle* [1970] A.C. 166.

nature of the deceased's occupation in life.[70] If the award is split into two parts, namely the loss from the date of death to trial, and the future loss, the multiplier may also have to be split.[71] In 1971 Parliament provided that in assessing the damages payable to a widow in respect of the death of her husband there should not be taken into account the remarriage of the widow or her prospects of remarriage.[72] This legislation shows that change is not equivalent to reform: it has led to gross injustice, not least in that the court may be obliged to disregard a vital fact which has happened, namely the widow's remarriage to a wealthy second husband.[73] But a deduction must be made for the immediate receipt of a lump sum. There are many other factors which may serve to increase or decrease the multiplier or the multiplicand. The courts usually fix the multiplier after taking contingencies into account and not before. One particular contingency which has caused great difficulty is that of continued inflation. The present English view is that neither the multiplier nor the multiplicand should be increased to take account of inflation, save in exceptional cases.[74] The right way to protect an award from the ravages of inflation is by investing it prudently.[75]

(2) *The dependency: the multiplicand*

There is no right of action on behalf of any relative who cannot show some pecuniary loss in consequence of the death of the deceased. A wife's companionship is to be ignored, likewise the grief and misery caused by her departure.[76] Nothing can be claimed merely by way of *solatium* for mental suffering and bereavement in England,[77] although it may in Ireland,[78] and Scotland. There is, however, a sufficient pecuniary loss if the claimant can show some reasonable expectation of pecuniary benefit from the continuance of the deceased's life.[79] The dependency begins to run from the date of the death[80]; and it is not necessary that the benefit should be derived from the deceased as a matter of right, for a reasonable expectation of voluntary bounty is enough.[81] Thus a husband can recover damages for the death of his wife in respect of the loss of the pecuniary value of her domestic services, and the law interprets the term "services" widely—a wife and mother does not normally work set hours.[82]

Damages can be assessed under two distinct heads.[83] First, in respect of

---

[70] *Bishop* v. *Cunard White Star Ltd.* [1950] P. 240, 248.
[71] *Cookson* v. *Knowles* [1979] A.C. 556.
[72] Law Reform (Miscellaneous Provisions) Act 1971, s. 4(1).
[73] *Report* (1973), the Pearson Commission, § 247, and Atiyah, *Accidents, Compensation and the Law* (3rd ed.), P. 184.
[74] *Young* v. *Percival* [1975] 1 W.L.R. 17. Nor should any attention be paid to the speculations of academic economists: *Mitchell* v. *Mulholland (No. 2)* [1972] 1 Q.B. 65.
[75] *Lim* v. *Camden Health Authority* [1980] A.C. 174, 193. Thus the equity market is unstable: but the gilts market in 1980 was so stable that money there invested might produce an income exceeding the annual inflation rate.
[76] *Regan* v. *Williamson* [1976] 1 W.L.R. 305.
[77] *Blake* v. *Midland Ry.* (1852) 18 Q.B. 93. But the Law Commission (*Report*, 1973, § 172) recommend that damages for bereavement should be awarded according to a legislative tariff.
[78] Civil Liability Act 1961, s. 49(1).
[79] *Baker* v. *Dalgleish Steam Shipping Co.* [1922] 1 K.B. 361.
[80] *K.* v. *J.M.P. Co. Ltd.* [1976] Q.B. 85.
[81] *Franklin* v. *S.E. Ry.* (1858) 3 H. & N. 211.
[82] *Regan* v. *Williamson* [1976] 1 W.L.R. 305.
[83] *Nance* v. *B.C. Electric Ry.* [1951] A.C. 601, 614.

the sums which the deceased would probably have applied out of his income to the maintenance of his dependants; and secondly, in respect of such portion of any additional savings which he might have accumulated during the period for which, but for the accident, he would have lived. Tax must be taken into account.[84]

On the other hand, the fact that the dependant has private means is irrelevant, except in so far as it shows the amount of pecuniary benefit received from the deceased.[85] Nor is it necessary that any benefit should have been actually received from the deceased during his lifetime.[86] The benefit must be derivable, however, from the claimant's relationship to the deceased, and not merely from a contract between them, as where husband and wife are in partnership together in some trade or profession.[87] But a merely speculative possibility of pecuniary benefit is not enough.[88] When the dependant himself dies subsequently to the death of the person in respect of whose death the action is brought but before judgment, the shortness of his tenure of life before dependence was terminated must be taken into account in determining the amount to be awarded.[89]

Funeral expenses may be recovered if they have been incurred by the parties for whose benefit the action is brought.[90]

(3) *The deductions*[91]

The onus is on the defendant to show that any pecuniary benefit or reasonable expectation of pecuniary benefit to the relatives resulting from the death of the deceased is taken into account in reduction of damages, which are given to compensate the recipient on a balance of gains and losses for the injury sustained by the death.[92] Thus the benefits which a wife and children take under a settlement upon the husband's death must be taken into account.[93] But it is surely paradoxical that if a deceased spends freely on, instead of saving for the benefit of, his family they should have a higher claim for dependency on his death. Again when the relatives are also entitled either under a will or on intestacy to a share of the deceased's estate any damages given under the Law Reform (Miscellaneous Provisions) Act 1934 will go in reduction of the amount awarded to them under the Fatal Accidents Act. A deduction must also be made for the inheritance of other assets, unless (for example) these consist of articles of which the claimant would have had the use when the deceased was alive and at home. The classic example is the family dwelling-house. In such a case the capitalised value of the acceleration would be very small.[94] Further, if the defendant can prove that the dependency originally lost has since been reduced or has

---

[84] *British Transport Commission* v. *Gourley* [1956] A.C. 185.
[85] *Sheils* v. *Cruickshank* [1953] 1 W.L.R. 533.
[86] *Taff Vale Ry.* v. *Jenkins* [1913] A.C. 1.
[87] *Burgess* v. *Florence Nightingale Hospital for Gentlewomen* [1955] 1 Q.B. 349. *Aliter* if the wife has been employed by the husband's one-man company: *Malyon* v. *Plummer* [1964] 1 Q.B. 330.
[88] *Barnett* v. *Cohen* [1921] 2 K.B. 461.
[89] *Williamson* v. *Thorneycroft & Co.* [1940] 2 K.B. 658.
[90] Fatal Accidents Act 1976, s. 3(3).
[91] See *Murray* v. *Shuter* [1976] Q.B. 972.
[92] *Davies* v. *Powell Duffryn Collieries* [1942] A.C. 601, 623.
[93] *Pym* v. *Great Northern Ry.* (1863) 4 B. & S. 396.
[94] *Heatley* v. *Steel Co. of Wales Ltd.* [1953] 1 W.L.R. 405.

ceased entirely, the damages may be reduced, as when the mother of a dependant child remarries, and the step-father accepts the child as one of his own family,[95] for in such a case there is in truth a substitute breadwinner.[96]

Pensions and insurance policies[97]

But the principle which requires deductions to be made for benefits received has been seriously eroded by statute as well as by judicial decision. Section 4 (1) of the Fatal Accidents Act 1976 provides that in assessing damages in respect of a person's death in any action under the Fatal Accidents Act there shall not be taken into account any insurance money,[98] benefit,[99] pension[1] or gratuity which has been or will or may be paid as a result of the death. The words "as a result of the death" may give rise to some difficult questions of causation.[2] The modern tendency is to interpret such words in a way favourable to the dependants: generosity does not result from death.[3]

(4) The apportionment

When all necessary deductions from the starting sum have been made, the resulting total is usually apportioned amongst the family, taking the family as a unit, when claims are made in respect of more than one dependant,[4] although each dependant is entitled to an individual judgment for a separate sum. The actual apportionment is no concern of the defendant. The court has power to control the investment and release of the sum awarded as damages when minors are dependants[5] although it has no such power in respect of Law Reform Act damages, or of the widow's own damages since the Law Reform (Miscellaneous Provisions) Act 1971, s.5. After the 1971 Act the courts will probably assess separately each child's damages. The sums so awarded can then be placed under the control of the court.

---

[95] *Reincke* v. *Gray* [1964] 2 All E.R. 687.
[96] *Aliter* if a grandmother voluntarily provides a home for the children: *Hay* v. *Hughes* [1975] Q.B. 790.
[97] See the full treatment by Fleming in *International Encylcopaedia of Comparative Law*, Chap. 11.
[98] Words which, by s. 4(2), include a return of premiums.
[99] This word means (by s. 4(2)) benefit under the National Insurance Acts and also any payment by a friendly society or trade union for the relief or maintenance of a member's dependants.
[1] This is an important innovation, as under the old law pensions were deductible, even though paid voluntarily or under a contributory scheme. The word "pension" includes a return of contributions, and any payment of a lump sum.
[2] See above, §§ 200–206.
[3] *Hay* v. *Hughes* [1975] Q.B. 790.
[4] *Bishop* v. *Cunard White Star Ltd.* [1950] P. 240.
[5] R.S.C., Ord. 80, r. 12. The average life of a fund in court is 5 years. Does this mean that awards are too low, or that dependants are extravagant? The Pearson Commission found that only one-fifth of the recipients of damages made any attempt to treat the money as capital as distinct from income.

CHAPTER 24

REMEDIES: MISCELLANEOUS MATTERS

§ 218. SUCCESSIVE ACTIONS ON THE SAME FACTS

More than one action will not lie on the same cause of action; therefore all damages resulting from the same cause of action must be recovered at one and the same time. The rule is designed to prevent the oppressive and vexatious litigation that might result if an injured person were at liberty to divide his claim and sue in successive actions for different portions of the loss sustained from a single cause of action. Thus in *Fitter* v. *Veal*[1] the plaintiff, after recovering damages for an assault and battery, discovered that his injuries were more serious than was at first supposed, and he found it necessary to submit to a surgical operation; whereupon he brought a second action for additional damage. But it was held that he had only one cause of action, which had been wholly extinguished by the judgment recovered in the first action. The application of this rule is not excluded or affected by the fact that when the first action was brought the damage in respect of which the second action is brought had not yet accrued to the plaintiff.[2] But if the damage in either action was unknown to him he may be able to obtain an extension of time under the Limitation Act 1975.[3]

If, however, there are two distinct causes of action, and not merely two distinct heads of damage, successive actions will lie in respect of each of them. This happens in the following classes of cases:
(1) When the same act amounts to a violation of two distinct rights;
(2) When the defendant has committed two distinct acts, even though in violation of the same right;
(3) When the cause of action is a continuing one;
(4) (Probably) When the wrong is only actionable on proof of actual damage and it produces damage at different times.

(1) Violation of distinct rights

When the wrongful act of the defendant has violated two distinct rights vested in the plaintiff, a separate action will lie to recover the damage suffered in respect of each of these rights. Thus in *Brunsden* v. *Humphrey*[4] the plaintiff, a cabdriver, having already recovered compensation in the county court for damage done to his cab by a collision with the defendant's van, was held entitled by a majority of the Court of Appeal to bring a second action in the High Court in respect of personal injuries suffered by him in consequence of the same accident. So a plaintiff who has already sued for damages in a personal capacity can subsequently bring another action for damages arising from the same wrongful act in a representative

---

[1] (1701) 12 Mod. 542; (*sub tit. Fetter* v. *Beale*) 1 Ld.Raym. 339, 692, approved in *Cartledge* v. *E. Jopling & Sons Ltd.* [1963] A.C. 758, 780. But it is possible that the Civil Liability (Contribution) Act 1978 s. 4 has indirectly altered the law in this area: see above, § 168.
[2] *Derrick* v. *Williams* [1939] 2 All E.R. 559.
[3] See below, § 220.
[4] (1884) 14 Q.B.D. 141.

character.[5] To justify two actions, however, there must be two distinct rights violated; it is not enough that the same act amounts to two distinct violations of the same right. Thus separate actions will not lie for two different personal injuries received from the same act of negligence or assault, as when the plaintiff has his leg broken, and also his arm.[6] The arguments in favour of the rule in *Brunsden* v. *Humphrey* are that there may be issues of identity or justification or measure of damages in one action which are irrelevant in the other, and that the notion of separate rights or interests is familiar in negligence. The arguments against[7] are that a cause of action now means a factual situation which gives a right to the plaintiff,[8] that a single factual situation cannot be split up into several legal situations, and that repetition and technicality in litigation are not to be encouraged.

(2) Distinct wrongful acts

So also two actions will lie when the defendant has committed two distinct wrongful acts, even against the same person in violation of the same right. Thus if he has on two different occasions entered upon the plaintiff's land, the plaintiff is not bound to sue for both these trespasses at once, but may bring separate actions for each of them. On the same principle, if the same libellous statement is published to two or more persons at different times, a separate action will lie for each publication.[9]

(3) Successive actions for continuing injuries

When the act of the defendant is a continuing injury, its continuance after the date of the first action is a new cause of action for which a second action can be brought, and so from time to time until the injury is discontinued. An injury is said to be a continuing one so long as it is still in the course of being committed and is not wholly past. Thus the wrong of false imprisonment continues so long as the plaintiff is kept in confinement; a nuisance continues so long as the state of things causing the nuisance is suffered by the defendant to remain upon his land; and a trespass continues so long as the defendant remains present upon the plaintiff's land. In the case of such continuing injury an action may be brought during its continuance, but damages are recoverable only down to the time of their assessment in the action.[10] Prospective damages for any further continuance of the injury are not recoverable by way of anticipation, for *non constat* that the defendant will not discontinue the wrong forthwith. This is so however permanent the source of the mischief may be, and however improbable it may be that the defendant will discontinue it: as when he has built a house which blocks the ancient lights of the plaintiff. There will be time enough to sue for future damage when it accrues.[11] Nor does it make any difference in this respect

---

[5] *Marginson* v. *Blackburn B.C.* [1939] 2 K.B. 426; *Randolph* v. *Tuck* [1962] 1 Q.B. 175. See Street, "Estoppel and the Law of Negligence" (1957) 73 L.Q.R. 358.
[6] *Conquer* v. *Boot* [1928] 2 K.B. 336, 340.
[7] See *Cahoon* v. *Franks* (1967) 65 D.L.R. (2d) 274.
[8] See above, § 1.
[9] See above, § 53. Any vexatious or oppressive exercise of this right of suing separately for a number of acts of the same kind will be restrained by the court in the exercise of its discretionary power to prevent the abuse of legal process, or by a refusal to award costs in the second action.
[10] Ord. 37, r. 6.
[11] *Darley Main Colliery Co.* v. *Mitchell* (1886) 11 App.Cas. 127.

that the known probability of the future continuance of the injury has diminished the present saleable value of the property affected by it.[12]

If the continuing injury is actionable *per se*, as in the case of trespass, or if it is the cause of fresh damage from day to day, as in the case of an obstruction of ancient lights, successive actions will lie *de die in diem* until the defendant chooses to relieve himself from this burden of litigation by discontinuing his wrong. If, on the other hand, a continuing injury is of a kind which is actionable only on proof of actual damage, and the damage caused is intermittent, as in the case of withdrawal of support, a new action will lie only when some new damage accrues. A continuing injury to property is actionable at the suit of a plaintiff whose title did not accrue until after the commencement of the injury, and such a plaintiff may recover damages in respect of the continuance of the act since the accrual of his title. Thus, he who buys land may sue for a continuing trespass or nuisance which existed at the time of his purchase.[13] Notwithstanding these rules as to the measure of damages in continuing injuries, when an action is brought for an injunction against such an injury, damages may be given in substitution for an injunction; such damages are given in full satisfaction for all future damage which may arise from a continuance of the injury complained of, and therefore no subsequent action will lie in respect thereof.[14]

(4) Successive actions for wrongs actionable only on proof of damage

Where the act of the defendant is actionable *per se*, there is no doubt that all damage, both actual and prospective, may and must be recovered in one action. But where the act of the defendant is not actionable *per se*, but is actionable only if it produces actual damage, and it produces damage twice at different times, is there one cause of action, or are there two? If, for example, the defendant by an act of negligence has created a source of danger which on two successive occasions causes personal harm to the plaintiff, is the plaintiff barred from recovery for the second harm because he has already recovered damages or accepted compensation for the first? Both on principle and on authority[15] it seems that when an act is actionable only on proof of actual damage, successive actions will lie for each successive and distinct accrual of damage.[16] But where the damage sued for in the second action is not in reality distinct from that sued for in the first, but is merely a part of it or consequential upon it, it cannot be recovered. For it is clear that the second damage in order to be recoverable in a second action must arise directly from the wrongful act of the defendant and not indirectly through the damage already sued for. In other words, compensation for the first damage includes compensation for all the ulterior consequences of that damage whether already accrued or not, but it does not include compensation for entirely distinct damage accruing from the defendant's act independently of the damage first sued for.[17]

---

[12] *West Leigh Colliery Co.* v. *Tunnicliffe and Hampson Ltd.* [1908] A.C. 27.
[13] *Konskier* v. *B. Goodman Ltd.* [1928] 1 K.B. 421.
[14] See below, § 219.
[15] *Maberley* v. *Peabody & Co.* [1946] 2 All E.R. 192.
[16] *O'Keefe* v. *Walsh* [1903] 2 I.R. 681, 700; *Johnson* v. *Mount Albert B.C.* [1979] 2 N.Z.L.R. 234, 243.
[17] *Bowen* v. *Paramount Builders Ltd.* [1977] 1 N.Z.L.R. 394, 424.

Accord and satisfaction

An accord and satisfaction is a destruction of the cause of action, just as a judgment is, and therefore it is equally a bar to any later action founded on the same cause of action, even though for further damage.[18] Yet if it can be shown that the real agreement between the parties was not to destroy the whole cause of action, but merely to pay and receive compensation for the damage accrued up to that time, that agreement will be effective, and an action will lie for any further damage.

§ 219. INJUNCTIONS

Under the Supreme Court of Judicature (Consolidation) Act 1925, s. 45, all Divisions of the High Court have power to issue injunctions whenever it shall appear to the court to be just and convenient that such order should be made.

Recently the jurisdiction has been greatly expanded. So a creditor may obtain what is known as a *Mareva*[19] injunction to restrain a foreign debtor removing assets out of the jurisdiction.[20] Or there may be an *Anton Piller* order[21] giving the plaintiff a power of entry and search.

Injunctions are either prohibitory or mandatory. A prohibitory injunction is an order restraining the defendant from committing or repeating an injurious act—for example, a trespass to land or the erection of a building which would obstruct the plaintiff's lights. A mandatory injunction is an order requiring the defendant to do some positive act for the purpose of putting an end to a wrongful state of things created by him—for example, an order to pull down a building which he has already erected to the obstruction of the plaintiff's lights.[22] A mandatory injunction ought to be in such terms that the person against whom it is granted knows exactly what he has to do.[23] Injunctions, whether prohibitory or mandatory, are either interlocutory or perpetual. An interlocutory (or interim) injunction is one issued provisionally before the hearing of an action, in order to prevent the commission or continuance of an alleged injury in the meantime,[24] pending an inquiry into the case and a final determination of the right of the plaintiff to a perpetual injunction.

Onus of proof. It was once thought that an applicant for an interlocutory injunction had to show that he had a prima facie case. But in *American Cyanamid Co.* v. *Ethicon Ltd.*,[25] an action for the infringement of a patent, the House of Lords laid down a more complex set of guidelines. The court should first consider whether damages would be an adequate remedy. If yes, then normally no interlocutory injunction should be granted. But if there is

---

[18] *Read* v. *Great Eastern Ry.* (1868) L.R. 3 Q.B. 555.
[19] *Mareva Compania Naviera S.A.* v. *International Bulkcarriers* [1975] 2 Lloyd's Rep. 509.
[20] Even a defendant within the jurisdiction may be enjoined: *Chartered Bank* v. *Daklouche* [1980] 1 W.L.R. 107. For the conditions to be satisfied by the plaintiff, see *Third Chandris Shipping Corporation* v. *Unimarine S.A.* [1979] Q.B. 645.
[21] For its form, see *New Law Journal*, November 9, 1978.
[22] See *Kelsen* v. *Imperial Tobacco Co. Ltd.* [1957] 2 Q.B. 334, above, § 13.
[23] *Redland Bricks Ltd.* v. *Morris* [1970] A.C. 652.
[24] *Hampstead and Surburan Properties Ltd.* v. *Diomedous* [1969] 1 Ch. 248.
[25] [1975] A.C. 396.

doubt as to the adequacy of damages,[26] the court, if satisfied that there is a serious question to be tried, should then consider any other factors relevant to the question whether the balance of convenience favours the grant of an injunction—*e.g.* the uncompensatable harm and convenience which may be suffered by the plaintiff if the injunction is refused.[27] These guidelines have not settled all problems.[28] They have not apparently affected the practice in defamation actions,[29] and have been seriously modified in labour disputes by the Trade Union and Labour Relations Act 1976 s. 17 (2),[30] which in effect provided for yet another factor to be taken into account.

Categories of injunctions. Injunctions are either against the continuance of an injury, against the repetition of one, or against the commission of one. The commonest and most important case is the first of these; and injunction is the ordinary and most effective remedy in all cases of continuing wrongs—for example, a nuisance. Even when the injury is not continuing, however, an injunction may be granted if there is any sufficient reason to believe that it will be repeated—for example, a trespass under a claim to a right of way. It is no answer to a claim for an injunction to restrain a trespass that no damage has been done to the plaintiff.[31]

Indeed, it is possible to say that every tort is redressible by an injunction except assault and battery,[32] negligence,[33] false imprisonment, and malicious prosecution. But an interlocutory injunction to restrain the publication of a libel will be granted only in the clearest cases (and probably not at all when justification or fair comment are pleaded[34]), in which any jury would say the matter was defamatory, and in which, if the jury did not so find, their verdict would be set aside on appeal as unreasonable.[35] So in *Bestobell Paints Ltd. v. Bigg*[36] the defendant posted a notice on his shabby house: "These premises have been painted with Carson's paint." A claim for an interlocutory injunction was refused when the defendant stated that he would plead justification at the trial.

But even if no complete injury or cause of action for damages yet exists, an injunction may be obtained in a *quia timet* action to prevent the commission of an injury in the future; as when the defendant threatens or intends to erect a building which will obstruct the plaintiff's lights. In all cases, however, it seems necessary that there shall be a sufficient degree of probability that the injury will be substantial and will be continued, repeated, or committed at no remote period, and damages will not be a sufficient or adequate remedy.[37]

No injunction will be granted in a case in which obedience to the order is impossible.[38] For there are cases in which a defendant is liable in law for the

---

[26] *e.g.* because the defendant is an immigrant worker: *De Falco* v. *Crawley B.C.* |1980| 1 All E.R. 913, 922.

[27] *NWL Ltd.* v. *Woods* [1979] 1 W.L.R. 1294.

[28] *Fellows & Son* v. *Fisher* [1976] Q.B. 122.

[29] Duncan and Neill, *Defamation*, § 19.08.

[30] See above, § 136.

[31] *Woollerton and Wilson Ltd.* v. *Costain Ltd.* |1970| 1 W.L.R. 411.

[32] But see *Egan* v. *Egan* [1975] Ch. 218.

[33] *BBC* v. *Hearn* |1977| 1 W.L.R. 1004. See *Miller* v. *Jackson* |1977| Q.B. 966, 980.

[34] *Wallersteiner* v. *Moir* [1974] 1 W.L.R. 991.

[35] *Sinclair* v. *Gogarty* |1937| I.R. 377.

[36] (1975) 119 S.J. 678.

[37] *Redland Bricks Ltd.* v. *Morris* [1970] A.C. 652.

[38] *Harrington (Earl)* v. *Derby Corporation* [1905] 1 Ch. 205, 220.

continuance of a wrongful state of things, and yet has no power to put an end to it. In such a case, unless the court grants an injunction but suspends its operation for such time as may seem necessary to enable the defendant to comply with the order,[39] the plaintiff's only remedy is damages. Suspending the operation of an injunction is a well-established practice when the defendant is a local authority, but in other cases the practice is not so clear.[40] Nor will an injunction be granted to restrain a trespass to person or property if its effect would be directly to maintain the party seeking it in an illegal position.[41]

Damages in lieu of injunction[42]

Since Lord Cairns' Act 1858,[43] the court has had jurisdiction, in all cases in which it might grant an injunction, to award damages either in addition to or in substitution for such an injunction. This jurisdiction seems to be at once wider and narrower than that of the High Court under the Judicature Act. It is wider in that damages can be given when they have not been asked for; narrower, in that they can only be given in a case where an injunction could be given. The discretion of the court to depart from the general rule of restraining an injury by injunction, and to compel a plaintiff to accept pecuniary satisfaction for his wrongs, is in theory unfettered. But "Ever since Lord Cairns' Act, the Court of Chancery has repudiated the notion that the legislature intended to turn that court into a tribunal for legalising wrongful acts; or, in other words, the court has always protested against the notion that it ought to allow a wrong to continue simply because the wrongdoer is able and willing to pay for the injury he may inflict."[44]

"In my opinion," said A.L. Smith L.J. in *Shelfer's* case,[45] "it may be stated as a good working rule that (i) if the injury to the plaintiff's legal rights is small, (ii) and is one which is capable of being estimated in money, (iii) and is one which can be adequately compensated by a small money payment, (iv) and the case is one in which it would be oppressive to the defendant to grant an injunction: then damages in substitution for an injunction may be given." These principles have constantly been cited with approval,[46] although their application to the facts of a particular case may cause difficulty,[47] and it may be that they do not apply to an action for trespass as distinct from nuisance.[48] The onus of proving special circumstances which would justify the award of damages is on the defendant.[49] At least three matters may be taken into account by the court, namely, (1) the magnitude of the injury complained of, (2) the conduct of the parties, and (3) the interests of the defendant and the public.

---

[39] *Pride of Derby and Derbyshire Angling Association Ltd.* v. *British Celanese Ltd.* [1953] Ch. 149.

[40] *Trenberth* v. *National Westminster Bank* (1979) 123 S.J. 388.

[41] *Boreham* v. *Commonwealth of Australia* (1953) 88 C.L.R. 518.

[42] See Jolowicz, "Damages in Equity—A Study of Lord Cairns' Act" [1975] C.L.J. 224.

[43] Although the Act has been repealed the jurisdiction so created is preserved by s. 37 of the Supreme Court of Judicature (Consolidation) Act 1925.

[44] *Shelfer* v. *City of London Electric Lighting Co.* [1895] 1 Ch. 287, 315, 316, *per* Lindley L.J.

[45] [1895] 1 Ch. 287, 322.

[46] Most recently in *Kennaway* v. *Thompson* [1981] Q.B. 88.

[47] *Redland Bricks Ltd.* v. *Morris* [1970] A.C. 652.

[48] *Woollerton and Wilson Ltd.* v. *Costain Ltd.* [1970] 1 W.L.R. 411.

[49] *McKinnon Industries Ltd.* v. *Walker* [1951] 3 D.L.R. 577, 581, *per* Lord Simonds.

(i) *Magnitude of the injury*

On this principle injunctions have been refused in the case of merely temporary or intermittent nuisances,[50] and in the case of repeated trespasses committed under a claim of right but causing no damage,[51] and in cases where the interest of the plaintiff in the property affected was about to determine.[52]

(ii) *Conduct of the parties*

If a plaintiff has knowingly stood by and made no objection while the defendant has in ignorance invaded his rights (as by erecting a building which obstructs an easement of light or a right of way), no injunction will be granted to him.[53] Conversely, if the defendant has himself acted with wilful and high-handed disregard of the plaintiff's rights, an injunction may be granted.[54]

(iii) *Effect on interests of defendant or of the public*

When the damage done or apprehended is substantial, and there is nothing in the conduct of the plaintiff sufficient to render him undeserving of this remedy, an injunction may be granted even though its effect will be to inflict upon the defendant or upon the public at large a loss that is greater than any benefit so conferred upon the plaintiff.[55] The court will not sanction, in the interest of individuals or of the public, any substantial invasion of private rights, even on the terms of paying full compensation for the injury so inflicted.[56] So Lord Sumner, dissenting, doubted[57] "whether it is complete justice to allow the big man, with his big building and his enhanced rateable value and his improvement of the neighbourhood, to have his way, and to solace the little man for his darkened and stuffy little house by giving him a cheque that he does not ask for."

When damages are awarded in substitution for an injunction in pursuance of the discretionary jurisidiction conferred by Lord Cairns' Act, such damages are given in respect of the future, and not merely, as at common law, in respect of damage already done in the past. Such an award of damage amounts, therefore, to a legalisation of the apprehended mischief; the defendant has thereby purchased a right to do the act in respect of which an injunction was asked, and in respect of which damages have been given instead. Further, it should be noted that a bare majority of the House of Lords has held[58] that the court has power to award damages in lieu of an injunction in a *quia timet* action when no actual harm or complete cause of action for damages already exists. The curious result of this decision is that a court of equity has power to award damages when a court of law could not. But apart from these exceptional cases the Act does not provide for the

---

[50] *Swaine* v. *G.N. Ry.* (1864) 4 De G.J. & S. 211.
[51] *Behrens* v. *Richards* [1905] 2 Ch. 614.
[52] *Jacomb* v. *Knight* (1863) 3 De G.J. & S. 533.
[53] *Gaskin* v. *Balls* (1879) 13 Ch.D. 324.
[54] *Sefton (Earl)* v. *Tophams Ltd.* [1964] 1 W.L.R. 1408.
[55] *Kennaway* v. *Thompson* [1981] Q.B. 88.
[56] *Bellew* v. *Cement Ltd.* [1948] I.R. 62.
[57] *Leeds Industrial Co-operative Society* v. *Slack* [1924] A.C. 851, 872.
[58] *Leeds Industrial Co-operative Society* v. *Slack* [1924] A.C. 851.

assessment of damages on any new basis.[59] The measure of damages is the same under Lord Cairns' Act as at common law, although in some cases under the Act the time at which such damages are assessed may be the date of the judgment rather than the date of the breach

§ 220. THE LIMITATION ACTS 1939 TO 1980[60]

The Limitation Act 1939, as amended by the Law Reform (Limitation of Actions, etc.) Act 1954, simplified the law relating to the limitation of actions for tort. Unfortunately the law again became complex, partly because of the Limitation Act 1963, which attempted to settle some difficulties by establishing a machinery which was at once flexible and elaborate,[61] and partly because of some decisions which took an unexpectedly benevolent view of the plaintiff's rights.[62] Two more complex statutes, the Limitation Act 1975 and the Limitation Amendment Act 1980, became necessary.[62a]

By the Act of 1939[63] no action founded on tort shall be brought after the expiration of six years from the date on which the cause of action accrued. By the Act of 1954 the limitation period for actions for damages in respect of personal injuries was reduced to three years. By the Act of 1975 new time limits for various types of personal injuries actions were prescribed, subject to an overriding power given to the court.[64]

When time begins to run

In calculating whether time (whether the period be six years or three years) has run against the plaintiff, the day on which the accident happened is excluded from the computation,[65] but the day on which the writ was issued is included.[66] In any event, it is important to observe that although the writ must be issued within the prescribed period, another year can elapse before it need be served.[67] So in practice the period of limitation may be seven or four, not six or three, years.

The period of limitation begins to run at the time when the cause of action

---

[59] *Johnson* v. *Agnew* [1980] A.C. 367.

[60] See the Fifth Interim Report of the Law Revision Committee (Cmnd. 5334); Report of Lord Justice Tucker's Committee on the Limitation of Actions, 1949 (Cmnd. 7740); Woolf, *The Time Barrier in Personal Injury Claims*; Goodman, "First Catch Your Defendant" (1966) 29 M.L.R. 366; Report of the Law Commission (Cmnd. 4532 ((1970))); Interim Report of the Law Reform Committee (Cmnd. 5630, 1974); Final Report of the Law Reform Committee (Cmnd. 6923, 1977); J. Pritchard, *Personal Injury Litigation*, Ch. XVII.

[61] The Act "has a strong claim to the distinction of being the worst drafted Act on the statute book": *Central Asbestos Co. Ltd.* v. *Dodd* [1973] A.C. 518, 529, *per* Lord Reid. But Lord Reid never had to consider the Rehabilitation of Offenders Act 1974 or the Limitation Acts of 1975 and 1980.

[62] As in *Knipe* v. *British Railways Board* [1972] 1 Q.B. 361, in which the plaintiff was entitled to sue in respect of an injury which had occurred 20 years previously.

[62a] Since the text was sent to the printers, the Limitation Act 1980 has been passed by Parliament. It is a pure consolidation Act, which came into force on May 1, 1981.

[63] s. 2 (1) (a). The Act must be pleaded; the court will not of its own motion take notice that the action is out of time: *Dismore* v. *Milton* [1938] 3 All E.R. 762.   [64] See below, § 221.

[65] *Marren* v. *Dawson, Bentley & Co. Ltd.* [1961] 2 Q.B. 135.

[66] *Trow* v. *Ind Coope (West Midlands) Ltd.* [1967] 2 Q.B. 899.

[67] R.S.C., Ord, 6 r. 8 (2). It is only in exceptional cases that the court will extend this period for a writ which has not been timeously served: *Chappell* v. *Cooper* [1980] 1 W.L.R. 958. In cases of personal injuries there are important practical reasons for speedy service: see above, § 214, n. 58.

accrued, *i.e.* "the earliest time at which an action could be brought."[68] Therefore, when a wrongful act is actionable *per se* without proof of actual damage, the statute runs from the time at which the act was committed—as in libel,[69] assault, or interference with goods. This is so even though the resulting damage does not happen or is not discovered until a later date; for such damage is not a new cause of action, but merely an incident of the old one.[70]

When, on the other hand, the wrong is not actionable without actual damage the period of limitation does not begin to run until that damage happens: as in the case of negligence,[71] fraud,[72] or wrongful interference with an easement[73] of support.[74] But it is sometimes very difficult to be sure of the moment of time when damage can be said to have happened. This is the problem of latent damage.

Latent damage: personal injuries

It was formerly held that once damage had occurred the cause of action accrued and that time began to run against the plaintiff even though he was unaware or mistaken as to the consequences of the damage,[75] or even though the defendant was unknown or untraceable.[76] This gave rise to grave injustice, *e.g.* in some cases of pneumoconiosis, in which substantial injury to the lungs may be suffered years before it can be discovered. A committee reported[77] in favour of a change in the law, and the Limitation Act 1963, ss. 1 and 2[78] made the change recommended. But these changes in turn revealed defects,[79] and on the advice of another committee[80] further changes were made by the Limitation Act 1975, which provide in effect that ignorance of matters of law should not of itself prevent time running in cases of personal injuries.

Latent damage: other cases

It is still uncertain how far absence of knowledge may suspend the running of time when the damage alleged is damage to house property. While it does seem that the former rule that the cause of action arose at the date of construction, or perhaps on the date of the conveyance of a building[81] is no longer accepted either in the Court of Appeal[82] or in the House of Lords,[83] it

---

[68] *Reeves* v. *Butcher* [1891] 2 Q.B. 509, 511, *per* Lindley L.J.
[69] *Brunswick (Duke of)* v. *Harmer* (1849) 14 Q.B. 185. See above, § 53.
[70] *Cartledge* v. *E. Jopling & Sons Ltd.* [1963] A.C. 758.
[71] *Watson* v. *Winget Ltd.* 1960 S.C. 92.
[72] Otherwise there might be great injustice in "a clock fraud"—one so timed as to explode and damage the plaintiff more than six years later: *Barber* v. *Houston* (1885) 18 L.R. Ir. 475, 481.
[73] *Backhouse* v. *Bonomi* (1861) 9 H.L.C. 503. As to the period of limitation when distinct damage results at different times from the same wrongful act, see above, § 218.
[74] *Long* v. *Western Propellers Ltd.* (1967) 65 D.L.R. (2d) 147, 149.
[75] *Cartledge* v. *E. Jopling & Sons Ltd.* [1963] A.C. 758.
[76] *R.B. Policies at Lloyd's* v. *Butler* [1950] 1 K.B. 76.
[77] Cmnd. 1829 (1961).
[78] Which received the royal assent on July 31, 1963, only 6 months after the decision in *Cartledge* v. *Jopling.* Law reform can be speedy.
[79] See *Central Asbestos Co.* v. *Dodd* [1973] A.C. 518.
[80] See Cmnd. 5630 (1974). For the complex details, see below, § 221.
[81] Put forward in *Dutton* v. *Bognor Regis Building Co.* [1972] 1 Q.B. 373.
[82] *Sparham-Souter* v. *Town & Country Developments Ltd.* [1976] Q.B. 858.
[83] *Anns* v. *Merton B.C.* [1978] A.C. 728.

is not possible at present to go beyond Lord Wilberforce's statement that the cause of action arises when the state of the property constitutes present or imminent danger to the occupier's person or property.[84] This statement does not expressly require that the damage should be perceived. Nor does it cover a situation in which some damage has been perceived, but its potential severity has not been appreciated.

The problem of latent damage is so difficult that Lord Hailsham of St. Marylebone L.C., told the House of Lords that it was premature to express a solution in the Limitation Amendment Act 1980.[85] Further cases will be required before Parliament enacts the fifth Limitation Act since 1939. On the one hand, it seems unreasonable that a plaintiff should lose his right of action before he knows that he has it. On the other hand, it seems equally unreasonable that a plaintiff should be entitled to wait for six years after he has discovered the damage before he issues his writ—especially as it is only in exceptional cases that his action can be dismissed for want of prosecution.[86] It also seems hard on a professional man such as an architect if he can be sued many years after he has committed the act which causes damage years later.[87] Perhaps the solution is to have a cut-off point (say 10 years) after which there is no liability.

Disability

If when a cause of action accrued, the person to whom it accrued was under a disability, the action may be brought within six years from the date when he ceased to be under a disability or died, whichever event first occurred.[88] In the case of an action for personal injuries[89] the period is three years from the cesser of the disability or death.[90] A minor has therefore a statutory right of which he cannot be deprived by the court to delay the issue of his writ until 3 years after his majority, however long that may be after the accident.[91] The Act of 1975 abolished (s. 2) the former rule that, whether the period be six years or three years, the plaintiff must prove that the person under the disability was not, at the time when the right of action accrued to him, in the custody of a parent. A person is of unsound mind if he is detained under any Act authorising the detention of persons of unsound mind or mental deficients,[92] or if he is, by reason of mental illness, incapable of managing his affairs in relation to the accident as a reasonable man would have done.

These disabilities must exist at the time when the cause of action first

---

[84] [1978] A.C. 728, 760. It should be noted that Lord Salmon ([1978] A.C. at 769–771) said that time began to run from the date when the damage first occurred. While all five Law Lords in *Anns* disapproved the statement in *Dutton*, the difficulty arises from the fact that Lord Wilberforce, and the three who concurred in his judgment, did not approve of, or even comment on, *Sparham-Souter*.

[85] 400 H.L. Deb. col. 1234 (20 October 1979).

[86] *Walkley* v. *Precision Forgings Ltd.* [1979] 1 W.L.R. 606.

[87] In the *Anns* case two of the plaintiffs were held entitled to sue in respect of a flat bought in 1962.

[88] Limitation Act 1939, s. 22.

[89] Below, § 221.

[90] Limitation Act 1975, s. 2.

[91] *Tolley* v. *Morris* [1979] 1 W.L.R. 592. According to *Birkett* v. *James* [1978] A.C. 297, such an action cannot be dismissed for want of prosecution unless the plaintiff's delay has been contumelious.

[92] Limitation Act 1939, s. 31 (3).

arises. If the statute has once commenced to run, the subsequent insanity of the plaintiff or the fact that the claim has passed to a person under a disability[93] will not have any effect.[94] When a person is under successive disabilities, *e.g.* insanity supervening on infancy, time does not run against him until the last of the disabilities has come to an end provided that there is no interval between any of the disabilities.[95] But, when a right of action which has accrued to a person under a disability accrues on his death to another person under a disability, no further extension of time is allowed.[96]

Fraud

The Limitation Act 1939, s. 26—as amended by section 7 of the Act of 1980—provides that when the action is based upon the fraud of the defendant or any fact relevant to the plaintiff's cause of action has been deliberately concealed from him by the defendant,[97] or the action is for relief from the consequences of a mistake, time does not run until the plaintiff has discovered the fraud, concealment or mistake, or could with reasonable diligence have discovered it. But the bona fide purchaser of property for valuable consideration or any person claiming through him[98] is not to be prejudiced by this provision.[99]

§ 221. SPECIAL PERIODS OF LIMITATION[1]

The general limitation period of six years established by the Limitation Act 1939 has been both extended and contracted by different statutes. It has been extended to thirty years by the Nuclear Installations Act 1965, s. 15. It has been contracted by other statutes in four special cases: (1) personal injuries; (2) accidents at sea and in the air; (3) actions arising out of death; (4) contribution between tortfeasors.

(1) Personal injuries

The primary limitation period

Section 2 (1) of the Law Reform (Limitation of Actions, etc.) Act 1954 amended the Limitation Act 1939 by reducing from six years to three years the period of limitation for actions for damages for negligence, nuisance or breach of duty (whether the duty exists by virtue of a contract or of a provision made by or under a statute or independently of any contract or any such provision), where the damages claimed by the plaintiff for the negligence, nuisance or breach of duty consist of or include damages in respect of personal injuries to any person. The reason for this change is that it is desirable in the interests of justice that actions for personal injuries

---

[93] Limitation Act 1939, s. 22(1)(a).
[94] *Rhodes* v. *Smethust* (1840) 6 M. & W. 351.
[95] *Borrows* v. *Ellison* (1871) L.R. 6 Ex. 128.
[96] Limitation Act 1939, s. 22(1)(b).
[97] By s. 7 (2) the concept of concealment has been extended to cover deliberate concealment of a breach of duty in circumstances in which it is unlikely to be discovered.
[98] *Eddis* v. *Chichester Constable* [1969] 2 Ch. 345.
[99] See the elaborate provisions of s. 7(4).
[1] See Law Reform Committee, 20th Report, Cmnd. 5630 (1974), and Law Com. No. 64 (1975), § 137.

should be brought to trial quickly, while the evidence is still fresh in the minds of parties and witnesses. The Court of Appeal has held[2] that the words "breach of duty" are wide enough to include causes of action for personal injuries which are framed in trespass as distinct from case. This is to be welcomed on the ground that it is undesirable that a plaintiff should be able to avoid the three-year period of limitation by taking advantage of the technicalities of the forms of action. Still, on the other side it may be said that the distinction between trespass and case has not yet been expressly abolished,[3] that the Limitation Acts have not impliedly done so, and that a plaintiff is entitled to the period of limitation appropriate to his cause of action until Parliament otherwise determines. So if the action is for breach of contract for failing to effect an insurance policy to cover personal injuries, the period is six years and not three.[4]

The effect of knowledge: latent damage

The simple three-year rule has become complex as the result of two efforts by Parliament to provide a solution for the problem of latent damage. The Limitation Act 1975 s. 1 did some complicated legislative surgery on the body of the 1939 Act by inserting four new sections numbered 2A–2D, after section 2.[5] Sections 2B and 2C can be put aside for the present as dealing with claims under the Fatal Accidents Act 1976.[6] Section 2A redefines the moment at which time begins to run against a plaintiff, and then section 2D gives the court power to "disapply"[7] the primary period, as so redefined, if it thinks it equitable to do so.

So it is necessary to set out much of section 2A. It runs as follows:

2A.—(1) This section applies to any action for damage for negligence, nuisance or breach of duty (whether the duty exists by virtue of a contract or of provision made by or under a statute or independently of any contract or any such provision) where the damages claimed by the plaintiff for the negligence, nuisance or breach of duty consist or include damages in respect of personal injuries to the plaintiff or any other person.

(2) Section 2 of this Act shall not apply to an action to which this section applies.

(3) Subject to section 2D below,[8] an action to which this section applies shall not be brought after the expiration of the period specified in subsections (4) and (5) below.

(4) Except where subsection (5) applies, the said period is three years from—

(a) the date on which the cause of action accrued, or

(b) the date (if later) of the plaintiff's knowledge.

(5) If the person injured dies before the expiration of the period in subsection (4) above, the period as respects the cause of action surviving for the benefit of the estate of the deceased by virtue of section 1 of the Law Reform (Miscellaneous Provisions) Act 1934 shall be three years from—

---

[2] *Letang* v. *Cooper* [1965] 1 Q.B. 232; *Long* v. *Hepworth* [1968] 1 W.L.R. 1299.
[3] See above, § 1.
[4] *Ackbar* v. *C.F. Green & Co. Ltd.* [1975] Q.B. 582.
[5] *Firman* v. *Ellis* [1978] Q.B. 886, 910
[6] See above, § 217.
[7] To use the verb recognised by the draftsman but not by the Oxford English Dictionary.
[8] See the next sub-section.

(a) the date of death, or

(b) the date of the personal representative's knowledge, whichever is the later.

(6) In this section references to a person's date of knowledge are references to the date on which he first had knowledge of the following facts—

(a) that the injury was significant,[9] and

(b) that that injury was attributable in whole or in part to the act or omission which is alleged to constitute negligence, nuisance or breach of duty, and

(c) the identity of the defendant, and

(d) if it is alleged that the act or omission was that of a person other than the defendant, the identity of that person and the additional facts supporting the bringing of an action against the defendant,

and knowledge that any acts or omissions did or did not, as a matter of law, involve negligence, nuisance or breach of duty is irrelevant.[10]

(7) For the purposes of this section an injury is significant if the plaintiff would reasonably have considered it sufficiently serious to justify his instituting proceedings for damages against a defendant who did not dispute liability and was able to satisfy a judgment.

(8) For the purposes of the said sections a person's knowledge includes knowledge which he might reasonably have been expected to acquire—

(a) from facts observable or ascertainable by him, or

(b) from facts ascertainable by him with the help of medical or other appropriate expert advice which it is reasonable for him to seek,

but a person shall not be fixed under this subsection with knowledge of a fact ascertainable only with the help of expert advice so long as he has taken all reasonable steps to obtain (and, where appropriate to act on) that advice.

The disapplication provisions of section 2D

The power to "disapply" the complex provisions set out above may be exercised, under section 2D (1), "if it appears to the court that it would be equitable to allow an action to proceed." As has been observed, the result is that "we have uncertainty deliberately built into the law on top of the minute detail provided".[11] The basic question which arose was whether the court's discretion was to be exercised only in exceptional cases. In favour of such a view was the existence of six guide-lines ("which present a curious hotch-potch")[11a] in the section itself, and the fact that the Law Reform Committee, on whose Report[12] the Act was based, had so recommended. But it has now been held by the House of Lords that section 2D should not be read in any restrictive sense so as to apply only to exceptional cases.[13]

To this proposition there is, however, a qualification arising from the fact that the court's discretion to "disapply" arises only if "the provisions of section 2A or 2B of this Act prejudice the plaintiff." If the plaintiff has been prejudiced by his own act, or his solicitor's act,[14] in failing to serve the writ

---

[9] See *McCafferty* v. *Metropolitan Police Receiver* [1977] 1 W.L.R. 1073.
[10] So it is knowledge of the facts, not of the law, which is critical.
[11] W.L. Dale, *Legislative Drafting—A New Approach* (1978), p. 216.
[11a] *Thompson* v. *Brown* [1981] 1 W.L.R. 744, 751.   [12] Cmnd. 5630, 1974.
[13] *Simpson* v. *Norwest Holst Southern Ltd.* [1980] 1 W.L.R. 968.
[14] *Thompson* v. *Brown* [1981] 1 W.L.R. 744.

in time or in discontinuing the action, then the section cannot operate.[15] Normally there is no power to dismiss an action for want of prosecution before the expiry of the statutory period.[16]

(2) Accidents at sea and in the air

By the Maritime Conventions Act 1911, s. 8, a period of limitation of two years is imposed upon claims in respect of damage to a vessel or her cargo, or in respect of loss of life or personal injuries suffered by any person on board a vessel, caused by the fault of any other vessel.[17] Under the same Act the period within which the owners of the vessels involved may enforce their right of contribution in cases of loss of life or personal injuries is one year from the date of payment. These periods may, however, be extended by the court in certain circumstances.[18] By the Carriage by Air Act 1961, s. 5 (1), a two-year limitation period applies to such proceedings against air-carriers as are governed by that Act.

(3) Statutes connected with death

(i) *Death of injured party*

Claims under the Fatal Accidents Act 1976 have a special period of three years since the Limitation Act 1975.[19] As to survival actions, the ordinary six- or three-year period applies. It runs from the accrual of the cause of action as if no death had occurred. But if the deceased could have applied to the court under the Limtiation Act 1963, s. 1, as amended by the Act of 1975,[20] for leave to bring the action out of time then his estate will have a similar right.

(ii) *Death of wrongdoer*

Under section 1 (3) of the 1934 Act no proceedings in respect of a cause of action in tort could be taken against the estate of a deceased person unless, either the proceedings were pending at the date of his death or the proceedings were taken not later than six months after his personal representatives took out representation.[21] But the "six-months rule" was criticised by the Law Commission[22] on the ground that a plaintiff might be seriously prejudiced if the tortfeasor was unknown to him, and died at the time of the accident or shortly thereafter, or even if known, the death occurred before a writ had been served. It therefore proposed the total repeal of the "six-months rule," leaving all claims against estates to be

---

[15] *Chappell* v. *Cooper* [1980] 1 W.L.R. 958.
[16] *Birkett* v. *James* [1978] A.C. 297. Aliter if the action has been commenced with the leave of the court: *Biss* v. *Lambeth B.C.* [1978] 1 W.L.R. 382.
[17] See *The Alnwick* [1965] P. 357.
[18] See Cmnd. 5334, § 29.
[19] See above, § 217.
[20] For which, see above, § 220.
[21] The Law Reform (Limitations of Actions) Act 1954, ss. 4, 8 (3), and Sched., repealed the former additional requirement of the 1934 Act that the cause of action must have arisen not earlier than 6 months before the death of the wrongdoer. This provision remains familiar to all who have read what is, perhaps, the best of all detective stories with a legal setting, Cyril Hare's *Tragedy at Law.*
[22] Law Com. No. 19 (Cmnd. 4010 (1969)). See Ogus, Note (1969) 32 M.L.R. 551.

governed by the general law of limitations. Parliament accepted this recommendation, and by the Proceedings Against Estates Act 1970, s. 1, repealed section 1 (3) of the 1934 Act.[23] The Act of 1970 therefore constitutes a significant exception to the general principle of "the executor's year."

Where the cause of action, as in the case of disturbance of the right of support, does not arise until the damage has been suffered, the Act of 1934 expressly provides[24] that if the wrongdoer dies before or at the same time as the damage is suffered, there shall be deemed to be subsisting against him such cause of action as would have subsisted if he had died after the damage was suffered.

(4) Contribution between tortfeasors

The limitation period in England[25] is two years under the Limitation Act 1939, s. 22, as amended by the Limitation Act 1975, s. 2.

§ 222. FELONIOUS TORTS[26]

At common law the rule was that when a tort was also a felony, no action could be brought in respect of the tort until the defendant had been prosecuted for the felony or a reasonable excuse had been shown for his not having been prosecuted.[27] But the rule has been abolished in England[28] by the Criminal Law Act 1967, s. 1. It is now possible to sue a thief for unlawful interference with goods before he has been prosecuted.

§ 223. ASSIGNMENT OF RIGHTS OF ACTION

The assignment of a right of action for damages for a tort is in general illegal and void.[29] The rule is based on considerations of public policy, and is designed to prevent the oppressive litigation that would result if a right of action for damages were recognised as a marketable commodity capable of purchase by way of a commercial speculation. The rule applies to torts of all kinds, whether they are injuries to property or to the person or otherwise. But there is an increasing tendency to uphold assignments when the assignee has a legitimate and genuine interest in the subject-matter of the suit.[30] So the rule is not applicable in the following six cases:

(1) Where the right assigned has some other source than an illegal act. It is on this principle that rights arising under a contract are assignable, as opposed to rights arising from the breach of a contract. So also with rights arising *quasi ex contractu*, as in the case of money paid by mistake. On the same principle, there should be no objection to the assignment of a judgment debt even in an action of tort, or to the assignment of money agreed to be paid by way of settlement of a claim in tort. (2) The rule does not prevent

---

[23] For Ireland, see s. 9 of the Civil Liability Act 1961, which neatly settles the doubts raised by Diplock J. in *Airey* v. *Airey* [1958] 1 W.L.R. 729 (see 15th ed., § 164).
[24] s. 1 (4). "Damage" in this subsection means injury: *Post Office* v. *Official Solicitor* [1951] 1 All E.R. 522.
[25] For Ireland, see s. 31 of the Civil Liability Act 1961.
[26] See Pannam "The Felonious Tort Rule" (1965) 39 Austr. L.J. 164.
[27] *Smith* v. *Selwyn* [1914] 3 K.B. 98.
[28] In Ireland it still exists: see *Dillon* v. *Dunne's Stores* (*No.* 1) (1966, unreported).
[29] *Glegg* v. *Bromley* [1912] 3 K.B. 474. See on the whole of this section Winfield, *Present Law*, pp. 67–69.
[30] See *Trendtex Trading Corporation* v. *Credit Suisse* [1980] Q.B. 629.

the assignment of property merely because it is the subject of litigation and cannot be recovered without an action. Thus, a sale of chattels by A to B while they are wrongfully detained by C is valid and confers upon B a right of action against C.[31] (3) Where a trustee in bankruptcy assigns the bankrupt's choses in action, even though they arise *ex delicto*, and even though the assignment is back to the bankrupt himself.[32] (4) The rule does not prevent the subrogation of an insurer to the rights of the assured, even though these rights are rights of action for damages for a tort, nor the subsequent express assignment of the assured's rights to the insurer. In such a case equity before the Judicature Act would have compelled the assignor to exercise his rights against the contract-breaker or tortfeasor for the benefit of the assignee. Since 1873 those rights can be the subject of an express assignment, provided that section 136 of the Law of Property Act 1925 is complied with.[33] (5) The rule does not apply to any other case in which the assignee has any lawful interest in the subject-matter sufficient to exclude the doctrine of maintenance—for example, an assignment by a trustee to his beneficiaries of a right of action for an injury to the trust estate.[34] (6) The rule does not prevent the assignment of the fruits of an action in tort, *i.e.* an assignment of the damages to be recovered in such an action—even though the assignment is made before the action has commenced or before judgment has been recovered.[35] This is not the assignment of an existing cause of action. It is merely the equitable assignment of future property defined or identified by reference to such a cause of action. It confers upon the assignee no right to institute or intervene in the action, and is therefore free from the objectionable element of maintenance.

§ 224. WAIVER OF TORTS[36]

In certain cases when the defendant has by means of a tort become possessed of a sum of money at the expense of the plaintiff, the plaintiff may at his election waive the tort. He may sue either for damages for the tort, or in quasi-contract for money had and received by the defendant to the use of the plaintiff. This is so, for example, if the defendant wrongfully takes by trespass or obtains by fraud the money of the plaintiff.[37] So also if the plaintiff's goods are wrongfully converted and sold by the defendant the plaintiff may choose between an action in tort for wrongful interference with goods and an action in quasi-contract for the price so received by the defendant.[38] It is obvious that in these cases there is no real waiver as where the forfeiture of a lease is waived by the receipt of rent. "If I find that a thief has stolen my securities and is in possession of the proceeds," said Lord Atkins,[39] "when I sue him for them I am not excusing him; indeed, he may be in prison upon my prosecution." The waiver is as fictitious as the con-

---

[31] *Dawson v. G.N. Ry.* [1905] 1 K.B. 260, 271.
[32] *Ramsey v. Hartley* [1977] 1 W.L.R. 686.
[33] *Compania Colombiana de Seguros v. Pacific S.N. Co.* [1965] 1 Q.B. 101.
[34] *Trendtex Trading Corporation v. Credit Suisse* [1980] Q.B. 629.
[35] *Glegg v. Bromley* [1912] 3 K.B. 474.
[36] See Goff and Jones, *The Law of Restitution*, Chap. 33; Beatson, "The Nature of Waiver of Tort" (1979) 17 Univ. W.A.L. Rev. 1. In view of the very full treatment in Goff and Jones, this section has been shortened.
[37] *Neate v. Harding* (1851) 6 Ex. 349.
[38] *Rodgers v. Maw* (1846) 15 M. & W. 444, 448.
[39] [1941] A.C. 1, 29.

tract. The phrase "waive the tort" is a picturesque one and has a pleasing sound and was (perhaps for that reason) regarded by the old common lawyers with affection,[40] but it is inaccurate. What is waived is not the tort but the right to recover damages for it. It is clear that there are torts to which the doctrine of waiver cannot be applied, for example, defamation and assault,[41] but it is not clear how far this doctrine does extend. The torts which it has been held can be waived are those of conversion, trespass to land or goods, deceit and the action for extorting money by threats. There are authorities which, if they could be relied on, would justify us in laying down a general rule to the effect that whenever the defendant has by his tort acquired a profit of any sort (whether it is the receipt of money or not) the tort may be waived, and an action of restitution brought to compel payment of a pecuniary equivalent for that profit.[42]

Effect of election

In those cases in which the waiver of a tort is permitted the two causes of action—delictual and quasi-contractual—are not cumulative but alternative. The plaintiff must make his election between them. Anything, therefore, which exhausts or extinguishes one of the causes of action destroys the other also. Accordingly, when the plaintiff's goods have been converted and sold and he obtains judgment in an action for money had and received he cannot thereafter resort to an action of conversion; and this is so even though the damages recoverable in conversion would far exceed the price for which the defendant sold the goods and for which judgment has been obtained against him.[43] But the mere commencement of an action in quasi-contract is no bar to a subsequent action in tort: such an action is not a waiver of the tort but merely a choice of one of two alternative remedies, and it is judgment alone in the first action which constitutes a bar to the second.[44]

When election to be made

Confusion has arisen from failure to distinguish between (1) election between inconsistent rights, and (2) election between alternative remedies. If a man is entitled to one of two inconsistent rights, when with full knowledge[45] he has done an unequivocal act showing that he has chosen the one, he cannot afterwards pursue the other[46]; which after the first choice is by reason of the inconsistency no longer his to choose. The commencement of an action is only evidence from which an election may be inferred: it is not conclusive.[47] Otherwise a plaintiff who issued a writ against one of two tortfeasors in order to prevent time running out would find that he was

---

[40] One of them was sufficiently moved to express his feelings in verse:
　　　　　"Thoughts much too deep for tears subdue the Court
　　　　　When I assumpsit bring, and god-like waive a tort."
　　　　—J.L. Adolphus, "The Circuiteers: an Eclogue" : (1885) 1 L.Q.R. 232.
[41] *United Australia* case [1941] A.C. 1, 12.
[42] See *Lightly* v. *Clouston* (1808) 1 Taunt. 112 (seduction).
[43] *Rice* v. *Reed* [1900] 1 Q.B. 54; *Re Simms* [1934] Ch. 1.
[44] *United Australia Ltd.* v. *Barclays Bank Ltd.* [1941] A.C. 1. And if there are two tortfeasors an unsatisfied judgment against one is no bar to proceedings against the other.
[45] [1941] A.C. 1, 30.
[46] *Re United Railways of the Havana and Regla Warehouses Ltd.* [1961] A.C. 1007, 1065.
[47] *Clarkson Booker Ltd.* v. *Andjel* [1964] 2 Q.B. 775.

barred from proceeding against the other. When the plaintiff's failure to elect becomes embarrassing to the defendant and the court he may be compelled to make his election during the trial.[48] But where there are alternative remedies on the same set of facts the plaintiff need not make his election until he applies for judgment.[49] It need hardly be necessary to add that if the same act constitutes two different torts the bringing of an action for both of them is no waiver of either.[50]

Two wrongdoers

The question remains: how far does the plaintiff's election to sue A in quasi-contract stand in the way of his subsequently bringing an action on the same facts against B for conversion? The answer was given in *United Australia Ltd.* v. *Barclays Bank.*[51] In that case the plaintiffs made out a cheque which was wrongfully endorsed by their secretary to the M.F.G. Co. The defendants collected it on behalf of that company. The plaintiffs brought an action against M.F.G. for money had and received, but before they had obtained judgment the company went into liquidation. The plaintiffs put in a proof in the winding up, but the company had no assets and the liquidator neither admitted nor rejected the proof. They then sued the defendants for conversion of the cheque. It was pleaded that by their action against M.F.G. and by their proof in the winding up they had waived their right to sue for the tort. But the House of Lords held that this was not so. The company and the bankers were not joint tortfeasors, though their independent acts had caused the same damage. Only satisfaction in the earlier proceedings would act as a bar to the second action. It was stressed that the bank and M.F.G. were not joint tortfeasors, but since the Law Reform (Married Women and Tortfeasors) Act 1935, the reasoning would seem to apply equally to the case of joint tortfeasors.

§ 225. FOREIGN TORTS[52]

Except in the case of injuries to interests in land, an action of tort will lie in England although the cause of action has arisen abroad or on the high seas.[53] Provided that the person of the defendant is within the jurisdiction of the English courts,[54] he can be sued in England for a libel published in New York, or for an assault committed in Turkey. But two conditions must be fulfilled as a general rule[55]:—

(1) The act must not have been justifiable by the law of the place where it was done;

---

[48] *British Ry. Traffic Co.* v. *Roper* (1939) 162 L.T. 217.
[49] *Maheson* v. *Malaysia Government Housing Society Ltd.* [1979] A.C. 374.
[50] *Caxton Publishing Co.* v. *Sutherland Publishing Co.* [1939] A.C. 178, 199; *United Australia* case [1941] A.C. 1, 18–19.
[51] [1941] A.C. 1.
[52] See Dicey and Morris, *Conflict of Laws*, Chap. 30; McGregor, "The International Accident Problem" (1970) 33 M.L.R. 1; Fridman, "Where is a Tort Committed?" (1974) 24 Toronto L.J. 247.
[53] *The Esso Malaysia* [1975] Q.B. 198 (under the Fatal Accidents Acts there is no requirement that the defendant should be of British nationality: see above, § 217).
[54] For the rules on jurisdiction, see R.S.C., Ord. 11, r. 1.
[55] Where it is against public policy to admit or exclude claims, the courts have a discretion to discourage "forum shopping": *Chaplin* v. *Boys* [1971] A.C. 356, 378, 383, 389.

(2) It must be of a kind which would have been actionable as a tort had it
   been done in England.[56]

A tort has not necessarily been committed in England merely because
damage flowing from a wrongful act done elsewhere has been suffered in
England, even in cases where damage is the gist of the action.[57] The tort
may be held to have been committed abroad, so that the leave of the court is
required to serve the writ. Each case must be considered on its own merits,[58]
but a generally accepted test is to look back over the series of events constituting the tort and ask where in substance the cause of action arose.[59]

(1) Act must not be justifiable where done

The meaning which is given to the word "justifiable" in our courts is well
illustrated by a comparison of some cases. In *Phillips* v. *Eyre*[60] an action for
false imprisonment was brought against the Governor of Jamaica, who
pleaded that the arrest was made in connection with the suppression of a
rebellion, and had been declared lawful subsequently by an act of the local
legislature. The Court of Exchequer upheld his plea. In *Machado* v. *Fontes*[61]
the Court of Appeal held that the act need not be actionable in the place
where it is done in order to be actionable in England. It is sufficient if it is
not legally justifiable and is punishable. But *Machado* v. *Fontes* has
apparently been overruled by the House of Lords in *Chaplin* v. *Boys*.[62]

(2) Act must be actionable by English law

The second condition that must be fulfilled before an action for a foreign
tort will lie in England is that an act of that sort must amount to an actionable tort in accordance with the law of England. This rule has been affirmed
in the House of Lords.[63] The substantive law of England plays a dominant
role in determining the cause of action, but there is now a tendency to search
for the relevant issue in the case and consider what law has the most significant relationship with that issue.[64]

Trespass. No action in tort will lie in England for any trespass or other
tort committed in respect of land situated out of England,[65] although it
might be possible to waive the tort and sue in quasi-contract.[66] This is so
even if no question as to the title to the land is in issue between the parties.
In the case of contracts and trusts, or admiralty actions *in rem*,[67] on the
other hand, the jurisdiction of the English court is not excluded by the fact
that the land is out of England.

---

[56] *Phillips* v. *Eyre* (1870) L.R. 6 Q.B. 1, where Willes J. formulated these two rules, which
were approved in substance by the H.L. in *Chaplin* v. *Boys* [1971] A.C. 356.
[57] *Distillers Co. (Bio-Chemicals) Ltd.* v. *Thompson* [1971] A.C. 458.
[58] *Diamond* v. *Bank of London & Montreal Ltd.* [1979] Q.B. 333.
[59] *Castree* v. *E. & R. Squibb & Sons Ltd.* [1980] 1 W.L.R. 1248.
[60] (1870) L.R. 6 Q.B. 1.
[61] [1897] 2 Q.B. 231.
[62] [1971] A.C. 356.
[63] *Chaplin* v. *Boys* [1971] A.C. 356.
[64] *Church of Scientology of California* v. *Police Commissioner* [1976] C.L.Y. 2174.
[65] *Hesperides Hotels Ltd.* v. *Aegean Hotels Ltd.* [1979] A.C. 508.
[66] *Att.-Gen.* v. *Nissan* [1970] A.C. 179, 213.
[67] *The Tolten* [1946] P. 135.

CHAPTER 25

EXTRAJUDICIAL REMEDIES

It is not necessary in all cases that a man should resort to judicial proceedings in order to seek protection or redress in respect of injuries threatened or committed against him. In many instances the law grants him liberty to help himself by his own act and strength. We shall deal in this chapter with self-redress; with self-defence and the prevention of trespass we have already dealt.[1]

§ 226. RE-ENTRY ON LAND[2]

He who is wrongfully dispossessed of land is not bound to proceed for its recovery by action at law,[3] for he may retake possession of it by his own act, if he can do so peaceably and without the use of force.[4] Even if he has obtained a judgment for possession he may still enter at his own risk without the aid of the sheriff.[5] A forcible entry, however, even by a person lawfully entitled to the possession, was an indictable misdemeanour under the Statutes of Forcible Entry 1381, 1429 and 1623.[6] These statutes have been repealed by the Criminal Law Act 1977 s. 13 and replaced by a number of specific criminal offences—e.g. under section 6 it is an offence without lawful authority to use or threaten violence to secure entry into premises against the known opposition of someone on the premises. There is an exception for a "displaced residential occupier."[7] Before the Act of 1977 it was established that forcible entry upon a person wrongfully in possession by a person entitled to the possession was, although a criminal offence, no civil injury for which the wrongdoer so ejected had any remedy.[8] If in the course of a forcible entry an assault is committed upon the occupier or other person defending the possession, or damage is done to chattels upon the premises, will an action for damages lie in respect of this independent injury, although none lies for the entry and eviction itself? After some conflict of opinion the Court of Appeal in *Hemmings* v. *Stoke Poges Golf Club*[9] held that it would not. So long as no more force was used than was justifiable at common law for the ejection of a trespasser[10] or the removal of his goods, the fact that the entry was a breach of the Statutes of Forcible Entry did not expose the true

---

[1] Above, § 46.
[2] See Law Commission Report (Law Com. No. 76), 1974, which is the basis of the Criminal Law Act 1977.
[3] Unless the premises have been let as a dwelling under a tenancy which is not a protected tenancy within the meaning of the Rent Act 1965, when a court order is required by s. 32 of the Act.
[4] *Taunton* v. *Costar* (1797) 7 T.R. 431.
[5] *Aglionby* v. *Cohen* [1955] 1 Q.B. 558.
[6] This "is the reason for the perenially comic spectacle, so dear to playwrights and novelists, of the patient or crafty bailiff trying to obtain entry without strong hand or multitude of people": Allen, *The Queen's Peace*, p. 48.
[7] So an occupier who is not within this category cannot apparently use force to recover his property unless he is "a protected intending occupier" under s. 7 (2).
[8] *Pollen* v. *Brewer* (1859) 7 C.B. (N.S.) 371.
[9] [1920] 1 K.B. 720.
[10] See above, § 46.

owner to an action for trespass to person or goods.[11] It is uncertain how far these rules are still law.

§ 227. RECAPTION OF CHATTELS[12]

Any person entitled to the possession of a chattel may retake the chattel either peaceably or by the use of reasonable force from any person who has wrongfully taken or detained it from him. Such a retaking, even though forcible, is neither a civil injury nor a criminal offence.[13] As to the amount of force which is permissible, and as to the necessity of a precedent request,[14] the defence and recaption of chattels is presumably governed by the same rules as the ejectment of trespassers upon land.[15] The remedy of forcible recaption is not limited to cases of the wrongful taking of chattels, but extends to all cases of the wrongful possession of them.[16] It is a matter of some doubt how far the right of retaking the chattels will serve to justify an entry on the land on which they are situated. It is clear that if the occupier of the land has himself wrongfully taken and placed the goods there, the owner of them may enter and taken them.[17] A similar rule applies if the occupier has permitted a wrongdoer to leave goods on the land.[18] But what if the occupier is in no way responsible for the presence of the goods on his land, but merely refuses to give them up, or to allow the owner to enter and take them; as in the case of a lessee who gives up possession of the land, but leaves a chattel behind him, and then seeks to recover it? This is a question that has more than once come before the courts, but has not succeeded in obtaining a definite and comprehensive answer.[19] The Law Reform Committee has suggested that the deciding factor should be whether the person retaking his chattel has acted reasonably in entering on another's premises

---

[11] *Aglionby* v. *Cohen* [1955] 1 Q.B. 558, 562.

[12] See Branston, "Forcible Recaption of Chattels" (1912) 28 L.Q.R. 263, and the 18th Report of the Law Reform Committee (Cmnd. 4774 (1971)), paras. 116–126.

[13] *Blades* v. *Higgs* (1865) 11 H.L.C. 621.

[14] The need for a prior request for return of the property before resorting to force was not accepted in *Whatford* v. *Carty* [1960] C.L.Y. 3258.

[15] See above, § 46.

[16] *Blades* v. *Higgs* (1861) 10 C.B. (N.S.) 713, 720. It has been doubted whether it extends to a mere wrongful detention of a chattel lawfully acquired: *Devoe* v. *Long* [1951] 1 D.L.R. 203.

[17] *Austin* v. *Dowling* (1870) L.R. 5 C.P. 534, 539.

[18] *Huet* v. *Lawrence* (1948) S.R. (Qd.) 168.

[19] As the authorities stand the position seems to be as follows. A man may enter another man's land to retake his own chattels if they came there (1) by accident, *e.g.* if a fruit tree grow in a hedge and the fruit fall on to another's land: *The Case of Thorns* (1466) Y.B. 6 Edw. IV, 7, p. 18; *Mitten* v. *Faudrye* (1626) Poph. 161; (2) by the felonious act of a third party: Blackstone, III, 5; *Higgins* v. *Andrewes* (1619) 2 Roll.Rep. 55. But it is not enough to prove that his property was on the land without proving the circumstances in which it came there: *Anthony* v. *Haney* (1832) 8 Bing. 186; still less does it suffice to justify the entry if the property came there by his own act—for example, by way of bailment. In such a case it has been held that the owner of the chattels may enter to retake them only if (1) the occupier's right of possession has been validly determined, and (2), no breach of the peace is committed: *Devoe* v. *Long* [1951] 1 D.L.R. 203; *Anthony* v. *Haney* (1832) 8 Bing. 186, 193. The occupier is not liable merely because he refuses to hand the chattels back to their owner: *Capital Finance Co. Ltd.* v. *Bray* [1964] 1 W.L.R. 323. He is not liable unless he has exercised dominion over the chattel: *Wilde* v. *Waters* (1855) 24 L.J.C.P. 193, 195; *Isaack* v. *Clark* (1614) 2 Bulstr. 306, 314; *Thorogood* v. *Robinson* (1845) 6 Q.B. 769; *British Economical Lamp Co.* v. *Empire, Mile End* (1913) 29 T.L.R. 386; *Ellis* v. *Noakes* (1930), [1932] 2 Ch. 98, 104.

or in using any degree of force.[20] It is settled[21] that a man who has hived bees has no right if they swarm to follow them on to another man's land, for when they get there they once more become *ferae naturae* and are the property of no one until they are again hived.

§ 228. ABATEMENT OF NUISANCE

It is lawful for any occupier of land, or for any other person by the authority of the occupier, to abate (*i.e.* to terminate by his own act) any nuisance by which that land is injuriously affected. Thus the occupier of land may without notice cut off the overhanging branches of his neighbour's trees,[22] or sever roots which have spread from those trees into his own land.[23] In these cases the abator can act without leaving his own land, but subject to certain requirements as to prior notice, which will be considered later, the right also extends to the cases in which it is necessary for the abator to enter upon the land of the other party.[24] In abating a nuisance any unnecessary damage done is an actionable wrong,[25] and therefore, where there are two ways of abating a nuisance, the less mischievous is to be followed, unless it would inflict some wrong on an innocent third party or the public.[26] The right of abatement is alternative to damages. If the nuisance is abated, no damages can be obtained in respect of the injury suffered.[27] It is sometimes said that the law does not regard the right of abatement with favour,[28] but this seems too strong. There is no reason to encourage litigation to deal with such trivial nuisances as overhanging branches. But as an abatement may give rise to a breach of the peace, caution is desirable.

It seems to be assumed that there is no right of entry and abatement in a case in which, although an actionable nuisance exists, an injunction against the continuance of it could not be obtained. If, for example, a house is built which obstructs ancient lights, but to so small an extent or under such circumstances that no mandatory injunction would be granted to pull the house down, it cannot be supposed that the owner of the obstructed light is nevertheless at liberty to attain the same end by the exercise of his right of abatement.[29] Strangely enough, however, there may apparently be a right of entry and abatement where there is no action for damages for the nuisance. So no damages can be obtained against a defendant who has allowed a tree to overgrow his boundary, unless it is the cause of actual damage[30]; for damage is of the essence of nuisance. But there is no reason to suppose that

---

[20] Cmnd. 4774 (1971), para. 126. But the Law Commission disagree—see Working Paper No. 54 (1974).
[21] *Kearry* v. *Pattinson* [1939] 1 K.B. 471.
[22] *Lemmon* v. *Webb* [1895] A.C. 1.
[23] *Butler* v. *Standard Telephones* [1940] 1 K.B. 399. He may not, however, appropriate to his own use the things so severed, and if he does so, he is liable in conversion for their value: *Mills* v. *Brooker* [1919] 1 K.B. 555.
[24] See Law Commission Working Paper No. 78, *Rights of Access to Neighbouring Land* (1980).
[25] *Roberts* v. *Rose* (1865) 4 H. & C. 103.
[26] *Lagan Navigation Co.* v. *Lambeg Bleaching Co.* [1927] A.C. 226, 245.
[27] *Baten's Case* (1610) 9 Co.Rep. 53b.
[28] *Lagan Navigation Co.* v. *Lambeg Bleaching Co.* [1927] A.C. 226, 244.
[29] This is discussed in *Lane* v. *Capsey* [1891] 3 Ch. 411.
[30] *Smith* v. *Giddy* [1904] 2 K.B. 448; *Lemmon* v. *Webb* [1894] 3 Ch. 1, 11. If damage has been caused, an injunction may also be obtained: *McCombe* v. *Read* [1955] 2 Q.B. 429.

the right of the neighbour to cut the encroaching roots and branches is subject to any such limitation.[31]

Necessity of notice before abatement

It is clear that there are at least two cases in which no notice is required: (1) When there is no entry on the land of the other party—e.g. cutting roots and branches.[32] (2) In case of emergency—i.e. where the nuisance threatens such immediate harm to person or property that the delay involved in giving notice would be unreasonable.[33]

It seems clear also that there are four cases in which notice must be given: (1) When the nuisance was committed, not by the present occupier, but by a predecessor in title.[34] (2) When the occupier is not responsible for the creation or continuance of the nuisance.[34] (3) When the abatement involves the demolition of a house which is actually inhabited.[35] (4) When the more mischievous of two ways of abating a nuisance is followed.[36]

Whether notice is required in other cases is a question to which no certain reply can be given. In *Lemmon* v. *Webb*[37] there is an obvious inclination to state the rule in the general form, that in all cases of entry and abatement notice is required except in case of emergency.

Abatement of public nuisance

It is lawful for any person to abate a public nuisance to a highway, so far as it is necessary to enable him to exercise his right of way thereon, or right of access thereto.[38] Thus if a fence is unlawfully erected across a highway or a gate wrongfully locked, any member of the public may in the exercise of his right of way remove the fence or break open the gate. And this is so even though the obstruction has been erected in the exercise of a bona fide but unfounded claim or right. Probably this right of abatement exists only when the abator can prove that he has sustained such special damage as is required to confer upon him a private right of action.[39] The right of abating a nuisance on a highway extends only to nuisances of commission, and not to those of omission so as to entitle any member of the public to undertake the repair of a highway or the creation thereon of a permanent structure such as a bridge, which he may consider necessary for the convenient

---

[31] Salmond regarded this as going further than a mere right of abating a nuisance—as simply a part of the occupier's exclusive right of possession, and of doing as he pleases with his own. But the overhanging branches and the enroaching roots are until severance realty, and realty which is the property of the owner of the tree: *Lemmon* v. *Webb* [1894] 3 Ch. 1, 20; *Mills* v. *Brooker* [1919] 1 K.B. 555. An overhanging roof or cornice has been held to be a nuisance to the land it overhangs because of the necessary tendency to discharge rainwater upon it: *Baten's Case* (1610) 9 Co.Rep. 53b. It is possible that in early days on a parity of reasoning overhanging branches were similarly regarded, and that the doctrine that in such cases special damage must be proved is of later growth.
[32] *Lemmon* v. *Webb* [1894] 3 Ch. 1; [1895] A.C. 1.
[33] *Jones* v. *Williams* (1843) 11 M. & W. 176, 182; *Lemmon* v. *Webb* [1894] 3 Ch. 1, 13.
[34] *Jones* v. *Williams* (1843) 11 M. & W. 176.
[35] *Davies* v. *Williams* (1851) 16 Q.B. 546.
[36] *Lagan Navigation Co.* v. *Lambeg Bleaching Co.* [1927] A.C. 226, 245.
[37] [1895] A.C. 1.
[38] *Webb* v. *Stansfield* [1966] C.I.Y. 2590 (opening door of car parked in front of garage: in such a case the defence of necessity may also be available: see § 185, but not that of distress damage feasant: see § 229).
[39] *Campbell Davys* v. *Lloyd* [1901] 2 Ch. 518, 524.

exercise of his right of passage. Such acts must be done by those who are charged with the common law or statutory duty of repairing or constructing highways.[40]

§ 229. Distress Damage Feasant[41]

It is lawful for any occupier of land to seize any chattels which are unlawfully upon his land and have done or are doing damage there, and to detain them until payment of compensation for the damage done. This right is known as that of distress damage feasant. Normally the things so distrained were cattle or other trespassing animals, but the Animals Act 1971, s. 7 has abolished the right to seize and detain any animal by way of distress damage feasant, and substituted a new remedy which gives the occupier a power of sale.[42] But distress damage feasant still exists, and it is established that the right extends to all chattels animate or inanimate. Thus a railway company has been held entitled to seize and detain a locomotive engine which was wrongfully encumbering its lines.[43] So an occupier is not obliged to return a cricket ball or football which has broken his window-pane. Distress damage feasant differs from other forms of distress in that it is a remedy which can be exercised out of hand, at any time of the day or night.[44] The right of distress damage feasant is vested, in general, only in the occupier of land. Mere use without exclusive possession is, it may be assumed, as insufficient to confer this right as it is to confer the right to eject a trespasser or to sue in an action of trespass.[45]

Limits of right of distress

(i) *Object's presence must be wrongful*

The thing distrained must be unlawfully on the land—*i.e.* it must be there under such circumstances that an action for damages will lie against the owner or some other person responsible for it.[46] The right of action, how-ever, need not be against the owner of the thing distrained. If the thing is present by the wrong of him who had the custody of it, or possibly even by the wrong of a mere stranger, it may be seized and detained as a security for compensation.[47]

(ii) *Actual damage*

There must be actual damage done by the thing distrained; for it is rightly taken and detained only as a security for the payment of compensation, and when there is no damage done there can be no compensation due.[48] Though

---

[40] *Campbell Davys* v. *Lloyd* [1901] 2 Ch. 518.
[41] See the exhaustive discussion of this topic in Williams, *Animals*, pp. 1–123.
[42] See above, § 124.
[43] *Ambergate Ry.* v. *Midland Ry.* (1853) 2 E. & B. 793.
[44] *Watkinson* v. *Hollington* [1944] K.B. 16.
[45] *Burt* v. *Moor* (1793) 5 T.R. 329.
[46] *Tillett* v. *Ward* (1882) 10 Q.B.D. 17.
[47] 1 Roll.Ab.665, *Distress*, D.
[48] *R.* v. *Howson* (1966) 55 D.L.R. (2d) 582—mere trespass by wrongfully parked car does not justify distress, though the removal of the car may be justified under abatement of nuisance (see § 228) or necessity (see § 185).

there can be no right of distress unless there has been an infringement of the right to land either by trespass or nuisance, once that infringement is established the damage need not be done to the land itself or to things forming part of the freehold, such as crops. It is sufficient if damage is done on the land to the property or, presumably, the person of the occupier.[49]

(iii) *Object must still be on land*

The thing must be seized while still on the land. There is no right of following it, even in fresh pursuit, and even if it is purposely removed by its owner in order to avoid distress.[50] In spite of some authority to the contrary it does not seem that the thing distrained need have been caught *flagrante delicto* doing damage,[51] but if the same thing comes more than once upon the same land it cannot be distrained or detained on a subsequent occasion in respect of damage done by it on a former visit.[52]

(iv) *No right of sale*

The right of distress damage feasant includes no right of sale, but merely a right to retain the thing until adequate compensation is made. Formerly the law was the same in the case of distress for rent also, but the statutes which confer a power of sale on landlords have left unaffected the common law as to distress damage feasant. But the right of the occupier is to detain only until compensation is paid for the damage done. It is the duty of the owner to form an estimate of the amount of the damage, and to make a tender of this sum, however extortionate the demand made by the distrainor.[53] Things distrained damage feasant may at the option of the distrainor be kept by him on the premises where they were seized, or kept in his own custody elsewhere, or impounded by him in a public pound.[54] By the Protection of Animals Act 1911, s. 7, he is bound to provide animals impounded by him with food and water.

(v) *Alternative to action*

The exercise of the right of distress damage feasant suspends the right of action for the damage complained of, so long as the detention of the property continues. Distress and action are alternative remedies which cannot be concurrently pursued. If, however, the property distrained perishes or is lost without the distrainor's fault, he is remitted to his right of action, and so also if the property is restored to the owner.

---

[49] *Boden* v. *Roscoe* [1894] 1 Q.B. 608.
[50] *Clement* v. *Milner* (1800) 3 Esp. 95.
[51] Williams, pp. 84–85.
[52] *Vaspor* v. *Edwards* (1701) 12 Mod. 658, 660.
[53] *Sorrell* v. *Paget* [1950] 1 K.B. 252, 265. In this case the distrainor's demand was for a sum as "salvage." Although "salvage by land is a legal chimera" (Asquith L.J.) this did not excuse the wrongdoer from making a tender.
[54] *Vaspor* v. *Edwards* (1701) 12 Mod. 658, 664. "As a public institution the, pound was commonly referred to in our literature of a hundred years and more ago. I hope that a good many people recollect that in, perhaps, the most celebrated of English novels, Mr. Pickwick was removed by Captain Boldwig to the village pound under the imputation of being a drunken plebeian": *Searle* v. *Wallbank* [1947] A.C. 341, 350, *per* Lord Maugham.

INDEX